Essentials of

PEDIATRIC INTENSIVE CARE

Section Editors

Nick G. Anas, M.D.

John M. Andersen, M.D.

Susan Ballard, R.R.T.

Brett P. Giroir, M.D.

Philip C. Guzzetta, Jr., M.D.

Catherine L. Headrick, R.N., M.S.

Christine A. Lindsay, Pharm.D., B.C.P.S.

Katherine Lipsky, A.C.S.W., L.M.S.W.-A.C.P.

Peter M. Luckett, M.D.

Thomas Wm. Mayo, J.D.

E. Steve Roach, M.D.

William A. Scott, M.D.

Mouin G. Seikaly, M.D.

Jane D. Siegel, M.D.

John F. Sommerauer, M.D.

Robert H. Squires, Jr., M.D.

Michael W. Stannard, M.D.

Luis O. Toro-Figueroa, M.D.

Perrin C. White, M.D.

Robert A. Wiebe, M.D.

Naomi J. Winick, M.D.

VOLUME TWO

Procedures, Equipment, and Techniques

Essentials of PEDIATRIC INTENSIVE CARE SECOND EDITION

Edited by

Daniel L. Levin, M.D.

Professor of Pediatrics, Dartmouth Medical School; Medical Director,
Pediatric Intensive Care Unit, Children's Hospital at Dartmouth, Lebanon,
New Hampshire; formerly Professor of Pediatrics, University of Texas
Southwestern Medical Center at Dallas, and staff physician,
Children's Medical Center of Dallas, Texas

Frances C. Morriss, M.D.

Associate Professor, Departments of Pediatrics and Anesthesia and
Pain Management, University of Texas Southwestern Medical Center
at Dallas, Texas

CHURCHILL
LIVINGSTONE

QUALITY MEDICAL
PUBLISHING, INC.

New York, Edinburgh, London, Madrid, Melbourne, San Francisco, Tokyo, St. Louis

LIBRARY OF CONGRESS CATALOGING IN PUBLICATION DATA

A catalog record for this book is available from the Library of Congress

ISBN 0-443-05931-4 (Volume 1)
ISBN 0-443-05932-2 (Volume 2)
ISBN 0-443-05930-6 (Volume 1 and 2 set)

Distributed in the United Kingdom by Churchill Livingstone, Robert Stevenson House, 1–3 Baxter's Place, Leith Walk, Edinburgh EH1 3AF, and by associated companies, branches, and representatives throughout the world.

Medical knowledge is constantly changing. As new information becomes available, changes in treatment, procedures, equipment, and the use of drugs become necessary. The editors/authors/contributors and the publishers have, as far as it is possible, taken care to ensure that the information given in this text is accurate and up to date. However, readers are strongly advised to confirm that the information, especially with regard to drug usage, complies with the latest legislation and standards of practice.

The Publishers have made every effort to trace the copyright holders for borrowed material. If they have inadvertently overlooked any, they will be pleased to make the necessary arrangements at the first opportunity.

Quality Medical Publishing, Inc. and Mosby–Year Book, Inc., mutually recognize and respect the contribution made by the authors to this work. In this spirit, Quality Medical Publishing, Inc., acknowledges and gratefully accepts the permission to use portions of this work that previously appeared in Mosby–Year Book's *A Practical Guide to Pediatric Intensive Care*.

PUBLISHER   Karen Berger

ASSISTANT EDITOR   Esha Gupta

PROJECT EDITOR   Carolita Deter

MANUSCRIPT EDITORS   George Mary Gardner, Carolita Deter

PRODUCTION   Judy Bamert

BOOK DESIGN   Susan Trail

COVER DESIGN   Jeannette Jacobs

ILLUSTRATORS   Scott Thorn Barrows, Kimberly Martens, Chris Peterson

Printed in the United States of America.

First published in 1997   7 6 5 4 3 2 1

Contributors

Thomas J. Abramo, M.D.
Assistant Professor, Division of Pediatric Emergency Medicine, Department of Pediatrics, University of Texas Southwestern Medical Center at Dallas; Director, Pediatric Transport Service, Children's Medical Center of Dallas, Texas

Perrie M. Adams, Ph.D.
Associate Dean for Research, University of Texas Southwestern Medical Center at Dallas, Texas

Steven R. Alexander, M.D.
Professor, Division of Pediatric Nephrology, Department of Pediatrics, University of Texas Southwestern Medical Center at Dallas; Medical Director, Dialysis and Renal Transplantation, Children's Medical Center of Dallas, Texas

Sana Al-Jundi, M.D.
Clinical Instructor, Department of Pediatric Critical Care, UCLA School of Medicine, Los Angeles, California

Anthony Amponsem, M.D.
Staff Pediatric Intensivist, Division of Pediatric Critical Care Medicine, Department of Pediatrics, King/Drew Medical Center, Los Angeles, California

Nick G. Anas, M.D.
Associate Clinical Professor, Department of Pediatrics, Harbor UCLA Medical Center, Torrance, California

John M. Andersen, M.D.
Professor and Director, Division of Pediatric Gastroenterology and Nutrition, Department of Pediatrics, University of Texas Southwestern Medical Center at Dallas, Texas

Barbara G. Anderson, Ph.D.
Professor Emeritus, Department of Anthropology, Southern Methodist University, Dallas, Texas

Walter S. Andrews, M.D.
Surgical Director, Pediatric Liver Transplant Program, Children's Medical Center of Dallas, Texas

David L. Anglin, M.D.
Chief, Pediatric Critical Care, Children's Hospital of Austin, Texas

Victor M. Aquino, M.D.
Research Fellow, Department of Pediatrics, University of Texas Southwestern Medical Center at Dallas, Texas

Antonio Arrieta, M.D.
Associate Director, Pediatric Infectious Disease; Medical Director, "KIDS" Clinic, Division of Pediatric Subspecialty Faculty, Department of Infectious Disease, Children's Hospital of Orange County, Orange, California

Grace M. Arteaga, M.D.
Assistant Professor, Division of Pediatric Critical Care, Department of Pediatrics, University of Illinois at Chicago, Illinois

Bassam Atiyeh, M.D.
Associate Professor, Division of Pediatric Nephrology, Department of Pediatrics, Wayne State University, Detroit, Michigan

Donna Badgett, C.R.T.T.
Systems Manager, Respiratory Care, Children's Medical Center of Dallas, Texas

David L. Bakken, M.D.
Fellow in Pediatric Emergency Medicine, Department of Pediatrics, University of Texas Southwestern Medical Center at Dallas, Texas

Susan Ballard, R.R.T.
Critical Care Team Leader, Respiratory Care Department, Children's Medical Center of Dallas, Texas

Lynn J. Banks, R.N., B.S.N., C.C.R.N.
Clinical Nurse IV, Children's Medical Center of Dallas, Texas

William Banks, M.D.
Assistant Professor, Division of Pediatric Radiology, Department of Radiology, University of Texas Southwestern Medical Center at Dallas, Texas

R. Phil Barton, M.D.
Pediatric Intensivist, Division of Pediatric Critical Care, Department of Pediatrics, Children's Hospital at St. Francis, Tulsa, Oklahoma

Michel Baum, M.D.
Professor of Pediatrics and Internal Medicine, Sarah M. and Charles E. Seay Chair in Pediatric Research; Director, Division of Pediatric Nephrology, Department of Pediatrics, University of Texas Southwestern Medical Center at Dallas, Texas

Nancy M. Bauman, M.D.
Assistant Professor, Department of Otolaryngology, University of Iowa College of Medicine, Iowa City, Iowa

Juan Carlos Bernini, M.D.
Senior Clinical Research Fellow in Pediatric Hematology-Oncology, University of Texas Southwestern Medical Center at Dallas, Texas

Michael J. Biavati, M.D.
Assistant Professor, Department of Otolaryngology, University of Texas Southwestern Medical Center at Dallas, Texas

Carol L. Bieler, R.N.
Ventilation Oxygenation Support Systems Coordinator, Children's Medical Center of Dallas, Texas

Dawne A. Black, B.S., R.R.T.
Clinical Care Coordinator, Children's Medical Center of Dallas, Texas

Sarah D. Blumenschein, M.D.
Assistant Professor, Division of Pediatric Cardiology, Department of Pediatrics, University of Texas Southwestern Medical Center at Dallas, Texas

Robert M. Bradley, M.D.
Staff, Transfusion Service, Baptist Memorial Hospital, Memphis, Tennessee

David R. Breed, M.D.
Staff Neonatologist, St. David's Hospital, Austin, Texas

William J. Bridge, J.D.
Associate Professor, Southern Methodist University School of Law, Dallas, Texas

Lela W. Brink, M.D.
Assistant Professor and Director, Pediatric Intensive Care Unit, Division of Pediatric Critical Care, Department of Pediatrics, University of North Carolina, Chapel Hill, North Carolina

John G. Brooks, M.D.
Professor and Chairman, Department of Pediatrics, Dartmouth Medical School; Medical Director, Children's Hospital at Dartmouth, Lebanon, New Hampshire

Mary C. Brower, M.D.
Assistant Professor, Division of Pediatric Neurology, Department of Neurology, University of Texas Southwestern Medical Center at Dallas, Texas

Orval E. Brown, M.D.
Associate Professor, Department of Otolaryngology, University of Texas Southwestern Medical Center at Dallas, Texas

Derek A. Bruce, M.B., Ch.B.
Clinical Associate Professor, Division of Pediatric Neurosurgery, Department of Neurological Surgery, University of Texas Southwestern Medical Center at Dallas, Texas

George R. Buchanan, M.D.
Professor and Director, Division of Pediatric Hematology-Oncology, Department of Pediatrics, University of Texas Southwestern Medical Center at Dallas; Director, Center for Cancer and Blood Disorders, Children's Medical Center of Dallas, Texas

Susan Burke, R.N., M.A., C.P.N.P.
Advanced Nurse Practitioner, Children's Medical Center of Dallas, Texas

H. Steven Byrd, M.D.
Professor and Vice Chairman, Division of Plastic Surgery, University of Texas Southwestern Medical Center at Dallas, Texas

Carolanne Capron, R.N., M.Ed.
Director, Department of Nursing, Columbia Wesley Medical Center, Wichita, Kansas

John J. Cheyney, R.N., B.S.N., C.C.R.N.
Clinical Nurse II, Children's Medical Center of Dallas, Texas

Gary D. Cieslak, M.D.
Staff Anesthesiologist, St. Luke's Regional Medical Center, Boise, Idaho

David C. Cleveland, M.D.
Clinical Assistant Professor, Department of Surgery, University of Texas Southwestern Medical Center at Dallas, Texas

Colleen A. Conlin, P.A.
Physician Assistant, Pediatric Liver Transplant Program, Children's Medical Center of Dallas, Texas

Dan Cooper, M.D.
Professor, Division of Respiratory and Critical Care, Department of Pediatrics, Harbor UCLA Medical Center, Torrance, California

Michelle Morris Copeland, R.N., M.S.
Clinical Nurse Specialist, Children's Medical Center of Dallas, Texas

Mark G. Coulthard, M.B., B.S., F.R.A.C.P.
Staff Specialist, Intensive Care Unit, Royal Children's Hospital, Herston, Queensland, Australia

Blair E. Cox, M.D.
Assistant Professor, Division of Neonatal-Perinatal Medicine, Department of Pediatrics, University of Texas Southwestern Medical Center at Dallas, Texas

Charles E. Curran, S.T.D.
Elizabeth Scurlock Professor of Human Values, Southern Methodist University, Dallas, Texas

Shermine Dabbagh, M.D.
Associate Professor and Chief, Division of Pediatric Nephrology, Department of Pediatrics, Wayne State University, Detroit, Michigan

John Darling, R.R.T.
Critical Care Therapist, Children's Medical Center of Dallas, Texas

Toni Darville, M.D.
Instructor, Division of Critical Care Medicine, Department of Pediatrics, University of Arkansas for Medical Sciences, Little Rock, Arkansas

Stan L. Davis, M.D.
Assistant Clinical Professor, Department of Anesthesiology and Pain Management, University of Texas Southwestern Medical Center at Dallas, Texas

Kathleen A. Delaney, M.D.
Associate Professor, Division of Emergency Medicine, Department of Surgery, University of Texas Southwestern Medical Center at Dallas, Texas

Mauricio R. Delgado, M.D., F.R.C.P.(C)
Associate Professor, Division of Pediatric Neurology, Department of Neurology, University of Texas Southwestern Medical Center at Dallas, Texas

Andreas Deymann, M.D.
Fellow in Pediatric Critical Care, Harbor UCLA Medical Center, Torrance, California

Bryan A. Dickson, M.D.
Assistant Professor, Division of Pediatric Endocrinology, Department of Pediatrics, University of Texas Southwestern Medical Center at Dallas, Texas

Paula Jean Dimmitt, R.N., M.S., C.P.N.P.
Ear, Nose, and Throat Nurse Practitioner, Ear, Nose, and Throat Clinic, Children's Medical Center of Dallas, Texas

Sheri Doster, R.N., M.S.N.
Clinical Nurse Specialist, Renal Transplantation, Children's Medical Center of Dallas, Texas

Mary Drury, R.N., M.N., C.P.N.P.
Pediatric Nurse Practitioner, Children's Medical Center of Dallas, Texas

Jim Eisenwine, R.Ph.
Pharmacist, Children's Medical Center of Dallas, Texas

Gary D. Elmore, R.R.T.
Administrative Director, Respiratory Care, Children's Medical Center of Dallas, Texas

Graham J. Emslie, M.D.
Associate Professor, Division of Child and Adolescent Psychiatry, Department of Psychiatry, University of Texas Southwestern Medical Center at Dallas; Director, Psychiatry Services, Children's Medical Center of Dallas, Texas

Trina M. Fabré, Pharm.D.
Pediatric Clinical Pharmacist, Children's Medical Center of Dallas, Texas

Linda Farley-Fisher, R.N., B.S.N.
Pacemaker-Electrophysiology Clinical Nurse III, Children's Medical Center of Dallas, Texas

Mary M. Farrell, M.D.
Critical Care Intensivist, Department of Critical Care Pediatrics, Orlando Regional Health Care System/Arnold Palmer Hospital, Orlando, Florida

Elizabeth Farrington, Pharm.D., B.C.P.S.
Clinical Assistant Professor, Division of Pharmacy Practice, Department of Pharmacy, University of North Carolina, Chapel Hill, North Carolina

Arleen C. Farrow, M.D.
Fellow in Pediatric Hematology-Oncology, University of Texas Southwestern Medical Center at Dallas, Texas

Robert D. Fildes, M.D.
Associate Professor and Director, Division of Pediatric Nephrology, Department of Pediatrics, Georgetown University Medical Center, Washington, D.C.

Vicki Fioravanti, R.N., C.C.T.C.
Liver Transplant Coordinator, Children's Medical Center of Dallas, Texas

Debra H. Fiser, M.D.
Professor and Chairman, Department of Pediatrics, University of Arkansas for Medical Sciences, Little Rock, Arkansas

Richard Thomas Fiser, M.D.
Instructor, Division of Pediatric Critical Care Medicine, Department of Pediatrics, University of Arkansas for Medical Sciences, Little Rock, Arkansas

David E. Fixler, M.D.
Director, Division of Pediatric Cardiology, Department of Pediatrics, University of Texas Southwestern Medical Center at Dallas, Texas

Dorothy C. Foglia, R.N., M.S., C.C.R.N.
Clinical Nurse Specialist, Children's Medical Center of Dallas, Texas

Bradley P. Fuhrman, M.D.
Professor, Division of Pediatric Critical Care, Department of Pediatrics, Children's Hospital of Buffalo and State University of New York at Buffalo, New York

Susan B. Garber, R.N., B.S., C.I.C.
Infection Control Nurse, Children's Medical Center of Dallas, Texas

Jorge A. Garcia, M.D.
Staff, Pediatric Cardiology, Department of Pediatrics, Texas Tech University, Amarillo, Texas

Thomas R. George, R.R.T.
Director of Education, Respiratory Care Services, Children's Medical Center of Dallas, Texas

G.E. Ghali, D.D.S., M.D.
Assistant Professor, Division of Oral and Maxillofacial Surgery, Department of Surgery, Louisiana State University Medical Center, Shreveport, Louisiana

Cole A. Giller, Ph.D., M.D.
Assistant Professor, Department of Neurological Surgery, University of Texas Southwestern Medical Center at Dallas, Texas

Brett P. Giroir, M.D.
Assistant Professor, Division of Pediatric Critical Care, Department of Pediatrics, University of Texas Southwestern Medical Center at Dallas, Texas

Jill S. Giroir, J.D.
Strasburger & Price, L.L.P., Dallas, Texas

Maggie Gonzales, R.N., B.S.N.
Clinical Nurse II, Children's Medical Center of Dallas, Texas

Jose L. Gonzalez, M.D.
Assistant Professor, Division of Pediatric Endocrinology, Department of Pediatrics, University of Texas Southwestern Medical Center at Dallas, Texas

Gary Goodman, M.D.
Clinical Professor, Division of Respiratory and Critical Care, Department of Pediatrics, Harbor UCLA Medical Center, Torrance, California

Collin S. Goto, M.D.
Assistant Professor, Division of Pediatric Emergency Medicine, Department of Pediatrics, University of Texas Southwestern Medical Center at Dallas, Texas

Juan A. Gutierrez, M.D.
Instructor, Division of Pediatric Critical Care, Department of Pediatrics, University of Arizona Health Sciences Center, Tucson, Arizona

Philip C. Guzzetta, Jr., M.D.
Professor and Chairman, Division of Pediatric Surgery, Department of Surgery, University of Texas Southwestern Medical Center at Dallas, Texas

Bill and Cathy Hare
Parents

Yaron Harel, M.D.
Assistant Professor, Department of Pediatrics, University of Medicine and Dentistry, New Jersey, Newark, New Jersey

Kathalene M. Harris, R.R.T., C.P.F.T.
Respiratory Care Coordinator, Texas Scottish Rite Hospital for Children, Dallas, Texas

Mary F. Harris, M.D.
Clinical Professor, Department of Anesthesiology and Pain Management, University of Texas Southwestern Medical Center at Dallas, Texas

Robert M. Haws, M.D., Major, U.S.A.F., M.C.
Section of Nephrology, Department of Pediatrics, Wilford Hall Medical Center, Lackland Air Force Base, Texas

Mary Fran Hazinski, R.N., M.S.N, F.A.A.N.
Clinical Specialist, Division of Trauma, Departments of Surgery and Pediatrics, Vanderbilt University Medical Center, Nashville, Tennessee

Catherine L. Headrick, R.N., M.S.
Clinical Nurse Specialist, Children's Medical Center of Dallas, Texas

John H. Herman, Ph.D.
Associate Professor, Department of Psychiatry, University of Texas Southwestern Medical Center at Dallas, Texas

Larry Herrera, M.D.
Fellow in Hematology-Oncology, University of Texas Southwestern Medical Center at Dallas, Texas

Mark J. Heulitt, M.D.
Associate Professor, Division of Critical Care Medicine, Department of Pediatrics, University of Arkansas for Medical Sciences, Little Rock, Arkansas

Barry A. Hicks, M.D.
Assistant Professor, Division of Pediatric Surgery, Department of Surgery, University of Texas Southwestern Medical Center at Dallas, Texas

David A. Hicks, M.D.
Pulmonologist and Director, Cystic Fibrosis Center, Children's Hospital of Orange County, Orange, California

Patricia Hicks, M.D.
Assistant Professor, Division of General Academic Pediatrics, Department of Pediatrics, University of Texas Southwestern Medical Center at Dallas, Texas

Omar M. Hijazi, M.D.
Assistant Professor, Division of Pediatric Critical Care, Department of Pediatrics, The Chicago Medical School, Finch University of Health Science; Co-Director, Pediatric Intensive Care Unit, Mount Sinai Hospital, Chicago, Illinois

Michele S. Holecek, R.N., M.S.N., C.C.R.N.
Clinical Nurse Specialist, Children's Hospital of Orange County, Orange, California

LeeAnn Howard, R.N., C.C.R.N.
Clinical Nurse II, Pediatric Intensive Care Unit, West Texas State University, Canyon, Texas

H.K. Huang, M.D.
Professor and Vice Chairman, Department of Radiology, University of California at San Francisco, California

Martina Christine Hum, M.D.
Fellow in Pediatric Hematology-Oncology, University of Texas Southwestern Medical Center at Dallas, Texas

John L. Hunt, M.D.
Professor, Department of Surgery, University of Texas Southwestern Medical Center at Dallas, Texas

Susan T. Iannaccone, M.D.
Professor, Division of Pediatric Neurology, Department of Neurology, University of Texas Southwestern Medical Center at Dallas; Director, Neuromuscular Disease and Neurorehabilitation, Texas Scottish Rite Hospital for Children, Dallas, Texas

Mary Elaine Jones, Ph.D, R.N.
Professor, School of Nursing, University of Texas at Arlington, Texas

Pedro A. Jose, M.D., Ph.D.
Professor and Vice-Chair, Division of Nephrology, Departments of Pediatrics and Physiology, Georgetown University Medical Center, Washington, D.C.

Barton A. Kamen, M.D., Ph.D.
Professor, Departments of Pediatrics and Pharmacology, Carl B. and Florence E. King Foundation Distinguished Professor of Pediatric Oncology Research, and American Cancer Society Clinical Research Professor, University of Texas Southwestern Medical Center at Dallas, Texas

Thomas G. Keens, M.D.
Professor, Division of Neonatology and Pediatric Pulmonology, Children's Hospital, Los Angeles, California

David J. Keljo, M.D., Ph.D.
Associate Professor, Division of Pediatric Gastroenterology and Nutrition, Department of Pediatrics, University of Texas Southwestern Medical Center at Dallas, Texas

Vicki D. Kelley, M.S.
Child Life/Child Development Specialist, Children's Medical Center of Dallas, Texas

D. Christopher Keyes, M.D., M.P.H.
Director, North Texas Poison Center, Division of Emergency Medicine, University of Texas Southwestern Medical Center at Dallas, Texas

Erica A. Kirsch, M.D.
Fellow in Pediatric Critical Care, University of Texas Southwestern Medical Center at Dallas, Texas

Louann Kitchen, R.N., M.S.
Clinical Research Coordinator and Adjunct Clinical Instructor, Division of Pediatric Critical Care, Department of Critical Care, University of Texas at Arlington, Texas

Amjad A. Kouatli, M.D.
Fellow in Pediatric Cardiology, University of Texas Southwestern Medical Center at Dallas, Texas

Dennis F. Landers, M.D., Ph.D.
Professor and Chairman, Department of Anesthesiology and Pain Management, University of Texas Southwestern Medical Center at Dallas, Texas

Regina Lantin-Hermoso, M.D.
Fellow, Department of Pediatrics, University of Texas Southwestern Medical Center at Dallas, Texas

Gerald J. Lavandosky, M.D.
Pediatric Intensivist, Division of Pediatric Critical Care Medicine, Department of Pediatrics, Joe Dimaggio Children's Hospital, Hollywood, Florida

Steven R. Leonard, M.D.
Clinical Assistant Professor, Division of Cardiothoracic Surgery, Department of Surgery, University of Texas Southwestern Medical Center at Dallas, Texas

Daniel L. Levin, M.D.
Professor of Pediatrics, Dartmouth Medical School; Medical Director, Pediatric Intensive Care Unit, Children's Hospital at Dartmouth, Lebanon, New Hampshire; formerly Professor of Pediatrics, University of Texas Southwestern Medical Center at Dallas, and staff physician, Children's Medical Center of Dallas, Texas

Christine A. Lindsay, Pharm.D., B.C.P.S.
Clinical Coordinator, Pharmacy; Director, Clinical Pharmacology, Critical Care, Children's Medical Center of Dallas, Texas

Katherine Lipsky, A.C.S.W., L.M.S.W.-A.C.P.
Director, Department of Social Work, Children's Medical Center of Dallas, Texas

Patricia Ann Lowry, M.D.
Associate Professor, Division of Pediatric Radiology, Department of Radiology, Temple University Medical School, Philadelphia, Pennsylvania

Lea Lua, M.D.
Fellow in Critical Care Medicine, University of Texas Southwestern Medical Center at Dallas, Texas

Paul S. Lubinsky, M.B., Ch.B.
Director, Department of Pediatric Intensive Care, Children's Hospital at Mission, Orange, California

Peter M. Luckett, M.D.
Assistant Professor, Division of Pulmonary Medicine/Critical Care Medicine, Department of Pediatrics, University of Texas Southwestern Medical Center at Dallas, Texas

Rebecca R. Lynn, M.D.
Fellow in Pediatric Emergency Medicine, University of Texas Southwestern Medical Center at Dallas, Texas

Julie A. Mack, M.D.
Assistant Professor, Division of Pediatric Radiology, Department of Radiology, University of Texas Southwestern Medical Center at Dallas, Texas

Lynn Mahony, M.D.
Associate Professor, Division of Pediatric Cardiology, Department of Pediatrics, University of Texas Southwestern Medical Center at Dallas, Texas

Dallas M. Manly, B.S., R.R.T.
Coordinator of Education and Advocacy, Respiratory Care, Children's Medical Center of Dallas, Texas

Scott C. Manning, M.D.
Associate Professor, Department of Otolaryngology, University of Washington Children's Hospital and Medical Center, Seattle, Washington

James F. Marks, M.D., M.P.H.
Associate Professor, Division of Pediatric Endocrinology, Department of Pediatrics, University of Texas Southwestern Medical Center at Dallas, Texas

Marcy A. Martinez, L.M.S.W.-A.C.P.
Clinical Social Worker, Department of Social Work, Children's Medical Center of Dallas, Texas

William F. May, Ph.D.
Director, Cary M. Maguire Center for Ethics and Public Responsibility, Southern Methodist University, Dallas, Texas

Thomas Wm. Mayo, J.D.
Associate Professor, Southern Methodist University School of Law, Dallas, Texas

Karin A. McCloskey, M.D.
Associate Professor, Division of Pediatric Emergency Medicine, Department of Pediatrics, University of Texas Southwestern Medical Center at Dallas, Texas

George H. McCracken, Jr., M.D.
Professor of Pediatrics and Sarah M. and Charles E. Seay Chair in Pediatric Infectious Diseases, Department of Pediatrics, University of Texas Southwestern Medical Center at Dallas, Texas

Deborah McCurdy, M.D.
Associate Director, Division of Pediatric Rheumatology, Department of Pediatrics, Children's Hospital of Orange County, Orange, California

Mary J. McDonald, R.N., M.S.N.
Pediatric Nurse Practitioner, Children's Medical Center of Dallas, Texas

Desiree Medeiros, M.D.
Fellow in Pediatric Hematology-Oncology, University of Texas Southwestern Medical Center at Dallas, Texas

Stephen M. Megison, M.D.
Clinical Assistant Professor, Division of Pediatric Surgery, Department of Surgery, University of Texas Southwestern Medical Center at Dallas, Texas

Geralyn M. Meny, M.D.
Assistant Professor, Department of Pathology, University of Texas Southwestern Medical Center at Dallas, Texas

Van S. Miller, M.D., Ph.D.
Assistant Professor, Division of Pediatric Neurology, Department of Neurology, University of Texas Southwestern Medical Center at Dallas, Texas

Stephen F. Mills, Ph.D.
Director, Multimedia Applications, Berkom USA, Austin, Texas

Lisa M. Milonovich, R.N., B.S.N., C.C.R.N.
Clinical Nurse IV, Children's Medical Center of Dallas, Texas

Charles E. Mize, M.D., Ph.D.
Associate Professor, Division of Genetics and Metabolism, Department of Pediatrics, University of Texas Southwestern Medical Center at Dallas, Texas

David Moromisato, M.D.
Assistant Professor, Division of Respiratory and Critical Care, Department of Pediatrics, Harbor UCLA Medical Center, Torrance, California

Frances C. Morriss, M.D.
Associate Professor, Departments of Pediatrics and Anesthesia and Pain Management, University of Texas Southwestern Medical Center at Dallas, Texas

Fernando R. Moya, M.D.
Professor, Division of Neonatal-Perinatal Medicine, Department of Pediatrics, University of Texas Southwestern Medical Center at Dallas, Texas

Joseph T. Murphy, M.D.
Assistant Instructor, Department of Surgery, University of Texas Southwestern Medical Center at Dallas, Texas

Mahmoud M. Mustafa, M.D.
Consultant Pediatric Hematologist-Oncologist, Department of Oncology, King Faisal Specialist Hospital and Research Center, Riyadh, Saudi Arabia

Thomas T. Mydler, M.D.
Assistant Professor, Division of Pediatric Emergency Medicine, Department of Pediatrics, University of Texas Southwestern Medical Center at Dallas, Texas

Mohan R. Mysore, M.B., B.S.
Assistant Professor, Division of Critical Care Medicine, Department of Pediatrics, University of Wisconsin Medical School, Madison, Wisconsin

John D. Nelson, M.D.
Professor, Division of Pediatric Infectious Diseases, Department of Pediatrics, University of Texas Southwestern Medical Center at Dallas, Texas

Bruce G. Nickerson, M.D.
Associate Clinical Professor, Division of Cardiothoracic Surgery, Department of Pediatrics, UCLA School of Medicine, Los Angeles; Director, Pulmonary Medicine, Children's Hospital of Orange County, Orange, California

Hisashi Nikaidoh, M.D.
Clinical Associate Professor, Division of Cardiothoracic Surgery, Department of Surgery, University of Texas Southwestern Medical Center at Dallas; Director of Thoracic Surgery, Children's Medical Center of Dallas, Texas

Mary Nixon, R.N., B.A.
Pulmonary Case Manager, Children's Hospital of Orange County, Orange, California

Michelle Norr, R.N., B.S.N.
Organ Recovery Coordinator/Pediatric Coordinator, Southwest Organ Bank, Dallas, Texas

Pamela J. Okada, M.D.
Fellow in Pediatric Emergency Medicine, University of Texas Southwestern Medical Center at Dallas, Texas

Richard Orr, M.D.
Associate Professor, Division of Pediatric Critical Care Medicine, Departments of Anesthesiology/Critical Care Medicine and Pediatrics, University of Pittsburgh School of Medicine, Pittsburgh, Pennsylvania

Maria Ortega, M.D.
Anesthesiologist, Children's Medical Center of Dallas, Texas

A. Maurine Packard, M.D.
Resident, Department of Neurology, New York Hospital/Cornell Medical Center, New York, New York

M. Heather Paterson, R.N., C.C.R.N.
Clinical Nurse IV, Children's Medical Center of Dallas, Texas

Michael P. Penick, J.D.
Adjunct Professor, Southern Methodist University School of Law, Dallas, Texas

Ronald M. Perkin, M.D.
Professor and Associate Chairman, Department of Pediatrics; Director, Critical Care Medicine and Inpatient Respiratory Care, Loma Linda University Children's Hospital, Loma Linda, California

Vicky L. Pierce, R.N., B.S.N.
Clinical Nurse II, Children's Medical Center of Dallas, Texas

Susan Prestjohn, R.N., B.S.N.
Clinical Nurse III, Children's Medical Center of Dallas, Texas

Patricia A. Primm, M.D.
Assistant Professor, Division of Pediatric Emergency Medicine, Department of Pediatrics, University of Texas Southwestern Medical Center at Dallas, Texas

Marcia A. Pritchard, M.D.
Assistant Professor, Division of Pediatric Radiology, Department of Radiology, University of Texas Southwestern Medical Center at Dallas, Texas

Gary F. Purdue, M.D.
Professor, Department of Surgery, University of Texas Southwestern Medical Center at Dallas, Texas

Albert H. Quan, M.D.
Assistant Professor, Division of Pediatric Nephrology, Department of Pediatrics, University of Texas Southwestern Medical Center at Dallas, Texas

Raymond Quigley, M.D.
Assistant Professor, Division of Pediatric Nephrology, Department of Pediatrics, University of Texas Southwestern Medical Center at Dallas, Texas

Donna S. Rahn, R.N., B.S.N., C.C.R.N.
Clinical Nurse IV, Children's Medical Center of Dallas, Texas

Bala Ramachandran, M.B., B.S.
Fellow in Pediatric Critical Care, University of Texas Southwestern Medical Center at Dallas, Texas

Octavio Ramilo, M.D.
Assistant Professor, Division of Pediatric Infectious Diseases, Department of Pediatrics, University of Texas Southwestern Medical Center at Dallas, Texas

Soledad S. Ureta Raroque, M.D.
Fellow in Pediatric Emergency Medicine, University of Texas Southwestern Medical Center at Dallas, Texas

Anthony R. Riela, M.D.
Associate Professor, Division of Pediatric Neurology, Department of Neurology, University of Texas Southwestern Medical Center at Dallas, Texas

W. Steves Ring, M.D.
Frank M. Ryburn, Jr., Professor and Chairman, Division of Thoracic and Cardiovascular Surgery, Department of Surgery, University of Texas Southwestern Medical Center at Dallas, Texas

E. Steve Roach, M.D.
Helen and Robert S. Strauss Professor, Division of Pediatric Neurology, Department of Neurology, University of Texas Southwestern Medical Center at Dallas, Texas

Cassandra Rochon-Bailey, R.N., M.S., C.C.R.N.
Pediatric Intensive Care Nurse, Children's Medical Center of Dallas, Texas

Zora R. Rogers, M.D.
Assistant Professor, Division of Pediatric Hematology-Oncology, Department of Pediatrics, University of Texas Southwestern Medical Center at Dallas; Associate Medical Director, Pediatric Sickle Cell Clinic, Center for Cancer and Blood Disorders, Children's Medical Center of Dallas, Texas

Nancy K. Rollins, M.D.
Professor, Division of Pediatric Radiology, Department of Radiology, University of Texas Southwestern Medical Center at Dallas, Texas

Kathleen M. Rotondo, M.D.
Assistant Professor, Division of Pediatric Cardiology, Department of Pediatrics, University of Texas Southwestern Medical Center at Dallas, Texas

James A. Royall, M.D.
Associate Professor and Director, Pediatric Intensive Care Unit, Division of Pediatric Critical Care, Department of Pediatrics, The University of Iowa Hospitals and Clinics, Iowa City, Iowa

Susan J. Russell, M.B., B.S., F.R.A.C.P.
Lecturer, Department of Paediatric Haematology/Oncology, School of Paediatrics, University of New South Wales, Sidney, New South Wales, Australia

Christy I. Sandborg, M.D.
Associate Adjunct Professor, Division of Pediatric Rheumatology, Department of Pediatrics, University of California, Irvine, California

Eric S. Sandler, M.D.
Assistant Professor, Division of Pediatric Hematology-Oncology, Department of Pediatrics, University of Texas Southwestern Medical Center at Dallas, Texas

David N. Schell, M.B., B.S., F.R.A.C.P.
Staff Physician, Intensive Care, Royal Alexandra Hospital for Children, Westmead, Sydney, New South Wales, Australia

Adam J. Schwarz, M.D.
Fellow in Pediatric Critical Care, Harbor UCLA Medical Center, Torrance, California

Susan M. Scott, M.D.
Assistant Professor, Division of Pediatric Emergency Medicine, Department of Pediatrics, University of Texas Southwestern Medical Center at Dallas, Texas

William A. Scott, M.D.
Associate Professor, Division of Pediatric Cardiology, Department of Pediatrics, University of Texas Southwestern Medical Center at Dallas, Texas

Mouin G. Seikaly, M.D.
Associate Professor, Division of Pediatric Nephrology, Department of Pediatrics, University of Texas Southwestern Medical Center at Dallas, Texas

Kathleen Seikel, M.D.
Postdoctoral Fellow in Pediatric Emergency Medicine, University of Texas Southwestern Medical Center at Dallas, Texas

Kenneth Shapiro, M.D.
Clinical Associate Professor, Department of Neurological Surgery, University of Texas Southwestern Medical Center at Dallas, Texas

Patrick C. Sharp, Pharm.D.
Pediatric Clinical Specialist, Children's Hospital of Orange County, Orange, California

Philip W. Shaul, M.D.
Associate Professor, Division of Neonatal-Perinatal Medicine, Department of Pediatrics, University of Texas Southwestern Medical Center at Dallas, Texas

Jane D. Siegel, M.D.
Professor, Division of Pediatric Infectious Diseases, Department of Pediatrics, University of Texas Southwestern Medical Center at Dallas, Texas

Balbir Singh, M.D.
Assistant Professor, Division of Pediatric Neurology, Department of Neurology, University of Texas Southwestern Medical Center at Dallas, Texas

Douglas P. Sinn, D.D.S.
Professor and Chairman, Division of Oral and Maxillofacial Surgery, Department of Surgery, University of Texas Southwestern Medical Center at Dallas, Texas

Frederick H. Sklar, M.D.
Clinical Associate Professor, Division of Pediatric Neurosurgery, Department of Surgery, University of Texas Southwestern Medical Center at Dallas; Director, Pediatric Neurosurgery, Children's Medical Center of Dallas, Texas

John F. Sommerauer, M.D.
Associate Professor, Division of Pediatric Critical Care Medicine, Department of Pediatrics, University of Texas Southwestern Medical Center at Dallas, Texas

Steven P. Sparagana, M.D.
Assistant Professor, Division of Pediatric Neurology, Department of Neurology, University of Texas Southwestern Medical Center at Dallas, Texas

Judy B. Splawski, M.D.
Associate Professor, Division of Pediatric Gastroenterology and Nutrition, Department of Pediatrics, University of Texas Southwestern Medical Center at Dallas, Texas

Janet E. Squires, M.D.
Associate Professor, Division of General Pediatrics, Department of Pediatrics, University of Texas Southwestern Medical Center at Dallas, Texas

Robert H. Squires, Jr., M.D.
Associate Professor, Division of Pediatric Gastroenterology and Nutrition, Department of Pediatrics, University of Texas Southwestern Medical Center at Dallas, Texas

Michael W. Stannard, M.D.
Associate Professor, Division of Pediatric Radiology, Department of Radiology, University of Texas Southwestern Medical Center at Dallas, Texas

Dusit Staworn, M.D.
Assistant Professor, Division of Pulmonary and Critical Care, Department of Pediatrics, Pramongkutklao Hospital, Bangkok, Thailand

Joel B. Steinberg, M.D.
Robert L. Moore Chair in Pediatrics, General Academic Pediatric Department, University of Southwestern Medical Center at Dallas, Texas

Richard R. Sterrett, M.D.
Adjunct Clinical Instructor, Department of Pediatrics, University of Nevada School of Medicine, Las Vegas, Nevada

Rocky Stone, R.R.T., R.C.P.
Clinical Coordinator, Respiratory Care, Children's Hospital of Orange County, Orange, California

Laurie J. Sutor, M.D.
Assistant Professor, Department of Pathology, University of Texas Southwestern Medical Center at Dallas, Texas

Dale M. Swift, M.D.
Assistant Clinical Professor, Department of Neurological Surgery, University of Texas Southwestern Medical Center at Dallas, Texas

James D. Swift, M.D.
Assistant Director, Pediatric Intensive Care Unit, Division of Pediatric Critical Care Medicine, The Columbia Children's Hospital/Medical City, Dallas, Texas

Jeanne S. Takano, M.D.
Fellow in Pediatric Critical Care, University of Texas Southwestern Medical Center at Dallas, Texas

Murat M. Tanik, Ph.D.
Professor, Department of Computer and Information Science, New Jersey Institute of Technology, Newark, New Jersey

Diana Hopkins Taylor, R.N., M.S.N.
Transport Coordinator, Transport Services, Children's Medical Center of Dallas, Texas

James A. Thomas, M.D.
Assistant Professor, Division of Pediatric Critical Care Medicine, Department of Pediatrics, University of Texas Southwestern Medical Center at Dallas, Texas

Marita T. Thompson, M.D.
Fellow in Pediatric Intensive Care, University of Texas Southwestern Medical Center at Dallas, Texas

W. Raleigh Thompson, M.D.
Assistant Professor, Division of Pediatric Surgery, Department of Surgery, University of Texas Southwestern Medical Center at Dallas, Texas

Lisa Thompson-Bush, R.N.
Pediatric Intensive Care Nurse, Children's Medical Center of Dallas, Texas

Cathleen A. Tipton, R.M.A., E.M.T.
Cardiovascular Technologist, Children's Medical Center of Dallas, Texas

Kory D. Toro, R.R.T.
Critical Care Team Leader, Children's Medical Center of Dallas, Texas

Luis O. Toro-Figueroa, M.D.
Associate Professor, Division of Pediatric Critical Care Medicine, Department of Pediatrics, University of Texas Southwestern Medical Center at Dallas; Medical Director, Respiratory Care, Children's Medical Center of Dallas, Texas

Monica Trujillo, M.D.
Fellow in Pediatric Infectious Diseases, University of Texas Southwestern Medical Center at Dallas, Texas

Amir Vardi, M.D.
Instructor, Division of Pediatrics, Tel-Aviv University Sackler School of Medicine, Sheba Medical Center, Tel-Aviv, Israel

Richard L. Vinson, C.R.T.T.
Respiratory Pulmonary Function Therapist, Pulmonary Function Laboratory, Children's Medical Center of Dallas, Texas

Theodore P. Votteler, M.D.
Clinical Professor, Departments of Surgery and Pediatrics, University of Texas Southwestern Medical Center at Dallas, Texas

Lewis J. Waber, M.D.
Associate Professor, Division of Genetics and Metabolism, Department of Pediatrics, University of Texas Southwestern Medical Center at Dallas, Texas

John Wallace, B.S.N., C.C.R.N., C.P.T.C.
Assistant Manager, Southwest Organ Bank, Dallas, Texas

David A. Waller, M.D.
Associate Professor, Departments of Psychiatry and Pediatrics; Director, Division of Child and Adolescent Psychiatry, Department of Psychiatry, University of Texas Southwestern Medical Center at Dallas, Texas

Patricia Walters, R.R.T., R.P.F.T.
Pulmonary Laboratory Technologist, Children's Medical Center of Dallas, Texas

Richard L. Wasserman, M.D., Ph.D.
Clinical Assistant Professor, Division of Allergy and Immunology, Department of Pediatrics, University of Texas Southwestern Medical Center at Dallas, Texas

Mehernoor F. Watcha, M.D.
Associate Professor and Director, Pediatric Anesthesia Research, Department of Anesthesiology and Pain Management, University of Texas Southwestern Medical Center at Dallas, Texas

Ellen M. Weinstein, M.D.
Assistant Professor, Division of Pediatric Cardiology, Department of Pediatrics, University of Texas Southwestern Medical Center at Dallas; Director, Echocardiography Laboratory, Children's Medical Center of Dallas, Texas

Laura A. Wells, R.N., B.S.N., C.C.R.N.
Clinical Nurse III, Children's Medical Center of Dallas, Texas

Linda White, R.N., B.S.N.
Electrophysiology Nurse, Children's Medical Center of Dallas, Texas

Perrin C. White, M.D.
Professor, Division of Pediatric Endocrinology, Department of Pediatrics, University of Texas Southwestern Medical Center at Dallas, Texas

Melissa J. Whitehead, R.N.
Staff Nurse, Children's Medical Center of Dallas, Texas

Robert A. Wiebe, M.D.
Professor, Division of Pediatric Emergency Medicine, Department of Pediatrics, University of Texas Southwestern Medical Center at Dallas, Texas

Joe K. Wieber
Systems Analyst, Information Services, Children's Medical Center of Dallas, Texas

Gary D. Williams, M.B., B.S., F.R.A.C.P.
Lecturer, Division of Paediatrics, Department of Intensive Care, University of New South Wales, Sidney, New South Wales, Australia

Penny G. Williams, R.N., M.S.
Education Specialist, Emergency Center, Children's Medical Center of Dallas, Texas

Naomi J. Winick, M.D.
Associate Professor, Division of Pediatric Hematology-Oncology, Department of Pediatrics, University of Texas Southwestern Medical School at Dallas, Texas

Janice W. Woods, M.D.
Assistant Professor, Division of Critical Care, Department of Pediatrics, Martin Luther King/Drew Medical Center, Los Angeles, California

Sheryl Wright, M.D.
Assistant Professor, Division of Pediatric Critical Care, University of Texas Health Science Center at San Antonio; Associate Medical Director, Pediatric Intensive Care Unit, University Hospital, San Antonio, Texas

Michael L. Wyman, M.D.
Assistant Professor, Division of Neonatal-Perinatal Medicine, Department of Pediatrics, University of Texas Southwestern Medical Center at Dallas, Texas

Raymond T. Yeh, Ph.D.
Distinguished Research Professor, Department of Computer and Information Science, New Jersey Institute of Technology, Newark, New Jersey

Stephanie H. Yeh
Account Manager, International Software Systems, Inc., Austin, Texas

Thomas M. Zellers, M.D.
Associate Professor, Division of Pediatric Cardiology, Department of Pediatrics, University of Texas Southwestern Medical Center at Dallas, Texas

R. Jeff Zwiener, M.D.
Associate Professor, Division of Pediatric Gastroenterology and Nutrition, Department of Pediatrics, University of Texas Southwestern Medical Center at Dallas, Texas

To

The Professional and Administrative Staff
Children's Medical Center of Dallas
1975-1996

and to

Our Departed Mentors and Colleagues:
William H. Tooley, M.D.
William T. Jenkins, M.D.
Steven J. Boros, M.D.
John C. Reedy, M.D.

and, as always, to

Micah, Brendan, Erin, and Laura

Preface

A review of the prefaces of the earlier versions of *Essentials of Pediatric Intensive Care* serves as a vivid reminder of the tremendous advances that have occurred in the field. When we began work on our first book in 1976, our goal was to address the need for an elementary review of organ system failure in pediatric patients since no useful collective body of information dealing with the sickest pediatric patients was available at that time. This culminated in the publication of a book representing the efforts of clinicians for all aspects of the pediatric health care community in 1979. Changes in the field prompted an update in 1984. By the time we published the first edition under the current title with QMP in 1990 the scope of interest and depth of technical expertise as well as the formal recognition by organized medicine were apparent. The publication of several excellent textbooks in pediatric critical care pointed to the growing interest in this field of medicine. However, in retrospect, we see that this heralded only the beginning of the multitude of changes we were to witness.

A speaker remarked recently that a high school science student today knows more physics than Sir Isaac Newton. By analogy, we believe that the average pediatric resident has a greater knowledge of pediatric critical care medicine than we did when we started the Pediatric Intensive Care Unit at Children's Medical Center of Dallas in July of 1975. Today medical students and residents routinely use therapeutic agents and technologies that we only dreamed of 20 years ago and the pace of development is accelerating. Hence the size and complexity of this book has grown enormously since we first tried to answer questions about why patients do not breath or maintain a blood pressure and describe the tools available for treatment. We now have a dazzling array of diagnostic, monitoring, and therapeutic approaches to choose from. For example, the inclusion of chapters on molecular intensive care, extracorporeal membrane oxygenation, liquid ventilation, and immunobiology of transplant medicine are evidence of recent progress. However, at least two major problems face us in the utilization of these new resources.

One is recognizing that the financial resources that can be devoted to health care are not without limits. The impact of managed health care on medicine in general and pediatric intensive care in particular has yet to be determined. This applies to education and research as well as patient care. We disagree with those experts who predict that fewer resources will be allocated to advanced technology. Without doubt, we will be compelled to provide more efficient medical care, and chapters dealing with process modeling and computerization have been added to help achieve this goal. Society may insist that we provide higher quality of care at lower cost, but we do not believe that it will condone jeopardizing our children and denying them aggressive care.

On a more philosophical level, we are faced with the task of learning how to logically and compassionately apply new diagnostic, monitoring, and therapeutic technologies. Efficient use of resources is one aspect of controlling costs; another, more difficult aspect is the appropriate application of our skills. Statements such as "One must do everything for the patient" or "We want you to do everything possible to save our child's life" that once reflected our collective mortality and ethics may not be appropriate in today's health care environment. In a way, our technical skill has outpaced our psychological and philosophical ability to deal with our physical capabilities. The layman certainly cannot understand the implications of "I want everything done." Therefore we need to be careful to define the difference between therapeutic efforts that will possibly benefit the patient and those that simply prolong death. The former is certainly our mission, but the latter may in reality prove to be the case. Medicine has become so complex that sometimes we may not even know when a patient is dead. We can have a patient who is alive, in a coma, without a functioning heart, lungs, kidney, or gastrointestinal tract, have a donor liver, a reversed coagulation system, a blocked immune system, and a pharmacologically paralyzed musculoskeletal system. Is he alive? We must learn to balance our knowledge and skill with compassion, respect for persons, and respect for death as well as respect for life. Chapters entitled "Bioethics," "Determination of Death, "Medical Futility," "Withholding and Withdrawing Life-Sustaining Care," and "Delivery of Culturally Sensitive Care" address these important issues.

In the current health care climate the dynamics of hospital care may change so dramatically in the foreseeable future that children's hospitals will become centers for treatment of children either as outpatients or as intensive care patients. If this occurs, the next edition may well be entitled *Pediatric Critical Care Medicine: A Texbook of In-Patient Medicine*. Whatever the title, it will include much new information if we are permitted and encouraged by society to continue to study in the laboratory and in the hospital and to use the knowledge gained to develop even better diagnostic, monitoring, and therapeutic skills. If we are given this charge, we must also devote at least as much time and energy to understanding when to apply these skills as to how to apply them.

Daniel L. Levin
Frances C. Morriss

Contents

Volume One: Pathophysiology, Monitoring, and Treatment

IV. Inflammation

V. Infection

VI. Hematology/Oncology

XI. Gastrointestinal

XII. Poisoning, Ingestions, and Toxins

XIII. Trauma and Environmental Hazards

Volume Two: Procedures, Equipment, and Techniques

XXI. Transfusions and Blood Products

XXII. Renal Replacement Therapy

Abbreviations

$A\text{-}aD_{O_2}$	alveolar-arterial oxygen difference		BPD	bronchopulmonary dysplasia
AAMS	Association of Air Medical Services		BPI	bactericidal/permeability increasing protein
AAP	American Academy of Pediatrics		BSA	body surface area
ABC	airway, breathing, and circulation		BSI	bloodsteam infections
ABG	arterial blood gas		BTPS	body temperature, ambient pressure, saturated
ABW	actual body weight			
AC	alternating current		BUN	blood urea nitrogen
ACE	angiotension-converting enzyme		BVM	bag-valve mask
ACh	acetylcholine			
AChe	actylcholinesterase		CAAMS	Commission for Accreditation of Air Medical Services
ACS	acute chest syndrome			
ACT	activated clotting time		CAH	congenital adrenal hyperplasia
ADH	antidiuretic hormone		CAM	cell adhesion molecules
ADP	adenosine diphosphate		cAMP	cyclic adenosine monophosphate
AG	abdominal girth		Ca_{O_2}	arterial O_2 content
AJD_{O_2}	arteriojugular difference for oxygen		CAPD	chronic ambulatory peritoneal dialysis
ALS	air leak syndrome		CAPP	coronary artery perfusion pressure
ALT	alanine aminotransferase		CAVH	continuous arteriovenous hemofiltration
ALTE	apparent life-threatening events		CBF	cerebral blood flow
AMP	adenosine monophosphate		CBG	capillary blood gas
ANA	antinuclear antibody		Cc_{O_2}	capillary O_2 content
APSAC	anisoylated plasminogen-streptokinase activator complex		C_{cr}	creatinine clearance
			C_{cw}	chest wall compliance
APTT	activated partial thromboplastin time		CDH	congenital diaphragmatic hernia
ARDS	acute respiratory distress syndrome		C_{Dyn}	dynamic lung compliance
ARF	acute respiratory failure		CGD	chronic granulomatous disease
ASA	American Society of Anesthesiologists		cGMP	cyclic guanosine monophosphate
ASD	atrial septal defect		CHEOPS	Children's Hospital of Eastern Ontario Pain Scale
AST	aspartate transaminase			
ATGAM	antithymocyte globulin		CHF	congestive heart failure
ATLS	acute tumor lysis syndrome		CI	cardiac index
ATN	acute tubular necrosis		CIMS	clinical information management systems
ATP	adenosine 5'-triphosphate		C_L	lung compliance
ATPase	adenosine triphosphatase		Cl	clearance
ATS	American Thoracic Society		cM	centimorgan
AUC	area under the curve		CMV	cytomegalovirus; conventional mechanical ventilation
AV	arteriovenous; atrioventricular			
$a\text{-}vD_{O_2}$	arteriovenous oxygen difference		CNP	c-type natriuretic peptide
AVM	arteriovenous malformation		CO	cardiac output
			Co_2	oxygen content of blood
BAEP	brain stem auditory evoked potential		COPD	chronic obstructive pulmonary disease
BAL	bronchoalveolar lavage		Cp	drug concentration in plasma
BCG	bacille Calmette-Guérin		CPAP	continuous positive airway pressure
BiPAP	bilevel positive airway pressure		CPB	cardiopulmonary bypass
BMI	body mass index		CPD	citrate phosphate dextrose
BMT	bone marrow transplantation		CPP	cerebral perfusion pressure

CPS	pulmonary system compliance		EVL	endoscopic variceal ligation
Cp_{ss}	steady-state plasma concentration			
CPT	chest physiotherapy		FAA	Federal Aviation Administration
CRC	catheter-related colonization		FAD	flavin adenine dinucleotide
CRP	C-reactive protein		FDP	fibrin degradation product
CRS	catheter-related sepsis		FENa	fractional excretion of sodium
CSF	cerebrospinal fluid		FF	filtration fraction
CVC	central venous catheter		FFP	fresh frozen plasma
Cv_{O_2}	mixed venous O_2 content		FHF	fulminant hepatic failure
CVP	central venous pressure		Fi_{O_2}	fraction of inspired O_2
CVVH	continuous veno-venous hemofiltration		FOC	frontal-occipital circumference
CW	continuous wave		FRC	functional residual capacity
CyA	cyclosporin A		FRF	filter replacement fluids
			FWD	free water deficits
DA	dopaminergic			
DAD	diffuse alveolar disease		GABA	gamma-aminobutyric acid
DAG	diacylglycerol		GASLV	gravity-assisted spontaneous liquid ventilation
DC	direct current			
DCM	dilated cardiomyopathy		GCS	Glasgow Coma Scale
DDAVP	desmopressin acetate		GDP	dimeric guanine nucleotide
DIC	disseminated intravascular coagulation		GER	gastroesophageal reflux
DKA	diabetic ketoacidosis		GFR	glomerular filtration rate
DMSA	dimercaptosuccinic acid		GGT	gamma-glutamyltransferase
DNase	deoxyribonuclease		Gi	inhibitory G protein
Do_2	total oxygen delivery		GM-CSF	granulocyte-monocyte colony stimulating factor
DORA	Dynamic Objective Risk Assessment		GMSPS	Glasgow Meningococcal Septicemia Prognostic Score
2,3-DPG	2,3-diphosphoglycerate			
DPPC	dipalmitoylphosphatidylcholine		Gs	stimulatory G protein
dsDNA	double-stranded DNA		GSB	group B *Streptococcus*
DTPA	diethylenetriamine pentaacetic acid		GSH	glutathione
			G6PD	glucose-6-phosphate dehydrogenase
EACA	epsilon-aminocaproic acid		GSSG	oxidized glutathione
EBV	Epstein-Barr virus		GTP	heterotrimeric guanine nucleotide
EBW	effective body weight		GVHD	graft-vs.-host disease
ECF	extracellular fluid			
ECLS	extracorporeal life support		Hb	hemoglobin
ECMO	extracorporeal membrane oxygenation		HBcAb	hepatitis B core antibody
EDHF	endothelial-dependent hyperpolarizing factor		HBsAg	hepatitis B surface antigen
			HC	heel-to-crown length
EDRF	endothelial-derived relaxing factor		Hct	hematocrit
EDTA	ethylenediaminetetraacetic acid		HCV	hepatitis C virus
EF	ejection fraction		HFFI	high-frequency flow interruption
EGD	esophagogastroduodenoscopy		HFJV	high-frequency jet ventilation
EIA	enzyme immunoassay		HFLOV	HFOV with liquid ventilation
ELAMs	endothelium-leukocyte adhesion molecules		HFOV	high-frequency oscillatory ventilation
ELISA	enzyme-linked immunosorbent assay		HFPPV	high-frequency positive pressure ventilation
ELSO	Extracorporeal Life Support Organization		HFV	high-frequency ventilation
EMD	electromechanical dissociation		Hib	*Haemophilus influenzae* type b
EOG	electro-oculography		HIE	hypoxic-ischemic encephalopathy
ERCP	endoscopic retrograde cholangiopancreatography		HIV	human immunodeficiency virus
			HLA	human leukocyte antigen
ERPF	effective renal plasma flow		HMD	hyaline membrane disease
ESR	erythrocyte sedimentation rate		HME	heat and moisture exchanger
ESRD	end-stage renal disease		HPLC	high-pressure liquid chromotography
$etco_2$	end-tidal carbon dioxide		HSP	Henoch-Schönlein purpura

HSV	herpes simplex virus
5-HT	5-hydroxytryptamine
HTR	hemolytic transfusion reaction
HUS	hemolytic-uremic syndrome
IABP	intra-aortic balloon pump
IBW	ideal body weight
ICAM	intercellular adhesion molecule
ICF	intracellular fluid
ICH	intracranial hemorrhage
ICP	intracranial pressure
I:E	inspiratory-expiratory time ratio
Ig	immunoglobulin
IL	interleukin
IMV	intermittent mandatory ventilation
INR	international normalized ratio
IO	intraosseous
IP_3	inositol phosphate
IPPB	intermittent positive pressure breathing
ISI	international sensitivity index
ITP	immune thrombocytopenic purpura
IVAD	intradermal venous access device
IVC	inferior vena cava
IVIg	intravenous immunoglobulin
IVOX	intravascular oxygenation
JCAHO	Joint Commission on Accreditation of Healthcare Organizations
JDM	juvenile dermatomyositis
JRA	juvenile rheumatoid arthritis
K_e	elimination rate constant
K_f	ultrafiltration coefficient
KUF	membrane ultrafiltration coefficient
LA	latex agglutination
LAN	local area network
LAP	left atrial pressure
LBM	lean body mass
LBP	lipopolysaccharide binding protein
LDH	lactic dehydrogenase
LIP	lymphoid interstitial pneumonia
LMA	laryngeal mask airway
LMWH	low molecular weight heparin
LPA	latex particle agglutination tests
LPD	lymphoproliferative disease
LPS	lipopolysaccharide
LTP	laryngotracheoplasty
LVEDP	left ventricular end-diastolic pressure
LVEDV	left ventricular end-diastolic volume
MAC	midarm circumference
MAI	*Mycobacterius avium-intracellulare*
MAMC	midarm muscle circumference
MAOI	monomine oxidase inhibitor

MAP	mean arterial pressure
MAS	meconium aspiration syndrome
MBC	minimum bactericidal concentrations
MCT	medium-chain triglyceride
MDI	metered dose inhaler
MH	malignant hyperthermia
MHAUS	Malignant Hyperthermia Association of the United States
MHC	major histocompatibility complex
MIC	minimum inhibitory concentration
MODS	multiple organ dysfunction syndrome
MOF	multiple organ failure
MOSF	multiple organ system failure
MRSA	methicillin-resistant *Stapylococcus aureus*
MUGA	multiple gated acquisition
NADH	*N*-methyl-D-aspartate
NADPH	nicotinamide adenine dinucleotide phosphate
NASPE	North American Society for Pacing and Electrophysiology
NAST	Neonatal Abstinence Scoring Tool
NCCLS	National Committee for Clinical Laboratory Standards
NE	norepinephrine
NEEP	negative PEEP
NMS	neuroleptic malignant syndrome
NNIS	National Nosocomial Infections Surveillance System
NO	nitric oxide
NREM	non-rapid eye movement
NSAID	nonsteroidal anti-inflammatory drug
NTSB	National Transportation Safety Board
OCR	oculocephalic reflex
β-OHB	beta-hydroxybutyric acid
OI	oxygenation index
OLT	orthotopic liver transplantation
OSAS	obstructive sleep apnea syndrome
OSHA	Occupational Safety and Health Administration
OTFC	oral transmucosal fentanyl citrate
P_{ACO_2}	alveolar CO_2 tension
Pa_{CO_2}	arterial CO_2 tension
PACU	postanesthesia care unit
PADP	pulmonary artery diastolic pressure
PAF	platelet activating factor
PAGE	perfluorocarbon-associated gas exchange
PAH	para-aminohippurate
PAI	plasminogen activator inhibitor
PALS	pediatric advanced life support
PAN	polyarteritis nodosa
P_{AO_2}	alveolar O_2 tension
Pa_{O_2}	arterial O_2 tension
PAoP	pulmonary arterial occlusion pressure
PAP	pulmonary arterial pressure

P$\overline{aw}$	mean airway pressure	RFI	renal failure index
P$_B$	barametric pressure	RIA	radioimmunoassay
PBLS	pediatric basic life support	RPF	renal plasma flow
PC	platelet concentrate	RPR	rapid plasma reagin
PCA	patient-controlled analgesia	RS	Reye's syndrome
PCP	*Pneumocystis carinii* pneumonia	RSV	respiratory syncytial virus
PCPC	Pediatric Cerebral Performance Category	rTPA	recombinant tissue plasminogen activator
PCR	polymerase chain reaction	RVEDP	right ventricular end-diastolic pressure
PCWP	pulmonary capillary wedge pressure	RVEDV	right ventricular end-diastolic volume
PDA	patent ductus arteriosus		
PDE	phosphodiesterase	SA	sinoatrial
PEEP	positive end-expiratory pressure	Sao$_2$	arterial O$_2$ saturation
PET	positron emission tomography	SCD	sickle cell disease
Petco$_2$	end-tidal CO$_2$ tension	SCFA	short-chain fatty acid
PFC	perfluorocarbon	SCIDS	severe combined immunodeficiency syndrome
PFCe	PFC emulsion	SCUF	slow continuous ultrafiltration
PG	prostaglandin	SDP	signal donor platelet
pH	hydrogen ion concentration	SIADH	syndrome of inappropriate secretion of anti-diuretic hormone
PICVC	peripherally inserted central venous catheter	SIDS	sudden infant death syndrome
Pio$_2$	inspired partial pressure of oxygen	SIMV	synchronized intermittent manadatory ventilation
PIP	peak inspiratory pressure		
PIP$_2$	phosphatidylinositol 4,5-biphosphate	SIRS	systemic inflammatory response syndrome
PKC	protein kinase C	SIV	simiam immunodeficiency virus
PLUG	plug the lung until it grows	Sjvo$_2$	jugular O$_2$ saturation
PLV	partial liquid ventilation	SLT	Shiga-like toxin
PMN	polymorphonuclear leukocyte	SLV	spontaneous liquid ventilation
POPC	Pediatric Overall Performance Category	SP	surfactant protein
PPD	purified protein derivative	SPAG	small-particle aerosol generator
PPF	plasma protein fraction	SSEP	somatosensory evoked potential
PPHN	persistent pulmonary hypertension of the newborn	SU	shoulder-to-umbilicus length
		SV	stroke volume
PRA	preformed reactive antibodies	SVR	systemic vascular resistance
PRBCs	packed red blood cells	SVC	superior vena cava
PRISM	Pediatric Risk of Mortality	SVCS	superior vena cava syndrome
PSI	Physiologic Stability Index	Svo$_2$	mixed venous oxygen saturation
PSS	progressive systemic sclerosis	SVT	supraventricular tachycardia
PT	prothrombin		
Ptcco$_2$	transcutaneous CO$_2$ tension	t$_{1/2}$	half-life
Ptco$_2$	transcutaneous O$_2$ tension	TBSA	total body surface area
PTH	parathyroid hormone	TBW	total body water; total body weight
PTT	partial thromboplastin time	TBX$_2$	thromboxane
PTU	propylthiouracil	tcco$_2$	transcutaneous CO$_2$
PVR	pulmonary vascular resistance	tco$_2$	transcutaneous O$_2$
PVL	pressure-volume loop	T$_e$	expiratory time
Pvo$_2$	mixed venous O$_2$ tension	TEE	transesophageal echocardiography
Pw	pulsed wave	TEN	total enteral nutrition
P$_x$	plasma drug concentration	TF	tissue factor
		TFVL	tidal flow volume loop
RAP	right atrial pressure	TGF	transforming growth factor
Raw	airways resistance	THAM	tris[hydroxymethyl]aminomethane; tromethamine
RBF	renal blood flow		
RDA	recommended dietary allowance		
RDS	respiratory distress syndrome	THFV	transthoracic high-frequency oscillation
REM	rapid eye movement	T$_i$	inspiratory time

TIA	transient ischemic attack	V_{comp}	circuit compressible volume
TIBC	total iron binding capacity	V_D	dead space ventilation
TISS	Therapeutic Intervention Scoring System	V_d	volume of distribution
TLV	total liquid ventilation	V_E	minute ventilation
TMP	transmembrane pressure	VEP	visual evoked potential
TMP/SMX	trimethoprim/sulfamethoxazole	$V_{O_2}I$	oxygen consumption index
TNF	tumor necrosis factor	VOSS	ventilation oxygenation support system
t-PA	tissue plasminogen activator	$\dot{V}/\dot{Q}$	ventilation-perfusion ratio
TPN	total parenteral nutrition	VRE	vancomycin-resistant enterococci
TSF	triceps skinfold	VSD	ventricular septal defect
TSH	thyroid-stimulating hormone	V_T	tidal volume
TTE	transthoracic echocardiography	VT_d	delivered tidal volume
TTKG	transtubular K concentration gradient	VV	veno-venous
TTP	thrombotic thrombocytopenia purpura	vWF	von Willebrand's factor
		VZIG	varicella immune globulin
UFR	ultrafiltration rate	VZV	varicella-zoster virus
UF_x	ultrafiltrate drug concentration		
UVC	umbilical venous catheter	ZDV	zidovudine
		ZEEP	zero PEEP
VA	venoarterial		
VAD	ventricular assist device		

XVI
General Considerations

121 The Physical Setting: Conceptual Considerations

Daniel L. Levin

BACKGROUND

The role that the actual physical environment plays in the successful management of critically ill children must not be underestimated. A well-designed unit facilitates the work of the entire health care team and supports both the child's and family's needs for privacy, quiet, and comfort. It is critical that the design of the unit addresses the needs of all these people.

Even in the most ideal circumstances, designers of PICUs inevitably face numerous constraints, including financial, geographic, personnel, and political issues. The challenge to the designers and planners is to identify and prioritize the major functions and requirements of the unit and choose among the many options to meet these objectives. Without careful ordering of objectives, optimal decisions about unit design cannot be made.

It is also critical that the design team adopt a long-range perspective of the unit's functions and requirements. This futuristic perspective must be based on a comprehensive strategic planning process and reflect a unit mission that has evolved from careful analysis of both internal and external factors. In today's rapidly changing health care environment, it is unwise to assume that patient populations, team composition and function, treatment modalities, and resources currently available will remain as they are in the future. Major changes in any one of these variables can drastically change the physical requirements of the unit. Therefore a unit designed for the future must be adaptable and expandable and must maximize the resources of space, time, equipment, communication, and personnel. Conduits, cables, and work surfaces need to be designed for easy adaptation.

ALLOCATION OF SPACE

One of the first decisions to make is about division and allocation of a limited amount of space. This is perhaps the most difficult decision and one that is essential to effective and efficient functioning of the unit (Fig. 121-1).

Patient Care Areas

Before decisions about allocation of space can be made, the number of beds to comprise the unit must be determined. The number of beds can be determined by analyzing the following data. Historical PICU occupancy statistics provide the starting point. In addition to looking at average daily census, it is important to look at the maximum daily census. If adequate systems are not in place to ensure efficient patient flow out of the unit, it is highly likely the maximum census will greatly exceed the average daily census. The number of beds available in the unit must accommodate this increased patient load, even if only for 6 hours of the day. Other important variables that will affect future bed use include the com-

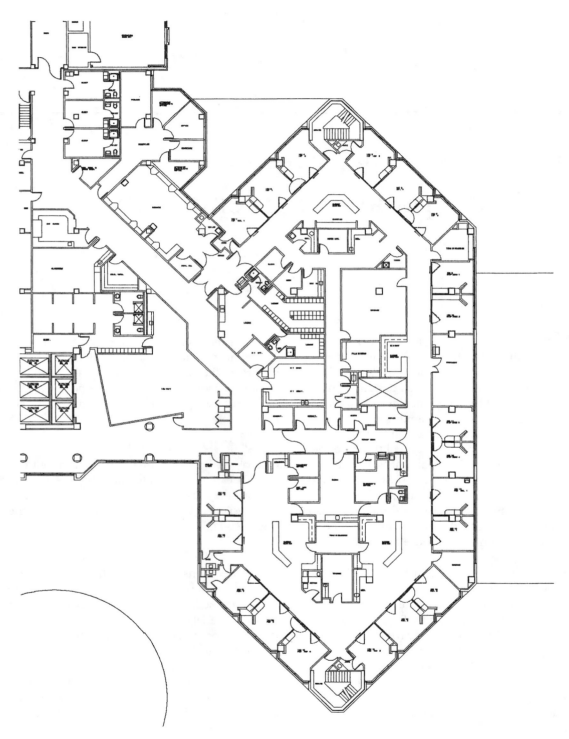

Fig. 121-1   Overall unit design. (Courtesy HKS, Inc., Dallas, Tex.)

petitive health care environment in the area, the planned addition or deletion of programs that involve a PICU stay, and demographic trend projections for the area. Finally, the number of beds in the unit may in part be determined by comparing space per patient required and desired with actual space available.

State codes govern the amount of space required per patient and the minimum distance required between patients. For example, in Texas the Hospital Licensing Standards stipulate that neonatal ICUs must have a minimum area of 100 square feet per bed and that the distance between beds must be at least 6 feet. For PICUs, a minimum square footage of 120 feet is required. Clearance between beds must be at least 4½ feet. The amount of space required by code may be much less than the amount of space desired. Technologically sophisticated units may need as much as 200 square feet per bed to accommodate routine (numerous IV poles and pumps and ventilator) and special patient care needs (hemodialysis, extracorporeal membrane oxygenation, and portable nuclear scans) (Fig. 121-2). Individual bed space requirements may limit the overall bed capacity of the unit.

Minimum requirements for isolation are also governed by state codes. In Texas one private room to be used for seclusion and/or isolation must be provided for each 10 beds or one for each unit if the

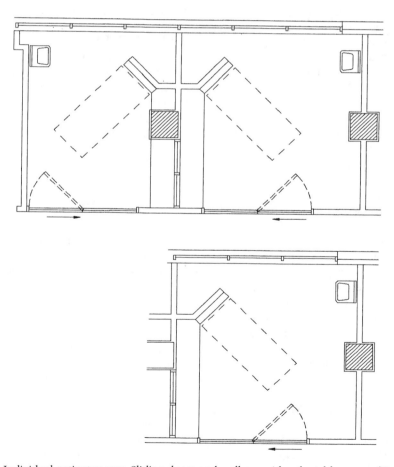

Fig. 121-2 Individual patient rooms. Sliding doors and walls provide adaptable space. (Courtesy HKS, Inc., Dallas, Tex.)

overall bed capacity is less than 10 beds. It is also necessary for planners to consider the isolation requirements or preferences for anticipated patient populations. For example, although not a universal practice, individual transplant surgeons may desire isolation rooms for their patients. Also to be considered are the recommendations of the Centers for Disease Control and Prevention for replacing traditional forms of isolation with body substance isolation, thereby decreasing the number of isolation rooms needed.

Support Services

State codes also govern the minimum requirements for kinds of support areas. For example, in Texas the Hospital Licensing Standards stipulate that a storage space of not less than 20 square feet be provided in neonatal ICUs. Other requirements include a workroom, examination and treatment room, formula room, janitor closet, and soiled workroom.

In addition to allocating space for support areas as required by state codes, planners must consult with all members of the PICU multidisciplinary team to discuss their individual space needs before making a final decision about allocation of space for support services. A systematic analysis of needed support areas can address the topics of equipment, services, communication, and personnel.

Regardless of what the codes suggest, a storage space of only 20 square feet is inadequate for a large, technologically sophisticated unit. The only way to determine how much storage space is needed is to measure equipment and carts, multiply by the exact quantities, add the totals, and include additional square footage to accommodate new equipment.

Space needs must be considered for respiratory therapy, surgery, pharmacy, radiology, dietary, social service, child life, pastoral care, materials management, education, biomedical engineering, and clerical support. A unit with an automated patient data management system will also need space allocated for that system.

Every unit must have space(s) allocated for electronic and human communications. This may be the central nursing station in a small unit or a separate communications center in addition to multiple nursing stations in a large unit. The central communications center will house the master telephone and intercom systems, contain computer and pneumatic tube terminals, and serve as the coordinating center for the entry and exit of staff, visitors, equipment, and supplies. It is also necessary to provide space away from the patient areas for staff communication with each other and with families.

Allocating space for unit personnel for both work-related activities and relaxation is essential. An adequate number of classrooms and conference rooms must be provided so that multiple functions can occur at once. It is also important that staff members have a comfortable and private lounge in which to relax and socialize. Locker facilities must be provided in or adjacent to the unit. Finally, office space needs to be located on the unit for all members of the multidisciplinary team.

It is also important to provide support areas such as on-call rooms, office space, small library facilities, and desk space for physicians who use the PICU.

Family Support Areas

In Texas the Hospital Licensing Standards require that PICUs provide an appropriately secure sleeping space for parents who must be in communication with the PICU staff. Space must also be allocated for other parent-support facilities such as a lounge, grieving rooms, quiet rooms, shower and lavatories, locker facilities, kitchenette, and vending areas. These facilities need to be near local and long-distance telephone facilities.

DESIGN OF SPACE

Although Hospital Licensing Standards and other accreditation organizations have certain requirements that guide the design of space, numerous options confront planners as they enter the process of spatial design. Prioritization of unit objectives will guide the decision process.

Patient Care Areas

When designing patient care areas, planners must consider the current trend of providing care with fewer people, a result of both personnel shortages and cost-containmant efforts. The acuity of the patients and the technologic sophistication of the unit also must be considered. A fast-paced, technologically sophisticated unit with a lean staffing component dictates that resources needed for the care of patients be in close proximity to those patients and that access to and visualization of patients be unimpeded by physical barriers and inefficient traffic patterns.

These considerations will guide the choice between an open bay arrangement or enclosed cubicles in the patient areas. If the general population of the unit is comprised of critically ill children who need extensive technology and personnel on a continuous basis, providing an open bay or cubicles with sliding walls is desirable. This design allows expansion of the space around the patient and its adaptation to accommodate a sudden and/or sustained influx of equipment and personnel (see Fig. 121-2). The nature and quantity of invasive monitoring devices also help establish the requirements for the spacial layout. All children undergoing invasive monitoring or who are aided by life support equipment need constant observation. This is more easily accomplished in an open bay arrangement than in an area with an enclosed cubicle design. When working with critically ill, unstable, or potentially unstable children, it is likely that the prioritized list of unit requirements places patient safety and quick access to patients ahead of patient privacy or infection control. Although individual cubicles are superior to the open bay arrangement for provision of privacy and quiet and for minimizing cross-contamination, supporting concerns that have a higher priority (e.g., ready access) require that the open bay or cubicles with sliding walls be chosen. If affordable, the cubicle with sliding walls appears to be the best solution since each state usually has regulations concerning the availability of windows in each patient area.

If space and finances allow, an additional patient area that is desirable is a special procedures room. The functions of this room can be multiple, including initial placement of catheters and tubes, performance of minor and/or major surgical procedures, and provision of a holding area for a patient whose own room is not yet ready. To accommodate these multiple functions, this room must contain the same design as the individual bed spaces in the rest of the unit but also must contain equipment and features needed in an operating room. This includes a surgical table that can accommodate fluoroscopy equipment (a portable C-arm), multiparameter monitoring capabilities, an anesthesia machine and electrosurgical unit, an overhead surgical light, a scrub sink, and blanket and solution warmers. The general lighting system can be zoned so that certain areas of the room can be illuminated while fluoroscopy is in progress. The headwall system must contain several more vacuum outlets and access to additional medical gases such as nitrous oxide and nitrogen. C-lockers at one end of the room can house supplies and small pieces of equipment.

In the design of individual bed spaces the overall patient population of the unit as well as the long-term plans for the unit must be considered. It is also imperative that designers consider the trends in current and future monitoring capabilities. A large technologically sophisticated PICU in a tertiary care facility has significantly different bedside requirements from those of a small PICU in a community hospital. Additionally, a unit committed to purchasing new monitors that provide modules to replace numerous stand-alone monitoring devices actually may have fewer electrical and space requirements at the bedside. Automated patient data management systems create specific requirements for each bedside (see Chapter 129).

Numerous vendors manufacture custom-made headwalls or columns capable of providing virtually every physical resource needed at the bedside. Numbers and location of electrical outlets, grounding inlets, vacuum, oxygen, and air outlets, alarm buttons, communications systems, lighting controls, equipment brackets, and storage capabilities can all be individually tailored (Fig. 121-3). Achieving the optimum arrangement of these systems necessitates collaboration of a multidisciplinary team comprised of physicians, nurses, respiratory therapists, biomedical engineers, and architects.

Key issues to address in the design of the bed space include provision of adequate access both to patients and to the resources at the bedside, unimpeded visualization of both the patient and the monitoring devices, expandability of space, and privacy. It is essential that electrical, vacuum, oxygen, and air outlets are positioned so that cables and tubings attached to them do not impede patient contact or visualization. Also, it is essential that patient position does not impede access to any of these outlets. There needs to be sufficient space to accommodate the parents at bedside in addition to health care workers. Additionally, the layout of the bed space must accommodate health care providers of varying heights. This becomes particularly important when choosing the height of cardiac monitors and computer screens, since they are typically placed at a height that allows

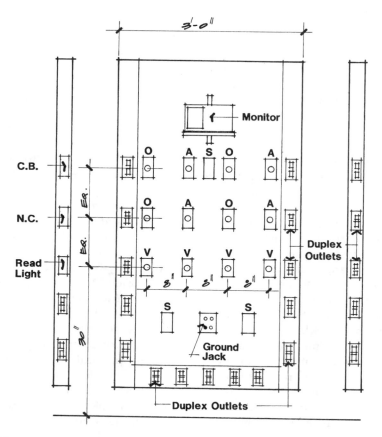

Fig. 121-3 Headwall for patient bed. (Courtesy HKS, Inc., Dallas, Tex.)

visualization from more distant positions. The large number of cables from the patient to the monitors can feed into a central transmission system rather than drape individually across the patient and his space.

Support Services

Storage space must be near the patient areas to facilitate efficiency. Movable furniture such as C-lockers on adjustable tracks will provide needed flexibility as storage needs change over time. Storage areas also must have numerous electrical outlets at both floor and counter height so that chargeable equipment can remain plugged in.

Support service areas can function as work areas or office areas. Services such as respiratory therapy, pharmacy, radiology, dietary, and clerical support need work areas designed specifically for them. The capabilities of the pharmacy and radiology satellite areas must mimic those provided in the central pharmacy and the radiology department. Other services such as social services, pastoral care, and child life will need offices of a standard design.

The communications areas must be designed to provide adequate space and seating for a variety of team members. If space allows, it is desirable to provide a separate area in which physicians can review charts, access hospital-wide computer systems, write orders, and talk on the phone. Nursing stations must be located and designed to facilitate visualization of numerous patients in the event nurses must leave the bedside to perform functions at the nursing station. The design of the family conference rooms must comfortably accommodate four to five family members and several health care team members and must provide privacy.

Staff conference rooms and classrooms must be designed to accommodate a variety of functions. It is desirable that each of these rooms have blackboards and projection screens. Storage space for in-service videotapes, audiovisual and teaching equipment, procedures manuals, and reference materials must either be provided in a small library in the unit or be incorporated into a conference room or classroom. The staff lounge needs to include comfortable sofas and chairs for relaxation. A small area of the lounge should be designed as a kitchenette with a refrigerator and microwave oven.

Family Support Areas

The parent sleeping area is preferably separate from the general visitors' lounge. The furniture in the lounge needs to be arranged so that the room is divided into numerous small sections to provide as much privacy as possible. If space allows, a game table can be provided at one end of the lounge. A message board will facilitate family and visitor communication with each other. Shower and lavatory facilities need to be accessible from both the sleeping and lounge areas. Grieving and quiet rooms need to be located away from the general family area so that privacy is maximized for particularly distraught family members.

ADDITIONAL READING

Fein IA, Strosberg MA. Managing the Critical Care Unit. Rockville, Md.: Aspen, 1987, pp 113-125.

Texas Department of Health. Hospital Licensing Standards. Hospital and Professional Licensure Division, sections 7-3 and 7-4. May 1986.

122 Anatomic and Physiologic Differences Between Children and Adults

Mary Fran Hazinski

BACKGROUND

The critically ill child is both physically and physiologically immature and differs from the critically ill adult in several important ways. Everyone caring for such a child must be able to approach the patient at a level appropriate to his psychosocial development and level of distress, modifying assessment techniques and interventions accordingly. In addition, equipment used must not only be smaller, but it must be designed to serve the unique characteristics of the child's maturing body.

Treatment of the critically ill child must include treatment and support of the family. This requires excellent communication among members of the health care team and clear, consistent, and frequent communication with the parents. For further information regarding the psychosocial support of the child and family, see Chapters 107 and 108.

Anyone working in the critical care environment must develop the ability to determine at a glance whether the child "looks good" or "looks bad" (Table 122-1). This determination involves rapid visual evaluation of the child's color and perfusion, level of activity, responsiveness, and position of comfort. The healthy child will have pink mucous membranes and nail beds and uniform skin color over the trunk and extremities. The child's skin will be warm, peripheral pulses strong, and capillary refill instantaneous (<1 to 2 seconds) when the ambient temperature is warm.

The adult in cardiorespiratory distress often will complain of dyspnea or chest pain. The critically ill or injured child, in comparison, usually acts ill, but this assessment is based on nonverbal rather than verbal clues. The child in cardiorespiratory distress may grimace or is unusually irritable or lethargic. The moderately ill infant or child usually does not demonstrate good eye contact, may be irritable when aroused, and often is unable to find a comfortable position. The extremely ill child is unresponsive to most stimulation and usually demonstrates flaccid muscle tone. A decreased response to painful stimulus is abnormal in the child of any age and usually indicates severe cardiorespiratory or neurologic deterioration.

CARDIOVASCULAR DIFFERENCES
Anatomic Differences

Cardiac location. The heart of the infant, child, and adult is located under the lower half of the sternum. Cardiac compression during resuscitative efforts necessitates compression one fingerbreadth below the nipple line in the infant and one fingerbreadth above the costosternal notch in the child and the adult.

Ventricular morphology. During postnatal adaptation to extrauterine life, systemic vascular resistance rises. As a result, the work load of the left ventricle increases, and hypertrophy and hyperplasia of left ventricular myocytes occur during the first 3 to 6 months of life. Left ventricular wall thickness nearly doubles during this time.

Pulmonary vascular resistance normally falls after birth at sea level, and the work load of the right ventricle decreases proportionately. Myocyte growth is slower in the right than the left ventricle during the first months of life, and right ventricular muscle thickness remains the same throughout childhood. Right and left ventricular weights are approximately equal at birth, but the right ventricular–left ventricular

Table 122-1   Initial Evaluation of the Seriously Ill or Injured Child*

Characteristic	"Looks Good"	"Looks Bad"
Color and perfusion	Pink mucous membranes	Pale or gray skin and mucous membranes
	Color consistent over trunk and extremities	Mottled color over trunk and extremities
Peripheral perfusion	Skin uniformly warm	Skin cool
	Capillary refill brisk	Capillary refill prolonged/sluggish despite warm ambient temperature
Activity	Age-appropriate (may be frightened, unhappy, or unwilling to be separated from parents)	Unusually irritable or fretful, then lethargic
	Will engage in play, sustain eye contact	Will not engage in play or sustain eye contact
Responsiveness	Age-appropriate	Very irritable (initially), then lethargic
		Decreased response to pain is a worrisome sign
Position of comfort	Can rest, sleep in several positions	Fretful, appears unable to rest
		May be most comfortable with head of bed elevated
		Ultimately unresponsive to any position change

*Modified from Hazinski MF. Postoperative care of the critically ill child. Crit Care Nurs Clin North Am 2:599, 1990.

NORMAL HEMODYNAMIC VARIABLES IN CHILDREN

Calculation of systemic vascular resistance (SVR)

$$\text{SVR (in index units)} = \frac{\text{Mean systemic arterial pressure} - \text{Mean right atrial pressure}}{\text{Cardiac index}}$$

Normal SVR (in index units) in neonates: 10-15 units
Normal SVR (in index units) in children: 15-30 units

Calculation of pulmonary vascular resistance (PVR)

$$\text{PVR (in index units)} = \frac{\text{Mean pulmonary artery pressure} - \text{Mean left atrial pressure}}{\text{Cardiac index}}$$

Normal PVR (in index units) in neonates: 8-10 units
Normal PVR (in index units) in children: 1-3 units

Normal oxygen consumption

Infants <2-3 wk of age: 180-270 ml/min/m² BSA
Children >2-3 wk of age: 150-160 ml/min/m² BSA *or* 5-8 ml/kg/min
Normal arterial oxygen content: 18-20 ml O_2/dl blood

NOTE: To convert index units to dynes · sec/cm^{-5}, change cardiac index to cardiac output in denominator of equation and multiply equation by 80.
BSA = body surface area.

weight ratio is only 0.5 to 0.6 by 2 months of age. These changes in right and left ventricular size produce corresponding changes in the infant's ECG. Right ventricular dominance is present during the first months of life, but left ventricular dominance is usually apparent by 3 to 6 months of age. During childhood the P wave duration, PR interval, QRS duration, and QRS magnitude increase.

Circulating blood volume. The child's circulating blood volume is higher per kilogram body weight than the blood volume of the adult (average 70 to 80 ml/kg). However, the child's absolute blood volume is still small, and relatively small amounts of blood loss may result in critical intravascular volume depletion. For this reason, a total of all blood lost or drawn for laboratory analysis (including any necessary "discard" samples) must be recorded on the nursing flow sheet and blood replacement therapy considered (in conjunction with other patient assessment variables) when acute unreplaced blood loss totals 5% to 7% of the child's circulating blood volume. Additional patient assessment variables to consider include heart rate, color, and evidence of end-organ perfusion. Excess blood loss can be virtually eliminated with use of careful sampling techniques.

Physiologic Differences

The differences between neonatal and adult cardiovascular function are largely the result of the transition from fetal to extrauterine circulation. For the most part, hemodynamic changes are only relevant during the first weeks or months of life. However, cardiopulmonary disease or altitude may delay or modify the transition and affect later changes in cardiac function and vascular resistance.

Cardiac output. At birth, cardiac output is higher per kilogram body weight than during any other time in life, averaging approximately 300 ml/kg/min. Cardiac output per kilogram body weight ultimately decreases to 100 ml/kg/min during adolescence and to 70 to 80 ml/kg/min during adulthood. Because the child's body weight is small, absolute cardiac output at birth is only approximately 0.7 L/min, but it increases to approximately 6.0 L/min in the large adolescent or adult male (Table 122-2). The cardiac index throughout childhood is slightly higher than in adulthood and is normally 3.0 to 4.5 L/min/m² BSA.

Cardiac output is the product of heart rate and stroke volume. During childhood heart rate is rapid and stroke volume small; thus cardiac output is directly proportional to heart rate.

Heart rate. Normal heart rate decreases as the child grows (Table 122-3). Tachycardia provides the most efficient method of increasing cardiac output in a patient of any age. An increase in heart rate should be observed when the child is active, anxious, in pain, or febrile or when cardiorespiratory disease is present. Since, however, the cardiac output in the neonate and young infant may be near maximal, an increase in heart rate may only marginally improve cardiac output during early life. In fetal lambs a 40% to 65% increase in heart rate is necessary to improve cardiac output 10% to 20%.

Some slowing of the heart rate should be expected when the child is asleep or sedated (see Table 122-3). However, a significant decrease in heart rate below normal may produce a substantial decrease in cardiac output, particularly if cardiorespiratory disease is present. In fetal lambs a decrease in heart rate of only 25% can be expected to produce a 20% decrease in cardiac output.

Arrhythmias. In the pediatric patient most arrhythmias are clinically insignificant; that is, they do not compromise cardiac output or systemic perfusion and are not likely to deteriorate into significant arrhythmias. These clinically insignificant arrhythmias do not require treatment.

The most common clinically significant arrhythmias in children are bradycardia and supraventricular tachycardia. The terminal cardiac rhythm in children is most often bradycardia, progressing to asystole. Bradycardia is usually an ominous clinical sign in critically ill or injured children. Slowing of the heart rate in the critically ill child is often caused by hypoxia, so this condition must be immediately identified and treated. Bradycardia may also result from vagal stimulation such as produced by suctioning.

Clinically significant ventricular arrhythmias are not common in children unless complex congenital heart disease, myocarditis, cardiomyopathy, electrolyte abnormalities, or asphyxia is present. In comparison, ventricular arrhythmias are fairly common in adult patients, and the terminal cardiac rhythm in the adult is likely to be ventricular tachycardia or fibrillation.

Myocardial function. Stroke volume is small in the infant and young child, averaging approximately 1.5 ml/kg. During maturation, stroke volume increases from approximately 5 ml in the neonate to approx-

Table 122-2 Normal Cardiac Output, Oxygen Delivery, and Oxygen Consumption in Neonates, Infants, and Children*

Age (weight/BSA)	Cardiac Output† (ml/min)	Heart Rate	Normal Stroke Volume (ml)	Oxygen Delivery‡ ($\dot{D}O_2$) (ml/min)	(ml/min/m²)	Oxygen Consumption ($\dot{V}O_2$) (ml/min)	(ml/min/m²)
Newborn (3.2 kg/0.2 m²)	700-800	145	5	133-200	665-1000	36-54	180-270
6 mo (8 kg/0.42 m²)	1000-1600	120	10	200-280	476-667	70-100	167-238
1 yr (10 kg/0.5 m²)	1300-1500	115	13	260-300	520-600	85-110	170-220
2 yr (13 kg/0.59 m²)	1500-2000	115	18	300-400	508-678	91-123	154-208
4 yr (17 kg/0.71 m²)	2300-2375	105	27	460-475	648-669	110-150	155-211
5 yr (19 kg/0.77 m²)	2500-3000	95	31	500-600	649-779	115-170	149-221
8 yr (28 kg/0.96 m²)	3400-3600	83	42	680-720	708-750	150-208	156-200
10 yr (35 kg/1.1 m²)	3800-4000	75	50	760-800	690-727	190-250	122-227
15 yr (50 kg/1.4 m²)	5000-6000	70	85	1200	857	300-400	120-200

NOTE: Cardiac index = $\dfrac{\text{Cardiac output}}{\text{m}^2 \text{ BSA}}$

*Reproduced by permission from Hazinski MF. Cardiovascular disorders. In Hazinski MF, ed. Nursing Care of the Critically Ill Child. St. Louis: Mosby, 1984, p 90; and Hazinski MF. Hemodynamic monitoring of children. In Daily EK, Schroeder JS, eds. Techniques in Bedside Hemodynamic Monitoring, 5th ed. St. Louis: Mosby, 1994, p 280.

†Cardiac index for children: 3.0-4.5 L/min/m².

‡Assuming a hemoglobin concentration of 15 g/dl normal arterial oxygen content.

Table 122-3 Normal Vital Signs in Children

Age	Heart Rate* (bpm)		Respiratory Rate (per min)
	Awake	Sleeping	
Infant	120-160	80-180	30-60
Toddler	90-140	70-120	24-40
Preschool age	80-110	60-90	22-34
School age	75-100	60-90	18-30
Adolescent	60-90	50-90	12-16

Age	Blood Pressure (mm Hg)†	
	Systolic	Diastolic
Neonate (1 mo)	85-100	51-65
Infant (6 mo)	87-105	53-66
Toddler (2 yr)	95-105	53-66
School age (7 yr)	97-112	57-71
Adolescent (15 yr)	112-128	66-80

*Extrapolated from Gillett PC, Garson A, Porter CJ, et al. Dysrhythmias. In Adams FH, Emmanouilides GC, eds. Moss' Heart Disease in Infants, Children, and Adolescents, 3rd ed. Baltimore: Williams & Wilkins, 1983; and Hazinski MF. Children are different. In Hazinski MF, ed. Nursing Care of the Critically Ill Child, 2nd ed. St. Louis: Mosby, 1992.
†Blood pressure tables taken from the 50th to 90th percentile ranges of the ages noted; extrapolated from graphs published by Horan MJ (Chairman). Task force on blood pressure control in children. Report of the Second Task Force on Blood Pressure in Children—1987. Pediatrics 79:1, 1987.

imately 70 to 90 ml in the adolescent (see Table 122-2). Ventricular end-diastolic volume increases from approximately 40 ml/m² BSA in infants to approximately 70 ml/m² BSA in children older than 2 years. Infant myocardium has a higher ejection fraction than that of the older child.

Most information about developmental changes in myocardial function is based on studies of isolated or nonhuman myocardium. These findings must therefore be applied with caution in humans. Newborn lamb myocardium is less compliant and contains a higher water content and less contractile mass than adult sheep myocardium. This finding is documented histologically in humans. Fetal animal myocardial fibers shorten less effectively than adult myocardial fibers, and immature canine myocardium demonstrates maximal contractility at smaller end-diastolic volume than in the mature dog. Neonatal lambs demonstrate a blunted cardiac output response to volume therapy.

This research has led to the widespread belief that infants need higher preload (higher ventricular end-diastolic pressure) to maximize cardiac output and may be incapable of increasing stroke volume and cardiac output even with fluid challenges. However, even infant lambs are capable of increasing cardiac output significantly (35% to 70%) in response to volume loading, particularly if systemic vascular resistance is low.

It is now clear that neonates and infants can increase cardiac output in response to volume therapy if systemic vascular resistance remains normal or low. Certainly by the time the infant is 3 to 8 weeks of age, myocardial response to volume therapy is similar to the response of the adult myocardium, and by 1 to 2 years of age the child's myocardial function is similar to adult myocardial function.

Oxygen supply and demand. Oxygen consumption per kilogram body weight and indexed to BSA is extremely high during the neonatal period (180 to 279 ml/min/m²). It decreases during infancy and childhood and reaches "adult" levels (122 to 220 ml/min/m²) by approximately 10 years of age. Oxygen delivery per kilogram body weight and indexed to BSA is also higher in neonates (665 to 1000 ml/min/m²), infants, and children than in adults. However, during the first weeks of life the oxygen delivery of the neonate and young infant is near maximal because the heart rate and cardiac output are near maximal even at rest. This leaves young patients with little oxygen "reserve." As a result, anything that increases oxygen demand (cold, stress, infection, or pain) or decreases oxygen delivery (cardiac or pulmonary disease or bradycardia) may result in rapid cardiorespiratory deterioration and development of progressive hypoxia and metabolic acidosis.

Vascular resistance. At birth, with the conversion from placental to pulmonary oxygenation of the blood, alveolar oxygen concentration increases and pulmonary vascular resistance begins to fall from 8 to 10 index units. It reaches the "adult" normal level of 1 to 3 units/m² BSA within the first 6 to 8 weeks of life (see p. 1113). Right ventricular muscle mass decreases, and a corresponding reduction in right ventricular ECG voltage is seen during infancy.

Even after the normal postnatal decrease in pulmonary vascular resistance, the neonatal pulmonary vascular bed may remain reactive, and reactive pulmonary vasoconstriction may also develop in children with pulmonary hypertension. Reactive pulmonary vasoconstriction may develop in response to alveolar hypoxia, acidosis, or hyperthermia and will produce elevated pulmonary vascular resistance and increased right ventricular afterload. Such reactive vasoconstriction may be particularly detrimental if pulmonary hypertension is already present.

Systemic vascular resistance and systemic arterial pressure begin to rise with separation of the circulation from the placenta (see p. 1113). Normal systemic vascular resistance is 10 to 15 index units in infants younger than 12 months, 20 to 30 index units after 12 to 18 months, and 30 to 40 index units in adults. The rise in systemic vascular resistance corresponds to an increase in left ventricular muscle mass and ECG voltage.

Effect of afterload on myocardial function. Stroke volume decreases dramatically in newborn lambs when ventricular afterload increases. However, human infants seem to be able to maintain normal cardiac output even with moderately elevated afterload (e.g., that produced by semilunar valve stenosis) unless the increase in afterload is severe or acute.

Response to catecholamines. The development of human adrenergic receptors and the response of normal infants and children to adrenergic receptor stimulation continue to be studied. Animal research has demonstrated that cardiovascular parasympathetic innervation and response are virtually the same in all age groups. Sympathetic nervous system innervation to the myocardium is, however, incomplete at birth. Although cardiac adrenergic receptors are present at birth, cardiac norepinephrine levels are lower than adult levels for the first 3 weeks of life. These findings suggest that during the first weeks of life vagal effects will predominate and cardiac rate and contractile response to endogenous β_1-adrenergic receptor catecholamine stimulation will be limited.

Research regarding the response of children to (exogenous) catecholamine administration has yielded conflicting information. Generalization of study conclusions has been impossible because the age and underlying cardiovascular function of the children in each study varied. It is imperative, therefore, that vasoactive drug administration be titrated at the bedside and the drug selection, dosage, and patient response be carefully and frequently evaluated.

Age-related changes in catecholamine metabolism continue to be studied in humans. Excretion of va-

soactive drugs is probably related more to the child's clinical condition, including hepatic and renal function, than to age. Catecholamine clearance is likely to be prolonged in patients of any age with hepatic or renal dysfunction. During catecholamine administration every patient must be closely monitored for adverse or toxic effects of each drug. Such effects may include extreme tachycardia or other arrhythmias, increased pulmonary artery or wedge pressure, and systemic hypotension or hypertension.

Historically, higher doses of cardiac glycosides (per kilogram body weight) have been administered in infants than in older children or adults; however, no data exist to support this differential dosage. The volume of distribution of digoxin is larger in infants and children than in adults because much of the drug is stored in skeletal muscle (which constitutes a larger portion of the body mass of the infant than of the adult). However, infant myocardium accumulates digoxin more than adult myocardium, particularly during administration of large "loading" doses of the drug. In addition, digoxin excretion is affected by the GFR, so the half-life of the drug is longest in neonates. For these reasons, premature neonates and infants less than 12 months of age need to receive *lower* digoxin doses per kilogram body weight than children or adults. Caution must be used when administering a digitalis derivative in *premature* neonates because the prevalence of clinical toxicity is highest (nearly 30%) in these patients.

PULMONARY DIFFERENCES

The five major components of the respiratory system include (1) the CNS, which serves as the controller of ventilation; (2) the airways, which conduct gas to and from the alveoli; (3) the chest wall, which encloses the lungs; (4) the respiratory muscles; and (5) the acinar tissue, which includes the alveolar space and capillaries. Since each of these major components is incompletely developed at birth, neonatal respiratory function is inefficient, and the infant is particularly susceptible to respiratory failure.

Anatomic Differences

CNS control of breathing. Central (e.g., carotid body) and peripheral chemoreceptors needed to control ventilation are present at birth, although peripheral chemoreceptors are less numerous in the infant than in the child. All of these receptors are functional at birth. Developmental changes in control of respiration are discussed under "Physiologic Differences" (p. 1119).

Airways. All conducting airways are present at birth, and their numbers do not increase after birth. By contrast, the alveolar epithelial and endothelial layers continue to develop until 10 to 12 years of age. Thus discrete lung injury early in life may not impair lung development during childhood, and compensatory alveolar growth may occur. However, diffuse neonatal lung injury (e.g., bronchopulmonary dysplasia) may disrupt or delay alveolar growth, resulting in pulmonary dysplasia.

The airway branching pattern is complete at birth, and the airways increase in size and length throughout childhood. Not only are the child's airways smaller than those in the adult, but supporting airway cartilage and elastic tissue are not developed until school age. In addition, small airways muscles may be incompletely developed during the first years of life. For these reasons, the child's airways are susceptible to collapse and may easily become obstructed as a result of laryngospasm, bronchospasm, edema, or mucous accumulation. Lack of development of the small airways muscles may render young infants less responsive than older children to bronchodilator therapy.

Airway resistance normally varies inversely and exponentially with airway radius. Poiseuille's formula states that airway resistance is inversely proportional to $1/\text{radius}^4$ during quiet breathing when airflow is laminar and $1/\text{radius}^5$ when airflow is turbulent (e.g., during crying or when work of breathing is increased). The clinical impact of this relationship is that small compromises in airway radius (e.g., bronchospasm, edema, and mucous accumulation) will result in significant increases in airway resistance and work of breathing.

Closing volume as a percent of total lung volume is higher in infants than in healthy adults. There is some evidence that some of the airways remain closed even during normal breathing in the young infant. The significance of this finding is unknown, but it may make the infant more susceptible to atelectasis.

The pediatric larynx is more anterior and cephalad than the adult larynx, and the stiff, cartilaginous epiglottis articulates at a more acute angle with the larynx than in the adult. Thus the epiglottis may obscure the glottic opening, making intubation difficult. Since the anterior attachment of the vocal cords is below the posterior attachment, a curved endotracheal tube can easily become caught in the anterior commissure, preventing proper advancement of the tube into the trachea. Application of pressure on the cricoid cartilage during intubation will displace the larynx posteriorly and may facilitate intubation.

The pediatric trachea is relatively short, so inadvertent endotracheal tube migration into either mainstem bronchus may easily occur. In addition, the orotracheal tube will move with changes in head position—flexion of the neck displaces the tip of the tube further into the trachea, and extension of the neck moves the tube farther out of the trachea.

Until approximately 8 years of age the narrowest part of the pediatric larynx is at the level of the nondistensible cricoid cartilage. This means that during infancy and childhood the larynx is funnel shaped. In comparison, the narrowest portion of the adolescent or adult larynx is at the vocal cords; thus the adult larynx is cylindric. The shape of the larynx must be considered in selection of endotracheal tubes. The child's endotracheal tube must be able to easily pass through the vocal cords and allow a slight air leak at the level of the cricoid cartilage when approximately 25 cm H_2O positive pressure is provided. Under most conditions, cuffed endotracheal tubes are probably best avoided in children less than 8 years because the cuff may damage the trachea.

During the first 5 to 8 years of age the growth of the distal airways is proportionately slower than the growth of the proximal airways; therefore the distal airways provide proportionally more resistance to airflow than do the distal airways of the adult. As a result, during infancy and childhood the distal airways and the alveoli they serve both fill and empty slowly.

Chest wall. The chest wall encloses and supports the lungs. The cartilaginous ribs of the infant and young child are twice as compliant as the bony ribs of the older child or adult. During episodes of respiratory distress the infant's chest wall will retract; this reduces the infant's ability to maintain functional residual capacity or increase tidal volume, and it increases the work of breathing.

The infant's ribs are oriented more horizontally than in the adult because they articulate linearly with the spinal column and sternum. The infant's chest has less anteroposterior displacement during inspiration than the adult chest. These factors tend to reduce the mechanical efficiency of respiratory muscle function during the first years of life because intercostal muscles do not have the leverage needed to lift the ribs effectively. As the child grows, the rib articulation changes to a 45-degree angle, and the intercostal muscles are able to elevate the ribs and contribute to chest expansion.

The diaphragm muscles insert horizontally on the inner surfaces of the ribs of the infant rather than obliquely as in the adult. If the infant is placed supine, diaphragm movement may be compromised since diaphragm contraction may well draw the ribs inward rather than expand the chest outward. Compared with the adult, the percentage of fatigue-resistant muscle fibers in the diaphragm is lower.

Respiratory muscles. The respiratory muscles consist of the muscles of the upper airway, the lower airways, and the diaphragm. They contribute to expansion of the lung and maintenance of airway patency. The respiratory muscles of the infant and young child may lack tone, power, and coordination; this reduces respiratory efficiency.

At any age the diaphragm is the chief muscle of inspiration. Anything that impedes diaphragm movement (e.g., abdominal distention) can result in respiratory failure in the young child. In the relaxed state the neonatal diaphragm is located higher in the thorax and has a smaller radius of curvature than the adult diaphragm, reducing the efficiency of diaphragm contraction. If a hemidiaphragm is paralyzed during infancy or early childhood, a type of flail chest results. The flaccid hemidiaphragm is pulled up into the chest during contraction of the functioning (contralateral) hemidiaphragm, and respiratory failure usually results.

The intercostal muscles are not fully developed until school age, so they act primarily to stabilize the chest wall during the first years of life. Since the intercostal muscles have neither the leverage nor the strength to lift the rib cage in the young child, generation of tidal volume depends on diaphragm function.

Lung tissue. Postnatal pulmonary growth consists of an increase in alveolar size and number, which produces a corresponding increase in alveolar surface area from 2.8 to 32 m^2 and an increase in lung volume from 200 ml to 2.2 L by 8 years of age. There is a smaller amount of elastic and collagen tissue in the neonatal lung than in the adult lung. As a result, liquid or air can easily enter the pulmonary interstitium; this may explain the increased tendency of infants to develop pulmonary edema, pneumomediastinum, pneumothorax, and interstitial emphysema. Reduced elastic fibers contribute to the tendency for small airway collapse. Because elastic recoil of the thorax and lung is low, pleural pressure is nearly atmospheric; this may also contribute to premature airway closure during this age. Elastic fibers increase in number, approaching adult quantities by approximately 4 years of age.

Physiologic Differences

CNS control of breathing. At birth all chemoreceptors, both central (in the ventral brain stem) and peripheral (in the carotid body), are present and functioning to control respiration, and chemoreceptor response is normal soon after birth. For unknown reasons, however, the premature infant and the neonate may demonstrate a biphasic response to hypoxemia, consisting of transient hyperpnea followed by hypoventilation. After the neonatal period, control of breathing usually resembles that of the adult.

Airways. The airways of the child are significantly smaller than those of the adult. Because resistance to airflow increases exponentially as the radius of the airway is reduced, a small reduction in airway radius from edema or mucous accumulation can produce substantial increases in resistance to airflow. For example, if the infant with a 4 mm trachea has 1 mm of circumferential laryngeal edema or inflammation, the airway radius will be reduced by 50% (from 2 to 1 mm) and resistance to airflow increased 16-fold during quiet breathing; the changes will be even more dramatic if airflow is turbulent. If the adult patient with a 10 mm larynx has 1 mm of circumferential edema, the airway radius will be reduced by only 20% (from 5 to 4 mm) and resistance to airflow increased only 2-fold during quiet breathing.

The peripheral airways of the adult provide approximately 20% of total airway resistance; these same airways contribute up to 50% of the total airway resistance in children up to 5 years of age. As a result, small airways diseases such as bronchiolitis may result in significant increases in resistance to airflow and severe respiratory distress.

During mechanical ventilation the high peripheral airway resistance and reduced lung compliance of the child must be considered. Not only must adequate inspiratory time be allowed, but adequate exhalation time must be provided or air trapping will develop. Air trapping is even more likely to develop in the presence of asthma or bronchiolitis.

Chest wall. The compliance of the infant's chest wall is approximately double that in the adult. Because the infant's lungs are stiff, it may be difficult for the spontaneously breathing infant to maintain adequate lung volume even at rest and particularly during periods of respiratory distress.

During effective positive pressure ventilation the infant's compliant chest wall normally expands outward easily. If the chest wall does not expand during positive pressure ventilation, it is likely that the lungs are not being adequately ventilated.

As the child grows, chest wall compliance decreases, and elastic outward recoil of the rib cage increases because of an increase in chest wall muscle tone. These changes improve the child's ability to maintain functional residual capacity, reducing the likelihood of atelectasis and small airway closure.

Respiratory muscles. Because respiratory muscles in the infant often lack the tone, power, and coordination of the adult respiratory system, respiratory failure is likely to develop during episodes of respiratory distress. Abdominal breathing is normal in infants and young children; typically the abdomen and chest wall rise together during inspiration. Therefore abdominal distention or decreased abdominal wall compliance (such as occurs with gastric distention or peritonitis) can interfere with diaphragm excursion and effective ventilation. Paradoxical abdominal motion during inspiration, with the abdomen protruding outward when the chest retracts inward, may be a sign of severe respiratory distress and will further impair the infant's ability to generate adequate tidal volume. Infants and young children in respiratory distress usually swallow air. This air may contribute to gastric distention and compromise diaphragm movement, and insertion of a nasogastric tube needs to be considered.

The infant with severe respiratory distress will often grunt during exhalation. Grunting results from closure of the glottis during active exhalation, which increases transpulmonary pressure, lung volume, and functional residual capacity. If grunting is observed, ventilatory support should be considered. The effect of grunting is mimicked by provision of continuous positive airway pressure or positive end-expiratory pressure during assisted ventilation.

Lung tissue. During childhood, lung distensibility or compliance (change in lung volume per centimeter H_2O change in pressure) increases from approximately 4 to 6 ml/cm H_2O in the neonate to approximately 77 ml/cm H_2O in the school-age child. Lung compliance in the adult averages approximately 150 ml/cm H_2O. Since the chest wall becomes progressively "stiffer" as lung compliance increases, ventilation becomes more efficient as the child grows.

The relative sizes of lung volumes and capacities remain the same throughout life. The tidal volume averages 6 to 7 cc/kg body weight and constitutes approximately 8% of total lung capacity. Because the absolute tidal volume of the child is small, mechanical ventilators for children must be capable of providing small tidal volumes in short inspiratory times at low pressures. This usually dictates use of ventilators that can be adjusted to provide flow characteristics different from the flow characteristics provided during mechanical ventilation in adults.

NEUROLOGIC DIFFERENCES
Anatomic Differences

At birth all major structures of the brain and all cranial nerves are developed, although neuronal dendritic arborization is incomplete until childhood. As the child grows, the brain increases dramatically in size and complexity. During the first years of life the brain achieves more than 90% of the adult number of brain cells, and it triples in weight as a result of the development of fiber tracts, synapses, and myelination. By 2½ years of age the brain has reached 75% of its mature adult weight, and by 6 years approximately 90% of the mature adult brain weight has been achieved.

The cranial nerves and some central neurons are myelinated at birth. At 1 year of age all major nerve tracts are myelinated.

The head of the infant and young child is large and heavy in proportion to the rest of the body. If the infant or child falls a significant distance or is thrown through or from an automobile or from a bicycle (e.g., after colliding with an automobile), the head will tend to lead (i.e., the infant or child will fly head first), and severe head injuries will result when the head ultimately strikes the ground or another object. Since the skull is relatively thin during infancy and childhood and provides little protection for the brain, head trauma can produce severe brain injury during this age. The cranial sutures do not fuse until approximately 16 to 18 months of age. As a result, if there is a gradual increase in intracranial volume during infancy, head circumference may increase. This potential for head expansion will not, however, prevent increased ICP from developing, particularly if intracranial volume increases acutely.

Normal cerebral blood flow and cerebral perfusion pressure values in infants and children are unknown. Cerebral blood flow has been estimated at 30 to 55 ml blood flow/100 g brain tissue/min and is primarily distributed in the temporal and occipital regions during infancy. Adult cerebral blood flow has been measured at 50 ml/100 g brain tissue/min and is distributed preferentially to the frontal lobes of the brain.

The blood-brain barrier is formed by supporting neuroglial cells and the tight junctions between endothelial cells in brain capillaries. The barrier prevents movement of some harmful molecules and substances from the blood into the brain. This barrier appears to be well developed at birth in the full-term infant, although it is more permeable to bilirubin than the adult blood-brain barrier. The blood-brain barrier is immature in the preterm infant, which may contribute to the higher incidence of intracranial hemorrhage and increased CNS effects of some drugs in preterm infants.

The normal volume of CSF production during childhood is unknown, although the average volume of CSF present in the neonatal CNS is estimated at 40 to 50 ml. Normal CSF content varies as the child matures. The normal neonatal CSF may demonstrate 1 to 4 white blood cells per milliliter and occasional polymorphonuclear leukocytes. However, after 6 months of age white blood cells are generally absent, and polymorphonuclear leukocytes should not be seen. Protein concentration is generally >90 mg/100 ml in the neonate and ranges from 15 to 40 mg/100 ml after 6 months of age.

Spinal cord injuries are less common after pediatric trauma than adult trauma because the child's spine, particularly the upper cervical spine, is more elastic and mobile than the adult spine. Pediatric ligaments are relatively lax, the neck and paraspinous and paravertebral muscles are incompletely developed, and the vertebral facets are more shallow than in the adult. This laxity of the spine can protect the child during minor trauma but may result in subluxation and spinal cord injury if major acceleration-deceleration forces are applied to the head, neck, or vertebral column. The pediatric vertebrae are softer and more cartilaginous than adult vertebrae and thus are less likely to fracture. As a result, when the child does sustain a spinal cord injury, it is often present without radiographic abnormality (spinal cord injury without radiographic abnormality, or SCIWORA). Cervical spine injuries observed in infants and young children tend to be higher in the cervical spine C1-5 than cervical spine injuries observed in adults (most commonly C5-7).

Physiologic Differences

At birth the infant functions largely at a subcortical level, and most responses are reflexive in nature. Many reflexes are primitive and will disappear with maturation. The term infant will demonstrate a dominance of flexor tone, and children of all ages will respond to touch.

The brain of the infant and child is less compartmentalized than the brain of the adult since the infant and child brain has higher water content and incomplete myelination. Since the brain of the young patient is more homogeneous, it is more susceptible to diffuse injury and gliding contusions than the adult brain. Such diffuse injury often results in loss of consciousness and pupil dilatation. These clinical signs are usually indicative of severe head injury in the adult but may be observed after mild, moderate, or severe head injury in children. The diffuse nature of pediatric closed head injuries provides one explanation for the higher survival associated with a Glasgow Coma Scale (GCS) score of 5 to 8 after head injury than that observed in adults with the same GCS score. A second possible explanation for higher pediatric survival may be that neuronal dendritic arborization and development of fiber tracts continue throughout childhood and may enable compensation for injured areas of the brain.

The GCS score has not been validated as a prognostic score or as a scoring system for use in infants and nonverbal patients. Several modifications of the GCS have been developed for use in infants and children, and some have been validated. Whenever the GCS or a modified version of the GCS is used in the unconscious patient, application of the motor component of the score is extremely important, yet this section of GCS is most often evaluated incompletely or incorrectly. As a result, every member of the health care team must be consistent in utilization of this scoring system so it may be useful for observing trends in the child's neurologic function.

Electrical activity in the brain is incompletely developed at birth. During infancy there is an increase in frequency and amplitude of resting electrical activity. Brief periods of flattening of the EEG have been reported in healthy neonates; this observation has led the Task Force on Brain Death Determination in Children to recommend an extended observation period (i.e., 48 hours) for infants 7 days to 2 months of age before brain death is pronounced, although this is controversial.

FLUID AND ELECTROLYTE BALANCE
Anatomic Differences

Water distribution. A major portion of a child's body weight is water, constituting approximately 75% of the full-term infant's weight and approximately 60% to 70% of the weight of the adolescent or adult. During the first months of life most body water is located in the extracellular compartment, and much of this water is exchanged daily. Both the infant and young child have a large surface area to volume ratio; thus they will lose a larger amount of water to the environment through evaporation than does the adult.

Renal development. At birth the neonate possesses the adult complement of nephrons, but only approximately 50% of nephrons are located in the renal cortex. After birth, however, tubular length and volume and glomerular size increase, and 85% of all nephrons are located in the cortex.

Renal blood flow accounts for only approximately 5% to 10% of total cardiac output at birth, and only approximately 50% of renal blood flow passes through the cortex because the cortical glomeruli are immature and renal vascular resistance is high. In the older child approximately 25% of cardiac output passes through the kidneys, and most (80% to 90%) of this blood flow passes through the renal cortex.

Absolute glomerular filtration rate (GFR) and GFR in relation to weight or BSA is low in the neonate. During the first weeks of life GFR increases rapidly as the result of the increase in renal blood flow and a decrease in renal vascular resistance. GFR in the neonate averages approximately 2.5 ml/min and rises to approximately 15.5 ml/min in the 6-month-old infant and to approximately 50 ml/min in the preschooler. By adulthood GFR has increased to approximately 131 ml/min.

Electrolyte balance. For the most part, maintenance of electrolyte balance is identical in children and adults.

Glucose homeostasis. Hypoglycemia often develops in young infants during episodes of stress (e.g., shock, seizures, or sepsis). Infants have high glucose needs and low glycogen stores, which makes hypoglycemia more likely to develop than hyperglycemia.

Physiologic Differences

Water distribution. The child's metabolic rate and evaporative losses are higher than those of the adult, so the child has higher maintenance fluid requirements per kilogram body weight. However, since the child's body weight is small, the absolute fluid volume administered will be small. All fluid administered in the PICU must be infused through a volume-controlled pump to enable precise regulation of fluid administration. Maintenance fluid requirements must be calculated for each child and modified by the health care team according to the child's clinical condition (see Chapter 55).

The young child may rapidly become dehydrated or fluid overloaded. It is imperative to record all sources of fluid intake (including oral intake, IV fluids, and all fluids used to flush monitoring lines or administer medications) and fluid loss (including urine, stool, emesis, and drainage). In the critically ill child fluid balance must be calculated hourly so that appropriate modifications in therapy may be made as needed.

Renal function. After birth there is a significant increase in renal blood flow and GFR as well as renal cortical blood flow. These changes are associated with a rapid rise in renal sodium reabsorption within the first days of life. Even at birth the kidney is capable of excreting a large volume load, although maximal volume excretion occurs when the GFR increases.

The fetal kidney produces large quantities of urine with a high sodium concentration. During the first 72 hours of life continued renal sodium and water excretion results in a normal weight loss equivalent to approximately 5% to 10% of birthweight. By the end of the first week of life in the term infant there is equilibration between sodium and water intake and excretion. Premature infants, however, may continue to demonstrate sodium wasting for several weeks as the result of immature tubular function and relative insensitivity to aldosterone.

The neonatal kidney is less capable of excreting

a solute load than is the kidney of the older child because of decreased availability of urea and decreased tubular length and responsiveness to antidiuretic hormone (ADH). The neonate uses nearly all dietary protein for growth; as a result, less protein is catabolized to urea, and less medullary urea is available in the loop of Henle to concentrate the urine. As the infant's protein intake increases, more urea is available in the urine, and urine osmolality increases. In addition, as the child grows, the tubules lengthen and become more responsive to ADH. For these reasons, renal concentrating ability increases.

During the first year of life the kidney has a lower threshold for bicarbonate reabsorption than during any other period of life. The ability to excrete acid is limited during the first weeks of life by low GFR; thus metabolic acidosis may develop rapidly in the infant with increased hydrogen ion production.

Normal minimal urine volume in the well-hydrated infant averages 2 ml/kg/hr, and normal minimal urine volume in the child averages 1 ml/kg/hr. The well-hydrated adult may excrete only 0.5 ml/kg/hr on average. Normal urine osmolality is hypotonic with respect to plasma during the first days of life but usually approaches adult values within the first month of life.

Glucose homeostasis. As noted previously, hypoglycemia may develop in critically ill infants. Therefore the infant's serum or heelstick glucose concentration must be closely monitored (hourly or more often if condition and marginal glucose levels indicate). The critically ill infant requires a continuous source of glucose intake to maintain an acceptable serum glucose level. Intermittent bolus administration of glucose in response to hypoglycemia will only perpetuate wide fluctuations in serum glucose concentration; therefore continuous glucose infusion is the preferred method of treatment of hypoglycemia. Hyperglycemia needs to be prevented during cardiopulmonary and trauma resuscitation because it has been linked with poor neurologic outcome.

GASTROINTESTINAL FUNCTION AND METABOLIC DIFFERENCES
Anatomic Differences

GI system. At birth all structures of the alimentary tract are present, although they increase in size and function during childhood. Infant pancreatic enzyme secretion is immature, but other digestive enzymes are present in higher quantities to compensate. For the most part, GI secretory function, enzyme activity, and carbohydrate and fat absorption are similar in the infant and adult. The mucosal barrier within the small intestine epithelium is incomplete in the neonate; thus ingested food antigens may be absorbed during the first weeks of life. In addition, the bacterial flora of the GI tract may be a source of bacteremia in the neonate.

At birth the liver synthesizes plasma proteins (except immunoglobulins); stores, synthesizes, and converts carbohydrates; and releases glucose from glucagon, just as in the adult. However, the neonatal liver is immature, and enzymatic synthesis and degradation do not reach adult levels until several weeks or months of age. Synthesis of vitamin K–dependent clotting factors is reduced significantly at birth, and prothrombin time is often dramatically prolonged on the second or third day of life; this decrease in clotting factor levels is prevented by the administration of vitamin K in the neonate.

Physiologic jaundice develops in newborn infants for a variety of reasons. Bilirubin production is higher than in the adult during the first days of life. Neonates also have lower plasma-binding capacity for bilirubin, reduced hepatic uptake of bilirubin, decreased hepatic conjugation of bilirubin, and limited hepatic bilirubin excretion compared with adults (see Chapter 87).

Nutritional requirements. The child's metabolic rate is higher than that of the adult, so the child's nutritional and caloric needs also are higher per kilogram body weight than in the adult.

Thermoregulation. Infants and young children have a large surface area to volume ratio and decreased insulating subcutaneous fat stores. As a result, they can lose a great deal of heat to the environment through evaporation and radiation. Additional heat loss occurs with administration of large volumes of room temperature IV or dialysis fluids. The infant cannot shiver to generate heat during episodes of cold stress and is forced to break down "brown fat," located around the kidneys, adrenal glands, between the scapulae, and around the large thoracic vessels (see below).

Physiologic Differences

GI system. Gastric motility is reduced and gastric emptying is more rapid in the neonate and infant than in the older child, and virtually all neonates have some degree of gastroesophageal reflux.

The neonatal liver is less able to metabolize toxic substances through oxidative detoxification or conjugation than is the liver of the older child or adult. Depression of these activities may result in prolongation of beneficial or toxic effects of drugs or their metabolites.

Conjugation of bilirubin by the newborn liver is less efficient than in older children or adults. During the neonatal period bilirubin load is increased as the result of more rapid erythrocyte turnover and bilirubin production and enhanced intestinal bilirubin reabsorption. These conditions result in transient hyperbilirubinemia even in healthy neonates and more profound hyperbilirubinemia in premature neonates.

Nutritional requirements. The child's maintenance caloric requirements are higher per kilogram body weight than the requirements of the adult. In addition, a large portion of the child's caloric requirements are needed for basal metabolism and cell growth. For this reason, even the comatose child needs high-calorie nutrition, and the child with cardiorespiratory distress, sepsis, wound healing, or multisystem disease or trauma may well need nearly double the average "maintenance" calories. Caloric requirements are increased approximately 10% per day for each degree elevation in temperature >37° C. The highest known caloric requirements are in burn patients.

Thermoregulation. When the infant is exposed to a cold environmental temperature, endogenous norepinephrine is secreted, stimulating the breakdown of brown fat and release of heat. However, this "nonshivering thermogenesis" is an energy-requiring process and results in increased oxygen consumption. To eliminate the need for nonshivering thermogenesis, a neutral thermal environment needs to be provided for the neonate and young infant. A neutral thermal environment is that environmental temperature at which the neonate maintains a rectal temperature of 37° C with the lowest oxygen consumption. The ranges of neutral thermal environment have been experimentally determined for infants of various ages and birthweights (see Chapter 56). Neutral thermal environments can be maintained most efficiently in the PICU with overbed warmers. These warmers heat the air around the infant or child yet allow ready access to the patient for observation or treatment. Such warmers are used only with servo-

controls, so the risk of excessive or inadequate warming and thermal injury is reduced (see Chapter 127), and drafts near the bedside need to be eliminated. Use of radiant warmers will increase evaporative fluid losses in young infants, and fluid administration rate needs to be evaluated accordingly.

IMMUNOLOGIC DIFFERENCES

Neonates are particularly vulnerable to infection for several reasons. Passive immunity is normally conveyed from the mother to the fetus through transmission of immunoglobulins during the last trimester. Thus the very premature neonate is immunoglobulin-deficient. The neonate has decreased polymorphonuclear leukocyte function and small polymorphonuclear leukocyte storage pools. Neonates also have a decreased ability to synthesize new antibodies, and they cannot make and deliver adequate numbers of phagocytes to sites of infection. Poor nutrition during hospitalization can lead to reduced protein synthesis and further reduction in antibody formation.

Infants have not yet built up their own immunoglobulin stores, and maternal immunoglobulin stores are depleted at approximately 2 to 5 months of age. As a result, infants are less able to phagocytize bacteria or form antibodies, which leaves them particularly vulnerable to polysaccharide-carrying bacteria (e.g., *Haemophilus influenzae*) between 4 to 18 months of age. Low immunoglobulin levels also render the infant susceptible to viral infection. Adult levels of immunoglobulins are achieved at approximately 4 to 7 years of age.

Although there is a widespread perception that children are also more susceptible to infection than adults, the prevalence of nosocomial infections in the PICU is actually lower than that of similar infections in adult ICUs. The sites of nosocomial infections differ between pediatric and adult patients. Nosocomial infections in children are most likely to develop as cutaneous infections, bacteremias, or pneumonias, whereas nosocomial infections in adults are most likely to be urinary tract or wound infections.

There is no question that the risk of nosocomial infection increases when the child remains in the PICU for more than 14 days or is subjected to prolonged intubation, arterial or CVP catheterization, or ICP monitoring. Thorough handwashing before and after patient contact is mandatory for every member of the health care team (see Chapter 39).

ADDITIONAL READING

Agostoni E, Mognoni P, Torri G. Relation between changes of rib cage circumference and lung volume. J Appl Physiol 20:1179, 1965.

Aherne W, Hull D. Brown adipose tissue and heat production in the newborn infant. J Pathol Bacteriol 91:223, 1966.

Berman WJ Jr. The relationship of age to the effects and toxicity of digoxin in sheep. In Heymann MA, Rudolph AM (Co-Chairpersons). The Ductus Arteriosus. Report of the Seventy-fifth Ross Conference on Pediatric Research. Columbus, Ohio: Ross Laboratories, 1978.

Bohn DJ, Poirier CS, Edmonds JF, et al. Hemodynamic effects of dobutamine after cardiopulmonary bypass in children. Crit Care Med 8:367, 1980.

Boyden EA. Development and growth of the airways. In Hodson WA, ed. Development of the Lung. New York: Marcel Dekker, 1977.

Brown RB, Hosmer D, Chen HC, et al. A comparison of infections in different ICUs within the same hospital. Crit Care Med 13:472, 1985.

Bruce DA, Schut L. Management of acute craniocerebral trauma in children. Contemp Neurosurg 10:1, 1979.

• Chameides I, Hazinski, MF, eds. Textbook of Pediatric Advanced Life Support. Dallas: American Heart Association, 1994.

Chernick V, Avery ME. The functional basis of respiratory pathology. In Kendig EL, ed. Disorders of the Respiratory Tract in Children. Philadelphia: WB Saunders, 1977.

Clyman RI, Roman C, Heymann MA, et al. How a patent ductus arteriosus affects the premature lamb's ability to handle additional volume loads. Pediatr Res 22:531, 1987.

• Clyman RI, Teitel D, Padbury J, et al. The role of beta-adrenoreceptor stimulation and contractile state in the preterm lamb's response to altered ductus atreriosus patency. Pediatr Res 23:316, 1988.

Committee on Trauma, American College of Surgeons. Advanced Trauma Life Support Course for Physicians, 5th ed. Chicago: American College of Surgeons, 1993.

• Coulter DL. Neurologic uncertainty in newborn intensive care. N Engl J Med 316:841, 1987.

Davis GM, Bureau MA. Pulmonary mechanics in newborn respiratory control. Clin Perinatol 14:551, 1987.

Deschpande JK, Tobias JD. The Pediatric Pain Handbook. St. Louis: Mosby, 1996.

Donn SM, Kuhns LR. Mechanisms of endotracheal tube movement with change of head position in the neonate. Pediatr Radiol 9:39, 1980.

Driscoll DJ. Use of inotropic and chronotropic agents in neonates. Clin Perinatol 14:931, 1987.

Edelman CM Jr, Barnett HL, Troupka V. Renal concentrating mechanisms in newborn infants. J Clin Invest 39:1062, 1960.

Eisenberg M, Bergner L, Hallstrom A. Epidemiology of cardiac arrest and resuscitation in children. Ann Emerg Med 12:672, 1983.

Finholt DA, Kettrick RG, Wagner HR, et al. The heart is under the lower third of the sternum. Am J Dis Child 140:646, 1986.

Freeman JM, Ferry PC. New brain death guidelines in children: Further confusion. Pediatrics 81:301, 1988.

Friedman WF. The intrinsic physiologic properties of the developing heart. In Friedman WF, ed. Neonatal Heart Disease. New York: Grune & Stratton, 1973.

Friedman WF, Pool PE, Jacobowitz D, et al. Sympathetic innervation of the developing rabbit heart. Circ Res 23:25, 1968.

Friss-Hansen B. Body water compartments in children. Pediatrics 28:169, 1961.

Gillette PC, et al. Dysrhythmias. In Adams FH, Emmanouilides GC, et al., eds. Moss' Heart Disease in Infants, Children, and Adolescents, 4th ed. Baltimore: Williams & Wilkins, 1989.

Godfrey S. Respiration. In Godfrey S, Baum J. Clinical Pediatric Physiology. Oxford: Blackwell, 1979.

Graef JW. Manual of Pediatric Therapeutics, 5th ed. Boston: Little, Brown, 1994.

Graham TP Jr, Jarmakani JM, Atwood GF, et al. Right ventricular volume determinations in children. Normal values and observations with volume or pressure overload. Circulation 47:144, 1973.

Harrison VC, de Hesse E, Klein M. The significance of grunt in hyaline membrane disease. Pediatrics 41:549, 1968.

Hazinski MF. Is pediatric resuscitation unique? The relative merits of early CPR and ventilation versus early defibrillation for young victims of prehospital cardiac arrest [editorial]. Ann Emerg Med 25:540, 1995.

• Hazinski MF. Hemodynamic monitoring of children. In Daily EK, Schroeder JS, eds. Techniques in Bedside Hemodynamic Monitoring, 5th ed. St. Louis: Mosby, 1995.

Hazinski MF. Pediatric advanced life support. In Cummins RO, ed. Textbook of Advanced Cardiac Life Support, Dallas: American Heart Association, 1994.

Hazinski MF. Postoperative care of the critically ill child. Crit Care Nurs Clin North Am 2:599, 1990

Hazinski MF. Nursing care of the critically ill child: The 7-point check. Pediatr Nurs 11:453, 1985.

Hellerstein S. Fluid and electrolytes: Clinical aspects. Pediatr Rev 14:103, 1993.

Hirschl RB. Oxygen delivery in the pediatric surgical patient. Curr Opin Pediatr 6:341, 1994.

Hogg JC, Williams J, Richardson JB, et al. Age as a factor in the distribution of lower-airway conductance and in the pathologic anatomy of obstructive lung disease. N Engl J Med 282:1283, 1970.

Jansen AH, Chernick V. Onset of breathing and control of respiration. Semin Perinatol 12:104, 1988.

Klopfenstein HS, Rudolph AM. Postnatal changes in the circulation and responses to volume loading in sheep. Circ Res 42:839, 1978.

Kirsch JR, Traystman RJ, Rogers MC. Cerebral blood flow measurement techniques in infants and children. Pediatrics 75:887, 1985.

Liebman J, Plonsey R. Electrocardiography. In Adams FH, Emmanouilides GC, eds. Moss' Heart Disease in Infants, Children, and Adolescents, 4th ed. Baltimore: Williams & Wilkins, 1989.

McBride JT, Wohl MEB, Strieder DJ, et al. Lung growth and airway function after lobectomy in infancy for congenital lobar emphysema. J Clin Invest 66:962, 1980.

Menon RK, Sperling MA. Carbohydrate metabolism. Semin Perinatol 12:157, 1988.

Meyers A. Fluid and electrolyte therapy for children. Curr Opin Pediatr 6:303, 1994.

Milliken J, Tait GA, Ford-Jones EL, et al. Nosocomial infections in a pediatric intensive care unit. Crit Care Med 16:233, 1988.

Morray JP, Tyler DC, Jones TK, et al. Coma scale for use in brain-injured children. Crit Care Med 12:1018, 1984.

Muller NI, Bryan AC. Chest wall mechanics and respiratory muscles. Pediatr Clin North Am 26:503, 1979.

Orlowski J. Optimum position for external cardiac compression in infants and young children. Ann Emerg Med 15:667, 1986.

Park MK. Use of digoxin in infants and children, with specific emphasis on dosage. J Pediatr 108:871, 1986.

Perkin RM, Levin DL, Webb R, et al. Dobutamine: A hemodynamic evaluation in children with shock. J Pediatr 100:977, 1982.

Portnoy JM, Olson LC. Normal cerebrospinal values in children: Another look. Pediatrics 75:484, 1985.

Robatham JL. Maturation of the respiratory system. In Shoemaker WC, Thompson WL, Holbrook PR, eds. Textbook of Critical Care, 2nd ed. Philadelphia: WB Saunders, 1988.

Roberts RJ. Drug Therapy in Infants: Pharmacologic Principles and Clinical Experience. Philadelphia: WB Saunders, 1984.

Robillard JE, Nakamura KT, Matherne GP, et al. Renal hemodynamics and functional adjustments to postnatal life. Semin Perinatol 12:143, 1988.

Romero TE, Friedman WF. Limited left ventricular response to volume overload in the neonatal period: A comparative study with the adult animal. Pediatr Res 13:910, 1979.

Romero T, Covell J, Friedman W. A comparison of pressure-volume relations of the fetal, newborn and adult heart. Am J Physiol 222:1285, 1972.

Rowlatt UF, Rimoldi HJA, Lev M. The quantitative anatomy of the normal child's heart. Pediatr Clin North Am 10:499, 1963.

Rudolph AM, ed. Pediatrics, 20th ed. Boston: Appleton & Lange, 1996.

Rudolph AM. Fetal circulation and cardiovascular adjustments after birth. In Rudolph AM, ed. Pediatrics, 20th ed. East Norwalk, Conn.: Appleton & Lange, 1996.

Rudolph AM. The changes in the circulation after birth. Circulation 41:343, 1970.

Rudolph AM, Heymann MA. Cardiac output in the fetal lamb: The effects of spontaneous and induced changes of heart rate on right and left ventricular output. Am J Obstet Gynecol 124:183, 1976.

Sarff LD, Platt LH, McCracken GH Jr, et al. Cerebrospinal fluid evaluation in neonates: Comparison of high-risk neonates with and without meningitis. J Pediatr 88:473, 1976.

Schreiber MD, Meymann MA, Soifer SJ. Increased arterial pH, not decreased $PaCO_2$ attenuates hypoxia-induced pulmonary vasoconstriction in newborn lambs. Pediatr Res 20:113, 1986.

Shelley HJ. Carbohydrate reserves in the newborn infant. Br Med J 1:273, 1964.

Spotnitz WD, Spotnitz HM, Truccone NJ, et al. Relation of ultrastructure and function. Sarcomere dimensions, pressure-volume curves, and geometry of the intact left ventricle of the immature canine heart. Circ Res 44:679, 1979.

• Task Force on Brain Death Determination in Children. Guidelines for the determination of brain death in children. Pediatrics 80:298, 1987.

Thornburg KL, Morton MJ. Filling and arterial pressures as determinants of RV stroke volume in the sheep fetus. Am J Physiol 244:H656, 1983.

Tooley WH. Lung growth in infancy and childhood. In Rudolph AM, ed. Pediatrics, 18th ed. East Norwalk, Conn.: Appleton & Lange, 1986.

Walsh CK, Krongrad E. Terminal cardiac electrical activity in pediatric patients. Am J Cardiol 51:557, 1983.

Wilson CB. Immunologic basis for increased susceptibility of the neonate to infection. J Pediatr 108:1, 1986.

Younkin D, Delivoria-Papadopoulos M, Reivich M, et al. Regional variations in human newborn cerebral blood flow. J Pediatr 112:104, 1988.

• Zaritsky A, Chernow B. Use of catecholamines in pediatrics. J Pediatr 105:341, 1984.

Zaritsky A, Lotze A, Stull R, et al. Steady-state dopamine clearance in critically ill infants and children. Crit Care Med 16:217, 1988.

Zuccarello M, Facco E, Zampieri P, et al. Severe head injury in children: Early prognosis and outcome. Childs Nerv Syst 1:158, 1985.

123 Admission and Discharge Criteria and Procedures

Donna S. Rahn · Laura A. Wells

ADMISSION CRITERIA

Patients admitted to a PICU vary in age from newborn infants to teenagers. Their illnesses are as varied as their ages and involve all major organ systems. The one thing they all have in common is they are critically ill and depend on the expertise and knowledge of the medical team. Patients may come from the operating room after surgery and need close observation by a staff skilled in caring for their particular needs. Patients may also be transferred from the nursing units because they need more aggressive care and closer supervision than can be provided on the unit or from another hospital that was unable to provide the necessary care. To be accepted for admission to the PICU, patients must meet specific criteria so that the advanced and highly skilled resources of the PICU are appropriately used. Specific admission and discharge criteria must be developed for each institution. A written hospital policy that details both admission and discharge criteria must be developed, routinely revised, and frequently monitored by a multidisciplinary team consisting of physicians, nurses, and hospital administrators. The policy needs to include guidelines for reconciling admission requests and limitations of care for the terminally ill. Many institutions detail exclusion criteria as well as specific guidelines for brain death and termination of care. Despite discharge criteria, consideration must be given to the quality and degree of care to be provided at the discharge destination.

When the designated admission criteria are met, the PICU attending physician, charge nurse, and respiratory team leader coordinate the patient's admission to the unit. All patients admitted to the PICU have specific problems; initial, thorough assessment is imperative to identify and treat these specific problems early, thoroughly, and aggressively.

The initial assessment is the basis of all further observations and is relied on throughout the hospital stay as a basis for comparison with later observations. Early observations, best noted by the admitting nurse, must be recorded accurately and completely with charting. Recording of the basic assessment and initial data is necessary for proper management of the patient and demonstrates the progress of that management by noting changes from the information recorded initially. Medications, fluid calculations, and placement of various catheters rely on the accuracy of the nurse in obtaining and charting the patient's weight and body measurements (e.g., frontal-occipital head circumference [FOC], abdominal girth, chest circumference, length or height, and shoulder-to-umbilicus length). The admission routine is performed as quickly and thoroughly as the patient's condition will allow. Patients admitted under emergency conditions who need more immediate attention undergo a brief assessment to identify the most critical needs followed by a complete assessment after the patient's condition has stabilized. A thorough assessment can enable identification of problems not related to the admitting diagnosis and other unrecognized or potential problems.

The PICU nurse and physician must rely on their instincts as well as the physical data in caring for the critically ill child. Physical data can be interpreted as critical or not, depending on the overall assessment of the patient. The health care specialists at the bedside need to look at the patient, review the entire process, and rely on past experiences to realize how sick these children really are. When children become ill, their condition tends to deteriorate rapidly until medical intervention slows or stops the process. Therefore, when patients are scheduled for admission to the PICU, all necessary preparation must be completed before their arrival.

ADMISSION CRITERIA

Cardiac

Life-threatening arrhythmias
Temporary cardiac pacing
Invasive hemodynamic monitoring
Frequent observation after cardiothoracic surgery
Unstable heart disease

Respiratory

Assisted ventilation
Airway protection
Respiratory treatments more frequently than every
  hour
Intubation with an endotracheal tube
Rising P_{CO_2}
Decreasing P_{O_2} and O_2 saturation despite increasing
  F_{IO_2}
Marked stridor
$F_{IO_2} > 0.50$

Neurologic

ICP monitoring
Increased ICP
Frequent neurologic assessments
After craniotomy
Unstable seizures and neurologic disease
Closed head injury

GI

Active GI bleeding
Advanced diarrhea and dehydration
Frequent observation after surgery

Other

Manual peritoneal dialysis with dwell times every hour
Vasoactive drug infusion
Medications with potential for severe reactions
Severe electrolyte or fluid imbalance
Potentially lethal ingestions
After tracheostomy

DISCHARGE CRITERIA

Cardiac

Stable cardiac rhythm
Invasive hemodynamic monitoring no longer re-
  quired
Stable hemodynamic assessments

Respiratory

F_{IO_2} requirement < 0.50
Respiratory treatments more frequently than every 2
  hours
Extubation
Stable artificial airway (tracheostomy)
Long-term mechanical ventilation once settings have
  been stabilized; frequently these patients will need
  home mechanical ventilation

Neurologic

ICP monitoring no longer needed
Normal ICP
Seizures controlled and stable neurologic disease

GI

No GI bleeding
Fluid shifts resolved

Other

Manual peritoneal dialysis with dwell times less frequent than every hour
Stable fluid and electrolyte balance
Vasoactive drug infusions not needed except in patients awaiting heart transplantation, if condition is
  otherwise stable

PREPARING FOR ADMISSION

The most important initial task when admission to the PICU is expected is to prepare for the patient's arrival. Having become familiar with all available information about the patient, the admitting nurse can anticipate the patient's needs and have all necessary equipment available and in working order for any emergency situation that might arise on or shortly after arrival.

Once the patient is accepted, the nurse must set up the patient care area. The appropriate size bed, isolette, or radiant warmer must be obtained. A cardiac-respiratory monitor with capability for pressure readings, an oxygen saturation monitor, and a noninvasive automatic blood pressure device (when available) must be checked for proper functioning. Essential emergency resuscitation equipment must be at all bedsides (e.g., anesthesia bag and appropriate size mask for hand ventilation, suction device and appropriate size catheters, tonsil suction equipment, oxygen, and IV equipment including infusion pump and tubing; see Chapter 125). A crash cart (including emergency medications), a procedure cart for intubation and/or cutdowns, a thoracentesis tray, and a defibrillator must be immediately available. A scale for weighing the patient must be at the bedside, and when indicated a mechanical ventilator or other respiratory equipment must be available. Possible procedures need to be anticipated and any necessary supplies collected (e.g., nasogastric or feeding tube, bladder catheterization set, transducers for pressure lines [arterial or CVP], materials for obtaining specimens for laboratory studies, and lumbar puncture tray). The bedside drawers are stocked with a stethoscope and appropriate size blood pressure cuff as well as necessary equipment for routine care. The necessary paperwork is assembled for routine admission: nursing assessment and narrative notes; medication and graphic records; physician admission, history, and progress notes; physician orders; and respiratory therapy records.

ADMISSION ASSESSMENT

On arrival the patient must be assessed for any distress or physiologic instability that must be taken care of immediately. If the child's condition seems stable, vital signs need to be taken, including heart rate, respiratory rate, systemic arterial blood pressure, temperature, and capillary refill time. After vital signs are measured, the patient can be transferred to the scales. While a patient is being weighed, every precaution

---

ESSENTIAL BEDSIDE ITEMS

Alcohol swabs
Povidone-iodine swabs
Adhesive bandages
Tape
Cotton balls
Adhesive remover
Syringe adapters
Blood specimen tubes
Stethoscope
Noninvasive blood pressure device
Temperature probe adhesive pads
Needleless needle-syringe system
Cotton-tipped applicators
Bedside glucose monitoring equipment
Personal protection equipment (gloves, masks, gowns, and eye protection)
Lancets
Electrodes
Tape measure
Safety pins
Rubber bands
Lubricant
Tongue blades
Urine dipsticks
Blood pressure cuff

ADMISSION ROUTINES

Weight
Temperature
Heart rate
Respiratory rate
Blood pressure
Glucose determination
Urine specimen
Urine dipstick or urinalysis
Specific gravity
Suction
Measurements (for infants <1 mo or <2500 g)
    Frontal-occipital circumference
    Abdominal girth
    Heel-to-crown length
    Chest circumference
    Shoulder-to-umbilicus length

must be taken to provide adequate oxygen and ventilatory support. After transfer to the PICU bed, the cardiac monitor must be attached, with appropriate alarm limits set for each patient and the alarms activated. Any tubes or catheters must be checked to ensure they are adequately secured and patent. The oxygen saturation monitor is applied when available. In many situations restraints may need to be placed on the patient's hands or feet to protect the child from removing catheters, drains, or tubes, particularly the endotracheal tube. The restraints need to be placed with caution, not too tight but secure enough to serve their purpose.

If an emergency situation arises during admission, the child must be placed on the PICU bed immediately. The weight and vital signs can be obtained after any critical problems are resolved and the patient's condition is more stable.

A complete assessment needs to be documented accurately and completely on the nursing records (Fig. 123-1). The assessment must include those parameters necessary for determination of morbidity and mortality scores (e.g., Pediatric Risk of Mortality score; see Chapter 124). The following items are to be included on every assessment. Those with an asterisk must be done immediately; the others can wait until the patient's condition is stabilized.

Cardiac System

* *Temperature:* Obtain the axillary temperature of infants who weigh <2500 g, are <1 month of age, or are at risk for rectal bleeding. Obtain the rectal temperature of larger infants and children, especially those who have had cardiac surgery or neurosurgery.
* *Heart rate:* Obtain rate for 1 full minute by means of auscultation over the precordium, assess strength and regularity, and listen for possible murmurs.
* *Blood pressure:* Determine value (with appropriate size cuff; see Chapter 125) by means of auscultation, palpation, or noninvasive blood pressure device. Include arterial systolic, diastolic, and mean blood pressure when available.
* *Other pressures:* Record values for any additional pressure values being measured such as CVP, pulmonary artery pressure, and ICP.
* *Pulses:* Palpate pulses in all four extremities for strength and regularity. Document any differences noted.
* *Capillary refill:* Count the number of seconds it takes

for color to return after pressing on skin or nail beds.

Venous access: Verify condition of present IV catheter. If no venous access has been established, place a peripheral IV catheter as soon as possible. If the patient's condition is unstable and venous access is unsuccessful, an interosseous catheter must be considered or a central venous catheter placed by an experienced physician (see Chapter 131).

Cardiac assessment is necessary to evaluate for adequate perfusion and cardiac output. A rapid heart rate, normal or low blood pressure, weak pulses, and prolonged capillary refill time of >3 seconds may indicate poor cardiac output and fluid resuscitation may be needed. An infant or child in shock will not always have low blood pressure. If the patient's temperature is low, take measures to warm the patient (i.e., use blankets to cover the child or place the patient under a radiant warmer with a temperature probe. Notify the physician of any concerns noted during cardiac assessment.

Respiratory System

* *Respiratory rate:* Count for 1 full minute, assessing respiratory effort; observe for distress, stridor, snoring, nasal flaring, grunting, retractions, audible wheezing, and chest asymmetry.
* *Color:* Note color of skin, lips, mucous membranes, and nail beds.
* *Breath sounds:* Auscultate for bilateral air movement; note any wheezes, crackles, or coarseness and document any dissimilar findings. If an endotracheal tube is in place, make certain it is taped securely and confirm the position of the tip of the tube by chest radiography.
* *Secretions:* Suction the nose, mouth, pharynx, and endotracheal tube when necessary, ensuring patency of the airway. Note color and consistency of secretions when suctioning is performed.
* *Protective airway reflexes:* Note the presence or absence of the gag or cough reflex.
* *Chest tubes:* Note the presence of any chest tubes and their location; assess the amount, color, and character of the drainage. Assess the drainage collection system for a proper underwater seal and ordered suction.

The respiratory evaluation is critical in assessment of a new patient. An oral or nasal airway and appropriate head position may be needed to maintain a patent airway in the neurologically depressed patient. If a patent airway has been established and the patient is still having difficulty breathing, other respiratory variables must be assessed. Oxygen saturation monitors and blood gas levels can be used to determine ventilation and oxygenation. Patients may need assisted oxygen and hand ventilation, either with a mask or endotracheal tube. Whether the patient arrives with an endotracheal tube or one is placed at admission, mechanical ventilatory assistance will be needed. Evaluate the effectiveness of mechanical ventilation by observing the patient for signs of distress and poor oxygenation. The ventilator settings may need to be adjusted and confirmed with determination of arterial or venous blood gas level and pH.

Neurologic System

* *Level of consciousness:* Determine alertness, awareness, and response to painful stimuli (nonpurposeful vs. purposeful). Determine the patient's Glasgow Coma Scale score (Fig. 123-1).
* *Pupils:* Observe the pupils with a bright light and determine their responsiveness and size.
* *Activity:* Note movement, including strength and symmetry of extremities, and any jitteriness or irritability.
* *Seizures:* Observe and describe any seizure activity; note areas affected by the seizure, eye deviation, duration of seizure, and response to any interventions.
* *Fontanel:* If applicable, palpate the fontanel; document whether it is full, tense, bulging, or depressed.

Joints: Document any contractures or immobilized limbs.

The neurologic examination may give insight into serious or even life-threatening problems. A change in the patient's level of consciousness is usually an early sign of neurologic or perfusion problems. Consult the patient's family to evaluate the significance of change in mentation or behavior. Changes in pupil size and reactivity may be a late sign of increasing ICP.

GI System

Abdomen: Inspect for distention; auscultate for presence or absence of bowel sounds; check placement of nasogastric tube; palpate for tightness and tenderness.

Drainage: Empty stomach contents with a feeding tube or nasogastric tube. If continuous suction is needed to the stomach, use a nasogastric tube. Note the position of any surgically placed drains (e.g., Hemovac or Jackson-Pratt drains, peritoneal dialysis catheter, or ostomies); note color, consistency, and quantity of all drainage; check drainage for presence of blood when any bleeding is suspected.

Stool: When stool is present, describe color, consistency, and amount; check for presence of blood when bleeding is a possibility.

Genitourinary System

Urine: Verify with transport team when the patient last voided. When necessary, place urine collection bag on patient to secure a sample for urinalysis; also check with a urine dipstick and measure specific gravity. Note color, clarity, odor, and quantity.

Palpate the bladder for fullness. If the patient is oliguric or anuric, insert a bladder catheter if one is not already in place. If a catheter is in place and there is little or no urine output, check the patency of the catheter, observing for kinks in the tubing and irrigating the catheter if necessary. Small amounts of urine may indicate hypovolemia or decreased kidney perfusion. Large amounts of urine may indicate diabetes insipidus or other endocrine imbalance.

Integument

Skin: Document the patient's skin temperature, skin turgor, muscle tone, and any edema noted. Assess moistness of the mucous membranes and document any lesions noted. Observe for any interruptions in skin integrity (e.g., rash, erythema, bruises, petechiae, burns, or areas of breakdown). Document size, color, location, and extent of affected area.

Wounds: Assess any wounds for drainage or hemorrhage, especially in the immediate postoperative period. Removal of the dressings may be necessary to fully assess the wound.

Serious bruising or petechiae may be indicative of bleeding disorders. When an integumentary or neurologic examination yields suspicious findings, the possibility of child abuse must be considered. Use caution and judgment when investigating a suspected child abuse case (see Chapter 102).

Intravascular Catheters

Document the sites of all intravascular catheters and assess for patency. Document the kind of IV fluid being infused. When catheters equipped with a pressure transducer are used, document the presence and description of the waveforms seen on the monitor.

DATE ___ / ___ / ___

CODES

T I M E		NEURO							CARDIAC				RESPIRATORY			
	PUPILS		COMA SCORE			F O N T	A C T I V		HEART SOUNDS	PERIPH PULSES	CAPIL REFILL		COLOR LIPS/NAILS	RESP QUALITY	BREATH SOUNDS
	L	R	E	V	M										

NEURO

Pupils

± — REACTS SLOWLY
+ — REACTS
‡ — REACTS BRISKLY
– — NO REACTION

Coma Score

E O 4 — SPONTANEOUSLY
Y P 3 — TO SPEECH
E E 2 — TO PAIN
S N 1 — NONE
    0 — CLOSED BY SWELLING

V R 5 — ORIENTED
E E 4 — CONFUSED, EASILY AROUSED
R S 3 — INAPPROPRIATE
B P   WORDS, CRIES TO STIMULUS
A O 2 — INCOMPREHENSIBLE
L N   SOUNDS
  S 1 — NONE
  E 0*— ETT, TRACH

M R 6 — OBEYS COMMANDS
O E 5 — LOCALIZE PAIN
T S 4 — WITHDRAWS IN
O P   RESPONSE TO PAIN
R O 3 — FLEXION TO PAIN
  N 2 — EXTENSION TO PAIN
  S 1 — NONE
  E   USUALLY RECORD
        BEST ARM RESPONSE

Mod. Infant Coma Score

V R 5 — COOS, BABBLES
E E 4 — IRRITABLE; CRIES
R S 3 — CRIES TO PAIN
B P 2 — MOANS TO PAIN
A O 1 — NONE
L N
  S
  E

M R 6 — NORMAL SPONTANEOUS
O E   MOVEMENTS
T S 5 — WITHDRAWS TO TOUCH
O P 4 — WITHDRAWS TO PAIN
R O 3 — ABNORMAL FLEXION
  N 2 — ABNORMAL EXTENSION
  S 1 — NONE
  E

Fontanel

S — SOFT   Fr — FIRM
F — FLAT   FI — FULL
D — DEPRESSED B — BULGING

Activity

SA — SPONTANEOUSLY ACTIVE,
      MOVES ALL EXTREMITIES
AS — ACTIVE WITH STIMULATION
I — IRRITABLE
J — JITTERY
S — SEIZURE *
↓ — DECREASED ACTIVITY
↑ — INCREASED ACTIVITY
N — NO RESPONSE

CARDIAC

Heart Sounds

S — STRONG
R — REGULAR
I — IRREGULAR
M — MURMUR
D — DISTANT

RESPIRATORY

Color

P — PINK
W — PALE
D — DUSKY
C — CYANOTIC

Respiratory Quality

N — EASY, UNLABORED
S — SHALLOW
R — RETRACTIONS
F — NASAL FLARING
P — PERIODIC
A — APNEIC
IP — IN PHASE

Breath Sounds

= — EQUAL
↓ — DECREASED
C — CLEAR
CO — COARSE
CR — CRACKLES
WH — WHEEZES
W — WET
A — ABSENT

SUCTIONING

Airway

NT — NASAL TRACHEAL TUBE
OT — ORAL TRACHEAL TUBE
T — TRACHEOSTOMY
H — HALO
F — FACE TENT
M — MIST TENT

Secretion Color

C — CLEAR
W — WHITE
Y — YELLOW
T — TAN
G — GREEN
B — BLOODY

Consistency

T — THIN
TH — THICK
F — FROTHY

G. I.

Abdomen

S — SOFT
F — FLAT
R — ROUNDED
FM — FIRM
D — DISTENDED

Bowel Sounds

+ — PRESENT
– — ABSENT
↑ — HYPERACTIVE
↓ — HYPOACTIVE

NG Color

C — CLEAR
G — GREEN
Y — YELLOW
CG — COFFEE GROUND
OB — OLD BLOOD
BR — BRIGHT RED
A — ANTACID

G. U.

Urine Source

D — DIAPER
F — FOLEY
UB — URINE BAG
O — OTHER *

Color

C — CLEAR
W — PALE
Y — YELLOW
A — AMBER
O — ORANGE
B — BLOODY

Clarity

C — CLEAR
CL — CLOUDY
S — SEDIMENT

OTHER

Skin Integrity

W — WARM   P — PETECHIAE
C — COOL   R — RASH
M — MOIST   S — SCALY
D — DRY   O — OTHER *

Skin Turgor

E — ELASTIC
TA — TAUT
TN — TENTING

Edema

P — PITTING
N — NON-PITTING

Muscle Tone

A — APPROPRIATE
F — FLACCID
E — EXAGGERATED

Patient Turned

R — RIGHT SIDE
L — LEFT SIDE
P — PRONE
S — SUPINE

*See Nurses Notes

*SEE NURSES NOTES

Fig. 123-1   PICU flow sheet for nursing assessment.

ASSESSMENT

SUCTION CATHETER SIZE____					G.I.					G.U.				OTHER					R.N. INIT
AIRWAY	AMOUNT	COLOR	SECRET	CONSIST	ABDOMEN	BOWEL SOUNDS	NG	COLOR		URINE SOURCE	COLOR	CLARITY		SKIN INTEG	SKIN TURGOR	EDEMA	MUSCLE TONE	PATIENT TURNED	

IV SITE CONDITION

N—PATENT, INFUSING WELL   H—HARD
R—RED   BL—BLANCHED
E—EDEMATOUS   RS—RED STREAKS
D—DRSG., DRY, INTACT

DAILY EQUIPMENT/CARE CHECKLIST

	07 to 14	15 to 22	23 to 06
C-R MONITOR, ALARMS ON			
SYRINGE PUMPS			
BLANKETROL			
MONATHERM			
GOMCO			
PHOTOTHERAPY LIGHTS			
DINAMAP / DOPPLER			
TRANSDUCERS IN USE			
CT TO SUCTION			
EXTERNAL PACEMAKER			
ISOLETTE, OHIO, CLINITRON			
MONITORS TcPO$_2$			
TcPCO$_2$			
O$_2$SAT			
END TIDAL CO$_2$			
EGGCRATE MATTRESS			
IV FLUID CHECKS			
IV SITE CHECKS			
BED CHECKS			
ISOLATION / TYPE _____			
HOB ↑			
RESTRAINTS ARMS			
LEGS			
HEAD			
IV PUMP / TUBING			
TRANSDUCER DOME Δ			
DRESSING Δ — CENTRAL LINE			
WOUND			
FOLEY CARE			
ORAL CARE			
TRACH CARE			
BATH / LINEN Δ			
ROM / PT			
PARENT CONTACT C / V			

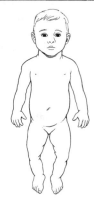

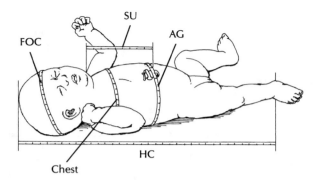

Fig. 123-2 Drawing showing correct placement of infant for measuring: *FOC,* frontal-occipital circumference; *SU,* shoulder-to-umbilicus length; *AG,* abdominal girth; *HC,* heel-to-crown length.

Measurements in Infants (Fig. 123-2)

Frontal-occipital head circumference (FOC): Measure daily in centimeters to detect any change in size. FOC is measured across the forehead, just above one ear, around the largest part of the back of the head, and above the other ear. Hydrocephalus is a common cause of steadily increasing FOC.

Abdominal girth (AG): Measure the abdomen in centimeters just above the umbilicus. An increase in size is one of the first signs of necrotizing enterocolitis in infants and denotes abdominal distention relative to intra-abdominal processes in older children.

Length (HC): Heel-to-crown measurement is used to determine the proper length of nasotracheal tube (length × 0.21 + 1 cm) and, with the weight, to determine body surface area:

$$\frac{(\text{Height [in]} \times \text{Weight [lb]})}{3131}$$

or

$$\frac{(\text{Height [cm]} \times \text{Weight [kg]})}{3600}$$

Shoulder-to-umbilicus (SU): Shoulder-to-umbilicus length (i.e., from the top of the shoulder to the umbilicus) is measured in centimeters. This measurement is used when an umbilical artery catheter is to be placed. The proper length of the catheter from tip to point of exit from the abdomen = SU × 0.65.

Chest circumference: The chest is measured in centimeters over the nipple line. Chest circumference is approximately the same as FOC.

Measurements are necessary to many functions performed in the PICU. Plotting the patient's weight, length, and FOC against standard growth charts can confirm significant growth abnormalities. Body surface area is used by clinicians for certain hemodynamic calculations and by pharmacy services to calculate drug doses.

Laboratory Tests on Admission

Bedside glucose determination: This reading indicates glucose homeostasis and is imperative in infants younger than 6 months and any patient with suspected hypoglycemia or hyperglycemia (e.g., coma, seizures, or hepatic failure). If the value is <45 mg/dl, an IV catheter must be placed immediately to administer glucose. After giving dextrose solution, the glucose value is checked every half hour until it is >45 mg/dl in infants or >90 mg/dl in older children.

Admission laboratory tests commonly include complete blood cell count and determination of electrolytes, glucose, calcium, and BUN concentrations. For any patient who might need blood products, a serum sample must be sent to the blood bank for crossmatching. Other laboratory tests will be ordered by the physician on the basis of the patient's condition. Anticipate drawing blood for testing and ensure that blood tubes and other necessary supplies are readily available.

PREPARING FOR DISCHARGE

When the patient meets discharge criteria and no longer needs the constant observation, skilled nursing care, and special PICU equipment, he or she can be discharged. The physicians, nurses, and respiratory therapists, with other members of the multidisciplinary team, must have completed discharge planning for the patient. Discharge planning needs to include preparation of the family and receiving unit for ongoing physiologic, rehabilitative, and emotional needs. The patient may need to be transferred to a "stepdown" unit or have special nursing care before being sent to a general care nursing unit. A thorough report of the patient's PICU admission, along with the medical record, must be communicated to the staff and the receiving physician who will be caring for the patient. Coordination with other services such as social work, pastoral care, physical and occupational therapy, child life workers, and home health care workers will be needed depending on the patient's discharge disposition. A multidisciplinary care conference is often necessary to accomplish a smooth transition from the PICU.

ADDITIONAL READING

Administrative Practice and Policy Manual. ICU Administrative Policies. Dallas: Division of Nursing, Children's Medical Center of Dallas.

Alspach JG, Williams SM. Core Curriculum or Critical Care Nursing. Philadelphia: WB Saunders, 1985.

Dawson JA. Admission, discharge, and triage in critical care: Principles and practice. Crit Care Clin 9:555-573, 1993.

• Hazinski MF. Nursing Care of the Critically Ill Child. St. Louis: Mosby, 1992.

Recommendations for intensive care unit admission and discharge criteria. Task Force on Guidelines, Society of Critical Care Medicine. Crit Care Med 16:807-808, 1988.

Silver HK, Kempe CH, Bruyn HB. Handbook of Pediatrics. Los Altos, Calif.: Lange Medical Publications, 1991.

• Whaley LF, Wong DL. Nursing Care of Infants and Children. St. Louis: Mosby, 1995.

124 Outcome and Risk Measures

Mark J. Heulitt · *Carolanne Capron* · *Debra H. Fiser*

BACKGROUND AND INDICATIONS

Clinical scoring systems are commonly used in clinical investigations and to compile comparison data within national databases. Scores that quantify clinical status to reflect probability of clinical outcomes include the Glasgow Coma Scale, Apgar score, croup score, and Pediatric Risk of Mortality (PRISM) score. Clinical scores are judged on their reliability, data requirements, and validity. To ensure maximum objectivity, the score must be based on routinely available information. Finally a valid score will be consistent with the clinician's common sense evaluation and perform as expected.

Risk measurements. Outcome cannot be interpreted without risk adjustment. Case-mix adjustments must account for the prognostic significance of the burden of illness that the patient brings to the hospital. There are a number of reasons to ascertain prognosis in the PICU environment. Individual patient decisions made by both the family and health care providers as well as allocation of resources, may be affected by knowledge of prognosis. In addition, prognosis is useful for risk adjustment for quality assurance purposes and for sample stratification for clinical research.

The clinical scoring systems discussed must not be confused with nursing-focused patient classification systems. Many of these classification systems are used to predict nurse staffing patterns based on validated time studies of nursing care provided. However, clinical scoring systems, acuity systems, and patient classification systems may be correlated because the patient with more acute illness needs more intensive nursing care but has a poorer prognostic score.

The Joint Commission on Accreditation of Healthcare Organizations (JCAHO) continues to challenge facilities to improve both their processes and outcomes through a multidisciplinary approach. Strong encouragement is also given to measurement with national comparisons. Therefore it is essential that medicine and nursing identify scoring systems that can be effectively taught and used within the clinical area.

TECHNIQUE

A designated space for recording clinical scoring information may be incorporated in the patient data record. This information may be collected at admission and discharge from the PICU or daily, depending on the scoring system used. A severity of illness score may also be used to estimate potential care needs for patients being transported to the PICU. The focus of the following discussion is on scoring systems that meet requirements of reliability, validity, and availability of routine information in the areas of risk measurements, outcome, and therapeutic interventions.

Pediatric Risk of Mortality

Severity of illness may be described in terms of disease stage classifications or with physiologic scores. Physiologic scores assigned at the time of PICU admission, such as PRISM, are preferred. PRISM, derived from the Physiologic Stability Index (PSI) (Table 124-1) and developed by Pollack et al., is a risk assessment score assigned at the time of PICU admission and is the most often used score in the PICU to predict risk of mortality. Its premise is that mortality risk assessment of PICU patients is proportional to the number of malfunctioning organ systems. The PRISM score (see Table 124-1) has 14 noninvasive variables and 23 ranges of these variables. The ranges of abnormality are weighted by their contribution to mortality risk. Variables not measured are assumed to be normal. The most deviant recorded variable for the admission day is used for scoring. The admission day time period used for scoring is a variable period of at least 8 hours. If less than 8 hours of time is accumulated, that time period is included in the next 24-hour period. Thus the admission day time period

Table 124-1 PRISM Score

Variable	Age Restrictions and Ranges		Score
Systolic blood pressure (mm Hg)	Infants: 130-160	Children: 150-200	2
	55-65	65-75	2
	>160	>200	6
	40-54	50-64	6
	<40	<50	7
Diastolic blood pressure (mm Hg)	All ages: >110		6
Heart rate (bpm)	Infants: >160	Children: >150	4
	<90	<80	4
Respiratory rate (breaths/min)	Infants: 61-90	Children: 51-70	1
	>90	>70	5
	Apnea	Apnea	5
Pao_2/Fio_2*	All ages: 200-300		2
	<200		3
$Paco_2$† (mm Hg)	All ages: 51-65		1
	>65		5
Glasgow Coma Scale score‡	All ages: <8		6
Pupillary reaction	All ages: Unequal or dilated		4
	Fixed and dilated		10
PT/PTT	All ages: 1.5 × control		2
Total bilirubin (mg/dl)	>1 month: >3.5		6
Potassium (mEq/L)	All ages: 3.0-3.5		1
	6.5-7.5		1
	<3.0		5
	>7.5		5
Calcium (mg/dl)	All ages: 7.0-8.0		2
	12.0-15.0		2
	<7.0		6
	>15.0		6
Glucose (mg/dl)	All ages: 40-60		4
	250-400		4
	<40		8
	>400		8
Bicarbonate§ (mEq/L)	All ages: <16		3
	>30		3

*Cannot be assessed in patients with intracardiac shunts or chronic respiratory insufficiency. Requires arterial blood sampling.
†May be assessed with capillary blood gas values.
‡Assessed only if there is known or suspected CNS dysfunction. Cannot be assessed in patients during iatrogenic sedation, paralysis, anesthesia, etc. Scores <8 correspond to coma or deep stupor.
§Use measured values.

ranges from 8 to 31 hours. If the patient dies during the admission day, all data, excluding those for the preterminal period, are included. The variable admission time period is used because the survivor's physiologic dysfunction is believed to remain stable, whereas nonsurvivors' physiologic instability is high and gets even higher during the period of interest. Mortality risks are calculated as indicated in Table 124-2. The total PRISM score indicates a relative scale of severity of illness. However, a more precise estimate of mortality risk can be computed with the following equation:

$$\text{Probability (PICU death)} = \exp (R)/[1 + \exp (R)]$$

where $R = 0.207 * \text{PRISM} - 0.005 * \text{age (mo)} - 0.433 * \text{operative status} - 4.782$. Operative status is scored as 0 if the admission day is not postoperative and 1 if it is postoperative. For examples of mortality for PRISM scores for a 60-month-old nonsurgical patient, see Table 124-2.

Dynamic Objective Risk Assessment

A limitation of the PRISM score is that it fails to assess the dynamic changes that occur during the course of worsening of or recovery from the illness. Using the PRISM score data, the Dynamic Objective Risk Assessment (DORA) can mirror the patient's changing disease and recovery status. The DORA score is calculated as follows:

$$P \text{ (death within 24 hr)} = \exp (R)/[1 + \exp (R)] = 0.160 \times \text{PRISM}_a - 6.427$$

if only an admission PRISM is available, *or*

$$R = 0.154 \times \text{PRISM}_t + 0.053 \times \text{PRISM}_a - 6.791$$

if more than one PRISM score is available.

Pediatric Cerebral Performance Category and Pediatric Overall Performance Category

Despite a great deal of productive work on health status and quality of life instruments that are useful in assessment of outcomes in adults, few instruments have been validated for use in children. The majority of instruments available for children measure only the level of disability in rehabilitation or developmental settings. Outcome can be viewed as a spectrum with survival and death at the ends and inter-

Table 124-2 Predicted Mortality Risk by PRISM Score for a 60-Month-Old Nonsurgical Patient

PRISM Score	Mortality Risk (%)
3	1.6
6	2.7
9	5.0
12	8.9
15	15.3
18	25.2
21	38.6
24	46.1
27	68.5
30	80.2

mediate outcomes existing with varying levels of disabilities in the middle. Until recently there was a lack of an intermediate outcome measure to assess outcomes in patients in the PICU. The Pediatric Cerebral Performance Category (PCPC) and the Pediatric Overall Performance Category (POPC) (Tables 124-3 and 124-4) are tools for assessing outcomes in PICU patients. Each is a six-point scale with scores that range from 1 (normal) to 6 (dead), with each interim point representing progressively greater functional impairment. Each scale category is accompanied by age-appropriate operational definitions. A baseline POPC and PCPC score may be assigned that describes the child's level of overall and cerebral function before the index illness or injury that brought the child to the PICU. This level of function can usually be determined from a typical admission history from parents and the referring physician. Note the POPC score may be worse (higher) than the PCPC score, but the PCPC score cannot be worse (higher) than the POPC score. For subsequent scores (discharge from the PICU, hospital, and follow-up), the worst level of performance for any single criterion is used for categorizing. Deficits are scored if they result from a neurologic disorder (PCPC) or from other diseases or conditions. Age-appropriate activities of daily living include those that all but the lowest 10th percentile of children at that age can perform (Table 124-5).

The PCPC and POPC scales were initially validated in a sample that included 1539 PICU admissions

Table 124-3 Pediatric Cerebral Performance Category Scale

Score	Category	Description
1	Normal	Age-appropriate level of functioning; preschool child developmentally appropriate; school-age child attends regular classroom at school
2	Mild disability	Able to interact at an age-appropriate level[1]; minor neurologic disease (e.g., seizure disorder) is controlled and does not interfere with daily functioning; preschool child may have minor developmental delays, but >75% of all activity of daily living developmental milestones are above 10th percentile[1]; school-age child attends regular school but grade is not appropriate for age or child is failing appropriate grade because of cognitive difficulties
3	Moderate disability	Below age-appropriate level of functioning; neurologic disease is not controlled and severely limits activities; in preschool child most activities of daily living developmental milestones are below 10th percentile[1]; school-age child can perform activities of daily living but attends special classroom because of cognitive difficulties or learning deficit
4	Severe disability	In preschool child activities of daily living milestones are below 10th percentile[1] and child is excessively dependent on others for provision of activities of daily living; school-age child may be so impaired as to be unable to attend school and depends on others for provision of activities of daily living; abnormal motor movements for both preschool and school-age child may include nonpurposeful, decorticate, or decerebrate responses to pain
5	Coma and vegetative state	Any degree of coma without presence of all brain death criteria; unawareness, even if appears awake, without interaction with environment; cerebral unresponsiveness and no evidence of cortex function (not aroused by verbal stimuli); may have some reflexive response, spontaneous eye opening, and sleep-awake cycles
6	Brain death	Apnea, areflexia, and/or EEG silence

[1]Frakenburg WK, Dodds J, Archer P, et al. The Denver II: A major revision and restandardization of the Denver Developmental Screening Test. Pediatrics 89:91-97, 1992. Reproduced by permission.

Table 124-4 Pediatric Overall Performance Category Scale

Score	Category	Description
1	Good overall performance	PCPC, normal; age-appropriate activities; medical and physical problems do not interfere with normal activity
2	Mild overall disability	PCPC, mild; minor chronic physical or medical problems; minor limitations (e.g., asthma), but are compatible with normal life; preschool child has physical disability consistent with future independent functioning (e.g., single amputation) and is able to perform >75% of age-appropriate activities of daily living[1]; school-age child is able to perform age-appropriate activities of daily living
3	Moderate overall disability	PCPC, moderate; medical and physical conditions are limiting, as described below; preschool child cannot perform most age-appropriate activities of daily living[1]; school-age child can perform most activities of daily living but is physically disabled (e.g., cannot participate in competitive physical activities)
4	Severe overall disability	PCPC, severe; preschool child cannot perform age-appropriate activities of daily living; school-age child depends on others for most activities of daily living
5	Coma or vegetative state	PCPC, coma or vegetative state
6	Brain death	Death

[1]Frakenburg WK, Dodds J, Archer P, et al. The Denver II: A major revision and restandardization of the Denver Developmental Screening Test. Pediatrics 89:91-97, 1992. Reproduced by permission.

from Arkansas Children's Hospital and later in a multi-institutional study of 11,000 admissions in 16 PICUs. Correlation between a change in PCPC or POPC and duration of stay, hospital charges, discharge disposition, and PRISM score has been demonstrated.

Subsequently the above-referenced scores have been validated with other previously validated instruments for assessing cognitive and general adaptive functional ability in infants and children (e.g., Bayley Developmental Quotient, Stanford Binet test, and Vireland Adaptive Behaviors Scale.

An example of the application of this score to clinical outcome has recently been completed for pediatric patients with acute respiratory failure supported with extracorporeal life support (ECLS). Of all of the children supported with ECLS and observed for

Table 124-5   Examples of Activities of Daily Living Developmental Items From the Denver II for Children Up to 5 Years of Age

Feeding	Feed self	Mobility—cont'd	
	Drink from cup		Stand alone
	Use fork, spoon		Walk well
	Prepare cereal		Walk backward
Toiletry	Brush teeth with little help		Run
	Wash and dry hands		Walk up steps
	Brush teeth with no help		Jump
Dressing	Remove garments		Hop
	Put on clothing	Language	Respond to noise
	Put on T-shirt		Vocalize
	Dresses with no help		Laugh
Mobility	Head up 45 degrees		Turn to voice
	Roll over		Dada and Mama specific
	Sit without support		One word
	Pull to standing		Name body part

Table 124-6   Therapeutic Intervention Scoring System (TISS) with Pediatric Adaptations*

Variable	Key	Variable	Key
4 points		*4 points—cont'd*	
Cardiac arrest ± countershock within 48 hr		Pressure-activated blood transfusion	4
Controlled ventilation (± PEEP)	1	G-suit	
Controlled ventilation with muscle paralysis	1	ICP monitor (any method)	
Balloon tamponade of varices		Platelet transfusion	
Continuous arterial infusion	2	Intra-aortic balloon assist	
Pulmonary artery catheter		Emergency surgical procedure (within past 24 hr)	5
Atrial ± ventricular pacing			
Hemodialysis (unstable patient)		Lavage for GI bleeding	
Peritoneal dialysis		Emergency endoscopy or bronchoscopy	
Induced hypothermia	3	≥2 continuous vasoactive drug infusions	

Key: 1, No spontaneous respiratory rate; 2, excluding arterial infusions to keep catheter patent; 3, active effort to keep temperature <33°C; 4, pump, bag, or manual pressure for rapid delivery; 5, therapeutic only (exclude diagnostic); 6, act of intubation only; 7, patients without endotracheal tubes; 8, includes efforts such as weighing diapers; 9, for example Stryker frame; 10, excluding parenteral nutrition catheters; 11, requires specific replacement orders; 12, any 2 hr consecutively; 13, after first 48 hr.
*Modified from Keene AR, Cullen DJ. Therapeutic Intervention Scoring System: Update 1983. Crit Care Med 11:1-3, 1983. © Williams & Wilkins.

Continued.

a year for development assessment, only 8% had significant morbidity (a change of >1 on the POPC and PCPC).

Therapeutic Intervention Scoring System

One of the original scoring systems used to assess severity of illness was the Therapeutic Intervention Scoring System (TISS) (Table 124-6). TISS quantified both therapeutic and monitoring interventions in an attempt to measure severity of illness. Because most diseases follow common pathophysiologic courses that are symptomatically treated, the score correlat-

ed with mortality risk. The score quantified 76 separate monitoring and therapeutic interventions, assigning points from 1 to 4 based on complexity and invasiveness. However, this scoring system could be heavily influenced by the diagnosis and physician-controlled variables.

RISKS AND COMPLICATIONS

The greatest risk of any scoring system is misapplication of data accumulated from large groups of patients to a single patient. It is necessary to validate time accuracy of scoring systems before their use as prognostic tools in individual patients.

Table 124-6 Therapeutic Intervention Scoring System (TISS) with Pediatric Adaptations—cont'd

Variable	Key	Variable	Key
3 points		*2 points*	
Central parenteral nutrition		CVP catheter	10
Pacemaker standby		≥2 peripheral IV catheters	
Chest tube(s)		Hemodialysis (stable)	
IMV or assisted ventilation		Fresh tracheostomy (within 48 hr)	
CPAP		Spontaneous respiration via tracheostomy or endotracheal tube	
Concentrated potassium infusion (>60 mEq/L)			
Naso- or orotracheal intubation	6	GI feedings	
Blind intratracheal suctioning	7	Replacement of excess fluid losses	11
Strict input and output	8	Parenteral chemotherapy	
>4 ABG, bleeding, or stat studies/(any) shift		Hourly neurologic vital signs	12
>20 ml/kg of blood products in 24 hr		Multiple dressing changes	
Bolus (unscheduled) IV medication		Pitressin infusion (IV)	
1 continuous vasoactive drug infusion			
Continuous antiarrhythmia infusion		*1 Point*	
Cardioversion for arrhythmia		ECG monitoring	
Hypothermia blanket		Hourly vital signs	
Arterial catheter		1 peripheral IV catheter	
Acute digitalization		Chronic anticoagulation	
Cardiac output determination		Standard input and output	
Active (IV) diuresis of fluid overload or cerebral edema		<5 stat studies/shift	
		Scheduled IV medications	
Active therapy for metabolic alkalosis		Routine dressing changes	
Active therapy for metabolic acidosis		Standard orthopedic traction	
Emergency thora-, para-, and pericardiocenteses		Tracheostomy care	13
		Decubitus ulcer care	
Anticoagulation (first 48 hr)		Urinary catheter	
>2 IV antibiotics		Supplemental oxygen (mask or nasal cannulas)	
Phlebotomy for volume overload		≤2 IV antibiotics	
Therapy of seizures or encephalopathy (within 48 hr of onset)		Chest physiotherapy	
		Extensive wound care	
		GI decompression	
Complicated orthopedic traction	9	Peripheral parenteral nutrition	

ADDITIONAL READING

Fiser D. Assessing outcome of pediatric intensive care. J Pediatr 121:68, 1992.

Fiser D. Outcomes evaluations as measures of quality in pediatric intensive care. Pediatr Clin North Am 44:6:1423, 1994.

Fiser D, Long N, Roberson P, et al. Validation of scales for measuring outcome in pediatric intensive care [abst]. Crit Care Med 24:A43, 1996.

Goldstein B, Fiser D, Kelly M, et al. Heart rate power spectral analysis: An index of physiologic stress and outcome in the pediatric intensive care unit [abst]. Crit Care Med 24:A127, 1996.

Keene AR, Cullen DJ. Therapeutic Intervention Scoring System: Update 1983. Crit Care Med 11:1, 1983.

Pollack MM, Getson PR, Ruttimann UE, et al. Efficiency of intensive care. A comparative analysis of eight pediatric intensive care units. JAMA 258:1481, 1987.

Pollack MM, Ruttimann UE, Getson PR. The pediatric risk of mortality (PRISM) score. Crit Care Med 16:1110, 1988.

Pollack MM, Ruttimann UE, Getson PR, et al. Accurate prediction of the outcome of pediatric intensive care. A new quantitative method. N Engl J Med 316:134, 1987.

125 Intensive Care Hemodynamic Monitoring and Daily Care

Donna S. Rahn · Vicky L. Pierce

BACKGROUND

Once admitted to the PICU, the patient will need close, constant supervision and monitoring by a multidisciplinary team of health care professionals. Alterations in the patient's internal environment defines the health care team's responsibilities. Highly sophisticated equipment has aided the health care profession in monitoring and caring for the critically ill child. *Monitoring* includes observing the patient and assessing all laboratory and technologic data. *Interpreting* involves using knowledge of the patient's history, physiology, and pathophysiology to determine whether the information gained from monitoring is normal or abnormal for the patient and to what degree. *Reporting* and *recording* provide the basis for quality care through communication to all caretakers. Patient data are primarily recorded on the chart, and the chart serves as a means of reporting pertinent clinical observations and measurements to all who are responsible for caring for the patient. The nursing records, including periodic assessments, are one of the most valuable tools for maintaining a current record of the routine and daily activities of the patient. *Intervening,* or action, is the essence of health care and the patient's state of health. *Evaluation* is performed to determine whether the action taken altered the patient's state of health.

An ongoing assessment of the PICU patient must be done simultaneously with constant monitoring. A comprehensive assessment, as described in Chapter 123, must be documented in the patient's chart at least daily by the patient's primary physician and by each nurse directly caring for the patient. In addition, patient assessment is often recorded by other members of the health care team (e.g., respiratory therapists, extracorporeal membrane oxygenation technicians, and consulting physicians). The nursing assessment is documented at least every 4 hours for all PICU patients and more frequently for the more critically ill patients, especially those receiving inotropic support. The assessment continues throughout the day, with each set of vital signs and when a medication or treatment is given, a dressing is changed, or the patient is turned or fed. All changes noted in the patient's condition must be documented or reported to the appropriate persons.

Despite the critical illness of all PICU patients, some need more monitoring and care than others. Routine monitoring can disclose important information that might alert caretakers of an impending problem, thus preventing serious complications. Daily care (e.g., tracheostomy, bladder catheter care, dressing changes, and bath) and equipment used by the patient must be documented (see Fig. 123-1). Charting this information communicates to other members of the health care team the care given, provides documentation of compliance with hospital policy and procedure, and supports patient charges. Certain daily measurements are recorded for many PICU patients. With few exceptions (see Chapter 6), every patient is weighed daily unless this is deemed a potentially unsafe procedure by the medical team. The frontal-occipital circumference (FOC) is measured daily in infants to rule out hydrocephalus. Abdominal girth is measured just above the umbilicus every 8 hours in infants with suspected necrotizing enterocolitis or with abdominal distention (Fig. 125-1; see also Chapter 83).

Each nurse caring for the PICU patient must be prepared at all times for emergency situations. On assuming responsibility for the care of the patient, it is advisable that the nurse devise a checklist for the essential bedside items needed to safely care for the critically ill child. *Text continued on p. 1148.*

WEIGHT_____ – ____

+ ____

FOC_____

DATE ___ / ___ / ___   AG____   ____   ____

PAGE A

	VITAL SIGNS											RESPIRATORY ASSISTANCE						
T I M E	TEMP		APICAL PULSE	RESP	PRESSURES							PEAK / V_T	CPAP / PEEP	RATE	FiO_2	Tc PO_2 / O_2 SAT	Tc PCO_2 / ET_v CO_2
	BED / SKIN	PT / SITE			CUFF	ART	MEAN	CVP									

® TRANSDUCERS RECALIBRATED

Fig. 125-1 PICU nursing flow sheet.

Children's Medical Center
of Dallas

PEDIATRIC INTENSIVE CARE UNIT
DEPARTMENT OF NURSING
PATIENT DATA RECORD

PAGE B

BLOOD GASES				
pO₂	pCO₂	pH	Δ	HCO₃ / O₂ SAT

LAB VALUES							HEMOGRAM					
HCT / TSP	CS / DXT	Na⁺ / K⁺	Cl⁻ / CO₂	GLUC	Ca⁺	BUN / CREAT	WBC	RBC	Hgb / Hct	PLTS	OTHER	

BLOOD PRODUCTS	
PRODUCT	AMT
07	
08	
09	
10	
11	
12	
13	
14	
T	
15	
16	
17	
18	
19	
20	
21	
22	
T	
23	
24	
01	
02	
03	
04	
05	
06	
T	

IV SOLUTIONS

A _____ _____   E _____ _____
B _____ _____   F _____ _____
C _____ _____   G _____ _____
D _____ _____   H _____ _____

PAGE C

	ALBUMIN		INTRAVENOUS FLUIDS													ARTERIAL			IV FLUSH	IV MEDS
	%	AMT	SOLN	RATE	AMT	SOLN	RATE	AMT	SOLN	RATE	AMT	SOLN	RATE	AMT	SOLN	RATE	AMT		
07																			
08																			
09																			
10																			
11																			
12																			
13																			
14																			
T																			
15																			
16																			
17																			
18																			
19																			
20																			
21																			
22																			
T																			
23																			
24																			
01																			
02																			
03																			
04																			
05																			
06																			
T																			

TOTALS

	BLOOD PROD./ALB	IV FLUIDS	ENTERAL	NUTRITION		DRAINAGE	BLOOD	EMESIS	STOOL	URINE
14					14					
22				CAL/KG/24°	22					
06				INTAKE ML/KG/24°	06					
T				OUTPUT ML/KG/24°	T					

Fig. 125-1, cont'd   PICU nursing flow sheet.

DATE ____ / ____ / ____

INTAKE   OUTPUT   PAGE D

ENTERAL FEEDINGS					OTHER				STOOL					URINE				
DIET	ORAL	TUBE	RESID	ANT-ACID			BLOOD	EMESIS	AMT	COLOR	TYPE/CONST	pH/HEME		AMT	SP GRAV	pH	LAB STIX	
																		07
																		08
																		09
																		10
																		11
																		12
																		13
																		14
																		T
																		15
																		16
																		17
																		18
																		19
																		20
																		21
																		22
																		T
																		23
																		24
																		01
																		02
																		03
																		04
																		05
																		06
																		T

TIME	TISS	PSI
___		
___		
___		

RN INIT	NAME	RN INIT	NAME

STOOL

COLOR
B—BROWN   Y—YELLOW
G—GREEN   BLD—BLOODY

TYPE/CONSISTENCY
S—SOFT   M—MECONIUM
F—FORMED   FR—FROTHY
SDY—SEEDY   C—CONSTIPATED
W—WATERY   L—LOOSE

BEDSIDE CHECKLIST

Patient monitors with alarm limits set, alarms on
Anesthesia bag, appropriate size mask, oxygen
Pneumothorax kit (for needle aspiration)
IV site and fluid
Calculation of drips for correct dose (μg/kg/min) and pump rate
Code sheet with correct doses for emergency drugs calculated by patient weight, signed by nurse and physician
Patient allergies
Gastric suction with appropriate settings
Siderails up and bed locked
Patient restraints
Universal precaution equipment (gowns, goggles, gloves, masks)

VITAL SIGNS

Recording vital signs documents the patient's status at any particular time (see Fig. 125-1). In the critically ill patient vital signs need to be checked every 1 to 2 hours and when there is significant change; in the chronically ill or more stable patient vital signs may need to be checked every 4 hours. All PICU patients need cardiac-respiratory monitoring and continuous oxygen saturation monitoring, with alarm settings appropriate for age and illness (see Chapter 122). Consideration must be given to "normal" values for age, trends in individual patient's vital signs, and vital signs appropriate for each child's illness or condition. Resting vital signs need to be obtained when possible and exceptions noted when indicated.

Temperature. Temperature can be measured at various sites, including the mouth, skin (axilla), rectum, tympanic membrane, and bloodstream (core). A variety of instruments are available for obtaining temperature. Careful consideration needs to be given to selection of the appropriate thermometer and site for temperature measurement. Axillary temperatures must be obtained in infants weighing <2500 g; axillary or tympanic membrane temperature may be obtained in patients with hematologic or oncologic disease or GI bleeding; and rectal or core temperature needs to be considered in patients with poor perfusion (e.g., patients after cardiac surgery, re-

ceiving inotropes, or in shock). In addition to recording the patient's temperature, the site where it was obtained is recorded. For infants in radiant warmers or isolettes, bed temperature and skin temperature are included (see Chapter 127).

Apical pulse. The apical heart rate and respiratory rate must each be counted for 1 full minute, assessed, and recorded with each set of vital signs. A cardiac rhythm strip needs to be obtained at the beginning of each nurse's shift and anytime there is a change in rhythm. Patients with temporary pacemakers must have the pacer mode and ordered settings documented in the chart as well as whether the pacemaker is sensing or pacing. Some monitor companies have special pacemaker modules to count the paced rate. Hypotension may be one of the first signs of pacemaker-related problems. The cardiac monitor will continue to count the paced beats even if the heart fails to respond to the pacemaker; thus in the pacemaker-dependent patient arterial catheter alarm limits must be set for the appropriate values and turned on.

Respiratory rate and respiratory assistance. The respiratory rate needs to be counted for 1 full minute and recorded with each set of vital signs. Lung status must be assessed at least with each set of vital signs and more frequently when the patient is receiving respiratory assistance. For each patient, whether receiving assisted ventilation or not, an Ambu bag or anesthesia bag with an oxygen source and appropriate size mask must be available at the bedside. With the high prevalence of spontaneous extubation in children, the endotracheal tube must be checked for stability and the tape changed when the tube becomes unstable. To manage the endotracheal tube, consideration must be given to sedating and restraining patients receiving assisted ventilation. A chest radiograph needs to be obtained daily to verify correct placement of the endotracheal tube.

In many institutions respiratory therapists are part of the multidisciplinary team and manage all ventilators and respiratory treatments. The nurse needs to verify ventilator orders and settings with the therapist, especially with the numerous modes of ventilation currently being used. Simultaneous recording of respiratory assistance with vital signs and when obtaining blood gas values and pH is beneficial for evaluation of respiratory status and changes that were made or need to be made. Important ventilator settings to be recorded include expired tidal volume or peak inflating pressure, positive end-expiratory pressure (PEEP) or continuous positive airway pressure, pressure above PEEP, ventilator rate, and mode of ventilation (e.g., pressure control or pressure support). The fraction of inspired oxygen must be recorded as well as the method of delivery (e.g., ventilator, face tent, or halo). All oxygen saturation, transcutaneous Po_2 and Pco_2, and end-tidal CO_2 values are recorded with vital signs, blood gas sampling, and any significant changes.

Blood pressure. Arterial blood pressure needs to be recorded with each set of vital signs. Blood pressure is not always one of the first indicators that a child is in trouble, and shock may be present despite normal blood pressure. Most PICUs have noninvasive blood pressure devices to measure systemic arterial blood pressure. Whether a noninvasive blood pressure device or a sphygmomanometer is used, the cuff must be the appropriate size and in the proper position to obtain an accurate blood pressure reading. The best sites for obtaining noninvasive blood pressure readings are, in order, the upper arm, the lower leg, and the upper leg. The cuff needs to cover approximately two thirds the length between the shoulder and elbow, the ankle and knee, or the groin and knee, respectively. Additional factors that may affect the accuracy of a noninvasive blood pressure measurement are impedance of peripheral blood flow, high pulmonary vascular resistance, obesity, and severe peripheral edema.

With a pressure transducer and monitor, an arterial catheter provides a continuous direct blood pressure reading in addition to a route for sampling the blood without sticking the child repeatedly. When an arterial catheter is present, a blood pressure reading needs to be obtained periodically with a cuff to compare the two values and to use as a baseline value when the arterial catheter is removed. Careful consideration must be given to the arterial catheter tracing on the bedside monitor when interpreting the arterial blood pressure measurement.

Modern technology has provided the health care staff with the means to monitor other pressures that have specific indications relative to a specific illness. Other pressure readings to be recorded with each set of vital signs, when monitored, include central venous blood pressure or right atrial blood pressure, pulmonary arterial blood pressure, pulmonary capillary wedge pressure, left atrial blood pressure, and ICP. When recording pressure readings, make certain

all transducers have been calibrated at least every 8 hours, the transducer is at the proper level to be read, and the tracing is adequate for the specific pressure. If the tracing is inaccurate or has changed from previous readings, notify the physician immediately. The catheter used for the pressure reading may have drifted and could be a source of potential danger to the child.

LABORATORY VALUES

Laboratory specimens are obtained from either an arterial catheter or puncture, heelstick, fingerstick, or venipuncture. Recording the method of sampling is important in evaluation of the laboratory result; for example, a heelstick sample may result in a hemolyzed specimen with a higher than normal potassium value. Common laboratory values routinely determined in the critically ill child include the following.

Glucose. A fingerstick sample must be obtained for measurement of glucose concentration in any patient younger than 6 months every 8 hours during the critical phase of illness and at least once a day when the patient's condition is stable. Frequent glucose determinations are also needed in any patient with suspected hypoglycemia or hyperglycemia, experiencing glucose intolerance, or receiving continuous insulin infusion (see Chapter 58), total parenteral nutrition (see Chapter 171), or peritoneal dialysis (see Chapter 168).

Electrolytes. Serum electrolytes must be measured as often as the patient's condition demands. In children receiving IV fluids only, electrolytes (Na, K, Cl, and Ca), CO_2, and Po_4 must be measured at least daily. Any patient who is critically ill, has renal or liver failure, is receiving diuretics, or has abnormal electrolyte values may need to have levels checked as often as every 2 to 4 hours. (Refer to chapters relating to specific disease entities or situations for guidelines.)

Hemogram (CBC). A blood sample is taken for a complete blood cell count in all new medical and surgical patients on arrival in the PICU, patients with suspected infection, and those receiving immunosuppressive therapy. In patients with documented or suspected bleeding, hemoglobin and hematocrit levels must be monitored frequently.

BUN and creatinine. In general the BUN and creatinine levels are checked in all patients receiving total parenteral nutrition and renal toxic agents (e.g., aminoglycosides) and patients with renal disease or suspected renal impairment. BUN levels are determined in all patients after heart surgery and patients admitted because of dehydration or hypovolemia.

INTAKE AND OUTPUT

Monitoring intake and output periodically throughout the day enables the nurse and physician to maintain a close watch on the patient's progress and alerts them to impending problems. The 24-hour totals and caloric intake provide an overall view and help the medical staff decide the course of treatment.

Intake

Accurate recording and reporting of fluid and nutritional intake and output can be critical in the pediatric patient. Even small amounts of fluid can push an already critically ill patient over the tolerable limit. The bedside clinician must constantly monitor the patient for signs of hypovolemia and hypervolemia and notify the physician caring for the patient.

Blood products. The blood product and the amount given on an hourly basis are recorded. Vital signs must be measured before starting the blood product, after 15 minutes, and hourly throughout the infusion. The patient is monitored for signs and symptoms of a transfusion reaction and the findings reported to the physician and the blood bank.

Albumin. The amount and percent (e.g., 5% or 25%) of albumin being given is recorded.

IV fluids. At the beginning of each shift the nurse needs to identify each IV fluid, check the label to ensure the correct solution, note the date and time it was started, follow the tubing to the insertion site, check for any loose connections, and inspect the site for infiltration or signs of infection. For patients receiving numerous IV fluids, it is advisable to label each pump with the site and type of fluid being infused, especially for vasopresser and analgesic drips. The dose (micrograms per kilogram per minute) must be calculated for each vasoactive drug infusion, labeled as such for easier accessibility when changes need to be made, and documented on the patient's record.

On the intake and output record each IV source (e.g., peripheral intravenous, CVP, or pulmonary artery catheter) is labeled and the solution and all additives documented. Both the rate of the IV infusion and the amount infused each hour is recorded. Many small patients are unable to tolerate any excess fluids; therefore it is important to record all IV flushes and volume of medications given so they can be incorporated into the 24-hour fluid intake volume.

Enteral feedings. The type of diet or fluids the patient is receiving is recorded as well as the amount and whether given orally or through a tube (e.g., gastrostomy, nasogastric, or oral gastric tube). There are different viewpoints about measurement of the amount of gastric residual a patient has while being fed. Many believe that a large amount of residual present before each tube feeding is indicative of whether the patient is tolerating oral intake. Others disagree, believing it advisable to continue feedings unless emesis or abdominal discomfort is present. Liquid antacids given are documented, although not counted in the total fluid intake for any given period.

Output

All sources of output must be recorded for each patient in the critical care setting. The characteristics of the drainage or output may be vital to identify a source of infection or active bleeding. Drainage sites and tubings must be given special care to prevent further complications such as infection.

Fluid loss. Many sources of fluid loss are not common to all patients but must be recorded (e.g., nasogastric tubes, chest tubes, surgical drains, intraventricular drains, or special bladder or kidney catheters). The source and amount of drainage are noted and whether the drain is connected to suction or to gravity drainage. Any changes in the characteristics of drainage (e.g., odor or color) are reported to the appropriate physician. The amount of all blood samples drawn from each patient is recorded. This reminds the physician of the quantity of blood the patient is losing and may be used as transfusion criteria when accompanied by a decrease in hemoglobin and hematocrit and other signs of compensation for decreased oxygen-carrying capacity (e.g., tachycardia). The estimated amount of emesis, if any, is recorded.

Stool. The amount of stool is charted as small, medium, or large. The amount of diarrhea or watery stool is recorded to aid in keeping track of fluid loss. The color, type, and consistency of the stool are charted. In patients with suspected bleeding, a Hematest or guaiac analysis of the stool is performed and the results recorded.

Urine. Hourly measurements are charted in patients with bladder catheters and infants' diapers weighed (1 g of increased weight equals 1 ml of fluid) to monitor urine output. When urine output has decreased or ceased, the bladder is palpated for fullness. A bladder catheter may need to be placed or if present may need to be irrigated using sterile technique, checked for patency, or replaced with a new catheter. Careful observation is mandatory after the bladder catheter has been removed. If the patient has not had any urine output for 8 hours after catheter removal, the physician is notified. It may be necessary to place another catheter to relieve bladder distention. Specific gravity, pH, and urine dipstick results (testing for protein, glucose, ketones, and blood) on a sample of urine are recorded at least daily.

CONCLUSION

Daily care is concluded with a thorough inspection of the patient's skin integrity and personal hygiene. The patient's skin is inspected for any areas of redness or breakdown. For patients with the potential for skin breakdown or those in whom it is already present, special beds are available that provide optimal conditions for healing and preventing further breakdown. Frequent repositioning of the patient, a preventive-type mattress (e.g., eggcrate), and clean, dry skin assist the health care worker in maintaining the patient's skin integrity and keeping the patient comfortable. Personal hygiene includes bathing and bed linen changes at least daily. Most PICU patients need some form of oral care, whether it is brushing the teeth or cleaning the mouth with prepackaged mouth swabs. Oral care may need to be done as often as every 2 to 4 hours in patients who are paralyzed, heavily sedated, or have oral endotracheal tubes. When the eyes are assessed, note drying or drainage and consider the use of artificial tears. Performing personal hygiene gives the caregiver an excellent opportunity to evaluate the patient's skin integrity. In addition, providing oral and skin care is a task parents and family members can do for the critically ill child.

The framework for delivery of patient care by the multidisciplinary team is vast and does affect the outcome of patient care. The chart can provide a continuous record of the patient's response to health care.

ADDITIONAL READING

Alspach JG, Williams SM. Core Curriculum for Critical Care Nursing. Philadelphia: WB Saunders, 1985.
• Hazinski MF. Nursing Care of the Critically Ill Child. St. Louis: Mosby, 1992.
Hudgins CL. Critical care competency-based orientation; ICU standards of nursing practice. Crit Care Nurse 11(9):58, 1991.
Kinney MR. AACN's Clinical Reference for Critical-Care Nursing, 3rd ed. St. Louis: Mosby, 1993.
Oski FA, DeAngelis CD, Fegin RD, McMillan JA, Warshaw JB. Principles and Practice of Intensive Care. Philadelphia: JB Lippincott, 1994.
Prestjohn S. Basic Nursing Care in the PICU. Dallas: Children's Medical Center of Dallas, 1994.
• Whaley LF, Wong DL. Nursing Care of Infants and Children. St. Louis: Mosby, 1995.

126 Infusion Pumps

Cassandra Rochon-Bailey · Bala Ramachandran

BACKGROUND AND INDICATIONS

Fluid delivery systems have been used since 1657, but it was not until the 1970s to 1980s that infusion techniques had evolved sufficiently to become practical and accurate.

Infusion pumps are used in the PICU to (1) maintain line patency in arterial or central venous catheters, (2) infuse hypertonic solutions (e.g., total parenteral nutrition), (3) deliver vasoactive and inotropic substances (e.g., epinephrine, dopamine, and sodium nitroprusside), (4) to permit continuous administration of sedatives, analgesics, and neuromuscular blocking agents (e.g., midazolam, fentanyl, and vecuronium), (5) ensure delivery of accurate volumes, especially in small patients, and (6) deliver intermittent drug doses over short, specific times (e.g., antibiotics and antineoplastic agents). Their use frees the nurses for other duties.

EQUIPMENT

The earliest infusion devices were simple flowmeters that relied on a gravity-fed system to regulate volume by counting and controlling the number of fluid drops per unit of time. These were soon replaced by infusion pumps that, unlike their predecessors, can generate pressure to overcome resistance to flow.

The three basic types of infusion pumps are peristaltic, cassette, and syringe pumps. Peristaltic pumps propel fluid by using rollers to sequentially compress tubing. The peristaltic mechanism may be either linear or rotary. In the linear type the IV tubing is held against a firm backplate and alternately compressed and released by "fingers" that move in a rippling fashion, forcing fluid to flow through the tubing. In the rotary type a section of tubing is held taut against a set of rollers that revolve to alternately compress and release the tubing, causing the fluid to flow.

The second type provides sequential low-volume filling from a volumetrically regulated cassette. The cassette itself may be of two types. One has a syringe-like chamber with a motorized plunger that moves in and out to fill the chamber with fluid and then pump it toward the patient. The other type of cassette uses a piston-actuated diaphragm mechanism to sequentially fill and empty the chamber.

The syringe pump has a motorized screw that depresses the plunger of a prefilled syringe. Most are easy to use and portable. They allow infusion of low fluid volumes at a constant rate over a preset time, providing greater patient safety than with the old, unregulated, hand-pushed method. In neonates and infants syringe pumps are also used for administration of blood products and enteral feedings.

All pumps have rechargeable battery capability, although in some this simply serves as an emergency backup in case of power failure. Most incorporate a variety of alarms to indicate the end of infusion, air in tubing, occlusion of tubing, empty IV bag, and low flow. In addition, some also monitor remaining battery life. There is usually an indicator that displays the actual volume delivered. Some pumps can use regular IV tubing; others require special administration sets specific to the pump. Available infusion rates range from 0.01 to 999 ml/hr.

Multichannel pumps. Multichannel pumps permit simultaneous infusion of more than one drug or solution through a single IV tube if the individual components are compatible. They can be programmed in a variety of ways to deliver medications at specified times, greatly simplifying the management of cases in which a large number of timed medications are necessary.

"Smart" syringe pumps. The new generation of syringe pumps are based on microprocessor technology and can accommodate programming of as many as 60 drugs with a wide range of concentrations. They accept syringe sizes of 1 to 60 ml, and infusion rates can be as low as 0.01 ml/hr. The user simply enters the patient's weight and desired infusion rate for the selected drug. The pump then calculates the volume to be infused per unit of time, thus minimizing the chance of human error due to miscalculation of infusion rates. These pumps also have a feature that allows bolus doses of medication to be delivered directly with the pump.

The solution to be administered must be carefully placed in a disposable syringe, taking appropriate precautions for drugs that spontaneously undergo pharmacologic changes (e.g., nitroglycerin). Before the device is connected to the patient, air must be purged from the tubing to minimize the possibility of an air embolism. A residual amount of fluid will remain in the tubing and cannot be infused. This amount must be calculated and added as extra volume when the syringe is initially filled, or the residual medication must be flushed from the tubing with 0.9% sodium chloride solution at the end of the infusion. Secure access must be established to the continuous infusion line or heparin-locked device. The needleless systems in use prevent any accidental dislodgment from the infusion port and reduce the risk of needlestick injuries to health care providers. The nurse must assess hourly that the volume set to be infused is actually being delivered.

Selection of the appropriate pump. Any type of pump can be used for constant infusions. Syringe pumps are preferred for intermittent infusions, especially if the volume to be given is small. They are also used to administer enteral feedings in small patients. Separate roller-head peristaltic enteral feeding pumps are available for use in larger patients. Syringe pumps are used to administer vasoactive and inotropic substances because of their greater accuracy; peristaltic pumps must not be used with these medications because the rate of infusion may vary with peristalsis, even though the total volume infused remains unchanged, and affect the patient's physiologic function. Syringe pumps, because of their small size, are also preferred for use during transport. Patient-controlled analgesia pumps have a separate cassette-type pump that incorporates a dedicated cassette prefilled with drug of a standard concentration.

Maintenance. Care must be taken to ensure that no fluid enters the pump mechanism. Syringe pumps, because they are small and portable, are easily damaged from mishandling or dropping. The pumps need to be inspected at least annually by the biomedical engineering department to ensure that there are no electrical current leaks from improper grounding and that the pump is functioning properly. The pumps are cleaned with a germicidal wipe after use in each patient.

RISKS AND COMPLICATIONS

Incorrect programming of the pump can result in overdosing or underdosing of medication. Allowing air to enter the tubing may cause an air embolism. A "runaway infusion" occurs when the infusion set is removed from the pump, allowing free flow of fluid into the patient. The IV site needs to be assessed frequently for signs of extravasation. Infiltration with certain medications or hypertonic solutions can result in severe tissue damage. The use of clear dressings allows more complete visualization of the site. Circumferential extremity dressings are not to be used, if possible, and restraints must be checked often. Failure to maintain an appropriate minimum flow rate can potentially lead to loss of IV access.

CURRENT RESEARCH AND FUTURE CONSIDERATIONS

Computer-assisted continuous infusion devices or computer-controlled infusion pumps represent the next generation of infusion devices. A computer incorporated into the pump is connected to a host computer through a communications port (RS232 port on currently available models). The computer provides a pharmacokinetic simulation of infusion requirements and continuously adjusts the infusion rate to maintain the desired drug concentration. These systems are useful to achieve and maintain a given depth of anesthesia with IV medications more rapidly and easily than with manual systems.

ADDITIONAL READING

• Gualtieri F. Safe use of syringe pumps: A word of caution. J Pediatr Nurs 7:356-357, 1992.

Holzman RS. Intravenous infusion equipment. Int Anesthesiol Clin 30:35-50, 1992.

• Milliam DA. Controlling the flow: Electronic infusion devices. Nursing 1990, 90:65-67, 1990.

• Miller D. Continuing medical education: Intravenous anaesthesia and delivery devices. Can J Anaesth 41:634-652, 1994.

Nobel J. Infusion pumps. Pediatr Emerg Care 7:242-243, 1991.

Rooke GA, Bowdle TA. Syringe pumps for infusion of vasoactive drugs: Mechanical idiosyncrasies and recommended operating procedures. Anesth Analg 78:150-156, 1994.

127 Temperature-Sensing and Temperature-Regulating Devices

Erica A. Kirsch · Lisa Thompson-Bush

Temperature-Sensing Devices

BACKGROUND AND INDICATIONS

Temperature is defined as the degree of heat in a substance generated by the movement of the molecules within the substance. Maintaining body temperature within the normal range is important for cells to operate efficiently and to avoid physiologic stresses that can occur with increased or decreased body temperature (see Chapter 56). The standard for normal mean human body temperature of 37° C (98.6° F), with a range of 36.2° to 37.5° C (97.2° to 99.5° F), was delineated by Carl August Wunderlich in 1860. Indications for monitoring body temperature in the PICU include detection of hypothermic and hyperthermic states that may benefit from medical intervention. Causes of elevated body temperature include changes in ambient temperature, fever, drugs, and hyperthermic syndromes such as heat stroke, malignant hyperthermia, and neuroleptic malignant syndrome. Causes of hypothermia include changes in ambient temperature, sepsis, shock, and extreme environmental exposure, as in trauma or submersion. Environmental factors are extremely important in the pediatric population because of the large ratio of body surface area to body mass in children.

TECHNIQUE

Alterations in body temperature are measured with devices that detect a change in the property of a substance that varies in direct proportion to the change in temperature of the body. There are several types of temperature-sensing devices. The glass mercury thermometer is a thermoexpansive thermometer. A thin-walled reservoir bulb is placed in contact with the patient's skin or mucous membrane. With increasing temperature, the mercury expands up a small capillary tube, and after adequate equilibration time (3 to 5 minutes), the temperature is read from a scale on the thermometer. The lower limit of most glass mercury thermometers is 34.4° C (94° F), which restricts their use in hypothermic states. Indwelling esophageal, pulmonary artery, bladder, or tympanic membrane probes, servomechanisms for warming and cooling devices, and electronic digital thermometers use thermistor or thermocouple technology. The thermistor is a metal oxide semiconductor that measures a change in electrical resistance with change in body temperature. The thermocouple is a circuit composed of two unlike metal elements that measures change in electrical current with change in body temperature. Both of these devices translate their measurements into digital readouts in 20 to 30 seconds. They are extremely sensitive to slight temperature variation and capable of monitoring extremes of hyperthermia and hypothermia. A liquid crystal thermometer contains cholesteric liquid crystals that alter their molecular structure and change color with changes in temperature. It is usually marketed as a disposable adhesive strip that is placed on the skin. The infrared thermometer, first introduced in 1986, measures the body's natural radiation of infrared energy, usually from the tympanic membrane, and converts this to digital display within seconds.

Intermittent Monitoring

The type of thermometer and site of temperature measurement used in the PICU will depend on the age and condition of the patient and the relative safety, accuracy, and convenience of the device. Although the primary temperature of interest is the core temperature, defined as the temperature of blood in the pulmonary artery or brain, temperature in most PICU patients can be adequately monitored with intermittent measurements from less invasive sites such as the sublingual, rectal, axillary, and tympanic membrane.

Although sublingual temperature quickly equilibrates with core temperature, this site is susceptible to external factors such as ingestion of hot or cold liquids and the physiologic effects of crying or hypertension. In addition, proper probe placement in the sublingual pocket may be difficult in some patients. Electronic thermometers are the best choice for sublingual use because they are faster and safer than glass mercury thermometers.

Rectal temperature is usually considered a better indicator of core temperature than oral or axillary measurements because it is less affected by ambient influences. Rectal probe placement may be difficult in large or uncooperative patients. Patient discomfort, infection control, and the potential for tissue injury also make this site undesirable. In addition, stool in the rectum may cause false readings. Electronic thermometers are the best choice at this site.

Axillary temperature is convenient and easy to obtain but is readily affected by ambient temperature and the patient's state of perfusion. Axillary temperatures may be more reliable in the neonate because of the smaller size and greater surface vasculature. Electronic probes are also recommended at this site.

Tympanic membrane temperature measurement with infrared thermometers is becoming a preferred method of temperature monitoring in the PICU. The tympanic membrane is in close proximity to the hypothalamus, the temperature regulatory center of the brain. It is relatively distant from ambient influences, and the temperature measured correlates well with pulmonary artery and esophageal temperature measurements. The infrared thermometer is easy to use and rapid and does not require contact with a mucous membrane. The accuracy of infrared tympanic membrane thermometry has not been established in infants younger than 3 months. Improper aiming of the probe, obstruction of the ear canal, or use of a radiant warmer may cause false measurements.

Continuous Monitoring

Continuous temperature monitoring in the PICU patient may be indicated in several cases: (1) patients such as neonates with potentially unstable low temperatures who need servomechanism warming devices, (2) patients in unstable cold environments such as in the operating room or during transport, (3) patients with existing moderate to severe hypothermia after trauma, exposure, submersion, or cardiopulmonary bypass surgery, (4) patients with states of low peripheral perfusion or extensive dermal injury, as in shock, use of α-agonists, or extensive burns, and (5) patients with hyperthermic syndromes such as heat stroke, malignant hyperthermia, and neuroleptic malignant syndrome. If large differences between surface and core temperature are anticipated, as may occur with rapid active cooling or warming, simultaneous monitoring of core and peripheral sites is recommended. Continuous core temperature monitoring can be performed with nasopharyngeal, esophageal, rectal, or tympanic membrane probes or with pulmonary artery or bladder catheter thermistor devices. Although pulmonary artery and bladder catheters are most accurate, temperature measurement at other sites is less invasive and may be more practical. Rectal temperatures can be affected by the presence of stool, and esophageal probes by warmed endotracheal tube gasses or cool nasogastric lavage solutions. Continuous skin temperature monitoring is most often used for servomechanism warming and cooling devices and is performed with a skin temperature probe placed over the liver. Probes must make full skin contact, avoiding bony prominences, and be insulated from radiant warming devices.

RISKS AND COMPLICATIONS

Risks and complications of temperature monitoring vary with the device and site of monitoring. Tissue damage, infection control, and measurement error are of primary concern. Tissue damage is most likely with a glass mercury thermometer as a result of lacerations or mercury granulomas after thermometer breakage. Broken glass mercury thermometers may also place hospital personnel at risk of mercury vapor inhalation. Hospitals must have appropriate policies and procedures for handling mercury spills and waste disposal. Rectal, esophageal, and tympanic membrane perforation have been reported with indwelling probes, glass mercury thermometers, and electronic digital thermometers. Neonates younger than 1 month or weighing <2500 g are at increased risk for rectal perforation. Infrared tympanic membrane probes present little risk of tissue damage because they are not in direct contact with the tympanic membrane. All probe sites must be checked routinely for tissue integrity. All indwelling probes provide a path for direct electrical access to a body cavity and must have isolated circuitry to prevent accidental defibrillation.

Infection control is an important consideration in the PICU. Bacterial contamination from improperly cleaned glass mercury thermometers has been reported, and these devices must be sterilized between patients or discarded after single patient use. Sterilization procedures increase the chance of thermometer breakage, and single patient use creates a hazardous waste disposal problem and is not economical. Disposable probe covers for digital thermometers decrease the infection risk, but reports of bacterial contamination from probe handles has been reported. Infrared tympanic membrane thermometers are probably less likely to cause infection because they do not contact mucous membranes and have disposable probe covers. Liquid crystal thermometers are disposable and without significant infection risk but are not usually cost effective.

False temperature readings are of great concern because they may lead to patient undertreatment or overtreatment. Errors in temperature measurement may result from improper technique (e.g., inadequate equilibration time or improper probe placement), incorrect choice of device in a specific patient, or device malfunction. It is recommended that all devices be used and maintained in accordance with operating manuals and that hospital personnel be trained in the correct use of devices and appropriate device choice in different patient populations. If a question of accuracy arises, patient temperature can be assessed by more than one method.

Temperature-Regulating Devices
BACKGROUND AND INDICATIONS

In the PICU it is often necessary to use specialized equipment to maintain the patient's temperature within the normal range. Both hypothermia and hyperthermia can cause increased metabolic rate and oxygen consumption, which can further compromise crit-

ically ill children if seizures, growth failure, poor wound healing, or arrhythmias develop (see Chapter 56). Therefore it is essential that a child's body temperature be maintained within normal limits.

Several devices are available for regulating patient temperature. Incubators, often used to maintain a normothermic environment for premature infants, are generally not used during the acute phase of illness because of the lack of accessibility to the infant and because they provide a less stable thermal environment when ports or access panels are opened for frequent interventions. Radiant warmers are routinely used in the critical care setting because they provide easy access to the infant. Hypothermia and hyperthermia blankets or specialty beds may be useful in older infants and children. Fluid warmers and heated ventilator circuits may be used in all age groups.

TECHNIQUE

Radiant warmers, frequently used for the critically ill neonate, consist of electrically heated elements positioned overhead that emit infrared rays onto the infant. This heating causes vasodilation, which allows transfer of heat to deeper tissues through conduction and blood circulation. The temperature can be controlled manually or with automatic servomechanism capabilities that adjust the heat output on the basis of the infant's temperature as read continuously with an abdominal skin probe. The probe is covered with a foam-backed, self-adhesive reflective shield. Covering the patient with clothing or blankets minimizes the benefits of the radiant heat source. In the extremely premature infant heat loss can be further prevented by stretching plastic food wrapping material across the warmer to reduce air turbulence around the infant and decrease convective and evaporative heat loss. To discontinue radiant warming, the set temperature of the warmer is slowly decreased over several hours while the patient's axillary temperature is frequently monitored. During this process warm blankets, dressing gowns, and socks are helpful in maintaining body temperature. Portable radiant warmers are available that can be placed over the patient's bed as needed and easily removed during procedures and as the patient's condition allows. These are useful in treating hypothermia in the older child.

Use of incubators is also standard practice to maintain body temperature in the neonate. Incubators operate by convection, circulating heated and humidified air around the infant. Air temperature may be controlled with a servomechanism or manual adjustment.

Hypothermia and hyperthermia blankets consist of a unit that pumps heated or cooled water through a blanket placed under or over the patient. The water is returned to the unit and continuously recirculated through the system, raising or lowering the patient's temperature by conductive transfer of heat. In the manually controlled mode the operator sets the temperature of the circulating water; in the automatic mode a probe is attached to the patient and connected to the heating or cooling device. The unit heats or cools the water to achieve the desired patient temperature. When the set point is reached, the device will automatically cease to operate. Safety features are available to automatically shut off the unit when the circulating water reaches excessively high or low temperatures.

In addition to directly cooling or warming the patient, other techniques available in the PICU to help maintain patient temperature include fluid warmers, ventilators, and specialty beds. IV fluids and blood products can be warmed to a desired temperature with a device that circulates these fluids by means of disposable tubing through a water bath. This water bath is precisely heated to a set temperature and warms the IV fluid or blood product before patient administration. Electronic circuitry continuously monitors the water temperature and will shut off the system and activate an alarm in the event of overheating. Most ventilators contain a heating and humidifying circuit that allows inspired gas to be warmed or cooled to the patient's thermoregulatory needs. Many specialty beds available in the PICU contain a heater that can be adjusted to meet thermoregulatory requirements. Some beds have a blower unit that circulates air through the mattress. Cooling this air by placing a container of ice in front of the blower unit is another method of cooling the patient.

RISKS AND COMPLICATIONS

Complications of temperature-regulating devices include hyperthermia and hypothermia and tissue damage. One of the primary problems associated with the use of radiant warmers is hyperthermia, which may be manifested by tachycardia, flushing, and lethargy with increased metabolism and oxygen consumption. Typically, hyperthermia is caused by

a loose skin probe; thus probe placement must be assessed regularly. Accuracy of the servomechanism, temperature probe, and radiant warmer power output are tested as part of a regular maintenance program and by frequently assessing the infant's vital signs (at least every 2 hours). The concomitant use of phototherapy increases the risk of hyperthermia and may necessitate adjustment of the heater set point. It is difficult to protect the infant in the radiant warmer from drafts. A normothermic environment is easier to achieve if radiant warmers are placed out of the way of heating or cooling vents or if vented air is redirected. Increased insensible water loss is another possible complication of radiant warmers. This problem is magnified in the preterm infant. In addition, basal metabolic rate and oxygen consumption are higher in the infant under a radiant warmer. Daily weight, strict intake and output, and serum sodium and urinary specific gravity must be monitored closely. Maintenance fluid requirements may increase from 20% to 50%. Plastic food wrapping material stretched across the warmer will decrease insensible water loss to some extent by reducing air turbulence and decreasing convective and evaporative heat loss. Extremes in body temperature are also a risk when the cooling or warming blankets or beds are used. The patient's temperature is monitored frequently when initiating therapy and hourly during therapy.

Tissue damage is another primary concern when heating or cooling devices are used. Premature infants with delicate skin and infants with poor peripheral circulation are at the greatest risk for cutaneous burns or excessive drying from radiant warmers. These patients must be monitored closely for areas of breakdown. Other adverse effects from infrared radiation include cataracts, flash burns of the skin, and heat stress. Skin damage from cooling or warming blankets and beds can often be prevented by placing dry linen between the device and the patient, although too many layers will limit the effectiveness of the therapy. The patient's skin must be frequently inspected for evidence of burns or breakdown and the position and placement of the temperature probe. When a blanket is used to induce hypothermia, shivering often results. This can cause the same increase in metabolism and oxygen consumption as does increased temperature, thereby defeating the purpose of the cooling unit. Shivering can be controlled with diazepam, chlorpromazine, or neuromuscular blockade, as clinically indicated. When warmed inspired respiratory gases are used for thermoregulation, care must be taken to maintain the temperature in the physiologic range of 25° to 37° C. Higher temperature can cause tracheal mucosal damage, whereas lower temperatures can cause drying of the airways. Blood or fluid warming devices may overheat and destroy blood products. High temperature alarms can be tested according to manufacturer's recommendations. Air vents on these units are necessary for the units to cool and must not be covered. Because several of these heating or cooling devices use water and electricity for operation, basic electrical safety measures are necessary. It is important to avoid placing pins or needles into blanket devices. If a water leak occurs, the unit must be turned off immediately and the power disconnected.

ADDITIONAL READING

Basham GA. Radiant warming devices. In Levin DL, Morriss FC, eds. Essentials of Pediatric Intensive Care. St. Louis: Quality Medical Publishing, 1990, pp 780-781.

Chamberlain JM, Grandner J, Rubinoff JL, Klein B, Waisman Y, Huey M. Comparison of a tympanic thermometer to rectal and oral thermometers in a pediatric emergency department. Clin Pediatr (Suppl)30:24-29, 1991.

Fraden J. The development of Thermoscan instant thermometer. Clin Pediatr (Suppl)30:11-12, 1991.

Fraden J, Lackey RP. Estimation of body sites temperatures from tympanic measurements. Clin Pediatr (Suppl)30:65-70, 1991.

Gildea JH. When fever becomes an enemy. Pediatr Nursing 2:165-167, 1992.

Hershler C, Conine TA, Hannay M. Assessment of an infrared non-contact sensor for routine skin temperature monitoring: A preliminary study. J Med Engineer Tech 16:117-122, 1992.

Kelly B, Alexander D. Effect of otitis media on infrared tympanic thermometry. Clin Pediatr (Suppl)30:46-48, 1991.

MacKenzie R, Asbury AJ. Clinical evaluation of liquid crystal skin thermometers. Br J Anaesth 72:246-249, 1994.

Mackowiak PA, Wasserman SS, Levine MM. A critical appraisal of 98.6° F, the upper limit of the normal body temperature, and other legacies of Carl Reinhold August Wunderlich. JAMA 268:1578-1580, 1992.

Medoff-Cooper B. Transition of the preterm infant to an open crib. J Obstet Gynecol Neonatal Nurs 5:329-335, 1994.

Nierman DM. Core temperature measurement in the intensive care unit. Crit Care Med 19:818-823, 1991.

Nobel JJ. Infrared ear thermometry. Pediatr Emerg Care 8:54-58, 1992.

Pilchak TM. Anesthesia and monitoring equipment for pediatrics. CRNA: Clin Forum Nurse Anesth 3:64-71, 1992.

Pransky SM. The impact of technique and conditions of the tympanic membrane upon infrared tympanic thermometry. Clin Pediatr (Suppl)30:50-52, 1991.

Romano MJ, Fortenberry JD, Autrey E, Harris S, Heyroth T, Parameter P, Stein F. Infrared tympanic thermometry in the pediatric intensive care unit. Crit Care Med 21:1181-1185, 1993.

Shenep JL, Adair JR, Hughes WT, Roberson PK, Flynn PM, Brodkey TO, Fullen GH, Kennedy WT, Oakes LL, Marina NM. Infrared, thermistor, and glass-mercury thermometry for measurement of body temperature in children with cancer. Clin Pediatr (Suppl)30:36-41, 1991.

Stein MT. Historical perspective on fever and thermometry. Clin Pediatr (Suppl)30:5-7, 1991.

Stewart JV, Webster D. Re-evaluation of the tympanic thermometer in the emergency department. Ann Emerg Med 21:158-161, 1992.

Talo H, Macknin ML, Medendorp SV. Tympanic membrane temperatures compared to rectal and oral temperatures. Clin Pediatr (Suppl)30:30-33, 1991.

Thomas K, Morriss FC. Temperature-sensing devices. In Levin DL, Morriss FC, eds. Essentials of Pediatric Intensive Care. St. Louis: Quality Medical Publishing, 1990, pp 783-785.

128 Interhospital Transport of the PICU Patient

Diana Hopkins Taylor · Karin A. McCloskey · Richard Orr

BACKGROUND

Technologic advancements and the increased complexity of caring for critically ill and injured children have led to regionalization of PICUs. Most pediatric illnesses and injuries do not occur near regional centers and therefore necessitate that children must often travel significant distances to reach definitive care. Use of specialized pediatric transport systems allows rapid delivery of expert pediatric care to any critically ill child. Appropriate initial stabilization followed by appropriate transport generally result in decreased morbidity and mortality.

Military experiences from World War II, the Korean War, and most dramatically the Vietnam War led to the development of transport systems for use by the civilian population. During the 1970s programs were developed for rapid transport of ill or injured patients from the nonhospital environment to available medical care and for interhospital transport and rapid transport of patients. Initially, interhospital transport was primarily via helicopter for victims of multiple trauma or via mobile ICUs for neonatal patients. The proliferation of neonatal transport programs is concomitant with the establishment of regional perinatal centers able to provide outreach education, comprehensive stabilization, and transport of critically ill neonates from referral centers. The importance of such systems in the pediatric population is well established.

As ICUs have become more specialized, so have transport systems. The emergency medical system (EMS) response to accident or injury is significantly different from that of specialized hospital-based providers who target specific populations. In addition, many transport options available for adult patients may not be appropriate for pediatric patients. EMS ambulance personnel and hospital-based all-age transport teams (usually helicopter programs) may not be trained, equipped, or experienced in managing pediatric emergencies with the same skill as in adult emergencies. Nonetheless, many rural areas are served primarily by all-age transport programs that must provide care for pediatric patients 5% to 15% of the time.

Over the past decade transport programs dedicated solely to the transport of pediatric patients have evolved in conjunction with the growth and development of PICUs. These specialized transport programs are capable of providing critical care to a wide variety of patients ranging in age from neonate to adolescent, with an appreciation for the physiologic changes that relate to growth and development and an understanding of the multitude of illnesses and injuries that affect children.

In the past few years guidelines have been established for the transport of pediatric patients. In 1986 the American Academy of Pediatrics (AAP) in collaboration with pediatricians and others with expertise in pediatric transport developed specific recommendations for pediatric transport systems. Awareness of and compliance with the guidelines was minimal, and a group of pediatricians convened a National Leadership Conference in 1990 to define and prioritize issues of major concern. This conference was attended by medical directors of pediatric transport programs and representatives from the AAP and the Association of Air Medical Services (AAMS). This group set forth recommendations for team composition, training requirements, and data collection:

1. *Pediatric transport team composition.* Pediatric patients are to be transported by staff with the cognitive and technical skills required for pediatric patients. Each critical care transport must be supervised by an attending physician with expertise in pediatric critical care or emergency medicine. Possession of appropriate skills

1159

by team members is more critical than the presence of a physician.

2. *Training requirements for pediatric transport teams*. Each team needs standardized training and teaching materials. Immediate, direct feedback from the medical control physician is to be provided before, during, and after transport. A quality improvement and case review process is necessary.

3. *Data collection*. It was suggested that pediatric transport programs would benefit from a national database that could be shared among programs. There was consensus that a task force be established to facilitate collection of information about operations, clinical, and financial data.

As a result of this leadership conference, the 1993 AAP guidelines for air and ground transport of pediatric and neonatal patients was written. In addition to the 1993 guidelines for pediatric transport services, broader regulations were set forth by the Federal Aviation Administration (FAA) and state and local agencies for operators of helicopters and fixed-wing aircraft. In addition, the AAMS supported the development of a voluntary certification process, the Commission for Accreditation of Air Medical Services (CAAMS), which certifies air medical programs in minimum operating standards for training, aviation, and safety aspects of air medical transport systems.

TECHNIQUE
Personnel

The selection of pediatric transport team members needs to be based on patient population needs, available personnel, and referral hospital expectations. Whether a physician is needed during transport has been controversial. Attempts have been made to determine a method to predict the need for a physician during transport based on the need for major interventions by transport personnel. In general the findings seem to suggest that team composition is less important than team members' experience in caring for critically ill pediatric patients, didactic education in pediatric critical care, and ongoing skills training with emphasis on airway management. The 1993 AAP guidelines emphasize the importance of skill levels and maintenance as opposed to educational background. It is probable that the value of a physician on a given transport team has to do with the cogni-

tive and decision-making processes, which may be difficult to quantitate and evaluate.

Personnel are classified as administrative, clinical, and vehicle operators. Each team member must meet certain standards and be able to safely and effectively perform assigned duties (Table 128-1). Nationally there is a multitude of team configurations, which have included emergency medical technicians (EMTs), paramedics, registered respiratory therapists (RRTs), registered nurses (RNs), advanced nurse practitioners, and physicians (both in training and attending). For most pediatric transport programs, team selection is determined on the basis of patient needs, and the majority function with either a two- or three-member team with a common configuration, including an RN, an RRT, and a physician at some level of training. At least two trained medical personnel, not including the vehicle operator, are necessary for most transports.

Specific personnel training requirements are determined by the needs of the individual program. All team members must have documented experience in pediatric critical care and must receive extensive orientation to the pediatric transport program policies, procedures, and protocols. Team members must be certified in basic life support and pediatric advanced life support, with at least one member of each transport team certified in advanced cardiac life support (Table 128-2). Training in specialized skills such as airway management, vascular access, immobilization, or other procedures used within the specific program must be incorporated into the initial and ongoing educational process. Clinical protocols must be developed to ensure care is provided consistently and uniformly within the transport environment.

It is clear that the experience of the transport team is important in determining the success of the transport. A team leader is identified for each transport, and whether a physician or nurse, this person is involved in pediatric transport on a regular basis to ensure optimal outcomes. Medical personnel must be well trained in the problems of the critically ill pediatric patient, potential complications during transport related to these problems, and operation of all equipment used during transport. In addition, the team leader must have an in-depth understanding of the aviation environment and potential physiologic stresses to the patient and team members. In general the pediatric transport team must consist of personnel who are experienced and well trained in car-

Table 128-1 Pediatric Transport Team Personnel

Personnel	Qualifications	Responsibilities
Medical director	Physician, specialist in pediatric critical care or pediatric emergency medicine (neonatology, if appropriate), trained in transport medicine and administration	Team training and education; develops clinical policies and protocols for transport program; responsible for medical quality assurance, peer review, and outreach education
Program director	Health care–related administrative training and experience	Nonmedical aspects of program; procures equipment and supplies for transport service; manages operations with regard to vehicle operators, communication, and hospital administration; develops and manages budget
Transport coordinator	Nurse, respiratory therapist, or other health care provider with PICU, transport, and management experience	Hiring, education, and coordination of non-physician team members; ensures appropriate staffing; active in outreach and quality assurance
Transport physician	Certified by medical director; trained in transport medicine	Coordinates team efforts, including patient stabilization and management
Transport nurse	Registered nurse with substantial experience in PICU or pediatric emergency care; trained in transport medicine	Participates as team member on physician-led team; functions as team leader, as appropriate, when no physician assigned to team
Respiratory therapist	Registered or registry-eligible; substantial experience in PICU or pediatric emergency medicine; trained in transport medicine	Assists in respiratory stabilization and airway management; involved in transport of intubated patients
Paramedic	Minimum of 1 year's experience as a paramedic; trained in transport medicine; additional specific training in pediatrics	Assists team leader with stabilization and management of patient; may be driver of ground transport
Emergency medical technician (EMT)	Minimum of 1 year's experience as EMT; trained in transport medicine; additional specific training in pediatrics	Assists team leader with stabilization and management of patient; driver of ground ambulance
Communication specialist	Usually an EMT or paramedic; trained in transport communications	Assists team in all phases of communication for each transport; maintains channels of communication; tracks and follows transport vehicle or aircraft for duration of transport

Table 128-2 Required Training for Transport Team Members at Children's Medical Center of Dallas

Fellow or Physician	Registered Nurse	Registered Respiratory Therapist
PICU or emergency department fellow	Basic life support	Basic life support
Basic life support	Pediatric advanced life support	Pediatric advanced life support
Pediatic advanced life support	Advanced cardiac life support	Advanced cardiac life support
Advanced cardiac life support	Emergency medical technician	Trauma nursing core course (audit)
Advanced trauma life support	Trauma nursing core course	

ing for critically ill and injured pediatric patients, possess excellent interpersonal communication skills, are flexible, and are able to perform under conditions of stress.

Triage

All transport programs that accept children must have written protocols for patient triage. Frequent triage dilemmas include whether a patient undergoing interhospital transfer needs a critical care transport team, whether a physician is needed during transport, and prioritization of multiple simultaneous transport requests. All of these dilemmas arise as a result of imperfect tools currently used in assessment of the level of illness of the patient.

Transport triage is complicated by multiple factors, primarily the patient's changing clinical condition and difficulty in assessing severity of illness by telephone. There is no widely used objective triage tool for pediatric critical care transport. It is important that pediatric transport systems develop triage protocols that balance their program's resources with the regional community's needs. Elements of current triage systems include (1) judgment of any receiving physician, (2) judgment of an experienced attending physician who knows the capabilities of the referring staff, (3) a system for classification of patient status, (4) a "common sense" approach, and (5) an objective scoring system, even though originally developed for another clinical purpose (e.g., Pediatric Risk of Mortality, Glasgow Coma Scale, Pediatric Trauma Score, and Apgar score).

The first element is not optimal because experience and consistency may be lacking. The second provides experienced decision making along with increased consistency. Many systems have functioned successfully for years with this triage tool.

With a patient classification system, severity of illness and level of intervention can be evaluated. Most classification systems use clinical or interventional variables to determine patient status. For example, patient status may be categorized on a scale of 1 to 3, with 1 being the most stable and 3 the most critical (Table 128-3). This classification system provides a more objective mechanism for making triage decisions. Classification systems with five or six levels and more in-depth variables exist. To date, however, no categorization system has been validated as a pediatric transport triage tool.

The "common sense" approach identifies patient

Table 128-3 Patient Classification System for Transport at Children's Medical Center of Dallas

Category	Patient Condition
1	Stable
	Vital signs within normal limits
	No respiratory distress
	O$_2$ saturation >95% with room air
2	Critical but stable
	Potential for hemodynamic instability
	Altered level of consciousness (GCS >8)
	Mild to moderate respiratory distress
	Oxygen delivery
	O$_2$ saturation <95% on room air
3	Critical and unstable
	Inotropic support required
	Hemodynamic instability
	Moderate to severe respiratory distress
	Intubation
	GCS <8

GCS = Glasgow Coma Scale.

needs based on certain criteria. These criteria may differ among programs but include the following variables: (1) Will the patient be admitted to the PICU? (2) Does the patient have potential for significant respiratory, cardiovascular, or neurologic deterioration during the anticipated duration of transport? (3) Does the patient have multiple traumatic injuries? Again, the problem with this option is that decisions may be made inconsistently.

The most likely triage tool to ultimately be developed and validated will include an objective scoring system that can be used to predict need for major interventions, PICU admission, or probability of morbidity or mortality and a patient status classification system that incorporates the need to consider local variables such as transport time, available vehicles, geography, and referral hospital capabilities.

We have developed a well-defined Transport Triage and Activation Protocol (Fig. 128-1). An EMT-trained transfer coordinator (TC) receives the initial call from the referral hospital or physician and asks a series of questions in an effort to categorize the patient:

1. What is the patient's name and age?
2. What is the referral hospital, who is the referral physician, and what is the phone number?

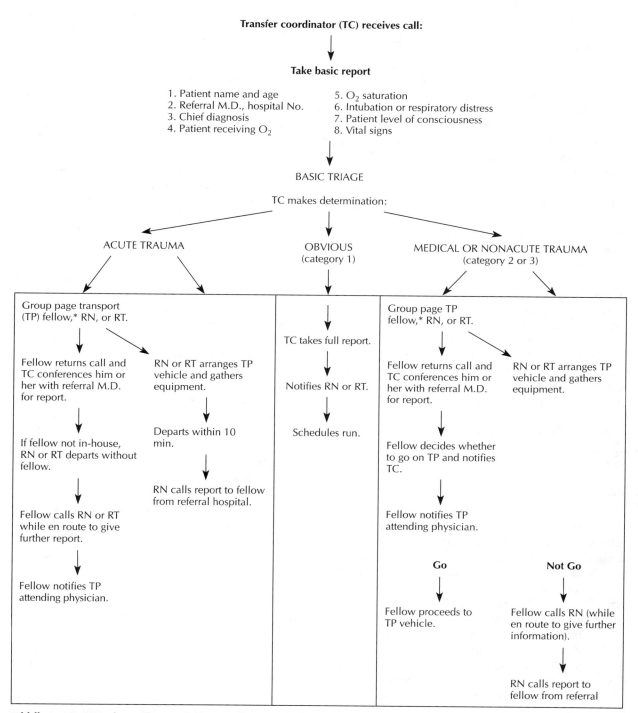

Fig. 128-1 Transport triage and activation protocol.

3. What is the chief diagnosis?
4. Is the patient being given oxygen?
5. Has an endotracheal tube been placed? Is the patient in respiratory distress?
6. What is the patient's oxygen saturation?
7. What is the patient's level of consciousness?
8. What are the patient's vital signs?

For obvious category 1 patients (stable and noncritical), the TC will continue to take report on the patient and schedule the transport to be done by the transport RN and RRT, with no involvement by the transport fellow or attending physician. For any patients that are identified a category 2 or 3 or with acute trauma, the TC will immediately page the on-call transport fellow and will conference the fellow with the referral physician for report and to provide consultation. The PICU and emergency department fellows rotate to provide 24-hour on-call coverage as the transport fellow. While the fellow is receiving report on the patient the transport RN and RRT gather their equipment, arrange for the appropriate vehicle, and are prepared to depart within 10 minutes. If after receiving report the patient is determined to be in category 3 (critical and unstable), the fellow will accompany the transport team. The team will depart within 10 minutes for any patients with acute trauma and will be accompanied by the fellow only if the fellow has finished receiving report and is immediately available to depart. No trauma transports are delayed so that a physician can attend the transport.

Mode of Transport

Three types of medically equipped vehicles are used by pediatric transport services: ground ambulance, helicopter, and fixed-wing aircraft. Modes of transport are decided on the basis of distance, severity of patient illness or injury, geographic terrain, vehicle availability, equipment needed, and crew member number and weight. Each mode of transport has advantages and disadvantages.

Ground ambulances vary in size and capabilities. They are relatively available and inexpensive and have virtually no restrictions on number of crew members or weight of equipment and personnel. The disadvantages are that they can be slow, especially if operating in metropolitan areas with heavy traffic flow, and they may have limited access to certain types of terrain. In normal circumstances ground ambulances are best used to transport critical, unstable patients up to 20 miles and noncritical, stable patients up to 100 miles.

Helicopters have the advantage of speed. Helicopters commonly used in air medical transport are capable of traveling 150 miles/hr and can fly from point to point, bypassing airports and thereby significantly decreasing transport time. In the mid-1980s there was significant concern about the safety of EMS helicopters. The National Transportation Safety Board (NTSB) undertook a safety study of helicopter operations and concluded that poor weather poses the greatest hazard to EMS helicopter operations. Since the publication of this NTSB study, EMS helicopter accident rates have decreased significantly. In addition, the AAMS has promoted the belief that pilots are the only ones qualified to make aviation decisions. Pilot teams must be isolated from patient information and thereby make "blind dispatch" decisions based solely on weather and aircraft conditions. Medical personnel must always defer to the pilot's authority with these decisions. The relative disadvantages to helicopter transport are cost, with an average rate of approximately $2980 per patient flight in 1994, and inability to operate on average 15% of the time because of weather conditions. Helicopter transport is of great benefit for patients with illnesses or injuries in which speed is of the utmost importance (e.g., pediatric trauma). Helicopter transport is most beneficial for transporting critical, unstable patients within 20 to 100 miles.

The advantages of transport with fixed-wing aircraft are less cost relative to helicopter transport and more rapid access to remote locations than with ground ambulance. The disadvantage is the requirement for ambulance transfer of the patient to and from the hospital to the airport. Weather and safety are less a factor with fixed-wing transport than with helicopter transport because of the controlled environment of airports. Noise and vibration are also less a problem than with helicopter transport, which makes patient care easier. Fixed-wing aircraft are most efficient and cost effective for long-distance transport, generally more than 100 miles. All transport vehicles must have on-board air, oxygen, suction, and electrical power to accommodate safe transport of any patient.

EQUIPMENT, THOMAS TRANSPORT PACK

General supplies

Syringes
    60 ml (3) Luer-Lok
    60 ml (1) catheter tip
    20 ml (5)
    10 ml (5)
    5 ml (5)
    3 ml (5)
    1 ml (5)
IV catheters
    24 gauge (4)
    22 gauge (4)
    20 gauge (2)
    18 gauge (2)
    16 gauge (2)
Butterfly needles
    25 gauge (1)
    23 gauge (1)
T-connectors (3)
Extension tubing (3)
Wrist restraints (4)
Armboards (2)
Intraosseous needles (3)
Heimlich valve (1)

BP cuffs
    Adult (1)
    Child (1)
    Infant (1)
    Neonatal No. 4 (1)
Foley catheters
    No. 6 (1)
    No. 8 (1)
    No. 10 (1)
    No. 12 (1)
    No. 14 (1)
Feeding tubes
    No. 5 (1)
    No. 8 (2)
Nasogastric tubes
    No. 10 (1)
    No. 12 (1)
    No. 14 (1)
Chest tube clamp (2)
Chest tubes
    No. 12 F (1)
    No. 10 F (1)
Tape measure (1)

Dextrostix (1 bottle)
K-Y jelly (2)
Povidone-iodine (Betadine) pads
    (10)
Alcohol pads (10)
Adhesive tape
Tegaderm (1)
Venigards (1)
Tourniquet (1)
Foley drainage bag (urimeter)
Stethoscope (1)
Calculator
Monitor
    ECG pads
    ECG lead wires (6)
Baxter infusion pump (2)
Transducer cable/tubing (1)
Pressure bag (1)
Sterile gloves (3)
Nonsterile gloves (6)
Pacifier (1)
Thermometer (1)
Portable phone

Respiratory therapy supplies

Endotracheal tubes
    2.5-5.0 mm (2)
    5.5-8.0 mm (1)
Stylets: Small, large (2)
Magill forceps: Small,
    large (1 each)
Laryngoscope handles (2)
Miller blades: 0, 1, 2,
    3 (1 each)
MacIntosh blades: 2, 3 (1 each)
Light bulbs (2)
AA batteries (2)
Resuscitation bags (Laerdal): In-
    fant, pediatric, adult (1 each)
Oral airways (graduated sizes) (1)

Resuscitation masks: 0, 1, 2, 3, 4,
    5, adult (1 each)
Suction catheters: 6, 8, 10, 12, 14
    gauge (2 each)
DeLee suction (1)
Yankauer suction (1)
Portable suction apparatus (1)
O_2 cannula: Infant, pediatric
    (2 each)
O_2 tubing (2)
O_2 mask: Infant, pediatric, adult
    (1 each)
Ventilation mask: Infant, pediatric,
    adult (1 each)
Pediatric ventilator circuit (1)

ABG kit (2)
ABG analyzer cartridges (4)
Nebulizer (2)
Tracheostomy adapters
Pulse oximetry probes: Neonatal,
    adult (2 each)
Capnography/$etco_2$ sensors (2)
Anesthesia bag setup (0.5 and 1 L
    bags)
O_2 tubing connector (1)
O_2 cylinder regulator (1)
PEEP valve (1)
Manometer (1)
Cylinder key (1)
Saline solution bullets (3)

PHARMACY SUPPLY LIST

Normal saline (NS) solution (10 ml) (3)
Sterile water (10 ml) (3)
IV fluids
   D₅W, 250 ml
   D₅ 1/4 NS, 250 ml
   NS, 500 ml (2)
   Lactated Ringer's solution, 500 ml (1)
5% albumin, 250 ml (1)
Resuscitation medications
   Atropine, 1 mg/10 ml (2)
   Epinephrine, 0.1 mg/ml, 10 ml (2)
   NaHCO₃, 8.4%
     50 ml (1)
     10 ml (2)
   CaCl, 10%, 10 ml (1)
   Dextrose, 50%, 50 ml (1)
   Naloxone, 0.4 mg/ml (1)
Vasoactive drugs
   Dopamine, 200 mg/5 ml (1)
   Dobutamine, 250 mg/20 ml (1)
   Epinephrine, 30 mg/30 ml (1)
   Nitroprusside, 50 mg vial (2)
   Prostaglandin E₁, 500 mg/ml (1) (prn)
   Propranolol, 1 mg/ml (1)
Controlled drug box
   Sodium thiopental, 500 mg vial (1)

Phenobarbital, 65 mg/ml, 2 ml vials (2)
Morphine, 10 mg/ml (2)
Fentanyl, 100 mg/2 ml (4)
Lorazepam, 2 mg/ml (2)
Midazolam, 5 mg/ml (1)
Ketamine, 10 mg/ml, 20 ml
Acetaminophen suppository
   650 mg (1)
   120 mg (1)
Ampicillin, 1 g vial (1)
Cefuroxime, 750 mg vial (2)
Diphenhydramine, 50 mg/ml (1)
Furosemide, 20 mg/2 ml (2)
Gentamicin, 80 mg/2 ml (1)
Lidocaine, 100 mg/5 ml (1)
Phenytoin, 100 mg/2 ml (2)
Potassium chloride, 2 mEq/ml IV (2)
Vecuronium, 10 mg vial (2)
Mannitol, 12.5 mg/50 ml (1)
Dexamethasone, 4 mg/ml (1)
Respiratory medications
   Atrovent, 500 μg/ampule (2)
   Atropine, 400 μg/ml (2)
   Racemic, epinephrine, 15 ml (1)
   Albuterol, 5 mg/ml (1)
   Breathine, 1 mg/ml (6)

All supplies and drugs necessary for use during transport are stocked and prepared in advance by the transport team.

Physiologic Stress of Transport

The physiologic stresses inherent in transport on both the patient and the team members must be planned for. The patient experiences transport-related stressors in addition to those related to the illness and treatment. Team stressors include physiologically difficult on-call schedules, irregular mealtimes, and having to work in unfamiliar hospitals without all the resources of the base hospital.

Stress occurring during both ground and air transport includes multiple patient transfers to and from stretchers and in and out of vehicles. During these transfers catheters and tubes can become dislodged, ventilation can be disrupted, and lifting or dropping heavy equipment may cause injury. Vibration, noise, electromagnetic interference, temperature variations, and motion sickness may cause physiologic derangements.

The physiology of air transport presents further challenges to the patient and team. A complete understanding of physical laws related to altitude, the stresses of flight, and the ability to understand and compensate for derangements inherent to human pathophysiology are key to safe and successful aeromedical transport. Specific stressors of unpressurized rotor or fixed-wing transport and pressurized fixed-wing transport include the effects of gravitational forces, hypoxia, gas expansion, and dehydration.

Several physical laws relate to aeromedical physiology. Boyle's law states that the volume of a given mass of gas varies inversely to the pressure of the gas;

that is, the same mass (number of gas molecules) has a smaller volume as pressure increases or a larger volume as pressure decreases. Charles' law describes the relationship between temperature and volume, showing that as gas molecules are compressed the temperature of the gas increases. Inversely, as the temperature of a gas increases, the volume increases because the gas molecules move faster and farther apart. Dalton's law states that the total pressure of a gas is the sum of all the individual (partial) pressures of all the gases in a mixture. Dalton's law describes the changes that occur within a gas mixture at different altitudes. Henry's law states that the amount of gas dissolved in a liquid is proportional to the partial pressure of the gas over the liquid and the solubility of the gas in a particular liquid. Henry's law primarily affects divers who ascend rapidly to above sea level during air transport.

Barometric pressure falls as altitude increases, resulting in predictable changes in gas expansion and oxygenation. Any gas-filled space in the human body or in medical equipment is affected by laws having to do with gases. Persons with air trapped in sinuses or ears may experience significant barotrauma and accompanying pain. An untreated pneumothorax at sea level will expand approximately 30% at cabin pressurization at 7000 to 8000 feet. Similarly, gas in normal or abnormal locations in the GI tract will expand 30%. These situations should be anticipated and avoided. Gas expansion in medical equipment must also be anticipated. Closed containers affected by gas expansion include endotracheal tubes and urinary catheter cuffs, pneumatic splints, and unvented glass IV bottles. Sudden aircraft decompression can result in explosive inflation of gas-filled structures such as isolette air mattresses.

Hypoxia can result from a variety of mechanisms. Hypoxic hypoxia results from decreased Po_2 at the alveolar level at altitude. Hyperemic hypoxia occurs in patients with decreased oxygen-carrying capacity of blood, as in anemia or carboxyhemoglobinemia. Stagnant hypoxia can occur in any area of reduced blood flow such as the brain during hyperventilation or an extremity under an expanding pneumatic splint. Histotoxic hypoxia results from impaired ability to use oxygen at the cellular level, most commonly from carbon monoxide or alcohol. Effects of such agents increase reduced oxygen tension. Hypoxia can profoundly affect the cardiopulmonary system and CNS and must be prevented with measures to increase available oxygen tension and oxygen delivery.

Communication

One of the most important components of the regionalization of pediatric critical care is the availability of a communications center to allow rapid access to the system. Whether a referral physician is calling for treatment recommendations or to activate the pediatric transport team, the communication center is a vital link to regional pediatric services.

An effective communication system must be well coordinated, with procedures and protocols understood by all who participate. It is important for communication to be maintained throughout all aspects of transport. This includes contact between referral and receiving hospitals, discussions between team members, and communication between the team and medical control center. In our program this is accomplished with an alpha-numeric computerized paging system that allows each team member to receive written and, if needed, simultaneous messages on their beepers regarding information about patients, vehicles, crew members, and other pertinent issues. Each team carries a pocket-sized portable telephone to communicate easily with the communication center, the transport physician, and the referral hospital if necessary. Many transport programs use two-way hand-held radios, which allow ease of communication between team members and the communication center.

Regional pediatric transport systems must have an established mechanism for rapid access to a physician who can provide treatment recommendations for stabilization of patients. Treatments recommended need to be within the scope and capability of the referring physician and hospital. Any advice given must be documented by both the referring and receiving hospitals, preferably with a tape recording. If physicians are not used as members of the transport team, verbal access to the transport physician must be ensured throughout the transport process.

The communication center needs to be located in a quiet place, with a direct telephone line for the local area and an additional toll-free line for the surrounding region. All telephone calls through the communication center either for patient transport or for consultation must be recorded. A two-way radio system, cellular phone, or advanced paging system is used to maintain access to team members, transport physicians, and vehicle operators. The individual answering the transport telephone must be able to devote full attention to taking the transport call and must not be distracted by other duties.

Preparation of Transport Team

Referral hospital preparation for transport can be divided into advanced preparation and immediate preparation. Advance preparation is an important part of an efficient transport process. All hospitals with emergency departments must have policies and procedures in place for interfacility transport. A list of receiving hospitals and phone numbers needs to be posted and easily accessible to emergency department staff. Information about systems for transportation of pediatric patients with an understanding of their team composition, speed, availability, and training and experience in pediatrics also needs to be accessible to the staff. A plan must be in place to access an alternate receiving center in the event that the nearest facility is not able to accept the patient. Pediatric resuscitation cards are posted for easy viewing, and pediatric equipment is kept readily available.

In immediate preparation the referring hospital can do a great deal to assist in efficient turnaround of the transport team. Radiographs, laboratory reports, and patient care records can be copied in advance for the receiving team. Catheters and tubes can be stabilized before moving the patient. The cervical spine and any suspected fractures must be stabilized in all trauma

---

**TRANSPORT PREPARATION
BY REFERRAL SERVICE**

Advance preparation

List of pediatric referral centers
List of transport systems for children
Pediatric resuscitation protocols
Pediatric resuscitation equipment
Administrative transfer protocols

Immediate preparation

Copy all records and radiographs
Phone number for pending laboratory results
Secure lines and tubes
Stabilize cervical spine and fractures
Prepare blood products

---

victims. In addition, any needed blood products can be ordered and prepared in advance. Any preparations performed before the team's arrival will allow the team to spend a minimum of stabilization time before departure from the referring hospital.

Transport Process

A history of the patient's illness or injury as well as current clinical status, vital signs, medications given, and interventions performed are provided to the team before departure. En route to the referral hospital the team can anticipate likely priorities and complications of the patient's management. Medication doses and drips can be calculated and an approach to initial patient assessment planned.

On arrival at the referring hospital a brief introduction to the staff and family is essential. The team immediately assesses the airway, breathing, and circulation. One of three conclusions can be drawn from this evaluation: the system is stable, so proceed; the system is unstable, so intervene as necessary; the assessment is unclear, so observe, reassess, and intervene as necessary. Assessment and interventions often must be performed simultaneously. It is important that all team members perform within their scope of practice and within the protocols set forth by the medical director of the transport service.

The patient must be efficiently but thoroughly stabilized before transport. Often a referring hospital, accustomed to a "swoop and scoop" approach for adults with multiple trauma, will perceive that neonatal or pediatric specialty teams demonstrate "excessive" delays in departure. However, because most pediatric transport systems bring the PICU to the patient, there is no need to rush to departure. This may be inconvenient for the referring hospital whose personnel and resources are being taken away from other patients, but it is certainly in the best interest of the patient to be stabilized appropriately before departure. One study of 2000 pediatric and neonatal patients treated by an experienced, efficient team showed an average 45- and 60-minute stay, respectively, at the referral center. To meet the needs of the referring hospital, the pediatric transport team must establish immediately that they are able to function independently, without requiring constant use of referring hospital personnel. The patient can also be moved out of what may be the emergency department's only critical care room. For certain patients such as victims of multiple trauma, speed in reaching the physical facilities of the tertiary care center may be a priority. Otherwise there is no reason to rush to depart without taking the time to fully stabilize the patient because any interventions will be more difficult in a moving vehicle. Stabilization times in children are usually longer than in adults because of lack of pediatric experience in a primarily adult emergency department. Increased time may be needed to comfort the patient, explain what to expect, and talk to the parents.

The referring physician is responsible for transfer of the patient to the care of the team. Written and verbal reports include any medications given, interventions performed, intake and output, laboratory values, and previous medical history. Typically the transport team leader communicates with the family, explaining the transport plan of care and giving directions to the regional center. In addition, the team leader obtains informed consent from the parent or legal guardian if it has not already been obtained by the referral staff. The transport team allows the family to see the child before leaving the referral hospital. Before departure from the referral hospital, a report on the patient's clinical status must be called in to the receiving unit.

When preparing the patient for transfer to the transport stretcher, each team member must pay close attention to assigned functions. Patients have a wide range of severity of illness and differing needs before and during transport. Interventions, as indicated by patient assessment, include the following:

1. Cardiorespiratory monitoring with alarm limits set to identify when vital signs are not within normal limits
2. Oxygen saturation monitoring to ensure maintenance of saturation >94%
3. Supplemental oxygen for any patient with a potential for instability
4. Vascular access with a minimum of one, and preferably two, peripheral IV catheters in patients with acute trauma or a potential for instability
5. Assessment of vital signs every 5 minutes until stable and every 30 minutes in the stable patient, including blood pressure and heart and respiratory rates
6. Temperature measured at least every hour; use of an overhead warmer, warming pads, and warmed blankets to keep body temperature within normal limits
7. Chest radiography and assessment of airway, breathing, and circulation in patients in res-

piratory distress or in need of respiratory evaluation
8. End-tidal CO_2 monitoring in intubated patients and those in respiratory distress
9. Pharmacologic agents, IV fluids, and blood as needed on the basis of the diagnosis and symptoms
10. A bladder catheter in patients with acute trauma and those needing monitoring of urine output
11. A nasogastric or orogastric tube in patients at risk of emesis or for relief of gastric distention

It is important that all patients be monitored continuously and that placement of tubes and equipment be checked and monitored. Pediatric patients, especially infants, have difficulty maintaining body temperature, and care must be taken to ensure proper warming techniques are used when needed. During transport the team must be prepared for any change in the patient's condition and have extra airway equipment, fluids, and medications readily available in case they are needed.

On arrival at the receiving unit it is important that the team coordinate the patient's move to the PICU bed. Individual assignments are designated for stretcher-to-bed transfer. Once the patient is transferred and assessment of catheter and tube placement is completed, a report is given to the receiving staff. Patient care is turned over directly to the receiving physician.

It is important that the transport team have a system for follow-up communication with the referral staff after the transport is complete. This can be done with a telephone conversation or a faxed message. Important information to relay is how the child tolerated the transport, any known treatment plans, where the child is located, and whom to call for further information. Legal considerations regarding patient confidentiality may preclude divulging detailed information about the patient without the written consent of the parents.

RISKS AND COMPLICATIONS

In two common situations pediatric transport errors are made. The first arises when the patient is deemed stable enough for local EMS transfer but has an unstable event for which the crew is untrained, inexperienced, or ill-equipped to handle. The second situation arises when a trained pediatric transport team is available to transport the patient and an all-age team with little pediatric training and experience is chosen instead because they will respond and transport the patient more quickly. In the first situation the patient's condition may deteriorate in a way that cannot be predicted. Often these two mistakes are made because of a misperception that the faster the patient is transported the better. Except for patients with surgical emergencies, there is no evidence that the speed of transfer, regardless of level of care en route, is beneficial to the pediatric patient. The referring hospital is legally responsible for assuring that the level of care en route is appropriate. The pediatric transport program has a responsibility to educate the community it serves about its capabilities in order to create reasonable expectations among referring hospitals.

Refer to "Mode of Transport" and "Physiologic Stress of Transport" for other risks and complications.

Medicolegal Issues

Transport of critically ill or injured children gives rise to a number of legal issues that may not initially seem obvious to those involved in the care of the patient. There are no well-defined parameters to determine who is legally responsible for a patient during transport. It is generally accepted that both the referring and receiving hospitals share some level of responsibility. It is well understood that when a patient arrives at the referring hospital all responsibility lies with that hospital until the receiving center is contacted. It is also understood that once a patient is transferred to the care of the receiving physician the receiving hospital is responsible for the patient. In between, or the transfer phase, is where there may be some cojoined responsibility, and liability increases as level of involvement with the patient's care increases. Additional gray areas are encountered during third-party transport, when the transport team is from a hospital not the referring or receiving hospital.

The Consolidated Omnibus Budget Reconciliation Act (COBRA) of 1986 was drafted to prevent hospitals from refusing, limiting, or terminating patient care for financial reasons. COBRA was revised and broadened in 1990. The act requires that the referring hospital evaluate all patients arriving at the hospital with emergency conditions and stabilize the patient appropriately before transferring the patient elsewhere. The patient (or parents) always maintains the right to refuse to consent to the proposed transfer or treatment. This law states that the transferring hospital is responsible for the medical integrity of the receiving hospital as well as the medical appropriateness of the patient transfer. It behooves referral hospital physicians and staff to have a good understanding of the capabilities (i.e., personnel, pediatric training and experience, and equipment) of transport providers to ensure provision of an appropriate mechanism for safe transfer of the patient.

ADDITIONAL READING

Ackerman N. Aeromedical physiology. In McCloskey KA, Orr RA, ed. Pediatric Transport Medicine. St. Louis: Mosby, 1995, pp 143-157.

American Academy of Pediatrics Committee on Hospital Care: Guidelines for air and ground transportation of pediatric patients. Pediatrics. 78:943-950, 1986.

American Academy of Pediatrics Task Force on Interhospital Transport. Guidelines for air and ground transport of neonatal and pediatric patients. Elk Grove Village, Ill.: The Academy, 1993.

Chance G, Matthew J, Gash J. Neonatal transport: A controlled study of skilled assistance. J Pediatr 93:662-666, 1978.

Collett H. 1989 Accident review. J Air Med Transport 9:12-19, 1990.

Day S, McCloskey K, Orr R, Bolte R, Notterman D, Hackel A. Pediatric interhospital critical care transport: Consensus of a national leadership conference. Pediatrics 88:696-704, 1991.

Dobrin RS, Block B, Gilman J. The development of a pediatric emergency transport system. Pediatr Clin North Am 27:633-646, 1980.

Frew S. Emergency medical services legal issues for the emergency physician. Emerg Med Clin North Am 8:41, 1990.

Hart HW. The conveyance of patients to and from hospital, 1720-1850. Med Hist 22:397-407, 1978.

Kanter RK, Tomkins JM. Adverse events during interhospital transport: Physiologic deterioration associated with pretransport severity of illness. Pediatrics 84:43-48, 1989.

Krug S. Staff and equipment for pediatric critical care transport. Curr Opin Pediatr 4:445-450, 1992.

Lam D. Wings of life and hope: A history of aeromedical evacuation. Probl Crit Care 4:477-494, 1990.

Lindebeck G. Reimbursement patterns in a hospital-based fixed wing aeromedical service. Am J Emerg Med 11:586-589, 1993.

Mayfield T. 1995 Annual transport statistics and fees survey. Air Med 1:41-45, 1995.

McCloskey K, Johnston C. Pediatric critical care transport survey: Team composition and training, mobilization time, and mode of transportation. Pediatr Emerg Care 6:1-3, 1990.

McCloskey K, Johnston C. Critical care interhospital transports: Predictability of the need for a pediatrician. Pediatr Emerg Care 6:89-92, 1990.

McCloskey K, King W. Variables predicting the need for major procedures during pediatric critical care transport [abst]. Ann Emerg Med 18:170, 1989.

McCloskey K, King W, Byron L. Pediatric critical care transport: Is a physician always needed on a team? Ann Emerg Med 18:247, 1989.

Omnibus Budget Reconciliation Act of 1989. Sec., 6018 42 USC and 1395 cc (West Suppl 1990).

Orr R, McCloskey K, Britten A. Transportation of critically ill children. In Rogers MC, ed. Textbook of Pediatric Intensive Care, vol 2. Baltimore: Williams & Wilkins, 1992.

Orr R, Venkataraman S, McCloskey K, et al. Pediatric risk of mortality score (PRISM): A poor predictor in triage of patients for pediatric transport. Crit Care Med 23:224, 1995.

Pace J. Air evacuation in the European theater of operations. Air Surg Bull 2:323, 1945.

Schanaberger C. Understanding COBRAS twist and turns. JEMS 14:101-104, 1991.

Smith D, Hackel A. Selection criteria for pediatric critical care transport teams. Crit Care Med 11:10-12, 1983.

Youngberg B. Medical-legal considerations involved in the transport of critically ill patients. Crit Care Clin 8:501-511, 1992.

129 PICU Computerization

Donna Badgett · Donna S. Rahn · Laura A. Wells · Joe K. Wieber

BACKGROUND AND INDICATIONS

Computers are becoming an increasingly important tool in the management of PICU patients. Bedside instruments such as patient monitors and infusion pumps incorporate computers to improve their capabilities for performing patient care such as measuring blood pressure, interpreting cardiac rhythms, and regulating IV infusions. The scope of PICU computerization, however, goes beyond its uses in instrumentation. Currently the major emphasis is on automation of the manual tasks involved in patient care documentation.

Two decades ago a few pioneering institutions began using computers to automate the collection of vital signs. Today's clinical information management systems (CIMS) automate many of the traditional medical records, including flow sheets, physician's orders, nursing care plans, assessments, and progress notes. Nurses and physicians are beginning to use electronic versions of the flow sheet and chart to record and review information. Hospitals are placing computer displays and keyboards at patient bedsides and nursing stations to replace paper and pencil.

As CIMS continue to gain functional capabilities and data storage, increasing emphasis is being placed on identifying, capturing, and storing relevant data and transmission and receipt of data among numerous and various CIMS. This increase in quantity and quality and access to data is not only assisting in the direct care of patients but provides an excellent foundation for many and various clinical research possibilities.

Although there are numerous benefits to adding CIMS in a health care institution, the process is not always easy. Change is often difficult; many staff may feel threatened by a machine recording much of their work for them. Often staff are concerned about the authenticity of the data entered. Most systems asso-ciate a given log in and password with a given individual staff member. Once that log in and password are entered and associated with a given piece of data, the staff member has "signed" that information. Strict adherence to security policies and procedures is the cornerstone of information management systems. Sharing one's log in and password is strictly forbidden. Policies and procedures must be in place to ensure a unique log in and password for all staff and to secure the confidentiality of patient information.

Objectives of PICU Computerization

The broad objectives of PICU computerization are to improve the quality of patient care and reduce hospital operating costs. Five specific objectives follow:

- To be the official version of the medical record for all of the clinical staff, including nurses, physicians, respiratory therapists, and others. To achieve this objective, the system must be accessible at all appropriate locations (e.g., the patient bedside and the nursing station) and must be highly reliable.
- To automate all steps in creating the chart, from physicians' orders to the Kardex to the flow sheet. The system cannot offer a partial solution such as automating half the flow sheet, nor can it require double charting such as recording an entry on paper and again into the computer.
- To collect data once from the person responsible for it and automatically transcribe it into all appropriate parts of the chart. Computers eliminate time-consuming and error-prone transcription steps such as copying a medication order onto both the Kardex and the medication administration record.
- To collect information automatically. As computers are used in more bedside instruments and hospital ancillary departments, the CIMS can acquire information automatically from them.

• To extend users' abilities. For example, computers can check ordered medications for drug interactions and inappropriate dosages, notify users when medications are overdue or new laboratory results are available, calculate doses of drugs on the basis of a patient's weight, and provide on-line reference information.

As these objectives are increasingly met, computers revolutionize the way information is managed in the critical care unit because paper and pencil cannot extend users' abilities in the way that computers can. A new generation of PICU computer systems based on the availability of high-performance bedside workstations is enabling this revolution.

TECHNIQUE
Equipment

The computer equipment used in PICUs can vary in cost and complexity from a simple personal computer at a nursing station to an interconnected network of high-performance workstations at every bedside. Regardless of the specific configuration or the manufacturer, however, all systems have most of the following components.

processor   Hardware that executes the software (computer programs) that control the system's operation.

display   Television-like monitor that presents text and graphics generated by the processor. The display is the primary output device for presenting information to users.

disk   Floppy or hard drive that is used for storing computer programs and data.

keyboard   Input device used as a major method to control the system and enter data.

mouse   Small "pointing" device placed next to the keyboard that contains one to three buttons for selecting items on the computer display. Other pointing devices include touch screen, light pen, and track ball.

printer   Output device that generates paper reports for backup and the permanent medical record. Printers are generally placed at the nursing station.

A workstation consists of a processor, disk, display, keyboard, and mouse. Workstations are interconnected by a local area network (LAN) so that the individual workstations function together as one system. The LAN enables users to review any patient's data from any bedside or nursing station. LAN technology can enable users to access a multitude of applications, running on various computers, all from a single workstation.

Applications

The applications provided by today's CIMS allow immediate access to patient clinical data from and for multiple disciplines. From physician orders to laboratory work to medications to collection of vital signs, virtually all of a patient's clinical information can be used to populate a single flow sheet. Data entered do not have to be reentered to populate multiple flow sheets. This eliminates redundancy and ensures accuracy. The process for gathering, displaying, and disseminating information can be accomplished by the following methods.

Vital signs flow sheet (Fig. 129-1). Computers acquire data automatically from patient monitors to document vital signs. The documentation process entails verifying that the monitored values are correct or modifying them if they are not before storing them. Data from other bedside instruments such as noninvasive blood pressure devices and oximeters can also be captured automatically. Some observations or measurements such as a Glasgow Coma Scale score must be assessed by the nurse and entered manually.

Graphs and trends. Manual flow sheets have either a tabular or graphic format for recording data; if another presentation is needed, the data must be recopied into the new format. Data entered into a computer can be presented in either tabular or graphic format without double entry. Trends of vital signs can be plotted automatically over various time intervals. These graphs can be presented on the computer display or printed on paper.

Respiratory flow sheet. Manual charting of ventilator settings, respiratory procedures, and measurements is time consuming, and there is no way to ensure that detailed changes are tracked. CIMS allows prompting of specific data elements required or desired as dictated by the procedure being performed. Computers can acquire ventilator data directly from the ventilators and blood gas results from the laboratory. Derived respiratory variables such as oxygen index or shunt fraction can be calculated without manual intervention. This information is combined to create a respiratory flow sheet.

Hemodynamic and other calculations. PICU systems provide calculations of cardiorespiratory vari-

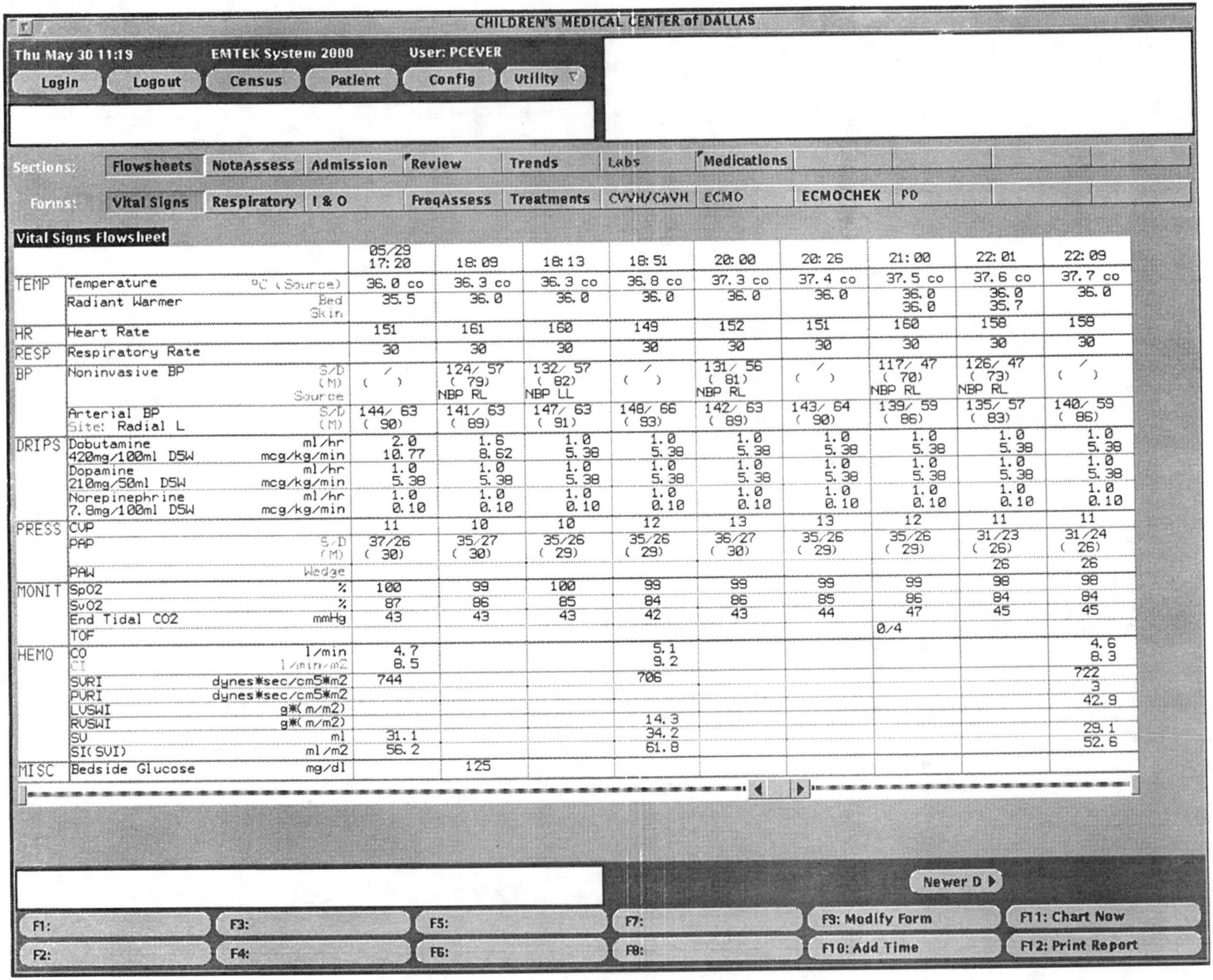

Fig. 129-1   Screen print from computer flow sheet.

ables such as vascular resistance and shunt fraction as a by-product of the charting process. Both the primary and derived data are included in the electronic record and provide valuable physiologic insight. Manual entry into a system with subsequent copying onto the flow sheet is no longer needed.

Intake and output. Critically ill patients often receive five or more IV infusions and have a comparable number of tubes, drains, and other output devices. Recording this information is difficult, and calculation of total volumes at the end of a shift is notoriously inaccurate. With a CIMS, this process is almost totally automated. Hourly volumes from infusion pumps and drainage devices can be acquired automatically with bedside device interfaces. From these interfaces, systems can calculate running, shift, and daily totals of various IV fluids and output and even compute nutritional intake such as daily caloric and protein intake. Thus maintaining the intake-output flow sheet can be entirely automated.

Medications. Ensuring that medications are administered correctly as scheduled is time consuming; infusions of vasoactive drugs may be changed and documented as frequently as every 5 minutes. When the physician's orders are entered into a computer, however, the system sends that information to the pharmacist for review, presents a chronologic list of medications to be administered, and alerts nurses when they are due. Systems are also commonly used to calculate patient-specific dosages and infusion rates for drugs on the basis of patient weight. Further, systems calculate the dosage for drugs such as gentamicin based on pharmacokinetic modules. Many systems incorporate checks for drug interactions, allergies, and inappropriate dosages. All of these warnings and notifications result in fewer medication errors.

Ancillary department communication. Whereas information used in the PICU is mainly generated there, PICU orders and requisitions are sent to ancillary departments such as the laboratory and pharmacy, and results from those departments are returned to and charted in the PICU. Currently laboratory results are reported by either telephone or printed result slip and the nurse transcribes them to the flow sheet.

Now that laboratory and other ancillary departments are computerized, the PICU system must interface with those departmental computer systems. With such interfaces, results can be directly trans- ferred and made immediately available at the bedside in a clinically useful format such as a flow sheet. Messages alert users to the availability of new results, particularly critical values.

Physician's orders. Physician's orders pose the greatest challenge in the documentation process because they drive most diagnostic and therapeutic interventions. After trying to decipher illegible handwriting or interpret incomplete orders, nurses or clerks must transcribe these orders to requisition forms, the Kardex, and the flow sheet (sometimes five or more documents) with an associated risk of error.

Computers enhance the creation of orders and ease the associated burden of documentation as follows:

- Providing standard order sets according to physician, unit, and problem such as sepsis evaluation, which can be entered quickly
- Transcribing orders to the appropriate departments and forms
- Requiring the complete entry of the order so that assumptions by the nurse are reduced
- Checking for the appropriateness of repetitive laboratory tests or medication doses
- Generating derivative orders for the nurse, such as invoking nursing protocols when assisted ventilation is to be administered

Perhaps the greatest benefit provided by computer systems is called "closing the order loop," implying that for every order a CIMS drives the documentation process so there is verification of whether the order was executed. For example, when a medication is ordered, the system ensures that all appropriate administration of the medication is accounted for. Closing the order loop has profound implications for improving the quality assurance process compared with the current manual system, in which no guarantees exist that a patient will receive an ordered treatment.

Assessment and procedure notes. In the past health care workers seeking information had to review one area of the chart for the physicians' notes, another for the nurses' assessment, and yet another for other assessments. Once implemented, a CIMS allows automated documentation of all patient assessments and procedure notes. These notes follow a standard set by the institution and contain required fields of data entry, allowing the health care worker to choose a set of descriptive words or phrases to document findings. These assessments can be in dexed by topic, discipline, or entry sequence. There is now both single point of entry and retrieval within the patient's medical record.

Reference information. A CIMS is much more than an automated version of the medical record. It is an information utility that offers capabilities well beyond the manual charting system. For example, systems are programmed with edit checks to reduce the possibility of erroneous entries. They can provide a drug formulary with dosage and administration information, which can be used as a reference when writing orders. They can contain reference information such as hospital policies and procedures (e.g., procedure for calibrating a transducer or inserting a catheter), which can be displayed on a workstation at the bedside whenever a nurse or physician needs this information. Use of CIMS as an information utility, a kind of online electronic library, promises ultimately to replace traditional textbooks.

Quality assurance and research. The medical record is the major legal reference for the care given a patient. Maintaining accurate records is critically important, both to assist with the ongoing care of patients and to protect personnel against unjustified legal claims. Computers provide many checks to ensure that care is given as ordered and according to policy. Further, an electronic medical record ensures that care is easily and clearly documented and can be systematically audited. Unlike manual records, in which chart reviews are difficult at best, the electronic record is a database that can be queried to study the efficacy of a particular procedure or to document outcomes.

CURRENT RESEARCH AND FUTURE CONSIDERATIONS

Health care computerization continues to expand, with innovations in both software and hardware. Many companies specialize in software development that will integrate with other software systems to provide a complete electronic medical record. In the future computers will facilitate sharing of patient information between physicians' offices, hospitals, laboratories, and insurance companies. Together with the exchange of information comes the challenge and responsibility of maintaining a confidential and priviledged medical record. Hospitals are also challenged in meeting the financial and resource-depleting endeavors of selecting and implementing a CIMS. Research continues in evaluation of the benefits of the CIMS as it relates to time savings, quality of documentation, and cost to the institution. Voice-activated, stylus, and radiofrequency hand-held computers are among the devices being developed to facilitate entry and retrieval of information in the clinical setting.

ADDITIONAL READING

Behrenbeck JG, Davitt P, Ironside P, Mangan DB, O'Shaughnessy D, Steele S. Strategic planning for a nursing information system (NIS) in the hospital setting. Comput Nurs 8:236-242, 1990.

Davis R. Online medical records raise privacy fears. USA Today, March 22:1-2, 1995.

Dawne U, Warnock-Matheron A, Ross S. Mapping the future of hospital information systems: Priorities for nursing applications. Comput Nurs 11:61-66, 1993.

• Kahl K, Ivancin L, Fuhrmann M. Automated nursing documentation system provides a favorable return on investment. J Nurs Adm 21:44-51, 1991.

• Lower MS, Nauert LB. Charting: The impact of bedside computers. Nurs Management 23:40-44, 1992.

Nauert LB, Lower MS, Cox KR. Bedside computers and quality documentation. Nurs Management 24:113-114, 1993.

130 Process Modeling

Stephen F. Mills · Raymond T. Yeh · Stephanie H. Yeh · Murat M. Tanik · H.K. Huang · Brett P. Giroir

BACKGROUND

A large health care facility such as a hospital generates massive volumes of data that must subsequently be recorded, processed, and stored to support treatment of patients, management of facility resources, and billing. These data are generally managed with a combination of manual hard copy systems and proprietary, special-purpose data processing systems. Evolution in data processing and management technologies and the increased availability of high-speed data networks have provided opportunities to improve the efficiency and effectiveness with which medical data are managed, both internal to health care facilities and among facilities. For health care administrators, this technologic growth could result in significant enhancement of monitoring and planning capabilities. For medical diagnosticians, there is the opportunity to develop valuable analytic tools and sources of support. For patients, the potential exists for higher quality of service, improved outcomes, and lower costs. For the various other participants and stakeholders in the health care enterprise, there is the potential for operational increases in quality and efficiency.

The realities of developing clinically acceptable applications and integrating them into operational health care facilities, however, present formidable obstacles to successful clinical deployment of evolving technologies. In addition to problems inherent in the development of any large software system, health care informatics is further complicated by the difficulties associated with integrating a number of such systems, each potentially quite different in structure and behavior, to form a single "seamless" and user-friendly environment for medical users. For service-based industries such as health care, evidence increasingly indicates that the quality of the services provided depends directly on the quality of the processes that produce these services. This implies the need to focus on understanding and improving the health care process as a means of improving the quality of delivered care. Insertion of enabling technologies and integration with existing and future applications to form a health care informatics system must thus be guided by an understanding of how the entire process that is performed by a health care enterprise will be affected.

HEALTH CARE INFORMATION MANAGEMENT: THE CURRENT ENVIRONMENT

Information management within health care facilities has often been attacked in "bottom up" fashion through the introduction of independent medical information systems at the department level. Frequently these are single-function systems intended to solve a specific data management problem for a particular user community. Examples include the following:

- Picture archival and communication systems or image management and communication systems that acquire, store, and subsequently retrieve diagnostic images for viewing by medical users
- Hospital information systems that maintain patient-specific data and track hospital resources for administrative and billing purposes
- Radiology information systems that maintain patient information and scheduling of resources related to radiologic examinations
- Laboratory systems that track order processing, specimen collection and processing, reporting of results, and billing information related to patient testing
- Pharmacy systems to manage inventories, track narcotics, perform drug interaction and allergy checks, and check dosage

- Nursing support systems to manage scheduling of staff and planning of patient care and for advanced clinical charting
- A variety of clinical information systems that address the special needs of ICUs, coronary care units, pediatric wards, and operating rooms
- Medline and Medlog medical information services

The approach taken in developing and installing these systems has generally been to focus on the problem to be solved, often without consideration for legacy systems within the same facility or the requirements of future systems. This approach often results in an informatics environment that comprises dozens of proprietary, stand-alone information systems that cannot share or exchange data. Not only do redundancy and conflict among the systems result, but the task of combining all data to get a global view of patient status is greatly complicated.

The user community for the various health care information systems is diverse, resulting in a large variety of data processing and reporting requirements. The health care environment encompasses such diverse stakeholders as physicians, nurses, and other primary caregivers; technologists and support personnel; vendors of disposable items; third-party payors; laboratories, pharmacies, and other service providers; manufacturers of medical equipment; patients; and health care administrators. Health care facilities generally manage the information required and produced by these groups with a combination of manual hard copy systems and proprietary, special-purpose data processing systems. Proprietary and incompatible data formats are often used, making integration of data virtually impossible. The "information explosion" resulting from enabling technologies in the data acquisition, storage, retrieval, and transfer areas has in many cases oversaturated the existing data management infrastructure. In an attempt to maintain some control over the processes within a health care facility, rigid multilayer hierarchies of management are often established.

THE FUTURE: A "SEAMLESS" INTEGRATED ENVIRONMENT

To maximize the effectiveness of medical information systems, data from a variety of sources must be integrated and presented to each user in a format matched to the needs and interests of that user. In addition to the data currently managed by health care information systems, data integrated and presented to users will likely include multimedia data combined with intelligent text retrieval capabilities. Expert systems and machine learning techniques will likely be used as diagnostic tools to assist physicians and as support tools to efficiently manage the huge volume of data that will result from improved collection and storage capabilities. Fig. 130-1 depicts a multimedia health care informatics environment capable of supporting a variety of medical users and stakeholders.

In the long term the replacement of virtually all hard copy information systems with soft copy versions is implied. To incorporate existing medical information systems, system integration within a health care facility will often be accomplished by adding "layers" of software that create interfaces between the boundaries of stand-alone proprietary systems. The establishment of universally accepted data format and interchange standards for health care applications and systems will be necessary to facilitate both internal integration and interconnection with external facilities.

Future improvements to medical information systems are likely to focus explicitly on providing the highest quality of care to each patient. This means improving the health care process so that the duration of patient stays within facilities is minimized, costs of procedures are minimized, redundant and unnecessary testing is eliminated, quality of diagnosis is maximized, and optimal patient outcomes result.

The integration of information from a variety of sources to provide a seamless environment appropriate to the needs of each user is contingent on the capability to filter out unnecessary information. To be effective in delivering needed information appropriately, such filtering capability must be based on the work flow and structure of activities and communication within the particular health care facility. If the processes executed within the facility are effective and clearly understood, the needed information flow will be obvious.

NEED FOR PATIENT-FOCUSED PROCESS MODELING IN HEALTH CARE

The implementation of a facility-wide health care informatics system is likely to create formidable new problems. Management of a large health care facility (or any other large enterprise) becomes increasingly more difficult as administrators are inundated by a profusion of data produced by a diverse array of information systems. A mechanism for selecting essential information appropriate to the particular task

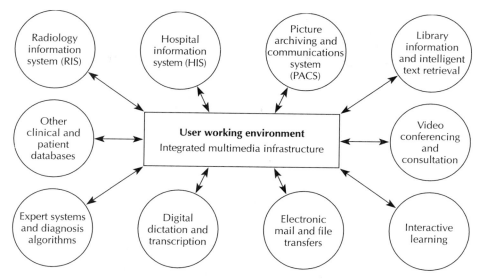

Fig. 130-1   Multimedia working environment for users and stakeholders throughout the health care facility. (From Mills SF, Yeh RT, Tanik MM, Huang HK. Towards process-oriented healthcare management. In Proceedings of the IEEE International Conference on Systems Integration, São Paolo, Brazil, 1994, pp 224-232.)

to be performed is necessary to support management of the various activities within the enterprise. Development of process models can provide such a mechanism.

Process modeling emerged as an identifiable area of research in the early 1980s. Process modeling efforts have historically tended to focus on the areas of software engineering and office automation; the concepts and methodologies are applicable to other complex business activities, however. The increasing use of information management technologies, organizational and structural changes, and increasing emphasis on cost reduction and quality improvement combine to make the health care environment an ideal candidate for application of these techniques.

In contrast to traditional information science modeling methods, process modeling focuses on interaction among agents, independent of whether a computer is involved in these interactions. Curtis et al. identify the following uses for process modeling:

- Representation of processes in a form understandable by humans to facilitate communication about and agreement on the nature of the described process
- Support of process improvement through identification, for example, of redundancies that

could be eliminated and points at which automation technologies could be introduced
- Support of administration and process management through introduction of mechanisms for measuring, monitoring, and planning
- Automated guidance for the persons that participate in the process
- Automated support during execution of the process by, for example, comparing collected performance data against predicted results

Yeh et al. defined a systematic approach to process modeling that is intended to address three essential areas for which stakeholders in an enterprise must perform trade-off analyses:

1. *Stability vs. flexibility:* Successful enterprise management depends on a degree of predictability and control. If stability is forced at the expense of flexibility, however, the enterprise may be ill-equipped to deal with a rapidly evolving environment.

2. *Modularity vs. interconnectivity:* There are huge potential gains from the interconnection of health care information systems, both within a facility and among independent facilities. It is desirable, however, to preserve a level of modularity for each enterprise to maintain control over internal systems.

3. *Long-term vs. short-term objectives:* In many cases enterprise administrators tend to focus on the

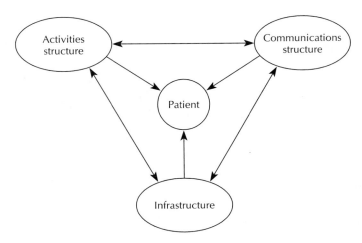

Fig. 130-2 Patient-focused process modeling.

narrow-scope objectives associated with execution of the process but fail to consider long-term organizational objectives such as improvement of the process itself. These objectives may include such concerns as retraining of employees, migration paths for information system components, and physical facility expansion and growth. The result of ignoring these objectives in favor of shorter term goals is likely to be long-term deterioration of the organization.

Because of the complexity and interdependency of these issues, Yeh et al. indicate that a three-dimensional approach to modeling is necessary for a complicated process. The three dimensions are as follows:

1. *Activity dimension:* Concerned with the determination of what tasks need to be performed and scheduling of these tasks. This dimension is essential in analyzing the trade-off between stability and flexibility but is insufficient to support analysis of more complicated trade-offs that involve human dynamics such as unexpected changes in key personnel and variation in individual performance.

2. *Communication dimension:* Concerned with the relationships among the various stakeholders in the enterprise, the agents that execute the process, and anyone else who can influence the process. This dimension is necessary for analysis of the trade-off between modularity and interconnectivity.

3. *Infrastructure dimension:* Concerned with resources, training, and ancillary needs of the organi-

zation within the enterprise. This dimension supports trade-off analysis of long-term vs. short-term objectives by introducing the support organizations required by the process and supports the activities and communications but also provides a mechanism for improving the process and tracking long-term goals.

The three-dimensional modeling approach supports development of a process model that explicitly addresses the various factors within an enterprise that can affect the process and thus provides a powerful and flexible management tool. This approach appears particularly well suited to the health care environment because of (1) the large number of distinct activities associated with each patient treated within a health care facility; (2) the extensive communication that takes place among the various caregivers and service providers for a given patient both within a health care facility and among different facilities; and (3) the huge infrastructure necessary to support and train personnel within a health care facility. As illustrated in Fig. 130-2, successful process modeling for the health care enterprise must employ a patient-focused approach.

IMPROVING PROCESSES IN THE HEALTH CARE ENTERPRISE

To be useful, health care process models must be able to support the existing health care informatics environment and serve as a guide for the future. The

Table 130-1 Process Redesign

Current Process	Redesigned Process
Activity structure	
Sequential	Concurrent
Ad hoc	Statistical quality control
Process dominated by non-value-added components	Non-value-added components negligible
Rework	Right the first time
Many handoffs	Few handoffs
Fragmented	Consolidated
Organizational and communications structure	
Functional division	Cross-functional collaboration
Managers as supervisors	Managers as coaches
Misalignment	Alignment
Hierarchical organization	Clustered organization
Internally focused	Patient focused
Lack of vision	Clarity of vision
Infrastructure	
Fragmented capacity	Integrated capacity
Duplicated functions	Consolidated functions
Limited information technologies	Extensive information technologies
Information not generally accessible	Information at worker's fingertips
Focus on individual achievement	Focus on team achievement
Skill-based job classifications	Team-based job classifications

ability to tailor the modeling process and perform trade-off analyses is critical in the health care informatics environment. In many cases it is impractical to dispose of existing information systems, even if they are independent and proprietary. The general approach to developing health care process models as a means to understand and improve the process within a health care facility should thus be similar to the following:

1. Conduct a detailed study of the existing processes within selected health care facilities.
2. Map the study results onto the process modeling formalism to create process models.
3. Determine where changes in the existing processes are needed.
4. Perform a trade-off analysis to determine where acceptable changes can be made.
5. Implement, monitor, and improve the processes and models in an operational environment.

Refinement of this general approach leads to the following specific methodology for process improvement that appears well suited to the health care environment:

1. Assess maturity level of the process within the target organization along each of the three dimensions:
   a. *Activity assessment:* How is work structured?
   b. *Communication assessment:* How is information created, distributed, and communicated?
   c. *Infrastructure assessment:* How are facility resources invested (e.g., training sessions conducted regularly and a facility-wide reuse policy)?
2. Identify core processes within the organization.
3. Select processes for innovation.
4. Redesign selected processes according to the three-dimensional framework:
   a. Redesign infrastructure.
   b. Redesign communications structure.
   c. Redesign activities structure.
5. Implement the improved process.
6. Monitor execution of the process and evaluate results.

Table 130-1 characterizes the results of the redesigning processes.

PROCESS MODELING IN THE PICU: A CASE STUDY

This section describes a process modeling research project using the techniques described. The goals of this project were to develop process models for a selected health care enterprise with process modeling tools and formalisms and to use these models to improve the efficiency of processes within that enterprise. The PICU was selected as the initial "enterprise" to be modeled. Although having a much smaller patient capacity than a hospital or other major health care facility, the PICU is a microcosm of the hospital, with its own radiology facilities, pharmacy, invasive procedure rooms, physician and nursing staff, and supply of disposable items. In addition to transfers from other patient areas within the hospital, patients enter the PICU from the emergency department and outside institutions, as is the case for hospitals and other large-scale health care enterprises. A variety of extreme medical problems are treated, possibly resulting in a more thorough exercise of process modeling technology than would be possible elsewhere in the hospital. The staff is smaller than in a full-scale medical center, which was expected to reduce the number of interviews necessary to collect process data.

Process data for construction of the models were collected in the PICU at Children's Medical Center of Dallas, a 28-bed multidisciplinary medical/surgical unit with more than 1500 admissions per year. Children's Medical Center operates in close coordination and physical proximity with University of Texas Southwestern Medical Center. Data for development of the initial models were collected through interviews with the PICU staff, including nurses, physicians, and administrators. Discussion during these interviews focused on tasks performed in the PICU, resources used to support these tasks, and communications among the participants (including any documentation associated with the PICU processes).

Because there were no historical data to indicate the validity of process modeling concepts for the health care environment, an informal analysis was first performed to validate these concepts in the PICU. The primary health care delivery processes associated with nursing activities were selected for this initial analysis. The PICU at Children's Medical Center depends heavily on the nursing staff, resulting in contention for the nurses' time. As a result, the nursing

processes were identified as both extremely critical to the success of the PICU and also likely, in the opinion of the research team, to be well suited to process modeling techniques. Interviews were conducted with the nursing staff, and the collected data were used to analyze nursing processes.

More detailed interviews were subsequently performed. In addition to the nursing staff, these interviews included other clinicians and some administrators. The results of the interviews were assessed and used as a basis to develop process models. The three-dimensional approach described was used to implement the models to ensure that infrastructure, activities, and communications were considered concurrently. The ProSLCSE process modeling and analysis tool, developed by International Software Systems, Inc., Austin, Texas, was used as the implementation platform and testbed for the process models. ProSCLSE provides a number of important capabilities, including explicit modeling of activities, communications, and infrastructure; simulation and execution of the models; substitution of empirical data in place of simulation data, where available; generation of reports that list process statistics for the agents involved or the product or service being generated, bottlenecks, and areas of resource contention; and support of various views (e.g., primary caregiver, administrator, or third-party payor) in support of the diverse interests within the enterprise.

Construction of detailed clinical and administrative process models for the PICU is currently being completed. Fig. 130-3 shows a ProSCLSE graphic representation of a process model that represents the top-level view of a subset of the PICU at Children's Medical Center. Figs. 130-4 through 130-10 show the hierarchy of subprocesses that compose this top-level view. The initial emphasis on billing and administrative functions in these models is primarily because of the abundance of data available in these areas and not their relative importance or complexity. Additional efforts are under way to develop a more detailed abstraction hierarchy for the other components of PICU operations. To date, a process abstraction hierarchy consisting of 30 such process models has been developed for the PICU at Children's Medical Center.

The entire hierarchy of process models can be executed for the purpose of analyzing the processes in a simulated operational environment. In addition, the hierarchy of PICU process models can eventually be used as a basis for or incorporated into a full enterprise model of Children's Medical Center.

Process analysis and modeling activities at Children's Medical Center have resulted in recommendations for changes in the staffing mix in the PICU.

The initial nursing process analysis activity resulted in recommendations for ways in which certain functions being performed by the nursing staff could be reallocated, thus reducing the demands on the nursing staff and freeing them to focus on clinical tasks that make better use of their clinical skills. Through

Text continued on p. 1187.

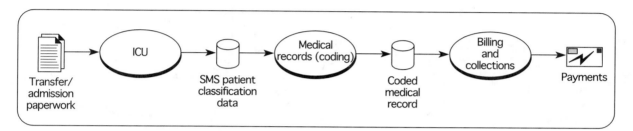

Fig. 130-3   Top-level model of the PICU.

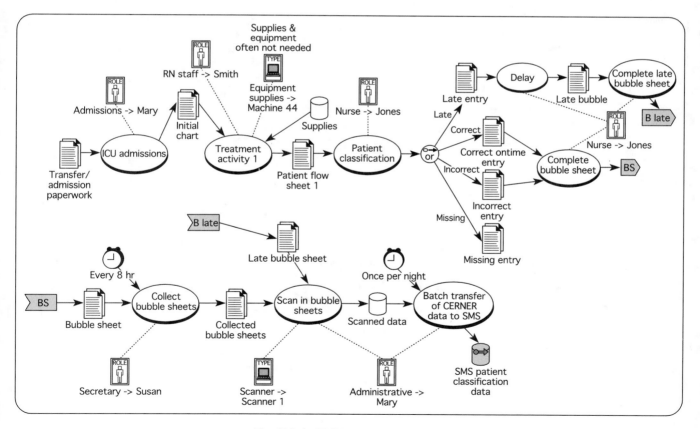

Fig. 130-4   PICU operations process.

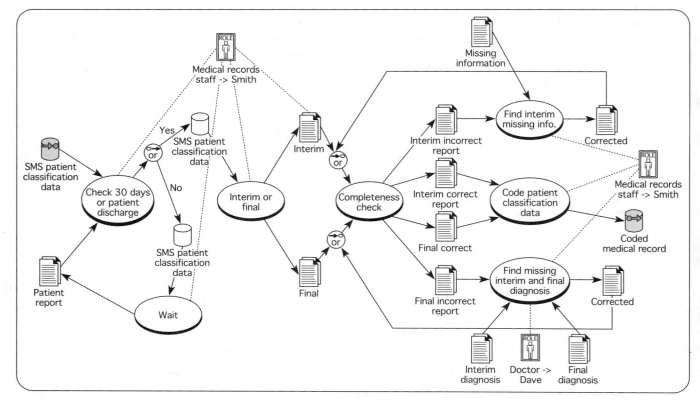

Fig. 130-5 Medical records coding process.

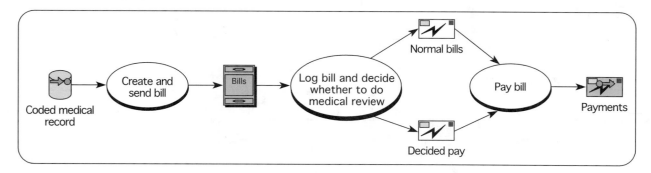

Fig. 130-6 Billing and collections process.

of the hand (dorsal metacarpal and dorsal venous network), (2) the foot (dorsal venous arch, venous plexus of the dorsum, and median and marginal vessels), (3) the forearm (median antebrachial and accessory cephalic veins), (4) the ankle (greater and lesser saphenous veins), (5) the antecubital fossa (median cephalic and basilic veins), (6) the arm (cephalic, basilic, and axillary veins), (7) the scalp in neonates and infants (superficial temporal, occipital, posterior auricular, frontal, and supraorbital veins), (8) the neck (external jugular vein), and (9) the thigh (greater saphenous and femoral veins).

The preferred sites for peripheral venous cutdown insertion are (1) the lesser saphenous vein (ankle), (2) the antecubital fossa (median cephalic and basilic veins), (3) the external jugular vein, and (4) the greater saphenous vein (thigh).

Equipment

All necessary equipment for the procedure must be set up before attempting cannulation to decrease the chances of accidental decannulation while attempting to locate equipment after catheterization of a vessel. The equipment necessary for percutaneous cannulation and a venous cutdown is listed below. A butterfly needle or cannula of appropriate size is chosen to correspond with the size of the vessel and clinical needs. Small catheters lead to vessel thrombosis and do not provide adequate access for rapid infusion of large amounts of fluids.

Equipment for peripheral venous cannulation

Armboards appropriate for patient's size (hand and foot immobilization)
Benzoin sticks and alcohol wipes
Infusion pump
IV fluid and IV tubing with a micro drip chamber
Needles or catheters and butterfly needle, 19, 21, 23, 25 gauge
Over-the-needle catheters, 14, 16, 18, 20, 22, 24 gauge
Povidone-iodine ointment
Povidone-iodine pads
Protective goggles (universal precaution)
Rubber bands
Small paper cup (protect scalp cannula)
Sodium chloride flush solution, 10 ml vial
Surgical gloves and mask (universal precautions)
Surgical tape, ½ and 1 inch
Syringes

3 ml syringe with ⅜-inch needle
10 ml syringe
T-connector
Tourniquet

Venous cutdown cannulation equipment

Catheters (short or long), 18- to 25-gauge selection (see also Table 131-1)
Lidocaine, 1%
Plastic catheter introducer
Surgical procedure lamp
Vascular access tray (see below)
Other equipment (same as above)

Vascular access tray (sterile)

Syringe for flush solution, 10 ml
Clear dermal tape
Draping towels
Five 4 × 4 inch gauze sponges
Four-inch curved eye-dressing forceps
Four-inch straight eye-dressing forceps
Needle holder
Scalpel blades, Nos. 11 and 15
Scalpel handle
Smooth forceps
Small scissors
Suture on needle, 4-0 nylon
Toothed forceps
Two 5-inch curved mosquito hemostats
Umbilical tape

Insertion

Percutaneous insertion. Using aseptic technique prepare the area in which the cannula will be inserted with povidone-iodine solution. Apply a tourniquet proximal to the insertion site. Anchoring a rubber band around the patient's head above the eyebrows to avoid any ocular damage may be useful for scalp venipuncture in infants. Allow the povidone-iodine solution to dry for 30 seconds. Visualize and palpate an appropriate vein. Straight vessels provide better insertion sites. Approach the vessel in the direction of blood flow. The use of nitroglycerin ointment (0.4 mg for infants <1 year old; 0.8 mg for children >1 year old) causes vasodilatation and may facilitate venous cannulation in children without causing systemic effects.

When using a butterfly needle, flush it with 0.9% sodium chloride solution before insertion to ensure that the needle and tubing are free of air and bubbles. Grasp the needle by the butterfly wings with the bevel up. Stretch the skin over the vessel with your free hand to anchor the vessel. Puncture the skin with the needle 0.5 to 1.0 cm distal to the desired vessel puncture site. Advance the needle along the vein's axis until vessel puncture is accomplished. At this point blood return into the butterfly tubing can generally be observed. Attach a 3 ml syringe filled with 0.9% sodium chloride solution to the needle and aspirate gently to corroborate blood return. After blood return is obtained, release the tourniquet and flush the tubing and needle. Fluid must flow freely. Some rely only on the ease of infusion rather than checking for blood return. Tissue swelling and/or discoloration is an indication of extravasation. If the line has good blood return and flushes properly, secure it with adhesive tape without covering up the skin insertion site. Connect it to the rest of the infusion system at this point. A small self-adhesive dressing that allows easy inspection can be applied to the skin insertion site to protect it from ambient contamination.

The approach with the over-the-needle catheter is similar except that there is no need to flush the catheter before insertion, even though some prefer to do so, and the insertion of the cannula is different. Once the vessel is pierced with the needle and blood returns into the hub, advance the needle slightly into the lumen of the vein until the cannula is within the vessel. At this point hold the needle in a stationary position while the catheter is slowly advanced over the needle. Some personnel prefer to advance the catheter while rotating it over the needle. After advancing the catheter carefully, remove the needle and allow blood to return through the catheter. Remove the tourniquet and flush the catheter. If the catheter flushes without signs of extravasation, secure it with adhesive tape, connect it to the infusion system, and cover it with a sterile dressing. To avoid the risk of catheter shearing and catheter material embolism, do not pull the catheter back over the needle once the catheter has been advanced beyond the needle tip.

Cutdown insertion. Only the lesser saphenous venous cutdown (Fig. 131-2) will be discussed here since the technique is basically the same for all locations. A description of the other cutdown sites can be found in Additional Reading. The saphenous vein at the ankle is located superior and anterior to the medial malleolus (Fig. 131-2, *A*). Using aseptic technique apply povidone-iodine to the surgical site three times and let dry. Infiltrate the area with lidocaine using a 25-gauge needle. Drape the surgical site and set up the necessary equipment (i.e., mount scalpel blade, draw flush solution, and mount the T-connector). Cut a cardboard wedge in a triangular shape with a base 1 cm from the cardboard to hold the surgical suture material. Recheck the patient for depth of analgesia. Make a 1 cm incision at the upper limit of the medial malleolus, starting at the most anterior quarter of the malleolus and extending anteriorly. Identify the saphenous vein by scraping the tibia from anterior to posterior with the hemostat closed and the curve down to pick up the tissue bundle that contains the saphenous vein and nerve. Open the hemostat wide to separate the nerve and the vein from the connective tissue. Use the two eye-dressing forceps, alternating them in an opening and closing fashion, to dissect the saphenous vein. The vein is round, pink, and elastic; the nerve is flat, white, and stringlike.

After dissecting the vein, place a 6 cm long stay suture distally and another proximally. Do not tie the suture around the vessel. Place a hemostat, holding the ends of each stay suture together (Fig. 131-2, *B*). Slip the triangular-shaped cardboard under the vessel. While exerting gentle traction on the distal stay suture, cannulate the vein using the same technique as for percutaneous insertion of over-the-needle catheters. For inserting long catheters, make a puncture incision with an 18- or 20-gauge needle in the middle of the vessel (Fig. 131-2, *C*). Introduce the plastic catheter introducer into the vessel lumen, opening the puncture incision. Pick up the tip of the long catheter with the eye-dressing forceps and introduce it gently into the vessel, or the angiocatheter may be introduced directly into the vessel. Advance the catheter gently until the length desired is introduced (Fig. 131-2, *D*).

After the catheter has been placed, connect it to a syringe with a T-connector and aspirate gently to check for blood return; flush the catheter with a 0.9% sodium chloride solution, observing the patient for signs of extravasation. Connect the T-connector to the IV set tubing and proceed to close the surgical wound with simple interrupted stitches. Suture the catheter to the skin and the T-connector (Fig. 131-2, *E*). Cleanse the wound of blood with 0.9% sodium chloride solution or povidone-iodine solution. Apply adhesive tape to the catheter and T-connector for more stability without covering the wound. Finally,

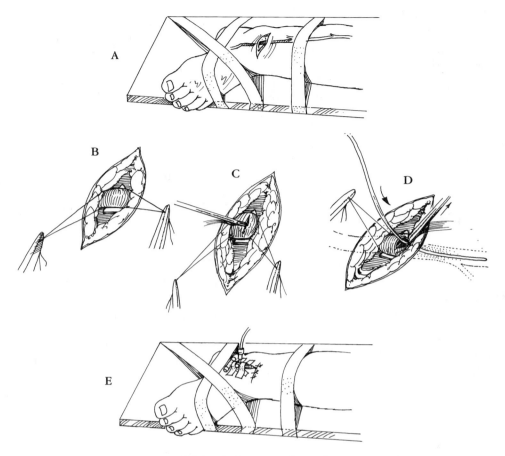

Fig. 131-2 Saphenous vein cutdown.

secure the stay sutures with tape distally and proximally. These sutures are helpful in stopping bleeding around the catheter. If bleeding occurs, gently pull the stay sutures to enhance hemostasis. The wound may be covered with any of the multiple occlusive and transparent dressings commercially available.

Maintenance

The dressing must be changed every 48 hours. The skin insertion site dressing must be small enough to allow inspection for signs of infiltration and infection (i.e., cellulitis and phlebitis) every hour and 8 hours, respectively. A transparent self-adhesive dressing can be used and must be changed when it is no longer occlusive. IV fluids must be changed every 24 hours and IV tubing every 72 hours.

Catheter Removal

The Centers for Disease Control and Prevention recommends that the insertion site be changed every 72 hours, but the availability of other sites may be limited. The risk of catheter-induced septicemia or suspected septicemia from peripheral Teflon catheters is small in general pediatric patients. In patients admitted to the general pediatric ward the risk of colonization and catheter-related septicemia may not be adequate reason for removing IV catheters at 72 hours when local or systemic signs of inflammation or infection are absent. At Children's Medical Center of Dallas the catheter is left in place longer than 72 hours in patients with minimal vascular access and no signs of local or systemic infection. This must be documented by the physician in the progress notes.

RISKS AND COMPLICATIONS

Peripheral venous cannulation has a low rate of complications, which can be separated into two categories: infectious and noninfectious. The infectious complications are local cellulitis, phlebitis, colonization, and septicemia. The noninfectious complications are arterial cannulation, chemical or mechanical phlebitis, extravasation, thrombosis, and embolus formation. Because stainless steel needles can produce many complications, including vessel abrasion, perforation, extravasation, thrombus formation, low flow rate, and scarring, Teflon and Silastic catheters are preferred.

Extravasation of some drugs may cause skin and deep tissue necrosis. The use of hyaluronidase decreases and in some cases prevents tissue injury by temporarily destroying the interstitial cement and increasing diffusion of extravasated fluid through the tissues. Investigators have used 15 units of hyaluronidase subcutaneously in infants and 300 units of hyaluronidase in rabbits without secondary effects. A dose of as many as 750,000 units has been used in animals with virtually no adverse effects. For optimal effect, hyaluronidase must be administered within 1 hour of extravasation. Hyaluronidase can be replaced with 1% lidocaine, a readily available medication. Lidocaine is administered without epinephrine into the wound to cause vasodilatation.

Central Venous Catheterization

A CVC is a catheter placed within the thoracic cavity, usually with the tip terminating in the superior or inferior vena cava. CVC is used for (1) central venous pressure (CVP) measurement, (2) CVP waveform analysis, (3) delivery of drugs to the central circulation, (4) administration of high-concentration parenteral alimentation, (5) rapid infusion of large volumes of fluids or blood products, (6) exchange transfusion, (7) chemotherapy, (8) blood sampling, (9) administration of vasoconstrictor inotropes, (10) an alternate route for parenteral fluids or drugs for patients in whom peripheral venous cannulation is no longer possible, (11) hemodialysis or hemofiltration, (12) plasmaphoresis, (13) delivery of thrombolytic therapy, or (14) removal of air embolism from the right atrium. A CVC is used in the care and monitoring of critical care patients and as an access route for home therapy in patients with malnutrition, malignancies, and infections who need prolonged courses of antibiotics. Rapid delivery of drugs to the central circulation during resuscitation is best achieved through a CVC.

There are three categories of CVCs: temporary, tunneled, and implanted. Catheterization can be accomplished by a percutaneous or cutdown technique. The advantages of the percutaneous technique over the cutdown technique are it leaves no disfiguring scar, it can be performed more quickly, it is simpler to learn, and the number of access sites are not limited. The advantage of the cutdown technique over the percutaneous technique is direct visualization of vessels in those patients who are in shock or who are difficult to cannulate percutaneously. To measure CVP, the catheter tip ideally is positioned at the atriocaval junction; however, it has been reported that a catheter terminating in the intrathoracic portion of the inferior vena cava reliably predicts right atrial pressure in pediatric patients after cardiac surgery. The tip of the CVC is placed at the atriocaval junction so that an accidental perforation would be above the reflection of the pericardium and thus continued infusion would result in hydrothorax and not cardiac tamponade.

TECHNIQUE
Access Sites (see Fig. 131-1)

Any peripheral vessel (see discussion of access sites under peripheral venous catheterization) can be used to access a central vein if a long enough catheter is used to reach the central circulation; however, long, small catheters that fit into small peripheral veins have high flow resistance. Usually the more peripheral the site, the smaller the catheter that may be used. Peripheral sites such as the scalp, hands, and feet generally do not lend themselves to cutdowns. In addition to the list of percutaneous peripheral insertion sites, the following deep veins are available for CVC placement: internal jugular vein, femoral vein, and subclavian vein. Other peripheral veins such as the external jugular, antecubital, and saphenous veins may be used to access the central circulation.

Peripheral access to the central circulation tends to be more technically difficult and usually necessitates smaller and longer catheters. In patients who have had frequent catheterization or in whom the above-mentioned vessels have posed problems, other veins such as the lumbar, inferior epigastric, intercostal, hepatic, and azygous and hemiazygous veins have been used for surgical catheterization.

Do not catheterize the internal jugular vein in patients with increased ICP since the catheter may impede venous return from the head and further increase ICP. In patients with high intrathoracic pressure and in small infants the subclavian approach is avoided when possible because of the high incidence of pneumothorax. The external jugular, facial, and saphenous veins in the thigh are almost exclusively used for cutdown.

Equipment

The variety of CVCs available has increased in the past few years, allowing physicians to select the catheter that best fits the patient's needs. From the perspective of length of time of implantation and construction characteristics, CVCs may be classified into two categories: short vs. long term and single vs. multiple lumens. Most short-term catheters (up to 3 weeks of use) are constructed from polyethylene or polyurethane. Polyurethane is preferred over polyethylene because of its elasticity and lesser thrombogenicity. Silicone is preferred for long-term catheters because it is less thrombogenic and more pliable than polyurethane. Polyurethane catheters coated with hydromer (isocyanate prepolymer or hydrogel interpolymer of polyvinylpyrrolidone) have been reported to be less thrombogenic than silicone, polyvinylchloride, and noncoated polyurethane. Multiple-lumen catheters have made simultaneous drug administration and monitoring possible. Catheters with up to three noncommunicating lumens are presently available in a single catheter body. Exit ports are usually separated to facilitate simultaneous use. Sizes vary from less than 1 to 14 F. Combining different materials and single- or multiple-lumen designs with the wide range of sizes that are available has resulted in a large number of catheters for use in pediatric patients. There are at least 18 catheter manufacturers; some make customized catheters and others have a standardized product line. Table 131-1 lists generic catheters that provide a wide range of options depending on the patient's age, the insertion site, the catheter size, and the length and number of lumens. Kits containing all the equipment needed, in-

Table 131-1　Generic Central Venous Catheter Guidelines

No. of Lumen	Minimum Size (F)	Maximum Length (cm)	Age (weight)	Vein
Single	3	10	Newborn (3 kg) to 6 mo (8 kg)	Neck/subclavian
Single	3	30	Newborn (3 kg) to 6 mo (8 kg)	Basilic/femoral
Single	4	15	6 mo (8 kg) to 2 yr (13 kg)	Neck/subclavian
Single	4	45	6 mo (8 kg) to 2 yr (13 kg)	Basilic/femoral
Single	5	20	2 yr (13 kg) to adult	Neck/subclavian
Single	5	60	2 yr (13 kg) to adult	Basilic/femoral
Double	4	10	Newborn (3 kg) to 6 mo (8 kg)	Neck/subclavian
Double	4	30	Newborn (3 kg) to 6 mo (8 kg)	Basilic/femoral
Double	5	15	6 mo (8 kg) to 2 yr (13 kg)	Neck/subclavian
Double	5	45	6 mo (8 kg) to 2 yr (13 kg)	Basilic/femoral
Double	7	20	2 yr (13 kg) to adult	Neck/subclavian
Double	7	60	2 yr (13 kg) to adult	Basilic/femoral
Triple	5	15	6 mo (8 kg) to 2 yr (13 kg)	Neck/subclavian
Triple	5	45	6 mo (8 kg) to 2 yr (13 kg)	Basilic/femoral
Triple	7	20	2 yr (13 kg) to adult	Neck/subclavian
Triple	7	60	2 yr (13 kg) to adult	Basilic/femoral

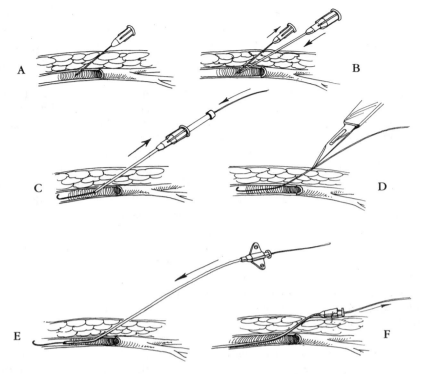

Fig. 131-3   Percutaneous venous access. Seldinger technique.

cluding local anesthetic, are available from a variety of catheter manufacturers.

Insertion

Percutaneous insertion. There are three percutaneous techniques: the Seldinger technique, the through-the-needle technique, and the combined technique. The Seldinger technique consists of locating the desired vessel percutaneously with a small-gauge search needle mounted on a syringe. The syringe is removed from the needle when blood is returned (Fig. 131-3, *A*), and a thin-walled needle is introduced following the same trajectory of the search needle until entry into the vessel is gained (Fig. 131-3, *B*). A guidewire is passed through the needle into the vessel, advancing one fourth to one third of the wire (Fig. 131-3, *C*). The thin-walled and search needles are removed, leaving the guidewire in place (Fig. 131-3, *D*). The skin opening is dilated with the set dilator. The dilator is taken out and the catheter is inserted over the wire, making certain the guide-

wire is visible through the proximal end of the catheter before advancing it into the vessel (Fig. 131-3, *E*). A twisting motion is used to advance the catheter. Slight enlargement of the entry site with a scalpel may be necessary. After the catheter is introduced into the proper position, the guidewire is removed gently (Fig. 131-3, *F*).

The through-the-needle technique of catheterization consists of venous cannulation with a needle or catheter large enough to accommodate a catheter once a vessel is cannulated (Fig. 131-4, *A*). The catheter is advanced into the vessel and the introducing needle or catheter removed (Fig. 131-4, *B*). To avoid catheter shearing, the catheter is not pulled through the needle. Usually these setups have some kind of protective device to cover the sharp end of the needle and protect the catheter or have a needle that can be broken in half longitudinally and removed (Fig. 134-4, *C* to *E*). This technique is especially useful in premature infants for placing small, long Silastic catheters into small vessels and ad-

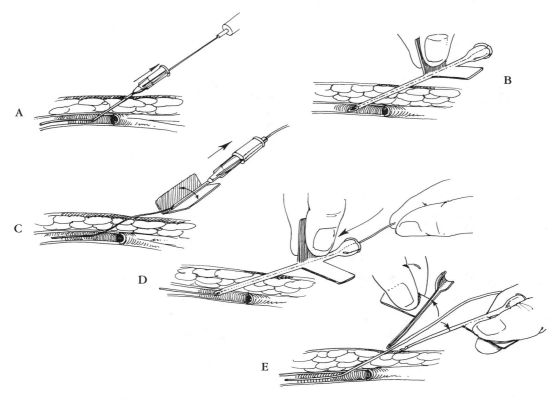

Fig. 131-4 Percutaneous venous access. Through-the-needle technique.

vancing them to the central circulation. This technique of insertion does not allow pulling back the catheter because of the possibility of shearing it with the needle.

The third technique is a combination of the Seldinger technique and the through-the-needle technique. Vascular access is obtained using the same guidewire approach (Fig. 131-5, *A*). A peel-away sheath is introduced over the wire into the vessel, and the wire is removed (Fig. 131-5, *B* and *C*). A catheter of smaller diameter than the peel-away sheath is introduced into the vessel, and after the catheter is positioned as desired, the sheath is pulled and peeled, leaving the catheter in place (Fig. 131-5, *D* to *F*). This technique is useful for placement of soft, large-diameter catheters (i.e., Broviac or Hickman type) because it allows the use of vessel dilators and the sheath offers little resistance to the advancement of a floppy catheter.

The percutaneous cannulation techniques for use in the internal jugular, external jugular, femoral, and subclavian veins will be discussed in detail. The percutaneous catheterization of the basilic vein is omitted since the technique is similar to that used with a peripheral IV catheter. The only modifications are the application of the Seldinger, through-the-needle, or combined technique.

According to the Food and Drug Administration and the Intravenous Nursing Society's Standard of Practice, CVC placement is to be performed under full aseptic technique, including surgical hand scrub, hair cover, mask, sterile gown, gloves, drapes, and appropriate skin antiseptics. Protective eyewear is required under universal precautions. Surgical skin preparation, including presurgical antiseptic scrub followed by the application of an antiseptic solution, is critical in the prevention of catheter-related infections. Two percent chlorhexidine gluconate was reported

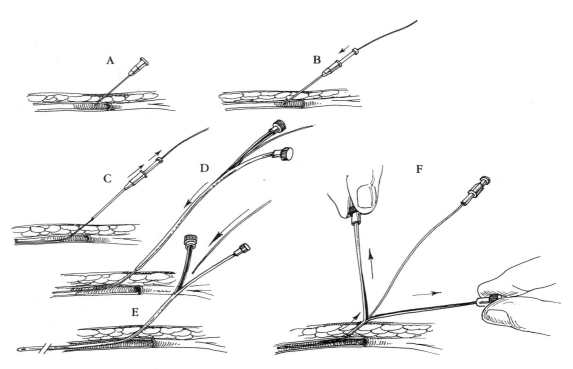

Fig. 131-5 Percutaneous venous access. Combination technique.

to be superior to 10% povidone-iodine and 70% alcohol in the reduction of catheter-related infections when used in preoperative and postoperative insertion site care. The use of full aseptic technique resulted in a greater than 50% reduction, and delay in the onset of catheter-related infections compared with the use of sterile gloves and small drapes limited aseptic technique. Jugular and subclavian approaches are performed with the patient's ECG monitored continuously to detect changes in rate or rhythm since the wire or catheter may enter the heart and trigger arrhythmias that necessitate removing the catheter or wire or treatment of the arrhythmia. Refer to Chapters 179 and 180 for appropriate sedation of the pediatric patient undergoing CVC placement.

External jugular vein cannulation (Fig. 131-6). Restrain the child's arms and legs and turn his head to the side opposite to the catheterization site (right side preferred). Place the child in a 20- to 30-degree Trendelenburg position and identify the external jugular vein (it is helpful to occlude it distally with a finger at the base of the neck). Use complete aseptic technique and give a local anesthetic. Cannulate the vessel using the Seldinger technique or through-the-nee-

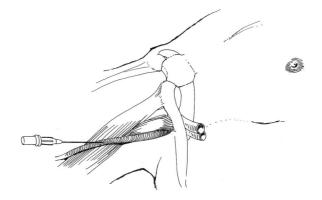

Fig. 131-6 Technique for external jugular vein catheterization.

dle technique, depending on the catheter desired. Passing the wire or catheter centrally may prove difficult since it may enter the subclavian vein following the trajectory into the arm or in some instances may not advance past the bifurcation. Use of the J end of the guidewire may help insert the wire in the

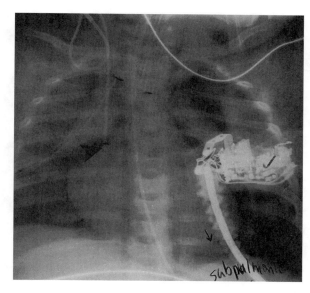

Fig. 131-7   Chest radiograph to confirm CVP placement (arrowhead).

central position. Check for proper catheter placement (Fig. 131-7) and suture the catheter in place. Catheters inserted through the external jugular vein preferentially go out toward the arm. A success rate of 53% has been reported in young children using the external jugular vein for CVC placement.

Suture the catheter after verifying its position. The sutures must be tight enough to stabilize the catheter and prevent catheter dislodgment, but loose enough to prevent skin necrosis. Nylon monofilament suture is preferred over silk. Silk sutures are irritating to the skin and support colonization of microorganisms between the braided strands, increasing the risk of catheter-related infection. Catheter stabilization also reduces the risk of microorganism entry by reducing the in-and-out movement of the catheter at the insertion site.

Internal jugular vein cannulation. The four different approaches to the catheterization of the internal jugular vein are anterior, central, posterior, and low. Only the central approach is discussed in this chapter since the anterior and posterior approaches are modifications of the same technique. A discussion of the low approach is also omitted since it is believed to have a higher incidence of pneumothorax than the other three approaches and in case of pulmonary vascular anomalies may lead to severe hemorrhage.

Immobilize the patient in the Trendelenburg position (Fig. 131-8); place a diaper roll between the shoulders and hyperextend the neck. The right-sided approach is preferred because of the lower position of the lung's apical pleura, there is less likelihood of injuring the thoracic duct and the vena cava, and it provides a straighter route to the right atrium. Identify the following landmarks: sternal notch, clavicle, all three heads of the sternocleidomastoid muscle, carotid artery, and cricoid cartilage (see Fig. 131-8). Cleanse the area surgically using sterile technique, including the use of cap, mask, and gloves. Infiltrate the area with lidocaine. When using the central approach for internal jugular vein cannulation (Fig. 131-9), identify the sternocleidomastoid muscle and the carotid artery. The two medial heads of the sternocleidomastoid muscle form a triangle, with the apex cephalad and the base caudad. The most medial head of the sternocleidomastoid muscle inserts in the sternum. Locate the apex of the triangle at approximately the level of the cricoid cartilage and introduce the search needle at a 30-degree angle to the coronal plane, directing the tip of the needle caudally and parallel to the sagittal plane or slightly down toward the ipsilateral nipple. Do not advance the needle past the level of the clavicle to avoid pleural puncture. Redirecting the needle 5 to 10 degrees laterally may be necessary to achieve cannulation. When venous blood is freely obtained with the search needle, leave the needle in place and remove the syringe. Introduce a thin-walled needle and complete the procedure following the instructions described for the Seldinger technique. Caution must be taken not to leave any port or needle open to air since negative intrathoracic pressure can pull air through the needle into the vein, resulting in air embolism. Once the catheter is in place, secure it with several stitches and check for proper catheter placement as described below.

Femoral vein cannulation (Fig. 131-10). Immobilize the patient in a frog-leg position. Identify the femoral pulse and surgically cleanse the area using sterile technique. Administer a local anesthetic. Insert the search needle medial to the femoral pulse and 1 to 2 cm below the inguinal ligament, advancing it cephalad at a 45-degree angle until blood flow is obtained (do not go past the inguinal ligament to avoid intra-abdominal puncture of a femoral vessel). After cannulation with the search needle, complete the Seldinger technique. Confirm the catheter position and secure the catheter as previously described.

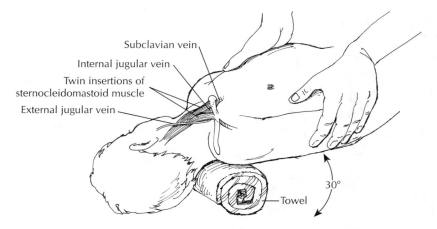

Fig. 131-8   Central venous catheterization. Trendelenburg position.

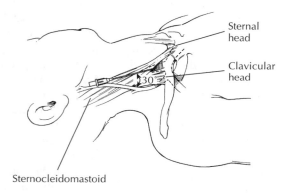

Fig. 131-9   Technique for internal jugular vein catheterization.

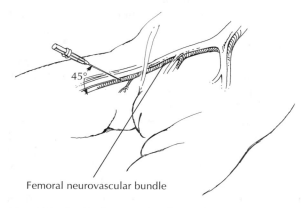

Fig. 131-10   Technique for femoral vein catheterization.

Subclavian vein cannulation (Fig. 131-11). The infraclavicular approach in small infants is recommended only when no other routes are available. In infants only 44% of the first needlesticks are successful and the complication rate is 12%. Meticulous attention to technique is necessary to avoid pneumothorax and injury to the subclavian or internal thoracic artery.

Immobilize the child in a 30-degree Trendelenburg position (see Figs. 131-8 and 131-9) with his head turned to the side opposite the area being cannulated and both arms down. Identify the following landmarks: suprasternal notch, junction of the middle and medial thirds of the clavicle, and pectoral shoulder groove (Fig. 131-11, *A*). Surgically scrub the area and apply a local anesthetic. Introduce a thin-walled needle at the junction of the middle and medial thirds of the clavicle, directing it toward a finger placed in the suprasternal notch. The syringe needs to be parallel to the frontal plane, lying in the pectoral shoulder groove. Advance the needle, applying gentle negative pressure under the clavicle toward the clavicular sternal junction at the level of the fingertip in the suprasternal notch. When there is free flow of blood, rotate the needle 90 degrees so the bevel faces caudad to facilitate the passage of the guidewire into the superior vena cava (Fig. 131-11, *B* and *C*). Remove the syringe carefully, occluding the needle to prevent air embolism; then complete the Seldinger technique for catheter placement. Secure the catheter and confirm the catheter position as previously de-

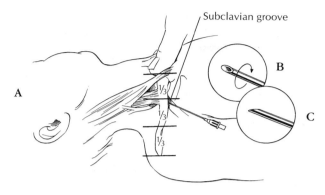

Fig. 131-11   Infraclavicular approach to subclavian vein cannulation.

scribed. Maintaining the angle of entry close to the horizontal plane and avoiding a lateral puncture site minimizes the risk of subclavian artery catheterization. To maintain a smooth curve for the catheter below the clavicle and avoid catheter kinking and occlusion, the skin needs to be entered at a point at least 1 to 2 cm below the clavicle. After confirming proper positioning, the catheter must be secured with single stitches and transparent dressing.

Cutdown insertion. The cutdown technique for CVC placement is similar to that for peripheral venous cutdowns. The preferred site is the basilic vein. The greater saphenous vein in the groin, the facial vein (a frequent choice in infants), the internal and external jugular veins, and the femoral vein may also be used but will not be discussed in this chapter. Only the anatomic considerations for basilic vein cannulation will be discussed here. See Additional Reading for more information. The rest of the technique combines the peripheral venous cutdown and percutaneous CVC techniques. The anatomic landmarks for the basilic vein are the brachial pulse, the medial epicondyle of the humerus, and the groove between the biceps and triceps muscles. A 1 cm incision transverse to the vessels is made approximately 1 cm above the antecubital fold medial to the brachial pulse and lateral to the epicondyle traversing the biceps/triceps groove. Blunt dissection reveals the basilic vein, the median nerve, and the brachial artery. The basilic vein lies deep within the groove and occasionally may be found behind the brachial artery or the median nerve. Cannulation of the vein may be performed using the Seldinger tech-

nique or directly into the vessel as previously described.

Broviac, Groshong, and *Hickman catheters* are used for long-term central venous catheterization. There is little difference between the three catheters except for the one-way occlusion valve in the Groshong catheter. The Groshong catheter has an antireflux mechanism, eliminating the need for catheter clamping and frequent heparin flushing. Normal venous pressure keeps the valve closed, whereas external infusion pressure opens the valve. Hickman and Broviac catheters are very similar to the short-term catheters except that these catheters are made of barium-impregnated silicone rubber (Silastic) and possess one, two, or three lumens. The single-lumen catheters come in 2.7 and 4.2 F sizes for pediatric patients and 6.6 and 9.6 F sizes for adults. Double-lumen catheters are available in 7, 9, 10, and 12 F sizes. The subcutaneous portion is coated with Dacron, which adheres to the scar tissue, thus securing the catheter and minimizing the risk of microorganisms spreading around the catheter. Some of these catheters have a silver-impregnated cuff that is positioned around the catheter under the skin at the insertion site.

Totally implanted catheters, also called intradermal venous access devices (IVADs), are completely covered with the skin, decreasing the risk of contamination, have a subcutaneous reservoir attached to the catheter, and allow venous access without disfigurement. The reservoirs are available in several designs and are made of stainless steel, titanium, or plastic. The reservoirs have a silicone diaphragm that requires a special needle (Huber) to preserve the life of the diaphragm. Catheter heparinization is necessary after each infusion and at monthly intervals when not used. The advantage of the IVAD is that it preserves the skin barriers and has been shown to have a lower incidence of colonization and infection. Another advantage of the IVAD is that it permits a near-normal lifestyle.

Guidelines for confirmation of proper placement. The available methods for confirming proper placement of a CVC include:

1. External surface measurement. The distance from the point of the insertion site to the point between the second and third rib at the costochondral junction is used to estimate the approximate distance the catheter must be inserted to reach the superior vena atriocaval junction. This method does not take

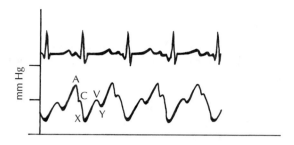

Fig. 131-12 CVP waveform (see text).

into account such factors as anatomic variations and abnormal growth; therefore it is only useful for approximation of appropriate placement. Methods 3 to 7 are more accurate for determining correct anatomic positioning.

2. Waveform analysis. A CVP waveform with its characteristic A, C, and V waves (Fig. 131-12) with the presence of respiratory cycle fluctuation ensures intrathoracic placement. Pressure is lower during spontaneous inspiration. This method only confirms intrathoracic position not anatomic position. Methods 3 to 7 are more accurate for determining correct anatomic positioning.

3. Chest radiography. An anteroposterior chest radiograph will confirm the presence of the tip of the catheter at the superior vena atriocaval junction (see Fig. 131-7). This method is considered the standard for confirming proper CVC placement. A lateral chest radiograph may be helpful in identifying the exact anatomic position when catheter malposition is suspected based on the anteroposterior radiograph.

4. IV dye contrast study. An IV dye study may be helpful when anatomic variations or thrombi formation are suspected or when malposition is suspected.

5. Sonography. This method is advocated by some authors as a noninvasive, nonradiation procedure to document proper catheter positioning. To date, prospective clinical studies have not been reported to support its accuracy.

6. Electrocardiography. ECG confirmation of catheter placement has been attempted using two techniques. One technique uses the ECG signal obtained through a guidewire and the other technique uses the ECG signal received through a saline solution–filled catheter with an ECG sensor attached to the outside port of the catheter. These methods also lack prospective clinical confirmation.

7. Fluoroscopy. This method is most often used in the operating room by surgeons as a "real-time" aid in guiding the proper placement of the catheter tip. This method has occasionally been used in the PICU in patients in whom access is difficult or who have suspected anatomic variations.

CVP Interpretation

CVP directly correlates with right atrial pressure (RAP), which reflects right ventricular end-diastolic pressure (RVEDP) when the physiologic and anatomic conditions of the right heart and lungs are normal. Clinically, CVP is used as an indicator of preload, although right ventricular end-diastolic volume (RVEDV) is a better indicator of preload. Physiologically, RVEDP is one of the variables that determine RVEDV. The variables that determine RVEDV are ventricular compliance and transmural ventricular distending pressure. The transmural distending pressure is the intracavitary pressure itself (RVEDP) minus the juxtacardiac pressure (i.e., intrathoracic pressure). An indirect clinical estimation of RVEDV can be made at the bedside by measuring the right ventricular end-diastolic dimensions with two-dimensional echocardiography. It provides better correlates of RVEDV. To date, this method has not been validated in critically ill children.

Waveform Analysis

A normal CVP waveform is composed of (1) the A wave, which represents atrial contraction; (2) the X descent, which represents atrial relaxation; (3) the C wave, which represents the closing and bulging of the tricuspid valve at the onset of ventricular systole; (4) the V wave, which represents passive venous filling of the right atrium during ventricular systole; and (5) the Y descent, which represents rapid atrial emptying after opening of the tricuspid valve (see Fig. 131-12).

The A wave follows the ECG P wave by 80 msec in adults. The distance between the A wave and the P wave is equal to the PR interval. When the PR interval is prolonged, the C wave becomes more accentuated. The V wave occurs near the ECG T wave. The relationship of the CVP waveform relationship to the ECG waveform is helpful in distinguishing it from other pressure tracings.

The CVP waveform analysis can be divided into (1) elevated A wave, (2) elevated V wave, (3) elevated A and V waves, and (4) abnormalities related to arrhythmia. An elevated A wave may be caused by tricuspid stenosis, pulmonary stenosis, pulmonary hypertension, and right ventricular failure. Tricuspid insufficiency causes elevation of the V wave. The causes of elevation of the A and V waves are volume overload, cardiac tamponade, constrictive pericardial disease, and left ventricular failure. The abnormalities associated with arrhythmia are no A waveform during atrial fibrillation, the summation of the A and V waveforms (cannon A waves) during junctional rhythm, and no A waves during ventricular pacing.

Maintenance

Transparent, water vapor–permeable plastic dressings or gauze and tape can be used to protect the catheter insertion site. Nonwater-permeable plastic dressings must be avoided because they have been shown to increase the skin colonization and infection rate at the insertion site. Antibiotic ointment has been reported to decrease the infection rate; however, some of these local antibiotics may result in a higher incidence of infection related to yeast.

To maintain the patency of venous catheters, fluids must be administered by constant infusion through an infusion pump. Since this is a low-pressure line, CVP lines can be satisfactorily maintained with infusion rates as low as 2 to 3 ml/hr. In addition, 1 unit of sodium heparin per 1 ml of fluid in the solution may be used to maintain patency. To maintain the patency of catheters with multiple ports, a continuous infusion can be used as previously described or the port can be "heplocked" with 100 units of heparin per milliliter of solution. Higher concentrations of heparin have been reported to heparinize patients when accidentally flushed.

Catheter blood sampling is useful except that it may not be considered representative of mixed venous blood gas since there are three major venous contributors to the atrium: the sinus venosum (lowest oxygen content), the superior vena cava (intermediate oxygen content), and the inferior vena cava (highest oxygen content). Depending on the area in which the catheter lies, the blood gas values will reflect different contributions to the right atrial blood volume.

When CVP readings are desired during fluid infusion, attach the catheter to a transducer system with a 30 ml/hr flow-directed device. If the fluid administration rate exceeds 30 ml/hr, the continuous display of pressure by the 30 ml/hr flow-directed device cannot be used. However, by deleting the flow-directed device, pressures may be obtained by turning the stopcock to the fluid source off to obtain intermittent CVP readings. Since the CVP is a low-pressure line, recalibration of the transducer every 12 hours is necessary. The administration of lipids through catheters in line with a continuous flow-directed device renders the CVP measurement unreliable unless the fluid source is occluded momentarily for CVP measurement.

Strict adherence to aseptic technique (mask included) during catheter manipulation and maintenance must be observed. To aid in the prevention of local and systemic infections, care of the CVC and site includes (1) changing the fluid every 24 hours, (2) changing the central dressing at least three times weekly (M, W, F) or when nonocclusive dressing is used, (3) observing the site for erythema, swelling, and/or drainage, (4) checking the dressing for any leakage of fluid, (5) routinely checking each port for patency, and (6) cleansing the delivery system connections for 30 seconds with iodine solution before opening them.

Regular dressing changes minimize the risk of insertion site colonization and subsequent septicemia. The need for pain medication and sedation must be considered before removing the dressing as well as the educational needs of the patient and family. CVC dressing changes include removal of the old dressing using aseptic technique (including masks and sterile gloves), cleansing around the catheter insertion site with acetone-alcohol in a 2- to 3-inch diameter circle without touching the catheter itself, and application of a povidone-iodine solution at the catheter site and along the catheter for 3 to 5 cm. The alcohol must be allowed to dry thoroughly to prevent the formation of a tincture that can cause skin burns. Alcohol works by denaturing proteins and is effective against gram-positive and gram-negative bacteria as well as some fungi and viruses. Some clinicians place a drop of iodine ointment on the insertion site. The dressing can be covered with a transparent water vapor–permeable membrane dressing. Sterile 2×2 inch gauze can be used if the site is leaking or oozing blood. When skin breakdown is noted, the frequency of dressing changes is decreased. Other antimicrobial cleansing agents are available for use in patients allergic to povidone-iodine solutions.

Catheter function must be reappraised continuously by pressure waveform analysis and blood return, and periodic documentation of the proper anatomic location of the tip of the catheter on a chest radiograph is necessary to avoid life-threatening extravasation.

Catheter Removal

Removal of venous catheters is indicated when the patient's condition no longer necessitates their use or when catheter clotting is suspected. Before removal of a clotted catheter, streptokinase or urokinase may be used to dissolve central line clots (see Chapter 181). Other indications for catheter removal include any signs of local infection, phlebitis, sepsis, and/or positive blood cultures obtained through the catheter (catheter colonization).

After the catheter is removed, continuous pressure must be applied to the catheter insertion site for 5 to 10 minutes until no bleeding is noted. The catheter must be inspected to confirm that it has been removed in its entirety and the tip sent for culture if the catheter was removed using a sterile technique. The site must be covered with povidone-iodine ointment, dressed with a small self-adhesive bandage or gauze pad, and inspected daily until healing occurs.

Peripherally Inserted Central Venous Catheters

Peripherally inserted CVCs (PICVCs) were first used in humans by Bleichroder, a German physician, in 1912. A PICVC is a catheter inserted through a peripheral vein (e.g., in the dorsum of the hand, the antecubital vein, or above the antecubital area) and advanced into the central circulation with the tip usually at the atriocaval junction. PICVCs are long, small catheters with high-flow resistance; thus they are not suitable when rapid fluid infusion or withdrawal is necessary. The advantages of the peripheral approach include elimination of the intrathoracic complications of needle puncture, decreased risk of infection, reduced risk of air embolism, cost reduction, and preservation of the venous anatomy. The patient does not have to be placed in a Trendelenburg position for insertion of a PICVC, which is especially advantageous in patients with increased ICP. The PICVC can be inserted in all age groups and has no diagnostic limitation.

In a series of 610 PICVC insertions in infants in the NICU, Hwang and Soong reported a successful catheterization rate of 92%. Catheters were inserted in neonates <1500 g in 45.2% of the cases. The dorsum of the hand was the insertion site in 48.8% and the antecubital vein in 25.1%. The mean duration of PICVC placement was 17.6 days (range 1 to 74 days), and the incidence of catheter-related sepsis was 2.1/1000 catheter days. PICVCs can be inserted by nurses as well as physicians.

The contraindications to PICVC placement include burns and dermatitis at or above the insertion site and previous ipsilateral venous thrombosis.

TECHNIQUE
Access Sites

The veins used for the insertion of the PICVC include the cephalic vein, the basilic vein, the medial cephalic vein, the medial basilic vein, and the veins on the dorsum of the hand. These veins are superficial and easily seen or palpated.

Equipment

The equipment necessary for the insertion of a PICVC is identical to the equipment needed for CVC insertion. A PICVC can be inserted with or without a guidewire. PICVCs are available commercially in multiple French sizes and lengths, in polyurethane, Silastic, and other materials, and with single or double lumens. Many PICVCs are made of polyurethane because this material has a higher burst pressure and greater shear resistance than Silastic catheters. All PICVCs are radiopaque; however, the density of the opacification varies, and the smaller the catheter, the more difficult it is to see on a radiograph. Although a single lumen is most commonly used, PICVCs are available as double-lumen catheters. Sizes ranging from 1.2 to 2.6 F that use an introducer needle between 24 and 19 gauge for insertion are available for pediatric or neonatal patients. Adult catheters range in size from 2.6 to 5.0 F and use a 19- to 14-gauge needle for insertion. For catheters placed in vessels near articulations, immobilizing the joint with a board may be desirable to prevent catheter kinking and/or occlusion.

Insertion

Before PICVC insertion, an anthropometric measurement is taken of the venous pathway from the insertion site to the second intercostal space and mid-arm circumference to serve as a baseline to assess future swelling. Gather and organize all the equipment necessary before starting the procedure. Position the arm at a 45-degree angle to the body. Aseptically prepare the insertion site. Introduce the PICVC catheter using the Seldinger, through-the-needle, or combined technique, and advance it to the premeasured length. Forceps may be of help in advancing the catheter. Once the catheter is in the desired position, it is secured with sutures to reduce the risk of malpositioning, total removal, dislodgment, and/or infection. Closely monitor the limb and insertion site for complications.

Risks and Complications of CVC and PICVC Placement

CVC and PICVC complications can be classified as infectious, thrombotic, mechanical, cardiopulmonary, and other types.

Infectious complications. Infection of intravascular catheters is one of the leading causes of bacteremia in the PICU. Catheter-related infections may be classified as local, systemic, or colonization. For example, site or wound cellulitis and/or phlebitis is a catheter-related local infection. Systemic manifestations of sepsis associated with CVCs are known as catheter-related sepsis (CRS). Catheter-related colonization (CRC) refers to localized colonization of a catheter without major associated systemic manifestations. CRS and CRC can be differentiated by comparing semiquantitative peripheral and through-the-catheter blood cultures. A negative peripheral blood culture with a positive catheter culture indicates CRC colonization, and when both cultures are positive, with a semiquantitative catheter blood culture 5-fold greater than the peripheral culture, CRS is the likely diagnosis. When the difference between semiquantitative cultures is less than 5-fold, the presence of noncatheter-related sepsis or bacteremia is most likely. The incidence of CRS has been reported to be 2.1 to 30.2/1000 central catheter days, and it has been implicated in case fatality in 20% to 40% of patients. Catheter-related infections are responsible for the removal of 20% of implanted right atrial catheters.

Catheters become colonized from microorganisms found on the skin, in the infusate, or from hematogenous spread. Skin colonization at the insertion site is the major source for catheter colonization. *Staphylococcus epidermidis* and *aureus,* which migrate from the skin, account for over half of these infections. *Candida* is another major exogenous or endogenous

causative agent. Enterobacteriaceae and *Pseudomonas* are typical causative agents in infusate contamination. When the catheter is colonized with yeast or enteric bacilli, the mechanism of catheter colonization is usually by hematogenous spread.

Exogenous contamination of the catheter during insertion or use is the major cause of catheter-related infection. Infusate contamination and hematogenous spread account for the remainder. The skin in the antecubital area has been shown to have a lower colonization rate as compared with the neck or the chest areas (10 CFU/10 cm² vs. 1000 to 10,000 CFU/10 cm², respectively). A similar study of the skin at CVC insertion sites in neonates showed colony counts ranging from 0 to 10 CFU/10 cm². Furthermore, jugular and femoral sites had higher counts than subclavian and umbilical sites. Based on these observations the authors recommended the subclavian approach to CVC placement to minimize the risk of infection in neonates who will have prolonged catheterization. Catheters inserted in the femoral area in adults had double the risk of catheter-related infection when compared with catheters inserted in the subclavian area; however, this difference was not substantiated in a study in pediatric patients. Increasing the moisture and temperature of the skin has been implicated as causing a higher colonization rate. If peripheral sites away from oral, nasal, anal, and endotracheal secretions are used, the opportunities for direct contamination are decreased. This may help explain the lower risk of catheter-related infection associated with the use of PICVCs.

Following insertion, the lumen of the catheter will be coated with plasma, tissue proteins, and a fibrin sleeve. This forms a biofilm rich in fibrin and fibronectin, to which *Staphylococcus* and *Candida* highly adhere. The incidence of fibrin sleeve formation is 55% to 100%. Once the microorganisms gain access to the catheter lumen, a glycocalyx material known as extracellular slime will form. The slime permits the exchange of nutrients and allows the microorganisms to adhere and to be isolated from the phagocytic cells, antibodies, and antibiotics. Studies designed to prevent the development of a fibrin sheath by changing the catheter over a guidewire every 3 to 4 days did not show a decrease in the incidence of catheter-related infection.

CRS is the most frequent of the serious CVC-related complications. The risk of catheter-related infection is influenced by many factors, including the age of the patient, most marked at both the extremes of life (<1 year and >60 year), immune status of the patient, site of insertion, central or peripheral access, presence of concurrent infection, type of catheter used, number of lumens, number of attempts at insertion, use of tunneled vs. nontunneled catheters, presence of defects in the catheter, duration of catheterization, presence of thrombus, insertion and suture technique, postinsertion care, and training of the health care provider.

CVC has been reported in at least one study to have a 64-fold risk of infection as compared with peripheral catheters (23 catheter-related infections/1000 catheter days vs. 0.36 catheter-related infections/1000 catheter days, respectively). Totally implantable catheters are associated with the least risk of catheter-related infections, with an incidence of 0 to 1 catheter-related infection/1000 catheter days. The bacteria adhere to the catheter's microscopic defects and scratches resulting from manufacturing materials and/or techniques as well as rough insertion procedures. Bacteria adhere in order of decreasing magnitude to such hydrophobic polymers as silicone, polyethylene, polytetrafluoroethylene, and Teflon.

The longer the catheter is in place, the more likely the patient will develop catheter-related infection. An association between CRS and duration of catheterization >5 days has been observed. Silver-coated catheters or cuffs release silver ions, which have been shown to be an effective antimicrobial agent against most bacteria and fungi associated with catheter-related infection and are presently commercially available for clinical use. The Children's Cancer Group, which prospectively studied pretreatment with antibiotics prior to CVC insertion, showed no decrease in the incidence of catheter-related infection. Triple-lumen catheters had four times the risk of infection (32%) compared with single-lumen catheters (8%).

Many strategies have been used to treat catheter-related infection. Some of these are catheter removal alone, combined catheter removal and antibiotic therapy, leaving the catheter in place and giving antibiotic therapy, and the use of urokinase as an adjuvant to any of the above combinations. More than 80% of cases of CRS can be cleared with antibiotic therapy without removing the CVC. Conventional therapeutic doses of antibiotics often kill disseminated bacteria, whereas organisms within the biofilm are not affected, therefore increasing the risk of catheter-re-

lated infection recurrence when conventional doses are given. CRS or CRC in a hemodynamically stable patient may be eradicated with the catheter left in place. However, if the patient does not improve, the catheter must be removed.

Candida accounts for 98% of fungemias associated with catheter-related infections in patients with cancer. Antifungal therapy and catheter removal are indicated in patients with a positive peripheral blood culture, neutropenia, or immunosuppression, patients with invasive candidal infection at other sites, or if signs of infection do not resolve with catheter removal. However, in immunocompetent patients with catheter-related infection caused by *Candida,* the simple removal of the catheter may suffice. Either persistently positive blood cultures or a hemodynamically unstable patient is always an indication for both catheter removal and antifungal therapy. Device removal is usually the most important step if the catheter-related infection is caused by a yeast.

Training of health care providers in the use of full aseptic technique for CVC insertion and insertion site care, the use of chlorhexidine antiseptics and patches, skin site protection with transparent, water vapor–permeable occlusive dressings, changing the IV fluid every 24 hours, the dressing every 48 hours, and the IV tubing every 48 to 72 hours, proper suturing technique, choice of insertion site, catheter stabilization, and use of antimicrobial-coated or negatively charged silver-coated catheters must all be incorporated in the strategy to minimize the risk of catheter-related infections.

Catheter occlusion. The causes of catheter occlusion include thrombus formation, fatty deposits, chemical occlusion from cements caused by calcium salts and other drugs, the catheter tip laying against the vessel wall, and catheter kinking.

Thrombotic complications are the most common cause of catheter occlusion. The incidence of catheter-related venous thrombosis ranges from 4% to 68%; however, clinical thrombosis occurs in only 1% to 5%. CVCs are the major cause of deep venous thrombosis in the upper extremity. Thrombotic complications have been reported in association with low blood flow states, decreasing size of the vessel, surgical glove powder, extended catheter life, sepsis, high glucose concentrations, high osmolarity of the infusate solutions (with osmolarity >600 mOsm/L resulting in 100% of cases of phlebitis and the lowest risk with osmolarity <450 mOsm/L), pH of the infusate (acidic or alkaline), systemic alteration in coagulation, catheter migration to a smaller blood vessel, and catheter material (the risk of thrombosis in decreasing order of prevalence was polyvinyl, polyethylene, polyurethane, and silicone). Use of guidewires is not associated with increased risk of thrombophlebitis.

Thrombus can occur as a result of occlusion on withdrawal, blunting of the transduced waveform, persistent bacteremia, edema, and/or increased resistance to infusion. When thrombus formation is suspected, it may be confirmed by a color-flow Doppler imaging, CT, MRI, and dye contrast study. If the presence of a thrombus is confirmed, the catheter needs to be treated with heparin or urokinase and thrombectomy needs to be considered. If the thrombus does not respond to treatment, the catheter must be removed. In many causes of partial occlusion conservative management with catheter removal and observation usually leads to clot reabsorption. In patients in whom access is difficult, obstruction by a fibrin sheath can be treated with urokinase in a concentration of 5000 IU/ml at a volume great enough to fill the catheter and left in the catheter for 5 to 10 minutes before being withdrawn. The catheter is checked for patency, and if still occluded, urokinase can be reinstilled and left for up to 12 hours. If the catheter is still not open, urokinase can be infused at a dose of 200 IU/kg/hr.

Thrombolytic therapy is followed by long-term heparinization. A success rate of 92% has been reported after urokinase infusion for a mean of 28.7 hours. Chemical occlusion does not respond to classic thrombolytic therapy. The treatment of choice for chemical obstruction is injection of 0.1 N HCl in combination with heparin. Use of a less thrombogenic material such as silicone, the addition of heparin to the infusate, proper flushing technique, monitoring the osmolarity and the pH of the infusate, and monitoring the position of the catheter tip can help reduce the incidence of thrombotic catheter occlusion.

Mechanical complications. Mechanical complication rates as high as 25% have been reported. These complications include migration, malposition, occlusions, fractures, curling inside the heart or the vessel, and dislodgment. Next to migration and malposition, occlusion is the most common complication. Clotting is the leading cause of catheter occlusion. Catheter fractures may be repaired using a blunt needle, sutures, and a glue technique. Catheter dislodgment can be prevented by securing the sutures, minimizing patient movement, and confirming

catheter placement on a radiograph or sonogram or by waveform analysis.

Catheter migration and malposition are the most common mechanical complications. The correct position of the tip of a CVC is at the atriocaval junction. Occlusion alarm from the infusion pump, inability to withdraw blood, increased external catheter length, local pain or swelling, and neurologic abnormalities may indicate catheter migration or malposition. Although the position of the catheter may be correct at insertion, it may migrate with increased intrathoracic pressure, coughing, sneezing, vigorous upper extremity movements, and forceful flushing. Venous thrombosis, inaccurate CVP readings, arrhythmias, chest or back pain, intravascular knotting and looping, venous or myocardial perforation, and chest wall and breast abscess are all serious complications of malpositioned catheters. The catheter position needs to be checked even if there are no apparent complications related to the catheter. Malpositioned catheters often can be corrected without removal. A "jet" injection technique, catheter exchange, and interventional radiologic techniques may be used to avoid catheter removal.

Arterial cannulation will generally be indicated by the return of bright blood and a pulsatile flow. In patients with hypoxia and hypotension, however, the color and the flow of blood are not dependable signs of arterial vs. venous cannulation. Observing for retrograde flow in the IV infusion, connecting the line to a pressure wave transducer, and checking the catheter course on a radiograph can help detect arterial cannulation. The use of appropriate technique as described for subclavian and jugular catheterization helps to decrease the risk of arterial catheterization. Arterial catheters are not used for infusion because of the risk of blindness and neurologic complications.

Other vascular mechanical complications are *arteriovenous fistula formation* and *stenosis of the catheterized vessel*.

Cardiopulmonary complications. The cardiopulmonary complications associated with CVC placement include pneumothorax, hydrothorax, hemothorax, arrhythmia, embolism, right atrial thrombus, infective endocarditis, and cardiac tamponade. These complications are responsible for the great majority of deaths associated with CVC placement.

Pneumothorax, hydrothorax, and *hemothorax* are more often associated with subclavian and internal jugular (low more frequently than high insertion) approaches, with the subclavian approach having the higher complication rate. However, it was reported that central venous catheterization for a mean of 13.5 months in pediatric patients did not have significant adverse effects on cardiopulmonary function testing.

Arrhythmias most frequently occur during catheter insertion, atrial placement, when the catheter is laying against the tricuspid valve, or when the catheter is dislodged into the right ventricle. These situations can be prevented by maintaining the catheter at the atriocaval junction. When catheter dislodgment causes arrhythmia, the catheter must be pulled back to the atriocaval junction. Pretreatment or treatment with antiarrhythmic drugs can be of clinical benefit in preventing some CVC-induced arrhythmias.

Embolism may be caused by air leaking into the system, a thrombus being dislodged, and/or catheter embolism. *Air embolism* most commonly occurs when the catheter is open to air, especially when the patient is spontaneously breathing. The intrathoracic pressure is negative, and air will travel through the catheter at a flow rate that is related to the catheter length, diameter, and the pressure gradient between the atmospheric and the intrathoracic pressures. Increasing the pressure gradient, increasing catheter diameter, and decreasing its length will decrease the flow resistance and increase the airflow rate. A 14-gauge needle with an internal diameter of 0.07 inch can transmit 100 ml of air per second. The average lethal rate in human is 70 to 150 ml/sec. External catheter breakage needs to be dealt with immediately to decrease the risk of air embolism. The site of entrance, the rate of airflow, and the position of the body when the air reaches the heart are the factors that modulate the outcome of air embolism. Air embolism may be minimized at the time of insertion by using the Trendelenburg position and positive airway pressure. A patient with air embolism needs to be placed into a steep left lateral Trendelenburg position to decrease the amount of air leaving the right ventricle until air aspiration by catheter or needle aspiration can be accomplished. *Thrombotic embolism* secondary to dislodgment is most frequently seen when catheters are removed prematurely before starting thrombolytic therapy. A thromboembolic phenomenon must be suspected in any patient with a CVC or after its removal when a patient has a sudden onset of hypoxia or respiratory distress. *Catheter embolism* is generally caused by catheter shearing, but rupture after forceful irrigation and catheter re-

traction after external breakage can cause embolism as well. To avoid catheter shearing, catheters must not be pulled through the needle. The initial management of catheter embolism includes application of a tourniquet proximal to the site, a radiograph to help localize the embolus, and a venous cutdown if the fragment is local. Transvenous removal is the method of choice if the embolus advances into the circulation. Transvenous removal is accomplished in the first 24 hours since the embolus can move deeper into the circulation with time or become more adherent to the vessel wall, decreasing the chance of successful retrieval. Thoracotomy and pulmonary arteriotomy are necessary when transvenous attempts fail. A mortality of 32% was reported in patients experiencing catheter embolism due to cardiac perforation, endocarditis, arrhythmias, and pulmonary embolism.

Right atrial thrombus is a potentially fatal, rarely symptomatic, and often underdiagnosed complication of CVCs. Right atrial thrombus may be manifested by a new murmur, fever, hepatomegaly, respiratory distress, protracted thrombocytopenia, cardiac calcification as seen on a chest radiograph, and persistent bacteremia or it may be discovered accidentally on echocardiography. If bacteremia or fungemia does not respond to therapy in a patient with a CVC, right atrial thrombus must be excluded. Pulmonary embolism is one of the serious complications of right atrial thrombus. Only 15% of cases of pulmonary embolism found at autopsy were diagnosed clinically. Although right atrial thrombus can resolve spontaneously, medical therapy, including streptokinase, urokinase, heparin, and tissue plasminogen activator, and/or surgical removal has been recommended. Infected atrial thrombi can be safely removed by cardiotomy even in small premature infants.

Infective endocarditis as a complication of CVC has been reported in patients with structurally normal hearts. In a patient with fever, heart murmur, persistent bacteremia, central catheter, and no apparent focus, echocardiography is included in the workup to detect vegetations. Removal of the catheter and use of antibiotics resulted in 67% full recovery in a series of 12 neonates. Coagulase-negative staphylococci were isolated in nine patients.

Cardiac tamponade is the most serious catheter-related complication and the most difficult to diagnose. A mortality rate of 50% to 100% has been reported and can be attributed to the difficulty in identifying the insidious onset of signs and symptoms that usually lead to a rapid drop in cardiac output and cardiac arrest. The clinical picture of cardiac tamponade includes sudden neck vein distention, increased CVP, sudden onset of duskiness or cyanosis, apnea, grunting, bradycardia, tachycardia, paradoxical pulse, increasing hypotension, decreasing pulse pressure, distant heart sounds, confusion, nausea, respiratory distress, loss of CVP waveform, and inability to draw blood back from the catheter. Although some cases of tamponade occur during catheter insertion, it most frequently has a delayed onset. Cardiac tamponade must be suspected in any patient who suffers cardiac arrest with a central catheter in place or who has a history of CVC removal close to the event. Any patient with these clinical features must be evaluated for the possibility of cardiac tamponade secondary to perforation. The same preventive measures described in the discussion of pneumothorax apply to cardiac perforation. The risk of perforation is greater with (1) intra-atrial placement of the catheter, specifically those placed from a jugular or subclavian approach, (2) a left-sided venous approach, (3) a subclavian approach, (4) stiff catheters, and (5) beveled catheters. Cardiac tamponade must be immediately treated with administration of a volume expander through another route, inotropic agents, cessation of infusions through the suspected catheter, aspiration through the suspected catheter, pericardiocentesis, and in some cases pericardial window or pericardial tube placement (see Chapter 144).

Other complications. Additional CVC complications include fluid extravasation, misplacement, Horner's syndrome, subdural collection of fat emulsion (neonates), superior vena cava syndrome, thoracic duct injury, and venostasis. Misplacement of the catheter tip into an ascending lumbar vein has been reported as a complication of femoral vein catheterization. A lateral radiograph can help confirm the catheter position. In general most catheter-related complications are recognizable; therefore mortality and morbidity are usually preventable. There tends to be a higher incidence of morbidity and mortality in infants because of their smaller anatomy and vague symptoms.

Umbilical Vein Catheterization

Umbilical vein catheterization into the central circulation of newborn infants is possible up to 7 days of age. The advantages of this procedure are easy access, simplicity, and ability to accommodate large-di-

ameter catheters. Disadvantages of the procedure are listed in Chapter 132. Umbilical vein catheterization can only be used over the short term. The principal indications for its use are exchange transfusion, administration of resuscitation drugs in the delivery room, CVP monitoring, and administration of high-concentration glucose.

TECHNIQUE
Access site
The umbilical stump contains a single large, thin-walled vein usually located cephalad to the umbilical arteries.

Equipment
See Chapter 132.

Insertion
Immobilize the patient, surgically scrub the umbilical stump, and place a fenestrated sterile drape around it. Prepare the equipment while the povidone-iodine solution dries (i.e., flush catheter, mount scalpel blade, and connect catheter to transducer and fluid source). Analgesia is not necessary since the umbilical stump has no innervation. Place a curved hemostat at the distal end of the umbilical stump; pull gently and turn it cephalad over the instrument. Slowly cut the cord with the scalpel blade superficially 2 cm above the skin margin. Advance toward the center of the cord until the vein is partially transected. Ideally, no more than half the vein's circumference is cut. Remove any visible clots within the vein. Introduce the catheter gently until a CVP waveform with respiratory fluctuations can be observed (Fig. 131-13, *A*). Be careful not to allow air into the fluid system since it can cause air embolism during inspiration. Secure the catheter with Dermick tape and suture it to the umbilical stump (Fig. 131-13, *B*). An H-type adhesive tape bridge can be used to further secure the catheter to the abdominal wall (Fig.131-3, *C*). An anteroposterior radiograph of the chest and abdomen must be taken before infusing any hypertonic solution to confirm that the catheter is properly positioned at the superior vena cava right atrium junction (Fig. 131-14). A double-lumen umbilical venous catheter has been used without increased risk of complication.

Maintenance
Refer to "Maintenance" in the discussion of central venous catheterization.

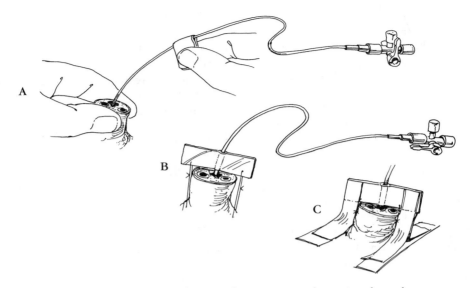

Fig. 131-13 Umbilical vein catheterization and securing the catheter.

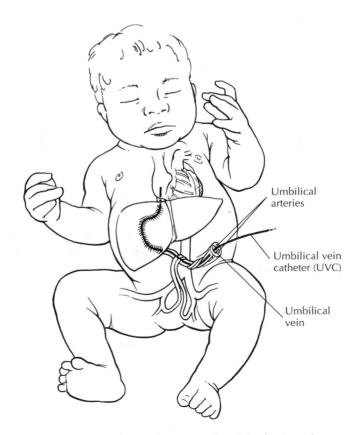

Umbilical
arteries

Umbilical vein
catheter (UVC)

Umbilical
vein

Fig. 131-14 Confirmation of umbilical vein catheter.

Catheter Removal

The umbilical vein catheter is removed when the indications for insertion are resolved or when there is evidence of omphalitis, catheter colonization, or sepsis. The catheter must be removed slowly and inspected for integrity. After removal of the catheter, pressure must be applied around the umbilical stump for 5 to 10 minutes to obtain hemostasis.

RISKS AND COMPLICATIONS

In addition to the complications listed in Chapter 132, some of the complications that may occur are necrotizing enterocolitis, hepatic infarction, hepatic abscesses, and bowel perforation during large-volume infusion or exchange transfusion. It is worth noting that malposition of the tip of the umbilical vein catheter within the liver is commonly associated with hepatic infarction abscesses and portal hypertension at a later age.

ADDITIONAL READING
General

Aaronson IA. Complications of central venous catheters used for parenteral nutrition. [letter]. J Pediatr Surg 18:657, 1983.

• Albanese GT, Wiener ES. Venous access in pediatric oncology patients. Semin Surg Oncol 9:467-477, 1993.

Alexander HR, Lucas AB. Long-term venous access catheters and implantable ports. In Alexander HR, ed. Vascular Access in the Cancer Patient. Philadelphia: JB Lippincott, 1994.

Alexander HR, Lucas AB. New technologies in long-term venous access and peripherally inserted central venous access catheters. In Alexander HR, ed. Vascular Access in the Cancer Patient. Philadelphia: JB Lippincott, 1994.

• Alvarado-Diez MA, Marquez-Enriquez LM, Troconis-Trens G, Serrano V, Vasquez-Gutierrez E, Rivera-Rebolledo JC, Villegas-Silva R. Experience in the use of central venous catheterization via subclavian puncture in a pediatric hospital. Bol Med Hosp Infantile Mexico 50:394-398, 1993.

• American Heart Association. Textbook of Pediatric Advanced Life Support, chap 5. Dallas: The Association, 1994, pp 1-14.

Brahos GJ. Central venous catheterization via the supraclavicular approach. J Trauma 17:872-877, 1977.

Brown RA, Millar AJ, Knobel J, Cywes S. Central venous catheters. Technique and experience at Red Cross War Memorial Children's Hospital, Cape Town, 1987-1990. South Africa Med J 80:11-13, 1991.

Dennis MJS, Hunter AE, Ryan JJ. Long-term indwelling Silastic central venous catheters: Clinical audit leading to improved surgical technique. J R Soc Med 83:620-622, 1990.

Durand M, Ramananathan R, Martinelli B, Tolentino M. Prospective evaluation of percutaneous central venous Silastic catheters in newborn infants with birth weights of 510 to 3920 grams. Pediatrics 78:245-250, 1986.

Greenspoon JS, Terrasi J. Central venous catheterization: Are complications related to the route? Am J Obstet Gynecol 155:1143, 1986.

Hodge D, Delgado-Paredes C, Fleisher G. Central and peripheral catheter flow rates in "pediatric" dogs. Ann Emerg Med 15:1151-1154, 1986.

Ikeda S, Schweiss JF. Maximum infusion rates and CVP accuracy during high-flow delivery through multi-lumen catheters. Crit Care Med 13:586-588, 1985.

Mactier H, Alroomi LG, Young DG, Raine PAM. Central venous catheterization in very low birth weight infants. Arch Dis Child 61:449-453, 1986.

Pegelow CH, Narvaez M, Toledano SR, Davis J, Oiticica C, Buckner D. Experience with a totally implantable venous device in children. Am J Dis Child 149:69-71, 1986.

Quan SF. Mixed venous oxygen. Am Fam Physician 27:211-215, 1983.

Ramachandran P, Cohen RS, Kim EH, Glasscock GF. Experience with double-lumen umbilical venous catheters in the low-birth-weight neonate. J Perinatol 14:280-284, 1994.

• Ryder MA. Peripherally inserted central venous catheters. Nurs Clin North Am 28:937-971, 1993.

Sharkey SW. Beyond the wedge: Clinical physiology and the Swan-Ganz catheter. Am J Med 83:111-122, 1987.

• Shepherd A, Williams N. Care of long-term central venous catheters. Br J Hosp Med 51:598-602, 1994.

Soong WJ, Hwang B. Percutaneous central venous catheterization: Five-year experiment in a neonatal intensive care unit. Acta Paediatr Sin 34:356-366, 1993.

Stark DD, Brasch RC, Gooding CA. Radiographic assessment of venous catheter position in children: Value of the lateral view. Pediatr Radiol 14:76-80, 1984.

Teplick RS. Measuring central vascular pressures: A surprisingly complex problem. Anesthesiology 67:289-291, 1987.

Verweij J, Kester A, Stroes W, Thijs LG. Comparison of three methods for measuring central venous pressure. Crit Care Med 14:288-290, 1986.

Wachs T, Watkins S, Hickman RO. "No more pokes": A review of parenteral access devices. Nutr Support Serv 7:12-18, 1987.

Wiener ES, McGuire P, Stolar CJH. The CCSG prospective study of venous access devices: An analysis of insertions and causes of removal. J Pediatr Surg 27:155-164, 1992.

Indications

Asaadi M, Seltzer MH. Subclavian intravenous catheterization for hyperalimentation. Resident Staff Physician August 1980, pp 53-58.

Birman H, Haq A, Hew E, Aberman A. Continuous monitoring of mixed venous oxygen saturation in hemodynamically unstable patients. Chest 86:753-756, 1984.

Cameron GS. Central venous catheters for children with malignant disease: Surgical issues. J Pediatr Surg 22:702-704, 1987.

Technique

Cobb LM, Vinocur CD, Wagner CW, Weintraub WH. The central venous anatomy in infants. Surg Gynecol Obstet 165:230-234, 1987.

Colley PS, Artru AA. ECG-guided placement of Sorenson CVP catheters via arm veins. Anesth Analg 63:953-956, 1984.

• Cote CJ, Jobes DR, Schwartz AJ, Ellison N. Two approaches to cannulation of a child's internal jugular vein. Anesthesiology 50:371-373, 1979.

DeFalqie RJ. Percutaneous catheterization of the internal jugular vein. Anesth Analg 53:116-121, 1974.

Diemer A. Central venous Silastic catheters in newborns: Localization by sonography and radiology. Pediatr Radiol 17:15-17, 1987.

Dronen SC, Yee AS, Tomlanovich MC. Proximal saphenous vein cut down. Ann Emerg Med 10:328-330, 1981.

• Filston HC, Johnson DG. Percutaneous venous cannulation in neonates and infants. A method for catheter insertion without "cut-down." Pediatrics 48:896-901, 1971.

• Filston HC, Grant JP. A safer system for percutaneous subclavian venous catheterization in newborn infants. J Pediatr Surg 14:564-570, 1979.

Gilhooly J, Lindenberg J, Reynolds JW. Central venous silicone elastomer catheter placement by basilic vein cut down in neonates. Pediatrics 78:636-639, 1986.

• Groff DB, Ahmed N. Subclavian vein catheterization in the infant. J Pediatr Surg 9:171-174, 1974.

• Hall DMB, Geefhuysen J. Percutaneous catheterization of the internal jugular vein in infants and children. J Pediatr Surg 122:719-722, 1977.

Hughes WT. Buescher ES. Pediatric Procedures, 2nd ed. Philadelphia: WB Saunders, 1980, pp 87-121.

• Kanter RK, Zimmerman JJ, Strauss RH, Stoeckel KA. Central venous catheter insertion by femoral vein: Safety and effectiveness for the pediatric patient. Pediatrics 77:842-847, 1986.

Kitterman JA, Phibbs RH, Tooley WH. Catheterization of umbilical vessels in newborn infants. Pediatr Clin North Am 17:895-912, 1970.

• Krausz MM, Berlatsky Y, Ayalon A, Freund H, Schiller M. Percutaneous cannulation of the internal jugular vein in infants and children. Surg Gynecol Obstet 148:591-594, 1979.

Marx JA, Rosen P, Jorden RC, Moore EE. Proximal saphenous vein cut down: When and why? Ann Emerg Med 11:167, 1982.

Meland NB, Wilson W, Soontharotoke CY, Koucky CJ. Saphenofemoral venous cut downs in the premature infant. J Pediatr Surg 21:341-343, 1986.

• Morgan WW, Harkins GA. Percutaneous introduction of long-term indwelling venous catheters in infants. J Pediatr Surg 7:538-541, 1972.

Pietsch JB, Nagaraj HS, Groff DB. Simplified insertion of central venous catheter in infants. Surg Gynecol Obstet 158:91-92, 1984.

• Prince SR, Sullivan RL, Hackel A. Percutaneous catheterization of the internal jugular vein in infants and children. Anesthesiology 44:170-174, 1976.

Puntis JWL. Percutaneous insertion of central venous feeding catheters. Arch Dis Child 61:1138-1140, 1986.

• Rao TLK, Wong AY, Salem MR. A new approach to percutaneous catheterization of the internal jugular vein. Anesthesiology 46:362-364, 1977.

Schug CB, Culhane DE, Knopp RK. Subclavian vein catheterization in the emergency department. A comparison of guidewire and nonguidewire techniques. Ann Emerg Med 15:769-773, 1986.

• Seldinger SI. Catheter replacement of the needle in percutaneous arteriography. Acta Radiol 39:368-376, 1953.

Simon RR, Hoffman JR, Smith M. Modified new approaches for rapid intravenous access. Ann Emerg Med 16:44-49, 1987.

Star DS, Cornicelli S. EKG-guided placement of subclavian CVP catheters using J-wire. Ann Surg 204:673-676, 1986.

Vaksmann G, Rey C, Breviere GM, Smadja D, Dupuis C. Nitroglycerine ointment as aid to venous cannulation in children. J Pediatr 111:89-92, 1987.

• Woo-Sup A, Joong-Shin K. An easy technique for long-term central venous catheterization and subcutaneous tunneling of the Silastic catheter in neonates and infants. J Pediatr Surg 21:344-347, 1986.

General Complications

Casado-Flores J, Valdivielso-Serna A, Perez-Jurado L, Pozo-Roman J, Monleon-Luque M, Garcia-Perez J, Ruiz-Beltran A, Garcia-Teresa MA. Subclavian vein catheterization in critically ill children: Analysis of 322 cannulations. Intensive Care Med 17:350-354, 1991.

Goutail-Flaud MF, Sfez M, Berg A, Laguenie G, Couturier C, Barbotin-Larrieu F, Saint-Maurice C. Central venous catheter-related complications in newborns and infants: A 587-case survey. J Pediatr Surg 26:645-650, 1991.

Hogan L, Pulito AR. Broviac central venous catheters inserted via the saphenous or femoral vein in the NICU under local anesthesia. J Pediatr Surg 27:609-611, 1992.

Laurie SWS, Wilson KL, Kernahan DA, Bauer BS, Vistnes LM. Intravenous extravasation injuries. The effectiveness of hyaluronidase in their treatment. Ann Plast Surg 13:191-194, 1984.

Lavandosky G, Gomez R, Montes J. Potentially lethal misplacement of femoral central venous catheters. Crit Care Med 24:893-896, 1996.

Lee SJ, Neiberger R. Subclavian vein stenosis: A complication of subclavian vein catheterization for hemodialysis. Child Neurol Urol 11:212-224, 1991.

Lemmer JH, Zwischenberger JB, Bove EL, Dick M. Lymph leak from a femoral cut down site in a neonate: Repair with fibrin glue. J Pediatr Surg 22:827-828, 1987.

Loughran SC, Edwards S, McClure S. Peripherally inserted central venous catheters. Guide-wire versus non-guide-wire use: A comparative study. J Intraven Nurs 15:152-159, 1992.

Malatack IJ, Wiener ES, Gartner JC, Zitelli BJ, Brunetti E. Munchausen syndrome by proxy: A new complication of central venous catheterization. Pediatrics 75:523-525, 1985.

Nicolson SC, Sweeney MF, Moore RA, Jobes DR. Comparison of internal and external jugular cannulation of the central circulation in the pediatric patient. Crit Care Med 13:747-749, 1985.

Pasquale MD, Campbell JM, Magnant CM. Groshung versus Hickman catheters. Surg Gynecol Obstet 174:408-410, 1992.

Rasuli P, Hammond DI, Peterkin IR. Spontaneous intrajugular migration of long-term central venous access catheters. Radiology 182:822, 1992.

Sherman BW, McNamara MP, Shen SJ. Inadvertent arterial administration of parenteral hyperalimentation solution resulting in generalized seizure activity. JPEN 16:284, 1992.

Shiu MH. A method for conservation of veins in the surgical cut down. Surg Gynecol Obstet 134:315-316, 1972.

Shulman RJ, Pokorny WJ, Martin CG, Petitt R, Baldaia L, Roney D. Comparison of percutaneous and surgical placement of central venous catheters in neonates. J Pediatr Surg 21:348-350, 1986.

· Smith-Wright DL, Green TP, Lock JE, Egar MI, Fuhrman BP. Complications of vascular catheterization in critically ill children. Crit Care Med 12:1015-1017, 1984.

Sterner S, Plummer DW, Clinton J, Ruiz E. A comparison of the supraclavicular approach and the infraclavicular approach for subclavian vein catheterization. Ann Emerg Med 15:421-424, 1986.

Stine MJ, Harris H. Subdural collection of intravenous fat emulsion in a neonate. Clin Pediatr 24:40-41, 1985.

Torramade JR, Cienfuegos JA, Hernandez JL, Pardo F, Bentio C, Gonzalez J, Balen E, de Villa V. The complications of central venous access systems: A study of 218 patients. Eur J Surg 159:323-327, 1993.

van Tets WF, van Dllemen HM, Tjan GT, van Berg Henegouwen D. Vertebral arteriovenous fistula caused by puncture of internal jugular vein. Eur J Surg 158:627-628, 1992.

Wagman LD, Konrad P, Schmit P. Internal fracture of a pediatric Broviac catheter. JPEN 13:560-561, 1989.

Wechsler RJ, Byrne KJ, Steiner RM. The misplaced thoracic venous catheter detailed anatomical consideration. Crit Rev Diagn Imaging 21:289-305, 1982.

Zenk KE, Dungy CI, Greene GR. Nafcillin extravasation injury. J Dis Child 135:1113-1114, 1981.

Infectious Complications

Andrivet P, Bacquer A, Ngoc CV, Ferme C, Letinier JY, Gautier H, Gallet CB, Brun-Buisson C. Lack of clinical benefit from subcutaneous tunnel insertion of central venous catheters in immunocompromised patients. Clin Infect Dis 18:199-206, 1994.

Ascher DP, Shoupe BA, Maybee D, Fischer GW. Persistent catheter-related bacteremia: Clearance with antibiotics and urokinase. J Pediatr Surg 28:627-629, 1993.

Balagtas RC, Bell CE, Edwards LD, Levin S. Risk of local and systemic infections associated with umbilical vein catheterization: A prospective study in 86 newborn patients. Pediatrics 48:359-367, 1971.

Bertone SA, Fisher MC, Mortensen JE. Quantitative skin cultures at potential catheter sites in neonates. Infect Control Hosp Epidemiol 15:315-318, 1994.

· Collignon PJ. Intravascular associated sepsis: A common problem. The Australian study on intravascular catheter associated sepsis. Med J Aust 161:374-378, 1994.

Dr. Charles A. Janeway Child Health Center, Memorial University of Newfoundland, St. John's. Subendocardial abscess as a complication of prolonged central venous access for parenteral nutrition. Can J Surg 35:91-93, 1992.

Elliott TSJ, Froqui MH. Infections and intravascular devices. Br J Hosp Med 48:496-497, 500-503, 1992.

· Flynn PM, Shenep JL, Stokes DC, Barrett FF. Differential quantitation with a commercial blood culture tube for diagnosis of catheter related infection. J Clin Microbiol 26:1045-1046, 1988.

Flynn PM, Shenep JL, Stokes DC, Barrett FF. In situ management of confirmed central venous catheter-related bacteremia. Pediatr Infect Dis 6:729-734, 1987.

Fraschini G, Jadeja J, Lawson M, Holmes FA, Carrasco HC, Wallace S. Local infusion of urokinase for the lysis of thrombosis associated with permanent central venous catheters in cancer patients. J Clin Oncol 5:672-678, 1987.

Garland JS, Nelson DB, Cheah TE, Hennes HH, Johnson TM. Infectious complications during peripheral intravenous therapy with Teflon catheters: A prospective study. Pediatr Infect Dis 6:918-921, 1987.

Garrison RN, Wilson MA. Intravenous and central catheter infection. Surg Clin North Am 74:557-570, 1994.

Holt RW, Heres EK. Creation of subcutaneous tunnel for Broviac and Hickman catheters. JPEN 9:225-226, 1985.

· Jarvis WR, Edwards JR, Culver DH, and the National Nosocomial Infections Surveillance System. Nosocomial infection rates in adult and pediatric intensive care units in the United States. Am J Med 91:185S-191S, 1991.

Jones GR, Konsler GK, Dunaway RP, Lacey SR, Azizkhan RG. Prospective analysis of urokinase in the treatment of catheter sepsis in pediatric hematology-oncology patients. J Pediatr Surg 28:350-355, 1993.

Knox WF, Hooton VN, Barson AJ. Pulmonary vascular candidiasis and use of central venous catheters in neonates. J Clin Pathol 40:559-565, 1987.

Larson E. Guidelines for the use of topical antimicrobial agents: APIC guidelines for infection control practices. Am J Infect Control 16:253-265, 1988.

Lecciones JA, Lee JW, Navarro EE, Witebsky FG, Marshall D, Steinberg SM, Pizzo PA, Walsh TJ. Vascular catheter associated fungemia in patients with cancer: Analysis of 155 episodes. Clin Infect Dis 14:875-883, 1992.

Levy JH, Nagle DM, Curling PE, Waller JL, Kopel M, Tobia V. Contamination reduction during central venous catheterization. Crit Care Med 16:165-167, 1988.

Maki DG, Ringer M, Alvarado CJ. Prospective randomized trial of povidone-iodine, alcohol, and chlorhexidine for the prevention of infection associated with central venous and arterial catheters. Lancet 338:339, 1991.

Maki DG, Stolz SS, Wheeler S, Mermal LA. A prospective, randomized trial of gauze and two polyurethane dressings for site care of pulmonary artery catheters: Implications for catheters management. Crit Care Med 22:1729-1737, 1994.

Maki DG, Cobb L, Garman JK, Shapiro J, Ringer M. Multicenter trial of an attachable silver-impregnated subcutaneous cuff for prevention of infection with central venous catheters [abstr]. Presented at the Interscience Conference on Antimicrobial Agents in Chemotherapy, 1987.

Maki DG, Cobb L, Garman JK, Shapiro J, Ringer M, Helgerson R. An attachable silver-impregnated cuff for prevention of infection with central venous catheters. A prospective randomized multicenter trial. Am J Med 85:307-314, 1988.

Mecrow IK, Ladusans EJ. Infective endocarditis in newborn infants with structurally normal hearts. Acta Paediatr 83:35-39, 1994.

Moro ML, Vigano EF, Cozzi Lepri A. Risk factors for central venous catheter-related infections in surgical and intensive care units. The Central Venous Catheter-Related Infections Study Group. Infect Control Hosp Epidemiol 15:253-264, 1994.

Paut O, Kreitmann B, Silicani MA, Wernert F, Broin P, Viard L, Camboulives J. Successful treatment of fungal right atrial thrombosis complicating central venous catheterization in a critically ill child. Intensive Care Med 18:375-386, 1992.

Raad I, Davis S, Khan A, Tarrand J, Elting L, Bodey GP. Impact of central venous catheter removal on the recurrence of catheter-related coagulase-negative staphylococcal bacteremia. Infect Control Hosp Epidemiol 13:215-221, 1992.

Raad II, Hohn DC, Gilbreath BJ, Suleiman N, Hill LA, Bruso PA, Marts K, Mansfield PF, Bodey GP. Prevention of central venous catheter-related infections by using maximal sterile barrier precautions during insertion. Infect Control Hosp Epidemiol 15:231-238, 1994.

• Ramanathan R, Durand M. Blood cultures in neonates with percutaneous central venous catheters. Arch Dis Child 62:621-623, 1987.

Ranson MR, Oppenheim BA, Jackson A. Double-blind placebo-controlled study of vancomycin prophylaxis for central venous catheter insertion in cancer patients. Am J Hematol 31:269-272, 1989.

Severien C, Nelson JD. Frequency of infections associated with implanted systems vs cuffed, tunneled Silastic venous catheters in patients with acute leukemia. Am J Dis Child 145:1433-1438, 1991.

Stamm WE. Prevention of infections. Infections related to medical devices. Ann Intern Med 89:764-769, 1978.

Williams N, Carlson GL, Scott NA, Irving MH. Incidence and management of catheter-related sepsis in patients receiving home parenteral nutrition. Br J Surg 81:392-394, 1994.

Thrombotic Complications

Bagnall HA, Gomperts E, Atkinson JB. Continuous infusion of low-dose urokinase in the treatment of central venous catheter thrombosis in infants and children. Pediatrics 83:963-966, 1989.

Borow M, Crowley JG. Prevention of thrombosis of central venous catheters. J Cardiovasc Surg 27:571-574, 1986.

De Schepper J, Hachimi-Idrissi S, Cham B, Bougatef A. Diagnosis and management of catheter-related infected intracardiac thrombosis in premature infants. Am J Perinatol 10:39-42, 1993.

Linder LE, Curelaru I, Gustavsson B, Hansson HA, Stenqvist O, Wojciechoiski J. Material thrombogenicity in central venous catheterization: A comparison between soft, antebrachial catheters of silicone elastomer and polyurethane. JPEN 8:399-406, 1984.

Mulvihill SJ, Fonkalsrud EW. Complications of superior vs. inferior vena cava occlusion in infants receiving central total parenteral nutrition. J Pediatr Surg 19:752-757, 1984.

Raad II, Luna M, Khalil SA, Costeron JW, Lam C, Bodey GP. The relationship between the thrombotic and infectious complications of central venous catheters. JAMA 271:1014-1016, 1994.

Wacker P, Oberhansli I, Didier D, Bugmann P, Bongard O, Wyss M. Right atrial thrombosis associated with central venous catheters in children with cancer. Med Pediatr Oncol 22:53-57, 1994.

Cardiovascular Complications

Agarwal KC, Ali Khan MA, Falla A, Amato JJ. Cardiac perforation from central venous catheters: Survival after cardiac tamponade in an infant. Pediatrics 73:333-338, 1984.

Beattie PG, Kuschel CA, Harding JE. Pericardial effusion complicating a percutaneous central line in a neonate. Acta Paediatr 82:105-107, 1993.

Demey HE, Colemont LJ, Hartoko TJ, Roodhooft AMI, Ysebaert DK, Bossaert LL. Venopulmonary fistula: A rare complication of central venous catheterization. JPEN 11:580-582, 1987.

Henderson AM, Sumner E. Late perforation by central venous cannulae. Arch Dis Child 59:776-789, 1984.

Iberti TJ, Katz LB, Reiner MA, Brownie T, Kwun KB. Hydrothorax as a late complication of central venous indwelling catheters. Surgery 94:842-846, 1983.

Krasna IH, Krause T. Life-threatening fluid extravasation of central venous catheters. J Pediatr Surg 26:1346-1348, 1991.

Maschke SP, Rogove HJ. Cardiac tamponade associated with a multi lumen central venous catheter. Crit Care Med 12:611-613, 1984.

Motte S, Wautrecht JC, Delcour C, Bellens B, Vincent G, Dereume JP. Vertebral arteriovenous fistula following central venous cannulation: A case report. J Vasc Dis 37:731-734, 1986.

O'Brodovich H, Adams M, Coates G, Way RC, Andrew M. Cardiopulmonary function during long-term central venous catheterization. Am J Pediatr Hematol-Oncol 13:148-151, 1991.

Sullivan CA, Knoefal SH. Cardiac tamponade in a newborn: A complication of hyperalimentation. JPEN 11:319-321, 1987.

Symchych PS, Krauss AN, Winchester P. Endocarditis following intracardiac placement of umbilical venous catheters in neonates. J Pediatr 90:287-289, 1977.

Tocino IM, Watanabe A. Impending catheter perforation of superior vena cava: Radiographic recognition. Am J Roentgenol 146:487-490, 1986.

Wirrel EC, Pelausa EO, Allen AC, Stinson DA, Hanna BD. Massive pericardial effusion as a cause of sudden deterioration of a very low birthweight infant. Am J Perinatol 10:419-423, 1993.

132 Arterial Access and Catheters

Lea Lua · Maggie Gonzales · Philip C. Guzzetta, Jr. · Luis O. Toro-Figueroa

Peripheral Arterial Catheterization

Peripheral arterial cannulation or catheterization for continuous monitoring was introduced into pediatric practice in the mid-1960s using the umbilical artery in neonates and later the peripheral arteries in infants and children. Over the past four decades indwelling arterial catheterization has become an increasingly safer procedure. The decision to use an arterial catheter for monitoring is based on careful clinical judgment and an assessment of the benefits and associated risks. The clinical interpretation of the data obtained must take into consideration that the accuracy of the data may vary during any monitoring period.

INDICATIONS

The four principal indications for placement of an indwelling arterial catheter in the PICU are as follows:

1. For continuous systemic arterial blood pressure and pulse waveform monitoring in patients in whom frequent assessment of cardiopulmonary status is necessary.
2. To guide clinicians in making proper dosage adjustments in patients in shock from any cause who need treatment of hypotension with either fluid or cardiovascular agents (e.g., dopamine, dobutamine, or norepinephrine) and patients in hypertensive crisis receiving antihypertensive medications (e.g., sodium nitroprusside or nitroglycerine).
3. For serial blood gas analysis to evaluate respiratory and acid-base status. Arterial cannulation avoids repeated arterial puncture, which leads to injury to the vessels and discomfort for the patient.
4. For calculation of cerebral perfusion pressure in patients with increased ICP and an ICP monitor in place.

Arterial cannulation is also performed for diagnostic and therapeutic reasons such as cardiac catheterization, angiography, embolization, indocyanine green cardiac output measurement, and exchange transfusion.

CONTRAINDICATIONS

Skin infections or interruptions (e.g., burn, blister, or abrasion) at the site where arterial catheter insertion is being contemplated is an absolute contraindication to the procedure. Arterial puncture must not be per-

---

ADVANTAGES AND DISADVANTAGES OF PERIPHERAL ARTERY CATHETERIZATION

Advantages

Lower prevalence of minor and serious complications

Multiplicity of available sites

Preductal blood sampling (right radial, right ulnar, and right temporal)

Precoarctation arterial blood pressure monitoring

Applicable in patients of any size or age

Disadvantages

Amplification of systolic blood pressure readings the more distal the catheter is placed along the arterial system (e.g., pedal arterial pressure as much as 25.1 ± 12.3 mm Hg greater than radial arterial blood pressure has been reported)

Scarring after catheter removal (especially with cutdown)

Inaccurate when peripheral vascular resistance is high

Inability to accommodate indwelling electrodes for continuous monitoring of pH or Pao_2

---

formed at any site at high risk for circulatory insufficiency (e.g., absent collateral circulation, signs of severe vascular obstructive disease such as arterial bruit and diminished pulses, or previous arterial embolic event). Severe hemorrhagic disorder and anticoagulation treatment, which could lead to massive hematoma formation and serious exsanguination, are relative contraindications to arterial puncture. Arterial puncture or cannulation must not be attempted in areas where there is a vascular prosthesis. Sites of previous surgical procedures are not used if possible.

TECHNIQUE
Equipment

Equipment needed for both percutaneous and cutdown arterial catheterization is as follows:

Percutaneous arterial catheterization equipment

Adhesive tape, ½ and 1 inch
Appropriate size catheter or catheter-over-stylet in a kit
   Adolescent to adult, 18-20 gauge
   School-aged child, 20-22 gauge
   Toddler to infant, 22 gauge
   Premature infant, 24 gauge
Armboard
Benzoin sticks
Povidone-iodine solution and ointment
Gloves (universal precaution)
Heparin, 1000 U/ml; add 1 U/ml of arterial line fluid
Lidocaine, 1%
Papaverine, 60 mg/ml; add 60 mg/500 ml of arterial line fluid
Protective goggles (universal precaution)
0.225%, 0.45%, and 0.9% sodium chloride solution, 500 ml
Suture, 4-0 nylon
Syringes
   3 ml syringe with ⅝-inch, 25-gauge needle
   10 ml syringe for flush solution
T-connector (with Luer-lok syringe in small infants, without in other children)
Transparent sterile dressing

Arterial cutdown catheterization equipment

Sterile surgical gown
Surgical procedure lamp
Vascular access tray (see below)
Other equipment (see below)

Vascular access tray (sterile)

Syringe with 20-gauge needle for flush solution, 10 ml
Clear dermal tape

Five 4 × 4 inch gauze sponges
Four-inch curved eye-dressing forceps
Four-inch straight eye-dressing forceps
Needle holder
Scalpel blades, Nos. 11 and 15
Scalpel handle
Smooth forceps
Small scissors
Suture on needle, 4-0 silk
Toothed forceps
Two 5-inch curved mosquito hemostats
Umbilical tape

Other equipment

Continuous flush device, 3 ml/hr
Four-foot high-pressure infusion set
Monitor with pressure module
Pressure transducer
Pressure infusion bag or infusion pump

Access Sites

The site chosen for continuous monitoring must (1) have adequate vascular caliber for the size of the catheter to ensure accurate monitoring without the catheter totally occluding the vessel, (2) have adequate collateral circulation, (3) be accessible for visual inspection and nursing care, and (4) not prone to contamination.

Sites available for cannulation in order of decreasing preference are the radial, posterior tibial, dorsalis pedis, ulnar, femoral, axillary, brachial, and superficial temporal arteries (Fig. 132-1).

Radial and ulnar arteries. The radial artery is a major branch of the brachial artery and extends along the lateral side of the forearm to the distal end of the radius. The radial artery pulse is palpable at the wrist between the groove formed by the flexor carpi radialis tendon medially and distal radius laterally. The ulnar artery is another major branch of the brachial artery and extends medially to the wrist lateral to the tendon of the flexor carpi ulnaris. The radial artery forms the deep palmar and dorsal arch; the ulnar artery forms the superficial palmar arch in 88% of the population. Twelve percent of the patients examined had either poor collateral flow or an incomplete palmar arch. A modified Allen test must be performed if possible before placing an arterial catheter in the radial or ulnar artery to assess adequacy of collateral circulation in the hand. Clench and compress the patient's hand to squeeze out the blood and then occlude both the ulnar and radial arteries. Open and re-

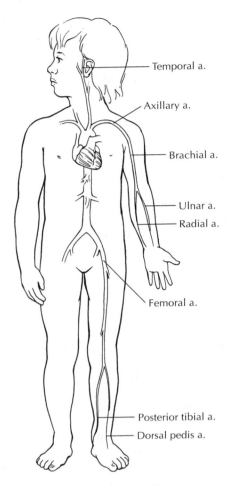

Fig. 132-1 Arterial sites.

The dorsalis pedis artery is a continuation of the anterior tibial artery. It can be felt on the dorsum of the foot parallel and lateral to the extensor hallucis longus tendon (or first interosseous space of the dorsum). The dorsalis pedis artery provides collateral circulation to the foot by anastomosing with the plantar arch of the foot derived from the terminal branch of the posterior tibial artery. It has been reported in the literature that about 12% of the population has congenital bilateral absence of the dorsalis pedis arteries. A procedure analogous to the modified Allen test is performed to establish the presence of collateral circulation in the foot. Blanch the great toe by compressing the toenail while the dorsalis pedis artery is being occluded. Release the pressure on the toenail and observe for return of color. Rapid return of color (within 5 seconds) indicates adequate collateral circulation. This test is almost never performed in emergency situations.

Femoral artery. The femoral artery, a continuation of the external iliac artery, enters the thigh, passing beneath the inguinal ligament at a point midway between the anterior superior iliac spine and the symphysis pubis. It lies medial to the femoral nerve and lateral to the femoral vein.

Axillary artery. The axillary artery, a terminal branch of the subclavian artery, begins at the lateral border of the first rib, enters the axilla, and leaves the area at the lower level of the teres major muscle to become the brachial artery. It gives off the most distal branch, the subscapular artery, which anastomoses with the thyrocervical trunk of the subclavian artery to provide collateral circulation to the distal part of the upper extremity in case of obstruction or thrombosis of the axillary artery.

Brachial artery. The brachial artery is a continuation of the axillary artery. Its pulsation is easily palpable at or slightly above the elbow crease. It lies medial to the biceps tendon and lateral to the median nerve. Because there is no collateral circulation to the forearm before the origin of the profunda brachii artery, vascular injuries in this segment of the brachial artery pose a significant risk for ischemic injury to the forearm. After the profunda brachii artery, the largest branch of the brachial artery, collateral circulation is provided to the forearm by its communication with the branches from the radial and ulnar arteries.

Temporal artery. The temporal artery is the ter-

lax the hand, which appears pale, then release the pressure over the ulnar artery. Return of color within 5 seconds indicates adequate collateral circulation from the ulnar artery. Repeat the test by releasing pressure over the radial artery to assess the radial collateral circulation. It is important to note that in patients in shock the Allen test may yield negative and/or confusing results. Often when emergency cannulation is necessary, the Allen test is not performed.

Posterior tibial and dorsalis pedis arteries. The posterior tibial artery lies deep to the posterior compartment muscles but becomes superficial in the lower part of the leg. Its pulsation can be best palpated posterior and inferior to the medial malleolus.

minal branch of the external carotid artery. It can be felt just above the zygoma of the temporal bone in front of the tragus of the ear.

Procedure

Before the arterial site chosen for the procedure is cannulated, the extremity needs to be placed in a stable and comfortable position. For the radial and ulnar arteries, place the patient's hand, wrist, and distal third of the forearm supine on an armboard of a size appropriate for the patient's size. Use 4 × 4 inch gauze pads under the wrist and proceed to secure the extremity with adhesive tape while maintaining the wrist in an extension angle of 30 degrees. Extending the hand at the wrist straightens the artery and places it in its most superficial position. Failure to position the wrist appropriately contributes to cannulation failure. Care must be taken to leave the fingertips free for visual inspection. Apply tape securely but gently to prevent pressure sores or occlusion of collateral circulation and venous drainage.

To immobilize the ankle for posterior tibial artery cannulation, place a well-padded board on the external aspect of the extremity, placing the ankle in the anatomic position (90-degree flexion). Extra padding may be added to prevent pressure sores around the external malleolus. When cannulating the dorsalis pedis artery, the same precautions are applied but the foot is maintained in a partial plantar flexion position and the well-padded board is placed on the inner aspect of the lower leg and foot, specifically the external maleolus. To immobilize the axilla, the arm must be hyperabducted by more than 90 degrees and externally rotated.

Sterile technique must be maintained at all times. The site must be surgically cleansed three times with povidone-iodine solution for 3 minutes. To obtain maximum bactericidal effect, the solution must be dry before proceeding. With a small-gauge needle, infiltrate the skin and deep tissue with lidocaine without epinephrine. Take care not to infuse lidocaine directly into a vessel (aspirate for blood before injecting the lidocaine). Infiltration must be gentle and the quantity sufficient to produce local analgesia but not so much as to impede palpation of the arterial pulse. Test for local analgesia before proceeding. Before attempting cannulation, ensure that all necessary equipment is readily available and the tubing and catheters are flushed with solution. Catheter flushing

is not necessary, but some clinicians claim this practice facilitates early detection of blood flashback when entering the arterial lumen.

Cannulation of a peripheral artery may be performed by means of a percutaneous catheterization or cutdown technique.

Percutaneous catheterization. In contrast to peripheral venous cannulation percutaneous catheterization is directed against the flow of blood in the artery; thus the catheter, while advancing, "sees" the arterial blood waveform. The two preferred methods of percutaneous peripheral artery catheter insertion are direct and transfixation techniques (Fig. 132-2). The direct method is similar to the technique used to start a peripheral IV catheter. Approach the artery directly at the point where the pulse is most prominently palpated (directing the bevel of the needle downward will prevent the tip of the needle from piercing the posterior wall of the vessel). Advance the catheter gradually at a 30-degree angle with the skin surface (parallel to the artery) until blood flushes into the catheter's inner needle-stylet clear hub, signifying entrance of the inner needle-stylet into the lumen after penetrating the anterior wall of the artery. As blood continues to flush back, the catheter over the needle is slowly advanced while the inner needle is held in a fixed position.

For the transfixation method, approach the artery at a 45-degree angle and penetrate both the anterior and posterior walls. After transfixation is achieved remove the inner needle and pull the catheter back slowly until blood returns to the catheter reservoir, then advance the catheter into the vessel wall.

When a catheter over the needle plus guidewire is available, cannulation is performed with the Seldinger-like technique. Either of the two percutaneous methods can be used. The guidewire is advanced past the end of the inner needle while blood continues to flush back into the reservoir. Advance the catheter over the needle into the vessel and remove the guidewire and the inner needle.

Connect a T-connector and a 10 ml syringe with flush solution free of air bubbles to the catheter to prevent unnecessary blood loss and test for patency. Patency can be documented by the free flow of blood into the syringe and by observing the arterial waveform once the catheter and tubing are connected to the transducer-monitor system (Fig. 132-3).

The catheter must be secured to the skin with su-

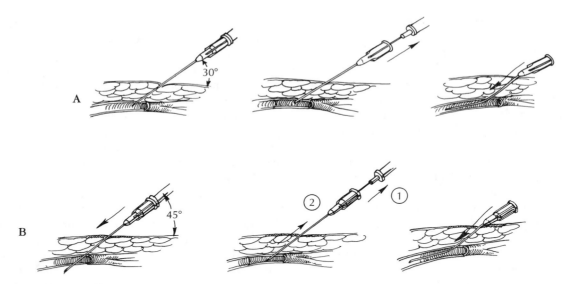

Fig. 132-2 Percutaneous catheterization techniques. **A,** Direct. **B,** Transfixation.

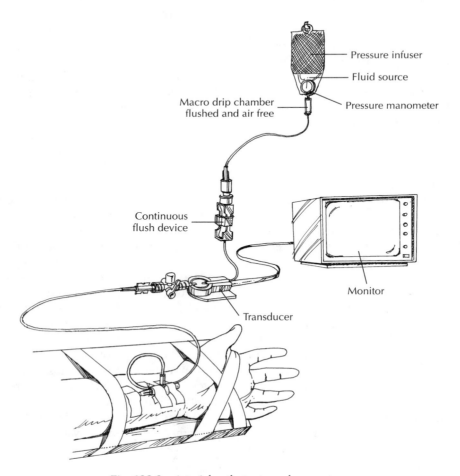

Fig. 132-3 Arterial catheter-transducer setup.

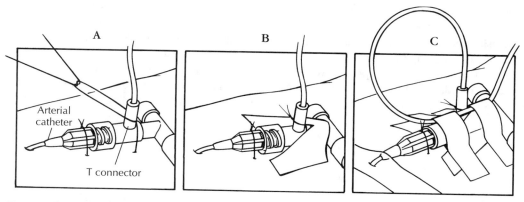

Fig. 132-4 A, Suture-secured arterial catheter. **B,** Adhesive tape–secured arterial catheter. **C,** Self-adhesive small bandage protects insertion site.

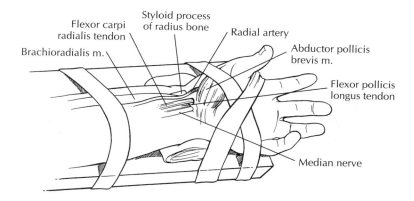

Fig. 132-5   Radial artery anatomy.

tures or a very adhesive dressing such as tincture of benzoin. Apply 2½-inch adhesive tape butterfly strips and cover them with a short strip of 1-inch adhesive tape. Take care to leave the skin insertion site visible for inspection. A small amount of povodine-iodine ointment may be applied to the skin insertion site. A small self-adhesive bandage may be used to dress the skin insertion site area because it is easily removable and therefore permits frequent examination of the skin site (Fig. 132-4).

Cutdown technique. The radial artery cutdown method is discussed in detail; the technique for cutdown of other sites is similar except for anatomic landmarks.

First, identify the anatomic landmarks. The radial artery is medial to the brachioradialis tendon and

proximal to the lower radial epiphysis on the volar side of the wrist. Palpation is best achieved proximal to the palmar branch. The flexor carpi radialis tendon lies medial to the radial artery, and the median nerve on the palmaris longus tendon is seen more medially (Fig. 132-5).

Drape the surgical site and set up the necessary equipment (i.e., mount scalpel blade, draw flush solution, and prime the T-connector). Cut a wedge with a base of approximately 1 cm from the cardboard that holds the suture material to use later during the procedure. Recheck the skin site for local analgesia.

Make an incision appropriate for the size of the child that is transverse to the artery's path. Use a single stroke to expose the subcutaneous tissue. With both mosquito hemostats, gently dissect parallel to the vessel using a blunt technique. Do not tear or cut any tissue within the operative field. Identify the structures by using the aforementioned landmarks. In general arteries are round, pulsating, elastic, and bright red (except in patients with hypoxia). Veins are flat, very pliable, and darker than arteries. Nerves are flat, pale, and stringlike. Tendons are white, round, and ropelike. Muscle tends to be beefy and friable. Bone tends to be solid and white.

After the artery is identified, elevate it gently with a curved hemostat. Place a 4-0 stay suture (6 cm long) distally and another proximally. Do not tie the vessel. Place a hemostat to hold the ends of each stay suture together (Fig. 132-6, *A*). Proceed gently to re-

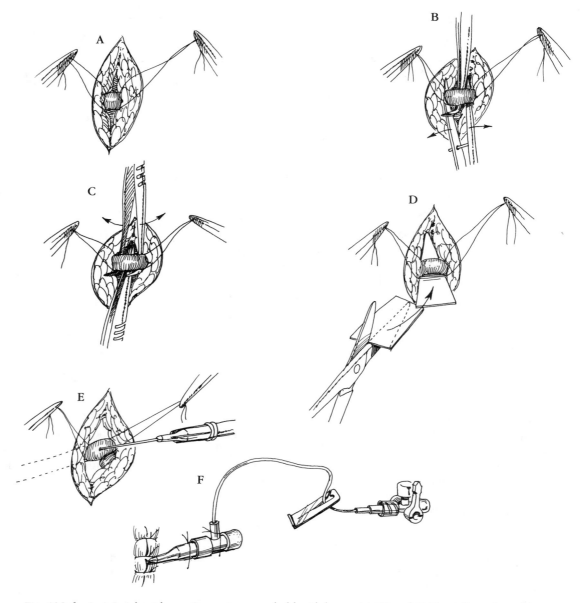

Fig. 132-6 A, Arterial cutdown. Stay sutures are held with hemostats. **B** and **C,** Blunt dissection with eye-dressing forceps. **D,** Cardboard wedge in position. **E,** Pull on stay suture and advance catheter. **F,** Close surgical wound and secure arterial catheter.

move from the vessel all connective tissue that may lead to "false channeling" when inserting the catheter. The best way to accomplish this is to stretch the artery carefully by opening the forceps in an alternating fashion from the underside of the vessel. Do not attempt to pick, pull, or cut any tissue off the artery because this may lead to arterial rupture (Fig. 132-6, *B* and *C*).

After removing all undesired tissue, pull on the distal stay suture and slip the cardboard wedge under the vessel (Fig. 132-6, *D*). Exert gentle traction on the distal stay suture and cannulate the vessel with the same technique described for percutaneous insertion (Fig. 132-6, *E*).

Advance the catheter slowly to decrease the likelihood of vasospasm. Attach the flushed T-connector and syringe and check for patency in a fashion similar to that used in the percutaneous technique. Do not connect the T-connector to the transducer until the surgical wound is sutured and the catheter is secured in place because this may lead to decannulation if the tubing is accidentally pulled.

Close the surgical wound with single stitches and suture the catheter hub securely to the skin and the T-connector (Fig. 132-6, *F*) to give the unit more stability. Clean the wound of blood with 0.9% sodium chloride solution or povodine-iodine solution. Apply adhesive tape as in the percutaneous technique. Wound and dressing care is also similar to that for percutaneous catheterization. Finally, secure the stay sutures by taping them to the skin both distal and proximal to the incision. If bleeding occurs around the catheter, pull the stay sutures gently to enhance hemostasis. The stay sutures must never be tied around the catheter. After 24 hours or when a bleeding diathesis has been corrected, the sutures may be removed by pulling them out through the wound.

Pressure Waveform

A continuous pressure waveform tracing must be displayed on the monitor screen at all times, and ideally a printout of the waveform with a simultaneous ECG tracing is available. A pressure waveform (Fig. 132-7) starts as the aortic valve opens and is followed by left ventricular ejection of a stroke volume that creates the initial rapid-rising portion of the waveform (systolic phase) referred to as the anacrotic limb. After peak systolic pressure, the gradual decelerating portion of the pulse pressure wave (descending limb) begins when ejection of blood slows at the same time

that blood "runs off" to the periphery during diastole. The descending limb is interrupted by a dip or incisura, which occurs during isovolumetric relaxation of the ventricle just before closure of the aortic valve when blood flows back from the aorta into the ventricle. This event coincides with ECG T waves, which represent ventricular repolarization. A second positive wave is formed after aortic valve closure as a result of elastic recoil of the aorta and reflected waves from distal arteries.

The waveform changes as pulse is propagated from the central to the peripheral arteries. The systolic phase is amplified, leading to a steeper ascending limb and higher peak systolic pressure. The dip in the descending limb of the peripheral waveform, now referred to as the dicrotic notch, is smoother and occurs later relative to the incisura of the central waveform. The dicrotic notch or wave is the summation of the incoming pulse wave and reflected waves from the peripheral vessels. Diastolic pressure is lower and pulse pressure is wider; however, mean arterial pressure is not substantially altered. The change in the contour of the pulses as they are transmitted peripherally is attributed to the following factors: (1) distortion of the components of the pulse wave as they travel, (2) different rates of transmission of various components of the pulse wave, (3) amplification and distortion of different components of the standing and reflected waves, (4) differences in the elastic behavior and caliber of arteries, and (5) conversion of some kinetic energy to hydrostatic energy. In summary, pressure wave-

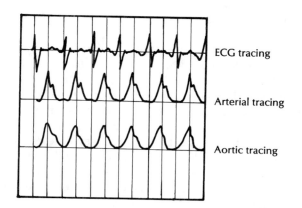

Fig. 132-7 Pressure waveform: aortic vs. peripheral artery.

form at the periphery appears narrower and has higher systolic pressure, lower diastolic pressure, and wider pulse pressure than the central pressure waveform.

Pressure waveforms also may be helpful in determining the severity of cardiac arrhythmias because the waveform will vary when cardiac output is altered by arrhythmia. Pulsus alternans, caused by diminished ventricular performance, and pulsus paradoxus, caused by high intrapleural pressure or high pericardial pressure, can be noted in the continuous waveform tracing. In patients with pulsus paradoxus the arterial pressure tracing will decrease during inspiration and rise during expiration in those who are spontaneously breathing and will increase during inspiration and will decrease during expiration in those receiving assisted ventilation. Hypovolemia may be diagnosed if the waveform is very narrow with a blunted systolic peak and loss of the diacrotic notch.

Directly measured systemic arterial blood pressure is higher than indirectly measured blood pressure when direct measurement is taken at a more distal artery; the patient has elevated systemic vascular resistance (the pressure gradient necessary to produce Korotkoff's sound is lost, thereby making auscultation more difficult); or there is overshoot of the systolic pressure, which occurs when the extension tubing has a low resonant frequency (long and compliant extension tubing). When pressures measured with the indirect method are higher than pressures obtained with the intra-arterial method, the error is most commonly technical. Check for improper cuff size or placement, uncalibrated transducer system, mechanical obstruction of the catheter from clots or air bubbles, and disconnection at any point in the system.

In patients with pacemakers the display of the arterial waveform is paramount to monitoring cardiac function because an ECG tracing or the pacemaker artifact will continue to appear on the monitor screen and can be counted as heart rate by the electronic sensing device without any corresponding cardiac output being generated. In an asystolic patient a low heart rate alarm will not be initiated in these circumstances. A decrease in pressure or a flat-line waveform may be the first sign of trouble because the heart rate is fixed at the preset pacing rate.

Maintenance

Arterial catheters allow routine blood specimens to be obtained from the catheter, which prevents the need for repeated needlesticks. Equipment needed includes:

Alcohol swab
1 to 3 ml syringe (waste)
1 to 3 ml syringe (sample)

Once the necessary equipment has been gathered, arterial blood for sampling can be obtained. Clamp the fluid source at the T-connector and clean the injection site with alcohol. After the alcohol is completely dry, insert a 1 to 3 ml syringe and aspirate 0.4 to 0.5 ml of fluid and blood to allow displacement of heparinized fluid from the catheter and T-connector. Attach another 1 to 3 ml syringe and draw the desired amount of blood needed for sampling. Use of a larger syringe can cause arterial spasm. Once the blood sample has been obtained, unclamp the T-connector; the volume of pressurized fluid that accumulated while the T-connector was clamped will be enough to flush the catheter adequately. If the catheter is on an infusion pump (with infusion rate less than the recommended 3 ml/hr) or fails to clear with back pressure, gently flush the system with 1 to 2 ml of heparinized fluid and observe the monitor for return of the arterial waveform. Do not use the continuous flow device to flush the catheter because it delivers a large amount of fluid rapidly. In addition, the flow generated by this device when released will cause arterial retrograde flow, which can reach the arch vessels and possibly cause CNS embolization or an acute increase in ICP. It is worth noting that this procedure needs to be modified in patients with latex allergy.

Only 0.225%, 0.45% or 0.9% sodium chloride solutions may be infused through an arterial catheter. Do not infuse any medications except heparin (1 to 5 U/ml) and papaverine (60 mg/500 ml) through any arterial catheter. Heparin may help prevent clot formation, and papaverine may prevent arterial spasm, thus increasing the longevity of the catheter. Papaverine is contraindicated in patients with ICP precautions because it could cause increased cerebral blood flow from vasodilation. Heparin may not be used in patients with severe bleeding diathesis or who are anhepatic. Patients with liver failure as well as neonates do not have the ability to degrade heparin.

In our unit, tubing and fluids are changed every 72 hours, and the catheter insertion site is inspected daily for signs of infection or ecchymotic changes in the skin above the catheter tip. The area is inspected for blanching, redness, cyanosis, and changes in temperature or capillary refill time every hour. The catheter must be removed if circulation becomes compromised or any signs of cellulitis are present. Blood is obtained for culture from the arterial catheter and at a peripheral site in patients who become febrile to help distinguish bacteremia or sepsis from catheter colonization.

Catheter Removal

Indications for catheter removal include (1) stabilization or resolution of the indications for cannulation of the artery; (2) catheter-related infection (local or systemic) or colonization by microorganisms; (3) evidence of clot formation (e.g., damped tracing or sluggish blood flow); and (4) any evidence of thrombosis or mechanical occlusion of the artery (e.g., edema, discoloration, cold extremity, poor capillary refill, or absent distal pulses). Thrombosis or mechanical occlusion of the artery is an indication for *immediate* removal of the catheter.

To remove a peripheral arterial catheter, cut the securing stitch, pull the catheter out gently, and hold pressure on the area for 5 to 10 minutes. The fluid source need not be clamped before removal of the catheter in the hope of preventing formation of clots with arterial circulation. Correcting the deficiencies and applying pressure hemostasis longer may be necessary in patients with bleeding disorders.

RISKS AND COMPLICATIONS

The recorded incidence of complications from peripheral artery catheterization varies from 0.3% to 51%. The most commonly reported complication is arterial thrombosis. Factors that increase the risk of thrombosis are low cardiac output states, lack of use of heparin, lack of continuous flush method, small wrist circumference, duration of catheterization (>4 to 7 days), lack of collateral circulation (modified Allen's test <5 seconds), inappropriately large catheter diameter and length relative to arterial diameter, tapered catheter, patient age <5 years, cannulator's lack of experience with the procedure, multiple arterial punctures, and size of the hematoma before insertion. Arterial recanalization has been reported in as many as 100% of occluded radial arteries up to 75 days after decannulation.

If thrombosis is suspected, the catheter must be removed and the extremity checked hourly for pulses, warmth, and perfusion and discoloration. Application of heat to the opposite extremity may cause reflex vasodilation and increase flow through an incomplete obstruction. IV heparin at a dose of 100 units/kg every 4 hours for 48 hours had been recommended for clinically significant arterial thrombosis (e.g., loss of pulse, decoloration, or coolness below the suspected site of thrombosis). Thrombolytic therapy with urokinase or streptokinase must be considered. Doppler ultrasonography can be performed to distinguish functional (vasospasm) from mechanical (thrombosis) obstruction and is advocated to aid in

---

COMPLICATIONS OF PERIPHERAL ARTERIAL CATHETERIZATION

Common

Arteriospasm
Hematoma
Bleeding
Colonization with a microorganism
Cellulitis
Bacteremia
Sepsis
Skin sloughing (ischemia)
Thrombosis
Embolization

Less common

Arteritis
Arterial-intimal flaps
Pseudoaneurysm
Peripheral nerve damage
Arteriovenous fistula formation
Cerebrovascular accident (especially with temporal site)
Necrosis of an extremity

evaluation of whether early consultation with a vascular surgeon is necessary.

Cerebral embolic events occur from retrograde flow, especially when the intermittent flushing method is used. Flush of as little as 7 ml can produce this complication. Because the tip of the catheter inserted into the temporal artery ends in the external carotid artery, there is the possibility of cerebral embolization from retrograde flow through the common carotid artery. The use of a temporal artery for continuous catheterization is discouraged for this reason.

Infection-related complications have been reported at a rate ranging from 1.27% to 25.0%. One study reported a colonization rate of 18% and a 4% rate of septicemia. Factors associated with increased risk of infection were insertion via surgical cutdown, cannulation for more than 4 days, and presence of local inflammation. Another study reported a colonization rate of 25%, with a rate of septicemia of only 0.6% in pediatric patients. When catheter-related infection is suspected, cultures must be obtained (see Chapter 131), use of the arterial catheter is discontinued, and broad-spectrum antibiotics are administered for both gram-negative and gram-positive (*Staphylococcus epidermidis* included) organisms. Antifungal therapy is used when fungal disease is suspected clinically.

When bleeding at the site of insertion occurs, one must make certain that all tubing connectors are tightly sealed and there are no cracks or defective materials. Interlocking tubing connectors are available, and their use decreases the potential for bleeding secondary to loose tubing connections. Bleeding abnormalities must be corrected if possible. Application of local pressure for a limited time can help achieve hemostasis and prevent excessive blood loss. The distal extremity must be carefully inspected during the application of local pressure to prevent too much pressure resulting in tissue ischemia. Circular bandages are not recommended because they may lead to ischemia. When an arterial cutdown is bleeding, the stay sutures may be pulled gently to achieve hemostasis. Do not tie these sutures. If bleeding persists, use of the catheter may have to be discontinued.

Vascular spasm necessitates discontinuation of an arterial catheter and may even lead to tissue necrosis. Generally during arterial spasm the arterial waveform is suddenly lost. Arterial spasm is most common in the youngest of patients because of the greater degree of arterial reactivity. Papaverine may be used as a continuous infusion, as previously described, to prevent vasospasm. Diluted lidocaine, 0.1 ml of 1% in 0.9 ml of 0.9% sodium chloride solution, infused very slowly may dilate the constricted artery. Warming the opposite extremity may also be helpful. If arteriospasm does not resolve, the arterial catheter must be removed.

Pressure waveform changes will also alert the health care team to mechanical problems with the system. Underdamping (decreased waveform amplitude) may be caused by an insensitive monitor or transducer, high-compliance tubing, air bubbles in the system, tube kinking, lipid deposition in the transducer dome, clot formation, tubing too long (>7 ft), compliant injection sites (T-connectors), leakage (e.g., in tubing, connections, stopcocks, or injection sites), or vasospasm. Overdamping (increased waveform amplitude) may occur when the monitor-transducer system is too sensitive or there is a faulty flush device or air bubbles within the system. With underdamping, first make certain the patient's vital signs are stable and a change in hemodynamic status is not responsible for the waveform change. Exsanguination from leakage or disconnection of the arterial catheter system may cause waveform underdamping and is life threatening. The entire system must be readily visible and the waveform constantly displayed to prevent a leak in the system from resulting in a fatal hemorrhage.

Use of very small catheters in and of themselves does not account for overdamping inasmuch as significant differences have not been found in pressures recorded with 22- and 24-gauge catheters.

Umbilical Artery Catheterization

TECHNIQUE

An indwelling umbilical artery catheter may be placed by either of two methods: direct placement or cutdown. Although no local anesthesia is needed for direct umbilical catheterization, anesthetic infiltration at the site of skin incision must be instituted for the umbilical cutdown technique. The infant must be monitored throughout the whole procedure, ideally with a cardiorespiratory monitor and pulse oximeter.

ADVANTAGES AND DISADVANTAGES OF UMBILICAL ARTERY CATHETERIZATION

Advantages

Rapid and easy access

Less skill needed

Larger catheter size can be used

Use of indwelling electrode for continuous monitoring of pH or Pao$_2$ is possible because a larger catheter can be used

No significant scarring after removal of catheter

Ability to monitor aortic pressure, which is more indicative of organ perfusion pressure than pressure measurements obtained from a peripheral arterial catheter when peripheral vascular resistance is high

Disadvantages

Higher incidence of minor and serious complications

Only postductal blood gas is obtainable

Only postcoarctation blood pressure is obtainable

Inaccessible route after approximately 10 days of life

Equipment

Equipment necessary for both direct and cutdown techniques is as follows:

Umbilical artery catheterization equipment

Blunt needle, 18 gauge

Catheters (polyvinylchloride with single end hole)
  Neonates <1500 g body weight, 3.5 F
  Neonates >1500 g body weight, 5 F

Continuous flush device, 3 ml/hr

Continuous infusion pump

IV fluid; add sodium heparin (1 U/ml)

Low compliance pressure tubing, 4 ft

Monitor with pressure module

Pressure transducer kit

Sterile measuring tape

Sterile surgical gown and gloves

Surgical mask, goggles, and cap

Surgical procedure lamp

Three-way interlocking stopcock

Vascular access tray (see p. 1217)

Access Site

The umbilical cord normally contains two arteries and one vein, with the vein at the center and the arteries arranged on either side and caudal to the vein to form a triangle. The single, large, thin-walled, oval vein is easily distinguished from the smaller, thick-walled, round arteries, which are usually constricted and pinpoint sized.

Sterile technique must be maintained at all times. The site must be surgically cleansed three times with iodine solution for 3 minutes. The povodine-iodine must be dry before proceeding to obtain maximum bactericidal effect.

Procedure

Direct technique. Set up the equipment and flush all tubing and the catheter. Immobilize the infant with arm and leg restraints and clean the umbilical site as previously described. Tie an umbilical tape loosely at the base of the cord without including skin. The tape may be tightened if bleeding occurs.

Two tip positions are considered safe locations: the high position, in the thoracic aorta below the ductus arteriosus, and the low position, above the bifurcation of the aorta at the level of L3 or L4. The low position is associated less often with serious complication and is preferred. Measure the distance between the umbilicus and the acromioclavicular junction. Two thirds of this measurement plus the length of the umbilical stump is generally the distance from the insertion site to the third or fourth lumbar vertebra. Mark this distance on the catheter with the sterile transparent dermal butterfly tape.

Remove the "dirty" umbilical clamp and place a curved hemostat at the distal end of the stump, pull gently, and turn the stump cephalad over the instrument (Fig. 132-8, *A*). With the scalpel blade, slowly cut the cord superficially 2 cm above skin level. Advance toward the center of the cord gently until an artery is partially transected. Ideally, no more than half the artery's circumference must be cut. The younger the infant the more likely retraction of the umbilical artery will occur with complete transection of the vessel.

Dilate the artery with the curved eye-dressing forceps. The curved forceps allows better control and visualization. Dilation must be gentle and progressive to minimize arterial rupture or spasm.

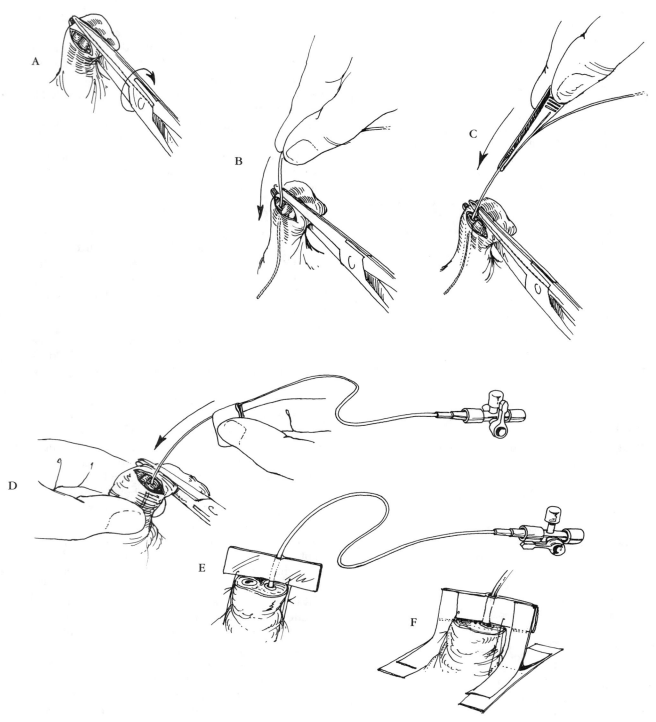

Fig. 132-8 Umbilical artery catheter placement. **A,** Pull stump gently and turn it cephalad over hemostat. **B,** Introduce and advance catheter. **C-F,** Insert and secure catheter.

After flushing the catheter free of air and all bubbles, insert it into the artery with the pincer or an eye-dressing forceps to grasp it (Fig. 132-8, *B* and *C*). Advance the catheter smoothly with gentle pressure to overcome the resistance met when passing from the hypogastric artery to the femoral artery (Fig. 132-8, *D*). Confirm placement by both aspirating blood and observing the waveform when connected to the transducer-monitor system. Secure the catheter by placing sutures from the butterfly tape to the umbilical skin. An H-type tape bridge is recommended to secure the catheter to the abdominal wall as an extra safety measure (Fig. 132-8, *E* and *F*).

Finally, the catheter tip position must be confirmed. An anteroposterior abdominal radiograph will show the catheter tip at the level of the third or fourth vertebra (Fig. 132-9).

Cutdown technique. The cutdown technique is used when direct umbilical cannulation is not possible, as when the stump has dried and vessels cannot be visualized or the catheter cannot be advanced because of obstruction at the bend of the cord at the abdominal wall.

Equipment setup, infant immobilization, and skin preparation can be done as in the direct technique. Catheter length is determined similar to the direct method but without considering the umbilical stump measurement.

A 1 cm skin incision is made below the umbilical stump–abdominal wall junction or 1 to 2 cm below this junction (Fig. 132-10). The sheath is identified as a tough white fascia and is cut carefully to expose the white cordlike urachus in the middle and the arteries on either side.

After the artery is identified, it can be isolated with stay sutures similar to the method used for peripheral arterial cutdown. A cardboard wedge under the artery may be helpful in immobilization, arteriotomy, and cannulation. Cannulation and confirmation can be done as in the direct technique. The surgical wound may be closed and dressed as in the peripheral cutdown method. The catheter must be secured as described.

Pressure Waveform

See the section "Pressure Waveform" for peripheral artery catheterization (p. 1223).

Maintenance

To draw blood from the umbilical artery catheter (Fig. 132-11), turn the stopcock so that the IV solution stops flowing. Aspirate 1 to 2 ml from the catheter in-

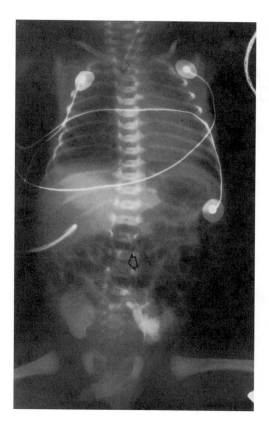

Fig. 132-9 Proper position of umbilical artery catheter as seen on thoracoabdominal radiograph.

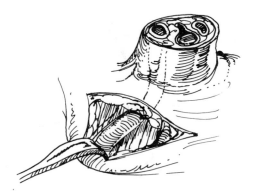

Fig. 132-10 Umbilical artery cutdown.

to the dry syringe. The IV fluid is prevented from infusing, and aspiration clears the catheter of IV fluid. Turn the stopcock to the neutral position. Remove the syringe and attach the sampling syringe. Turn the stopcock off to the fluid source and aspirate the desired amount of blood. Turn the stopcock to the neutral position and remove the sampling syringe, then attach a syringe with 1 to 2 ml of heparinized solution. Turn the stopcock off to the IV fluid source. Slightly aspirate to remove any air in the stopcock and slowly insert the flush solution. Return the stopcock to the neutral position, remove the flush syringe, and place a sterile injection cap on the sampling port. Observe the monitor for return of the arterial waveform. In small infants it is necessary to monitor closely the amount of discarded blood and record it as

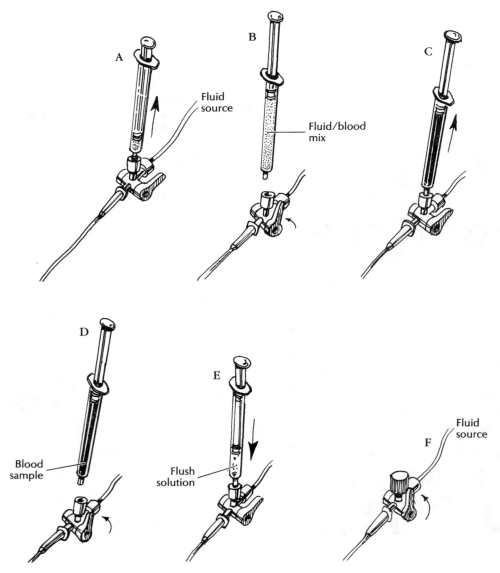

Fig. 132-11 Umbilical artery catheter blood sampling. **A,** Turn stopcock off to fluid source. **B,** Turn stopcock off to all ports. **C,** Draw blood sample. **D,** With stopcock off to all ports, remove sample syringe. **E,** Flush catheter. **F,** Turn stopcock off to sampling port.

blood loss. If it is necessary to return blood to the infant, it must be given only through a venous catheter.

D_5W or $D_{10}W$ solution, in addition to sodium chloride solutions, may be infused through umbilical artery catheters. No medications but heparin may be infused through an umbilical artery catheter. A small amount of heparin (1 to 5 U/ml) may help prevent clot formation, although heparin may not be used in those patients with a severe bleeding diathesis or in anhepatic patients. Tubing and fluid changes must be done following the same guidelines as for peripheral arterial catheterization.

Blanching, mottling, cyanosis, pallor, decreased pulses, or cooling of the legs must be reported to a physician immediately. Such developments usually indicate arterial obstruction, and removal of the catheter may be necessary.

The catheter is always taped securely in place to prevent accidental dislodgment. The nurse measures the distance from the umbilicus to the first tubing connection and records this distance on the nursing care plan so that catheter migration can be easily detected.

If any signs of cellulitis are present, the catheter must be removed, and blood drawn from the catheter must be sent for culture. Umbilical stump culture is also indicated if there is cellulitis in the stump area. In febrile patients blood must be drawn for culture from the arterial catheter and from a peripheral site to help distinguish bacteremia or sepsis from colonization.

Catheter Removal

Indications for removal of the umbilical artery catheter include (1) stabilization or resolution of the indications for cannulation of the artery; (2) catheter-related infection (local or systemic) or colonization by microorganisms; (3) evidence of clot formation (e.g., damped tracing or sluggish blood flow); and (4) evidence of thrombosis or mechanical occlusion of the artery.

The umbilical artery catheter must be removed over 20 to 30 minutes to allow the umbilical artery to constrict to prevent free bleeding on removal of the catheter. All catheters must be inspected for thrombus formation and for integrity on removal.

RISKS AND COMPLICATIONS

The reported rate of complications from umbilical artery catheterization ranges from 8.6% to 95%.

Nonclinically significant thrombus formation is the most common and probably the least diagnosed complication. It may develop in as many as 95% of patients when thrombus formation is diagnosed at aortography in infants with umbilical artery catheters. The incidence of clinically significant thrombosis formation secondary to use of umbilical artery catheters is 3.3% to 6%. As in patients with peripheral arterial catheters, these thrombi resorb over time, or there may be pericatheter fibrin formation. The concern is that when an organ distal to the occlusion is affected, the outcome is usually dismal because there is no collateral circulation to the abdominal aorta unless prompt surgical embolectomy is performed. Reported complications include loss of an extremity, transverse myelitis, renovascular hypertension (renal artery thrombosis), and skin necrosis. Whenever thrombus formation is suspected, use of the umbilical catheter must be discontinued. Abdominal ultrasonography, CT, or aortography and early medical treatment with streptokinase or urokinase can be considered (see Chapter 181), and early consultation with a vascular surgeon is necessary.

The rate of umbilical artery catheter colonization has been reported to be as high as 62%. The incidence of septicemia is similar to that with peripheral arterial catheters, 2.6% in one series. Colonized or

---

COMPLICATIONS OF UMBILICAL ARTERY CATHETERIZATION

Thrombosis
Bleeding
Bacteremia
Cellulitis
Sepsis
Renal failure (secondary to aortic thrombosis)
Necrotizing enterocolitis
Congestive heart failure (secondary to aortic thrombosis)
Embolization
Infectious arthritis
Ischemia (to internal organs or lower extremities)
False abdominal aortic aneurysm
Osteomyelitis
Vascular perforation
Pelvic exsanguination
Electrocution

infected umbilical arterial catheters must be managed similar to peripheral arterial catheters.

Bleeding around the catheter can be successfully stopped by gently tightening the umbilical tape around the stump. Once the bleeding has stopped, do not leave the tape tied permanently because this may lead to tissue necrosis. Bleeding from faulty or untightened tubing or connectors can be managed similar to that for peripheral arterial catheters.

Administration of any medications, including antibiotics, or direct mechanical trauma secondary to catheter insertion may lead to intimal damage. Any of these causes may lead to internal flap formation, which in time serves as a site for thrombus formation.

Spasm of the iliac artery may be stopped by warming the opposite extremity when the spasm is unilateral. If blanching persists, use of the catheter must be discontinued.

ADDITIONAL READING
Technique

Au-Yeung YB, Sugg VM, Kantor NM, et al. Percutaneous catheterization of scalp arteries in sick infants. J Pediatr 91:106, 1977.

• Barr PA, Sumners J, Wirtschafter D, et al. Percutaneous peripheral arterial cannulation in the neonate. Pediatrics 59(Suppl 6, Pt 2):1058, 1977.

• Benz JJ, Gallo BM, Hudak CM. Hemodynamic monitoring. Crit Care Nurs 5:124, 1990.

Butt W, Shann F, McDonnell G, et al. Effect of heparin concentration and infusion rate on the patency of arterial catheters. Crit Care Med 15:230, 1987.

Butt W, Whyte H. Blood pressure monitoring in neonates: Comparison of umbilical and peripheral artery catheter measurements. J Pediatr 105:630, 1984.

Cheng EY, Lauer KK, Stommel KA, et al. Evaluation of the palmar circulation by pulse oximeter. J Clin Monitor 5(10):1, 1989.

Cilley RE. Arterial access in infants and children. Semin Pediatr Surg 3:174, 1992.

Clark JM, Jung AL. Umbilical artery catheterization by a cut down procedure. Pediatrics 59:1036, 1977.

Cole FS, Todres ID, Shannon DC. Technique for percutaneous cannulation of the radial artery in the newborn infant. J Pediatr 92:105, 1978.

Ferguson SG, Huddleston SS. Hemodynamic monitoring. Springhouse notes. Crit Care Emergency Nurs p 54, 1990.

• Fiser DH, Grayes SA, van der Aa J. Catheters for arterial pressure monitoring in pediatrics. Crit Care Med 13:580, 1985.

Gordon LH, Brown M, Brown OW, et al. Alternative sites for continuous arterial monitoring. South Med J 77:1498, 1984.

• Hazinski MF. Hemodynamic Monitoring of Children: Techniques in Bedside Monitoring. St. Louis: Mosby, 1989, pp 151-178, 247-314.

Husum B, Palm T. Before cannulation of the radial artery: Collateral arterial supply evaluated by strain-gauge plethysmography. Acta Anaesthesiol Scand 24:412, 1980.

Morray JP, Brandford HG, Barnes LF, et al. Doppler-assisted radial artery cannulation in infants and children. Anesth Analg 63:346, 1984.

• Pfenninger J, Bernasconi G, Sutter M. Radial artery catheterization by surgical exposure in infants. Intensive Care Med 8:139, 1982.

Spahr RC, MacDonald HM, Holzman IR. Catheterization of the posterior tibial artery in the neonate. Am J Dis Child 133:945, 1979.

Wall PM, Kuhn LR. Percutaneous arterial sampling using transillumination. Pediatrics 59:1032, 1977.

Zerella JT, Trump DS, Dorman GW. Access for neonatal arterial monitoring. J Pediatr Surg 14:270, 1979.

Interpretation

Chyun DA. A comparison of intraarterial and auscultatory blood pressure readings. Heart Lung 14:223, 1985.

• Galvis AG, Donahoo JS, White JJ. An improved technique for prolonged arterial catheterization in infants and children. Crit Care Med 4:166, 1976.

• Goldenheim PD, Kazemi H. Cardiopulmonary monitoring of critically ill patients. N Engl J Med 3311:776, 1984.

Husum B, Palm T. Before cannulation of the radial artery: Collateral arterial supply evaluated by strain-gauge plethysmography. Acta Anaesthesiol Scand 24:412, 1980.

Kaye W. Invasive monitoring techniques: Arterial cannulation, bedside pulmonary artery catheterization, and arterial puncture. Heart Lung 12:395, 1983.

Rutten AJ, Ilsley AH, Skowronski GA, et al. A comparative study of the measurement of mean arterial blood pressure using automatic oscillometers, arterial cannulation and auscultation. Anaesth Intensive Care 14:58, 1986.

• Venus B, Mathru M, Smith RA, et al. Direct versus indirect blood pressure measurements in critically ill patients. Heart Lung 14:228, 1985.

Wiedemann HP, Matthay RA. Cardiovascular-pulmonary monitoring in the intensive care unit. Part 1. Chest 85:537, 1984.

Complications

• AACN Thunder Task Force. Arterial catheter complications and management problems: Observations from AACN's Thunder Project. Crit Care Nurs Clin North Am 3:557, 1993.

Abramowsky CR, Chrenka B, Fanaroff A. Wharton jelly embolism: An unusual complication of umbilical catheterization. J Pediatr 96:739, 1980.

Adams JM, Speer ME, Rudolph AJ. Bacterial colonization of radial artery catheters. Pediatrics 65:94, 1980.

Arnow PM, Costas CO. Delayed rupture of the radial artery caused by catheter-related sepsis. Rev Infect Dis 10:1035, 1988.

Bedford RF. Wrist circumference predicts the risk of radial arterial occlusion after cannulation. Am Soc Anesthesiol 48:377, 1978.

• Bedford RF, Wallman H. Complications of percutaneous radial artery cannulation: An objective prospective study in man. Anesthesiology 38:228, 1973.

Bull MJ, Shreiner RL, Garg BP, et al. Neurological complications following temporal artery catheterization. J Pediatr 96:1071, 1980.

• Caeton AJ, Goetzman BW. Risky business: Umbilical arterial catheterization. Am J Dis Child 139:120, 1985.

Cochran WD, Davis HT, Smith CA. Advantages and complications of umbilical artery catheterization in the newborn. Pediatrics 42:769, 1968.

Cohen A, Reyes R, Kirk M, et al. Osler's nodes, pseudoaneurysm formation, and sepsis complicating percutaneous radial artery cannulation. Crit Care Med 12:1078, 1984.

Cronin KD, Davies MJ, Domaingue CM, et al. Radial artery cannulation: The influence of method on blood flow after decannulation. Anaesth Intensive Care 14:400, 1986.

Feldman BH. Arterial cannulation in the newborn infant. J Pediatr 93:161, 1978.

• Fletcher MA, Brown DR, Landers S, et al. Umbilical arterial catheter use: Report of an audit conducted by the study group for complications of perinatal care. Am J Perinatol 11:94, 1994.

• Furfaro S, Gauthier M, Lacroix J, et al. Arterial catheter–related infections in children: A one-year cohort analysis. Am J Dis Child 145:1037, 1991.

Harris MS. Umbilical artery catheters: High, low, or no. J Perinat Med 6:15, 1978.

Henry CG, Gutierrez F, Lee JT, et al. Aortic thrombosis presenting as congestive heart failure: An umbilical artery catheter complication. J Pediatr 98:820, 1981.

Kirkpatrick DMBV, Kodroff M, Erlich FE, et al. Pelvic exsanguination following umbilical artery catheterization in neonates. J Pediatr Surg 14:264, 1979.

• Klein MD, Coran AG, Whitehouse WM Jr, et al. Management of iatrogenic arterial injuries in infants and children. J Pediatr Surg 17:933, 1982.

Lim MO, Gresham EL, Franken EA, et al. Osteomyelitis as a complication of umbilical artery catheterization. Am J Dis Child 131:142, 1977.

Lindsay SL, Kerridge R, Collett BJ. Abscess following cannulation of the radial artery. Anaesthesia 42:654, 1987.

Lowenstein E, Little JW, LO HH. Prevention of cerebral embolization from flushing radial artery cannulas. N Engl J Med 285:1414, 1977.

Malloy MH, Nichols MM. False abdominal aortic aneurysm: An unusual complication of umbilical arterial catheterization for exchange transfusion. J Pediatr 90:285, 1977.

• Mandel MA, Dauchot PJ. Radial artery cannulation in 1,000 patients: Precautions and complications. J Hand Surg 2A:482, 1977.

Marshall AG, Erwin DC, Wyse RK, et al. Percutaneous arterial cannulation in children: Concurrent and subsequent adequacy of blood flow at the wrist. Anaesthesia 39:27, 1984.

Mathieu A, Dalton B, Fischer JF, et al. Expanding aneurysm of the radial artery after frequent puncture. Anesthesiology 38:401, 1973.

Morris T, Bouthoutsos J. The dangers of femoral artery puncture and catheterization. Am Heart J 89:260, 1975.

Nagel JW, Sims JS, Aplin CE, et al. Refractory hypoglycemia associated with a malpositioned umbilical artery catheter. Pediatrics 64:315, 1979.

Naguib M, Hassan M, Farag H, et al. Cannulation of the radial and dorsalis pedis arteries. Br J Anaesth 59:482, 1987.

Pape KE, Armstrong DL, Fitzhardinge PM, Peripheral median nerve damage secondary to brachial arterial blood gas sampling. J Pediatr 93:852, 1978.

Prian GW, Wright GB, Rumack CM, et al. Apparent cerebral embolization after temporal artery catheterization. J Pediatr 93:115, 1978.

• Raad I, Umphrey J, Khan A, et al. The duration of placement as a predictor of peripheral and pulmonary arterial catheter infections. J Hosp Infect 23:17, 1993.

• Rajani K, Goetzman BW, Wennberg RP, et al. Effect of heparinization of fluids infused through an umbilical artery catheter on catheter patency and frequency of complications. Pediatrics 63:552, 1979.

Randel SN, Tsang BHL, Wung JT, et al. Experience with percutaneous indwelling peripheral arterial catheterization in neonates. Am J Dis Child 141:848, 1987.

Seibert JJ, Northington FJ, Miers JF, et al. Aortic thrombosis after umbilical artery catheterization in neonates: Prevalence of complications on long-term follow-up. AJR 156:567, 1991.

• Sellden H, Nilsson K, Larsson LE, et al. Radial arterial catheters in children and neonates. A prospective study. Crit Care Med 15:1106, 1987.

Shinfeld A, Ofer A, Engleberg I, et al. Septic emboli from a radial artery catheter with local manifestations of subacute bacterial endocarditis (review). J Vasc Surg 16:293, 1992.

Spahr RC, Macdonald HM, Holzman IR. Catheterization of the posterior tibial artery in the neonate. Am J Dis Child 133:945, 1979.

Wilkins RG. Radial artery cannulation and ischaemic damage: A review. Anaesthesia 40:896, 1985.

Youngberg JA, Miller ED. Evaluation of percutaneous cannulations of the dorsalis pedis artery. Anesthesiology 44:80, 1976.

133 Advanced Hemodynamic Monitoring: Pulmonary Artery and Left Atrial Catheterization

Jeanne S. Takano · LeeAnn Howard · Luis O. Toro-Figueroa

Pulmonary Artery Catheterization

BACKGROUND AND INDICATIONS

The first clinical application for catheterization of the right heart with a flow-directed, balloon-tipped catheter was described by Swan and Ganz in 1970. The Swan-Ganz catheter (pulmonary artery catheter) has since been modified, adding functions in an effort to obtain additional accurate physiologic information. Catheters currently in use provide information about intracardiac pressure, cardiac output, and continuously monitored mixed venous oxygen saturation and allow access for ventricular pacemaker therapy. Each of these functions necessitates a separate lumen within the catheter. Four- and five-lumen catheters are available. The most commonly used configuration is a four-lumen catheter, available in both 5 and 7 F sizes for use in pediatric and adult patients. A distally placed thermodilution sensor (for thermodilution cardiac output), a balloon lumen (for flotation and occlusion), a distal lumen (for pulmonary arterial blood pressure and pulmonary arterial occlusion pressure), and a proximal lumen (for right atrial blood pressure) are the most common components of the four-lumen pulmonary artery catheter.

In a five-lumen catheter, now used in adults, the additional lumen provides either a right ventricular (middle) port or a distally placed fiberoptic line for continuous measurement of mixed venous oxygen saturation. The right ventricular port may be used to monitor pressure within the ventricle or as access to the ventricular muscle mass for placement of endocardial pacing wires. The mixed venous oxygen saturation can be continuously monitored to provide a "real time" estimate of cardiac output, provided hemoglobin concentration, arterial oxygen saturation,

and oxygen consumption remain constant. No studies are available that provide data about the efficacy or safety of either of these new applications of the pulmonary artery catheter in pediatric patients.

The standard distance between the proximal and distal lumens is 10, 15, 20, or 30 cm. Special-order pulmonary artery catheters are available for pediatric use with shorter distances between distal and proximal ports. A two-dimensional plot (Fig. 133-1) using

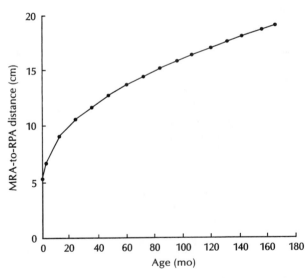

Fig. 133-1 MRA-to-RPA distance = 1.504 + 0.156 × Length − 0.117 × SSSP. (MRA = Middle right atrium; RPA = right pulmonary artery; SSSP = distance from suprasternal notch to suprapubis.) (From Borland LM. Allometric determination of the distance from the central venous port to the wedge position of the balloon-tip catheter in pediatric patients. Crit Care Med 14:974-976, 1986.)

the square root of age compared with the middle right atrium to right pulmonary artery distance is available to predict proximal to distal port distance. The clinical validity of these equations is still being studied, but the graph may be helpful to clinicians with patients who may need special-order catheters.

Cardiac Pressure Monitoring

Catheterization of the pulmonary artery through the right side of the heart provides the following direct pressure measurements: (1) right atrial blood pressure (RAP) or central venous blood pressure (CVP), (2) pulmonary arterial blood pressure (PAP), (3) pulmonary arterial occlusion pressure (PAoP), and (4) right ventricular blood pressure (RVP), as measured through the fifth lumen or using single measurements during insertion or withdrawal of a four-channel catheter. See Fig. 133-2 for normal pressures.

Clinicians have used PAoP as an indirect reflection of left ventricular end-diastolic pressure (LVEDP). During ventricular diastole the mitral valve is open and the left ventricle is in direct communication with the left atrium and the pulmonary veins. Pressure is transmitted to the pulmonary capillaries (wedge pressure) and is determined without influence of the PAP by the PAoP. This continuous closed circuit allows the clinician to use PAoP as a reflection of LVEDP, but only under certain conditions. PAoP is not

equivalent to pulmonary hydrostatic pressure, especially in patients with increased pulmonary vascular resistance.

Criteria for proper PAoP measurement are as follows: (1) a and v waves must be present in the PAoP waveform (Fig. 133-3, *A*) and must appear and disappear quickly with inflation and deflation of the balloon, and PAoP must have the least respiratory variability; (2) catheter patency must be documented by

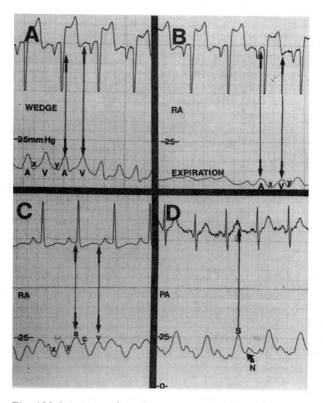

Fig. 133-3 A, Normal wedge pressure waveform. Peak of the a wave follows peak of the ECG P wave by 240 msec, whereas peak of the v wave occurs after the ECG T wave. **B,** Normal RAP waveform. Peak of the a wave follows peak of the ECG P wave by 80 msec, whereas peak of the v wave occurs at end of the ECG T wave. During inspiration RAP falls and a and v waves become more prominent. **C,** RAP waveform from a patient with first-degree atrioventricular block. The c wave is clearly visible. The RAP is elevated because of right ventricular infarction. **D,** Normal PAP waveform. Peak systolic pressure *(S)* occurs within the ECG T wave. Note dicrotic notch *(N).* (From Sharkey SW. Beyond the wedge: Clinical physiology and the Swan-Ganz catheter. Am J Med 83:111-122, 1987.)

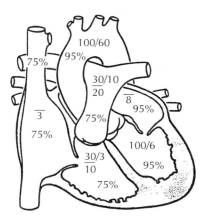

Fig. 133-2 Catheterization data in the normal pediatric heart with pressure (torr) and oxygenation saturation (%). (From Ream AK, Fogdall RP. Acute Cardiovascular Management: Anesthesia and Intensive Care. Philadelphia: JB Lippincott, 1982.)

CONDITIONS IN WHICH PAoP DOES NOT REFLECT LVEDP

Decreased left ventricular compliance
(PAoP = LVDP/LVEDV)
Two physiologic causes

With decrease in volume there is a left shift along a single Frank-Starling curve.
With increased intrinsic stiffness there is a left shift along the family of Frank-Starling curves.

Intrinsic causes of decreased ventricular compliance

Principal causes
    Ventricular hypertrophy
    Ventricular ischemia
    Ventricular fibrosis
    Ventricular tumors
    Ventricular infiltrative processes (e.g., amyloidosis)
    Pericardial disease
Other causes
    Increased temperature
    Increased osmolality
    Increased heart rate

Eccentric balloon occlusion
(PAoP > LVEDP)

Balloon occludes distal port directly or by placing port against vessel wall.

Incorrect transducer placement

Check for correct position (see Technique, p. 1238).

Increased pulmonary vascular resistance
(PAoP > LVEDP)

Causes
    Alveolar hypoxia
    Chronic obstructive pulmonary disease
    Hypercarbic states
    Recent open heart surgery
    Pulmonary embolism

Overwedging (overocclusion)
(PAoP > LVEDP)

Occurs with distention of the pulmonary vasculature or occlusion of the catheter tip.

Pulmonary venous obstruction
(PAoP > LVEDP)

Causes
    Atrial myxomas
    Increased intrathoracic pressure
    Mediastinal fibrosis
    Pulmonary venous thrombosis
    Thoracic tumors

Respiratory effects
(PAoP > LVEDP)

Record PAoP and respiratory cycle simultaneously:
    Spontaneous breathing: Read PAoP at end inspiration; if using digital readout, read systolic PAoP.
    Mechanical ventilation: Read PAoP at end expiration; if using digital readout, read diastolic PAoP.
West's zones (see Fig. 133-6):
    Zone I: $P_A > P_a > P_v$; PAoP > LVEDP
    Zone II: $P_a > P_A > P_v$; PAoP > LVEDP
    Zone III: $P_a > P_v > P_A$; PAoP = LVEDP
PEEP
    May convert a West's zone III into a zone II or I; (PAoP > LVEDP) (usually when PEEP ≥ 15 cm H_2O, or lower if hypovolemia is present).
    When PAoP increases by more than 50% of increase in applied PEEP, non–zone III placement should be suspected.
    PEEP will increase pericardial pressure (PP). PP will be transmitted to the LV, elevating LVEDP and decreasing LVEDV (left shift of the Frank-Starling curve).
    Effects of PEEP on pleural pressure decrease in lungs with low compliance.
    PEEP effect on pleural pressure may be assessed by:
        Direct measurement of pleural pressure
        Midesophageal pressure in the lateral decubitus position

Valvular heart disease

Mitral valve disease (PAoP > LVEDP)
    Mitral stenosis (large a wave)
    Mitral insufficiency (large v wave)
Aortic regurgitation (PAoP = LAP > LVEDP)

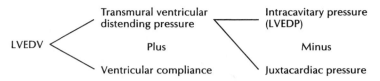

Fig. 133-4   *Relation of LVEDV to LVEDP.*

free flow of blood with the balloon inflated; (3) the occlusion blood sample oxygen tension must be 10 mm Hg greater than pulmonary arterial blood oxygen tension ($P_{PAoP}O_2 - PaO_2 > 10$ mm Hg), although this criterion may not hold true when the catheter tip is in a low $\dot{V}/\dot{Q}$ zone (e.g., in a patient with pneumonia); (4) PAoP must be less than or equal to pulmonary artery diastolic pressure (PADP) (i.e., when large v waves are present [e.g., in mitral valve disease], the area between the a and v wave must be used to determine PAoP); and (5) the catheter tip must be below the left atrium on the lateral chest radiograph.

Even if the above criteria are met and the clinical situations in which PAoP does not reflect LVEDP (see p. 1236) are not present, one cannot necessarily assume that LVEDP reflects left heart preload. Preload correlates better with left ventricular end-diastolic volume (LVEDV). LVEDP is a major component of LVEDV, but juxtacardiac pressure and ventricular compliance also have a significant effect on LVEDV. Changes in these components may shift the ventricular pressure-volume curve to the right or left with or without changing LVEDP (Fig. 133-4). There is no consistent correlation between PAoP and LVEDV. Two-dimensional echocardiography provides left ventricular end-diastolic dimensions that better assess LVEDV.

Pulmonary arterial blood pressures and waveform must be monitored continuously (with the distal balloon deflated) to detect catheter migration and accidental wedging. A normal pulmonary arterial pressure waveform is composed of a systolic phase, a dicrotic notch, and a diastolic phase (Fig. 133-3, *D*). Simultaneous ECG and PAP waveforms must be available for interpretation.

Pulmonary arterial systolic blood pressure normally reflects right ventricular systolic blood pressure. In the absence of most of the factors mentioned, PADP reflects left atrial blood pressure (LAP) within 4 mm Hg (see Fig. 133-2). When PADP and PAoP are

within 4 mm Hg, there is no need to occlude the pulmonary artery by inflating the balloon. PADP may be elevated by any clinical disorder or therapeutic intervention that increases pulmonary vascular resistance (e.g., recent cardiopulmonary bypass graft, chronic obstructive pulmonary disease, alveolar hypoxia, hypercarbic states, or pulmonary embolism), pulmonary venous blood pressure (e.g., pulmonary venous obstruction, mitral valve disease, or left ventricular failure), and pulmonary blood flow (e.g., left-to-right intracardiac shunt and some aortopulmonary shunts).

Misinterpretation of pulmonary arterial catheter data can be minimized with careful evaluation of the patient's clinical status, knowledge of the disease process, meticulous use of PAoP criteria for measurement, and frequent reexamination of the patient and reevaluation of pulmonary arterial catheter data after therapeutic interventions.

Indications for placement of a pulmonary arterial catheter are as follows: (1) as a guide to treatment of shock or any low cardiac output state unresponsive to initial fluid, inotropic, or vasodilator therapy; (2) for pulmonary arterial hypertension monitoring and management; (3) as a tool to assess and manage cardiopulmonary interactions in any pulmonary process in which high intrathoracic pressures are used to maintain alveolar recruitment (e.g., PEEP >10 to 15 cm H_2O in patients with acute respiratory distress syndrome [ARDS]); and (4) to assist in perioperative management in patients who have undergone complicated procedures (e.g., complex heart defect repair or liver transplantation) or have complex diseases (e.g., multiorgan system failure) who are at risk for cardiopulmonary instability or systemic inflammatory response syndrome (SIRS).

No absolute contraindications to pulmonary artery catheterization have been established, but the following may be considered relative contraindications: (1) cardiopulmonary instability with rapidly changing vital signs (near-arrest state); (2) cardiac arrhythmias or ventricular irritability that may be worsened by direct catheter stimulation of the endocardium; (3) intracardiac shunting, which renders the thermodilution technique inaccurate because of loss of indicator (e.g., cold fluid); (4) tricuspid or pulmonary valve insufficiency, which prevents the flow-directed catheter forward movement, making placement difficult, and renders the thermodilution technique inaccurate because of loss of indicator; and (5) congenital or acquired abnormalities of systemic venous circulation (e.g., Glenn shunt or superior vena cava syndrome).

TECHNIQUE
Catheter Insertion

Vascular access for pulmonary artery catheter placement can be established with either the percutaneous or cutdown methods. Preferred insertion sites are the internal or external jugular, femoral, subclavian, basilic (most commonly used in adolescent patients), or axillary veins. The jugular and subclavian veins must not be used in patients with increased ICP because the catheter may impede venous return from the head and thereby increase ICP further. In small infants and patients with high intrathoracic pressure the subclavian approach is not used because of the increased risk of pneumothorax.

Percutaneous vascular access with the Seldinger technique and a flexible polyurethane or Teflon sheath-dilator provides a rapid and safe method for catheter placement (see Chapter 131). The Trendelenburg position must be used for upper extremity, thoracic, and neck approaches to reduce the risk of air embolism. Other advantages of the percutaneous approach are better hemostasis, more aesthetically pleasing appearance after removal, and more vascular sites available. In addition, some authors report a lower incidence of infections.

A Teflon vascular sheath with a side port or T-connector (for fluid administration) and an airtight valve (allowing introduction, repositioning, removal, and replacement of the catheter) is recommended and is secured with sutures. Assistance is needed to handle catheter connections with cables and fluid sources and to monitor the patient's vital signs throughout the procedure. Before pulmonary artery catheter insertion, balloon patency must be tested by attaching a syringe and injecting the prescribed volume of air (0.5 ml for a 5 F and 1.5 ml for a 7 F catheter). Exceeding the maximum recommended balloon inflation

volumes may rupture the balloon and result in air embolism. The thermodilution thermistor is tested by connecting it to the appropriate connection cable to the cardiac output computer; a temperature reading confirms circuit integrity. Transducers are connected to monitor CVP and PAP continuously. These steps can be done as part of the sterile procedure by the person inserting the catheter with the help of an identified assistant.

Pulmonary arterial blood pressure is monitored using a transducer with a 3 ml flush device and low-compliance tubing. The flush device may be omitted if the flow rate is >30 ml/hr, but the infusion pump pressure will introduce an artifact and increase pressure readings. Standard heparinized fluids (1 to 5 units/ml) can be used to prime the tubing. The lower the flow rate, the higher the concentration of heparin needed to prevent clotting. Care must be used in priming the tubing, the pulmonary artery, right atrial, and right ventricular lumens, and all stopcocks. Air in the system represents a potential embolus or may dampen pressure readings.

The transducer must be placed at the intersection of the midaxillary line and the intermammary line at the level of the left atrium. Zeroing and calibration of the transducer must be performed according to the monitor manufacturer specifications. Mechanical calibration can be confirmed by holding the tip of the catheter 27 inches above the transducer; the PAP should then read 20 mm Hg. The catheter can be wiggled to demonstrate an appropriate waveform amplitude on the monitor screen. When the catheter has been properly calibrated and tested, a sterile sleeve is placed over the catheter but is not extended until proper placement of the catheter has been accomplished. The extended sterile sleeve permits maintenance of catheter sterility while allowing later repositioning of the catheter.

Placement of the tip of the catheter into the pulmonary artery may be accomplished at the bedside with the flotation method with or without fluoroscopic assistance. Continuous ECG and pressure monitoring is necessary.

The flotation method uses the flow of blood to move the catheter (with balloon inflated) through the right side of the heart. The clinician must follow pressure and waveform changes closely to determine catheter position. The catheter is advanced with the balloon deflated into the superior or inferior vena cava and advanced further until respiratory fluctuations are observed in the venous pressure tracing, indicating intrathoracic position of the catheter tip. The pulmonary arterial catheter is marked in centimeters to show distance from the tip, allowing the operator to estimate the length of the catheter placed. While mean pressure is monitored, the balloon is inflated with air or sterile CO_2 (0.5 ml for a 5 F and 1.5 ml for a 7 F catheter according to manufacturer's volume specifications) and floated into the right ventricle. A ventricular waveform and stepup in mean blood pressure will be detected as the catheter tip enters the ventricle. Flow-directed guidance of the pulmonary artery catheter through the right side of the heart needs adequate blood flow to maneuver the tip of the catheter into the pulmonary artery. As diastolic pressure readings are monitored, the catheter is guided into the pulmonary artery while the widening and rounding of the waveform and the stepup in blood pressure are observed. The dicrotic notch in the waveform corresponds to closure of the pulmonary

valve. The catheter is advanced until a PAoP tracing is observed and the balloon deflated (see Fig. 133-2 for intracardiac blood pressures and Fig. 133-5 for a sequential pressure tracing of right heart catheterization). When the balloon is deflated, the waveform generally returns to that characteristic of the pulmonary artery. Optimally, the balloon, when in pulmonary artery occlusion position, does not remain inflated for more than two respiratory cycles.

Flow-directed guidance of the pulmonary artery catheter may be difficult in low cardiac output states and is facilitated by use of bedside fluoroscopy and any maneuver that improves right ventricular stroke volume. Correct placement through the right internal jugular or left subclavian vein is often easier than through the basilic or femoral vein because of the shorter catheter being manipulated. Other helpful maneuvers include positioning the patient with the head slightly elevated and the left side up, increasing the catheter stiffness by injecting iced sterile fluid through

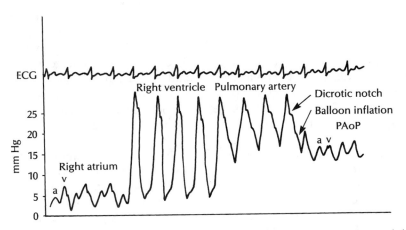

Fig. 133-5 Representative recording of pressures as a Swan-Ganz catheter is inserted through the right side of the heart into the pulmonary artery. First waveform is a right atrial tracing with characteristic a and v waves. Right ventricular, pulmonary artery, and pulmonary artery wedge tracings follow in sequence. The pressures and waveforms shown are normal. Note that the wedge tracing shows a and v waves transmitted from the left atrium. In addition, the wedge pressure (mean) is less than pulmonary artery diastolic pressure. The wedge tracing is not always distinct, but a very damped tracing or mean wedge pressure greater than pulmonary artery diastolic pressure usually indicates a mechanical problem in the system (e.g., air bubble in the connecting tubing, catheter tip "overwedged," balloon inflated over distal orifice, or catheter tip in zone 1 or zone 2). In a patient with severe mitral regurgitation the large transmitted left atrial v waves occasionally may cause the wedge tracing to resemble a pulmonary artery tracing. In such cases careful analysis of the waveforms and attention to where peak pressure occurs in relation to the ECG complex usually will avoid misinterpretation. (Redrawn from Matthay MA. Invasive hemodynamic monitoring in critically ill patients. Clin Chest Med 4:233-249, 1983.)

PAoP RELIABILITY CRITERIA

Balloon inflated until a PAoP waveform is obtained or its capacity reached

PAoP equal to or less than PADP

a and v waves present in PAoP waveform

PAoP waveform appears and disappears quickly with balloon inflation and deflation

Distal lumen patency during PAoP documented by free flow of blood

Less respiratory variability during PAoP than during PAP.

PAoP oxygen tension must be 10 mm Hg greater than PAP oxygen tension

Catheter tip below left atrium (West's zone III) on lateral chest radiograph

Transducers must be zeroed and recalibrated with any change in patient position or sudden change in pulmonary artery pressure

Transducers, lines, stopcocks, and catheter lumens air and clot free

---

the catheter immediately before insertion, gently rotating the catheter to take advantage of the preformed curve, advancing the catheter during an end-expiratory pause to take advantage of the transient increase in stroke volume, and using half the prescribed balloon volume.

Once the catheter is in position and the balloon deflated, the sterile sleeve is extended over the catheter and secured to the side port of the sheath. The length of catheter in the patient is noted and the catheter secured with surgical tape or a locking device provided by the manufacturer. Once the catheter is secured, the list of criteria for proper PAoP measurement must be rechecked. Anteroposterior and lateral chest radiographs must also be obtained to determine whether there is a redundant catheter loop in the right ventricle and the catheter tip is below the left atrium (West's lung zone III, where $Pa > Pv > PA$). Only zone III provides free communication between the distal lumen of the catheter and the left atrium, and zone III is physiologically defined by intrathoracic pressure and patient position (Fig. 133-6).

Careful monitoring is necessary to detect changes in the pulmonary artery waveform. The pulmonary artery catheter must be recalibrated with any change

in patient position or sudden change in pulmonary artery pressure. Air bubbles or clot formation may dampen the pulmonary artery waveform. Any air bubbles in the catheter must be aspirated through the stopcock and the catheter flushed. After air is aspirated, heparinized 0.9% sodium chloride solution may be used to flush the catheter to clear any blood from the tubing. If a wedged waveform persists, the catheter must be repositioned. A wedged waveform may also occur if the catheter is lodged against the vessel wall.

The insertion site dressing is inspected every hour and the sterile dressing changed every 7 days or more frequently if necessary. The site is assessed for redness, edema, or leakage. Skin site and blood cultures are recommended whenever the patient is febrile, sepsis is suspected, or signs of cellulitis are present at the insertion site.

PAoP is obtained by slowly inflating the balloon while observing the pulmonary artery waveform for a wedge tracing (see Fig. 133-3, *A* and *D*). The balloon is inflated only until the waveform changes to a wedged waveform. Overinflation may result in balloon rupture, pulmonary artery rupture, pulmonary infarction, or falsely high PAoP readings. Normal resistance will be felt when inflating the balloon. To deflate the balloon, remove the syringe from the lumen and let it deflate spontaneously. The air must not be aspirated because this may lead to balloon rupture. Blood seen in the balloon lumen indicates the balloon has ruptured, and this port must not be used again.

Indications for removal of the catheter are as follows: (1) when the indication for its placement has resolved or is static, (2) there is evidence of fibrin sheath or clot formation (e.g., damped tracing, after ruling out wedging and air bubble in the system, or echocardiographic evidence), (3) a pulmonary embolism exists that can be traced to the pulmonary artery catheter, (4) intractable arrhythmias are present, and (5) the catheter is colonized by microorganisms.

When a pulmonary artery catheter is removed, the balloon must be completely deflated. Pressure recordings and waveform inspection can be carried out as the catheter tip is withdrawn through the different cardiac chambers. Blood gases may also be drawn from the different chambers to assess left-to-right intracardiac shunts after open heart surgery. Mixing in the right atrium is incomplete; therefore the venous saturation along the jet streams from the coronary sinus, the superior vena cava, and the inferior vena ca-

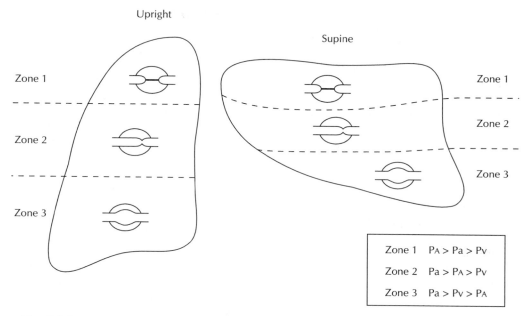

Fig. 133-6 West's zones. (P_A = Alveolar pressure; Pa = arterial pressure; Pv = venous pressure.)

va decrease in order, respectively. Once the catheter is removed, the balloon must always be inspected for evidence of rupture.

Thermodilution

It is often important to measure cardiac output in a child in shock or with low cardiac output state. Changes in cardiac output are useful to assess the effect of inotropic and vasoactive agents and assisted ventilation. Thermodilution indicators have proved satisfactory because the indicator (change in temperature) is easily detectable, nontoxic, and produces no cardiorespiratory changes.

In this method a known volume of sterile normal saline solution or D_5W at a known temperature is introduced at one point in the circulation (in the right atrium) and the change in intravascular blood temperature is measured distally (at the catheter tip in the pulmonary artery). Currently available instruments electronically integrate the area under the thermodilution curve and display the cardiac output in liters per minute. This value is divided by body surface area to give the cardiac index.

The thermodilution technique can provide accurate and reproducible values if several conditions are met: (1) the duration of the injection must be <2 seconds, (2) the volume and temperature of the injec-

tate must be accurately determined, (3) the temperature of the injectate must be preserved, (4) the temperature of the pulmonary artery blood is determined, (5) the injection site and thermistor recording site must be located in areas where the injectate is completely mixed with the blood (this is best accomplished with a central venous or right atrial injection site and a thermistor site in the main pulmonary artery or a proximal branch), and (6) the heart rate and systemic arterial blood pressure need to be in a relatively steady state.

Abrupt changes in these variables during the injection may result in an invalid determination. The thermodilution technique is not an accurate measure of cardiac output when there is tricuspid insufficiency or intracardiac mixing.

It is important to accurately measure the temperature of the injectate. When injecting solutions at room temperature 2 vials of the injectate must be available: one used for a reservoir from which the injectate is withdrawn, the other used to monitor the temperature of the injectate with an external thermistor probe. When using iced injectate, several vials of injectate solution are placed in an ice bath; in 40 minutes the vials will cool to approximately 0° C. One of the vials serves as a site to monitor the injectate temperature. Just before injection the fluid is rapidly drawn up into the syringe with minimal handling of the syringe barrel. Injectate-filled syringes are not placed directly into the ice bath because of the potential for bacterial contamination of the injectate.

The syringe is attached to the proximal port and injected as quickly (<2 seconds) and evenly as possible. The injection catheter must not contain any medications. An alternative to using vials of injectate is a commercially available in-line system (e.g., American Edwards CO-Set closed injectate system) in which the cardiac output may be determined without opening the tubing system and a more consistent injectate temperature is maintained.

Manufacturer-specific computation constants are provided in the catheter package inserts to compensate for catheter size, injectate temperature, and injectate volume when calculating cardiac output. Reproducible, accurate thermodilution-measured cardiac output determinations depend on the following conditions being met:

1. Proper mixing of injectate and blood
2. Stable temperature of injectate
3. Duration of injection <2 seconds
4. Appropriate distance between injection site and thermistor
5. Accurate determination of volume and temperature of injectate
6. No medications in injection lumen
7. No concurrent infusion of other solutions or medications
8. Absence of tricuspid or pulmonary insufficiency or intracardiac mixing
9. Relative steady state as reflected by heart rate and systemic arterial blood pressure
10. Cardiac output measurements obtained in duplicate or triplicate within several minutes
11. Values within 10% to 15% of each other

Reproducibility of the cardiac output determinations is ensured by performing them in triplicate. These replications must be done within several minutes and must yield values within 10% to 15% of each other. The third may replace the first or second determination if the difference between the first two is >10%. The first three determinations may be off by more than 15% as a result of temperature changes within the catheter and therefore may be eliminated and the subsequent two determinations averaged. Normal values for hemodynamic and oxygenation measurements and derived variables are listed in Table 133-1.

RISKS AND COMPLICATIONS

Prospectively collected data that document the prevalence of complications of pulmonary artery catheterization in the pediatric population are lacking. A retrospective study in 1980 assessed the safety vs. risks of placement of 22 pulmonary artery catheters in 19 pediatric patients with catheterization performed at the patient's bedside. The following complications were reported: catheter malposition (4), balloon rupture (3), dislodgment (2), pneumothorax during vascular access attempted in an internal jugular vein (1), femoral cutdown site bleeding (1), hypotension with balloon inflation (1), transient premature ventricular contractions (14), spontaneous "wedging" (3), and failure to "wedge" balloon (9).

In another study of 774 vascular catheterizations (of which 47 were pulmonary artery catheters) in 467 children, 4.1% of patients had complications of bleeding, arterial obstruction, or sepsis. A knot in one pulmonary artery catheter was reported, with no effect on patient outcome. No other significant complications related to pulmonary artery catheters were mentioned.

A composite list of complications reported in the medical literature in adult patients include catheter migration, arrhythmias (including premature atrial or ventricular depolarizations, ventricular tachycardia, complete heart block, and right bundle branch block), bacteremia, pulmonary embolus, thrombosis (subclavian vein), valvar perforation (pulmonic), thrombocytopenia, "wedge" pressure errors, microbial colonization, pneumothorax, failure to "wedge," inadvertent arterial catheterization, balloon rupture, "overwedging," pulmonary hemorrhage, pulmonary artery false aneurysm, intravascular or intracardiac knot formation, pulmonary infarction, pulmonary artery perforation, interobserver variability in measurements, and air embolism (including paradoxical CNS air embolization).

Continuous Mixed Venous Oxygen Saturation Monitoring
BACKGROUND AND INDICATIONS

Continuous mixed venous saturation is measured with reflectance spectrophotometry, in which multiple wavelengths of light reflected through red blood cells measure oxyhemoglobin and deoxyhemoglobin

Table 133-1 Normal Values for Hemodynamic and Oxygenation Measurements and Derived Variables

	Source	Value
Directly measured variables		
Core temperature, heart rate (HR)	Preferably measured directly from patient but can be obtained from monitor	Normal range for age
Systolic, mean, and diastolic arterial pressure	Can be obtained from indwelling arterial catheter (monitor), automated blood pressure device, or manually measured with manual pressure manometer	Normal range for age
CVP or mean right atrial pressure	Directly measured through pulmonary artery catheter proximal port and displayed on monitor	Mean, 3 mm Hg
Systolic, mean, and diastolic pulmonary artery pressure	Directly measured through pulmonary artery catheter distal port and displayed on monitor	Normal range for age
PAoP	Directly measured through pulmonary artery catheter distal port and displayed on monitor during occlusion	Mean, 8 mm Hg
Cardiac output (CO)	Directly measured through the catheter's thermistor with thermodilution method ($CO = HR \times SV$)	Normal, 4-8 L/min
Arterial blood gases and pH	Arterial blood sample is drawn directly from a catheter with standard technique and precautions, carefully labeled, and sent for analysis of blood gases and hemoglobin level; draw must always be simultaneous with mixed venous blood sample if intrapulmonary shunt or other derived variable calculation is to be performed	pH, 7.35-7.45 P_{CO_2}, 35-45 mm Hg tc_{CO_2}, 23-29 mmol/L HCO_3, 18-24 mmol/L P_{O_2}, 80-95 mm Hg S_{O_2}, 96%-100%
Mixed venous blood gas and pH	Mixed venous blood sample is drawn as for arterial blood sample; mixed venous hemoglobin sample is necessary because results of two samples can differ significantly	pH, 7.28-7.42 mm Hg P_{CO_2}, 38-52 mm Hg tc_{CO_2}, 24-30 mmol/L HCO_3, 22-28 mmol/L P_{O_2}, 37-42 mm Hg S_{O_2}, 60%-80%
Derived variables		
Cardiac index (CI)	Reflects capacity of ventricle to mobilize a given volume (liters) over time (1 minute) indexed to subject's body surface area (square meters) ($CI = CO/BSA$)	Normal, 3.3-6.0 L/min/m²
Stroke volume (SV)	Amount of blood pumped by ventricle during one contraction: ($SV = [CO/HR]$ [1000 ml/L])	Normal, 60-100 ml/beat
Stroke volume index (SVI) (or stroke index)	Stroke volume indexed to patient's body surface area ($SVI = CI/HR$) *or* ($SVI = SV/BSA$)	Normal, 33-47 ml/beat/m²
Systemic vascular resistance index	Resistance against which left ventricle must work to eject its volume; resistance is equal to pressure difference across a circuit divided by flow or cardiac output across that circuit; can be indexed by substituting cardiac index for cardiac output; clinically, represents ventricular afterload across systemic circulation: $SVR = ([MAP - CVP] \times 80)/CI$	To convert from Wood's units to units of force, use factor of 80 Normal, 800-1600 dyne · sec/cm⁻⁵/m²

Continued.

Table 133-1   Normal Values for Hemodynamic and Oxygenation Measurements and Derived Variables—cont'd

	Source	Value
Derived variables—cont'd		
Pulmonary vascular resistance	Represents right ventricular afterload across pulmonary circuit: $PVR = ([MPAP - PAoP] \times 80)/CI$	Normal, <250 dyne $\cdot$ sec/cm^{-5}/m^2
Stroke work (SW) and stroke work index	Represents external work during single ventricular contraction; average pressure generated by ventricle ($MAP - VEDP$) multiplied times stroke volume and conversion factor for converting pressure into work, which is 0.0136: $SW = SV [MAP - VEDP] \times 0.0136$	Normal, 45-75 g $\cdot$ m/m^2/beat
	LVEDP reflected by PAoP; value can also be indexed by BSA: $LVSWI = SVI [MAP - PAoP] \times 0.0136$	
	For right ventricle, average pressure generated by ventricle is $MPAP - CVP(MRAP)$: $RVSWI = SVI [MPAP - MRAP] \times 0.0136$	Normal, 5-10 g $\cdot$ m/m^2/beat
Oxygen delivery index (Do_2I)	Measure of global oxygen delivery to tissue beds; depends on adequate oxygenation, hemoglobin concentration, and cardiac output: $Do_2I = [Cao_2][CI][10]$; $Cao_2 =$ Arterial oxygen content $= [1.34][aHb][So_2] + [0.003][Pao_2]$	Normal, 570-670 ml/min/m^2
Oxygen consumption index (Vo_2I)	Represents amount of oxygen consumed globally by tissues; $Vo_2I = [Cao_2 - Cvo_2][CI]$; $Cvo_2 =$ Mixed venous oxygen content $= [1.34][mvHb][So_2] + [0.003][P_{mv}o_2]$	Normal, 120-200 ml/min/m$_2$
Arteriovenous oxygen content difference ($C[a-v]Do_2$)	Average amount of oxygen extracted per unit of blood volume; stable oxygen consumption inversely related to cardiac output: $avDo_2 = Cao_2 - Cvo_2$	Normal, 3.0-5.5 ml/dl
Oxygen utilization ratio (OUR) (or extraction ratio)	Amount of delivered oxygen consumed by tissues: $OUR = [Cao_2 - Cvo_2]/Cao_2$	Normal, 0.24-0.28
Venoarterial admixture (or intrapulmonary shunt fraction) ($\dot{Q}s/\dot{Q}t$)	Fraction of cardiac output not oxygenated during passage through lungs, resulting in right-to-left shunting: $\dot{Q}s/\dot{Q}t = [Cco_2 - Cao_2]/[Cco_2 - Cvo_2]$; $Cco_2 =$ Pulmonary end capillary O_2 content $= [1.34][aHb][1.0$ for $So_2] + [0.003][Pao_2]$; ($Pao_2 = [Fio_2][P_B - P_{H_2O}] - Paco_2/R$; $R =$ Respiratory quotient $= 0.8$	Normal, $>5\%$
Coronary artery perfusion pressure (CAPP)	Represents CAPP during diastole: $CAPP = DAP - PAoP$	Normal (adults), >40 mm Hg

to determine the mixed venous blood oxygen saturation (Svo_2). Transmitting and detecting fiberoptic filaments embedded in a distal lumen of a flow-directed pulmonary artery catheter are exposed to the pulmonary blood flow. Advantages of fiberoptic catheters are that they provide a measure of adequacy of signal and the reflected light intensity. The light intensity warns of catheter tip migration and validates the displayed Svo_2. The clinical value of continuous Svo_2 monitoring, however, is controversial.

The determinants of Svo_2 are arterial oxygen saturation (Sao_2), cardiac output, hemoglobin concentration, and oxygen consumption. When these are stable, continuous Svo_2 properly reflects cardiac output. The physiologic range for Sv_{O_2} is 65% to 80%. A decrease in Sv_{O_2} usually implies decreased Sa_{O_2} or cardiac output, development of relative anemia, or increased oxygen consumption. An increase in Sv_{O_2} may be difficult to interpret. Therapeutic interventions that lead to high Pa_{O_2} or pathologic and nonpathologic conditions that impair oxygen consumption (e.g., sepsis or anesthesia) or increase oxygen delivery (e.g., early hypermetabolic compensated septic shock, cirrhosis, or inotropic or vasoactive therapy) may be responsible for increased Sv_{O_2}.

A theoretical advantage of continuous Sv_{O_2} monitoring is that it provides continuous feedback for evaluation of therapeutic interventions. The theoretical disadvantages are that (1) cardiac output correlates poorly with Sv_{O_2} in clinical disorders in which there is dissociation between oxygen delivery and oxygen consumption, (2) a critical Sv_{O_2} level for specific organ dysfunction is not known, and (3) the accuracy of the technology itself is questioned. To date, no prospective, randomized studies in adult or pediatric patients clearly validate the use of continuous Sv_{O_2} monitoring.

There currently are no established indications for continuous Sv_{O_2} in pediatric patients. It seems logical to assume that some indications proposed in adult patients will apply to pediatric patients. The proposed indications for use in adults include diseases that affect oxygen transport and delivery (e.g., shock and other low cardiac output states), therapies or operative procedures in which oxygen transport or delivery may be affected (e.g., cardiac surgery, posttransplantation therapy, multiple organ system failure, SIRS, high mean airway pressure, or pentobarbital coma), and diseases in which oxygen use may be impaired (e.g., sepsis or ARDS).

TECHNIQUE

Various Sv_{O_2} catheters and monitors are available, including 7.5 and 8.5 F five-lumen catheters, 5.5 F four-lumen catheters, and a 4 F single-lumen catheter with oximetry. Most monitoring devices must be calibrated before insertion, and calibration must also be verified after insertion. (Insertion technique is described on p. 1238.) Recalibration is usually not necessary if the measured value from a pulmonary arterial sample is within 4% of the monitored Sv_{O_2} value. Continuing surveillance for catheter tip migration or wedging is necessary because appropriate placement of the catheter tip is essential to obtain accurate re-

sults. Signs of migration include diminished light intensity as displayed by the monitor, decreasing PAP waveform that may simulate a PAoP waveform, or increased or high Sv_{O_2} value.

RISKS AND COMPLICATIONS

The risks and complications from continuous Sv_{O_2} monitoring are similar to those with flow-directed pulmonary artery catheters. An additional theoretical concern is that therapeutic interventions will be made on the basis of inaccurately obtained data or uninterpretable numbers rather than physiologic applicability to the pathophysiologic process.

Left Atrial Catheterization
BACKGROUND AND INDICATIONS

Left atrial blood pressure reflects LVEDP when there is no mitral valve disease or aortic regurgitation. Open heart surgery increases pulmonary vascular resistance, thereby rendering PAoP a poor indicator of left atrial pressure. Mitral valve disease (regurgitation or stenosis) will also render PAoP inaccurate. Many thoracic surgeons prefer direct placement of a left atrial catheter during cardiac surgery to obtain a more reliable reflection of LVEDP.

TECHNIQUE

A polyurethane 16-gauge Sentinel single-lumen catheter is inserted through the chest or abdominal wall left of the midline, and an incision is made in the tip of the left atrial appendage. After insertion the catheter is secured to the atrium with a pursestring suture. By convention, left atrial catheters usually exit from the left side of the chest so as not to be confused with a similar surgically placed right atrial catheter on the right side.

Extreme care must be taken to maintain the catheter free of air bubbles because any air embolism to the systemic circulation has great potential for catastrophic complications.

Left atrial catheters are always set up with a 3 ml continuous-flush transducer and low-compliance tubing with a pressure bag for fluid delivery. Stopcocks are never placed in left atrial catheters to decrease the possibility of accidental disconnection or iatrogenic blood loss. Placing this system on a pump involves a much higher risk of air entering the system. A 0.9% or 0.45% sodium chloride heparinized (1 unit/ml) solution is infused through these catheters. The system must be cleared of all air bubbles before the left atrial catheter is attached.

RISKS AND COMPLICATIONS

Medication administration and blood sampling are not done through the left atrial catheter because this increases the likelihood of air embolism or clot formation, the two most common complications noted. In addition, bleeding from the atrial incision can complicate removal of the left atrial catheter. The mediastinal chest tube must not be removed until all surgically placed atrial catheters have been removed. If bleeding occurs at a rate of more than 3 ml/kg/hr, thoracotomy and insertion site repair must be considered. Inability to remove the left atrial catheter may result if the catheter becomes trapped by the suture at the atrial appendage or breaks below the skin level. In either case, a thoracotomy may be necessary to remove the catheter.

ADDITIONAL READING
Advanced Hemodynamic Monitoring

• Abou-Khalil B, Scalea TM, Trooskin SZ, Henry SM, Hitchcock R. Hemodynamic responses to shock in young trauma patients: Need for invasive monitoring. Crit Care Med 22:633-639, 1994.

Dalen JE. Bedside hemodynamic monitoring. N Engl J Med 301:1176-1178, 1979.

• Krovetz LJ, McLoughlin TG, Mitchell MB, Schiebler GL. Hemodynamic findings in normal children. Pediat Res 1:122-130, 1967.

• Saarela E, Kari A, Nikki P, Rauhala V, Iisalo E, Kaukinen L. Current practice regarding invasive monitoring in intensive care units in Finland. A nationwide study of the uses of arterial, pulmonary artery and central venous catheters and their effect on outcome. The Finnish Intensive Care Study Group. Intensive Care Med 17:264-271, 1991.

Stopfkuchen H. Hemodynamic monitoring in childhood. Intensive Care Med 15(Suppl 1):527-531, 1989.

Pulmonary Artery Catheterization

Colgan FJ, Stewart S. An assessment of cardiac output by thermodilution in infants and children following cardiac surgery. Crit Care Med 5:220-225, 1977.

Dean JM, Wetzel RC, Rogers MC. Arterial blood gas derived variables as estimates of intrapulmonary shunt in critically ill children. Crit Care Med 13:1029-1033, 1985.

Dhainault JF, Burnet F, Monsallier JF, Villemant D, Devaux JY, Konno M, DeGournay JM, Armaganidis A, Iotti G, Huyghebarert MF. Bedside evaluation of right ventricular performance using a rapid computerized thermodilution method. Crit Care Med 15:148-152, 1987.

• Eisenberg PR, Jaffe AS, Shuster DP. Clinical evaluation compared to pulmonary artery catheterization in the hemodynamic assessment of critically ill patients. Crit Care Med 12:549-553, 1984.

Fanconi S, Burger R. Measurement of cardiac output in children. Intensive Care World 9:8-12, 1992.

• Freed MD, Keane JF. Cardiac output measured by thermodilution in infants and children. J Pediatr 92:39-42, 1978.

• Ganz WW, Forrester JS, Chonette D, Donoso R, Swan J. A new flow-directed catheter technique for measurement of pulmonary artery and capillary wedge pressure without fluoroscopy. Am J Cardiol 25:96, 1970.

• Grabenkort W. A cardiopulmonary physiologic profile for use with the Swan-Ganz catheter. Resident Staff Physician 29(7):80-85, 1983.

• Hebert KA, Glancy DL. Indications for Swan-Ganz catheterization. Heart Dis Stroke 3:196-200, 1994.

• Iberti TJ, Fischer EP, Leibowitz AB, Panachek EA, Silverstein JH, Albertson TE. A multicenter study of physicians' knowledge of the pulmonary artery catheter. JAMA 264:2928-2932, 1990.

• Mimoz O, Rauss A, Rekik N, Brun-Buisson C, Lemaire F, Brochard L. Pulmonary artery catheterization in critically ill patients: A prospective analysis of outcome changes associated with catheter-prompted changes in therapy. Crit Care Med 22:573-579, 1994.

Morris AH, Chapman RH. Wedge pressure confirmation by aspiration of pulmonary capillary blood. Crit Care Med 13:756-759, 1985.

Morris AH, Chapman RH, Gardner RM. Frequency of wedge pressure errors in the ICU. Crit Care Med 13:705-708, 1985.

• Nadeau S, Noble WH. Misinterpretation of pressure measurements from the pulmonary artery catheter. Can Anaesth Soc J 33:352-363, 1986.

• O'Dwyer JP, King JE, Wod CE, Taylor BL, Smith GB. Continuous measurements of systemic vascular resistance. Anaesthesiology 49:587-590, 1994.

O'Malley K, Rhame FS, Cerra FB, McComb RC. Value of routine pressure monitoring system changes after 72 hours of continuous use. Crit Care Med 22:1424-1430, 1994.

Parlow JL, Milne B, Cervenko FW. Balloon flotation is more important than flow direction in determining the position of flow-directed pulmonary artery catheters. J Cardiothorac Vasc Anesth 6:20-23, 1992.

• Pollack MM, Reed TP, Holbrook PR, Fields AI. Bedside pulmonary artery catheterization in pediatrics. J Pediatr 96:274-276, 1980.

Quintana E, Sanchez JM, Serra C, Net A. Erroneous interpretation of pulmonary capillary wedge pressure in massive pulmonary embolism. Crit Care Med 11:933-935, 1983.

Raper R, Sibbald WJ. Misled by the wedge? The Swan-Ganz catheter and left ventricular preload. Chest 89:427-434, 1986.

• Steingrub JS, Celoria G, Vickers-Lahti M, Teres D, Bria W. Therapeutic impact of pulmonary artery catheterization in the medical/surgical ICU. Chest 99:1451-1455, 1991.

• Swan HJC, Ganz W. Use of balloon flotation catheters in critically ill patients. Surg Clin North Am 55:501-520, 1975.

• Swan HJC, Ganz W, Forrester J, Marcus H, Diamond G, Chonette D. Catheterization of the heart in man with use of a flow-directed balloon-tipped catheter. N Engl J Med 283:447-451, 1970.

Equipment

• Armagandis A, Dhainaut JF, Billard JL, Klouche K, Mira JP, Brunet F, Dinh-Xuan AT, Dall'Ava-Santucci J. Accuracy assessment for three fiberoptic pulmonary artery catheters for Svo₂ monitoring. Intensive Care Med 20:484-488, 1994.

• Bilen Z, Weinberg PF, Gowani Y, Cohen IL, Socaris S, Fein IA. Clinical utility and cost-effectiveness of protective sleeve pulmonary artery catheters. Crit Care Med 19:491-496, 1991.

• Bourland LM. Allometric determination of the distance from the central venous pressure port to wedge position of balloon-tip catheters in pediatric patients. Crit Care Med 14:974-976, 1986.

Colardyn F, Vandenbogaerde J, De Niel C, Jordaens L. Ventricular pacing via a Swan-Ganz catheter: A new mode of pacemaker therapy. Acta Cardiol 41:233-239, 1986.

Heard SO, Davis RF, Sherertz RJ, Mikhail MS, Gallagher RC, Layon J, Gallagher TJ. Influence of sterile protective sleeves on the sterility of pulmonary artery catheters. Crit Care Med 15:499-502, 1987.

Hecker BR, Brown DL, Wilson D. A comparison of two pulmonary artery mixed venous catheters during changing conditions of cardiac surgery. J Cardiothorac Anesth 3:269-275, 1989.

Ruiz BC, Tucker WK, Kirby RR. Laboratory report: A program for calculation of intrapulmonary shunts, blood-gas and acid-base values with a programmable calculator. Anesthesiology 42:88-95, 1975.

Simoos ML, Demey HE, Bossaert LL, Colordijn F, Essed CE. The paceport catheter: A new pacemaker system introduced through a Swan-Ganz catheter 15:66-70, 1988.

• Yonkman CA, Hamory BH. Sterility and efficiency of two methods of cardiac output determination: Closed loop and capped syringe method. Heart Lung 17:121-128, 1988.

Mixed Venous Oxygen Saturation

• Birman H, Haq A, Hew E, Aberman A. Continuous monitoring of mixed venous oxygen saturation in hemodynamically unstable patients. Chest 86:753-755, 1984.

Gettienger A. Mixed venous saturation: The puzzle is still incomplete. Chest 94:786-787, 1990.

Kandel G, Aberman A. Mixed venous oxygen saturation. Arch Intern Med 143:1400-1402, 1983.

Martin WE, Cheny PW, Johnson CC, Wong KC. Continuous monitoring of mixed venous oxygen saturation in man. Anesth Analg 52:784-793, 1973.

• Pier AF. Using mixed venous oxygen saturation data to trend overall oxygenation in cardiothoracic surgical patients. Crit Care Nurs Q 16:72-85, 1993.

Rouby JJ, Poète P, Bodin L, Bourgeois J, Arthaud M, Viars P. Three mixed venous saturation catheters in patients with circulatory shock and respiratory failure. Chest 98:954-958, 1990.

• Vaughn S, Puri VK. Cardiac output changes and continuous mixed venous oxygen saturation measurement in the critically ill. Crit Care Med 16:495-498, 1988.

Left Atrial Catheterization

• Leitman BS, Naidich DP, McGuinness G, McCauley DI. The left atrial catheter: Its uses and complications. Radiology 185:611-612, 1992.

Risks and Complications

• Benson J, Patla V. Real or apparent entrapment of a Swan-Ganz pulmonary artery catheter after cardiac surgery? Intensive Care Med 20:309-310, 1994.

Bernardin G, Milhaud D, Roger PM, Pouliquen G, Corcelle P, Mattei M. Swan-Ganz catheter-related pulmonary valve infective endocarditis: A case report. Intensive Care Med 20:142-144, 1994.

Cooper JP, Jackson J, Walker JM. False aneurysm of the pulmonary artery associated with cardiac catheterization. Br Heart J 69:188-190, 1993.

• Elliott CG, Zimmerman GA, Clemmer TP. Complications of pulmonary artery catheterization in the care of critically ill patients. Chest 76:647-652, 1979.

• Ewer MS, Ali MK, Gibbs HR, Swafford J. Nodus migrans: The case of the migrating knot. Am J Crit Care 1:108-110, 1992.

Fairfax WR, Thomas F, Orme JF. Pulmonary artery catheter occlusion as an indication of pulmonary embolus. Chest 86:270-271, 1984.

Feinberg BI, LaMantia KR, Addonizio P, Geer RT. Pulmonary artery catheter-associated thrombocytopenia: Effect of heparin coating. Mt Sinai J Med 54:147-149, 1987.

Greeno E, Parenti C. Pulmonary artery rupture from Swan-Ganz catheter insertion: Report of two cases [review]. Crit Care Nurs Q 15:71-74, 1992.

Mermel LA, McCormick RD, Springman SR, Maki DG. The pathogenesis and epidemiology of catheter-related infection with pulmonary artery Swan-Ganz catheters: A prospective study utilizing molecular subtyping. Am J Med 91:197S-205S, 1991.

Myers ML, Austin TW, Sibbald WJ. Pulmonary artery catheter infections. A prospective study. Ann Surg 201:237-241, 1985.

Nelson LD, Martinez OV, Anderson HB. Incidence of microbial colonization in open versus closed delivery systems for thermodilution injectate. Crit Care Med 14:291-293, 1986.

• Rello J, Coll P, Net A, Prats G. Infection of pulmonary artery catheters. Epidemiologic characteristics and multivariate analysis of risk factors [review]. Chest 103:132-136, 1993.

• Smith-Wright DL, Green TP, Lock JE, Egar MI, Fuhrman BP. Complications of vascular catheterization in critically ill children. Crit Care Med 12:1015-1017, 1984.

• Sise MJ, Hollingsworth P, Brimm JE, Peters RM, Virgilio RW, Shackford SR. Complications of the flow-directed pulmonary-artery catheter: A prospective analysis in 219 patients. Crit Care Med 9:315-318, 1981.

Thomson IR, Dalton BC, Lappas DG, Lowenstein E. Right bundle-branch block and complete heart block caused by the Swan-Ganz catheter. Anesthesiology 51:359-362, 1979.

Traeger SM. Failure to wedge and pulmonary hypertension during pulmonary artery catheterization: A sign of totally occlusive pulmonary embolism. Crit Care Med 13:544-547, 1985.

134 Intraosseous Infusions

Mary J. McDonald · Robert A. Wiebe

BACKGROUND AND INDICATIONS

In 1922 Drinker first described the anatomy of the bone marrow and suggested it could be used for infusion of blood products and other fluids. Tocantins is credited with demonstrating the rapid absorption of intraosseous injections and of popularizing this technique in the 1940s. A report by Heineld et al. demonstrated the safety and effectiveness of intraosseous infusions in almost 500 patients. Ninety-eight percent of these infusions were successful, and the only reported complication was subsequent osteomyelitis in five patients. Further refinements in technique and equipment led to increasing use of this procedure through the late 1950s. The technique gradually fell into obscurity in the late 1950s and throughout the next decade following the introduction of more sophisticated plastic intravenous cannulas and refinements in intravenous access techniques.

Intraosseous infusion enjoyed a resurgence of popularity after a report of its use in venography in 1977. Turkel and many others championed the use of intraosseous infusion in critically ill patients and documented the effectiveness of this technique, particularly in pediatric patients. Numerous studies demonstrated that this route could be used for infusion of many different medications and also allowed delivery of fluids at high flow rates with the use of pressure infusion devices. Over the last decade intraosseous infusions have been used effectively in prehospital, emergency department, PICU, and inpatient settings. This technique is now recognized as an important alternative in children when vascular access is imperative but in whom routine intravenous access is not feasible in a timely manner.

Intraosseous infusions are indicated in life-threatening situations in which intravascular access is essential for treatment and in which routine intravenous access is not readily obtainable. Pediatric applications of this technique have been widely used, perhaps be-cause of the inherent difficulty in establishing intravenous access in small children with correspondingly small veins. The procedure is also used in adults, both historically and currently; however, the increased density of adult bones makes the procedure technically more difficult. Common clinical indications for intraosseous access include cardiopulmonary arrest, shock, major trauma, extensive burns, status epilepticus, and overwhelming sepsis.

Because of the gravity of the typical situation in which intraosseous access is considered, there are relatively few absolute contraindications. Placement of the needle through an area of cellulitis or a burn is avoided if possible. Ipsilateral fractures, vascular injuries, or a previously unsuccessful attempt at intraosseous infusion in the same bone precludes reliable venous outflow. The risk of iatrogenic fractures is increased in osteogenesis imperfecta and osteoporosis. Dense bone associated with conditions such as erythroblastosis fetalis may make penetration of the bone more difficult.

TECHNIQUE
Equipment

Specially designed needles are available for intraosseous infusions. Commercially available needles include the Illinois sternoiliac bone marrow aspiration needle and the Jamshidi modified Illinois disposable sternoiliac aspiration needle (American Pharmaseal, Glendale Calif.), the Sur-Fast intraosseous needle (Cook Critical Care, Bloomington, Ind.), and the SAVE (sternal *access venous entry*) device (Biologix, Sausalito, Calif.). Spinal and bone marrow biopsy needles have been used previously and are still considered an acceptable alternative if other devices are not available. However, these needles have a longer shaft and are difficult to stabilize and easily dislodged. All of these devices are designed with a stylet to prevent occlusion of the needle with bone marrow. In children younger than 18 months

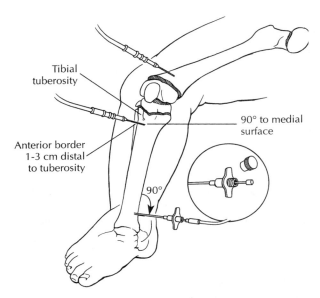

Fig. 134-1 Placement of intraosseous infusion needle in the medial malleolus. Inset shows removal of the obturator for attachment of the IV tubing for fluid administration.

16- to 20-gauge needles are recommended, and 12- to 16-gauge needles are suggested in older children and adults.

Procedure

The preferred site for intraosseous infusion in pediatric patients up to 5 years of age is the anteromedial aspect of the proximal tibia. This site is considered ideal because it is free from significant musculature and neurovascular structures and is anatomically easy to locate. After 5 years of age this site is less desirable because diffusion into the vascular spaces is diminished as a result of gradual replacement of the highly vascular red marrow by less vascular yellow marrow. Common alternative sites in pediatric patients include the distal tibia at the medial malleolus and the femur (Fig. 134-1). Other sites that have been used for children include the humerus, iliac crest, and sternum. The two sites recommended for use in adults are the sternum and the distal medial malleolus.

The proximal tibial site is located by palpating the tibial tuberosity and placing the needle 1 to 3 cm below this landmark on the flat anteromedial aspect of the bone. On the distal tibia the needle is inserted proximal to the medial malleolus. The access site on the femur may be more difficult to locate because of thick overlying muscle and soft tissue. If this site is used, the needle is inserted in a midline position on the lower third of the bone about 3 to 4 cm above the femoral condyle.

Once the site has been selected, the leg is restrained and the site cleaned with an antimicrobial solution. A sandbag placed behind the knee will aid in stabilization. If the patient is conscious and time permits, the skin and periosteum are infiltrated with a local anesthetic. The intraosseous needle is inserted with a boring or screwing motion until a decrease in resistance is felt. The use of the screwing motion decreases the chance of inadvertently bending the needle during insertion and decreases the risk of fracture. The angle of needle placement is 10 to 15 degrees from the vertical position when accessing either the proximal tibia or femur. To avoid damage to the epiphyseal plate, the needle needs to be directed caudally when using the proximal tibia, cephalad when using the femur, and vertically when accessing the distal tibia.

A sudden decrease in resistance is felt when the needle enters the bone marrow. If placement is correct, the needle will remain upright in the bone without support. The stylet is removed, and placement can usually be confirmed by aspiration of marrow. The needle is flushed with 0.9% sodium chloride solution and the site carefully observed for leakage. After placement is confirmed, the needle needs to be carefully secured with tape to prevent accidental dislodgment. Medications or fluids can be administered with a standard infusion pump or pressure infusion device. The intraosseous catheter is considered a short-term solution for vascular access, and a generally accepted guideline is that intraosseous infusions be limited to ≤12 hours. A more permanent venous access route can be established as soon as possible.

The intraosseous route can be used to infuse emergency medications and fluids at essentially the same dosage and rate as when given intravenously. Products that have been administered successfully are listed on p. 1251. It is recommended that strong alkaline and hypertonic solutions be diluted before infusion. Administration of a 0.9% sodium chloride solution flush after each medication will speed delivery to the systemic circulation.

The technique of intraosseous catheter insertion is considered relatively simple and easy to learn. Intraosseous needles have been successfully placed by

---

**MEDICINES AND FLUIDS ADMINISTERED
VIA INTRAOSSEOUS INFUSIONS**

Antibiotics	Insulin
Antitoxins	Isoproterenol
Atracurium besylate	Levarterenol
Atropine sulfate	Lidocaine
Calcium chloride	hydrochloride
Calcium gluconate	Lorazepam
Contrast media	Morphine
Colloids	Plasma
Dexamethasone	Phenytoin sodium
Dextran 40	Propranolol
Diazepam	hydrochloride
Diazoxide	Lactated Ringer's
Digoxin	solution
Dobutamine	Sodium bicarbonate
Dopamine	Suxamethonium
Epinephrine	chloride
Glucose	Succinylcholine
Heparin	chloride
Hypertonic saline	Thiopental sodium
solution	Whole blood

---

physicians, nurses, and paramedics with minimal technical training. Both Glaeser et al. and Anderson et al. demonstrated that a 1-hour standardized training session, including both lecture and skill practice on manikins, is enough to successfully train prehospital providers such as emergency medical technicians and paramedics in the procedure of intraosseous infusion. Both of these groups showed that proficiency was maintained over time (5 years and 1 year, respectively), with a success rate of almost 80% in actual field application.

RISKS AND COMPLICATIONS

Intraosseous infusions have long been considered a safe procedure with a relatively low prevalence of complications. Rosetti et al. reviewed 4270 cases and found a complication rate of less than 1%. Osteomyelitis was the most frequent complication, with an incidence of 0.6%. Recent reports substantiate that osteomyelitis continues to be a problem, although an infrequent one. Most cases are associated with prolonged infusions of several days' duration, placement of an intraosseous catheter in a patient with preexisting bacteremia, and infusion of hyper-

tonic solutions. Both bacterial and fungal infections have been documented.

Other complications of intraosseous infusions are unusual. However, recent case reports indicate that although serious complications are rare, they can have devastating consequences to the child. Moscati and Moore and Vidal et al. reported compartment syndrome after intraosseous infusions that necessitated amputation of the involved extremity. Other cases of compartment syndrome have required emergency fasciotomy; although none of these cases resulted in amputation, residual damage to the involved extremity was described. The exact mechanism leading to the development of compartment syndrome is unclear. Contributing factors may include prolonged infusion, multiple punctures into the same bone, incomplete penetration of the needle through the cortical bone, inadvertent puncture of the posterior cortex, accidental dislodgment of the needle during resuscitation, and use of pressure infusion devices. They key to prevention of compartment syndrome is meticulous attention to proper placement technique and diligent and frequent observation of the site to allow early recognition of early signs and symptoms. Early signs and symptoms may include edema, weakness and pain on passive stretch of muscles, hypoesthesia and tenseness of the fascial boundaries of the compartment, diminished pulses, and increased resistance to infusion. If this complication is suspected, compartment pressure needs to be measured. If pressures are >35 to 40 mm Hg, early surgical fasciotomy must be undertaken to preserve tissue perfusion.

Extravasation of fluids and drugs into the subcutaneous tissue is a common and usually benign complication. However, this may lead to tissue damage necessitating debridement and skin grafting. Many drugs associated with tissue necrosis are used during resuscitation, including epinephrine, potassium chloride, pressor agents, hypertonic glucose, calcium, and sodium bicarbonate. Care must be taken to ensure patency of the intraosseous catheter before infusion of medications.

Tibial fractures have been documented after intraosseous catheter placement. Symptoms include swelling of the lower leg and pain. Consideration needs to be given to obtaining radiographs routinely after intraosseous infusion attempts, particularly in infants, in whom fractures are difficult to detect clinically. The use of smaller needles (18 to 20 gauge) and a gentle rotating motion during needle insertion may help to decrease the risk of fracture in infants.

Awareness of the potential risks and use of appropriate precautions will decrease the incidence of problems and provide early recognition of complications. The following strategies are recommended:

1. Use sharp needles of appropriate gauge to decrease the pressure necessary for cortical perforation.
2. Emphasize a rotary, screwing motion during placement, with gentle but firm downward pressure.
3. Stabilize the tubing and splint the involved limb to prevent accidental dislodgment.
4. Avoid use of dressings on the site that can obscure visualization of fluid extravasation.
5. Assess the site continuously for signs of extravasation, leaking, swelling, or pain.
6. Measure the leg circumference at least hourly during prolonged infusions.
7. Set a low pressure limit on the infusion pump whenever possible to allow early recognition of increased resistance.
8. Check the catheter carefully for patency before infusing medications known to cause tissue irritation. Patency can be evaluated by flushing the catheter with 0.9% sodium chloride solution or by aspiration of bone marrow.
9. Consider obtaining radiographs to rule out fracture and evaluate the limb if displacement of the needle into the soft tissue is suspected.
10. Remove the catheter within 12 hours to prevent development of osteomyelitis.

CURRENT RESEARCH AND FUTURE CONSIDERATIONS

In animal studies infusion rates differed substantially between vascular access sites. The highest infusion rate was obtained in a peripheral venous access site followed in descending order in the humerus, femur, malleolus, and tibia. Additional studies would help to determine whether these findings have clinical significance in humans and if perhaps the malleolus or the distal femur is the preferred site in young infants.

Although case reports offer excellent insight into the potential problems associated with intraosseous infusion, prospective studies are needed to evaluate the actual incidence of problems and to help clarify the most common and important complications. Additional refinements in equipment and techniques may also help to decrease complications.

ADDITIONAL READING

Anderson TE, Arthur K, Kleinman M, Drawbaugh R, Eitel DR, Ogden CS, Baker D. Intraosseous infusion: Success of a standardized regional training program for prehospital advanced life support providers. Ann Emerg Med 23:52-55, 1994.

Barron BJ, Tran HD, Lamki L. Scintigraphic findings of osteomyelitis after intraosseous infusion in a child. Clin Nucl Med 19:307-308, 1994.

Begg AC. Intraosseous venography of the lower limb and pelvis. Br J Radiol 27:318-324, 1954.

Burke T, Kehl DK. Intraosseous infusion in infants. J Bone Joint Surg 75A:428-429, 1993.

Chameides L, Hazinski M. Textbook of Pediatric Advanced Life Support. Chicago: American Heart Association, 1994.

Drinker CK. Drinker KR, Lund CC. The circulation in the mammalian bone marrow. Am J Physiol 62:1-92, 1922.

• Evans RJ, McCabe M, Thomas R. Intraosseous infusion. Br J Hosp Med 51:161-164, 1994.

Galpin RD, Kronick JB, Willis RB, Frewen TC. Bilateral lower extremity compartment syndromes secondary to intraosseous fluid resuscitation. J Pediatr Orthop 11:773-776, 1991.

• Glaeser PW, Hellmich TR, Szewczuga D, Losek JD, Smith DS. Five year experience in prehospital intraosseous infusions in children and adults. Ann Emerg Med 22:1119-1124, 1993.

Glaeser PW, Losek JD. Emergency intraosseous infusions in children. Am J Emerg Med 4:34-36, 1986.

Heinild S, Sondergaard T, Tudvad F. Bone marrow infusion in childhood: Experiences from a thousand infusions. J Pediatr 30:400-412, 1947.

Katz DS, Wojtowycz AR. Tibial fracture: A complication of intraosseous infusion. Am J Emerg Med 12:258-259, 1994.

• McNamara RM, Spivey WH, Unger HD, Malone DR. Emergency applications of intraosseous infusion. J Emerg Med 5:97-101, 1987.

Moscati R, Moore GP. Compartment syndrome with resultant amputation following intraosseous infusion. Am J Emerg Med 8:470-471, 1990.

Platt SL, Notterman DA, Winchester P. Fungal osteomyelitis and sepsis from intraosseous infusion. Pediatr Emerg Care 9:149-150, 1993.

Ponaman ML, White L. Intraosseous infusions. In Levin D, Morriss F, eds. Essentials of Pediatric Critical Care. St. Louis: Quality Medical Publishers, 1990, pp 845-848.

Ribeiro JA, Price CT, Knapp R. Compartment syndrome of the lower extremity after intraosseous infusion of fluid. J Bone Joint Surg 75A:430-433, 1993.

Rosetti VA, Thompson BM, Miller J, Aprahamian C. Intraosseous infusion: An alternative route of pediatric intravascular access. Ann Emerg Med 14:885-888, 1985.

• Sawyer RW, Bodai BI, Blaisdell FW, McCourt MM. The current status of intraosseous infusion. J Am Coll Surg 179:353-360, 1994.

Shoor PM, Berryhill RE, Benumof JL. Intraosseous infusions: Pressure-flow relationships and pharmacokinetics. J Trauma 19:772-774, 1979.

Simmons CM, Johnson NE, Perkin RM, Stralen DV. Intraosseous extravasation complication reports. Ann Emerg Med 23:363-366, 1994.

Spivey WH. Intraosseous infusion. In Roberts J, Hedge J, eds. Clinical Procedures in Emergency Medicine, 2nd ed. Philadelphia: WB Saunders, 1991.

Tocantins LM, O'Neill JF, Jones HW. Infusions of blood and other fluids via the bone marrow: Applications in pediatrics. JAMA 117:1229-1234, 1941.

Turkel H. Intraosseous infusion [editorial] Am J Dis Child 137:706, 1983.

Vidal R, Kissoon N, Gayle M. Compartment syndrome following intraosseous infusion. Pediatrics 91:1201-1202, 1993.

• Warren DW, Kissoon N, Sommerauer JF, Rieder MJ. Comparison of fluid infusion rates among peripheral intravenous and humerus, femur, malleolus and tibial intraosseous sites in normovolemic and hypovolemic piglets. Ann Emerg Med 22:183-186, 1993.

Wright R, Reynolds SL, Nachtsheim B. Compartment syndrome secondary to prolonged intraosseous infusion. Pediatr Emerg Care 10:157-159, 1994.

• Zenk KE. Use of intraosseous infusions in infants and children. Clin Pharm 9:90-91, 1990.

135 Jugular Bulb Monitoring

Derek A. Bruce · Dale M. Swift

BACKGROUND AND INDICATIONS

Preservation of brain function is one of the most important aims of PICU care. Many disease processes that necessitate multisystem support in the PICU can produce potentially fatal injury to the brain. If the patient survives, quality of life is often predicated on the presence or absence of brain injury. Methods of monitoring the adequacy of major substrates to the brain are limited; systemic arterial pressure, ICP, arterial blood gas levels and pH, blood metabolites, and electroencephalographic findings are the most frequently measured variables. Measurements of cerebral blood flow (CBF) are possible but are available in only a few research-oriented units. They are cumbersome to perform because there is no simple on-line system for repeated CBF studies. Methods available include cold xenon scanning and CT, radioactive xenon and external detectors, nitrous oxide inhalation with arterial and jugular venous blood samples, positron emission tomography (PET), single photon emission CT, and focal techniques such as local heat clearance in which the probe must be in contact with the cerebral tissue. Transit time of cerebral blood, velocity of flow, and implied resistance can be obtained from transcranial Doppler measurements.

Measurement of cerebral rates of metabolism have been made, usually in conjunction with CBF measurements using PET or one of the other techniques accompanied by arterial and jugular bulb blood sampling. A considerable body of data has been generated, mainly in adults, on the reliability and value of intermittent jugular venous blood sampling for measurement of cerebral uptake of oxygen and glucose plus cerebral output of lactate. Current technology makes it possible to obtain continuous oxygen saturation measurements from the jugular bulb. These correlate well with jugular Pa_{O_2} content and have the advantage that blood does not have to be drawn.

Patient Selection

Any child in whom there is significant concern about whether the supply of oxygen and glucose to the brain is adequate for the level of brain metabolism is a potential candidate for jugular bulb catheterization and monitoring of the arteriovenous difference of oxygen, glucose, and possibly pyruvate and lactate metabolism. These measurements are always accompanied by the current routine monitoring of ICP, mean arterial pressure (MAP), Pa_{O_2}, Sa_{O_2}, and Pa_{CO_2}. Ideally, CBF is measured at the time of the initial transbrain measurement of metabolite difference to establish true metabolic rate. Without this information it is difficult to infer the cause of any changes in the measured arteriovenous differences. Transcranial Doppler ultrasound, while not providing a direct measurement of flow, does supply useful information about the state of the cerebral circulation and is an acceptable substitute for true CBF measurement. In practice this technique has been used most frequently in patients with traumatic brain injury and increased ICP. The technique of measurement of arteriojugular oxygen differences can be helpful even in the absence of CBF measurements, but interpretation of any changes is more difficult.

Pathophysiology

The local rate of cerebral metabolism controls the local CBF in different areas of the brain. The delivery of substrate for metabolism, primarily oxygen and glucose, is through the CBF. CBF normally exhibits pressure autoregulation. This is the ability to maintain constant flow despite changes in cerebral perfusion pressure (CPP). CPP is the driving force for perfusion of the brain by blood and clinically is approximated by MAP minus mean ICP:

$$CPP = MAP - ICP$$

Poiseiulle's law has been used to approximate factors that control CBF:

$$CBF = \frac{\pi R^4 (MAP - ICP)}{8\theta l}$$

where R = arteriolar radius, θ = blood viscosity, and l = length of vascular bed. The two most important factors in control of CBF are arteriolar radius and CPP. CBF is constant, if pressure autoregulation is intact, between CPP of 55 to 60 and 170 mm Hg in adults. Recent studies in adults who had sustained head injury suggest that CBF may fall at CPP as high as 70 mm Hg. The exact values in children are unknown and almost certainly vary with age; in the newborn, normal CPP is

$$CPP = 50 - 5 = 45 \text{ mm Hg}$$

The upper limits in children are not known. Suffice it to say that the delivery of oxygen and glucose to the brain is maintained despite variations in ICP and MAP to some value of CPP, after which CBF starts to fall. Despite a decrease in CBF the delivery of oxygen and glucose to the brain is still preserved by increased extraction of substrate from blood. The amount of oxygen extracted from the blood can be increased as CBF falls until Pv_{O_2} has decreased to >20 to 23 mm Hg, after which there may be decreased oxygen in the brain tissues with resultant metabolic disturbance. When the patient's lungs are being hyperventilated, the oxyhemoglobin dissociation curve is displaced to the left, making it harder for oxygen to be released at the blood tissue interface. This might result in an apparently adequate Pv_{O_2} but inadequate tissue oxygen content. Whether this changes the level of Pv_{O_2} at which potential tissue ischemia may result is not known. Glucose extraction is maintained to low blood glucose levels by facilitated transport of glucose from the blood to the brain, and except when there is severe hypoglycemia or extremely low CBF, delivery of glucose to cerebral tissue is rarely impaired. In most human and animal studies CBF can decrease to approximately 20% to 25% of normal before infarction results.

The cerebral circulation has excellent homeostat-ic mechanisms to ensure adequate supply of oxygen and glucose to the brain under normal and pathologic circumstances; after trauma, hypoxia, ischemia, or infection, however, the pressure autoregulatory mechanism can be impaired such that alterations in CPP either by increasing ICP or lowering MAP can result in increases or decreases in CBF within the normal range of presumed pressure autoregulation (defective autoregulation). The reason for cerebral monitoring is to identify deleterious changes in the variables most important in controlling delivery of substrate to the brain and if possible to maintain them in the normal range or restore them to normal values as soon as a significant change occurs. These variables are CBF, MAP, ICP, CPP, and metabolic rate. MAP, ICP, and CPP are the simplest and most frequently monitored. CBF and cerebral metabolism are rarely measured. The clinical dilemma is that the level of CPP necessary in any given child is unknown because cerebral metabolic rate is not known; neither therefore is the required delivery of substrate or the state of pressure autoregulation and the appropriate CBF. In the PICU an effort is made to maintain ICP <20 mm Hg and MAP just above the mean for age so that CPP is above the estimated normal for age. Current arguments differ as to whether ICP, MAP, or CPP is the most important value. In children data are inadequate to answer that question, and monitoring of the jugular bulb oxygen levels and cross-brain oxygen extraction have been proposed as methods to increase the knowledge of the relationship between the delivery of substrate to the brain and its use. The assumption is that the more information available, the better the therapy that can be delivered.

The jugular bulb sits at the base of the brain immediately outside the jugular foramen and is the point of exit of the blood draining most of the cerebral hemispheres. In most children the right jugular vein is dominant and therefore is usually the one chosen for cannulation. It has been estimated that only 2% to 3% of the blood in the jugular bulb is from extracranial sources. This is not necessarily true when CBF is low or when suction is placed on the catheter in the jugular bulb, and the error is likely maximal when these conditions coexist. The normal arterio-jugular difference for oxygen (AJD_{O_2}) is 4 to 9 vol%; thus a level <4 vol% is a possible indicator of hyperemia, and levels >10 vol% may indicate ischemia.

The absolute level of jugular bulb P_{O_2} that may represent inadequate oxygen delivery is 20 to 23 mm Hg. Current methods allow continuous measurement of jugular venous oxygen saturation. The lower limit of normal is in dispute but generally is considered to be ≤50%.

The relationship between the arteriojugular differences (AJD), CBF, and cerebral metabolic rate (CMR) is as follows:

$$CMR = AJD \times CBF \div 100$$

$$AJD = CMR \div CBF \times 100$$

The arteriojugular difference is a measure of the balance between cerebral metabolism and cerebral substrate delivery. If the cerebral metabolism remains constant, any changes in arteriojugular difference reflect changes in either cerebral perfusion or systemic variables such as Pa_{O_2} or Pa_{CO_2}. After traumatic injuries the cerebral metabolic rate for oxygen (CMR_{O_2}) has been reported to be stable after 24 hours; therefore changes in AJD_{O_2} can be assumed to be due to changes in cerebral perfusion if the blood gas levels remain constant. Thus AJD_{O_2} or jugular oxygen saturation (Sjv_{O_2}) can serve as an objective measure to help decide which therapy is likely to be of most value when the implied perfusion changes. Decreased AJD_{O_2} or increased Sjv_{O_2} suggests an excess of flow over metabolism, and increased hyperventilation may be the best therapy to match the flow to metabolism or lower ICP if elevated. If AJD_{O_2} increases or Sjv_{O_2} decreases, lowered perfusion with possibly inadequate delivery of substrate for current metabolism may be occurring and suggests the best therapy is to manipulate CPP by either decreasing ICP or increasing MAP or both. The other alternative is to decrease metabolic requirements.

If metabolism is not stable, measurements of CBF are needed to clarify what is occurring because an increase in metabolism (e.g., a seizure) could increase AJD_{O_2} or decrease Sjv_{O_2} without the balance between perfusion and metabolism having changed. The literature contains many reported episodes of changes in AJD_{O_2} without a clear cause, although as many as 70% can be directly related to changes in Pa_{CO_2}, arterial pressure, or ICP. In addition, it is certain that not all episodes of ischemia are reflected by AJD_{O_2} or Sjv_{O_2}. Certainly local ischemia may well be overlooked if the contribution of venous blood from that area to the total jugular bulb volume is low. The use of transcranial Doppler measurements in conjunction with jugular values can help interprete the changes. Many episodes of change are associated with systemic changes (e.g., decrease in Pa_{O_2}, Pa_{CO_2}, or MAP). The distribution of cerebral venous blood into the two jugular veins is variable from person to person, and it is important to understand that a change in jugular oxygenation is only one measure of the ongoing intracranial events that must be viewed in context with other monitors and findings at clinical examination. These limitations aside, the continuous measurement of jugular venous oxygen content is likely to be a valuable adjunct in treatment of children with increased ICP and disturbed intracranial homeostasis.

Measurements of other aspects of cerebral metabolism including glucose, pyruvate, and lactate, can be made with intermittent arterial and jugular venous sampling. These values, however, show greater errors in measurement, and the handling of samples is more complex. The cerebral metabolic rate of glucose can be measured fairly easily and compared with CMR_{O_2} to produce an oxygen-glucose index as a relative measure of aerobic metabolism. Cerebral metabolic rates of pyruvate and lactate are less reliable indicators of metabolism because local intracellular pH can affect the enzymes that control glycolysis, and the relative blood-brain barrier permeability of pyruvate is better than that of lactate. There has been a proposed direct relationship between ischemia and decreased oxygen glucose ratio, that is, increased anaerobic metabolism and increased CBF as measured by increased Sjv_{O_2}.

Therapy

In association with ICP and MAP, alterations in AJD_{O_2} or Sjv_{O_2} can be used to select appropriate therapy to manipulate the inferred relationship between cerebral metabolic rate and CBF. If the systemic arterial blood gas levels are unchanged and AJD_{O_2} increases or Sjv_{O_2} decreases without evidence of seizure activity, MAP and ICP must be evaluated. If MAP has fallen, an increase in MAP may restore the cerebral circulation. If the ICP has risen, therapy to lower ICP without lowering CBF is important (e.g., mannitol or less hyperventilation). The other therapeutic option is to lower the metabolism (e.g., with barbiturate). Decreased AJD_{O_2} or increased Sjv_{O_2} occurring with increased ICP suggests vasodilatation in response to decreased CPP or autoregulation, and in this setting decreasing ICP by decreasing CBF and cerebral blood

Table 135-1 Possible Alterations in ICP, MAP, $AJDo_2$, and by Inference CBF, and Suggested Therapy

ICP	MAP	$AJDo_2$	CBF	Therapy	Metabolism
+	0	−	+	Lower $Paco_2$	0
−	+	−	+	Lower $Paco_2$, lower MAP	0
+	+	No change	No change	No therapy, lower ICP	
+	0	+	−	Lower ICP, raise $Paco_2$	Decrease
+	−	+	−	Lower ICP, raise MAP	Decrease
−	−	+	−	Raise MAP, raise $Paco_2$	Decrease

volume is appropriate. This is achieved by lowering $Paco_2$. Thus, with the additional information from the jugular oxygen catheter, more selective therapeutic decisions can be made as to which of the variables making up CPP needs to be changed and whether drugs that lower metabolic rate might be appropriate therapy (Table 135-1).

Additional monitoring with transcranial Doppler ultrasound and more recently with near-infrared spectroscopy has been evaluated to try to further improve the identification of cerebral tissue ischemia at the earliest possible time and thus permit early intervention to improve the relationship between CBF and cerebral metabolic rate.

TECHNIQUE

The internal jugular vein runs parallel and immediately lateral to the common and then the internal carotid artery in the neck, and its course is from the mastoid eminence to a point just lateral to the sternoclavicular joint. A short beveled needle with a guidewire and catheter are necessary for cannulation. In general a 20-gauge needle is adequate. Many techniques can be used to cannulate the vein. The simplest is to turn the neck to the opposite side and place a small roll under the neck. It is helpful to lower the head, but this may have to be limited if ICP rises with this position change. A point is selected approximately halfway between the mastoid tip and the sternoclavicular joint overlying the sternomastoid muscle. The pulsations of the carotid artery are noted and a point just lateral to the pulsations is selected. A short beveled needle on a syringe is aimed superiorly at an angle of about 30 degrees to the skin. With gentle aspiration on the syringe, the point of the needle is deepened until blood is obtained. It is usually obvious whether this is venous or arterial blood,

but if there is any question, the syringe can be disconnected and the flow of blood observed. If the artery has been punctured, the blood flow will be pulsatile. If this occurs, the needle is withdrawn and *gentle* pressure placed over the artery for a few minutes (about 4) to prevent a hematoma. Another attempt at cannulation can be made slightly more lateral to the carotid pulsation. Once venous blood is obtained, the syringe is removed and the guidewire placed into the vein in a cephalad direction. A sheath can be passed over the guidewire and a cannula placed. In small children it rarely is necessary to use a sheath. The catheter is inserted over the wire until resistance is felt, usually at the jugular bulb. The wire is removed and blood aspirated to ensure patency, and the catheter is connected to a transducer with low-compliance tubing filled with sodium chloride solution. A continuous flush is set up to deliver 1 ml/hr of 0.9% sodium chloride solution containing 1 unit of heparin per milliliter of solution. It is helpful to transduce the waveform and record the pressure required to flush because this visual and pressure record helps forewarn of impending occlusion. Once the catheter is in place, a lateral radiograph of the neck, including the base of the skull, is needed to check the location of the catheter. The catheter must be fixed with a suture at the skin so that it cannot be accidentally dislodged. If there are changes in $AJDo_2$ or $Sjvo_2$ values after a period of stability, especially if the difference decreases, it is important to recognize that this may be because the catheter tip is no longer in the jugular bulb. A repeat radiograph needs to be obtained to check the position.

RISKS AND COMPLICATIONS

Most risks are from bleeding and vessel trauma during catheter insertion. Once the catheter is in place, reported complications are rare and the catheter may be left as long as necessary, certainly up to a week or more. When the catheter is removed, it is necessary to apply pressure to the vein for 5 minutes.

ADDITIONAL READING

Andrews PJD, Dearden NM, Miller JD. Jugular bulb cannulation: Description of a cannulation technique and validation of a new continuous monitor. Br J Anaesth 67:553-558, 1991.

• Chan KH, Miller JD, Dearden NW, et al. The effect of changes in cerebral perfusion pressure upon middle cerebral artery blood flow velocity and jugular bulb venous oxygen saturation after severe brain trauma. J Neurosurg 77:55-61, 1992.

• Cruz J. Continuous versus serial global hemodynamic monitoring: Applications in acute brain trauma. Acta Neurochir 42(Suppl):35-39, 1988.

Cruz J. Contamination of jugular bulb venous oxygen measurements. J Neurosurg 77:975-976, 1992.

• Cruz J, Miner ME, Allen SJ, et al. Continuous monitoring of cerebral oxygenation in acute brain injury: Injection of mannitol during hyperventilation. J Neurosurg 73:725-730, 1990.

• Fortune JB, Feustal PJ, Weigle CGM, et al. Continuous measurement of jugular venous oxygen saturation in response to transient elevation of blood pressure in head injured patients. J Neurosurg 80:461-468, 1994.

Kirkpatrick PJ, Smielewski P, Czosnyka M, et al. Near-infrared spectroscopy use in patients with head injury. J Neurosurg 83:963-970, 1995.

Lewis SB, Myburgh JA, Reilly PL. Detection of cerebral venous desaturation by continuous jugular bulb oximetry following acute neurotrauma. Anaesth Intensive Care 23:307-314, 1995.

Matta BF, Lam AM, Maygerg TS. The influence of arterial saturation on cerebral venous oxygen saturation during hyperventilation. Can J Anaesth 41:1041-1046, 1994.

Moss E, Dearden NM, Berridge JC. Effects of changes in mean arterial pressure on Sjo_2 during cerebral aneurysm surgery. Br J Anaesth 75:527-530, 1995.

• Robertson C, Narayan RK, Gokaslan ZL, et al. Cerebral arteriovenous oxygen difference as an estimate of cerebral blood flow in comatose patients. J Neurosurg 70:222-230, 1989.

Schneider GH, von Helden A, Lanksch WR, et al. Continuous monitoring of jugular bulb oxygen saturation in comatose patients—Therapeutic implications. Acta Neurochir (Wein) 134:71-75, 1995.

Sheinberg M, Kanter MJ, Robertson CJ, et al. Continuous monitoring of jugular venous oxygen saturation in head injured patients. J Neurosurg 76:212-217, 1992.

Stocchetti N, Paparella A, Bridelli, F, et al. Cerebral venous oxygen saturation studied with bilateral samples in the internal jugular veins. Neurosurgery 34:38-44, 1994.

Sutton LN, McLaughlin AC, Dante S, et al. Cerebral venous oxygen content as a measure of brain energy metabolism with increased intracranial pressure and hyperventilation. J Neurosurg 73:927-932, 1990.

Yoxall CW, Weindling AM, Dawani NH, et al. Measurement of cerebral venous oxyhemoglobin in children by near-infrared spectroscopy and partial jugular venous occlusion. Pediatr Res 38:319-323, 1995.

XVIII
Neurology and Neurosurgical Devices

136 Intracranial Pressure Monitoring

Cole A. Giller · Frederick H. Sklar

BACKGROUND AND INDICATIONS

An understanding of the methods of monitoring ICP is a prerequisite for detection and treatment of PICU patients with intracranial hypertension. A variety of ICP monitoring systems are available to the clinician: some are reliable, most are invasive, and none is perfect. Noninvasive techniques are also used and range from palpating the fontanel to sophisticated Doppler evaluation. In this chapter techniques and problems related to the most commonly used ICP monitoring devices will be discussed.

ICP monitoring may be important in the PICU care of children with presumed intracranial hypertension as a result of head trauma, hydrocephalus, cerebral tumor, and metabolic disorders. For example, marked elevation of ICP can occur after head trauma, and use of pressure monitoring guides ICP reduction therapy. Changes in pressure measurements may suggest development of an expanding hematoma. A reasonable guideline for treatment of trauma is to monitor those patients whose mental status is less than purposeful and those who need tracheal intubation. Because cerebral edema and ventricular effacement are frequent CT findings after trauma, ventricular puncture may be difficult.

Hydrocephalus occasionally produces rapid and potentially life-threatening elevation of ICP. Monitoring by ventriculostomy can document pressure changes, and CSF drainage will bring pressure back into safe ranges. Similarly, monitoring intracranial tumors can provide warnings of increasing edema, hem-

orrhage, or hydrocephalus. ICP is sometimes elevated in children with craniosynostosis and, if detected, may alter the surgical strategy. Disorders such as metabolic disturbances, Reye's syndrome, and lead intoxication can result in cerebral edema, and ICP monitoring can guide intensive pressure reduction therapy.

TECHNIQUE
Ventriculostomy

The standard technique for monitoring ICP is ventriculostomy. A fluid-filled catheter is positioned within a ventricle, and pressure is monitored with a transducer.

Procedure (Fig. 136-1)

The patient is sedated if necessary and placed supine with the head in neutral position. The nondominant right side is usually chosen for catheter insertion. The scalp is shaved, prepared, and draped with sterile towels. The skin is generously infiltrated with lidocaine in the midpupillary line at the coronal suture.

In infants it is sometimes easier and safer to make the twist drill hole just anterior to the coronal suture or fontanel rather than attempt to pass a catheter through the suture of fibrous fontanel. In this way the rigid skull stabilizes the ventriculostomy catheter.

A 4 mm transverse skin incision is made. In older children the incision is continued through the periosteum, and a twist drill hole is made while the drill

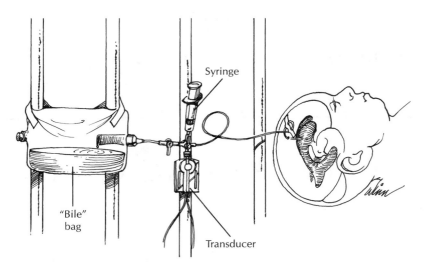

Syringe

"Bile"
bag

Transducer

Fig. 136-1 Standard apparatus for ICP monitoring and CSF drainage at ventriculostomy.

is firmly supported to avoid accidental penetration of the dura and brain. Some twist drill devices have adjustable safety stops. In infants the skull may be very thin, and gentle rotatory pressure with a hand-held drill bit may suffice to create a hole.

The dura is penetrated several times with an 18-gauge needle, and the subdural space is checked for fluid. A ventriculostomy catheter fitted with a stylet is introduced through the twist drill hole and directed toward the medial canthus of the ipsilateral eye while the catheter is held perpendicular to the skull. A gentle "pop" is often felt as the catheter punctures the ependymal surface of the ventricle. These landmarks are meant only as estimates for the surgeon to use while guiding the catheter into the frontal horn. It may be more appropriate to visualize the ventricular system in relation to the coronal suture and to aim appropriately. CT is helpful in case of ventricular shift or effacement.

Alternative procedure

In an alternative technique, a No. 14 or No. 16 Cone needle is introduced into the frontal horn. The needle is removed and replaced with a No. 5 pediatric feeding tube filled with 0.9% sodium chloride solution. The tube is slowly threaded into the frontal horn along the needle tract. Tapping the ventricle first with a Cone needle is sometimes easier, especially when the ventricles are small.

CSF will flow from the catheter if the ventricle has been successfully cannulated, although flow may be nearly absent if the ventricles are small or the pressure is low. Nevertheless, the fluid in the catheter must pulsate and flow freely into the ventricle when the distal end of the catheter is elevated. A stopcock is attached, with ports connecting to a pressure transducer and drainage bag. The catheter is secured to the scalp with sutures, and a sterile occlusive dressing is applied (see Fig. 136-1).

Use

ICP may be monitored with the transducer at the level of the foramen of Monro. The stopcock can be used to drain CSF intermittently. Alternatively, CSF can be drained continuously; pressure can be regulated by the height of the drainage bag or the in-line valve to the bag available in some systems. The bag must be drained when full and sampled for cell counts or culture when clinically indicated. CSF drainage may not be possible if the ventricles are small because the ventricular walls may collapse around the tube and occlude the catheter. Pressure readings are not accurate if fluid is draining while the readings are being made.

Technical difficulties

Small ventricles may be difficult to cannulate. Visible CSF pulsations within the catheter or a pulsatile waveform may be the only evidence of successful puncture.

The ICP waveform may become dampened at any time, and flow of CSF may decrease, indicating either a decrease in ICP or an obstructed system. Application of light pressure over a jugular vein usually will elevate ICP if it is decreased and may help to distinguish the two situations. Small volumes (0.1 to 0.2 ml) of 0.9% sodium chloride solution (without preservative) may be used to flush the catheter. An improved waveform that rapidly damps indicates an intraparenchymal position of the catheter tip or a collapsed ventricular system. Finally, a CT scan can confirm catheter position. All tubing must be checked for patency and kinking. The proper position of the drainage bag must be determined at catheter insertion to ensure consistency when draining the system.

When replacing ventriculostomy catheters, removal of the used catheter before introducing the new one permits untoward CSF leakage, possibly making retapping the ventricle difficult or impossible. Accordingly, the new catheter must be placed before the old one is removed.

Risks and complications

The infection rate for intraventricular catheterization is 3% to 5% and remains low as long as the catheter is replaced every 4 or 5 days. Meticulous attention to aseptic insertion and occlusive dressing can lower the infection rate farther. The most common infection is ventriculitis. The new catheter is generally positioned on the opposite side. Some surgeons tunnel the catheter under the scalp a considerable distance from the twist drill hole and insist that this procedure protects against infection and decreases the urgency to change ventriculostomy catheters. Prophylactic antibiotic therapy is not used. Scalp IV catheters are contraindicated because of increased risk of local infection.

The risk of intracranial hemorrhage during insertion is <2%. Anticoagulation and untreated coagulopathies are contraindications to invasive ICP monitoring. The occasional CSF leak is easily stopped with either a suture or a collodion-soaked cotton ball.

Intraparenchymal Recordings

In the last decade thin fiberoptic probes have been developed that allow pressure measurements directly from cerebral tissue without the inconvenience of a fluid-filled system. These devices rely on measurement of deviation of a pressure-sensitive diaphragm and yield measurements that compare favorably with those obtained with ventriculostomy. The probe itself is thin and flexible, causing little morbidity because it is placed directly into cerebral tissue or, if desired, the ventricles. Because use of these catheters does not necessitate ventricular puncture, they are not prone to produce obstruction or ventricular collapse. These systems are technically easier to insert and maintain than ventricular catheters, and concern about significant signal or baseline drift over several days has been alleviated with design changes. CSF drainage is not possible with these fiberoptic devices.

Procedure

A twist drill hole is made with a bit supplied in the kit. The drill allows adjustment for pediatric skull thickness. A hollow metal connector is screwed firmly into the hole, and a probe is used to pierce the dura. The fiberoptic tube is calibrated and passed through the connector into the brain tissue to a depth of 2 to 3 cm and withdrawn 1 mm. A connection hub connects over the catheter to seat it in place. An ICP waveform is generally apparent on the monitor.

Use

Flushing and recalibration are not necessary. Care must be taken not to bend or break the fiberoptic catheter.

Risks and complications

Complications are the same as for ventriculostomy except for a lower incidence of ventriculitis. However, insertion of both these devices and ventriculostomy catheters is associated with a high risk of hemorrhage in the setting of hepatic failure and secondary coagulopathy.

Ventricular Tap

Occasionally it is desirable simply to tap the ventricle to obtain samples of CSF for laboratory tests or emergency CSF drainage and ICP reduction. In older children the procedure is the same as that for ventriculostomy using a Cone needle. In infants an 18-gauge spinal needle can be used to puncture the ventricle percutaneously through the fontanel or coronal suture. Gentle twisting of the needle may be needed to pass through the coronal suture. A suture and collodion-soaked cotton ball may be placed after the procedure to manage CSF leakage.

VENTRICULAR TAP TRAY

1 Children's Hospital hand drill
1 Burton-Blacker hand drill
1 Adson forceps *with* teeth
1 sponge forceps
1 suture scissors
1 needle holder
1 No. 11 and 1 No. 15 knife blade
1 custard cup
1 18-gauge 1½-inch spinal needle (metal)
1 18-gauge 3½-inch spinal needle (metal)
1 18-gauge 3½-inch Cone needle
1 20-gauge 3½-inch Cone needle
4 green surgical towels
20 4 × 4 inch sponges
1 Weitlaner retractor
1 Lampert rongeur
1 knife handle
1 3½-inch Gelpi retractor
1 16-gauge 3½-inch Cone needle (new)
30-inch extension set
Povidone-iodine ointment and Tegaderm
1 three-way stopcock
1 18-gauge needle, disposable
1 22-gauge needle, disposable
1 25-gauge needle, disposable
1 10 ml Luer-Lok syringe, disposable
1 package bone wax
1 straight ventricular catheter
1 bile bag
1 package 3-0 Ethilon suture (31663)
1 package 4-0 Ethilon suture (699)
1 T-connector
1 vial 1% lidocaine
1 No. 5 pediatric feeding tube
1 10 ml vial 0.9% sodium chloride solution (without
    preservative)

Shunting

A ventricular shunt with a reservoir or pumping device can be tapped to measure ICP, obtain CSF for laboratory samples, or drain CSF in an emergency. The scalp over the shunt is shaved, prepared, and draped. A 23-gauge butterfly needle is introduced into the shunt. In the case of sudden neurologic or cardiopulmonary deterioration from shunt malfunction, tapping the shunt may not yield fluid. A spinal needle can be introduced through the shunt directly into the ventricle as a lifesaving procedure.

Subdural Recordings

If the ventricles are small and difficult to tap, a subdural catheter may be used to measure pressure. This technique works well only in patients with thin skulls and has been almost entirely replaced with intraparenchymal monitoring.

Procedure

The insertion site for the subdural catheter is chosen in the midpupillary line directly over bone at or near the coronal suture. A twist drill hole is made as in ventriculostomy, and a small rongeur is used to enlarge the hole. A small skin retractor and some bone wax are useful to maintain hemostasis. The dura is sharply incised, and a No. 5 feeding tube filled with 0.9% sodium chloride solution is slipped beneath the dura with the aid of a venous catheter introducer. Alternatively, a fiberoptic pressure transducer can be used in the subdural space. The tube is directed anteriorly and advanced several centimeters. In practice, the subdural catheter is introduced after attempts at tapping the ventricle have failed.

Use

The catheter usually needs to be flushed with 0.1 to 0.2 ml of 0.9% sodium chloride solution (without preservative). Damping of the pressure tracing may indicate partial occlusion of the catheter and inaccurate pressure measurements. The subarachnoid space is frequently entered, permitting slow CSF drainage in approximately a third of cases. The catheter is attached to the collection system as indicated previously for intraventricular catheters in cases in which CSF drainage is possible.

Risks and complications

Complications are the same as for ventriculostomy except for a lower incidence of ventriculitis.

Subarachnoid Bolt

Although some clinicians use subarachnoid bolts as ICP monitors, it is believed that readings from these devices are frequently unreliable. Moreover, the previously described systems offer compelling advantages over the bolt. However, a discussion of subarachnoid bolts is included for completeness.

Procedure

After a twist drill hole is made, a No. 11 knife blade is used to incise the dura in a cruciate fashion. A small curette can be used to scrape the dura against the bone edge to widen the opening. A hollow stainless steel bolt is screwed into the skull until the tip of the bolt is presumed to be in the subarachnoid space and the bolt is secure. The bolt is flushed with 0.9% sodium chloride solution (without preservative) with a 20-gauge needle and connected to a pressure transducer. A waveform is generally apparent on the monitor. The skull must be thick enough to support the bolt; some bolts with wider threads have been adapted for use in the thin skulls of infants.

Use

Damping of the waveform is a persistent problem and may indicate obstruction of the bolt. Flushing with 0.1 to 0.2 ml of 0.9% sodium chloride solution (without preservative) or gentle probing of the bolt with a lumbar puncture needle may clear the obstruction. If the bolt is partially obstructed, recorded pressures may be entirely erroneous. Screwing the device farther into the skull may also restore the waveform.

Risks and complications

The complications are the same as with ventriculostomy except for decreased risk of ventriculitis.

Applanation Devices

The open fontanel provides a mechanical linkage into the cranium and has been used to measure ICP using the applanation principle. The force necessary to slightly flatten the membranous fontanel is measured to provide ICP trend measurements. Problems with position and drift remain unresolved, although new technology is promising.

Transcranial Doppler Ultrasound

Blood velocity can be measured noninvasively through bone in children and adults by means of transcranial Doppler ultrasound. An ultrasound probe is held to the head, and a waveform is obtained that yields measurements of velocity during systole and diastole. The relative difference between systolic and diastolic velocities (usually calculated as [systolic − diastolic]/mean velocity) is defined as the pulsatility and varies directly with ICP. Although pulsatility is also affected by other variables such as P_{CO_2} and medications, its sudden increase has been successfully used to detect hydrocephalus and ICP accompanying traumatic cerebral edema. Daily monitoring of transcranial Doppler ultrasound velocities therefore provides another method of detection of ICP elevation.

$\cdot\ \cdot\ \cdot$

A proper working knowledge of the equipment is needed to ensure accuracy of the readings obtained from these monitoring devices. Orders must be specific about positioning the patient's head; whether it should be kept elevated or flat must be determined so that consistency of care is maintained.

ADDITIONAL READING

Allen R. Intracranial pressure: A review of clinical problems, measurement techniques and monitoring methods. J Med Eng Technol 10:299-320, 1986.

Bader MK, Littlejohns L, Palmer S. Ventriculostomy and intracranial pressure monitoring: In search of a 0% infection rate. Heart Lung 24:166-172, 1995.

Blei AT, Olafsson S, Webster S, Levy R. Complications of intracranial pressure monitoring in fulminant hepatic failure. Lancet 341:157-158, 1993.

Gambardella G, Zaccone C, Cardia E, Tomasello F. Intracranial pressure monitoring in children: Comparison of external ventricular device with the fiberoptic system. Childs Nerv Syst 9:470-473, 1993.

Goraj B, Rifkinson-Mann S, Leslie DR, et al. Correlation of intracranial pressure and transcranial Doppler resistive index after head trauma. Am J Neuroradiol 15:1333-1339, 1994.

Jenkins JG, Glasgow JFT, Black CW, et al. Reye's syndrome: Assessment of intracranial monitoring. Br Med J 294:337-338, 1987.

Kaiser AM, Whitelow AGJ. Intracranial pressure estimation by palpation of the anterior fontanelle. Arch Dis Child 62:516-517, 1987.

Kakis JV. An introduction to monitoring intracranial pressure in critically ill children. Crit Care Q 3:1-8, 1980.

Lundberg N, Kjalluist A, Kullberg G, et al. Non-operative management of intracranial hypertension. In Kuayenbuhl H, ed. Advances and Technical Standards in Neurosurgery, vol 1. Berlin: Springer-Verlag, 1974.

McGraw CP. Continuous intracranial pressure monitoring: Review of techniques and presentation of method. Surg Neurol 6:149-155, 1976.

McGraw CS, Alexander E Jr. Durometer for measurement of intracranial pressure. Surg Neurol 7:293-295, 1977.

Mitchell P. Intracranial hypertension: Implications of research for nursing care. J Neurosurg Nurs 12:145-154, 1980.

Mollman HD, Rockswald GC, Ford SE. A clinical comparison of subarachnoid catheters to ventriculostomy and subarachnoid bolts: A prospective study. J Neurosurg 68:737-741, 1988.

Nadvi SS, DuTrevou MD, Van Dellen JR, et al. The use of transcranial Doppler ultrasonography as a method of assessing intracranial pressure in hydrocephalic children. Br J Neurosurg 8:573-577, 1994.

Ostrop RC, Luerssen TG, Marshall LF, et al. Continuous monitoring of intracranial pressure with a miniaturized fiberoptic device. J Neurosurg 67:206-209, 1987.

Peters RJA, Hanlo PW, Gooskens RHJM, Braun KPJ, Tulleken CAF, Willemse J. Noninvasive ICP monitoring in infants: The Rotterdam teletransducer revisited. Childs Nerv Syst 11:207-213, 1995.

Raju TWK, Vidysager D, Papazafiraton C. Intracranial pressure monitoring in the neonatal ICU. Crit Care Med 8:575-581, 1980.

Robinson RO, Rolfe P, Sutton P. Non-invasive method for measuring intracranial pressure in normal newborn infants. Dev Med Child Neurol 19:305-308, 1977.

Sundbarg G, Nordstrom CH, Messeter K, et al. A comparison of intraparenchymal and intraventricular pressure recording in clinical practice. J Neurosurg 67:841-845, 1987.

Thompson DNP, Harkness W, Jones B, et al. Subdural intracranial pressure monitoring in craniosynostosis: Its role in surgical management. Childs Nerv Syst 11:269-275, 1995.

Vries JK, Becker DP, Young HF. A subarachnoid screw for monitoring intracranial pressure: Technical note. J Neurosurg 39:416-419, 1973.

Zeidelman C. Increased intracranial pressure in the pediatric patient: Nursing assessment and intervention. J Neurosurg Nurs 12:7-10, 1980.

137 Neurophysiologic Monitoring

Balbir Singh · Anthony R. Riela · Mauricio R. Delgado

BACKGROUND AND INDICATIONS

Currently most body systems are closely monitored in PICUs with frequent clinical observations as well as numerous monitoring devices to detect minor subclinical abnormalities before they can cause further damage. However, progress in CNS monitoring has been slow. Patients with neurologic disease are usually observed with serial clinical examinations, which can be unreliable for detection of minor but often significant changes. Clinical evaluations become useless in patients who have been given paralytic agents or heavy sedation. Neurophysiologic monitoring with electroencephalography (EEG) and evoked potentials can provide useful objective information about the overall functional integrity of the CNS. Recent advances in monitoring techniques, including computerization, have made data compression, presentation, and interpretation simpler for clinical use.

TECHNIQUE

Electroencephalography

The EEG waveforms are generated primarily from the pyramidal cortical neurons and represent the summation of cortical postsynaptic excitatory and inhibitory electrical potentials. Thus the waveforms reflect the state of cerebral metabolism defined by multiple intracellular and interneuronal processes such as phosphorylation, axonal transport, and enzyme synthesis. The EEG is a sensitive but often nonspecific indicator of cerebral dysfunction. Changes in the EEG can appear long before cerebral tissue adenosine triphosphate (ATP) levels start to drop. These abnormalities appear when cerebral blood flow (CBF) falls to 20 to 25 ml/100 g/min, whereas synaptic activity continues until CBF drops to 17 ml/100 g/min. Energy failure and cell death do not occur until CBF drops to 10 ml/100 g/min. Thus timely intervention based on EEG findings can possibly prevent irreversible ischemic CNS injury.

Multiple electrodes are applied to the head according to the standardized international 10-20-electrode placement system (Fig. 137-1). Cerebral activity is best recorded on a 16- to 20-channel machine. Each channel measures the potential difference between two points on the scalp. Application of a full complement of electrodes may not be possible in some patients with head injury or who have undergone brain surgery, and modification of electrode placement may be necessary. Additional electrodes to record respiration, ECG, and eye movements can improve the accuracy of EEG interpretation.

Artifacts produced by various mechanical and electrical appliances are a major problem in the interpretation of EEGs recorded in the PICU. Ventilators

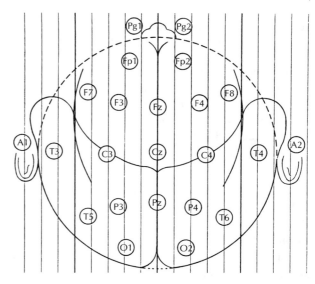

Fig. 137-1 Location of EEG electrodes according to international 10-20-electrode system.

and IV infusion pumps are some sources that generate artifacts in the recording. Some artifacts can be eliminated with electronic filters. In addition to these instrumental and external artifacts, physiologic artifacts are more common in young infants and neonates. Pulse, ECG, sucking, swallowing, posturing, and nystagmus commonly cause confusion in interpretation of the EEG. Scalp muscles and cardiac muscle generate electrical activity several hundred times higher in amplitude than EEG signals. Head injury and craniotomy can cause asymmetric scalp edema, leading to unilateral suppression of EEG activity simulating ipsilateral cerebral disease.

Relevant clinical information (e.g., gestational age in neonates, age, a brief history of the illness, reason for the study, level of consciousness, medications, skull defects, and any scalp lesions) is helpful for appropriate interpretation. An EEG that is normal for an infant can indicate severe cerebral dysfunction in an older child. Similarly, slowing related to sleep or drowsiness can be confused with EEG changes of encephalopathy. Benzodiazepines, barbiturates, and other drugs can have a significant effect on background activity.

EEG patterns

Alpha frequency (8 to 13 Hz) is the normal EEG background rhythm in older children, adolescents, and adults (Fig. 137-2). In infants the normal background ranges between 3 and 5 Hz and gradually reaches the older child's normal range (8 Hz) by 4 to 6 years of age. Beta frequencies (>13 Hz) are also normal; these frequencies increase with administration of sedative drugs such as benzodiazepines and barbiturates. Slower frequencies, or delta (<4 Hz) and theta (4 to 8 Hz) rhythms, are normal during drowsiness but can also indicate diffuse cerebral dysfunction caused by disorders such as encephalitis, hypoxic-ischemic injury, drug injection, and metabolic encephalopathy. Alternatively, focal destructive lesions cause focal slowing.

EEG Findings in Specific Clinical Disorders

Coma

The EEG can provide an objective measure of the severity of encephalopathy. Even before consciousness is impaired, the background rhythm slows. As the child's condition deteriorates, delta waves replace the faster frequencies. With severe encephalopathy, brain waves become unresponsive to external stimuli. Normal sleep patterns associated with favorable outcome are not seen in deeper stages of coma. With worsening, there is a progressive decrease in the voltage of the delta activity, and finally flattening of the EEG occurs with electrocerebral inactivity. In some patients a suppression burst pattern may develop before electrocerebral inactivity. Low-amplitude delta, suppression burst pattern, and electrocerebral inactivity carry a grave prognosis (except perhaps in a child in coma from drug overdose). The EEG changes may continue to be seen several days after clinical recovery from the underlying disease.

In children in deep coma or those who have been given paralytic agents the EEG may provide the first clue of brain death. In these patients a timely diagnosis of brain death can prevent unnecessary use of resources and aid in an opportune decision about organ donation.

Cardiac surgery during hypothermia has provided extensive information about the effect of low body temperature on the EEG. No changes occur with mild hypothermia, but generalized slowing appears with core temperature of 30° C followed by suppression burst pattern at 20° C. Electrocerebral inactivity occurs as the temperature drops below 17° to 18° C. Rarely electrocerebral inactivity may not develop until the temperature drops to 7° C. Because hypothermia can cause reversible electrocerebral inactivity, this finding does not necessarily indicate irreversible cerebral injury.

After cardiac arrest, EEG changes are predictable. In the experimental model of cardiac arrest no changes occur for 5 to 10 seconds, after which delta activity is seen. This is followed by a rapid decrease in amplitude and electrocerebral inactivity. If cardiac arrest is brief, the EEG recovers promptly in reverse sequence. Continued hypoxia for 5 to 10 minutes can lead to irreversible cerebral damage. An EEG is usually obtained after an hypoxic episode to assess the severity of damage. Some changes carry a good prognosis; others correlate with poor outcome. A normal or near-normal EEG indicates a high likelihood of intact survival. Children with electrocerebral inactivity or suppression burst pattern often do not survive. The outcome of patients with intermediate changes is less predictable. Children with severe generalized slowing that does not improve over 24 hours have a high rate of mortality or significant neurologic morbidity. Following successful resuscitation after cardiac arrest, EEG activity may return after electrocerebral inactivity for up to 1 hour. Therefore it is recommended that

EEG be performed no sooner than 5 to 6 hours after the acute injury.

Encephalitis

Generalized slowing is the most common EEG finding in viral encephalitis (Fig. 137-3). The degree of slowing is usually proportionate to the severity of the illness. In contrast to the generalized slowing seen in nonherpetic viral encephalitis, unilateral slowing is usually seen in herpes encephalitis (Fig. 137-4) and is most pronounced in the temporal area. Periodic lateralizing epileptiform discharges (sharp and slow wave complexes that repeat at 1- to 5-second intervals) are seen in more than 50% of children with her-

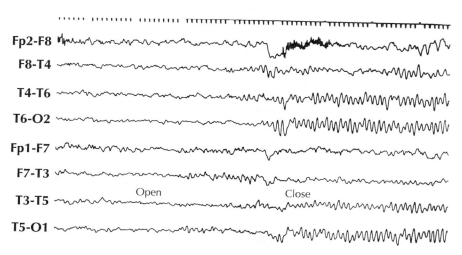

Fig. 137-2 Normal alpha rhythm with patient's eyes open and closed.

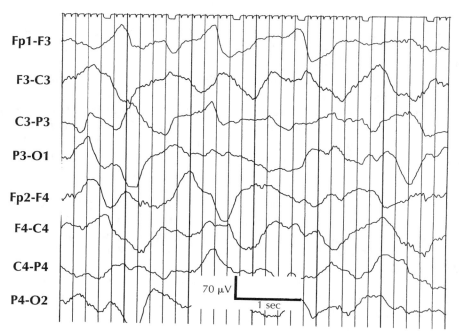

Fig. 137-3 Generalized slowing with 0.5 to 1 Hz delta waves in a patient with viral encephalitis.

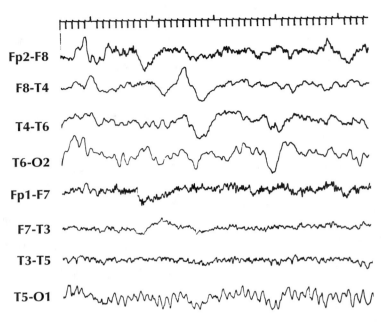

Fig. 137-4 Right-sided temporal slowing in a patient with herpes encephalitis (channels 1 to 4, top).

pes encephalitis. These periodic complexes generally are associated with a poor prognosis. As the disease progresses, periodic complexes may be seen bilaterally or may disappear from the initial location and reappear on the opposite side. Neonatal herpes typically affects the brain difusely; thus the periodic discharges are often bilateral from the onset. Focal EEG changes in a child with clinical features of encephalitis are strongly suggestive of herpes simplex encephalitis. These changes can frequently be seen before any radiologic changes. Compared with encephalitis, bacterial or viral meningitis tends to produce milder EEG changes. In bacterial meningitis the appearance of focal slowing late in the disease suggests the possibility of cerebral infarction or abscess.

Drug ingestion

In drug-induced coma the degree of alteration of sensorium and EEG changes correlate with the severity of intoxication. Excessive beta frequencies in a patient in coma suggest drug overdose. With mild overdose, delta and theta frequencies are intermixed with a normal alpha background. As the depth of coma increases, the EEG shows an increasing degree of slowing. Finally, a suppression burst pattern may be followed by gradual attenuation of the slow frequencies, ending in electrocerebral inactivity. Children with a suppression burst pattern or electrocerebral inactivity caused by intoxication have a much better prognosis than those with the same changes caused by coma due to hypoxia or infection. Therefore every effort needs to be made to exclude intoxication as the cause of electrocerebral inactivity.

Alpha coma

Rarely in children in coma the EEG may show predominant activity in the alpha range. This has been reported in patients with brain stem lesions, hypoxic encephalopathy, and drug overdose. In these children alpha frequencies are distributed more widely than the physiologic alpha activity (which tends to occur posteriorly). Patients with alpha coma from a brain stem lesion or hypoxic injury usually die or survive in a vegetative state. In contrast, children with alpha coma due to drug intoxication usually survive without serious sequelae. Children with hypoxic-ischemic encephalopathy in whom alpha coma develops in the first 24 hours fare better than those in whom it appears after the first day. Alpha coma pattern has been reported in infants, with the normal background slower than alpha frequencies, which suggests the generator of this alpha pattern is different from the physiologic alpha of normal background seen in older children.

Reye's syndrome

Reye's syndrome can cause mild slowing to suppression burst pattern, depending on the severity of the disease. An EEG can be of help in predicting the outcome of the disease. EEG changes in Reye's syndrome can be divided into five grades. In children with grade I and II EEG findings (mild slowing in the theta and delta ranges) the prognosis is usually good; children with intermediate changes (grade III) have 50% survival; and patients with severe changes consisting of severe slowing or suppression burst pattern (grades IV and V) usually die or survive with severe neurologic sequelae.

Locked-in syndrome

In locked-in syndrome the EEG is diagnostically helpful. This syndrome is caused by extensive damage to the brain stem at the level of the pons, resulting in quadriplegia and total mutism, which is a state superficially resembling coma. Because the cerebral hemispheres are not affected, mental function may be normal. Many patients may be able to communicate with preserved eye movements, and, as expected, the EEG is normal. In an apparently unconscious patient a normal EEG should prompt a detailed neurologic examination to see whether the patient can communicate with vertical eye movements. Once the diagnosis of locked-in syndrome is made, the patient needs to be included in decision making and kept informed about the disease process.

Seizures

An EEG is typically obtained between seizures (interictal) and thus may not provide diagnostic information for episodic symptoms. Interictal spikes have a high correlation with epileptic seizures but are rarely seen in patients without seizures. Alternatively, in many patients with epileptic seizures the EEG is normal between seizures. Despite these limitations, routine EEGs can provide useful information that can improve management of seizures in most patients. Interictal epileptiform discharges can be broadly classified as partial (focal) or generalized. Focal spikes correlate with focal cortical dysfunction, whereas generalized epileptic discharges suggest a diffuse onset, often the result of a genetically inherited primary generalized epilepsy. This information can aid in the selection of the most appropriate anticonvulsant therapy.

Seizures are common in patients with acute cerebral injury. Acute seizures occur in 10% to 25% of adult patients with subarachnoid hemorrhage, head injury, and ischemic stroke. In one study in adults the incidence of electrographic seizures in patients admitted to an ICU with a neurologic diagnosis was as high as 35%; three fourths of these patients had nonconvulsive status epilepticus. Nonconvulsive status epilepticus developed most often in patients with nonspecific metabolic encephalopathy. In some of these patients nonconvulsive status epilepticus was the predominant cause of coma.

Unrecognized seizures can be a serious problem in the critical care setting. Animal studies have shown that even electrographic seizures in paralyzed animals receiving mechanical ventilation can increase cerebral metabolic rate, increase ICP, and cause neuronal damage. Studies have shown a worse prognosis in ICU patients with neurologic disease who have nonconvulsive seizures. For these reasons, both clinical and electrographic seizures need to be treated.

After treatment of convulsive status epilepticus, only EEG findings can differentiate postictal stupor from nonconvulsive status epilepticus. An EEG can also help differentiate epileptic from nonepileptic episodes; posturing, positional clonus, nonepileptic myoclonus, and movement disorders can sometimes be confused without an EEG.

Video-EEG

With the help of video-EEG equipment, clinical expression of an epileptic episode and associated EEG changes can be recorded on the same videotape. Simultaneous playback of this information can help the physician correctly interpret the data. Partial epileptic seizures generate a focal rhythmic activity that increases in amplitude and spreads to the adjoining areas of the brain (Fig. 137-5). After the seizures stop, transient slowing often occurs over the same areas. In patients with primarily generalized tonic-clonic seizures, spike or spike-and-wave activity occurs in all areas of the brain. After the seizures, diffuse slowing is seen. Only rarely does a child with tonic-clonic seizures that affect all extremities fail to

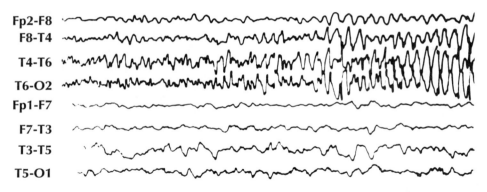

Fig. 137-5   Partial seizure beginning in the right temporal region (channels 3 and 4).

show epileptiform activity on a simultaneous video-EEG recording. In contrast, patients with nonepileptic episodes never show an epileptiform discharge; at times rhythmic movement artifact may be difficult to differentiate from an epileptic discharge. However, postictal slowing is never seen in children with nonepileptic seizures.

In children with altered mental status or when the diagnosis of epileptic seizures is reasonably certain, a routine EEG is generally adequate. In patients with acute neurologic disease and a high possibility of electrographic seizures or patients who have been given paralytic agents, continuous EEG or video-EEG is more appropriate. In children in barbiturate coma for treatment of status epilepticus or due to increased ICP, intermittent paper EEG monitoring for 2 to 5 minutes every half-hour to hour is adequate to monitor the duration of suppression burst pattern intervals. Alternatively, continuous EEG recording on videotape or an optical disk can be used. This provides a continuous display of the EEG, and the nursing staff does not have to manipulate the equipment at regular intervals.

For optimal management of acute neurologic injury and seizures, continuous EEG provides more valuable information. With the help of continuous EEG, the appropriate amount of anticonvulsant can be given to stop clinical and electrographic seizures, avoiding the risks of underdosing or overdosing. An inadequate dose may control the clinical seizure, but electrographic seizures may continue, leading to neuronal injury. Alternatively, overdose of anticonvulsant agents can cause serious and unnecessary compli-

cations such as respiratory arrest, hypotension, and cardiac arrhythmias. In children undergoing barbiturate coma for control of status epilepticus or of increased ICP, continuous EEG helps monitor the depth of coma. In these children tolerance to the effects of barbiturates may result in poor correlation between serum barbiturate levels and depth of coma. Infusion rates capable of producing a suppression burst pattern should be achieved and maintained for 24 to 48 hours (Fig. 137-6). Following this, the infusion rate is gradually decreased and then stopped unless electrographic or clinical seizures recur. With deepening barbiturate coma, duration of the suppressions gradually increases, leading to reversible electrocerebral silence, which is associated with higher morbidity and mortality. In patients with neurologic diseases who are given paralyzing agents to facilitate ventilation, seizure surveillance with continuous EEG is the only technique that can detect seizures.

Automation of EEG

A major problem in the routine use of EEG in the PICU is the difficulty of real-time interpretation. In the past an analog EEG signal was recorded on paper or videotape. The main disadvantage of the analog signal is that it cannot be manipulated after the recording is completed. Because of the complexity of EEG waveforms, an electroencephalographer is needed to provide reliable interpretation of the study. However, electroencephalographers are not available on site at all times, even in large neurologic PICUs. Digitized EEG has overcome most of these difficulties. Once

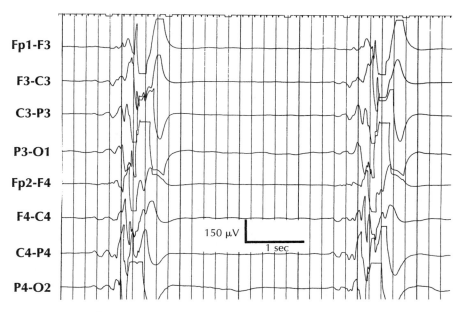

Fig. 137-6 Suppression burst pattern in a patient in barbiturate coma.

the signal is digitized and stored, it can be manipulated at the time of review and also can be transmitted to remote sites for expert opinion. Availability of computerized spike detection systems has made it easier for the nonexpert to diagnose seizures with subtle clinical manifestations. These techniques can be used for automatic detection of electrographic seizures. False positive and negative rates are high even under ideal conditions of an epilepsy monitoring unit. The reliability of these systems in the PICU setting has not been assessed but is likely to be low as a result of abundant artifacts. For this reason, close supervision of these systems is essential. Long-term EEG monitoring is extremely labor intensive. To solve this problem, digitized EEG data can be manipulated statistically and presented as maps that display EEG frequencies in various head regions. These maps can be compared to determine a trend in EEG changes indicating improvement or deterioration of cerebral functions. The advantage of this technique is its simplicity, which makes it possible for PICU personnel to react to changes in EEG. In practice, the PICU staff can be trained to monitor simple and common EEG patterns. Any unusual activity can be transmitted to the EEG laboratory or office for the elec-

troencephalographer's opinion. Centralized EEG services may be developed in the future that will be manned by a team of technicians specialized in monitoring and data will be reviewed by an expert located at the laboratory, office, or home.

Evoked Potentials

Evoked potentials are the electric responses of the central and peripheral nervous system to sensory stimulation. Evoked potentials have some advantage over EEG monitoring in that the interpretable potentials are more resistant to sedative medications and anesthesia sufficient to produce isoelectric ("flat") EEGs. Evoked potential testing is more sensitive to irreversible hypoxic-ischemic neuronal damage than EEG.

Different sensory pathways can be evaluated with evoked potentials, including visual (visual evoked potentials [VEPs]), auditory (brain stem auditory evoked potentials [BAEPs]), and somatosensory sytem (somatosensory evoked potentials [SSEPs]). Special techniques are necessary to elicit interpretable waveforms from the background electrical "noise" generated by the heart (ECG), brain (EEG), and muscle (electromyography). Because the am-

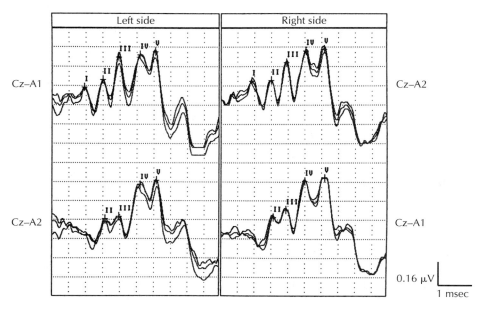

Fig. 137-7 Normal BAEPs showing normal waves I-V.

plitude of the evoked potential waves is small compared with other electrical activity in the body, computer averaging is necessary to obtain reproducible time-locked responses. Abnormalities are related to absence, latency delay, or low amplitude of the required waveforms.

BAEPs and SSEPs are the evoked potentials most commonly used in the PICU. Their clinical use stems from the close relationship between the evoked potential waveforms and their specific anatomic generators. This specificity allows localization of conduction defects in different areas of the nervous system. BAEPs are usually produced by a clicking sound transmitted through earphones. Function from the auditory nerve to the lower portion of the midbrain can be assessed with this technique (Fig. 137-7). Absence of waveforms without significant change of the auditory nerve signal carries a poor prognosis in a variety of conditions.

SSEPs are produced by electrical stimulation of sensorimotor peripheral nerves. Most commonly used are the median, ulnar, peroneal, and posterior tibial nerves. SSEPs assess the function of the peripheral nerve being stimulated, the posterior columns of the spinal cord, sensory pathways in the brain stem, thalamus, and cortical reception areas in the parietal re-

gions (Fig. 137-8). Thus SSEPs can be helpful in the diagnosis of lesions in the peripheral nerve, spinal cord, brain stem, and certain brain regions. However, abnormalities demonstrated by evoked potentials are etiologically nonspecific and must be carefully correlated with the clinical findings.

Coma

The resistance of BAEPs to metabolic, pharmacologic, and physiologic changes makes this test a valuable tool in assessing comatose patients. For example, children in coma from barbiturate overdose sufficient to produce the clinical and EEG impression of brain death may still have interpretable BAEPs. Because BAEPs reflect only the function of the auditory pathways in the brain stem, it is possible that BAEPs will be normal in a child completely paralyzed from a brain stem lesion sparing the auditory tracts. Inasmuch as BAEPs assess only function of auditory pathways below the midbrain, progressive supratentorial lesions will not produce BAEP changes until structures below the midbrain are involved. SSEP waveforms, like BAEPs, are extremely resistant to metabolic and pharmacologic changes. Children given high-dose barbiturate therapy for increased ICP may have an isoelectric EEG but unaltered SSEPs (except

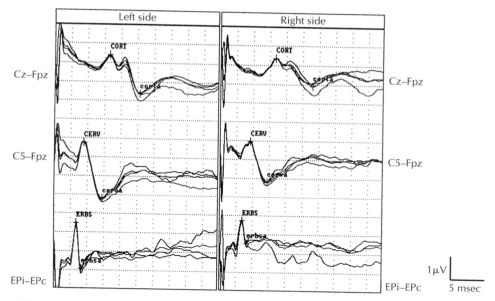

Fig. 137-8 Normal median nerve SSEPs showing Erb's point and cervical (N13) and cortical (N20) potentials.

for the cortical response). A poor prognosis is associated with bilateral absence of SSEPs in comatose patients.

Head injury

BAEPs have been used in the early prediction of outcome in patients in coma secondary to head injury. If damage to the peripheral hearing apparatus is excluded, the absence of BAEPs strongly correlates with poor outcome. This information cannot be used in isolation, but must be correlated with other prognostic indicators and overall clinical findings. Several investigators have found that abnormalities of upper extremity SSEPs after closed head injury are also associated with poor outcome. Although SSEPs may be a useful assessment tool in sedated or paralyzed patients, in others this test does not contribute significantly to the accuracy of prognosis beyond that offered by clinical examination alone.

Brain death

Several investigators have used BAEPs to study the functional integrity of the brain stem in patients with suspected brain death. BAEPs are of special value in children with possible drug overdose and help exclude brain death. Deafness or ear disease can

cause absence of all BAEP waves. Hence, in the absence of an auditory nerve signal (wave I), no inferences can be made as to the presence or absence of brain stem function. For this reason, although BAEPs are abnormal in patients who meet the criteria for brain death, it has not been proposed as a standard procedure to determine brain death. Median nerve SSEPs can also be used to assess brain death. Brachial plexus and cervical waveforms will be the only responses present in brain-dead patients. However, similar changes may be rarely seen in children with severe diffuse CNS injury who are not brain dead. Therefore, similar to BAEPs, although the presence of SSEPs can rule out brain death, their absence has limited value in assessment of suspected brain death.

ADDITIONAL READING

Aoki Y, Lombroso CT. Prognostic value of electroencephalography in Reye's syndrome. Neurology 23:333-343, 1973.

Daly DD, Pedley TA. Current Practice of Clinical Electroencephalography, 2nd ed. New York: Raven Press, 1990.

Firsching R, Frowein RA. Multimodality evoked potentials and early prognosis in comatose patients. Neurosurg Rev 13:141-146, 1990.

Gastaut H, Fischer-Williams M. Electroencephalographic study of syncope: Its differentiation from epilepsy. Lancet 2:1018-1025, 1957.

• Jordan KG. Continuous EEG and evoked potential monitoring in the neuroscience intensive care unit. J Clin Neurophysiol 10:445-475, 1993.

Jordan KG. Nonconvulsive status epilepticus in the neuro-ICU detected by continuous EEG monitoring. Neurology 42(Suppl 1):194, 1992.

Kurtz D. The EEG in acute and chronic drug intoxications. In Remond A, ed. Handbook of Electroencephalography and Clinical Neurophysiology, vol 15. Amsterdam: Elsevier, 1976, pp 88-104.

Markand ON. Electroencephalography in diffuse encephalopathies. J Clin Neurophysiol 1:357-407, 1984.

Meyer JS, Sakamoto K, Akiyama M, et al. Monitoring cerebral blood flow, metabolism and EEG. Electroencephalogr Clin Neurophysiol 23:497-508, 1967.

Niedermeyer E, Lopes Da Silva F. Electroencephalography: Basic Principles, Clinical Applications, and Related Fields, 3rd ed. Baltimore: Williams & Wilkins, 1993.

• Nuwer MR. Electroencephalograms and evoked potentials. Monitoring cerebral function in the neurosurgical intensive care unit. Neurosurg Clin North Am 5:647-659, 1994.

Pagni CA, Courjon J. Electroencephalographic modification produced by moderate and deep hypothermia in man. Acta Neurochir (Wien) 13(Suppl):35-49, 1964.

Robertson CS, Simpson RK Jr. Neurophysiologic monitoring of patients with head injury. Neurosurg Clin North Am 2:285-294, 1991.

Rogers AT, Stump DA. Cerebral physiologic monitoring. Crit Care Clin 5:845-861, 1989.

Sclabassi RJ, Kalia KK, Sekhar L, Janetta PJ. Assessing brainstem function. Neurosurg Clin North Am 4:415-431, 1993.

Spehlmann R. Evoked Potentials Primer. Boston: Butterworth-Heinemann, 1985.

• Stone JL, Ghaly RF, Hughes JR. Evoked potentials in head injury and states of increased intracranial pressure. J Clin Neurophysiol 5:135-160, 1988.

138 Sleep Studies

John H. Herman · Joel B. Steinberg

BACKGROUND

The increasing recognition and treatment of sleep disorders in children has resulted from studies in adults showing that sleep apnea is related to the state of sleep and to specific sleep stages and techniques developed to evaluate risk for sudden infant death syndrome (SIDS). Sleep disorders are defined here as conditions that are related to sleep, occur only during sleep, or are exacerbated by sleep.

Sleep and Intensive Care Medicine

In the PICU polysomnography is used to monitor respiratory disorders and other sleep-related events that are life-threatening or associated with significant morbidity and contributes objective data as to which therapeutic interventions are indicated (e.g., whether tracheostomy is necessary). Certain medical conditions and medical symptoms are state dependent; that is, sleep or one of its stages exacerbates the condition or is necessary for it to occur. The polysomnogram allows the clinician to examine the relationships between physiologic variables such as state of consciousness (wakefulness vs. sleep and its stages), ventilatory behavior, and a wide variety of other variables that are monitored electrophysiologically (Table 138-1). A second major attribute of the polysomnogram is its flexibility. Variables to be monitored are individually selected on the basis of their clinical relevance in a specific patient. The variables recorded on a respiratory polysomnogram may vary significantly depending on the clinical symptoms being evaluated. A polysomnogram designed to assess sleep-related movement disorders or sleep-related seizure disorders might differ considerably from one that is designed to evaluate disordered breathing during sleep.

Significance of Studying Sleep

Sleep has a critical impact on some medical conditions and symptoms because it reduces innervation of skeletal muscles, affects the sympathetic-parasympathetic balance of the autonomic nervous system, and affects control of respiration. Because of the increased amplitude of cortical synchrony in association with non–rapid eye movement (NREM) sleep, some seizure disorders occur more frequently or exclusively during sleep. Sleep per se and REM sleep to a greater extent compromise respiratory function under normal conditions and especially in a variety of medical conditions (e.g., central and obstructive respiratory syndromes), and it is this interaction that necessitates polysomnography for adequate evaluation. Gastroesophageal reflux (GER) or apparent life-threatening events of infancy frequently are observed only during sleep. Objective evidence that sleep occurred is crucial if the medical event being investigated occurs principally or exclusively during sleep or only in one stage of sleep. The polysomnogram alone is capable of demonstrating that a sufficient amount of sleep and its stages occurred during monitoring (e.g., respiratory monitoring) to confirm or rule out a sleep-related condition.

Stages of Sleep

According to standardized scoring criteria, sleep is divided into two principal states that alternate cyclically in a regular and predictable pattern: REM sleep and NREM sleep. The term "states" is used because the physiology of REM and NREM sleep are more distinct from each other than either is from wakefulness. NREM sleep is subdivided into four stages, each characterizing progressively "deeper" sleep status. The stages of sleep and wakefulness, including the moment of transition between stages, may be monitored with three electrophysiologic techniques: electroencephalography (EEG), electro-oculography (EOG), and electromyography (EMG).

Chronologic organization of sleep stages. REM and NREM sleep alternate cyclically throughout the sleep period. At the beginning of sleep the deeper stages (slow-wave sleep, or stages III and IV) are prevalent. In the second half of the sleep period as awakening approaches, sleep is principally light (stage II) NREM and REM sleep. This pattern is evident by 1 year of age and persists throughout life.

Sleep stages in the neonate. REM and NREM sleep are distinguishable on polysomnograms in the first 6 months of life but less so than in adults. They are referred to as active and quiet sleep, respectively. By 6 months of age sleep stages may be identified by adult criteria. After the first year of life sleep is initiated by NREM stages. In the newborn infant active sleep (REM sleep) may occur immediately after wakefulness (Figs. 138-1 and 138-2). Active sleep and quiet sleep (NREM sleep) alternate in a 50- to 60-minute cycle in infants, which lengthens to 90 to 120 minutes in adolescents (REM-NREM cycle).

Table 138-1   Polysomnographic Monitoring

Technique	Data Obtained
Electroencephalography (EEG) 10-20 system, C3 and C4	Measures cortical synchrony or waveforms characteristic of different sleep stages and cortical indicators of state of consciousness
Electro-oculography (EOG)	Detects saccadic eye movements (rapid eye movements [REM]) of waking and REM sleep and pursuit (slow) eye movements of drowsiness and light sleep
Electromyography (EMG)	Records movements (phasic activity) and resting background (tonic activity) of skeletal muscles; demonstrates atonia of REM sleep
Electrocardiography (ECG)	Detects heart rate changes (e.g., bradycardia or tachycardia)
Nasal and oral airflow (with a thermistor)	Senses temperature changes with expired (heated) and inspired (room temperature) air
Chest and abdominal respiratory motion (with impedance, resistive measurements, inductive plethysmography, piezoelectric recording, or other techniques)	Assesses quality of expansion and contraction of chest and abdomen with each breath
Intercostal and diaphragmatic EMG	Detects presence or absence of activity in these muscle groups with inspiration and indicates quality of respiratory effort
Pneumotachogram with sealed face mask	Measures airflow with each breath
Endoesophageal balloon or water catheterization at the midthoracic level	Measures effort of breathing
Respiratory microphone	Transforms respiratory sounds into frequencies recordable on polysomnogram
Noninvasive blood gas monitoring, including transcutaneous gas analysis and spectral analysis, to estimate oxygen hemoglobin and blood CO_2	Estimates hypoxemia, hypercapnea, and hypocapnea; end-tidal CO_2 may also be used to monitor airflow; Sao_2 and end-tidal CO_2 are printed out continuously along with respiratory recordings
Additional 10-20 EEG system electrodes in 4- to 20-channel array	Detects sleep-related seizure disorders
pH probe, 1 or 2 channels, at L7 and laryngeal levels	Monitors gastroesophageal reflux
Limb EMG electrodes from anterior tibialis or forearm muscles or both	Detects periodic limb movements and other sleep-related movement disorders
Laryngeal EMG	Monitors laryngeal spasms
Arterial catheterization	Used to obtain arterial blood gas levels during sleep
Audio and video monitoring	Permits observation of movement disorders, paradoxical movements, retractions, abnormal respiratory sounds, and parasomnias

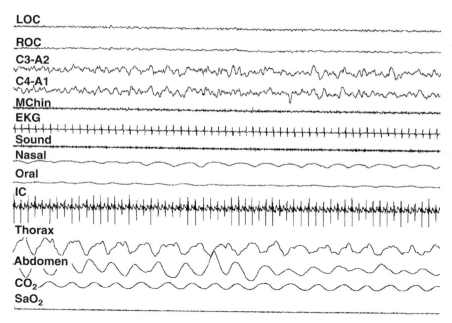

Fig. 138-1 Quiet sleep in a 6-week-old girl being evaluated for apnea of infancy. Thirty-second polysomnogram showing the typical low-voltage, mixed-frequency EEG, lack of eye movements or twitches, regular respiration, and decreased heart rate variability typical of quiet sleep in the neonate. Note paradoxical respiration is not present. High end-tidal CO_2 is 32 mm Hg and SaO_2 is 100%. (LOC = Left outer canthus EOG; ROC = right outer canthus EOG; C3-A2 = left hemisphere central EEG; C4-A1 = right hemisphere central EEG; MChin = skeletal EMG; EKG = right to left clavicle; sound = respiratory microphone; nasal = nasal airflow; oral = oral airflow; IC = intercostal EMG; thorax = thoracic expiration-inhalation from respiratory band; abdomen = abdominal expiration-inspiration from respiratory band; CO_2 = end-tidal CO_2; SaO_2 = transcutaneous oxygen saturation.)

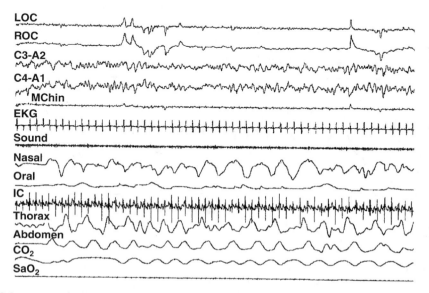

Fig. 138-2 Active sleep in same infant. Thirty-second polysomnogram displays typical characteristics of active sleep, including EEG similar to that of quiet sleep, presence of REM, irregular respiratory amplitude and rate, and paradoxical respiration. High end-tidal CO_2 is 37 mm Hg and SaO_2 varies between 98% and 96%. Channel labels identical to those in Fig. 138-1.

Breathing Patterns and Effort

The majority of polysomnographic studies recorded under hospital conditions are performed to assess respiration or address medical conditions with a suspected respiratory cause. Control of breathing is affected by both sleep and the states of sleep. For example, the ventilatory response to reduced oxygen or increased carbon dioxide is blunted somewhat by NREM sleep and is virtually absent in REM sleep, and innervation of muscles that hold the upper airway patent is decreased in NREM sleep and further diminished in REM sleep.

Paradoxical breathing

During normal breathing inspiration is achieved by synchronous enlargement of the thorax and outward movement of the abdominal wall; that is, the motions are in phase. In contrast, expansion of one compartment is accompanied by contraction of the other in conditions in which there is loss of tone of either the rib cage or abdomen or with partial or complete upper airway obstruction. In each of these instances movements of the two compartments are out of phase, referred to as paradoxical breathing. With partial or complete airway obstruction, the diaphragm pushes the abdomen out, resulting in greater negative intrathoracic pressure that causes the rib cage to move inward. This is especially common in infants, who have more pliable rib cages. Paradoxical movement is indicative of increased airway resistance or obstructive apnea. In the presence of paradoxical movement a pathologic increase in the effort of breathing may be observed in children in the absence of discrete apnea or hypopnea.

Apnea

Obstructive sleep apnea. In obstructive sleep apnea the flaccid tissue of the upper airways is pulled shut by negative inspiratory pressure, much like a straw collapsing from excessive suction. Obstructive apnea is defined as greatly reduced or absent airflow with continuation of respiratory effort. Oxygen pressure drops and carbon dioxide pressure rises rapidly as the airway remains shut, which leads to arousal, allowing the airway to reopen (Fig. 138-3). This apnea-arousal-apnea cycle may be repeated

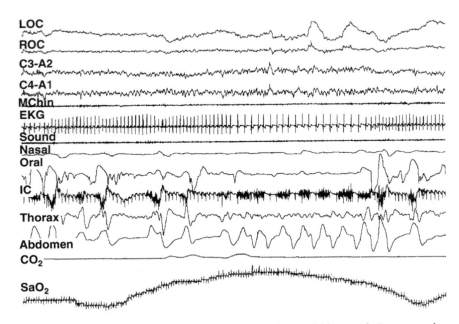

Fig. 138-3   Twelve-second obstructive sleep apnea in a 4-year-old boy with Down syndrome. The recording shows almost total cessation of nasal and oral airflow in the presence of increased amplitude of IC EMG and abdominal respiratory band excursion. Note the rapid drop in SaO_2 from 91% to 78% at the end of the 30-second recording associated with the obstructive apnea illustrated, the large-amplitude oral gasps at the end of the apnea, and the bradycardia accompanying the apnea. Channel labels identical to those in Fig. 138-1.

throughout the entire sleep period or it may occur in only one stage of sleep or only in the supine position.

Central sleep apnea. Central sleep apnea is defined as prolonged cessation of the effort of breathing: no activity is seen in thermistors or other devices that monitor airflow and movement of the chest or abdomen or the intercostal muscles. Prolonged central sleep apneas include apnea of prematurity and apnea of infancy and are seen less frequently in children and adults. All infants, children, and adults demonstrate a normal number of central apneas during sleep. If they are preceded by a deep breath, they are termed sighs. Normal central apneas are self-limiting, but the events are significant when associated with hypoxemia, bradycardia, or severely disrupted sleep.

Criteria to assess sleep apnea. In adults obstructive or central sleep apnea is considered clinically significant if its duration is >10 seconds. In an infant or child, who has a greater respiratory rate and smaller oxygen reserve, apnea of a duration of 2½ breaths is considered significant, as are briefer events accompanied by hypoxemia or bradycardia. Obstructive and central sleep hypopnea occur when the amplitude of airflow is reduced by an amount significant enough to result in hypoxemia but airflow is still present. Mixed apneas and hypopneas contain both central and obstructive components. Apnea of infancy may be central, obstructive, or mixed. These will be isolated events that are interspersed with normal respiration. If respiration is continuously obstructive in an infant, the diagnosis is obstructive sleep apnea as opposed to apnea of infancy, obstructive variety; the latter term is reserved for isolated obstructive events.

Monitoring of Blood Gases

Estimating blood gas levels with noninvasive techniques such as pulse oximetry establishes the degree of hypoxemia or hypercapnea that occurs in conjunction with central or obstructive sleep apneas. In children with cardiac or other pulmonary conditions the polysomnogram may demonstrate whether sleep-related hypoxemia or hypercapnea is associated with discernible changes in respiration. Polysomnograms may be recorded to demonstrate that hypoxemia and/or hypercapnea occur without central or obstructive apnea. A PICU setting is preferred when an arterial catheter is deemed critical to determine blood gas values more accurately.

INDICATIONS

Polysomnographic monitoring is indicated to determine whether a patient's medical condition worsens during sleep (e.g., decline in Sa_{O_2}) or to determine the pathophysiology of sleep-related symptoms (e.g., sleep-related cyanotic episodes) (Table 138-2). Polysomnography may also help determine whether a variety of surgical procedures are indicated, including Nissen fundoplication, tonsillectomy, adenoidectomy, or tracheostomy, or whether closing a tracheotomy is medically indicated.

Each polysomnogram is preceded by an initial evaluation in which the patient's physician and the sleep specialist agree on the critical questions to be addressed by the sleep study and the variables to be monitored. Too often a generic polysomnogram or a two- to four-channel recording is obtained without prior determination of the specific diagnosis or diagnoses to be defined, evaluated, or excluded. The questions to be answered by a sleep study dictate the montage. Polysomnograms may be obtained needlessly when there is failure to specify a priori the clinical consequences of a positive or negative study.

Infants

Polysomnographic studies are frequently performed in infants who have had an apparent life-threatening event or are observed to have difficulty breathing while asleep. Indications in infants include a wide range of significant but inexplicable phenomena involving sleep and the cardiopulmonary system such as cyanotic episodes ("blue spells"), GER, possible seizures related to an apparent life-threatening event, or sleep-related bradycardia. Polysomnograms are often obtained as part of the evaluation in an infant who has experienced an apparent life-threatening event in whom previous hospital evaluation yielded normal results. These studies are effective in documenting symptoms or conditions that need medical intervention, such as apnea of infancy. A normal polysomnogram, although not predictive of the absence of any risk for SIDS, may be helpful in that it removes the infant from the high-risk category that would be conferred by a positive cardiac or pulmonary finding.

Cardiopulmonary monitors placed on infants during sleep at home typically trigger inexplicably, and monitors with "downloading" recording devices frequently demonstrate apneic or bradycardic events in an otherwise healthy and normally developing infant or child. Cardiopulmonary monitor alarms and recorded results from unattended monitoring may be

Table 138-2   Sleep-Related Diagnoses and Symptoms and Sleep Disorders to be Ruled out by Polysomnographic Evaluation

Diagnosis/Symptoms	Suspected Sleep Disorder
Episodic nocturnal arousals with screaming and unusual movements but child is not responsive	Night terrors, confusional arousals, sleep-related seizures, anxiety dreams, nocturnal paroxysmal dystonia
Sleep-related coughing or choking	Sleep-related abnormal swallowing syndrome, sleep-related asthma, sleep-related GER, laryngospasm, sleep-related choking syndrome
Unexplained apneic or cyanotic episodes with spitting up in an infant	Apnea of infancy, obstructive or central sleep apnea, sleep-related GER
Neuromuscular or cranial facial abnormalities (e.g., myotonic dystrophy, spina bifida, cerebral palsy, spinal motor atrophy, scoliosis, Down syndrome, Hurler's syndrome, or hydroencephally); snoring or excessive daytime sleepiness	Obstructive sleep apnea, obstructive respiratory process, central alveolar hypoventilation, central sleep apnea, periodic limb movements, major depressive disorder
Hypersomnolence, nonrestorative sleep, excessive daytime sleepiness	Narcolepsy, idiopathic hypersomnolence, chronic fatigue syndrome, Kline-Levin syndrome, disordered circadian rhythm syndromes, major depressive disorder, insufficient sleep syndrome, periodic limb movements
Excessive movement during sleep, rhythmic or nonperiodic	Head banging or rhythmic movement disorders, nocturnal paroxysmal dystonia, periodic limb movement disorder, REM sleep movement disorder, sleep-related seizure disorder, kinetic arousal disorder
Surgical high risk, history of obstructive sleep apnea with no anatomic abnormalities, evaluation for tracheostomy	Establish severity of obstructive apnea to help determine risk-benefit ratio
Evaluation for discontinuation of tracheotomy	Demonstrate obstructive apnea to be no longer present
Nasal CPAP or bipressure PAP, negative pressure ventilator titration studies	Establish efficacy of respiratory assistance mode and effective pressure setting
Pulmonary hypertension	Obstructive sleep apnea, obstructive respiratory process
Unexplained hypoxemia	Obstructive or central sleep apnea, obstructive respiratory process, central alveolar hypoventilation
Evaluation of apparent life-threatening event in an infant	Apnea of infancy with hypoxemia or bradycardia or both
Evaluation for cardiopulmonary monitor discontinuation	Exclude apnea of infancy
Failure to thrive with obstructed respiration	Obstructive sleep apnea, obstructive respiratory process, chronic alveolar hypoventilation
Stridor during sleep	Obstructive sleep apnea, obstructive respiratory process with hypoxemia
Sleep-related sickle cell anemia pain crises	Sleep-related hypoxemia with or without central or obstructive apnea
Sleep-related hypoxemia without explanation	Central or obstructive sleep apnea, obstructive respiratory process, chronic alveolar hypoventilation
Sleep-related hypercapnea	Central or obstructive sleep apnea, obstructive respiratory process, chronic alveolar hypoventilation
Depression with hypersomnolence and excessive daytime sleepiness or hyposomnolence that does not respond to appropriate antidepressant treatment	Disrupted sleep with high stage 1 and low stages III and IV, periodic limb movements, narcolepsy, idiopathic hypersomnolence, obstructive sleep apnea
Generalized anxiety disorder accompanying sleep disorder	Disrupted sleep with high stage I, frequent arousal from all stages of sleep, low stages III and IV, periodic limb movements, idiopathic hypersomnolence, obstructive sleep apnea
Attention deficit disorder (ADD) with disrupted sleep or ADD with hyperactivity and impaired vigilance	Kinetic arousal disorder, periodic limb movements, obstructive sleep apnea

impossible to interpret. However, a respiratory polysomnogram may be recorded in conjunction with the home monitor to determine the significance of alarms. Typically, all variables are within normal limits on the polysomnogram at the moment the home monitor triggers, but demonstrating this may be of critical significance to the patient's pediatrician and family in evaluating whether to discontinue the home monitor.

Children

Polysomnography is used in children when a sleep-related medical disorder is suspected or medically significant events have been witnessed during sleep, such as cyanosis, erratic breathing, apnea, or possible seizures. Frequently a polysomnogram is indicated if snoring and apneic pauses are described by parents but physical examination fails to demonstrate hypertrophy of the tonsils or adenoids. Sleep studies are also useful when surgery is indicated to aid respiration during sleep but the patient is a high-risk candidate for surgery. Sleep studies are indicated in children with chronic hypersomnolence or excessive daytime sleepiness or those in whom sleep appears to be nonrefreshing.

Evaluation of Tracheostomy and Decanulation

A polysomnogram provides objective evidence that helps determine the risk-benefit ratio of performing a tracheostomy. Similarly, a polysomnogram recorded with a patient's tracheotomy plugged helps determine whether removing the tracheotomy is medically indicated. Polysomnography is necessary because a closed tracheotomy may prevent the deeper stages of sleep and thereby inhibit the apnea or hypoxemia that occurs only in these sleep stages.

Ventilatory Assistance

When nasal continuous positive airway pressure (CPAP) is a possible treatment option for obstructive sleep apnea or nasal inspiratory and expiratory changes in pressure (nasal BiPAP) is a treatment option for central sleep apnea, a titration study is indicated. First, the polysomnogram in conjunction with nasal CPAP or BiPAP establishes whether these are indeed viable treatment options. Second, in the case of nasal CPAP, the study determines the minimal pressure setting necessary to treat the respiratory disorder; in the case of BiPAP it determines inspiratory and expiratory pressures.

TECHNIQUES
Polysomnography

Polysomnography is performed with a polygraph with 10 to 64 alternating-current amplifiers and pre-amplifiers and several direct-current amplifiers. This equipment amplifies bioelectric signals with potentials from ± 5 to 500 μV to a range of -1 to $+1$ volts, after which the signal is printed out on paper or digitized and displayed on a computer monitor. The input to the polygraph is derived from electrodes or sensing devices affixed to the patient's scalp, face, and body.

Electrophysiology and Stages of Sleep and Wakefulness

The EEG is recorded from surface central electrode sites, C3 and C4, measured according to the 10- to 20-electrode placement system. Slow, rolling eye movements, recorded with EOG, signal the onset of sleep, along with relaxed EMG potentials, and the dropout of alpha (8 to 12 Hz) brain waves on the EEG, a rhythm characteristic of the relaxed awake state. During NREM sleep higher voltage and a slower EEG are observed compared with wakefulness or REM sleep, and eye movements are absent. Recorded from jaw and chin muscles, the EMG continues to show relaxed tonus during NREM sleep. During REM sleep the EEG is more similar to that during wakefulness (low voltage), the EMGs show atonia (total absence of muscle tone), and the EOG shows rapid eye movements.

Monitoring
State of consciousness

State of sleep and wakefulness may be assessed by recording EEG, EOG, and EMG. All additional channels permit the monitoring of clinically relevant variables. Placement of scalp electrodes for EEG are determined according to the 10- to 20-electrode placement system recommended by the International Federation of Societies for Electroencephalography and Clinical Neurophysiology. Typically, signals are recorded in a unipolar format from left and right central cortex (C3 and C4) referred to the contralateral mastoid. Eye movements are recorded by placing electrodes lateral to the outer canthi of each eye, also referred to the contralateral mastoid. This enables the clinician to monitor the corneofundal potential, or the electropotential difference between the cornea and the retina. The signal thus derived is the EOG. The EMG is obtained by placing electrodes superficial to the masseter and mandibular muscles and recording the continuous (tonic) level of background muscle activity.

Sleep and wakefulness in infants

Sleep stages are not readily distinguishable at birth. Therefore polysomnographic recordings, behavioral observation, and monitoring of motility patterns have been used to assess sleep stages and wakefulness in the infant, and all three techniques show reasonable concordance.

Respiration

Respiratory recordings minimally necessary to evaluate obstructive and central apnea syndromes are qualitative and include assessment of airflow from both nares and the mouth and monitoring of thoracic and abdominal expansion and contraction to measure respiratory motion.

Qualitative respiratory monitoring. Airflow is typically monitored with temperature-sensitive thermistors. The tips of the wires are placed directly over the nostrils and the corner of the mouth, and the voltage induced by temperature changes associated with each breath is then amplified. Airflow may also be assessed by monitoring tracheal breath sounds with a microphone placed on the sternal notch. The microphone output may be amplified for recording or connected to a speaker to permit an auditory signal. Snoring and other breath sounds are typically monitored with a low-frequency miniature microphone placed near the patient's mouth; the amplified output is recorded by analog or digital techniques.

Detection of respiratory motion is the standard polysomnographic technique for qualitatively assessing respiratory effort. When properly placed, bands over the thoracic and abdominal surface show expansion with inspiration and contraction with expiration. The expansion-contraction is detected with piezoelectric sensors, strain gauges, or changes in impedance, inductance, or magnetic fields. In each case the signal is converted to voltage, amplified, and recorded on paper or stored digitally. During normal respiration the thoracic and abdominal bands move synchronously with each inspiratory-expiratory cycle. In obstructive apnea respiratory bands move out of phase, that is, paradoxical breathing; during central apnea no movement is detected in either band.

Activity of intercostal and diaphragmatic EMG activity may be recorded from surface electrodes placed in pairs, the former at the eighth intercostal space and the latter over the parasternal region. If properly placed, the recordings will show nearly simultaneous EMG discharge during normal respiration and alternate discharge during the paradoxical movement associated with obstructive apnea or Müller's maneuver.

Quantitative respiratory monitoring. The above qualitative measurements of airflow in addition to movement of the chest wall and abdomen fail to assess two additionally important respiratory variables: airflow volume and respiratory effort. Thermistor and respiratory band polysomnographic amplitude depend on the position of the monitoring device with respect to the position of the signal being assessed. For example, slight displacement of the nasal thermistor from the nares will result in a large increase or decrease in signal amplitude.

Quantitative measurement of airflow rate and tidal and minute volume may be obtained with a pneumotachograph in conjunction with a face mask and a differential pressure transducer. Volumetric measurements of ventilation as part of a polysomnogram are useful to evaluate hypoventilation and upper airway resistance but are impractical in children because the necessary equipment is cumbersome and not well tolerated.

A quantitative technique to measure effort of breathing is to insert a balloon or a catheter filled with air or water through the nares to the esophagus. The catheter is open at the distal end, which is situated at the midthoracic level. The proximal end of the catheter is covered with a pressure transducer calibrated for negative and positive readings. When the catheter is properly inserted, a respiratory waveform with an amplitude relative to ventilatory exertion is seen.

Blood Oxygen Saturation

With the exception of the highly invasive procedure of placing an indwelling arterial catheter, oxygen pressure is estimated noninvasively by a variety of techniques (see Table 138-1). Pulse oximetric estimation of blood oxygen pressure is by far the most widely used method.

Seizures

When seizures are suspected to be contributing to a sleep disorder such as night terrors, apnea, or hypoxemia, a standard 10- to 20-electrode system montage may be recorded in conjuction with the polysomnogram to ascertain the relationship between hypersynchronous events and the observed sleep-related symptoms. Digital storage techniques permit recording of up to 32 electrode sites and displaying up to 32 EEG channels in addition to the polysomnogram on a monitor at 10 to 30 mm/sec.

Gastroesophageal reflux

A catheter with one or two pH monitoring probes may be placed to record GER only or reflux at the level of the larynx as well, the latter to estimate the risk of laryngomalacia. This is typically performed in conjunction with a respiratory polysomnogram to ascertain the relationship between reflux and apnea.

Periodic limb movement

Sleep may be severely disrupted by rhythmic discharges of the anterior tibialis muscles, each discharge associated with arousal or awakening. This phenomenon can occur in the equivalent muscles in the arms. Superficial electrodes placed in pairs over these muscles provide an electromyographic signal of these contractions during sleep.

Hypercapnia and hypocapnia

Transcutaneous or end-tidal CO_2 can be measured in conjunction with a polysomnogram to assess levels of this gas during obstructive or central respiratory disorders. End-tidal CO_2 is used by some sleep laboratories as a measurement of airflow. Transcutaneous CO_2 does not correlate well with arterial P_{CO_2} in our experience, and end-tidal CO_2 underestimates P_{CO_2}.

Arterial blood gas levels

When accurate assessment of P_{O_2} or P_{CO_2} is essential, an arterial catheter may be placed to determine whether hypoxemia or hypercapnia is present during sleep. Blood samples are obtained if there is a pronounced decrease in Sa_{O_2} or elevation in end-tidal CO_2, providing validation of noninvasive estimates of blood gas levels.

RISKS AND COMPLICATIONS

Because the purpose of a polysomnogram is to document known or suspected sleep-related diseases and elucidate their mechanisms (e.g., obstructive sleep apnea that causes observed cyanosis during sleep), the recording situation creates a medical conundrum.

To observe the events in question, which frequently can be severe (e.g., Sa_{O_2} <50% or heart rate <50 bpm in an infant), they must be allowed to occur without interruption. However, the dictum of doing no harm mandates intervention before any event becomes severe. The knowledge that such events have been occurring in the hospital or at home without medical intervention does not solve this dilemma because, once observed, medical ethics and legal responsibility necessitate higher accountability.

The night technician recording the polysomnogram cannot be abandoned without written instructions on when to intervene, when to notify nursing, or when to notify the medical staff. The polysomnographer and attending physician need to decide beforehand what respiratory or cardiac values are acceptable and which dictate intervention. In adult sleep disorders centers, typically intervention does not occur at any level of Sa_{O_2} desaturation if bradycardia is not observed. Clearly, the situation is different in children. The agreed on permissible levels of desaturation or bradycardia need be written in the chart. In addition, a written policy and procedure statement from the sleep disorders center regarding permissible levels of hypoxemia or bradycardia must be adhered to by the night technician, and the attending physician or the physician who ordered the polysomnogram must be informed of these values.

In certain instances during polysomnography (e.g., in infants or children known to be incapable of maintaining normal blood gas values during sleep without ventilatory assistance and in whom the mechanism of ventilatory dependency is being explored with polysomnography), it may be best to remove ventilatory assistance with the polysomnographer and physician present.

Even under conditions of suitable medical coverage and continuous monitoring, polysomnography performed while the medical, sleep-related event in question transpires involves some degree of risk. This risk must be discussed by the physician and polysomnographer and a decision made that the risk-benefit ratio is not harmful to the patient.

ADDITIONAL READING

Chase MH. Synaptic mechanisms and circuitry involved in motoneuron control during sleep. In Bradley RJ, ed. International Review of Neurology, vol 24. New York: Academic Press, 1983, pp 213-358.

Guilleminault C. Sleep and breathing. In Guilleminault C, ed. Sleeping and Waking Disorders: Indications and Techniques. Boston: Butterworths, 1982, pp 155-182.

Janz D. Epilepsy and the sleeping-waking cycle. In Vincken P, Bruyn G, eds. The Epilepsies, vol 15. Handbook of Clinical Neurology. Amsterdam: North Holland, 1974, pp 457-490.

Orem J. Respiratory neurons and sleep. In Kryger M, Roth T, Dement W, eds. Principles and Practice of Sleep Medicine. Philadelphia: WB Saunders, 1994, pp 177-193.

Parmeggiani P. The autonomic nervous system in sleep. In Kryger M, Roth T, Dement W, eds. Principles and Practice of Sleep Medicine. Philadelphia: WB Saunders, 1994, pp 194-203.

Phillipson E, Sullivan CE, Read TJC, et al. Ventilatory and waking responses to hypoxia in sleeping dogs. J Appl Physiol 44:512-520, 1977.

Rechtshaffen A, Kales A. A Manual of Standardized Terminology, Techniques and Scoring System for Sleep Stages of Human Subjects. Washington, D.C.: U.S. Government Printing Office, 1968.

Strohl K, Chester C. Polysomnography for breathing disorders during sleep. In Nochomovitz M, Cherniaack N, eds. Noninvasive Respiratory Monitoring, vol 3. Contemporary Issues in Pulmonary Disease. New York: Churchill Livingstone, 1986, pp 153-166.

Thoman E, Acebo C. Monitoring of sleep in neonates and young children. In Ferber R, Kryger M, eds. Principles and Practice of Sleep Medicine in the Child. Philadelphia: WB Saunders, 1995, pp 55-68.

139 Near-Infrared Spectroscopy

Richard R. Sterrett

BACKGROUND AND INDICATIONS

Absorption of light through biologic tissues depends on the wavelength of the light and the properties of the tissue. Water and hemoglobin absorb visible light effectively, preventing it from penetrating more than a few millimeters into tissue. Conversely, biologic tissue does not absorb light in the near-infrared spectrum, allowing it to penetrate several centimeters into tissues. Organometallic compounds such as hemoglobin, oxyhemoglobin, and oxidized cytochrome *c* oxidase have characteristic infrared absorption spectra, and attenuation of infrared light in biologic tissue can be attributed almost solely to these compounds. Analysis of the spectra generated can reveal relative changes in these compounds. Spectra can be acquired repetitively, allowing continuous analysis.

Infrared light penetrates several centimeters into the human head. Early studies in infants used a near-infrared light source placed on one side of the infant's head with the sensor placed on the opposite side. As will be shown, analysis of spectra is similar to pulse oximetry performed routinely for continuous monitoring of Sao_2.

Currently spectral analysis has been focused largely on the ratio of saturated hemoglobin to total hemoglobin (i.e., brain oxygen saturation) and on the relative changes in total hemoglobin in the area of the brain being studied. When infrared light passes through cerebral tissue, it encounters a largely venous (estimated at 70% to 80%) vascular bed. Hence near-infrared spectroscopy provides a cerebral oximetry value that reflects predominantly venous and capillary saturation.

Near-infrared spectroscopy has been compared with xenon-133 clearance and jugular bulb saturation with good correlation. In initial studies instruments were used that directed light from a source on one side of the head to a sensor on the other side and limited application in human neonates. It has since been shown that similar information can be obtained by analyzing the spectra of light as it reflects off the brain tissue back toward its source. Current instruments have a light source surrounded by detectors that obtain spectra from the underlying brain tissue. Analysis of the spectra obtained supplies information about the tissue only in the area where the light penetrates and returns, and tissue saturation obtained is referred to as the regional saturation of hemoglobin.

Other aspects of cerebral oxygen metabolism have been investigated with near-infrared spectroscopy. The relative changes in the total hemoglobin in the area being studied can be measured, supplying information about changes in regional brain blood volume. Currently the absolute total volume of hemoglobin cannot be ascertained. In addition, the regional cerebral blood flow may be characterized. By injection of indocyanide green into the systemic circulation and simultaneous monitoring of an arterial vessel and cerebral tissue, the changes in indocyanide green concentration can be used to calculate regional cortical transit time. Another application is use of changes in the spectra of cytochrome *c* oxidase to obtain information about regional cellular glucose metabolism.

Current clinical applications are investigational. Studies have examined the effect of suctioning on cerebral oxygenation and blood volume, the effects of circulatory arrest on cerebral reperfusion, the effects of thought on cerebral oxygenation, and the detection of intracranial hematomas. It is hoped this technology will allow noninvasive early detection of changes in cerebral metabolism, thereby allowing timely changes in therapy that improve patient outcomes.

RISKS AND COMPLICATIONS

Near-infrared spectroscopy is a totally noninvasive technique and therefore its use poses no additional risks to the patient. Because this technique is not yet clinically available, its use and difficulties in interpretation are not yet known.

ADDITIONAL READING

• Beretta SL, Citerio G, Gemma M. Noninvasive cerebral regional saturation monitoring: Comparison with jugular bulb saturation in patients in coma [abst]. Crit Care Med 23:76, 1995.

Bucher HU, Edwards AD, Lipp AE, Duc G. Comparison between near infrared spectroscopy and ^{133}xenon clearance for estimation of cerebral blood flow in critically ill preterm infants. Pediatr Res 33:56, 1992.

Gopinath SP, Robertson CS, Chance B. Delayed traumatic intracranial hematomas: Early detection in ICU using near infrared spectroscopy [abst]. Crit Care Med 23:77, 1955.

Hampson NB, Camporesi EM, Stolp BW, Moon RE, Shook JE, Griebel JA, Piantadosi CA. Cerebral oxygen availability by NIR spectroscopy during transient hypoxia in humans J Appl Physiol 69:907, 1990.

Hoshi Y, Tamura M. Detection of dynamic changes in cerebral oxygenation coupled to neuronal function during mental work in man. Neurosci Lett 150:5, 1993.

• McCormick PW, Stewart M, Goetting MG, Dujovny M, Lewis G, Ausman J. Noninvasive cerebral optical spectroscopy for monitoring cerebral oxygen delivery and hemodynamics. Crit Care Med 19:89, 1991.

Shah AR, Kurth CD, Gwiazdowski SG, Chance B, Delivoria-Papadopoulos M. Fluctuations in cerebral oxygenation and blood volume during endotracheal suctioning in premature infants. J Pediatr 20:769, 1992.

• Smith DS, Levy W, Maris M, Chance B. Reperfusion hypoxia in brain after circulatory arrest in humans. Anesthesiology 73:12, 1990.

XIX

Cardiac Procedures

140 Cardiopulmonary Arrest and Resuscitation

Penny G. Williams · Patricia A. Primm

BACKGROUND AND INDICATIONS

Unlike adult cardiopulmonary arrest, children rarely suffer sudden cardiac events. In children a cascade of physiologic changes culminates in a final common pathway to cardiac arrest. Respiratory conditions are by far the most common cause of cardiac arrest in children. Usually primary respiratory arrest leads to hypoxemia and acidosis and culminates in bradycardic or asystolic arrest. Of all the arrhythmias associated with cardiac arrest, asystole accounts for 78%, bradyarrhythmias account for 12%, and ventricular arrhythmias account for the remaining 10%.

In respiratory arrest a prolonged phase of tissue hypoxia leads to multiple organ failure. This multiorgan failure complicates the outcome of pediatric resuscitation. Consider the heart an end organ; by the time it stops, irreparable damage has occurred to the brain, kidney, and liver.

Survival rates of children having cardiac arrest are dismal, and most who do survive have significant neurologic impairment. The survival rate from out-of-hospital pediatric cardiac arrest ranges from 10% to 34%. These statistics represent apneic and pulseless arrest victims brought to a pediatric emergency department. Survival rates following in-hospital cardiac arrest are 10%.

Resuscitation from isolated respiratory arrest is more successful, with survival rates approaching 95% among trauma and nontrauma victims treated in a pediatric emergency department. Early recognition of the arrest coupled with quick response time and early entry to the emergency medical service (EMS) system can improve resuscitation outcomes.

The mechanism by which blood moves during cardiopulmonary resuscitation is the subject of ongoing investigation. Both the traditional model of heart compression and the newer model of the thoracic pump theory probably play a part in the actual mechanism in children. The traditional view assumes that chest compression over the ventricles moves blood by direct cardiac compression. The thoracic pump model suggests that the movement of blood is caused by an increase in cardiothoracic pressure and expulsion of blood from the lungs through the left heart with simultaneous opening of both mitral and aortic valves.

Cardiopulmonary arrest in children occurs most commonly at either end of the pediatric age spectrum—younger than 1 year and teenagers. The most common causes during infancy are sudden infant death syndrome, respiratory diseases, submersion, sepsis, neurologic disease, and airway obstruction, including foreign body aspiration. After 1 year of age the leading cause of pediatric cardiopulmonary arrest is injuries. Children in the PICU are always at risk of cardiopulmonary arrest because of the relative in-

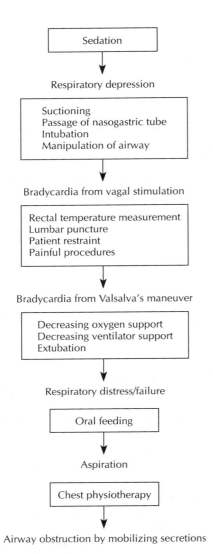

Sedation

↓

Respiratory depression

Suctioning
Passage of nasogastric tube
Intubation
Manipulation of airway

↓

Bradycardia from vagal stimulation

Rectal temperature measurement
Lumbar puncture
Patient restraint
Painful procedures

↓

Bradycardia from Valsalva's maneuver

Decreasing oxygen support
Decreasing ventilator support
Extubation

↓

Respiratory distress/failure

Oral feeding

↓

Aspiration

Chest physiotherapy

↓

Airway obstruction by mobilizing secretions

Fig. 140-1 High-risk procedures that may lead to cardio-pulmonary arrest.

stability of their conditions. Fig. 140-1 outlines several conditions or procedures that place pediatric patients at risk for cardiopulmonary arrest.

TECHNIQUE

Monitoring for early signs of cardiopulmonary deterioration is critical in recognizing and managing impending cardiopulmonary arrest. A rapid cardiopulmonary assessment using the *a*irway, *b*reathing, and *c*irculation approach (ABCs) yields key physical findings on which to base clinical decisions (Table 140-1).

Pulse oximetry, end-tidal carbon dioxide ($etco_2$) detection, and ECG monitoring can be useful noninvasive tools for clinical evaluation. Pulse oximetry permits evaluation of oxygenation through continuous measurement of arterial oxygen saturation and is used to diagnose poor peripheral perfusion. In most cases an oxygen saturation of ≤90% indicates the beginning of hypoxia. Since this measurement depends on pulsatile blood flow, pulse oximetry may not be useful in low-perfusion states.

$etco_2$ detection can be helpful in verifying endotracheal tube placement in infants >2 kg by monitoring pulmonary artery carbon dioxide concentration ($Paco_2$). This technique may not be reliable in pulseless arrest since low $etco_2$ levels may be indicative of decreased pulmonary blood flow rather than esophageal tube placement.

ECG monitoring allows for continuous assessment of the patient's heart rate and gives a tracing of the electrophysiologic conduction. Since ECG monitoring does not reflect the quality of myocardial contraction or tissue perfusion, ECG analysis must be correlated to the clinical assessment of the patient.

Although laboratory tests may be helpful in determining the severity of a condition, they are not the basis for initial clinical decisions. Arterial blood gas determination and serum blood levels such as glucose, calcium, or other electrolytes may be helpful in guiding resuscitation and in evaluating response to therapy.

Pediatric Basic Life Support

Pediatric basic life support (PBLS) is used to describe the sequential assessments and psychomotor skills used to support or regain effective ventilation and circulation in respiratory or cardiopulmonary arrest. A combination of artificial ventilations and external cardiac compressions comprise PBLS techniques. Table 140-2 summarizes the standards and guidelines for PBLS maneuvers as established by the American Heart Association. For the purpose of PBLS, an infant is defined as younger than 1 year of age and a child is defined as between the ages of 1 and 8 years. These are guidelines only, and children often differ from the norm in a health care setting. Judgment must be exercised in choosing the technique that will produce the best result.

PBLS maneuvers must be integrated and coordi-

Table 140-1   Rapid Cardiopulmonary Assessment

Respiratory Assessment	Cardiovascular Assessment
A. Airway patency	C. Circulation
Able to maintain independently	Heart rate
Adjuncts/assistance necessary to maintain	Blood pressure
B. Breathing	Volume/strength of central pulses
Rate	Peripheral pulses
Mechanics	Present/absent
Retractions	Volume/strength
Grunting	Skin perfusion
Accessory muscles	Capillary refill time (consider ambient temperature)
Nasal flaring	Temperature
Air entry	Color
Chest expansion	Mottling
Breath sounds	CNS perfusion
Stridor	Responsiveness
Wheezing	Awake
Paradoxical chest movement	Responds to voice
Color	Responds to pain
	Unresponsive
	Recognizes parents
	Muscle tone
	Pupil size
	Posturing

Reproduced with permission. Textbook of Pediatric Advanced Life Support, 1994. Copyright American Heart Association.

Table 140-2   Summary of PBLS Maneuvers in Infants and Children

Maneuver	Infant (<1 yr)	Child (1 to 8 yr)
Airway	Head tilt–chin lift (if trauma is present, use jaw thrust)	Head tilt–chin lift (if trauma is present, use jaw thrust)
Breathing		
Initial	Two breaths at 1 to 1½ sec/breath	Two breaths at 1 to 1½ sec/breath
Subsequent	20 breaths/min (approx.)	20 breaths/min (approx.)
Circulation		
Pulse check	Brachial/femoral	Carotid
Compression area	Lower half of sternum	Lower half of sternum
Compression width	2 or 3 fingers	Heel of 1 hand
Depth	Approximately ⅓ to ½ depth of chest	Approximately ⅓ to ½ depth of chest
Rate	At least 100/min	100/min
Compression-ventilation ratio	5:1 (pause for ventilation)	5:1 (pause for ventilation)
Foreign body airway obstruction	Back blows/chest thrusts	Heimlich maneuver

Reproduced with permission. Textbook of Pediatric Advanced Life Support, 1994. Copyright American Heart Association.

nated with advanced life support procedures in a health care setting. The same guidelines and standards for PBLS are followed during resuscitation efforts.

Airway

The most important component of PBLS in the pediatric population is establishing and maintaining a patent airway. The airway may become obstructed as a result of edematous tissue, blood or secretions, or more commonly from the tongue being displaced posteriorly into the airway.

The head tilt–chin lift maneuver is the easiest technique to open the airway, lifting the tongue away from the posterior pharynx. Care must be taken not to hyperextend the neck since this may cause the cartilaginous trachea to collapse. If neck or spinal injury is suspected, the jaw thrust maneuver is used. Ideally, one person immobilizes the spine while another person lifts the jaw upward and outward without any extension of the neck.

A large-bore suction device (tonsil suction) and suction must be readily available to clear the airway of blood or secretions and to respond to procedures that stimulate a gag reflex and subsequent vomiting. A suction force of 80 to 120 mm Hg is usually necessary to provide effective suction.

Artificial airways can be used as airway adjuncts to maintain airway patency. Oropharyngeal airways are used in unconscious patients since the rigid nature of the airway may stimulate gagging and vomiting in the conscious patient. Nasopharyngeal airways are better tolerated in the conscious patient since the airway is made of soft pliable material. Because of the small diameter of this airway, it needs to be evaluated frequently to ensure it is not obstructed with blood or secretions.

Breathing

If the airway has been opened and the patient is not spontaneously breathing, rescue breathing must be performed. A mouth-to-mask device with a one-way valve can create a barrier between the health care provider and the patient.

Bag-mask ventilation systems are readily available in the acute care setting, eliminating the need for prolonged rescuer ventilation. Resuscitation bags used for infants and children need to have a minimum volume of 450 ml to ensure delivery of an appropriate

tidal volume. When larger volume bags are used, only the force and volume necessary to expand the chest wall must be used. A wide variety of mask sizes are available. A mask is selected that contours to the child's face and does not apply pressure to the eyes. Bag-mask ventilations are delivered using the same guidelines delineated in the PBLS standards (see Table 140-2). Bag-mask ventilations are coordinated carefully with chest compressions to ensure that appropriate chest expansion occurs with each ventilation.

Self-inflating bag-valve mask (BVM) ventilation devices function independently from an inflow of a gas source and therefore provide a quick means to ventilate a patient in an emergency. BVM devices deliver room air unless supplemental oxygen is connected. At an oxygen flow rate of 10 L/min this system will deliver 30% to 80% oxygen. Oxygen reservoirs are available with this BVM system to allow higher concentrations of oxygen to be delivered (from 60% to 95%). A flow rate of 10 to 15 L/min is necessary to maintain an adequate oxygen supply in the reservoir bag. Since the BVM device contains a one-way valve, the bag must be compressed to permit the flow of gas. Thus this system cannot be used in spontaneously breathing patients to deliver blow-by oxygen support. BVM systems are available with a pressure activated pop-off valve. However, pressures needed during resuscitation may exceed the limit on the pop-off valve. Therefore bags must also be available that do not have pop-off valves or valves that can easily be occluded with a finger or by taping or twisting the valve into a closed position.

Anesthesia ventilation systems consist of a reservoir bag, oxygen port, and an overflow valve. In this system gas flow is necessary to inflate the bag, and the overflow valve must be adjusted to control the volume of gas in the bag and the pressure delivered. Thus the anesthesia system is best used by skilled practitioners who have had experience in regulating the flow of gas and the volume of gas needed for the patient. The advantage of an anesthesia system is that it can deliver 100% oxygen, whereas many BVM devices are limited in the amount of oxygen delivery.

Circulation

Cardiac chest compressions are indicated when the pulse is not palpable or when the heart rate is <60 bpm with signs of poor perfusion. The carotid pulse is easiest to palpate, but because infants have short necks, the brachial or femoral pulse is more accessible to palpation in infants. Chest compressions are coordinated with ventilations providing a breath between each set of five compressions.

The mechanism of blood flow during chest compressions in infants and children is most likely the result of direct compression of the heart. The thin chest wall in children offers less resistance and makes compression easier than in adults. Accordingly, it is important to ensure that placement of the finger and hand for chest compression is accurate and that the infant or child is on a flat surface. When the head of an infant is tilted, the shoulders may elevate off the hard surface, creating a gap between the back and the hard surface. This gap can easily be filled with the palm of the rescuer's hand, creating a firm surface (Fig. 140-2).

In the newborn or small infant the preferred method for performing chest compressions is to place two thumbs side by side on the sternum just below the nipple line with the fingers encircling the chest and supporting the back (Fig. 140-3). If the rescuer's hands are large, it may be necessary for the thumbs to be superimposed one on top of the other. If encircling the chest causes a restriction in chest expansion during ventilations or if the rescuer's hands are too small to encircle the chest and provide support to the spine, this technique must not be used. Mechanical devices to compress the sternum are not currently recommended for use in infants or children. These devices have been designed for adults and have not been redesigned or tested in children.

The effectiveness of cardiac compressions need to be monitored periodically throughout resuscitation. Central pulses are palpated during chest compressions to ensure that the quality and depth of compressions are adequate. Peripheral pulses can be assessed as well by tracings noted on the ECG monitor to better assess cardiac output and response to resuscitation efforts.

Pediatric Advanced Life Support

Pediatric advanced life support (PALS) refers to the assessment and support of pulmonary and circulatory function in the critically ill infant or child. Oxygen is administered to all children with cardiopulmonary arrest or compromise via a BVM device or face mask. Self-refilling bags must be readily available in child

and adult sizes with appropriate masks for infants, children, and adults. The bag must not have a pop-off valve, and a minimum volume of 450 ml is delivered with oxygen flow at 10 to 15 L/min.

Ventilation via an ET tube is the most effective and safest route for airway management. Once the prop-

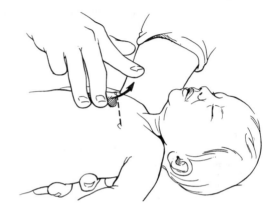

Fig. 140-2 Placement of rescuer's hand to support spine during cardiac compressions. (Redrawn from Guidelines for Cardiopulmonary Resuscitation and Emergency Cardiac Care: Recommendations of the 1992 National Conference. JAMA 268:2256, 1992. Copyright 1992, American Medical Association.)

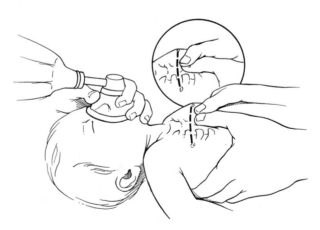

Fig. 140-3 Hand position for chest encirclement technique for external chest compressions in neonates. (Redrawn from Guidelines for Cardiopulmonary Resuscitation and Emergency Cardiac Care: Recommendations of the 1992 National Conference. JAMA 268:2279, 1992. Copyright 1992, American Medical Association.)

er placement of the ET tube is verified, positive pressure ventilation with a bag-valve device is continued with the head maintained in a neutral position. Continued monitoring via auscultation, visualization of chest movement, pulse oximetry, and etco$_2$ monitoring will ensure the patency of the airway.

Acquiring vascular access is the second step in PALS. The intravenous (IV) or intraosseous (IO) route for fluid and drug administration is far preferable to the ET route because all drugs and fluids delivered will be reliably absorbed. The ET route of drug delivery is limited to a few lipid-soluble drugs (epinephrine, atropine, lidocaine, and naloxone). This route has the theoretical advantage of more rapid distribution of drugs to the arterial site of action, but animal studies show that, at least for epinephrine, ET administration delivers only about one-tenth that of equivalent IV epinephrine doses. Optimal ET doses of atropine, lidocaine, and naloxone in pediatric patients have not been determined. Without definitive

TYPE OF ARRHYTHMIA

TREATMENT

Asystole

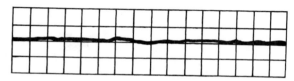

Rate: complete absence of any ventricular
    electrical activity
P waves: In some cases P waves may be seen
Pulse: absent

CPR
Epinephrine: 0.01 mg/kg IV, IO 1st dose
        0.1 mg/kg ET 1st dose
        0.1 mg/kg IV, IO, ET 2nd and
           subsequent doses

Electromechanical dissociation

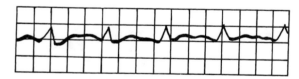

Rate: irregular
Rhythm: irregular but electrical activity present
Pulse: absent

CPR
Epinephrine: 0.01 mg/kg IV, IO 1st dose
        0.1 mg/kg ET 1st dose
        0.1 mg/kg IV, IO, ET 2nd and
           subsequent doses
Consider causes: Acidosis, cardiac tamponade,
           tension pneumothorax,
           hypothermia, hypovolemia,
           hypoxemia

Sinus bradycardia

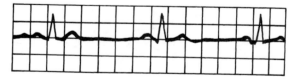

Rate: less than 60 bpm
Rhythm: regular
P waves: upright
QRS: following each P wave

Epinephrine: 0.01 mg/kg IV, IO
        0.1 mg/kg ET
Atropine: 0.02 mg/kg IV, IO, ET
Consider pacing

Fig. 140-4   Treatment of arrhythmias.

data, the currently recommended IV dose for at-ropine, lidocaine, and naloxone is the minimum dose for ET administration. Epinephrine is given endotra-cheally at a dosage 10 times the IV dose. If a reliable IV or IO line cannot be achieved in 3 to 5 minutes, ET delivery of resuscitation drugs can be instituted. Delivery of ET drugs is best achieved by direct in-stillation into the ET tube via a syringe. All drugs, whether delivered by the IV, IO, or ET route, need to be flushed with 3 to 5 ml of 0.9% sodium chloride solution to move the drug into the circulation or dis-tal airways, respectively.

Resuscitation therapy for bradycardia

Sinus bradycardia, atrioventricular block, and sinus node arrest with a slow junctional or idioventricular rhythm are the most common preterminal rhythms in infants and children (Fig. 140-4). All slow rhythms re-sulting in cardiopulmonary instability need immediate treatment (Fig. 140-5).

TYPE OF DYSRHYTHMIA	TREATMENT

Supraventricular tachycardia

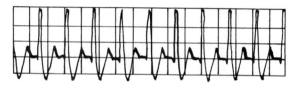

Rate: >220 bpm
Rhythm: regular
P waves: may be difficult to see
QRS: narrow

Synchronized cardioversion : 0.5 J/kg
　　　　　　　　　　　　　　　 1.0 J/kg 2nd dose
Adenosine: 0.05-0.1 mg/kg IV

Ventricular fibrillation

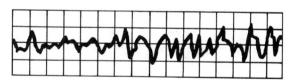

Rate: rapid; usually too disorganized to count
Rhythm: irregular, waveforms vary in size and shape
No P wave, QRS, ST segment, or T wave discernable
Pulse: absent

CPR
Defibrillation: 2 J/kg, 4 J/kg, 4 J/kg
Epinephrine: 0.01 mg/kg IV, IO 1st dose
　　　　　　　 0.1 mg/kg ET 1st dose
　　　　　　　 0.1 mg/kg IV, IO, ET
　　　　　　　 2nd and subsequent doses
Lidocaine: 1 mg/kg IV, IO, ET

Ventricular tachycardia

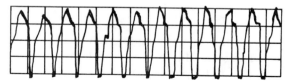

Rate: close to normal to >400 bpm
Rhythm: usually regular
P waves: often not recognizable
QRS: wide

If no palpable pulse treat as per ventricular fibrillation

If pulse present:
　Lidocaine: 1 mg/kg IV, IO, ET
　Synchronized cardioversion: 0.5 to 1.0 J/kg
　Lidocaine infusion: 20 to 50 µg/kg/min

Fig. 140-4, cont'd

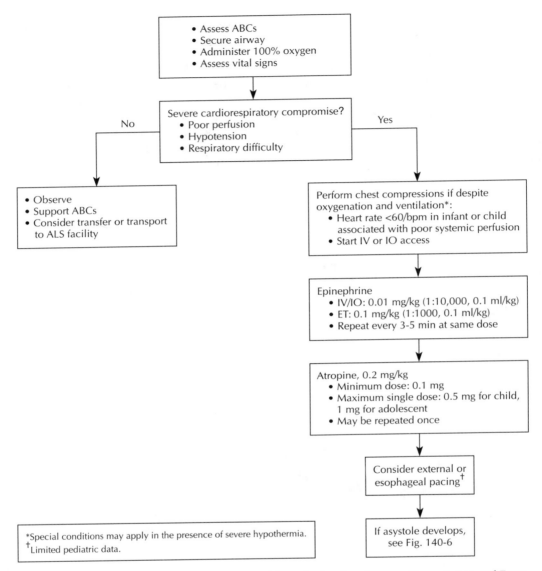

Fig. 140-5 Bradycardia decision tree. (From Guidelines for Cardiopulmonary Resuscitation and Emergency Cardiac Care: Recommendations of the 1992 National Conference. JAMA 268:2266, 1992. Copyright 1992, American Medical Association.)

Epinephrine. In bradycardic patients with a detectable pulse but poor perfusion or hypotension who fail to improve with adequate oxygenation and ventilation, epinephrine is administered in a dose of 0.01 mg/kg. Higher doses of epinephrine are indicated for cardiac arrest or rhythms without a pulse but not for bradycardia with a pulse (i.e., a perfusing rhythm). When the ET route is the only route available, epinephrine is given at an initial dose of 0.1 mg/kg. This higher dose is recommended because of the poor absorption of endotracheally delivered epinephrine. Subsequent doses of epinephrine are not increased if the patient maintains a perfusing rhythm.

Atropine. Bradycardia seen in children resulting in cardiovascular compromise usually reflects the ad-

RESUSCITATION EQUIPMENT

Drugs

Adenosine: 6 mg vial
Atropine: 10 ml prefilled syringe (0.1 mg/ml) (2)
Benadryl: 1 ml ampule (1)
Calcium chloride: 10 ml prefilled syringe (100 mg/ml) (2)
Calcium gluconate: 10 ml ampule (2)
50% dextrose: 50 ml vial (2)
Digoxin: 1 ml ampule (2)
Dilantin: 2 ml ampule (2)
Dopamine: 5 ml ampule (2)
Epinephrine (1:10,000): 10 ml prefilled syringe (0.1 mg/ml) (2)
Epinephrine (1:1000): 30 ml vial (1 mg/ml)
Heparin: 10 ml vial (1000 units/ml) (2)
Isuprel: 5 ml ampule (2)
Lasix: 2 ml ampule (2)
Lidocaine: 10 ml prefilled syringe (2% intracardiac) (2)
Methylprednisolone: 2 ml vial (125 mg) (2)
Narcan: 1 ml ampule (2)
Potassium chloride: 10 ml vial (2)
Sodium bicarbonate: 10 ml prefilled syringe (1 mEq/ml) (2)
0.9% sodium chloride solution: 10 ml vial (nonpreservative) (4)
Valium: 2 ml ampule (2)
Vecuronium: 10 mg vial
Versed: 2 ml ampule (2)

IV equipment

Lactated Ringer's solution: 250 ml (1)
5% dextrose: 250 ml (1)
5% dextrose in 0.45% sodium chloride: 250 ml (1)
0.9% sodium chloride solution: 250 ml (1)
IV Solusets (microdrip and maxidrip) (2)
Extension tubing (2)
Three-way stopcocks (4)
T-connectors
Latex tourniquet
Alcohol and povidone-iodine swabs
Protective IV catheter (catheter-over-needle): 24 to 16 gauge
Winged needle device: 21 to 25 gauge
Armboards: small and large
Adhesive tape: ½″ to 2″

Suctioning equipment

Bulb syringe
Tonsil-suction tip
Suction catheters: tip sizes 6.5 to 16 F
Feeding tube: size 8 F
Salem sump: 10-14 F
Catheter adapter
50 ml syringe
Adhesive tape: 1″

Airway equipment

Mouth-to-mask device with one-way valve
1 L hyperinflation bag
Oxygen flowmeter
Oxygen face masks: sizes neonate to large adult
Oral airways: 40 to 100 mm
Magill forceps: child and adult
Nasal airway, 12 to 34 F
Laryngoscope handle: standard size
Straight (Miller) laryngoscope blades: sizes No. 0 to 3
MacIntosh laryngoscope blades: size No. 2 and 3
Extra bulbs and batteries
Endotracheal tubes: uncuffed, sizes 2.5 to 6.0
Endotracheal tubes with cuff: sizes 6.0 to 8.0
Benzoin stylet in swabs
0.9% sodium chloride solution for suctioning
Stylet

Miscellaneous

Needleless syringe system
Syringes, TB: 3, 10, 20 ml (4 each)
Needles: 25 to 18 gauge (5 each)
IO needles: 18-gauge or bone marrow aspiration needles
Blood collection tubes
Arterial blood gas puncture kit
Cotton balls
2″ × 2″ gauze
Medication labels
Isolation supplies (gloves, goggles, gowns, masks)
Cardiac arrest board
Lubricating jelly

weight using a computer program (Tables 140-3 and 140-4). Supplies needed for monitoring and defibrillation, such as electrodes, paste or gel, and extra ECG paper must be readily accessible to the defibrillator.

To ensure that the resuscitation equipment is ready for use and functioning properly, routine checks must be made. Expiration dates of drugs and IV fluids are noted and a system established for replacing these drugs once expired. The defibrillator must be checked daily based on manufacturer recommendations.

Record of Resuscitation

The resuscitation record is an essential component of the resuscitation process and serves as the official and legal document of the arrest. Its purpose is to account for the events that occur during a code. It is impor-

Table 140-3   CPR Drug Calculations for 10 kg Patient

Drug and Concentration	Dosage	Calculated Dose	
Atropine sulfate (0.1 mg/ml syringe)	0.02 mg/kg IV or ET; may repeat in 5 min	0.2 mg	2.0 ml
Calcium chloride, 10% (100 mg/ml)	20 mg/kg IV; may repeat in 10 min	200.0 mg	2.0 ml
Dextrose, 50% (0.5 g/ml); dilute to $D_{25}W$	0.5 g/kg ($D_{25}W$) IV, 2 ml/kg ($D_{25}W$)	5.0 g	20.0 ml
Epinephrine, 1:10,000 (0.1 mg/ml syringe)	0.01 mg/kg IV; repeat q 5 min	0.1 mg	1.0 ml
Epinephrine, 1:1000 (1 mg/ml 30 ml vial)	0.1 mg/kg ET or 2nd dose IV in pulseless arrest (may use up to 0.2 mg/kg IV)	1.0 mg	1.0 ml
Lidocaine, 2% cardiac (20 mg/ml)	1 mg/kg IV or ET, then 0.5 mg/kg q 10 min	10.0 mg 5.0 mg	0.5 ml 0.25 ml
Sodium bicarbonate (1 mEq/ml)	1 mEq/kg IV; may repeat in 10 min	10.0 mEq	10.0 ml
Cardioversion	0.5-1 J/kg	5 to 10 J	
Defibrillation	2-4 J/kg	20 to 40 J	

Table 140-4   IV Drips for 10 kg Patient

Drug and Concentration	Dosage Range	Concentration Formula	Calculated Dose
Dobutamine (12.5 mg/ml)	5-15 μg/kg/min	6 mg/kg/100 ml at 1 ml/hr = 1 μg/kg/min	60.0 mg/100 ml (4.8 ml/100 ml)
Dopamine (40 mg/ml)	2-20 μg/kg/min	6 mg/kg/100 ml at 1 ml/hr = 1 μg/kg/min	60.0 mg/100 ml (1.5 ml/100 ml)
Epinephrine (1 mg/ml vial)	0.1-1 μg/kg/min (up to 20 μg/kg/min in pulseless arrest)	0.6 mg/kg/100 ml at 1 ml/hr = 0.1 μg/kg/min	6.0 mg/100 ml (6.0 ml/100 ml)
Lidocaine (20 mg/ml)	20-50 μg/kg/min	120 mg/100 ml at 1 ml/kg/hr (10.0 ml/hr) = 20 μg/kg/min	120 mg/100 ml) (6 ml/100 ml)
Nitroprusside (50 mg/vial)	0.5-8 μg/kg/min	6 mg/kg/100 ml at 1 ml/hr = 1 μg/kg/min	60.0 mg/100 ml
Norepinephrine (1 mg/ml vial)	0.05-0.1 μg/kg/min	0.6 mg/kg/100 ml at 1 ml/hr = 0.1 μg/kg/min	6.0 mg/100 ml (6.0 ml/100 ml)

tant that a form be developed so that documentation can be quick, efficient, and accurate. Team members often refer to the record when responding to a code to verify when procedures were last performed. The resuscitation record captures demographic information about the patient, beginning and ending times of the code, sequence of events and procedures, drugs and fluids administered, vital signs, laboratory values, treatment, and patient outcome. The names of the participants involved in the resuscitation are recorded. The physician and recording nurse must sign the form to verify that the information recorded is accurate and can be referred to as the actual medical orders.

ECG strips can be affixed to the back of the resuscitation record to provide further documentation. The resuscitation record can be a valuable tool in evaluating the appropriateness of care and the effectiveness of training.

Training

The performance demonstrated in response to a code reflects the education and training of personnel. It is beneficial to use continuous quality improvement indicators to evaluate actual code events. Code critiques performed immediately following a code or retrospectively can provide information about trends in locations of arrests and any problems with personnel resources, equipment, or the communication system.

Physicians, nurses, respiratory therapists, and other health care professionals must maintain proficiency at all times in CPR skills. Nationally standardized courses are available to train individuals in basic life support and in advanced concepts of resuscitation. Basic life support is recommended for all health care professionals who are involved in direct patient care. Advanced life support standards and guidelines and hospital policies and procedures related to codes can be included in hospital employee and residency orientation programs and in annual competency programs. Simulated mock codes can be a useful teaching method to allow personnel the practical experience in cardiac arrest procedures.

Administrative Coordination

Close observation and evaluation are essential for a successful CPR program. A committee composed of multidisciplinary members can provide the expertise for evaluation and critique. Disciplines most commonly included in such committees are critical care medicine, anesthesiology, cardiology, nursing, hospital administration, respiratory therapy, pharmacy, central supply, nursing, and medical education. The function of such a committee is to:

1. Provide ongoing monitoring and evaluation of resuscitation
2. Develop policies and protocols for resuscitation (i.e., communication system for announcing arrests, function of arrest team members, documentation on CPR record, staff training requirements, and do not resuscitate orders)
3. Standardize resuscitation equipment
4. Design, implement, and evaluate educational programs in basic and advanced life support

CURRENT RESEARCH AND FUTURE CONSIDERATIONS

Since survivors of pediatric cardiopulmonary arrest often have significant neurologic impairment, a major goal is resuscitation of the brain as well as the heart. Some brain cells are damaged during the primary insult, but a cascade of processes follows arrest that can lead to further loss of brain cells in the hours following arrest. At the cellular level ion pump failure causes influxes of calcium, sodium, and chloride ions and leads to intracellular swelling. Free radicals generated during and after cardiac arrest are also believed to cause membrane damage during reoxygenation.

Experimental treatment modalities aimed at preventing or ameliorating secondary injury are the focus of ongoing research. Hyperventilation is commonly used to decrease ICP with carbon dioxide levels maintained between 25 and 30 torr. Excessive hyperventilation can cause a drastic reduction of cerebral blood flow, resulting in brain ischemia. Other promising modalities include induction of mild hypothermia and the use of pharmacologic agents such as thiopental, calcium channel blockers, and free radical scavengers.

Other current research efforts focus on improving the outcome of resuscitation. Higher doses of epinephrine in pulseless states are currently being evaluated in regard to improved outcomes. A new waveform for transthoracic defibrillation using sequential overlapping pulse shock waveforms is being studied to facilitate defibrillation. Active compression-decompression and high-impulse CPR are being studied as alternatives to standard manual CPR.

ADDITIONAL READING

• American Heart Association. Textbook of Advanced Pediatric Life Support. Dallas: The Association, 1994.

Berg RA, Oho CW, Kern KB, Sanders AB, Hilwig RW, Hansen KK, Ewy GA. High-dose epinephrine results in greater mortality after resuscitation from prolonged cardiac arrest in pigs: A prospective, randomized study. Crit Care Med 22:282-290, 1994.

Brown CG, Werman HA. Adrenergic agonists during cardiopulmonary resuscitation. Resuscitation 19:1-16, 1990.

Chameides L. CPR challenges in pediatrics. Ann Emerg Med 22:388-392, 1993.

Chang MW, Coffeen P, Lurie KG, Shultz J, Bache RJ, White CW. Active compression-decompression CPR improves vital organ perfusion in a dog model of ventricular fibrillation. Chest 106:1250-1259, 1994.

• Emergency Cardiac Care Committee and Subcommittees, American Heart Association. Guidelines for cardiopulmonary resuscitation and emergency cardiac care. JAMA 268:2251-2281, 1992.

Goetting MG, Paradis NA. High-dose epinephrine improves outcome from pediatric cardiac arrest. Ann Emerg Med 20:22-26, 1991.

Kerber RE, Spencer KT, Kallok MJ, Birkett C, Smith R, Yoerger D, Kieso RA. Overlapping sequential pulses: A new waveform from transthoracic defibrillation. Circulation 89:2369-2379, 1994.

Lewis LM, Stothert JC Jr, Gomez CR, Ruoff BE, Hall IS, Chandel B, Standeven J. A non-invasive method for monitoring cerebral perfusion during cardiopulmonary resuscitation. J Crit Care 9:169-174, 1994.

Lurie KG. Active compression-decompression CPR: A progress report. Resuscitation 28:115-122, 1994.

Rudikoff MT, Maughan WL, Effron M, Freund P, Weisfeldt ML. Mechanisms of blood flow during cardiopulmonary resuscitation. Circulation 61:345-352, 1980.

• Safar P. Cerebral resuscitation after cardiac arrest: Research initiatives and future directions. Ann Emerg Med 22:324-349, 1993.

Tucker KJ, Khan J, Idris A. Savitt MA. The biphasic mechanism of blood flow during cardiopulmonary resuscitation. A physiologic comparison of active compression-decompression and high-impulse manual external cardiac massage. Ann Emerg Med 24:895-906, 1994.

Van Seggern K, Egar M, Fuhrman BB. Cardiopulmonary resuscitation in a pediatric ICU. Crit Care Med 14:275-277, 1986.

Zaritsky A. Pediatric resuscitation pharmacology. Ann Emerg Med 22:445-455, 1993.

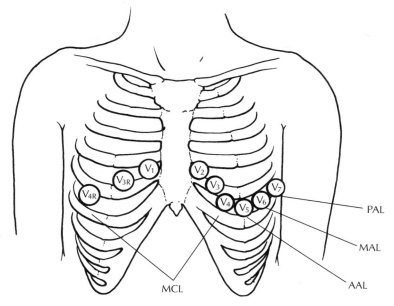

Fig. 141-3 Pediatric ECG chest lead placement. (AAL = Anterior axillary line; MAL = midaxillary line; MCL = midclavicular line; PAL = posterior axillary line.)

ECG Interpretation in Pediatric Patients

The normal components of the ECG are shown in Fig. 141-4. ECG standards of measurements for pediatric patients differ greatly from those for adults, and normal values vary with age (Table 141-1). Interval measurements are made in seconds and amplitude measurements in millivolts. The intervals of interest are the resting heart rate, PR interval, QRS duration, and corrected QT (QT_c) interval ($QT_c = QT/\sqrt{RR}$ interval).

Rhythm abnormalities are discussed in Chapter 27. Although abnormally short PR intervals may represent a normal variation, they are also associated with low atrial or junctional ectopic pacemakers, accessory connection inserting into the bundle of His, Duchenne's muscular dystrophy, Pompe's disease, Fabry's disease, and mannosidosis.

The electrical axis, or the average QRS vector, is calculated from the limb leads. The frontal plane can be divided into four 90-degree quadrants, and the axis assigned to one of these quadrants depends on the predominant forces in leads I and aVF. Once the quadrant is known, the axis is approximated as perpendicular to the most isoelectric limb lead (i.e., the lead with the most equivalent R and S waves), with the perpendicular directed into the quadrant previ-

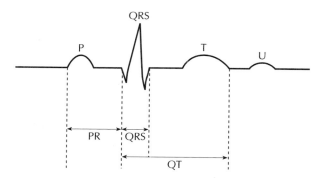

Fig. 141-4 Normal components of the ECG.

ously determined. The normal QRS axis shifts from right to left with age (see Table 141-1). In most, but not all cases, axis deviation is secondary to hypertrophy or hypoplasia of one of the ventricles. Other causes include cardiac malposition, conduction system abnormalities, thoracic deformities, and lung abnormalities.

The axis may also be calculated for P and T waves. In sinus rhythm with normal anatomy P waves generally have an axis of 0 to 90 degrees, which does not change with age. Deviation usually suggests an ec-

Table 141-1 Summary of Normal Values

| Age | Intervals | | | Axis of QRS (°) | Amplitudes | | | | | | | | | |
	HR (bpm) II	PR (sec) II	QRS (sec) V5		Q Wave (mV) III	Q Wave (mV) V6	R Wave (mV) V3R	R Wave (mV) V1	R Wave (mV) V5	R Wave (mV) V6	S Wave (mV) V3R	S Wave (mV) V1	S Wave (mV) V5	S Wave (mV) V6
0 to ≤3 days	90-160	0.08-0.16	0.02-0.08	60-195	≤0.50	≤0.20	0.2-2.0	0.5-2.7	0.1-2.3	0-1.2	0-1.5	0.1-2.3	0.1-1.9	0-1.0
3 to ≤30 days	90-180	0.07-0.14	0.02-0.08	60-195	≤0.55	≤0.30	0.1-1.9	0.3-2.5	0.2-2.4	0-1.6	0-1.1	0-1.7	0.2-1.8	0-1.0
1 to ≤3 mo	120-180	0.07-0.13	0.02-0.08	30-115	≤0.65	≤0.25	0.2-1.5	0.3-1.8	1.0-3.3	0.5-2.1	0-0.7	0-1.2	0.2-1.4	0-0.7
3 to ≤6 mo	105-185	0.07-0.15	0.02-0.08	5-105	≤0.65	≤0.25	0.1-1.2	0.3-2.0	1.0-3.4	0.6-2.2	0-1.1	0-1.7	0.1-1.7	0-1.0
6 to ≤12 mo	110-170	0.07-0.16	0.02-0.08	5-100	≤0.85	≤0.30	0.1-1.2	0.1-2.0	1.0-3.1	0.6-2.3	0-1.1	0.1-1.8	0.1-1.5	0-0.7
1 to ≤3 yr	90-150	0.08-0.15	0.03-0.08	5-100	≤0.55	≤0.30	0.1-1.1	0.2-1.8	1.0-3.2	0.6-2.3	0-1.2	0.1-2.1	0.1-1.2	0-0.7
3 to ≤5 yr	70-140	0.08-0.16	0.03-0.07	5-105	≤0.40	≤0.35	0.1-1.0	0.1-1.8	1.1-3.7	0.8-2.4	0.1-1.4	0.2-2.1	0-1.0	0-0.5
5 to ≤8 yr	65-130	0.09-0.16	0.03-0.08	10-135	≤0.30	≤0.45	0-0.9	0.1-1.4	1.5-3.8	0.8-2.6	0.2-1.5	0.3-2.3	0-1.0	0-0.4
8 to ≤12 yr	60-130	0.09-0.17	0.03-0.08	10-120	≤0.25	≤0.30	0-0.9	0.1-1.2	1.5-3.8	0.9-2.6	0.1-1.8	0.3-2.5	0-0.8	0-0.4
12 to ≤16 yr	60-120	0.09-0.18	0.03-0.09	10-130	≤0.30	≤0.30	0-0.7	0.1-1.0	0.8-3.5	0.7-2.3	0.1-1.6	0.3-2.1	0-0.8	0-0.4

CRITERIA FOR ATRIAL AND VENTRICULAR ABNORMALITIES

Right atrial enlargement
  P-wave amplitude >(+)0.25 mV in lead II
  Initial component of P wave peaked and >(+)0.30 mV in lead V_1
Left atrial enlargement
  P-wave duration >0.10 second in lead II
  Biphasic P wave with negative terminal component >0.04 second and >(−)0.1 mV
  P wave is "double humped" in lead I, II, or V_6 with peaks >0.04 second apart
Right ventricular hypertrophy
  R-wave amplitude >98th percentile in V_1, V_{3R}, or V_{4R} (>1.5 mV in V_1 at >1 yr of age)
  S-wave amplitude >98th percentile in V_5 or V_6 (>0.9 mV in V_6 at <1 mo of age)
  qR pattern in V_1, V_{3R}, or V_{4R} (R usually >1 mV)
  Upright T wave in V_1 >1 wk of age and <8 yr of age
  qR pattern in a V_R with R >0.6 mV
  rSR' pattern in V_1, V_{3R}, or V_{4R} with R' >1 mV
  Pure R wave (i.e., no S or Q waves in V_1, V_{3R}, or V_{4R})
  R/S ratio >1 in V_{3R} >3 yr of age
  R/S ratio >1 in V_1 >16 yr of age
Supportive of right ventricular hypertrophy
  Rightward axis for age
  Preservation of normal right-sided amplitudes in the presence of clear left ventricular hypertrophy

Left ventricular hypertrophy
  R amplitude >98th percentile for age in V_5, V_6, or V_7 (>3.5 mV in V_6)
  S amplitude >98th percentile for age in V_1, V_{3R}, or V_{4R} (>2.0 mV in V_1)
  R amplitude in V_6 + S amplitude V_1 >98th percentile for age
  Absent Q wave or abnormally large Q wave in V_6 or V_7 (>0.45 mV)
  qS pattern in V_1
  Asymmetric T-wave inversion with terminal upward convexity in V_5 and V_6
  Wide angle (>100 degrees) between QRS and T axes
Supportive of left ventricular hypertrophy
  Leftward axis for age
  Preservation of normal left forces in the presence of clear right ventricular hypertrophy
Biventricular hypertrophy
  Both criteria for right and left ventricular hypertrophy are satisfied
  Right or left hypertrophy exists with preservation of normal contralateral forces
  Two consecutive midprecordial leads have a combined R + S amplitude >6.5 mV

topic atrial pacemaker. The T-wave axis is generally aligned with the QRS axis, except in hypertrophy with strain, ischemia, infarction, and conduction abnormalities.

Systematic assessment for atrial, ventricular, and repolarization abnormalities follow. In general the P waves are low in amplitude (<0.25 to 0.3 mV) and have a duration of <0.1 second. Specific criteria for right and left atrial enlargement are found in leads II and V_1. Commonly the atria enlarge secondary to decreased ventricular compliance or in response to volume overload, as is seen with left-to-right shunts and AV valve regurgitation.

Abnormalities of intraventricular conduction may be inherited, may be secondary to progressive disease, or may occur following open heart surgery. Most if not all of the criteria for hypertrophy and repolarization are invalid in the presence of significant conduction abnormalities because the delayed activation distorts the normal activation sequence. The common patterns are right, left anterior, left posterior, and complete left bundle branch block.

Right bundle branch block is characterized by a QRS duration greater than the 98th percentile for age, but >0.12 second at any age. Late activation may be rightward and anterior, with a characteristic rsR' pattern in V_1 with a prominent wide R' wave, and there is a wide S wave in leads I and V_6.

Left bundle branch block is also characterized by a prolonged QRS associated with a loss of the initial septal depolarization (no Q in lead I, aVL, or V_6), a prominent S wave in V_1, and a prominent notched R in V_6.

Only one of the two fascicles of the left bundle

may be impaired. Left anterior fascicular block is characterized by initial forces to the right and inferior, but the mean axis is left of -30 degrees. The QRS duration is slightly prolonged. Left posterior fascicular block is rare in children. The initial forces are superior, with a mean axis that is rightward for age in the absence of right ventricular hypertrophy. Again, the QRS is slightly prolonged.

Bifascicular block refers to impaired conduction in any two of the three main fascicles, but for pediatric patients, this usually occurs as a combination of right bundle branch block with left anterior fascicular block. Most commonly bifascicular block occurs after cardiac surgery. There are rare inherited disorders in which this represents part of the progression to complete heart block.

Ventricular hypertrophy is assessed in the precordial leads. Right ventricular forces are reflected by the R wave in leads V_1, V_{3R}, and V_{4R} and the S wave in V_5, V_6, and V_7, whereas left ventricular forces are better evaluated with the R wave in V_5, V_6, and V_7 and the S wave in V_1, V_{3R}, and V_{4R}. Since the ECG represents a summation of electrical activity, there are usually diminished forces in the leads away from the hypertrophied chamber. When generalized low voltage exists (i.e., the QRS amplitude is <1.0 mV in all the precordial leads and <0.5 mV in all the limb leads), it is suggestive of pericardial effusion, myocarditis, or anasarca.

The ST segment is normally at the isoelectric baseline. Elevation of the ST segment is associated with injury such as trauma or myocardial infarction (see below) or inflammation, as might be seen with pericardial diseases. An early "take-off" of the ST segment, also known as J-point elevation, is normal in adolescence.

Repolarization of the ventricle is represented by the T wave. T-wave changes may be noted in any lead, but those seen in leads II and V_5 are particularly useful. The T wave may be upright in V_1, V_{3R}, and V_{4R} during the first few days of life and in adolescence, but at other ages this indicates right ventricular hypertrophy. Inverted, asymmetric T waves, particularly in the presence of hypertrophy, suggest ventricular strain. T-wave abnormalities are often present when electrolytes are given (see below).

The U wave follows the T wave, but it is not always present. It is believed to result from repolarization of the Purkinje fibers or possibly from diastolic relaxation of the ventricles. Usually U-wave amplitude is $<50\%$ of the T wave. When it merges with the T wave and its amplitude is $>50\%$ of the T wave, it is included in the measurement of QT_c.

Specific Abnormalities

Ischemia or infarction occur infrequently in pediatric patients. Common causes include direct injury, low-output states, myocarditis, and anomalous left coronary artery, and it may be a sequela of Kawasaki syndrome. Very early there are T-wave changes consisting of prolongation and increase in amplitude with or without inversion. Next, ST elevation is observed in the leads overlying the area of injury, often with reciprocal depression in leads facing the opposite side of the heart. Over a period of hours to days the ST elevation transitions to symmetric inversion. There is loss of the R wave over the area of infarction, and a pathologic Q wave (>0.03 second and >0.5 mV) may evolve. The complete spectrum of ECG changes is not seen in all patients; many may manifest ST- and T-wave changes only. Prominent Q waves are also present with conduction abnormalities, ventricular inversion or malposition of the heart, and neuromuscular disorders or as a consequence of cardiac surgery. In the inferior leads (II, III, and aVF) prominent, but narrow Q waves up to 0.85 mV are normal in young children (see Table 141-1).

Pericarditis is typified by more diffuse ST elevation with a pattern that is concave upward. Elevation is often seen in all leads except aV_R and V_1, which may show a depression. Usually there is an associated sinus tachycardia. The T waves usually remain upright throughout the acute phase of the illness in contrast to the inversion often present in myocardial ischemia. There is often late T-wave inversion, but it is not associated with loss of the R wave or the development of a Q wave. Frequently there is associated PR-segment depression. T-wave elevation may be due to early repolarization, but a ST- to T-wave amplitude ratio that exceeds 0.25 suggests pericarditis.

Electrolyte abnormalities may significantly alter the ECG. Some of the more common derangements are listed below.

1. Potassium: Hyperkalemia initially results in peaking of the T wave; however, in the absence of serial studies, this is often difficult to discern. With further increases, conduction is impaired and the T

waves flatten. Further increases may result in loss of the P wave and finally ventricular arrhythmias and AV block. Hypokalemia initially causes a decrease in T-wave amplitude with an increased prominence of the U wave. Arrhythmias are rare except for the potentiation of digitalis-related arrhythmias.

2. Calcium: Hypercalcemia may shorten the QT interval and cause sinus node dysfunction. There is also a potential for aggravation of digitalis-induced arrhythmias. Hypocalcemia is primarily manifested as prolongation of the interval between the QRS and the onset of the T wave with a normally configured T wave.

3. Magnesium: Hypermagnesemia rarely causes AV conduction delay. Hypomagnesemia often co-exists with and prevents the correction of, hypocalcemia. The direct effects are similar to hypokalemia in that there are combined derangements of the T wave.

Neuromuscular diseases are often associated with ECG abnormalities. Duchenne's muscular dystrophy is associated with prominent, but narrow Q waves in the lateral precordium and tall R waves over the right precordium. A significant proportion of these patients also has a short PR interval. In Friedreich's ataxia there is a cardiomyopathic process leading to a high incidence of ECG abnormalities. Commonly there is an inappropriate sinus tachycardia, but any arrhythmia may occur. Left ventricular hypertrophy is frequently seen with increased voltage and T-wave changes. Criteria for right and or biventricular hypertrophy may be present. Diffuse ST changes with prolonged QT_c intervals are often present following CNS injury, frequently associated with arrhythmias.

Other systemic diseases associated with ECG abnormalities are discussed in their respective chapters in Volume I.

HOLTER MONITORING
Indications

Holter monitoring is a continuous recording of a patient's heart rate and rhythm, usually of 24 hours' duration. All patients in the PICU are monitored continuously, but because of imperfect algorithms within the monitors, irregular rhythms may not be detected. The indications for continuous recording in the PICU include:

1. New-onset arrhythmia or suspected arrhythmia
2. Quantification of heart rate or arrhythmias

3. Follow-up of drug or device therapy to treat rhythm disturbance or that may cause a rhythm abnormality

Technique

The standard Holter is a cassette or digital device that is battery powered and continuously records one to three channels of ECG data for up to 24 hours. It attaches to the patient's chest with five lead wires. As is necessary for standard ECG, good lead location and skin preparation are of utmost importance. Correctly preparing the skin surface will significantly reduce the chances of unreadable tapes due to artifact caused by the patient and nearby equipment. A diary is maintained to list any symptoms that may occur while wearing the unit. Either the staff or the patient may note symptoms, medications, and interventions that could affect the interpretation. In addition, a patient event button can be used to mark the recording to correlate precisely the time of any symptoms. At the end of the monitoring period the unit is removed from the patient and the recording is scanned. A beat-by-beat analysis is computed based on parameters for age criteria by the system analyzer.

A more efficient system directly archives all ECG data from the bedside monitor for a predetermined period (e.g., 72 hours) on all patients. This obviates the need for a separate recording device. These systems continuously update to keep the most current data accessible. This type of system also allows for instantaneous review of heart rate and rhythm as well as automated analysis and quantification of heart rate. The summary data are presented in a format identical to standard Holter monitoring. All the prospective analyses that may be performed with a standard Holter monitor are available. Further, retrospective review of suspected arrhythmias or episodes of clinical deterioration are possible since all the patient data are continuously archived. This type of review is particularly useful in attempting to reconstruct events leading to a patient's change in status. An additional feature of this system is remote access that allows overview of patient's rhythm from areas outside of the ICU using standard telephone lines.

RISKS AND COMPLICATIONS

Electrocardiography and Holter monitoring are painless procedures. Occasionally a skin irritation develops from the electrode adhesive. All electrical equipment within the PICU must be properly grounded to avoid electrical injury to the patient.

CURRENT RESEARCH AND FUTURE CONSIDERATIONS

At present investigation is being conducted using serial ECG recordings on heart transplant recipients. Diminished voltages on lead V_6 may be an early indicator of rejection.

Analysis of heart rate variability, or the patterns of change in beat-to-beat intervals, has been used in adults as a predictor of well-being after myocardial infarction. Whether similar patterns can be found in children who are critically ill or recovering from open heart surgery is currently under investigation.

Signal averaging is a process of summing several hundred QRS complexes to reduce the electrical interference and allows for detailed examination of the recording, particularly the terminal portion of the QRS complex. The technique has assisted in predicting the risk of ventricular arrhythmias in adult patients. The experience in pediatric patients is limited.

ADDITIONAL READING

• Benson DW. The normal electrocardiogram. In Emmanouilides GC, Reimenschneider TA, Allen HD, Gutgesell HP, eds. Moss and Adams' Heart Disease in Infants Children and Adolescents Including the Fetus and Young Adult, 5th ed. Baltimore: Williams & Wilkins, 1994, pp 152-164.

Davignon A, Rautaharju P, Boisselle E, Soumis F, Megelas M, Choquette A. Normal ECG standards for infants and children. Pediatr Cardiol 1:123-131, 1979/80.

Dubins D. Rapid Interpretations of EKGs, 5th ed. Tampa: Cover Publishing, 1996.

• Garson A Jr. Electrocardiography. In Garson A Jr, Bricker JT, McNamara DG, eds. The Science and Practice of Pediatric Cardiology. Philadelphia: Lea & Febiger, 1990, pp 713-767.

Helfant, RH. Essentials of Cardiac Arrhythmias. Philadelphia: WB Saunders, 1980.

Schlant RC, Adolph RJ, DiMarco JP, Dreifus LS, Dunn MI, Fisch C, Garson A Jr, Haywood LJ, Levine HJ, Murray JA, Noble RJ, Ronan JA. Guidelines for electrocardiography: A report of the American College of Cardiology/American Heart Association Task Force on Assessment and Therapeutic Cardiovascular Procedures (Committee on Electrocardiography). J Am Coll Cardiol 19:473-481, 1992.

142 Cardiac Pacing

Linda Farley-Fisher · Susan Prestjohn · Linda White

BACKGROUND

Cardiac pacing provides a mechanism for optimizing cardiac output. Since cardiac output is determined by heart rate and stroke volume, interventions that increase heart rate will usually enhance cardiac output unless the heart rate becomes so fast that ventricular filling is reduced. In addition, maintaining synchrony between atrial and ventricular contraction augments cardiac output.

Temporary pacing is a definitive therapy for patients with transient or sustained arrhythmias until a stable rhythm returns or a permanent pacemaker system is implanted. Other applications of temporary pacing are termination of tachycardia with the use overdrive pacing (Chapter 27) and assessment of the conduction system with programmed stimulation.

In 1952 noninvasive transcutaneous pacing was introduced for the treatment of Stokes-Adams attacks associated with heart block. Patient discomfort and inability to adequately assess capture limited its application. New electrodes and ECG filtering have largely overcome early problems of extreme discomfort and interpretation of capture on the ECG. This technique has subsequently reemerged as an emergency therapy for bradycardia and asystole; it has also been integrated with many defibrillator systems. Since its introduction in 1957 percutaneous placement of a pacing wire for transthoracic pacing has remained a controversial procedure. Because of frequent complications and low success rates, it is not widely used today. Transvenous pacing, developed in 1959, is the most commonly used method of temporary pacing. Catheterization of the central venous system is a common hospital practice, and technologic advancements have facilitated rapid and simple insertion of one or more electrode catheters into the heart. Transesophageal pacing, used since the late 1970s, takes advantage of the proximity of the esophagus to the atria. Advances in electrode design,

including a pill electrode that can be swallowed by cooperative older patients, and development of a soft 4 F bipolar electrode catheter for infants have facilitated use of this technique. Epicardial pacing wires have been implanted during cardiothoracic surgery since the 1980s, when it was recognized that arrhythmias were a frequent complication of heart surgery.

Pacing Modes

The North American Society for Pacing and Electrophysiology (NASPE) and the British Pacing and Electrophysiology group have developed a standardized pacemaker code (NBG code) to describe various types of pacing modes (Table 142-1). The first letter indicates chamber paced, the second letter indicates the chamber sensed, and the third letter indicates the response algorithm to sensed events. The fourth letter deals with programmability and rate modulation; the letter R is the most common and indicates an increase in the lower rate in response to a physiologic sensor. The fifth letter concerns the antitachycardia function of some advanced pacemakers. From a practical point of view, the classification of temporary pacing modes uses only the first three letters of the code. The choices for temporary pacing modes are now nearly as numerous as those available for permanent pacing. The most common modes of pacing are noted in Table 142-2. The single-chamber pacemaker (Fig. 142-1) can be used to perform either atrial or ventricular asynchronous (fixed rate) pacing (AOO or VOO); more commonly it is used for atrial demand (AAI) or ventricular demand (VVI) pacing that responds to sensing the patient's intrinsic rhythm by inhibition of pacing. Older temporary dual-chamber pacemakers (Fig. 142-2) offer DVI but not DDD pacing and an important distinction exists; however, newer models offer both DVI and DDD pacing. Temporary dual-chamber pacemakers (Fig.

Table 142-1   NBG Pacemaker Code

I Chamber Paced	II Chamber Sensed	III Response to Sensing	IV Programmability Rate Modulation	V Antitachyarrhythmia Function
V = ventricle A = atrium D = dual (A + V) O = none	V = ventricle A = atrium D = dual (A + V) O = none	T = triggers pacing I = inhibits D = dual (T + I) O = none	P = simple program- mable M = multiprogram- mable C = communicating R = rate modulation O = none	P = pacing (antitachy- cardia) S = shock D = dual (P + S) O = none

Table 142-2   Common Temporary Pacing Modes

NBG Code* and Function	Indications	Characteristics	Contraindications and Limitations
AAI Atrial demand Atrial inhibited Atrial synchronous 	Sinus bradycardia Maintains adequate car- diac output with "atrial kick" Increases cardiac output in patients with im- paired left ventricular function Electrophysiology diag- nostics	Atrium is paced only when intrinsic rate falls below preset rate; when atrial activity is sensed, pacemaker is inhibited from firing	Atrial tachycardia Atrial fibrillation/flutter AV block High atrial thresholds
VVI Ventricular demand Ventricular inhibited Ventricular synchronous 	Bradycardia AV block Sick sinus syndrome Electrophysiology diag- nostics Prophylactically with medications or after surgery "Overdrive" suppression of ectopic beats	Ventricle is paced only when intrinsic rate falls below predeter- mined level; when ventricular activity is sensed, pacemaker is inhibited from firing	No AV synchrony No rate variability
DDD Dual-chamber demand Universal pacing 	AV block Noncompliant ventricle in which atrial contri- bution to ventricular filling is essential Restores AV synchrony, which may augment cardiac output	Both atrial and ventricu- lar pacing occurs when intrinsic rate falls below preset rate; atrial synchronous ventricular pacing be- tween programmed lower and upper rate; may be programmed to VVI, AAI, DVI, or VDD mode	Atrial fibrillation/flutter Atrial tachycardia Slow retrograde conduction

O = sensing; ☐ = output circuit; * = pacing; ◁ = amplifier; AV = atrioventricular; T = triggers; I = inhibits.
*See Table 142-1.

Fig. 142-1 Medtronic single-chamber temporary pacemaker generator.

Fig. 142-3 Medtronic temporary dual-chamber pacemaker.

Fig. 142-2 Medtronic temporary pacemaker generator.

142-3) can be used to provide AV synchrony by pacing in the DOO, DVI, VDD, or DDD mode when appropriate. DVI and DDD both are considered dual-chamber pacing and require an electrode in the atrium and the ventricle. Both modes allow pacing in the atrium and ventricle, but they differ in sensing capabilities and responses. DDD senses in both chambers, inhibits atrial or ventricular pacing based on the sensed atrial or ventricular activity, and follows sensed atrial events with ventricular output pulses (triggered output) unless inhibited by a sensed ventricular event. In the DVI mode both outputs can be inhibited only by ventricular and not by atrial events. Therefore AV sequential pacing is (fixed) at the programmed lower rate, whereas in the DDD mode sensed atrial events will trigger ventricular pacing to maintain AV synchrony between the programmed lower and upper rates. The DDD mode ensures pacing with AV synchrony over a wide range of heart rates; in the DVI mode only one paced rate is available. Also, since atrial events are not sensed in DVI pacing, the potential exists for competition between intrinsic events and an atrial paced event, which may initiate an atrial arrhythmia. Another benefit of DDD pacing is that the patient's sinus rate is readily known and can be used for ongoing assessment of cardio-vascular status. The only contraindication to DDD pacing is the presence of an atrial arrhythmia (i.e., sick sinus syndrome or atrial flutter/fibrillation), which could result in inappropriate ventricular responses.

INDICATIONS

Temporary cardiac pacing may be used for therapeutic or prophylactic indications. Therapeutic cardiac pacing is warranted in virtually any patient with sustained symptomatic or hemodynamically compromising arrhythmia that is unresponsive to medical therapy or in which medical therapy is not tolerated. Prophylactic pacing is warranted when there is potential for significant bradycardia. Specific indications for temporary pacing vary with different clinical situations. A complete list of indications for temporary pacing provides an overview of its potential use.

CONTRAINDICATIONS

Cardiac pacing by any method is unequivocally contraindicated in the setting of severe hypothermia despite profound bradycardia and hypotension. In this situation cardiac pacing may induce refractory ventricular fibrillation or alter compensatory physiologic mechanisms to the hypothermia. Bradycardia or asystolic arrest of >20 minutes' duration represents a relative contraindication to pacing because of the extremely poor prognosis for survival. Another contraindication is digitalis toxicity with recurrent ventricular tachycardia. Contraindications relative to transvenous pacing include congenital heart defect repairs in which venous access to the atrium or ventricle is not possible (i.e., Fontan operation or an impassible tricuspid valve prostheses) and bleeding disorders. Temporary transvenous atrial pacing is contraindicated in multifocal atrial tachycardia, atrial fibrillation, and significant AV conduction system disease.

Permanent Pacemakers

The miniaturization and sophistication of permanent pacing systems has made cardiac pacing an acceptable treatment for infants and children. Approximately 100,000 pacemakers are implanted annually in the United States; of these, 1% to 2% are implanted in pediatric patients.

Surgically acquired heart block is an infrequent but important complication of intracardiac surgery for

---

> ### INDICATIONS FOR TEMPORARY PACING
>
> Bradycardia
> Sinus node dysfunction, atrial flutter with slow ventricular response, permanent pacemaker failure, carotid syndrome, drug induced
> Second-degree AV block
> Type I (AV nodal), symptomatic, type II (His-Purkinje), symptomatic
> Complete AV block
> Congenital (AV nodal) and acquired (His-Purkinje) symptomatic; surgical, asymptomatic, and symptomatic; left bundle branch block during right heart catheterization (prophylactic)
> Arrhythmia suppression and/or termination (see Chapter 27)
> Supraventricular tachycardia (AV nodal reentry, Wolff-Parkinson-White syndrome), atrial flutter, junctional ectopic tachycardia, ventricular ectopy
> Diagnostics
> Assessment of sinoatrial node or AV node, arrhythmias

---

congenital heart disease. Most patients with surgical complete heart block that is transient have return of normal or near-normal conduction within 2 weeks of the procedure. At Children's Medical Center of Dallas the patient with surgical compete heart block is evaluated on a daily basis, and if the heart block does not resolve within 14 days, the patient undergoes permanent pacemaker implantation.

A child with a previous cardiac repair and a permanent pacemaker is occasionally admitted to the PICU. The clinician who understands permanent pacing technology and current pacing modes (see Table 142-1) can accurately interpret pacemaker function and malfunction and thereby safely manage these patients. The patient's history and indication for pacing are important considerations. The majority of pacemakers are implanted for second- or third-degree heart block and sinus bradycardia. Patients are classified as "pacemaker dependent" when there is no evidence of intrinsic rhythm, which is manifested as a period of asystole longer than 3 to 4 seconds after sudden inhibition of pacemaker output. A past history of syncope or near syncope would also suggest pacemaker dependence.

Additional programmable features of permanent pacemakers that aid in the management of these patients are rate response, automatic antitachycardia pacing, and programmed stimulation for tachycardia termination. Programming is achieved externally with pulsed magnetic fields or a radio frequency signal that is sent through the patient's skin and received by the generator. If a magnetic field is applied, it can cause a small, thin, flat piece of metal called a reed switch to bend slightly, touch another metal terminal, and thus complete an electrical circuit. This allows the pacemaker to receive programming information. The pacemaker may also be interrogated to determine current programming and operating status.

Rate-responsive pacing has been developed to help a patient adapt to physiologic stress with an increase in heart rate. One device in use measures body motion. A flat sheet of piezoelectric material can be placed inside the pacemaker generator. Changes in body movement and muscle motion cause deformation of a piezoelectrode crystal, a quartz-like substance that, when bent, generates electrical energy. That signal is routed through the sensors, filters, and other electrical components, causing the pacemaker to increase or decrease its rate, depending on the amount of activity or motion sensed. A lower rate limit is set to allow a reasonable baseline when no activity is sensed and a maximum rate is set when the pacemaker is sensing considerable motion.

Antitachycardia pacemakers are used automatically to terminate reentrant arrhythmias with overdrive pacing. The most sophisticated device senses tachycardia automatically based on preprogrammed rate criteria and automatically initiates a preselected termination therapy. Other pacemakers allow the physician to use the external programmer to perform noninvasive programmed stimulation. Rapid pacing as well as single and multiple premature beats at individually programmable cycle lengths are available to attempt to terminate tachycardia.

TECHNIQUES
Choice of System

Before therapy is begun, the goals to be achieved by pacing must be determined (Fig. 142-4). The patient's sinus node and AV conduction status play a major role in pacing mode selection. AAI pacing may be adequate for patients without AV block that have

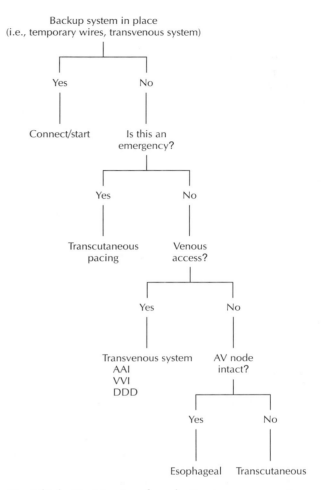

Fig. 142-4 Decision tree for selecting temporary pacing modality.

bradycardia. DVI is rarely used since the advent of the DDD mode. For the patient in complete heart block, the DDD pacing system may be chosen to allow for AV synchrony, thereby increasing cardiac output. If a patient returns from the operating room and has the potential for heart block, a VVI system may be considered as a backup.

A second consideration in determining the mode of therapy is the availability of pacing access and pacing hardware (Table 142-3). Transvenous ventricular pacing may not be possible because of the patient's anatomy (i.e., following the Fontan operation). If epicardial wires are unavailable, transcutaneous and esophageal pacing become the options.

Table 142-3 Clinical Features of Pacing*

	Transvenous	Transcutaneous	Epicardial	Transesophageal
Time to initiate	3-10 min	<1 min	<1 min	Minutes
Training required	+++	+	+	++
Chambers paced	A, V	V	A, V	A ± V
Emergency use	+	+	+	±
Prophylactic use	+	+	+	−
Prolonged use	+	−	+	−
Treat VT	+	+	+	−
Treat SVT	+	−	+	+
Vascular trauma	+	−	−	−
Arrhythmias	+	+	+	+
Visceral trauma	+	−	−	−
Infection	+	−	±	−
Discomfort	−	+	−	+
Comments	Most versatile and reliable	Fast and easy	Postoperative only, early lead failure	Primarily atrial pacing

A = atria; SVT = supraventricular tachycardia; V = ventricles; VT = ventricular tachycardia.
*Modified from Wood MA. Temporary cardiac pacing. In Ellenbogen KA, Kay GN, Wilkoff BL, eds. Clinical Cardiac Pacing. Philadelphia: WB Saunders, 1995, pp 687-700.

System Placement

Epicardial lead wires are placed in the operating room at the time of open heart repair (Fig. 142-5, *A*). Location and/or color coding may be used to differentiate the chambers to which each wire attaches. At our institution the wires on the right side of the chest are atrial, and the wires on the left side of the chest are ventricular. It is best to clarify with the surgeons which wires belong to which chamber.

With transvenous pacing, the placement of the catheters is similar to that of a central catheter (Chapter 131). The preferred site is the subclavian vein to achieve greater catheter stability and increase patient mobility. If the patient is very small, the most immediate access is the femoral vein. Achieving appropriate atrial sensing is more difficult from this site. Balloon-tipped pacing catheters may be used with ECG monitoring during insertion rather than fluoroscopy. If fluoroscopy is used, the ventricular lead is placed at the right ventricular apex and the atrial lead is in the right atrial appendage (Fig. 142-5, *B*). Balloon-tipped plastic catheters and semirigid catheters without balloons allow for flotation without fluoroscopy. A J-tip catheter is available for atrial pac-

ing. There are pulmonary artery catheters with one to five pacing electrodes to allow for ventricular and atrial pacing. During insertion and removal the patient's rhythm on the monitor must be meticulously monitored.

A third option for pacing is through the esophagus. An esophageal pacing and recording catheter, lubricated with viscous lidocaine, is inserted through the nares. The catheter insertion depth is determined by the height of the patient (Fig. 142-6). Older patients may be able to swallow a pill electrode. The position is verified by maximizing the amplitude of the atrial or ventricular electrogram or by successful pacing. Pacing is achieved using a stimulation system designed for transesophageal pacing, which outputs higher energy than transvenous pacing systems. Transesophageal pacing may cause significant patient discomfort and is not routinely used for sustained pacing. Its primary use is for diagnosis and termination of arrhythmias.

Transcutaneous pacing may be the most accessible means of pacing in emergency settings (Fig. 142-7). It is noninvasive and relatively easy to implement. Because of the amount of current needed to pene-

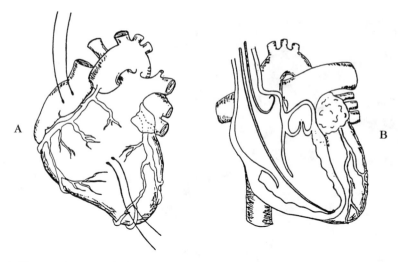

Fig. 142-5 A, Temporary epicardial atrial and ventricular leads. Two unipolar lead wires are placed on both the right atrium and right ventricle creating a bipolar lead system. **B,** Temporary transvenous atrial and ventricular bipolar placing catheters. The atrial J lead is positioned in the right atrial appendage and the ventricular lead is in the right ventricular apex.

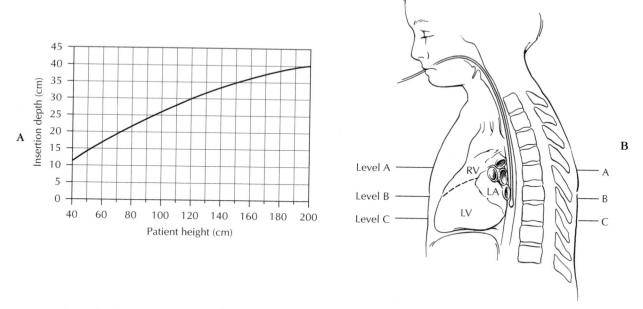

Fig. 142-6 A, Esophageal catheter insertion depth. **B,** Left sagittal view showing relationship of pill electrode to the heart. (LA = Left atrium; LV = left ventricle; RV = right ventricle.) (Modified from Arzbaecher RC, Jenkins JM, Collins S, Berbari E. Atrial electrical activity: The view from the esophagus. In Proceedings of the IEEE/EMBS First Annual Conference, 1979, pp 314-318.)

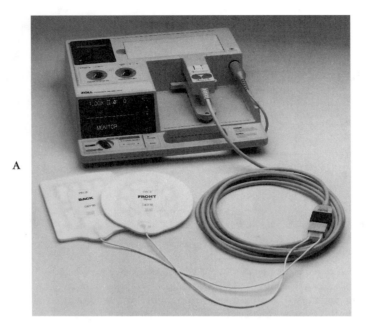

Fig. 142-7 **A**, Pediatric noninvasive electrodes. **B**, Anterior and posterior placement. **C**, Alternative placement.

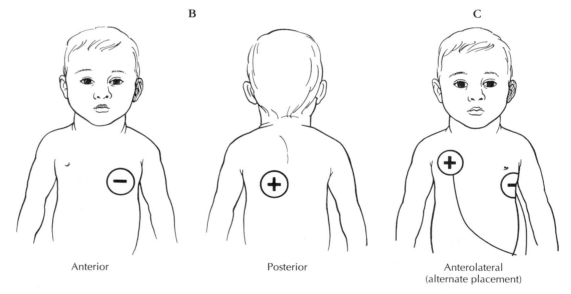

Anterior

Posterior

Anterolateral
(alternate placement)

trate bone and muscle mass, this method can sometimes be painful. Sedation is suggested if time permits. Electrodes are available in adult and pediatric sizes. The electrodes contain low-impedance gel to facilitate transmission of the electrical impulses. For proper capture, the negative electrode needs to be placed anteriorly at the point of maximum impulse on the chest. The positive electrode is placed on the posterior portion of the chest. It is centered between the thoracic spinous processes and the inferior aspect of the left scapula. The electrodes may need readjustment periodically to ensure proper skin integrity. The output energy is set above the minimum settings to obtain capture consistently. Transcutaneous pacing is only used until the patient receives either a transvenous or an epicardial system or has a permanent pacemaker implanted.

Epicardial electrodes and transvenous electrodes

are connected to a temporary pacemaker in essentially the same way. Proper connection of the wires to the pacing system is imperative for adequate sensing, capture, and patient comfort. Gloves must be worn when handling pacing wires to decrease the possibility of causing an electrical shock to the patient and to observe universal precautions.

System Assessment

The stimulation threshold is the minimum amount of energy for consistent pacing. The sensing threshold is the maximum setting at which consistent sensing occurs. These thresholds need to be checked when the pacemaker is connected to the patient and daily thereafter. Thresholds are affected by many factors, including edema, electrolyte imbalance, medications, and integrity of the pacing system. To ensure a safety margin that will avoid loss of capture, the pacing amplitude needs to be set at two to three times the threshold value for transvenous systems. It may not be possible to achieve this magnitude of safety margin with other pacing modalities. To determine the sensitivity threshold, the patient must have an intrinsic rhythm. For an adequate safety margin, the sensitivity is preferably programmed to one half of the threshold value, but at least one setting more sensitive than the threshold value. Appropriate upper and lower rates depend on the patient's age, diagnosis, and goal of therapy. If a dual-chamber system is used, an AV delay appropriate for the patient is also programmed.

Continuous monitoring is necessary in patients who need temporary pacing. In addition to the ECG, a pulse oximeter is used to assess oxygenation and cardiac output. The ECG, the patient's intrinsic rhythm, whether the pacemaker is pacing or sensing, the ordered settings, and observation of the exit site for infection are documented on every shift.

RISKS AND COMPLICATIONS

The incidence of complications related to temporary cardiac pacing is low. The most common complications are fever, phlebitis, and arrhythmia. Infections and pulmonary emboli occur primarily in patients with femoral vein entry sites and are common when catheters are in place for longer than 72 hours.

Myocardial perforation can occur during the placement of a transvenous pacing catheter. Symptoms may be precordial chest pain, skeletal muscle stimulation, dyspnea (with tamponade), and shoulder pain. Clinical signs of pericardial tamponade are

---

COMPLICATIONS OF TEMPORARY PACING

Cough
Catheter dislodgment
Infection
Bleeding (arterial or venous)
Hematoma
Arrhythmia
Pain (transcutaneous and transesophageal)
Pneumothorax
Air or foreign body embolus
Phlebitis and/or thrombosis
Tamponade
Nerve injury
Thoracic duct injury
AV fistula
Myocardial perforation
Diaphragmatic pacing
Skin burns
Pacemaker malfunction
   Oversensing
   Undersensing
   Loss of capture

---

hypotension and pulsus paradoxus. The ECG may exhibit a change in the paced QRS axis or morphology, and a radiograph will show a change in lead position, extracardiac location of lead tip, and a new pericardial effusion. Risks of removing the transvenous catheter are similar to placement, including bleeding, infection, and arrhythmias.

Complications from transcutaneous pacing are exceptionally rare in the clinical setting. The most frequent problems are the induction of coughing and severe pain during pacing. Pain results from activation of cutaneous nerves and intense skeletal muscle contraction. The degree of discomfort appears to be directly related to the stimulus amplitude and mass of muscle activated. The current necessary to produce severe pain is highly variable among patients, but most patients can be paced at least briefly at tolerable levels of discomfort with sedation.

Complications from transesophageal pacing are oral or nasopharyngeal trauma during the passing of the electrode, perforation of the esophagus, electrical burning of the mucosa, and esophageal discomfort or "heartburn" during pacing.

Table 142-4   Troubleshooting During Temporary Pacing

Loss of Capture	No Output	Undersensing	Oversensing

Ineffective stimulus
  Lead dislodgment
  Myocardial perforation
  Insulation break
  Lead conductor failure
  Threshold elevation
  Programmed settings
	Nondelivery of stimulus
	  Loose connection
	  Lead fracture
	  Battery depletion
	  Component failure
	  Oversensing
		Lead dislodgment
		Inadequate PR wave
		Lead fracture
		Insulation break
			Lead fracture
			Muscle inhibition
			T wave
			Lead dislodgment

At Children's Medical Center epicardial wires are generally removed in postoperative patients before transfer from the PICU to the ward. Prior to removal of the wires a complete blood count may be obtained to monitor the platelet count and allow time to correct the count. If a chest tube is in place, the wires can be removed first so that the chest tube can evacuate any blood, thereby avoiding cardiac tamponade.

Problems related to pacemaker system malfunction are noted in Table 142-4. Electrode displacement may cause intermittent loss of pacing and or sensing capabilities. Failure to stimulate is recognized by an absence of paced impulses at the programmed intervals and occurs due to interruption in delivery of the pacing stimulus to myocardial tissue. The most frequent cause is either a loose connection, wire fracture, or oversensing (see below). Failure to capture is the inability of the stimulus to depolarize the chamber of the heart. This problem is manifested on the ECG by a pacing stimulus that is not followed by evidence of conduction of the impulse through the paced chamber. Failure to capture may be due to battery depletion, lead fracture, or improper connection. In temporary pacing systems the myocardial lead interface deteriorates so rapidly that failure to capture usually occurs in 7 to 14 days. Both failure to pace and capture warrant immediate attention. An initial step to correct this problem is to increase the output (amplitude or pulse width), change the battery, and check all connections. If these corrective measures fail, the transcutaneous or transvenous system is used in emergency situations.

Sensing problems may be the result of either oversensing or undersensing of electrical events and can occur within 3 to 5 days of epicardial lead placement. Oversensing is usually the result of myopotential inhibition, a situation in which electrical events originating in skeletal muscle are sensed. When this occurs, the pacemaker is inhibited from discharging and the rhythm strip shows no pacing output. Environmental current also may be sensed, resulting in inhibition of pacing. This can be corrected by making the system less sensitive (i.e., a higher millivolt level). Undersensing is recognized by the premature appearance of a paced event. The pacing stimulus is inappropriate since the intrinsic electrical event was not recognized and may lead to atrial and/or ventricular arrhythmias. This is corrected by making the system more sensitive to the intrinsic electrical events (i.e., a lower millivolt level). Battery depletion is a common problem; one of the first signs of waning energy source is usually the loss of sensing function. A new battery must always be used at the beginning of pacing. Most temporary pacing devices have a mechanism for indicating battery status.

One final area of concern of permanent pacemakers is related to environmental hazards that involve electromagnetic interference. Environmental damage or disruption of pacing and pacing circuitry is rare but can occur with the use of MRI, irradiation (cobalt machines or linear accelerators used in cancer treatment), lithotripsy, diathermy, defibrillation, and electrocautery. If exposed to these energy sources, the pacemaker may be damaged or reprogrammed in an unpredictable manner. This represents an emergency situation that must be assessed by a cardiologist immediately.

ADDITIONAL READING

Bartecchi CE. In Bartecchi CE, Mann DE, eds. Temporary Cardiac Pacing. Chicago: Precept Press, 1990, pp 35-51.
Benefits of DDD mode for temporary pacing. Technical Concept Paper. Medtronic, Inc., 1993.

Crockett P, Grose McHugh L. Noninvasive pacing. What you should know. Redmond, Wash.: Physiocontrol, 1988.

Ferguson TB, Cox JL. Temporary external DDD pacing after cardiac operations. Ann Thorac Surg 51:723, 1991.

Garson A, Bricker JT, McNamara DG. The Science and Practice of Pediatric Cardiology. Malvern, Pa.: Lea & Febiger, 1990, pp 2135-2173.

• Haffajee CI. Temporary cardiac pacing: Modes, evaluation of function, equipment, and trouble shooting. Cardiol Clin 3:515, 1985.

Hickey C, Baas LS. Temporary cardiac pacing. AACN Clin Issues Crit Care Nurs 2(1):107-117, 1991.

Intermedics Inc. Concepts of permanent cardiac pacing. Angleton, Tex.: Intermedics Inc., 1994.

• Luceri RM, Stafford WJ, Castellanos A, Myerburg RJ. In Platia EV, ed. Management of Arrhythmias: The Nonpharmocological Approach. Philadelphia: JB Lippincott, 1987, pp 219-235.

• Moses HW, Schneider JA, Miller BD, Taylor GJ. A Practical Guide to Cardiac Pacing, 3rd ed. Boston: Little Brown, 1991, pp 43-46.

Owen A. Keeping pace with temporary pacemakers. Nursing 91 April, 58-64.

Silver MD, Goldschager N. Temporary transvenous pacing in the critical care setting. Chest 93:607, 1988.

• Wood MA. Temporary cardiac pacing. In Ellenbogen KA, Kay GN, Wilkoff BL, eds. Clinical Cardiac Pacing. Philadelphia: WB Saunders, 1995, pp 687-700.

Zoll PM. Noninvasive cardiac stimulation revisited. PACE 13:2014, 1990.

143 Cardiac Assist Devices

David C. Cleveland

BACKGROUND

The use of mechanical circulatory support devices in patients with intractable ventricular failure is becoming increasingly common. During the past decade the vast clinical experience accumulated in the adult population has led to many new options for mechanical ventricular assistance, including some completely implantable systems that are compatible with outpatient care. All the devices currently approved for adults can be used in adolescents of adult size. Unfortunately these devices have not been sufficiently miniaturized for use in infants and children. The intra-aortic balloon pump (IABP), extracorporeal membrane oxygenation (ECMO), and ventricular assist devices (VADs) have been used for circulatory support of children in the PICU setting.

In 1962 Moulopoulos et al. introduced the IABP as a method of circulatory support, and it has become the most widely used device to support the failing left ventricle. The IABP increases myocardial oxygen supply by increasing coronary blood flow in diastole and decreases myocardial oxygen demand by reducing afterload (Fig. 143-1). Its effectiveness in children has been questioned because of the increased elasticity of the aorta, rapid heart rates, and small stroke volumes. Experience in the pediatric age group is varied. In 1980 The Hospital for Sick Children in Toronto reported its use in 38 patients with 14 survivors. All but four of these patients were over 5 years of age and all patients younger than 5 years of age died. A similar experience was reported at Primary Children's Hospital of Salt Lake City. Of 29 children who received an IABP, 12 (41%) survived and survival rates were higher for patients over 5 years of age. Del Nido et al., however, reported the successful use of an IABP in a 2 kg infant, indicating that success is possible even in the smallest patient. Because most pediatric cardiac centers do not use the IABP as a primary method of cardiac assist, overall experience is limited. At Children's Medical Center of Dallas the IABP has been used in two patients over the past 5 years with one long-term survivor, a child supported after cardiac transplantation. The other child received an IABP in an attempt to bridge to transplant. With the availability of pediatric balloon catheters and the improvements in console technology, it may be possible to use the IABP for primary left ventricular failure in children.

The concept of ECMO support for a child with cardiac failure is attractive. It was first used in 1965 by Spencer et al. at New York University to support a 6-year-old child after repair of a ventricular septal defect. This child ultimately died of cardiac arrhythmia. Results of venoarterial support for postoperative cardiac failure over the next decade were discouraging, Bartlett et al., who had championed the use of ECMO for respiratory failure in infants and children, believed it was ineffective as a technique for cardiac support. Most clinicians had abandoned the idea of using venoarterial bypass to support the failing circulation when Pennington at the Cardinal Glennon Children's Hospital in St. Louis began a program for ECMO support of pediatric patients with postoperative cardiac failure in 1982. Over the next 11 years 81 children with postoperative cardiac failure were treated; there were 28 survivors and results improved with time. From 1988 to 1993, 44 children were treated and there were 20 survivors (45%). A majority of clinicians now depend on ECMO as the technique of choice for cardiac support in infants and children. As of January 1995, 1401 pediatric patients had been listed by the Extracorporeal Life Support Organization (ELSO) as receiving ECMO primarily for cardiac support. The majority of these children (1084) had undergone cardiac repairs and, of these, 42% survived. Since 1990 we have managed cardiac failure with ECMO in 24 children with nine long-term survivors (38%). Fifteen of these patients were given ECMO after cardiac surgery and five of these survived. Long-term survivors appear to be functionally normal. Overall it

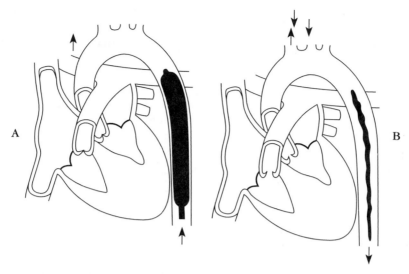

Fig. 143-1   The IABP works by inflating at the onset of diastole **(A)**, which results in increased coronary blood flow, and deflating just prior to the onset of systole **(B)**, which results in decreased afterload. This decreases myocardial oxygen consumption and improves cardiac output.

appears that ECMO can provide successful temporary cardiac assistance in selected patients.

The experience with the VAD as a method of cardiac assist in children is limited. In 1971 DeBakey reported the successful use of a left VAD in a 16-year-old who could not be weaned from cardiopulmonary bypass after mitral valve replacement. However, the overall results of VAD as a method of circulatory support in children have been disappointing and there continues to be controversy surrounding the use of a VAD in this setting. Recent experience by Karl at the Royal Children's Hospital in Melbourne is more encouraging. A conscious attempt was made to use a VAD instead of ECMO when possible. In a child who cannot be weaned from cardiopulmonary bypass a cannula is placed in the left atrium and it is gradually converted to a left VAD. Once cardiopulmonary bypass is discontinued, hemodynamic values and pulmonary function are assessed. If they are adequate, the patient is maintained on a left VAD rather than ECMO. With this approach, 29 children have been supported with a left VAD and 14 have been long-term survivors. This experience indicates that VAD support is a viable alternative to ECMO for cardiac support.

INDICATIONS
Severe Ventricular Dysfunction After Cardiac Surgery

Ventricular dysfunction is the most common reason for instituting circulatory support in the pediatric population. Many operations to repair congenital heart defects involve prolonged work inside the cardiac chambers with incisions into one or both ventricular chambers. During this period of time (aortic cross-clamp time) the myocardium is ischemic. Many strategies of myocardial protection have been attempted to limit myocardial damage during this period. Most of these strategies depend on maintaining the heart in a hypothermic and depolarized state by delivering cardioplegic solutions. Despite the cardiac surgeon's attempt to "protect" the myocardium, almost all complicated repairs result in some myocardial damage. Fortunately cardiac reserves are usually adequate to maintain the circulation while the myocardium repairs itself. When the myocardial damage sustained at operation surpasses myocardial reserves, the child cannot be weaned from cardiopulmonary bypass. The surgeon must first decide if the technical repair is satisfactory. An inadequate technical repair is usually a contraindication to circulatory support. Imperfections of the repair must be corrected before mechanical support is considered.

The decision as to which type of support to use is based on the age and size of the patient and on measurements made in the operating room. In patients over 5 years of age who have primarily left ventricular failure, an IABP can be placed. Once actuated, systemic and atrial filling pressures must be reevaluated. If myocardial performance is still inadequate, left VAD support can be considered. In a patient with biventricular failure the options are usually limited to separate right and left VADs or ECMO support. In general ECMO support has been used instead of biventricular VADs. When the patient is younger than 5 years of age, the IABP is not likely to be successful. The decision to use a VAD or ECMO is based on measurements of filling pressures and on the experience with the techniques at the institution. If myocardial failure is predominately localized to one ventricle, the right or left VAD can be used during the initial period of VAD support. Dysfunction of the other ventricle is often unmasked. Careful, early reassessment of ventricular function is therefore mandatory. When bleeding has been a problem during surgery, institution of VAD support is preferable to ECMO. With heparin bonding of circuit components, heparinization can be completely reversed during VAD support.

Ventricular Dysfunction Not Associated With Cardiac Surgery

Some children present with reversible ventricular dysfunction and can be considered for mechanical ventricular support. Acute myocarditis and acute rejection after cardiac transplantation refractory to maximum conventional support have been successfully treated with mechanical support at Children's Medical Center of Dallas. The goal is to give the myocardium time to recover from the acute insult.

Bridge to Cardiac Transplantation

Currently the least common indication for circulatory support in the pediatric population is stabilization of the patient before cardiac transplantation. Patients considered for this modality of treatment must meet all the criteria for cardiac transplantation, and there must be a realistic expectation that an organ can be obtained within a 2-week time frame. This has become more difficult to predict since the waiting time for organs has increased substantially in the past few years in the United States. With the present state of

technology, complication rates increase significantly after 2 weeks on circulatory support. These factors must be considered before placing a potential transplant candidate on mechanical support. Despite the controversy surrounding ECMO as a bridge to cardiac transplant, it is a viable alternative for some patients. Del Nido et al. from The Children's Hospital of Pittsburgh reported the use of ECMO as a bridge to transplant in 14 children. Nine of these patients received a heart and seven survived.

TECHNIQUES
IABP

Before the balloon pump is placed, the standard safety chamber on the Datascope System 90 must be replaced with a pediatric safety chamber and hose. Lead placement is extremely important in children because of rapid heart rates. The leads are checked before placement of the balloon to ensure an accurate signal. The appropriate balloon for the age and size of the patient is selected (Table 143-1). In general balloon volume is 40% to 60% of estimated stroke volume. Helium is used as the inflation gas in all cases. Percutaneous insertion of the IABP is indicated in adolescents but is not possible in infants and children. Instead, the femoral artery is exposed, and with adequate proximal and distal control, a longitudinal arteriotomy is made and a Gore-Tex or Dacron side-arm graft is placed. The balloon catheter is then inserted through the side arm. Once in the descending aorta, the balloon is positioned immediately below the left subclavian artery and a chest radiograph is obtained to verify correct positioning before initiating support.

Anticoagulation is usually not necessary, but if distal pulses are 1+ and capillary refill is sluggish, it may be initiated to achieve a PTT that is twice normal. A

Table 143-1   Estimated Balloon Volume for Age and Size

Balloon Volume (cc)	Approximate Age Range (yr)	Approximate Weight Range (kg)
2.5	<1	3-8
5.0	1-2.5	8-13
7.0	2.5-5	13-18
12.0	5-12	18-40
20.0	>12	>40

1/1 pumping frequency is attempted in all patients. The inflation point and duration are timed to achieve maximal diastolic augmentation and optimal reduction of afterload by maximally reducing the presystolic and peak systolic pressures. The circulation is assessed at regular intervals and the character, volume, and strength of the pulses are recorded every hour in the feet and in the left arm. It is not uncommon for the lower extremities to demonstrate mild circulatory compromise. However, as long as pulses are present, the balloon may be safely left in place. Rapid heart rates and use of helium inflation gas lead to rapid diffusion from the balloon. It is important to monitor augmentation closely so the balloon can be refilled when necessary.

As the patient's hemodynamic values begin to improve, inotropes are decreased to moderate levels (e.g., dobutamine and dopamine <10 μg/kg/min and epinephrine <0.04 μg/kg/min). At this point the frequency of balloon inflation can be decreased to one half and eventually to one third. If hemodynamic val-

ues remain stable, the balloon catheter is removed. With the operating team present, the femoral artery is reexposed, the IABP is stopped, and the balloon catheter is disconnected from the safety chamber. A 60 ml syringe with a three-way stopcock is used to create negative pressure on the balloon catheter. All snares are removed from the graft and the catheter withdrawn through the graft. The graft is occluded with a vascular clamp, trimmed, and sutured, leaving a small cuff on the femoral artery. The limb must be monitored closely for signs of ischemia after catheter removal. If ischemia persists, the femoral artery must be surgically explored for thrombosis.

ECMO

The circuit used for postoperative circulatory support is virtually identical to the circuit used for pulmonary support in neonates and children (Fig. 143-2). The method of cannulation depends on the timing of institution of support. At our institution we generally

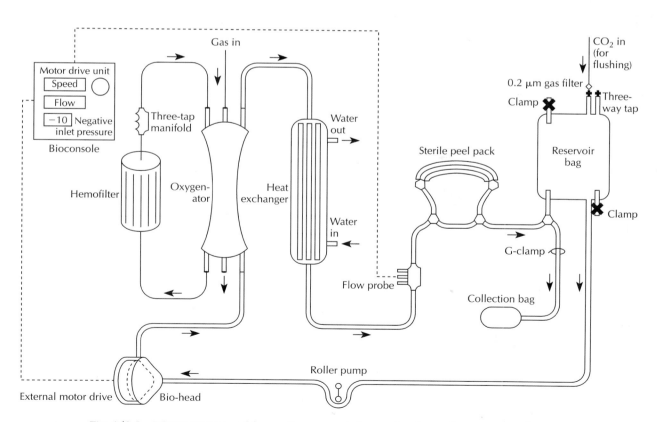

Fig. 143-2 ECMO circuit used for cardiac support. A centrifugal or roller pump may be used and hemofiltration may be added to the circuit as illustrated.

prefer to cannulate the aorta and right atrium directly, bringing the cannulas out through stab wounds in the skin and leaving the sternum open. If the sternum has been closed and the patient decompensates in the PICU, the sternum is reopened in an initial attempt to increase cardiac output and avoid the use of mechanical circulatory support. Alternatively, if the patient has only the skin closed and needs increasing levels of support or has a cardiac arrest in the PICU, the right carotid artery and internal jugular vein may be cannulated and ECMO support initiated. Cannulas that allow flows up to 150 ml/kg/min are selected. Pursestring sutures are placed in the aorta and in the right atrial appendage. Short soft rubber tourniquets are placed and the cannulas are inserted. ECMO support is initiated slowly. Once full flow is achieved, the adequacy of left atrial decompression is assessed. If left atrial pressures are consistently >12 mm Hg, a second venous drainage cannula is placed in the left atrium via the right superior pulmonary vein or the left atrial appendage. During the period of mechanical support the patient must be paralyzed and sedated, inotropic support weaned to a minimum level, and ventilation reduced. As myocardial function improves, ventricular ejection will be observed

on the arterial tracing. It is often necessary to insert a hemofiltration device in the circuit to aggressively remove fluid volume that has collected in the first 48 to 72 hours of support. As fluid balance is restored, the ECMO flow is gradually weaned. During the weaning process, inotropic support is added. When an absolute flow of 250 to 300 ml/min is reached, the circuit is occluded to determine if adequate circulation can be maintained. When successful, decannulation can be performed. If the cervical vessels were used for cannulation, they must be repaired.

VAD

The circuit for a VAD is much simpler than an ECMO circuit (Fig. 143-3). No oxygenator or heat exchanger is needed. The prime volume is kept to a minimum by mounting the Biomedicus pump head as close to the patient as possible. The circuit consists only of an inlet to the pump and out to the patient with an in-line flow probe. Only minimal levels of heparinization are indicated (activated clotting time of 150 seconds), and with the new heparin-bonded equipment, a VAD can be used without heparinization. However, this is recommended only when bleeding is difficult to control. The left atrial cannula may be

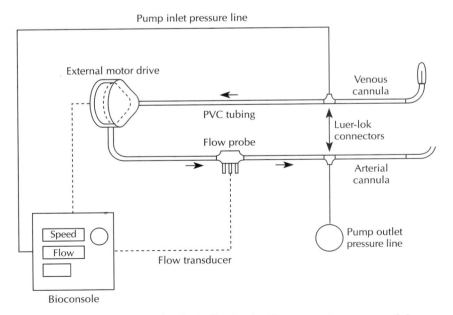

Fig. 143-3 The VAD circuit is technologically simple. No oxygenator or reservoir is necessary. A centrifugal pump is generally used in a VAD circuit.

placed via the right superior pulmonary vein, the roof of the left atrium, or through the left atrial appendage. Usually the same aortic cannula used for cardiopulmonary bypass can be used for a left VAD. The left VAD is instituted slowly and flows are quickly increased to 100 ml/kg/min. Atrial pressures and adequacy of ventilation are monitored carefully and, if they deteriorate, the patient is converted to ECMO. During support with a left VAD the patient is maintained on continuous fentanyl and vecuronium infusions. Full flows are maintained over the first 24 hours, but flow is reduced as early as possible and the left heart is allowed to eject. As flows are reduced, left atrial pressure is maintained below 10 mm Hg. Aggressive diuresis is begun as recovery of the myocardium proceeds, and if not accomplished with diuretics alone, hemofiltration is added to remove excess volume. When flows are 50 ml/kg/min, the circuit can be occluded to determine if the VAD can be safely removed. The cannulas are removed in the PICU by the operating room team.

RISKS AND COMPLICATIONS

The major risk of IABP is vascular compromise that may be manifested as limb, renal, or mesenteric ischemia. Correct balloon position and continuous monitoring are the best methods to avoid serious complications. IABP is an invasive procedure and carries a risk of serious infection. The balloon catheter must be placed under operating room conditions, even when it is performed in the PICU. Strict aseptic techniques are used during dressing changes. When the length of support is <5 days and these conditions are met, significant complications from infection are rare.

Bleeding from surgical sites is a frequent complication with ECMO support in the postoperative cardiac surgical patient and may be extremely difficult to control. When bleeding persists at a rate >10 ml/kg/hr, the patient must be returned to the operating room for reexploration. Renal function is often inadequate on ECMO. Of 1401 patients supported by ECMO for cardiac indications in the international registry, 391 underwent hemodialysis or hemofiltration. Infection can also be a major problem with ECMO support and has been documented in 118 patients. The risk of major complications increases as the time on ECMO increases.

The use of a VAD is associated with similar risks and complications as ECMO except that the tendency for bleeding complications is significantly reduced.

CURRENT RESEARCH AND FUTURE CONSIDERATIONS

Improved methods of mechanical circulatory support in the pediatric population are needed. The present systems available for this group of patients necessitate that the patient remain in the PICU sedated and usually ventilated. The systems are limited in both the adequacy of support they provide and the length of time they can be used. Because of these limitations, they are usually reserved for use in the postoperative cardiac surgical patient. Their use as a bridge to transplantation is rare. Important benefits of long-term VAD support have been realized in the adult population. Devices such as the Novacor or Heartmate have enabled patients to ambulate and exercise actively. Reversal of organ dysfunction and improved nutrition have also been documented.

It is estimated that 3000 children are born in North America every year who could benefit from cardiac replacement whereas fewer than 100 cardiac transplantations are actually performed. As the waiting list for organs increases, the time on the list also increases. Many patients with hypoplastic left heart syndrome die or have serious complications while awaiting a donor organ. There is an immediate need to miniaturize the devices now available to allow implantation in infants. Some preliminary work is being done at the University of Utah, but clinical applications are still remote.

ADDITIONAL READING

Arabia FA, Rosada LJ, Sethi GK, Smith RG, Copeland JG. From balloon pumps to total artificial hearts. CHF March/April, pp 31-39, 1995.

Bartlett RH, Gazzaniga AB, Fong SW, Rookh HB, Haidue N. Extracorporeal membrane oxygenator (ECMO) for cardiorespiratory failure: Experience with 28 cases. J Thorac Cardiovasc Surg 73:375-386, 1977.

· Christensen DW, Veasy LG, McGough EC, Dean JM. Intra-aortic balloon counterpulsation in children: A review of 29 patients. Crit Care Med 19(Suppl):S75, 1991.

DeBakey ME. Left ventricular bypass for cardiac assistance: Clinical experience. Am J Cardiol 27:3-11, 1971.

Del Nido PJ, Swan PR, Benson LN, Bohn D, Charlton MC, Coles JG, Trusler GA, Williams WG. Successful use of intra-aortic balloon pumping in a 2-kilogram infant. Ann Thorac Surg 46:574-576, 1988.

• Del Nido PJ, Armitage JM, Fricker FJ, Shaver M, Cipriani L, Dayal G, Park SC, Siewers RD. Extracorporeal membrane oxygenation support as a bridge to pediatric heart transplantation. Circulation 90(Pt 2):1166-1169, 1994.

• Karl TR. Extracorporeal circulatory support in infants and children. Semin Thorac Cardiovasc Surg 6:154-160, 1994.

Koppert E, Holfert GW, Dew PA. Preliminary in vitro evaluation of the first neonatal total artificial heart. Trans Am Soc Artif Intern Organs 36:M122-M128, 1991.

McCarthy PM, Sabik JF. Implantable circulatory support devices as a bridge to heart transplantation. Semin Thorac Cardiovasc Surg 6:174-180, 1994.

McCarthy PM, James KB, Savage RM, Vargo R, Kendall K, Harasaki H, Hobbs RE, Pashkow FJ. Implantable left ventricular assist device. Approaching as alternative for end-stage heart failure. Implantable LVAD study group. Circulation 90(Pt 2):1183-1186, 1994.

Moulopoulos SD, Topaz S, Kolff WJ. Diastolic balloon pumping (with carbon dioxide) in the aorta. Mechanical assistance of the failing circulation. Am Heart J 63:669-675, 1962.

Pennington DG. Commentary on circulatory support in infants and children. Semin Thorac Cardiovasc Surg 6:161-162, 1994.

Pollock JC, Charlton MD, Williams WG, Edmonds JF, Trusler GA. Intra-aortic balloon pumping in children. Ann Thorac Surg 29:522-528, 1980.

Spencer FC, Eiseman B, Trinkle JK, Rossi NP. Assisted circulation for cardiac failure following intracardiac surgery with cardiopulmonary bypass. J Thorac Cardiovasc Surg 49:56-73, 1965.

Vetter HO, Kaulback HG, Schmitz C, Forst A, Uberfuhr P, Kreuzer E, Pfeiffer M, Dewald O, Reichert B. Experience with the Novacor left ventricular assist system as a bridge to cardiac transplantation, including the new wearable system. J Thorac Cardiovasc Surg 109:74-80, 1995.

Weiss BM, von Segesser LK, Turina MI, Vetter W, Seifert B, Pasch T. Assisted circulation without systemic heparinization. J Cardiothorac Vasc Anesth 8:168-174, 1994.

144 Pericardiocentesis

Steven R. Leonard · *Hisashi Nikaidoh*

BACKGROUND AND INDICATIONS

The pericardial space is normally little more than a potential space containing a small amount of serous pericardial fluid for lubrication. Many disease processes can cause pericardial effusions, and accumulation of pericardial fluid can be acute or chronic. In either event compression of cardiac chambers with impaired diastolic filling may result in decreased cardiac output (cardiac tamponade). If left untreated, death may ensue.

Pericardiocentesis is a technique for aspirating pericardial fluid for diagnostic or therapeutic purposes. Any pericardial effusion of uncertain etiology must be evaluated by microbiologic and biochemical analyses. Diagnostic pericardiocentesis must be carried out under optimal conditions by an experi-

enced physician. However, when cardiac tamponade is present, emergency pericardiocentesis must be performed by the most experienced and appropriately trained individual immediately available to provide hemodynamic stabilization before the effusion can be drained more thoroughly.

A significant pericardial effusion (see Chapter 21) may be suspected based on the history (retrosternal pain that may be improved by leaning forward) and physical examination (dyspnea, tachycardia, pericardial friction rub, jugular venous distention, and paradoxic pulse). The chest radiograph may demonstrate cardiomegaly with a globular heart shadow, especially when compared to previous radiographs. Echocardiography has become the standard for diagnosis. It is a simple, relatively inexpensive test that

---

CAUSES OF PERICARDIAL EFFUSIONS

Infectious pericarditis

Viral (coxsackie, influenza, mononucleosis)
Pyogenic (especially *Staphylococcus,* pneumococcus, *Haemophilus influenzae*)
Tuberculous
Human immunodeficiency virus

Related to systemic illnesses

Uremia
Rheumatic fever
Collagen vascular diseases
    Rheumatoid arthritis
    Systemic lupus erythematosus
    Scleroderma
Myxedema
Sarcoidosis

Related to cardiac injury

Postmyocardial infarction (Dressler's syndrome)
Postpericardiotomy syndrome

Hemopericardium

Postoperative
Trauma

Drug-induced

Procainamide
Hydralazine

Idiopathic
Iatrogenic (e.g., perforation of central venous line)

---

can be easily done at the bedside. It may provide valuable information about the size and location of the effusion.

TECHNIQUE
Equipment

The following equipment is needed:

Pericardiocentesis equipment

Surgical cap and mask
Sterile gloves
Protective eyewear
Povidone-iodine solution, 10%, and applicators (or sterile gauze sponges)
Lidocaine without epinephrine, 1%
Sterile drapes
Needles, 25 and 22 gauge
Syringes for local anesthetic (3 or 5 ml) and aspiration of fluid (30 or 60 ml)
Spinal needle or IV catheter (Angiocath or Jelco) with a metal hub, 20 gauge
Sterile ECG lead with alligator clip
ECG machine
Laboratory tubes for culture and chemistry analyses

Procedure

Appropriate consent must be obtained before beginning the procedure. For a diagnostic pericardiocentesis, the child may be premedicated with morphine sulfate, 0.1 mg/kg, or fentanyl, 1 to 2 µg/kg. In addition, midazolam, 0.1 mg/kg, may be used for sedation. If pericardiocentesis is being performed as an emergency for cardiac tamponade, premedication is contraindicated since sedation may cause cardiovascular collapse. If the patient is younger than 6 to 7 years of age or uncooperative and if pericardiocentesis is not an emergency procedure for cardiac tamponade, it is probably more safely performed in the operating room with the patient under general anesthesia. Alternatively, if the patient is mechanically ventilated, he may be sedated and pharmacologically paralyzed for a short period of time.

The patient is positioned in either the supine position or with the head of the bed slightly elevated. The ECG machine is attached for monitoring of the limb leads.

The clinician dons cap, mask, and protective eyewear. After scrubbing, the surgeon dons sterile gloves, and the patient's skin is widely prepared with povidone-iodine solution, including the anterior chest and upper abdomen. Sterile drapes are placed. Lidocaine is injected with the 25-gauge needle to raise a skin wheal in the notch just to the left of the xiphoid process where the lowest costal cartilage joins the sternum. More local anesthetic is injected into the subcutaneous tissue using the 22-gauge needle. The total lidocaine dose must not exceed 6 mg/kg.

The sterile alligator clip is attached to the hub of the 20-gauge needle for use during aspiration. The other end is attached to lead V of the ECG machine, and the machine is adjusted to monitor the precordial lead continuously (Fig. 144-1). The 30 ml syringe is attached to the needle, and the needle is inserted through the skin wheal. The needle is held at a 45-degree angle to the skin surface and directed toward the left midscapular area (Fig. 144-2).

The needle is carefully advanced while gentle suction is maintained on the syringe and the ECG is monitored. The needle must not be advanced beyond the point at which pericardial fluid is obtained or when an injury current is noted on the ECG. If an IV catheter is being used, the external sheath can be advanced further into the pericardial cavity, the inner needle removed, and the syringe replaced on the hub of the outer sheath for aspiration of fluid.

Alternatively, pericardiocentesis can be performed using echocardiography for guidance. Advancement of the needle into the pericardial space is continuously visualized, and the proximity of the needle to the heart is carefully monitored. One must be certain that sterile technique is not broken while using this method.

In some cases (e.g., a postoperative effusion, tuberculous effusion, or traumatic hemopericardium) a bloody aspirate may be obtained. If so, the needle must not be withdrawn immediately. A portion of the fluid is placed in a glass tube. If the blood clots, the needle is likely within a cardiac chamber. It can be withdrawn and the patient monitored closely for signs of cardiac tamponade. If the bloody fluid does not clot, the fluid is probably a defibrinated clot within the pericardium, and the appropriate volume of fluid can be aspirated. In addition, the hematocrit of the aspirated fluid can be compared to that of the patient to help differentiate intracardiac from intrapericardial blood.

If air is aspirated during pericardiocentesis for an effusion, it must be assumed that the pleural space has been entered and pneumothorax may have resulted. If the patient's condition permits, the pericardiocentesis is delayed and a chest radiograph is obtained to exclude pneumothorax. Occasionally pericardiocentesis can be performed for pneumopericardium that has caused cardiac tamponade. In this case the procedure is performed as described above. When air is aspirated through the needle, the external sheath is advanced into the pericardial cavity to aspirate the air.

Usually pericardiocentesis is done for diagnostic purposes, and it is not necessary to attempt to aspirate "dry" the pericardial cavity. A sufficient volume of fluid can be obtained for the necessary analyses and the procedure terminated. If pericardiocentesis is being performed to relieve cardiac tamponade, enough fluid must be aspirated to improve the patient's hemodynamic status until more definitive

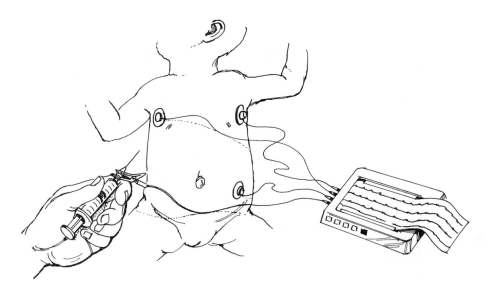

Fig. 144-1 Position of patient for pericardiocentesis. The alligator clip is attached to the metal hub of the needle and the ECG recorder.

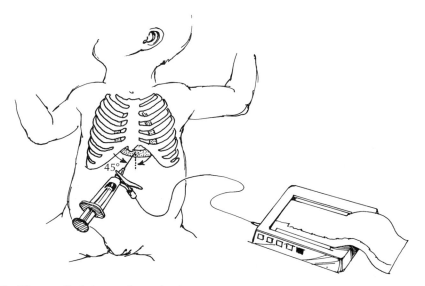

Fig. 144-2 The needle is inserted at a 45-degree angle to the skin surface and directed toward the left midscapular area.

drainage can be performed in the operating room.

If it is likely that continued accumulation of fluid will cause hemodynamic compromise, a guidewire may be inserted through the needle into the pericardial cavity and a soft pigtail catheter (e.g., Starszel) or a small chest tube advanced over the wire. The catheter may then be attached to gravity or low suction drainage. Catheter placement must be confirmed on a chest radiograph.

RISKS AND COMPLICATIONS

Laceration of the myocardium or coronary artery may result in cardiac tamponade. Coronary artery injury may also result in myocardial infarction.

If the needle is inserted or directed too inferiorly, it may cause intra-abdominal injury, especially to the liver. If the needle is inserted or directed too laterally, it may cause bleeding from the superior epigastric vessels or injury to the lung with subsequent pneumothorax.

The patient who has had previous cardiac surgery is at increased risk for cardiac injury because the acute margin of the heart is likely to be adherent to the pericardium. A postoperative pericardial effusion is best drained in the operating room where insertion of a pericardial tube can be performed under direct vision.

Attempted diagnostic pericardiocentesis in a young or uncooperative child may result in a cardiac injury. Such patients are best treated in the operating room under general anesthesia.

ADDITIONAL READING

Beland MJ, Paquet M, Gibbons JE, Tchervenkov CI, Dobell ARC. Pericardial effusion after cardiac surgery in children and effects of aspirin for prevention. Am J Cardiol 65:1238, 1990.

Duvernoy O, Borowiec J, Helmius G, Erikson U. Complications of percutaneous pericardiocentesis under fluoroscopic guidance. Acta Radiol 33:309, 1992.

Eisenberg MJ, Gordon AS, Schiller NB. HIV-associated pericardial effusions. Chest 102:956, 1992.

Feldman WE. Bacterial etiology and mortality of purulent pericarditis in pediatric patients: Review of 162 cases. Am J Dis Child 133:642, 1979.

Fiser DH, Walker WM. Tension pneumopericardium in an infant. Chest 102:1888, 1992.

• Kirkland LL, Taylor RW. Pericardiocentesis. Crit Care Clin 8:699, 1992.

Sahni J, Ivert T, Herzfeld I, Brodin L. Late cardiac tamponade after open-heart surgery. Scand J Thorac Cardiovasc Surg 25:63, 1991.

Shabetai R, Fowler NO, Guntheroth WG. The hemodynamics of cardiac tamponade and constrictive pericarditis. Am J Cardiol 26:480, 1970.

• Stewart JR, Gott VL. The use of a Seldinger wire technique for pericardiocentesis following cardiac surgery. Ann Thorac Surg 35:467, 1983.

• Susini G, Pepi M, Bortone F, Salvi L, Barbier P, Fiorentini C. Percutaneous pericardiocentesis versus subxiphoid pericardiotomy in cardiac tamponade due to postoperative pericardial effusion. J Cardiothorac Vasc Anesth 7:178, 1993.

XX

Respiratory Care Procedures

145 Oxygen Therapy

Rocky Stone · Gary D. Elmore

BACKGROUND AND INDICATIONS

Oxygen was discovered approximately two centuries ago. Since then, oxygen has been widely used in the treatment of various cardiopulmonary disorders. Supplemental oxygen is commonly prescribed to treat cardiac and respiratory diseases in infants and children. Oxygen is used to treat or prevent hypoxemia, decrease myocardial workload, and reduce the work of breathing.

Hypoxemia results from a variety of pathophysiologic mechanisms and varies with patient age and disease state. Clinicians accept lower Pao_2 values in premature infants and in children with congenital heart disease or chronic pulmonary disease. Oxygen therapy is indicated when arterial hypoxemia is present to prevent development of tissue damage, metabolic acidosis, and pulmonary vasoconstriction. Children with symptomatic pulmonary hypertension need increased levels of Fio_2 to reduce vascular tone. However, this may be contraindicated in children with hypoplastic left heart syndrome before surgical repair when reduced pulmonary vascular resistance may be undesirable.

Many techniques and devices are available to deliver supplemental oxygen in neonatal and pediatric patients, but no single way is best. The selection of a particular method must be individualized to the patient and the clinical situation. When selecting an oxygen device, the clinician needs to consider Fio_2 requirement, required inspiratory flow, patient comfort (essential in treatment compliance), and humidification needs.

TECHNIQUE
Incubators

Closed incubators may be used to provide a humidified neutral thermal environment for newborn infants, but they are poor devices for administration of oxygen. Oxygen can be administered through a flowmeter to a port at the back of the incubator. The majority of incubator units are designed with air-entrainment ports that restrict the Fio_2 within the incubator to a maximum of 40% unless the red safety flag is raised and the air-entrainment ports are closed. Higher Fio_2 concentrations may be obtained by closing the air-entrainment ports to allow oxygen concentrations up to 85% with appropriate oxygen liter flow. A pop-off valve limits the oxygen flow into the incubator at 8 L/min. With most incubators a red flag in the vertical position indicates an oxygen concentration of >40% and in the horizontal position indicates an oxygen concentration of ≤40%.

Stable Fio_2 levels in incubators are not often obtained because of patient care activities (Fio_2 concentrations decrease rapidly when ports are opened) and leaks in the system. Combined use of an oxygen hood or nasal cannula with the incubator will provide more reliable oxygen delivery. When possible, oxygen concentrations are monitored with an oxygen analyzer with high and low alarms set.

Oxygen Hoods and Tot Huts

Oxygen hood devices are made of clear Plexiglas and are designed to deliver stable oxygen concentrations to neonates and small infants who are not intubated; the hood is placed just over the infant's head. The Tot Hut is a small disposable tent frame with a canopy that envelops the upper half of an infant's torso, and like oxygen hoods it provides a controlled oxygen environment. An Fio_2 of up to 100% is attainable with an appropriate oxygen flow rate. Total gas flow into a small hood or Tot Hut needs to be >7 L/min to prevent a buildup of carbon dioxide within the hood or hut. In larger hoods and Tot Hut tents flows of 10 to 12 L/min are recommended.

The oxygen hood and Tot Hut tents are devices that provide delivery of medical gas to the patient. To ensure the desired oxygen concentration and provide adequate humidification to the patient, a large-volume nebulizer or humidifier must be used with these devices. The oxygen concentration inside a hood or hut can be regulated with a large-volume nebulizer by adjusting the Fio_2 setting on the nebulizer collar, which controls air entrainment into the system, or by placing the nebulizer on the 100% setting and attaching it to an air-oxygen blender. With the nebulizer on the 100% source gas setting, entrainment of room air is prevented; thus all Fio_2 adjustments are controlled by the air-oxygen blender. This setup is the most desirable for delivery of precise oxygen concentrations and reduced noise levels within the hood or hut, a common complaint associated with nebulizers.

Oxygen hoods are available in various shapes and sizes. Some hood designs are thought to generate more turbulent gas flow than others, making it difficult to maintain a stable Fio_2. Also, laboratory measurements have shown that when 100% oxygen is used some hood designs can have "layering," with the highest concentration of oxygen near the bottom. Therefore an oxygen analyzer needs to be placed as close as possible to the infant's nose and mouth to accurately reflect inspired oxygen concentration. Standard openings in the hoods or tents must not be covered or taped over, as this may lead to carbon dioxide retention.

Mist Tents

Mist tents or croup tents, as they are frequently called, were once commonly used to deliver supplemental oxygen to infants and toddlers. Mist tents provide a cool aerosol and low to moderate oxygen concentrations (21% to 50%). An often cited advantage of mist tents is greater patient mobility. The clear plastic tent canopy may cover either the entire child or just the head and chest. However, mist tents are limited for oxygen administration simply because they are cumbersome, they are difficult to maintain, patient access is limited, and they may be poorly tolerated by some children. Older children and toddlers are frequently uncomfortable with the isolation from their families that is imposed by the tent. Bedding and pajamas need to be changed frequently to keep the child dry and comfortable.

The oxygen concentration of a mist tent is a function of three factors: gas flow, canopy volume, and system leaks. A minimum flow rate of 10 to 15 L/min is necessary to maintain maximum oxygen concentrations and flush out exhaled carbon dioxide. Oxygen concentrations must be monitored continuously with an analyzer placed near the patient's face. Stable oxygen concentrations may be difficult to maintain because of leaks and will drop rapidly if the tent is kept opened.

Tents must be equipped with a cooling unit to provide a comfortable temperature of 5° to 7° C below room temperature. Families need to be instructed that electrical items such as radios, compact disk players, toys, and call buttons may pose a fire hazard inside the tent.

Masks

Several types of masks are manufactured to deliver varying concentrations of oxygen. Most masks are available in infant, pediatric, and adult sizes. They need to be soft, made of pliable plastic, and transparent to ensure that the patient's face is visible. The simple oxygen mask (Fig. 145-1) delivers a low to moderate oxygen concentration depending on flow rate. This mask is not the ideal choice if a stable Fio_2 is desired because the concentration is directly affected by the oxygen flow rate and patient inspiratory flow rate. Aerosol masks may deliver up to 100% oxygen provided the flow adequately meets inspiratory demand. Nonrebreathing masks are designed with one-way leaf valves and a reservoir bag that partially collapses during inspiration, and they deliver moderate to high concentrations of oxygen. Partial rebreathing masks are designed similarly to the simple oxygen mask but are equipped with a reservoir bag like the nonrebreathing mask and are capable of delivering up to 60% oxygen. Venturi masks deliver precise concentrations of oxygen that vary from 24% to 50%. In general masks allow easy access to the patient on a temporary basis but usually are not tolerated for long-term use.

Face Tents

Face tents are loose fitting and generally well accepted by children. With adequate flow rates, a stable oxygen concentration can usually be administered. When properly set, the oxygen concentration given must equal the source of gas. Because face tents are made only in adult sizes, they are often inverted to accommodate smaller patients (Fig. 145-2). This creates a smaller reservoir and better fits the pediatric patient.

Nasal Cannulas and Catheters

Nasal cannulas and catheters are used to deliver low flow rates and low doses of oxygen. The oxygen concentration delivered with the nasal cannula and catheter varies with changes in patient inspiratory flow rate. Because infants are obligate nose-breathers, one needs to make sure not to occlude the infant's nares by fitting the cannula or catheter too snugly. Most nasal cannulas and catheters are available in neonatal, pediatric, and adult sizes to provide a more custom fit and increase tolerance in smaller patients. These devices enable easy access to the patient, and oxygen therapy need not be circumvented for feed-ings. Oxygen flow >1 to 6 L/min is needed with these devices. Nasal catheters are not well tolerated by most patients because they are inserted to the level of the uvula. However, patients generally adapt well to cannulas (Fig. 145-3).

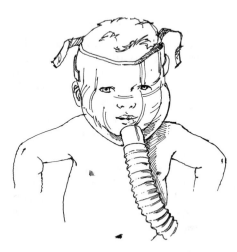

Fig. 145-2 Face tent.

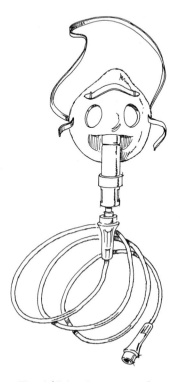

Fig. 145-1 Oxygen mask.

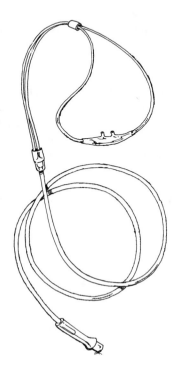

Fig. 145-3 Nasal cannula.

T-Bars and Tracheostomy Masks

The most direct method of delivering oxygen is through an endotracheal or a tracheostomy tube. These devices are capable of delivering precise oxygen concentrations when adequate flow is used. The flow must be high enough to meet patient inspiratory flow demands yet not allow room air entrainment. In some instances a short reservoir tube placed on the expiratory side of a T-bar can be used to stabilize Fio_2, as opposed to increasing flow rate. Concentrations of up to 100% oxygen are possible with both devices. The apparatus of choice must be examined closely to prevent unnecessary tension, which may cause inadvertent extubation. T-bars alone are not suggested for use in children younger than 4 years because the patient's airway is at zero end pressure, a nonphysiologic condition. Absence of continuous positive airway pressure at this age leads to increased work of breathing secondary to small airway collapse. Instead, a device capable of maintaining positive airway pressure for even short periods of time is recommended.

RISKS AND COMPLICATIONS

As with other drugs, oxygen has potential toxicity. When administering oxygen therapy to relieve hypoxemia, potential effects of toxicity must be minimized by use of arterial blood gas analysis, pulse oximetry, and transcutaneous oxygen monitoring. The respiratory therapist must closely monitor and analyze the oxygen concentration at least every 4 hours and with changes in flow rates or Fio_2.

Toxic effects of oxygen therapy in the neonate can lead to bronchopulmonary dysplasia. Infants with low birthweight and prematurity are at increased risk for retinopathy of prematurity. Although the exact pathogenesis of this disease is unknown, it seems to be partially related to elevated oxygen tension in immature retinal arteries. The condition has also been diagnosed in many infants exposed to room air. Bronchopulmonary dysplasia is a chronic disease that develops from a combination of oxygen toxicity and positive pressure ventilation. The disease results in excessive mucous production, air trapping, lobar atelectasis, hypercarbia, and an altered ventilation-perfusion ratio. Pulmonary oxygen toxicity can be further characterized by decreased or absent ciliary activity, decreased surfactant production, and destruction of type I pneumocytes.

The development of oxygen toxicity depends on the duration of oxygen exposure and the oxygen concentration administered. A Pao_2 of 60 to 80 mm Hg (Sao_2 90% to 95%) is considered a reasonably safe level in most patients to reduce the risk of oxygen toxicity.

As the patient's condition improves, weaning from oxygen support can begin. In patients who have received long-term oxygen therapy, oxygen flow rate must be reduced in small decrements, no more than 5% at a time. Oxygen delivery must also be decreased slowly in patients with reactive pulmonary vasculature to prevent undesirable pulmonary arterial constriction.

ADDITIONAL READING

Burgess WR, Chernick V. Respiratory Therapy in Newborn Infants and Children. New York: Thieme, 1986.

Burton GC, Hodgkin JE. Respiratory Care: A Guide to Clinical Practice, 2nd ed. Philadelphia: JB Lippincott, 1984, pp 407-410, 700-702.

Committee on Oxygen Therapy, American Association of Respiratory Care. Oxygen therapy in the acute care hospital. Respir Care 36:1410-1413, 1991.

Koff PB. Neonatal and Pediatric Respiratory Care, 2nd ed. St. Louis: Mosby, 1993, pp 226-239.

Levin DL, Frances CM, eds. Essentials of Pediatric Intensive Care. St. Louis: Quality Medical Publishing, 1990, pp 884-887.

McPherson SP. Respiratory Therapy Equipment, 2nd ed. St. Louis: Mosby, 1981, pp 92-95.

146 Inhaled Medications

Thomas R. George

BACKGROUND AND INDICATIONS

Inhalation of therapeutic agents is the optimal method of delivering many of the drugs used in pulmonary medicine and is safe, well tolerated, and in certain circumstances more effective than oral or parenteral administration. Medications delivered directly to the lung have a rapid onset of action and fewer systemic side effects. An aerosol is a suspension of liquid or solid particles in a gas. Major factors that influence penetration (depth within the tracheobronchial tree that particles of a given size may reach) and deposition (factors that influence aerosol settling in the airway) include the following:

1. Particle size: Particles 10 to 15 μm in diameter will deposit primarily in the mouth and nose, whereas those in the range of 5 to 10 μm will deposit primarily within the first 6 generations of the airways. Aerosol particles are optimally 1 to 5 μm in diameter to penetrate the lower respiratory tract.

2. Inertial impaction: This process describes the tendency of a moving body to resist change. Deposition occurs as a result of the abrupt changes caused by branching of the tracheobronchial tree.

3. Ventilation: Ventilatory patterns can affect the deposition site and quantity of aerosol deposited. Rapid shallow breathing decreases overall deposition, whereas slow deep breathing increases the amount of aerosol deposited and the amount of deposition at the bronchiolar level.

4. Gravitational settling: Sedimentation from gravity primarily influences deposition of particles 1 μm or larger, and settling rate is proportional to the square of the particle size.

5. Humidity: Because aerosols are generated in a relatively dry environment, particles may increase in size as under body temperature, ambient pressure, and saturated (BTPS) conditions.

Other factors that may influence particle penetration and deposition are concentration of particles (particles may coalesce to form larger particles) and brownian movement, although primarily particles smaller than 1 μm are affected.

Bronchodilators are the most commonly administered inhaled medications and include agents that affect sympathetic (adrenergic) and parasympathetic (cholinergic) airway receptors. Other inhaled medications are ribavirin, mucolytic, steroid, and antibiotic agents, and cromolyn sodium. The latter four are infrequently used in the PICU and are not discussed here.

Medications

β-Adrenergic bronchodilators. Inhaled β-agonist drugs (Table 146-1) are sympathomimetic agents that stimulate bronchial smooth muscle receptors, primarily β_2-receptors. Most are analogs of the naturally occurring catecholamines epinephrine and norepinephrine. The primary action of these agents is to stimulate adenylate cyclase activity, which increases production of intracellular levels of cyclic 3'5-adenosine monophosphate from adenosine triphosphate. In addition to relaxation of bronchial smooth muscle, β-agonists inhibit mast cell degranulation, reduce mucous gland secretion, augment mucociliary clearance, and improve intrinsic respiratory muscle contractility.

Because these agents stimulate both β_1- and β_2-receptors, side effects include tachycardia, arrhythmias, vasodilation, and rarely myocardial ischemia. Other side effects associated with medications that contain β-agonists are elevated blood glucose and insulin levels and hypokalemia, although this is most often associated with high-dose continuous nebulization and parenteral administration. However, pharmacologic advances have produced agents with increased β_2 selectivity, longer duration of action, and fewer side effects.

Table 146-1 Commonly Used β-Adrenergic Agents

Drug and Concentration	Dose	Site of Action (receptors)	Peak Onset (min)
Epinephrine, 1%	0.25-0.5 ml	α, β	5-20
Isoproterenol, 0.5%	0.25-0.5 ml	β	5-30
MDI, 130 μg/puff	1-2 puffs		
Isoetherine, 1%	0.25-0.5 ml	$\beta_2 > \beta_1$	5-30
MDI, 0.34 mg/puff	1-2 puffs		
Bitolterol, 0.2%	0.5-1.5 ml	β_2	15-30
MDI, 0.37 mg/puff	1-2 puffs		
Metaproterenol, 5%	0.2-0.3 ml	β_2	30-60
MDI, 0.65 mg/puff	1-2 puffs		
Terbutaline, 0.1%	1.0-3.0 ml	β_2	30-60
MDI, 0.2 mg/puff	1-2 puffs		
Albuterol, 0.5%	0.25-0.5 ml	β_2	30-60
MDI, 180 μg/puff	1-2 puffs		
Pirbuterol		β_2	30-60
MDI, 200 μg/puff	1-2 puffs		

Solution needs to be diluted with 0.9 sodium chloride to a total volume of at least 2.5 ml.

Of the catecholamine adrenergic agents, epinephrine and isoproterenol are less selective. Epinephrine activates all three types of receptors, and isoproterenol activates both β_1- and β_2-sites. Isoetherine is more β_2-selective than epinephrine and isoproterenol. Catecholamines tend to have a rapid onset, short duration, and increased incidence of systemic side effects.

Bitolterol has a unique action: when inhaled, it is converted by esterase hydrolysis to the active catecholamine colterol. This reaction results in a duration of action of up to 8 hours.

Newer agents such as albuterol, pirbuterol, and terbutaline are more β_2-selective and have a longer duration of action and fewer side effects than epinephrine and isoproterenol.

Salmeterol, a recently developed long-acting catecholamine bronchodilator, has a duration of action as long as 12 hours. Its use is limited to maintenance therapy for bronchospasm. The dosage in patients younger than 12 years has not been established, and administration for treatment of acute bronchospasm is not recommended. It is currently available in a metered dose inhaler (MDI) only.

Many respiratory disorders are characterized by bronchospasm that is reversed by inhaled β-adrenergic agents. These disorders include acute severe asthma, bronchiolitis, cystic fibrosis, bronchopulmonary dysplasia, and congenital cardiac lesions with left-to-right shunting. Inhaled β-adrenergic agents also are indicated in the management of mucous plugging because they enhance mucociliary activity and for respiratory muscle fatigue because they augment diaphragmatic contractility.

Anticholinergic bronchodilators. Anticholinergic agents (Table 146-2) inhibit the action of acetylcholine at cholinergic receptor sites, reducing intracellular levels of guanyl cyclase and inhibiting intracellular increases of cyclic 3'5'-guanylmonophosphate. Whereas β-adrenergic agents appear to affect distal bronchioles, anticholinergic agents act on proximal airways because of the larger number of cholinergic receptor sites. Relative to β-adrenergic agents, they have a delayed onset but longer duration of action. Both atropine and ipratropium bromide may be delivered simultaneously with inhaled β-adrenergic agents and may have a synergistic effect. They are less effective in treating acute bronchospasm alone compared with inhaled β-adrenergic agents.

Racemic epinephrine. Racemic epinephrine is a

Table 146-2 Commonly Used Anticholinergic Agents

Drug	Dose	Peak Onset (min)	Duration of Action (hr)
Atropine	0.05 mg/kg (maximum dose 2.5 mg)	60	3-4
Ipratropium (solution)	0.25-0.5 mg	60	4-6

Solution needs to be diluted with 0.9 sodium chloride to a total volume of at least 2.5 ml.

Table 146-3 Racemic Epinephrine Dosage Guidelines (solution concentration 2.25%)

Body Weight (kg)	Dose (ml)
0-20	0.25
>20	0.50

Solution needs to be diluted with 0.9 sodium chloride to a total volume of at least 2.5 ml.

preparation that contains equal amounts of dextrorotatory and levorotatory forms of epinephrine. Its activity is mediated by the stimulation of α-sympathomimetic receptors. Racemic epinephrine reduces mucosal swelling by inducing vasoconstriction and is useful in the management of conditions characterized by upper airway obstruction and inspiratory stridor (e.g., viral croup, mucosal edema after extubation, smoke inhalation, and angioneurotic edema). Racemic epinephrine may be indicated for worsening upper airway function in disorders of chronic obstruction such as tracheomalacia. It has also been used to reduce mucosal edema during bronchoscopy to remove impacted foreign bodies. Its onset of action is immediate, and dosing may be repeated as indicated by physical examination (e.g., every 2 to 3 hours but as often as every 15 minutes).

All children need to be hospitalized after treatment with racemic epinephrine because it has a short duration of action, may produce rebound symptoms, and does not alter the natural course of disease. Dosing guidelines for racemic epinephrine are outlined in Table 146-3.

Ribavirin. Ribavirin is a virustatic agent with a broad spectrum of activity against RNA and DNA viruses; respiratory syncytial virus (RSV) infection has been most thoroughly studied. Its indications and clinical efficacy are controversial, but ribavirin reduces the morbidity and mortality related to RSV infections in high-risk groups (e.g., infants with congenital heart disease, immunosuppression, bronchopulmonary dysplasia, and cystic fibrosis) and al-

so is widely used in the management of RSV bronchiolitis and pneumonia. Aerosol administration appears to be effective against viral respiratory pathogens because high concentrations are achieved in airway secretions. There is minimal systemic absorption, and no significant side effects have been documented. The dosage is 6 mg of ribavirin in 300 ml of sterile water (20 μg/ml) aerosolized continuously for 12 to 18 hours over 3 to 7 days.

TECHNIQUE
Aerosol Administration

Of the various methods of aerosol delivery to both spontaneously breathing patients and those receiving mechanical ventilation, no method has proven superior. Selection of the method and delivery device depend on many factors, including the following:

1. Type of nebulizer: Small-volume nebulizers and MDIs are most commonly used.
2. The efficiency of drug delivery is less with mechanical ventilation compared with spontaneous breathing, most commonly because of the endotracheal tube.
3. Patient cooperation: Aerosols are most effective when given to cooperative, spontaneously breathing patients.

Small-volume nebulizer. Small-volume nebulizers generate an aerosol by passage of a high-velocity gas stream (usually oxygen) across a tube, which creates a Bernoulli effect; the medications are pulled from the reservoir and become nebulized. A baffle in front of the jet stream removes the larger particles and returns them to solution for renebulization, and the small particles (1 to 5 μm in diameter) are delivered to the patient's airway. The aerosol is administered in the spontaneously breathing patient with a mouthpiece (Fig. 146-1), mask, or "blow-by" technique. The nebulizer typically holds a maximum of 8 to 10 ml of solution, and drugs are usually diluted with 0.9% sodium chloride solution to reach a volume of 2 to 3 ml. A gas flow of 6 to 8 L/min is commonly used, and treatment duration is 10 to 15 minutes. If possible, instruct the patient to breath slowly and deeply to peak inspiration with an end-inspiratory pause and passive exhalation. Even under ideal conditions only a small proportion (9% to 12%) of the drug placed in the nebulizer actually reaches the patient. Intermittent positive pressure breathing may be used to augment tidal volume and deliver aerosols to patients who are unable to inspire adequately, although this is difficult in the pediatric patient in respiratory distress because patient compliance is necessary for proper administration.

The endotracheal tube acts as a barrier to the aerosol, resulting in premature deposition of particles. When aerosol administration is used in patients receiving mechanical ventilation, various techniques are used. When using the assisted aerosol technique, the nebulizer is attached to a manual ventilation device, most commonly a non-self-inflating bag. The solution is nebulized into the bag and manually delivered to the patient. Aerosols may also be administered "in-line" with mechanical ventilation. With this technique, the nebulizer is placed in the inspiratory limb of the circuit, and the aerosol is nebulized and delivered with the mechanical breaths. Several factors that must be considered when medication is administered with this technique include the following:

1. Nebulizer location: Optimal location is controversial but is probably no closer than 18 inches from the Y-connector.
2. Continuous vs. intermittent flow: Intermittent gas flow administering nebulizer medication during the inspiratory phase only results in increased deposition of aerosol medications. This technique may be technically difficult and increases treatment duration.
3. Addition of supplemental flow from the nebulizer may alter ventilation variables. Careful attention must be given to peak and end-expiratory pressure levels, tidal volume, and Fio_2 when administering aerosols along with mechanical ventilation.

Metered-dose inhaler: An MDI is an aerosol-generating device that consists of a canister containing the drug and a propellant, usually with a mouthpiece or spacer device (Fig. 146-2). Most particles produced are 2 to 5 μm in diameter. When actuated, the drug is dispersed in a specific quantity along with the propellant. The propellant, usually a chlorofluorocarbon, dissipates rapidly after actuation, leaving the drug as an aerosol. MDIs are usually used with a spacing device, particularly in pediatric patients. This may have a mask attached, depending on the patient's age. Spacing devices are preferred in pediatric patients because they eliminate the need for coordinated action and reduce the amount of large particles deposited in the upper airway. Aerosolized drugs are administered as follows:

1. Shake canister vigorously.
2. Assemble MDI and spacer.
3. Hold MDI upright and actuate.
4. Place spacer in mouth or cover mouth and nose with mask.
5. If the patient is cooperative, have him inspire slowly to total lung capacity. If a mask is used,

Fig. 146-1 Patient receiving aerosolized medication via jet nebulizer.

a one-way valve is placed between the mask and the chamber to minimize dead space, and the mask is held in place for 5 seconds if possible.

6. Repeat if needed, with a minimum of at least 3 minutes between subsequent doses.

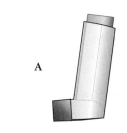

Fig. 146-2   **A,** Metered dose device. **B,** Spacer device.

MDIs are not used in patients who are severely fatigued, unable to tolerate a mask, or in severe respiratory distress.

With mechanical ventilation, MDIs can be used as described above or in-line with mechanical ventilators. A spacer is recommended because it acts as an aerosol reservoir; timing of the actuation depends on the type of spacer used. The spacer is placed in-line on the inspiratory limb of the ventilator and the drug is delivered just before or during the inspiratory phase of ventilation, with at least 1 minute between doses. Care must be taken with administration in very small pediatric patients and neonates with high oxygen requirements because actuation of the MDI may result in a transient reduction in Fio_2.

Continuous aerosol therapy. As larger and more frequent doses of β-adrenergic agents have been used, continuous nebulization (Fig. 146-3) has been studied for safety and efficacy of delivery. With continuous nebulization, the specific nebulizer output must be known, and medication and diluent are added to the nebulizer. Flow is adjusted to deliver the desired dose. For example, if the known nebulizer output is 0.25 ml/min (15 ml/hr) and a 10 mg dose (5 mg/ml) is desired, 2 ml of the drug must be diluted with 13 ml of 0.9% sodium chloride solution to

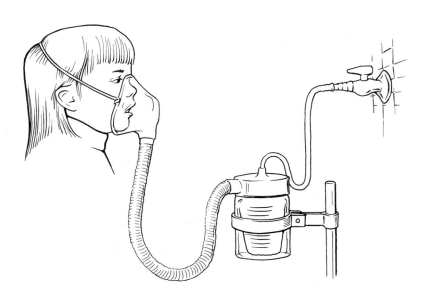

Fig. 146-3   Continuous medication nebulizer setup.

achieve the desired dose. This technique may offer technical advantages, and continuous nebulizer therapy may provide a more consistent dose than intermittent administration. This method can be adapted for use with mechanical ventilators, but the following factors need to be considered:

1. Nebulizer flow alterations may be observed due to physical changes within the circuit, such as pressure levels and higher humidity levels.
2. Fluids and other substances may enter the nebulizer, affecting drug delivery and concentration.
3. Additional flow from the nebulizer as well as the drugs themselves may adversely affect ventilator performance and needs to be closely observed.
4. No clear clinical advantage has been demonstrated over intermittent nebulizer therapy.

• • •

To summarize delivery methods for aerosolized medications in critically ill patients, consider the following:

1. It is unclear which method is superior, and each patient needs to be frequently evaluated for response to therapy.
2. With mechanical ventilation, the amount of medication delivered is decreased (2% to 6%). This needs to be considered when determining drug dosage (2% to 6% vs. 9% to 12%). In general 2% to 6% of aerosolized medications are deposited in the airways when patients are receiving ventilatory support vs. 9% to 12% in spontaneous breathing patients.

Ribavirin Administration

Technical aspects of ribavirin administration are important because of its propensity to deposit in ventilator circuitry or other apparatus. Spontaneously breathing patients can be given ribavirin by means of a tent, hood, or face mask using the small-particle aerosol generator nebulizer. Fig. 146-4 summarizes the setup for ribavirin administration with a mechanical ventilator.

Important considerations are as follows:

1. Circuit inspection is frequent, with careful checks for crystalline deposits associated with ribavirin administration. Circuits are changed at least every 48 hours.

2. A pressure relief valve is placed in the isolated small-particle aerosol generator (SPAG) circuitry and set just above baseline pressure.
3. Filters are placed in strategic locations to prevent ribavirin from entering the mechanical ventilator apparatus (e.g., valves and electronics).
4. As with other aerosols, it is likely that less drug is delivered with mechanical ventilation than in spontaneously breathing patients.

In addition, all caregivers must familiarize themselves with institutional guidelines for potential risks to the care giver.

RISKS AND COMPLICATIONS

Side effects of sympathomimetic agents are most commonly from overdosage but may also result from idiosyncratic responses. Side effects of these agents involve the cardiovascular system (e.g., tachycardia, palpitations, arrhythmias, and hypertension) and CNS (e.g., anxiety, tremor, restlessness, headache, dizziness, emesis, and nausea). A decrease in heart rate may also occur with relief of airway obstruction. Adrenergic agents stimulate mobilization of glucose from the liver, producing hyperglycemia. Transient reduction in Pa_{O_2} may be observed as a result of temporary worsening of ventilation-perfusion ratios.

Atropine must not be used for nonpulmonary disorders because they may be exacerbated by blockade of parasympathetic innervation (e.g., narrow-angle glaucoma, gastric outlet obstruction, or bladder outlet obstruction). As with systemic use, atropine may be associated with tachycardia, blurred vision, and drying of pulmonary secretions, although these occur less frequently with aerosolized atropine. Ipratropium has a relatively high therapeutic index and is seldom associated with side effects. Most complaints seem to be a bad taste and dryness of the mouth and throat.

Hazards associated with administration techniques such as inappropriate use of MDIs and salmeterol in patients with severe symptoms include variations of ventilator volumes, pressures, and Fi_{O_2}.

CURRENT RESEARCH AND FUTURE CONSIDERATIONS

Clinical trials with agents are ongoing or in development. β-Adrenergic agents currently being evaluated include procaterol and eformoterol.

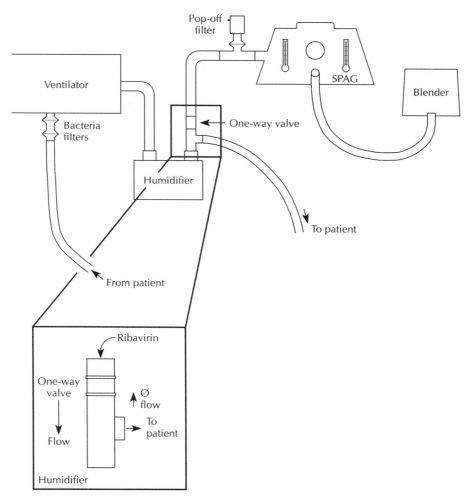

Fig. 146-4 Setup for ribavirin administration via mechanical ventilator. One-way valve is placed to close on inspiration and open on expiration.

Future considerations involving administration are ongoing; most involve identifying the superior methods of aerosol administration. One technique involves placement of an intratracheal cannula for MDI use just below the endotracheal tube, allowing the aerosol to bypass the tube. Preliminary studies are promising, although more clinical trials need to be initiated.

ADDITIONAL READING

American Academy of Pediatrics, Committee on Infectious Diseases. Use of ribavirin in the treatment of respiratory syncytial virus infection. Pediatrics 92:501-504, 1993.

Colacone A, Wolkove N, Stern E, et al. Continuous nebulization of albuterol in acute asthma. Chest 97:693-697, 1990.

• Consensus Conference on Aerosol Delivery. Aerosol consensus statement. Chest 100:1106-1109, 1991.

Everard M, Clark A, Milner A. Drug delivery from holding chambers with attached facemask. Arch Dis Child 67:74-78, 1992.

Grigg J, Arnon S, Jones T, et al. Delivery of therapeutic aerosols to intubated babies. Arch Dis Child 67:25-30, 1992.

• Hess D. Inhaled bronchodilators during mechanical ventilation: Delivery techniques, evaluation of response and cost effectiveness. Respir Care 32:105-119, 1994.

Manthous C, Hall J. Administration of therapeutic aerosols to mechanically ventilated patients. Chest 106:560-571, 1994.

Pierson D, Kacmereck R. Foundations of Respiratory Care. New York: Churchill Livingstone, 1992.

• Rau J. Respiratory Care Pharmacology, ed 4. St. Louis: Mosby, 1993.

Westley RC, Cotton EK, Brooks JG. Nebulized racemic epinephrine administered by IPPB for treatment of laryngotracheobronchitis. Am J Dis Child 132:484, 1978.

147 Suctioning

Melissa J. Whitehead · *Richard L. Vinson*

BACKGROUND AND INDICATIONS

Sputum is a complex fluid consisting of mucoproteins, water, electrolytes, cellular debris, and blood. The volume, consistency, color, odor, and presence of foreign substances in the sputum may be of diagnostic value in the child with respiratory disease (Table 147-1). An ET tube acts as a foreign body and may increase mucous production. In addition, the ET tube interferes with the mucociliary apparatus and therefore clearance of secretions. Mobilization of secretions may be affected by pharmacologic agents, after some surgical procedures, and as a result of many neurologic disorders. For these reasons, suctioning is a vital part of routine care in pediatric patients with an ET tube or tracheotomy. Suctioning may also be indicated in patients without an ET tube but with an ineffective cough or with excessive or tenacious secretions (Table 147-2).

TECHNIQUE
Endotracheal Suctioning Equipment

The ideal suctioning technique removes the greatest amount of secretions with the least amount of risk to the patient. The need for suctioning is based not only on the presence of an artificial airway but also on patient symptoms. Patients with increased secretions in the nose, pharynx, or artificial airway lumen; increased cough; ausculatory evidence of airway secretion; or signs of artificial airway obstruction can benefit from suctioning (see Table 147-2). Once the need for suctioning has been determined, the equipment is assembled. When the intubated patient is suctioned, the appropriate size hyperinflation or self-inflating bag and suction catheter must be readily available at the bedside (Table 147-3). Suction catheter size for the various tracheotomy tubes depends on each manufacturer. In general the largest catheter that can easily pass through the tube is used. The patient

---

SUCTIONING EQUIPMENT

Stethoscope
Adjustable vacuum regulator
Suction catheter kit
Hyperinflation or self-inflating bag with manometer
0.9% sodium chloride solution
Water-soluble lubricant (for nasotracheal suctioning only; not recommended for ET tube)
Oxygen source with adjustable flowmeter
Appropriate size mask
Universal precautions equipment

---

monitor is checked to ensure that alarms and limits are set and functional. The hyperinflation or self-inflating bag is connected to a manometer to appropriately monitor the pressure used to ventilate the lungs. Manual ventilation is performed at approximately the same peak pressures as used with conventional mechanical ventilation. The same positive end-expiratory pressure (PEEP) as for conventional mechanical ventilation is used to maintain alveolar recruitment, prevent atelectasis, and provide proper oxygenation. The suction apparatus must have an adjustable vacuum system regulator to prevent excessive negative pressure. The recommended maximum negative pressure for different sized patients is listed in Table 147-4. The equipment must be tested to ensure it is turned on and functioning properly before the suctioning procedure is initiated. An explanation of the procedure and what will be experienced must be given to the patient (depending on age) or family before the suctioning procedure is begun, even if the patient is apparently unconscious.

Table 147-1 Characteristics of Sputum

Disease	Bloody	Fetid	Frothy	Mucoid	Muco-purulent	Purulent
Acute bronchitis	X				X	X
Aspiration pneumonia		X				X
Asthma				X		
Bronchiectasis	X	X				X
Cystic fibrosis		X			X	
Lung abcess		X				X
Pneumonia	X					X
Pulmonary edema			X			
Pulmonary infarction	X					
Respiratory syncytial virus/bronchiolitis				X		
Tuberculosis	X					

Table 147-2 Indications for Suctioning

Physiologic Condition	Associated Symptoms	Observed Monitored Variables
Excessive upper airway secretions	Inability to swallow Drooling Coughing Gagging Emesis Rhinitis	Tachycardia Hypertension
Excessive pulmonary secretions	Coughing or inability to cough Agitation Fighting ventilator Wet crackles Change in breath sounds Visible secretions in ET tube	Tachypnea Tachycardia Hypertension Increased ventilator pressure Increased $etco_2$ or $tcco_2$ Decreased exhaled tidal volume
Inspissated pulmonary secretions	Coughing or inability to cough Agitation Fighting ventilator Decreased or absent breath sounds Retractions	Apnea Bradycardia Cyanosis Decreased $etco_2$ Decreased Sao_2

Table 147-3 Recommended Catheter Sizes for ET Suctioning*

Tube Size (mm)	Suction Catheter (mm)
2.0	5
2.5	6.5
3.0	6.5
3.5	6.5-8
4.0	8
4.5	8-10
5.0	10-12
5.5	10-12
6.0	12-14

*From Children's Medical Center of Dallas procedure manual.

Table 147-4 Maximum Negative Pressure for Airway Suctioning*

Age	Negative Pressure (cm H_2O)
Infant	60-90
Child	90-110
Older child	110-150

*From Hazinski MF. Nursing Care of the Critically Ill Child. St. Louis: Mosby, 1984.

Artificial Airway Suctioning

Aseptic technique must be maintained when opening a commercial suction catheter package. Two gloves are provided for suctioning; one must remain sterile throughout the procedure and the other protects the caregiver from the patient's secretions. The hand with the sterile glove is used to remove the catheter from the suction catheter package and connect it to the suction tubing. If needed, minimal amounts (<3 ml) of 0.9% sodium chloride solution may be instilled in the artificial airway with the nonsterile gloved hand. In all patients manual ventilation must be used for a minimum of 10 breaths, with continual assessment for tolerance of the procedure (i.e., heart rate, systemic arterial blood pressure, skin color, respiratory rate, Sao_2). In general an Fio_2 0.10 high-er than the patient's therapeutic Fio_2 requirement is used. In selected patients, particularly those with pulmonary artery hypertension, an Fio_2 of 1.0 and hyperventilation are used to facilitate dilation of the pulmonary arteries or protect against a pulmonary artery hypertensive crisis. Hyperventilation is used in patients with increased ICP to constrict the cerebral vasculature and reduce blood flow to the brain, therefore reducing the likelihood of increasing ICP during suctioning. These patients usually tolerate suctioning better when premedicated with either sedatives, narcotics, or other agents to control ICP. Also, in patients at risk for increased ICP, lidocaine can be given intravenously to prevent or decrease the cough reflex.

The patient with a tracheotomy tube needs to be positioned with the neck flexed. The suction catheter is gently inserted to 0.5 to 1.0 cm below the tip of the artificial airway before suction is applied. Graduated catheters are used to approximate the depth the suction catheter is to be introduced by comparing the marked length of the artificial airway to the marked length of the suction catheter. If marked graduated catheters are unavailable, a suitable depth can be marked in centimeters on a suction catheter posted at the bedside. The measured catheter can be used by the caregiver to approximate the depth for insertion of the sterile suction catheter. The sterile catheter is inserted without applied negative pressure and withdrawn while twirling it between the fingers during continuous application of suction. Suctioning must not last longer than 5 to 10 seconds. Manual ventilation is used while tolerance to the procedure is reassessed. At least two or more passes of the catheter may be necessary. Remember to always interpose manual ventilation between catheter insertions and suctioning.

After the final ET or tracheotomy tube insertion, the nares and mouth are cleared of secretions. Once again, complete assessment is performed, including but not limited to breath sounds, vital signs, skin color, Sao_2, transcutaneous O_2 (tco_2), transcutaneous CO_2 ($tcco_2$), and end-tidal CO_2 ($etco_2$). This procedure may be modified in patients who need relatively high ventilator settings, especially high PEEP or mean airway pressure ($P\overline{aw}$). Under these circumstances the patient may tolerate suctioning better if mechanical ventilation is maintained throughout the procedure by suctioning through a PEEP-sustaining device rather than performing manual ventilation between passes of the suction catheter. This is also a serious consideration when suctioning a patient receiving high-frequency oscillatory ventilation (HFOV). (See Chapter 156 for the specific description of ET suctioning during HFOV.) When suctioning a patient receiving mechanical ventilation with PEEP of ≥6 cm H_2O, a PEEP-sustaining device is used to prevent loss of PEEP during the suctioning procedure. Also, in-line or closed-circuit suction catheters are available in all sizes and may be used when disconnection of ventilation is undesirable. Currently there is debate about whether closed vs. open suctioning is the safest and most cost-effective technique.

Each institution needs to evaluate and choose the technique that best suits its needs. The amount of suctioning needed by patients may vary greatly. Because suctioning to ensure artificial airway patency must be performed when necessary, assessment of the need for suctioning, rather than a schedule, is used to determine such need. Suctioning must be performed whenever secretions are visible in the tube, secretion accumulation is evident, or any artificial airway obstruction is suspected clinically (see Table 147-2).

Nasotracheal Suctioning

Nasotracheal suctioning provides a means of removing excessive or thick secretions from the upper and lower airways in patients without an artificial airway who have an ineffective cough mechanism. Before beginning the procedure, the need for suctioning and the procedure is explained to the patient or parent. The equipment, similar to that for artificial airway suctioning, is assembled. The oxygen flowmeter, with hyperinflation bag and appropriate size mask, is set to 6 to 7 L/min. In some instances higher flow rates may be necessary to achieve adequate hyperoxygenation. With aseptic technique, the catheter package is opened, a moderate amount of water-soluble lubricant is dispensed onto a sterile part of the package, and two gloves are donned. The lubricant is applied to the tip of the suction catheter.

The patient must be positioned properly, with the head of the infant or small child in the sniffing position and the older cooperative child in a semisitting position at approximately 45 degrees with the jaw thrust forward. The patient is allowed to breathe oxygen for approximately 10 breaths or ventilation is assisted with a hyperinflation or self-inflating bag before insertion of the catheter for suctioning. Patients with a history of pulmonary artery hypertension must breathe oxygen at an FiO_2 of 1.0 for at least 1 minute before and after each suctioning attempt or successful completion. The catheter is gently inserted into the nare and advanced toward the patient's earlobe. If resistance is felt, the catheter is gently twisted and the direction changed. If resistance persists, the catheter must be removed and placement attempted in the other nare. The patient is encouraged to cough or attempt to stimulate a cough to open the epiglottis to allow entry of the catheter into the trachea. When the trachea is entered, the patient's face will flush red and his lips will purse.

The catheter is removed by twirling it between the fingers while applying continuous suction. This must be accomplished within 5 to 10 seconds. Manually ventilation is used while patient tolerance is again assessed. At least two additional passes of the catheter may be necessary. Finally, the patient is stabilized with oxygen as needed and reassessed.

Contraindications to routine nasal suctioning are thrombocytopenia, recent facial or craniofacial surgery or trauma, epistaxis, and immunosuppression in patients with mucosal denudation.

RISKS AND COMPLICATIONS

Suctioning is a physiologically noxious stimulus, and many of the associated complications are related to evoking the patient's protective airway reflexes or sympathetic reflexes. Others are inherent to the technique itself and include hypoxemia, arrhythmias, pulmonary artery hypertension, atelectasis, gagging, vomiting, bleeding, mucosal damage, bronchospasm, airway obstruction, reflex vagal stimulation, bacterial contamination, and accidental extubation. Hypoxemia during the suctioning procedure may result in the removal of alveolar gas or obstruction from the instilled 0.9% sodium chloride solution. Patients who need supplemental oxygen are at greater risk of hypoxia during the suctioning procedure. Careful monitoring of their tolerance during the procedure and assisting them with hand ventilation immediately after each pass of the suction catheter will decrease the risk of hypoxemia during the course of the suctioning procedure or afterward as a result of vagal stimulation by the suction catheter (Table 147-5). Atelectasis, mucosal damage, and bleeding are best avoided by maintaining the negative suctioning pressures within the suggested guidelines (see Table

Table 147-5 Possible Respiratory Reflexes During Suctioning

Reflex	Area Stimulated
Spasm	Larynx, trachea
Gag, emesis	Pharynx
Cough	Pharynx, larynx, trachea, bronchi
Sneeze	Nasopharynx
Swallow	Pharynx
Apnea	Pharynx

147-3). Insertion of the catheter no farther than 1 cm below the artificial airway and use of an appropriate size suction catheter will also prevent tissue injury and airway obstruction. Limiting the time and number of passes to a minimum needed for airway patency will decrease obstructive side effects. Maintenance of strict sterile technique and use of no or a limited amount of saline solution will decrease the risk of bacterial contamination. Extubation during suctioning can occur if the artificial airway is not secure or the patient is not properly restrained.

CURRENT RESEARCH AND FUTURE CONSIDERATIONS

For many years 0.9% sodium chloride solution has been the standard solution instilled into the airway before suctioning. Recently this practice has been challenged; current studies have demonstrated adverse effects including decreased Sao_2 and increased risk of nosocomial pneumonia. Saline solution can act as a vehicle for bacteria to travel from the contaminated artificial airway to the patient's lower airway. Although saline solution and mucus do not mix, saline solution acts as a vehicle for transport of thick mucoid secretions and an agent to elicit the cough reflex. The majority of data collected regarding the use of saline solution with suctioning have been from adult populations, and few data from the pediatric population are available. More research is needed in critically ill pediatric patients and other populations before standardization of this technique can be achieved.

ADDITIONAL READING

· Ackerman MH. The effect of saline lavage prior to suctioning. Am J Crit Care 2:326-330, 1993.
· Bostick J, Wendelgass ST. Normal saline instillation as part of the suctioning procedure: Effects on Pao_2 and amount of secretions. Heart Lung 16:532-537, 1987.
Deppe SA, Kelly JW, Thoi LL, Chudy JH, Longfield RN, Ducey JP, Truwit CL, Anatopol MR. Incidence of colonization, nosocomial pneumonia, and mortality in critically ill patients using a Trach Care closed-suction system versus an open suction system: Prospective randomized study. Crit Care Med 18:1389-1393, 1990.
Hagler DA, Traver GA. Endotracheal saline and suction catheters: Source of lower airway contamination. Am J Crit Care 3:444-447, 1994.
McIntosh D, Baun MM, Rogge J. Effects of lung hyperinflation and presence of positive end expiratory pressure on arterial and tissue oxygenation during endotracheal suctioning. Am J Crit Care 2:317-325, 1993.
Runton N. Suctioning artificial airways in children: Appropriate technique. Pediatr Nurs 18:115-118, 122-123, 1992.

148 Bronchial Hygiene

Kathalene M. Harris · Dallas M. Manly

BACKGROUND AND INDICATIONS

In a patient with normal lungs certain physiologic mechanisms maintain clean airways for adequate ventilation. These mechanisms—normal cough and the mucociliary escalator, or unified beating action of the cilia of the epithelial cells as they move mucus toward the larger airways—clear the airways of typical secretions.

Certain pulmonary diseases, air pollutants, and surgical processes can affect normal mucus transport by altering the cough mechanism or the consistency of mucus. When this occurs, techniques are needed to aid in clearing retained secretions. These adjuncts may be used in both acute and chronic disease states. One of the most commonly used therapies to achieve adequate bronchial hygiene is chest physiotherapy (CPT).

CPT consists of a variety of therapies to mobilize pulmonary secretions and promote greater use of respiratory muscles, resulting in more physiologic distribution of ventilation. Therapies used in CPT at Children's Medical Center of Dallas include postural drainage and positioning, chest percussion, chest vibration or tussive squeeze, and coughing and breathing instructions. Each of these techniques may be used alone or in any combination to meet the patient's needs.

Pediatric patients who benefit most from CPT are those at risk for retained secretions, atelectasis, and pneumonia; patients who have undergone thoracoabdominal surgery; and comatose patients with neuromuscular or preexisting chronic lung disease.

When determining which modality is best for the patient, several factors are considered. The motivation of the patient must be considered because of the importance of independent performance of all techniques. These adjuncts provide more autonomy in patient care; however, compliance with performing the procedure appropriately is of great importance.

The goals of both the patient and the physician must be considered, along with which therapy will be most effective in clearing the patient's secretions. Finally, individual factors must be considered, such as age, ease of learning, and preexisting conditions.

Indications for CPT have generated controversy over the last 15 years. The American Association for Respiratory Care has reevaluated CPT and found the need for a standardized guideline for CPT delivery.

The decision to use CPT includes assessment of potential benefits vs. potential risks. Therapy is provided for no longer than necessary to obtain the desired results. The following indications and contraindications are widely accepted by the profession and will assist the practitioner in tailoring bronchial hygiene therapy to their patients' needs.

A. Indications
  1. Evidence or suggestion of difficulty with secretion clearance:
     a. Excessive sputum production with decreased effectiveness of cough
     b. Evidence or suggestion of retained secretions in presence of artificial airway
  2. Presence of atelectasis caused by or suspected of being caused by mucous plugging
  3. Diagnosis of disease such as cystic fibrosis, bronchiectasis, or cavitating lung disease
  4. Foreign body aspiration (after bronchoscopy only)
B. Contraindications
  1. Absolute contraindications:
     a. Head and neck injury until stabilized
     b. Active hemorrhage with hemodynamic instability
  2. Relative contraindications:
     a. Four to 24 hours after operative tracheostomy
     b. Twenty-four hours after operative cardiac prosthesis
     c. Before bronchoscopic foreign body aspiration
     d. Active seizures

3. Relative contraindications to positioning:
   a. Increased ICP (>20 mm Hg)
   b. Recent spinal surgery (e.g., laminectomy) or acute spinal injury
   c. Active hemoptysis
   d. Pulmonary edema associated with congestive heart failure
   e. Large pleural effusions, not drained
   f. Pulmonary embolism
   g. Rib fracture, with or without flail chest
   h. Surgical wound or healing tissue
4. Relative contraindications to Trendelenburg positioning:
   a. ICP >20 mm Hg
   b. Situations in which increased ICP is to be prevented (e.g., neurosurgery, aneurysms, and eye surgery)
   c. Uncontrolled hypertension and pulmonary artery hypertension precautions
   d. Distended abdomen
   e. Esophageal surgery (e.g., before and immediately after tracheal-esophageal fistula repair)
   f. Uncontrolled airway at risk for aspiration (tube feeding or recent meal)
   g. Gastroesophageal reflux
   h. Premature infants (head of bed must remain elevated ≥30 degrees if ordered)
5. Relative contraindications for percussion therapy:
   a. Subcutaneous emphysema
   b. Recent conductive, spinal, or epidural anesthetic
   c. Recent skin grafts or flaps on thorax
   d. Burns, open wounds, and skin infections on thorax
   e. Recently placed transvenous pacemaker or subcutaneous pacemaker (particularly if mechanical devices are to be used)
   f. Suspected pulmonary tuberculosis
   g. Lung contusion
   h. Severe bronchospasm
   i. Osteomyelitis of ribs
   j. Severe osteoporosis (particularly in children receiving long-term steroid therapy)
   k. Complaint of chest wall pain
   l. Conditions prone to hemorrhage (e.g., platelets <30,000/μl)
   m. Osteogenesis imperfecta and conditions predisposing to bone fragility

TECHNIQUE
Postural Drainage

Postural drainage is a method of bronchial hygiene used to remove secretions by positioning the patient and allowing gravity to assist in the movement of se-

cretions. The various segmental bronchi are positioned to be as vertical as possible. Gravity assists the downward flow of secretions into the central airways, where they may be coughed up or suctioned out of the tracheobronchial tree.

Various drainage positions are necessary because the various segmental bronchi are directed superiorly, inferiorly, anteriorly, posteriorly, laterally, and medially (Figs. 148-1 to 148-9).

Percussion

Percussion is a technique of rhythmically clapping the chest wall to free secretions from the walls of the airway. It is generally applied to patients in postural drainage positions. When a certain segmental bronchus is being posturally drained, percussion is applied to that portion of the chest wall where the underlying segment is located. It is administered with a light cloth placed over the patient's chest to prevent a stinging sensation. Care must be taken not to clap over bony structures such as the scapulae and clavicles or over the kidney area.

Percussion can be accomplished with the cupped hand or three-finger tenting techniques. The cupped hand technique (Fig. 148-10) is used for large areas. Air is trapped between the therapist's hand and the patient's chest wall and causes the secretions to

Fig. 148-1 Upper lobes, posterior segment. Bed or drainage table flat. Patient leans over folded pillow at 30-degree angle. Percuss over upper back on each side of chest.

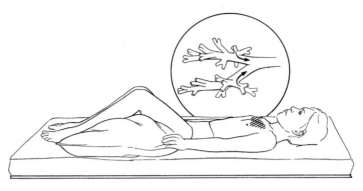

Fig. 148-2 Upper lobes, anterior segment. Bed or drainage table flat. Patient lies on back with pillow under knees. Percuss between clavicle and nipple on each side of chest.

Fig. 148-3 Upper lobes, apical segment. Patient sits on bed or drainage table and leans back on pillow at 30-degree angle against the therapist. Percuss with a cupped hand over the area between the clavicle and top of the scapula on each side.

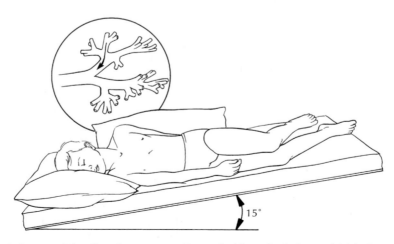

15°

Fig. 148-4 Left upper lobe, lingular segment. Foot of table or bed elevated 14 inches, or about 15 degrees. Patient lies head down on right side and rotates one-fourth turn backward. Pillow may be placed behind patient from shoulder to hip. Knees are flexed. Percuss over left nipple area.

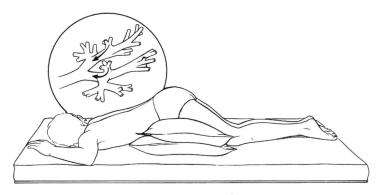

Fig. 148-5 Lower lobes, superior segment. Bed or table flat. Patient lies on abdomen with pillows under hips. Percuss over middle of back below tip of scapula on either side of spine.

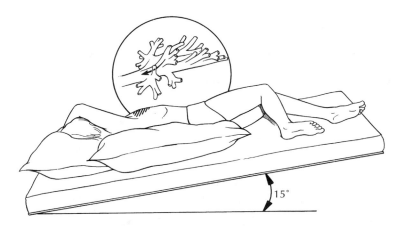

Fig. 148-6 Right middle lobe, lateral segment or medial segment. Foot of table or bed elevated 14 inches, or about 15 degrees. Patient lies head down on left side and rotates one-fourth turn backward. Pillow may be placed behind patient from shoulder to hip. Knees are flexed. Percuss over right nipple area.

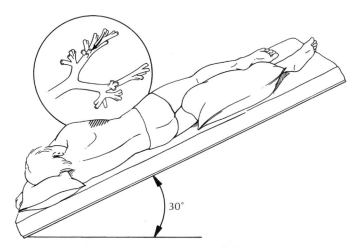

Fig. 148-7 Lower lobes, right or left anterior basal segment. Foot of table or bed elevated 18 inches, or 30 degrees. Patient lies on appropriate side and rotates 30 degrees backward, head down, pillow under knees. Percuss over lower ribs just beneath axilla.

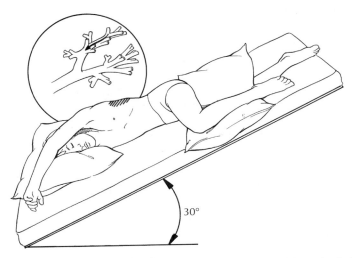

Fig. 148-8 Lower lobes, right or left lateral basal segment. Foot of table or bed elevated 18 inches, or 30 degrees. Patient lies on abdomen and rotates one-fourth turn upward. Upper leg can be flexed over pillow for support. Percuss over uppermost portion of lower ribs.

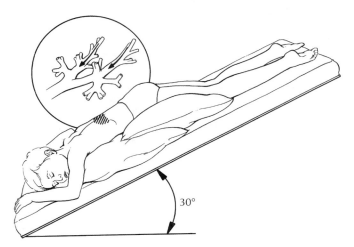

Fig. 148-9 Lower lobes, right or left posterior basal segment. Foot of table or bed elevated 18 inches, or 30 degrees. Patient lies on abdomen with head down. Percuss over lower ribs close to spine on each side of chest.

Fig. 148-10 Cupped hand percussion technique.

Fig. 148-11 Three-finger tenting percussion technique.

loosen. The three-finger tenting technique (Fig. 148-11) is used for smaller surface areas. The first three fingers are cupped with the middle finger slightly elevated. The same loosening of secretions occurs as with the cupped hand technique.

Vibrations and Tussive Squeeze

Vibrations are rapid shaking motions applied to the chest wall during expiration. This is another useful manual technique to loosen and mobilize (with postural drainage) secretions from the peripheral airways. Vibrations can be performed with the hand or a mechanical vibrator. Mechanical vibration may be beneficial for patients who absolutely cannot tolerate hand percussion or who are likely to hemorrhage as a result of direct trauma to the chest wall. Caution is observed in patients with cardiac pacemakers. The electromechanical vibrator must not come in direct contact with external pacer wires.

Tussive squeezing is gentle upward and inward pressure exerted on the chest wall during expiration, following the natural movement of the rib cage. It can be applied in combination with vibrations or segmental breathing. Segmental breathing is a specialized technique for use on problem areas in the lungs. This is accomplished by placing the hand over the area to be emphasized, which causes proprioceptive input for selected muscular movement. The techniques that produce the most secretions are used.

Cough Instructions or Assistance

A practitioner first assesses the reason the cough is ineffective. A cough has four stages, and each needs to be evaluated:

1. Deep inspiration: The patient's inspiratory capacity must be at least 75% of predicted or vital capacity >15 cc/kg to produce an effective cough.
2. Closure of glottis: Adequate glottic function is part of an effective cough mechanism.
3. Contraction of abdominal muscles: Contraction of these muscles along with glottic closure permits an increase in intrapulmonary pressure.
4. Glottic opening: This allows for rapid forceful expiration.

If a patient has an ineffective cough, dysfunction of one or a combination of the four components may be the cause. Inspiratory volume can be increased by intermittent positive pressure breathing; glottic closure can be enhanced with one-way valves or substituted by huff-coughing. In the patient older than 1 year weak abdominal muscles can be assisted with abdominal thrusts. Certainly good nutrition with inspiratory and expiratory muscle strengthening can improve cough effectiveness.

Patients with known airway obstruction (e.g., reactive airways disease) can use alternative coughing, such as multistage or staccato cough. This decreases the tendency for the unstable airways to collapse during coughing.

Patients to be examined for effectiveness of cough may need a stimulus to cough. Tracheal tickle, sterile water instillation (artificial airway), tickling to induce laughing, or stimulating an infant to cry may cause a cough reflex. Any patient who needs to cough after postural drainage position changes can be stimulated by one of these methods if a spontaneous cough cannot be induced.

Extracorporeal Membrane Oxygenation

CPT has been performed in patients receiving ECMO in various centers in the United States. In these instances the goal of therapy is to aid in preventing and correcting atelectasis while the patient receives mechanical ventilation. Because of the increased risk of hemorrhage in a heparinized patient, vibratory CPT is performed without repositioning the patient.

Once the procedure is completed, suctioning is performed, followed by lung conditioning. Lung conditioning consists of a series of sigh breaths administered with a peak pressure of 35 cm H_2O or 10 cm H_2O above the ventilator peak pressure for 5 seconds. When the vital signs return to normal, these long sigh breaths are repeated four to six times after suctioning has been completed. Mechanical ventilation is resumed with resting ventilator settings. To allow healing of air leak and prevent worsening of a pneumothorax, lung conditioning is discouraged.

Liquid Ventilation

During ventilation with perflurocarbon the lung is filled with fluid that significantly increases the weight of the lung. This precludes turning and positioning the patient for therapy. Frequent and abrupt turning may cause contusions or laceration of lung tissue. Movement of secretions into the proximal airways is common, and the secretions must be suctioned frequently to prevent obstruction of the airways. (See Chapter 159 for more information on this subject.)

Nitric Oxide Administration

There is no contraindication to performing CPT in patients receiving nitric oxide. However, as in any aspect of patient care, caution must be used by monitoring for elevation in pulmonary artery pressure, desaturation, or variances in systemic arterial blood pressure.

High-Frequency Oscillator Ventilation

Because of internal oscillatory movement in the airways during high-frequency oscillatory ventilation, percussion is generally not necessary. Changes in positioning may be useful in alveolar recruitment but need to be tailored to patient tolerance.

Key Points

Always consider the patient's condition when delivering therapy. Give CPT for a minimum of 20 minutes, approximately 1½ to 2 minutes in each position. Patient positions and percussion technique may need modification as patient tolerance dictates.

Concentrate more time on consolidated, atelectatic areas or areas with adventitious breath sounds and prophylactically treat the rest of the lung.

Remember to percuss and vibrate over ribs, following their natural contour. Do not percuss over developed breast tissue, the sternum, fractured ribs, open wounds, recent incisions, central catheters, chest drainage tubes, cannulas used for ECMO, or the abdomen. For posterior positions, separate the scapulae by abducting the child's arms with the elbows near the ears if the extremities can be positioned in this manner.

Do not disturb maintenance oxygen therapy or thermal environment to provide therapy. In infants coordinate timing of treatments and feedings with nursing personnel.

After each postural drainage position and percus-sion, encourage the patient to cough. Assisted cough or suction may be indicated. Always assist the patient in a head-up position when coughing.

Monitor vital signs, work of breathing, $Spao_2$, $tcco_2$, or any other variables available. If the patient becomes unstable, call for help and attempt to stabilize. Place the patient in a head-up position if not already in that position.

At the end of therapy assist with secretion evacuation and expectoration as necessary. Return the patient to an upright position. Inspect, palpate, and auscultate the patient's chest, comparing before and after therapy. Be certain all monitors are attached and alarms functional.

Special Considerations in Chest Physiotherapy

Patients with endotracheal tubes need to be cautiously positioned to prevent accidental extubation. Whenever tolerated, the ventilator circuit can be disconnected momentarily while the patient is repositioned. In some instances (e.g., patients dependent on high end-expiratory pressure) disconnection may not be feasible. In these patients extreme caution must be taken to not dislodge the endotracheal tube. Also, excessive condensation in the ventilator circuit must be drained to prevent accidental lavage during therapy. CPT can be beneficial in patients with artificial airways, but always with an eye toward safety.

RISKS AND COMPLICATIONS

Because of the delicate condition of many patients, the hazards and adverse reactions of these therapies must be a primary consideration for the practitioner. Reactions may include but are not limited to hypoxemia, increased ICP, acute hypotension, pulmonary hemorrhage, pain or injury to muscles, ribs, or spine, vomiting or aspiration, bronchospasm, and arrhythmias. In the event of an adverse reaction stop treatment and call for help while attempting to stabilize the patient.

CURRENT RESEARCH AND FUTURE CONSIDERATIONS

Several new therapies that have become routine in adult respiratory care have some significant indications in clearance of the airway in pediatric patients.

Forced Expiratory Technique

Forced expiratory technique is a method of modifying a cough to achieve maximal mobilization of airway secretions. These coughs originate from relaxed diaphragmatic breathing from middle to low lung volumes. After a large inspiration a rapid succession of short coughs is performed. These "huffing" coughs are performed with other adjuncts of bronchial hygiene to promote maximal secretion removal.

High-Frequency Chest Wall Oscillation

High-frequency chest wall oscillation enhances clearance of the peripheral airways. In this technique a vest apparatus is connected to a pump that when activated applies oscillations from 3 to 25 Hz. These oscillations create rapid changes in pressure exerted on the chest. When transmitted to the airways, this produces airflow patterns similar to those achieved with a huffing maneuver. This therapy is useful in patients with cystic fibrosis.

Positive Expiratory Pressure

Positive expiratory pressure therapy is a method to administer positive pressure with a mask to the airways, increasing the transmural pressure and dilating the central and peripheral airways so that secretions, previously obstructive, are mobilized. Moving secretions into the larger airways enables better gas exchange. Positive pressure is administered through a resistance valve attached to a face mask. Relaxed, diaphragmatic breathing with large tidal volumes is used, followed by active, nonforceful exhalation. An end pressure of 10 to 20 cm H_2O is maintained. Exhalation is two to three times longer than inspiration. This therapy lasts 15 minutes and consists of 10 to 20 breaths, followed by huffing maneuvers. Positive end pressure mask therapy is simple to perform and provides an alternative to CPT. Patients with cystic fibrosis and bronchiectasis have responded favorably to this therapy.

Flutter Valve

The Flutter Valve (distributed by Scandipharm, Birmingham, Ala.) is effective in patients with cystic fibrosis and may be beneficial in the PICU for the older alert patient. It could be especially useful in the older patient who has had some significant chest wall surgery but needs more aggressive therapy than incentive spirometry and vibratory CPT.

This technique is easy to learn and its portability has been a distinct advantage. It could improve patient compliance and comfort and reduce cost of care. It has proved three times more effective than conventional techniques in clearing mucus from the airways.

A Flutter Valve combines the benefits of high-frequency oscillations in the airway and positive end pressure techniques. The device resembles a pipe with a steel ball inside. The patient actively exhales through the Flutter Valve, and an end pressure of 10 to 25 cm H_2O is generated. During exhalation the ball flutters in the pipe and oscillations are generated and transmitted to the airways. The patient can alter the end pressure by changing the flow rate and the rapidity of oscillations with the angle of the device in the mouth. The modulating pressure gradient vibrates the bronchial walls, and mucus is loosened and moved up into the airways to be expectorated. The Flutter Valve is used for a minimum of 5 minutes.

ADDITIONAL READING

American Association for Respiratory Care. Clinical practice guidelines, postural drainage therapy. Respir Care 36:1418-1426, 1991.

• Andersen JB, Falk MF. Chest physiotherapy in the pediatric age group. Respir Care 36:545-554, 1991.

Constan MW, Stern RC, Doershuk CF. Efficacy of the flutter device for airway mucus clearance in patients with cystic fibrosis. J Pediatr 124:689-693, 1994.

Frownfelter DL. Chest Physical Therapy and Pulmonary Rehabilitation, 2nd ed. Chicago: Year Book, 1987, pp 271-276.

Kendig EL. Disorders of the Respiratory Tract in Children, 3rd ed. Philadelphia: WB Saunders, 1977.

Levitzky MG, Cairo JM, Hall SM. Introduction to Respiratory Care. Philadelphia: WB Saunders, 1990, pp 469-485.

Mahlmeister MJ, Fink JB, Hoffman GL, Fifer LF. Positive-expiratory-pressure mask therapy. Theoretical and practical considerations and a review of the literature. Respir Care 36:1218-1229, 1991.

• Pierson DJ. Foundations in Respiratory Care. New York: Churchill Livingstone, 1992.

• Sutton PP, Parker RA, Webber BA. Assessment of the forced expiration technique, postural drainage and directed coughing in chest physiotherapy. Eur J Respir Dis 64:62-68, 1983.

Tyler ML. Complications of positioning and chest physiotherapy. Respir Care 27:458-465, 1982.

149 Noninvasive Respiratory Monitoring: Oxygen Saturation, Transcutaneous Oxygen and Carbon Dioxide, and End-Tidal Carbon Dioxide

Andreas Deymann · David Moromisato

Technologic advances in the practice of critical care have resulted in dramatic changes over the past two decades. In particular, the technology for monitoring respiratory status is relatively new and continues to improve. The importance of respiratory monitoring in infants and children stems from the fact that the majority of patients in the PICU are admitted because of primary cardiopulmonary disease or because respiratory problems in the course of acute illness are anticipated. Approximately half of patients are admitted to the PICU for efficient, intensive monitoring rather than specific interventional therapy.

Historically, respiratory function was monitored using blood gas and pH analyses in conjunction with intermittent physical examinations to observe for signs of impaired respiratory function. However, in the small infant or child these techniques are not only painful and difficult to perform but depend on the experience and skill of the bedside caregiver. Thus the development of continuous, reliable, painless, and easily interpretable monitoring techniques was especially appealing to individuals caring for patients with acute respiratory illness. In this chapter the noninvasive techniques commonly used to monitor the respiratory status of the critically ill infant and child are discussed. Because pulse oximetry and end-tidal CO_2 monitoring are most extensively used, they are discussed in depth.

Oxygen Saturation Monitoring

BACKGROUND AND INDICATIONS

Although the technology for pulse oximetry has been available since 1934, not until the 1980s did its use in the ICU become standard for monitoring potential problems of oxygenation. Now the pulse oximeter is so ubiquitous in the ICU that Sao_2 has sometimes been referred to as the "fifth vital sign." Measurements of Sao_2 and arterial Pao_2 are routine in the management of a variety of cardiac and pulmonary disorders in the PICU to assess the adequacy of systemic oxygenation. In conjunction with cardiac output and hemoglobin concentration, Sao_2 monitoring enables determination of O_2 availability or delivery to the vital organs; Pao_2 represents the maximal tension driving O_2 to its mitochondrial sites of use. Hypoxemia (see discussion of normal values, p. 1361) can result from reduced alveolar O_2 concentration (Pao_2), alterations in ventilation-perfusion ($\dot{V}/\dot{Q}$) matching, disruption of diffusion of O_2 across the alveolar-capillary membrane, or depression of cardiac output.

The relationship of Sao_2 to Pao_2 is expressed by the oxyhemoglobin dissociation curve (Fig. 149-1). The dissociation curve is sigmoidal. At $Pao_2 > 60$ mm Hg the curve flattens and demonstrates that hemoglobin is maximally saturated; therefore hemoglobin molecules exposed to the high concentration of O_2 within the alveoli will be transported to peripheral

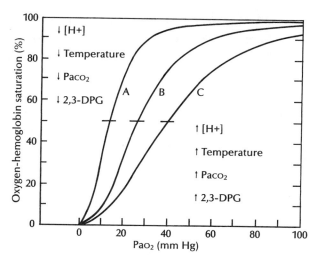

Fig. 149-1 Oxyhemoglobin saturation. Curve *B,* normal adult hemoglobin. Curves *A* and *C* show, respectively, increased and decreased affinity of the hemoglobin molecule for oxygen, accompanied by causes. The 50% saturation value for each curve is represented by horizontal dashed line.

vascular beds nearly 100% saturated. At Pao_2 <60 mm Hg the curve is steep and demonstrates that small changes in O_2 tension result in large changes in hemoglobin saturation. Therefore a small reduction in Pao_2 results in greater unloading of oxygen from hemoglobin and increases the gradient for O_2 delivery to tissue vascular beds.

The position of the oxyhemoglobin dissociation curve may shift to the right or left, reflecting changes in the affinity of hemoglobin for O_2. The quaternary structure of the hemoglobin molecule regulates its affinity for O_2 and is altered by several factors, including $Paco_2$, hydrogen ion concentration (pH), body temperature, hemoglobin concentration of 2,3-diphosphoglycerate (2,3-DPG), and type of hemoglobin. The value at which the hemoglobin molecule is 50% saturated (P_{50}) is used as an index of the relative position of the oxyhemoglobin dissociation curve. "Normal" P_{50} is 27 mm Hg (i.e., assuming normal body temperature, pH, $Paco_2$, red blood cell 2,3-DPG content, and normal adult hemoglobin chains). A shift of the curve to the right (i.e., increased P_{50}) implies lower affinity of O_2 for hemoglobin; conversely, a shift to the left (i.e., decreased P_{50}) means that O_2 is bound more avidly to hemoglobin.

Acidosis, hypercapnia, and hyperthermia (variables that reflect stress or disease) shift the curve to the right (see Fig. 149-1); thus Sao_2 is reduced at any given Pao_2. This shift allows O_2 unloading to tissues under stress to occur more readily. In contrast, alkalosis, hypocapnia, and hypothermia increase the affinity of O_2 for hemoglobin, thereby reducing P_{50}. This results in reduced Pao_2 relative to Sao_2 and limits the delivery of O_2 to cellular mitochondria. For example, when alkalosis is induced to reduce pulmonary arterial blood pressure or when hypocapnia is used to treat intracranial hypertension, O_2 delivery and consumption may be impaired by the leftward shift of the oxyhemoglobin dissociation curve.

2,3-DPG also regulates oxygen affinity for hemoglobin. It lowers hemoglobin affinity by binding to beta chains of hemoglobin A or gamma chains of hemoglobin F (fetal hemoglobin). For example, anemia leads to increased 2,3-DPG levels (increased P_{50}), whereas storage of bank blood with acid-citrate-dextrose results in depletion of 2,3-DPG (reduced P_{50}).

The type of hemoglobin determines O_2 binding. For example, fetal and sickle cell hemoglobins bind O_2 more avidly than does hemoglobin A. The correlation between Pao_2 and Sao_2 in infants with fetal hemoglobin levels comprising 75% or more of the blood is good, with a mean difference of 3.6% ± 2.3%. The reason for this minimal effect of fetal hemoglobin on the accuracy of Sao_2 is that fetal hemoglobin is indistinguishable from adult hemoglobin with the red and infrared wavelength used by most pulse oximeters. Methemoglobin is a hemoglobin molecule in which iron is oxidized, and therefore it cannot bind O_2. Thus tissue hypoxia and acidosis occur when methemoglobin levels exceed 30%. Finally, O_2 binding may be inhibited by substances with greater affinity for hemoglobin such as carbon monoxide (therefore the actual Sao_2 is reduced). Carbon monoxide also limits O_2 delivery by reducing P_{50} (i.e., shifting the oxyhemoglobin dissociation curve to the left).

Sao_2 monitoring (in conjunction with assessment of cardiac output, hemoglobin concentration, pH, urine output, and mental status) is invaluable in determining the adequacy of systemic oxygenation. If Sao_2 monitoring is used along with mixed venous saturation (Svo_2) measurements, the relationship of O_2 consumption to O_2 delivery can be used to observe and dictate therapeutic interventions. In the absence of technology capable of measuring Pao_2 and O_2 consumption in specific tissue beds (e.g., brain, myocardium, and kidney), continuous systemic O_2 measurements provide the most reliable description of the cardiorespiratory state and responses to therapy. As a generalization, Sao_2 monitoring provides a gauge of pulmonary function by demonstrating trends that reflect the adequacy of oxygenation.

An ideal monitoring system must include the following capabilities. First, it must be continuous; intermittently obtained information in critically ill patients may not accurately reflect trends and changes in clinical status and is less useful than continuous data in assessing the response to a therapeutic intervention. Second, monitoring must be as noninvasive as possible and painless and depend on minimal patient cooperation. Invasive monitoring procedures often cause discomfort to the patient and increase the risk of complications such as infection. Finally, the data collected must be valuable and interpretable to the medical staff in terms of management. Continuous pulse oximetry meets these criteria and explains its widespread acceptance in the PICU. Over the past 10 years noninvasive continuous Sao_2 monitoring has decreased intermittent intra-arterial sampling as the optimal method to determine the adequacy and trend of systemic oxygenation in critically ill patients.

Indications for continuous pulse oximetry are as follows:

1. Management of critically ill patients in the PICU
2. Interhospital and intrahospital transport of patients
3. Assessment of systemic oxygenation before and after surgery
4. Perioperative manipulations to improve systemic oxygenation
5. Polysomnography (sleep) studies
6. Radiographic or invasive monitoring procedures that place the patient at high risk
7. Home care of O_2-dependent children
8. Minor procedures that require use of conscious sedation

TECHNIQUE

The technique of continuous pulse oximetry is based on the following three principles: the color of blood is a function of Sao_2, the optical properties of hemoglobin determine the color of blood at various Sao_2 levels, and the total absorption of a system of absorbers is the sum of their individual absorbances (Beer-Lambert law). All commercially available pulse oximeters currently use two wavelengths of light (red and infrared) to determine the ratio of oxygenated hemoglobin to deoxygenated hemoglobin. Visible red light (660 nm) is absorbed more by deoxygenated hemoglobin than by oxyhemoglobin; infrared light (940 nm) is absorbed more by oxyhemoglobin than deoxygenated hemoglobin. These two wavelengths of light are passed through the chosen arterial bed (e.g., finger, toe, or earlobe), and the percent oxyhemoglobin and deoxygenated hemoglobin is determined by measuring the ratio of infrared and red light transmitted to the photodetector (Fig. 149-2). The direct-current (DC) component of this ratio is the absorbance of the tissue bed; the alternating cur-

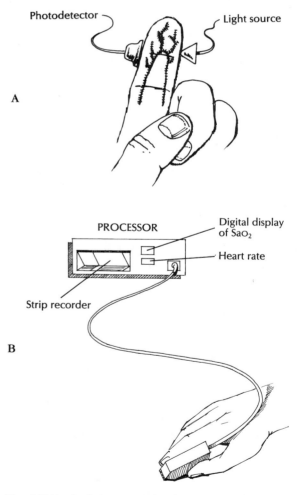

Fig. 149-2 **A,** Oximeter probe detector and light source. **B,** Finger pickup and oximeter. The chart can be useful for the permanent record.

rent (AC) is represented by the pulsatile arterial bed. The formula used to calculate the ratio is $R = (AC_{660}/DC_{660})/(AC_{940}/DC_{940})$. The ratio obtained from this formula is calibrated with the absorbance ratios measured in human volunteers while simultaneously sampling arterial blood. This type of analysis excludes the measurement of other hemoglobin molecules that may be present, such as methemoglobin or carboxyhemoglobin (two conditions, for example, in which continuous pulse oximetry provides misleading or inaccurate information) (Fig. 149-3).

Continuous pulse oximetry also provides measurement of heart rate independent from that obtained with impedance chest wall leads. The pulsating vascular bed in the site chosen for monitoring creates a change in the light path length that modifies the amount of the light detected. The oximeter determines the pulse rate from the change in the amount of light that is absorbed from systole to diastole. The SaO_2 value is accurate only if the heart rate as measured with the pulse oximeter correlates with the heart rate as determined either by chest wall impedance or palpation.

Application of the continuous pulse oximeter is simple. The use of digits (or the heel in a newborn) provides easy access and multiple sites. No heat pretreatment to "arterialize" the bed is necessary, as is the case with transcutaneous O_2 and CO_2 monitoring systems. A microprocessor performs the calibration, measurements, and readout functions, making it easy to use. The initial reading occurs within 10 to 15 seconds of application of the probe. The probes available are small, relatively inexpensive, disposable, and durable (see Fig. 149-2).

Continuous pulse oximetry has obviated the need for intra-arterial monitoring in many circumstances. The use of arterial blood samples for SaO_2 measurements is indicated when noninvasive measurement is not possible or is inaccurate.

RISKS AND COMPLICATIONS

For the purposes of this discussion, risks and complications of continuous, noninvasive SaO_2 monitoring are defined as those situations in which the technique provides inaccurate, misleading, or insufficient information or normal variations are misinterpreted by health caregivers.

The definition of hypoxemia remains arbitrary. Most often PaO_2 <60 mm Hg is used in clinical practice, and respiratory failure is defined as PaO_2 <50 mm Hg. However, normal values for PaO_2 are estimated by the formula created by Mellengaard (PaO_2 = 104.2 mm Hg − 0.27 × age). Mellengaard's formula takes into consideration the normal decline in PaO_2 that occurs with age. Another tool used to estimate PaO_2 is the alveolar gas equation. It can be used to estimate the alveolar-arterial gradient (A-a), which is normally <10 mm Hg in children. However, Mellengaard's formula and the normal values for the A-a gradient do not reflect the physiologic post-

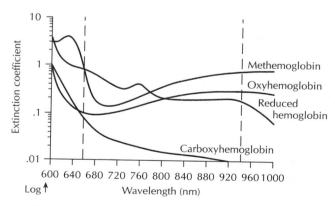

Fig. 149-3 Oxyhemoglobin absorbs relatively more light in the infrared region and reflects light. Carboxyhemoglobin also reflects light effectively. Deoxyhemoglobin absorbs more red light than does oxyhemoglobin and reflects infrared light. Methemoglobin appears more like reduced hemoglobin at the red wavelength (660 nm) but has an absorbance similar to that of oxyhemoglobin in the infrared wavelength (940 nm). Thus high levels of methemoglobin tend to reduce pulse oximeter value to 85% regardless of actual oxyhemoglobin concentration. (Courtesy Ohmeda Medical Systems Division, Louisville, Colo.)

natal adaptation period, during which normal O_2 saturations are slightly lower than during childhood. In addition, the frequency of naturally occurring desaturation is significantly higher and must be taken into account when interpreting pulse oximeter readings. With regular breathing during quiet sleep, O_2 saturations measured with pulse oximetry are ≥95% in preterm infants and ≥96% in full-term infants. Episodic desaturation normally occurring in infants decreases with age and maturity. Episodic decreases in Sao_2 lasting >4 seconds in *preterm* infants at discharge can occur as many as 61 times over 12 hours (95th percentile) and at 6 weeks of age occur only three times in 12 hours. For *full-term* infants at 6 weeks of age these relatively prolonged episodes of desaturation are also rare, but desaturation to ≤80% for <4 seconds occurs a median of 0.7 times per hour.

Inaccurate measurements occur in situations of significant reduction in vascular pulsation, which is detected by a discrepancy between the oximeter heart rate measurement compared with that obtained by chest wall impedance, palpation, or auscultation. These situations include hypotension, hypothermia, peripheral vasoconstriction, and motion artifact. Motion artifact limits the use of oximetry in circumstances in which the patient and monitor are unobserved and a hard-copy readout of Sao_2 values is obtained (e.g., home sleep studies). Newer technologies will soon be available that measure heart rate independent of vascular pulsation, allowing detection of motion artifact as a cause of a reduced Sao_2. An additional source of error is introduced by extraneous light sources that consist of wavelengths near the measured frequencies (e.g., infrared radiation heaters and ultraviolet phototherapy for treating hyperbilirubinemia). Injection of dyes such as methylene blue, indigo carmine, indocyanine green, and fluorescein also interfere with Sao_2 measurements. Finally, the present technology does not provide accurate data when Sao_2 falls below 50%.

Misleading information is obtained in the following situations. Because only oxyhemoglobin and reduced hemoglobin are detected with pulse oximetry, the presence of abnormal hemoglobin types such as carboxyhemoglobin or methemoglobin can lead to overestimation of true Sao_2. In these circumstances intra-arterial sampling and measurement of Sao_2 with co-oximetry is necessary for accurate determinations. In addition, several problems are related to the shape of the oxyhemoglobin dissociation curve (i.e., Sao_2 and Pao_2 are not linearly related through-

out the wide range of possible Pao_2 values). A significant reduction in Pao_2 (e.g., from 300 to 90 mm Hg) may occur without a change in Sao_2 (i.e., Sao_2 will remain at 98% to 100%). In this situation a physiologically significant event is not detected with pulse oximetry. More commonly, a reduction in Sao_2 from 98% to 92% will not be appreciated as significant even though it reflects a decrease in Pao_2 (e.g., from 100 to 70 mm Hg) and represents a position much closer to the steep portion of the oxyhemoglobin dissociation curve. Although several studies have demonstrated the accuracy and precision of pulse oximetry, its failure rate was as high as 7% in the most critically ill patients. In addition, when saturation is <80%, pulse oximeters tend to underread Sao_2, and bias of −12% to 18% has been reported. Caution is warranted because confidence limits for saturation >70% are up to 4% and most oximeters have a bias of <1% and precision of <2% above 90% O_2 saturation. Another situation in which the shape of the curve may be responsible for misleading information is when hypoxemia results from hypoventilation. As a rule, the reduction in Pao_2 that results from hypoventilation is inversely proportional to the increase in $Paco_2$, according to the alveolar gas equation ($[P_{barometric} - P_{water}] \times Fio_2) - Paco_2 = Pao_2$. For example, in a patient breathing room air an increase in $Paco_2$ from 40 to 60 mm Hg results in a reduction in Pao_2 from about 100 to 80 mm Hg (see alveolar gas equation above), with little change in Sao_2 value. Hypoventilation will be further masked by administration of supplemental O_2, which may allow a reduction of Pao_2 from 150 to 130 mm Hg but no change in Sao_2 when hypoventilation has resulted in a 20 mm Hg increase in $Paco_2$.

Misleading information also occurs because of changes in the position of the oxyhemoglobin dissociation curve. Reduced P_{50} indicates that O_2 is bound to hemoglobin more avidly; therefore, for any given Pao_2 value, Sao_2 will be higher than if the curve were in the normal position. A patient in whom alkalosis or hypocapnia has been induced will demonstrate greater Sao_2 relative to Pao_2, and the degree of intrapulmonary shunt will not be appreciated (or accurately calculated) with Sao_2 measurements as a guide.

Conditions in which insufficient information is provided by noninvasive pulse oximetry may result in misapplication of the data. Specifically, O_2 delivery depends on cardiac output, hemoglobin concentration, and Sao_2. A reduction in Sao_2 may be accompanied by an increase in cardiac output sufficient to maintain adequate O_2 delivery. In addition, O_2 delivery and O_2 consumption are not consistently related in all circumstances (e.g., O_2 consumption is reduced relative to delivery in patients with acute respiratory distress syndrome [ARDS]); thus simultaneous determination of Svo_2 may be necessary to evaluate the adequacy of Sao_2.

CURRENT RESEARCH AND FUTURE CONSIDERATIONS

Invasive devices such as a pulmonary artery catheter with oximeter probes attached have been developed to assess Svo_2 saturation continuously. Continuous monitoring of jugular bulb saturation may be helpful in assessing cerebral O_2 consumption in situations of increased ICP. Transcranial measurements of O_2 saturation in the cerebral cortex might become an exciting tool to assess local O_2 saturation and, it is hoped, even more helpful than venous jugular bulb saturation.

Transcutaneous Oxygen Monitoring

BACKGROUND AND INDICATIONS

Transcutaneous O_2 (tco_2) monitoring became possible in the early 1970s with development of a small device that incorporates a membrane-covered electrode, a heater, and a temperature-sensing thermistor. Measurement of blood gas tensions at the surface of the skin is made possible by a technique that is simple to use and painless for the patient. In contrast, with $Paco_2$, a determination in which the value reflects the partial pressure of the gas dissolved in blood, transcutaneous O_2 tension ($Ptco_2$) and CO_2 tension ($Ptcco_2$) values reflect both gas exchange (i.e., Pao_2 and $Paco_2$) and skin perfusion (i.e., cardiac output). This disadvantage has reduced their initial widespread use because in stages of poor perfusion and tissue hypoxia the transcutaneous value poorly approximates the arterial value.

Today this technique is primarily used in the NICU and shows good correlation between $Ptco_2$ and Pao_2 values. Because skin thickness increases with age, in the pediatric population $Ptco_2$ is proportionately but unpredictably lower than Pao_2. In addition, to prevent local burns the electrodes require frequent calibration and a change of site because of heat produced by the electrode. Because of these difficulties,

the use of tco_2 monitoring has fallen out of favor in most PICUs and been replaced with pulse oximetry and end-tidal CO_2 monitoring.

Transcutaneous Carbon Dioxide Monitoring

BACKGROUND AND INDICATIONS

$Ptcco_2$ must exceed the capillary and arterial Pco_2 to provide the gradient necessary to transport CO_2 out of the tissue beds and into the venous circulation. $Ptcco_2$ exceeds $Paco_2$ in neonates by a mean of 15 to 20 mm Hg and in adults by 10 to 35 mm Hg. If the gradient between $Ptcco_2$ and $Paco_2$ remains constant, $Ptcco_2$ becomes an accurate monitor of $Paco_2$. The correlation between $Ptcco_2$ and $Paco_2$ is greater than for $Ptco_2$ and Pao_2; the linear correlation coefficient approximates 0.8 to 0.9 in patients with adequate cardiovascular function. A reduction in cardiac output increases $Ptcco_2$ but has a minimal effect on $Paco_2$. In adults, when the cardiac index falls to ~1.5 L/min/m², $Ptcco_2$ is inversely related to the cardiac index, and quantitatively the $Ptcco_2$ and $Paco_2$ changes correlate poorly. As in $Ptco_2$ monitoring, the degree of shock can be assessed by measuring the $Ptcco_2$-$Paco_2$ gradient; a larger gradient reflects poor peripheral perfusion. Acidosis and hypoxemia will also increase $Ptcco_2$ out of proportion to an increase in $Paco_2$.

The $Ptcco_2$ response to changes in $Paco_2$ is slow, 3 to 4 minutes. Nonetheless, in the presence of stable hemodynamic and metabolic function, $tcco_2$ monitoring provides a useful gauge of alveolar ventilation. Clinical circumstances in which $tcco_2$ monitoring is valuable include ventilator management in the patient with respiratory distress or shock, transport of the critically ill neonate or infant, and performance of invasive procedures such as bronchoscopy and cardiac catheterization. Newborn and young infants with respiratory distress and shock syndromes benefit most from $Ptcco_2$ monitoring because these are the groups in whom the correlation between $Ptcco_2$ and $Paco_2$ is greatest and in whom invasive blood gas monitoring is often more difficult and tedious.

TECHNIQUE

The $tcco_2$ probe applied to the patient's skin contains a heater, an electrode, and a thermistor. Similar to the tco_2 system, warming softens the skin, thereby making the physical barrier to diffusion more permeable, and also results in capillary dilatation and augments CO_2 production locally. Warming the skin to 44° C increases the response time to $Paco_2$ changes and is necessary to obtain clinically useful $Ptcco_2$ values. The electrode is an outgrowth of the Severinghaus modification of the Stowe electrochemical sensor commonly used in blood gas analyzers. The typical $tcco_2$ sensor consists of a pH-sensitive glass electrode, a silver chloride reference electrode, a membrane permeable to CO_2, and a bicarbonate electrolyte solution. After the skin is warmed, CO_2 diffuses through the Teflon membrane into the bicarbonate solution. The CO_2 reacts with water to form H_2CO_3, which dissociates into H^+ and HCO_3^-; the H^+ production alters the pH of the solution, increasing the electrical potential between the glass electrode and the reference electrode. This change in electrical potential is converted to millimeters of mercury and displayed as the $Ptcco_2$ value.

A new probe needs a warmup period of approximately 1 hour to allow the electrolyte solution to distribute evenly over the glass electrode, which is fragile and expensive. Calibration of the equipment generally is performed in vitro at high and low CO_2 concentrations (e.g., 5% and 10%) and in vivo by comparing the $Ptcco_2$ value with a simultaneously obtained $Paco_2$ value.

RISKS AND COMPLICATIONS

As with Pto_2 monitoring, $Ptcco_2$ monitoring is inaccurate or invalid if the observer is unaware of the physiologic determinants of its value. Therefore changes in $Ptcco_2$ must be compared with $Paco_2$ and to the state of peripheral perfusion. Burns of the skin surface occur if the site is not changed every 2 to 4 hours, the thermostat that controls skin temperature fails, or hypotension reduces peripheral perfusion, resulting in poor dissipation of heat. Limitations of this technique include limited use if breath-to-breath monitoring is needed; clinical studies revealed that uniform directional changes of $Ptcco_2$ and $Paco_2$ only occurred consistently for $Paco_2$ changes >5 (16% of changes between $Ptcco_2$ and $Paco_2$ were in different directions).

In summary, $Ptco_2$ and $Ptcco_2$ monitoring is a noninvasive means of observing blood gas exchange and tissue perfusion in critically ill children. Electrodes that simultaneously monitor $Ptco_2$ and $Ptcco_2$ are available, but warming of the skin, scrupulous attention to details such as calibration, frequent chang-

ing of the monitoring site to prevent burns, and a comparison with arterial blood gas tensions and tissue perfusion are necessary. These techniques have provided a way to assess gas exchange status and patient response to therapeutic intervention. The transcutaneous approach for CO_2 monitoring is limited by slow response time, which includes physiologic and instrument response time. Finally, end-tidal CO_2 monitors and pulse oximetry have replaced $Ptcco_2$ and $Ptco_2$, although both techniques increase patient safety during such procedures as transport, bronchoscopy, cardiac catheterization, and weaning from mechanical ventilation.

End-Tidal Carbon Dioxide Monitoring
BACKGROUND AND INDICATIONS

End-tidal CO_2 ($etco_2$) monitoring, or capnography, is the measurement and display in waveform of CO_2 concentration in exhaled gases. In contrast, capnometry provides only a quantitative measurement. The value of noninvasive monitoring of blood gas tension is the ability to continuously observe the patient's pulmonary function (i.e., gas exchange) and to assess immediately the response to therapeutic interventions. The $etco_2$ concentration is a function of the following four factors: $Paco_2$, cardiac output, dead space in percent of tidal volume (V_D/V_T), and airway time constants. Thus $etco_2$ monitoring can be used to observe adequacy of alveolar ventilation, estimate changes in metabolic status (i.e., production of CO_2), evaluate the adequacy of cardiac output, and assess pulmonary perfusion relative to alveolar ventilation (i.e., percent dead space ventilation). The limitations of capnography are related to the multiple determinants of the $etco_2$ value. The validity of capnography in assessing alveolar ventilation is highest when $Petco_2$ approximates $Paco_2$. However, even in healthy persons the $Petco_2$ is 1 to 5 mm Hg lower than $Paco_2$ because of the contribution of nonventilated and poorly ventilated lung units to the $Petco_2$ measurement. Indeed, whereas the $Paco_2$ value is determined by the Pco_2 of perfused alveoli (whether or not they are ventilated), the $Petco_2$ value represents the Pco_2 of all ventilated alveoli (whether or not they are perfused). This limitation must always be considered when using $etco_2$ monitoring to assess alveolar ventilation. Thus any condition that reduces pulmonary perfusion of ventilated alveoli (i.e., increases dead space ventilation) will increase the disparity between $Paco_2$ and $Petco_2$; this is the basis for the calculation of dead space ventilation with the following equation: $VD/VT = Paco_2 - Petco_2/Paco_2$. Therefore, as dead space increases, $Petco_2$ increasingly underestimates $Paco_2$. Conditions that decrease perfusion to the lungs (increase VD/VT and decrease $Petco_2$) can be categorized into those that reduce cardiac output (hypovolemia, depressed myocardial contractility, cardiac arrest, and increased systemic afterload), increase pulmonary vascular resistance (pulmonary vasospasm, excessive PEEP), reduce the cross-sectional area of the pulmonary vascular bed (ARDS and multiple pulmonary emboli), or obstruct blood flow in large pulmonary arteries (air and thrombotic emboli) or divert blood flow (extracorporeal membrane oxygenation or cardiac bypass). In all of these situations the $Paco_2$-$Petco_2$ gradient will increase, making capnography not a measurement of alveolar ventilation but a marker of pulmonary perfusion. Alternatively, conditions that increase $Paco_2$ (either reduced alveolar ventilation or increased CO_2 production) will be reflected by increased $Petco_2$, provided pulmonary perfusion remains constant.

$Petco_2$ monitoring of critically ill children in the PICU can be used as follows. A change in the $Petco_2$ value is an indication for measurement of $Paco_2$ and reevaluation of pulmonary and hemodynamic status. A reduction in $Petco_2$ with concomitant reduction in $Paco_2$ (i.e., constant gradient) is consistent with either improved alveolar ventilation (VA) or reduced CO_2 production (Vco_2). A reduction in $Petco_2$ in the presence of unchanged or increased $Paco_2$ reflects increased dead space ventilation. If simultaneously obtained Svo_2 demonstrates increased CO_2 ($Paco_2$) and reduced O_2 (Pao_2), a critical reduction in cardiac output has occurred such that alveolar blood flow is reduced and cannot keep pace with CO_2 production, and O_2 extraction has increased, resulting in a widened arteriovenous oxygen difference (a-vDo_2). An increase in $Petco_2$ with a concomitant increase in $Paco_2$ is consistent with either reduced VA or increased Vco_2 (e.g., associated with malignant hyperthermia syndrome). An increase in $Petco_2$ with an unchanged $Paco_2$ (i.e., reduced gradient) is an unusual circumstance that occurs when dead space ventilation is minimal and the time constants of the airway (either resistance or compliance) are increased. In the pediatric population this situation is present in patients with severe small airways obstruction (e.g., bronchiolitis) in whom the slowest emptying lung units

Table 149-1 Comparison of $Petco_2$ and $Paco_2$ Values in Critically Ill PICU Patients

$Petco_2$	$Paco_2$	Differential Diagnosis
Reduced	Reduced	Improved alveolar ventilation
		Reduced CO_2 production
Reduced	Unchanged or increased	Reduced cardiac output or cardiac arrest
		Increased pulmonary vascular resistance
		Reduced cross-sectional area of pulmonary vascular bed
		Pulmonary embolus
Increased	Increased	Reduced alveolar ventilation
		Increased CO_2 production
Increased	Unchanged	Increased airway resistance
		Excessive alveolar compliance
Unchanged	Unknown	No guarantee of cardiopulmonary stability

may have $Petco_2$ values that exceed $Paco_2$ as a result of the pendelluft effect (i.e., back-and-forth movement of gas between neighboring gas exchange units). Table 149-1 summarizes the clinical use of simultaneous measurements of $Petco_2$ and $Paco_2$. During a respiratory cycle the concentration of CO_2 is low during the initial phase of expiration because the gas comes from the anatomic dead space (trachea and bronchi plus tubing and instrument). In the midportion of exhalation CO_2 rises sharply to a plateau. The plateau is defined as peak $Petco_2$ during the terminal 20% of the expiratory volume (Fig. 149-4).

Monitoring of $etco_2$ is used in several situations. First, it has become an invaluable tool in verification of endotracheal intubation. In animal studies $Petco_2$ measurements identified either endotracheal or endoesophageal intubations always correctly. The only false positive result noted was after carbonated soft drink ingestion. Second, it can assist in titration of PEEP by observation of the lowest $Paco_2$-$Petco_2$ gradient, indicating that recruitment of alveoli is maximal. Minimizing the gradient may prevent overdistention of the alveoli. In clinical studies the usefulness has been limited to patients that had recruitable alveoli, as identified by an inflection point on the

Fig. 149-4   Normal $Petco_2$ pattern. Left side of tracing of exhaled Pco_2 is obtained with reduced paper speed; $Petco_2$ value of 40 mm Hg is demonstrated with each breath. Right side demonstrates four sections of an entire cycle *(A-E)*. Segment *AB* is the initiation of the expiratory phase of the respiratory cycle, during which gas is removed from the anatomic dead space. As perfused alveoli empty, $Petco_2$ increases rapidly to a peak *(BC)*. A plateau *(CD)* is achieved and must be evident to ensure accurate $Petco_2$ determination. Segment *DE* represents initiation of the inspiration phase of the respiratory cycle.

pressure-volume curve exerted by PEEP. Third, its use has been advocated in assessing effectiveness of cardiopulmonary resuscitation and cardiac output. Finally, measuring $etco_2$ can be used to calculate physiologic dead space. $Petco_2$ is also used to identify rebreathing of CO_2 when a nonrebreathing circuit is being used (i.e., transport of a patient), in which the $Petco_2$ tracing never reaches baseline, indicating the elevated inspired CO_2 level.

TECHNIQUE

For all practical purposes, $etco_2$ monitoring in critically ill patients can be performed only in those with either an endotracheal tube or tracheostomy in place. Pco_2 in an exhaled gas mixture may be determined either with infrared absorption analysis or mass spectrometry. A chemical method is now used to determine endotracheal rather than endo-esophageal intubation by color change assessing the exhaled air semiquantitatively for CO_2. This discussion focuses on the use of the infrared technique since mass spectrometry has limited use in the PICU because of its expense, slow response time, bulkiness, and labor-intensive upkeep.

The molecules that define the structure of a gas exhibit characteristic absorption spectra determined by their composition and configuration. Infrared energy reacts with these molecules. In expired air only two constituents (CO_2 and water) react with infrared light, and the degree of absorption depends on the reactivity and number of molecules present. CO_2 strongly absorbs infrared light at a wavelength of 4.28

nm; thus this wavelength is used to measure gaseous CO_2. The infrared energy is passed through a chamber that contains a sample of exhaled CO_2, and a lens directs the unabsorbed radiation onto a detector. The higher the Pco_2 in the exhaled gas mixture, the more the radiation is absorbed and the less it is directed to the detector. The detector creates an electrical signal proportional to the intensity of incidental radiation and thus the $Petco_2$ of the sample. The signal is processed to display a continuous waveform of the $Petco_2$ values. Fig. 149-4 shows a normal pattern of exhaled CO_2 over time. Different display modes are also available besides observing a number displayed by the capnometer. Capnography allows the clinician to evaluate the characteristics of a breath-to-breath tracing or a more compressed capnogram to follow trends in $Petco_2$. Breath-to-breath monitoring is desirable in states of rapid change because it allows visualization of characteristics of each breath.

The gas to be analyzed can reach the sample chamber in one of two ways (Fig. 149-5). *Sidestream* analyzers pump the exhaled gas sample from the trachea in the distal breathing circuit through small-bore tubing to a remote analyzer. This method adds little weight or dead space to the breathing circuit. However, the narrow lumen of the sample tube often becomes obstructed by airway secretions or water from humidified gas. The response time is slow compared with that of mainstream analyzers. *Mainstream* analyzers are attached directly to the endotracheal tube or tracheostomy. Because the analyzer is part of the breathing circuit, the response time is rapid. However, the analyzer is heavy and must be supported to prevent endotracheal tube kinking or dislodgment.

Changes in $Petco_2$ must be compared with the $Paco_2$ value to determine the cause of the gas exchange derangement. If it is assumed they correlate (i.e., dead space ventilation is constant), hypoventilation can be diagnosed by an increase in the height of the capnogram (Fig. 149-6) and hyperventilation by reduction in the height of the capnogram (Fig. 149-7). Apnea, disconnection from a ventilator circuit, or esophageal intubation results in reduction of $Petco_2$ toward zero (Fig. 149-8). If reduction in $Petco_2$ occurs in the presence of unchanged or increasing $Paco_2$, increased dead space ventilation can be inferred. Fig. 149-9 shows a capnogram typical of cardiac arrest in which the $Petco_2$ value progressively falls and ends in small waves that result from CO_2 production by the lungs. Fig. 149-10 demonstrates a more subtle reduction in $Petco_2$ caused by reduced pulmonary per-

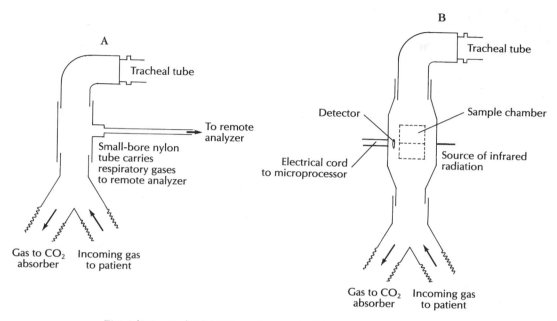

Fig. 149-5   End-tidal CO_2 analyzers. **A**, Sidestream. **B**, Mainstream.

Fig. 149-6 Increase in $Petco_2$ is consistent with hypoventilation. Diagnosis is confirmed by demonstrating increased $Paco_2$.

Fig. 149-7 Reduction of $Petco_2$ is consistent with hyperventilation.

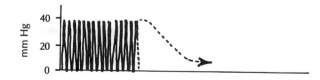

Fig. 149-8 Reduction in $Petco_2$ from 40 to 0 mm Hg is consistent with situations in which no alveolar ventilation is occurring (apnea) or the endotracheal tube is malfunctioning or improperly placed.

Fig. 149-9 $Petco_2$ tracing demonstrates progressive reduction as cardiac arrest occurs, resulting in decreased pulmonary perfusion.

Fig. 149-10   Petco$_2$ tracing is consistent with compromised pulmonary perfusion by hypovolemia, increased pulmonary vascular resistance, or administration of excessive PEEP.

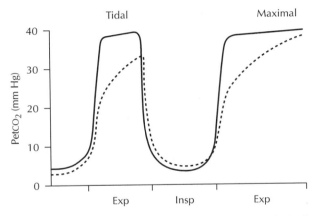

Fig. 149-11   Petco$_2$ tracing in airway obstruction (dashed line) and normal subject (solid line). Normal plateau at end expiration is not reached in obstructive airways disease because poorly ventilated lung regions still empty air with high Pco$_2$. (From Marini JJ. Monitoring during mechanical ventilation. Clin Chest Med 9:73-100, 1988.)

fusion. The shape of the breath-to-breath curve is influenced by many factors (e.g., sampling rate, tubing length and size, sensor location, and patient pathophysiology). Use of a breath-to-breath diagram (Fig. 149-11) shows the influence of obstructive airway disease on the shape of the Petco$_2$ curve. In obstructive airway disease air empties slower as poorly ventilated lung regions continue to empty after end expiration.

RISKS AND COMPLICATIONS

For purposes of this discussion, complications of etco$_2$ monitoring are defined as misinterpretation of the displayed data. This can occur because of misunderstanding of the physiologic principles or as a result of mechanical malfunction of either the monitoring or ventilating apparatus. The former situation occurs when the changing Petco$_2$ value is not compared with a simultaneously obtained Paco$_2$ value. It cannot be assumed that pulmonary perfusion and CO$_2$ production have remained constant. The second category includes situations in which a change in the Petco$_2$ value is the result of mechanical malfunction and not an abnormality in the patient. A sudden reduction in Petco$_2$ to zero may indicate one or more of the following mechanical defects: obstructed endotracheal tube, defective CO$_2$ analyzer, ventilator malfunction, or endotracheal tube malposition. A sudden increase in the Petco$_2$ baseline may be the result of a saturated CO$_2$ absorber, the presence of water in the analyzer, or a calibration error.

The accuracy of etco$_2$ measurements allows only limited reliance on the measured value. The Canadian Working Group on Critical Care found in a comparison of Petco$_2$ and Pco$_2$ a bias (mean difference between Petco$_2$ and Paco$_2$) of 2.35 to 18.0 mm Hg and a precision (standard deviation from the bias) of 5.3 to 10.0 mm Hg. Furthermore, Petco$_2$ did not accurately predict directional changes in Pco$_2$. Indeed, studies in adults lead to the conclusion that capnography as a tool to monitor weaning of ventilatory support is useful only in healthy, hemodynamically stable patients.

In summary, etco$_2$ monitoring of the intubated patient may provide a means of observing alveolar ventilation or CO$_2$ production or pulmonary perfusion, provided a changing Petco$_2$ value is compared with a simultaneously obtained Paco$_2$ value. In addition, it is valuable for assessing the patency or proper placement of an endotracheal tube, perhaps for adjusting PEEP by determining adverse effects on dead space ventilation, and for observing the effectiveness of cardiopulmonary resuscitation.

CURRENT RESEARCH AND FUTURE CONSIDERATIONS

Current research in this field includes development of a Petco$_2$ monitoring setup from a nasal cannula.

ADDITIONAL READING

Oxygen Saturation Monitoring

Barker SJ, Tremper KK. Advances in oxygen monitoring. Pulse oximetry: Applications and limitations. Int Anesthesiol Clin 15:3, 1987.

Brown M, Vender JS. Noninvasive oxygen monitoring. Crit Care Clin 4:493, 1988.

Bryan-Brown CW, Baek SM, Makebali G, et al. Consumable oxygen: Availability in relation to oxyhemoglobin dissociation. Crit Care Med 1:17, 1973.

Cohen DE, Downes JJ, Raphaely RC. What difference does pulse oximetry make? Anesthesiology 68:181, 1988.

Jurban A. Pulse oximetry. In Tobin MJ, ed. Respiratory Monitoring in Contemporary Management in Critical Care. New York: Churchill Livingstone, 1991, p 79.

• Levine RL, Fromm RE Jr. Critical Care Monitoring from Pre-hospital to the ICU. St. Louis: Mosby, 1995, p 215.

Marin JJ. Monitoring during mechanical ventilation. Clin Chest Med 9:73, 1988.

• Moller JT, Pedersen T, Rasmussen LS, et al. Randomized evaluation of pulse oximetry in 20,802 patients. II. Perioperative events and postoperative complications. Anesthesiology 78:445, 1993.

Nichols DG, Rogers MC. Developmental physiology of the respiratory system. In Rogers MC, ed. Textbook of Pediatric Intensive Care. Baltimore: Williams & Wilkins, 1991, p 100.

• Poets CF, Southall DP. Noninvasive monitoring of oxygenation in infants and children: Practical considerations and areas of concern. Pediatrics 93:737, 1994.

Wahr JA, Tremper KK. Noninvasive oxygen monitoring techniques. Crit Care Clin 11:199, 1995.

Transcutaneous Oxygen Monitoring

Brown M, Vender JS. Noninvasive oxygen monitoring. Crit Care Clin 4:499, 1988.

• Hansen TN, Tooley W. Skin surface carbon dioxide tension in sick infants. Pediatrics 64:942, 1979.

Martin RJ, Pultusker M, Lough M, Ferrano A, Kerrel N. Optimal temperature for the measurement of transcutaneous carbon dioxide tension in the neonate. J Pediatr 97:114, 1980.

Merritt T, Liyamasawd S, Boettrich C, et al. Skin surface CO_2 measurements in sick preterm and term infants. J Pediatr 99:782, 1981.

Stock MC. Noninvasive carbon dioxide monitoring. Crit Care Clin 4:522, 1988.

Tabata BK, Kirsch JR, Rogers MC. Transcutaneous blood gas measurements. In Rogers MC, ed. Textbook of Pediatric Intensive Care. Baltimore: Williams & Wilkins, 1987, p 1423.

Tremper KK, Shoemaker WC. Transcutaneous oxygen monitoring of critically ill adults with and without low flow shock. Crit Care Med 9:706, 1981.

Tremper KK, Mentelos RA, Shoemaker WC. Effect of hypercarbia and shock on transcutaneous carbon dioxide at different electrode temperatures. Crit Care Med 8:608, 1980.

Tremper KK, Shoemaker WC, Shippy CR, et al. Transcutaneous P_{CO_2} monitoring on adult patients in the ICU and the operating room. Crit Care Med 9:752, 1981.

Transcutaneous Carbon Dioxide Monitoring

• Hansen T, Tooley W. Skin surface carbon dioxide tension in sick infants. Pediatrics 64:942, 1979.

Herrell N, Martin RJ, Pultusker M, et al. Optimal temperature for the measurement of transcutaneous carbon dioxide tension in the neonate. J Pediatr 97:114, 1980.

Levine RL, Fromm RE Jr. Critical Care Monitoring from Pre-Hospital to the ICU. St. Louis: Mosby 1995, pp 214-215.

Mahutte CK, Midriels TM, Kessel KT, Trueblood DM. Evaluation of a single transcutaneous P_{O_2}-P_{CO_2} sensor in adult patients. Crit Care Med 12:1063-1066, 1984.

Stock MC. Noninvasive carbon dioxide monitoring. Crit Care Clin 4:522, 1988.

Tremper KK, Mentelos RA, Shoemaker WC. Effect of hypercarbia and shock on transcutaneous carbon dioxide at different electrode temperatures. Crit Care Med 8:608, 1980.

End-Tidal Carbon Dioxide Monitoring

Baudendistel L, Goudsouzion N, Cote C, et al. End-tidal CO_2 monitoring: It use in the diagnosis and management of malignant hyperthermia. Anaesthesia 39:1000, 1984.

Falk IL, Rackow EC, Weil MH. End-tidal carbon dioxide concentration during cardiopulmonary resuscitation. N Engl J Med 318:607, 1988.

• Kesten S, Chapman KR. In Tobin MJ, ed. Respiratory Monitoring in Contemporary Management in Critical Care. New York: Churchill Livingstone, 1991, pp 79-100.

• Levine RL, Fromm RE Jr. Critical Care Monitoring from Pre-Hospital to the ICU. St. Louis: Mosby, 1995, pp 210-213.

Marini JJ. Monitoring during mechanical ventilation. Clin Chest Med 9:73, 1988.

May WS. Respiratory monitoring. Int Anesthesiol Clin 163:159, 1986.

Murray JP, Modell JM. Early detection of endotracheal tube accidents by monitoring carbon dioxide concentration in respiratory gas. Anesthesiology 59:344, 1983.

Nunn JF, Hill DW. Respiratory dead space and arterial to end-tidal CO_2 tension differences in anesthetized man. J Appl Physiol 15:383, 1960.

Raemer DB, Francis D, Philip JH, et al. Variation in P_{CO_2} between arterial blood and peak expired gas during anesthesia. Anesthesiol Analg 62:1065, 1983.

Stock MC. Noninvasive carbon dioxide monitoring. Crit Care Clin 4:511, 1988.

Technology Subcommittee of the Working Group on Critical Care. Noninvasive blood gas monitoring: A review of the use in the adult critical care unit. Can Med Assoc J 143:703, 1992.

Weft MH, Bitera J, Trevino RP, et al. Cardiac output and end-tidal carbon dioxide. Crit Care Med 13:907, 1985.

150 Bedside Pulmonary Function Testing of Patients Receiving Mechanical Ventilation

Patricia Walters · Peter M. Luckett

BACKGROUND AND INDICATIONS

Traditional pulmonary function tests are based on the ability of an awake patient to perform forced expiratory maneuvers. Pediatric performance standards for children able to perform forced maneuvers have been established by the American Thoracic Society (ATS), and a number of regression equations exist in the literature for predicted normal reference values. Pulmonary function cannot be tested in a large group of patients incapable of generating forced maneuvers on command. Techniques to test tidal breath in infants with use of a mask were developed to meet this need. No regression reference equations exist to predict normal values in these patients. Target values for curve morphology, compliance, resistance, and functional residual capacity (FRC) have been established and are debated in the literature. A joint committee of the ATS and European Respiratory Society continues to develop procedural guidelines and equipment standards for infant testing. These methods may be applied to pulmonary function testing during mechanical ventilation in infants and other pediatric patients.

Routine pulmonary function testing in adults and older children has been used for decades to diagnose pulmonary disease, determine the degree of illness, and evaluate therapeutic interventions. Testing is based on quantitative measurement of gas flow into and out of the lungs. It is affected by the mechanical properties of the lungs, the airways, the respiratory muscles, and the rib cage. In addition to these properties, once intubation is accomplished and mechanical ventilation started, gas flow is also affected by the endotracheal tube, ventilator mode, and pharmacologic alterations. Ventilator pulmonary

function tests allow evaluation of the effects of various therapies on lung function that include (1) pulmonary responsiveness to pharmacologic agents such as bronchodilators and diuretics, (2) ventilator settings when ventilation is difficult, (3) lung function in patients difficult to wean from mechanical ventilation, and (4) extraordinary ventilator techniques such as high-frequency ventilation, extracorporeal membrane oxygenation, or partial liquid ventilation.

The four basic components of ventilator pulmonary function tests are evaluation of tidal flow volume loop, pressure-volume loop, passive mechanics, and FRC. Each component test has calculated subdivisions. Commercial brands of pulmonary function equipment are programmed to calculate various aspects of gas flow for a single breath. The most common patient tests are summarized on p. 1371. Optimally, each test is performed for both ventilator and spontaneous breaths. Comparing ventilator and spontaneous breath values is useful in evaluating patient response. Not all components can be tested under all patient conditions. Ventilator pulmonary function tests appropriate to each ventilator mode are summarized in Fig. 150-1.

TECHNIQUE
Tidal Flow Volume Loops

Pneumotachometers are the measuring devices used for tidal flow volume loops (TFVLs) and report values for flow rate, volume, and time. This device measures flow by analyzing the change in pressure across a fixed resistance. Each pneumotachometer has a known resistance, and flow traveling across that resistance generates a decrease in pressure as it exits the pneumotachometer. This pressure difference is di-

COMMON VENTILATOR PULMONARY FUNCTION TEST COMPONENTS

Tidal flow volume loop

Delivered tidal volume, inspiratory
Delivered tidal volume, expiratory
Delivered tidal volume per kilogram
Inspiratory time
Expiratory time
Respiratory rate
Mean expiratory flow rate divided by mean inspiratory flow rate (ME/MI) (spontaneous nonventilator-assisted breaths only)

Pressure-volume loop (ventilator-assisted breaths only)

Delivered tidal volume, inspiratory
Delivered tidal volume, expiratory
Delivered tidal volume per kilogram
Inspiratory time
Expiratory time
Respiratory rate
Delivered peak inspiratory pressure
Delivered end pressure
Dynamic compliance
Dynamic compliance per kilogram
Terminal compliance ratio (%C-20)

Passive mechanics

Static compliance
Static compliance per kilogram
Resistance
Time constant

Functional residual capacity

FRC
FRC per kilogram

rectly proportional to flow. Pneumotachometer resistance is constant, pressure change is measured across the pneumotachometer, and flow is calculated. Flow is defined as volume of gas per unit time; therefore volume is calculated from the integration of measured flow. All calculations are performed by a computer interfaced to the pneumotachometer.

TFVLs are obtained during initial ventilator pulmonary function evaluation to ensure correct use of pneumotachometer size. Pneumotachometers in sizes 10, 30, and 100 L/min are necessary to measure the full range of pediatric patients. It is essential that patient peak tidal inspiratory flow and peak tidal expiratory flow as measured on TFVLs does not exceed the flow range limitation of the pneumotachometer. This is necessary for accurate reporting of volume and other component tests that produce calculations based on flow. Pneumotachometer "clipping" refers to flow that exceeds pneumotachometer range (Fig. 150-2). As a rule of thumb the smallest pneumotachometer possible is used to reduce mechanical dead space and increase pneumotachometer resolution without sacrificing flow accuracy. During mechanical ventilation elastic recoil of the respiratory system may be increased as a result of neuromuscular blockade or restrictive lung disease. An increase in elastic recoil increases peak tidal expiratory flow rate, which in turn may necessitate a larger pneumotachometer than would be needed for routine mask testing.

TFVLs measure tidal volume and inspiratory time at the endotracheal tube. This volume is the true delivered tidal volume and may vary greatly from that monitored with the ventilator. Most ventilators measure tidal volume inside the ventilator, which includes volume lost to ventilator tubing compliance and tidal volume actually delivered to the patient. Equations exist to calculate the volume lost to ventilator tubing compliance. Factors that may affect this volume are tubing age, temperature, and changing lung function. The lungs of pediatric patients with severe disease are often less compliant than the ventilator circuit, and it is not unusual to measure delivered tidal volume that is less than half the ventilator setting. Volume measures obtained with ventilator pulmonary function tests are corrected to body temperature and pressure standards, whereas ventilators measure volume in terms of ambient temperature and pressure standards. In addition, ventilator pulmonary function test equipment is routinely calibrated to a known volume before each patient test, whereas ventilator monitors are calibrated infrequently if at all. TFVLs also distinguish between inspiratory and expiratory volume. In patients with large leaks (>8%) around the endotracheal tube the inspiratory volumes will be much greater than expiratory volumes, compromising the accuracy of ventilator pulmonary function tests. The pneumotachometer must be left in line between the endotracheal tube and ventilator Y-connector for several minutes to allow temperature and

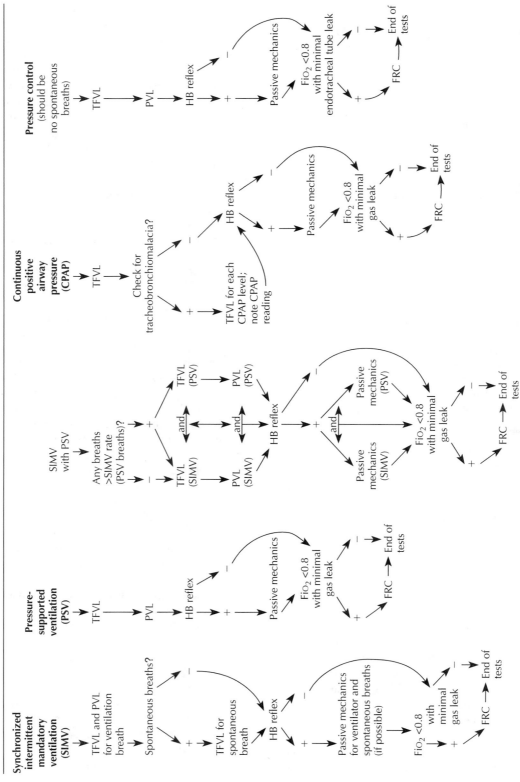

Fig. 150-1   Ventilator pulmonary function tests. Appropriate ventilator modes are presented in algorithmic form. Maximum information is obtained by performing ventilator pulmonary function tests for both ventilator- and nonventilator-assisted breaths before and after pharmacologic intervention or ventilatory setting change. (HB = Hering-Breur; PVL = pressure-volume loop; TFVL = tidal flow volume loop; + = positive; − = negative.)

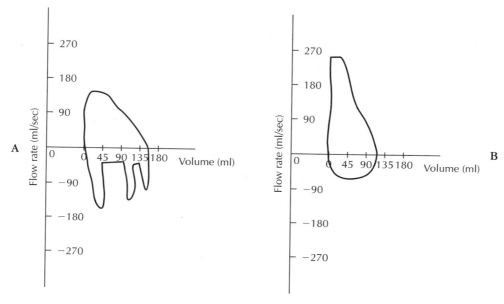

Fig. 150-2   Flow rate is plotted against volume to generate TFVLs. Note 2:1 ratio of flow rate to volume. Flow moves clockwise from zero volume to maximal volume with positive expiratory flow above the x-axis representing exhalation and from maximal volume to zero volume with negative flow below the x-axis representing inhalation. Both loops were measured with a 10 L/min pneumotachometer with a maximal flow range of 220 ml/sec. **A,** TFVL shows irregular inspiratory flow outside of pneumotachometer range. This is inspiratory pneumotachometer "clipping." **B,** TFVL demonstrates expiratory flow that peaks and flattens outside of pneumotachometer range. This is expiratory pneumotachometer "clipping." Whenever flow is outside pneumotachometer range, the volume measured on the x-axis is inaccurate, and a larger pneumotachometer must be used.

pressure to equilibrate. Patient conditions in which expiratory volume exceeds inspiratory volume are rare. Inadequate equilibration time is likely when expiratory volume exceeds inspiratory volume as measured by ventilator pulmonary function tests. Generally inspiratory volume equals or exceeds expiratory volume before any measurements are recorded.

During an inspiratory plateau flow stops for the duration of the plateau as pressure is held constant inside the lungs until the end of inspiratory time as set on the ventilator. A plateau may be set on the ventilator or established by the patient with decreased pulmonary compliance. Inspiratory time measured by a pneumotachometer in ventilator pulmonary function tests is a function of inspiratory flow only and does not reflect plateau time. Consequently, when an inspiratory plateau is present, pneumotachometer-measured inspiratory time will be less than the ventilator setting for inspiratory time. The difference between inspiratory flow time and ventilator inspiratory time setting is the duration of the plateau and may change as the patient's condition changes (Fig. 150-3). Pneumotachometers cannot distinguish between inspiratory plateau time and pause time between exhalation and inhalation. As a result, the expiratory time reported on ventilator pulmonary function tests is a combination of the time allotted to expiratory flow, the pause between breaths, and inspiratory plateau. Therefore pressure measured during expiratory time on ventilator pulmonary function tests when an inspiratory plateau is present is erroneously high compared with ventilator PEEP settings.

Gas flow measures on the expiratory side of TFVLs during mechanical ventilation are a function of elastic recoil of the lung, respiratory system resistance, and resistance of the expiratory limb of the ventilator circuit. Gas flow on the inspiratory side of TFVLs during mechanical ventilation is a function of resis-

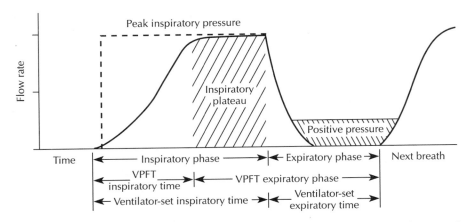

Fig. 150-3 Relationship of flow rate, time, and pressure as gas enters the lungs from mechanical ventilation and with an inspiratory plateau. Note the different inspiratory time measures with mechanical ventilation vs. pneumotachometer. End pressure must be interpreted with caution when an inspiratory plateau is present. (VPFT = Ventilator pulmonary function tests.)

tance of the endotracheal tube and ventilator flow pattern. Lesions associated with extrathoracic obstruction such as laryngomalacia are bypassed by the artificial airway. As a result, ventilator pulmonary function tests cannot be used to diagnose extrathoracic obstruction. The presence of intrathoracic obstruction produced by anatomic anomalies such as tracheobronchiomalacia may be diagnosed during spontaneous breaths that are not ventilator assisted (and in the absence of PEEP).

On TFVLs, normal spontaneous tidal breathing is sinusoidal, and mean expiratory flow is equal to mean inspiratory flow (ME/MI). An ME/MI ratio with abnormal expiratory-inspiratory flow deviates from 1.0. With intrathoracic obstruction such as tracheobronchiomalacia, loss of large airway support structures during expiration results in premature closure of the airways. Expiratory flow is obstructed in relation to inspiratory flow, generating a reduced value for ME/MI. An ME/MI value <0.65 that is unresponsive to bronchodilator therapy suggests the presence of intrathoracic obstruction. PEEP or CPAP will effectively splint the airway open, masking an intrathoracic obstruction. Therefore the end pressure level may need to be incrementally decreased before an ME/MI value <0.65 is apparent on TFVLs. Conversely, end pressure may be incrementally increased to normalize ME/MI at 0.7 to 1.0. Young pediatric patients in whom extubation fails need to be evaluated for intrathoracic obstruction. Extended use of CPAP may be necessary to maintain airway patency when the need for mechanical ventilation has past.

A ventilator-assisted breath with a positive response to bronchodilator therapy is accompanied by an increase in delivered tidal volume for both volume-cycled and pressure-cycled ventilation. During a volume-cycled ventilator breath the inspiratory pressure needed to deliver that breath will decrease as patient resistance improves in response to bronchodilator therapy. This decrease in pressure decreases the volume lost to ventilator tubing compliance and increases the true tidal volume delivered to the patient, whereas the ventilator continues to register the same set volume. During a pressure-cycled ventilator breath the ventilator pressure setting remains unchanged, whereas the tidal volume delivered by that amount of pressure increases as patient resistance decreases.

The variations in TFVLs are presented in Fig. 150-4. It is important to note that not all brands of pulmonary function equipment follow ATS guidelines for a 2:1 ratio of flow rate to volume on TFVLs. Some brands of equipment plot all ventilator pulmonary function test data points in a square box; thus ventilator and spontaneous breaths look alike. Without the ATS standard for presentation, evaluation of curve morphology is difficult.

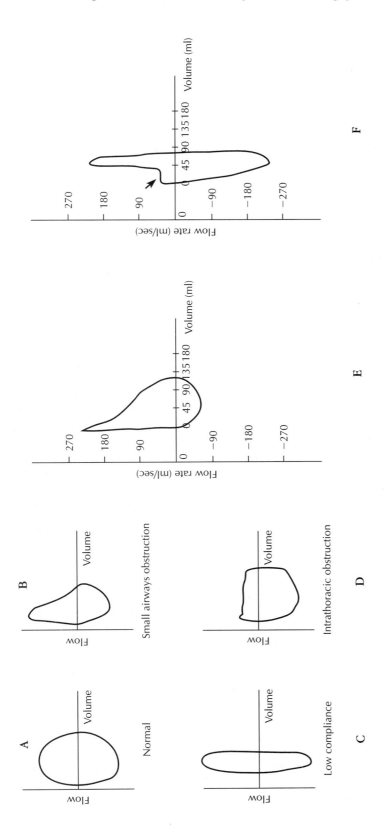

Fig. 150-4   TFVLs show variations in curve morphology as measured with ventilator pulmonary function tests. Loops represent nonventilator-assisted breaths **(A-D)** and ventilator-assisted breaths **(E and F)**. **A,** Normal egg-shaped curve of a spontaneous breath at normal respiratory rates. Normal sinusoidal movement of gas flow in and out of the lungs produces this shape. Note: Inhalation is below the x-axis, exhalation is above the x-axis; the x-axis is volume, the y-axis is flow; and there is a 2:1 ratio of flow to volume. **B,** Reduction in expiratory flow that accompanies small airways obstruction often associated with bronchospasm. **C,** High inspiratory and expiratory flow with a small volume. This pattern is associated with decreased compliance but may also be noted in a patient with normal compliance who is breathing at a rapid respiratory rate. **D,** Reduction in mean expiratory flow compared with inspiratory flow. This pattern produces an ME/MI <0.65 and is associated with intrathoracic obstruction. **E,** Inspiratory flow limitation produced by the endotracheal tube and ventilator mode during a volume-limited ventilator breath. Also note the comparatively higher peak expiratory flow followed by rapid deceleration of flow. This is indicative of the higher elastic recoil associated with neuromuscular blockade used during mechanical ventilation and should not be confused with the pattern of small airways obstruction for a nonventilator-assisted breath. **F,** Characteristic pattern of inspiratory plateau (arrow). In this instance the ventilator inspiratory time setting is longer than the inspiratory time measured with ventilator pulmonary function tests. Note that the inspiratory plateau is drawn on the expiratory side of the curve. This is the result of the inability of the computer software (interfaced to the pneumotachometer) to distinguish inspiratory plateau from expiratory pause.

Pressure-Volume Loops

Once it has been established that the patient inspiratory and expiratory flow is in range for pneumotachometer size, pressure-volume loops (PVLs) are collected with the same equipment used to obtain TFVLs. Like TFVLs, PVLs refect bulk gas flow into and out of the lungs. In general the computer software interfaced to the pneumotachometer will activate an additional pressure reading taken from the junction of the ventilator circuit and the endotracheal tube to plot against volume creating the PVL. Positive airway pressure generated by the ventilator is used as a measure of transpulmonary pressure and is required for this plot. Spontaneous breaths that are not ventilator assisted must not be used for PVLs. The common parameters taken from a PVL are dynamic compliance, terminal compliance ratio, tidal volume, inspiratory time, and inspiratory and expiratory pressures.

Compliance is defined as the change in volume achieved for a given change in pressure. Static compliance is the slope of the relationship of change in volume vs. change in pressure when measurements are made as the result of occlusion and at zero flow. Static compliance is measured without the influence of the expiratory limb of the ventilator circuit and is an assessment of the elastic properties of the lungs. Measurement of static compliance is discussed on p. 1378. Dynamic compliance is calculated during tidal breathing at the point of no flow during the switch from inhalation to exhalation. Respiratory rate affects dynamic compliance measurement. At a low respiratory rate dynamic and static compliance values are the same. At a high respiratory rate dynamic compliance may decrease and become less than static compliance. This is referred to as frequency dependency of compliance and is the result of nonuniformly distributed gas flow through the lungs. Dynamic compliance is used to evaluate the patient-ventilator interface to help determine ventilator settings. Pediatric compliance values are normalized to body weight in kilograms.

Compliance measures taken at different lung volumes established by ventilator settings produces an S-shaped pressure-volume curve (Fig. 150-5, *A*). At the lower section of the curve the patient is breathing at low lung volume (well below normal FRC), and major pressure changes produce only minor increases in tidal volume. The steeper midsection of the curve represents compliance measures taken at near-normal FRC, where minor changes in pressure produce maximum changes in tidal volume. This midsection represents a more compliant lung in which dynamic compliance and ventilator settings (lung volumes) are maximized. The top section of the curve represents breathing at high lung volume (well above normal FRC), and again major pressure changes produce minor tidal volume changes. At this top section of the pressure-volume curve the elastic limit of the lungs is reached and compliance decreases. The patient is at risk for overdistention of lung units at these lung volumes.

Depending on the method of ventilation, several assumptions may be made from the PVL that are useful in evaluating the patient-ventilator interface. Fig. 150-5 shows several patterns for PVLs measured during mechanical ventilation. During the pressure-support ventilation mode (unlike the time-cycled pressure-limited mode), inspiration terminates in response to reduction in inspiratory flow. In this instance ventilator flow is sinusoidal and typically generates a rectangular PVL. Little information can be deduced from this type of loop. However, during volume- or pressure-limited ventilation the PVL becomes more characteristically elliptic. The base of the inspiratory side of the loop shows how much pressure must be generated before any volume can enter the lungs. An inflection point occurs in the midportion of the loop for both inspiration and expiration, showing where there is maximal volume change for minimal pressure change. The pressure value plotted at the inspiratory inflection point may be used to determine the setting for ventilator inspiratory pressure. The pressure value plotted at the expiratory inflection point may be used to determine PEEP settings if no inspiratory plateau is present. The top part of the PVL shows the point at which there is minimal volume change for a large amount of pressure change and is used to assess the risk of overdistention.

To calculate the terminal compliance ratio (%C-20), an additional dynamic compliance is measured at 20% from the end of inspiration. If this value is greater than the standard dynamic compliance measure, the ratio of dynamic compliance to terminal compliance will fall to <1.0. A PVL with a %C-20 <0.8 is flattened at the top and has a "duck bill" appearance, suggesting overdistention (Fig. 150-6, *A*). Overdistention may be prevented by manipulating ventilator settings for inspiratory time, peak pressure, volume, rate, or PEEP.

Areas of the lung that have low compliance with

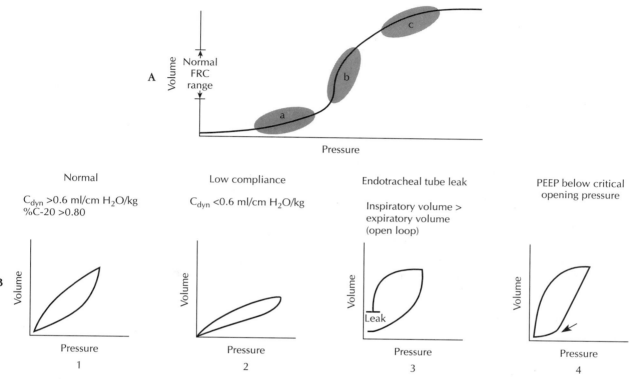

Fig. 150-5 A, Pressure-volume curve demonstrates the relationship between pressure and volume when compliance is determined at different lung volumes. Pressure is measured on the x-axis and volume on the y-axis. In the highlighted area labeled *a* large pressure changes produce only small volume changes in a patient breathing below normal FRC. Compliance is reduced at this low lung volume. In the highlighted area labeled *b* small pressure changes produce large volume changes in a patient breathing at near-normal FRC. Compliance is maximized in this portion of the pressure-volume curve. In the highlighted area labeled *c* again large pressure changes produce only small volume changes in a patient breathing well above normal FRC. Compliance is reduced at this high lung volume. When mechanically ventilating at high lung volumes, decreasing compliance indicates lung overdistention. **B,** PVLs *1* through *4* demonstrate variations in curve morphology as measured with ventilator pulmonary function tests. Loop *1* is the normal shape generated by volume- or pressure-limited mechanical ventilation with normal dynamic compliance and a normal terminal compliance ratio. Loop *2* shows the pattern of decreased dynamic compliance. Loop *3* shows the open loop pattern associated with a large leak around the endotracheal tube. The percentage of leak may be estimated by comparing inspiratory and expiratory volumes. Loop *4* shows a flattened area on the inspiratory side of the PVL (arrow); critical opening pressure must be reached before volume can readily enter the lungs. This flattened portion will take on a more normal appearance if PEEP is increased.

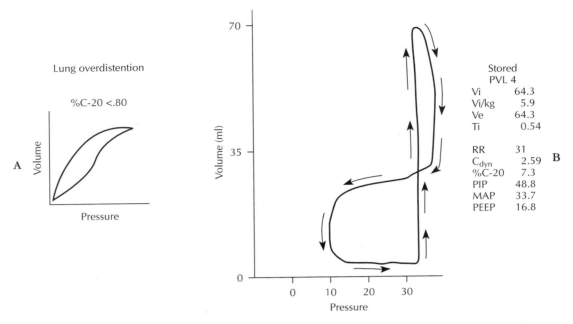

Fig. 150-6 **A,** PVL demonstrates the characteristic "duck bill" appearance that accompanies lung overdistention and terminal compliance ratio <0.8. **B,** PVL demonstrates the pendeluft phenomenon. Arrows show the irregular motion of pressure and volume during inhalation and exhalation as measured with a pneumotachometer during the pendeluft phenomenon. The loop was captured during pressure-control ventilation with a 1-second inspiratory time *(Ti).* Inspiratory time recorded by the pneumotachometer is 0.54 second, denoting an inspiratory plateau. End-pressure (PEEP) readings obtained during inspiratory plateau are invalid.

normal or elevated resistance require more time to fill than do areas that have normal or increased compliance with normal or decreased resistance. If inspiratory time is long enough, ventilation inside the lung will redistribute gas flow from an area that fills quickly to an area that fills slowly. This is the pendeluft phenomenon. During pressure-control ventilation or any mode of ventilation in which ventilator inspiratory time is set long enough to generate an inspiratory plateau, the end pressure value obtained from a PVL will be erroneously high and is not to be interpreted as auto-PEEP. If the inspiratory plateau is long enough, the pendeluft phenomenon will occur; pressure and volume measures at the pneumotachometer are disrupted and normal PVL morphology is altered. A characteristic pattern develops (Fig. 150-6, *B*). Lung diseases such as acute respiratory distress syndrome (ARDS), with differential ventilation of compliant and noncompliant areas, may

benefit from ventilator mode and inspiratory time settings that generate the pendeluft phenomenon.

A positive response to bronchodilator therapy will alter the PVL. The increased delivered tidal volume associated with a positive response to bronchodilator will generate higher dynamic compliance. Inspiratory and expiratory inflection points may also change. In addition, the duration of inspiratory plateau may decrease as airway resistance decreases.

Passive Mechanics and FRC

Passive mechanics by occlusion technique is primarily used to determine static compliance, airway resistance, and time constants of the total respiratory system for both ventilator-assisted and nonventilator-assisted breaths. In the occlusion technique a low dead space sliding valve with pneumotachometer is used to capture plateau pressure at zero flow during occlusion followed by expiratory flow and volume measurements. Test reliability depends on muscle relaxation on occlusion. This condition is met if the Hering-Breuer reflex is present (expiratory time after occlusion at least 25% longer than average expiratory time of the four previously unoccluded breaths). This condition may also be met during sedation or neuromuscular blockade, which is routinely used during mechanical ventilation. It is important to note that not all patients will maintain sufficient relaxation with sedation. A patient may respond positively one day and negatively on another day, often as a function of the level of consciousness. All patients need to be tested for the presence of the Hering-Breuer reflex or adequate relaxation before testing for passive mechanics. During the passive mechanics procedure the patient receives routine ventilator breaths through the sliding valve until a switch is manually activated that allows the ventilator pulmonary function test computer interface to locate and occlude the beginning of the next exhalation for 0.1 second. After occlusion the exhaled gas is directed through the pneumotachometer and outside the ventilator circuit for computer analysis. These measurements are made without the influence of the expiratory limb of the ventilator circuit and therefore are more representative of pure respiratory mechanics. The sliding valve reconnects ventilator gas flow to the patient for the next inspiration. PEEP, which helps to maintain FRC during mechanical ventilation, is bypassed for the single exhalation following occlusion. The change from mechanical ventilation to occlusion and back to mechanical ventilation is rapid but still may precipitate alveolar derecruitment secondary to loss of PEEP. The patient is allowed to re-recruit alveoli by maintaining PEEP with several mechanical breaths before further data collection. Measurements from multiple occluded breaths are computer analyzed for static compliance, resistance, and time constant. The acceptable mean value for each parameter carries a coefficient of variation <0.2 for at least six breaths.

Normal values for pediatric passive mechanics are listed. Pediatric static compliance is normalized to body weight. Normal adult compliance is 100 to 200 ml/cm H_2O. Normal pediatric compliance is 1 to 2 ml/cm H_2O/kg. ARDS is associated with a compliance of <20 to 30 ml/cm H_2O in adults and less than 0.2 to 0.3 ml/cm H_2O/kg in pediatric patients. Successful weaning from mechanical ventilation usually accompanies pediatric compliance of at least 0.6 to 0.7 ml/cm H_2O/kg.

NORMAL VALUES FOR PEDIATRIC PASSIVE MECHANICS

Static compliance 1 to 2 ml/cm H_2O/kg
  0.6 to 0.7 associated with successful weaning from mechanical ventilation
  Less than 0.3 associated with ARDS
Resistance 0.03 to 0.07 cm H_2O/ml/sec (infant value; value decreases with increase in age)

In children airway resistance decreases as airway diameter increases during lung growth until adult values are reached. Passive mechanics measures total respiratory system resistance, which is the result of airway resistance and tissue resistance of the chest wall and lung parenchyma. Consequently, a positive response to bronchodilator therapy does not always accompany a decrease in resistance as measured by passive mechanics. A significant improvement in tidal volume delivery and compliance may be enough to identify a positive response to bronchodilator therapy.

A time constant is the time required to fill or empty a lung unit to 65% of capacity and is calculated by multiplying compliance times resistance; therefore time constants vary as compliance and resistance change. It is estimated that time equal to three to five time constants is needed for complete emptying or filling of the lung unit. These data are useful in determining inspiratory and expiratory time settings for mechanical ventilation. Diseases such as obstructive airways disease with increased resistance necessitate longer than normal lung emptying time, whereas diseases such as hyaline membrane disease with decreased compliance necessitate a shorter filling time.

FRC is the volume of gas left in the lungs at the end of a tidal breath. Physiologically, it is the resting point between the opposing forces of the chest wall and lung parenchyma. Atelectasis decreases FRC, whereas air trapping increases it. PEEP helps to maintain FRC within the lungs during mechanical ventilation. Optimal PEEP may be defined as the level that accompanies the best compliance and best FRC values. Either the nitrogen washout or helium dilution technique is used for FRC measurement in patients receiving assisted ventilation. Both techniques measure only FRC that is in contact with patent airways and not FRC trapped behind plugged airways. A mechanical valve is used to switch from the ventilator circuit to the FRC test gas for ventilation until equilibration with the test gas. Test reliability depends on accurate equilibration with the test gas. Consequently, FRC cannot be measured in a patient with obvious gas leaks either around the endotracheal tube or through a chest tube. In addition, FRC cannot be tested in patients being given ≥80% oxygen for mechanical ventilation. The test gas used for FRC by nitrogen washout is 100% oxygen. Caution must be exercised in FRC testing in infants. Use of 100% oxygen may precipitate a transient increase in Pao_2, which may be of concern in premature infants at risk for retinopathy of prematurity or infants with ductal-dependent congenital cardiac disease in whom pulmonary blood flow may be adversely affected by elevated Pao_2. Normal infant values for FRC are 20 to 25 ml/kg. Predicted normal reference equations (based on gender, age, and height) are used in older patients taller than 100 cm.

RISKS AND COMPLICATIONS

Procedures for ventilator pulmonary function tests during conventional mechanical ventilation carry minimal risk for the patient. Care must be taken not to alter patient status with the addition of test circuits. All such circuits induce a small increase in mechanical dead space. It is often useful to remove capnography sensors during ventilator pulmonary function tests to reduce dead space. Fio_2 may need to be increased slightly to maintain a stable oximetry value. Improvement of pulmonary mechanics as measured by ventilator pulmonary function tests may not always accompany a change in arterial blood gases.

Care must be taken to ensure patient stability and test integrity whenever standard test circuits are modified for unusual testing situations such as high-frequency ventilation. The clinician must remain cognizant of what is measured, how it is measured, and why it is measured. High-frequency positive-pressure ventilation is administered with conventional ventilators at rates >60 cycles/min, maintaining bulk gas flow into and out of the lungs. Therefore ventilator pulmonary function tests can be performed as usual. High-frequency jet ventilation combines conventional bulk gas flow ventilation with high-velocity jets of gas injected through the distal end of the endo-

tracheal tube. Because these jets of gas do not pass through the pneumotachometer for ventilator pulmonary function tests, accurate testing cannot be accomplished. In addition, any occlusion of the endotracheal tube during jet ventilation by test circuits eliminates the safety outlet for pressure relief, and life-threatening injury can result. TFVLs and PVLs are measures of bulk gas flow and are not applicable to high-frequency oscillation. FRC may be measured during high-frequency oscillation; however, the value obtained will be the mean lung volume generated by pulsating airway pressure around the set mean airway pressure rather than FRC. Mean lung volume is slightly higher than true FRC under these conditions. The sliding valve used for occlusion during passive mechanics can be modified for testing during high-frequency oscillation to provide for measures of static compliance and airway resistance. These measures are made from exhalation outside the ventilator circuit and are not reliant on bulk gas flow. Each manufacturer of ventilator pulmonary function test equipment needs to provide specifications for circuit modifications. To date little has been published regarding the use of ventilator pulmonary function tests during extracorporeal membrane oxygenation or partial liquid ventilation. Further investigation is needed before guidelines can be established for the interpretation of ventilator pulmonary function tests performed during these ventilation techniques.

ADDITIONAL READING

Abramson AL, Goldstein MN, Stenzler A, Steele A. The use of tidal breathing flow volume loop in laryngo-tracheal diseases of neonates and infants. Laryngoscope 92:922-926, 1982.

American Thoracic Society and European Respiratory Society, eds. Respiratory mechanics in infants: Physiologic evaluation in health and disease (statement). Am Rev Respir Dis 147:474-496, 1993.

Boros SJ, Bing DR, Mammel MC, Hagen E, Gordon M. Using conventional infant ventilators at unconventional rates. Pediatrics 74:487-492, 1984.

• Denjean A, Guimaraes H, Migdal M, Miramand JL, Dehan M, Gaultier C. Dose-related bronchodilator response to aerosolized salbutamol in ventilator-dependent premature infants. J Pediatr 120:974-979, 1992.

England SJ. Current techniques for assessing pulmonary function in the newborn and infant: Advantages and limitations. Pediatr Pulmonol 4:48-53, 1988.

Farstad T, Bratlid D. Effects of endotracheal tube size and ventilator settings on the mechanics of a test system during intermittent flow ventilation. Pediatr Pulmonol 11:15-21, 1991.

• Fisher JB, Mammel MC, Coleman JM, Bing DR, Boros SJ. Identifying lung overdistension during mechanical ventilation by using volume-pressure loops. Pediatr Pulmonol 5:10-14, 1988.

Guslits BG, Wilkie RA, England SJ. Comparison of methods of measurement of compliance of the respiratory system in children. Am Rev Respir Dis 136:727-729, 1987.

Heaf DP, Turner H, Stocks J, Helms P. Comparison of occlusion and inflation techniques for measuring total respiratory compliance in sick intubated infants. Pediatr Pulmonol 3:78-82, 1987.

Hirschl RB, Parent A, Tooley R, McCracken M, Johnson K, Shaffer TH, Wolfson MR, Bartlett RH. Liquid ventilation improves pulmonary function, gas exchange, and lung injury in a model of respiratory failure. Ann Surg 221:79-88, 1995.

Lesouef PN, England SJ, Bryan AC. Passive respiratory mechanics in newborns and children. Am Rev Respir Dis 129:552-556, 1984.

Lesouef PN, England SJ, Bryan AC. Total resistance of the respiratory system in preterm infants with and without an endotracheal tube. J Pediatr 104:108-111, 1984.

Mammel MC, Boros SJ, Bing DR, Holloman KK, Connett JR. Determining optimum inspiratory time during intermittent positive pressure ventilation in surfactant-depleted cats. Pediatr Pulmonol 7:223-229, 1989.

Mammel MC, Fisher JB, Bing DR, Gatto CW, Boros SJ. Effect of spontaneous and mechanical breathing on dynamic lung mechanics in hyaline membrane disease. Pediatr Pulmonol 8:222-225, 1990.

• Marini JJ. New options for ventilatory management of acute lung injury. New Horizons 1:489-503, 1993.

• Rosen WC, Mammel MC, Fisher JB, Coleman JM, Bing DR, Holloman KK, Boros SJ. The effects of bedside pulmonary mechanics testing during infant mechanical ventilation: A retrospective analysis. Pediatr Pulmonol 16:147-152, 1993.

Seear M, Wensley D, Werner H. Comparison of three methods for measuring respiratory mechanics in ventilated children. Pediatr Pulmonol 10:291-295, 1991.

Simbruner G, Gregory GA. Performance of neonatal ventilators: The effects of changes in resistance and compliance. Crit Care Med 9:509-519, 1981.

Sivan Y, Deakers TW, Newth CJL. An automated bedside method for measuring functional residual capacity by N_2 washout in mechanically ventilated children. Pediatr Res 28:446-450, 1990.

• Sivan Y, Deakers TW, Newth CJL. Functional residual capacity in ventilated infants and children. Pediatr Res 28:451-454, 1990.

Tepper RS, Asdell S. Comparison of helium dilution and nitrogen washout measurements of functional residual capacity in infants and very young children. Pediatr Pulmonol 13:250-254, 1992.

151 Oxygen Consumption Measurements

Gary Goodman · Anthony Amponsem · Dan Cooper

BACKGROUND AND INDICATIONS

Oxygen is essential for cellular respiration. A wide range of diseases (e.g., cardiorespiratory arrest, acute respiratory distress syndrome, and shock) affect the body as a result of impaired oxygen delivery or impaired oxygen utilization. Understanding oxygen delivery and measuring oxygen consumption are therefore central principles in critical care medicine. Oxygen is the most important substrate carried by the circulation, and compared with its rate of use has the lowest stores. The amount of oxygen available to the body declines as the gas moves from the atmosphere to the individual cell. This decremental decline has been described as the oxygen cascade. Barometric pressure, humidity, minute ventilation, diffusion of gas across the pulmonary capillary, ventilation-perfusion matching, blood flow, and hemoglobin concentration all affect the efficiency of oxygen delivery and can reduce the availability of oxygen to the tissues. In addition, the metabolic rates of different organs and tissues can vary, altering oxygen consumption. The three central components of oxygen delivery are oxygen saturation, hemoglobin concentration, and blood flow (cardiac output). The body can tolerate a reduction of 50% in any of these components individually. Smaller declines, however, in more than one component will have serious and often permanent consequences if not rapidly corrected.

The transport of oxygen to tissues is a paradigm in critical care. The free oxygen molecule, however, does not dissolve easily in blood; rather, nearly 99% of oxygen is carried bound to hemoglobin, which has a great affinity for oxygen. The amount of oxygen bound by hemoglobin is determined not by Pa_{O_2} but directly as the percent saturation of hemoglobin. This is measured either with co-oximetry in the blood gas laboratory or noninvasively with pulse oximetry. Thus oxygen content is the product of hemoglobin concentration, percent saturation of hemoglobin with oxygen, and amount of oxygen each gram of hemoglobin can carry:

$$Ca_{O_2} = Hb \times 1.34 \times Sa_{O_2}$$

The amount of oxygen dissolved in the blood is insignificant (except under circumstances of hyperbaric oxygen therapy) and is the product of Pa_{O_2} and the solubility of oxygen in blood:

$$Dissolved\ O_2 = Pa_{O_2} \times 0.003$$
$$(ml\ of\ oxygen/1\ mm\ Hg\ P_{O_2})$$

Oxygen content can be determined from any blood sample: arterial, venous, or mixed venous (pulmonary artery).

Oxygen delivery, in turn, is the product of oxygen content (oxygen bound to hemoglobin plus dissolved oxygen) and cardiac output:

$$D_{O_2} = Ca_{O_2} \times CO$$

Cardiac output is measured directly by thermodilution with a pulmonary artery catheter. With samples of arterial and mixed venous (pulmonary artery) blood and the cardiac output determination, oxygen consumption can be inferred by measuring the arteriovenous oxygen content difference: $Ca_{O_2} - Cv_{O_2}$.

Oxygen consumption can be determined either indirectly using the Fick relationship, in which oxygen consumption is inferred from the product of cardiac output and arteriovenous oxygen content difference, or directly by respiratory gas analysis.

TECHNIQUE

Assessment of oxygen consumption begins at the bedside with physical examination of the patient.

Temperature, heart rate, work of breathing, and agitation all contribute significantly to oxygen consumption. Clinical assessment of tissue perfusion by such indicators as skin color and temperature, pulse volume, capillary refill time, urinary output, and mental status can suggest states of decreased tissue perfusion and oxygenation (Table 151-1). Laboratory findings of metabolic acidosis and lactic acidosis suggest global inadequacy of oxygen delivery. Indirect measurement of oxygen consumption requires specific information determined at the bedside and in the laboratory. Arterial and mixed oxygen content are calculated by measurement of S_{O_2} and P_{O_2} with co-oximetry from appropriate blood samples and determination of hemoglobin concentration (Table 151-2). Cardiac output is determined by thermodilution. Oxygen consumption can be estimated using the Fick relationship:

$$O_2 \text{ consumption} = V_{O_2} = CI \times a\text{-}vD_{O_2} \times 10$$

Oxygen extraction can also be expressed as a percentage of the delivered oxygen that is consumed and is normally about 30%. Oxygen extraction defines the balance between oxygen supply (delivery) and demand (consumption). The oxygen extraction ratio is another method to determine trends in oxygen use and adequacy of oxygen delivery.

Oxygen consumption can also be measured directly with respiratory gas analysis and direct calorimetry. Original measurements were through collection of expired gases with a Douglas bag or a Tissot spirometer. More recently pneumotachometers or gas exchange analyzers have been developed to measure mixed expired oxygen and carbon dioxide concentrations for calculation of oxygen consumption. These systems measure the respiratory tidal volume via a collection compartment, which is used at the same time as an expiratory mixing chamber to measure expired oxygen and carbon dioxide concentration from the mixed gas. Oxygen consumption is obtained from the following calculation:

$$V_{O_2} = VE \left[(1 - F_{E_{O_2}} - F_{E_{CO_2}}/1 - F_{I_{O_2}}) \times F_{I_{O_2}} - F_{E_{O_2}} \right]$$

where VE = expired volume of gas in liters per minute at standard temperature and pressure dry con-

Table 151-1 Clinical Assessment of Tissue Oxygenation

Organ System	Clinical Sign or Laboratory Measurement	Alteration
Metabolic	Core temperature	Hypothermia
	pH	Acidosis
	Serum lactate	Elevation
CNS	Mental status	Confusion or depression
Cardiac	Perfusion	Delayed capillary refill
	Systemic arterial blood pressure	Hypotension
Pulmonary	Pa_{O_2}, Pa_{CO_2}	Hypoxemia, hypercapnia
	Respiratory muscle function	Hyperpnea, apnea
Renal	Urinary output	Decreased

Table 151-2 Clinical Measurement and Calculation of Oxygen Variables

Variable	Measurement or Calculation	Normal Range
Arterial blood gas	Pa_{O_2}	80-100 mm Hg
	Sa_{O_2}	90%-100%
Hemoglobin	Oxygen content = Ca_{O_2} = $(Sa_{O_2} \times Hb \times 1.34) + (0.003 \times Pa_{O_2})$	17-20 ml/dl
Cardiac index	Oxygen delivery = D_{O_2} = $Ca_{O_2} \times CI \times 10$	570-670 ml/min/m²
Mixed venous blood gas	$P\overline{v}_{O_2}$	37-43 mm Hg
	$S\overline{v}_{O_2}$	70%-76%
Ateriovenous oxygen difference	$a\text{-}vD_{O_2}$ = $Ca_{O_2} - C\overline{v}_{O_2}$	4-5 ml/dl
Oxygen consumption	$\dot{V}_{O_2}$ = $CI \times a\text{-}vD_{O_2} \times 10$	120-200 ml/min/m²
Oxygen extraction ratio	$\dot{V}_{O_2}/D_{O_2}$	20%-30%

ditions, FE_{O_2} = proportion of oxygen in mixed expiratory gas, FE_{CO_2} = proportion of carbon dioxide in mixed expiratory gas, and FI_{O_2} = fractional inspired oxygen.

With the availability of commercial metabolic carts, indirect calorimetry is being used increasingly at the bedside for direct patient management. Limitations to the technique include the following: gas sensors must be frequently calibrated; measurements are only for a limited period, generally 20 to 60 seconds; and large errors are expected when patients need an FI_{O_2} of 1.0.

Continuous monitoring of arterial and mixed venous oxygen saturations can be performed by a combination of noninvasive pulse oximetry and an indwelling fiberoptic pulmonary artery catheter. Changes in mixed venous oxygen saturation imply a changing relationship between oxygen delivery and consumption. A high mixed venous oxygen saturation implies either increased oxygen delivery or decreased extraction; a low mixed venous oxygen saturation suggests decreased oxygen delivery or increased extraction. Interval measurement of oxygen delivery and consumption can confirm such trends. However, many experts believe this is too indirect and global an assessment of tissue oxygenation to be clinically useful. Individual organs have different values of oxygen extraction that may vary with stress and in different disease states. Newer approaches to this problem are being focused on assessment of specific tissue oxygenation such as measurement of interstitial gastric pH with balloon tonometry. Sophisticated techniques, including near-infrared and magnetic resonance spectroscopy, may also provide important information about energy production.

Interventions that positively influence the oxygen delivery–oxygen consumption relationship are intended to decrease oxygen consumption and increase oxygen delivery. Oxygen consumption can be decreased by decreasing metabolic expenditures (e.g., maintaining normothermia, correcting metabolic abnormalities, sedation and muscle relaxation, and assisted ventilation). Oxygen delivery is augmented by optimizing the determinants of oxygen content and cardiac output (e.g., hemoglobin concentration, arterial oxygenation, preload, contractility, afterload, and heart rate).

The focus of much research has been on the re-

lationship between oxygen delivery and consumption. Normally, oxygen delivery exceeds oxygen consumption 3-fold. In healthy persons oxygen delivery can be increased 5-fold during exercise. In contrast, a state of supply-dependent oxygen consumption or pathologic supply dependency has been described in critically ill patients. Some authorities have recommended increasing oxygen delivery to supranormal levels to attempt to improve oxygen consumption. Recent studies in critically ill adults and in children after cardiac surgery could not confirm an increase in oxygen consumption with increasing oxygen delivery and did not alter morbidity or mortality. Early resuscitation and in particular rapid and adequate volume expansion are crucial in patients in shock. Delays in treatment are associated with development of refractory tissue hypoxia.

Table 151-3 reviews the pathophysiology of different disease states that may affect oxygen content, delivery, or use. Optimizing oxygen consumption involves treating the underlying disease process and augmenting compensatory mechanisms that balance the pathophysiologic derangement. Table 151-4 illustrates various manipulations that favorably affect oxygen delivery and consumption. It is important not only to improve oxygen content, delivery, and uptake but also to reduce oxygen use by lowering metabolic demands. Monitoring clinical signs of end-organ function in addition to periodic invasive measurements of hemodynamic and oxygen variables allows the clinician to determine the response to different interventions and the changing physiology of the patient.

RISKS AND COMPLICATIONS

Therapeutic interventions based on measurement of cardiopulmonary variables can be instituted safely in a PICU in which the nursing and medical staff are knowledgeable about their significance as well as limitations of the technology. Noninvasive bedside monitoring of heart rate, respiratory rate, and temperature, Doppler measurement of systemic blood pressure, and continuous pulse oximetry can be accomplished with few risks and complications. Invasive measurement of arterial blood pressure with indwelling vascular catheters may be complicated by infection, bleeding, thrombosis, vasospasm, or emboli. Potential risks of pulmonary artery catheters include bleeding, infection, arrhythmias, and emboli. See ap-

Table 151-3 Derangements of Oxygen Transport

Mechanism	Pathophysiology	Clinical Examples
Decreased oxygen content	Hypoxemia	Pneumonia
	Anemia	Hemorrhage
	Reduced hemoglobin-binding sites	Sickle cell hemoglobin, methemoglobin, carbon monoxide poisoning
Decreased oxygen delivery	Decreased cardiac output	
	Inadequate preload	Hypovolemia
	Diminished contractility	Cardiomyopathy, heart surgery, congenital heart disease
	Excessive systemic afterload	Systemic hypertension
	Excessive pulmonary afterload	Pulmonary hypertension
	Reduced regional blood flow	Elevated ICP
	Increased Hb affinity for oxygen	Alkalosis, hypothermia, carbon monoxide poisoning
Altered oxygen use	Increased tissue oxygen requirements	Burns, hyperpyrexia, hyperthyroidism
	Inability of tissues to use oxygen	Septic shock

Table 151-4 Manipulation of Oxygen Parameters

Goal	Method
Oxygen content	
Increase oxygen-carrying capacity	Transfusion of packed RBCs: Hct 35%-45%
	Maintenance of normal pH
	Maintenance of normothermia
Increase Hb saturation	Administration of supplemental oxygen
	Continuous positive airway pressure
	PEEP
	Positive pressure ventilation
Increase dissolved oxygen	Hyperbaric oxygen
Oxygen delivery	
Optimize cardiac output	
Heart rate	
Low	Administration of atropine, isoproterenol; placement of cardiac pacemaker
High	Provision of sedation, volume, pharmacologic therapy
Preload	Maintenance of optimum cardiac filling pressures
Contractility	Administration of glucose, calcium, oxygen, inotropic agents
Afterload	
Pulmonary	Maintenance of increased alveolar oxygen, hyperventilation, alkalosis; administration of pharmacologic vasodilators
Systemic	Administration of pharmacologic vasodilators
Oxygen uptake	
Optimize unloading of oxygen	Maintenance of normothermia, acid-base balance, Sa_{O_2} >85%
Optimize regional blood flow	
Renal	Administration of low-dose dopamine (3-5 μg/kg/min)
Cerebral	Decrease ICP
	Maintenance of cerebral perfusion pressure
Cardiac	Support of diastolic blood pressure
Decrease oxygen use	Administration of sedatives, muscle relaxants, paralysis
	Mechanical ventilation (to decrease work of breathing)
	Maintenance of normothermia

propriate chapters for details on these procedures. Respiratory gas analysis requires experienced respiratory therapists. These devices should not interfere with ongoing ventilatory support.

ADDITIONAL READING

• Dantzker DR. Adequacy of tissue oxygenation. Crit Care Med 21:S40-S43, 1993.

Edwards JD, Shoemaker WC, Vincent JL, eds. Oxygen Transport: Principles and Practice. Philadelphia: WB Saunders, 1993.

Gattinoni L, Brazzi L, Pelosi P, et al. A trial of goal-directed hemodynamic therapy in critically ill patients. N Engl J Med 333:1025-1032, 1995.

• Leach RM, Treacher DF. The relationship between oxygen delivery and consumption. Dis Mon 40:303-368, 1994.

Seear M, Wensley D, MacNab A. Oxygen consumption-oxygen delivery relationship in children. J Pediatr 123:208-214, 1993.

Snyder JV, Pinsky MR, eds. Oxygen Transport in the Critically Ill. Chicago: Year Book, 1987.

Westenskow DR, Cuttler CA, Wallace WD. Instrumentation for monitoring gas exchange and metabolic rate in critically ill patients. Crit Care Med 12:183-187, 1984.

152 Intubation and Difficult Airway Management

Sheryl Wright · Frances C. Morriss · Kory D. Toro

INDICATIONS FOR INTUBATION

Despite the often emergent nature of airway problems in children, placement of an ET tube must be approached in a deliberate and calm manner if trauma to the airway and patient instability are to be avoided. Regardless of the indications for intubation, airway control must be established immediately with the use of bag and mask ventilation while equipment, personnel, and supplies are being readied. Intubation will proceed more safely in an oxygenated and physiologically stable patient. Although establishing a patent airway and providing adequate ventilation are not synonymous with intubation, intubation provides a closed system of ventilation while ensuring patency and protection of the airway. Specific indications for intubation are listed below:

Apnea

Acute respiratory failure (PaO_2 <50 mm Hg in patient with FiO_2 >0.5 and PaCO_2 >55 mm Hg acutely; see Chapter 9)

Need to control oxygen delivery (e.g., institution of PEEP, accurate delivery of FiO_2 >0.5)

Need to control ventilation (e.g., to decrease work of breathing, to control PaCO_2, to provide muscle relaxation)

Inadequate chest wall function (e.g., in patient with Guillain-Barré syndrome, poliomyelitis, flail chest)

Upper airway obstruction

Need to protect the airway of a patient whose protective reflexes are absent

INTUBATION TECHNIQUE

The process of intubation involves placement of a flexible tube into the opening of the upper airway, the larynx, from the oropharyngeal or nasopharyngeal route using a lighted blade to assist visualization.

The soft tissues of the oral cavity (tongue, tonsils, and uvula) must be displaced and the axis of the pharyngeal airway aligned with the axis of the larynx to accomplish tube placement (Fig. 152-1). Laryngoscopy and intubation elicit a number of physiologic

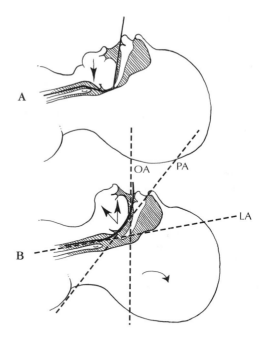

Fig. 152-1 Axis of oral pharyngeal and laryngeal airways. **A,** Normal airway with head at neutral position. (Note that tongue tends to obscure opening to laryngeal airway.) **B,** Alignment of pharyngeal and laryngeal airway to permit visualization with laryngoscopy from pharynx by placing head in sniffing position. (OA = Oral axis; PA = pharyngeal axis; LA = laryngeal axis.) (Redrawn from Salem MR, Wong AY, Collins VJ. The pediatric patient with a full stomach. Anesthesiology 39:435-440, 1973.)

responses and reflexes that must be recognized and managed appropriately:

Airway protective reflexes (neurologically mediated via glossopharyngeal and vagal nerves)
  Glottic closure (laryngospasm)
  Cough
  Gag and retch
  Sneeze
Cardiovascular responses
  Sinus bradycardia (direct vagal stimulation)
  Tachycardia and hypertension (neuroendocrine mediation via sympathetic efferents)
  Arrhythmias, especially if patient becomes hypoxic

Equipment

All necessary equipment for airway support including intubation must be available and functional before attempting intubation. The equipment may be placed in a portable cart or tool box to facilitate portability for emergency situations in which speed may be essential. Minimal equipment needs are listed below:

Intubation equipment

Laryngoscope handles and blades of various sizes and types
Oral or uncut ET tubes of various sizes with standard 6 mm connectors, cuffed and uncuffed, single use preferred
Suction equipment (source of vacuum, tonsil suction, catheters)
Nasogastric or large-bore, soft red-rubber catheters
Bag and mask of appropriate sizes
Oxygen source
Atropine
Supplies for securing ET tube
Oral and nasal airways of various sizes
Personal protection equipment
Stethoscope
Optional equipment
  Nasotracheal tubes
  Magill forceps
  Stylets (tip protection preferred)
  Specialized tubes
  Manometer to measure airway pressure
  Afrin nasal spray
  Intubation pillow

Straight laryngoscope blades (Miller, Phillips, or Seward) are more useful in neonates and infants because the angulation of the infantile epiglottis hampers the use of a curved blade (MacIntosh), which is usually placed in the vallecula behind the epiglottis.

A short, stubby handle can be particularly useful for intubation of a patient with a short neck and/or a prominent chest.

Uncut *oral* ET tubes should range in size from 2.0 to 6.0 mm uncuffed and 5.5 to 8.0 mm cuffed. Although cuffed tubes of sizes smaller than 5.5 mm are available, they are not recommended because the addition of a cuff to an ET tube decreases the tube's internal diameter. Since the resistance for laminar flow is related inversely to the fourth power of the tube's radius, a small decrease in the internal diameter results in a larger increase in resistance. Cuffs, if used, must be the low-pressure, high-volume type to minimize circumferential tracheal mucosal trauma. The material composing the tube must be biologically compatible with human tissue; polyvinylchloride tubes have low tissue toxicity and suitable malleability without being rigid. Tubes with a shoulder (Cole) are not recommended because their use is associated with increased trauma to the glottis, particularly the arytenoid cartilages. Desirable characteristics of tube design include transparent material, beveled tip, sequential centimeter indicators along the length, identification of tube size on the connectors or cuff pilot tube, and a radiopaque marking to assess position. A lateral fenestration at the tip (Murphy eye) opposite to the bevel allows an alternate pathway for gas flow should the tip become occluded. Some clinicians believe the eye creates an additional nidus for accumulation of secretions.

The tonsil suction is the most effective device for removing blood and thick mucus from the airway. Catheters are more effective for removing secretions from the ET tube. As with other procedures that expose the operator to body secretions, gloves and glasses or goggles must be worn during intubation.

Assistants

Training a specific group of personnel, usually respiratory care specialists, from the PICU staff to assist with intubation will ensure appropriate support for the intubator and increased safety since all health care workers present will have predetermined tasks and responsibilities. The assistant to the intubator is responsible for assembling and checking function of necessary equipment, positioning the patient, applying cricoid pressure if needed, managing bag and mask ventilation if needed, securing the ET tube, and determining the amount of leak around the tube. The patient's nurse administers the IV medication and assesses vital signs throughout the procedure. If hypoxia or hemodynamic instability occur, the procedure must be stopped for appropriate treatment to stabilize the patient. In addition, the assistant group can be responsible for care, organization, and maintenance of equipment between uses and for transporting it to distant locations.

Continuous cardiorespiratory monitoring (EEG, systemic arterial blood pressure, heart rate, and oxygen saturation) is desirable throughout the procedure; if such monitoring is unavailable, one assistant must be responsible for monitoring pulse by palpation and oxygenation by visual assessment and reporting any changes to the intubator. If it is practical, secure an IV line for drug administration.

Procedure

Quickly assess the patient's airway for obvious anatomic abnormalities, including the ability to move the neck and open the mouth (see p. 1399). If time allows, assess for presence of protective airway reflexes, empty the stomach with a large-bore nasogastric tube, soft oral red-rubber catheter, or suction catheter and remove the tube. This step is particularly important if the patient has been fed recently or has gastric distention.

Oxygenate the patient with 100% oxygen for 2 to 3 minutes to replace alveolar air with oxygen and thus provide an added source of oxygen should the patient become apneic. Optimal saturation for intubation is 100% or the same as the patient's normal saturation. If the patient is a premature infant, optimal saturation is 96% to 97%.

While the patient receives oxygen, select the appropriate laryngoscope and appropriate type and size of tube. Proper tube diameter for children over 2 years of age may be estimated by the formula.

$$\text{Tube size} = \frac{\text{Age in years}}{4} + 4.5$$

Often the diameter of the patient's fifth finger correlates well with airway size. In children over 6 to 8 years of age cuffed tubes are appropriate, especially if sealing the airway to prevent an air leak is desirable. Most children this age need a 6.0 to 6.5 mm tube; often the presence of an uninflated cuff is sufficient to prevent an air leak around the tube. Select a tube one size larger and one size smaller than the expected size. *For emergency situations oral tube placement is technically easier to perform and there-*

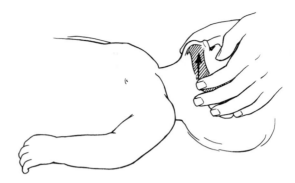

Fig. 152-2   Sniffing position. Head is slightly extended; jaw is elevated and pulled forward.

fore safer and faster. If a cuffed tube is selected, test the cuff for patency and absence of leaks. Consider the use of atropine (0.02 mg/kg IV) to block the vagus nerve, especially in neonates and infants in whom bradycardia is common.

Position the child with the intubator at his head, removing the head of the bed if necessary. The patient's head must be in the sniffing position (i.e., head slightly extended with the jaw thrust forward) (Fig. 152-2). The normal occipital prominence of a neonate will maintain a sniffing position. Hyperextension of the head will obstruct the airway and interfere with visualization of the larynx (the axes of the laryngeal and oropharyngeal airways diverge with hyperextension). An assistant must gently restrain the patient's arms, shoulders, and head and direct a flow of oxygen over his face. Open the patient's mouth widely and insert the laryngoscope blade (grasped firmly in the left hand) in the right side of the mouth. Move the blade to the midline, keeping the tongue trapped to the left of the blade. Place a curved blade in the vallecula behind the epiglottis and a straight blade in front of the epiglottis (Fig. 152-3). Lift superiorly with a motion from the shoulder. Do not bend the wrist since this forces the blade against the teeth and gums and elevates the blade tip, pushing the larynx out of the line of vision. As the blade is lifted and withdrawn slightly, the larynx should drop into view.

From the right side of the mouth insert the ET tube under direct vision several centimeters through the vocal cords. Insertion of the tube down the blade may entrap the tube in the blade groove, preventing easy placement. Gentle posterior or downward pressure over the cricoid cartilage may be helpful in vi-

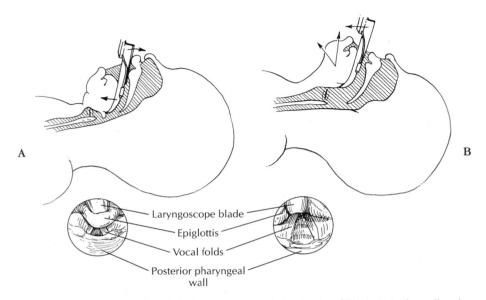

A

B

Laryngoscope blade
Epiglottis
Vocal folds
Posterior pharyngeal
wall

Fig. 152-3   Proper position of straight laryngoscope blade. **A,** Tip of blade is in the vallecula and is being used as a lever to push against upper alveolar ridge. (Inset: Epiglottis is pushed down obscuring opening. **B,** Tip of blade has picked up epiglottis and head is lifted, not lowered. (Inset: Soft tissue is trapped by blade and view of larynx is improved.)

sualizing a larynx that appears to be displaced anteriorly (Fig. 152-4). Alternatively, a stylet can direct the tip of tube anteriorly (Fig. 152-5). In a neonate cricoid pressure can be applied by the intubator using the fifth finger; however, in older infants and children an assistant must apply the pressure. Since the axis of the infantile larynx is angled anteriorly away from the tracheal axis, the tube tends to abut anteriorly as it is advanced; this may be corrected by flexing the patient's head slightly or by twisting the tube in a corkscrew motion.

If the patient becomes desaturated or bradycardic at any time, institute bag and mask ventilation with 100% oxygen immediately. The smallest diameter of the infant airway is at the cricoid cartilage; thus a tube may pass through the vocal cords and then meet resistance. Do not force the tube if this occurs: reintubate with a smaller sized tube. Inflate the cuff (if present) with the smallest amount of air necessary to eliminate an air leak around the tube. Should the patient regurgitate stomach contents, quickly place him in the lateral head-down position and suction the pharynx with the tonsil sucker. See Table 152-1 for common problems during intubation and possible solutions.

Once the patient's trachea is intubated, ventilate him with a breathing bag and check for bilaterally equal breath sounds. Use a rapid rate of bag compressions so the person listening can easily distinguish this respiratory pattern from air movement in a spontaneously breathing but esophageally intubated patient. Louder or absent breath sounds on one side indicate that the tube lies in a mainstem bronchus and must be withdrawn until the breath sounds become equal. Breath sounds are generally absent over the stomach; with esophageal intubation, transmitted breath sounds can be heard over the chest but will be louder over the stomach. In addition, the child will be able to phonate. The chest wall will move with pressure on the breathing bag; absent movement suggests an obstructed tube or esophageal intubation. If the child is breathing spontaneously, look for corresponding movement of the bag. If any doubt exists about the tube position, use the laryngoscope to visualize the patient's vocal cords and check the tube position visually. If the patient's condition deteriorates, remove the tube, reestablish bag and mask ventilation, and check for plugging or other mechanical problems. See p. 1392 for ways to verify correct tube placement.

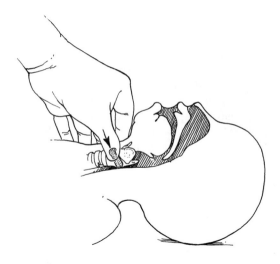

Fig. 152-4 Application of cricoid pressure. Gentle pressure, applied perpendicularly over cricoid cartilage, will occlude the esophagus, protecting against passive regurgitation, and will push the larynx inferiorly.

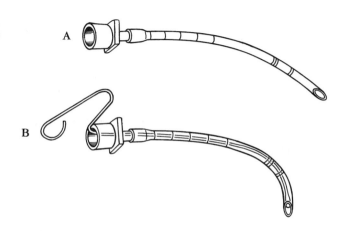

Fig. 152-5 **A,** Usual curvature of ET tube. **B,** Styleted ET tube with tip directed anteriorly. (Note tip of stylet does not protrude from end of tube.)

Table 152-1 Intubation Problem Solving

Problem	Strategies
Difficulty identifying anatomic features	Check head position; need sniffing position, not extreme hyperextension of neck
	Suction secretions from airway
	Open mouth widely
	Afrin for epistaxis
Inability to see glottic opening	Check light for brightness
	Lift epiglottis with straight blade
	Check blade position with respect to base of tongue; use conger blade to bypass base of tongue
	Patient not paralyzed; ventilate and wait for relaxation
Inability to see vocal cords	Lift laryngoscope blade; levering displaces larynx superiorly and away from intubator's line of vision
	Gentle cricoid pressure
	Stylet in "hockey stick" position
Inability to pass tube	Tube diameter too large
	Tube abutting anteriorly, bring head slightly forward
	Use Magill forceps with nasal tube

Check the tube for appropriate size by assessing the amount of air leakage present when graded positive pressure (using a manometer in the circuit) is applied. A leak of air that occurs around the tube at 15 to 25 cm H_2O pressure indicates proper tube diameter. With leaks occurring at >25 cm H_2O pressure, laryngeal and tracheal mucosal damage is more likely. With leaks of <15 cm H_2O pressure, mechanical ventilation may be difficult because of volume loss. The leak is best heard by auscultation, with a stethoscope placed over the larynx or the open mouth.

Stabilize the tube with adhesive tape and tincture of benzoin (Figs. 152-6 and 152-7). Do not release the tube until it is secure and the patient is restrained.

METHODS OF ASSESSING CORRECT TUBE PLACEMENT

Auscultation over anterior lung fields and stomach
Observation of appropriate chest wall movement with bagging
Appropriate curve on capnograph
Appropriate movement of bag if patient is breathing spontaneously
Direct visualization of tube in larynx by laryngoscopy or intraluminal fiberoptic device
Chest radiograph

Finding	*Cause*
Breath sounds heard loudest over stomach; enlarging stomach, absent capnograph tracing with ventilation	Esophageal intubation
Asymmetric movement of chest with bagging	Mainstem bronchial intubation, pneumothorax, bronchial obstruction
Unequal breath sounds	Mainstem bronchial intubation, pneumothorax, bronchospasm
No breath sounds over lungs or stomach, abnormal saturation, increased inflating pressure	Plugged ET tube, severe bronchospasm, tracheal obstruction below ET tube

When in doubt, take out the tube and ventilate patient. Try again.

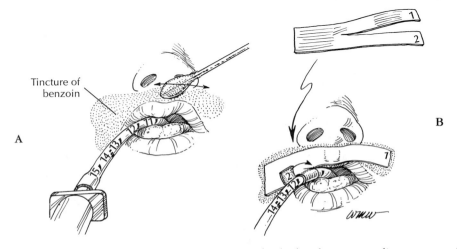

Fig. 152-6   Securing an oral tube. **A,** Tube position is checked with respect to lip or gum and tincture of benzoin applied to upper lip. **B,** Tape is torn in half in approximately half of its length. Upper portion of tape is applied to upper lip and lower portion is wrapped securely around the tube.

Obtain a chest radiograph to check tube position; the tip should lie in the trachea, midway between the carina and the clavicles. Accidental extubation is much more likely when the tip is above the clavicles. Check for pneumothorax as well. Once the correct position is established, cut the tube to an appropriate length to minimize dead space. Record size, length of tube referenced to patients' lips or gum, and pressure at which leak is heard in the chart or Kardex or on the respiratory care flow sheet.

DIFFICULT AIRWAY MANAGEMENT

Ideally, intubation is performed in the operating suite in a healthy patient undergoing planned, controlled tracheal intubation for an elective procedure. This is not the case in the PICU where intubation is necessary for airway control in the acute situation. Known

and predictable anatomic obstacles to successful intubation must be given special consideration. A pharmacologic approach tailored to the patient's intercurrent illness will streamline the procedure and minimize the stress of intubation on the patient as well. In addition, a predetermined plan for alternate airway maintenance in the event difficulty is encountered will minimize morbidity and mortality.

Tracheal intubation depends on the ability to establish a line of vision from the alveolar ridge to the glottic opening. Two anatomic obstacles must be overcome to accomplish this: alignment of airway axes (see Fig. 152-1) and displacement of soft tissue structures. To align the three airway axes (oral, pharyngeal, and laryngeal) in older children, the neck is extended and the head tilted backward with a small pillow under the occiput and the jaw thrust forward

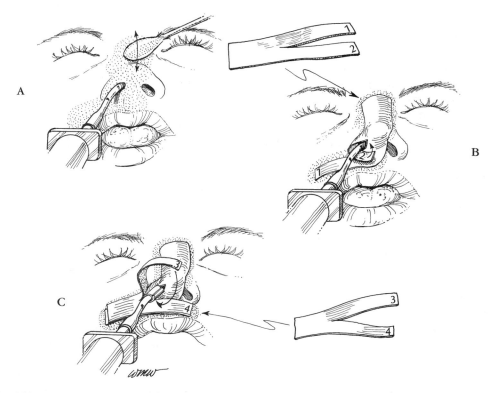

Fig. 152-7   Securing a nasotracheal tube. **A,** Tube position is noted in centimeters along the tube and tincture of benzoin is applied to bridge of nose and upper lip. **B,** Tape is prepared in same manner as for oral tube and is applied to the bridge of nose. One end *(1)* is applied to upper lip and the second *(2)* to the shaft of tube. **C,** A second piece of tape is prepared. The untorn end is applied to the cheek with the lower piece *(4)* laid securely along the upper lip; the other *(3)* is wrapped around the tube with the first piece of tape underlying the wrap. (Note that the area where the tube and its connector meet is left unobscured for observation.)

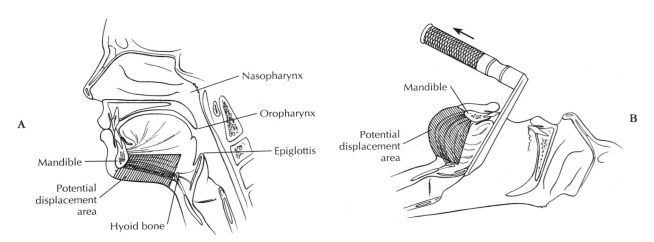

Fig. 152-8 **A,** Diagram of airway demonstrating potential displacement area of soft tissue intubation. **B,** Laryngoscopy with displacement of tongue and soft tissue into potential displacement area. (Redrawn from Berry FA, Yemen TA. Pediatric airway in health and disease. Pediatr Clin North Am 41:153-180, 1994.)

(sniffing position) (see Fig. 152-2). In younger children and infants the occiput is large in relation to the upper torso and the pillow is placed under the neck and shoulders to prevent flexion of the head on the chest while maintaining the neck in a slightly extended position. Anything that interferes with the ability to position the head and neck in this manner will make intubation more difficult.

The tongue and related soft tissues need to be displaced into an area called the potential displacement area (Fig. 152-8). This area is a bony box in the hypopharyngeal and inframandibular area and is bound by the anterior ramus of the mandible, the lateral rami of the mandible, and the hyoid bone.

Anatomic Considerations
Dysmorphic syndromes

Several dysmorphic syndromes that include any of the following features will present anatomic obstacles to intubation as a consequence of the inability to align airway axes or to displace the tongue and soft tissues (see Appendix, p. 1404)

   Micrognathia (small mandible)
   Retrognathia (underdevelopment of the mandible)
   Glossoptosis (posterior displacement of the tongue)
   Macroglossia (large tongue)
   Microstomia (small mouth)

   Short or fixed neck
   Poor mandibular mobility
   Atlantoaxial instability

Normal growth and development of the airway

The size of the head in relation to the torso, the shape of the larynx, and its position relative to surrounding structures contribute to the difficulty of intubation in the very young. The normal newborn head and tongue are relatively large and the neck is short compared with older children. Anatomic features of the larynx are significantly different from those of the adult: the younger the patient the more anterior and superior is the glottic opening. The lower border of the cricoid cartilage is opposite the fourth cervical vertebra in the newborn. With growth, it moves relative to surrounding structures and can be found at the level of the fifth cervical vertebra by age 6. The larynx of the infant and small child is more funnel shaped, terminating in the cricoid ring, which is the narrowest diameter of the infant airway. The narrowest diameter of the adult airway is at the glottic opening; therefore visual estimation of appropriate tube size is possible. Since the cricoid cartilage cannot be visualized with laryngoscopy, appropriate tube size must be estimated for infants without visual confirmation. Up to the age of 8 years the diameter of cricoid cartilage is smaller than the opening to the vocal cords. The vocal cords attach lower anteriorly than posteriorly, appearing slanted in relation to the axis of the trachea, and visualization of the anterior commissure is often not possible. With maturation of the thyroid cartilage, the vocal cords are perpendicular to the tracheal axis and the larynx is more cylindric. Compared with the adult epiglottis, the infantile epiglottis is angled away from the axis of the trachea. At the time of laryngoscopy it appears to fall forward and obscure the opening of the glottis. The vocal cords are stiffer because the cuneiform cartilages occupy a greater proportion of the vocal cord length. Finally, the loosely attached laryngeal mucosa is more vulnerable to edema formation.

As maturation proceeds, the airway anatomically becomes that of the adult, with final growth occurring at puberty when male thyroid cartilage growth surpasses that of the female. For this reason, females of the same size and weight compared to males often need a half size smaller ET tube. Other changes in airway include development of luxurious lymphoid tissue in the oral and nasal pharynx during early childhood, loss and replacement of teeth at ages 5 to 7 years, and increasingly presence of dental appliances in the mouth of the preadolescent and adolescent child.

CONSIDERATIONS FOR USE OF PHARMACOLOGIC AGENTS FOR INTUBATION

1. Always use oxygen.
2. Will neuromuscular blockade facilitate intubation?
   - Is there a contraindication to paralysis? (Can patient be ventilated after paralysis?)
   - Is airway trauma likely?
   - Is this a difficult airway?
3. Will the usual reflexes associated with intubation put the patient at risk?
   - Parasympathetic (bradycardia)
   - Sympathetic (hypertension, tachycardia)
4. Should patient be amnestic for the procedure?
5. Are special techniques indicated? (Consider gastric protection, local anesthetic agents, drying agents, osmotic diuresis as adjuncts for specific identified needs.)
6. Are pathophysiologic processes present (e.g., hypovolemia, allergic phenomena, myocardial depression, bronchospasm) that must be considered before appropriate pharmacologic agents can be chosen?

Trauma and burns

Blunt and penetrating trauma can produce a spectrum of laryngotracheal injury ranging from simple laceration or contusion to complete transection. Hemoptysis, stridor, wheezing, or presence of subcutaneous air following trauma raises the suspicion of tracheal injury. Absence of these signs is not a reliable indicator of absence of injury. In fact, proximal soft tissue injury without actual airway injury can compromise the airway (hematoma, swelling, etc.)

Until evaluation of the cervical spine is complete, neck immobilization after any trauma is necessary. This can greatly affect the intubator's ability to visualize the vocal cords since neck extension cannot be used to align the divergent airway axes. The cervical collar can be removed if an assistant is available to maintain in-line cervical stabilization during laryngoscopy. Visualization can be further augmented by jaw thrust or manual chin lift (a second assistant is occasionally necessary for this maneuver). If cricoid pressure is used, caution must be exercised since this pressure is transmitted directly to the cervical spine

and can aggravate an unstable bony injury. If trained personnel and equipment are available, fiberoptic intubation needs to be considered early when cervical spine injury is suspected. If oral intubation is difficult or impossible and trained personnel and equipment are available, a surgical airway can be considered early.

In the burned patient, if the total body surface area is large enough to indicate fluid resuscitation (>10% total body surface area in children) with any facial or neck component or significant facial or neck burns are present regardless of the total burn size, early intubation is indicated because significant swelling and possible airway compromise can be anticipated in the first 24 hours after the burn injury.

When facial burns are present, the mechanism of injury must also be elucidated. Superheated fluids (steam) carry significant thermal energy and can pass deeply enough into the tracheobronchial tree to cause thermal injury to the lung. However, the usual inhalation injury is secondary to chemical irritants that cause immediate direct trauma to the airway.

The upper airway must be carefully inspected for mucosal inflammation, ulcers, or carbon deposits. Mirror laryngoscopy may facilitate the examination in the cooperative patient. The lower airway is inspected by flexible fiberoptic bronchoscopy after the airway has been protected by an ET tube.

Physiologic Considerations and Pharmacologic Approach

After the decision is made to proceed with intubation, the next decision that needs to be made is whether pharmacologic adjuncts are appropriate.

Unless intubation is part of airway management in the cardiopulmonary arrest situation or in patients with airway obstruction, most clinicians will prefer to intubate using some form of deep sedation or induced unconsciousness. Intubation in the awake state can elicit protective reflexes that trigger tachycardia, bradycardia, elevation of blood pressure, increased intracranial pressure, intraocular pressure, cough, and bronchospasm. Increased intracranial pressure, reactive airways disease, and reactive pulmonary vascular states are associated with changes in heart rate and blood pressure or presence of protective reflexes that produce undesirable side effects such as cerebral tissue shifts, increased airways resistance, or changes in pulmonary blood flow.

Pharmacologic control promotes a smoother intubation with less physiologic stress for the patient, who often is already in a compromised state. Loss of consciousness can be induced with an anesthetic induction agent in combination with a neuromuscular blocking agent to provide muscle relaxation. Neuromuscular blockade can greatly facilitate intubation and ventilation but must not be used unless the clinician is absolutely certain that adequate ventilation can be provided or that the patient can be intubated. Induction of paralysis under any other condition can be fatal because relaxation of airway muscles and soft tissues will obstruct the airway. Narcotics used in combination with anxiolytics can provide adequate intubating conditions when neuromuscular blockage is undesirable. Pharmacologic control also blunts the autonomic responses to the stimulus of intubation. In infants atropine (0.02 mg/kg IV) is often added to the drug regimen because instrumentation of the airway itself can directly stimulate vagal receptors and induce bradycardia. Lidocaine (1 to 1.5 mg/kg) may be given intravenously to blunt airway protective reflexes elicited by instrumentation.

Often drug choices are made based on the clinician's experience with a particular drug and the drug's immediate availability; however, the drug regimen chosen must be based on the patient's physiologic state. Agents with side effects that would exacerbate the pathophysiology involved must be avoided if possible. Useful agents are listed in Table 152-2.

Regardless of the drugs chosen, doses must be used that will induce the desired effect, particularly neuromuscular blocking agents. Reduction of doses from those recommended can cause incomplete paralysis, increase the difficulty of intubation, and lead to hypoxia from airway obstruction. The drugs recommended in Table 152-2 are appropriate to produce deep sedation with apnea and/or complete neuromuscular blockade. Allow sufficient time for drug effect to occur; a nurse or assistant can keep track of the time elapsed since administration of the drugs. Intubation attempts before complete sedation has occurred predispose to laryngospasm; blunting of autonomic reflexes will be incomplete.

Clinical Examples (Table 152-3)

In the patient with a full stomach risk of aspiration of gastric contents is high. After loss of protective airway reflexes most clinicians use rapid IV sequence with immediate acting drugs and cricoid pressure preceded by 3 minutes of preoxygenation with Fio_2 1.0 since bag and mask ventilation causes gastric distention and cannot be used until the ET tube is in place. Cricoid pressure must be maintained until the ET tube is in place and confirmed to provide adequate protection from aspiration. Conditions predisposing to aspiration of stomach contents include:

1. Recent meal (within 4 hours)
2. Trauma, shock, and pain
3. Delayed gastric emptying (pyloric stenosis, small bowel obstruction, ileus, narcotics, pregnancy, abdominal masses)
4. Esophageal motility disorders (history of tracheoesophageal fistula, diverticula, scleroderma)
5. Gastroesophageal reflux and hiatal hernia
6. Loss of protective airway reflexes (coma, CNS injuries, general anesthesia)
7. Airway obstruction

In the asthmatic patient the clinician must avoid drugs that release histamine (morphine, curare, or thiopental). The clinician might even choose to use the side effects of ketamine (bronchodilation) to

Table 152-2 Pharmacologic Agents Used for Intubation

Drugs	Dose*	Onset	Duration	Side Effects
Morphine	0.1-0.2 mg/kg IV (max 15 mg) Neonates: 0.05 mg/kg IV	Peak:20 min	2-4 hr in neonates	Histamine release, hypotension, peripheral vasodilation, euphoria, dysphoria, itching, sphincter of Oddi spasm, central nausea and vomiting, decreased response to hypercarbia
Fentanyl	1-3 μg/kg IV	1-3 min	30-90 min	Bradycardia, decreased response to hypercarbia, chest wall rigidity, itching
Diazepam	0.1-0.2 mg/kg IV	0.5-2 min	3 hr	Local irritation, pain
Midazolam	0.05-0.15 mg/kg IV	1-2.5 min	<2 hr	Nausea and vomiting, hiccoughs
Ketamine	1-2 mg/kg IV 4-5 mg/kg IM	1-3 min 3.5 min	10-15 min	Increased upper airway secretions, increased ICP, increased cerebral metabolic rate, emergence hallucinations, laryngospasm, hypertension, tachycardia, increased cardiac output, increased pulmonary artery pressures, decreased airways resistance, direct myocardial depressant
Thiopental	4-6 mg/kg IV	1-2 circulation times	10-30 min	Histamine release with hypotension and vasodilatation, decreased cerebral metabolism, oxygen consumption, and blood flow, decreased myocardial contractility, myoclonus
Propofol	2-3 mg/kg IV	<30 sec	4-8 min	Pain on injection, decreased mean systemic arterial pressure, decreased cardiac output
Etomidate	0.3-0.4 mg/kg IV	<30 sec	3-5 min	Suppressed adrenocortical function and (?) decreased cerebral blood flow, decreased ICP, nausea and vomiting on emergence
Succinylcholine	2 mg/kg IV 4 mg/kg IM	10-20 sec	3-5 min	Fasciculations, increased ICP, increased intraocular pressure, hyperkalemia (especially with old burns, denervating motor neurologic disorders, massive muscle trauma), malignant hyperthermia trigger, bradycardia
Pancuronium	0.01 mg/kg IV	2-4 min	45-60 min	Tachycardia, hypertension
Vecuronium	0.10-0.20 mg/kg IV	2-3 min	35-55 min	—
Atracurium	0.4-0.5 mg/kg IV	2-2.5 min	20-40 min	Histamine release
d-Tubocurarine	0.3-0.6 mg/kg IV	2-4 min	45-60 min	Histamine release with hypotension, rash
Rocuronium	0.7-1.0 mg/kg IV	60-75 sec	15-85 min	Prolonged paralysis

*The dose given is calculated to induce unresponsiveness and apnea or to provide rapid and intense neuromuscular blockade satisfactory for intubation (>95% receptor occupancy).

Table 152-3   Management Examples of Complicated Airway Cases

Condition	Treatment Goal During Intubation	Drugs Used*	Other Considerations
Full stomach	Prevention of passive regurgitation after airway protective reflexes lost	Thiopental, rocuronium, or succinylcholine	1. Oxygen for 3 min 2. No ventilation during procedure 3. Rapid injection of all drugs 4. Rapidly acting drugs to minimize period of apnea 5. Cricoid pressure
Bronchospasm	Eliminate or treat stimuli that would induce or increase bronchospasm (i.e., pharmacologic stimuli of airway protective reflexes, especially cough)	Ketamine, vecuronium, lidocaine, atropine	1. Complete paralysis is only effective to eliminate cough-related bronchospasm 2. Oxygen for 3 min 3. IV anesthetic will blunt cough reflex
Increased ICP	No increase in heart rate or blood pressure	Pentothal or etomidate, vecuronium, rocuronium lidocaine	1. Oxygen for 3 min 2. Hyperventilate to induce protective effects of hypocarbia on cerebral blood flow 3. Intubate only after full paralysis achieved (patient cannot cough) 4. Choose agents without sympathomimetic characteristics
Pulmonary vascular hypertension	Avoid decreased pulmonary blood flow	Midazolam, fentanyl, vecuronium	1. Maintain hyperoxia and hypocarbia to promote pulmonary vasodilation 2. Ensure patient is paralyzed and deeply sedated before instrumentation 3. Fio_2 1.0 throughout procedure
Hypovolemia or depressed cardiac output	Maintain blood pressure without heart rate changes	Etomidate or midazolam with fentanyl	1. Avoid vasodilators and myocardial depressants 2. Volume infusion available 3. Monitor ECG

*See Table 152-2 for doses.

counter the pathophysiology at hand. Sufficient time must be allowed for the depth of anesthesia needed to minimize responses to instrumentation.

In the patient with increased intracranial pressure the choice of induction agent depends on the patient's hemodynamic status. Thiopental is an excellent choice in the hemodynamically stable patient. If the patient is unstable or hypovolemia is suspected, etomidate is a useful alternative since it also decreases intracranial pressure. As always, preoxygenation is carried out, but in this instance the patient can be hyperventilated to provide additional cerebral protection. Drugs that increase intracranial pressure (e.g., ketamine or pancuronium) are to be avoided.

The presence or potential for increased pulmonary artery pressure is another instance in which hypocarbia and hyperoxia are desirable. A drug regimen aimed at minimizing reflex autonomic stimulation while maintaining cardiovascular stability is optimal.

Awake intubation with or without a topical anesthetic (to nose, pharynx, and vocal cords) must be strongly considered in airway obstructive processes. These clinical situations include extrinsic airway compression, as might be seen with intrathoracic or neck tumors, neck swelling from burns or trauma, infections involving the pharynx or larynx, and bronchospastic disease. In these instances sedation or neuromuscular blockade may cause complete obstruction where a partial obstruction existed in the spontaneously breathing patient. Alternatively, consider taking the patient to the operating room for a general anesthetic, which preserves spontaneous ventilation and allows evaluation and instrumentation.

Airway Assessment
Schwartz hyoid maneuver

If the mandible is normal and the hyoid bone is in the normal position, the potential displacement area will usually be adequate. This can be assessed with the Schwartz hyoid maneuver by placing two fingers (3 cm) between the anterior ramus of the mandible and the hyoid bone. In infants this distance is 1.5 cm. Visualization by direct laryngoscopy may be impossible if the potential displacement area is reduced.

Mallampati grading

Mallampati et al. suggested that the size of the base of the tongue is an important factor in determining the degree of difficulty in directly visualizing the larynx. The clinical sign is the concealment of faucial pillars and uvula by the base of the tongue when the latter is maximally protruded in the seated patient. Clinical assessment reveals the following classes:

Class 1   Faucial pillars, soft palate, and uvula can be visualized.

Class 2   Faucial pillars and soft palate can be visualized but uvula is masked by the base of the tongue.

Class 3   Only soft palate can be visualized.

Glottic Exposure Adequate

Grade 1   Glottis (including anterior and posterior commissures) can be fully exposed.

Grade 2   Glottis can be partially exposed (anterior commissure cannot be visualized).

Glottic Exposure Inadequate

Grade 3   Glottis cannot be exposed (only corniculate cartilages can be visualized).

Grade 4   Glottis, including corniculate cartilages, cannot be exposed.

In the series of 210 adult patients reported by Mallampati et al., all patients with class 1 anatomy had adequate exposure of the glottis on laryngoscopic visualization. Only two thirds of class 2 patients had adequate exposure. Of the class 3 patients, only 7% had adequate exposure (all grade 2), the remainder having inadequate exposure (grade 3 or 4).

Difficult Airway Algorithm

Preparation of the patient with a difficult airway is essential if known anatomic obstacles exist, but a predetermined plan for alternate airway maintenance in the event difficulty is encountered in any intubation attempt will minimize morbidity and mortality. The commonly accepted difficult airway algorithm was established by the American Society of Anesthesiologists (Fig. 152-9).

Special Adjuncts for Difficult Airway Management

The intubating bronchoscope, the laryngeal mask airway (LMA), and antegrade or retrograde wire placement have been used individually or in combination to achieve tracheal intubation. All require an experienced operator for placement. In cases where a surgical airway is not mandatory for anatomic reasons,

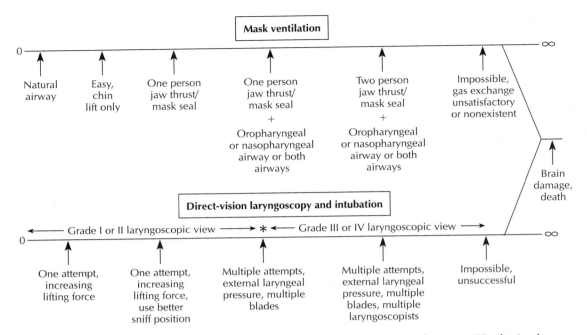

Fig. 152-9   Difficult airway algorithm. Airway refers to either mask ventilation or ET tube intubation by direct vision laryngoscopy. The degree of difficulty can range from zero, which is extremely easy, to infinite, which is impossible. When mask ventilation and direct vision laryngoscopy are impossible and no other maneuver is successful, brain damage and/or death will ensue. In between these extremes there are several well-defined, commonly encountered degrees of difficulty. (From American Society of Anesthesiologists' Task Force on Management of the Difficult Airway. Practice guidelines for management of the difficult airway. Anesthesiology 78:597-602, 1993.)

Table 152-4   Difficult Airway Equipment Cart*

Equipment	Size	Comment
Fiberoptic bronchoscope with light source	2.5, 3.5, 4.5 mm	Provides direct visualization of larynx without manipulating neck
Airway management adjuncts		
Laryngeal mask airway		Inserted blindly into pharynx to form low-pressure seal around laryngeal inlet, permitting gentle positive pressure ventilation
	Size 1: Neonates ≥6.5 kg	Inflates 2-4 ml
	Size 2: Pediatric, 6.5-20 kg	Inflates up to 10 ml
	Size 2½: Pediatric, 20-30 kg	Inflates up to 15 ml
	Size 3: Small adult >30 kg	Inflates up to 20 ml
	Size 4: Large adult	Inflates up to 30 ml

*The difficult airway equipment cart should be used in conjunction with a standard airway equipment care. Some supplies needed may be found on either cart. The purpose is not to duplicate equipment.

Table 152-4   Difficult Airway Equipment Cart*—cont'd

Equipment	Size	Comment
Airway management adjuncts—cont'd		
Combitube	Large and small	Plastic double-lumen tube with tracheal channel (open distal end) and esophageal channel (occluded distal end with openings in pharyngeal section); depending on position of tube, inflated distal cuff seals either esophagus or trachea; auscultation confirms placement
Retrograde intubation kit with angiocath	Pediatric	Epidural catheter with flexible guidewire used as a stylet traversing cricothyroid membrane to exit oral cavity; ET tube advances over catheter with wire into trachea
Cricothyroidotomy kit	14 g angiocath, barrel of a 3 ml syringe, No. 7.0 ET tube connector	O_2 insufflation possible, CO_2 elimination impeded
Percutaneous transtracheal ventilation	14 g catheter, high-pressure tubing, manual interruptor	System for jet ventilation or barrel of 3 ml syringe and No. 7.0 ET tube connector provide connection between catheter and standard O_2 delivery apparatus
Open-fronted oral airways	Adult and pediatric sizes	Facilitate passage of fiberoptic devices
Intubation aids		
Trachlight/light wand		Lighted stylet using transillumination of soft tissues of neck to guide tip of ET tube into trachea
Bullard intubation laryngoscope	Two sizes	L-shaped blade with fiberoptic bundles for viewing and light source with attachable stylet
Oxyscope laryngoscope blades and oxygen tubing	Various sizes available	Blades with nipple designed to attach O_2 tubing directly to laryngoscope blade
Tube changers		Stabilize airway without ET tube; O_2 insufflation possible
Stubby laryngoscope handle		
Stylets (coated)	Various signs	Redirect ET tube tip
Miscellaneous		
Swivel connector with adapter for fiberoptic scope		
Extra bulbs	Small and large	
Extra wires		
Extra batteries		
Lubricant		
Nasal trumpets		
Extension set		
Medication		
2% viscous lidocaine		
1% or 2% lidocaine solution		
4% topical solution		
20% benzocaine spray		
½% Neo-Synephrine spray		

these can be useful adjuncts for tracheal intubation. Equipment for difficult airway management can be stored in a cart for ease of use and mobility. See Table 152-4 for suggested contents. Topical anesthetic agents for local airway use must also be included.

Surgical airway

In blunt injuries of the face, bone fragments, hematoma, or soft tissue swelling can make oral intubation impossible. In blunt or penetrating trauma to the neck the airway can be fractured, disrupted, or obstructed by tissue flaps or hematoma. These injuries are best managed by tracheostomy or (single or multiple) needle cricothyroidotomy. Tracheostomy is preferred over surgical cricothyroidotomy in patients younger than 13 years of age or when tracheal disruption is suspected. If either needle or surgical cricothyroidotomy is accomplished, a formal operative tracheostomy needs to be performed within 1 to 2 hours. Any injury to the face or neck severe enough to necessitate surgical airway intervention has an increased risk of association with cervical spine injury. Care must be taken to ensure cervical spine stabilization.

In either needle or open cricothyroidotomy the cricothyroid membrane is first identified (the space between the lower edge of the thyroid cartilage and the upper edge of the cricoid ring) and trapped between the index finger and thumb of the nondominant hand. For needle access, a needle or catheter over the needle assembly is passed through the membrane, aspirating while advancing the needle. When air is encountered, advancement is stopped, and if using a catheter, the catheter is slipped over the needle and the needle is removed. A No. 3.0 ET connector can then be placed on the hub of the catheter (or needle) for insufflation or attachment to a jet ventilating device. If open cricothyroidotomy is performed, the membrane is identified in the same manner and localized with the index finger and thumb of the nondominant hand. A vertical midline incision is made down to the cricothyroid membrane. An assistant can then grasp the lateral tissues to provide exposure. The cricothyroid membrane is opened transversely with the scalpel, and a tracheostomy tube or ET tube is inserted into the trachea. If needed, the membrane opening can be dilated with hemostats prior to insertion of the tube. A special trocar and tube assembly for cricothyroidotomy in adults is available as a kit.

Fiberoptic laryngobronchoscopy

The intubating fiberoptic bronchoscope can be invaluable for patients with anatomic abnormalities that make direct laryngoscopy and intubation difficult or impossible. After selecting an ET tube of appropriate size for the patient, the tube is threaded over the bronchoscope and the bronchoscope is passed into the trachea and positioned above the carina via the oral or nasal route. The ET tube is passed over the bronchoscope and into the trachea. The bronchoscope is withdrawn and the ET tube secured.

The procedure may be augmented by passage of the loaded bronchoscope through a previously placed LMA. The disadvantage of this procedure is that an (adapterless) ET tube small enough to also pass through the LMA must be used or the LMA must be modified so that it can be "peeled off" once the ET tube is in place. The advantage of the LMA is that ventilation can be carried out during the intubation procedure.

Alternatively, a wire can be passed through the suction port of the bronchoscope and into the trachea. The bronchoscope and LMA are then withdrawn, and an ET tube is passed over the wire and into the trachea. The obvious disadvantage is that the airway is left unsecured and unprotected between wire placement and ET tube placement.

Laryngeal mask airway

The LMA has a role in the management of the difficult airway. The LMA is a rigid tube that is fused at a 30-degree angle to a distal elliptical spoon-shaped mask with an inflatable rim. The cuff is inflated through a small lumen with a pilot balloon. The shaft opens into the concavity of the ellipse via a fenestrated aperture with three orifices to prevent the epiglottis from falling back and blocking the lumen. After the cuff is completely deflated and the posterior aspect of the LMA lubricated, it is inserted with the distal aperture facing anteriorly into the open mouth, applying the tip of the cuff to the hard palate and using the index finger of the inserting hand to guide the tube along the palate over the back of the tongue. The tube is then advanced in one smooth movement until resistance is felt as the upper esophageal sphincter is engaged. Without holding the tube, the cuff is inflated. This maneuver will cause the tube to move outward as the cuff seats around the laryngeal inlet. It is secured in a manner similar to that used for the ET tube. The LMA can only be used for short periods of time (hours) and thus is a bridge to a more secure airway. Aspiration of gastric contents is the most serious problem with use of the LMA since no esophageal occlusion occurs.

Retrograde wire placement

Puncture of the cricothyroid membrane with a small needle angled cephalad provides access to the trachea for placement of a retrograde wire. The wire is passed cephalad into the pharynx for retrieval out the mouth or passage out the nose. An ET tube of appropriate size for the patient can then be passed over the wire and into the trachea. When the tube passes the cords and the tip enters the trachea, the wire is withdrawn while gentle pressure is exerted on the ET tube to prevent displacement.

CONCLUSION

A planned approach to every intubation as if it were a difficult intubation will ensure the operator is prepared for the occasional difficult airway. Airway assessment is helpful in predicting some difficult intubations so that special preparations can be made. The choice of pharmacologic assistance based on the patient's underlying pathophysiology can facilitate intubation for the patient and the operator. A predetermined plan, based on the operator's level of experience, for alternate airway maintenance in the event difficulty is encountered will help minimize morbidity and mortality.

ADDITIONAL READINGS

Abrams KJ. Airway management and mechanical ventilation. New Horiz 3:479-487, 1995.

• American Society of Anesthesiologists' Task Force on Management of the Difficult Airway. Practice guidelines for management of the difficulty airway. Anesthesiology 78:597-602, 1993.

Audenert SM, et al. Retrograde-assisted fiberoptic tracheal intubation in children with difficult airways. Anesth Analg 73:660-664, 1991.

Bancek CD, Gunnerson HB, Tulloch WC. Percutaneous transtracheal high-frequency jet ventilation as an aid to fiberoptic intubation. Anesthesia 67:247-249, 1987.

Bentz WE, Tatro DS. The Pediatric Drug Handbook, 2nd ed. Chicago: Year Book, 1988.

• Benumof JL. Management of the difficult adult airway with special emphasis on awake tracheal intubation. Anesthesiology 75:1087-1110, 1991.

Berry FA, Yemen TA. Pediatric airway in health and disease. Pediatr Clin North Am 41:153-180, 1994.

Borland LM, Swan DM, Heff S. Difficult pediatric endotracheal intubation: A new approach to retrograde technique. Anesthesia 55:577-578, 1981.

Hasan MA, Black AE. A new technique for fiberoptic intubation in children. Anesthesia 49:1031-1033, 1994.

Inaba AS, Seward PN. An approach to pediatric trauma. Emerg Med Clin North Am 9:523-548, 1991.

Jones LK. Smith's Recognizable Patterns of Human Malformation, 4th ed. Philadelphia: WB Saunders, 1988.

Lopez-Viego MA, ed. The Parkland Trauma Handbook. St. Louis: Mosby, 1994.

Mallampati SR, Gatt SP, Gugino LD, Desai SP, Waruksa B, Freiberger D, Liu PL. A clinical sign to predict difficult tracheal intubation: A prospective study. Can Anesth Soc J 32:429-434, 1985.

Marshall TA, Deeder R, Pai S, Berkowitz, Austin T. Physiologic changes associated with endotracheal intubation in preterm infants. Crit Care Med 12:501-503, 1984.

Maves SS, Mirenda JV. Anesthesia interventions in the emergency room. Probl Anesth 6:329-340, 1992.

McEnvoy GK, ed. American Hospital Formulary Service '95 Drug Information. Bethesda: American Society of Health-System Pharmacists, 1995.

Pennant JH, White PF. The laryngeal mask airway: Its uses in anesthesiology. Anesthesiology 79:144-163, 1993.

Rouse TM, Eichelberger MR. Trends in pediatric trauma management. Surg Clin North Am 72:1347-1364, 1992.

Salem MR, Wong AY, Collins VJ. The pediatric patient with a full stomach. Anesthesiology 39:435-440, 1973.

Smith SJ. Combined use of laryngeal mask airway and fiberoptic laryngoscope in difficult intubation. Anesth Intensive Care 19:471-472, 1991.

Wood RE, Postma D. Endoscopy of airway in infants and children. J Pediatr 112:1-6, 1988.

APPENDIX

Syndromes Associated With Known Anatomic Obstacles to Adequate Laryngoscopic Visualization

Micrognathia

Achondrogenesis syndromes
Amyoplasia congenita disruptive sequence
Aniridia–Wilms' tumor association
Bloom syndrome
Camptomelic dysplasia
Cat-eye syndrome
Cerebrocostomandibular syndrome
Cerebrooculofacioskeletal syndrome
Cohen syndrome
de Lange syndrome
Dubowitz syndrome
Escobar syndrome
Facioauriculovertebral spectrum
Femoral hypoplasia–unusual facies syndrome
Fetal aminopterin effects
Fetal trimethadione effects
Frontometaphyseal dysplasia
Hajdu-Cheney syndrome
Hallermann-Streiff syndrome
Hurler-Scheie compound syndrome
Langer-Giedion syndrome
Langer mesomelic dysplasia
Lethal multiple pterygium syndrome
Marshall-Smith syndrome
Maternal phenylketonuria fetal effects
Meckel-Gruber syndrome
Melnick-Needles syndrome
Metaphyseal chondrodysplasia, Jansen type
Miller syndrome
Miller-Dieker syndrome
Möbius sequence
Mohr syndrome
Nager syndrome
Neu-Laxova syndrome
Oral-facial-digital syndrome
Oromandibular–limb hypogenesis spectrum
Otopalatodigital syndrome, type II
Pallister-Hall syndrome
Pena-Shokeir phenotype
Progeria syndrome
Pyknodysostosis
Retinoic acid embryopathy

Roberts-SC phocomelia syndrome
Robin sequence
Russell-Silver syndrome
Schwartz-Jampel syndrome
Seckel syndrome
Shprintzen syndrome
Smith-Lemli-Opitz syndrome
Stickler syndrome
Treacher Collins syndrome
Trichorhinophalangeal syndrome
Triploidy syndrome
Trisomy 8 syndrome
Trisomy 9 mosaic syndrome
Trisomy 18 syndrome
Weaver syndrome
XO syndrome
XXXX syndrome
Zellweger syndrome
4p-syndrome
5p-syndrome
9p-syndrome
13q-syndrome
18p-syndrome
Beals syndrome
CHARGE association
Chondrodysplasia punctata, Conradi-Hunermann type
Diastrophic dysplasia
Fetal alcohol effects
Killian/Teschler-Nicola syndrome
Lenz-Majewski hyperostosis syndrome
MURCS association
Noonan syndrome
Radial aplasia-thrombocytopenia syndrome
Rubinstein-Taybi syndrome
Trisomy 13 syndrome

Microstomia

Fetal valproate effects
Hallermann-Streiff syndrome
Hecht syndrome (limited opening)
Oromandibular–limb hypogenesis spectrum
Otopalatodigital syndrome, type I
Otopalatodigital syndrome, type II
Pena-Shokeir phenotype

Rapp-Hodgkin ectodermal dysplasia syndrome
Robinow syndrome
Ruvalcaba syndrome
Trisomy 18 syndrome
Treacher Collins syndrome

Macroglossia

Athyrotic hypothyroidism sequence
Beckwith-Wiedemann syndrome
Down syndrome (prominent)
Generalized gangliosidosis syndrome, type I
Hurler syndrome
Killian-Teschler-Nicola syndrome
Maroteaux-Lamy mucopolysaccharidosis syndrome
Robinow syndrome
Scheie syndrome
Schinzel-Giedion syndrome
Triploidy syndrome
Trisomy 4p-syndrome

Abnormalities of larynx

Cerebro-costo-mandibular syndrome (trachea)
Chondrodysplasia punctata, Conradi-Hunermann type (tracheal stenosis)
Diastrophic dysplasia (stenosis)
Facioauriculovertebral spectrum
Fraser syndrome (atresia)
Fronto-metaphyseal dysplasia (subglottic narrowing)
Larsen syndrome (mobile arytenoid cartilage)
Marshall-Smith syndrome
Multiple neuroma syndrome (neuromas)
Nager syndrome (hypoplasia upper airway)
Opitz syndrome (cleft)
Pachyonychia congenita syndrome (obstructed)
Pallister-Hall syndrome (cleft)
Robin sequence (glossoptosis)
Shprintzen syndrome (web)

Short rib–polydactyly, Majewski type (hypoplasia)

Treacher Collins syndrome (pharyngeal hypoplasia)

Short neck

Albright hereditary osteodystrophy
Beals syndrome
CHARGE association
Chondrodysplasia punctata, Conradi-Hunermann type
Down syndrome
Fetal alcohol effects
Fetal hydantoin effects

Frumann-Sheldon syndrome
Fibrochondrogenesis
Hurler syndrome
Iniencephaly sequence
Jarcho-Levin syndrome
Killian-Teschler-Nicola syndrome
Klippel-Feil sequence
Koslowski spondylometaphyseal dysplasia
Meckel-Gruber syndrome
Morquio syndrome
MURCS association
Neu-Laxova syndrome
Noonan syndrome

Roberts–SC phocomelia syndrome
Scheie syndrome
Schwartz-Jampel syndrome
Spondyloepiphyseal dysplasia congenita
Spondyloepiphyseal dysplasia tarda
Trisomy 4p-syndrome
9p-syndrome
Trisomy 18 syndrome
XXXXY syndrome
XXXXX syndrome
XO syndrome
5p-syndrome

153 Extubation and Fiberoptic Examination

*Orval E. Brown · Frances C. Morriss · Michael J. Biavati ·
Scott C. Manning*

Extubation

INDICATIONS

The primary indication for removal of an endotracheal tube is resolution of the process that necessitated intubation. If an endotracheal tube has been in place a short time and the patient is relatively healthy (e.g., patient with an overdose), resolution of the primary process is all that is required before considering extubation. If the tube has been in place for a long time, other factors that might contribute to failure of extubation must be considered. Those organ systems or conditions in which preexisting or ongoing abnormalities might contribute to or increase the work of breathing must be considered. The function of the cardiovascular and respiratory systems must be as normal and stable as possible. There may be increased work of breathing after extubation, and any conditions (e.g., hypermetabolic state or anemia) that may exacerbate cardiac or respiratory work must be corrected.

There are no acute pulmonary changes, particularly those associated with newly acquired infection or loss of lung volume. Physical examination reveals no new findings, and tracheal secretions are thin and clear. Ventilatory support needs to be minimal (i.e., the patient needs infrequent suctioning), end-expiratory pressure is low (2 to 3 cm H_2O), ventilatory rate and the degree of pressure support are minimal or ventilation is not needed, and Fio_2 is <0.4. Respiratory support in the previous 24 hours, including increases in the frequency of bronchodilator administration, has not been increased. A stable chemical status must be documented by either noninvasive respiratory monitoring (transcutaneous oxygen and carbon dioxide determination, Sao_2, or end-tidal carbon dioxide determination), or arterial blood gas and pH determination.

Not all patients will demonstrate normal oxygenation and carbon dioxide elimination, but all must have stable levels of Pao_2 and $Paco_2$ that are normal for their particular diagnosis. For example, the infant with cyanotic congenital cardiac disease will not have normal Sao_2 levels, and the patient with chronic pulmonary disease may have a physiologic pH only because renal compensation and retention of bicarbonate ion has balanced the inability to eliminate carbon dioxide. In patients who have needed prolonged support because of respiratory failure, adequate time must be allowed after that support has become minimal to assess whether respiratory fatigue will occur. This implies observation for at least 24 hours. If respiratory muscle fatigue is a problem, theophylline in doses to achieve a serum level of 10 to 20 mg/ml may be tried to improve respiratory muscle (particularly diaphragmatic) function. Therapy (e.g., aerosolized bronchodilators or chest physiotherapy) must be scheduled so that the patient receives maximum benefit, yet is not exhausted at extubation.

Increased cardiovascular work can contribute to failure of extubation. Patients must demonstrate adequate cardiac output as judged by such clinical indications as normal systemic arterial blood pressure, adequate urinary output, good capillary refill, stable cardiac rhythm, and, if present, control of congestive heart failure. Ongoing tachypnea and tachycardia are of particular concern because they correlate with increased amount of effort and pulmonary work. Pharmacologic augmentation of cardiac output is minimal, and the need for diuretic, cardiac glycoside, and an-

---

EVALUATION BEFORE EXTUBATION

Resolution of primary process
Respiratory stability

Chest radiograph
Arterial blood gas and pH determination
Complete blood cell count
Tracheal secretion culture, Gram's stain
Chest physiotherapy, bronchodilator therapy, or suctioning, as needed
Satisfactory pulmonary examination

Cardiovascular stability

Adequate cardiac output
Stable rhythm
Minimal pharmacologic cardiac support
Adequate oxygen-carrying capacity (Hct)

Neurologic stability

Usual state of consciousness
Presence of airway protective reflexes (gag, swallow, cough)
Absence of apnea
Adequate control of seizures
Absence of central respiratory depressants (discontinue or decrease narcotics, tranquilizers, sedatives)
Good neuromuscular function of respiratory muscles

Metabolic stability

Absence of fever
Normal electrolytes and minerals (Na, K, Cl, PO_4, Mg, Ca)
Normal serum glucose
Adequate hydration
Adequate caloric intake to support work of breathing

---

tihypertensive agents is stable. Even though the respiratory status may have been unchanged for some time, upper airway obstruction and hypoxia after extubation are possible. Either of these conditions coupled with unstable cardiovascular status such as may occur after major cardiac surgery can cause serious complications.

CNS stability is necessary to ensure good reflex protection of the airway after extubation and ade-quate respiratory drive and respiratory muscle function. Physical examination and observation must demonstrate absence of apnea and presence of normal gag and cough reflexes. Central respiratory depressants such as narcotics, sedatives, tranquilizers, and antihistamines must be either discontinued or given in doses low enough to ensure consciousness after extubation. All neuromuscular blocking agents must be discontinued or pharmacologically reversed to ensure adequate muscle strength to sustain breathing. In patients with primary neuromuscular disease (e.g., hypotonia, muscular dystrophies, spinal cord dysfunction, or myasthenia gravis), direct evaluation of respiratory function can be useful to determine ability to sustain respiratory effort unassisted; inspiratory pressure must be >22 cm H_2O negative pressure, and vital capacity must be at least 10 to 15 cc/kg body weight. These simple tests can be repeated as needed to evaluate ongoing neuromuscular function. In comatose patients the ability to swallow and to handle oropharyngeal secretions may also need assessment. Seizures, particularly those associated previously with cyanosis or apnea, must be controlled.

Hypermetabolic states will increase oxygen consumption, placing increased demands on the cardiorespiratory system. Fever is the one most frequently seen in the PICU. The fever is controlled, and the cause identified and treated. In neonates and premature infants many abnormalities of electrolytes and glucose are associated with apnea and electrical dysfunction of the neuromuscular membrane; serum Na, K, Cl, PO_4, Ca, Mg, pH, and glucose must be maintained within the normal range. In the patient with increased fluid requirements or who is young, intravenous hydration with an appropriate solution must be provided for the period when nothing can be taken by mouth. Patients with chronic disease processes, particularly those with prolonged respiratory failure, may have inadequate caloric intake. Caloric requirements will increase as the patient assumes more control of breathing. If nutritional supplementation is inadequate, the patient may not be able to sustain the work of breathing and thrive; this is particularly true in small and premature infants.

TECHNIQUE
Preparation

All oral feedings are withheld for a minimum of 4 hours before extubation. Glottic closure is incomplete immediately after extubation, predisposing the patient to aspiration of both stomach contents and oropharyngeal secretions. If reintubation is necessary, an empty stomach reduces this risk. All pain medication, muscle relaxants, and respiratory depressant drugs are withdrawn or significantly decreased long enough before extubation to eliminate any depressant effects. Oxygen and suction must be available, and the patient must have cardiac rhythm and oxygen saturation monitoring. A complete selection of intubation equipment including laryngoscopes and a varied selection of endotracheal tubes must be available at the bedside. Appropriate drugs for intubation must be immediately available (see Chapter 152).

Procedure

The endotracheal tube and pharynx are suctioned to clear all secretions. The stomach is emptied, and if present, the nasogastric tube is removed. Tape or other endotracheal tube securing devices are released and the tube is secured manually. Hyperventilation is performed with 100% oxygen (or an appropriate Fio_2 if the patient is a premature infant), and extubation is accomplished at peak inspiration. This induces a cough, and any secretions in the airway are expelled. Humidified oxygen is administered with a delivery system (e.g., mask, croup tent, or face tent) that is most comfortable for the patient at a concentration that will keep Sao_2 >92%. The patient must be monitored carefully by the physician at the bedside for at least 10 to 15 minutes after extubation to ensure that rapid deterioration, if it occurs, can be treated promptly.

Monitoring After Extubation

The problems that most commonly necessitate reintubation are laryngeal edema, particularly in the subglottis, thick secretions that obstruct the airway, fatigue from the increased work of breathing, apnea, cardiovascular instability, and inadequate pulmonary function. Patients are monitored closely in the PICU for at least 24 hours after extubation. Any signs of respiratory distress or air hunger necessitate immediate reevaluation for possible reintubation. The patient is given nothing by mouth for at least 4 hours after extubation to reduce the risk of aspiration if reintubation is necessary. Sedatives or pain medications that depress respiratory drive usually are not given in the immediate period after extubation.

Fiberoptic Examination With Extubation

INDICATIONS

Fiberoptic nasolaryngoscopy is a safe and effective method to evaluate the larynx in infants and children (Fig. 153-1). It is a valuable tool to help differentiate upper airway obstruction from lower airway disease as a cause of extubation failure. This technique provides excellent noninvasive visualization of the pharynx, epiglottis, and vocal cords. Although fiberoptic examination does not visualize the subglottis well, it can give a strong indication of subglottic disease; the trachea is not visualized. The technique is generally used in patients who have had a failed extubation and in whom upper airway problems are suspected. Other indications for fiberoptic nasolaryngoscopy include stridor, aphonia, increasing respiratory rate, deteriorating blood gas values, or other high-risk factors such as prolonged intubation.

TECHNIQUE
Preparation

The patient is prepared and extubation performed as described. In patients undergoing a second or third trial of extubation steroids are usually used to reduce laryngeal edema. Dexamethasone (Decadron), 0.5 mg/kg/dose for four doses, is administered. Steroid

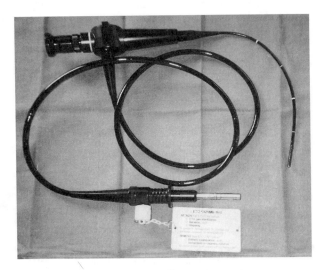

Fig. 153-1 Olympus ENF-P fiberoptic nasolaryngoscope.

administration starts at midnight the night before extubation and is given at 6:00 A.M., noon, and 6:00 P.M. Extubation is performed early in the morning so that observation can be continued during the day.

Procedure

Immediately after extubation, if the patient's condition is stable, fiberoptic nasolaryngoscopy is performed. The patient is prepared with several drops of 0.25% oxymetazoline and a few drops of 2% to 4% lidocaine in the nose. The patient is carefully restrained, and intubation and suction equipment is immediately available. Sao$_2$ monitoring is mandatory. The fiberscope is inserted through the nose in patients weighing >1500 g or through the oral cavity in patients weighing <1500 g. The small outer diameter of the fiberscope (~3.5 mm) permits the procedure to be performed safely with only local anesthesia; sedation, which might interfere with respiratory effort, is not necessary. The fiberscope is advanced through the nasal or oral cavity until the epiglottis and laryngeal airway are identified. The major positive findings may include mass lesions (e.g., granulation tissue or cysts), subglottic edema, or decreased mobility or paralysis of the vocal cords. Slight bowing of the true vocal cords from the endotracheal tube is common. Subglottic edema may not be immediately evident because the stenting effect of the endotracheal tube may mask the edema. Subglottic edema, if it develops, will become evident 3 to 4 hours after extubation, and repeated fiberoptic nasolaryngoscopy may be necessary. Patients in whom progressive stridor, air hunger, or deteriorating blood gas values develop after extubation are reexamined. When the examination is concluded, the fiberscope is withdrawn and aerosolized racemic epinephrine is given.

Patients who fail extubation are managed on the basis of findings of fiberoptic examination. Mass lesions are managed with microlaryngoscopy and bronchoscopy and with laser treatment if indicated. Subglottic edema is managed in the same way as croup. True vocal cord paralysis may necessitate a tracheotomy if the patient's airway is inadequate. Laryngeal granulation is treated with steroids, antibiotics, and racemic epinephrine. Occasionally suspension microlaryngoscopy with carbon dioxide laser excision of granulation is indicated if granulations are excessive and obstructing the airway.

ADDITIONAL READING

Fan LL, Flynn JW. Laryngoscopy in neonates and infants: Experience with flexible fiberoptic bronchoscope. Laryngoscope 921:451-456, 1981.

Fox WW, Berman LJ, Dinwiddie R, et al. Tracheal extubation of the neonate at 2 to 3 cm H$_2$O continuous positive airway pressure. Pediatrics 59:257-261, 1977.

• Frageus L. Difficult extubation following nasotracheal intubation. Anesthesiology 49:43-44, 1978.

• Morriss FC, Brown OE, Manning SC, Wade B. Extubation and fiberoptic examination. In Levin DL, Morriss FC, eds. Essentials of Pediatric Intensive Care. St. Louis: Quality Medical Publishing, 1990, pp 945-948.

Nussenbaum E. Flexible fiberoptic bronchoscopy and laryngoscopy in infants and children. Laryngoscope 93:1033-1035, 1983.

Pransky SM, Grundfast KM. Differentiating upper from lower airway compromise in neonates. Ann Otol Rhinol Laryngol 94:509-515, 1985.

• Wallar P, Forte V. Failed extubation in the neonatal intensive care unit. Am Otol Rhinol Laryngol 102:489-495, 1993.

154 Fiberoptic Bronchoscopy

Bruce G. Nickerson

BACKGROUND AND INDICATIONS

Fiberoptic flexible bronchoscopy is the examination of the airways from the nose to the fourth or fifth generation of the airways with a flexible fiberoptic bronchoscope. Over the last 15 years this procedure has become common in most PICUs in North America. Technical improvements in bronchoscopes and their optics, medications for sedation, and monitoring methods have made bronchoscopy feasible and safe in nearly all patients if performed by a skilled bronchoscopist and can provide useful information or improve the patient's condition. Successful bronchoscopy in a critically ill child necessitates good clinical judgment, a clear understanding of the limitations of the bronchoscopist and support team, laboratory, and PICU, and close monitoring and management of the patient's airway and ventilation before, during, and after the procedure.

Rigid and flexible fiberoptic bronchoscopy are the two types of bronchoscopy, and most pediatric hospitals offer both types, depending on the goals of the procedure. For rigid bronchoscopy, general anesthesia is used and it is usually performed by a surgeon or otolaryngologist. After the patient is anesthetized, a rigid steel tube fitted with a telescope and anesthesia circuit is used to intubate the lungs. Rigid bronchoscopes have the best optics, the ability to suction larger and thicker secretions, and special instruments to remove foreign bodies. Some may have attachments for laser ablation of granulomas or polyps. The disadvantages of rigid bronchoscopy are its expense, requirement of general anesthesia and an operating room, and positive pressure ventilation may distend and distort the shape of the airway so that malacia or airway collapse may be missed.

Flexible fiberoptic bronchoscopy is performed with a fiberoptic bronchoscope that is passed through the nose so that the upper airway can be viewed with less distortion. Flexible bronchoscopes come in a variety of sizes, some as small as 2 mm in diameter. They may be passed through endotracheal tubes or tracheostomies without removing the patient from mechanical ventilation. Flexible bronchoscopy is performed with the patient under conscious sedation. It is usually carried out in a treatment room with appropriate monitoring or in a PICU. Thus it may be performed without moving a critically ill patient and at considerably less expense than rigid bronchoscopy. Flexible bronchoscopy is an excellent technique for obtaining lower airway secretions in children who do not cough up sputum.

Flexible bronchoscopy allows a dynamic view of the airway with less distortion of the tissues than rigid bronchoscopy. Because the patient is breathing spontaneously, generating negative pressure in the chest, it allows visualization of areas of malacia or collapse. Specimens can also be taken from more peripheral sites, in particular the left upper lobe, which is difficult to visualize with a rigid bronchoscope. Flexible bronchoscopes may be helpful for difficult intubations, as in patients with Pierre Robin sequence and those unable to open their jaws or who have unstable cervical spines.

The disadvantages of flexible bronchoscopy are that the airway and sedation are less rigidly controlled; thus more skill is needed to manage these crucial aspects. Flexible bronchoscopes have smaller suction channels, which may make it more difficult to manage thick secretions. Flexible bronchoscopes are generally not used to remove foreign bodies because the airway is less well controlled and the smaller flexible bronchoscopes lack the ability to grasp or hold.

Indications for bronchoscopy are either diagnostic or therapeutic. As with all procedures, bronchoscopy is indicated only if it is likely to provide benefits that outweigh the risks. These may be either direct such as lysis of mucous plugs for treatment of atelectasis or indirect such as diagnosis of an infection that can be treated with specific therapy.

Diagnostic Bronchoscopy

Fiberoptic bronchoscopy may be performed to diagnose anatomic or physiologic airway problems.

Diagnosis of congenital stridor is a common indication for flexible bronchoscopy. The most common cause of congenital stridor is laryngomalacia. Typically the infant has a history of increasing, noisy breathing, particularly during activity and wakefulness, while lying supine and possibly when crying. The usual onset is in the first 4 weeks of life but is usually not noticed at birth. Laryngomalacia can be classified into three types. The most common type is prolapse of one or both arytenoid cartilages into the airway, which then vibrate during inspiration. This may be due to poor tone of the posterior cricoarytenoid muscles or redundancy of the arytenoid cartilages themselves. Usually this condition causes stridor that may vary markedly from breath to breath, depending on the degree of arytenoid prolapse. Occasionally only one arytenoid cartilage is involved. This type of laryngomalacia is usually benign. Typically the stridor becomes louder as the infant's strength increases. After 6 months of age the stridor gradually decreases as the caliber of the airway grows and usually resolves by age 2 years.

A more severe form of laryngomalacia is caused by a stove pipe– or omega-shaped epiglottis. Instead of the normal quarter moon, or C shape, the epiglottis, as viewed from above, curves in on itself in the shape of the Greek letter omega. During inspiration the epiglottis may collapse or even twist, causing stridor. Often infants with an omega-shaped epiglottis have more severe stridor, which occasionally necessitates tracheostomy or supraglottiplasty.

In "trap door" laryngomalacia the epiglottis folds from anterior to posterior over the larynx. This type is more commonly associated with other congenital anomalies and may have a more severe course.

Laryngeal polyposis may also be noted in the first 2 months of life, with increasing stridor. The stridor may be more constant or vary more directly with the force of inspiration. This condition is often associated with a history of maternal genital warts and vaginal delivery. It is possible that the virus that causes genital warts may infect the neonate's airway. Laryngeal polyposis can be difficult to treat and may necessitate tracheostomy and recurrent laser treatment or interleukin-2 to remove the polyps and maintain a patent airway.

Paralysis of one or both vocal cords may also cause congenital stridor. There may be an associated history of dystocia, traumatic delivery, or Erb's palsy. Vocal cord paralysis may also develop after cardiac, chest, or neck surgery from trauma or damage to the recurrent laryngeal nerves that control motion of the vocal cords. Paradoxical motion of the vocal cords into the airway during inspiration or failure of the vocal cords to completely abduct or adduct must be carefully noted. Diagnosis of vocal cord palsy may take time and careful examination, noting motion of the cords during inspiration and expiration.

Congenital laryngeal webs may occur just below the vocal cords in the neonate and cause severe respiratory distress. Prolonged intubation, intubation with a large endotracheal tube, or secondary bacterial infection of the airway may lead to tracheal stenosis at the level of the cricoid cartilage, the narrowest segment of the airway. The bronchoscopist must proceed with caution if a tight tracheal web is seen because trauma to the tissues may cause inflammation and edema, worsening the airway obstruction. Because resistance to flow is inversely proportional to the fourth power of the radius, 15% narrowing leads to doubling of airway resistance. Treatment may involve tracheostomy, cricoid split, or anterior or posterior tracheoplasty.

Bronchoscopy is useful for examining the anatomy of the airways. In addition to tracheomalacia and bronchomalacia, the takeoff and bifurcations of each of the lobar bronchi can be evaluated. Anomalous bronchi such as the origin of the right upper lobe bronchus from the trachea ("pig" bronchus), absence of one of the segmental bronchi, tracheoesophageal fistula, or external compression of one or several of the airways are occasionally found.

Tracheomalacia is a relatively rare cause of respiratory distress in infancy. It is often associated with vascular compression of the airways in conjunction with congenital heart disease or an anomalous vessel; the cartilaginous deformities or tracheoesophageal fistula, mucopolysaccharidosis, or pulmonary anomalies; or prolonged intubation and mechanical ventilation. Symptoms usually include episodes of cyanosis with vigorous crying or agitation. The onset of symptoms may be as late as 6 to 9 months of age, when the infant cries with enough force to collapse the airways.

Infections of the airways such as tracheitis and recurrent pneumonias may be diagnosed from specimens obtained at flexible bronchoscopy. The procedure may be particularly useful for obtaining airway cultures in young children who do not cough up sputum, in immune compromised hosts who may be infected with unusual organisms, and in children with recurrent chronic or severe pneumonia or anatomic abnormalities such as stenosis or malacia. Transbronchial biopsy specimens may be used to diagnose infection vs. rejection after lung transplantation. Immotile cilia syndrome may also be diagnosed with specimens obtained with a brush technique or scraping of the nasal or bronchial mucosa. Ciliary movement can be evaluated with direct visualization of the epithelial cells under a microscope. Care must be taken to ensure that the cilia are not exposed to medications such as lidocaine or to excessive cooling. Ultrastructure evaluation with electron microscopy is performed on specimens fixed in glutaraldehyde.

Therapeutic Bronchoscopy

Therapeutic bronchoscopy may be performed to relieve atelectasis or inspissated secretions. Usually rigid bronchoscopy is performed to remove foreign bodies.

Video cameras are extremely helpful for recording the bronchoscopic procedure so that the patient, parents, and caretakers can review the findings and understand the information obtained.

TECHNIQUE

Flexible bronchoscopy is performed in a well-equipped setting by a trained bronchoscopy team. Although the bronchoscopist may have attended a formal course, it usually takes 2 to 3 years of participation on an active bronchoscopy service to function independently. This allows time to not only acquire the necessary mechanical skills but also to develop problem-solving abilities and judgment for managing difficult airways. It is also necessary for acquiring experience in visualizing a large number of different pathologic entities. The bronchoscopist must be skilled in bag and mask ventilation and intubation before attempting bronchoscopy.

Equipment

The site for flexible bronchoscopy includes equipment for monitoring conscious sedation (e.g., ECG and pulse oximeter and blood pressure monitors; two sources of suction, one for the patient's mouth and one for the bronchoscope; and two oxygen sources, one for the bag and mask and one for the patient. Emergency equipment for intubation and placement of chest tubes and medications for treatment of reversal of sedation, seizures, bronchospasm, airway edema, and allergic reactions must be immediately available.

Preparation of Patient and Family

The risks and goals of bronchoscopy are thoroughly reviewed and the patient's and family's questions answered. This is usually best done in a relaxed setting before scheduling the procedure. The clinical history and laboratory tests are reviewed.

At bronchoscopy the patient must have an empty stomach. This usually means nothing by mouth for at least 3 hours for infants and 4 to 6 hours for older patients. Intravenous access is established for administration of sedatives. Occasionally adequate sedation may be achieved with intranasal medications, but in my experience this is often less than satisfactory: if the first dose does not result in adequate sedation, a second dose may be hazardous because there may be delayed absorption of the first dose.

It is helpful to maintain a hypnotic atmosphere in the bronchoscopy room. Turning the lights down, helping the patient to relax, allaying anxieties, and maintaining a peaceful mood that everything is being taken care of often allows a lower dose of sedative to be used.

Adequate sedation is crucial to the success of bronchoscopy in children. The level of sedation is titrated using several small doses of IV medications (see below). The goal is to obtain a level of amnesia and analgesia that permits the procedure to proceed with minimal reaction to the irritation of the bronchoscope while maintaining protective airway reflexes and adequate ventilation. A number of different drugs may be used, and it is best to become familiar with the details and side effects of several medications.

Midazolam is the most commonly used sedative

EQUIPMENT AND MEDICATION NECESSARY FOR FIBEROPTIC BRONCHOSCOPY

Equipment

Bag and masks of various sizes
Light source
Oxygen for bag and mask
Oxygen for patient
Specimen labels
Suction for bronchoscope
Suction for mouth
Suction traps
Tube thoracostomy tray
Various sized bronchoscopes
Various sized endotracheal tubes and laryngoscopes

Medications

Albuterol
Atropine
Calcium gluconate
Epinephrine, 1:10,000
Flumazenil

Furosemide
Lavage medium, sterile (0.9% sodium chloride solution, Plasma-Lyte, isotonic bicarbonate)
Lidocaine, 1%
Lidocaine, 2% jelly
Lidocaine IV solution
Naloxone
Phenobarbital
Phenylephrine
Racemic epinephrine
Sodium bicarbonate, 1 mEq/ml

Sedative drugs (one from each class)

Diazepam
Fentanyl
Ketamine
Meperidine
Midazolam
Morphine

because of its rapid onset of action and resolution. Children sedated with this drug usually have no recall of the experience. The usual dosage is 0.1 to 0.2 mg/kg repeated every 5 minutes until adequate sedation is achieved. A narcotic analgesic such as fentanyl, meperidine, or morphine may be used in conjunction with midazolam. These drugs provide pain relief. The usual dosage of fentanyl is 2 μg/kg repeated every 5 minutes until adequate sedation is achieved; meperidine, 1 mg/kg, and morphine, 0.1 mg/kg, give similar results but more frequently produce side effects and may take longer to wear off.

Intranasal midazolam may occasionally be used, usually at about twice the IV dose. This is more difficult to control because the onset of sedation is more variable, and with repeated dosage, excessive sedation may occur from delayed absorption.

Ketamine may also be used for short-acting sedation, particularly in a child who is difficult to sedate with other agents or has previously received benzodiazepines with narcotics. However, the disadvantage of ketamine is that it increases the volume of oral secretions and may predispose to laryngospasm, which may make bronchoscopy more difficult.

Topical anesthesia is equally as important as the level of sedation. Application of a vasoconstricting agent such as phenylephrine to the nares shrinks the mucosa, which facilitates passage of the bronchoscope and decreases bleeding from the nasal mucosa. Some bronchoscopists use aerosolized 4% lidocaine. I prefer to apply 2% lidocaine jelly to the nose repeatedly, then insert a soaked cotton-tipped applicator into the posterior nares. This is followed by instillation of 1% lidocaine solution into the nasal cavity and the posterior pharynx. Usually it takes at least 60 seconds of continuous instillation for the lidocaine to adequately anesthetize the mucosa. The presence of upper airway rhonchi suggests adequate numbing, and the bronchoscopist can proceed. In patients undergoing lower airway lavage, spraying small aliquots of 1% lidocaine through the suction port of the bronchoscope can be helpful. The lidocaine is left in the airway for at least 60 seconds before it is suctioned so there is adequate time to anesthetize the airway receptors.

The total dose of lidocaine is limited to <5 to 6 mg/kg because much of it is absorbed through the mucosa.

Procedure

It is helpful to have two assistants during the procedure. One assists with manipulation of the bronchoscope, light source, lavage solutions, and collection of specimens; the other is responsible for monitoring the patient's state of sedation, ventilation, and color and checking the ECG, blood pressure, and pulse oximeter monitors. The second assistant may also administer medications and steady the patient's head if needed. In an emergency one assistant manages the airway while the other administers emergency medications.

The patient is placed on an adjustable bed that can be positioned at a height comfortable for the bronchoscopist. A neck roll to maintain the patient's head and neck in the "sniffing" position is extremely helpful for proper positioning of the airway and adequate visualization of the larynx.

Most bronchoscopists hold the instrument in the right hand and use the right thumb to manipulate the lever that curves the scope. The left hand is positioned on the patient's left cheek and used to twist and direct the scope in and out of the airway. Before the bronchoscope is passed, the distance from the nose to the larynx is estimated, and the left hand grips the bronchoscope at this point. This prevents the bronchoscope from being advanced past the larynx and into the esophagus if the larynx is not visualized.

If an endotracheal tube is in place and the patient is receiving mechanical ventilation, a Bodi attachment may be used so that the bronchoscope can be inserted through the tube while ventilation is maintained.

A tracheostomy may be used for mechanical ventilation while the bronchoscope is passed through the nose and the upper airway visualized. Thus the size of the tracheostomy and any associated granulomas or scar tissue above it may be visualized. If the tracheostomy tube is not too large, the bronchoscope can usually be passed posterior to it along the pars membranosa and the distal airway observed while ventilation is maintained through the artificial airway.

At the beginning of the bronchoscopic procedure the nasal turbinates are seen first followed by the posterior pharynx; often the opening to the eustachian tube may be seen. Movement and closure of the soft palate can be evaluated and the size of the arytenoid cartilages and lingual tonsils noted. The bronchoscopist then views the epiglottis. If there is difficulty visualizing the vocal cords, use of a neck roll to change the patient's position can often make this easier. Occasionally suction is necessary to clear the posterior pharynx of secretions. In a patient with a small mandible the jaw or tongue may need to be pulled forward to obtain adequate exposure of the larynx. If the room lights are turned down, the assistants may note the position of the bronchoscope's light in the upper airway and help the bronchoscopist find the larynx.

In patients with laryngomalacia the larynx and epiglottis typically move inferosuperiorly with each breath, which may make insertion of the bronchoscope through the vocal cords more challenging. Unless there is significant arytenoid cartilage prolapse, the vocal cords can usually be visualized by placing the bronchoscope above the epiglottis. Movement of the vocal cords both in abduction and adduction, time during expiration and inspiration, and any asymmetry are carefully studied.

The bronchoscope is inserted through the vocal cords. The posterior commissure is much wider and results in less trauma than a more anterior approach. The bronchoscope is passed into the upper trachea and the reversal of motion of the pars membranosa noted at the thoracic inlet. Any external compression or malacia of the trachea is noted. Secretions and the condition of the mucosa are also important. For example, the patient with recurrent aspiration may have significant erythema of the upper trachea and decreasing evidence of inflammation as the bronchoscope is advanced more distally.

If there is known infection in one lung, the other is inspected first to avoid cross-contamination. The bifurcations and anatomy of each of the lobar bronchi are visualized. Specimens are taken for culture and microscopic analysis. Bronchoalveolar lavage is usually done with aliquots of 1 to 10 ml of nonbacteriostatic sodium chloride solution or Plasma-Lyte. If too large a lavage aliquot is used, the patient usually coughs it into the posterior pharynx and suctioning of the pharynx is necessary.

LABORATORY ANALYSIS OF BRONCHOSCOPIC SPECIMENS

Bacterial culture and sensitivity
Gram's stain
Fungal stain and culture
Acid-fast stain and culture
Direct smear for parasites
Viral culture
Vital stain with direct florescent antibodies
Gomori's silver stain for *Pneumocystis carinii*
Viral cultures and florescent antibodies
Oil red O stain for fat-laden macrophages and fat globules from emboli
Wright's stain for eosinophils
Iron stain for hemosiderin-laden macrophages
Cell count and differential

Care is taken to avoid prolonged suctioning because it may result in trauma to the mucosa, collapse of the distal airways, and decreased oxygen saturation as it interferes with ventilation. Withdrawing the bronchoscope a few millimeters before suctioning may make lavage less traumatic. Usually only about 50% of the infused volume is returned; the rest is absorbed or coughed out.

Specimen Analysis

If the airway is being inspected because of anatomic problems, specimens may not be necessary. However, if there is significant suspicion of infection, cultures for bacterial, fungal, or acid-fast organisms are obtained. If aspiration is suspected, specimens may be stained for fat-laden macrophages. Eosinophils may indicate an allergic component. Cultures may also be taken for viruses. Presence of free fat globules may indicate bone marrow aspiration, as in patients with sickle cell anemia or bone marrow infarct. Direct preparation may reveal parasites such as lung flukes. Gomori's silver stain may reveal the presence of *Pneumocystis carinii*. Hemosiderin-laden macrophages may indicate old hemorrhage or idiopathic

pulmonary hemosiderosis. A cell count and differential may be helpful to indicate an inflammatory reaction or interstitial pneumonitis. Levels of medications such as deoxyribonuclease, antibiotics, or bronchodilators may also be determined.

After the procedure the patient is carefully observed until sedation has worn off. Often the level of sedation may increase when the bronchoscope is withdrawn; therefore monitoring is continued until the patient is fully awake and able to protect the airway. The patient is given nothing by mouth for approximately 1 hour after lidocaine has been administered to the upper airway and return of protective airway reflexes has been documented.

The assistants obtain the patient's vital signs and prepare specimens for laboratory analysis. If wheezing or stridor are noted after bronchoscopy, administration of an aerosolized bronchodilator or vasoconstrictor is necessary.

RISKS AND COMPLICATIONS

Common complications include reaction to sedation, small amounts of blood from the nose, wheezing, or stridor. These can usually be easily treated with appropriate agents. Some patients complain of a sore throat later in the day. Occasionally fever develops several hours after bronchoscopy.

Rare complications include allergic reactions to the medications used, seizures, pneumothorax, significant bleeding, infection, and death. In a few patients with impending respiratory failure bronchoscopy may precipitate respiratory failure and intubation may be needed.

ADDITIONAL READING

American Academy of Pediatrics, Committee on Drugs. Guidelines for monitoring and management of pediatric patients during and after sedation for diagnostic and therapeutic procedures. Pediatrics 89:1110-1115, 1992.

Green CG, Eisenberg J, Leong A, et al. Flexible endoscopy of the pediatric airway. Am Rev Respir Dis 145:233-235, 1992.

Wood RE. Spelunking in the pediatric airways: Explorations with the flexible fiberoptic bronchoscope. Pediatr Clin North Am 31:785-799, 1984.

155 Mechanical Ventilation and Oxygen Support Systems

*Luis O. Toro-Figueroa · R. Phil Barton · Peter M. Luckett ·
Ronald M. Perkin*

BACKGROUND

Assisted ventilation may be defined as the movement
of gas into and out of the lung provided by an external device connected directly to the patient. The
device may be a resuscitation bag, a continuous distending pressure apparatus, or a mechanical ventilator. It may be connected to the patient by way of
a face mask, an ET tube, tracheostomy, or the chest
(e.g., negative pressure mechanism).

Assisted ventilation is a supportive technique; it is
not curative. It can only maintain blood gas tension
homeostasis within acceptable physiologic limits for
a period of time. Its purposes are to provide alveolar ventilation (i.e., CO_2 removal), optimal systemic
oxygenation, and decreased work of breathing.

In patients with severe cardiopulmonary distress
for whom the effort of breathing is intolerable or ineffective, mechanical ventilation substitutes for the action of the respiratory muscles. In some patients with
respiratory failure respiratory muscle work accounts
for as much as 50% of total oxygen consumption. In
such circumstances mechanical ventilation allows
stores of oxygen to be rerouted to other tissue beds
that may be vulnerable to hypoxia. In addition, reversal of respiratory muscle fatigue, which may
have a role in the development of acute ventilatory
failure, depends on adequate rest. Positive pressure
ventilation can reverse and prevent atelectasis and by
allowing inspiration at a more compliant and therefore favorable region of the pulmonary pressure-volume curve can decrease the work of breathing. Improvements in pulmonary gas exchange and pressure-volume relations and relief from excessive respiratory work provide an opportunity for the lungs,
airways, and other tissue beds to heal.

Positive pressure ventilation can also decrease cardiac output and initiate or aggravate alveolar damage.
The dangers of ventilator-induced lung injury have
led to reappraisal of the objectives of mechanical ventilation. Rather than strive for normal arterial blood
gas values, it is probably better to accept a certain degree of respiratory acidosis, and possibly even hypoxemia, to avoid high inflation pressure and excessive delivered tidal volume. Similarly, it may be better to risk oxygen toxicity than to use high pressure
to achieve decreased FiO_2 at the expense of increased
volutrauma and barotrauma.

Terminology

To operate a mechanical ventilator appropriately, a
thorough understanding of conventional terminology is imperative. Terms commonly used with mechanical ventilation are defined below.

air leak percent (AL%) Proportion of inspiratory tidal
  volume (V_{Ti}) lost from the ventilator circuit around
  the ET tube and from the patient compared with expiratory tidal volume (V_{Te}): $AL\% = V_{Ti} - V_{Te}/V_{Ti} \times$
  100. Ideally, AL% is maintained at <10%.
continuous flow Continuous flow of gas through a mechanical ventilator and circuit throughout respiratory cycle.
dead space (V_D) Volume of gas that is unable to be delivered for gas exchange. Dead space usually consists
  of the ventilator tubing, artificial airway (ET tube or
  tracheostomy), and large, non-gas exchange conducting airways of the patient.
delivered tidal volume (V_{Td}) Total gas volume delivered during the inspiratory phase of the mechanical
  breath. V_{Td} is the result of V_{Ti} minus the circuit com-
  pressible volume (V_{comp}): $V_{Td} = V_{Ti} - V_{comp}$. V_{Td} is usu-

ally quantitatively expressed in a volume that ranges between 5 and 15 cc/kg.

demand flow Intermittent flow of gas through a mechanical ventilator and circuit; occurs only when patient's inspiratory efforts open the ventilator gas flow demand valve.

expiratory hold Feature on certain ventilators that holds both inspiratory and expiratory valves closed after exhalation until they are released manually by the clinician.

expiratory tidal volume (V_{Te}) Total gas volume returned by the patient to the expiratory transducer of the ventilator during the expiratory phase of the mechanical breath. V_{Te} is the result of V_{Td} minus the volume leaked (V_{leak}) from the circuit around the ET tube and from the patient plus the V_{comp}: $V_{Te} = V_{Td} - V_{leak} + V_{comp}$. V_{Te} is usually quantitatively expressed in a volume that ranges from 5 to 20 cc/kg.

expiratory time (T_e) Time allotted for completion of the expiratory phase of the respiratory cycle.

flow triggering Mechanism by which patient's inspiratory efforts trigger an inspiratory phase to begin secondary to a preset amount of flow generated from the patient.

fraction of inspired oxygen (Fio_2) Concentration of oxygen being delivered to the patient.

inspiratory-expiratory ratio (I:E) Fractional proportion of time spent on each phase of the respiratory cycle. Depending on the cycling mechanism of a mechanical ventilator, inspiratory time may determine I:E ratio.

inspiratory flow rate (FR_i) Preselected parameter in volume-cycled ventilation that determines how quickly tidal volume (V_{Td}) is delivered. $V_{Td} \div FR_i = T_i$.

inspiratory hold Feature on certain ventilators that holds inspiratory and expiratory valves closed after inspiration until they are released manually by the clinician.

inspiratory pause Percent of inspiratory phase following end inspiration in which occlusion of the expiratory port is set for a preselected period to prevent exhalation. Inspiratory pause percent of inspiratory time may be selected by the clinician to promote inspiratory pressure plateaus and pendelluft.

inspiratory rise time percent Time in inspiratory phase during which change or increase in pressure is most marked, usually during the initial 20% to 25% of inspiration. Abrupt increases in delivered positive pressure during initial phase of inspiration may be uncomfortable, and prolonging the inspiratory rise time percent may be beneficial.

inspiratory sensitivity (S_i) Preselected variable that establishes pressure (below PEEP) or flow (below inspiratory flow) at which patient effort may start an inspiratory phase.

inspiratory tidal volume (V_{Ti}) Total gas volume generated by the ventilator during the inspiratory phase of the mechanical breath. V_{Ti} is usually quantitatively expressed in a volume that ranges from 7 to 20 cc/kg.

inspiratory time (T_i) Time allotted for completion of the inspiratory phase of the respiratory cycle.

mean airway pressure ($\overline{Paw}$) Averaged pressure derived from a complete inspiratory and expiratory cycle waveform. $\overline{Paw}$ is transmitted to the airways and alveoli from the beginning of one inspiration to the next. Parameters that affect $\overline{Paw}$ are PIP, PEEP, RR, T_i, and T_e.

minute ventilation Product of respiratory rate and delivered tidal volume. Minute ventilation needed for a certain level of CO_2 removal is an important determinant of the work of breathing (amount of pressure needed to move a certain volume of air). Two factors determine minute ventilation during mechanical ventilation: dead space gas volume/tidal volume ratio (V_D/V_T) and CO_2 production.

negative PEEP (NEEP) Occurs when negative pressure is applied to airway during entire respiratory cycle.

peak inspiratory pressure (PIP) Preselected maximally sustained positive pressure during the inspiratory phase of the mechanical respiratory cycle. PIP is partially responsible for the generation of tidal volume delivered.

peak end-inspiratory (plateau) pressure Airway pressure measured from the end of the inspiratory phase to the beginning of the expiratory phase of respiration. Peak end-inspiratory pressure is prolonged when the clinician has added inspiratory pause to the inspiratory phase and in pressure control modes of ventilation. Pendelluft (see Cycling Mechanisms, p. 1429) is promoted with inspiratory pause and longer peak inspiratory plateaus.

positive end-expiratory pressure (PEEP) Level of positive pressure throughout completion of the expiratory phase.

pressure above PEEP Preset pressure above the preset PEEP level. Pressure above PEEP = PIP − PEEP.

pressure triggering Mechanism by which patient's inspiratory efforts trigger an inspiratory phase to begin secondary to a preset amount of pressure generated from the patient.

respiratory cycle Time elapsed from the beginning of one mechanical inspiration to the beginning of the next ($T_i + T_e$).

respiratory rate (RR) Frequency of automatically mechanically cycled breaths.

zero PEEP (ZEEP) Occurs when no pressure (zero) is applied to airway during entire respiratory cycle.

Physiologic Principles of Mechanical Ventilation

The American College of Chest Physician's Consensus Conference held in 1993 provided several general principles that guide the use of mechanical ventilation:

- There is no optimum mode of ventilation for any disease state or optimum method of weaning patients from mechanical ventilation.
- The underlying pathophysiology of various disease states varies with time, and thus the mode, settings, and intensity of ventilation need to be reassessed.
- Mechanical ventilation is associated with a number of diverse consequences, and measures to minimize such complications need to be implemented when possible.
- To minimize side effects, the physiologic targets need not be in the normal range. For example, at times it may be beneficial to allow Pa_{CO_2} to increase (i.e., controlled hypoventilation or permissive hypercapnia) rather than risk the dangers of lung hyperinflation.
- Alveolar overdistention can cause alveolar damage or air leaks. Hence maneuvers to prevent development of excess alveolar or transpulmonary pressure need to be instituted if necessary. It is probably unwise to use large-volume and high-pressure mechanical ventilation.
- Dynamic hyperventilation such as gas trapping, auto-PEEP, or intrinsic PEEP often is unnoticed and needs to be measured or estimated, especially in patients with airway obstruction.

In addition to these general principles, physiologic principles must always be considered in the patient who needs mechanical ventilation.

Pulmonary compliance

Compliance of the lung is defined as the change in volume per unit change in distending airway pressure ($\Delta V/\Delta P$) and is determined by elastic forces within the lung such as the surface tension generated by the air-tissue interface within the alveoli. Lung compliance (C_L) therefore is a measure of "stiffness" and is described by a sigmoid curve with a diminishing slope at either end where large and small lung volumes exist (Fig. 155-1). Chest wall compliance (C_{cw}) is related to the lungs' supporting structures such as the rib cage, parietal pleura, diaphragm, and intra-abdominal cavity pressure. Respiratory system compliance (C_{RS}) is defined as the total lung and chest wall compliance. Because greater negative intrapleural pressure must be generated to inflate a less compliant lung, the work of breathing increases and becomes less efficient. Disease states associated with reduced lung, chest wall, or pulmonary system compliance are listed on p. 1419.

In a child receiving mechanical ventilation, calculation of static (C_{St}) and dynamic lung compliance (C_{Dyn}) provides diagnostic information and a parameter to monitor the course of pulmonary function over time. Static compliance is determined by divid-

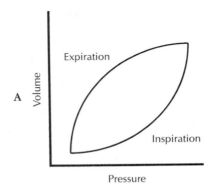
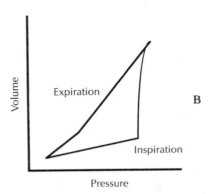

Fig. 155-1 **A,** Normal pressure-volume curve. **B,** Restrictive pressure-volume curve. In the restrictive lung mechanics a larger inspiratory pressure is needed to initiate a significant delivery of volume.

CONDITIONS ASSOCIATED WITH DECREASED PULMONARY COMPLIANCE

Increased elastic recoil forces

Hyaline membrane disease
Severe bronchiolar-alveolar pneumonia (any cause)
Diffuse pulmonary edema (cardiogenic, hydrostatic, neurogenic)
Acute respiratory distress syndrome (increased permeability pulmonary edema)
Diffuse atelectasis
Interstitial inflammation (fluid or fibrotic process)
Radiation pneumonitis
Chronic lung disease

Reduced chest wall, lung, and diaphragmatic excursion

Thoracic trauma, abdominal surgery
Pleural effusions (blood, chyle, exudates, transudates)
Pneumothorax
Reduced diaphragmatic excursion caused by abdominal distention
Paralysis or injury of diaphragm
Thoracic bone deformities (severe kyphoscoliosis)

Alveolar overdistention

Asthma
Bronchiolitis
Meconium aspiration
Bronchopulmonary dysplasia
Laryngotracheobronchomalacia
Excessive PEEP or CPAP
Inadequate assisted expiratory time

ing the tidal volume by the plateau or static inflation pressure, which can be obtained by occluding the exhalation port just before exhalation. This measurement provides an estimate of actual pulmonary system compliance (C_{PS}). Dynamic compliance is determined by dividing tidal volume by peak inspiratory pressure (PIP). The pressure required for the same change in volume to occur is always greater in dynamic compliance than in static compliance, and this difference, or lower compliance numeric value

of dynamic compliance, reflects resistance within the airways to airflow.

Functional residual capacity

Functional residual capacity (FRC) is the volume of gas retained in the lung at the end of the expiratory phase of the respiratory cycle after exhaling the tidal volume inhaled. In patients with respiratory failure from alveolar or interstitial disease, FRC usually is decreased. With atelectasis, FRC and the number of alveolar units that participate in gas exchange decrease. Acute functional loss of alveoli leads to systemic arterial hypoxemia. A major goal of assisted ventilation is to return FRC toward normal and thereby improve systemic arterial oxygenation.

Airways resistance

Airways resistance (R_{AW}) is the pressure difference between mouth and alveoli or the driving pressure needed to move respiratory gases through the airways at a constant flow rate. Airway resistance is determined by four factors: flow rate or velocity of airflow, length of the airways, physical properties such as viscosity and density of the gas inhaled, and radius of the airways. The most important determinant of airways resistance is the airway radius. Because resistance is inversely related to the fourth power of the radius, as defined by Poiseuille's law, even minor decreases of airway lumen size from bronchospasm, collapse related to interstitial edema or emphysema, narrowing from swelling, or obstruction from mucous accumulation can cause a significant increase in airways resistance.

Time constants

The time constant of the respiratory system is a measure of how quickly the lungs can inhale or exhale or how long it takes for alveolar and proximal airway pressures to equilibrate. The product of airways resistance and pulmonary compliance defines the time constant. A knowledge of time constants aids greatly in choosing the safest, most effective ventilator inspiratory time (T_i) and expiratory time (T_e) for an individual patient. Various diseases can alter the time constant, depending on the pathologic site. In addition, different segments of the lung may have different time constants. In diseases that cause increased airways resistance, such as asthma or bronchopulmonary dysplasia (BPD), the time constants of alveolar units increase, causing slower filling and emptying of the diseased alveolar unit. In diseases that result in decreased compliance, such as acute respiratory distress syndrome (ARDS), the time constant decreases, causing faster filling and emptying time of the alveolar unit. Under normal conditions, three to five time constants are necessary to allow complete filling or emptying of an alveolar unit. In a healthy infant one time constant equals approximately 0.15 second; therefore three time constants, or 0.45 second, allow approximately 75% to 80% filling of all alveolar units. Increasing the inspiratory time beyond five times the time constant does not yield much greater than 95% alveolar filling and results in inadequate expiratory time.

Inadequate expiratory time in mechanically ventilated lungs can lead to air trapping and occult end-expiratory pressure (auto-PEEP, inadvertent PEEP, or intrinsic PEEP). Auto-PEEP is relatively common but seldom appreciated. The patient with increased airways resistance is at risk for gas trapping, and appropriate ventilator settings must be selected to prolong the expiratory phase as much as possible to allow the inhaled tidal volume to be exhaled completely. Signs of gas trapping include overexpansion of the chest, decreased chest wall movement, CO_2 retention, and cardiovascular dysfunction. A simple method for detecting auto-PEEP is to occlude the ET tube at end expiration and measure the equilibration pressure distal to the occlusion. In the presence of gas trapping the pressure distal to the airway occlusion will remain higher than the measured PEEP unless there is a leak around the ET tube or the patient makes a spontaneous respiratory effort during the occlusion.

A large proportion of airways resistance in an infant or child receiving assisted ventilation may be secondary to the use of an ET tube or its connectors. When an artificial airway is partially kinked or obstructed by secretions, airways resistance becomes exaggerated and may be responsible for clinically significant gas trapping and auto-PEEP.

Work of breathing

Spontaneous ventilation in the presence of cardiopulmonary disease may significantly increase work of breathing. Although ventilation normally consumes <5% of total oxygen delivery (Do_2) to meet the respiratory pump's oxygen demand (Vo_2), in lung disease the work of breathing is markedly increased. In disease states such as those characterized by pulmonary edema or bronchospasm, oxygen demand may increase to 25% or 30% of total oxygen delivery. This increase in oxygen demand causes a redistribution of oxygen delivery, resulting in increased lung blood flow to maintain adequate perfusion and oxygen extraction to the respiratory muscles. When cardiac output is limited, such increased work of breathing can divert blood from other vital organs or tissues and thereby induce metabolic lactic acidosis. Intubation and mechanical ventilation adjusted to patient demand may dramatically decrease work of breathing, resulting in redistribution of oxygen delivery to other vital organs. The accompanying increase in mixed venous oxygen saturation (Svo_2) may result in increased Pao_2 and arterial blood saturation percent (Sao_2) if significant ventilation-perfusion ($\dot{V}/\dot{Q}$) inequality is present.

It is often assumed that when mechanical ventilation is administered in the assist-control mode work of breathing has been greatly reduced, if not eliminated. However, recent studies have demonstrated that patients with dyspnea continue to breathe voluntarily through the ventilator-generated breaths regardless of whether they initiated the breath and may actually demonstrate increased work of breathing and worsening dyspnea. Proper matching of the mechanical ventilator–generated flow pattern, threshold sensitivity, and tidal volume is essential to decrease the patient's sensation of dyspnea and work of breathing. Recently some of the new methods and strategies for ventilatory and oxygenation support have been used in an attempt to address this issue by automatically matching patient-driven ventilatory patterns with a minimal amount of patient-derived effort.

Hypercapneic respiratory failure or ventilatory failure

The ventilatory pump, which consists of the bones and muscles of the chest wall, conducting airways, and diaphragm, is responsible for providing adequate alveolar ventilation to achieve effective gas exchange. The hallmark of ventilatory failure is CO_2 retention. The most common causes of ventilatory failure are listed on p. 1421.

CAUSES OF VENTILATORY FAILURE

Increased CO_2 production

Fever, shivering, drug withdrawal
Exercise and/or seizures, pain, agitation causing excessive movement
Trauma
Sepsis
Hyperthyroidism
Burns
Excessive glucose administration
Malignant hyperthermia

Decreased alveolar ventilation with normal lungs
Depressed ventilatory drive

Sedation (narcotics, tranquilizers)
Brain injury or illness
Abnormal control of breathing
Alkalosis
Seizures

Neuromuscular disease or weakness

Spinal cord
  Tetanus
  Trauma
Anterior horn cell
  Poliomyelitis
  Werdnig-Hoffmann disease
Peripheral nerve
  Acute inflammatory polyneuropathy
  Diphtheria
Neuromuscular junction
  Myasthenia gravis
  Botulism
  Organophosphate poisoning
  Tick paralysis
  Snake bite
  Pharmacologic effects
Muscle
  Polymyositis
  Hypokalemia
  Hypophosphatemia
  Fatigue
  Muscular dystrophies

Sleep apnea

Upper airway obstruction

Secretions
Head position
Pharyngeal hypotonia
Subglottic edema or mass
Infections: croup and epiglottitis
Tracheomalacia
Foreign body
Laryngospasm
Large tonsils or adenoids

Thorax, pleura, abdomen

Trauma, flail chest
Pneumothorax
Pleural effusion
Chest or abdominal surgery
Abdominal distention
Burn eschar

Decreased alveolar ventilation with abnormal lungs
Obstructive diseases

Asthma
Bronchitis
Bronchopulmonary dysplasia
Bronchiolitis
Cystic fibrosis

Alveolar diseases

Pneumonia
ARDS
Congestive heart failure
Pulmonary contusion

Increased dead space ventilation
Reduced pulmonary blood flow

Pulmonary hypertension
Shock
Pulmonary emboli

Alveolar overdistention

Asthma
Bronchiolitis
Foreign body
Excessive PEEP

Because most patients can augment minute ventilation to eliminate the additional CO_2, increased CO_2 production by itself rarely causes ventilatory failure. However, increased CO_2 production may precipitate ventilatory failure in patients with poor neurologic, pulmonary, or muscle function that prevents them from increasing minute volume.

In most patients with ventilatory failure, increased $Paco_2$ is the result of alveolar hypoventilation.

Hypoxemic respiratory failure

Traditionally hypoxemic respiratory failure has been described as $Pao_2 \leq 50$ mm Hg in the absence of intracardiac right-to-left shunting. Hypoxemia is a primary manifestation of gas exchange failure. CO_2 elimination may also be affected but usually can be compensated for by increases in alveolar ventilation. Elimination of CO_2 is much more efficient across the alveolar capillary membrane than is exchange of oxygen because CO_2 is dissolved, not carried. Because an increase in basement membrane thickness is uncommon, abnormalities in diffusion that affect CO_2 removal are uncommon. Thus, in the absence of superimposed ventilatory pump failure, hypercapnia is not a feature of gas exchange failure. In fact, in most cases of gas exchange failure, because of the significant increase in ventilatory drive, which causes tachypnea, and increased minute ventilation, efficient CO_2 compensation with a low $Paco_2$ and associated respiratory alkalosis is common in the early stages of hypoxemic respiratory failure. The basic mechanisms that are most responsible for hypoxemia are listed in the next column.

Most cases of hypoxemia in gas exchange failure are due to combinations of right-to-left shunting and $\dot{V}/\dot{Q}$ inequality. Because one component of the hypoxemia is $\dot{V}/\dot{Q}$ inequality, usually an increase in Fio_2 results in some improvement. When a large shunt (>25%) is present, Pao_2 is not significantly improved by increasing Fio_2. In these cases a diffuse pulmonary disease process is usually present, and positive airway pressure (PAP) is needed to maintain adequate FRC for adequate gas exchange. Even in the absence of parenchymal disease, severe impairment of chest wall mechanics from rib fractures, pain, weakness, or other causes may necessitate ventilatory assistance to reverse gas exchange abnormalities. Under these circumstances, Fio_2 <0.5 is preferred to

---

BASIC MECHANISMS RESPONSIBLE FOR HYPOXEMIA

Inadequate inspiratory oxygen partial pressure (Pio_2)
Global alveolar hypoventilation
Right-to-left shunting
Ventilation-perfusion ($\dot{V}/\dot{Q}$) mismatch
Incomplete diffusion equilibrium
Excessive systemic oxygen consumption
Low cardiac output with or without right-to-left shunting
Perfusion of poorly ventilated (low $\dot{V}/\dot{Q}$) regions with a reduction in Svo_2

---

minimize the risk of oxygen toxicity. An extensive list of therapeutic measures to improve respiratory function is presented on p. 1423.

INDICATIONS

Mechanical ventilation can be lifesaving in patients with acute severe hypoxemia or worsening respiratory acidosis refractory to more conservative measures. Most of the indications for assisted ventilation in patients with respiratory failure are listed on p. 1423.

TECHNIQUE
Goals and Objectives

In general the ideal mechanical ventilator provides the short-term or long-term support necessary to achieve adequate gas exchange, minimize oxygen consumption, optimize CO_2 elimination, significantly reduce the risks of volutrauma, barotrauma, and oxygen toxicity, diminish untoward cardiopulmonary interactions, and facilitate independent spontaneous breathing. Although the newer generation of ventilators more closely meets these ideal goals and objectives, the ideal ventilator that will fulfill all of them is not yet available. Nevertheless, these goals and objectives can serve as guidelines for the clinician to develop a comprehensive management plan, to set obtainable pathophysiologic therapeutic targets, and to consider a change in ventilatory strategy, method, or

THERAPEUTIC MEASURES TO IMPROVE RESPIRATORY FUNCTION

Improve ventilatory function
Decrease CO_2 production

Reduce fever
Control infection
Control seizures
Careful sedation
Relieve pain
Neuromuscular blockade if indicated

Increase alveolar ventilation

Airway control
  Correct head position
  Pulmonary toilet, secretion removal
  Racemic epinephrine
  Oral or nasal airway placement
  ET tube placement
Remove foreign body
Relieve bronchospasm
  β-Adrenergic agonists
  Theophylline
  Anticholinergic agents
  Corticosteroids
Improve ventilation regulation
  Naloxone
  Respiratory stimulants

Improve lung compliance and volume
  Diuretics
  Positive airway pressure
Mechanical ventilation

Decrease physiologic dead space

Improve pulmonary blood flow
Optimize lung volume; reduce hyperinflation
Increase cardiac output

Improve arterial oxygenation
Provide supplemental oxygen

Face mask
Nasal cannula
ET tube

Improve ventilation

See above

Decrease intrapulmonary shunt

Patient position
Positive airway pressure
Diuretics

Optimize cardiac output

INDICATONS FOR ASSISTED MECHANICAL VENTILATION

Respiratory "pump" failure: muscular or skeletal
Increased CO_2 production
Ineffective respiratory drive
Obstructive airway diseases
Low cardiac output states
Upper airway obstruction
Drugs and intoxications
Neuromuscular diseases
Postoperative recovery
Alveolar diseases
Anesthesia
Apnea

ventilation oxygenation support system. Some specific goals and objectives of mechanical ventilation are listed on p. 1424.

Artificial Airways Management

A stable airway must be established before positive pressure ventilation can be instituted. This is usually accomplished with an artificial airway (i.e., ET tube or tracheostomy) or with a tightly sealed nasal or face mask (see Chapters 152 and 162). Like the normal upper airway, an artificial airway has nonlinear pressure-flow characteristics; therefore with increasing flow rates the airway resistance progressively increases. In addition, for any given flow rate the pressure loss across an artificial airway depends primarily on its internal radius: as the tube size (radius) decreases, re-

SPECIFIC GOALS AND OBJECTIVES OF
MECHANICAL VENTILATION

Improve pulmonary gas exchange

Relieve acute respiratory acidosis or ventilatory failure

Reverse hypoxemia or hypoxemic respiratory failure

Change pressure-volume relations in lung

Optimize pulmonary compliance

Prevent or reverse atelectasis

Reduce or otherwise modulate work of breathing

Decrease oxygen cost of breathing

Reverse respiratory muscle fatigue

Use anesthesia, sedation, or neuromuscular blockade

Avoid complications

Decrease and prevent anoxic-hypoxic events

Reduce and prevent barotrauma, volutrauma, and oxygen toxicity

Support lung and airway healing

Allow time for specific therapeutic intervention to succeed

Allow time for lung repair to evolve

Promote independent breathing or independent lifestyle

Facilitate discontinuing ventilatory dependence

Provide partial, complete, ambulatory, permanent, or temporary assisted ventilation to support chronic debilitating illness or lung disease

sistance increases exponentially to the fourth power.

Positive pressure ventilation usually overcomes the effect of the increased resistance to gas flow caused by the artificial airway. This increased resistance may also act as a low-pass filter, diminishing the resultant alveolar pressure. During the process of discontinuing mechanical ventilation it may also add significantly to resistive work of breathing and minute ventilation requirements.

Small amounts of mucous secretions or plugs may decrease the radius of a small ET tube significantly and further increase the resistive work of breathing or impede adequate gas flow, resulting in hypoventilation, fatigue, and subsequent respiratory pump failure. Therefore frequent suctioning of the ET tube and proper humidification of inspired gases are essential (see Chapters 145 and 147).

The normal anatomic narrowing caused by the subglottic ring in the airway of infants and children younger than 8 years has made use of uncuffed ET tubes the current clinical standard. In theory, to minimize laryngeal damage in children in this age range, a small air leak around the ET tube needs to be maintained with a maximum sustained PIP of 20 cm H_2O (range 15 to 35 cm H_2O). When pulmonary compliance is decreased, the presence of air leak around an ET tube >10% of inspired tidal volume may pose a challenge in sustaining adequate minute ventilation and FRC because of loss of volume from the breathing circuit.

Negative Pressure Ventilators

Although far less common than positive pressure mechanical ventilation, negative pressure ventilation may be used in the PICU under appropriate conditions. Negative pressure ventilation is the oldest form of artificial ventilatory assistance. The first widely used negative pressure ventilator was developed by Drinker in 1928 and used extensively during the poliomyelitis epidemic of the 1950s. A number of types of negative pressure ventilators are available, and all work by applying intermittent negative pressure to the thorax, which leads to a concomitant decrease in transpulmonary pressure. This simulates normal tidal breathing more closely than positive pressure ventilation and is particularly useful in respiratory insufficiency due to pump failure.

The three basic types of negative pressure ventilators are tank, jacket, and cuirass ventilators. The advantages of tank ventilators are that they do not need to be fit to the patient, require only one tight seal around the neck, and are the most efficient type of negative pressure ventilators, providing the largest tidal volume for a given pressure change. The plastic Portalung (Lifecare) is made in three sizes, allowing its use in infants as well as older children. Airtight seals may be difficult to obtain, and access to the patient is limited although more readily available than with jacket or cuirass ventilators. Jacket ventilators include a rigid internal framework and a suit that must be sealed at the arms, neck, and legs. Good fit is important and often difficult to achieve. These ventilators may be more useful for home use. Standard sized cuirass ventilators are available, but the cuirass is most efficient when individually molded for the patient. When a good fit is achieved, it is easy to care for, and most older patients find it easy to get into and out of, unlike the jacket ventilator. Cuirass ventilators are useful for home ventilation but need to be remade when the child grows or gains weight.

To begin negative pressure ventilation, the patient is placed in the device, the pressure is lowered to 5 to 10 cm H_2O, and the seal at the neck is checked for leaks. The rate is set below the spontaneous breathing rate of the patient, and the pressure is lowered gradually until a desirable tidal volume is achieved as assessed by the adequacy of chest rise. Mask pulmonary function testing may also be performed to quantitate tidal volume. With most machines, the end-expiratory pressure can be set to a negative value to support FRC. Pressure between -15 and -30 cm H_2O is usually adequate. The rate is adjusted as needed to maintain adequate minute ventilation.

A number of cautions are in order. Upper airway obstruction may become a problem. This is true in patients without previous evidence of obstruction as well as those with preexisting upper airway anomalies or obstructive sleep apnea. In some patients CPAP will need to be added to maintain upper airway patency. In addition, the airway is not protected as it is when an ET tube is present, and aspiration is a danger, especially in patients with bulbar dysfunction. Finally, negative pressure ventilators have limited usefulness in patients who need continuous ventilation or who have significantly increased respiratory system impedance from severe lung disease or chest wall deformity.

The general objectives for selecting patients for noninvasive methods of ventilatory support are (1) to maintain a sense of well-being free of signs and symptoms such as irritability, diaphoresis, or use of accessory muscles; (2) to maintain adequate gas exchange; (3) to allow spontaneous respirations and periods of respiratory muscle training; and (4) to allow for continued growth of the child. Children with acute or chronic respiratory insufficiency may be appropriate candidates for negative pressure ventilation. It is especially useful in patients with neuromuscular and skeletal disorders and patients with chronic lung

disease who do not need full and continuous respiratory support. In may also be useful as a bridge to full liberation from ventilatory support and in patients whose parents are opposed to tracheostomy tube placement.

Continuous Distending Pressure

Ineffective oxygenation in patients with acute respiratory failure, despite the use of high-concentration oxygen supplementation, led to the application of continuous distending pressure in an attempt to normalize FRC. PEEP and CPAP are two techniques that provide continuous distending pressure for management of restrictive pulmonary disorders in which the reduction of FRC is clinically evident. PEEP is defined as residual pressure above atmospheric pressure maintained at the airway opening at end expiration. Although it may be used during spontaneous ventilation, it is most commonly used in conjunction with mechanical ventilation. CPAP is usually defined as pressure above atmospheric pressure maintained at the airway opening throughout the respiratory cycle during spontaneous breathing. Thus pressure in the airway is always positive when CPAP is used.

Technical considerations

Many devices and systems have been developed to deliver CPAP and PEEP. All work on the same principle: use of a continuous gas inflow source or generator, a reservoir, a valve to restrict outflow of gas to produce above ambient expiratory pressure, and a humidification device. To prevent rebreathing of exhaled gases, the system needs gas flow rates sufficient to provide two to three times the patient's minute volume requirements. CPAP is most commonly applied to the airways via an ET tube, but application devices, including face mask or nasal prongs, are also used. Systems to deliver PEEP are usually more complex, and their operation characteristics depend greatly on the specific mechanical ventilator involved. PEEP can be generated by either continuous flow or intermittently with a servomechanism that maintains it at a preset level by providing flow when the PEEP level falls below the level prescribed. Recent technologic developments have made both types available in some ventilator models and have created servomechanisms more sensitive and responsive to patient demand, resulting in reduced work of breathing required to trigger the servomechanism.

Physiologic effects of PEEP and CPAP

Pulmonary system. Arterial oxygenation improves with PEEP or CPAP. The mechanisms believed important in improving oxygenation during continuous distending pressure are summarized in the next column.

The increase in FRC that results from PEEP or CPAP depends on both lung compliance and chest wall compliance. The efficacy of continuous distending pressure is influenced by factors such as position, presence of pleural effusion, abdominal distention, and muscular tone as well as the inflation characteristics of the lung. When FRC is increased, ventilation to poorly recruited or collapsed alveoli improves, lung compliance improves, intrapulmonary shunting decreases, and Pao_2 increases. However, when PEEP or CPAP results in overdistention of alveoli, lung compliance may decrease and dead space ventilation may increase, resulting decreased oxygenation.

In unilateral lung disease redistribution of blood flow in relation to ventilation of the affected lung may also cause decreased Pao_2 because of increased intrapulmonary shunting. Application of PEEP or CPAP to the normal lung may cause overdistention of alveoli, increased pulmonary vascular resistance, or diversion of pulmonary blood flow to the sick lung, all of which can affect gas exchange unfavorably.

A beneficial effect attributed to PEEP or CPAP is redistribution of alveolar fluid, both within the alveolus itself and through transfer of fluid from the alveolus to the interstitial compartment. Continuous distending pressure neither reduces lung water nor speeds lymphatic clearance rates; in fact, most studies have shown that it increases total lung water content. The redistribution of lung water is presumed to be the effect of interstitial space distention and increase in venous and lymphatic pressure. Redistribution of lung water from alveoli to interstitial spaces may provide valuable reductions in diffusion distance and increased efficiency for oxygen exchange.

Cardiovascular system. Although PEEP can increase FRC and improve Sao_2, it is well established in animal models and human subjects that excessive PEEP depresses cardiac output by reducing venous return, increasing right ventricular afterload, and shifting the interventricular septum into the left ventricle. The reduction in left ventricular volume that results from change of the right ventricular geometry and size is termed ventricular interdependence. Because

---

> ### MECHANISMS THAT IMPROVE OXYGENATION WITH CPAP AND PEEP
>
> Increase FRC by recruitment of collapsed alveoli
> Redistribute lung water from alveoli to interstitium
> Optimize $\dot{V}/\dot{Q}$ relationship
> Volume maintenance of recruited alveoli
> Prevent small airways closure during exhalation

---

oxygen delivery to peripheral tissues predominately depends on cardiac output under conditions in which arterial hemoglobin saturation approaches 90%, even modest reductions in cardiac output can have dramatic effects on oxygen delivery.

That aggressive medical management with fluid supplementation and vasopressor agents can overcome these adverse hemodynamic consequences of PEEP or CPAP need not serve as the impetus for use of excessive levels. Although poorly documented, levels of PEEP or CPAP sufficient to affect right ventricular performance can produce intracardiac shunting through a patent foramen ovale. In addition, profound reductions in cardiac output may result in excessive oxygen extraction by peripheral tissues; this results in return of severely desaturated venous blood to the right heart. The consequent lower mixed venous oxygen content may contribute to profound arterial desaturation, particularly when $\dot{V}/\dot{Q}$ abnormalities are prominent.

Renal system. Significant water retention, as manifested by weight gain, positive water balance, hyponatremia, decreased hematocrit, and pulmonary edema without signs of cardiac failure, is frequently seen when positive pressure is applied to the airways and lungs. The effects of continuous distending pressure on renal function are complex and may involve one or a combination of the following factors: elevation of antidiuretic hormone level, activation of the renin-angiotension-aldosterone axis, redistribution of intrarenal blood flow to juxtamedullary nephrons, and reduction in atrial natriuretic peptides. As a result of the complexity of this interaction between continuous distending pressure and renal function, a large number of mechanisms have been postulated, and conflicting results have been reported in multiple studies in animals and humans. To date there is lack of consensus on the true effects of CPAP or PEEP on renal function. For these reasons, it may be best to evaluate the interaction between continuous distending pressure and the renal system in each patient.

Central nervous system. The use of PEEP or CPAP may result in or intensify intracranial hypertension or cerebral ischemia. As continuous distending pressure is increased, venous return to the thorax is obstructed and mean venous pressure in the cerebral veins increases. These effects are directly related to the amount of continuous distending pressure applied and vary inversely with lung compliance. Changes in increased ICP correlate well with changes in continuous distending pressure and pleural pressure. Decreased cerebral perfusion pressure may be related to decreased cardiac output or mean systemic arterial blood pressure as well as increased ICP.

Indications and applications of PEEP and CPAP

PEEP and CPAP are commonly used in the treatment of restrictive lung diseases, specifically, ARDS and hyaline membrane disease.

Many of the therapeutic goals of other uses of PEEP or CPAP are quite different from the goals in patients with ARDS or hyaline membrane disease. In some cases continuous distending pressure is used to treat airway disease rather than alveolar disease. PEEP or CPAP is most likely to benefit patients with acute or diffuse lung disease associated with reduced FRC. If hypoxemia persists despite supplemental oxygen administration of >50%, a trial of continuous distending pressure is indicated.

PEEP or CPAP is generally increased in small increments of 2 to 3 cm H_2O while monitoring oxygenation and hemodynamic performance. As Pa_{O_2} or Sa_{O_2} improves, Fi_{O_2} may be reduced. Assuming normal oxygen-hemoglobin dissociation, Pa_{O_2} >60 mm Hg results in Sa_{O_2} >90%, which provides more than adequate oxygen delivery in most patients. A "safe" Fi_{O_2} level has not been determined; however, a value below 0.6 is well tolerated by most patients for extended periods. The optimal levels of PEEP and CPAP remain controversial. Although continuous distended pressure improves oxygenation and allows reduction in Fi_{O_2}, it may impair cardiac performance and expose a patient to pulmonary barotrauma or volutrauma. Thus continuous monitoring is necessary

---

INDICATIONS FOR PEEP AND CPAP

Acute lung injury

ARDS
Hyaline membrane disease
Aspiration syndromes
Diffuse pneumonias

Other conditions

Reducing or discontinuing mechanical ventilation
Intracardiac left-to-right shunting
Central or obstructive apnea
Asthma and bronchiolitis
Chronic lung diseases
Tracheobronchomalacia
Postoperative care
Artificial airways
Pulmonary edema

---

to evaluate the benefits of PEEP or CPAP and to prevent or minimize its adverse effects and complications.

After the patient's condition has improved, continuous distending pressure must be carefully reduced by 1 or 2 cm H_2O in a deliberate fashion. Premature withdrawal or sudden discontinuation of PEEP or CPAP may lead to a precipitous decrease in oxygenation and FRC. Procedures such as tracheal suctioning that temporarily result in removal of PEEP must be kept to a minimum when possible. Such derecruitment and desaturation events can be prevented with a "PEEP-port" or "PEEP-keep" device or an in-line suction catheter (see Chapter 147).

Two other variations of continuous distending pressure include zero PEEP (ZEEP) and negative PEEP (NEEP). ZEEP occurs when no pressure (zero) is applied to the airway during the entire respiratory cycle. ZEEP is most commonly used in patients with obstructive pulmonary disease or with increased ICP to augment cerebral venous drainage. NEEP occurs when negative pressure is applied to the airway during the entire respiratory cycle. This maneuver was designed to minimize the effects of positive pressure ventilation and reduction of airway pressure. NEEP has been associated with airway collapse, especially in patients with obstructive pulmonary disease, and is no longer considered efficacious.

Bilevel Positive Airway Pressure

Noninvasive positive pressure ventilation with a nasal mask, eliminating many of the complications or problems associated with an ET tube or tracheostomy, has been developed for treatment of chronic respiratory failure. Such intermittent or nocturnal conventional volume-cycled or pressure-cycled positive pressure ventilation has been used successfully to treat hypoventilation associated with upper airway obstruction, laryngotracheobronchomalacia, obstructive apnea, congestive heart failure, neuromuscular disease, chronic lung disease, and kyphoscoliosis. The method employs quiet, portable, easy-to-use equipment and allows considerable patient independence.

The bilevel positive airway pressure system (BiPAP; Respironics, Murrysville, Pa.) delivers positive pressure and ventilatory assistance in a spontaneously breathing patient. It is pneumatically powered and electrically controlled and uses a moderate gas pressure supply source. The electronic control down regulates the gas pressure to a low level, and positive pressure is then supplied to the patient. Unlike nasal CPAP, the unit can deliver different pressures during inspiration and exhalation or can be set up to deliver CPAP only. With BiPAP, when the patient initiates a breath the device delivers a small assist to ventilation along a positive pressure gradient, increasing tidal volume and minute ventilation. Oxygenation and CO_2 elimination are improved without increased risk of infection or airway trauma directly related to an artificial airway.

Limitations of BiPAP include lack of a comprehensive alarm system, humidification delivery system, and ventilation backup system. Ancillary monitors or personnel are needed if patient surveillance is desired. The efficacy of BiPAP in the treatment of severe hypoxemia has not been demonstrated. Patients who have difficulty handling tracheobronchial secretions would not be expected to benefit from BiPAP. The tight seal needed at the nasal area for BiPAP application can cause irritation and skin breakdown. Diligent local skin care is needed to prevent this complication, especially during the initial application.

BiPAP-assisted breathing has been successfully used in individually selected patients with chronic lung disease, tracheostomies, intact respiratory drive, and low to moderate oxygen and ventilation requirements. Because this device is not approved by the FDA for use with artificial airways, it is imperative that informed consent be obtained before its application in patients with ET tubes or tracheostomies, for example. Most of the scientific knowledge about BiPAP is derived from adult studies. Prospective, randomized studies of its use in pediatric populations are overdue.

Positive Pressure Ventilators

Maintenance of intact end-organ function is the fundamental goal for using mechanical ventilatory support in patients with severe cardiorespiratory dysfunction. Currently many different mechanical ventilation modalities are available for the clinician to choose from. To provide adequate gas exchange and avoid potential complications, these choices must be carefully and properly tailored to match ventilatory method and strategy with each specific disease process.

When used appropriately, mechanical ventilation can be lifesaving. However, it carries risks of severe complications. Even the delivery of oxygen may be harmful to the lung. Cellular metabolism involves a sequential reduction of oxygen to water, resulting in the generation of free radicals (e.g., H_2O_2, O_2^-, and HO_2). These oxygen radicals are highly toxic, reactive molecules capable of damaging cell membranes and intracellular structures. In normal lungs exposure to high P_{AO_2} for <24 hours does not result in clinically significant lung tissue abnormalities. However, when lungs with parenchymal injury are exposed to F_{IO_2} >0.6, lung tissue structure and function can become abnormal (oxygen toxicity). In general continuous exposure to F_{IO_2} <0.6 is considered safe and not thought to cause further lung injury. No controlled pediatric or adult studies exist to validate this recommendation or guideline.

Over the past few years a growing body of literature has supported the idea that mechanical ventilation may cause alveolar changes identical to those found in ARDS. During mechanical ventilation lung distention may induce tissue fluid balance alterations, increased endothelial and epithelial lung cell permeability, and altered lung parenchymal ultrastructure, resulting in tissue damage similar to what has been described in ARDS. Both exposure to positive pressure and mechanical distention of the pulmonary parenchyma may be important in causing parenchymal lung injury.

In most acute lung insults, injuries to the lung parenchyma are nonhomogeneous, with alveolar collapse in some areas of the lung and relatively normal architecture and function in the remainder. The effects of mechanically generated gas flow during inspiration in the noninjured areas of the lung may cause alveolar overdistention, resulting in injury to or rupture of the normal alveoli (volutrauma). This same gas flow to injured areas may cause excessively high pressure within the proximal airways, leading to distal alveolar collapse and resulting in rupture of or injury to involved airways or adjacent alveoli (barotrauma).

Extensive knowledge of the available methods of mechanical ventilation is imperative to develop strategies that will support adequate oxygenation and ventilation and promote lung healing, regeneration, remodeling, and recovery while preventing oxygen toxicity, volutrauma, and barotrauma.

Cycling mechanisms

During the inspiratory phase the only function of a ventilator is to force gas flow into the airways and lungs. Usually by the time the inspiratory phase ends a certain gas pressure, volume, and flow rate have been achieved. When a number of preset variables is reached, a changeover process is initiated and active mechanical inspiration ends. This allows exhalation, usually a passive process, to occur. Exhalation is terminated when the active mechanical inspiratory tidal breath starts. A ventilator's cycling mechanism may be used to classify it. According to which factor of the cycling mechanism controls the end of a mechanical ventilatory cycle, ventilators are classified into four types: time cycled, pressure cycled, volume cycled, and flow cycled (Table 155-1).

The inspiratory period (inhalation) for a *time-cycled ventilator* is terminated when the predetermined inspiratory time is completed. This cycling mechanism is independent of any inspiratory tidal volume delivered or the pressure required to deliver it. Time-cycled ventilators do not control inspiratory tidal volume directly; therefore it is proportional to the product of the flow rate and inspiratory time and will remain constant as long as these factors remain constant. Conversely, to increase inspiratory tidal volume, inspiratory time or flow rate must be increased. When inspiratory time increases, respiratory rate decreases unless expiratory time is decreased. With a time-cycled ventilator, when PIP increases to deliver a set flow rate, lung compliance may have decreased. Sudden decreases in PIP may result from a gas leak in the ventilator or circuit, a large air leak in the patient, or changes in patient position that cause increased ET tube leak.

Pressure-limited time-cycled mechanical ventilators are a variation of time-cycled ventilators. The unique characteristic of this type of ventilator is that by setting a constraint on PIP, a pressure limit is achieved at the preselected PIP value. When the preset pressure limit is reached, the gas flow rate is diverted from the inspiratory circuit and the airway pressure is held at a constant level until the ventilator cycle time is completed. This inspiratory pressure hold is also known as inspiratory plateau pressure.

Table 155-1 Mechanical Ventilator Cycling Characteristics

Variable	Ventilator Type (cycle)			
	Pressure	Volume	Time	Flow
Flow	Controlled	Controlled	Controlled	Controlled
Volume	Determined	Controlled	Determined	Determined
Pressure	Controlled	Determined	Determined	Controlled
Frequency	Controlled	Controlled	Controlled	Controlled
I:E ratio	Determined	Determined	Controlled	Determined
Fio$_2$	Controlled	Controlled	Controlled	Controlled

Gas actively flows from the ventilator, through the circuit, and to the patient during the pressure limit or inspiratory plateau period. This limit in PIP has been proposed as a strategy to reduce the risk of barotrauma. The inspiratory plateau period is also responsible for facilitating the pendelluft effect. Alveolar units with short time constants (low compliance, low resistance) fill and empty more rapidly. At end expiration, when units with short time constants (fast units) are empty and ready to fill, slow units are still emptying; thus gas moves from the slow to the fast units (pendelluft effect). During inspiration fast units have filled and start to empty, whereas slow units are still filling; thus gas moves from fast to slow units (pendelluft effect). This phenomenon is responsible for the redistribution of gas within the lung through intraregional mixing of alveolar gas.

With a *volume-cycled mechanical ventilator,* inspiration is terminated when the predetermined inspiratory tidal volume has been delivered into the patient circuit, irrespective of PIP, inspiratory time, and inspiratory flow rates. The preset inspiratory tidal volume is determined by the clinician; however, the proportion that the lungs actually receive compared with that preselected may not always be equal or constant. For example, when pulmonary compliance decreases or airways resistance increases, PIP increases to deliver the predetermined tidal volume. As PIP increases, some volume will be lost from the ventilator circuit as a consequence of the system's compliance, the compressibility of the gas volume, air leak around the ET tube, or direct loss of gas volume from the ventilator or circuit. The most common mechanism for correcting a decrease in delivered tidal volume is to slowly increase inspiratory tidal volume until the desired expiratory tidal volume is achieved. Factors that may cause increased PIP during volume-cycled ventilation include decreased respiratory system compliance, malposition, kinking, or obstruction of the ET tube, water condensation in ventilator tubing, and increased airways resistance.

Pressure-cycled ventilators terminate mechanical inspiration when a preselected PIP is reached. The preselected PIP will be achieved irrespective of the inspiratory tidal volume, inspiratory time, or flow rate. Passive exhalation occurs when the expiratory valve opens only after the predetermined PIP is reached. During pressure-cycled ventilation, inspiratory tidal volume can be mathematically described as $V_{Ti} = T_i \times$ flow rate, where V_{Ti} is inspiratory tidal volume and T_i is inspiratory time. Changes in inspiratory time affect the delivered tidal volume, whereas changes in respiratory system compliance affect inspiratory tidal volume and inspiratory time directly and airways resistance affects both of them inversely. For example, a significant decrease in the duration of the inspiratory time (time needed to reach preset PIP) may result from decreased respiratory system compliance and increased airways resistance; therefore delivered tidal volume will be decreased. To reestablish adequate inspiratory tidal volume, PIP can be increased to compensate for the decrease in respiratory system compliance and flow rates adjusted to compensate for the increase in airways resistance.

With *flow-cycled ventilators,* mechanical inspiration is terminated when the inspiratory flow rate decreases to a predetermined critical value. Inhalation will be terminated regardless of inspiratory tidal volume, inspiratory time, or PIP generated. While a flow-cycled breath is being delivered, the PIP and flow rates increase rapidly. The inspiratory phase continues until the flow rate decreases to the predetermined critical value. At this point the passive exhalation phase begins with opening of the expiration valve.

Patterns of gas flow

Pressure is the measure of the impedance to gas flow in a ventilator circuit, a patient's airways, or lung units. The patterns of gas flow characteristic of ventilators depend on the driving pressure generated by and the driving mechanisms in a specific type of conventional ventilator. Four main types of flow patterns have been described: constant flow, sinusoidal flow, decelerating flow, and accelerating flow (Fig. 155-2).

With *constant flow,* the driving pressure is high relative to the airway pressure and is limited by an adjustable resistance control. Because gas flow remains constant throughout inspiration, airway pressure and lung volume continue to increase linearly. Changes in respiratory system compliance or airways resistance usually do not affect the inspiratory flow waveform and inspired tidal volume.

A *sinusoidal flow* pattern, or sine-wave flow, is characterized by a progressively increasing inspiratory flow rate, gradually falling to zero just before onset of exhalation. Airway pressures and inspiratory tidal volume increase gradually and decrease gradually, also forming a sinusoidal waveform.

A *decelerating flow* profile results from ventilators that generate gas flow with a nonconstant flow gen-

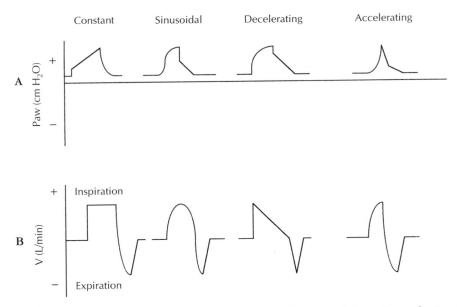

Fig. 155-2   Patterns of gas flow. Airway pressure *(Paw)* and flow rate *(V)* are shown for inspiratory flow waveforms.

erator. A decelerating flow pattern is seen when the driving pressure is relatively low compared with the proximal airway pressure, and the result is characterized by reaching maximal flow early in the inspiratory phase that gradually declines to zero at the end of inspiration. Airway pressure and pulmonary volume rise exponentially, and finally fall before commencement of exhalation.

With *accelerating flow,* flow rate increases exponentially throughout the inspiratory phase and decelerates immediately before the beginning of exhalation. Airway pressures and inspiratory tidal volume also increase exponentially during inspiration, and decrease rapidly before expiration. There is much controversy about which type of inspiratory flow is best to improve oxygenation, ventilation, and $\dot{V}/\dot{Q}$ matching with the least deleterious effects. Several mechanical ventilatory strategies have been used to decrease iatrogenic lung injury, including use of decreased tidal volume, limited PIP, increased inspiratory time, and increased airways pressure; by-passing dead space; and use of permissive hypercapnia or relative hypoxemia. Because an accelerating inspiratory flow waveform has been associated with generating high PIP, the consensus currently is

not to use it when high PIP is needed to recruit and ventilate the alveoli. Decelerating waveforms generate lower PIP and more constant airways pressure over the inspiratory cycle and are recommended to promote the pendelluft effect. The decelerating flow pattern is often recommended as the best to use in disease states associated with decreased compliance. Results of many of the studies performed to investigate the benefits of the different inspiratory flow patterns have been inconclusive because of the number of variables considered (e.g., altered inspiratory time, I:E ratios, delivered tidal volume, and flow rates). In a recent study the tidal volume and flow rate were held constant and different types of inspiratory waveforms were compared with a series of prolonged inspiratory times. The results supported prolonged inspiratory time, not the inspiratory waveform, as the variable that most improves gas exchange.

Modes of positive pressure mechanical ventilation

Airway pressure release ventilation. This mode (Fig. 155-3) uses a CPAP circuit to generate two levels of pressure during spontaneous breathing. The

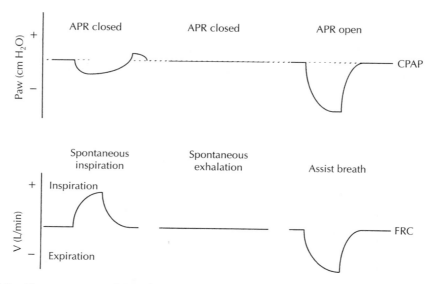

Fig. 155-3 Airway pressure release *(APR)* ventilation. In this mode high gas flow is provided to maintain a constant level of CPAP during spontaneous inspiration and exhalation. To assist breathing, CPAP is briefly interrupted to allow a transient decrease in FRC and elimination of CO_2 from the lungs.

theory is to recruit alveoli with long time constants and keep them open with a sustained high airway pressure. CPAP is maintained at a predetermined level, and periodically decreased to a lower, baseline level with a timer that cycles the valve controlling the end pressure. The clinician sets the initial pressure level, lower pressure level, respiratory rate, and duration of pressure releases. Usually the duration of airway pressure release (i.e., baseline end pressure) is ≥1.5 seconds and is timed to occur during expiration. During airway pressure release ventilation intrathoracic pressure decreases with every inspiratory effort, theoretically minimizing hemodynamic compromise. Few studies have established the indications of this method in adult or pediatric populations. One of the proposed advantages is its use in patients with mild to moderate lung injury and adequate respiratory drive.

Assist control ventilation. Mechanical breaths are activated by the patient's spontaneous inspiratory effort. If the patient's inspiratory efforts are insufficient, the preset mechanical respiratory rate is maintained automatically.

Assisted ventilation. The ventilator, triggered by each inspiratory effort the patient makes, assists each tidal breath.

Continuous positive pressure ventilation. A positive pressure breath is followed by a decrease in airway pressure that does not return to the zero atmospheric pressure baseline. An example of this method is controlled mandatory ventilation used in combination with PEEP.

Controlled mandatory ventilation. This mode delivers a preset mechanically generated breath regardless of the patient's inspiratory effort. It does not provide gas flow for tidal breathing between mechanical breaths.

Intermittent mandatory ventilation. This is a modification of controlled mandatory ventilation in which the patient is allowed to take spontaneous breaths and inhale gas flow through the ventilator circuit.

Intermittent positive pressure breathing. This technique uses bag-valve-mask ventilation with positive pressure breaths. It is usually administered in patients with inadequate tidal breathing or severe or refractory atelectasis.

Pressure control ventilation. In this mode (Fig. 155-4) the inspiratory phase ends when the preset pressure limit is achieved. Pressure control ventilation may be either pressure cycled, time cycled, or pressure limited and time cycled, with or without syn-

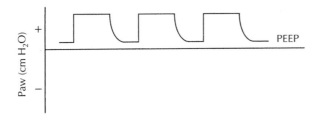

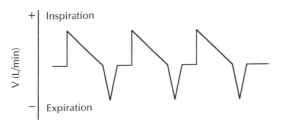

Fig. 155-4 Pressure control ventilation. The ventilator delivers breaths with a preset inspiratory pressure and decelerating flow.

chronized intermittent mandatory ventilation. The inspiratory waveform depends on the type of ventilator used; constant or decelerating flow generators are most commonly used. Inspiratory time and delivered inspired tidal volume may vary depending on changes in respiratory system compliance or airways resistance. The clinician presets the FiO_2, inspiratory time, respiratory rate, PIP, and PEEP. The pressure control method allows the patient to trigger the inspiratory breath, with either flow or pressure mechanism, but once the breath is initiated, the preset values are administered. This method is used in patients with severe disease in whom neuromuscular blockade is necessary. Contrary to the volume control mode, change in respiratory rate affects inspiratory time, which will have to be adjusted if the same time is to be maintained. Compared with volume control, the pressure control mode requires lower PIP to generate a similar inspiratory tidal volume and higher airway pressure for the same minute ventilation. In theory, this is an advantage of pressure control over volume control because it prevents ventilator-induced volutrauma and barotrauma in patients with lung compartments with different respiratory system compliance, airways resistance, and time constants. By producing higher airway pressure at lower PIP,

pressure control ventilation restores or maintains FRC with lower risk of further iatrogenic trauma by more efficiently recruiting alveoli without overdistending them and improving $\dot{V}/\dot{Q}$ matching.

Pressure control or volume control synchronized intermittent mandatory ventilation plus pressure support ventilation. As with any synchronized mode, the patient receives a set number of synchronized mandatory ventilator breaths that may be triggered by flow (Fig. 155-5) or pressure (Fig. 155-6). During the synchronized ventilation cycle the patient may trigger a preset controlled breath. If the time during which a mandatory breath should occur passes without any breathing effort, a mandatory controlled breath is initiated by the ventilator. Between preset controlled ventilator breaths the patient may breathe spontaneously with assistance from pressure support ventilation. Because both of these are "synchronized" modes, they can be used only in spontaneously breathing patients. These combined modes of ventilation provide transition from volume control or pressure control ventilation to pressure support ventilation alone. In theory, they may increase the success rate of discontinuing mechanical ventilation and decrease the time needed to do it.

Pressure-regulated volume control ventilation. This is a relatively new mode of controlled mechanical ventilation in which the ventilator analyzes expiratory tidal volume on a breath-by-breath basis and resets the PIP level needed to assure the targeted volume (Fig. 155-7). The ventilator accomplishes this by regulating inspiratory pressures to a value based on the volume-pressure relation derived from the previous breath and compared with the targeted volume. As with volume control ventilation, the pressure is allowed to change ±3 cm H_2O from one breath to the next. A decelerating inspiratory flow waveform is generated. The clinician sets the FiO_2, respiratory rate, PEEP, inspiratory time, and desired tidal volume. The advantage of this mode is that the desired tidal volume can be guaranteed at the lowest PIP necessary to achieve it, thus minimizing barotrauma and variations in tidal volume that occur as respiratory system compliance and airways resistance change.

Pressure support ventilation. In this mode (Fig. 155-8) the patient must trigger every breath to receive the predetermined pressure assist from the ventilator. Preset values include FiO_2, PEEP, and pressure above PEEP or PIP, depending on the device. The patient determines the respiratory rate, I:E ratio, and part

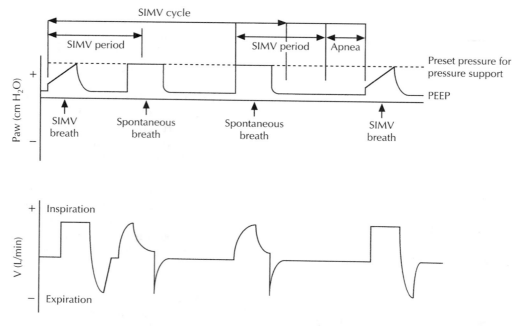

Fig. 155-5 Volume control synchronized intermittent mandatory ventilation plus pressure support. A combination of volume control and pressure support is used. The ventilator delivers mandatory breaths (volume control) and assisted breaths triggered by the patient (pressure support). SIMV period is time window during which ventilator, sensing no breath, will deliver a breath; encompasses one respiratory cycle. SIMV cycle is set length of time between mandatory synchronized breaths. It is applied at different times in cycle, depending on patient's intrinsic respiratory rate.

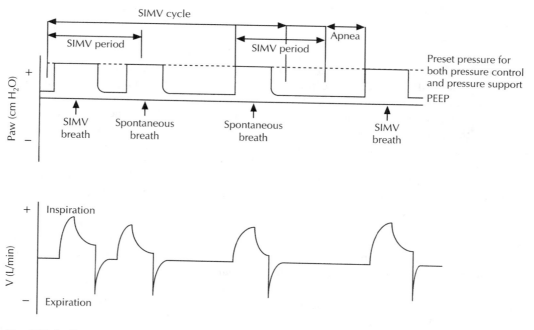

Fig. 155-6 Pressure control synchronized intermittent mandatory ventilation (SIMV) plus pressure support. A combination of pressure control and pressure support is used. The ventilator delivers mandatory breaths (pressure control) and assisted breaths triggered by the patient (pressure support.)

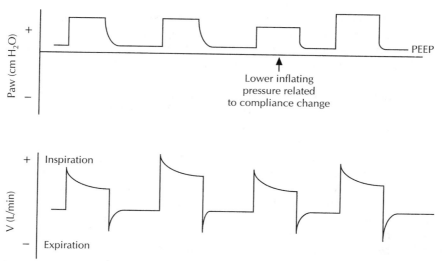

Fig. 155-7   Pressure-regulated volume control. Breaths are delivered at the lowest possible inflating pressure to deliver the preset tidal volume according to the dynamic changes in lung-thorax mechanical properties. The pressure is kept constant, and inspiratory flow is decelerating.

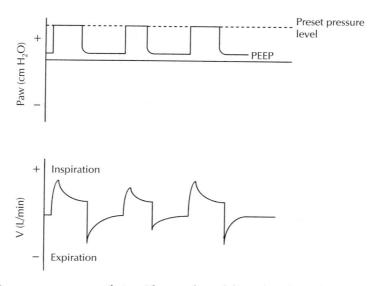

Fig. 155-8   Pressure support ventilation. The ventilator delivers breaths with a preset pressure kept constant during inspiration and with decelerating flow. All breaths are triggered by the patient. Therefore the breath-to-breath interval may vary.

of the resultant inspiratory tidal volume, all of which depend on the patient's intact respiratory drive and respiratory pump fitness. The patient's respiratory efforts may vary from breath to breath. When the upper pressure limit is reached, pressure assist is maintained at the preset level until the inspiratory flow rate decreases to 25% of maximum and the inspiratory phase ceases. At this point passive exhalation begins when the flow rate reaches zero. It must be stressed that in patients with acutely worsening pulmonary compliance or increasing airways resistance, the delivered inspiratory tidal volume will decrease and the potential for hypoventilation will increase. Pressure support ventilation is ideally suited for use in patients in whom prolonged mechanical ventilation is being discontinued slowly. To decrease the work of breathing in patients with respiratory muscle weakness or fatigue, the pressure support mode is used in combination with synchronized intermittent mandatory ventilation. As the patient becomes stronger, the rate of synchronized intermittent ventilation is decreased rapidly, allowing the patient to assume more of the work of breathing and depend on pressure support ventilation to supplement respiratory efforts and maintain an adequate minute volume. As the di-

aphragm and other respiratory muscles are retrained by increasing respiratory work load, the patient generates a greater part of the inspiratory tidal volume, and pressure support is slowly decreased.

Proportional assist ventilation. In this method (Fig. 155-9) ventilator output is modified to meet the patient's respiratory demands. This mode can function only in the spontaneously breathing patient. The ventilator senses and monitors the patient's respiratory efforts and provides the pressure support needed to meet demands. For example, in a spontaneously breathing patient, the pressure support provided at the airway is changed in proportion to the inspiratory tidal volume (elastic assist) or the inspired flow (resistive assist) or a combination of both. In other words, as the patient creates more negative pressure during inspiration, the ventilator increases its pressure support level to deliver a higher tidal volume, and as the patient relaxes, the ventilator decreases pressure support, also decreasing inspiratory tidal volume. This process depends on a feedback sensor that takes into account both volume and flow signals. Compared with synchronized intermittent mandatory ventilation methods, proportional assist ventilation decreases the PIP needed to deliver an

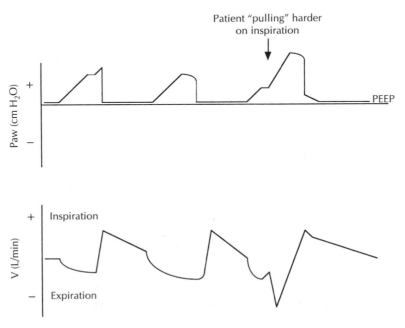

Fig. 155-9 Proportional assist ventilation. The patient generates more negative inspiratory force, and the ventilator increases its pressure support level to increase flow and deliver volume accordingly.

equivalent tidal volume, thus decreasing the potential for barotrauma. Because this device relies on patient feedback, the chance of hypoventilation in a patient with progressive respiratory failure always exists, and therefore caution must be used. This method is currently in the developmental stages, with a few human trials completed. This mode is very promising and may be the only method of mechanical ventilation that will allow the patient to have complete control of the respiratory pattern.

Synchronized intermittent mandatory ventilation. The patient's own inspiratory efforts are used in synchrony with intermittent mechanical ventilation.

Volume control ventilation. This method (Fig. 155-10) delivers preselected inspiratory tidal volume and inspiratory time. Flow waveform characteristics depend on which type of ventilator is used; constant or sinusoidal flow generators are most commonly used. The volume control mode may be either volume cycled or time cycled and may be set up with or without synchronized intermittent mandatory ventilation. This mode controls all inspiratory variables of the mechanical breaths except when the patient is allowed to trigger the beginning of the mechanical inspiratory phase. For all mechanically generated breaths, including those triggered, Fio_2, inspiratory time, respiratory rate, inspiratory tidal vol-

ume, and PEEP values are preset by the clinician. Changes in flow rate, airways resistance, respiratory system compliance, and ventilator circuit compliance and resistance that occur during volume control ventilation may cause PIP to increase or decrease. Therefore the delivered inspiratory tidal volume is usually not constant. For example, when the patient's respiratory system compliance decreases beyond ventilator circuit compliance, some of the delivered inspiratory tidal volume with each volume control breath will be "lost" or compressed within the ventilator circuit. When there is a leak in the ventilator system, the delivered inspiratory tidal volume is less than the preset value; therefore the expiratory tidal volume must be closely monitored because it will approximate the actual delivered tidal volume more closely.

Volume support ventilation. This is another type of spontaneously breathing assisted ventilation (Fig. 155-11) and guarantees the patient a targeted inspiratory tidal volume. The clinician sets the Fio_2, PEEP, and targeted inspiratory tidal volume as well as the mandatory backup respiratory rate. The patient determines the respiratory rate, inspiratory time, I:E ratio, and minute volume. After each mechanical breath triggered by the patient's inspiratory effort, the ventilator, by way of a servomechanism, adjusts the PIP or pressure above PEEP by ± 3 cm H_2O in an attempt to maintain the preset desired inspiratory tidal volume. When the patient breathes above or below the preset inspiratory tidal volume, the ventilator will decrease or increase the PIP or pressure above PEEP to maintain the targeted volume. If apnea develops, the ventilator will automatically switch to a mandatory control mode. Like pressure support ventilation, the volume support mode is suitable for use while weaning patients from mechanical ventilation. It may also provide a way to maintain mechanical support for extended periods, with minimal unloading and weakening of the respiratory muscle pump. In theory, volume support ventilation may be suitable in patients with normal respiratory function who are recovering from anesthesia. To date, studies that validate use of this method in any pediatric age population have not been published.

Positive pressure ventilatory and oxygenation strategies

Maintenance of arterial blood gas levels within the "normal" range has always been the main objective

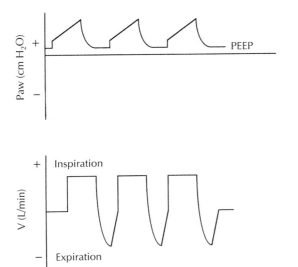

Fig. 155-10 Volume control ventilation. The ventilator delivers the preset tidal volume at a constant flow rate.

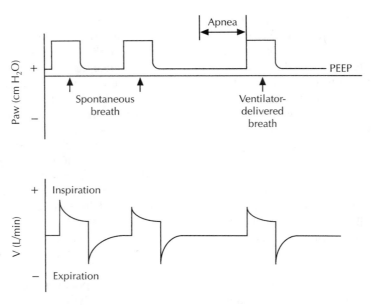

Fig. 155-11 Volume support ventilation. The ventilator delivers support for spontaneous patient-triggered breaths to achieve a preset volume with constant pressure and decelerating flow. In case of apnea, automated backup rate in the form of pressure-regulated volume control is provided.

of traditional conventional mechanical ventilation, whether this technique is applied in support of patients with acute lung injury, ARDS, or normal lung function. This strategy has come under significant scrutiny in the 1990s. With traditional conventional mechanical ventilation, all ventilator variables are aggressively adjusted to high settings if necessary to achieve normal values for Pao_2 and $Paco_2$. Therefore attempts to maintain normal values during treatment of acute lung injury exposes the airways and lung parenchyma to excessive volume, pressure, respiratory rate, and Fio_2. These high settings are believed to further injure the airways and parenchyma and result in pathologic changes characteristic of volutrauma, barotrauma, or oxygen toxicity.

Permissive hypercapnia and relative hypoxemia. These treatment strategies were conceived to prevent development of ventilator-induced injuries by adequately using the "baby lung" model, as described by Gattinoni, to support the patient with acute lung injury and the initial disease process while allowing the lung to heal and repair itself. Acute lung injury is characterized by patchy areas of consolidated, poorly compliant lung tissue adjacent to areas of relatively normal, compliant lung tissue. Similar to hyaline membrane disease, acute lung injury manifests three

distinct alveolar populations: normal, irreversibly consolidated, and atelectatic but potentially recruitable. In this lung model application of conventional mechanical ventilation with large inspiratory tidal volume, high PIP, and high PEEP can overinflate the normal alveoli, leading to volutrauma and barotrauma. Lowering PIP and therefore delivering a smaller inspiratory tidal volume at lower respiratory rate can decrease transmission of inflation pressure, modify shear forces, and prevent alveolar overdistention. During the acute and recovery phases of ARDS or acute lung injury use of permissive hypercapnea allows for respiratory acidosis with metabolic compensation, and a progressive increase in $Paco_2$ to 60 to 100 mm Hg and higher may result. If the rate of development of hypercapnia is 5 to 10 mm Hg/hr, metabolic compensation of pH occurs through renal buffering systems. Slow onset of renal compensation or failure of mechanical ventilation to further eliminate CO_2 can cause an acute elevation in $Paco_2$ and decrease pH to <7.20. Because acute-onset respiratory acidosis induces CNS, cardiovascular, and renal dysfunction, a rapid increase in $Paco_2$ must be avoided. In the presence of other organ dysfunction, a rapid decrease in pH, or extremely low pH (≤ 6.9), administration of a buffer such as bicarbonate or

THAM (tris[hydroxymethyl]aminomethane) will correct the pH to a more desirable level (≥ 7.2). In the spontaneously breathing patient with respiratory acidosis, work of breathing needs to be continuously assessed. If the work of breathing becomes significant, as indicated by increasing tachypnea, dyspnea, and retractions, sedation and/or neuromuscular blockade must be considered. Although permissive hypercapnea has been used since the late 1980s, prospective, randomized, controlled trials of this treatment strategy in adult or pediatric patients have not been completed. Despite this, it is considered the standard of care in some of the leading national pediatric critical care centers.

Recently there has been a renewed interest in actively preventing oxygen toxicity in patients with severe acute lung injury and ARDS. As a result of a perceived need to limit exposure of lung tissue to oxygen, clinicians have elected to maintain Fio_2 at <0.50 despite the potential for hypoventilation or relative hypoxemia. This strategy is based on the theory that the normal oxygen delivery to oxygen consumption balance provides a large "oxygen surplus" that consists of hemoglobin-bound and dissolved oxygen. In normal circumstances oxygen delivery is four to five times greater than oxygen consumption, and most of the delivered oxygen content consists of oxygen bound to hemoglobin, not oxygen dissolved in plasma. Because the amount of oxygen that can be dissolved in plasma is small, increasing Pao_2 does not significantly increase the oxygen content of blood if the hemoglobin binding sites are near complete saturation. Therefore the degree of saturation becomes more important than Pao_2 with respect to the amount of oxygen available to tissues. Maintenance of lower Pao_2 with fairly adequate Sao_2 ($\geq 85\%$) allows ventilation with lower Fio_2 and pressures. Some clinicians have elected to apply this strategy in patients with acute lung injury to decrease oxygen toxicity and the effects of the high distending pressures necessary to maintain "normal" Pao_2 values. Neonates and children with cyanotic congenital heart disease demonstrate a tolerance to hypoxemia. Increased saturation of hemoglobin from arteriopulmonary shunts and increased red blood cell mass create an increased blood oxygen content despite abnormal Pao_2 and Sao_2.

As with permissive hypoxemia, prospective, randomized, controlled trials of relative hypoxemia in adult and pediatric patients have not been completed. Despite this, its clinical application is considered standard in some of the leading national pediatric critical care centers. Although there is no accepted national consensus, most practitioners elect to decrease Fio_2 aggressively while accepting a Pao_2 near 50 mm Hg and Sao_2 near 85%.

Permissive hypercapnea and relative hypoxemia are useful in patients with ARDS or acute lung injury to decrease total time required for ventilatory support. In less ill patients or during periods of tapering support, guidelines for Sao_2 can be relaxed (85% to 90%). The two strategies may be used separately to allow normal Po_2 and hypercapnia or lower oxygen and normal Pco_2 if clinical circumstances suggest the need for normal values. Superphysiologic oxygen levels may be desirable in patients with identified CNS injury, sickle cell anemia, shock, or after solid organ transplantation. Patients with moderate lung injury and no other significant organ failure may not need such stringent control of pH as patients with more severe disease. This modified strategy seems to maintain pH of 7.25 to 7.3 regardless of $Paco_2$ in the absence of hypochloremic metabolic acidosis. Patients receiving drugs such as catecholamines, which are ineffective at abnormal pH, will need pH adjusted to the normal range (i.e., close to 7.35). Alkaline pH, if necessary for treatment of cerebral or pulmonary vascular bed constriction, can be maintained with exogenous buffer, not by changing ventilatory parameters.

The next goal is to determine the true indications for permissive hypercapnea and relative hypoxemia, alone or in combination. Some of the potential indications and contraindications for these techniques are listed on p. 1440. Further research in this field is warranted.

Inverse ratio ventilation. Inverse ratio ventilation, or reverse I:E ventilation, is a strategy that can be carried out with most commercially available ventilators. To achieve an inverted I:E ratio, the clinician must increase the duration of inspiration to greater than the duration of expiration for an I:E ratio of more than 1:1. Inspiratory time may be adjusted by increasing the ventilator setting or adding inspiratory pause or hold. Either of these maneuvers recruits alveoli by increasing the mean airway pressure within airway segments and lung units with prolonged time constants. The relatively short expiratory time additionally increases airway pressure by causing intrinsic PEEP (auto-PEEP), which can lead to further alveolar recruitment. Alveolar recruitment improves

---

PERMISSIVE HYPERCAPNIA AND RELATIVE HYPOXEMIA: POTENTIAL INDICATIONS AND CONTRAINDICATIONS

Indications

Prevention of volutrauma, barotrauma, and oxygen toxicity
Postoperative recovery
Acute lung injury or ARDS
Weaning from or discontinuation of mechanical ventilation
Treatment or support in patients with air leak syndrome or bronchopleural fistulas
Status asthmaticus in respiratory failure

Contraindications

Suspected intracranial hypertension
Cerebrovascular disease
Cardiac arrhythmias
Severe pulmonary hypertension
Severe systemic hypertension
Severe cardiac failure or dysfunction
Sickle cell disease

$\dot{V}/\dot{Q}$ matching and enables the clinician to decrease PIP, PEEP, and Fio_2. Inverse ratio ventilation may be of benefit in refractory hypoxemic ARDS that does not respond to other modes or strategies of conventional mechanical ventilation.

Inverse ratio ventilation is technically feasible with either pressure control or volume control modes, but because this strategy shortens expiratory time, air trapping may become clinically significant. Volume control is not the preferred mode. Because inverse ratio ventilation creates a nonphysiologic respiratory pattern, adequate sedation and neuromuscular blockade are usually needed. Smaller tidal volumes (5 to 8 cc/kg) with PIP <35 to 40 cm H_2O and PEEP <10 cm H_2O are used during inverse ratio ventilation to achieve adequate gas exchange. During inspiration the lungs are held fully expanded for a longer time, exposing them to higher intrathoracic pressure and volume (i.e., increasing risks of barotrauma and volutrauma). Cardiac output may be decreased as preload is reduced (see Chapter 20). A pulmonary artery catheter for advanced hemodynamic monitoring is recommended in patients undergoing inverse ratio ventilation. No prospective, randomized, controlled investigation has demonstrated a significantly favorable risk-benefit effect on morbidity or mortality of adult or pediatric patients given inverse ratio ventilation compared with those given conventional mechanical ventilation. The recent success of high-frequency oscillatory ventilation in supporting pediatric patients with ARDS who weigh <35 kg has made the role of inverse ratio ventilation less clear. This treatment method may be confined to patients who weigh >35 kg, but even this indication may be precluded by the FDA approval of high-frequency oscillatory ventilation without a weight limit, rapid development of other high-frequency devices, use of nitric oxide as a specific pulmonary vasodilator, and promising preliminary results of the multicenter phase I and II partial liquid ventilation trials (see Chapters 156, 158, and 159).

Pharmacologic Adjuncts to Mechanical Ventilation

To facilitate mechanical ventilation and invasive procedures associated with care of pediatric patients receiving mechanical ventilation, some form of sedation is generally needed. Indications for sedation are listed in Table 155-2.

The specific drugs and routes of administration appropriate for use as sedatives are discussed in Chapter 179. Most care given in the PICU is foreign, threatening, and incomprehensible to the critically ill child who often has little ability to process explanations of such care. Although the patient and family need to be educated about ongoing care, use of sedative agents will relieve anxiety, reduce physiologic signs of stress (e.g., tachycardia, hypertension, crying, tearing, nonspecific muscle activity, tachypnea, diaphoresis, and pupillary dilation), and prevent development of disturbed psychological states (psychosis). It is especially important to adequately sedate any patient in whom catecholamine release that accompanies stress is undesirable. Although pharmacologic sedation cannot substitute for the normal sleep state, its use may change perception of the highly stimulatory and constantly noisy PICU environment enough to promote sleep.

Patients who need neuromuscular blockade also need a sedative agent that provides amnesia as well as anxiolysis. An appropriate sedation regimen can also assist with retention of ET tubes, drains, IV

Table 155-2   Indications for Sedation

Indications	Rationale
Demonstrated agitation or anxiety unrelieved by adequate analgesia	Prevention of anxiety, physiologic stress, and development of psychosis
Multiple invasive procedures within 24 hours	Prevention of anxiety, physiologic stress, and development of psychosis
Requirement for artificial airway other than established tracheostomy	Prevention of anxiety, physiologic stress, and development of psychosis
	Prevention of accidental extubation
	Decreased trauma to upper airway
Requirement for mechanical ventilation without neuromuscular blockade	Prevention of anxiety, physiologic stress, and development of psychosis
	Facilitation of ventilator control of respiratory variables
Requirement for neuromuscular blockade	Prevention of anxiety, physiologic stress, and development of psychosis and sleep disorders
	Facilitation of ventilator control of respiratory variables
	Assurance of amnesia

catheters, and other indwelling devices; appropriate ventilator management; and performance of invasive procedures such as renal replacement therapy, plasmaphoresis, and extracorporeal membrane oxygenation. Patient agitation, in particular, often has adverse respiratory effects (e.g., increased dyspnea, work of breathing, and desaturation episodes) when patient and ventilator are not in synchrony. Dysynchrony is more likely with use of any controlled mode or when spontaneously breathing patients experience obstruction of airflow. Remember that agents commonly used for sedation have no analgesic properties and will not treat or prevent pain.

Presence of ongoing pain or frequent painful procedures is the primary reason for addition of analgesic agents to the sedation regimen. The most obvious need is in the immediate postoperative period or in the critically ill patient early in the course of care when multiple invasive procedures are necessary to establish appropriate monitoring and treatment. Failure of sedation alone to achieve a quiet, comfortable patient may warrant a trial of analgesia because nonobvious sources of pain may be present. Certainly addition of analgesia will significantly modify the physical signs of stress. If there are appropriate indications for use of sedative agents, substitution of an analgesic is inappropriate. Addition of analgesic agents should be based on specific indications related to the presence or likelihood of pain.

In many patients the goals of chosen ventilatory strategies are accomplished without the use of neuromuscular blockade. In a number of clinical conditions, however, severity of the pulmonary injury or the need to tightly control ventilatory parameters mandates respiratory muscle paralysis. Table 155-3 lists indications for neuromuscular blockade, and Chapter 180 describes use of appropriate agents.

In several studies the prolonged use of neuromuscular blocking agents has been associated with a significant incidence of persistent neuromuscular dysfunction that may hinder extubation or simulate neurologic abnormalities. In some cases patients have had residual muscle weakness that does not resolve for months.

A number of these patients received high doses of corticosteroids, which suggests an adverse interaction between these two classes of drugs. Until more is known, it is prudent to limit neuromuscular blocking agents to patients in whom adequate ventilation cannot be achieved despite appropriate administration of sedation or analgesia or both. Corticosteroids must not be given during neuromuscular blockade unless there are clear indications for their use. Also, prolongation of neuromuscular blockade and augmentation of dose response have been reported with concomitant use of neuromuscular blocking agents and aminoglycosides.

Tables 155-4 and 155-5 list additional drugs and

Table 155-3   Deep Sedation, Amnesia, and Neuromuscular Blockade During Mechanical Ventilation

Indications	Rationale
Poorly controlled pain with adequate sedation and high-dose analgesics	Prevents volutrauma, barotrauma, and psychosis Reduces oxygen consumption and toxicity
Nonconventional strategies Permissive hypercapnea or relative hypoxemia	Same as above Decreases altered respiratory drive caused by hypoxemia and hypercapnea
Inverse ratio ventilation	Same as above Allows passive lung recoil Prevents auto-PEEP
Nonrespiratory indications Increased ICP	Reduces work of breathing and intrathoracic pressure Same as nonrespiratory indications Aids hyperventilation Treats increased ICP
Shock	Same as nonrespiratory indications Decreases oxygen consumption Improves cardiac function
Postoperative	Control for reasons other than pain (e.g., open wound, physiologic stability)

Table 155-4   Systemic Conditions That Affect Neuromuscular Blockade*

Condition	Physiologic Effect	Effect on Neuromuscular Blockade
Hypoalbuminemia	Decreased binding of neuromuscular blockage agent	Augments
Hyper-α_1-acid glycoproteinemia	Increased binding of neuromuscular blocking agent	Opposes
Hypoperfusion	Decreased delivery of neuromuscular blockage agent to liver	Augments
Hypothermia	Decreased hepatic drug metabolism	Augments
Hyperthermia	Increased hepatic drug metabolism	Opposes
Acidosis	Increased drug affinity for receptor and protein binding sites	Augments
Liver failure	Decreased hepatic drug metabolism	Augments
Malnutrition	Decreased muscle strength as a consequence of tissue loss	Augments
Obesity	Toxicity from weight-based dosing	Augments
Pregnancy	Change in volume of distribution and cardiac output, higher drug clearance, hepatic enzyme induction	May oppose or augment
Neonate, premature infant	Decreased hepatic metabolism, increased volume of distribution, altered drug binding, immature acetylcholine receptors	May oppose or augment
Renal failure	Decreased elimination	Augments

*May depend on specific agent chosen.

Table 155-5   Abnormalities of Nerve Conduction and Transmission and Effect

Abnormality of Transmission or Conduction	Pathologic Condition	Physiologic Condition	Effect on Neuromuscular Blockade
Absence of nerve impulse	Central axonal degeneration, denervation, burns	Up regulation (increase) of ACH receptors	Opposes
Inability of impulse to propagate	Demyelination, tetrodotoxism, immobilization	Up regulation of ACH receptors	Opposes
Failure to release ACH into synapse	Blocked ACH release by hydantoins, carbamazepine, clostridial toxins, and aminoglycosides; hypermagnesemia	Up regulation	Opposes
Failure to bind ACH to receptor	Nondepolarizing neuromuscular blockade (clindamycin, polymyxin, α-bungarotoxin)	ACH receptor channel blockade	Augments
Abnormalities of membrane depolarization	Myasthenia gravis	Down regulation (reduced) of ACH receptors	Augments
	Electrolyte abnormality (hypocalcemia, hypophosphatemia, severe hypokalemia)	Muscle membrane stabilization	Augments
	Drug action (hydantoins, chlorpromazine), hypermagnesemia	Muscle membrane stabilization	Augments
Abnormalities of contractile process	Muscular dystrophy, myotonia	Decreased and abnormal motor units	Unpredictable
Abnormalities of termination of contraction	Malignant hyperpyrexia	Reuptake of calcium by sarcoplasmic reticular blockade	Nondepolarizing agents, no effect; depolarizing agents trigger
Abnormalities of ACH breakdown	Deficiency of cholinesterase, drug inhibition of cholinesterase, organophosphate toxicity, metaclopropamide, oral contraceptive, cyclophosphamide	ACH receptor down regulation	Augments

ACH = acetylcholine.

disease states that affect neuromuscular blockade. Many of these augment neuromuscular blockade, creating relative overdose or tolerance, a consequence of neuromuscular junction acetylcholine receptor down regulation. Many of the physiologic abnormalities commonly seen in PICU patients (e.g., perfusion, temperature and electrolyte abnormalities, disuse muscular atrophy, poor nutrition, and multiple organ failure) affect nerve transmission to muscle, and therefore it is particularly important to monitor the state of neuromuscular blockade. Periodic evaluation of muscle response to an applied standard electrical impulse allows dose adjustment while maintaining adequate relaxation and is presently the best method

to prevent overdose and subsequent toxicity. Because of multiple factors involved in adequate neuromuscular junction function, myopathy may develop despite adequate monitoring of neuromuscular blockade and appropriate drug doses.

Weaning From Mechanical Ventilation
Guidelines for starting "transfer" process

These guidelines are written to provide a protocol that may be clinically useful to facilitate the withdrawal of the pediatric patient from conventional mechanical ventilation. To date there are no conclusive studies in the pediatric population to support specific recommendations about which methods are the best in specific patients. Thus the clinician needs to adapt these guidelines to the particular patient population on the basis of unique experiences with various techniques.

Withdrawal of ventilatory support may be initiated under the following circumstances:

1. Significant improvement or reversal of the condition for which mechanical ventilation was started
2. Discontinuation of neuromuscular blocking agents (nerve stimulation used to verify adequate muscle response)
3. Signs of or potential for effective respiratory efforts
4. FiO_2 requirements ≤ 0.50 and PEEP <8 to 10 cm H_2O
5. Vital signs appropriate for age and disease process
6. Cardiovascular support with vasoactive drugs at a minimum (dopamine, dobutamine, or equivalent agent ≤ 5 $\mu g/kg/min$)
7. Absence of significant compensatory hypochloremic metabolic alkalosis, hypokalemia, hypocalcemia, hypomagnesemia, or marked hypophosphatemia
8. Appropriate nutritional state, in the opinion of the attending physician, including but not necessarily limited to fluid balance and caloric and protein balance (carbohydrate and protein contribution to CO_2 production needs to be evaluated)
9. Patient-ventilator synchrony and appropriate respiratory pump muscle retraining
10. Absence of symptoms and signs of acute benzodiazepam or opiate withdrawal (this does not imply the patient is not receiving these medications)

Withdrawal methods

All the methods listed are commonly used to withdraw ventilatory support successfully, and preference for any one method is an individual decision. Lack of progress is an indication that the method chosen needs to be reevaluated and the patient's ability to tolerate transfer of the work of breathing from the ventilator to the native ventilatory pump reexamined. Another method may be more successful and needs to be considered.

One or any combination of the following methods can be used:

1. Volume-limited, time-cycled, accelerating-flow, synchronized intermittent mandatory ventilation
2. Pressure-limited, time-cycled, continuous-flow, synchronized intermittent mandatory ventilation
3. Pressure-limited, time-cycled, decelerating-flow, synchronized intermittent mandatory ventilation or pressure control
4. Pressure support ventilation
5. Volume support ventilation
6. Volume-limited synchronized intermittent mandatory ventilation plus pressure support ventilation
7. Pressure control synchronized intermittent mandatory ventilation plus pressure support ventilation

Withdrawal strategies

General oxygenation

1. *Ventilator settings:* FiO_2, PEEP, airway pressure, I:E ratio, and inspiratory time weaning will be defined by the patient's physiologic state, disease process, and ability to progress with parameters chosen.
2. *Physiologic outcome:* Maintain SaO_2 $>85\%$ and PaO_2 >50 mm Hg. Adjustments in airway pressure and FiO_2 are made for low saturation or SaO_2.

General ventilation

1. *Ventilator settings:* Tidal volume, peak pressures, respiratory rate, and minute ventilation weaning will be defined by the patient's physiologic state, disease process, and ability to progress with parameters chosen.
2. *Physiologic outcome:* Maintain pH >7.25 regardless of $PaCO_2$. Adjustments in minute ventilation or alkaline buffer solution administration may be necessary to compensate for low pH.

Transfer of work of breathing from ventilator to patient

Patients will be assessed for tolerance using the following guidelines:

1. Tachypnea is not so critical an indicator as dyspnea.
2. Desaturation. (SaO_2 $<85\%$ to 90% for <15 minutes) is tolerated.

3. Respiratory acidosis with pH <7.25 for <30 minutes, regardless of Pa_{CO_2}, is tolerated.
4. There are no signs of respiratory distress.
5. Pulmonary function testing may be performed in difficult clinical scenarios (see Chapter 150).

Respiratory distress is defined by the presence of two or more of the following criteria:

1. Diaphoresis
2. Presence of paradoxical abdominal muscle movement during respiratory cycle
3. Marked use of the accessory muscles of respiration
4. Sustained tachycardia (e.g., >15 minutes at >120% of baseline heart rate)
5. Marked subjective dyspnea
6. Depression in mental status or increasing irritability (inability to be consoled)

Discontinuation of mechanical ventilation

The patient must be able to sustain unassisted breathing, that is, spontaneous breathing without an artificial airway except a tracheostomy. Oxygen or low-level CPAP (≤ 5 cm H_2O) may be administered. There are few truly objective criteria to ensure successful extubation in any pediatric patient (see Chapter 153). In general a patient has demonstrated the potential to sustain unassisted breathing when the supported minute ventilation is at least $\leq 25\%$ of the combined minute ventilation (i.e., ventilator plus spontaneous breathing). These criteria may not apply to patients who have received prolonged mechanical ventilatory support. They may need even small amounts of support for longer periods. Remember to consider pressure support and breaths in such patients. After assessing the patient's ability to sustain work of breathing and removing the ET tube successfully, a trial of spontaneous breathing is initiated with oxygen or CPAP ≤ 5 cm H_2O, as appropriate. The following criteria are frequently used: (1) Sa_{O_2} >90% or Pa_{O_2} >60 mm Hg, (2) spontaneous tidal volume >4 ml/kg ideal body weight, (3) respiratory rate <35 breaths/min, and (4) pH >7.30, if measured. If these criteria are met for longer than 2 hours, the trial of unassisted breathing is continued. Inability to meet the specified criteria for 48 hours or less indicates need for resumption of ventilatory support. The degree to which upper airway obstruction contributes to the need for continued ventilatory sup-

port must be appreciated because this problem is treated differently.

Monitoring and Laboratory Tests

Provision of artificial respiratory support exposes the critically ill child to a number of risks. Mechanical ventilation must be accomplished in a way that provides optimal (or acceptable) support for the patient while minimizing these risks. Therefore, although ventilatory strategies may differ depending on the disease process, the general goals of mechanical ventilation remain the same: to ensure adequate gas exchange, prevent or minimize the damaging effects and complications of mechanical ventilation, and limit the duration that ventilation is needed. To accomplish these goals, mechanical ventilation must be actively monitored and managed. The continuous possibility of changing conditions demands frequent reassessment of the patient. Attention to detail and timely responses to changes in the patient-ventilator unit will determine whether these goals are successfully achieved.

Desired end points may vary depending on the ventilatory strategy being used, but in general they include blood oxygenation, CO_2 elimination, hemodynamic stability, and patient comfort. Many of the tools used to monitor artificial ventilation are discussed elsewhere (e.g., see Chapters 132, 133, 149, and 150). Methods may be categorized as noninvasive and invasive. The most important noninvasive monitoring tool is direct observation. Physical examination of the patient, with the focus on inspection and auscultation, will usually give a first approximation that the desired goals are being achieved. In addition, close attention to the interaction of the patient with the ventilator can be important. In the patient who is not paralyzed, increased respiratory rate is an important early sign of a change in the adequacy of respiratory support. Symmetry and depth of chest movement, use of accessory muscles, and asynchronous breaths or breaths of inconsistent quality may indicate the need to change ventilator settings. Auscultation of breath sounds allows assessment of the evenness of air delivery and examination for air leakage. In addition, listening to the function of the ventilator can reveal information about the efficiency of ventilation that is not available on the bedside data sheet.

Radiologic examination of the chest provides important supportive information while the patient is receiving mechanical ventilation. It allows confirmation of ET tube placement (when done with a consistent technique), detection of complications (e.g., atelectasis, localized overinflation, presence of extra-alveolar air, and excess fluid), position of the diaphragms, heart size, and assessment of the course of the underlying disease. The position of the diaphragms can be particularly important when using PEEP and is critical information when setting mean airway pressure for high-frequency oscillatory ventilation. In the critically ill child a chest radiograph must be obtained daily or after an acute change in the patient's condition that is not well understood. A daily chest radiograph is not necessary in patients with resolving illness.

Invasive methods include blood gas analysis, pulmonary artery catheterization, and pulmonary function testing. Blood gas analysis is used to assess the adequacy of alveolar ventilation, arterial oxygen, and acid-base status (see Chapter 9). Pa_{O_2} is important not only because it is the major determinant of Sa_{O_2} and therefore oxygen content (see Chapter 151) but also because it reflects alveolar oxygen pressure. Alveolar oxygen pressure can be estimated using the simplified form of the alveolar air equation: $PA_{O_2} = Fi_{O_2}(P_B - 47) - 1.25\ Pa_{CO_2}$. The efficiency of oxygen exchange in the lung can be monitored with the alveolar-arterial oxygen tension difference, $P(A-a)_{O_2}$, or an arterial oxygen index such as Pa_{O_2}-Fi_{O_2} ratio, Pa_{O_2}-PA_{O_2} ratio, or oxygen index ($OI = [P\overline{aw} \times Fi_{O_2}]/Pa_{O_2}$). None of these is accurate over the entire range of Fi_{O_2} but they are useful adjuncts to monitor the evolution of a lung injury or the response to therapeutic interventions. Calculation of shunt fraction (Qs/Qt), using Sv_{O_2} obtained from a pulmonary artery catheter, can be useful to estimate the effect of increasing Fi_{O_2} on venous admixture. Pa_{CO_2} is used to assess the adequacy of alveolar ventilation (V_A). The relationship $Pa_{CO_2} = V_{CO_2} \times 0.863/V_A$ illustrates that the fundamental cause of hypercapnia is decreased alveolar ventilation relative to CO_2 production. Alveolar ventilation may be decreased as a result of decreased minute ventilation (V_E) or increased dead space (V_D), and Pa_{CO_2} must be interpreted in conjunction with these parameters. Dead space consists of anatomic dead space and physiologic dead space. Physiologic dead space (V_D/V_T) can be increased by $\dot{V}/\dot{Q}$ mismatch in acute lung injury or in vascular lesions such

as embolic disease. In acute lung injury, with use of PEEP, V_D/V_T may increase as relatively compliant lung units become overdistended, leading to an increase in the number of low $\dot{V}/\dot{Q}$ lung units. V_D/V_T may be estimated with the Bohr equation: $V_D/V_T = (Pa_{CO_2} - Pet_{CO_2})/Pa_{CO_2}$ (Pet_{CO_2} = end-tidal CO_2). In infants and small children the dead space in the ventilator circuit may also be significant.

RISKS AND COMPLICATIONS

Positive pressure ventilation is associated with numerous physiologic and mechanical complications. Most adverse physiologic responses to positive pressure ventilation result from inappropriately high mean airway pressure. Elevation of airway pressure may decrease venous return and cardiac filling and output. Depressed cardiac output and changes in peripheral vascular resistance and blood flow can lead to hypotension, oliguria, and fluid retention, all of which tend to aggravate pulmonary disease and de-

---

COMPLICATIONS OF MECHANICAL VENTILATION

Positive mean airway pressure

Decreased cardiac filling and output
Altered $\dot{V}/\dot{Q}$ matching
Extravascular water accumulation
Pulmonary parenchymal damage
GI malfunction
Cerebral ischemia
Intracranial hypertension
Decreased central venous return
Alveolar hypoventilation or hyperventilation
Alveolar rupture with extra-alveolar free air

ET or tracheostomy tubes

Mucosal damage (tracheal and laryngeal)
Accidental malposition or extubation
Partial or complete tube obstruction
Pneumonia

Operation of ventilator

Mechanical failure
Alarm failure
Inadequate nebulization or humidification

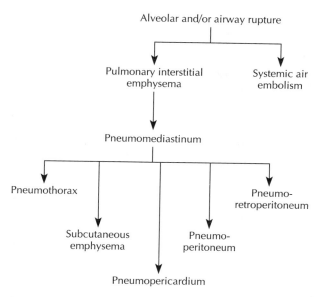

Fig. 155-12 Barotrauma or volutrauma complicating mechanical ventilation.

crease systemic oxygen transport. Hemodynamic monitoring, intravascular volume expansion, and pharmacologic therapy for myocardial support are commonly indicated during positive airway pressure ventilatory support.

Positive pressure ventilation may also adversely affect the distribution of alveolar ventilation and pulmonary arterial perfusion. Inappropriately high levels of airway pressure can lead to overinflation of alveoli, increased dead space ventilation, decreased pulmonary compliance, increased fluid accumulation in the lungs, and decreased pulmonary arterial blood flow through the capillary beds of overdistended alveoli. This may result in increased dead space ventilation and intrapulmonary shunting respectively. The beneficial effects and optimal level of positive airway pressure depend on the underlying pulmonary disease.

Airway and alveolar rupture and their sequelae constitute the most frequent life-threatening complication of ventilatory assistance. Airway pressure >40 to 50 cm H_2O causes barotrauma, with development of air leak syndrome, which includes parenchymal interstitial emphysema, pneumomediastinum, pneumothorax, pneumopericardium, pneumoperitoneum, pneumoretroperitoneum, and sub-

cutaneous emphysema (Fig. 155-12). All pediatric critical care personnel must be able to immediately recognize and treat different manifestations of air leakage (see Chapter 161).

A number of studies have shown high ventilatory pressures resulting in large distending volumes (>12 cc/kg) cause increased regional lung stretch in the healthier alveoli that can damage the lung structure. This type of injury has been termed volutrauma. Ventilation with large tidal volumes or high PIP can induce lung injury in previously healthy lungs or worsen acute lung injury. This traumatic lung injury is characterized by granulocyte infiltration, hyaline membrane formation, and increased vascular permeability, with evidence of diffuse alveolar damage often occurring without evidence of severe barotrauma. The specific mechanisms of this type of lung injury have not been completely elucidated, but the absolute pressure transmitted to the alveoli (or airway pressure) is not the fundamental cause. Minimizing alveolar overdistention by "strapping" the chest wall (mechanically restricting chest wall movement) prevents lung injury even at very high pressures. One goal is to minimize regional peak lung inflation to prevent alveolar overdistention. Because there is no adequate way to measure this clinically, a reasonable guideline is to try to maintain plateau pressure <35 cm H_2O and limit ventilator-generated tidal volume to ≤10 cc/kg. Today most practitioners advocate that inspiratory tidal volume be kept at about 7 cc/kg, as measured at the proximal airway. This approach has also been used as part of the permissive hypercapnea strategy.

The occurrence of mechanical misadventures such as ET tube obstruction, disconnected tubes, unplanned extubation, and apparatus malfunction are largely preventable and underscore the need for continuous electrical and human monitoring of both the machine and the patient. Among the wide variety of noncardiopulmonary complications that have been described for mechanical ventilation, perhaps the most important involve dysfunction of the renal, GI, and CNS systems, including emotional distress.

Emotional distress during mechanical ventilation is exceedingly common and needs to be diagnosed and managed accordingly. Inattention to distress or to the patient's emotional needs may lead to PICU psychosis. Patient agitation can cause patient-ventilator dyssynchrony and increase the possibility of self-extubation, air leak syndrome, cardiovascular instability, hypercapnea, and hypoxemia. Means for communication with the patient must always be provided. Sedatives that have anxiolytic as well as amnestic properties may be of benefit. The use of analgesics is warranted before any painful or even potentially painful procedure and when the clinical condition or state is known to have associated pain. Analgesics are not a substitute for sedatives and vice versa (see Chapter 179).

Renal dysfunction during positive pressure ventilation is believed to be a consequence of reduced effective circulating blood volume. This results from impairment of venous return to the right side of the heart caused by the high intrathoracic pressure generated during mechanical ventilation. Perfusion of the renal parenchyma is altered, intrarenal blood flow redistributed, ADH released, and atrial natriuretic peptide secretion inhibited. Reduced free water clearance and generalized fluid retention are the consequences.

GI problems include luminal gut distention from air swallowing, hypomotility, obstipation related to pharmacologic agents and immobility, vomiting related to pharyngeal stimulation and motility disturbances, mucosal ulceration, and bleeding. Serious dysfunction of the liver as a direct consequence of mechanical ventilation is extremely rare and when present is usually part of multiple organ system failure.

Increased intrathoracic pressure can elevate jugular venous pressure and ICP and thereby reduce cerebral perfusion pressure. Such effects assume particular importance when reduced mean arterial pressure or reduced intracranial compliance result from head injury or surgical intervention. The risk of intracranial hypertension in patients receiving mechanical ventilation with high airway pressure is attenuated by conditions that limit transmission of alveolar pressure to the pleural space, such as low ratio of lung to chest wall compliance.

Problem Management

Acute respiratory distress in the patient receiving ventilatory support may be caused by the disease or by ventilator malfunction. Common ventilatory dilemmas and their possible causes are listed in Table 155-6.

Acute hypoxemia

Hypoxemia or worsening systemic oxygenation is a common problem in the PICU patient. Ventilator-related problems, patient-related problems including progression of the underlying disease, superimposed

---

CAUSES OF HYPOXEMIA

Ventilator-related problems

ET tube obstruction or malposition
Ventilator or breathing circuit malfunction
Improper ventilator settings

Progression of underlying disease process

Pneumothorax
Atelectasis
Aspiration
Bronchospasm
Retained secretions
Pulmonary edema
Nosocomial pneumonia
Decreased cardiac output

Interventions and procedures

Suctioning
Position change
Chest physiotherapy
Thoracentesis
Dialysis
Inappropriate ventilator settings

Drug therapies

Bronchodilators
Vasodilators
Vasopressors
Sedation, neuromuscular blockade

---

disorders, interventions, procedures, and medications can all adversely affect oxygenation. However, impaired oxygenation is not always the result of worsening lung problems. In fact, after pathophysiologic or mechanical problems have been excluded (e.g., pneumothorax, bronchial intubation, change in Fio_2, or ventilator malfunction), sudden changes in Pao_2 are usually circulatory (e.g., pulmonary arterial hypertension or decreased cardiac output) or metabolic (e.g., increased oxygen demand) in origin.

Acute hypercarbia

The adequacy of ventilation of the lungs is assessed by $Paco_2$. A frequent problem that develops in patients receiving mechanical ventilation is hypercarbia (i.e., $Paco_2$ >55 mm Hg in acute conditions).

An increase in CO_2 production will necessitate an

Table 155-6 Ventilator Dilemmas

Problem	Possible Causes
Normal plateau and high peak airway pressures	High peak inspiratory flow rate
	High resistance in ET tube or circuit
	Small ET tube
	Kinking
	Obstruction
	Secretions
	High airway resistance
	Secretions
	Bronchospasm
	Edema
	Foreign body
	Tracheobronchomalacia
	Tracheostenosis
High plateau and high peak pressures	Alveolar overdistention
	Pulmonary edema
	Consolidation
	Atelectasis
	Mainstem bronchus intubation
	Pneumothorax
	Chest wall constriction
	Abdominal distention
	Agitation, seizures
Auto-PEEP	Obstructed airways or circuit
	Insufficient expiratory time
Low exhaled volumes	Leak from circuit
	Air leak: ET tube, or chest tube, ventilatory circuit
	Insufficient delivered tidal volume
	Bronchopleural fistula
Increased respiratory rate	Change in clinical status
	Low tidal volume
	Insufficient flow rate
No spontaneous breaths	Respiratory alkalosis
	Sedation
	CNS malfunction
	Unrecognized neuromuscular blockade

increase in ventilation to prevent hypercarbia. Occasionally excessive carbohydrate administration results in hypercarbia in critically ill patients. Although the administration of adequate calories is essential, excessive calories administered as carbohydrates leads to formation of fat and liberation of CO_2. The process is readily reversed by decreasing the carbohydrate load. A few pathophysiologic conditions that can cause increased CO_2 production are hyperthyroidism, malignant hyperpyrexia, and drug withdrawal syndrome.

Patient-ventilator interaction

With all modes and levels of ventilatory assistance, variable degrees of interaction are needed between the spontaneously breathing patient and the ventilator. In certain circumstances these interactions may not occur properly (dyssynchrony) and can have deleterious consequences. One common example is the development of intrinsic PEEP or auto-PEEP in patients with airflow obstruction.

When the patient and machine work in synchrony, inspiratory effort is sensed and adequate respiratory support is provided to meet patient demand. When patient-ventilator dyssynchrony develops and this demand is not met, the patient may perform a significant amount of additional work of breathing, which can impede adequate ventilation during respiratory failure support or weaning.

Inadequate expiratory time and subsequent incomplete exhalation of inspired tidal volume can cause development of auto-PEEP. With auto-PEEP the work of breathing will increase and hemodynamic compromise is possible. To reduce the level of auto-PEEP, the airflow obstruction must be relieved, and expiratory time increased, and application of extrinsic PEEP to overcome the effect of the obstructed airway must be considered.

Several other factors may markedly increase the work of breathing in mechanically ventilated patients with airflow obstruction. Trigger insensitivity and a relatively insensitive demand valve can contribute to dyssynchrony. Muscular effort and continued diaphragmatic contraction may also promote dyssynchrony during inspiration in patients with limited ventilatory reserve. Potential methods to avert dyssynchrony include use of large ET tubes, administration of high-demand minute volume, and delivery of adequate gas flow.

CURRENT RESEARCH AND FUTURE CONSIDERATIONS

During the last decade the technologic advances made by mechanical ventilator manufacturers have been remarkable. The versatility, accuracy, and sensitivity of most microprocessor servocontrol devices on the market have created new options to fit patient needs. These options have outstripped our ability as investigators to discern which patients benefit best from each of the new modes or even the new strategies that these innovative devices make possible.

There are no well-designed prospective, randomized studies in pediatric patients to validate any mode of conventional mechanical ventilation as safe and efficacious. This is further complicated by the rapid evolution of other techniques and devices such as high-frequency ventilation, nitric oxide, partial liquid ventilation, and extracorporeal membrane oxygenation.

CAUSES OF HYPERCARBIA

Mechanical problems

Failure to deliver tidal volume
    Malfunction
    Compression volume losses
    Air leak: ET tube, chest tube, ventilatory circuit
    Occluded ET tube
    Disconnection
Failure to sense respirations
    Malfunction
    Large ET tube or circuit leak
    Complete disconnections
    Dyssynchrony
    Sensitivity too low
Inadequate inspiratory time
    Malfunction
    Set too short
    Set too long
    Dyssynchrony
Inadequate expiratory time

Patient problems

    Decreased respiratory drive
    Metabolic alkalosis
    Sedation
    CNS insult
    Apnea
    Respiratory muscle fatigue
Increased CO_2 production
    Fever
    Shivering
    Sepsis
    Trauma
    High carbohydrate load
    Hypermetabolic state
Increased dead space ventilation
    Hypovolemia
    Shock
    Pulmonary hypertension
    Excessive PEEP
Low respiratory compliance

A series of systematic large-population studies through collaborative multicenter studies similar to the recently completed study that compared high-frequency oscillatory ventilation with conventional mechanical ventilation is needed.

Because of the complexity and rapid evolution

of the traditional and nontraditional techniques and strategies currently being used to support patients with ARDS, a consensus about universal definitions of these techniques and strategies will be necessary. Over the past few years the boundaries between conventional and nonconventional mechanical ventilation have become indistinct, and conventional therapy is defined differently at different institutions. Only when we can agree on what we are comparing will multicenter studies be feasible and meaningful.

At our institution we are in the process of developing a computerized system to record our observations and collect data from all patients who undergo mechanical ventilation or any of the other new respiratory support therapies. Luis O. Toro-Figueroa coined the term "ventilation oxygenation support systems" (VOSS) to bring all these therapies under one umbrella for this purpose.

ADDITIONAL READING

· Al-Saady N, Bennett ED. Decelerating inspiratory flow waveform improves lung mechanics and gas exchange in patients on intermittent positive-pressure ventilation. Intensive Care Med 11:68-75, 1985.

Arnold JH, Hanson JH, Toro-Figueroa LO, et al. Prospective, randomized comparison of high-frequency oscillatory ventilation and conventional mechanical ventilation in pediatric respiratory failure. Crit Care Med 22:1530-1539, 1994.

Banner MJ, Lampotang S. Mechanical ventilators: Fundamentals. In Perel A, Stock MC, eds. Handbook of Mechanical Ventilatory Support. Baltimore, Md.: Williams & Wilkins, 1992, pp 7-30.

Bergbom-Engberg I, Haljamae H. Assessment of patients' experience of discomforts during respirator therapy. Crit Care Med 17:1068-1071, 1989.

Bone RC, Gravenstein N, Kirby RR. Monitoring respiratory and hemodynamic function in the patient with respiratory failure. In Kirby RR, Manner MJ, Downs JB, eds. Clinical Applications of Ventilatory Support. New York: Churchill Livingstone, 1990, pp 301-336.

Bricker MB, Morris WP, Allen SJ, et al. Venous air embolism in patients with pulmonary barotrauma. Crit Care Med 22:1692-1698, 1994.

Brochard L, Rauss A, Benito S, et al. Comparison of three methods of gradual withdrawal from ventilatory support during weaning from mechanical ventilation. Am J Respir Crit Care Med 150:896-903, 1994.

Brochard L, Rua F, Lorino H, et al. Inspiratory pressure support compensates for the additional work of breathing caused by the endotracheal tube. Anesthesiology 5:739-745, 1991.

Demling RH, Knox JB. Basic concepts of lung function and dysfunction: Oxygenation, ventilation, and mechanics. New Horizons 1:362-370, 1993.

· Esteban A, Alia I, Ibanez J, et al. Modes of mechanical ventilation and weaning: A national survey of Spanish hospitals. Chest 106:1188-1193, 1994.

Fields AI. Mechanical ventilation for acute respiratory failure. In Stidham GL, Weigle CGM, eds. Pediatric Critical Care Review Series. II. Fullerton, Calif.: Society of Critical Care Medicine, 1993, pp 45-58.

· Gattinoni L, Pesenti A. ARDS: The non-homogenous lung. Facts and hypothesis. Intensive Crit Care Dig 6:1-4, 1987.

· Gattinoni L, Pesenti A, Avalli L, et al. Pressure-volume curve of total respiratory system in acute respiratory failure: Computed tomographic scan study. Am Rev Respir Dis 136:730-736, 1987.

Glauser FL, Polatty RC, Sessler CN. Worsening oxygenation in the mechanically ventilated patient. Am Rev Respir Dis 138:458-465, 1988.

Hansen-Flaschen J, Cowen J, Raps EL. Neuromuscular blockade in the intensive care unit. Am Rev Respir Dis 147:234-236, 1993.

· Lachman B. Open up the lung and keep the lung open [editorial]. Intensive Care Med 18:319-321, 1992.

· Lachman B, Handly B, Schultz H, et al. Improved arterial oxygenation, CO_2-elimination, compliance and decreased barotrauma following changes of volume-generated PEEP-ventilation with inspiratory/expiratory (I/E)-ratio of 1:2 to pressure-generated ventilation with I/E-ratio of 4:1 in patients with severe adult respiratory distress syndrome. Intensive Care Med 6:67, 1980.

· MacIntyre NR. Respiratory function during pressure support ventilation. Chest 89:677-683, 1986.

· MacIntyre NR. Weaning from mechanical ventilatory support: Volume-assisting intermittent breaths versus pressure-assisting every breath. Respir Care 33:121-125, 1988.

Marcy TW, Marin JJ. Respiratory distress in the ventilated patient. Clin Chest Med 15:55-73, 1994.

· Marini JJ. Monitoring during mechanical ventilation. Clin Chest Med 9:73-98, 1988.

· Mercat A, Graini L, Tebul JL, Lenique F, Richard C. Cardiorespiratory effects of pressure-controlled ventilation with and without inverse ratio in the adult respiratory distress syndrome. Chest 104:871-875, 1993.

Nahum A, Marini JJ. Alternatives to conventional mechanical ventilation in acute respiratory failure. In Current Pulmonology, vol 15. St. Louis: Mosby, 1994, pp 157-207.

· Passos Amato MB, Valente Barbas CS, Bonassa J, et al. Volume-assured pressure support ventilation: A new approach for reducing muscle workload during acute respiratory failure. Chest 102:1225-1234, 1992.

Perkin RM, Anas NG. Acute respiratory failure. In Grossman M, Dieckmann RA, eds. Pediatric Emergency Medicine. Philadelphia: JB Lippincott, 1991, pp 84-88.

• Perkin RM, Levin DL. Adverse effects of positive pressure ventilation in children. In Gregory G, ed. Respiratory Failure in the Child. Clinics of Critical Care Medicine, vol 3. New York: Churchill Livingston, 1981.

• Rappaport SH, Shpiner R, Yoshihara G, et al. Randomized, prospective trial of pressure-limited versus volume-controlled ventilation in severe respiratory failure. Crit Care Med 22:22-32, 1994.

Sanchez CA, Hinson JM. What to do when patient-ventilator interactions increase work of breathing. J Crit Illness 8:491-504, 1993.

Schuster DP. A physiologic approach to initiating, maintaining, and withdrawing mechanical ventilatory support during acute respiratory failure. Am J Med 88:268-277, 1990.

Shikora SA, Bistrian BR, Borlase BC, et al. Work of breathing: Reliable predictor of weaning and extubation. Crit Care Med 18:157-162, 1990.

• Slutsky AS. Mechanical ventilation: ACCP consensus conference. Chest 104:1833-1859, 1993.

Spearman CB, Sanders HG. The new generation of mechanical ventilators. Respir Care 32:403-418, 1987.

Stock MC, Downs JB, Frolicher DA. Airway pressure release ventilation. Crit Care Med 15:462-466, 1987.

• Suter PM. Permissive hypercapnia. In Parker MM, Shapiro MJ, Porembka DT, eds. Critical Care: State of the Art, vol 15. Fullerton, Calif.: Society of Critical Care Medicine, 1995, pp 347-360.

• Tobin MJ. Mechanical ventilation. N Engl J Med 330:1056-1061, 1994.

• Tuxem DV. Permissive hypercapneic ventilation. Am J Respir Crit Care Med 150:870-874, 1994.

van Uffelen R, Rommes JH, van Saene HKF. Preventing lower airway colonization and infection in mechanically ventilated patients. Crit Care Med 15:99-102, 1987.

• Weinberger SE, Schwartzstein RM, Weiss JW. Hypercapnia. N Engl J Med 321:1223-1231, 1989.

Yang KL, Tobin MJ. A prospective study of indexes predicting the outcome of trials of weaning from mechanical ventilation. N Engl J Med 324:1445-1450, 1991.

Younes M, Puddy A. Roberts D, et al. Proportional assist ventilation: Results of an initial clinical trial. Am Rev Respir Dis 145:121-129, 1992.

156 High-Frequency Oscillatory and Jet Ventilation

Juan A. Gutierrez · Kory D. Toro · Dawne A. Black · M. Heather Paterson · David L. Anglin · Luis O. Toro-Figueroa

BACKGROUND

Conventional mechanical ventilation (CMV) has been used extensively and successfully to support breathing in patients with respiratory failure. Although its effect on survival has never been evaluated or quantified, it is generally accepted that many lives have been saved with CMV. Although CMV is effective in the majority of patients, a significant number develop severe respiratory failure that is refractory to CMV. When CMV is the only support available for these patients, the outcome is usually chronic lung disease or death.

Use of high pressure or volume during CMV produces severe secondary lung injury associated with development of stress fractures of capillaries, epithelium, and basement membrane, which leads to increase in vascular permeability and secondary inflammation that further injures the lung. It has also been well demonstrated that exposure of lung tissue to high Fio_2 results in formation of free radicals and further injures the lung, also producing lung fibrosis. All these events lead to progressive mismatch of alveolar and capillary flow, worsening hypoxemia and hypercarbia. The usual clinical response is to increase Fio_2, ventilatory rate, pressure, and/or volume. This creates a negative effect that perpetuates oxygen toxicity, barotrauma, and volutrauma.

With high-frequency ventilation (HFV), the clinical approach to treatment of severe respiratory failure that does not respond to CMV is shifting. HFV encompasses a mixed group of unique ventilatory techniques that can be defined by two common elements: use of supraphysiologic ventilatory rates, usually >60 cpm (1 Hz), and use of tidal volume smaller than the anatomic dead space.

Sjostrand in 1967 accidentally discovered high-frequency positive pressure ventilation (HFPPV) while attempting to eliminate variations induced by spontaneous respiration during blood pressure measurements. By using high ventilatory rates and low tidal volumes close to dead space volume, he found that oxygenation and ventilation could be maintained for a prolonged period.

Subsequently in 1972 Lunkenheimer, in an effort to measure mediastinal impedance in dogs, proved that oxygenation and ventilation with high-frequency oscillatory ventilation (HFOV) was feasible by oscillating the chest wall in these animals with a loudspeaker connected at the airway with an ET tube.

In 1976 Smith introduced a third technique, known as high-frequency jet ventilation (HFJV). In this technique high-velocity jets of gas are moved through a small-bore cannula built parallel to the ET tube, and both are placed within the trachea. The high-velocity jet of gas entrains additional gas flow from the ET tube, thereby augmenting the tidal volume and accelerating gas movement into the alveoli. One technique that evolved from the HFJV technique is high-frequency flow interruption (HFFI). In HFFI the source of highly pressurized gas used to entrain gas flow through the ET tube is built in the ventilator circuit, as opposed to being parallel to the ET tube as in HFJV. In HFFI the source of this gas is controlled by a wheel with small openings that allows cycling of gas flow into the airways.

Mechanisms of Gas Transport During HFV

Conventionally the lungs are viewed as a two-compartment model. The first compartment is composed of the airways, which do not participate in gas exchange, and is referred to as anatomic dead space.

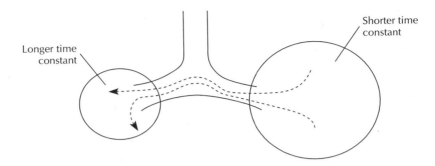

Fig. 156-1   Pendelluft effect. In inspiration, gas flows from the alveolar units with a shorter time constant (rapid filling) to those with a longer time constant (slow filling), thus producing interalveolar gas mixing. The flow is reversed in expiration.

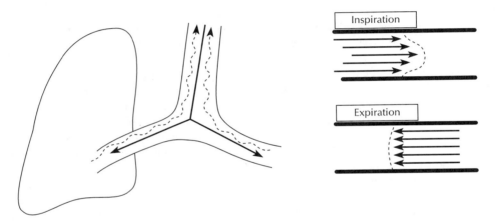

Fig. 156-2   Convective streaming. During inspiration the gas flows faster at the center of the airway than close to the walls. During exhalation the gas flows at almost the same velocity in the center and close to the walls. The end result is augmented dispersion of the gas. A pattern is generated in which the gas flows preferentially through the center of the airway during inspiration and close to the walls during exhalation.

The second compartment, formed by the aggregate of alveolar units, is responsible for gas exchange. To achieve effective ventilation, the volume of gas entering and exiting this compartment, or tidal volume, needs to be higher than the volume of gas within the anatomic dead space; otherwise all the gas would be wasted in dead space ventilation and never reach the alveoli to participate in gas exchange.

During normal spontaneous breathing, and in CMV, bulk (convective) gas exchange is responsible for most of the movement of gas in and out of the lungs. A gradient of pressure similar in spontaneous breathing and CMV is present within the airways, with higher pressure at the proximal airway and lower pressure at the alveoli. At the alveolar level the gas moves in and out of the capillaries through molecular diffusion across the alveolocapillary membrane according to a concentration gradient.

During HFV at least six different mechanisms of gas transport have been described: direct alveolar ventilation, pendelluft effect (Fig. 156-1), convective streaming (Fig. 156-2), augmented dispersion (Tay-

Table 156-1   Mechanisms of Gas Exchange During HFV

Mechanism	Description
Direct alveolar ventilation	Some of the proximal alveoli, which are close to the airways, receive direct bulk flow in similar fashion to flow to most of the lung during CMV. The overall importance of this mechanism is thought to be probably minimal.
Pendelluft effect (see Fig. 156-1)	Some bronchoalveolar units have low resistance and high compliance; others have high resistance and low compliance. The former (rapid) units fill before the latter (slow) units. The rapid units then empty into the slow units during inhalation. The slow units may empty into the rapid units during exhalation. The whole process constitutes intrapulmonary gas transport.
Convective streaming (see Fig. 156-2)	During inspiration the gas at the center of the airway moves faster than the gas in contact with the airway walls, which is slowed by friction. During expiration the flow is slower and the friction reduced; thus both streams of gas move at the same pace (slowly). A pattern of gas flow develops toward the alveoli in the center of the stream and away from the alveoli along the airway walls.
Augmented (Taylor) dispersion	As a result of convective streaming, some gas disperses radially and a swirling flow is created, increasing the gas mixing. The front column of gas dispersion is affected by eddies, airways bifurcations, and turbulence.
Cardiogenic mixing	The heart beating induces some oscillation of gas within the airways, which increases peripheral gas mixing. This mechanism is probably of minor importance.
Molecular diffusion	As in normal breathing and CMV, gas diffuses across the alveolocapillary membrane following the concentration gradients.

lor dispersion), cardiogenic mixing, and molecular diffusion (Table 156-1).

Which mechanism is most important during HFV is yet to be elucidated, and most likely a combination of all these mechanisms accounts for gas exchange during HFV. The result is a complex interaction between the geometry of the airways and the high-frequency flow of gas traveling longitudinally along the airways into the alveoli. Pedley et al. in 1994 reviewed the complexity of gas flow in the airways during HFV. The relatively short expiratory times and diminished dependence on gas bulk flow predispose to dangerous hyperinflation, specifically in the presence of gas flow limitation, as in obstructive airways disease (e.g., asthma and bronchiolitis). The higher the frequency the more pronounced this effect seems to be.

Classification

Three main groups of HFV are used clinically and provide the simplest and most commonly accepted HFV classification:

1. High-frequency positive pressure ventilation (HFPPV)
2. High-frequency oscillatory ventilation (HFOV)
3. High-frequency jet ventilation (HFJV)

Another way to group HFV devices is by the type of exhalation mechanism they provide: active or passive. Only true HFOV devices provide an active exhalation phase. HFPPV, HFJV, and HFFI devices all rely on lung recoil, or passive exhalation. Most HFV devices provide total ventilatory and oxygenation support, whereas most HFJV devices require the use of a conventional mechanical ventilator in tandem to generate a mean airway pressure ($P\overline{aw}$) and provide gas flow through the ET tube for entrainment.

High-frequency positive pressure ventilation

HFPPV devices are relatively simple and usually consist of a flow interrupter that produces positive pressure waves at frequencies of 60 to 120/min (1 to 2

Hz) with small tidal volumes (3 to 4 cc/kg), close to the dead space volume (Fig. 156-3). During the inspiratory phase gas is insufflated toward the airways, usually through a side arm and an open pneumatic valve, while the expiratory airway (main channel) remains open. During the exhalation phase the valve is closed and lung deflation is passive. To achieve effective tidal volume and prevent circuit dead space ventilation, it is imperative that a noncompliant circuit is used. This technique of HFV can be simulated with most CMV devices.

High-frequency oscillatory ventilation

HFOV devices require a source for continuous flow of fresh gas (bias flow), an oscillator mechanism capable of generating high-frequency oscillations of the column of gas in the circuit and airways, typically a piston or loudspeaker, and an exhalation port that exerts a low-pass filter effect to maintain $P\overline{aw}$ during the entire respiratory cycle (Fig. 156-4). This phenomenon, called low-pass filter effect, is the result of the peak pressure generated during inspiration, which may be as high as 90 cm H_2O when measured at the proximal airway, but this high-amplitude pressure waveform is rapidly dampened by the resistive forces generated by the HFOV circuit and the conductive airways. As a result of this effect, the alveoli are exposed to significantly lower amplitude pressure waves during the whole respiratory cycle, and peak inspiratory and expiratory pressures at the alveolar level are also markedly reduced (Fig. 156-5). Finally, the continuous flow of gas washes out the CO_2 and creates the predetermined airway pressure.

The active to-and-fro movement of the HFOV piston, transmitted through the column of gas, generates a positive inspiratory pressure and a negative expiratory pressure, respectively. Because of this, true HFOV devices are the only devices in the HFV group with an active expiratory phase. Although frequencies between 1 and 60 Hz are possible, the FDA has approved only frequencies between 3 (180 bpm) and 15 (900 bpm) Hz for clinical use. The tidal volume generated by an HFOV device is usually well below anatomic dead space volume, typically 1 to 3 cc/kg, but must always be greater than half the dead space volume to prevent CO_2 retention.

Compared with CMV and HFJV, HFOV usually requires a significantly higher $P\overline{aw}$ to achieve similar levels of oxygenation. Typically, the objective of HFOV is to reduce peak airway pressure while generating appropriate $P\overline{aw}$ to achieve and maintain ad-

equate lung expansion, resulting in a more favorable pressure-volume relationship, improved compliance, and gas exchange. This is usually accomplished by increasing $P\overline{aw}$ until the lung is "opened" and Fio_2 is weaned to <0.60. This has been defined as optimal alveolar recruitment.

Effects on oxygenation. Similar to CMV, HFOV produces a direct relationship between lung volume and oxygenation. During HFOV, practically all oxygenation is exclusively determined by changes in Fio_2 and $P\overline{aw}$ (Fig. 156-6). As lung volume is recruited, oxygenation increases; therefore Fio_2 requirements

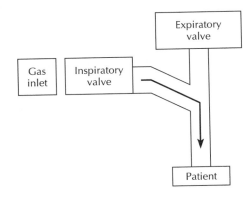

Fig. 156-3 Schema of HFPPV device. An inspiratory valve on the side arm acts as a flow interrupter. Gas flows to the airways when the valve is open. When the valve is closed, the elastic lung recoil pushes the gas through the expiratory valve.

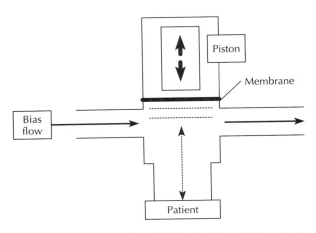

Fig. 156-4 Schema of HFOV device. The piston moves back and forth, producing oscillations in the membrane that are transmitted to the column of gas. Bias flow maintains the $P\overline{aw}$ and provides fresh gas.

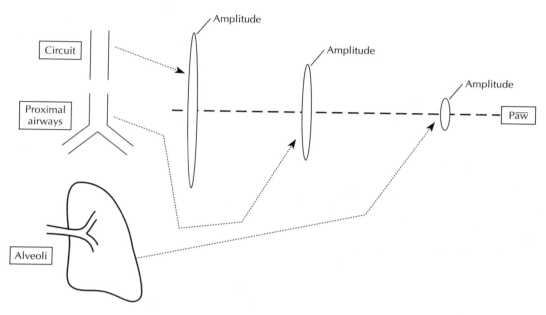

Fig. 156-5 Schema of low-pass filter effect. A high-amplitude pressure waveform is generated in the ventilator circuit. As the pressure wave travels down the airways and into the alveoli, the amplitude progressively decreases.

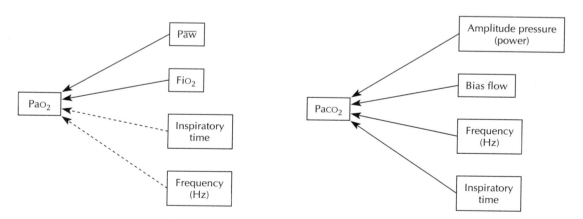

Fig. 156-6 Factors that affect oxygenation (Pa_{O_2}) and ventilation (Pa_{CO_2}) during HFOV. Pa_{O_2} is affected mainly by Fi_{O_2} and $\overline{Paw}$. In some circumstances inspiratory time and frequency may also affect oxygenation. Pa_{CO_2} is affected by diverse factors, but clinically the amplitude pressure is most used to manipulate ventilation.

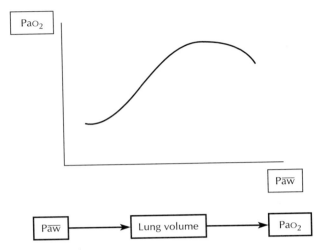

Fig. 156-7   Relationship between $\overline{Paw}$ and PaO_2. As $\overline{Paw}$ increases, so does PaO_2. At very high levels of $\overline{Paw}$ PaO_2 actually decreases. $\overline{Paw}$ exerts its effect on PaO_2 through changes in lung volume. At very high $\overline{Paw}$ the lung can be overdistended, with an increase in the functional dead space as the blood flow to the overdistended alveoli is impeded.

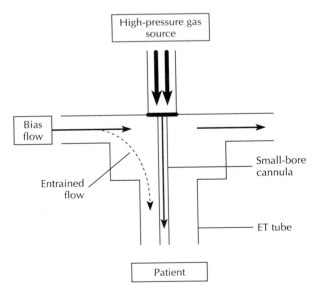

Fig. 156-8   Schema of HFJV. A high-pressure gas source is connected to the airway with a small-bore cannula inside the ET tube. Part of the bias flow is entrained by the high-velocity jet of gas.

usually decrease. When SaO_2 can be maintained at 90%, with FiO_2 of 0.60, equilibrium between lung volume, wall tension, and gas exchange has been reached. It is generally accepted that the risks of oxygen toxicity decrease when FiO_2 is <0.60. Inspiratory time and frequency can also affect oxygenation, but usually to no major clinically important degree.

Effects of modifying mean airway pressure. The $\overline{Paw}$ determines the lung volume and therefore oxygenation. $\overline{Paw}$ is one of the main determinants of oxygenation in HFOV. Increasing $\overline{Paw}$ will increase PaO_2 to a point. When hyperinflation is reached and the alveolar capillaries are compressed, PaO_2 will start to decrease with any further increases in $\overline{Paw}$ (Fig. 156-7). If the lung is hyperinflated, decreasing $\overline{Paw}$ will increase PaO_2. Once optimal alveolar recruitment is obtained and lower transpulmonary pressures are needed to maintain the lung open, the $\overline{Paw}$ can be further decreased without affecting PaO_2 or derecruiting alveoli until the "critical opening pressure" is reached. At this point further decreasing $\overline{Paw}$ will result in derecruitment. Clinically, the adequacy of the relationship between $\overline{Paw}$ and lung volume is assessed by the sufficiency of gas exchange, FiO_2, and lung expansion on the chest radiograph.

Effects on ventilation. During HFOV most of the ventilation depends on the amplitude pressure (power or ΔP), rate (frequency), inspiratory and expiratory times, and bias flow (fresh gas supply). $\overline{Paw}$ may affect CO_2 elimination by improving alveolar recruitment and decreasing the ventilation-perfusion ($\dot{V}/\dot{Q}$) mismatch.

Effects of modifying amplitude pressure. The power knob on the model 3100A HFOV (SensorMedics, Yorba Linda, Calif.) is a linear potentiometer that controls how much displacement the piston will have. Displacement of the piston generates a specific change in amplitude pressure, resulting in increased tidal volume. Therefore increasing the amplitude pressure will increase minute ventilation and decrease $PaCO_2$. It is worth noting, however, that the greater the increase in amplitude the greater the risk of barotrauma. The clinical adequacy of amplitude pressure is assessed and adjusted according to the degree of chest wall oscillations and the resulting arterial blood gas levels. Chest wall oscillation is assessed by means of visual inspection or tactile palpation. Factors that influence vibratory excursions of the chest wall during HFOV include the following:

Pulmonary system mechanics
Lung and chest wall compliance
Airways resistance
Airways dimension
Intrapulmonary secretions
ET tube lumen size and patency
Ventilator circuit alignment and patency
Ventilatory frequency
Pressure amplitude

Effects of modifying frequency. The effects of modifying respiratory frequency (rate) are complex. In general, at rates <200 breaths/min (3.33 Hz), CO_2 elimination is proportional to the product of tidal volume times respiratory rate, as in CMV; at rates >3.33 Hz, which are commonly used in HFOV clinical practice, CO_2 elimination is proportional to the product of the square of tidal volume times respiratory frequency. However, with the 3100A model, piston displacement decreases as frequency increases, decreasing the effective amplitude pressure and delivered tidal volume. With HFOV, a small change in amplitude pressure has a marked effect in the resulting tidal volume and minute ventilation.

Also, because active expiration during HFOV is time limited, increasing the frequency shortens the absolute inspiratory and expiratory times. This results in decreased tidal volumes because of less piston displacement time and less time for the gas to travel along the airways. The end result is CO_2 retention from the decreased absolute expiratory time and tidal volume. It is worth noting that the inverse is also true: when the frequency is decreased, absolute inspiratory and expiratory times, tidal volume, and minute ventilation increase. Compared with CMV, these effects create a paradox in which increasing the rate may result in increased Pa_{CO_2} whereas decreasing the rate may decrease Pa_{CO_2}. Understanding this paradox is essential when carrying out any HFOV oxygenation and ventilation strategies. Most of the time Pa_{CO_2} is manipulated through changing the amplitude, which tends to give more predictable results than changing the frequency.

Effects of modifying bias flow. Bias flow is one of the determinants of $P\overline{aw}$ and is important in "washing out" CO_2. An increase in bias flow while the $P\overline{aw}$ adjust valve is maintained at a constant setting produces an immediate increase in $P\overline{aw}$, resulting in alveolar recruitment, improvement in the resulting tidal volume, and decreased Pa_{CO_2}. However, any increase in $P\overline{aw}$ can be counteracted by opening the $P\overline{aw}$ adjust valve farther, maintaining the $P\overline{aw}$ the same, and increasing the CO_2 washout from the circuit and the patient, resulting in greater CO_2 elimination. Typically, the bias flow necessary to build adequate $P\overline{aw}$ and maintain appropriate minute ventilation in pediatric patients is 15 to 20 L/min. The larger the patient the greater the bias flow required. When additional bias flow beyond the capacity of the HFOV built-in flowmeter (50 L/min) is needed, a second flowmeter can be connected. The supplemental flow is added before the humidification systems. This modification has allowed us to use bias flow as high as 60 L/min in large pediatric patients.

Effects of modifying inspiratory time. Animal studies tend to disprove any important effects of changing the inspiratory time–expiratory time ratio (I:E). Clinically, increasing the inspiratory time results in increased tidal volume, which usually enhances CO_2 elimination and eventually increases Pa_{O_2}, in contrast to what has been described in animal models. When the lung is fully recruited, decreasing expiratory time by increasing inspiratory time percentage may induce CO_2 retention. Alternatively, when the lung is not fully recruited and $P\overline{aw}$ and power are set at maximum, gradually increasing inspiratory time to a maximum of 50% may improve alveolar recruitment and gas exchange. Keep in mind, however, that the combination of higher tidal volume and decreased expiratory time increases the likelihood of air trapping and hyperinflation. This situation must be monitored frequently with chest radiographs. Also, any event of cardiovascular instability or oxygenation-ventilation decompensation must lead the clinician to rule out hyperinflation or pneumothorax.

High-frequency jet ventilation

During the inspiratory phase, HFJV provides high-pressure gas flow through a small-bore cannula built in along the ET tube. The cannula is connected to a high-pressure (50 psi) gas source regulated by a solenoid valve (interrupter system). The resistance generated by the small diameter of the cannula reduces the gas pressure at the tip of the ET tube. The intermittent high-velocity jet of gas is delivered into the trachea, where it entrains the mainstream gas flow coming through the ET tube (Fig. 156-8). The entrainment may account for as much as 50% of the tidal volume generated. An additional port, used to monitor P$\overline{aw}$ within the trachea, also runs through the tip of the ET tube and is connected to the servo-control mechanism that maintains the preset value of airway pressure. The operational frequencies used during HFJV are usually between 4 and 11 Hz. The tidal volume generated ranges from 3.0 to 4.5 ml/kg. Typically, I:E is 1:6, with an inspiratory time of 0.02 second. The exhalation phase during HFJV is a passive process.

Compared with CMV and HFOV, HFJV usually requires a significantly lower P$\overline{aw}$ to achieve similar levels of oxygenation. HFJV dictates the use of a CMV in tandem to provide periodic tidal breaths and PEEP and to achieve adequate lung volume. The usual objective of HFJV is to minimize barotrauma. In normal lungs HFJV can achieve adequate oxygenation and ventilation at relatively low P$\overline{aw}$. In a lung with decreased compliance, HFJV can sustain oxygenation and ventilation at a much lower P$\overline{aw}$ than most techniques but cannot maintain adequate lung volume by itself. This is also desired in circumstances in which right ventricular venous return impediment is not warranted or when right ventricular dysfunction is present. Also, HFJV has been used to improve access to the airways during diagnostic or surgical bronchoscopy.

Other high-frequency ventilation techniques

High-frequency flow interruption evolved from HFJV. The difference is that the source of high-pressure gas used to entrain gas flow through the ET tube is built in within the ventilator circuit, as opposed to parallel to the ET tube, and this source of high-pressure gas is controlled by a wheel with small openings that allows cycling of gas flow into the airways.

In *transthoracic high-frequency oscillation* (THFV) an external oscillatory device produces high-frequency chest wall movement. To date, THFV is considered experimental and is not discussed here.

Many other modifications and hybrids of these techniques have been marketed as HFV systems. Each has specific performance and operational differences, which mean that the clinician must develop specific protocols and strategies. The scope of this chapter does not allow more detailed discussion of these specific differences.

INDICATIONS

The goal of HFV is to maximize oxygenation and ventilation with adequate lung volume while minimizing barotrauma, volutrauma, and oxygen toxicity. However, the two most widely used modes, HFOV and HFJV, generally are applied with two different strategies. This difference stems in part from the distinct mechanical and operational properties of the two devices.

HFV has been used in two relatively different populations: neonatal and pediatric patients. The neonatal population has been arbitrarily defined as any infant younger than 44 weeks postconceptional age or 1 month of age for a term infant; the pediatric population lower limit of age is defined by these criteria, and the upper age limit is 18 years. The spectrum of diseases and physiologic characteristics that typically separate these two populations of patients and which type of HFV device and strategy is chosen have a marked effect on efficiency, efficacy, and final outcome for each distinct age and patient population.

Neonatal Respiratory Distress Syndrome

High-frequency oscillatory ventilation. Neonatal respiratory distress syndrome (RDS) is the disease in which most of the HFV experience has been accumulated. The HIFI Study Group published a randomized multicenter study in 1989 that failed to demonstrate any advantages of HFOV compared with CMV, and indeed the prevalence of barotrauma and intracranial hemorrhage was higher in the HFOV-treated group. However, this study has been heavily criticized because of its lack of intercenter management strategy consistency, use of long and fixed inspiratory times, and most important, because the ventilatory strategy used was directed toward minimizing total pressure rather than achieving optimal alveolar recruitment. A second randomized study using a lung recruitment strategy with higher P$\overline{aw}$ and therefore greater mean lung volume demonstrated a lower prevalence of bronchopulmonary displasia in the HFOV-treated group, with no differences in mortality, barotrauma, or intracranial hemorrhage compared with CMV. After that, other randomized studies have confirmed the safety and potential advantages of HFOV in the neonatal population with RDS. Over the last few years HFOV has become part of the standard care for neonates with severe respiratory failure in many neonatal ICUs. In a recent study the main predictor for failure of HFOV in patients with RDS was the severity of the disease and lack of improvement in oxygenation after 6 hours of HFOV. Specifically, Pa_{O_2}/PA_{O_2} ratio <0.05 at the start and ≤0.08 after 6 hours were predictive of HFOV failure and need for extracorporeal membrane oxygenation (ECMO). Recently the combined use of HFOV and exogenous surfactant has proved superior to HFOV or surfactant alone in experimental models. Jefferies et al. demonstrated better distribution of the exogenous surfactant when HFOV was used.

High-frequency jet ventilation. In 1989 Spitzer et al. published a noncontrolled study of 176 neonates with RDS managed with HFJV. They concluded RDS could be successfully treated with lower P$\overline{a}$w and peak airway pressure, although no definitive improvement in outcome was observed. In 1990 Carlo et al. published a prospective, randomized study that compared early institution of HFJV with CMV. They concluded HFJV did not reduce morbidity or mortality and therefore was not superior to CMV. The combination of HFJV and surfactant administration has been evaluated in pilot studies and showed satisfactory results.

Persistent Pulmonary Hypertension of the Newborn

High-frequency oscillatory ventilation. Kohelet et al. in 1988 demonstrated that in 34 of 41 neonates persistent pulmonary hypertension of the newborn (PPHN) responded to HFOV. The high response rate to HFOV in this population of patients may be the result of its ability to recruit alveoli, improve Pa_{O_2}, improve CO_2 elimination, and achieve an alkaline pH most effectively and efficiently. Several studies place the success rate of HFOV in PPHN at approximately 50%, success or failure depending mainly on the presence or absence of pulmonary hypoplasia. Compared with the national registry survival rate for infants with PPHN managed with ECMO, which is about 83%, HFOV seems to be inferior, but it is not clear what the prevalence of pulmonary hypoplasia was in those patients given ECMO and how many of those patients would not have survived had they not responded to HFOV.

High-frequency jet ventilation. Carlo et al. in 1989 published results of a study in a small series of infants with PPHN treated with HFJV. Although there was improvement in most clinical measures, no differences in outcome were observed. Other case reports and small series also point to the potential benefits and support the use of HFJV in PPHN.

Neonatal Meconium Aspiration Syndrome

High-frequency oscillatory ventilation. In theory, use of HFOV in infants with meconium aspiration syndrome (MAS) may create problems. The physical presence of meconium in the airways and its propensity to cause air trapping in the small airways can lead to further hyperinflation and development of air leak syndrome (ALS). In neonates with MAS in whom the predominant clinical finding is diffuse alveolar disease (DAD) with or without PPHN and with mild to moderate air trapping, HFOV typically maintains small airways open, relieving obstruction and hyperinflation while facilitating reexpansion of collapsed or hypoventilated alveoli, therefore improving hypoxemia and hypercarbia. In MAS with DAD and moderate obstructive airway disease it is recommended that HFOV be attempted only in a facility where ECMO is available. The ELSO registry survival rate for infants with MAS is 80% and even greater in individual institutions.

High-frequency jet ventilation. Small series and individual case reports have documented the feasibility and safety of HFJV to support neonates with MAS.

Congenital Diaphragmatic Hernia and Neonatal Lung Hypoplasia

High-frequency oscillatory ventilation. Studies in animal models of congenital diaphragmatic hernia (CDH) supported with HFOV have yielded mixed results. The limitation in response to improved oxygenation seems to depend on the degree of pulmonary hypoplasia. In a study of infants with CDH treated with HFOV after meeting criteria for ECMO, approximately a third of infants responded favorably to HFOV without ECMO and survived to discharge. Of the two thirds that did not respond to HFOV and subsequently received ECMO, the survival rate was similar to that in infants who were ECMO near-misses. The ELSO registry survival rate for infants with CDH approximates 90%, and even greater in individual institutions. A recent retrospective study documented that in patients in whom CMV was not successful the presence of CDH and lung hypoplasia was an independent predictor of failure of HFOV. HFOV may be attempted in patients with CDH and lung hypoplasia, but the sickest of these patients (arbitrarily defined as having Pa_{O_2}/PA_{O_2}

≤0.08, oxygen index ≥30, or both) need to be managed in a facility in which ECMO can be initiated if HFOV fails.

High-frequency jet ventilation. Small series and individual case reports have documented the feasibility and safety of HFJV to support neonates with CDH and hypoplastic lungs.

Neonatal Air Leak With Pulmonary Interstitial Emphysema

High-frequency oscillatory ventilation. The possibility of using lower peak pressure to support patients with ALS makes both HFOV and HFJV theoretically good alternatives to CMV. However, because of the high lung volume used during HFOV, it has a greater potential to cause air trapping, hyperinflation, and worsening ALS. To date there is no evidence to support this possibility, and most studies have shown that ALS during HFOV does not worsen. Indeed, the trend is toward lesser prevalence of ALS and improvement of symptoms during HFOV compared with CMV. There are anecdotal case reports of successful treatment of lobar emphysema, a condition with high potential for development of ALS, with HFOV. Definitive studies are yet to be carried out. One caveat regarding the development or worsening of air leak after starting HFOV is that if $P\overline{aw}$ is not appropriately decreased after achieving adequate lung volume, which typically coincides with improvement in lung compliance and decrease in Fio_2 requirements, the likelihood of ALS developing or worsening is markedly increased.

High-frequency jet ventilation. Keszler et al. in 1991 published a prospective, randomized study that compared HFJV and CMV in newborns with interstitial emphysema. Use of HFJV resulted in faster resolution of ALS. However, no differences in mortality or prevalence of chronic lung disease were documented.

Pediatric Acute Lung Injury and Acute Respiratory Distress Syndrome

High-frequency oscillatory ventilation. In the late 1980s and early 1990s pediatric acute lung injury rescue studies demonstrated the feasibility and safety of HFOV in successfully supporting pediatric patients with severe acute lung injury and respiratory failure nonresponsive to CMV. In this heterogeneous group of patients with acute lung injury the severity, cause,

stage, and prognosis are all diverse. The reports are anecdotal and tend to review rescue attempts rather than prospective trials.

Traditionally, an oxygen index* ≥13 and the presence of severe ALS have been considered qualifying criteria for HFOV in pediatric patients. These criteria are still treatment dependent; for example, level of PEEP applied, Sao_2 value accepted by the clinician, and type of ventilator or method used can influence the oxygen index. Most of these rescue studies are noncontrolled or use historical controls, use nonstandardized management strategies, and are biased toward not reporting all instances in which HFOV has been used, especially if it fails.

In 1993 Arnold et al. reported the first series (n = 7) of pediatric patients with severe respiratory failure in whom CMV failed and were subsequently given HFOV. Six of seven patients survived. These authors concluded that HFOV can be used safely in pediatric patients and can be an effective alternative to CMV. That same year Cappon et al. described 12 pediatric patients with severe respiratory failure supported with HFOV. In seven patients HFOV was considered successful, four died, and one was given ECMO and survived. These authors noted that the improvement in oxygenation after switching to HFOV was more marked in survivors than in nonsurvivors.

Also in 1993 Rosenberg et al. published a retrospective study of 12 patients aged 4 months to 15 years who received HFV, five with HFFI and seven with HFOV. Seven of these patients survived, six with HFOV and one with HFFI. Finally, unpublished data collected from 27 pediatric centers in the early 1990s on pediatric patients with acute lung injury and severe respiratory failure assessed as failing CVM with the model 3100 HFOV device were pooled and analyzed by the manufacturer (SensorMedics). The survival rate for this pooled group of 82 pediatric patients was approximately 60%.

In 1994 Arnorld et al. published the first prospective, randomized comparison of HFOV and CMV in pediatric respiratory failure. This multicenter trial was corporate sponsored and led to FDA approval of HFOV for pediatric respiratory failure in late 1995. The study included pediatric patients with acute lung injury and severe respiratory failure, all of whom

---

*Oxygen index is defined as $P\overline{aw}$ multiplied by Fio_2 and a factor of 100 divided by Pao_2.

were older than 1 month and weighed <35 kg. Severe respiratory failure was defined by an oxygen index ≥13 and/or air leak. A balanced randomization was used to assign patients to receive HFOV or CMV. The study design allowed for crossover whenever specific criteria (i.e., intractable respiratory failure, shock secondary to ventilatory management strategy or mode, or progressive ALS) were met.

Of the 70 patients enrolled, 58 patients equally randomized to receive CMV or HFOV completed the study. Of the 12 patients eliminated from the final analysis, treatment was changed to ECMO in six, on family request; four exited secondary to protocol violations; and two were transferred to another institution. The patients assigned to the HFOV treatment group needed a higher $P\overline{aw}$ and had increased Pao_2/P_{AO_2}, decreased oxygen index over time, and significantly less prevalence of oxygen requirement at 30 days (21% in the HFOV group vs. 59% in the CMV group).

A 30-day outcome analysis showed no differences in survival between the two groups. Ranked outcome analysis demonstrated that the HFOV-only group (no crossover) had significantly better outcome than the CMV-only group: 83% survival without severe lung disease vs. 30%, respectively. Patients who crossed over from CMV to HFOV had a better outcome than did patients who crossed over from HFOV to CMV: 21% survival without severe lung disease vs. 0%, respectively. In addition, the authors noted that an oxygen index >42 at 24 hours identified patients who did not respond to HFOV. Mortality in this group was high.

The results of this study are encouraging; however, because data for 12 patients were eliminated from the final analysis and because of inherent variability in the course and outcome of acute severe respiratory failure in pediatric patients, final judgment cannot be made regarding the effectiveness or efficiency of HFOV compared with CMV. Nevertheless, HFOV is becoming a valid therapeutic alternative to CMV and ECMO and has influenced favorably the outcome in many pediatric patients. Presently the simplified indications for HFOV in pediatric patients, as approved by the FDA, are (1) any pediatric patient (no weight restriction) with severe respiratory failure in whom, in the opinion of a second independent physician, CMV has failed; (2) DAD or air leak; and (3) oxygen index >13 for at least 6 hours.

High-frequency jet ventilation. Although HFJV has

been used to support neonates and adults for several years, information about its pediatric application is scarce. In 1991 Berner et al. described findings in six children with refractory respiratory failure treated with HFJV. All six patients achieved adequate gas exchange with HFJV, but two died of multiple system organ failure. In 1993 Smith et al. reviewed 29 pediatric case reports of severe ARDS and progressive acute lung injury. In this noncontrolled study the objective was to oxygenate and ventilate the airways in these patients with the lowest $P\overline{aw}$ possible and to improve ALS. Twenty of the 29 patients survived, all with some degree of improvement of ALS. HFJV devices have also been used in adult trials with results that thus far have not been convincing enough to elicit widespread acceptance.

Respiratory Syncytial Virus

High-frequency oscillatory ventilation. An increase in expiratory resistance tends to induce air trapping and overdistention with all types of HFV; therefore any type of obstructive airway disease, including asthma and bronchiolitis, is considered a contraindication to use of HFOV. However, HFOV has been successfully used in patients with pneumonia from respiratory syncytial virus (RSV) with clinical symptoms consistent with acute respiratory distress syndrome (ARDS). Many infants with RSV pneumonia and ARDS-like symptoms do not have a predominant component of airway obstruction (e.g., bronchiolitis), although they may have evidence of mild to moderate air trapping, which can be confirmed by mild to moderately elevated airways resistance at pulmonary function testing. In addition, in some patients with severe bronchiolitis treated with high peak pressure, volume, respiratory rate, and Fio_2 during CMV management, development of DAD and ARDS is inevitable. In these patients lung volume maintenance usually becomes a major problem during CMV.

Gutierrez et al. published a report in five small infants with RSV pneumonia with evidence of mild to moderate airway obstruction, severe respiratory failure, and ARDS-like symptoms who received HFOV. Pulmonary function tests performed before initiation of HFOV demonstrated increased airways resistance and low lung compliance in all five infants. HFOV was effective in improving oxygenation and maintaining adequate ventilation in all infants. Four of these patients survived. In the one patient who did not survive, unilateral hyperinflation of the left lung developed and treatment was changed back to CMV. During CMV multiple severe air leaks developed, and blood culture proved septic shock; the infant died of intractable shock and respiratory failure.

This subset of patients with RSV pneumonia, very low lung compliance, and mild to moderately increased airways resistance may benefit from a trial of HFOV when CMV is failing and while ECMO is being considered. HFOV in patients with bronchiolitis with severe air trapping is not recommended. Large prospective, randomized studies are needed to confirm these observations and determine whether there is a specific degree of airway obstruction that predicts which patients with RSV pneumonia will benefit from HFOV.

Pediatric Air Leak Syndrome and Pulmonary Interstitial Emphysema

High-frequency oscillatory ventilation. Because of the high lung volume strategy during HFOV, the method has greater potential to cause air trapping, hyperinflation, and worsening ALS. To date, however, no evidence supports this possibility and most studies have shown that ALS during HFOV does not worsen. Although no statistically significant data support the use of HFOV in pediatric patients at risk for ALS, in the multicenter prospective, randomized comparison of HFOV and CMV in pediatric respiratory failure a trend toward improvement of ALS during HFOV was observed. The number of patients and the prevalence of ALS were not large enough to yield statistical significance. Definitive prospective, randomized studies are needed to establish the role of HFOV in preventing ALS and supporting respiration in pediatric patients with ALS.

High-frequency jet ventilation. Only a few case reports have been published of pediatric patients with ALS who have received respiratory support with HFJV. To date no prospective, randomized studies have been performed to help establish the role of HFJV in preventing ALS and supporting pediatric patients with ALS.

CONTRAINDICATIONS

Obstructive airways disease is usually considered a contraindication to use of most HFV devices. All such devices have relatively limited expiratory times and are most effective when used in conjunction with aggressive lung volume recruitment strategies, which are undesirable when attempting to provide respiratory support in patients with obstructed airways, high airways resistance, and a tendency to develop air trapping, which result in lung hyperinflation, barotrauma, or volutrauma. Therefore any of the obstructive lung diseases (e.g., asthma, reactive airways disease, emphysema, and bronchiolitis) are considered contraindications for most types of HFV, and especially HFOV. However, when the predominant component of the lung disease is restrictive, the presence of an obstructive component becomes a relative contraindication. Careful risk-vs.-benefit analysis is necessary, and if the clinician believes that the benefit of reversing hypoxemia outweighs the risk for hyperinflation and its associated consequences, a careful trial of HFV can be undertaken. For a related discussion of this subject, see p. 1463.

Cardiovascular system dysfunction (e.g., shock) or palliative vascular shunts and procedures that passively augment pulmonary blood flow are typically considered contraindications to HFV. Typically, patients are not able to maintain adequate blood flow at the high P$\overline{aw}$ needed to reexpand the lungs during HFV. Compensating cardiovascular function by optimizing preload and contractility can overcome these untoward effects. Shock is a contraindication to initiating or continuing HFV, especially HFOV. The shock state should always be reversed and the patient's condition stable before HFV is initiated. For a related discussion of this subject, see p. 1474.

TECHNIQUE
High-Frequency Oscillatory Ventilation
Switchover from conventional mechanical ventilation to high-frequency oscillatory ventilation

When switching from CMV to HFOV in pediatric patients, the following ventilator settings are used: Fio_2, 1.00; P$\overline{aw}$, 2 to 6 cm H_2O higher than for CMV; bias flow, at least 15 L/min; frequency, 10 to 15 Hz in neonates or 6 to 10 Hz in older patients; inspiratory time, 33%; and power, 2.0 to 4.0 (amplitude pressure ~30 cm H_2O) depending on patient size (Table 156-2). P$\overline{aw}$ and amplitude pressure are modified according to gas exchange and chest wall oscillations (chest wiggle factor). To some extent this transition is an art and a person experienced in HFOV must be at the bedside to quickly modify the settings according to the patient's response to the initial settings.

Table 156-2 Initial Settings Power and Frequency in Pediatric Patients According to Weight

Weight (kg)	Power	Frequency (Hz)
0.5-2.0	0.00	15
2.0-12	0.00-4.00	13-12
13-20	4.00	10
21-30	5.00	8
≥31	6.00	6

Diffuse alveolar disease

Oxygenation management. Immediately after the switch to HFOV the P$\overline{aw}$ is progressively increased until SaO_2 as measured by pulse oximetry reaches ≥90%. At this point progressive and aggressive decrease of FiO_2 is begun. The goal is to decrease FiO_2 to ≤0.60. During this process, if SaO_2 drops below 90%, P$\overline{aw}$ is increased until SaO_2 of ≥90% with FiO_2 <0.60, if possible, is reached and maintained. For an algorithm of the DAD oxygenation strategy, see Fig. 156-9. When SaO_2 is stabilized at 90% with FiO_2 <0.60, and if specifically the SaO_2 starts to increase, P$\overline{aw}$ *must* be decreased. Keep in mind Laplace's law, which indicates that as alveolar recruitment occurs, lung compliance and lung volume improve. Therefore the P$\overline{aw}$ that before was adequate now becomes excessive, resulting in alveolar overdistention, cardiovascular dysfunction, or volutrauma. Frequent chest radiographs are warranted to detect early signs of hyperinflation, which sometimes may occur without a discernible period of improved oxygenation or may manifest as sudden respiratory or cardiovascular deterioration after a period of improved oxygenation (see Fig. 156-9).

Ventilation management. The goal of HFOV in patients with DAD is to maintain $PaCO_2$ of 40 to 50 mm Hg with arterial pH of ≥7.30. However, the presently used practice of permissive hypercarbia suggests it may be safer to accept higher $PaCO_2$ levels and lower pH during HFOV. How much the piston is displaced during each oscillation (set with the HFOV power knob) is the most important determinate of the tidal volume generated. From an arbitrary value range of 0.0 to 10.0, the power is started as low as 0.0 for HFOV in premature infants and as high as 4.0 in pediatric patients. The power and its resulting pressure amplitude are usually adjusted to the level necessary

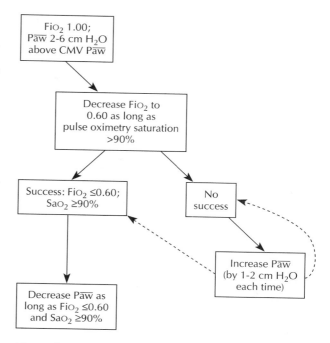

Fig. 156-9 Algorithm for oxygenation management in diffuse alveolar disease.

to produce a visible or palpable chest wall oscillation. Usually the pressure amplitude generated at these initial settings is 25 to 30 cm H_2O but rises immediately as the power is adjusted to the level necessary to produce adequate gas exchange. The frequency is set at 6 to 10 Hz (360 to 600 breath cpm) for pediatric patients and 10 to 15 Hz (600 to 900 breath cpm) for infants. Inspiratory time is always set at 33%. Bias flow is set at 15 to 20 L/min and is increased only when the adjust valve is maximized and more gas flow is needed to maintain the desired P$\overline{aw}$. If in the first arterial blood gas sample the $PaCO_2$ is above the target value, the power (the potentiometer that governs the amplitude pressure) is increased to a maximum value of 10. If $PaCO_2$ remains elevated, the following steps can be taken sequentially: decrease frequency progressively to 3 Hz; if no response, increase bias flow progressively to about 60 L/min; if no response, progressively increase inspiratory time to 50%.

Because of the potential dangers of negative cardiopulmonary interactions and the development of ALS, increasing inspiratory time must be accomplished with extreme caution. It is recommended that prolongation of inspiratory time to 50% be used only as long as is necessary to achieve and sustain alveolar recruitment. During this maneuver chest radiographs to detect hyperinflation must be obtained more frequently.

Air leak syndrome

Oxygenation management. The ALS strategy is based on accepting Fio_2 as high as 1.0 for as short a time as possible to compensate for derecruitment caused by the lower $P\overline{aw}$ and allow the air leak to heal. The goal of oxygenation during ALS is to maintain Sao_2 at ≤85%, as long as overall oxygen delivery is adequate, lactic acidosis does not develop, and hemodynamics remain stable. When ALS strategy does not support oxygenation in patients with severe diffuse alveolar disease due to hypoxemia, the oxygenation strategy for DAD must be used.

Ventilation management. As in permissive hypercapnia, the emphasis of the ALS strategy is on reducing the $P\overline{aw}$ and the pressure amplitude or power to the lowest values necessary to maintain adequate alveolar ventilation. High $Paco_2$ values (60 to 70 mm Hg or higher) and low pH (≤7.2) are well tolerated by most patients; therefore it is unnecessary to take the risks of increasing $P\overline{aw}$ and pressure amplitude or power to maintain "normal" $Paco_2$ values. Decreasing $P\overline{aw}$ and pressure amplitude may result in lower tidal volume, excessive CO_2 retention, and profound acidosis. Two options are available to maintain adequate CO_2 elimination at lower $P\overline{aw}$ and pressure amplitude: (1) Increase the frequency to relatively higher values in an attempt to increase minute ventilation while decreasing $P\overline{aw}$ and power (pressure amplitude). This maneuver is associated with the risk of decreasing absolute inspiratory and expiratory times and may lead to even smaller tidal volume and predispose to air trapping. (2) Decrease the frequency to a relatively lower value in an attempt to increase absolute inspiratory and expiratory times to compensate for the decrease in tidal volume and resulting minute ventilation. This maneuver has the associated risk of increasing tidal volume significantly, but this can be compensated for by further decreasing the power (pressure amplitude) and $P\overline{aw}$ to achieve the desired smaller tidal volume and mean lung volume, respectively. Typically, this results in adequate oxygenation and ven-

tilation. Which of the two maneuvers is superior remains controversial.

The ALS strategy is continued until the air leak has healed (i.e., no air leak is documented for at least 24 hours), after which the ALS strategy is abandoned and the DAD strategy reimplemented. To date no studies are available to validate the efficiency or effectiveness of the ALS strategy.

Switchover from high-frequency oscillatory ventilation to conventional mechanical ventilation

While HFOV support is being reduced, the above process is being reversed. Reversing the process by which support was escalated is the safest, most efficient and effective way to withdraw HFOV. Occasionally, depending on specific patient needs, one may alter the order in which these procedures are reversed.

In small infants HFOV has been successfully withdrawn by gradually reducing the power until the oscillator can be turned off, using the HFOV circuit as a CPAP generator, and gradually reducing the $P\overline{aw}$ setting to lower levels that allow extubation directly from HFOV. In older patients technical limitations (e.g., not being able to sustain low and stable $P\overline{aw}$ during support reduction and while the oscillator operates at minimal settings) make it more difficult to meet extubation criteria without switching to CMV. Most older children do not tolerate very low HFOV settings without sedation long enough to safely remove the ET tube.

A typical approach in pediatric patients has been to switch to CMV once $P\overline{aw}$ has been reduced to 18 ± 3 cm H_2O in larger children or 15 ± 3 cm H_2O in smaller infants, with Fio_2 ≤0.50, evidence of adequate gas exchange, and improving pulmonary function. The amplitude pressure settings (power) must be gradually reduced over the course of HFOV, although there is no minimum amplitude pressure or power criterion necessary for deciding to attempt to change to CMV. Also, it is important to note that little or no attention is given to the set frequency once its adequacy has been determined early during HFOV. Typically, the change to CMV is made on a trial basis at the same frequency at which ventilation has been successful in the particular patient. A change from HFOV to CMV is considered successful when oxygenation and ventilation during CMV are adequate with Fio_2 ≤ 0.60, rate ≤ 30 bpm, and peak pressure ≤ 30 cm H_2O.

Special Considerations in Larger Pediatric Patients

Experience with HFOV in patients weighing >35 kg is limited. Most larger pediatric patients have received HFOV rather than HFJV. For reasons that are not yet clear, to achieve adequate CO_2 elimination in older patients with any HFV device has proved more difficult and in some cases not possible. Proposed explanations for this failure include the limitation of the power that generates the amplitude pressure, relatively small displacement volume, and insufficient absolute expiratory time.

One approach to inadequate CO_2 elimination in older and larger patients receiving HFOV is to use relatively lower rates (e.g., as low as 3 Hz), high-amplitude pressures (e.g., maximum power of 10), high $\overline{Paw}$ (e.g., as high as 45 cm H_2O), high levels of bias flow (e.g., to 60 L/min), and prolonged inspiratory times (e.g., as high as 50%). This strategy may include relative hypoxemia with Sao_2 as low as 85%, or even lower, as long as adequate oxygen delivery and the absence of significant metabolic acidosis are ensured. Relative hypoxemia along with permissive hypercapnia, in the absence of hemodynamic instability and profound acidosis, may enable greater success with HFOV in larger patients. To date all larger patients have needed heavy sedation and neuromuscular blockade to achieve adequate ventilatory support.

Management

The following may reflect unproved but not unsupported biases. Many clinicians believe that in the patient with diffuse alveolar disease early institution of HFOV may result in less cumulative barotrauma than conventional ventilation at high peak inflating pressures. Improved outcome was noted in a large series of ECMO-eligible HFOV rescue patients when HFOV was instituted early in the course of the disease. In most animal studies HFOV is most effective when initiated early and with a strategy designed to recruit and maintain lung inflation. Histologic analysis of animal lungs has demonstrated that use of HFOV after 8 hours of CMV improves gas exchange and lung aeration compared with use of CMV only. However, use of HFOV relatively late is not so effective in re-

ducing the pathologic findings of acute lung injury as is use immediately after delivery or early development of acute lung injury. The use of an HFOV strategy that achieves optimal lung inflation seems to be equally important because the beneficial effects of HFOV in surfactant-deficient adult rabbits occur only if lung volume is maintained at levels that prevent development of generalized atelectasis. Some empiric management guidelines on how to correct abnormal arterial blood gas levels and clinical troubleshooting methods that can be of general benefit are listed on p. 1468.

Patient Care

Each pediatric critical care team must develop a set of operational guidelines, readily available to all other members, that provide the framework and set the expectations necessary to use HFOV safely and efficiently. Some issues to be addressed are team composition and responsibilities, education and training, policy and procedures, patient assessment and monitoring, respiratory care, patient positioning, analgesia, sedation, and neuromuscular blockade, and patient-parent interactions.

Team composition and responsibilities

The team must be multidisciplinary and include a physician, nurse, and respiratory care practitioner at a minimum. The team is responsible for establishing a comprehensive care plan for the patient receiving HFOV, with all members having direct input in its development. This joint effort includes even basic procedures such as strategy, frequency of monitoring, weighing, bathing, skin care, positioning, and airway care.

Education and training

To develop an adequate understanding of HFOV all team members must participate at some level in education, research, innovation, or application of the technique. It is our opinion that all team members must have experience with HFOV in didactic and practical laboratory settings before attempting to clinically provide ventilatory support in pediatric patients. The potential dangers of HFOV use are many and occur specifically when there is a lack of understanding of the differences between HFOV and CMV. Although knowledge and experience in CMV management principles and cardiopulmonary physiolo-

MANAGEMENT DURING HIGH-FREQUENCY OSCILLATORY VENTILATION

Management objectives

Use high mean lung volume with minimal Fio_2.

Permissive hypercarbia may be of significant value, specifically in ALS or patients who weigh >35 kg.

Make hemodynamic management a priority, with emphasis on high hemoglobin level, oxygen delivery, and extraction and consumption rather than absolute Po_2.

Titrate diuretic therapy and carefully manage fluid therapy to improve lung compliance.

Aggressively detect and evacuate air leaks and prevent ALS.

Optimize nutrition, preferably enterally, while avoiding excessive glucose and protein intake with resultant increased CO_2 production.

Patients who meet the indications for HFOV usually tolerate it well.

Do not force HFOV in clinical situations when there are no clear indications, contraindications are present, or the patient is not tolerating it well.

If an optimal CMV strategy is already being used, do not expect dramatic, immediate improvement in oxygenation, although generally ventilation improves dramatically. ("HFOV can shake CO_2 from a stone."—*A. Bryan*)

Measuring and determining optimal mean lung volume can be a problem during all forms of assisted ventilation, especially HFOV.

Guidelines for correcting abnormal arterial blood gas levels
CO_2 retention: Ventilation

Increase amplitude pressure by increasing the power until the chest seems to be vibrating.

Watch transcutaneous CO_2 for trend and determine gas level within a few minutes to see if Pco_2 warrants change.

Decrease frequency (rate) gradually when tidal volume is suspected as cause of inadequate minute ventilation.

Verify that airways are patent by aggressively lavaging and suctioning. Use right-angle adapter to avoid disconnecting circuit, losing $\overline{Paw}$ and lung volume, and worsening $\dot{V}/\dot{Q}$ matching in $\overline{Paw}$-dependent patients.

Reducing $\overline{Paw}$ may decrease CO_2 if signs of hyperinflation exist or when alveolar overdistention and reduced pulmonary blood are clinically suspected.

Verify patency of circuit, free of water and secretion accumulation, and proper circuit connections free of gas leaks.

Desaturation: Oxygenation

Adjust Fio_2

Titrate $\overline{Paw}$ according to Sao_2 and observe arterial blood gas levels; examine thorax for signs of hyperinflation; and check for evidence of air trapping with periodic chest radiographs.

Optimize oxygen delivery, including cardiac performance and hemoglobin.

Decrease frequency (rate) gradually when inadequate tidal volume is suspected as cause of alveolar hypoventilation and inadequate mean lung volume.

Reducing $\overline{Paw}$ may improve oxygenation if signs of hyperinflation exist or when alveolar overdistention and reduced pulmonary blood are clinically suspected.

Prolong inspiratory time gradually when inadequate tidal volume is suspected as cause of alveolar hypoventilation and inadequate mean lung volume.

Troubleshooting during HFOV
Rapid increase in Pco_2 or rapid decrease in Po_2

Tension pneumothorax: Evacuate.

ET tube obstruction may be noted as change of chest vibration intensity and decreased pressure amplitude (mainly secondary to secretions or ET tube displacement): Suction or reposition.

Decreased pulmonary blood flow or systemic arterial blood pressure: Optimize hemodynamics.

Continued.

MANAGEMENT DURING HIGH-FREQUENCY OSCILLATORY VENTILATION—cont'd

Gradual increase in P_{CO_2} or gradual decrease in P_{O_2}

Pulmonary interstitial emphysema.
Atelectasis
Patent ductus arteriosus
Slow nontension pneumothorax
Changes in patient sedation or comfort level
Worsening of lung disease
Need for suctioning
Chest wall rigidity
Oscillator drift in amplitude with increased P_{CO_2}.
Oscillator drift in $\overline{P_{aw}}$ with decreased P_{O_2}.
Gradually diminishing perfusion.
Apnea or decreased minute ventilation with increased P_{CO_2}.
Change in F_{IO_2} with decreased P_{O_2}.

---

gy are helpful, inappropriately applied $\overline{P_{aw}}$, inspiratory time, power, or frequency can have completely different effects than those predictable from previous CMV experience. A complete understanding of the different HFOV strategies is imperative to achieve the desired therapeutic goals and minimize the potential for iatrogenic injury. Comprehensive preclinical training combined with further clinical bedside training will reinforce the team's knowledge base, enhance their skills, and ensure the best possible utilization of HFOV while potentially avoiding multiple complications and pitfalls.

The HFOV educational and training process at Children's Medical Center of Dallas is divided into three phases. Phase 1 encompasses 8 hours of didactic classroom work. All aspects of HFOV and its differences from other nonconventional and conventional devices are covered. Variations of the different strategies in all patient populations are addressed. Lung simulators and clinical case histories are combined with hands-on experience to emphasize the critical pathways of each strategy. Phase 2 encompasses 4 hours of realistic hands-on clinical laboratory simulation with an animal model of acute lung injury. In phase 3 of the training process a preceptor is used to model for and train a new team member. This process applies across all disciplines

represented by the critical care health team. A multidisciplinary continuing education process has been developed and integrated with other therapies (e.g., ECMO, nitric oxide, and partial liquid ventilation), also known as ventilation and oxygenation support systems (VOSS), for the purpose of better understanding their specific interrelationships and applications.

Policy and procedures

Each pediatric critical care team must develop a specific HFOV policy and manual to address their institutional needs, such as device operating and maintenance procedures, humidifier and oxygen analyzer assembly and operation, circuit assembly and calibration, device performance check, alarm setting, valve testing, setting patient parameters, troubleshooting, and cleaning.

Patient assessment and monitoring

In critically ill children a great variety of conditions can lead to acute lung injury that can progress to ARDS and may benefit from HFOV. These conditions make delivery of care, ongoing systems assessment, laboratory and radiologic tests, medication administration, treatments, procedures, comfort measures, phychosocial interventions, and other therapeutic or supportive care difficult to standardize. As with

CMV, care of the child receiving HFOV is usually determined by the disease process and not the device used for ventilatory support during the process. The HFOV device, however, may place quite different and unique physical, physiologic, and psychological demands on the patient and caregivers. Physical assessment of pediatric patients receiving HFOV presents special challenges to the critical care practitioner. Although reliance on conventional assessment skills is important, the need to modify the techniques necessary for processing auditory, visual, and tactile sensory input places unique demands on caregivers.

To monitor these patients more closely, other supplemental clinical assessment tools must be more heavily relied on. For example, although visual assessment is essentially unchanged from that with CMV, the constant vibrating of the patient, and specifically of the chest, requires adjustments in classic clinical assessment skills. Frequently observing chest symmetry and spontaneous respiratory pattern, feeling or observing chest vibration (chest wiggle factor), evaluating lung expansion on chest radiographs, checking capillary refill time, skin color, and temperature, comparing central vs. peripheral pulses, and monitoring a continuous ECG tracing are some of the ways a clinician can compensate for the difficulties in assessment of the patient receiving HFOV. Chest vibration provides an adjunctive assessment of the adequacy of ventilation, and learning to detect changes in the vibratory pressure amplitude of the chest is important because small changes may affect CO_2 elimination. For example, ET tube displacement, mucous and other types of airway obstruction, lung overinflation, and pneumothoraces are common complications that may be discovered when assessing chest vibration in a child receiving HFOV.

Frequent neurologic checks must be part of a complete assessment during HFOV. Not all patients receiving HFOV need neuromuscular blockade. For example, small infants seem to experience a sedative effect from the oscillatory vibrations. Patients receiving HFOV may have spontaneous minute ventilation ranging from irregular hypoventilation to hyperventilation or have normal breathing patterns or apnea. Pain, agitation, hypoxia, elevated CO_2 level, rapid eye movement sleep, and lung injury all increase the spontaneous breathing frequency during HFOV. Excessive spontaneous movement or respi-

rations may jeopardize the overall safety of the patient and precipitate increased oxygen demand, create or worsen ALS, and even cause the oscillator to stop. In these circumstances increasing sedation or neuromuscular blockade is considered, although not always needed. Because of the risk of intraventricular hemorrhage in neonates, neurologic examinations, including pupillary checks, must be performed every 1 to 2 hours. This is not necessary in older pediatric patients.

Auscultation is the aspect of patient assessment most affected by HFOV. Loud rapid vibratory sounds are generated by movement of the piston and the air cooling mechanism and can be heard over the patient's entire torso. Heart, respiratory, and bowel sounds are essentially impossible to assess. The clinician needs to acquire an appreciation for the vibratory breath sounds produced by the oscillator; these may be characterized as bright, dull, or squeaky reflections of sounds transmitted through the lungs. Changes in the character of sound may reflect changes in lung compliance. Assessment of breath sounds during HFOV includes documentation of air entry, symmetry, and intensity and differences in perceived acoustic characteristics (pitch and rhythm) of breath sounds, all of which may indicate ET tube malposition, pneumothorax, atelectasis, or the need for suctioning. Breath, heart, and abdominal sounds may be auscultated during brief periods when HFOV is not being used, as during bagging or suctioning.

In our experience many children who are $P\overline{aw}$ dependent may not tolerate short periods of bagging or even the briefest period without HFOV. In these patients the setbacks associated with alveolar derecruitment and deoxygenation far outweigh the benefits of bagging, suctioning, and chest auscultation, and the clinician must rely on the other aspects of physical assessment. When direct evaluation of breath sounds, heart tones, and bowel sounds is imperative, assessment may be accomplished during short periods of 5 to 10 seconds with the oscillator in standby (oscillatory amplitude or power off) while the $P\overline{aw}$ continues to be applied or during times that oscillation must be interrupted (e.g., for suctioning or routine circuit change). When a patient is removed from continuously applied $P\overline{aw}$, the alveoli may collapse; therefore disconnection of HFOV is discouraged and must be limited to very short periods. The procedure for interruption of oscillation for patient assessment is as follows:

Deactivate alarm (45-second duration).

Engage stop switch (oscillator stops) but do not disconnect the patient from the circuit.

Do not disconnect the patient from the oscillator (maintain Paw and mean lung volume).

Perform assessment (5-second increments).

Press reset button.

Activate start switch (oscillation resumes).

Reactivate alarm.

Because of vibration, some practitioners find it difficult to palpate patient pulses during HFOV. Initially the vibrations seem to affect this assessment skill; however, it simply takes a little time and practice to regain mastery of palpation. Skin temperature, turgor, and perfusion are also frequently assessed, as in the care of any seriously ill child. In addition, the chest must be palpated for intensity and symmetry of oscillations and the abdomen palpated and abdominal girth measured regularly to assist in GI assessment and to alert the practitioner to any signs of pneumoperitoneum.

Frequent or continuous monitoring of vital signs will provide information about cardiac performance and respiratory status. A complete clinical assessment of cardiac function must include heart rate, blood pressure, capillary refill time, skin temperature, pulse volume and character, cardiac filling pressure, urinary output, and acid-base balance. Because of the inability to easily auscultate cardiac sounds, the heart rate obtained is typically recorded from the monitor. Delayed capillary refill, pale or cool extremities, hypotension, metabolic acidosis, decreased pulse pressure, tachycardia, and oliguria may be signs of cardiac dysfunction. Sudden changes in heart rate and perfusion, blood pressure, Sao_2, and CO_2 elimination necessitate immediate assessment and intervention. Desaturation and hypotension are classic signs of pneumothorax or lung overinflation. Although these two complications of HFOV do not occur frequently, they are severe and common enough to warrant constant surveillance and must always be considered medical emergencies. Desaturation and hypotension can also be signs of a low effective circulating volume or poor myocardial contractility. Other available hemodynamic data such as arterial pulse waveform and pressure and measured and derived variables from Swan-Ganz catheters may be useful in assessing the patient during HFOV. Occasionally apparent sudden tachyarrhythmia may develop that is determined to be an artifact of vibratory interaction with the ECG leads.

The critical care team must also become familiar with lung volume assessment with chest radiographs. These are more frequently obtained during the initial phase of establishing an optimum lung volume and during reduction of HFOV support. Radiographic signs of lung derecruitment (hypoventilation) or collapse (atelectasis) include radiopaque (white) lung fields, indistinct heart and diaphragm borders, lung expansion to the eighth posterior rib or higher, diffuse air bronchograms, and distinctly domed diaphragm. Chest radiographic signs of lung overinflation include radiolucent (black) lung fields, distinct or even sharp heart and diaphragm borders, lung expansion to the tenth posterior rib or lower, and flattened diaphragm. In neonates the ideal diaphragmatic position on an anteroposterior chest radiograph is at T9. Pediatric patients may need lung inflation at T10. During any phase of HFOV, chest radiographs can be useful to determine optimal lung inflation as well as to ensure proper ET tube position (i.e., tip of the ET tube at T1-3 in infants and T3-4 in older pediatric patients).

When absolutely necessary, weighing during HFOV can be accomplished. Maintenance of adequate mean lung volume is the most important objective when weighing a patient during HFOV. If weighing must be performed, the ventilator is disconnected but mean lung volume must be preserved or reestablished with a brief period of hand ventilation. Two or more persons are necessary to safely accomplish weighing. However, because of the inflexibility of the HFOV circuit and the tendency for lung derecruitment, most children receiving HFOV can not be weighed.

The HFOV circuit is a rigid tube that must be cautiously positioned to prevent kinking of the ET tube and thereby decreasing pressure amplitude or causing complete obstruction. The circuit and the ET tube must be supported by a stack of linen or other padding and secured to the mattress. Even the smallest movement of the HFOV circuit or the patient can change ET tube position and result in obstruction or extubation.

Monitoring devices must include a pulse oximeter and transcutaneous CO_2 ($tcco_2$) and cardiorespiratory monitors. The patient care flow sheet must include at a minimum vital signs, type of ventilator, Fio_2, $P\overline{aw}$, power, pressure amplitude, frequency (in hertz units), inspiratory time, bias flow, arterial blood gas levels, Sao_2, $tcco_2$, and any other pertinent laboratory data and assessment findings.

Respiratory care

Combination and delivery of some other respiratory care modalities with HFOV have been successfully and safely achieved. For example, delivery of bronchodilators through the respiratory tract is safe during HFOV, although how much lung deposition of drug is achieved is not known. Patients who can tolerate withdrawal of HFOV for short periods may benefit from hand bagging in the bronchodilator. To date there are no published articles on delivery of ribavirin during HFOV. At our institution we do not attempt delivery of ribavirin during HFOV.

Indications for suctioning in patients during HFOV are similar to those during CMV and include changes in respiratory status such as upward trend in $tcco_2$ tension; changes in blood gas levels, heart rate, respiratory rate, color, or respiratory effort; visible secretions in the ET tube; or perceived change in chest wall vibration. Frequency of suctioning is determined by individual patient needs rather than predetermined schedule. No matter how skillfully suctioning is carried out in patients who are $P\overline{aw}$ dependent, protracted periods of desaturation will follow. During the first 24 hours of HFOV, most patients need frequent suctioning, as often as every hour for the first 8 hours. Subsequently, suctioning requirements decrease dramatically. Suctioning is considered at least every 24 hours to maintain patency of the ET tube and the main airways. For safety, suctioning during HFOV is performed by two persons.

The need for hand bagging with PEEP must also be judged on an individual basis. Extensive hand ventilation in patients with interstitial emphysema or ALS is unwarranted. In a surfactant-deficient lung the larger tidal breaths generated by hand ventilation with a bag may cause excessive stretching of the more compliant airways and alveoli and result in volutrauma. Although hand ventilation may aid in preventing derecruitment during suctioning at lower lung volumes, the desaturation can be compensated for after suctioning by increasing Fio_2 or $P\overline{aw}$ or both. The strategy for suctioning during HFOV is disease specific. Patients with severe DAD and no evidence of PAH who need a prolonged recovery period after suctioning (slow return to baseline) may be candidates for empiric increase in $P\overline{aw}$ or Fio_2 before, during, and briefly after suctioning. In patients with PAH, preoxygenation with an Fio_2 of 1.0 is provided for approximately 5 minutes before suctioning. In patients with air leaks, increasing $P\overline{aw}$ can perpetuate or worsen ALS; therefore it is preferable to increase the Fio_2 to achieve presuctioning Sao_2. After quick single-pass suctioning, HFOV must be reestablished and the lungs allowed to rerecruit and stabilize. This process can be repeated as many times as necessary to clear the airways of secretions. Once presuctioning Sao_2 is achieved, $P\overline{aw}$ or Fio_2 are returned to baseline. IV sedation or analgesia or endotracheal lidocaine given before suctioning and other noxious procedures may ameliorate potential adverse effects.

Because of the potential risk of increased air trapping during HFOV, development of a sleeve seal leak with significant loss of gas flow and use of closed tracheal suction systems (e.g., Ballard in-line suctioning catheter) is generally discouraged. However, some patients seem to tolerate suctioning only when performed through a right-angle bronchoscope adapter or with the use of the closed tracheal suction system and without interrupting HFOV. The procedure for suctioning patients during HFOV is as follows:

Determine suctioning frequency based on clinical status.

Preoxygenate when necessary (in $P\overline{aw}$-dependent patients and PAH).

Pass suction catheter to 1 cm below tip of the ET tube.

Avoid hand ventilation when possible; compensate with increased $P\overline{aw}$ and/or Fio_2.

Use single-pass suctioning.

Allow recovery before the next intervention.

Repeat as many times as necessary.

Document type and amount of secretions.

Modify suctioning procedure according to patient tolerance and pathophysiology.

Use of conventional bronchial hygiene techniques (e.g., chest physiotherapy) must be individually evaluated. Because of chest wall vibration generated by HFOV, most patients do not need or benefit from chest physiotherapy.

Patient positioning

Similar to CMV, some patients prefer a specific position during HFOV. This preference may be due to the distribution of the pulmonary process or to the up and down migration of the ET tube that can occur with position changes. Because the DAD strategy is directed toward maintaining a constant lung volume, initial position changes must be accomplished without disconnecting the ET tube. HFOV usually is initiated with the patient supine, and positional changes must be gradual. In the early hours after transition to HFOV generally few or no position changes with ET tube disconnection are attempted. After 24 to 72 hours of HFOV, position changes are generally attempted at least every 12 hours. Initial position changes include supine, decubitus, prone, and reverse Trendelenburg if needed. The clinical response after each position change is assessed with oxygenation and CO_2 elimination and with clinical examination.

Analgesia, sedation, and neuromuscular blockade

Providing comfort for an infant or child during HFOV can be a true test of clinical skills and inventiveness. Most patients are generally less anxious during HFOV than CMV. Even though the loud cadence of HFOV along with other critical care device noises may result in altered day and night or sleep and rest patterns, the constant vibration of HFOV seems to have a calming effect, especially in infants. The use of developmentally appropriate interventions and behaviorally oriented care facilitates comfort and may help modulate the need for a pharmacologic approach to comfort. Conventional approaches for pain assessment and management (e.g., swaddling, nesting or containment, pacifiers, earmuffs, light reduction, soothing music, nurturing touch, and interaction with parents or caregivers) are useful.

Typically, the requirement for analgesia, sedation, and neuromuscular blockade is influenced more by patient condition than by HFOV. Use of muscle relaxants in neonates is not routine and must be individualized for all ages. The pressure sensors in HFOV devices are sensitive to the movement or respiratory efforts of most large children, creating pressure fluctuations within the circuit, triggering the alarm, and even stopping oscillation. For these reasons, most pediatric patients receiving HFOV need heavy sedation or neuromuscular blockade. For a complete discussion of strategies for analgesia, sedation, and neuromuscular blockade during the support of severe respiratory failure with CMV, see Chapters 179 and 180.

Patient-parent interactions

Psychosocial support and appropriate education of the child and family members facilitate trust and communication and assisting them in feeling supported, knowledgeable, and in control of the child's care. The physical characteristics of the oscillator can be daunting to families and can result in parental hesitancy and even withdrawal. Explaining the purpose and function while stressing the safety of the device frequently eases their concern. It is prudent to explain to parents that they may not detect their child's respirations during HFOV and that other types of ventilators may be used as the patient's condition changes. The family is encouraged to interact with or hold the child whenever possible. Bonding and parental interaction clearly benefit both child and parents, but they must be aware of some potential problems during HFOV. The rigidity of the ventilator circuit may inadvertently alter ET tube position, force water vapor condensation from the circuit to flow into the patient, and easily disconnect the patient from the device. Simple and safe holding methods have been devised for stable patients receiving HFOV and can be used safely with proper preparation. Always encourage other types of parental involvement when possible.

High-Frequency Jet Ventilation

Most of the experience with HFJV has been gathered in the neonatal population, and experience in older pediatric patients comes from individual case reports or small retrospective series. The FDA has not approved HFJV for ventilatory support in older pediatric patients, and its use remains empirical.

A common problem with HFJV is that it requires reintubation with a special triple-lumen ET tube. The risk involved in this procedure may be significant in many patients with pulmonary compromise. Recently a new modified ET tube connector that allows use of HFJV without the need to reintubate has been developed, field tested, and marketed for use in the neonatal population. To date no studies demonstrate the feasibility and safety of this modified ET tube connector in the older pediatric population.

Historically, the philosophy behind HFJV placed more emphasis on use of relatively low P$\overline{aw}$ to maintain oxygenation and ventilation. The typical ventilatory frequencies used during HFJV are between 4 and 11 Hz, and usually the lower rates are more efficient. During HFJV the simultaneous use of a conventional mechanical ventilator in tandem is necessary to provide PEEP and intermittent breaths, which assists with CO_2 removal and alveolar recruitment. Initial peak pressures delivered by HFJV are typically 80% to 90% of peak pressures delivered in an infant during CMV. The P$\overline{aw}$ is not directly controlled but is the result of pressure generated by the jet gas flow, inspiratory time (usually 20 to 30 msec), and PEEP generated through the CMV circuit.

Similar to HFOV, oxygenation depends on factors that affect P$\overline{aw}$. When P$\overline{aw}$ needs to be increased, changes in inspiratory time and PEEP are the most effective interventions. Ventilation during HFJV has some similarities with HFOV. During HFJV minute ventilation can be improved by adjusting the jet pressure, frequency, or inspiratory and expiratory times. The regulation of minute ventilation is greatly affected by the percentage of minute ventilation provided by CMV. Therefore all known factors that affect minute ventilation during CMV have a significant effect on CO_2 elimination during HFJV.

RISKS AND COMPLICATIONS
Lung Overdistention and Air Leak Syndrome

The most common adverse events during HFV are mechanical, especially the risk of ALS. During the process of alveolar recruitment the "spared" lung units may become hyperinflated because compliance of these units is normal. This alveolar hyperinflation may extend the lung injury and eventually lead to development of ALS. Also, once the abnormal lung units are reexpanded, the necessary distending pressure to maintain alveolar units decreases (Laplace's law). Clinically, alveolar recruitment is believed to occur when improvement in oxygenation is noted after increasing P$\overline{aw}$. With marked improvement in oxygenation, consider decreasing P$\overline{aw}$ to maintain adequate lung volume and prevent hyperinflation and to reduce the potential for further lung injury or ALS.

Although lower peak pressures reduce the risk of barotrauma during HFV, extreme care must be taken to observe the patient closely. This does not mean that the prevalence of ALS during HFV is greater than during CMV. To date no definitive study shows the prevalence of ALS during ventilatory support with either HFV or CMV. However, a trend toward a lower prevalence of recurrent ALS has been noted, and available clinical experience shows that the rate of ALS does not increase during HFOV when used properly.

Cardiopulmonary Interactions

The high P$\overline{aw}$ necessary to obtain alveolar recruitment may induce cardiovascular depression. Results from rescue and other studies do not support this concern. Clinical practice has demonstrated that in the well-resuscitated pediatric patient or the "cardiovascularly healthy," application of high P$\overline{aw}$ with HFOV to lungs with acute lung injury have not shown deleterious cardiovascular interactions. However, in patients with the potential for or who have cardiovascular instability, maintaining adequate preload and support of cardiovascular function with inotropic agents when necessary is essential to achieve appropriate $\dot{V}/\dot{Q}$ matching during HFOV. When alveolar recruitment is obtained, lung compliance improves, as shown by better oxygenation and ventilation; therefore P$\overline{aw}$ must be decreased to prevent hyperinflation and subsequent ALS or decrease of venous return. Any change in respiratory status, particularly of sudden onset, is suggestive of hyperinflation, ALS, or decrease of venous return, which must be promptly diagnosed and treated.

Necrotizing Tracheobronchitis

Necrotizing tracheobronchitis was associated mainly with the early HFV devices, especially HFFI and HFJV. All HFV devices require high gas flow, some as high as 60 L/min. Such high flow uses significant amounts of water vapor to achieve adequate inspired gas humidity and the combination of dry gas and high inspiratory flow can cause necrotizing tracheobronchitis. Modifications to the built-in HFJV humidification system provide adequate humidity of the inspiratory gases. Currently the prevalence of necrotizing tracheobronchitis during HFJV is no greater than during CMV, and during CMV is no greater than during HFOV. Because of the high inspiratory gas flow, anticipatory monitoring of any HFV humidification system must be carried out to recognize malfunction or early signs of inspissated secretions.

Unplanned Patient Disconnection or Extubation

The model 3100A (SensorMedics) HFOV circuit is rigid, and if manipulated without anchoring and protecting the ET tube the patient can be disconnected from the HFOV circuit or the ET tube dislodged. The circuits of other HFV devices do not pose similar problems. Because most patients receiving HFV are P$\overline{aw}$ dependent, vigilance against unplanned disconnection and extubation is necessary. Even short periods of disconnection for suctioning can lead to rapid loss of volume and poor oxygenation.

CURRENT RESEARCH AND FUTURE CONSIDERATIONS

In the last few years there has been a rapid, almost explosive, increase in available therapies for treatment of severe respiratory failure. The critical care practitioner no longer has to face the dilemma and frustration of having to accept failure of CMV management with its sequelae or death. Today the practitioner needs to consider, at least theoretically, which of the numerous available VOSS gives the patient the best chance for survival with the least iatrogenic disease. Available VOSS modalities include newer methods and strategies for positive pressure ventilation, such as pressure-regulated volume control, pressure control plus pressure support, volume support, HFPPV, inverse ratio ventilation, permissive hypercapnia, venoarterial or veno-venous ECMO, HFOV, HFV plus nitric oxide, and HFOV plus partial liquid ventilation. In addition, experimental therapies include airway pressure release ventilation, extracorporeal CO_2 removal, intravascular oxygenation, HFJV, and HFFI, among many others. The rapidly expanding number of VOSS modalities has created a dilemma for the critical care physician. Among the unanswered questions asked are: Which device should I choose as the first line of support? Which VOSS therapy prevents chronic lung disease? Which strategy is best to prevent ALS? How long do I stay with this VOSS therapy? When is it too late for any of the VOSS therapies to be effective?

High-Frequency Positive Pressure Ventilation

In 1991 Nielsen et al. demonstrated that HFPPV was more effective than volume-controlled CMV to obtain alveolar recruitment and improve oxygenation. The model used was surfactant-depleted piglet lungs. The experience with HFPPV in neonatal respiratory distress is more limited. In 1991 a multicenter randomized study in 346 infants reported less incidence of pneumothorax in the group treated with HFPPV, with no differences in mortality or prevalence of chronic lung disease. To date HFPPV has not gained widespread use.

High-Frequency Flow Interruption

Closely related to HFJV, HFFI has been successfully used in newborn infants, although with the low P$\overline{aw}$ approach used in the available studies no significant advantages over CMV were reported. Experimental evidence in animal models suggests that HFJV and HFFI may be of advantage in meconium aspiration syndrome.

High-Frequency Jet Ventilation

The issues that need to be clarified regarding use of HFJV in pediatric patients are broad. First, the effectiveness and efficiency of HFJV in safely providing respiratory support in pediatric patients with respiratory failure is yet to be established. Second, FDA approval is needed before perusing questions similar to those about HFOV. HFJV may have a role in respiratory support in patients with passive or shunt-dependent filling or right heart myocardial dysfunction. Interesting work by Meliones et al. in infants immediately after the Fontan procedure or with similar physiology documented that cardiac output doubled at half the P$\overline{aw}$ needed to maintain comparable gas exchange with CMV.

High-Frequency Ventilation and Nitric Oxide

According to experimental evidence, HFOV and nitric oxide may be synergistic. In 1993 Kinsella and Abman pioneered the simultaneous use of HFOV and nitric oxide. They proposed and demonstrated that combining HFOV with the delivery of nitric oxide resulted in further improvement in oxygenation. They postulated that by enhancing alveolar recruitment with HFOV and therefore making more alveoli available to deliver nitric oxide to the pulmonary vasculature, an overall improvement in oxygenation would occur. These same results have been reported in two infants with bronchopulmonary dysplasia and RSV infection, respectively. In addition, both small series and individual case reports that describe the feasibility and effectiveness of combined HFJV and nitric oxide have been recently published.

High-Frequency Oscillatory Ventilation and Surfactant

In 1994 Jackson et al. administered surfactant to premature monkeys and then initiated HFOV. They concluded that the combination therapy was superior to either therapy alone.

High-Frequency Oscillatory Ventilation and Partial Liquid Ventilation

In 1995 Harel et al. reported the use of partial liquid ventilation with an HFOV device (HFLOV). They concluded that compliance improved from least to most with CMV only, HFOV only, partial liquid ventilation plus CMV, and HFLOV.

Although it is difficult to delineate the exact role of HFOV and HFJV in supporting respiration in pediatric patients with respiratory failure from multiple causes, it seems both modes will continue to be important options among the VOSS therapies. It is imperative that studies be designed to answer questions about more specific indications and contraindications, timing, duration of therapy, and combination and sequencing of VOSS therapies and strategies.

ADDITIONAL READING

al-Alaiyan S, Katan A. Pulmonary interstitial emphysema treated by selective bronchial obstruction and high-frequency oscillatory ventilation. Am J Perinatol 11:433-435, 1994.

• Arnold JH, Truog RD, Thompson JE, Facler JC. High-frequency oscillatory ventilation in pediatric respiratory failure. Crit Care Med 21:272-278, 1993.

• Arnold JH, Hanson JH, Toro-Figueroa LO, Gutiérrez JA, Berens RJ, Anglin DL. Prospective randomized comparison of high-frequency oscillatory ventilation and conventional mechanical ventilation in pediatric respiratory failure. Crit Care Med 22:1530-1539, 1994.

Berner ME, Rouge JC, Suter PM. Combined high-frequency ventilation in children with severe adult respiratory distress syndrome. Intensive Care Med 17:209-214, 1991.

• Bond DM, Froese AB. Volume recruitment maneuvers are less deleterious than persistent low lung volume in the atelectasis-prone rabbit lung during high-frequency oscillation. Crit Care Med 21:402-412, 1993.

• Boros SJ, Mammel MC, Coleman JM, Horcher P, Gordon MJ, Bing DR. Comparison of high-frequency oscillatory ventilation and high-frequency jet ventilation in cats with normal lungs. Pediatr Pulmonol 7:35-41, 1989.

Bryan AC, Froese AB. Reflections on the HIFI trial. Pediatrics 87:565-567, 1991.

Cappon J, Anas N. High-frequency oscillatory ventilation in ECMO-eligible children with severe respiratory failure. Am Rev Respir Dis 147(Suppl):A887, 1993.

Carlo WA, Beoglos A, Chatburn RL, Walsh MC, Martin RJ. High-frequency jet ventilation in neonatal pulmonary hypertension. Am J Dis Child 143:233-238, 1989.

Carlo WA, Siner B, Chatburn RL, Robertson S, Martin RJ. Early randomized intervention with high-frequency jet ventilation in respiratory distress syndrome. J Pediatr 117:765-770, 1990.

Chan V, Greenough A. Determinants of oxygenation during high frequency oscillation. Eur J Pediatr 152:350-353, 1993.

Chan V, Greenough A. The effect of frequency on carbon dioxide levels during high frequency oscillation. J Perinat Med 22:103-106, 1994.

Chan V, Greenough A, Milner AD. The effect of frequency and mean airway pressure on volume delivery during high-frequency oscillation. Pediatr Pulmonol 15:183-186, 1993.

Chan V, Greenough A, Gamsu HR. High frequency oscillation for preterm infants with severe respiratory failure. Arch Dis Child 70:F44-F46, 1994.

Chan V, Greenough A, Dimitriou G. High frequency oscillation, respiratory activity and changes in blood gases. Early Hum Dev 40:87-94, 1995.

• Clark RH, Gerstmann DR, Null DM, de Lemos RA. Prospective randomized comparison of high-frequency oscillatory and conventional ventilation in respiratory distress syndrome. Pediatrics 89:5-12, 1992.

• Clark RH, Gerstmann DR, Null DM Jr, de Lemos RA. A prospective randomized comparison of high-frequency oscillation and conventional ventilation in candidates for extracorporeal membrane oxygenation. J Pediatr 124:447-454, 1994.

• Clark RH, Gerstmann DR, Null DM, Yoder BA, Cornish JD, Glasier CM, Ackerman NB, Bell RE, de Lemos RA. Pulmonary interstitial emphysema treated by high-frequency oscillator ventilation. Crit Care Med 14:926-930, 1986.

• Davis JM, Richter SE, Kendig JW, Notter RH. High-frequency jet ventilation and surfactant treatment of newborns with severe respiratory failure. Pediatr Pulmonol 13:108-112, 1992.

Froese AB, McCulloch PR, Sugiura M, Vaclavik S, Possmayer F, Moller F. Optimizing alveolar expansion prolongs the effectiveness of exogenous surfactant therapy in the adult rabbit. Am Rev Respir Dis 148:569-577, 1993.

• Gutierrez JA, Levin DL, Toro-Figueroa LO. Successful high-frequency oscillatory ventilation in small infants with respiratory syncytial virus infection. Presented at the Eleventh Conference on High-Frequency Ventilation, Snowbird, Utah 1994.

• Gutierrez JA, Levin DL, Toro-Figueroa LO. Hemodynamic effects of high-frequency oscillatory ventilation in severe pediatric respiratory failure. Intensive Care Med 21:505-510, 1995.

• Gutiérrez JA, Toro K, Vinson R, Jaramillo MA, Margraf L, Arteaga G, Black D, Walters P, Toro-Figueroa LO. High frequency oscillatory ventilation compared to pressure control: Alveolar pressures, lung volume, and alveolar cell count. Presented at the Sixty-first Annual International Scientific Assembly of the American College of Chest Physicians, New York, 1995.

• Hamilton PP, Onayemi JA, Smyth JA, Gillan JE, Cutz E, Froese AB, Bryan AC. Comparison of conventional and high-frequency ventilation: Oxygenation and lung pathology. J Appl Physiol 55:131-138, 1983.

• Harel Y, Toro-Figueroa LO, Vinson R, Toro KD, Black D, George T, Elmore G, Bieler C, Headrick C, Margraf L, Luckett PM, Levin DL. High-frequency liquid oxygenation ventilation (HFLOV): A perfluorocarbon associated gas exchange (PAGE) utilizing high-frequency oscillatory ventilation (HFLOV) is feasible and may improve synergistically lung compliance in a near drowning piglet model. Presented at the Pediatric Critical Care Colloquim, St. Simon Island, Ga., 1995.

HIFI Study Group. High-frequency oscillatory ventilation compared with conventional mechanical ventilation in the treatment of respiratory failure in preterm infants. N Engl J Med 320:88-93, 1989.

HIFO Study Group. Randomized study of high-frequency oscillatory ventilation in infants with severe respiratory distress syndrome. J Pediatr 122:609-619, 1993.

Imai Y, Kawano T, Miyasaka K, Takata M, Imai T, Okuyana K. Inflammatory chemical mediators during conventional ventilation and during high-frequency ventilation. Am J Respir Crit Care Med 150:1550-1554, 1994.

• Jackson JC, Truog WE, Standaert TA, Murphy JH, Juul SE, Chi EY, Hildebrandt J, Hodson WA. Reduction in lung injury after combined surfactant and high-frequency ventilation. Am J Respir Crit Care Med 150:534-539, 1994.

Jefferies AL, Dunn MS, Possmayer F, Tai KFY. 99mTc-DTPA clearance in preterm lambs: Effect of surfactant therapy and ventilation. Am Rev Respir Dis 143:845-851, 1993.

Keszler M, Klappenbach RS, Reardon E. Lung pathology after high frequency jet ventilation combined with low rate intermittent mandatory ventilation in a canine model of meconium aspiration. Pediatr Pulmonol 4:144-149, 1988.

Keszler M, Donn SM, Bucciarelli RL, Alverson DC, Hart M, Lunyong V, Modanlou HD, Noguchi A, Pearlman SA, Puri A, et al. Multicenter controlled trial comparing high-frequency jet ventilation and conventional mechanical ventilation in newborn infants with pulmonary interstitial emphysema. J Pediatr 119:85-93, 1991.

• Kinsella JP, Abman SH. Inhalational nitric oxide therapy for persistent pulmonary hypertension of the newborn. Pediatrics 91:997-998, 1993.

• Kocis KC, Meliones JN, Dekeon MK, Callow LB, Lupinetti FM, Bove EL. High-frequency jet ventilation for respiratory failure after congenital heart surgery. Circulation 86(Suppl II):II-127–II-132, 1992.

Kohelet D, Perlman M, Kirpalani H, Hanna G, Koren G. High-frequency oscillation in the rescue of infants with persistent pulmonary hypertension. Crit Care Med 16:510-516, 1988.

• Kohlhauser C, Popow C, Helbich T, Hermon M, Weninger M, Herold CJ. Successful treatment of severe neonatal lobar emphysema by high-frequency oscillatory ventilation. Pediatr Pulmonol 19:52-55, 1995.

Maynard RC, Wangensteen OD, Connett JE, Holloman KK, Boros SJ, Mammel MC. Alterations in feline tracheal permeability after mechanical ventilation. Crit Care Med 21:90-97, 1993.

McBride WT, McMurray TJ. Prolonged high frequency jet ventilation and milrinone therapy following modified Fontan procedure. Anaesthesia 49:312-314, 1994.

• McCulloch PR, Forket PG, Froese AB. Lung volume maintenance prevents lung injury during high-frequency oscillatory ventilation in surfactant-deficient rabbits. Am Rev Respir Dis 137:1185-1192, 1988.

Meliones JN, Bove EL, Dekeon MK, Custer JR, Moler FW, Callow LR, Wilton NC, Rosen DB. High-frequency jet ventilation improves cardiac function after the Fontan procedure. Circulation 84(Suppl III):364-368, 1991.

Miguet D, Lapillonne A, Bakr A, Claris O, Chappuis JP, Salle BL. Congenital diaphragmatic hernia: Results of the association of preoperative stabilization and oscillation ventilation (a prospective study of 17 patients). Cah Anesthesiol 42:335-338, 1994.

Nielsen JB, Sjostrand UH, Edgren EL, Lichtwarck-Aschoff M, Svensson BA. An experimental study of different ventilatory modes in piglets in severe respiratory distress induced by surfactant depletion. Intensive Care Med 17:225-233, 1991.

Ogawa Y, Miyasaka K, Kawano T, Imura S, Inukai K, Okuyama K, Oguchi K, Togari H, Nishida H, Mishina J. A multicenter randomized trial of high frequency oscillatory ventilation as compared with conventional mechanical ventilation in preterm infants with respiratory failure. Early Hum Dev 32:1-10, 1993.

Oxford Region Controlled Trial of Artificial Ventilation (OCTAVE) Study Group. Multicentre randomised controlled trial of high against low frequency positive pressure ventilation. Arch Dis Child 66:770-775, 1991.

Paranka MMS, Clark RH, Yoder BA, Null DM Jr. Predictors of failure of high-frequency oscillatory ventilation in term infants with severe respiratory failure. Pediatrics 95:400-404, 1995.

Pardou A, Vermeylen D, Muller MF, Detemmerman D. High-frequency ventilation and conventional mechanical ventilation in newborn babies with respiratory distress syndrome: A prospective randomized trial. Intensive Care Med 19:406-410, 1993.

• Parker JC, Hernandez LA, Peevy KJ. Mechanisms of ventilator-induced lung injury. Crit Care Med 21:131-143, 1993.

Pedley TJ, Corieri P, Kamm RD, Grotberg JB, Hydon PE, Schroter RC. Gas flow and mixing in the airways. Crit Care Med 22(Suppl):S24-S36, 1994.

• Peters EA, Engle WA, Yoder MC. Pulmonary hypoplasia and persistent pulmonary hypertension: Favorable clinical response to high-frequency jet ventilation. J Perinatol 12:21-24, 1992.

Rettwitz-Volk W, Schlosser R, von Loewenich V. One-sided high-frequency oscillating ventilation in the treatment of neonatal unilateral pulmonary emphysema. Acta Paediatr 82:190-192, 1993.

Revillon Y, Sidi D, Chourrout Y, Martelli H, Ghnassia D, Piquet J, Isabey D, Harf A, Jaubert F. High-frequency ventilation in newborn lambs after intra-uterine creation of diaphragmatic hernia. Eur J Pediatr Surg 3:132-138, 1993.

• Rosenberg RB, Broner CW, Peters KJ, Anglin DL. High frequency ventilation for acute pediatric respiratory failure. Chest 104:1216-1221, 1993.

Smith DW, Frankel LR, Derish MT, Moody RR, Black LE III, Chipps BE, Mathers LH. High-frequency jet ventilation in children with the adult respiratory distress syndrome complicated by pulmonary barotrauma. Pediatr Pulmonol 15:279-286, 1993.

• Spitzer AR, Butler S, Fox WW. Ventilatory response to combined high frequency jet ventilation and conventional mechanical ventilation for the rescue treatment of severe neonatal lung disease. Pediatr Pulmonol 7:244-250, 1989.

• Thompson MW, Bates JN, Klein JM. Treatment of respiratory failure in an infant with bronchopulmonary dysplasia infected with respiratory syncytial virus using inhaled nitric oxide and high frequency ventilation. Acta Paediatr 84:100-102, 1995.

• Traverse JH, Korvenranta H, Adams EM, Goldthwait DA, Carlo WA. Impairment of hemodynamics with increasing mean airway pressure during high-frequency oscillatory ventilation. Pediatr Res 23:628-631, 1988.

Venegas JG, Tsuzaki K, Fox BJ, Simon BA, Hales CA. Regional coupling between chest wall and lung expansion during HFV: A positron imaging study. J Appl Physiol 74:2242-2252, 1993.

Wiswell TE, Foster NH, Slayter MV, Hachey WE. Management of a piglet model of the meconium aspiration syndrome with high-frequency or conventional ventilation. Am J Dis Child 146:1287-1293, 1992.

157 Surfactant Therapy

Fernando R. Moya · David R. Breed · Mohan R. Mysore

BACKGROUND
Surfactant Components and Functions

Lung surfactant is a conglomerate composed predominantly of phospholipids and proteins but also contains smaller amounts of neutral lipids and cholesterol. Its most important function is to reduce surface tension at the air-liquid interface of the alveolar lining, thus reducing alveolar collapse on expiration. Surfactant also contributes to the immune functions and host defense mechanisms of the lung.

Phospholipids

The most abundant phospholipid of alveolar surfactant is phosphatidylcholine, followed by phosphatidylglycerol, phosphatidylethanolamine, and sphingomyelin (Table 157-1). Most of the phosphatidylcholine is found in its disaturated form, that is, with two saturated fatty acids, usually palmitic acid, in positions 1 and 2 of the glycerol backbone. Lung surfactant is able to reduce surface tension primarily because of dipalmitoylphosphatidylcholine (DPPC). This and other surfactant phospholipids are synthesized in alveolar type II pneumocytes with precursors obtained from the circulation, such as glucose, choline, and fatty acids. During fetal life the glycogen accumulated in type II pneumocytes also serves as a substrate for surfactant phospholipid biosynthesis. Most of the cholesterol of surfactant is derived from lipoproteins in the circulation.

Several of the enzymes involved in phospholipid biosynthesis are developmentally regulated and can be stimulated by hormones such as glucocorticoids. In this poorly understood process the surfactant phospholipids are transported to the Golgi system and eventually are stored as intracellular lamellar bodies, which subsequently are released into the alveolar spaces (Fig. 157-1).

Proteins

Surfactant contains four specific surfactant proteins (SP): SP-A, SP-B, SP-C, and SP-D. Collectively they amount to about 5% of surfactant by weight. Much progress has been made in characterizing the structure and functions of these proteins (Table 157-2).

SP-A. The most abundant surfactant protein (about 3% by weight), SP-A has a monomeric molecular mass of 28 to 36 kD, depending on its degree of post-translational modification. Two genes and a pseudogene for human SP-A are located on chromosome 10. The SP-A molecule has a collagen-like region that allows it to fold into a triple helix with two other SP-A molecules. It also has a lipid-binding domain and a globular carbohydrate recognition domain where glycosylation and addition of sialic acid occur. These characteristics give SP-A hydrophilic properties.

SP-A is synthesized in alveolar type II pneumocytes and nonciliated bronchiolar epithelial cells, but the relative contribution of each cell type to the alveolar pool of SP-A is unknown. The synthesis of SP-A is developmentally regulated in the fetus, with maximal expression at term. Glucocorticoids can either increase or decrease expression of SP-A. The func-

Table 157-1 Phospholipid Composition of Human Alveolar Surfactant

Phospholipid	Percent of Total
Phosphatidylcholine	70
Phosphatidylglycerol	10-12
Phosphatidylethanolamine	3
Phosphatidylinositol	3
Phosphatidylserine	3
Sphingomyelin	4
Other	2

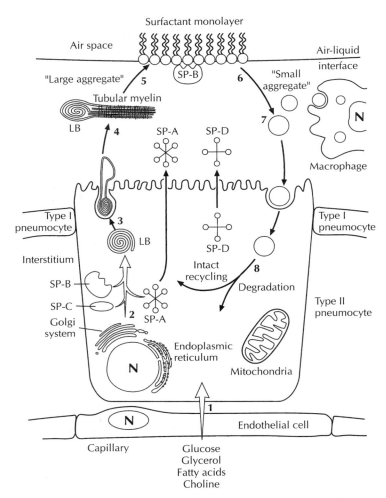

Fig. 157-1   Life cycle of pulmonary surfactant. *(1)* Precursors for the synthesis of surfactant components are supplied to type II pneumocyte through the circulation. *(2)* After synthesis and processing, these components, including some proteins (SP-A, SP-B, and SP-C), are stored in lamellar bodies. *(3)* Lamellar bodies are secreted by action of various stimuli. SP-A can be secreted with lamellar bodies or independently; virtually all SP-B and SP-C are secreted with lamellar bodies; and secretion of SP-D is completely independent of surfactant components. *(4)* Lamellar bodies unravel to generate tubular myelin. Both of these structures can be separated as "large aggregate," or heavy forms, by means of ultracentrifugation. *(5)* Tubular myelin is the precursor of the surfactant monolayer, which lowers surface tension at the air-fluid interface. The structural integrity of the monolayer is probably maintained in part by SP-B. *(6)* After repeated cycling as well as catabolism, surfactant components "squeezed out" of the monolayer form smaller vesicles. These can be separated as "small aggregates," or light forms, by means of ultracentrifugation and have poor ability to lower surface tension. *(7)* Some of these forms undergo endocytosis by the type II pneumocyte; others are taken up by alveolar macrophages. *(8)* Some surfactant components are returned to lamellar bodies through intact recycling; others undergo degradation into their precursor molecules.

Table 157-2   Surfactant Proteins

Protein	Molecular Weight (kD)	Chromosome	Hydrophobic	Main Function
SP-A	28-36	10	No	Surfactant adsorption and recycling Immune function
SP-B	8	2	Yes	Surfactant adsorption Formation of lamellar bodies
SP-C	4	8	Yes	Surfactant adsorption
SP-D	43	10	No	Immune function

tional form of SP-A is a complex of six trimers of SP-A (18 monomers). SP-A can be secreted into the alveoli by an independent mechanism or in conjunction with lamellar bodies. It is taken up by type II pneumocytes through receptor-mediated endocytosis. In conjunction with SP-B and Ca^{2+}, SP-A participates in formation of the lattice-like structure called tubular myelin, which is the precursor of the phospholipid monolayer at the air-fluid interface. This protein seems to be involved in regulation of surfactant recycling because it can inhibit phosphatidylcholine release from isolated type II pneumocytes. SP-A also appears to contribute to host defense mechanisms in the lung. It can bind to gram-negative bacteria, lipopolysaccharide, herpes simplex type 1 and influenza A viruses, and *Pneumocystis carinii* and can interact with alveolar macrophages.

SP-B. This hydrophobic protein accounts for about 1% of surfactant by weight and has a monomeric molecular mass of 8 kD. It may also be found as a dimer or an oligomer. The gene for human SP-B is located on chromosome 2. It is synthesized primarily in alveolar type II pneumocytes, but its gene is also expressed in bronchiolar epithelial cells. The primary translation product of the SP-B gene is a pre-pro–SP-B with a mass of about 40 kD. The mature protein of 79 amino acids is produced after several cleavage steps. SP-B has several cysteine residues that allow it to form intrachain disulfide bridges that are critical for its function. The synthesis of SP-B is developmentally regulated and can be stimulated by glucocorticoids.

A congenital SP-B deficiency caused by a 121ins2 mutation in its gene has been described recently. In this autosomal recessive disorder progressive respi-

ratory failure develops in affected newborns, with radiographic findings like those of respiratory distress syndrome (RDS) of preterm neonates. Microscopic examination of lung tissue demonstrates marked reduction in the number of intracellular lamellar bodies and poor organization of these structures. Furthermore, evidence of basolateral rather than predominantly apical secretion of lamellar bodies by type II pneumocytes has been observed. These findings suggest that the presence of SP-B is critical to formation of lamellar bodies and their properly polarized secretion into the alveolar surface of the type II pneumocyte. It appears that SP-B is secreted only with surfactant phospholipids. Along with SP-A and Ca^{2+}, SP-B participates in tubular myelin formation and enrichment of DPPC in the monolayer at the air-fluid interface. The adsorption of surfactant is markedly enhanced by SP-B. This surfactant protein can be internalized by type II cells and recycled into lamellar bodies. A serine protease, convertase, which is closely associated with the surfactant phospholipids, degrades SP-B.

SP-C. This is the most hydrophobic surfactant protein. In its mature form it has a molecular mass of 4 kD and comprises only 23 amino acids. The gene for human SP-C is located on chromosome 8. The synthesis of SP-C occurs only in type II pneumocytes and is also developmentally regulated. Of all surfactant proteins, SP-C is the first to be expressed by the fetal lung, and its expression is enhanced by glucocorticoids. Initially SP-C is synthesized as a much larger pro–SP-C, which is modified further by amino acid cleavage and palmitoylation to yield the mature product. SP-C is incorporated into lamellar bodies and secreted along with surfactant phospholipids. This protein enhances adsorption of phospholipids in the air-fluid interface, but to a lesser extent than SP-B. Little is known about the metabolism of SP-C.

SP-D. SP-D is a hydrophilic protein with a monomeric molecular mass of 39 kD initially, which increases to 43 kD after glycosylation and hydroxylation. Like SP-A, this monomer interacts through disulfide bonds to form trimers, which associate to form a larger structure of 12 monomers of SP-D. The gene for human SP-D is located on chromosome 10, in close proximity to the SP-A genes. This protein is synthesized in alveolar type II pneumocytes and Clara cells. Its synthesis is developmentally regulated, and its expression can be stimulated by glucocorticoids. However, unlike the other surfactant proteins, SP-D is not detectable in lamellar bodies. Secretion of SP-D is probably independent of surfactant phospholipids. For these reasons, it has been questioned whether SP-D is truly a surfactant protein.

The proposed functions of SP-D are related more to host defense mechanisms than to reducing surface tension at the alveolar level. SP-D binds to *Escherichia coli* and lipopolysaccharide and interacts with alveolar macrophages.

Surfactant Metabolism

Lung surfactant has a complicated life cycle (see Fig. 157-1). After intracellular synthesis of its various components in alveolar type II pneumocytes, surfactant is packaged into lamellar bodies. These are secreted through a process involving microtubules and microfilaments that is regulated by several factors such as alveolar stretch, β-adrenergics, adenosine, and SP-A. This is a slow process, particularly in immature animals and human neonates, which probably explains the slow and gradual clinical improvement in infants with RDS not treated with exogenous surfactant. Once in the alveolar space, the lipid layers of lamellar bodies unravel to form the three-dimensional lattice structure called tubular myelin. This structure is the precursor of the phospholipid monolayer, which lowers surface tension in the alveolar lining. Surface tension is the force in the surface film of a fluid that resists expansion or attempts to contract the surface. The thin film of fluid present in the alveolar lining is subjected to surface tension forces. The polar head of DPPC, which corresponds to the carbon molecule bound to the phosphate and choline molecules, interacts with water molecules at the air-fluid interface of the alveolar surface, and the saturated fatty acids

bound to the remaining two carbons of DPPC stand out to the surface. On compression of this monolayer film, such as during expiration, the hydrophobic fatty acids do not generate interactions between them and reduce surface tension. Formation of tubular myelin depends on the presence of DPPC, phosphatidylglycerol, SP-A, SP-B, and Ca^{2+}. In tubular myelin, SP-A is preferentially located in the corners of this three-dimensional structure, which suggests it may provide the basic framework for its formation.

In the alveolar lumen surfactant is found in various subfractions, which can be separated with ultracentrifugation. Heavy, or "large aggregates," contain tubular myelin and the highest proportion of SP-A, SP-B, and SP-C found in surfactant. These large aggregates adsorb easily on an air-fluid interface and are the precursors of the phospholipid monolayer, which lowers surface tension. The collapsed monolayer and surfactant components that are "squeezed out" of this monolayer form lighter, or "small aggregate," subfractions of surfactant. These are relatively devoid of surfactant proteins and probably represent catabolic forms. The small aggregates adsorb less well than large aggregate forms, although their phospholipid composition is similar. The conversion from large to small aggregate forms probably takes repeated contractions and expansions of the surface area of the surfactant layer and seems to be facilitated by SP-B degradation from the action of a serine protease. In term fetuses the surfactant found initially in the alveolar lumen is almost completely in large aggregate form. This pattern changes to an approximate equal proportion of large and small aggregate forms during the first days after birth. Various forms of lung injury can alter the distribution of surfactant into these subfractions.

Many of the surfactant components are taken up by the alveolar type II pneumocytes and recycled, whereas a proportion of them undergo phagocytosis by alveolar macrophages. The efficiency of recycling can amount to almost 90% of phosphatidylcholine in young animals compared with less than 50% in adults. Recycling of SP-A may be less efficient than that of phosphatidylcholine.

The estimated pool (alveolar plus intracellular) of surfactant at birth in neonates with RDS is 1 to 10 mg/kg. This surfactant pool is greatly enlarged by the common doses of exogenous surfactant used clinically, which vary between 50 and 200 mg/kg.

Surfactant Replacement Trials
Respiratory distress syndrome

The first attempts at surfactant replacement in the 1960s used aerosolized DPPC, which had no demonstrable benefits. Fujiwara et al. reported the first successful clinical use of surfactant replacement therapy with a modified bovine surfactant. Subsequently, numerous randomized, controlled clinical trials of various surfactant formulations have been published. Many trials have reported significant reductions in the prevalence of RDS when surfactant is given prophylactically to populations of neonates at risk for this disease. Many studies that show clinical improvement in neonates with established RDS (rescue therapy) have also been reported. Interpretation of the numerous surfactant trials is complicated by use of different surfactant preparations, variations in the method of administration, timing and repetition of dosing, and diversity of reported outcome variables.

However, in virtually all surfactant trials, short-term improvements in arterial oxygenation and arterial-alveolar oxygen gradients and reduced need for ventilatory support have been noted. In addition, when the data are collectively examined with meta-analysis, several definite conclusions can be made regarding the advantages of surfactant replacement therapy in neonates. With either natural or synthetic surfactant preparations, these benefits include a marked decrease in the occurrence of pneumothoraces and substantial improvement in survival (Fig. 157-2). However, no consistent beneficial effect of surfactant therapy in preventing or decreasing other complications associated with RDS and prematurity such as intracranial hemorrhage, retinopathy of prematurity, necrotizing enterocolitis, and patent ductus arteriosus have been noted.

In both in vitro and animal models of RDS, preparations of surfactant that contain SP-B and SP-

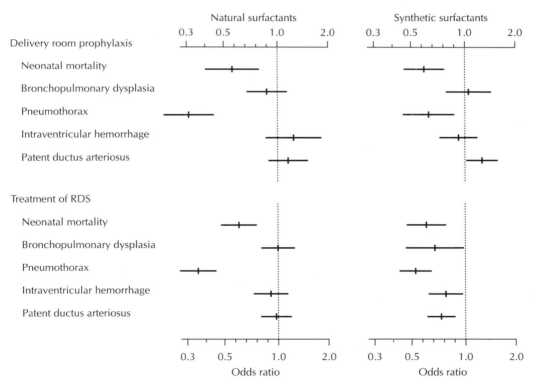

Fig. 157-2 Odds ratios (small vertical lines) and 95% confidence intervals (horizontal lines) from meta-analyses of clinical trials of natural and synthetic surfactants. Values not overlapping 1.0 indicate statistically significant reduction or increase for that specific complication compared with the control group. (From Jobe AH. Pulmonary surfactant therapy. N Engl J Med 328:861-868, 1993.)

C exhibit better function and faster responses than do synthetic products devoid of these proteins. Nonetheless, when the efficacy of a bovine-derived surfactant that contains SP-B and SP-C (Survanta, Ross Laboratories, Columbus, Ohio) and a synthetic surfactant (Exosurf, Burroughs Wellcome, Research Triangle Park, N.C.) was compared in large controlled clinical trials, only slight reductions were noted in average Fio_2 and average mean airway pressure ($\overline{Paw}$) needed and reduced risk of pneumothoraces that favored the bovine surfactant. However, no differences in death, bronchopulmonary dysplasia, or other common complications of RDS were found. Recently similar findings were reported by Hudak et al. in a large controlled trial that compared a bovine-derived surfactant (Infasurf, ONY, Amherst, N.Y.) with Exosurf.

Neonatal diseases other than respiratory distress syndrome

Because surfactant replacement therapy has shown convincing evidence of efficacy in treatment of RDS of the premature infant, this therapy might offer similar benefits in other diseases associated with surfactant deficiency or inactivation of surfactant because of plasma proteins, cytokines, and other inflammatory mediators present in the alveolar lumen in injured lungs.

Meconium aspiration can cause diffuse lung disease from obstruction of the airways and chemical pneumonitis. It has also been suggested that the surfactant system is altered in this disease. In vitro studies have demonstrated that increasing the concentration of surfactant results in reduction of the inhibitory effect of meconium on the surfactant system. In addition, some, but not all, studies of surfactant use in animal models of meconium aspiration have demonstrated beneficial effects. Auten et al. demonstrated improvements in the $A\text{-}aDo_2$ ratio and oxygenation index after surfactant replacement therapy in 14 term neonates with acute respiratory failure from either meconium aspiration or pneumonia. Similar findings were reported by Khammash et al. in 49 term neonates with severe respiratory failure from RDS or meconium aspiration syndrome. Recently Findlay et al. reported the findings of a small placebo-controlled trial of surfactant administration in neonates with severe meconium aspiration syndrome. Neonates who received Fio_2 >0.5 during mechanical ventilation were given either bovine-derived surfactant (Survanta) (6 ml/kg, a higher dose than used for

RDS) or air placebo. Treatment with the surfactant was initiated before 6 hours after birth. Neonates given surfactant had improved oxygenation and reduced prevalence of air leaks as well as shorter hospitalization compared with a control group of neonates. Collectively these limited data suggest that surfactant therapy may provide substantial benefits in neonates with severe forms of meconium aspiration syndrome.

In very sick neonates receiving maintenance extracorporeal membrane oxygenation (ECMO) evidence of progressive atelectasis and "whiteout" of the lungs on chest radiographs is often observed. From measurements of surfactant components in tracheal fluid samples obtained from these infants, it has been suggested that a transient surfactant deficiency develops. Results of limited uncontrolled trials in small numbers of these neonates suggest that administration of exogenous surfactant may be helpful, especially during the process of decreasing ECMO support. Both qualitative and quantitative abnormalities of the surfactant system have been demonstrated in animal models and in humans with congenital diaphragmatic hernia (CDH). The pathophysiology of CDH also includes lung hypoplasia and pulmonary hypertension. Surfactant replacement therapy has shown promise in the management of high-risk CDH in preliminary uncontrolled clinical reports.

Recently surfactant replacement therapy has been used in neonates with congenital SP-B deficiency. However, only transient improvement in their clinical condition was noted, even with multiple dosing of an SP-B–rich surfactant preparation.

Diseases of older infants and adults

Surfactant replacement therapy has been more difficult to study in children after the neonatal period because acute respiratory failure in the pediatric population is caused by a heterogeneous group of diseases that may differ in pathophysiology and clinical course. This makes it difficult to identify patients who could potentially benefit from surfactant administration and to pinpoint the optimal time in the course of the disease for institution of surfactant replacement therapy.

Acute respiratory distress syndrome (ARDS) is a disease process with various causes that affects pediatric and adult patients. The pathophysiologic findings of ARDS include leakage of plasma proteins, cytokines, phospholipases, arachidonic acid intermediates, and proteolytic enzymes into the alveolar

er children and adults needs to be studied further in well-controlled clinical trials.

The knowledge gained from surfactant research has enabled development of newer and potentially useful surfactant preparations. A synthetic surfactant preparation currently under study is KL$_4$, which is a mixture of DPPC and phosphatidylglycerol plus a synthetic peptide (KL$_4$) that mimics the action of SP-B. Studies in animal models and preliminary data in preterm neonates with RDS have demonstrated beneficial effects in gas exchange and lung distensibility after treatment with KL$_4$. If this surfactant proves clinically useful and comparable to or better than preparations currently used, it could provide an alternative that would alleviate concern about sensitization to animal proteins from use of natural surfactants.

In several disease processes (e.g., ARDS and pneumonia) surfactant inactivation is a major pathogenic mechanism that contributes to the severity of clinical findings. Inactivation of surfactant phospholipids is mediated in part by the action of phospholipases that cleave the fatty acid in position 2 of the glycerol backbone. Phospholipids in which this chemical bond has been substituted for one more resistant to the action of phospholipases can be used as surfactant components. Such modifications may permit development of a surfactant preparation uniquely effective in clinical conditions in which enhanced surfactant inactivation is occurring or is anticipated.

Surfactant administration could also be used as a vehicle to deliver drugs and viral vectors for gene therapy. However, an emerging therapy, partial liquid ventilation, may rival the usefulness of surfactant for this purpose.

ADDITIONAL READING

Amirkhanian JD, Bruni R, Waring AJ, Navar C, Taeusch HW. Full-length synthetic surfactant proteins, SP-B and SP-C, reduce surfactant inactivation by serum. Biochim Biophys Acta 1168:315-320, 1993.

Auten RL, Notter RH, Kendig JW, Davis JM, Shapiro DL. Surfactant treatment of full-term newborns with respiratory failure. Pediatrics 87:101-107, 1991.

Berry DD, Pramanik AK, Phillips JB III, Buchter DS, Kanarek KS, Easa D, Kopelman AE, Edwards K, Long W, American Exosurf Neonatal Study Group. Comparison of the effect of three doses of a synthetic surfactant on the alveolar-arterial oxygen gradient in infants weighing ≥1250 grams with respiratory distress syndrome. J Pediatr 124:294-301, 1994.

Bui KC, Walther FJ, David-Cu R, Garg M, Warburton D. Phospholipid and surfactant protein A concentrations in tracheal aspirates from infants requiring extracorporeal membrane oxygenation. J Pediatr 121:271-274, 1992.

Choukroun ML, Llanas B, Apere H, Fayon M, Galperine RI, Guenard H, Demarquez JL. Pulmonary mechanics in ventilated preterm infants with respiratory distress syndrome after exogenous surfactant administration: A comparison between two surfactant preparations. Pediatr Pulmonol 18:273-278, 1994.

Cochrane CG, Revak SD. Pulmonary surfactant protein B (SP-B): Structure-function relationships. Science 254:566-568, 1991.

Corbet A, Bucciarelli R, Goldman S, Mammel M, Wold D, Long W, American Exosurf Pediatric Study Group. Decreased mortality rate among small premature infants treated at birth with a single dose of synthetic surfactant: A multicenter controlled trial. J Pediatr 118:277-284, 1991.

Cowan F, Whitelaw A, Wertheim D, Silverman M. Cerebral blood flow velocity changes after rapid administration of surfactant. Arch Dis Child 66:1102-1109, 1991.

Cummings JJ, Holm BA, Hudak ML, Hudak BB, Ferguson WH, Egan EA. A controlled clinical comparison of four different surfactant preparations in surfactant-deficient preterm lambs. Am Rev Respir Dis 145:999-1004, 1992.

da Silva WJ, Abbasi S, Pereira G, Bhutani VK. Role of positive end-expiratory pressure changes on functional residual capacity in surfactant treated preterm infants. Pediatr Pulmonol 18:89-92, 1994.

Davis JM, Veness-Meehan K, Notter RH, Bhutani VK, Kendig JW, Shapiro DL. Changes in pulmonary mechanics after the administration of surfactant to infants with respiratory distress syndrome. N Engl J Med 319:476-479, 1988.

deMello DE, Nogee LM, Heyman S, Krous HF, Hussain M, Merritt TA, Hsueh W, Haas JE, Heidelberger K, Schumacher R, Colten HR. Molecular and phenotypic variability in the congenital alveolar proteinosis syndrome associated with inherited surfactant protein B deficiency. J Pediatr 125:43-50, 1994.

• Dizon-Co L, Ikegami M, Ueda T, Jobe AH, Lin WH, Turcotte JG, Notter RH, Rider ED. In vivo function of surfactants containing phosphatidylcholine analogs. Am J Respir Crit Care Med 150:918-923, 1994.

Enhorning G, Shennan A, Possmayer F, Dunn M, Chen CP, Milligan J. Prevention of neonatal respiratory distress syndrome by tracheal instillation of surfactant: A randomized clinical trial. Pediatrics 76:145-153, 1985.

Findlay RD, Taeusch HW, Walther FJ. Surfactant replacement therapy for meconium aspiration syndrome. Pediatrics 97:48-52, 1996.

Froese AB, McCulloch PR, Sugiura M, Vaclavik S, Possmayer F, Moller F. Optimizing alveolar expansion prolongs the effectiveness of exogenous surfactant therapy in the adult rabbit. Am Rev Respir Dis 148:569-577, 1993.

Fujiwara T, Chida S, Watabe Y, Maeta H, Morita T, Abe T. Artificial surfactant therapy in hyaline-membrane disease. Lancet 1:55-59, 1980.

Garland J, Buck R, Weinberg M. Pulmonary hemorrhage risk in infants with a clinically diagnosed patent ductus arteriosus: A retrospective cohort study. Pediatrics 94:719-723, 1994.

Gilliard N, Richman PM, Merritt TA, Spragg RG. Effect of volume and dose on the pulmonary distribution of exogenous surfactant administered to normal rabbits or to rabbits with oleic acid lung injury. Am Rev Respir Dis 141:743-747, 1990.

Gitlin JD, Soll RF, Parad RB, Horbar JD, Feldman HA, Lucey JF, Taeusch HW. Randomized controlled trial of exogenous surfactant for the treatment of hyaline membrane disease. Pediatrics 79:31-37, 1987.

Glick PL, Stannard VA, Leach CL, Rossman J, Hosada Y, Morin FC, Cooney DR, Allen JE, Holm B. Pathophysiology of congenital diaphragmatic hernia. II: The fetal lamb CDH model is surfactant deficient. J Pediatr Surg 27:382-388, 1992.

• Gregory TJ, Longmore WJ, Moxley MA, Whitsett JA, Reed CR, Fowler AA III, Hudson LD, Maunder RJ, Crim C, Hyers TM. Surfactant chemical composition and biophysical activity in acute respiratory distress syndrome. J Clin Invest 88:1976-1981, 1991.

Gross NJ, Schultz RM. Requirements for extracellular metabolism of pulmonary surfactant: Tentative identification of serine protease. Am J Physiol 262:L446-L453, 1992.

• Gunkel JH, Banks PLC. Surfactant therapy and intracranial hemorrhage: Review of the literature and results of new analyses. Pediatrics 92:775-786, 1993.

Hall SB, Venkitaraman AR, Whitsett JA, Holm BA, Notter RH. Importance of hydrophobic apoproteins as constituents of clinical exogenous surfactants. Am Rev Respir Dis 145:24-30, 1992.

Hallman M, Merritt TA, Pahjavuori M, Gluck L. Effect of surfactant substitution on lung effluent phospholipids in respiratory distress syndrome: Evaluation of surfactant phospholipid turnover, pool size, and the relationship to severity of respiratory failure. Pediatr Res 20:1228-1235, 1986.

Hallman M, Merritt TA, Jarvenpaa AL, Boynton B, Mannino F, Gluck L, Moore T, Edwards D. Exogenous human surfactant for treatment of severe respiratory distress syndrome: A randomized prospective clinical trial. J Pediatr 106:963-969, 1985.

Hoekstra RE, Jackson JC, Myers TF, Frantz ID, Stern ME, Powers WF, Maurer M, Raye JR, Carrier ST, Gunkel JH, Gold AJ. Improved neonatal survival following multiple doses of bovine surfactant in very premature neonates at risk for respiratory distress syndrome. Pediatrics 88:10-18, 1991.

Holm BA, Keicher L, Liu M, Sokolowski J, Enhorning G. Inhibition of pulmonary surfactant function by phospholipases. J Appl Physiol 71:317-321, 1991.

Horbar JD, Wright LL, Soll RF, Wright EC, Fanaroff AA, Korones SB, Shankaran S, Oh W, Fletcher BD, Bauer CR, Tyson JE, Lemons JA, Donovan EF, Stoll BJ, Stevenson DD, Papile LA, Philips J III. A multicenter randomized trial comparing two surfactants for the treatment of neonatal respiratory distress syndrome. J Pediatr 123:757-766, 1993.

Hudak ML, Farrell EE, Rosenberg AA, Jung AL, Auten RL, Durand DJ, Horgan MJ, Buckwald S, Belcastro MR, Donohue PK, Carrion V, Maniscalco WW, Balsan JM, Torres BA, Miller RR, Jansen RD, Graeber JE, Laskay KM, Matteson EJ, Egan EA, Brody AS, Martin DJ, Riddlesberger MM, Montgomery P. A multicenter randomized, masked comparison trial of natural versus synthetic surfactant for the treatment of respiratory distress syndrome. J Pediatr 128:396-406, 1996.

• Ikegami M, Jobe AH. Surfactant metabolism. Semin Perinatol 17:233-240, 1993.

Ikegami M, Jacobs H, Jobe A. Surfactant function in respiratory distress syndrome. J Pediatr 102:443-447, 1983.

Ikegami M, Agata Y, Elkady T, Hallman M, Berry D, Jobe A. Comparison of four surfactants: In vitro surface properties and responses of preterm lambs to treatment at birth. Pediatrics 79:38-46, 1987.

Ikegami M, Ueda T, Absolom D, Baxter C, Rider E, Jobe AH. Changes in exogenous surfactant in ventilated preterm lamb lungs. Am Rev Respir Dis 148:837-844, 1993.

Jobe AH. Pulmonary surfactant therapy. N Engl J Med 328:861-868, 1993.

Kääpä P, Seppänen M, Kero P, Saraste M. Pulmonary hemodynamics after synthetic surfactant replacement in neonatal respiratory distress syndrome. J Pediatr 123:115-119, 1993.

Kattwinkel J, Bloom BT, Delmore P, Davis CL, Farrell E, Friss H, Jung AL, King K, Mueller D. Prophylactic administration of calf lung surfactant extract is more effective than early treatment of respiratory distress syndrome in neonates of 29 through 32 weeks' gestation. Pediatrics 92:90-98, 1993.

Kendig JW, Notter RH, Cox C, Reubens LJ, Doris JM, Maniscolea WM, Sinkin RA, Bartoletti A, Dweck HS, Horgan MJ, Rosenberg H, Phelps DL. Shapiro DL. A comparison of surfactant as immediate prophylaxis and as rescue therapy in newborns of less than 30 weeks' gestation. N Engl J Med 324:865-871, 1991.

Khammash H, Perlman M, Wojtulewicz J, Dunn M. Surfactant therapy in full-term neonates with severe respiratory failure. Pediatrics 92:135-139, 1993.

Kwong MS, Egan EA, Notter RH, Shapiro DL. Double-blind clinical trial of calf lung surfactant extract for the prevention of hyaline membrane disease in extremely premature infants. Pediatrics 76:585-592, 1985.

• Lewis JF, Jobe AH. Surfactant and the adult respiratory distress syndrome. Am Rev Respir Dis 147:218-233, 1993.

Lewis JF, McCaig L. Aerosolized versus instilled exogenous surfactant in a nonuniform pattern of lung injury. Am Rev Respir Dis 148:1187-1193, 1993.

• Lewis JF, Tabor B, Ikegami M, Jobe AH, Joseph M, Absolom D. Lung function and surfactant distribution in saline-lavaged sheep given instilled vs. nebulized surfactant. J Appl Physiol 73:1256-1264, 1993.

Long W, Corbet A, Cotton R, Courtney S, McGuiness G, Walter D, Watts J, Smyth J, Bard H, Chernick V, American Exosurf Neonatal Study Group I, Canadian Exosurf Neonatal Study Group. A controlled trial of synthetic surfactant in infants weighing 1250 g or more with respiratory distress syndrome. N Engl J Med 325:1696-1703, 1991.

Lotze A, Knight GR, Anderson KD, Hull WM, Whitsett JA, O'Donnell RM, Martin G, Bulas DI, Short BL. Surfactant (Beractant) therapy for infants with congenital diaphragmatic hernia on ECMO: Evidence of persistent surfactant deficiency. J Pediatr Surg 29:407-412, 1994.

Mendelson CR, Alcorn JL, Gao E. The pulmonary surfactant protein genes and their regulation in fetal lung. Semin Perinatol 17:223-232, 1993.

Merritt TA, Kheiter A, Cochrane CG. Positive end-expiratory pressure during KL_4 surfactant instillation enhances intrapulmonary distribution in a simian model of respiratory distress syndrome. Pediatr Res 38:211-217, 1995.

Merritt TA, Hallman M, Berry C, Pohjavuori M, Edwards DK, Jaaskelainen J, Grafe MR, Vaucher Y, Wozniak P, Heldt G, Rapola J. Randomized, placebo-controlled trial of human surfactant given at birth versus rescue administration in very low birth weight infants with lung immaturity. J Pediatr 118:581-594, 1991.

Moya FR, Hoffman DR, Zhao B, Johnston JM. Platelet-activating factor in surfactant preparations. Lancet 341:858-860, 1993.

Moya FR, Montes HF, Thomas VL, Mouzinho AM, Smith JF, Rosenfeld CR. Surfactant protein A and saturated phosphatidylcholine in respiratory distress syndrome. Am J Respir Crit Care Med 150:1672-1677, 1994.

Moya FR, Thomas VL, Romaguera J, Mysore MR, Maberry M, Bernard A, Freund M. Fetal lung maturation in congenital diaphragmatic hernia. Am J Obstet Gynecol 173:1401-1405, 1995.

• Nogee LM, Garnier G, Dietz HC, Singer L, Murphy AM, deMello DE, Colten HR. A mutation in the surfactant protein B gene responsible for fatal neonatal respiratory disease in multiple kindreds. J Clin Invest 93:1860-1863, 1994.

Ogawa A, Brown CL, Schlueter MA, Benson BJ, Clements JA, Hawgood S. Lung function, surfactant apoprotein content, and level of PEEP in prematurely delivered rabbits. J Appl Physiol 77:1840-1849, 1994.

OSIRIS Group. Early versus delayed neonatal administration of a synthetic surfactant—The judgement of OSIRIS. Lancet 340:1363-1369, 1992.

• Pandit PB, Dunn MS, Colucci EA. Surfactant therapy in neonates with respiratory deterioration due to pulmonary hemorrhage. Pediatrics 95:32-36, 1995.

Pappin A, Shenker N, Hack M, Redline RW. Extensive intraalveolar pulmonary hemorrhage in infants dying after surfactant therapy. J Pediatr 124:621-626, 1994.

• Perlman JM, Rollins N, Burns D, Risser R. Relationship between periventricular intraparenchymal echodensities and germinal matrix–intraventricular hemorrhage in the very low birth weight neonate. Pediatrics 91:474-480, 1993.

Pison U, Max M, Neuendank A, Weissbach S, Pietschmann S. Host defense capacities of pulmonary surfactant: Evidence for "non-surfactant" functions of the surfactant system. Eur J Clin Inves 24:586-599, 1994.

Poulain FR, Allen L, Williams MC, Hamilton RL, Hawgood S. Effects of surfactant apolipoproteins on liposome structure: Implications for tubular myelin formation. Am J Physiol 262:L730-L739, 1992.

• Raju TNK, Langenberg P. Pulmonary hemorrhage and exogenous surfactant therapy: A meta-analysis. J Pediatr 123:603-610, 1993.

Revak SD, Merritt TA, Hallman M, Heldt G, La Polla RJ, Hoey K, Houghten RA, Cochrane CG. The use of synthetic peptides in the formation of biophysically and biologically active pulmonary surfactants. Pediatr Res 29:460-465, 1995.

• Rider ED, Jobe AH, Ikegami M, Sun B. Different ventilation strategies alter surfactant responses in preterm rabbits. J Appl Physiol 73:2089-2096, 1992.

• Rooney SA. The surfactant system and lung phospholipid biochemistry. Am Rev Respir Dis 131:439-460, 1985.

Rooney SA, Young SL, Mendelson CR. Molecular and cellular processing of lung surfactant. FASEB J 8:957-967, 1994.

Schwartz RM, Luby AM, Scanlon JW, Kellogg RJ. Effect of surfactant on morbidity, mortality, and resource use in newborn infants weighing 500 to 1500 g. N Engl J Med 330:1476-1480, 1994.

Segerer H, van Gelder W, Angenent FWM, van Woerkens LJPM, Curstedt T, Obladen M, Lachmann B. Pulmonary distribution and efficacy of exogenous surfactant in lung-lavaged rabbits are influenced by the instillation technique. Pediatr Res 34:490-494, 1993.

Seppänen M, Med B, Kääpä P, Kero P. Acute effects of synthetic surfactant replacement on pulmonary blood flow in neonatal respiratory distress syndrome. Am J Perinat 11:382-385, 1994.

Shapiro DL, Notter RH, Morin FC III, Deluga KS, Golub LM, Sinkin RA, Weiss KI, Cox C. Double-blind, randomized trial of a calf lung surfactant extract administered at birth to very premature infants for prevention of respiratory distress syndrome. Pediatrics 76:593-599, 1985.

Sherman MP, Campbell LA, Merritt TA, Long WA, Gunkel JH, Curstedt T, Robertson B. Effect of different surfactants on pulmonary group B streptococcal infection in premature rabbits. J Pediatr 125:939-947, 1994.

Soll RF, Hoekstra RE, Fangman JJ, Corbet AJ, Adams JM, James LS, Schulze K, Oh W, Roberts JD Jr, Dorst JP, Kramer SS, Gold AJ, Zola EM, Horbar JD, McAuliffe TL, Lucey JF, Ross Collaborative Surfactant Prevention Study Group. Multicenter trial of single-dose modified bovine surfactant extract (Survanta) for prevention of respiratory distress syndrome. Pediatrics 85:1092-1102, 1990.

Spragg RG, Gilliard N, Richman P, Smith RM, Hite RD, Pappert D, Robertson B, Curstedt T, Strayer D. Acute effects of a single dose of porcine surfactant on patients with the adult respiratory distress syndrome. Chest 105:195-202, 1994.

• Tarnow-Mordi WO, Soll RF. Artificial versus natural surfactant—Can we base clinical practice on a firm scientific footing? Eur J Pediatr 153:S17-S21, 1994.

Thornton CM, Halliday HL, O'Hara MD. Surfactant replacement therapy in preterm neonates: A comparison of postmortem pulmonary histology in treated and untreated infants. Pediatr Pathol 14:945-953, 1994.

Ueda T, Ikegami M, Rider ED, Jobe AH. Distribution of surfactant and ventilation in surfactant-treated preterm lambs. J Appl Physiol 76:45-55, 1994.

van de Bor M, Ma EJ, Walther FJ. Cerebral blood flow velocity after surfactant instillation in preterm infants. J Pediatr 118:285-287, 1991.

Vaucher YE, Harker L, Merritt TA, Hallman M, Gist K, Bejar R, Heldt GP, Edwards D, Pohjuvuori M. Outcome at 12 months of adjusted age in very low birth weight infants with lung immaturity: A randomized, placebo-controlled trial of human surfactant. J Pediatr 122:126-132, 1993.

• Vermont-Oxford Neonatal Network. A multicenter randomized trial comparing synthetic surfactant to modified bovine surfactant extract in the treatment of neonatal respiratory distress syndrome. Pediatrics 97:1-6, 1996.

Weg JG, Balk RA, Tharratt S, Jenkinson SG, Shah JB, Zaccardelli D, Horton J, Pattishall EN. Safety and potential efficacy of an aerosolized surfactant in human sepsis-induced adult respiratory distress syndrome. JAMA 272:1433-1438, 1994.

Wilkinson A, Jenkins PA, Jeffrey JA. Two controlled trials of dry artificial surfactant: Early effects and later outcome in babies with surfactant deficiency. Lancet 2:287-291, 1985.

Willson DF, Jiao JH, Bauman LA, Zaritsky A, Craft H, Dockery K, Conrad D, Dalton H. Calf's lung surfactant in acute hypoxemic respiratory failure in children. Crit Care Med 24:1316-1322, 1996.

Wright JR, Dobbs LG. Regulation of pulmonary surfactant secretion and clearance. Annu Rev Physiol 53:395-414, 1991.

Yee WFH, Scarpelli EM. Surfactant replacement therapy. Pediatr Pulmonol 11:65-80, 1991.

• Zola EM, Gunkel JH, Chan RK, Lim MO, Knox I, Feldman BH, Denson SE, Stonestreet BS, Mitchell BR, Wyza MM, Bennett KJ, Gold AJ. Comparison of three dosing procedures for administration of bovine surfactant to neonates with respiratory distress syndrome. J Pediatr 122:453-459, 1993.

158 Nitric Oxide Delivery

Philip W. Shaul · Thomas M. Zellers · Thomas R. George

BACKGROUND AND INDICATIONS

Nitric oxide (NO) is a ubiquitous free radical compound produced by a large number of cell types in the body. In its natural state NO exists as a gas, and it was initially studied as a component of air pollution. It is found in cigarette smoke in concentrations ranging from 400 to 1000 ppm. In mammalian cells NO is produced by the enzyme NO synthase on conversion of the amino acid L-arginine to L-citrulline. NO is synthesized in vascular beds by endothelial cells and diffuses intraluminally and abluminally to cause vascular smooth muscle relaxation through interaction with the vascular smooth muscle enzyme guanylate cyclase and synthesis of the second messenger cyclic guanosine monophosphate (cGMP). The focus of this chapter is the function of NO in the pulmonary vascular bed and its potential therapeutic use in pulmonary hypertensive disorders.

Nitric Oxide and Pulmonary Circulation

Pulmonary vascular tone is controlled by a complex interaction between the endothelial cell layer and the underlying vascular smooth muscle. The endothelial cell synthesizes and secretes at least three endothelial-derived vasoactive substances: endothelin, which is a vasoconstrictor, and prostacyclin and endothelium-derived relaxing factor, both of which are vasodilators and inhibitors of platelet aggregation. Endothelium-derived relaxing factor is an endogenous nitrovasodilator and is thought to be NO or a nitrosothiol that donates NO. Of these agents, NO appears to be most important in mediating vascular relaxation and maintaining vascular tone in the pulmonary circulation.

Pulmonary arterial and venous endothelium produce NO under both basal and stimulated conditions. Basally released NO attenuates vascular smooth muscle contraction in response to a number of endogenous vasoconstrictors, including epinephrine, norepinephrine, histamine, and endothelin-1. This at-

tenuation can be as large as 10 log molar inhibition. In addition, a variety of endogenously produced agonists, including acetylcholine, adenosine triphosphate (ATP), adenosine diphosphate, bradykinin, substance P, and thrombin, all activate release of NO from pulmonary endothelium. Furthermore, pulmonary endothelial NO production is augmented by increased flow and depressed by hypoxia.

NO in pulmonary endothelial cells is produced primarily by a presumed constitutive isoform of NO synthase. An inducible isoform of NO synthase is expressed in human pulmonary endothelial cells, but its relative function in those cells is yet to be determined. Constitutive endothelial NO synthase activity depends on the presence of molecular oxygen, calcium, calmodulin, and the cofactors NADPH, tetrahydrobiopterin, and flavin nucleotides. ATP may also be necessary for flow-induced NO release.

Rationale for Nitric Oxide Therapy

Four important concepts provide the rationale for NO as an inhalational therapeutic agent in pulmonary vascular disorders: (1) NO plays a critical role in the modulation of pulmonary vasomotor tone, acting as a potent endogenous vasodilator. (2) NO in its natural state exists as a gas and thereby has the capacity to be administered directly to the target organ. (3) Diminished NO-mediated pulmonary vasodilation associated with pulmonary hypertensive disorders has been demonstrated in both animal models and in humans. (4) The potential exists for a selective effect of inhaled NO on the pulmonary vascular bed based on the following postulated events. Inhaled NO can diffuse directly into the vascular smooth muscle of the pulmonary circulation to produce vasodilation. On entry into the vascular lumen, NO binds with hemoglobin and other hemoproteins with great affinity to form nitrosylhemoglobin, abolishing its biologic activity and preventing systemic vasodilation. Nitrosylhemoglobin subsequently forms nitrate and nitrite, which are excreted in the urine, and methemoglobin. Methemoglobin is rapidly converted back to hemoglobin by methemoglobin reductase contained in erythrocytes.

General considerations

With this rationale in mind, NO was first evaluated as a selective pulmonary vasodilator in animal models. Studies in healthy lambs revealed that the inhalation of 80 ppm of NO has no effect on pulmonary vascular resistance, systemic vascular resistance, cardiac output, left atrial pressure, or CVP. However, acute pulmonary hypertension induced by either infusion of a vasoconstrictor agent or inhalation of a hypoxic gas mixture was rapidly reversed by NO inhalation at 5 to 80 ppm. Systemic vasodilation did not occur. In addition, the pulmonary vasodilation produced by NO persisted for at least 1 hour without evidence of tolerance, and breathing 80 ppm for 3 hours did not increase methemoglobin or extravascular lung water, and lung histologic analysis also revealed no changes.

Persistent pulmonary hypertension of the newborn

Animal studies. Studies performed in older lambs were extended to include newborn lambs and reveal that inhalation of 20 ppm of NO fully reverses the 65% increase in pulmonary vascular resistance induced by a hypoxic gas mixture. Inhaled NO was also effective in the presence of hypoxia plus respiratory acidosis. As in the older lambs, NO inhalation did not cause elevation of methemoglobin levels, and there was no evidence of systemic effect.

The lamb model has also been used in studies of the transition of the pulmonary circulation at birth. In late-gestation fetal lambs there is an immediate and dramatic increase in pulmonary blood flow and a decrease in pulmonary artery pressure with cesarean section delivery and ventilation with 100% oxygen. These responses are markedly attenuated if delivery and ventilation are performed after infusion of an inhibitor of NO production into the pulmonary artery. These findings indicate that NO is critically involved in the birth-related decline in pulmonary vascular resistance.

Inhaled NO therapy has also been evaluated in animal models of persistent pulmonary hypertension of the newborn (PPHN) secondary to a variety of primary processes. In a model of neonatal sepsis, 2-week old piglets given an infusion of group B *Streptococcus* (GSB) demonstrated doubling of pulmonary artery pressure. This pulmonary hypertension was completely reversed by inhalation of 150 ppm NO. NO did not exacerbate GBS-induced impairment of cardiac output or ventilation-perfusion ($\dot{V}/\dot{Q}$) mismatch, and systemic blood pressure was not adversely affected. In a sheep model of congenital diaphragmatic hernia, NO inhalation in the presence of perfluorocarbon-associated gas exchange (PAGE) improved both pulmonary hypertension and hypoxemia. The response to inhaled NO has also been evaluated in a sheep model of PPHN induced by ligation of the ductus arteriosus 10 days before delivery near term. NO administration (6 to 100 ppm) for up to 30 minutes caused a dose-dependent decline in pulmonary arterial pressure and resistance and an increase in systemic oxygenation. Furthermore, continuous NO administration at 80 ppm increased survival from 0% to 83% over the first day of life during ventilation with Fio_2 0.92, and no histologic evidence of increased acute lung injury was noted with NO therapy.

Human studies. The first reports of the therapeutic use of inhaled NO in term infants with PPHN were published in 1992. In a study of six patients that focused on the acute effects of NO, inhalation of up to 80 ppm of NO at Fio_2 0.9 for as long as 30 minutes caused a rapid increase in postductal oxygenation. Systemic hypotension and methemoglobinemia were not observed. One infant who received NO for 23 days demonstrated no evidence of tolerance. In a second series of nine term neonates with PPHN, lower doses of NO (10 to 20 ppm) resulted in rapid improvement in oxygenation without systemic effects. In six of these patients clinical improvement was sustained for 24 hours at 6 ppm of NO. This latter report was extended to reveal that low dose NO (6 ppm) yielded persistent improvement in eight of nine consective patients treated in that manner. In a larger study reported in 1993 the acute response to NO (5 to 80 ppm administered in random order) was evaluated in 23 hypoxic near-term infants with an oxygenation index of ≥ 20 (oxygenation index = % O_2 inspired $\times$ mean airway pressure/Pao_2) after treatment with exogenous surfactant. Overall, 14 infants had an improved Pao_2 of >10 mm Hg or increased Sao_2 $>10\%$ in response to NO administration.

In patients who responded there was no difference in the effect of any of the doses from 5 to 80 ppm. Eleven of 13 infants with echocardiographic evidence of PPHN responded to NO compared with only three of 10 without such findings. The acute response to inhaled NO has also recently been evaluated in a small group of neonates with congenital diaphragmatic hernia (n = 8) before and after support with extracorporeal membrane oxygenation (ECMO) for 5 to 17 days. Before ECMO, postductal oxygenation did not improve with NO. However, there was a dramatic acute improvement in oxygenation with NO inhalation after ECMO support. NO therapy was also reported in a 28-week-gestation infant with severe hyaline membrane disease and GBS sepsis. It is important to note that all studies reported to date focused on acute responses and were not controlled.

Pulmonary hypertension secondary to cardiac disorders

Use of inhaled NO in patients with congenital heart disease and pulmonary hypertension has gained interest recently. In a small group of nonsurgical patients who underwent acute cardiac catheterization, all had significantly decreased pulmonary artery pressure and resistance and increased pulmonary blood flow in response to 80 ppm of NO. In addition, oxygen augmented the effects of NO. No adverse effects were noted, and no changes in systemic arterial hemodynamics were found. It has more recently been shown that a lower concentration of NO (12 vs. 60 ppm) yields the same effects, with decreased pulmonary vascular resistance that is augmented with coadministration of oxygen.

The use of NO in the postoperative period after cardiac surgery in adults and children is the subject of 11 studies or case reports since 1993. The effects of short-term treatment (eight studies) and long-term treatment (three studies) with NO (15 to 80 ppm) in 26 adults and 73 children have been reported, with a 22% to 42% reduction in pulmonary vascular resistance. Most studies in children report a 33% to 37% decrease in mean pulmonary artery pressure or calculated pulmonary vascular resistance. In one series of patients it was observed that acetylcholine-induced relaxation was less than that seen with inhaled NO. This finding may suggest pulmonary endothelial dysfunction with decreased endogenous NO release in the first 24 hours after cardiopulmonary bypass surgery. It is unknown whether this observation is specific to acetylcholine or if it applies to all receptor-mediated agonists that cause NO release. Although not all patients responded to inhaled NO, those with the most severe pulmonary hypertension seemed to respond best. Patients with initial mean pulmonary artery pressures <25 mm Hg had little response to the inhaled vasodilator. No methemoglobin levels >5% were reported. It is critical to realize that in patients with congenital heart disease only one study described NO inhalation given for more than 3 days in patients with pulmonary hypertension, and no investigation has been performed to determine its efficacy compared with conventional therapy.

Pulmonary hypertension secondary to acute respiratory distress syndrome

Several studies have recently described the effects of inhaled NO on pulmonary artery pressure and hemodynamics in adults and children with acute respiratory distress syndrome (ARDS). In a study of adults significant improvement in oxygenation and decreased intrapulmonary shunting were noted with inhaled NO, even at doses as low as 18 ppm. It was postulated that NO produces microselective vasodilation in areas of the lung ventilated, whereas vasodilation does not occur in areas poorly ventilated, decreasing $\dot{V}/\dot{Q}$ mismatch. No significant toxicity was noted, and the survival rate was 80% in a cohort of patients with expected survival of 50%. Selected patients received NO for more than 50 days. The noncontrolled, nonrandomized use of NO has also been reported in pediatric patients with severe hypoxemic failure. Half of the patients had bronchopulmonary dysplasia and infection with respiratory syncytial virus, and the others had ARDS from multiple causes. All patients with bronchopulmonary dysplasia and 50% with ARDS survived; the duration of therapy ranged from 1 to 24 days. The concentration of the gas used was 20 to 40 ppm, and no significant methemoglobinemia developed even with prolonged exposure.

• • •

In summary, of the various reports of NO therapy for pediatric pulmonary hypertension associated with PPHN, congenital heart disease, and ARDS, many have yielded encouraging results. However, the true efficacy of inhaled NO for treatment of these disorders and the effect on morbidity and mortality are yet to be determined.

TECHNIQUE
Chemistry and Toxicology

Before discussing the techniques involved in provision of inhaled NO, it is necessary to briefly review the chemistry and pulmonary toxicology of the molecule. NO is one of several oxides of nitrogen of biologic relevance. NO does not persist as a free radical for any length of time in biologic systems (e.g., the lungs). Redox reactions can occur in the presence of oxygen, yielding nitrogen dioxide, which is a higher oxide of nitrogen and a toxic free radical that facilitates lipid peroxidation. Reactions of NO with superoxide result in formation of peroxynitrite and its decomposition products, hydroxyl radicals and nitrogen dioxide. Peroxynitrite is a strong oxidizing agent, and similar to nitrogen dioxide, hydroxyl radicals facilitate lipid peroxidation. Controlled generation of these compounds in the lung may contribute to antimicrobial defense mechanisms, whereas excess production may contribute to lung injury.

Although early reports implicated NO as toxic to pulmonary tissues, subsequent carefully controlled investigations in animals suggest that there is minimal risk of lung injury from breathing low levels of NO for short periods. It has recently been demonstrated that the exposure of rats to 1000 ppm of NO for 30 minutes and 1500 ppm for 15 minutes does not produce changes in lung wet weight or histologic findings on light or electron microscopic study. In addition, rabbits breathing 43 ppm of NO and 3.6 ppm of nitrogen dioxide for 6 days were not found to have any pathologic effects on light or electron microscopic evaluation. Furthermore, NO in concentrations of 30 to 50 ppm has been used to assess alveolar-capillary diffusion in humans. Impure gas mixtures containing high levels of nitrogen dioxide and dinitrogen tetraoxide were the likely causes of the previously reported pulmonary toxicity. However, because data are not yet available regarding pulmonary toxicity in humans and there is potential for nitrogen dioxide and preoxynitrite formation when NO is delivered to the patient along with oxygen, extreme caution is warranted when NO therapy is under consideration. The ceiling for NO exposure set by the Occupational Safety and Health Administration (OSHA) is 25 ppm/8 hr (time-weighted average); for nitrogen dioxide it is 5 ppm.

Administration

No gas is currently available with FDA approval in various concentrations ranging from 450 to 800 ppm balanced in nitrogen. Medical-grade NO is typically contaminated <1% with nitrogen dioxide. Federal and local safety guidelines must be followed regarding storage, transport, and handling. Because NO has corrosive properties, noncorrosive metals such as stainless steel are used in regulators, blenders, and other gas delivery devices. When delivering inhaled NO, the potential for nitrogen dioxide formation must be minimized. The rate of nitrogen dioxide formation depends on the NO and oxygen concentrations being delivered to the patient and the time interval of mixing of the two gases. As a result, delivery systems need to be designed so that NO enters the inspired gas circuitry as close to the patient as possible while allowing for thorough mixing of the gases.

NO may be administered in spontaneously breathing patients in a controlled environment. An oxygen hood can be used for infants and small children (Fig. 158-1). NO gas is bled into the continuous gas flow supplying the hood. The concentration of NO achieved, as with any continuous flow system, depends on the NO source concentration, NO flow, and mainstream flow. The concentration of NO delivered to the patient can be estimated with the following formula:

$$\frac{\text{NO source gas ppm}}{\text{NO flow} + \text{Mainstream flow}} = \text{NO concentration}$$

After the patient is placed in the hood, an additional larger enclosure such as an oxygen tent can be used as a scavenger system to collect delivered NO that is not inhaled by the patient. This minimizes the unnecessary exposure of care providers to NO gas. Oxygen, NO, and nitrogen dioxide concentrations must be monitored frequently, both in the hood and in the immediate environment. A nonrebreathing mask with NO entering into the mainstream flow may be used for older patients. Caution is warranted to ensure that gas concentrations are analyzed as close to the mouth or nose as possible.

When administering NO in conjunction with mechanical ventilation, the delivered NO concentration can also be estimated with the formula above. NO must enter the ventilator circuit on the inspiratory limb approximately 25 to 50 cm proximal to the endotracheal tube (Fig. 158-2). This meets the criteri-

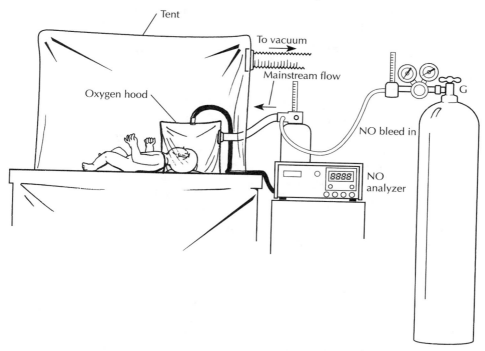

Fig. 158-1 NO delivery with an oxygen hood.

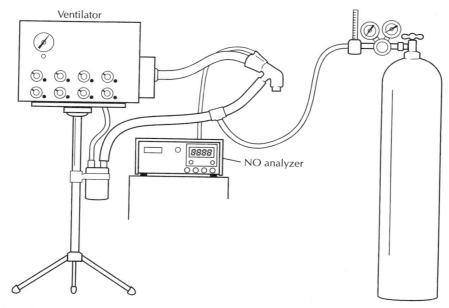

Fig. 158-2 NO delivery in conjunction with pressure-limited mechanical ventilation.

on of minimizing exposure time for oxygen and NO and allows adequate mixing of the gases. The inspired NO, nitrogen dioxide, and oxygen concentrations need to be analyzed at the patient connection. With this method, NO concentration is independent of ventilator settings, with the exception of flow. Most volume ventilator delivery systems mix NO with source gas and use blenders to adjust gas concentrations. The delivered NO concentration is relatively constant and unaffected by ventilator settings with this method. Considerable caution is needed when bellows or gas reservoirs are present within the ventilator because they may potentiate formation of excessive levels of nitrogen dioxide. When NO is delivered with mechanical ventilation, exposure of care providers to the gas is minimized by vacuum scavenging the expired gases exiting the ventilator. As in the spontaneously breathing patient, environmental concentrations of NO and nitrogen dioxides must be monitored at regular intervals.

Monitoring of Nitric Oxide and Nitrogen Dioxide

Two methods are currently available for NO and nitrogen dioxide analysis. The chemiluminescence method uses a technique in which NO reacts with ozone (O_3), releasing energy in the form of light. The amount of light energy produced is directly proportional to the concentration of NO in the sample. The light energy produced is then measured with a photomultiplier tube:

$$NO + O_3 \rightarrow NO_2 + O_2 + h\nu$$

Other oxides of nitrogen, including nitrogen dioxide (NO_2), can also be measured when the sample is introduced into a heated molybdenum converter, producing the following reaction:

$$3NO_2 + Mo \rightarrow 3NO + MoO_3$$

The resultant NO can then be detected through the reaction with ozone (see above), and a signal is generated for the total amount of oxides of nitrogen present in the sample. Elevated oxygen concentrations and excessive water vapor may result in underestimation of NO with this technique, a phenomena known as quenching. Chemiluminescence analyzers are sidestream analyzers and may affect mechanical ventilator performance, particularly with noncontinuous flow ventilators. Most chemiluminescence analyzers are currently designed for industrial applications and are difficult to use because of their large size and the noise generated.

Electrochemical analyzers provide an alterative method for measuring NO and nitrogen dioxide levels. In contrast to chemiluminescence analyzers, electrochemical analyzers are small, lightweight mainstream analyzers. Separate electrochemical cells are needed for NO and nitrogen dioxide. At the electrochemical cell the gas sample passes through a semipermeable membrane into an electrolyte solution. An electrical current is produced, and this current is compared with a reference electrode. The amount of electrical current generated is directly proportional to the NO or nitrogen dioxide concentration in the sample. Electrochemical analyzers are more convenient and considerably less expensive than chemiluminescence analyzers.

Laboratory Tests

Additional laboratory tests are indicated to monitor for possible side effects of NO therapy. There is potential for methemoglobinemia with NO administration. However, mice exposed to 10 ppm of NO for 6.5 months had methemoglobin levels identical to that in controls. In addition, the numerous noncontrolled human studies in both adults and children report minimal changes in methemoglobin levels when modest doses of NO are administered for relatively short durations. These observations are consistent with evidence that methemoglobin reductase is present even in the newborn period to rapidly reconvert methemoglobin to hemoglobin. However, determinations of methemoglobin levels are necessary during NO administration to assess this potential side effect, particularly in light of rare instances of methemoglobin reductase deficiency.

An additional effect of NO in the vasculature is inhibition of platelet aggregation. However, under in vivo conditions NO is rapidly scavenged. In studies of the pulmonary toxicity of NO in rats and rabbits there has been no evidence of pulmonary hemorrhage, and hemorrhage into the lung was not noted in studies of NO inhalation in newborn and older lambs. Until further studies are performed to evaluate platelet function in patients receiving inhalational NO therapy, it seems prudent to evaluate platelet count before considering NO treatment, and caution would be appropriate in patient populations at risk for bleeding diatheses or specific hemorrhagic disorders such as intraventricular hemorrhage in the preterm infant.

CURRENT RESEARCH AND FUTURE CONSIDERATIONS

Noncontrolled studies of the therapeutic use of inhaled NO suggest that in some pediatric patients with pulmonary hypertension this technique may be beneficial. However, there is a paucity of data regarding short-term and long-term toxicity of inhaled NO in humans, and its true efficacy and effects on morbidity and mortality remain to be determined. As a result, controlled, randomized, blinded studies of inhaled NO therapy are warranted in select populations of pediatric patients with pulmonary hypertension. Only after issues of safety and efficacy are addressed can definitive recommendations be made regarding therapeutic use of NO in the pediatric patient with pulmonary hypertension.

ADDITIONAL READING

Abman SH, Kinsella JP, Schaffer MS, Wilkening RB. Inhaled nitric oxide in the management of a premature newborn with severe respiratory distress and pulmonary hypertension. Pediatrics 92:606-609, 1993.

· Abman SH, Griebel JL, Parker DK, Schmidt JM, Swanton D, Kinsella JP. Acute effects of inhaled nitric oxide in children with severe hypoxemic respiratory failure. J Pediatr 124:881-888, 1994.

Adnot S, Raffestin B, Eddahibi S, Braquet P, Chabrier PE. Loss of endothelium-dependent relaxant activity in the pulmonary circulation of rats exposed to chronic hypoxia. J Clin Invest 87:155-162, 1991.

Adnot S, Kouyoumdjian C, Defouilloy C, Andrivet P, Sediame S, Herigault R, Fratacci MD. Hemodynamic and gas exchange responses to infusion of acetylcholine and inhalation of nitric oxide in patients with chronic obstructive lung disease and pulmonary hypertension. Am Rev Respir Dis 148:310-316, 1993.

Berger JI, Gibson RL, Redding GJ, Standaert TA, Clarke WR, Truog WE. Effect of inhaled nitric oxide during group B streptococcal sepsis in piglets. Am Rev Respir Dis 147:1080-1086, 1993.

Day RW, Lynch JM, Shaddy RE, Orsmond GS. Pulmonary vasodilatory effects of 12 and 60 ppm inhaled nitric oxide in children with ventricular septal defect. Am J Cardiol 75:196-198, 1995.

· Dinh-Xuan AT, Higgenbottam TW, Clelland CA, Pepke-Zaba J, Cremona G, Butt AY, Large SR, Wells FC, Wallwork J. Impairment of endothelium-dependent pulmonary artery relaxation in chronic obstructive lung disease. N Engl J Med 324:1539-1547, 1991.

· Finer NN, Etches PC, Kamstra B, Tierney AJ, Peliowski A, Ryan CA. Inhaled nitric oxide in infants referred for extracorporeal membrane oxygenation: Dose response. J Pediatr 124:302-308, 1994.

Frostell C, Fratacci M-D, Wain JC, Jones R, Zapol WM. Inhaled nitric oxide: A selective pulmonary vasodilator reversing hypoxic pulmonary vasoconstriction. Circulation 83:2038-2047, 1991.

Gaston B, Drazen JM, Loscalco J, Stamler JS. The biology of nitrogen oxides in the airways. Am J Respir Crit Care Med 149:538-551, 1994.

Girard C, Lehot J-J, Pannetier J-C, Filley S, French P, Estanove S. Inhaled nitric oxide after mitral valve replacement in patients with chronic pulmonary artery hypertension. Anesthesiology 77:880-883, 1992.

· Journois D, Pouard P, Mauriat P, Malhere T, Vouhe P, Safran D. Inhaled nitric oxide therapy for pulmonary hypertension after operations for congenital defects. J Thorac Cardiovasc Surg 107:1129-1135, 1994.

· Kinsella JP, Neish SR, Shaffer E, Abman SH. Low-dose inhalational nitric oxide in persistent pulmonary hypertension of the newborn. Lancet 340:819-820, 1992.

· Kinsella JP, Neish SR, Ivy DD, Shaffer E, Abman SH. Clinical responses to prolonged treatment of persistent pulmonary hypertension of the newborn with low doses of inhaled nitric oxide. J Pediatr 123:103-108, 1993.

Miller C, Miller J. Pulmonary smooth muscle relaxation: The role of inhaled nitric oxide. Respir Care 37:1175-1185, 1992.

Miller OI, Celermajer DS, Deanfield JE, Macrae DJ. Very low dose inhaled nitric oxide: A selective pulmonary vasodilator after operations for congenital heart disease. J Thorac Cardiovasc Surg 108:487-494, 1994.

Miller OI, Celermajer DS, Deanfield JE, Macrae DJ. Guidelines for the safe administration of inhaled nitric oxide. Arch Dis Child 70:F47-F49, 1994.

Moncada S, Higgs A. The L-arginine-nitric oxide pathway. N Engl J Med 329:2002-2012, 1993.

Pepke-Zaba J, Higgenbottam TW, Dinh-Xuan AT, Stone D, Wallwork J. Inhaled nitric oxide as a cause of selective pulmonary vasodilatation in pulmonary hypertension. Lancet 338:1173-1174, 1991.

Rich GF, Murphy GD, Roos CM, Johns RA. Inhaled nitric oxide. Selective pulmonary vasodilation in cardiac surgical patients. Anesthesiology 78:1028-1035, 1993.

Roberts JD, Shaul PW. Advances in the treatment of persistent pulmonary hypertension of the newborn. Pediatr Clin North Am 40:983-1004, 1993.

Roberts JD, Polander DM, Lang P, Zapol WM. Inhaled nitric oxide in persistent pulmonary hypertension of the newborn. Lancet 340:818-819, 1992.

· Roberts JD, Lang P, Bigatello LM, Vlahakes GJ, Zapol WM. Inhaled nitric oxide in congenital heart disease. Circulation 87:447-453, 1993.

· Roberts JD, Chen T-Y, Kawai N, Wain J, Dupuy P, Shimouchi A, Bloch K, Polander D, Zapol WM. Inhaled nitric oxide reverses pulmonary vasoconstriction in the hypoxic and acidotic newborn lamb. Circ Res 72:246-254, 1993.

• Roissant R, Falke KJ, Lopez F, Slama K, Pison U, Zapol WM. Inhaled nitric oxide for the adult respiratory distress syndrome. N Engl J Med 328:399-405, 1993.

Seitz WR, Neary MP. Chemiluminescence and bioluminescence. Contemp Top Anal Clin Chem 1:49-125, 1977.

Stamler JS, Loh E, Roddy MA, Currie KE, Creager MA. Nitric oxide regulates basal systemic and pulmonary vascular resistance in healthy humans. Circulation 89:2035-2040, 1994.

Stavert DM, Lehnert BE. Nitrogen oxide and nitrogen dioxide as inducers of acute pulmonary injury when inhaled at relatively high concentrations for brief periods. Inhal Toxicol 2:53-57, 1990.

Wessel DL. Inhaled nitric oxide for the treatment of pulmonary hypertension before and after cardiopulmonary bypass. Crit Care Med 22:930-938, 1994.

Wessel DL, Adatia I, Thompson JE. Delivery and monitoring of inhaled nitric oxide in patients with pulmonary hypertension. Crit Care Med 22:930-938, 1994.

• Wessel DL, Adatia I, Giglia TM, Thompson JE, Kulik TJ. Use of inhaled nitric oxide and acetylcholine in the evaluation of pulmonary hypertension and endothelial function after cardiopulmonary bypass. Circulation 88:2128-2138, 1993.

• Winberg P, Lundell BPW, Gustafsson LE. Effect of inhaled nitric oxide on raised pulmonary vascular resistance in children with congenital heart disease. Br Heart J 71:282-286, 1994.

Zayek M, Cleveland D, Morin FC. Treatment of persistent pulmonary hypertension in the newborn lamb by inhaled nitric oxide. J Pediatr 122:743-750, 1993.

Zayek M, Wild L, Roberts JD, Morin FC. Effect of nitric oxide on the survival rate and incidence of lung injury in newborn lambs with persistent pulmonary hypertension. J Pediatr 123:947-952, 1993.

159 Liquid Ventilation

Luis O. Toro-Figueroa · Yaron Harel · Dawne A. Black · Carol L. Bieler · Bradley P. Fuhrman

BACKGROUND AND INDICATIONS
Early Developments

In the early 1960s the quest to find a kinder, gentler way to assist ventilation in patients with acute lung injury led to experimental use of intrapulmonary salt solutions to enhance lung function, resulting in the development of the concept of liquid ventilation. Sodium chloride solution, which possesses a relatively low surface tension of approximately 70 dyne/cm², acts as a surfactant in the airways and alveoli to lower surface tension and abolish the hysteresis of the respiratory system. Lung compliance improves as a result. However, one of the limitations of sodium chloride solution is relatively poor oxygen solubility (2 to 3 ml of oxygen per 100 ml of solution).

To overcome the poor oxygen solubility of salt solutions, animal experiments were carried out in a hyperbaric oxygen chamber pressurized at 8 atm. For up to 18 hours mice were submerged in tromethamine (THAM, tris[hydroxymethyl]aminomethane) enriched with hyperbaric oxygen and allowed to swim and breath spontaneously while remaining submerged (Fig. 159-1). This experiment demonstrated that spontaneous liquid ventilation (SLV) was feasible for a limited time. In a similar experiment in which gravity was used to infuse the salt solution through an ET tube, adequate oxygenation was feasible for up to 50 minutes. Because of the high resistive work of breathing caused by both SLV and gravity-assisted spontaneous liquid ventilation (GASLV), all animals developed respiratory pump muscle fatigue that resulted in inadequate minute ventilation. Marked CO_2 retention and severe respiratory acidosis ensued. The unexplainable development of lactic acidosis during GASLV, although it responded to intravascular volume expansion, was considered an undesirable complication if liquid ventilation was to be used successfully in clinical medicine.

Perfluorocarbons

In 1966 Clark and Gollan demonstrated that use of stable perfluorocarbons (PFCs) to achieve SLV in small animals under normobaric conditions was feasible. PFCs are generally colorless, clear, odorless, hydrophobic, electrically resistant, chemically and biologically inert fluids that also act as poor solvents for most biologic solutes. PFCs typically consist of seven or eight fluorinated carbon atoms arranged in a straight chain. They have a high molecular weight, twice the density of water, and are radiopaque. Most of these qualities make PFC an ideal radiologic con-

Fig. 159-1 Spontaneous liquid ventilation of mouse submerged in tromethamine.

trast medium. Recently a PFC known as perflubron (Imagent) has been approved by the FDA as a radiologic contrast medium for use in ultrasonography, CT, and MRI. Its properties make it an ideal agent for use in imaging the sinuses, airways, GI tract, and pelvis.

PFC is also a remarkable liquid with a relatively low surface tension (10 to 15 dyne/cm^2) and an extraordinary ability to dissolve oxygen and CO_2 (approximately 50 ml of oxygen and 200 ml of CO_2 in 100 ml of PFC). Some PFCs can dissolve 20 times as much oxygen as water and 60 times as much CO_2. PFC has low viscosity and relatively high vapor pressure. These properties act to decrease the effect of PFC on resistance and facilitate its evaporation from the airways. The high coefficient of spreadability of PFC, together with its relatively low surface tension, allows it to function as a surfactant. Thus the liquid is liberally distributed throughout the airways and alveoli, improving compliance, facilitating alveolar recruitment, and maintaining open alveoli. Ventilation-perfusion ($\dot{V}/\dot{Q}$) matching improves with reduced airways pressure and better gas exchange.

PFC appears to cross the lung-epithelial barrier in small quantities and is scavenged by macrophages. It is well distributed throughout the body but not catabolized. The absence of excess inorganic PFC in the urine supports the hypothesis that PFC does not undergo biotransformation. The mechanisms for biodistribution and elimination are not well defined yet; it is known that volatilization from the lung and transpiration from the skin are important in its elimination. Variables that affect the rate of elimination of PFC are tissue lipid content, organ perfusion, $\dot{V}/\dot{Q}$ matching, and vapor pressure of a particular PFC. Although PFC may be present in tissues 3 years after liquid ventilation, it does not appear to exert any toxic effects. Morphologic, biochemical, and histologic examinations of numerous immature and mature animal species subjected to PFC liquid ventilation have failed to show any adverse effects. At histologic analysis liquid-ventilated lungs were more homogeneously expanded and free of hemorrhages and hyaline membrane in contrast to those ventilated conventionally. The aftereffects of PFC liquid ventilation in mammals have been extensively studied, and safe resumption of conventional ventilation after long periods of liquid ventilation is possible.

Early experimental work also showed that PFC facilitated gas exchange in PFC-filled lungs during deep sea diving and the high acceleration experienced in a space flight simulator. Other experimental medical uses for PFCs have focused on the armed forces' need to develop a blood substitute that can be stored without refrigeration in large quantities without significant risk of contamination or degradation and that can be easily administered on the battlefield. Perflubron has been formulated as a sterile egg protein–based emulsion that can be infused intravenously to provide oxygen-carrying capacity when blood loss has been significant. This may provide an alternative for intraoperative blood replacement in patients with religious objections to blood product transfusions as well as an infectious-free alternative to blood. Multiple experiments in animal models of acute lung injury demonstrated that the greatest potential of PFC was in acute restrictive lung diseases such as respiratory distress syndrome (RDS) and acute respiratory distress syndrome (ARDS) and in preventing barotrauma, volutrauma, and oxygen toxicity.

Total Liquid Ventilation

Shortcomings of SLV and GASLV led to the introduction of total liquid ventilation (TLV), in which PFC is instilled in the lungs through an ET tube (~20 to 30 ml/kg) and the patient is connected to a complex mechanical ventilation-oxygenation device (Fig. 159-2). Ventilator settings necessary to allow intrapulmonary movement of PFC include tidal volume (V_T) of 10 to 15 ml/kg and rate of 5 to 9 breaths/min with long inspiratory and expiratory times. Limitations of this system are its cost and degree of engineering and operational complexity.

Compared with conventional mechanical ventilation (CMV), TLV supported adequate gas exchange, acid-base balance, and cardiovascular stability and improved survival in premature lambs with RDS. Experimental data from a lamb model of meconium aspiration supported with TLV demonstrated that PFC facilitates pulmonary toileting and improves survival compared with CMV. The microsphere technique to demonstrate blood flow has been used in lambs undergoing TLV to show the redistribution of pulmonary blood flow from the dependent to the nondependent areas of the lung (Fig. 159-3). This effect is believed secondary to the selective distribution of PFC to the dependent areas of the lung, with subsequent physical displacement of blood volume; increased vascular resistance of the dependent area vessels may occur.

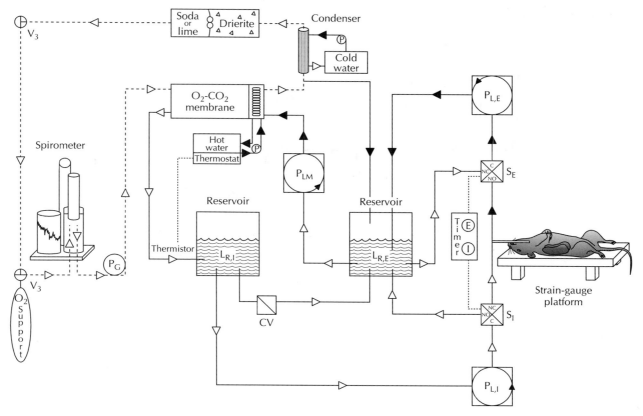

Fig. 159-2 Total liquid ventilation system. (Dashed line = gas circuit; solid line = fluorocarbon [FC] liquid; CV = check valve; $L_{R,I}$ and $L_{R,E}$ = inspiratory and expiratory FC reservoirs; $P_{L,I}$ and $P_{L,E}$ = inspiratory and expiratory FC roller pumps; P_{LM} = FC-oxygenator roller pump; P_G = gas oxygenator pump; P = circulating water pump; S_I and S_E = expiratory three-way solenoid valves [C, NO, NC = common, normally opened, and normally closed ports, respectively]; V_3 = manually operated three-way valve.) (Modified from Wolfson MR, Tran N, Bhutani VK, et al. A new experimental approach for the study of cardiopulmonary physiology during early development. J Appl Physiol 65:1436-1443, 1988.)

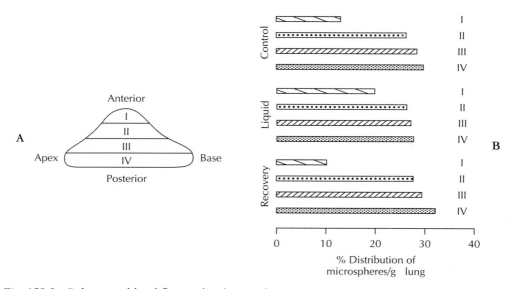

Fig. 159-3 Pulmonary blood flow redistribution during total liquid ventilation. **A,** Coordinate system for lung sections with lambs in supine position. **B,** Regional distribution of pulmonary blood flow (mean values).

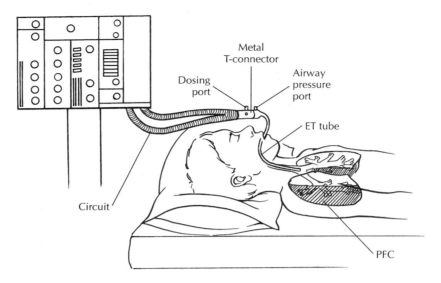

Fig. 159-4   Partial liquid ventilation.

The redistribution effect of pulmonary blood flow causes better $\dot{V}/\dot{Q}$ matching and results in better gas exchange. Finally, TLV in volume-expanded piglet lungs slightly increased oxygen consumption but did not cause lactic acidosis, and in healthy cats oxygen consumption and CO_2 production were well maintained.

Partial Liquid Ventilation
Animal experiments

In 1991 Fuhrman et al. developed PFC-associated gas exchange, which is now known as partial liquid ventilation (PLV). In this technique CMV is used to enhance gas exchange after filling the alveoli with PFC (Fig. 159-4). Compared with TLV, PLV requires at least 65% less PFC. During PLV gas exchange in the liquid medium occurs through in vivo bubble oxygenation (Fig. 159-5).

In multiple animal and species models of lung injury PLV has provided effective gas exchange, stable acid-base balance, hemodynamic stability, lower peak inspiratory pressure (PIP), increased compliance, and decreased airway resistance. Oxygenation during PLV is dose dependent: the higher the dose of PFC, the higher the Pao_2, whereas pH, Pco_2, mean airway pressure ($P\overline{aw}$), and compliance reach steady state after doses as small as 3 ml/kg. The weight of the PFC causes it to be deposited predominantly in the dependent portion of the lungs; surfactant-like properties predominate in the nondependent areas of lungs.

Human trials

In 1989 the first human trial was conducted in three premature infants (23 to 28 weeks of gestation) with probability of mortality >90%. Each infant was given preoxygenated PFC, as in GASLV, for two periods of 3 to 5 minutes each. During the two periods of liquid ventilation the following findings were noted: improved compliance and oxygenation (all three infants), improved ventilation and decreased airway resistance (two infants each), and worsening oxygenation, CO_2 retention, and decreasing compliance (one infant each). All patients tolerated the procedure hemodynamically. As expected, none of these infants survived.

Under the sponsorship of the manufacturer, eight university-affiliated pediatric medical centers examined the safety and efficacy PLV with LiquiVent (perflubron, Alliance Pharmaceutical Corp., San Diego, Calif.) in 10 children, ages 1 to 17 years, with ARDS. The protocol was approved by the FDA and participating hospital institutional review boards, and parental consent was obtained. In this open-label, multicenter, phase I/II pilot study each subject served as his or her own control. The primary study objective was to assess the safety and tolerance of perflubron as an intratracheally administered agent

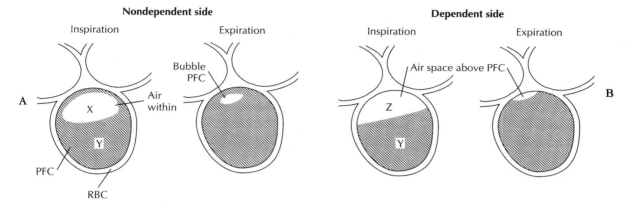

Fig. 159-5   Schema of in vivo bubble oxygenation during PFC-associated gas exchange. **A,** Bubble growth within the fluid on inspiration and expiration. **B,** Bubble growth against the alveolar lining, on inspiration and expiration. (X = gas/PFC surface; Y = alveolar lining/PFC surface; Z = alveolar/gas surface.)

for treatment of ARDS. The secondary objectives were to obtain preliminary efficacy data and use those data to design future dosing and ventilator management strategies.

The treatment period extended to a maximum of 96 hours from the start of initial dosing followed by a 48-hour posttreatment observation period. Follow-up extended to day 28. Long-term follow-up is being conducted at 3-, 6-, 12-, and 24-month visits to assess safety, occurrence of any adverse events, morbidity, and mortality. The entry criteria consisted of a clinical diagnosis of ARDS, three or more lung quadrants with radiographic findings consistent with ARDS, and a Pao_2/Fio_2 ratio of 75 to 200. Exclusion criteria consisted of cardiogenic pulmonary edema as confirmed by pulmonary artery occlusion pressure >18 mm Hg, evidence of chronic lung disease, heart disease, acute renal or hepatic failure, status epilepticus, multiple system organ failure, pregnancy, use of an experimental drug within 30 days before entry into the study, or any illness in which critical care is considered futile. After baseline assessment, PFC was instilled into the trachea through an ET tube (Fig. 159-6) and PLV initiated; evaporative losses were replaced every 1 to 2 hours during PLV.

Nine of the 10 patients tolerated initial perflubron dosing well. The average loading dose was 18 ± 8.1 ml/kg. The supplemental dose was 142 ± 86 ml/kg and was continued for 80 ± 25 hours, or approximately 3.5 ml/kg every 2 hours. Gas exchange improved in 9 of 10 patients, but lung mechanics were

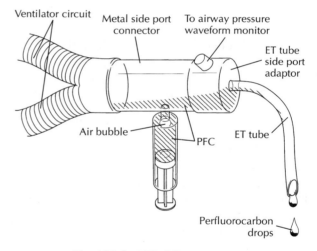

Fig. 159-6   PFC delivery system.

comparable before, during, and 48 hours after PLV (Table 159-1). One patient's condition deteriorated rapidly during the enrollment period, and that patient received only 6 ml/kg of PFC before extracorporeal membrane oxygenation (ECMO) was necessary because of further deterioration only 6 hours after entry into the study. Five patients had arterial desaturation attributed to secretions, but all responded to instillation of approximately 1 ml/kg of sodium chloride and suctioning. In three patients pneumothoraces developed after supplemental dosing had

Table 159-1 Lung Function Indices During First 48 hours of PLV

Measurement Interval	No. of Patients	A-aDo$_2$ (mm Hg)	Pao$_2$/Fio$_2$ Ratio	Paw (cm H$_2$O)	Oxygen Index
Baseline	10	457 ± 42	127 ± 22	20.6 ± 1.7	21.7 ± 4.8
Hours after PLV					
4	10	392 ± 48	144 ± 29	20.4 ± 2.1	22.5 ± 7.1
8	9	322 ± 49	156 ± 23	18.8 ± 1.3	14.5 ± 2.7
12	9	305 ± 45	148 ± 20	18.8 ± 1.3	15.7 ± 2.9
24	9	286 ± 46	146 ± 20	18.0 ± 1.5	14.2 ± 1.9
48	9	240 ± 6+	199 ± 42	17.0 ± 2.4	17.5 ± 7.1

been stopped and only CMV was being administered. Two patients died, 9 and 13 days, respectively, after cessation of PLV; one patient died of progressive respiratory failure, and the other of a cerebral hemorrhage during ECMO. Neither death was thought to be related to PLV. The results of this phase I/II study suggest that perflubron PLV may be safe and efficacious in pediatric ARDS and have led to implementation of the currently ongoing multicenter phase II/III study, a randomized controlled trial comparing PLV with CMV in pediatric patients with acute lung injury.

Ongoing and subsequent studies will determine indications for use of PLV. In theory, any acute lung injury from any cause may be an indication for PLV.

TECHNIQUE

Ongoing and subsequent studies will determine the best techniques for administration of PLV, which are likely to be similar to those used in the phase I/II and II/III studies.

A thorough baseline assessment of the patient is essential and needs to include assessment of hemodynamic variables, respiratory status including lung sounds, oxygenation, ventilation, acid-base balance, conventional ventilator settings, chest radiographs, lung mechanics, and oxygen delivery and consumption, as well as the usual assessments of end-organ function. Chest radiographs enable assessment of the degree of lung disease before PLV therapy (any infiltrates will be obscured by the radiopaque PFC). Assessment and documentation of all variables must be performed hourly to ensure the patient is tolerating PLV.

Appropriate levels of sedation, analgesia, and neuromuscular blockade are critical during PLV. Train-of-four monitoring is essential to ensure optimal neuromuscular blockade. During PFC instillation the patient must be supine and the liquid instilled so as to not occlude the airways. Occlusion of the airways leads to inadequate oxygenation and ventilation as a result of inappropriate V$_T$. During the early phases of PFC instillation one can observe improved alveolar recruitment of the dependent areas of the lungs and improved compliance in the nondependent areas. Both of these improvements typically lead to increased V$_T$ during the pressure control mode and decreased PIP during the volume control mode. As PFC continues to be instilled, further adjustments in the ventilator settings may be necessary: oxygenation typically improves as the loading dose is increased, and Fio$_2$ can often be decreased to 0.45 to 0.55.

Two methods of filling have been used. With bolus doses, several large aliquots are pushed through the ET tube until the FRC is filled. The advantage of this method is that it is less time consuming; the disadvantage is that it has a tendency to occlude the airways and cause loss of V$_T$, resulting in hypoxemia, hypercarbia, and hemodynamic instability. The trickle method is safer and more deliberate, especially when the airway pressure waveform is continuously monitored to determine how fast the dose can be instilled without causing excessive swings in pressure or loss of V$_T$. The FRC may be measured directly with bedside pulmonary function testing by using a standard FRC formula to calculate the value or by slowly filling the lung with the trickle method until a meniscus is seen when the ET tube, by rotating the patient's head, is at the level of the trachea under zero PEEP conditions, V$_T$ decreases by 30%, Sao$_2$ drops below 85%, hemodynamic instability develops, cardiac output decreases by ≥30%, or a total of 30 ml/kg of PFC is instilled.

Connect the PFC-filled (1 to 5 ml/kg) glass syringe to the metal straight airway connector, which is placed between the ET tube and the ventilator connectors. As the ventilator cycles, it forces air into the syringe and PFC into the airways (see Fig. 159-6). The amount and rate of PFC infused or trickled may be regulated or even halted by the degree of angulation at which the syringe and the air-fluid level are held. The main disadvantages of this method are longer filling time and need for repetition. The trickle method is a simple, easy way to instill PFC with minimal compromise of gas exchange and hemodynamic stability. The critical care team continuously monitors Sao_2 with a pulse oximeter and end-tidal CO_2 during PLV initial dosing. Arterial blood gas level is determined after the initial dosing is complete. Subsequent arterial blood gas sampling can be done as clinically indicated.

Breath sounds must be assessed after PFC filling of the lung; typically they are markedly different from those before filling. Coarse rhonchi become the predominant breath sound, but in smaller children it is not uncommon for breath sounds to become muffled. During PLV scrupulous attention to pulmonary toilet is necessary because large quantities of secretions are mobilized to the larger airways and necessitate frequent removal with suctioning. Secretions are often tenacious, and symptoms of acute airway obstruction may develop even if adequate suctioning has been provided. Usually these events respond to instillation of sodium chloride solution (1 ml/kg) and aggressive deep suctioning or tussive squeezing. If the obstruction is not relieved easily, abdominal thrusts and manual ventilation with pressure high enough to overcome the obstruction and push the plug away from the main airways into peripheral airways may be necessary. Replacement of the ET tube may be needed. If an acute hypoxemic episode occurs that is not related to secretions, a number of factors need to be assessed. Constant attention and assessment from a skilled critical care team will allow early identification of problems and intervention during PLV. At our institution pressure-controlled ventilation is used in pediatric patients during PLV. This mode generates a decelerating gas flow waveform, which results in constant preset peak pressure and variable V_T. As lung compliance and alveolar recruitment improve, close monitoring of V_T is imperative because excessive V_T causes volutrauma. Evaporation of PFC from the patient's lungs also causes

---

FACTORS ASSOCIATED WITH ACUTE HYPOXEMIA DURING PLV

Airway obstruction
Inadequate sedation, analgesia, or neuromuscular blockade
Inproper ET tube position
Inadequate cardiac output (assess preload and inotropes)
Inadequate oxygen-carrying capacity
Inadequate V_T
Inadequate minute ventilation (hypoventilation)
Inadequate Fio_2

V_T to increase. A low level of PFC in the ET tube suggests that dosing may be necessary, particularly if it has been several hours since administration of the previous dose.

PLV may be decreased when peak pressure and Fio_2 requirements are decreasing and compliance is increasing (i.e., V_T increases as PFC evaporates). Usually Pao_2/Fio_2, $(A-a)Do_2$, and oxygen index have improved dramatically and are closer to normal. Work is still in progress to determine how reliable these indices, which are based on the alveolar gas equation, are. When the patient can maintain optimal arterial blood gas values during the period immediately before the next supplemental dose is scheduled, no further PFC dosing is needed and all PFC in the lungs is allowed to evaporate. The rate of evaporation varies among patients and can be determined with daily chest radiographs.

Caution is necessary while reinstituting chest physiotherapy because lung contusion may occur when large amounts of the PFC are still present. The force generated by chest physiotherapy in conjunction with heavy PFC may predispose to tissue injury. Once 90% to 95% of the PFC has evaporated, the standard care regimen may be resumed.

RISKS AND COMPLICATIONS

The risks and complications associated with PLV in pediatric patients are still under investigation. The follow-up for the phase I/II study has not been concluded and the phase II/III study is in its early stages at this point.

CURRENT RESEARCH AND FUTURE CONSIDERATIONS
High-Frequency Liquid Oscillatory Ventilation

High-frequency oscillatory ventilation (HFOV), compared with CMV, improves gas exchange, incidence of oxygen dependency, pulmonary barotrauma, and chronic lung disease at 30 days and long-term outcome in pediatric patients with ARDS. Because PLV, which utilizes CMV, is superior to CMV alone in animal models of acute lung injury, could HFOV, which is superior to CMV, be combined with liquid ventilation (termed HFLOV by Toro-Figueroa) to achieve safer, more effective, and more efficient oxygenation and ventilation than with PLV? Harel et al. demonstrated in a pig near-drowning model that HFLOV is feasible, supports gas exchange, and improves static lung compliance beyond the effect of CMV (314% to 405%), HFOV (218% to 236%), or PLV (96% to 169%).

PLV Plus Nitric Oxide

The effects of PLV (perflubron loading dose of 5 ml/kg and maintenance dose of 2 ml/kg/hr) plus nitric oxide inhalation (NO at 80 ppm) and PLV alone were studied in a lamb model of congenital diaphragmatic hernia. Both groups showed improvement in compliance and Vт. With PLV plus NO inhalation a significant increase in oxygenation accompanied by a significant reduction in pulmonary hypertension was observed, both of which were reversed after cessation of NO therapy.

PLV Plus ECMO

Because of the advantages of liquid ventilation, CMV ("rest settings"), TLV (30 ml/kg loading dose and Vт 10 ± 10 ml/kg of perflubron at 5 bpm), and PLV (perflubron 30 ml/kg at CMV settings) were studied as adjuvants to ECMO (decreasing flows by 25% from a maximum of 80% of estimated cardiac output) while supporting neonatal lambs with acute lung injury induced with oleic acid and saline solution washout. Both TLV and PLV plus ECMO improved oxygenation and pulmonary compliance compared with CMV plus ECMO. TLV plus ECMO resulted in greater and sustained improvements compared with PLV plus ECMO. It was also concluded that the greater and sustained improvements experienced by the TLV plus ECMO group may have been related to greater clearance of pulmonary debris.

Pulmonary Administration of Antibiotics

Pulmonary administration and IV administration of gentamicin (5 mg/kg) was studied in newborn lambs during liquid ventilation. Intratracheal PFC gentamicin delivery achieved comparable serum levels as those achieved with IV administration. The lung tissue levels were higher and more homogeneous with pulmonary administration.

The feasibility of treating pneumonia by directly delivering antibiotics to the lung has been studied with a PFC emulsion (PFCe) as a delivery vehicle. In one study Wistar rats with pneumoccocal pneumonia were given either no treatment, a single dose of penicillin intramuscularly, or a similar dose of penicillin in PFCe instilled into the lungs. The 10-day survival rate for both treatment groups was 100% compared with 0% for the no-treatment group. The investigators concluded that penicillin in PFCe was as effective as intramuscular penicillin for treating lethal pneumonia in rats and that PFCe may be a viable therapeutic alternative for delivery of antibiotics to the lung.

Pulmonary Administration of Other Drugs

Neonatal lambs receiving liquid ventilation were used to study intravenously administered vasoactive drugs, including acetylcholine (0.01 to 1.0 mg/kg), epinephrine (0.001 to 0.5 mg/kg), and tolazoline HCl (0.5 to 2.0 mg/ml) vs. intrapulmonary administration of the same drugs and similar doses with PFC as a carrier. The measured heart rate, systemic arterial blood pressure, and CVP were plotted against the dose ranges studied (dose-response curves). The feasibility of delivering all these drugs was established, and all the intrapulmonary dose-response curves except for tolazoline HCl CVP shifted to the left compared with the IV curves. The tolazoline HCl CVP dose-response curve converged at doses <1.0 ml/kg.

PLV and Nosocomial Pneumonia

Because PLV requires instillation of sterile PFC through a commonly contaminated or colonized ET tube, concern about contamination of the airways and pulmonary parenchyma that can lead to nosocomial pneumonia led to a study examining the possibility of whether PLV with perflubron predisposes to nosocomial pneumonia. Investigators studied the viability and growth of *Pasteurella multocida* exposed to perflubron after 1, 2, and 3 hours at 37° C both in vitro (PFC plus *P. multocida* plus broth vs. *P. multocida* plus broth) and in vivo in pathogen-free rabbits (*P. multocida* plus PLV vs. *P. multocida* plus CMV). It was concluded that perflubron does not appear to have a bactericidal effect. These investigators also observed that PLV with perflubron does not increase the number of viable bacteria per gram of tissue and may even decrease colony counts. From these findings it was speculated that PLV with perflubron does not increase the risk for nosocomial pneumonia.

Other Potential Applications of Perfluorocarbons

Investigators have studied the potential of SLV with PFC (FC-77) for 20- and 30-minute periods in reducing bacterial growth and its effectiveness in treating Swiss-Webster mice 4, 8, and 12 hours after inoculation with pneumoccoci to cause lethal pneumonia compared with similarly inoculated control animals not exposed to PLV. They found no difference in survival rate or number of colony-forming units in SLV-treated animals compared with control animals. Also, no bacteria were recovered from the PFC drained from the lungs of the study animals. The same authors compared a series of blood agar plates freshly streaked with pneumococci and covered with PFC or a combination of PFC and saline solution or left uncovered and measured pneumococcal growth after 24 hours. Compared with the control plates, PFC and PFC plus saline solution did not prevent the growth of pneumoccoci on the experimental plates. This group of scientists concluded that FC-77 does not inhibit growth of pneumoccoci and that SLV by itself is not an effective treatment for lethal pneumococcal pneumonia in Swiss-Webster mice.

Anti-inflammatory Effects of Perfluorocarbons

Studies in several animal species, models, and cell lines have demonstrated that after in vivo and in vitro exposure to PFC (perflubron) there is a decrease in phytohemagglutinin responsiveness of lymphocytes and also in superoxide anion production, phagocytosis, and NO production by alveolar macrophages. Histologic inspection of PLV-supported lungs has shown that pulmonary tissue inflammation is reduced. Also it has been shown that perflubron emulsion does not activate endothelial cells (human umbilical vein), as measured by adhesion molecular expression, and does not prevent or modulate their activation by tumor necrosis factor or interleukin-1 but inhibits their activation by endotoxin and the liposaccharide-induced activation of RAW cells and their generation of tumor necrosis factor.

Physiology of PLV

Work is under way in an attempt to understand how the classic equations and indices used to describe gas exchange during gas ventilation compare with data observed and calculated in subjects undergoing PLV. One example of such work demonstrated that the alveolar gas equation overestimates PAO_2, intrapulmonary shunting, and risk of oxygen toxicity during PLV. In piglet (normal and meconium) models undergoing PLV with FiO_2 randomly varied at 0.45 to 1.0, the PaO_2 was calculated with the alveolar gas equation and by directly measuring Po_2 of the perflubron. These experiments demonstrated that during PLV functional FiO_2 is predictive of the PFC PaO_2 and is more accurate for prediction of PaO_2, risk of oxygen toxicity, $(A-a)DO_2$, and intrapulmonary shunting.

ADDITIONAL READING
Early Developments
• Kylstra JA, Paganeli CV, Lanphier EH. Pulmonary gas exchange in dogs ventilated with hyperbarically oxygenated liquid. J Appl Physiol 21:177, 1966.
• Kylstra JA, Tissing MO, Maen A. Of mice as fish. Trans Am Soc Artif Intern Organs 8:378, 1962.

Perfluorocarbons
• Clark LC, Gollan F. Survival of mammals breathing organic liquids equilibrated with oxygen at atmospheric pressure. Science 152:1755, 1966.
Gollan F, Clark LC. Prevention of bends by breathing an organic liquid. Trans Assoc Am Physician 80:102, 1967.
• Goodin TH, Grossbard EB, Kaufman RJ, et al. A perfluorochemical emulsion for hospital resuscitation of experimental shock: A prospective, randomized, controlled study. Crit Care Med 22:680-689, 1994.
Mattrey RF. Perfluorooctylbromide: A new contrast agent for CT, sonography and MR imaging. AJR 152:247-252, 1989.
Sass DJ, Ritman EL, Caskey PE, et al. Liquid breathing: Prevention of pulmonary arterio-venous shunting during acceleration. J Appl Physiol 32:451, 1972.
Thomas SR, Clark LC, Ackerman JL, et al. MR imaging of the lung using perfluorocarbons. J Comput Assist Tomog 10:1-9, 1986.

Total Liquid Ventilation

• Shaffer TH, Douglas PR, Lowe CA, et al. The effects of liquid ventilation on cardiopulmonary function in preterm lambs. Pediatr Res 17:303-306, 1983.

• Shaffer TH, Lowe CA, Bhutani VK, et al. Liquid ventilation: Effects on pulmonary function in meconium-stained lambs. Pediatr Res 18:47-52, 1984.

Shaffer TH, Tran H, Bhutani VK, et al. Cardiopulmonary function in very preterm lambs during liquid ventilation. Pediatr Res 17:680-684, 1983.

• Shaffer TH, Wolfson MR, Clark LC. Liquid ventilation—State of the art review. Pediatr Pulmonol 14:102-109, 1992.

• Wolfson MR, Greenspan KS, Rubenstien SD, et al. Comparison of gas and liquid ventilation: Clinical, physiological, and histological correlates. J Appl Physiol 72:1024-1031, 1992.

• Wolfson MR, Tran N, Bhutani VK, et al. A new experimental approach for the study of cardiopulmonary physiology during early development. J Appl Physiol 65:1436-1443, 1988.

Partial Liquid Ventilation: Animal Experiments

Curtis S. Perfluorocarbon-associated gas exchange: A hybrid approach to mechanical ventilation [editorial]. Crit Care Med 19:600-601, 1991.

• Curtis SE, Fuhrman BP, Howland DF, et al. Cardiac output during liquid (perfluorocarbon) breathing in newborn piglets. Crit Care Med 19:225-230, 1991.

• Curtis SE, Peek JT, Kelly DR. Partial liquid breathing with perflubron improves arterial oxygenation in acute canine lung injury. J Appl Physiol 75:2696-2702, 1993.

• Fuhrman BP, Paczan PR, DeFrancisis M. Perfluorocarbon-associated gas exchange. Crit Care Med 19:712-722, 1991.

Fuhrman BP, Papo MC, Hernan LJ, et al. Oxygenation and lung mechanics during 24h trials of perfluorocarbon associated gas exchange (PAGE) in piglets [abstr 226]. Pediatr Res 33(4, Pt 2):40A, 1993.

Leach CL, Fuhrman BP, Morin FC. Perfluorocarbon associated gas exchange (PAGE) with perflubron (LiquiVent) in respiratory distress syndrome (abstr 1309]. Pediatr Res 33(4, Pt 2):221A. 1993.

• Leach CL, Fuhrman BP, Morrin FC, et al. Perfluorocarbon-associated gas exchange (partial liquid ventilation) in respiratory distress syndrome: A prospective, randomized, controlled study. Crit Care Med 21:1270-1278, 1993.

Nesti FD, Fuhrman BP, Papo MC, et al. Perfluorocarbon associated gas exchange (PAGE) in gastric aspiration [abstr 215]. Pediatr Res 33(4, Pt 2):38A, 1993.

• Nesti FD, Fuhrman BP, Stienhorn DM, et al. Perfluorocarbon-associated gas exchange in gastric aspiration. Crit Care Med 22:1445-1452, 1994.

Notterman DA. A new PAGE in mechanical ventilation? Crit Care Med 21:1257-1259, 1993.

Overbeck MC, Pranikoff T, Yadao C, et al. Efficacy of partial perflurocarbon liquid ventilation in an adult model of acute respiratory distress syndrome [abstr]. Crit Care Med 23:A264, 1995.

Papo MC, Paczan P, Holm B, et al. A medical grade perfluorocarbon used during PAGE improves oxygenation and ventilation in a model of ARDS [abstr 219]. Pediatr Res 33(4, Pt 2):39A, 1993.

Parent AC, Overbeck MC, Hirschl RB. Measurement of cardiac output during partial liquid ventilation [abstr]. Crit Care Med 23:A243. 1995.

Thompson AE, Fuhrman BP, Alan J. Perfluorocarbon associated gas exchange (PAGE) in experimental meconium aspiration [abstr 1418]. Pediatr Res 33(4, Pt 2):239A, 1993.

• Tutuncu AS, Faithful NS, Lachmann B. Comparison of ventilatory support with intratracheal perfluorocarbon administration and conventional mechanical ventilation in animals with acute respiratory failure. Am Rev Respir Dis 148:785-792, 1993.

• Tutuncu AS, Faithful NS, Lachmann B. Intratracheal perfluorocarbon administration combined with mechanical ventilation in experimental respiratory distress syndrome: Dose-dependent improvement of gas exchange. Crit Care Med 21:962-969, 1993.

Partial Liquid Ventilation: Human Trials

• Greenspan JS, Wolfson MR, Rubinstien SD, et al. Liquid ventilation in preterm babies. Lancet 2:1095, 1989.

• Greenspan JS, Wolfson MR, Rubinstien SD, et al. Liquid ventilation in human preterm neonates. J Pediatr 117:106-111, 1990.

Hirschl RB, Grover B, McCraken M, et al. Oxygen consumption and carbon dioxide production during liquid ventilation. J Pediatr Surg 28:513-518, 1993.

Hirschl RB, Pranikoff T, Overbeck MC, et al. Pulmonary distribution and elimination of perfluorocarbon (PFC) during partial liquid ventilation in adult patients with respiratory failure [abstr]. Crit Care Med 23:A121, 1995.

Richman PS, Wolfson MR, Shaffer TH. Lung lavage with oxygenated perfluorochemical liquid in acute lung injury. Crit Care Med 21:768-774, 1993.

• Toro-Figueroa LO, Meliones JN, Curtis SE, et al. Perflubron partial liquid ventilation (PLV) in children with ARDS: A safety and efficacy pilot study [abstr 381]. Crit Care Med 24:A151, 1996.

High-Frequency Liquid Oxygenation Ventilation

Harel Y, Toro-Figueroa LO, Vinso R, et al. High frequency liquid oxygenation ventilation (HFLOV), a perfluorocarbon assisted gas exchange (PAGE) utilizing high frequency oscillatory ventilation (HFOV), is feasible and may improve synergistically lung compliance in a near drowning pig model [abstr]. Presented at the Eighth Annual Pediatric Critical Care Colloquium, St. Simon Island, October 1995.

PLV Plus Nitric Oxide

Wilcox DT, Glick PL, Karamonukian, et al. Perfluorocarbon associated gas exchange (PAGE) improves pulmonary mechanics and ventilation and assists in nitric oxide delivery in the hypoplastic congenital diaphragmatic hernia lamb model [abstr 50]. Extracorporeal Life Support Organization, October 1994.

PLV Plus ECMO

Wolfson MR, Friss HE, Billmire D, et al. Combined technologies: Liquid ventilation (LV) and extracorporeal life support (ECLS) for treatment of severe neonatal lung injury [abstr 49]. Extracorporeal Life Support Organization, October 1994.

Pulmonary Administration of Antibiotics

Dickson EW, Heard SO, Goodin T, et al. Use of a penicillin containing perfluorocarbon emulsion in the treatment of rats with lethal pneumococcal pneumonia [abstr 6]. Crit Care Med 24:A29, 1996.

Zelinka MA, Wolfson MR, Caligaro I, et al. Direct pulmonary administration of gentamicin during liquid ventilation of lamb: Comparison of lung and serum levels to IV administration [abstr 1723]. Pediatr Res 29(4, Pt 2):290A, 1991.

Pulmonary Administration of Other Drugs

Fox WW, Cox C, Farina C, et al. Liquid ventilation (LV) for pulmonary administration of gentamicin (G) in acute lung injury. Pediatr Res 35(4, Pt2):1362A, 1994.

Wolfson MR, Greenspan JS, Shaffer TH. Pulmonary administration of vasoactive drugs (PAD) by perfluorocarbon liquid ventilation. Pediatr Res 29(4, Pt 2):336A, 1991.

Wolfson MR, Shaffer TH. Pulmonary administration of drugs (PAD): A new approach for drug delivery using liquid ventilation. FASEB J 4:A1105, 1990.

Other Potential Applications of Perfluorocarbons

Dickson EW, Heard SO, Goodin T, et al. Spontaneous perfluorocarbon ventilation as a treatment for lethal pneumococcal pneumonia in mice [abstr 230]. Crit Care Med 24:A106, 1996.

Sjan I, Steihorn DM. The risk of nosocomial pneumonia is not increased during partial liquid ventilation (PLV) with perflubron (PFB) [abstr 232]. Crit Care Med 24:A106, 1996.

Anti-inflammatory Effects of Perfluorocarbons

Lane T, Smith D, Wancewicz E, et al. Inhibition of endotoxin-mediated activation of endothelial cells by a perfluorocarbon emulsion. Biomater Artif Cells Artif Immunobiol Biotech 21:163-172, 1993.

Nesti FD, Fuhrman BP, Ballow M, et al. Modulation of PHA (phytohaemagglutination) responsiveness with perflubron in acid aspiration pneumonitis [abstr]. Crit Care Med 23:A213, 1995.

Steinhorn DM, Smith TM, Fuhrman BP. Liquid perfluorocarbon (PFC) affects phagocytosis by alveolar macrophages (AM) after in vitro exposure [abstr]. Crit Care Med 23:A213, 1995.

Physiology of PLV

Herman LJ, Penfil S, Fuhrman BP, et al. Functional Fio_2 ($fFio_2$) predicts alveolar Po_2 (Pao_2) during perfluorocarbon associated gas exchange (PAGE) [abstr 375]. Crit Care Med 24:A149, 1996.

160 Extracorporeal Membrane Oxygenation

Carol L. Bieler · Amir Vardi · John Darling · Nick G. Anas

BACKGROUND

Extracorporeal membrane oxygenation (ECMO) for support of cardiopulmonary function is a direct extension of cardiopulmonary bypass (CPB) technology developed for cardiothoracic surgery. Initially CPB was accomplished with bubble oxygenators, which are characterized by a direct blood-gas interface. These are still used today and have the advantages of rapid setup time and relatively low expense but the disadvantage that the blood-gas interface produces physical stress on the red blood cells, resulting in hemolysis if used for more than a few hours. ECMO became possible with the advent of membrane oxygenators, which separate the blood and gas phases with a semipermeable membrane. This protects the red blood cells and prevents significant hemolysis, allowing safe extracorporeal oxygenation for longer periods.

Clinical reports of long-term membrane CPB for pulmonary support in patients with acute respiratory failure (ARF) were first published in the early 1970s; by 1974 CPB had been used in 150 adult patients with ARF. The growing interest in the clinical application of this technology resulted in the National Institutes of Health (NIH) multicenter, randomized study designed to compare the efficacy of ECMO vs. conventional mechanical ventilation in adult patients with severe ARF. The results of this study had a large impact on the future of ECMO: although ECMO could support gas exchange, there was no difference in survival rate; therefore use of ECMO was discouraged.

Critics of the NIH study suggested that it was doomed to failure because the clinical entry criteria selected patients who already had irreversible lung disease with fibrotic changes. They believed that at the time ECMO was offered to these patients the lungs were damaged to a degree that obviated lung repair and survival. It was suggested that ECMO be reevaluated in a group of patients who clearly had reversible lung disease. Neonates with persistent pulmonary hypertension of the newborn (PPHN) were identified as such a group. In the first days of life these infants can have life-threatening ARF that generally resolves as pulmonary vascular resistance decreases. Improvement in patient survival among these neonates established ECMO as a therapy for PPHN. Over the past two decades ECMO has become an accepted therapy for ARF in neonates. In addition, ECMO has evolved as a potential alternative to conventional medical management for pediatric respiratory failure also. However, defining maximal conventional therapy, determining cardiopulmonary variables that predict mortality, and identifying patients with reversible lung disease are still controversial.

INDICATIONS

The largest single group of patients receiving ECMO support is infants with PPHN secondary to meconium aspiration syndrome, congenital diaphragmatic hernia, pneumonia, sepsis, or idiopathic causes. ECMO is presently offered only when conventional mechanical ventilation fails and the patient meets criteria for predicted mortality of ≥80% (most predicted mortality is based on Extracorporeal Life Support Organization (ELSO) registry data and recent pediatric reviews). The international neonatal ECMO experience has shown an overall survival rate of 81%, according to the most recent report distributed by ELSO. Infants with meconium aspiration syndrome have the highest survival rate (94%), whereas infants with congenital diaphragmatic hernia have lower survival rates (58%), most likely secondary to associated pulmonary hypoplasia. Pediatric patients given ECMO have an overall survival rate of 51% despite advances in pulmonary support for ARF.

ECMO is being used for cardiac support as well, most commonly in patients with cardiac failure after cardiothoracic surgery. The outcome in these patients correlates with the cause of the cardiac failure, with a survival rate of 48%. Patients in whom ECMO was offered immediately after surgery because of inability to be weaned from CPB have many bleeding complications and little improvement in survival. In contrast, patients who are able to be weaned from CPB but who have progressive cardiac failure in the hours after surgery have had better results with ECMO support. The number of patients in these groups remains small, and more experience is needed before specific guidelines for ECMO inclusion or exclusion can be formulated. In addition, ECMO may be used as a bridge to cardiac transplantation.

Before ECMO therapy is initiated, patients must meet two basic criteria: they must have reversible primary disease and their degree of illness must be severe enough that their prognosis with standard conventional therapy is poor. ECMO may only postpone death if the disease process is irreversible.

TECHNIQUE
Apparatus

The two basic types of ECMO are venoarterial (VA) and veno-venous (VV). This terminology describes the direction of blood flow: outflow is always from the venous system, whereas inflow can be either into the arterial (VA) circulation or the venous (VV) circulation. Variants of artificial membrane gas exchange techniques include extracorporeal CO_2 removal and intravascular oxygenation (see p. 1516).

Over the last few years VV bypass has gained wider acceptance in both the neonatal and pediatric noncardiac populations. This mode of bypass eliminates use and possible ligation of the carotid artery, maintains blood flow to the lungs, and preserves a normal pulsatile blood flow. In addition, VV bypass eliminates potential obstruction of the left outflow tract and coronary circulation. Before choosing VV ECMO, the physician must consider the patient's age and size, the underlying disease process, and whether cardiac support is necessary. VV ECMO is difficult to perform in the absence of adequate intrinsic cardiac function.

Outflow of blood in VA or VV ECMO is through a catheter placed in the right atrium through the right internal jugular vein. A number of catheter types can be used, but to maximize venous return, large-bore (12 to 27 F) catheters tooled with multiple side holes are used. The diameter of the venous catheter and the height of the patient are the rate-limiting factors for gravity drainage of venous blood. The resistance to flow is directly proportional to the fourth power of the radius of the catheter and inversely proportional to its length. Thus the catheter needs to have as wide an inner diameter as the vessel will accommodate and be as short as possible. If adequate blood return to the ECMO circuit cannot be achieved, it may prove beneficial to elevate the patient's bed on blocks or add an additional venous cannula for increased blood return. Because the maintenance of adequate venous flow is often the most difficult part of ECMO, proper catheter size, design, and placement are critical as well as adequate patient intravascular volume.

From the catheter the blood enters a small collapsible bladder in the ECMO circuit (Fig. 160-1) that is attached to a servoregulated box connected to the roller pump. Inadequate blood return triggers an alarm on the bladder box and the pump shuts off. Once the bladder refills, the pump restarts. This safety mechanism is important in case of a kinked cannula or circuit and in the event hypovolemia develops. If a centrifugal pump is used and blood return is inadequate, the pump may generate increased negative pressure. Such negative pressure forms when blood inflow to the pump is slower than the flow enforced by the pump. Negative pressure may create air emboli from dissolved blood gases or severe hemolysis and may damage the tissues in contact with the cannula tip. Operating room bypass systems overcome this problem by means of a large blood reservoir placed between the patient and the pump. This solution is impractical when full anticoagulation is not used, as in ECMO.

After exiting the bladder, the blood is actively pumped by an occlusive pump or a centrifugal pump. Roller pumps are most commonly used, but in patients in whom >300 ml flow rates are necessary, use of a centrifugal pump is just as common. The flow generated by the pump depends on cannula size (both diameter and length), tubing size, and revolutions per minute.

Immediately beyond the pump is the membrane oxygenator (Fig. 160-2). The oxygenator is a hollow silicone rubber envelope rolled around a spool and

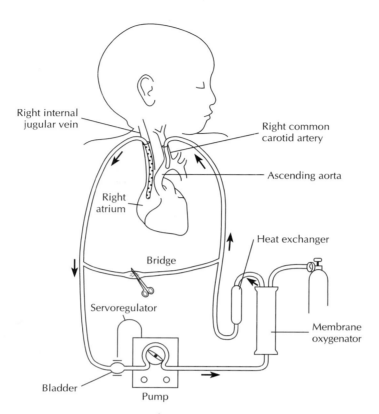

Fig. 160-1 Venoarterial ECMO.

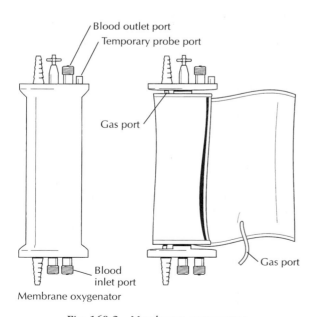

Fig. 160-2 Membrane oxygenator.

placed inside a fitted silicone sleeve. Blood flows on the outside of the coiled envelope, and gas flows in a countercurrent direction inside the membrane. Oxygen and carbon dioxide diffuse across the semipermeable membrane, and carbon dioxide is flushed from the gas compartment by the gas flow. Membranes are available in sizes ranging from 0.4 to 4.5 m^2 and are chosen depending on the size of the patient. Each membrane lung has specified blood and gas flow rates that enable the user to achieve optimal gas exchange. Next the blood flows through a heat exchanger, where countercurrent servoregulated heated water compensates for heat loss in the extracorporeal circulation.

Finally, blood is infused into the patient through a single end-hole catheter. In VA ECMO the catheter is placed in the right common carotid artery and advanced into the ascending aorta. This site is used to return the oxygenated blood as close to the aortic root as possible to guarantee delivery of well-oxygenated blood to the cerebral and coronary circulations. The arterial cannula is the main resistor to flow from the ECMO circuit to the patient. A short catheter with a relatively large inner diameter is indicated. Increased resistance at this point will cause increased postoxygenator pressure, creating back pressure and decreased oxygenator efficiency as well as hemolysis. In VV ECMO blood is returned to either the internal jugular vein (double-lumen cannula) or the femoral vein.

The ECMO circuit is designed with a bridge that allows the child and the circuit to be isolated from one another.

Use of an arterial filter is optional. Early experience suggests a filter on the arterial limb may cause microemboli after long-term use. However, some centers do use an air trap.

ECMO circuit priming volume varies among medical centers. Before a patient is given ECMO, the circuit is primed with packed red blood cells, albumin, calcium gluconate, and heparin, and the fluid is corrected to normal pH (Table 160-1). The prime is heparinized to avoid thrombus formation and embolization to the patient; this is critical in VA ECMO, in which blood is returned to the carotid artery, allowing direct access to the coronary and cerebral circulations. Anticoagulation is achieved in most cases with heparin. The whole-blood heparin effect is measured and maintained at an activated clotting time (ACT) of 180 to 220 seconds, which prevents clotting in the extracorporeal circulation (normal ACT, 90 to 120 seconds). Heparinization is monitored by ACT testing, which can be done easily at the bedside. Antithrombin III has recently been recommended to enhance the effect of heparin and limit the amount of heparin necessary to achieve adequate anticoagulation.

Procedure

When ECMO support is initiated, the clinician must select the rates for ECMO flow and gas flow through the oxygenator.

In both the neonatal and pediatric populations adequate ECMO flow can be reliably assessed clinically by evaluating arterial blood gas and pH values and the adequacy of perfusion. Attempts to document ECMO flow as a percentage of cardiac output have proved difficult because normal cardiac output is variable. Therefore most clinicians express ECMO flow as milliliters per kilogram per minute. Cardiac output

Table 160-1 Blood Prime Protocol at Children's Medical Center of Dallas*

Circuit	Dose	Priming Volume (ml)
Neonatal		600
THAM	75 ml	
Calcium gluconate	400 mg	
Albumin, 5%	60 ml	
Beef lung heparin	500 U	
Packed RBCs	400-480 ml	
Pediatric		800
THAM	85 ml	
Calcium gluconate	500 mg	
Albumin, 5%	80 ml	
Beef lung heparin	500 U	
Packed RBCs	600-650 ml	
Adult		1000
THAM	100 ml	
Calcium gluconate	600 mg	
Albumin, 5%	100 ml	
Beef lung heparin	500 U	
Packed RBCs	750-800 ml	

*Before the ECMO circuit is primed with the premixed blood prime, it is primed with a Normasol and heparin solution to eliminate air in the circuit.

may be as high as 300 ml/kg/min in the neonate and decrease to around 100 ml/kg/min as the child approaches adolescence. The percentage of cardiac output supported by ECMO is therefore estimated by evaluating the systemic arterial tracing. Because VA ECMO flow is nonpulsatile, the systemic arterial tracing will appear blunted or flattened when a large percentage of the cardiac output is captured during ECMO. As ECMO flow becomes a smaller portion of the cardiac output the tracing will become more pulsatile. Some clinicians suggest that a totally flattened arterial tracing correlates with ECMO flow rates >80% of cardiac output. This phenomenon is different with VV ECMO because normal pulsatile flow is maintained in the arterial circulation.

The flow and composition of gases through the membrane oxygenator are adjusted to achieve desired arterial blood gas values. During ECMO a combination of oxygen, air, and carbon dioxide flow through the oxygenator countercurrent to blood flow.

The correct ratio of gases is determined by the following patient and ECMO circuit features:

1. Age, and hence efficiency of the membrane
2. Size of membrane oxygenator
3. Amount of ECMO flow
4. Patient metabolic rate
5. Patient cardiac output

Any alteration in gas composition needs to be assessed with either in-line blood gas monitoring equipment or direct laboratory analysis.

Management

When the patient is stable and adequate arterial blood gas values have been obtained, the conventional ventilator settings are decreased to minimize acute lung injury. At our center we use peak end-expiratory pressure (PEEP) of 10 to 12 cm H_2O and peak inspiratory pressure (PIP) of 20 cm H_2O to minimize atelectasis or "lung whiteout" after initiation of ECMO. If ECMO flow is inadequate to sustain normal arterial blood gas values, the patient's own lungs must also participate in gas exchange, and the ventilator settings are adjusted accordingly.

Use of muscle relaxants is discontinued. The patient is allowed to move but is sedated to keep the amount of spontaneous movement within a safe range so as not to dislodge the cannula. In addition, the patient is given analgesia to eliminate pain. The patient remains supine with the head of the bed adjusted to maintain maximum blood flow to and from the cannula.

Duration

The duration of ECMO support depends on the primary disease and patient age. The risk of complications increases when no improvement in pulmonary function is noted within the first week of ECMO therapy. The decision to extend ECMO beyond 14 days must be considered individually for each patient in exceptional cases.

Neonates with ARF commonly undergo ECMO for 7 to 10 days. In these children ECMO is continued until the patient's lungs can support gas exchange with minimal to moderate ventilator support, typically PIP <30 cm H_2O, PEEP <8 cm H_2O, Fio_2 <0.50, and respiratory rate <35 breaths/min. ECMO in the pediatric patient is not yet well defined, and lung recovery (i.e., increased lung compliance) by the end of the first week of ECMO may prove to be a good prognostic indicator in this population as well. The readiness of the patient's lungs can be evaluated radiographically or with a documented increase in lung compliance or increased ability to sustain gas exchange. The ability to sustain gas exchange is assessed by determining arterial blood gas values while ventilator settings are increased and ECMO flow is weaned or by short trials without ECMO.

Other life-support techniques may be regarded as variants of ECMO. Extracorporeal CO_2 removal ($ECco_2R$) is a technique used for support of ventilatory failure. Extracorporeal flow is veno-venous and significantly less than that with ECMO. The purpose is to decrease the volutrauma caused by mechanical ventilation. Apneic oxygenation is achieved through the native lungs with low-rate, low-pressure positive pressure ventilation. In Europe (much more than in North America) experience is growing with use of $ECco_2R$ for treatment of acute respiratory distress syndrome.

Intravascular oxygenation (IVOX) is another technique for support of oxygenation. The membrane oxygenation concept is used, but rather than diverting the patient's blood to an extracorporeal circulation, a small membrane oxygenator is inserted into the inferior vena cava. Oxygenator size and efficiency limit this technique to adult patients in need of limited support. The IVOX technique is presently used mainly under research protocols.

Neither of these techniques supports cardiac function, and support provided to the pulmonary system is limited. However, these support systems are beneficial in many patients in whom conventional mechanical ventilation fails.

RISKS AND COMPLICATIONS

Risks and complications associated with ECMO do not differ in the neonatal and pediatric populations.

Hemorrhage. Hemorrhage is one of the most life-threatening complications associated with ECMO; heparinization is thought to be the most likely cause. Bleeding can occur in any organ, including the CNS, lungs, GI tract, kidneys, and subcutaneous tissue, and at the cannulation site. Children in whom ECMO is initiated after surgery (e.g., because of congenital diaphragmatic hernia) may have significant blood loss at the surgical site.

Although bleeding can occur anywhere, intracranial hemorrhage is the most devastating. In the case of intracranial bleeding the cause is most likely multifactorial (e.g., heparinization; ligation of the right

TECHNIQUE
Thoracentesis
Equipment

Equipment necessary for safe diagnostic or therapeutic thoracentesis includes the following:

Thoracentesis equipment

Surgical mask and cap
Sterile gloves
Goggles
Povidone-iodine solution, 10%
Lidocaine without epinephrine, 1%
Sterile drapes
Syringes, 5 and 30 ml
Needles, 25 and 22 gauge
Collection basin
IV catheter assembly, 20 or 18 gauge
Three-way stopcock
IV extension tubing
Sterile occlusive dressing
Culture tubes
Laboratory tubes for blood cell count and chemistry analysis

Procedure

Appropriate analgesia and sedation are needed. Because of the potential for respiratory depression, the child must be closely observed during and for several hours after the procedure. SaO_2 monitoring is prudent, and an assistant needs to be present to help maintain patient position and help with equipment.

The patient is placed in a comfortable position that ensures adequate exposure to the chest. Infants and small children may be placed supine with a small roll under the affected hemithorax and the arm positioned above the head. Alternatively, the child can be held in an adult's lap with the head over the shoulder and the legs about the waist. Older children may sit upright with their arms supported on a bedside table (Fig. 161-1).

The thoracentesis site is determined by correlating results of physical examination and radiologic studies. The fluid level can be determined by dullness to percussion or demonstrably marked on ultrasound scans. In general the best site is just inferior to the tip of the scapula, between the posterior axillary line and the edge of the paraspinous muscles. It is often helpful to mark the site with a pen before draping since surface landmarks may be obscured.

Cap, mask, and sterile gloves are donned after scrubbing, and goggles must be worn. The patient's skin is widely painted with povidone-iodine solution and draped with sterile towels. The site is anesthetized with use of a 5 ml syringe and 25-gauge needle to raise a skin wheal with 1% lidocaine. The subcutaneous tissue and chest wall (including the rib periosteum and pleura) are anesthetized with a longer 22-gauge needle. This needle is advanced into the pleural space while gently aspirating the syringe to locate the air or fluid collection. Both the anesthesia needle and the subsequent thoracentesis catheter must pass over the top of the rib to prevent injury to the neurovascular bundle located along the inferior border of each rib. If fluid or air cannot be aspirated, it may be necessary to use a site one intercostal space higher or lower and repeat the process.

Once the fluid collection is located, the IV catheter assembly is placed on a syringe and inserted through the anesthetized tissue into the pleural space. When the needle passes through the pleura a "pop" is generally felt and fluid or air will return to the syringe. The outer catheter is advanced into the pleural space and the needle extracted. The 30 ml syringe with an attached stopcock is rapidly placed on the catheter hub to prevent air from entering the pleural space. During the brief time while removing the inner needle and attaching the stopcock, the hub must be covered with a gloved finger. Some commercially available kits contain a catheter that can be advanced through the needle, which eliminates the need to change syringes and reduces the risk for pneumothorax.

For diagnostic thoracentesis, only enough fluid is aspirated to perform necessary laboratory analyses. For therapeutic thoracentesis, the largest possible amount of air or fluid is aspirated. Complete evacuation is facilitated by attaching the IV extension tubing to the third arm of the stopcock. When the syringe is full, the stopcock can be turned so the fluid is emptied through the extension tubing into the collection basin. By returning the stopcock to its initial position, further aspiration can be carried out without disconnecting the syringe and catheter. When the air or fluid is completely aspirated, the catheter is withdrawn with continuous suction, and a sterile occlusive dressing is applied. The pleural fluid is sent for appropriate studies, and a chest radiograph is obtained to access the effectiveness of the thoracentesis and to exclude pneumothorax.

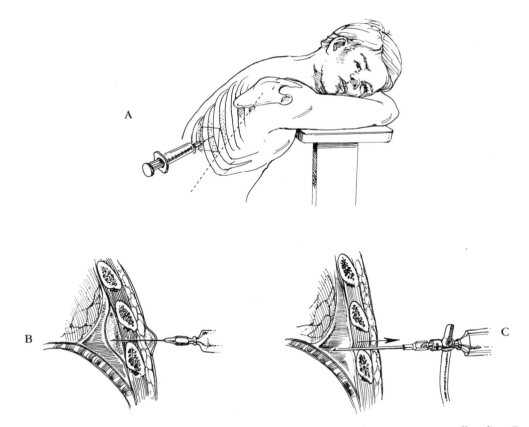

Fig. 161-1 Thoracentesis. **A,** Infiltration of skin site. Dashed line indicates posterior axillary line. **B,** Infiltration of intercostal tissues and pleura. **C,** Aspiration of fluid.

Chest Tube Insertion
Equipment

For tube thoracostomy the following equipment is needed:

Chest tube insertion equipment

Surgical mask and cap
Sterile gloves
Goggles
Povidone-iodine solution, 10%
Lidocaine without epinephrine, 1%
Sterile drapes
Syringes, 5 and 10 ml
Needles, 25 and 22 gauge
No. 15 scalpel blade
Suture for securing chest tube to skin (e.g., 2-0 silk)
Chest tube (see Table 161-2 for suggested sizes)

Chest tube drainage system
Thoracostomy tray
   Hemostats
   No. 3 scalpel handle
   Sponges
   Needle holder
   Tube clamp
   Scissors
Sterile occlusive dressing

Open tube thoracostomy

The patient is premedicated as described and positioned supine with a small roll below the affected hemithorax, and the arm is raised above the head if possible.

The insertion site is determined by physical ex-

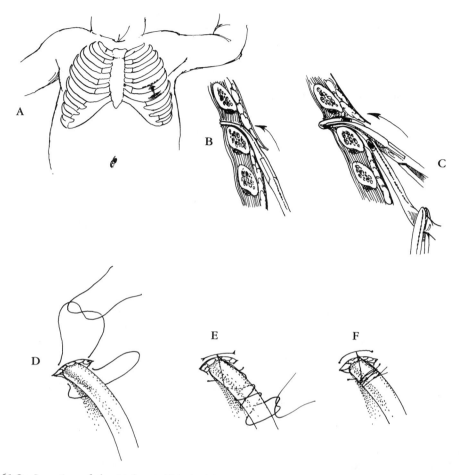

Fig. 161-2   Insertion of chest tube. **A,** Skin incision. **B,** Hemostat dissection. **C,** Insertion of chest tube. **D-F,** Securing of chest tube.

amination and correlation with radiographic studies. Because a supine patient lies on more posterior tubes, most chest tubes are placed anterior to the posterior axillary line. A tube used primarily to drain fluid is placed low in the chest (between the fifth and seventh intercostal spaces). The nipple is located at the level of the fourth intercostal space and is a useful surface landmark. Insertion lower than the seventh rib may cause injury to the diaphragm, liver, spleen, or other abdominal viscera. Chest tubes placed to evacuate a pneumothorax may be placed higher (second or third intercostal space) to prevent injury to the diaphragm. Tubes placed in the midclavicular line at

the second intercostal space are effective, but the more lateral position may be more cosmetically acceptable and more easily accomplished.

Cap, mask, and sterile gloves are donned after scrubbing, and goggles must be worn. The patient's skin is widely painted with povidone-iodine solution and draped with sterile towels. The skin incision is made with a No. 15 blade at least one interspace below the intercostal space through which the tube will enter the pleural cavity (Fig. 161-2). This creates a subcutaneous tunnel that helps prevent contamination from the skin and reduces the likelihood that a pneumothorax will develop during chest tube re-

Table 161-2   Choice of Chest Tube

| Patient Weight (kg) | Chest Tube Size (F) | | |
| | Pneumothorax* | Pleural Effusion† | |
		Transudate	Exudate
<3	8-10	8-10	10-12
3-8	10-12	10-12	12-16
9-15	12-16	12-16	16-20
16-40	16-20	16-20	20-28
>40	20-24	24-28	28-36

*With pneumothorax, the chest tube must be inserted high in the chest (second or third intercostal space) in the anterior or midaxillary line and directed anteriorly and superiorly.

†With pleural effusion, the chest tube must be inserted low in the chest (fifth through seventh intercostal space) in the midaxillary or posterior axillary line and directed posteriorly and inferiorly.

moval. A skin wheal is raised with a 25-gauge needle and lidocaine. The subcutaneous tissue, rib periosteum, chest wall muscle, and pleura are anesthetized with use of the longer 22-gauge needle. It is important to give adequate anesthesia because this procedure can be quite painful.

An appropriately sized chest tube is selected (Table 161-2), and the approximate depth of insertion is determined. It is important that the proximal fenestration of the tube comes to rest well within the pleural cavity. If necessary, the distal end of the tube can be trimmed.

The skin and subcutaneous tissue are incised with a No. 15 scalpel, and the tract of the tube is dissected by inserting a hemostat through the incision over the rib and into the pleural cavity. Considerable force is often needed, and a definite "pop" is generally felt. Entry into the pleural space is confirmed by a rush of air or fluid. The jaws of the hemostat are spread to dissect a tract adequate for insertion of the tube.

The tip of the chest tube is placed between the tips of the hemostat and advanced through the tunnel into the pleural space. When the hemostat is released, the tube can be advanced to the level previously determined. If the tube is being inserted because of pneumothorax, an anterior position is ideal. If it is being placed to drain fluid, a posterior and inferior direction is desirable.

Heavy silk or nylon suture material is used to secure the chest tube to the skin. The chest tube is connected to the drainage system, and connections are secured with tape to prevent accidental disconnection. Regulated suction (-20 cm H_2O) is applied to the system to fully reexpand the lung.

A small occlusive sterile dressing is applied, and a chest radiograph is obtained to confirm chest tube position and expansion of the lung.

Percutaneous tube thoracostomy

Pure pneumothorax or transudative effusion may be adequately evacuated with the Seldinger technique and specially designed catheter kits. This approach is quicker and less painful than traditional chest tube insertion. Skin preparation and administration of anesthesia are the same as with the open technique. When the insertion site has been determined, a seeker needle is passed over the rib into the pleural space with continuous aspiration. After air or fluid is obtained, a guidewire is inserted into the pleural space through the seeker needle. The skin incision is enlarged, and after dilation of the tract the chest tube is inserted over the guidewire to the predetermined depth. The chest tube is secured and attached to the collection system. Application of an occlusive dressing and procurement of a confirmatory radiograph complete the procedure.

Chest Tube Care

It is unwise to clamp a chest tube. Tube occlusion may cause tension pneumothorax or hydrothorax.

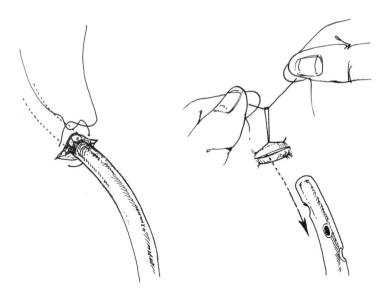

Fig. 161-3   Removal of the chest tube. **A,** First throw of a knot in the mattress suture. **B,** Removal of chest tube and tying of pursestring suture.

For similar reasons, the tubing between the chest tube and drainage system must not become kinked. Securing the tubing to bed sheets averts kinking and prevents the weight of the tubing pulling on the securing sutures. To prevent occlusion, tubes that drain blood or fibrinous material are occasionally stripped. Sterile water must be added periodically to the suction control chamber and the underwater seal chamber. As air bubbles escape through the chamber, water evaporates and the level of suction decreases.

If the patient is to be transferred or transported to another bed, the drainage system must remain below the level of the chest; the chest tube is not clamped during transport. Even without suction, the water seal mechanism allows air to escape from the pleural space and prevents entry of external air.

Chest Tube Removal

Sedation is provided if indicated. The securing suture is untied and unwound from about the chest tube. The first throw of a square knot is placed in the suture (Fig. 161-3). During a deep Valsalva maneuver or during inspiration if the patient is receiving positive pressure ventilation, the chest tube is *rapidly* withdrawn, and the pursestring suture is tied. An assistant holds pressure over the subcutaneous tract while the tube is removed and the suture is secured. A dry sterile dressing is placed over the wound. If the pursestring suture is not used, a petroleum jelly dressing or other occlusive dressing is used to cover the insertion site to prevent air entry and possible pneumothorax. A chest radiograph is obtained to exclude pneumothorax after chest tube removal.

RISKS AND COMPLICATIONS

During dissection or insertion of a tube the lung parenchyma may be entered, resulting in bleeding or pneumothorax. The diaphragm, liver, spleen, or other abdominal viscera may be injured if thoracentesis or chest tube placement is attempted too inferiorly. Pressure of an apical chest tube on the sympathetic chain may cause pain, temporary Horner's syndrome, or vascular compression.

Pleural contamination and empyema can result from interruption of sterile technique. If the proximal fenestration in the tube is not within the pleural space, subcutaneous emphysema and inadequate evacuation of the pleural space may result. Insertion too close to the inferior margin of the rib may cause injury to the neurovascular bundle. Abnormal breast development may result from a tube placed too near the areola in a female patient.

ADDITIONAL READING

Andrews CO. Pleural effusions: Pathophysiology and management. Ann Pharmacother 28:894-903, 1994.

Gross SB. Current challenges, concepts, and, controversies in chest tube management. AACN Clin Issues Crit Care Nurs 4:260-275, 1993.

Harriss DR, Graham TR. Management of intercostal drains. Br J Hosp Med 45:383-386, 1991.

Iberti TJ, Stern PM. Chest tube thoracoscopy. Crit Care Clin 8:879-895, 1992.

Lewis KT, Bukstein DA. Parapneumonic empyema in children: Diagnosis and management. Am Fam Physician 46:1443-1455, 1992.

McCartney JP, Adams JW, Hazard PB. Safety of thoracentesis in mechanically ventilated patients. Chest 103:1920-1921, 1993.

Quigley RL. Thoracentesis and chest tube drainage. Crit Care Clin 11:111-126, 1995.

162 Tracheotomy

Orval E. Brown · Michael J. Biavati · Scott C. Manning ·
Paula Jean Dimmitt · Susan Ballard

BACKGROUND AND INDICATIONS

Tracheotomy as a treatment for airway obstruction has been known since antiquity. The first successful tracheotomy is attributed to Brasavola in 1546, and Alexander the Great allegedly performed a tracheotomy in the 4th century B.C. The use of tracheotomy was characterized by poor success until the early 1900s, when Chevalier Jackson introduced a systematic approach to the management of airway obstruction with endoscopy and tracheotomy. Recent studies have revealed a changing set of indications for tracheotomy, standardization of the surgical procedure, appropriate management of early and late complications, and a systematic approach to in-hospital and home care.

In the early 1900s tracheotomy was primarily performed because of infectious causes of upper airway obstruction (e.g., diphtheria). In recent decades a marked shift has taken place in the indications for tracheotomy in pediatric patients. Infections such as diphtheria have largely been controlled with immunization and antimicrobial therapy, and many children with complex CNS, cardiac, and respiratory problems survive who would have died in the early 1900s. The increasing survival of these patients with their attendant multiple medical problems has resulted in an increased number of tracheotomies performed in patients without primary airway problems. The most common indication is prolonged ET intubation with mechanical ventilation, most frequently in patients with cardiac and CNS disorders, craniofacial surgery, or respiratory distress syndrome. Patients with CNS disorders usually have neurologic deficits after head trauma, intracranial tumor, or cardiac resuscitation. Prolonged ET intubation can cause significant laryngeal damage and result in acquired subglottic stenosis; proper tube management helps minimize this problem. Patients who will likely need prolonged ventilatory support are candidates for tracheotomy. In general patients who need ET tubes for longer than 2 weeks may be candidates for evaluation; neonates, however, tolerate intubation longer than older children, and the decision for tracheotomy in these patients is individualized.

Laryngeal problems can necessitate tracheotomy. Vocal cord paralysis with an inadequate airway may be an indication for tracheotomy. Congenital subglottic stenosis usually is manifested early in life with significant airway obstruction compared with acquired subglottic stenosis secondary to intubation or laryngeal injury. In many of these patients a tracheostomy is needed until laryngeal reconstruction can be performed. Neonates with congenital laryngeal malformations such as hemangioma or cystic hygroma may need a tracheostomy. Traumatic injuries such as severe facial fractures or facial and airway burns or laryngeal fractures may necessitate tracheotomy along with expedited repair of the injury; however, such severe injuries in pediatric patients often are fatal. Patients with severe laryngomalacia, which results in failure to thrive or CO_2 retention or may result in cor pulmonale, may need a tracheostomy for a year or so. Patients with severe obstructive sleep apnea and CO_2 retention despite previous treatment with tonsillectomy and adenoidectomy may need a tracheostomy. This is more common in patients with underlying conditions such as Down syndrome with a large tongue and hypotonia and cerebral palsy with hypertonic airway reflexes. Some patients with Pierre Robin syndrome with severe upper airway obstruction that does not respond to positioning may require a tracheostomy. In many of these patients the tracheostomy tube can be removed after about a year as their condition improves. Tracheotomy performed because of laryngeal papillomas is extremely uncommon now because CO_2 laser suspension microlaryngoscopy is used to control the disease. Also, it is believed that tracheotomy may result in implantation of papilloma in the trachea and tracheal stoma, and the procedure is generally considered only when absolutely necessary.

Some conditions previously treated with tracheotomy may be managed successfully with other methods. Epiglottitis is treated with intubation in the operating room, and patients are observed for about 48 hours in the PICU. This procedure is associated with less morbidity and mortality than tracheotomy in this patient population, and tracheotomy is almost never used at our institution to manage acute epiglottitis. Viral laryngotracheobronchitis (croup) that does not respond to maximum medical management is treated with intubation with a small ET tube for 2 to 5 days. Tracheotomy is considered in patients with croup that persists after extubation. It is believed by some authors that patients younger than 1 year with croup who need airway support need to undergo tracheotomy because of a high prevalence of acquired subglottic stenosis. This approach is controversial, and in our clinical experience some of these patients with croup will do well with short-term intubation.

TECHNIQUE

Tracheotomy in the infant and small child is performed in the operating room under proper lighting and magnification, including the use of 2.5× loupes. In unusual circumstances when a patient is too unstable to be transported to the operating suite, tracheotomy may be performed in the PICU. In this instance the complete surgical team and proper instruments are brought to the patient's bedside in the PICU to provide proper support.

Patients undergoing tracheotomy are initially managed with ET intubation or the airway is secured with a bronchoscope, and appropriate anesthesia is administered. Tracheotomy in a young struggling infant who has been given a local anesthetic agent is a hazardous procedure fraught with complications, particularly pneumothorax. The patient is placed in the supine position with a head roll under the shoulders and with the head extended. The patient's head and neck are positioned absolutely straight to assist in identifying midline anatomic landmarks such as the trachea and the cricoid and thyroid cartilages. Nasogastric tubes and esophageal stethoscopes are removed so that a rigid tube in the esophagus cannot be mistaken for the trachea (Fig. 162-1).

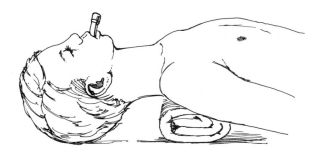

Fig. 162-1 Position of patient for tracheotomy.

Surgery

After routine sterile preparation the patient is draped, leaving the face and ET tube or bronchoscope exposed. This exposure facilitates management of the ET tube during placement of the tracheostomy tube and prevents accidental kinking and dislodgment of the tube. Since tracheotomy is a clean but not sterile procedure, this presents no serious break in surgical technique. The landmarks of the hyoid bone, cricoid cartilage, and sternal notch must be easily palpable.

A small transverse skin incision is made at approximately the level of the third tracheal ring (Fig. 162-2, *A*). Dissection is carried down through the subcutaneous tissue to the strap muscles, and excessive subcutaneous tissue may be excised to provide a cleaner wound. The strap muscles are separated in the midline and grasped with an Allis forceps. Midline dissection and absolute hemostasis are essential.

The thyroid isthmus and thymus gland are identified, and the thymus gland is retracted inferiorly with a vein retractor. The thyroid isthmus is dissected from the trachea with a small hemostat and is clamped, divided, and suture ligated. The cricoid cartilage and tracheal rings are identified. Two tracheal stay sutures (3-0 or 4-0 silk) are placed lateral to the incision through rings 2, 3, and 4 (Fig. 162-2, *B*). At this point the previously selected proper size tracheostomy tube is checked, and the anesthesia team is notified that the tracheotomy incision is about to be made. Coordination between surgeon and anesthesiologist is essential for smooth placement of the tracheostomy tube.

In most patients a noncuffed tracheostomy tube is used. The proper size (diameter and length) depends

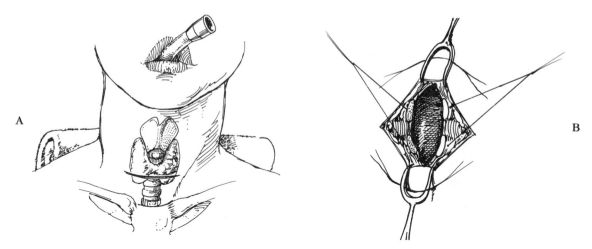

Fig. 162-2 **A,** Initial skin incision. **B,** Retraction sutures and tracheal incision.

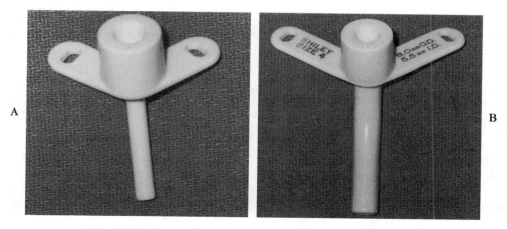

Fig. 162-3 Neonatal **(A)** and pediatric **(B)** tracheostomy tubes.

on the size of the patient. Neonatal tubes with short flanges and short tube length are used in very young infants (Fig. 162-3, *A*), and standard pediatric tubes with larger flanges and longer tube length are used in older patients (Fig. 162-3, *B*). As a general rule, the diameter of the tracheotomy tube selected is the same or 0.5 mm larger than that of the indwelling ET tube, if this is the proper size. Usually one tube is opened and prepared for the surgeon's use; however, if there is any question about the proper size tube, several different sized tubes are select-

ed and immediately available for use. A variety of special tubes, including pediatric cuffed tracheostomy tubes, are available for use in patients in whom ventilation with usual uncuffed tubes cannot be accomplished (e.g., extremely obese patients or patients undergoing tracheotomy with severe respiratory insufficiency requiring high ventilatory pressure). In general the use of cuffed tracheostomy tubes in the pediatric patient is restricted to special clinical circumstances.

A single midline vertical incision is made at tra-

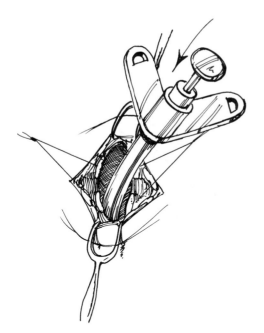

Fig. 162-4   Insertion of tracheostomy tube.

cheal rings 3 and 4, and the wound is suctioned clear of secretions. The ET tube is withdrawn to just above the incision. The wound is opened with a small hemostat, and the tracheostomy tube is placed in the lumen (Fig. 162-4). The obturator is withdrawn, and the tracheostomy tube is connected to the anesthesia circuit with a standard 15 mm adapter. The anesthesiologist confirms bilateral breath sounds and the presence of CO_2 on the capnographic monitor tracing. The tracheostomy tube is secured with placement of 3-0 or 4-0 silk stay sutures through the skin and the flanges of the tracheostomy tube. The tracheostomy tube ties are tied on one side of the neck, not directly posteriorly. The proper tension is reached when one finger slides easily beneath the ties. When the airway is secured, the ET tube may be removed. The shoulder roll is removed, and the previously placed stay sutures are taped to the chest with 1-inch wide paper tape. The stay sutures are separated and labeled "right" and "left" to ensure that the right and left sides are not inadvertently crossed during an emergency.

Postoperative Care

The chest radiograph is obtained while the patient is on the operating table to ensure tracheostomy tube tip placement above the carina and to check for possible pneumothorax. The patient is then transported to the PICU.

Tracheotomy ties are usually changed after 24 to 48 hours by the surgeon. After this, the ties are routinely changed daily and as needed by nursing personnel. The patient is kept in the PICU until the first tracheostomy tube change, done by the surgeon. In addition, the tracheal and tracheostomy tube flange stay sutures are generally removed at this time, usually 5 to 7 days after surgery. This allows adequate formation of the tracheal stoma and decreases the chance of accidental decannulation with loss of the surgical channel for the tracheostomy tube, which can result in severe complications. Specific orders for tracheostomy care are written by the surgeon with the postoperative orders. Routine hospital tracheostomy care policies may be instituted depending on the individual situation.

Tracheostomy dressings are not placed after the procedure because they maintain a moist environment at the surgical site, increasing the opportunity for infection. The site must remain as dry as possible, a goal that may create a challenge for the nursing staff when caring for an infant with a short neck. Maintaining slight extension of the infant's neck and turning his or her head every hour or two will assist in maintaining a dry environment. In addition, changing tracheostomy dressings in the immediate postoperative period increases the risk of accidental decannulation. This can be disastrous if the wound has not matured enough to provide a patent stoma for reinsertion. After tracheotomy, patients are usually observed in the PICU for 5 to 7 days unless one-on-one nursing care can be provided elsewhere in the hospital. In some older patients (10 to 12 years or older) the tracheostomy tube can be changed and the patient transferred to the nursing floor several days earlier.

Routine tracheostomy tube care

The tracheostomy wound must be thoroughly cleansed every 4 hours with half-strength hydrogen peroxide and sterile cotton-tipped swabs. Cleansing and complete drying of the wound are necessary to prevent infection and skin breakdown. After the initial tracheostomy tube ties are changed by the surgeon 24 to 48 hours after surgery, they must be changed every 24 hours or when wet or soiled. If two nurses are available, one nurse cuts the old ties while the other nurse holds the tracheostomy tube in place until the new ties are secured. To prevent dislodgment of the tracheostomy tube when only one nurse is available, new ties must be added before the old ties are cut. The ties must be snug enough that only one adult little finger can fit beneath the tie comfortably. A triple knot is tied on the side of the neck to prevent a pressure point. Placement of the knot can be altered from side to side with each change. If the skin underneath the ties begins to break down, foam padding can be placed underneath the ties. The cotton ties can also be replaced by a manufactured foam tracheostomy tie. Key to preventing skin breakdown is keeping the area clean and dry.

The initial tracheostomy tube is changed 5 to 7 days after surgery by the surgeon. If an inner cannula is used, it must be removed and cleaned with hydrogen peroxide or liquid soap and pipe cleaners every 8 hours and rinsed in sterile water before reinsertion. If disposable inner cannulas are available, a new one is inserted every 8 hours. After the initial change, tracheostomy tube replacement is recommended at least every 7 days or every day if preferred by the surgeon or family. The inner cannula can be changed once a day or more often if necessary. The outer cannula must be changed once a month or more often if necessary.

The infant's or child's vital signs and behavior must be closely monitored for signs of inadequate oxygenation or discomfort. During tracheostomy tube care the caregiver must assess the skin area and stoma for signs of breakdown or infection, including rash, redness, foul odor, or drainage. The nurse must maintain the following routine equipment at the patient's bedside: appropriate size suction catheters, wall or portable suction machine, humidification system, appropriate size bag and mask, and oxygen. In addition, the following special supplies are needed: clean tracheostomy tubes (one of the same size and another a size smaller), the obturator for the tracheostomy tube that is in the child, half-strength hydrogen peroxide, sterile water, sterile cotton-tipped applicators, tracheostomy ties, vials of saline solution, and bandage scissors.

Other considerations

Head position. The patient's head position must be carefully monitored to prevent occlusion of the tracheostomy tube by the chin, bedding, or clothing. Adapters such as a tracheostomy tube guard or swivel adapter can be placed over the tube orifice to prevent occlusion. If mechanical ventilation is being used, the swivel adapter will not add appreciable dead space or tubing weight. Erosion of the neck by the tracheostomy tube flanges can be prevented by placing a small roll under the child's shoulders to slightly extend the neck during sleep. Specialized thin foam dressings can also be applied to bony prominences to prevent skin breakdown from the flanges or base of the tracheostomy tube.

Tube length. Neonatal and pediatric tracheostomy tubes are of a standard length and may be too long for use in some patients, primarily neonates. Shortening the tube may be necessary. Rough edges must be smoothed to prevent traumatic injury or tracheal mucosal irritation with subsequent formation of obstructive granulation tissue. An anteroposterior radiograph must be obtained immediately after tube insertion to check its position in the trachea. Two companies supply tracheostomy tubes with adaptable length as well as custom-designed neonatal and pediatric tracheostomy tubes (Bivona tubes, Bivona Medical Technologies, Gary, Ind., and Shiley tubes, Mallinckrodt Medical TPI, St. Louis, Mo.).

Tube obstruction. In the event of acute airway obstruction from secretions, food, or foreign body aspiration, the first intervention is suctioning with sodium chloride solution as a lubricant. If the obstruction is not relieved, the tracheostomy tube ties must be cut, the obstructed tube removed, and a new tracheostomy tube of the same size inserted. Breath sounds must be auscultated to ensure proper tube placement. An anteroposterior chest radiograph also needs to be obtained after the tracheostomy tube is changed.

Parent education

Initially parental anxiety may stem from several factors, including the loss of the child's ability to speak or make noises, changes in the child's appearance, fear about ability to meet the child's care needs, and upheaval of family routine (e.g., work and day care arrangements). These concerns are best addressed by consistent and individualized education of the parents and the child if 2 years or older, beginning before the surgery, by the surgeon, nurse specialist, and PICU and floor nurses. Early participation of the parents and child in daily care of the tracheostomy also encourages bonding between the child and parent. A physician's orders to begin tracheostomy care teaching communicates the prospective plan to the entire health care team and the insurance company. Some insurance companies will reimburse the providers of specialty services involved in teaching the parents, other family members, and child in preparation for discharge to home. Formal teaching materials can include videos, slides, pictures or drawings, dolls with tracheostomies, sample tracheostomy equipment, and printed instructions with checklists. Formal teaching can be accomplished while daily care is performed by the PICU and floor nurses and at appointed times with the nurse specialist or surgeon. The parents and other family members and child need time with staff members so their questions and concerns can be fully answered. Tracheostomy wound care and suctioning techniques are good skills to learn first to encourage confidence and diminish fears. Other skills that need to be learned include changing of the tracheostomy tube tie and the tracheostomy tube itself, cleaning and storage of the tracheostomy tube, and where and how to obtain supplies. In addition, knowledge of how to perform cardiopulmonary resuscitation and chest physiotherapy, if necessary, as well as how to recognize signs and symptoms of respiratory distress are necessary. Child life workers need to work with elementary school–aged and adolescent patients regarding changing body image and activity restrictions. A speech therapist can help the child and parents develop a technique to communicate (see p. 1533). Social workers can help the parents arrange and adjust to lifestyle changes. Before the child is discharged from the hospital, parents and other family members must be able to handle all phases of tracheostomy tube care.

Home care

Home care equipment needs vary with each patient, and an adequate amount of time must be given to plan for and train parents how to use each piece of equipment. The suction machine operates on battery and AC and DC power. A representative of the home care equipment company visits with the parents in their home to arrange adequate space and safe electrical hookups for the equipment. Letters to the electric, phone, gas, and local police and fire companies informing them of the special needs of this child are provided for the parents to mail. Home nursing may need to be arranged to help the parents during transition from hospital to home care of the child.

Humidity-oxygen therapy. The patient's condition after surgery dictates the type of humidity-oxygen device needed (e.g., ventilator, tracheostomy cradle, or collar). For spontaneously breathing patients, a tracheostomy collar or mask is used rather than a T-bar attachment, which may inadvertently dislodge the tube from the airway. For patients who need mechanical ventilation, the ventilator tubing is secured to the child's clothing to prevent tension on the tracheostomy tube as the child moves. The artificial airway bypasses the patient's upper airway, which normally heats and humidifies inspired air to body temperature and 100% relative humidity by the time the air reaches the carina. It is essential, therefore, to provide heat and humidity in these patients to prevent the deleterious effects of breathing dry, cool gas. Inadequate heating and humidification may result in thickening of secretions, decreased ciliary activity, drying of the respiratory mucosa, and diminished patient ability to clear mucus and debris. Decreased pulmonary compliance and functional residual capacity may also be observed. Careful regulation of humidity output will prevent excessive condensation, movement of water into the trachea, and overhydration. Signs of excessive condensation include the need for frequent tracheal suctioning, watery and thin secretions, and increased coughing without sputum production. Excessive condensation may hinder stoma healing, produce a growth medium for bacteria, and cause skin rash or skin breakdown beneath the dressings or ties. Overhydration may result in atelectasis from condensation of water, with obstruction of the small airways, increased airways resistance, fluid and electrolyte imbalance, and diminished ciliary activity. The use of sterile water with a heated humidifier that provides molecular rather than particulate water is recommended for patients with tracheostomies. This may be delivered through a ventilator circuit or a tracheostomy collar or mask.

For the spontaneously breathing, actively mobile child, a heat and moisture exchanger (HME) is an alternative to a heated humidifier (Fig. 162-5). This device, also known as a regenerative humidifier or artificial nose, offers many features, including small size, low compliance and resistance, no water reservoir, no water source requirement, no electrical power requirement, passive operation, and decreased infectious potential. An HME captures exhaled water vapor and returns it to the patient in the next breath. Water condenses on the HME surfaces during expiration, and the heat that kept water in a gaseous state is released and warms the HME. When the patient inhales, the HME transfers the collected heat and moisture to the cool, dry inspired air passing through it.

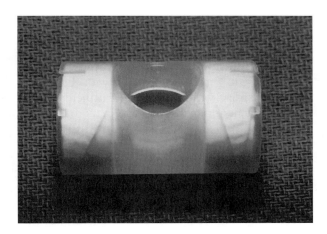

Fig. 162-5   Heat and moisture exchanger.

The efficiency of the HME is limited by the ambient temperature and humidity, the speed with which the gas passes through the HME, the internal volume of the HME, the thermal conductivity and hygroscopic quality of the material in the HME, and the hydration of the patient. Ideally, a cyclic effect is established, with cooling of the HME during inspiration by means of transfer of heat and humidity to inspired gas condensation of moisture and collection of heat from the next exhaled breath. An HME is not used with heated humidifiers or nebulizers or with aerosol medications because they could block delivery of the drug. An HME may not provide adequate moisture levels for patients with preexistent thick secretions or impaired mucociliary clearance. Also, an HME is replaced with heated humidity if the patient exhibits evidence of inadequate airway humidification. Mucus coughed into the HME may partially or completely occlude the device, and it must be changed immediately; therefore careful observation of the patient is necessary. If the HME is not tolerated, a gauze cover may be used.

Communication

When a tracheostomy is present, exhaled air follows the path of least resistance through the tracheostomy tube rather than the upper airway. This limits the vibratory movement of the vocal cords and in turn vocal intensity. Voice may be inaudible in some patients. These patients must be closely observed because they will be unable to vocally alert caregivers to distress, pain, or other problems. Patients who could speak before surgery will have the greatest anxiety from loss of vocalization; however, attention must also be given to infants too young to speak and their need to communicate. It is vital that all children have some means to make contact with staff and family after surgery. An older child may use a bell, buzzer, writing pad and pencil, picture board, or sign language.

After the acute phase of recovery, use of tracheostomy talk, instruction in covering the tracheostomy during exhalation, or a Passy-Muir speaking valve will allow resumption of some vocal communication. The Passy-Muir valve allows airflow through it into the tracheostomy tube during inspiration. During exhalation the valve closes, and air is directed through the larynx, vocal cords, nasal passages, and oral cavity, thereby allowing vocalization. Other benefits of speaking valves include improvements in olfaction and swallowing as well as better socialization. Sign language may be useful and has been identified as a way to facilitate communication for infants. Before use of any augmentive device, medical approval and consultation with speech-language pathologists and respiratory care practitioners are necessary. More than half of all children with tracheostomies referred for speech therapy have moderate to severe communication deficits. Early, routine referral to a speech-language pathologist offers potential for better monitoring and outcome. With appropriate care, most patients with normal hearing and neurologic development will be able to communicate well when the tracheostomy tube is removed.

Suctioning

A tracheostomy tube reduces the effectiveness of the cough reflex, and inasmuch as children are at greater risk than adults for mucous plugging because of smaller airways, suctioning is part of routine care. Initially, suctioning may be needed every 10 to 15 minutes, then slowly tapered to an as-needed basis as indicated at individual assessment. Attention must be given to depth of catheter insertion, suction pressure, number of times the catheter is passed, duration of suctioning, and hyperoxygenation and hyperinflation between suction passes (see Chapter 147). Sodium chloride lavage during suctioning may ease removal of dried or retained secretions and stimulate cough. Blood-streaked secretions are normal during the first 24 hours. This is also seen occasionally with deep suctioning or if the tracheal mucosa becomes dry. Frank hemorrhage is a medical emergency. The amount, color, consistency, and odor of secretions must be noted because changes could signal the beginning of infection. If chest physiotherapy and aerosol bronchodilator therapy are indicated, they may be started immediately after surgery. After the tracheal stoma heals and the tract forms, children are encouraged to expectorate secretions as often as possible. However, suctioning is still recommended to ensure a patent airway.

Decannulation

Decannulation is considered when the medical process that necessitated the tracheostomy tube is resolved. Patients are first examined with fiberoptic nasolaryngoscopy to assess the supraglottis and vocal cord mobility. If findings are satisfactory, direct laryngoscopy and bronchoscopy are performed in the operating room to assess the airway completely. The tracheostomy tube is removed and the entire airway assessed via endoscopy. If the airway is deemed adequate, the patient is admitted to the hospital for a trial decannulation, usually about a week after bronchoscopy to allow the child to recover from that procedure.

The tracheostomy tube is removed in the outpatient clinic, and the tracheal stoma is taped with an adhesive bandage. The patient is carefully observed by physicians and nurses for several hours before admission to the ward. An apnea monitor is used overnight, and if the airway is adequate, the patient is discharged the following morning.

Decannulation panic is almost invariably related to an inadequate airway and necessitates careful evaluation of the patient's airway. It is usually not necessary to decannulate in the PICU if the airway is adequate. Only occasionally are stepdown procedures indicated (e.g., daytime tracheostomy tube plugging or use of progressively smaller tracheostomy tubes).

RISKS AND COMPLICATIONS

The mortality rate associated with tracheotomy may be as high as 50%, but if deaths from intercurrent disease are eliminated, the mortality rate from tracheotomy alone is 2% to 8%. The mortality rate in the hospital or home does not differ significantly. The rate of other reported complications is 20% to 50%.

Complications may be considered early (occurring in the first week) or late (occurring after 1 week). The duration of tracheostomy tube use has risen from, on average, 2 weeks when necessary because of infectious disease to 6 months in patients with chronic respiratory, cardiac, or CNS disease. This increased duration of tracheostomy has resulted in more late complications.

Early Complications

The prevalence of intraoperative complications was as low as 0.5% in a series from a large pediatric center where tracheotomies were performed by experienced surgeons. Meticulous anesthesia and surgical technique reduce these complications, which are primarily subcutaneous emphysema and pneumothorax. Hemorrhage from the great vessels, esophageal perforation, recurrent laryngeal nerve injury, and tracheostomy tube placement in the pretracheal space are exceedingly rare in experienced major pediatric centers. Major complications encountered in the first week after tracheotomy include accidental decannulation and mucous plugging. Mucous plugging is managed with adequate humidification and suctioning.

Accidental decannulation

Accidental decannulation is most dangerous in the first 4 or 5 days after tracheotomy because a fistulous tract between the trachea and the skin has not yet been established and recannulation may be difficult or fatal if the tube is replaced in the subcutaneous tissue or the pretracheal space. For this reason, the first tracheostomy tube change is always done by the surgeon. Signs of accidental decannulation include oxygen desaturation, respiratory distress, air hunger, and changes in vital signs.

If accidental decannulation occurs, oxygen must be administered using a bag-and-mask technique with the patient's neck extended and a roll placed beneath the back. This will place the trachea in approximately the same position as during the operative procedure so that the skin incision overlies the tracheal incision. The stay sutures on either side of the incision must be grasped firmly and the trachea pulled gently upward to expose the tracheal incision (see Fig. 162-2, *B*). The tracheostomy tube can then be inserted easily, and ventilation resumed. A radiograph must be obtained to ensure the tube is in the proper position.

Delayed Complications

The most common delayed complication is persistent tracheocutaneous fistula, which reflects long duration of tracheostomy tube use with ingrowth of skin lining the fistulous tract to the trachea. This complication is managed by cauterizing the fistulous tract after decannulation when a stable airway is ensured. Inadvertent decannulation and tube obstruction from mucous plugging are other late complications. With proper hospital and home care, the mortality rate is reported as low as 13% per 100 patient-months. Careful home care management reduces the prevalence and risk of these complications. Granulation tissue of the tracheostoma is an occasional complication but it easily treated with silver nitrate application to the tracheostoma. Suprastomal tracheal granulation or fibroma is treated with bronchoscopic excision or stoma revision. Subglottic and tracheal stenosis is infrequent. Innominate artery erosion is exceedingly rare with the use of flexible plastic tracheostomy tubes.

CURRENT RESEARCH AND FUTURE CONSIDERATIONS

Current research is focused on the controversy regarding the best tracheal incision for tracheotomy: a single midline incision, as is most commonly used in our institution, or a flap incision. Animal studies indicate that both procedures are well tolerated with a low prevalence of stomal stenosis and stomal tracheomalacia. Future research will help clarify the issue, particularly as regards long-term tracheomalacia and stenosis at the tracheostoma, which are rare.

Further development of tracheostomy tubes will provide a wider choice for the surgeon. The development of pediatric cuffed tubes has been extremely beneficial in the management of respiratory insufficiency with high ventilation pressure. Further experience will indicate the best type of cuffed tube to use in this critically ill patient population. Further experience will also clarify the issue of tracheotomy in very young patients with severe laryngotracheal bronchitis unresponsive to medical therapy. Substantial controversy exists as to the efficacy of tracheotomy or intubation in these patients.

ADDITIONAL READING

Arvedson JD, Brodsky L. Pediatric tracheotomy referrals to speech-language pathology in a children's hospital. J Pediatr Otorhinolaryngol 23:237-243, 1992.

Berry DR. Suctioning an endotracheal or tracheostomy airway. In Smith DP, ed. Comprehensive Child and Family Nursing Skills. St. Louis: Mosby, 1991, pp 555-560.

Black RJ, Baldwin DL, Johns AN. Tracheostomy decannulation panic in children: Fact or fiction? J Laryngol Otol 96:297-304, 1984.

Bourland CM, Stool SC. Anesthesia for tracheotomy in children. In Myers EN, Stool SC, Johnson JT, eds. Tracheotomy. New York: Churchill Livingstone, 1985, pp 99-111.

Boyd SW, Benzel EC. The role of early tracheotomy in the management of the neurosurgical patient. Laryngoscope 102:559-562, 1992.

Brown OE, Manning SC, Blount G, Hatfield N. Tracheotomy. In Levin DL, Morriss FC, eds. Essentials of Pediatric Intensive Care. St. Louis: Quality Medical Publishing, 1990, pp 949-954.

Davis DA, Tucker JA, Russo P. Management of airway obstruction in patients with congenital heart defects. Ann Otol Rhinol Laryngol 102:163-166, 1993.

Davis HW, Johnson JT. Decision making in airway management of children and adults. In Myers GA, Stool SC, Johnson JT, eds. Tracheotomy. New York: Churchill Livingstone, 1985, pp 13-39.

Eavey RP. The evolution of tracheotomy. In Myers EN, Stool SC, Johnson JT, eds. Tracheotomy. New York: Churchill Livingstone, 1985, pp 1-11.

• Fitton C. Nursing management of the child with a tracheotomy. Pediatr Clin North Am 41:513-522, 1994.

• Fitton CM, Myer CM III. Practical aspects of pediatric tracheotomy care. J Otolaryngol 21:409-413, 1992.

Fry TL, Fischer NP, Jones RO, Pillsbury NC. Comparison of tracheotomy incision in a pediatric model. Ann Otol Rhinol Laryngol 94:450-453, 1985.

Gaudet PT, Peerless A, Sasaki C, Kirchner JA. Pediatric tracheostomy and associated complications. Laryngoscope 88:1633-1641, 1978.

• Gerson CP, Tucker GF. Infant tracheotomy. Ann Otol Rhinol Laryngol 91:413-416, 1982.

Hall SS, Weatherly KS. Using sign language with tracheotomized infants and children. Pediatr Nurs 15:362-367, 1989.

Hawkins DB, Williams EH. Tracheostomy in infants and young children. Laryngoscope 56:331-340, 1976.

• Hotaling AJ, Robbins WK, Madgy DN, Belenky WM. Pediatric tracheotomy: A review of technique. Am J Otolaryngol 13:115-119, 1992.

Jackson D, Albamonte S. Enhancing communication with the Passy-Muir valve. Pediatr Nurs 20:149-153, 1994.

Johnson JT, Reilly JS, Mallory GB. Decannulation. In Myers EN, Stool SC, Johnson JT, eds. Tracheostomy. New York: Churchill Livingstone, 1985, pp 201-210.

Kenna MA, Reilly JS, Stool SE. Tracheotomy in the preterm infant. Ann Otol Rhinol Laryngol 96:68-71, 1986.

Lichtman SW, Birnbaum IL, Sanfilippo MR, Pellicon JT, Damon WJ, King JL. Effect of a tracheostomy speaking valve on secretions, arterial oxygenation and olfaction: A quantitative evaluation. J Speech Hearing Res 38:549-555, 1995.

MacRae DL, Rae RE, Heeneman U. Pediatric tracheotomy. J Otolaryngol 13:309-311, 1984.

Myer CM III. The heat and moisture exchanger in post-tracheotomy care. Otolaryngol Head Neck Surg 69:209-210, 1987.

• Myers EN, Stool SC. Complications of tracheotomy. In Myers EN, Stool SC, Johnson JT, eds. Tracheotomy. New York: Churchill Livingstone, 1985, pp 147-169.

Myers EN, Carran RL. Early complications of tracheotomy. Incidence and management. Clin Chest Med 12:509-595, 1991.

Myers EN, Stool SC, Johnson JT. Technique of tracheotomy. In Myers EN, Stool SC, Johnson JT, eds. Tracheotomy. New York: Churchill Livingstone, 1985, pp 113-124.

Practice guideline: Tracheostomy. Otolaryngol Head Neck Surg 12:26-28, 1994.

Roberts N. The selective approach to successful stomal management at home. Otolaryngol Head Neck Surg 13:12-16, 1995.

Roemer NR. The tracheotomized child: Private duty nursing at home. Home Healthcare Nurse 10:28-32, 1992.

Rogers BM, Rooks JJ, Talbert JL. Pediatric tracheostomy: Long-term evaluation. J Pediatr Surg 14:258-263, 1979.

• Ruben RJ, Newton L, Chambers H, et al. Home care of the pediatric patient with a tracheotomy. Ann Otol Rhinol Laryngol 91:633-640, 1982.

Swift AC, Rogers JH. The outcome of tracheostomy in children. J Laryngol Otol 101:936-939, 1987.

• Teppas JJ, Herouy JH, Shermeta DW, et al. Tracheostomy in neonates and small infants: Problems and pitfalls. Surgery 89:635-639, 1988.

Testi C. Maintaining a tracheostomy site and airway. In Smith DP, ed. Comprehensive Child and Family Nursing Skills. St. Louis: Mosby, 1991, pp 604-611.

Wak EY, Madgy DN, Zablock U, Belenky WM, Hotaling AJ. An analysis of the inferior based tracheal flap for pediatric tracheotomy. Int J Pediatr Otorhinolaryngol 27:42-54, 1993.

Warnock C, Porpora K. A pediatric trach card: Transforming research into practice. Pediatr Nurs 20:186-188, 1994.

• Wetmore RF, Handler SD, Potsic WP. Pediatric tracheostomy: Experience during the past decade. Ann Otol Rhinol Laryngol 91:628-632, 1982.

Wood DE, Mathison DJ. Late complications of tracheotomy. Clin Chest Med 12:597-609, 1991.

Zeitouni A, Manoukion J. Tracheotomy in the first year of life. J Otolaryngol 22:431-434, 1993.

Zulliger JJ, Garvin JP, Schuller DE, et al. Assessment of intubation in croup and epiglottis. Ann Otol Rhinol Laryngol 91:403-406, 1982.

163 Discharge of the Technology-Dependent Child

Michele S. Holecek · Mary Nixon · Thomas G. Keens

BACKGROUND AND INDICATIONS

Advances in medical technology have enabled many children with potentially fatal illnesses to survive. However, many of these children remain technology dependent for years or even life. The increasing trend to discharge children who need a variety of specialized treatments, medications, and services poses new challenges for the health care team. Home medical care can be relatively simple (e.g., parenteral nutrition) to extremely complex (e.g., mechanical ventilation). The successful transition of these technology-dependent children from acute care settings to home necessitates a systematic, multidisciplinary approach that addresses all aspects of the child's and family's needs.

Discharge planning for ventilator-assisted children varies with patient needs, disease state, treatments, equipment, family needs, and financial status, among other factors. Although the primary focus of this chapter is discharge planning for ventilator-assisted infants and children, the information may be applicable to less complex cases. For example, children with tracheostomy tubes may need some, but not all, of the teaching, equipment, and support needed for children receiving assisted ventilation. Definitions of key terms used in this chapter are as follows:

chronic respiratory failure Impaired ability to exchange oxygen and CO_2 caused by disorders that affect respiratory function. Respiratory failure is generally deemed chronic after 1 month of continuous mechanical ventilation without acute respiratory disease.

long-term ventilation Continuous mechanical ventilation for >1 month.

assisted ventilation Use of mechanical ventilation to augment or support respiratory function.

ventilator dependent Need for mechanical ventilation daily. The duration (hours) will vary according to individual patient needs.

technology dependent Need for medical equipment and care to sustain life because of failure of normal physiologic function.

home care Care associated with patient maintenance, provided in the family dwelling, separate from an institutional setting. Care is provided by trained, competent caregivers, which may include family members, nurses, unlicensed assistive personnel, babysitters, or other identified caregivers.

Respiratory failure occurs when central respiratory drive or ventilatory muscle power are inadequate to overcome the respiratory load. Long-term support of ventilation will be necessary if the cause of this imbalance is not reversible. Many ventilator-assisted children do well at home, and home care of these patients can be safe and, compared with hospitalization, relatively inexpensive. The high motivation of parents to care for their children in the home often results in high-quality care. After the transition from hospital to home, parent-child relationships and child development are enhanced. The potential for rehabilitation in all aspects of daily living is increased, and many children have a near-normal lifestyle.

Chronic respiratory failure implies that there is an ongoing, perhaps irreversible, underlying respiratory disorder that results in inadequate ventilation or hypoxia. The diagnosis of chronic respiratory failure is made when attempts to wean from assisted ventilation have failed for 1 month in a patient without superimposed acute respiratory disease or unstable exacerbation of respiratory disease.

If relatively stable ventilator settings can be maintained, children with chronic respiratory failure are candidates for home mechanical ventilation. Physiologic criteria for home mechanical ventilation emphasize medical stability. The pulmonary component of the disorder is usually the most likely to provide instability. Therefore the pulmonary disease must not necessitate frequent adjustments in ventilator settings to maintain adequate gas exchange. In general Fio_2 needs to be ≤ 0.40. Peak inspiratory pressure (PIP) needs to be <40 cm H_2O, and if possible positive end-expiratory pressure (PEEP) is not used since home ventilators do not provide continuous flow of gas and the technique for providing PEEP is cumbersome. In addition to physiologic criteria, a number of criteria related to caregivers, financial considerations, home environment, and community support need to be met to optimize the chances of successful home care.

Chronic respiratory failure is classified in four basic diagnostic categories: ventilatory muscle weakness and neuromuscular diseases, central hypoventilation syndrome, chronic obstructive pulmonary disease (COPD), and restrictive lung disease.

Ventilatory Muscle Weakness and Neuromuscular Diseases

Ventilatory muscle weakness has three physiologic consequences. Inspiratory muscle weakness prevents deep inspiration, resulting in atelectasis and microatelectasis. Expiratory muscle weakness prevents effective coughing, resulting in decreased removal of pulmonary secretions and foreign material from the lungs. Both of these increase the prevalence and severity of pulmonary infections, which are the leading cause of morbidity and mortality in children with neuromuscular disease. When weakness of the ventilatory muscles progresses sufficiently, hypoventilation and inadequate gas exchange result. The two types of ventilatory muscle weakness are progressive and nonprogressive. In progressive neuromuscular diseases (e.g., spinal muscular atrophy and muscular dystrophy) muscle weakness worsens over time, resulting in inevitable and predictable development of chronic respiratory failure. In nonprogressive neuromuscular diseases, the neurologic lesion does not progress. However, in many children with static neuromuscular disorders functional progression of the impairment occurs because muscle strength cannot increase to overcome the increasing functional demands from increased body mass due to growth. Many children with static neuromuscular disorders become nonambulatory and ventilator dependent at or near puberty because of the marked increase in body mass associated with the pubertal growth spurt.

DISEASE STATES ASSOCIATED WITH CHRONIC RESPIRATORY FAILURE

Ventilatory muscle weakness and neuromuscular diseases

Muscular dystrophy
Myotonic dystrophy
Werdnig-Hoffmann disease
Progressive infantile spinal muscle atrophy
Spinal cord injury or atrophy
Myasthenia gravis
Phrenic nerve paralysis
Infant botulism
Guillain-Barré syndrome
Multiple sclerosis

Chronic obstructive pulmonary disease

Bronchopulmonary dysplasia
Cystic fibrosis

Central hypoventilation syndrome

Ondine's curse
Arnold-Chiari malformation
Acquired diseases that affect the respiratory centers (e.g., tumors, cerebrovascular accident, infections, trauma, hemorrhage)

Restrictive lung disease

Pulmonary hypoplasia
Diaphragmatic hernia

Other conditions

Congenital heart defects
Thoracic deformities (e.g., kyphoscoliosis)

Children with ventilatory muscle weakness are good candidates for prolonged ventilatory support at home. Because the cause of their respiratory failure is primary muscle weakness, they usually do not have significant lung disease that would necessitate frequent changes in ventilator settings. These children usually are much more stable at home with long-term ventilatory support and have less frequent pneumonias and hospital admissions than before the institution of prolonged ventilatory support. Some children will require continuous ventilatory support; others may require only sleeping or nocturnal ventilatory support.

Central Hypoventilation Syndrome

The cause of chronic respiratory failure in children with central hypoventilation syndrome is inadequate central respiratory drive, which can be congenital or acquired. The congenital form may be idiopathic (e.g., congenital central hypoventilation syndrome or Ondine's curse) or due to an identifiable brain stem lesion (e.g., Arnold-Chiari malformation with myelomeningocele). Acquired forms of central hypoventilation syndrome may be caused by brain stem trauma, tumor, hemorrhage, cerebrovascular accident, or infection. Although central respiratory drive is impaired, the lungs and ventilatory muscles may be nearly normal. This group of children may not have significant pulmonary disease, which permits reasonably stable ventilator settings to achieve adequate gas exchange. Some of these children will need continuous ventilatory support; others will need ventilatory support only while sleeping. Because the ventilatory muscles are normal and the respiratory load is not substantially increased, this group of patients can be offered a variety of methods for ventilatory support, including positive pressure ventilators, negative pressure ventilators, and diaphragm pacing.

Chronic Obstructive Pulmonary Disease

Chronic obstructive pulmonary disease increases the work of breathing to a level higher than can be sustained by the child. Often the underlying lung disease is intrinsically unstable and frequent adjustments in ventilator settings are necessary. However, in some children COPD stabilizes enough that chronic ventilatory support at home is possible. The most common chronic lung disease in which home ventilation has been used in children is bronchopulmonary dysplasia. Many of these children can be weaned from home mechanical ventilation over several months to years as lung growth results in gradual resolution of the lung disease.

Restrictive Lung Disease

Children with restrictive lung disease are generally poor candidates for home ventilation. Their lung disease is generally unstable, and oxygen and PIP pressure needs are high.

TECHNIQUE
Methods of Long-Term Ventilatory Support Used at Home

Home ventilation devices are different from those used in hospitals to treat acute respiratory failure. Six basic types of assisted ventilation can be used in the home: (1) portable positive pressure ventilation through a tracheostomy tube, (2) portable positive pressure ventilation through a nasal mask, (3) negative pressure ventilation with a chest shell (cuirass) or wrap ventilator, (4) negative pressure tank ventilation, (5) diaphragm pacing, and (6) ventilation with a rocking bed. Each of these devices has indications, advantages, and disadvantages that must be carefully considered in the selection process. Portable positive pressure ventilation through a tracheostomy tube is the most common method of providing home assisted ventilation for infants and children and is the focus of this chapter.

Decision-Making Process

Once it is determined that the child must have long-term respiratory support, a conference is held with the family to explore available options. During this conference all appropriate treatment methods are presented. The family is encouraged to consider the advantages and disadvantages of these options as they relate to the child's well-being and the potential effect on the family. Some patients and families choose not to use all technology available to them because of ethical, quality-of-life, religious, cultural, financial, or other issues. As in the case of all difficult decisions, discussion must focus on the child's best interest. A thorough examination of issues must include input from family members and the health care team.

In addition to selecting the treatment method, the family must also choose the best location for the long-term care of their child. The options available will vary according to community resources, financial reimbursement, patient needs, and family situation. The majority of families with ventilator-dependent children choose to care for them in their own homes. Placement in a foster care home is an alternative for some children. Placement in a long-term care facility (e.g., inpatient rehabilitation center, "stepdown" unit, residential school, board and care home, skilled nursing facility, or other facility designed to care for ventilator-assisted patients) may be necessary if home care is not an option because of the patient's needs, family resources, or community resources. Long-term hospitalization in a PICU is the only option for children who are too medically unstable to be transferred to a lower level of care. However, most children who need long-term ventilation remain hospitalized for a long time after they are medically stable because of delays in obtaining financial support for alternative care settings. This process may take weeks to months, particularly if public funding is needed.

The initial conference includes a frank discussion of the extent of the child's needs, responsibilities associated with each option, financial implications, and the effect on family members. The effect on the home environment and change in the activities of daily living are discussed in detail with all families who are considering home care. The family needs to have a clear understanding of the goals of home ventilation while considering the options. Realistic information about the lengthy and complex discharge process will help prepare the family for future events. Family members need time to hold private discussions and formulate questions before making decisions and beginning the discharge process.

The option of positive pressure ventilation in the family home offers many advantages. The most obvious benefit is the child is at home and out of a hospital setting. This decreases the risk of nosocomial infections, provides consistent caregivers, provides an environment more conducive for growth and development, and does not separate the family and child. The majority of caregivers surveyed reported a greater sense of satisfaction and control with the child at home.

Disadvantages vary according to each family. Problems related to equipment, financial burden, caregiver stress and fatigue, role issues, lack of privacy, and crowding are common. Discharge planning for the ventilator-assisted child occurs under the as-

---

GOALS OF HOME VENTILATORY SUPPORT

Promote the child's physical safety
Prevent or minimize complications
Optimize growth and development potential
Minimize separation from other family members
Decrease stress on the primary caregivers
Optimize quality of life
Extend life expectancy
Decrease the cost of care

---

sumption that the patient and family will demonstrate the ability to overcome obstacles and meet home ventilation program criteria. The home must have adequate space to meet the needs of the child, equipment, and assistive personnel. The family may need to find new housing if current living arrangements do not provide the needed space and utilities to adequately and safely care for the child.

Psychosocial Stresses

The family must have adequate resources to effectively cope with the problems associated with home ventilation. Financial issues are an important source of stress for families caring for ventilator-assisted children at home. Home care of ventilator-assisted children is also associated with major alterations in lifestyles that affect all family members. Not only are day-to-day activities disrupted but also long-term family goals such as parents' careers. A survey of parents of 34 ventilator-assisted children showed that 71% of parents were unable to pursue career choices, education, or job changes because of care requirements of their ventilator-assisted child. More than 51% of parents were unable to change employers because new employer medical insurance would not cover the ventilator-assisted child's preexisting condition. The stresses of caring for ventilator-assisted children at home may cause marital discord. Although divorces and separations are infrequent, the majority of families demonstrate marital discord on objective psychometric testing. Some caregivers report lower self-esteem, lower satisfaction, and less family closeness after caring for their ventilator-assisted child in the home for prolonged periods. This was attributed

---

HOME VENTILATION PROGRAM CRITERIA

Medical stability

$Fio_2 \leq 0.40$
Minimal ventilator settings without PEEP
Infrequent need to adjust ventilator settings
Nutritional stability with acceptable pattern of weight gain
No acute illness

Caretaker requirements

Primary caregiver committed to caring for the child whenever necessary
Backup caregiver committed to replacing or assisting the primary caregiver as needed
Willingness to assume responsibility and risks of the child's care
Willingness to learn all skills and knowledge necessary for home management
Ability to demonstrate competent care of the child before discharge

Financial requirements

Financial assistance to support home care (e.g., private insurance or public funding)
Ability to provide essential service and equipment not covered by insurance or public funding

Home environment

Electricity and water with essential service agreement
Telephone for emergency service
Ample space for the child, equipment, and assistive personnel (e.g., home nurse)

Community support

Physician willing to provide ongoing medical supervision
Transportation to accommodate the child and equipment
Friends, family, public health nurse, or others who can provide assistance if needed

---

to burnout and exhaustion related to prolonged, unrelieved intervals of caring for the ventilator-assisted child.

Despite these difficulties, most parents caring for ventilator-assisted children at home do not experience significant stress. Stress is inversely related to coping resources. In some situations the longer ventilator-assisted children are at home the less stress parents experience as they develop coping strategies. Nearly all parents state that having their ventilator-assisted child at home is predominantly a positive experience and less stressful than separation when their child is in the hospital. Nearly all parents believe that they provide better medical care for the ventilator-assisted child at home than was received in the hospital. The diversity of responses to providing care at home underscores the need for continued reevaluation of the family's individual needs. Assisting families to identify strategies to meet their needs is an ongoing challenge.

Discharge Planning Team

After the patient and family have chosen the home ventilator program, a team is organized to help the family prepare for discharge. This comprehensive multidisciplinary team consists of members from the hospital and the community chosen to meet the complex needs of the child and family. In some settings the functions of some of the roles will need to be completed by alternate members because of limited resources and personnel shortages.

One member of the team, usually a nurse or social worker, must act as the case manager. This coordinator is responsible for organizing and imple-

---

DISCHARGE PLANNING AND HOME CARE MANAGEMENT TEAM

Hospital based

Primary pulmonary physician
Clinical nurse specialist*
Associate nurse
Discharge planner*
Case manager*
Social worker*
Registered respiratory therapist
Physical therapist
Occupational therapist
Speech therapist
Clinical dietitian
Child life specialist
Clinical pharmacist

Community based

Primary care physician
Family members
Private and public insurers
Home care agency
Durable medical equipment vendor
Outpatient therapist
School teacher and school nurse
Public health nurse

---

*Suggested coordinator.

menting the discharge plan during hospitalization and acts as a liaison after discharge. The pulmonary physician is responsible for the medical plan and the physiologic stability of the patient. The associate or primary nurse provides teaching and continuity of care. The social worker provides emotional support and acts as a resource for the family to obtain emotional and financial support within the community. The clinical nurse specialist provides assistance and guidance with teaching, discharge planning, and follow-up care. The respiratory therapist instructs the family in respiratory care, equipment, and administration of treatments. The occupational therapist, child life specialist, physical therapist, speech therapist, and dietitian provide support based on the patient's needs and make recommendations for ongoing treatment after discharge.

The home care agency, the durable medical equipment vendor, and other community agencies provide services to ensure a smooth transition from the hospital to the home. Helping the family develop a rapport with the home care agency and equipment vendor is essential because these team members will become a major source of support after the child's discharge. The home care agency and vendor must provide surveillance of their staff and equipment and must be able to provide timely, effective assistance with problems.

The public or private insurers inform the family of their benefits and responsibilities. Families with private insurance can request a case worker from the insurance company to coordinate benefits and monitor expenditures. Ideally, a case worker provides consistency, informs the family about the use of their benefits on an ongoing basis, and assists the family in maximizing their benefits. For families who need public funding, a case worker will help the family to understand their responsibilities, restrictions, and the limits of their benefits. This information must be clearly outlined before discharge. For example, provision of a safe environment in which to care for the child is one of the family's responsibilities. Families need to be aware that case workers will make home visits to assess the child's environment and care. In addition, some public funding sources restrict travel to other states without prior authorization. Families need to be aware of such restrictions so that they do not inadvertently jeopardize their benefits.

Patient and Family Education

Early discussion introducing the concept of education to the family serves to reassure family members they will learn the skills to safely and successfully care for their child at home and assists them in understanding their roles in the discharge process. Family members must be aware that they will be expected

FAMILY LEARNING NEEDS

Tasks	Assessments	Home management
Basic skills	*Altered respiratory status*	*Coping with stress*
Suctioning	Color change (e.g., pallor, cyanosis)	Identify anticipated stress (e.g., financial burden, privacy, fatigue, child care)
Tracheostomy tube change	Neurologic changes associated with hypoxia and hypercarbia (e.g., agitation, irritability, lethargy)	Develop coping strategies
Tracheostomy tie changes		Identify resources
Tracheostoma care		
Ventilator adjustment		
Equipment use, maintenance, and troubleshooting	Increased work of breathing (e.g., retractions, nostril flaring, grunting)	*Community resources*
Cardiopulmonary resuscitation	Tachypnea	Access and use support systems (e.g., primary care physician, home nursing agency, local paramedics, therapists, school)
Accessing emergency services	Diaphoresis	
Administering medication	Decreased chest expansion	
	Exercise intolerance	
Optional skills		*Financial resources*
Aerosolized treatments	*Fluid and electrolytes*	Anticipate out-of-pocket expenses
Oxygen delivery	Edema or excess weight gain	Access and use financial support
Enteral feedings	Dehydration (e.g., sunken eyes and fontanel, decreased urine output, dry membranes, lethargy)	
Gastrostomy site care	Diarrhea	
Home therapy routine	Vomiting	
Chest physiotherapy	Fever	

to demonstrate proficiency in independently providing both routine and emergency care for their child. A lack of commitment to learning the skills is considered a serious problem and must be addressed as early as possible.

Early initiation of teaching gives caregivers adequate time to learn at their own pace, provides maximal opportunities for skill mastery, and allows rest periods from teaching as needed. Assessment of learning needs is a dynamic interaction between members of the discharge planning team and caregivers. This exchange of information serves to promote the family's involvement in the child's care. Family input into the teaching plan is critical because health care professionals and family members may have differing perceptions of learning needs. Unresolved disagreements about teaching priorities could result in conflict and issues of control. Use of a mutually developed learning contract may be helpful in providing structure and a means of communication for all members of the discharge planning team.

The discharge plan includes a comprehensive checklist. A teaching checklist assists the discharge planning team to quickly identify areas of mastery and focus on areas where additional teaching is needed. Individuals responsible for patient and family education must be competent in assessing learning needs, readiness to learn, and motivation and barriers to learning. Teaching sessions are structured according to caregivers' individual learning styles and pace. A survey of family members revealed that the preferred teaching session lasts 30 minutes, includes one or two family members, occurs at the bedside, and includes demonstration of the technique. Ample time for return demonstration and practice, with positive reinforcement and encouragement, is critical to develop caregivers' confidence and competence.

The types of educational activities used are tailored

to the caregivers' learning needs. Use of mannequins and teaching aids are helpful tools that allow caregivers to practice skills without fear of injuring the child. Providing written information for caregivers to read before demonstration is a widely used practice. The advantage of written materials is that they are available for future reference; thus caregivers need not memorize all information taught. The use of written materials must always be supplemented with discussion and demonstration. Barriers to traditional educational methods (e.g., language or illiteracy) pose challenges because innovative approaches to meet learning needs must be used.

Education focuses on teaching the child's care rather than complex details of the disease process. Teaching sessions begin in a nonthreatening manner with discussion and demonstration, focusing on simple, routine care (e.g., skin care, play, or bathing) and basic assessment (e.g., skin redness). Caregivers are given the opportunity to build confidence, develop a sense of mastery, and interact with the child at each level of the educational process. Teaching gradually progresses to increasingly more difficult skills (e.g., changing tracheostomy tube) and more complex assessment (e.g., signs of hypoxia). Topics ranked by caregivers as essential or very important are given priority and initiated according to caregivers' needs.

Before discharge, family members practice assuming the role of primary care provider for extended periods. During this time the PICU staff promote the family's autonomy and assume an assistive role. Caregivers must demonstrate skill proficiency, problem solving, familiarity with the child's routine, assessment of the child's status, and ability to respond appropriately in emergency situations. When caregivers are competent, they may take the child on short excursions from the PICU without a member of the health care team.

Equipment and Supplies

Careful selection of durable equipment vendors is essential. A vendor that is able to provide all durable medical equipment and disposable supplies is preferred. Optimally, the vendor has recent experience with pediatric home ventilator–assisted patients. The vendor must be reliable and able to provide emergency service within 1 hour. This is especially critical if the family does not have a backup ventilator or has limited supply stores. Scheduled equipment assessment (monthly) and 24-hour availability are essential. Routine home visits provide an opportunity to check equipment functioning, perform maintenance, provide ongoing education to caregivers, assist with problem solving, and assess safety concerns. Other considerations when selecting a vendor include supply delivery schedules, cost, availability of direct third-party billing, and provider status with appropriate state and federal agencies. Feedback from health care team members familiar with the vendor can be extremely valuable.

After a vendor is selected, a list of home care equipment is developed. Equipment lists are customized to meet the child's individual needs. The task of assembling the equipment list is a collaborative effort of the discharge planning team.

An important aspect of the teaching process includes use of the equipment. Caregivers must be able to demonstrate competence in assembling, operating, and maintaining all equipment. Most vendors are willing to provide the equipment and assistance with education during the transition phase from hospital to home. The equipment must function safely and the child's condition remain stable for at least 72 hours before discharge. On the day of discharge all equipment must be set up in the home. Ideally, the equipment vendor and the home care nurse are in attendance to assist with transfer of care from the hospital to the home.

Financial Reimbursement

When the caregivers have mastered key educational objectives, the child is ready to be discharged. However, securing funding for home support is generally a lengthy and cumbersome process that frequently delays discharge for substantial periods. Managed care and reductions in reimbursements have resulted in fewer resources available for shift nursing and durable medical equipment in the home. Early and continuous communication with the patient's insurance company is imperative. Establishing a relationship with the insurance company case manager will assist in identifying the limitations set by the insurer. For situations in which insurers provide 100% coverage for contracted providers, the family must understand that using alternate vendors may jeopardize coverage. If the family has limited coverage for home nursing and equipment, the insurance case manager may be helpful in negotiating these services with the insurance company. If the insurance company is covering 100% of the hospitalization, comparison of this cost with home care costs

HOME EQUIPMENT

Basic supplies
Tracheostomy supplies

Tracheostomy tubes
Twill tape (½ inch)
Cotton-tipped applicators
Hydrogen peroxide
Sterile water

Ventilation supplies

Portable ventilator
Backup ventilator (in home or immediately accessible)
Resuscitation bag and mask
Ventilator circuits
Filters
Ventilator power source (battery and generator)
Cascade humidifier

Suction supplies

Suction machine (convertible or portable and stationary)
Suction connection tubing
Suction catheters
0.9% sodium chloride solution

Optional or additional supplies
Monitoring equipment

Apnea monitor
Intercom system
Manual call system
Pulse oximeter

Treatment supplies

Medication nebulizer
H cylinder oxygen tank
Oxygen tubing
Air compressor

Transportation

Double stroller
Wheelchair with ventilator tray

Nutritional supplies

Continuous feeding pump
Formula bags
Large syringe
Gastrostomy tube connector
Site care supplies (same as tracheostomy site supplies)
Enteral formula
Refrigerator

INFORMATION FREQUENTLY REQUESTED BY HOME CARE PAYORS

History and physical examination that reflects the child's current status
Current progress notes including medical plan
List of equipment and supplies needed for home care
Identified equipment vendors and home nursing agency
Assessment of home nursing need, including number of hours and level of care
Nursing treatment plan for home care
Hospital or long-term care costs vs. home care costs
Detailed assessment of psychosocial status of child and family

may hasten the approval process. It may be possible to negotiate with the payor to provide the services and equipment needed in lieu of hospitalization because ventilator dependence frequently can generate hospital bills of $300,000 a year.

If the insurance company is not willing to negotiate or the family has no funding, the hospital case manager must then pursue public funding. This long and complex process must be started early in the child's hospitalization because the child is usually medically stable and ready for discharge long before funding is approved. Public funding and specialized financial programs that may include middle and upper income families vary according to geographic area. The goal of these programs is to enable children who would otherwise have to remain in an acute-care hospital to be cared for at home.

Although the cost of home care for the ventilator-dependent child is less than the hospital cost, it is expensive. Costs have been estimated at $110,000 annually, with skilled nursing service accounting for 60% of the total cost. In some cases the cost of home and hospital care is nearly equal for some third-party payors because of capitated contracts and restrictions on the type of nursing care used. Changing existing policy and procedure related to discharging ventilator-dependent children to home is an arduous and time-consuming process.

Home Environment and Community Resources

Members of the discharge planning team work simultaneously to achieve and maintain medical stability of the child, secure funding, educate families, and prepare the home environment. The home environment needs to be assessed early to allow time to implement any necessary changes. Some families may need to move or change their living arrangements to meet their child's needs. The home environment must have adequate space for equipment and supplies, electricity and adequate and available electrical outlets, a telephone, a bathroom, a refrigerator, a smoke or fire alarm, and accessibility for the patient (e.g., wheelchair ramps).

RISKS AND COMPLICATIONS

An essential part of the educational process is to emphasize the child's continued vulnerability. The family must be aware of the increased risk of morbidity and mortality associated with the underlying disease and dependence on medical technology. The risk of injury and accidental death must be explained carefully to caregivers. Emphasis is placed on the importance of the tracheostomy tube as the child's airway. Caregivers must understand that airway obstruction is the greatest risk for children and that cardiac arrest is usually secondary to unresolved airway complications.

The most frequent airway emergencies experienced by ventilator-assisted children include tracheal decannulation, airway obstruction, ventilator disconnection, alarm failure, and power failure. The educational process must include strategies to prevent these occurrences and essential steps needed in emergency interventions. If the tracheostomy tube appears to be occluded, caregivers are taught to first quickly attempt to suction. If unsuccessful, they must

be prepared to immediately replace the tracheostomy tube. Emergency equipment, including an extra tracheostomy tube, scissors, ties, and suction equipment, must always be available wherever the child is. In the event of an unplanned visit to an unfamiliar emergency department, caregivers who have developed expertise in the child's care must be prepared to share the specialized equipment and information necessary to meet the child's needs.

CURRENT RESEARCH AND FUTURE CONSIDERATIONS

Current health care trends reveal increasing use of home care. Surveys conducted in the United States and Britain document a growing population of ventilator-assisted pediatric patients effectively cared for in the home setting by their families. This population poses new challenges for the future. Because of changes in financial reimbursement and managed care, processes and solutions that were once effective are unusable.

The high cost of ventilator-assisted support cannot be overlooked. As the availability of technology continues to increase, health care professionals must evaluate their practices. Questions regarding what will be offered to patients and families must be addressed. Members of the health care team must address ethical issues and develop a unified approach to caring for patients with chronic respiratory failure. There must be constant emphasis on finding innovative ways to provide quality care, meet patient needs, and practice in a fiscally responsible manner.

ADDITIONAL READING

Adams AB, Whitman J, Marcy T. Surveys of long-term ventilatory support in Minnesota: 1986 and 1992. Chest 103:1463-1469, 1993.

Aday LA, Wegener DH. Home care for ventilator-assisted children: Implications for the children, their families, and health policy. Child Health Care 17:112-120, 1988.

Allen N, Simone JA, Wingenbach GF. Families with a ventilator-assisted child: Transitional issues. J Perinatol 14: 48-55, 1994.

DeWitt PK, Jansen MT, Ward SD, Keens TG. Obstacles to discharge of ventilator-assisted children from hospital to home. Chest 103:1560-1565, 1993.

Fields AI, Rosenblatt A, Pollack MM, Kaufman J. Home care cost-effectiveness for respiratory technology–dependent children. Am J Dis Child 145:729-733, 1991.

Liquid plasma and plasma	Deficit of stable coagulation factors	Source of nonlabile factors	Deficit of labile coagulation factors or volume replacement	Should be ABO compatible	Infectious diseases; allergic reactions	<4 hr
Cryoprecipitated antihemophilic factor	Hemophilia A, von Willebrand's disease, Hypofibrinogenemia, Factor XIII deficiency	Provides factor VIII, fibrinogen, von Willebrand's factor, factor XIII	Conditions not deficient in contained factors	Frequent repeat doses may be necessary	Infectious diseases; allergic reactions	<4 hr
Platelets: Platelets, pheresis	Bleeding from thrombocytopenia or platelet function abnormality	Improves hemostasis	Plasma coagulation deficits and some conditions with rapid platelet destruction (e.g., idiopathic thrombocytopenic purpura)	Do not use some microaggregate filters (check manufacturer's instructions)	Infectious diseases; septic/toxic, allergic, febrile reactions; GVHD	<4 hr
Granulocytes: Pheresis	Neutropenia with infection	Provides granulocytes	Infection responsive to antibiotics	Must be ABO compatible; do not use depth-type microaggregate filters	Infectious diseases; allergic reactions; febrile reactions; GVHD	One unit over 2- to 4-hr period—closely observe for reactions

*From American Association of Blood Banks, American Red Cross, Council of Community Blood Centers. Circular of Information for the Use of Human Blood and Blood Components. Bethesda: American Association of Blood Banks, 1994, pp 14-15.

sis raises the potassium content to three times that normally found in serum, and 2,3-DPG decreases, causing a shift in the oxygen dissociation curve to the left.

Packed red blood cells

Transfusion with packed red blood cells (PRBCs) is indicated for the anemic patient who needs increased tissue oxygen delivery. The diagnosis of anemia depends on the hemoglobin value and the patient's clinical condition. For example, if a child with sickle cell disease who is seen for a well child care visit has a hemoglobin level of 6 to 7 g/dl, no treatment is indicated. However, when the same child is hospitalized 2 months later with pneumonia, necessitating oxygen and ventilatory support, and his hemoglobin value is 7 g/dl, transfusion therapy may be indicated.

Packed red blood cell products. PRBCs are usually prepared with CPDA-1 solution or an additive solution. The additive solution is 100 ml of sodium chloride solution, glucose, and other components that enhance red cell function and survival. One unit of PRBCs has a volume of approximately 300 ml. The PRBCs are stored at 1° to 6° C. CPDA-1–prepared PRBCs have a shelf life of 35 days, whereas additive solution–prepared PRBCs have a shelf life of 42 days. The use of leukocyte-reduction filters decreases the incidence of febrile, nonhemolytic transfusion reactions due to contaminating WBCs. Irradiating blood products is the only way to prevent donor lymphocytes from proliferating and causing graft-vs.-host disease (GVHD) in recipients with severe defects in cell-mediated immunity.

Packed red blood cell dose. With CPDA-1–prepared PRBCs, a 10 ml/kg transfusion will increase the hemoglobin level by 2.5 to 3 g/dl and the hematocrit level by approximately 10%. With additive solution–prepared PRBCs, a 15 ml/kg transfusion will produce a similar increase. A standard transfusion is given over 2 to 4 hours. A 15 ml/kg transfusion is considered maximal, even when the child is hemodynamically stable. The treatment of severe anemia (Hb <4 g/dl) is discussed in detail in Chapter 50.

Platelets

Platelet transfusions can be used to stop or prevent severe hemorrhage in patients with thrombocytopenia and, less commonly, platelet dysfunction. Without major trauma or surgery, adequate hemostasis is generally maintained with a platelet count of ≥20,000/mm³, assuming platelet function is normal.

The decision to administer platelets must be based on factors in addition to the platelet count. Bleeding will be greater than that predicted by the platelet number when the patient has concomitant platelet dysfunction, vascular or coagulation abnormalities, or uremia or is receiving certain medications (e.g., aspirin). Hypertension, fever, trauma, and sepsis may also exacerbate bleeding in the thrombocytopenic patient. Additionally, thrombocytopenia in certain clinical situations (e.g., active bleeding, surgery, trauma, disseminated intravascular coagulation [DIC], intracranial malignancies, and intrinsic platelet dysfunction) may necessitate more intensive platelet transfusion support. Furthermore, when the patient has platelet dysfunction secondary to uremia or thrombocytopenia secondary to splenic sequestration, mechanical injury, or immune-mediated platelet destruction, the efficacy of transfused platelets will be markedly diminished. Finally, the decision to administer platelets must be based on an understanding of the attendant risks. Serious and even fatal infections can be transmitted via transfusion therapy, and patients may become sensitized to cellular antigens, forming antibodies that will later interfere with the efficacy of subsequent platelet transfusions.

After all of these data are considered, the following general recommendations are made for platelet transfusion support. For patients with life-threatening or clinically significant bleeding, give platelets when thrombocytopenia of any degree or platelet dysfunction exists. For patients without significant bleeding, give platelets under the following circumstances: before major surgery if the platelet count is <50,000/mm³ or if dysfunction is documented and before arterial catheter placement, lumbar puncture, or minor surgical procedures if the platelet count is <20,000/mm³. Transfusion is considered in a child with fever or sepsis whose platelet count is <20,000/mm³ or in any child with a platelet count of <5000/mm³ whose abnormal bone marrow is not likely to recover within the next 48 hours. A patient undergoing cardiovascular surgery with unexplained bleeding or in whom a cardiopulmonary bypass pump is being discontinued needs to receive platelets for hemostasis regardless of platelet count. The cardiopulmonary bypass pump causes platelet dysfunction; thus adequate platelet counts do not ensure hemostasis. Adjuvant support for thrombocytopenic patients and therapies for those conditions that do not normally respond to platelet transfusions are described in Table 164-2.

Table 164-2 Alternatives to Platelet Transfusion

Disorder	Therapy
Idiopathic thrombocyto-penic purpura	Steroids, IV gamma globulin, splenectomy
Uremia	Desmopressin (DDAVP), cryoprecipitate, RBC transfusions to correct anemia
Epistaxis	Local pressure, nasal packs
Oral mucosal bleeding	Gelfoam, desiccated collagen preparation, topical thrombin, aminocaproic acid

Platelet products. Two types of platelet products, random donor platelet concentrates and single-donor platelets (SDPs), are usually available. They may be obtained either from whole blood or by apheresis. Both types of platelet products are stored at 20° to 24° C with constant agitation for up to 5 days.

One random donor platelet concentrate (PC) is derived from 1 unit of whole blood. Each PC prepared in this manner will contain approximately 5.5×10^{10} platelets suspended in 40 to 70 ml of plasma. This volume can be decreased if necessary, but the process is time consuming and may interfere with platelet function. Various numbers of PCs are usually pooled together (see discussion of platelet dose below) for transfusion. This product is more readily available than single-donor apheresis platelets; however, multiple donor exposure usually results because pooling is necessary to achieve adequate dosing.

SDPs are obtained by apheresis from a single donor. The number of platelets obtained in this fashion (at least 3×10^{11} platelets suspended in 200 to 250 ml of plasma) approximately equals those in five to eight pooled PCs. SDPs may be more difficult to obtain since apheresis donors must be located. Their use is usually restricted to those patients refractory to pooled PCs or to those undergoing bone marrow transplantation when excessive antigen exposure would be harmful.

Platelet dose. As a suitable starting dose, one PC per 10 kg body weight can be expected to elevate the platelet count by 50,000/mm³. An equivalent increase in platelet count can be expected using 5 ml/kg of SDPs. Generally a minimum of 2 units of PC must be

ordered for infants, 3 units for toddlers, 4 units for young children, and 6 to 8 units for preadolescents and adolescents. The platelets must be transfused over 30 minutes or as rapidly as volume constraints allow through a standard 170 μm blood filter. Filters with a smaller pore size may filter out the platelets. Appropriate filters are usually provided by the blood bank.

It is important to document the response to platelet transfusion therapy in all patients. Less than expected increases in the posttransfusion platelet count may be due to a variety of factors such as alloimmunization, infection, DIC, splenomegaly, or injury to the platelets during procurement, storage, or transfusion. Obtaining platelet counts 1 and 24 hours after transfusion may help differentiate alloimmunization (low 1-hour platelet count) from other reasons for increased platelet consumption (1-hour count adequate, but 24-hour count low). SDPs, especially from family members, or HLA-matched platelets may be of benefit in the alloimmunized patient, whereas increasing the number of random donor units may benefit the patient with increased platelet consumption secondary to infection or bleeding. In cases associated with bleeding due to infections or DIC, 4 units of PC also provides the additional benefit of coagulation factors equivalent to 1 unit of FFP. In the case of massive PRBCs and platelet requirements, crucial coagulation factors may become diluted. Coagulation parameters need to be followed, including PT/PTT levels and platelet counts, and corrected as needed with the appropriate blood component to control bleeding.

Fresh frozen plasma

FFP is plasma that has been separated from anticoagulated whole blood within 8 hours of donation and rapidly frozen. All clotting factors are present, including 200 units of factor VIII per unit of FFP. It is used to replace depleted clotting factors in patients with acquired bleeding disorders such as occur in liver disease or DIC. A dose of 10 to 15 ml/kg is given over 30 minutes to 2 hours every 8 to 12 hours as needed. Do not use FFP as a source of colloid for volume replacement. Albumin or plasma protein fraction are used for this purpose since these products are less expensive and do not carry the same risk of transfusion-related infections.

FFP must be thawed at 36° to 38° C in a water bath or an approved microwave unit before administration. It must be transfused immediately or stored up to 24 hours at a temperature of between 1° and 6° C. No filter is necessary for FFP administration.

Factor concentrates

The use of these products is usually restricted to the treatment of patients with congenital deficiencies of a clotting factor. Cryoprecipitate, prepared in the blood bank, contains fibrinogen (approximately 150 mg per bag), factor VIII (approximately 80 units per bag), von Willebrand's factor activity, and factor XIII. Cryoprecipitate will benefit patients with hemophilia A, von Willebrand's disease, afibrinogenemia, and rarely DIC. Once thawed, cryoprecipitate is stored at room temperature and transfused within 4 hours of thawing.

Factor VIII and IX concentrates are commercially produced products containing known amounts of factor activity. In general 1 unit/kg of factor VIII concentrate will increase the factor VIII level by 2% and 1 unit/kg of factor IX concentrate will increase the factor IX level by 1%. Their use is restricted to patients with hemophilia and must be directed by a pediatric hematologist.

TECHNIQUE

Blood products are administered as soon as possible after they are obtained from the blood bank. Blood may be returned to the blood bank and reissued if the container closure has not been accessed and the blood temperature remains between 1° and 10° C. If the blood will not be used for several hours, it must be stored in a monitored refrigerator to ensure properly controlled refrigeration and decrease the risk of bacterial contamination. A check system must be used to ensure that the patient's name, hospital number, and blood type are correct.

A standard 170 μm blood filter must be used to retain blood clots and other debris in nonplatelet blood products. This filter is included in most routine blood administration sets. Standard filters can ordinarily be used for 2 to 4 units of blood. Platelets come from the blood bank with a special administration set because the use of the standard 170 μm blood filter may actually remove platelets. With FFP, no filter is necessary.

Special filters include Micropore filters and leukocyte-reduction filters. Micropore filters, which have an effective pore size of 20 to 40 μm, can eliminate the smaller microaggregates. Their use in combination with the standard 170 μm blood filter may de-

crease the likelihood of respiratory distress in postoperative cardiac patients and for patients in whom massive transfusions are anticipated. Leukocyte reduction filters are used to reduce WBC contamination of PRBCs and PCs. Leukocyte reduction of blood products is commonly performed in the blood bank. The leukocyte filters for PRBCs and PCs differ; therefore the appropriate filter must be used if leukocyte reduction is performed at the bedside.

Blood must be administered through as large a needle as possible to avoid hemolysis, particularly at rapid rates of infusion. Access to central circulation is needed for transfusions of ≥1 blood volume.

The IV catheter must be flushed with 0.9% sodium chloride solution to avoid hemolysis or agglutination of the RBCs and platelets. Intermittent flushing with small volumes of 0.9% sodium chloride solution may be needed to keep IV lines patent. Only 0.9% sodium chloride may be added to blood or blood components. Medications, lactated Ringer's solution, or dextrose solutions are not compatible with blood products because they may induce hemolysis or clotting. Blood products may be administered with a constant infusion pump to maintain vein patency and regulate infusion rate. All blood products must be infused in <4 hours.

A blood warmer must be used when transfusions are given to small infants or children in whom temperature control is a problem. Transfusions of ≥1 blood volume must also be warmed. Cold blood must never be given through a right atrial catheter since this may cause arrhythmias.

During transfusion a neonate must be watched closely for signs of hypoglycemia since he may not have adequate glycogen or glucose stores.

RISK AND COMPLICATIONS
Informed Consent

As stated in Chapter 115, the law mandates that informed consent be obtained for medical and surgical procedures, including the use of blood products. The physician must address the specific diagnosis that necessitates the use of blood or blood products and the steps used to arrive at that diagnosis. The procedure of transfusing must be explained as well as the expected benefits. The risks must also be addressed, specifically the following:

Allergic reactions, including hives, itching, and anaphylaxis
Fever and chills

165 White Blood Cell Transfusions

Larry Herrera · Richard L. Wasserman

BACKGROUND AND INDICATIONS

Granulocyte transfusion therapy continues to be a controversial modality. If, however, the key elements of granulocyte physiology are understood and the available information critically examined, the use of granulocyte transfusions in specific situations is rational, supported, and potentially lifesaving. Granulocytes are crucial in the defense against most bacterial and fungal infections. They function by attaching to the surface of a microorganism, ingesting it, and killing it. This interaction at the granulocyte surface triggers a complex series of intracellular events necessary for "cidal" activity. Once sufficiently stimulated, the granulocyte is incapable of being restimulated and loses its functional ability. Early studies of WBC transfusions did not appreciate the fragile nature of functional granulocytes, and many studies used nonfunctional granulocytes. Earlier studies also used too few absolute numbers of granulocytes in their transfusions and the number of transfusions given may have been inadequate. Harvesting granulocytes using filtration techniques, storing them for more than 6 hours, and administering them through a filter all inactivate granulocytes. Studies using appropriately collected and promptly administered granulocytes have demonstrated their effectiveness in reducing mortality in the presence of life-threatening infection.

WBC transfusions are indicated for patients with life-threatening infection whose neutrophil defenses are inadequate because of reduced neutrophil numbers or abnormal function. There are many trials in adults that reflect a marked advantage in survival in patients who received granulocyte transfusions in addition to standard antimicrobial therapy for the treatment of bacterial sepsis. At this time data are insufficient to recommend prophylactic granulocyte transfusions. Finally, there is no clear-cut proof that granulocyte transfusions are of benefit to patients with fungal infections, although there is evidence in a dog

---

> ### POTENTIAL INDICATIONS FOR WBC CELL TRANSFUSIONS
>
> *Neonates (up to 2 mo)*
> Suspected sepsis *plus* an absolute neutrophil count <1500/mm^3 *or* an immature/total neutrophil ratio >0.6
>
> *Neutropenia (congenital or secondary)*
> Absolute neutrophil count <250/mm^3 in a patient with culture-proven bacterial or fungal infection *and* inadequate response to 72 hr of broad-spectrum antibiotics and amphotericin B
>
> *Neutrophil function disorder*
> Significant infection (usually involving head and neck, chest, or abdomen) in a patient with known granulocyte function

---

model that granulocyte transfusions can decrease the severity of experimentally induced systemic candidal infection.

Neutropenia/Neutrophil Storage Pool Depletion

The most common cause of significant neutropenia is antineoplastic therapy. Patients undergoing chemotherapy for leukemia, bone marrow transplant recipients, and patients receiving treatment for solid tumors often have absolute neutrophil counts <500/mm^3 and occasionally have no detectable neutrophils at all. Congenital neutropenia and aplastic anemia are other causes of markedly reduced neutrophil numbers.

The neutrophil storage pool is composed of those elements in the bone marrow responsible for the production of functional neutrophils. At birth the neonate's neutrophil storage pool is considerably smaller than that of an older child and may be rapidly depleted by excessive demand. The neutrophil storage pool depletion occurs in the presence of neonatal sepsis caused by any organism but is a particular feature of group B streptococcal sepsis.

Several inherited disorders of neutrophil dysfunction have been described. The most well known of these is chronic granulomatous disease, which is a deficiency of oxidative metabolism that renders the neutrophil unable to kill certain bacteria and fungi. Staphylococci, *Escherichia coli, Serratia marcescens,* and various fungal species are particular problems. Other less common disorders of granulocyte function in which cell movement, phagocytosis, and killing are defective have also been described.

The decision to use granulocyte transfusion therapy in a particular patient is based on clinical judgment.

TECHNIQUE

It is crucially important to begin mobilizing the blood transfusion service to supply granulocytes as soon as the possibility of giving WBC transfusions is considered. A minimum of 4 to 8 hours is needed to harvest granulocytes and prepare the product for administration. ABO and Rh compatibility are mandatory. Although tissue typing is not a necessity, matching of granulocytes is likely to be of benefit in alloimmunized recipients. Alloimmunization must be suspected in patients who show a poor response to platelet transfusions. A parent or other family member is often the most suitable donor for the first day's transfusion since he or she is usually readily available. In the event that the recipient is a candidate for bone marrow transplantation, a family member is excluded as a donor. A routine type and crossmatch on the child must be sent for analysis, and the donor needs to be referred to the transfusion center. It is prudent to recommend that the family recruit several potential donors immediately since a given individual may be unable to serve as a donor because of incompatibilities or personal health problems.

Neonates usually need a single dose of 0.5 to 1.0 $\times$ 10^9 granulocytes/kg body weight. Depending on the patient's clinical status and response, multiple doses may be necessary. Some blood banks can harvest this number of granulocytes from a single fresh donation of whole blood using cell separators. Older children need to receive the entire harvest from a routine granulocytophoresis. Except in neonates, granulocyte transfusions must be given daily for at least 5 days. It is recommended that a minimum daily infusion of 2 to 3 $\times$ 10^{10} granulocytes per transfusion be administered. The total duration of therapy depends on the nature of the infection and the underlying defect in granulocytes. Some patients with chronic granulomatous disease have received granulocyte transfusions daily for 6 weeks or more. In the more common situation of chemotherapy-induced neutropenia, granulocyte transfusions may be stopped when the patient's bone marrow recovers. A total neutrophil count >250/mm^3 for 2 consecutive days in a patient who is recovering from infection is probably appropriate justification for ceasing transfusion. Patients with granulocyte functional disorders are often more difficult to assess, and granulocyte transfusions are usually continued until there is clinical evidence of recovery. It is seldom appropriate to give granulocyte transfusions for <5 days.

Granulocytes need to be administered as soon as possible after harvest because they begin to deteriorate immediately after they leave the donor's body. Under no circumstances should granulocytes >12 hours old be administered. Since granulocytes may be activated by rough treatment, the use of peristaltic pumps or other devices that may fragment the granulocytes must be avoided. The use of syringe pumps is ideal, but in most situations no pump is necessary. The rate of administration must be rapid. Although it is unwise to push a granulocyte transfusion over a few minutes, the granulocytes cannot be allowed to sit for long periods for the reasons mentioned previously, and 30- to 60-minute infusions are usually well tolerated. If an apparent mild transfusion reaction occurs, the rate of administration may be slowed as needed. Whether the WBC transfusion is stored in a blood bag or a syringe, it needs to be gently mixed every 10 to 15 minutes to prevent the high local concentrations of granulocytes that occur by gravity sedimentation. Mixing can be accomplished by gently squeezing the blood bag or rotating the syringe. Under no circumstances should granulocytes be passed through a filter <160 μm pore size.

RISKS AND COMPLICATIONS

The most predictable risk of granulocyte transfusion is hepatitis. The risk is related to the total number of transfusions. Given the total unit exposure of the typical granulocyte transfusion recipient, the likelihood of developing hepatitis is greater than in the typical RBC or platelet transfusion recipient. The risk of other blood-borne infections is modest, with a low risk of hepatitis B or immunodeficiency virus infection. Cytomegalovirus (CMV) infection is transmitted by blood and may be a significant issue in CMV-negative immunocompromised neutropenic patients. It is recommended that donors be prescreened to avoid discovery of infectious diseases after granulocyte infusion. Often these test results are not available until after administration. Therefore it is imperative that the physician explain this to the recipient's parents and obtain appropriate consent.

In addition to granulocytes, leukocyte transfusions also contain immunocompetent lymphocytes with resultant well-documented cases of acute graft-vs.-host disease (GVHD). These cases were acute in onset (6 to 10 days), and the typical manifestations of GVHD, including rash, liver dysfunction, diarrhea, and pancytopenia, were seen. As with other blood products, although irradiation is not a universally accepted procedure, it eliminates this complication. Patients with granulocyte functional disorders are not at risk for GVHD. Granulocyte transfusions for those patients need not be irradiated.

The immediate mild and severe transfusion reaction risks are similar to those for other blood products (see Chapter 164). Because damaged granulocytes release vasoactive mediators, the likelihood of a febrile or vasoactive transfusion reaction is higher with granulocytes than with other blood products. Transfusion reactions that do not resolve when the infusion rate is slowed may be treated with antihistamines, antipyretics, glucocorticoids, or meperidine. Some physicians choose to treat all recipients with antihistamines and antipyretics. Leukocyte transfusions carry a significant risk of alloimmunization (i.e., the production of antibodies against WBC antigens). This is a greater problem with multiple granulocyte transfusions but rarely interferes with their use.

Perhaps one of the most important complications related to granulocyte transfusions are the effects on the pulmonary system. Acute reactions may include bronchospasm, wheezing, and cough. Patients with significant pulmonary disease, particularly interstitial pneumonia or a widespread fungal pneumonitis, may experience significant deterioration of pulmonary function following the transfusion. Numerous mechanisms for this have been postulated. This should not be considered a contraindication to granulocyte therapy since patients with that degree of microbial invasion are at high risk for death without granulocyte transfusion. Initial reports of severe pulmonary reactions to the combination of amphotericin B and granulocyte transfusions have been refuted; therefore the use of amphotericin B need not be limited in patients also receiving granulocyte transfusions. Nevertheless, it is prudent to separate the transfusions by intervals of 6 to 8 hours.

CURRENT RESEARCH AND FUTURE CONSIDERATIONS

Other therapeutic advances may limit the need for granulocyte transfusions. The most recent of these advances is the availability and use of colony-stimulating factors that are produced through recombinant DNA technology. In patients undergoing chemotherapy such factors are widely being used to stimulate marrow regeneration and decrease the duration of severe neutropenia, thereby lessening the risk of sepsis. Although these agents decrease the duration of severe neutropenia, they do not totally eliminate the infection risk; therefore clinical situations will arise in which granulocyte transfusions will be considered as part of the therapeutic armamentarium. Even more recently there has been a resurgence of interest in the administration of granulocyte colony-stimulating factor to granulocyte transfusion donors in an effort to increase the yield of granulocytes and increase the functional life expectancy of the granulocyte once in the recipient.

ADDITIONAL READING

Cairo MS. The use of granulocyte transfusions in neonatal sepsis. Transfus Med Rev 4:14-22, 1990.

Freireich EJ. White cell transfusions born again. Leuk Lymphoma 11:161-165, 1993.

Tobias JD, Schleien C. Granulocyte transfusions—A review for the intensive care physician. Anaesth Intensive Care 19:512-519, 1991.

166 Therapeutic Apheresis

Robert M. Bradley · Laurie J. Sutor

BACKGROUND AND INDICATIONS

"Apheresis" is a term used to describe a procedure in which a particular component of the blood is separated and removed. For example, in plasmapheresis the cellular components are returned to the donor or patient while the plasma is either saved for transfusion or fractionation (donor apheresis) or replaced by colloid solutions (therapeutic plasma exchange). Cytapheresis is the inverse of this process in that the plasma is returned to the patient and a specific cellular component is removed. Removal of blood for therapeutic purposes has a long history, but the current practice of plasma exchange has its roots in the early part of this century. Automated techniques were developed in the late 1960s and early 1970s, and the use of this treatment modality has increased significantly over the past 25 years.

The goal in therapeutic plasma exchange is to remove pathologic factors such as toxins, antibodies, or immune complexes from the patient while replenishing the patient's intravascular volume with crystalloid or colloid solutions or donor plasma. In some clinical situations such as thrombotic thrombocytopenic purpura (TTP) and hemolytic-uremic syndrome (HUS), the replacement solution may also provide a substance that the patient lacks in sufficient quantity. There are two basic techniques for plasmapheresis: manual and automated.

The manual withdrawal of blood is time consuming and subjects the patients to large volume shifts. A unit of blood is withdrawn from the patient and then physically taken to a centrifuge to spin off the plasma. The cellular components are subsequently returned to the patient. This method thus introduces the potential for severe transfusion reactions in the event of the inadvertent return of the wrong unit of red cells to the patient. However, it does not involve expensive technology or specially trained personnel and is still used in special circumstances. Automated techniques are most common now and allow quicker, safer, and more efficient removal of plasma. Centrifugation, the predominant method of plasma separation in these machines, will be discussed in more detail below.

The services that provide apheresis vary. The regional blood donor center provides donor and therapeutic apheresis in some areas. Within the hospital, it can be provided by the blood bank, neurology, or hematology. Nephrologists also sometimes provide this service. The difference between dialysis and plasmapheresis is that dialysis removes mainly small molecules, whereas plasmapheresis removes larger molecules, including proteins and protein-bound molecules. Plasma exchange is typically performed by registered nurses and/or specially trained technicians. No matter who provides the service, however, quality patient care depends on the concerted efforts of the referring clinician, the apheresis physician, nurses, and other technical personnel.

Many of the indications for therapeutic apheresis have been difficult to define because of the lack of well-designed studies. In 1985 the American Medical Association Panel on Therapeutic Plasmapheresis published the results of its assessment of the status of the indications for this procedure. A second review of the topic was produced by the American Society for Apheresis in 1993, modifying the previous groups of indications established in 1985. These groups are defined as (1) indications for which therapeutic hemapheresis is standard and acceptable; (2) indications for which therapeutic hemapheresis is generally accepted, but is a second-line procedure to more conventional therapy; (3) conditions for which the reported evidence is insufficient to establish the efficacy of therapeutic apheresis; and (4) conditions for which the available controlled trials have shown a lack of therapeutic efficacy for hemapheresis. These categories are to be regarded as provisional, and therapy must be individualized for patient care needs. To date, most of the studies on plasmapheresis

INDICATIONS FOR THERAPEUTIC HEMAPHERESIS

Standard, accepted treatment

Goodpasture's syndrome
Thrombotic thrombocytopenic purpura
Acute Guillain-Barré syndrome
Myasthenia gravis
Cryoglobulinemia
Hyperviscosity syndrome
Posttransfusion purpura
Refsum's disease
Homozygous familial hypercholesterolemia
Chronic inflammatory demyelinating polyneuropathy
Eaton-Lambert myasthenic syndrome
HIV-related syndromes
　　Polyneuropathy
　　Hyperviscosity
　　Thrombotic thrombocytopenic purpura

Generally accepted, but second-line procedure to more conventional therapy

ABO-incompatible marrow transplant recipient
Immune thrombocytopenia (with staphylococcal protein A adsorption)
Bullous pemphigoid
Pemphigus vulgaris
Raynaud's disease
Systemic lupus erythematosus
Systemic vasculitis
Coagulation factor inhibitors
Poisonings
Paraproteinemic peripheral neuropathy

Hemolytic-uremic syndrome
Myeloma and paraproteinemias
Rapidly progressive nephritis (without antiglomerular basement membrane antibody disease)
Autoimmune hemolytic anemia

Insufficient evidence for efficacy

Juvenile rheumatoid arthritis
Progressive systemic sclerosis
Rheumatoid arthritis
Aplastic anemia/red cell aplasia
Nonhematologic cancer
Red cell alloantibodies and hemolytic disease of newborn
Immune thrombocytopenia (with staphylococcal protein A adsorption)
Platelet alloimmunization and refractoriness
Acute hepatic failure
Fabry's disease
Graves' disease
Multiple sclerosis
Paraneoplastic syndromes
Polymyositis/dermatomyositis
Organ allograft rejection (with photopheresis)

Available trials show lack of efficacy

Psoriasis
Amyotrophic lateral sclerosis
Functional psychotic disorders

have been in adults; applying the same data to the pediatric population may not be acceptable in some cases.

TECHNIQUE

Although a nurse must be available for blood sampling and volume and drug administration, most aspects of plasmapheresis can be performed by well-trained technicians. A number of technical points must be carefully considered for pediatric patients undergoing therapeutic hemapheresis. One of the first that has to be addressed is vascular access. The peripheral veins of children are not able to withstand the large-bore needles and high-flow rates used during automated plasma exchange procedures. Thus the use of a central venous catheter is essential. The catheter must have a double lumen and be thick walled; hemodialysis-type catheters are favored in these situations. In most cases a 7 F catheter is the smallest size used. Several brands are available, including Medicomp, Quinton, VasCath, and Cook.

The extracorporeal volume of the plasmapheresis machines is another important issue in pediatric hemapheresis. In general withdrawal of >10% of the total blood volume, or about 140 ml in a 20 kg (45 pound) child, is to be avoided. The extracorporeal volume of the Cobe Spectra, an automated continuous flow machine, is approximately 175 ml. This means that 175 ml of the child's total blood volume must be removed before the machine begins to return the red cells back to the patient. If the hematocrit is low, an even larger volume of blood will be withdrawn before the red cells are returned. Thus the extracorporeal circuit of continuous flow machines must be primed with packed RBCs for children weighing <20 kg (45 pounds) or in those with hematocrit levels <20%. The blood used for priming the circuit usually mimics the hematocrit of whole blood; however, this hematocrit can be adjusted, depending on the severity of the child's anemia.

Typically, 1 to 1.5 plasma volumes are exchanged per procedure. The American Society for Apheresis recommends that 1 patient plasma volume be exchanged per procedure; minor variations in this amount are not believed to be clinically important. The efficiency of the procedure is greatest in the first volume removed and decreases rapidly thereafter. Processing 1 total blood volume removes approximately 65% of the patient's plasma; 2 volumes, 85%; and 3 volumes, 95%. The patient's plasma volume is calculated from the patient's height, weight, and hematocrit and is easily performed on the software provided on automated instruments. The typical plasmapheresis procedure is completed in 1 to 4 hours, depending on the volume of plasma to be exchanged and the flow rate through the extracorporeal circuit. The number and frequency of procedures to be performed is heavily influenced by the type of disease, the patient's clinical status, and the response to the initial procedure. Although no set guidelines are available, one procedure per day for sick patients is reasonable. Critically ill patients may need two procedures in the first 24 hours, but this is the exception rather than the rule.

The replacement fluids used in plasmapheresis procedures may include 0.9% sodium chloride solution, plasma protein fraction (PPF), 5% albumin, and fresh frozen plasma (FFP). The exact component to be used has to be tailored to the patient's circumstances. Half and half mixtures of colloid and 0.9% sodium chloride solution are recommended for most procedures. However, some patients will become hypotensive while receiving this mixture. In these cases the percentage of PPF or albumin can be increased to maximize the oncotic pressure of the solution. PPF contains roughly 90% of plasma albumin and is often in greater supply than purified plasma albumin preparations. Both albumin and PPF are heat-treat-ed to inactivate viruses. FFP replacement is specifically indicated for patients with TTP; it may also be selected in those patients with conditions predisposing to bleeding, such as severe liver disease or disseminated intravascular coagulation. The potential for viral transmission from this component, however, tempers its use for other indications.

Monitoring and Laboratory Tests

The complete blood count, prothrombin time (PT) and activated partial thromboplastin time (APTT), electrolytes, calcium, and total protein are measured before the first procedure. Transient alterations in electrolytes and coagulation times can be expected after the procedure. These are rarely of clinical consequence, however. Whenever possible, the specific factor being removed (i.e., antiglomerular basement membrane antigen in Goodpasture's disease) or other initially abnormal laboratory values (i.e., platelet count in TTP) need to be followed for objective documentation of disease remission.

Some clinicians monitor ionized calcium but many do not. Often a complete blood count is obtained at the end of the procedure. The vital signs (systemic blood pressure, pulse rate, respiratory rate, and temperature) are checked every 15 to 20 minutes.

Equipment

There are two types of automated plasmapheresis equipment: centrifugation-based technology and membrane filtration technology. Centrifugation is predominantly used in the United States and depends on the differing densities of the various components of blood for separation. Centrifugation equipment can be further classified into continuous flow and discontinuous flow machines. Discontinuous or intermittent flow machines are more commonly used in donor pheresis. Only a single vascular access catheter is needed since the blood is processed in cycles. Disadvantages of discontinuous flow equipment include their larger extracorporeal volume (up to 600 ml in some instances) and their longer processing times. Alternatively, continuous flow machines have much smaller extracorporeal volumes and consequently are better for individuals who cannot tolerate large volume shifts.

Membrane filtration plasmapheresis retains the cellular elements of the blood inside hollow fiber membranes while the plasma passes out through pores and is collected separately. A major limitation of this equipment is that these machines are typically only able to perform plasma exchange procedures, whereas machines employing centrifugation technology may be used for both cell and plasma separation. This lack of versatility has made membrane filtration technology less popular in the United States in recent years.

Medications

The most important factors in drug removal from the plasma during plasma exchange are the volume of distribution of the drug and the percent that is bound to protein (see Chapter 175). However, the variability of drug kinetics in sick patients makes accurate prediction of plasma drug levels during pheresis difficult. In general it is best to withhold most medications until the procedure is completed if possible.

Recently it has been observed that anaphylactic-type reactions, characterized by hypotension and flushing, can occur in plasma exchange patients on angiotensin-converting enzyme inhibitor therapy. This has only been seen in patients receiving protein colloid replacement (albumin or PPF) during their plasma exchange procedure. Withholding these medications for 24 to 48 hours prior to plasma exchange has been recommended in these cases.

RISKS AND COMPLICATIONS

The most frequently encountered complications of therapeutic apheresis are hypocalcemia, hypovolemia, and allergic reactions to FFP and albumin. Complications related to infections and coagulation abnormalities are also seen. Mechanical hemolysis and equipment failures are rare.

Citrate is the anticoagulant of choice for most plasmapheresis procedures and is usually administered in the extracorporeal circuit in an acid-citrate-dextrose formulation. The anticoagulant effect of citrate depends on the binding of calcium and thus can potentially cause hypocalcemia in some patients. Most of the citrate added to the extracorporeal circuit is eventually discarded with the patient's plasma. However, a small amount will be infused into the patient, and children may be especially sensitive to this. If FFP is used as a replacement fluid, the amount of citrate infused will be much greater because the plasma also contains citrate as an anticoagulant.

The hypocalcemia seen in these procedures can be manifested in perioral and distal extremity pares-

thesias, abdominal pain, pallor, bradycardia, and hypotension. It may also be associated with QT prolongation on the ECG. Prophylactic oral calcium supplementation (i.e., milk or calcium-based antacid tablets) has been shown to be effective in decreasing the incidence of hypocalcemic symptoms. Acute episodes may also respond to this therapy; as additional measures, the plasmapheresis technician can decrease the rate of blood flow through the extracorporeal circuit or decrease the citrate to blood ratio in the circuit. Since the half-life of citrate is thought to be only a few minutes, stopping the procedure for 10 to 15 minutes may allow the patient to metabolize enough citrate to relieve the symptoms. IV calcium administration may be necessary in cases in which the above maneuvers are not successful.

Hypotensive episodes can occur during plasmapheresis as a result of vasovagal reactions, hypovolemia, and anaphylaxis. Hypovolemia may be due to inadequate volume return or hypo-oncotic fluid replacement. Discontinuous flow machines may also produce intermittent hypovolemia. If hypovolemia occurs, the procedure is stopped and fluids (crystalloids or colloids, 20 ml/kg) administered until the patient is stable.

Urticaria, nausea, wheezing, and hypotension signify a probable allergic reaction, and these are found in up to 20% of patients receiving FFP as replacement fluid. The incidence with albumin or PPF is considerably less. Diphenhydramine, administered intravenously or orally, is useful in mild reactions; severe reactions with anaphylactic shock will necessitate emergency resuscitative therapy. If the patient is known to be particularly sensitive to plasma or albumin, premedication with diphenhydramine (1.25 mg/kg/dose PO, IV, or IM), prednisone (1 mg/kg/dose PO), and ephedrine (1 mg/kg/dose PO, IV, or SQ) may be used.

Viral transmission from blood components is rare. Albumin and PPF are heat-treated and have been demonstrated over many years to be safe from viral contamination. The primary concern is with FFP, but even with this component, the risk of transfusion-acquired HIV is approximately 1 in 493,000 units; hepatitis B and hepatitis C occur at rates of 1 in 63,000 units and 1 in 103,000 units, respectively. The risk of bacterial infection after plasmapheresis is controversial, and conflicting reports have been published. However, plasmapheresis does reduce circulating levels of immunoglobulins and complement, and it would seem prudent to exercise caution in performing this procedure on septic patients. Meticulous care of the catheter is extremely important in the prevention of infection.

Laboratory coagulation abnormalities are often documented immediately after plasmapheresis. There is evidence to suggest that plasmapheresis removes both procoagulant and anticoagulant factors, however, and this may account for the paucity of published reports of significant bleeding in these situations. The APTT and PT are initially prolonged after pheresis, but usually return to near baseline values within 24 hours. Activation of the fibrinolytic system, with increased D-dimer and fibrin split product levels, has also been described. The platelet count may drop 25% to 30%. If the patient has an underlying hemorrhagic diathesis, replacement with FFP at the end of the procedure may be warranted.

Fortunately equipment failures are not often seen. Kinks in the tubing, low flow rates, malfunctioning blood warmers, and mechanical deformation from roller pumps can cause hemolysis of red cells. The appearance of pink or reddish plasma in the lines signals immediate cessation of the procedure and investigation into possible causes. Air bubbles must be removed from the lines to prevent air embolism. Hematomas may complicate catheter insertion. Chills or even hypothermia may result from the infusion of cooled blood or fluids that have been circulated without a blood warmer.

CURRENT RESEARCH AND FUTURE CONSIDERATIONS

New applications of therapeutic apheresis are being developed for use clinically. Some of the most promising examples thus far include selective protein removal, immune modulation techniques, and gene therapy. Special columns have been developed and just recently licensed in the United States for the removal of low-density lipoprotein from the plasma of patients with familial hypercholesterolemia. Columns that remove anti-A and anti-B antibodies have been developed for ABO-incompatible organ and marrow transplantation. Extracorporeal photoactivation of lymphocytes, with subsequent modulation of the immune system, has been used with success in mycosis fungoides and Sézary syndrome. In the future this technology may be expanded to the treatment of a number of other conditions, including rejection in ABO-incompatible heart transplant patients and a host of autoimmune or collagen-vascular disorders. Finally, the ability of apheresis technology to harvest cells has been used in gene therapy with exciting results. A recent review of the topic describes the progress of two children with subacute combined immunodeficiency syndrome secondary to adenosine deaminase deficiency. Their peripheral blood lymphocytes were removed by apheresis and genetically modified to contain the deficient gene. After these altered cells were infused, the children showed significant improvement in immune function. These examples highlight the continuing utility and broad scope of therapeutic apheresis in the delivery of medical care in the United States.

ADDITIONAL READING

Haire W, Sniecinski I. Venous access, anticoagulation, and patient care during apheresis. In Kessinger A, McMannis JD, eds. Practical Considerations of Apheresis in Peripheral Blood Stem Cell Transplantation. Lakewood: COBE Laboratories, 1994, pp 17-21.

Hemapheresis. In Walker RH, ed. The Technical Manual of the American Association of Blood Banks, 11th ed. Bethesda: American Association of Blood Banks, 1993, pp 29-49.

Kambic HE, Nose Y. Plasmapheresis: Historical perspective, therapeutic applications, and new frontiers. Artif Organs 17:850-881, 1994.

Kasprisin DO. Techniques, indications, and toxicity of therapeutic hemapheresis in children. J Clin Apheresis 5:21-24, 1989.

Klein HG. Cellular gene therapy: An overview. J Clin Apheresis 9:139-141, 1994.

• Mokrzycki MH, Kaplan AA. Therapeutic plasma exchange: Complications and management. Am J Kidney Dis 23: 817-827, 1994.

Owen HG, Brecher ME. Atypical reactions associated with use of angiotensin-converting enzyme inhibitors and apheresis. Transfusion 34:891-894, 1994.

Simon TL. Apheresis: Principles and practices. In Rossi EC, Simon TL, Moss GS, eds. Principles of Transfusion Medicine. Baltimore: Williams & Wilkins, 1991, pp 521-525.

Strauss RG. Current status of hemapheresis in the United States. J Clin Apheresis 6:95-98, 1991.

• Strauss RG, Ciavarell D, Gilcher RO, Kasprisin DO, Kiprov DD, Klein HG, McLeod BC. An overview of current managament. J Clin Apheresis 8:189-194, 1993.

Withdrawal of blood. In Mollision PL, Engelfriet CP, Contreras M. Blood Transfusion in Clinical Medicine. Cambridge: Blackwell, 1993, pp 1-47.

absorbed at this site under the influence of ADH.

These calculations are approximations of what may occur in specific nephron segments. For example, micropuncture studies suggest that fluid delivery to the diluting segments is at least twice that estimated from C_{H_2O} calculations. However, clearance techniques are the only methods for quantitating kidney function as a whole and for approximating transport at specific nephron sites. These techniques cannot distinguish variations among nephrons, cannot precisely localize function to specific nephron segments, and may not distinguish reabsorption or secretion for substances that undergo both processes.

Clearance Methods to Determine GFR

For the clearance rate of a substance to equal the GFR, the substance must be freely filtered and neither reabsorbed nor secreted. In addition, the substance must be physiologically inert, nontoxic, not protein bound, and not subject to metabolism, synthesis, or storage by the kidney. It must also have a clearance that is constant over a wide range of plasma concentrations.

Several substances have been suggested as markers for GFR, including inulin, polyfructosan, urea, creatinine, vitamin B_{12}, chelating substances (ethytenediamine tetraacetic acid [EDTA], and diethylenetriamine pentaacetic acid [DTPA]), contrast media (iothalamate and diatrizoate), and mannitol, among others. Inulin, a fructose polymer with a molecular weight of 5200 and molecular radius of 15 Å (Einstein-Stokes radius), meets all the criteria set by Smith and is the standard substance used in the measurement of GFR. Polyfructosan is a synthetic fructose polymer with a molecular weight of 3000. Its clearance does not differ significantly from inulin, and its greater solubility may offer an advantage over inulin when high concentrations in urine and plasma are necessary.

Creatinine, derived entirely from muscle creatine and phosphocreatine and routinely measured in clinical laboratories, has been used as an index of GFR. About 1.6% of the total body creatine pool is converted to creatinine daily. Creatine turnover rate is relatively constant in normal subjects, but little is known about turnover rate in disease. The major determinants of the creatine pool are the total muscle mass, which is influenced mainly by sex and age, and dietary (mainly meat) intake of creatine. About 1 g of urinary creatinine is excreted per 17.9 kg of mus-

cle mass. There is a greater generation of creatinine in males than females and in young adults compared with preadolescent and geriatric populations. Conditions associated with muscle wasting such as malnutrition, hyperthyroidism, muscular dystrophy, muscular paralysis, dermatomyositis, and others are causes of negative creatinine generation. In the adult creatine intake is about 500 to 800 mg/day; cooking converts creatine to creatinine and can greatly influence endogenous creatinine clearance. The generation of creatinine is reduced in patients with renal disease and elevated serum creatinine. Adding to the problem in patients with renal insufficiency is the fact that up to 60% of the creatinine generated may be removed by extrarenal means.

The clearance of creatinine can be used as an index of GFR in those species in which creatinine is not secreted (e.g., dog, cat, turtle, and rabbit). However, in man and primates creatinine is secreted in the proximal tubule. In normal humans about 10% to 40% of the excreted creatinine can be derived from tubular secretion; this increases to 50% to 60% in patients with renal disease. Moreover, certain substances (cimetidine, trimethoprim, and probenecid) can interfere with creatinine secretion.

When urine flow is <0.5 ml/min, significant amounts of creatinine may be reabsorbed within the kidney or from the lower urinary tract. Reabsorption of creatinine has also been demonstrated in congestive heart failure and uncontrolled diabetes mellitus. Depending on the methodology used to measure creatinine (Jaffe vs. modified Jaffe reactions or enzymatic), the presence of noncreatinine chromogens (e.g., protein, glucose, acetoacetate, pyruvate, uric acid, fructose, ascorbic acid, cephalosporins, and bilirubin) in the plasma may make the measurement of plasma creatinine imprecise. Schwartz et al. have modified the Technicon procedure, allowing accurate measurements of creatinine, especially at lower concentrations. These measurements are not affected by bilirubin.

The measurement of GFR using the ideal markers inulin and polyfructosan is not practical in the clinical setting. Very few laboratories are set up to measure inulin or polyfructosan routinely and radioactive markers may not be a well-accepted alternative. Thus the clearance of creatinine has been used in the clinical setting despite the uncertainties of using creatinine as a marker of glomerular filtration. The clearance of creatinine approximates inulin clearance, especially when the kidney function is within the normal range; the correlation coefficient between the clearance of inulin and clearance of creatinine from 3 to 192 ml/min/1.73 m² was 0.94. When GFR was <20 ml/min/1.73 M², creatinine clearance overestimated the clearance of inulin by 20%. Nonetheless, an absolute reduction in creatinine clearance is a specific but not a sensitive indicator of reduced GFR. In general a progressive decline in creatinine clearance indicates a decrease in GFR unless the patient is taking drugs that inhibit the tubular secretion of creatinine or the serum creatinine is falsely elevated.

TECHNIQUE
Glomerular Filtration Rate

The clearance of GFR markers such as inulin can be determined by several methods. The classic method involves the infusion of the marker substance until a steady-state concentration of the marker is attained in the plasma. Thereafter multiple samples of blood and urine are collected over a 2- to 4-hour period. The clearance of the marker substance is calculated as described above and the average of the determinations reported. The clearance of the marker is usually corrected for body surface area (e.g., milliliter per minute per 1.73 m²) to facilitate comparison among subjects of different sizes. Single-injection and constant-injection techniques of inulin without urine collection can also be used to assess GFR. However, these latter methods may greatly overestimate the GFR in the early postnatal period.

Endogenous creatinine clearance is traditionally measured by collecting urine over 24 hours, obtaining serum creatinine at the middle or the end of the urine collection, and calculating the clearance, as in any other clearance method. Inaccurate measurements of urine volume, whether the collection of urine is performed over 24 hours or shorter time intervals, can give erroneous results.

Isotope methods. Sodium iothalamate, EDTA, sodium diatrizoate, and DTPA among others can be radioisotopically labeled and used to measure GFR. The advantage of these methods is that the GFR of each kidney can be estimated. DTPA is associated with a relatively low radiation dose for the patient and provides an estimate of GFR that is 3% to 5% less than inulin-measured GFR. Radionuclides may be used to perform estimates of GFR as continuous infusion, single-injection, or simplified single-injection methods. In addition, external counting methods and scintigraphy allow for estimation of the GFR for each kidney individually and provide information of a comparative nature, which is particularly helpful in assessing unilateral renal parenchymal diseases or disorders, bilateral renal disease with planned surgical intervention, and evaluation of renal function after intervention or during periods of growth.

Serum creatinine clearance. Serum creatinine has been used as an index of GFR to obviate the problems associated with urine collection. However, as indicated above, serum creatinine is not only influenced by GFR but also by other variables, including age, meat intake, and muscle mass. Serum levels reflect not only renal excretion but also the generation, intake, and metabolism of creatinine. Serum creatinine reflects only GFR under steady-state conditions. When GFR decreases or increases abruptly, a steady state may not be achieved for several days. Serial measurements of serum creatinine may be the only reliable means of monitoring GFR. In the perinatal period serum creatinine is also influenced by maternal creatinine. In term infants serum creatinine increases by 0.09 ± 0.04 mg/dl within a few hours of birth, apparently due to a decrease in extracellular fluid volume, and decreases to about 0.4 mg/dl by the second week. Rudd et al. have shown that the decrease in serum creatinine after birth is related to gestational age; it is fastest in term infants and slowest in the most premature infants. From 2 months to 2 years of age, serum creatinine remains stable, reflecting proportional increases in GFR and muscle mass. Beyond 2 years of age serum creatinine increases in both sexes, but to a greater extent in males than females.

During maturation (1 to 20 years) serum creatinine (S_{cr}) may be estimated from the formula

$$S_{cr} \text{ (males)} = 0.35 + 0.025 \times \text{age (yr)}$$
$$S_{cr} \text{ (females)} = 0.37 + 0.018 \times \text{age (yr)}$$

In adult males (18 to 92 years) creatinine clearance (C_{cr}) can be calculated from the formula

$$C_{cr} = (140 - \text{Age in years}) \times \text{weight (kg)/serum creatinine (mg/dl)} \times 72$$

In females it is 85% that of males.

These and other formulas overestimate creatinine clearance in obese and edematous patients. Schwartz et al. and Counahan et al. have derived formulas that

Table 167-2   Mean and Ranges of k Used in Calculating GFR*

Age Group	k Mean	k Range
Low birthweight infants (<1 yr)	0.33	0.2-0.5
Term infants (<1 yr)	0.45	0.3-0.7
Children (2-12 yr)	0.55	0.4-0.7
Females (13-21 yr)	0.55	0.4-0.7
Males (13-21 yr)	0.70	0.5-0.9

*Modified from Schwartz GJ, Brion LP, Spitzer A. The use of plasma creatinine concentration for estimating glomerular filtration rate in infants, children, and adolescents. Pediatr Clin North Am 34: 571-590, 1987.

yield values of GFR in children that approximate those obtained from creatinine and inulin clearances:

$$\text{GFR (ml/min/1.73 m}^2) = k \cdot \text{Body length (cm)}/S_{cr} \text{ (mg/dl)}$$

where k is a constant that is a function of urinary creatinine per unit of body size. Table 167-2 gives the values and ranges of k in infants under 1 year of age up to subjects 21 years of age. The k values have to be adjusted downward in patients with moderate to severe malnutrition, obesity, and limb amputation and in subjects with heart and renal failure. Body length may not be a true indicator of muscle mass in subjects with gross musculoskeletal deformities. For example, arm span rather than body length may be a better indicator of muscle mass in patients with myelomeningocele.

Serum creatinine and progression of renal failure. The reciprocal relationship between serum creatinine and creatinine clearance has led investigators to use the reciprocal of serum creatinine concentration to relate it to the decline in creatinine clearance.

Although the reciprocal of serum creatinine appears to decline at a constant rate in most patients with renal disease, the rate of decline may be influenced not only by GFR but also by tubular secretion, generation, intake, and extrarenal elimination of creatinine. Some investigators suggest that determining the decline of renal function with time may be best studied by GFR measurements.

GFR during development. GFR is variable after birth but generally increases in the first 2 hours followed by a decrease at 4 hours. In the first 24 hours of life GFR may be as low as 2 ml/min/1.73 m² in infants of 25 weeks' gestation and reaches term values of 25 ml/min/1.73 m² by 34 to 36 weeks. The GFR is the same in infants of similar conceptional ages, even if their postnatal ages are different. The rise in GFR after birth depends on gestational age. In term infants GFR may increase 3- to 5-fold within a week. The GFR rises less rapidly in premature infants; the more premature the infant, the less GFR will increase during the neonatal period. In preterm infants undergoing diuresis in the first few days of life GFR may increase almost 2-fold by the second to the third postnatal day. In a minority of preterm infants who do not undergo diuresis after birth, the GFR does not change in the first week of life.

Renal Blood Flow

Ultrasonographic methods. Recently clinical experience and ease of availability have increased the use of duplex Doppler ultrasound and color-flow Doppler ultrasound in the diagnosis of a variety of vascular disorders and diseases of the kidneys. Their noninvasive nature coupled with the accumulation of clinical data on blood velocity waveforms, pulsatility indices, resistive indices (often with comparison studies using traditional angiography, isotope renography, etc.) have made Doppler ultrasound a highly useful and respected clinical tool. This is particularly apparent in the evaluation of the transplanted renal allograft, suspected renovascular hypertension, or following pharmacologic manipulation of blood pressure and cardiac output but also more recently in many unilateral and bilateral renal diseases. At present it is possible to measure flow variables in the segmental, interlobar, and interlobular arteries and veins. The relative portability makes these methods of renal vascular assessment potentially useful for the critically ill child.

Isotope methods. A large number of inexpensive effective renal plasma flow (ERPF) radioisotopic agents are currently available to estimate ERPF. These agents are excreted by tubular secretion, and each one has variable advantages and disadvantages (Table 167-3). Technetium-99m-mercaptoacetylglycylglyclglycine (^{99m}Tc MAG3), already widely used in Europe, is currently used in many centers in the United States as the clinical agent of choice for estima-

Table 167-3 Radionuclide Agents Used for Estimation of Renal Function

Agent	Disorder/Disease*	Advantages	Disadvantages
^{131}I OIH	Trauma, transplant, ARF, HTN, RAT, OU, UTI, CRF	Measures ERPF High target/background Renal uptake >DTPA High extraction efficiency Imaging down to 2% normal	Relatively high radiation Free iodide Poorly radiolabeled for camera
^{123}I OIH	Same as ^{131}I OIH	Same as ^{131}I OIH *plus* Lower radiation burden Excellent imaging agent	Expense Availability ? Radiocontamination
^{99m}Tc MAG3	Same as ^{123}I OIH	Same as ^{123}I OIH	Some liver uptake Expense >DTPA
^{99m}Tc DTPA	Trauma, transplant, OU, HTN, RAT, UTI	Measures GFR Low radiation dose Availability, inexpensive	Lower extraction efficiency Poor uptake in ARF/CRF Poor image quality in ARF Higher background/target

ARF = acute renal failure; HTN = suspected renovascular hypertension; UTI = pyelonephritis; RAT = renal artery embolism; OU = obstructive uropathy; transplant = renal allograft; CRF = chronic renal insufficiency/failure.
*List not all inclusive.

tion of ERPF. ERPF may be estimated by single-injection clearances of MAG3 or ^{131}I orthoiodohippurate (^{131}I OIH) or by external counting with scintigraphy. In the latter technique ERPF values for the right and left kidneys may be used to provide relative renal function. As in the estimation of GFR by camera imaging, the absolute values of ERPF are not as accurate as those obtained with single-injection or other infusion-clearance methods. However, reproducibility in a given patient is highly precise, with correlations >0.98. Unfortunately lack of portability for most camera/computer systems may limit their applicability in the PICU setting.

Clearance methods. The most commonly used agent to measure RPF is para-aminohippurate (PAH). This agent is used because it is almost completely extracted by the kidney in a single pass. The use of clearance to measure RPF is based on the Fick principle and for PAH the equation is written as

$$RPF = U_{PAH} \cdot V/(RA_{PAH} - RV_{PAH})$$

where RPF is renal plasma flow in ml/min, U_{PAH} is the concentration of PAH in the urine, V is urine flow in milliliters per minute, RA_{PAH} is the concentration of

PAH in the renal arterial blood, and RV_{PAH} is the concentration of PAH in the renal venous blood. Determining the renal venous extraction of PAH is not usually necessary in the clinical setting in adults since the renal venous extraction of PAH is almost 100%. In this situation $RA_{PAH} - RV_{PAH}$ is the same as RA_{PAH}. Renal blood flow (RBF) can thus be calculated from the formula

$$RBF = RPF/(1 - Hematocrit)$$

As in the case for GFR, for comparison of subjects of different sizes, the values can be corrected to 1.73 m^2 body surface area.

The Fick formula is not precisely applicable to measurement of RPF because renal venous outflow is less than the arterial inflow by an amount equal to urine flow and lymph flow. This problem increases with increasing urine flow, especially when the extraction of the marker substance is <50%. The extraction of PAH may reach this critical level in infants under 3 months of age.

The washout of radioactive gases such as xenon-133 (^{133}Xe) from the kidney and single-shot clearances of iodine-125 (^{125}I) PAH externally monitored have been used to determine RPF as well. Perfusion of each kidney can be determined with these methods.

Renal Plasma Flow During Development

The clearance of PAH is not a true estimate of RPF in the newborn because the renal venous extraction of PAH may be as low as 60% compared with over 90% in older infants (>3 months). As with GFR, the most rapid increase in RPF occurs in the first 3 months of age. The filtration fraction (GFR/RPF) is similar in newborns and adults.

Fractional Excretion

Under certain circumstances it may be necessary to determine the fractional excretion of a given substance, that is, the amount excreted ($U_s V$) as a function of the filtered load (GFR · P_s). This can be determined by the formula

Fractional excretion (%) = (U_s · V)/GFR · P_s · 100%

where U_s is the concentration of any substance in the urine, V is the urine flow, and P_s is the plasma concentration of the substance in question. The formula can be rearranged so that fractional excretion of any substance can be measured without determining GFR or timing the urine collection.

Fractional excretion (%) = (U_s · V)/U_{cr} · (V · P_s)/P_{cr} · 100%
= (U_s/P_s)/(U_{cr}/P_{cr}) · 100%

Fractional excretion of a substance can be used to evaluate tubular function. Fractional excretion of Na is decreased in hypovolemia and Na depletion states and increased in acute tubular necrosis and Na repletion states. Fractional excretion of phosphate is increased in hypophosphatemic rickets and decreased in hypoparathyroidism. Fractional potassium (K) excretion is low in hypoaldosteronism. Fractional excretion of chloride (Cl) is decreased when the intake of Cl is low and increased in Bartter's syndrome. Fractional reabsorption can also be used to assess renal tubular function:

Fractional reabsorption = 100 − Fractional excretion

In this regard, for some time now, lithium clearance has been suggested as a marker for proximal tubule Na reabsorption. Lithium transport was pre-

viously thought to occur exclusively in the proximal tubule; however, it is now apparent that fractional excretion of lithium (FE_{Li}) represents lithium reabsorption in Henle's loop and in the late distal and collecting tubules as well as proximal tubular reabsorption. Nonetheless, of any clinically available indirect methods, estimations of proximal tubular Na reabsorption from FE_{Li} appear to come the closest to direct measurements. In the PICU setting lithium clearance studies will remain in the hands of investigators until more is known about the renal effects of changes in renal perfusion pressure, changes in vasopressin activity, and use of diuretics, on FE_{Li}.

Renal function can also be evaluated, even when serum values are not available. The ratio of the concentration of a substance and creatinine in the urine (U_s/U_{cr}) has been used to assess renal function. For example, $U_{protein}$/U_{cr} >0.2 indicates significant proteinuria and $U_{uric\ acid}$/U_{cr} >1 indicates that hyperuricemia may be the cause of renal failure; $U_{calcium}$/U_{cr} >0.2 indicates hypercalciuria.

In the evaluation of disorders of K metabolism the fractional excretion of K (FE_K) has been used as a diagnostic tool in hyperkalemia or hypokalemia to assess the tubular secretion of K. However, the FE_K has to be interpreted using a normogram related to the GFR, which limits its practical value in many clinical settings. Recently a simple, semiquantitative test called the transtubular K concentration gradient (TTKG) has been proposed to evaluate the activity of the K secretory process in the cortical distal nephron. The TTKG provides an approximation of the concentration of K in the terminal cortical collecting duct and therefore provides some information about the K secretory process in the cortical distal nephron, that is, the TTKG permits the differentiation of the effects on overall K excretion of total urine volume (flow) from the distal K secretory process. The TTKG is calculated as follows:

$$\text{TTKG} = \{[K_{urine}]/(U/P)_{osm}\}/[K_{plasma}]$$

In adults, during hypokalemia, the TTKG needs to be <2 and in hyperkalemia >10. However, apparently inappropriate values for the TTKG need to be interpreted with caution. The urine must be at least isoosmolar. If the urinary flow rate is very high, TTKG may be low because of inadequate equilibration time of the urine in the cortical distal nephron. Under these conditions the rate of potassium excretion as well as the TTKG is calculated to help clarify the issue of defective K secretion.

Serum Urea Nitrogen and Renal Function

A relationship between serum urea nitrogen levels and renal function was noted before the concept of clearance evolved. Urea clearance is now rarely used as an index of GFR because of complex factors influencing the production and excretion of urea. A low serum urea nitrogen level is seen in overhydration, liver failure, malnutrition, and inborn errors of urea metabolism. High serum urea nitrogen levels may be seen in hypovolemia, acute parenchymal renal failure, obstructive uropathy, inborn errors of urea excretion, and states of increased urea production.

ADDITIONAL READING

Babcock DS. Sonographic evaluation of suspected pediatric vascular diseases. Pediatr Radiol 21:486-489, 1991.

Bauer JH, Brooks CS, Burch R. Clinical appraisal of creatinine clearance as a measurement of glomerular filtration rate. Am J Kidney Dis 2:337-346, 1982.

Bidiwala KS, Lorenz JM, Kleinman LI. Renal function correlates of postnatal diuresis in preterm infants. Pediatrics 82:50-58, 1988.

Briscoe DM, Hoffer FA, Tu N, et al. Duplex doppler examination of renal allografts in children: Correlation between renal blood flow and clinical findings. Pediatr Radiol 23:365-368, 1993.

Britton KE, Hoffer FA, Tu N, et al. Renal radionuclide studies. In Maisey MN, Britton KE, Gilday DL, eds. Clinical Nuclear Medicine. Philadelphia: JB Lippincott, 1991, pp 91-130.

Cockroft DW, Gault MH. Prediction of creatinine clearance from serum creatinine. Nephron 16:31-41, 1976.

Counahan R, Chantler C, Ghazali S, et al. Estimation of glomerular filtration rate from plasma creatinine concentration in children. Arch Dis Child 51:875-878, 1976.

Ethier J, Kamel K, Magner P, et al. Evaluation of the renal response to hypokalemia and hyperkalemia. Am J Kidney Dis 15:309-315, 1990.

Friedman DM, Schact RG. Doppler waveforms in the renal arteries of normal children. J Clin Ultrasound 19:387-392, 1991.

Guignard JP, John EG. Renal function in the tiny, premature infant. Clin Perinatol 13:377-401, 1986.

Hankins DA, Babb AL, Uvelli DA, et al. Creatinine degradation 1: The kinetics of creatinine removal in patients with chronic kidney disease. Int J Artif Organs 4:35-39, 1981.

Heymsfield SB, Arteaga C, McManus C, et al. Measurement of muscle mass in humans: Validity of the 24-hour urinary creatinine method. Am J Clin Nutr 37:478-494, 1983.

Hoyer PF, Melter M, Offner G, et al. Significance of duplex and color encoded Doppler sonographic monitoring in children with renal transplants. Transplant Proc 25:2571-2575, 1993.

Jose PA, Stewart CL, Tina LU, et al. Renal disease. In Avery GB, ed. Neonatology: Pathophysiology and Management of the Newborn. Philadelphia: JB Lippincott, 1987, pp 795-849.

Kassirer JP, Gennari FJ. Laboratory evaluation of renal function. In Early LE, Gottschalk CW, eds. Strauss and Weit's Diseases of the Kidney. Boston: Little, Brown, 1979, pp 41-91.

Koomans HA, Boer WH, Dorhout Mees EJ. Evaluation of lithium clearance as a marker of proximal tubule sodium handling. Kidney Int 36:2-12, 1989.

• Levey AS, Perrone RD, Madias NE. Serum creatinine and renal function. Ann Rev Med 39:465-490, 1988.

Levinsky NG, Levy M. Clearance techniques. In Orloff J, Berliner RW, eds. Renal Physiology. Washington, D.C.: American Physiological Society, 1973, pp 103-117.

Macy RL Jr, Naumann HD, Bailey ME. Water-soluble flavor and odor precursors of meat: 5. Influence of heating on acid-extractable non-nucleotide chemical constituents of beef, lamb and pork. J Food Sci 35:83-87, 1970.

McCrory WW. Developmental Nephrology. Cambridge: Harvard University Press, 1972.

O'Malley JP, Ziessman HA. Quantitation of renal function using radioisotopic techniques. In Preuss HG, ed. Clinics in Laboratory Medicine Renal Function. Philadelphia: WB Saunders, 1993, pp 53-68.

Patriquin H. Doppler examination of the kidney in infants and children. Urol Radiol 12:220-227, 1991.

Pieps Z, Denis R, Ham HR, et al. Determination of the 99mTcMag-3 overall clearance in children by means of one single blood sample: A multicentre study. In O'Reilly P, Taylor A, Nally JV, eds. Radionuclides in Nephrology. Blue Bell, Pa.: Field and Wood Medical Periodicals, 1994, pp 113-117.

• Rosendahl W, Grunert D, Schoning M. Duplex sonography of renal arteries as a diagnostic tool in hypertensive children. Eur J Pediatr 153:588-593, 1994.

• Rudd PT, Hughes EA, Placzek MM, et al. Reference ranges for plasma creatinine during the first month of life. Arch Dis Child 58:212-215, 1983.

• Schwartz GJ, Brion LP, Spitzer A. The use of plasma creatinine concentration for estimating glomerular filtration rate in infants, children, and adolescents. Pediatr Clin North Am 34:571-590, 1987.

Schwartz GJ, Haycock GB, Spitzer A, et al. Plasma creatinine and urea concentration in children: Normal values for age and sex. J Pediatr 88:828-830, 1976.

Shemesh O, Goibetz H, Kriss JP, et al. Limitations of creatinine as a filtration marker in glomerulopathic patients. Kidney Int 28:830-838, 1985.

Smith HW. The Kidney—Structure and Function in Health and Disease. New York: Oxford University Press, 1951.

Vade A, Subbaiah P, Kalbhen CL, et al. Renal resistive indices in children. J Ultrasound Med 12:655-658, 1993.

West ML, Bendz O, Chen CB, et al. Development of a test to evaluate the transtubular potassium concentration gradient in the cortical collecting duct in vivo. Miner Electrolyte Metab 12:226-233, 1986.

West ML, Marsden P, Richardson RM, et al. New clinical approach to evaluate disorders of potassium excretion. Miner Electrolyte Metab 12:234-238, 1986.

168 Peritoneal Dialysis

Albert H. Quan

BACKGROUND
Physiology

Peritoneal dialysis involves the exchange of water and solutes between the peritoneal membrane capillary blood vessel and the dialysate solution within the peritoneal cavity. Dialysate solution is first placed into the peritoneal cavity by means of a catheter, allowed to "dwell" for a specified period of time, and later drained and replaced with fresh dialysate to complete one cycle. The exchange of solutes and removal of uremic toxins occurs during this dwell time. The electrolyte composition of the dialysate solution mimics that of plasma to provide for stable serum electrolytes while allowing diffusion of uremic toxins from the capillary blood to the dialysate. The physiology of peritoneal dialysis is less understood than that of hemodialysis, but knowledge of peritoneal physiology is necessary to provide optimal and efficient dialysis.

Peritoneal Membrane

The peritoneal membrane envelopes all loops of bowel and reflects over the abdominal wall to form a large potential space, the peritoneal cavity. It is the largest serous membrane of the body, and its surface area is directly proportional to body surface area. Because children have a body surface area to body weight ratio higher than that of adults, peritoneal surface area per kilogram of weight in children is higher than that in adults. This may account for the higher transfer rates of solute and fluid observed in children. The structure of the peritoneal membrane, as depicted in Fig. 168-1, consists of a fenestrated capillary surrounded by interstitial connective tissue and covered on its outer layer by a thin layer of mesothelial cells. All solutes that traverse the peritoneal membrane must pass through all three structural layers, each of which provides an intrinsic "resistance" to solute and fluid flow. Solute and water both flow across the capillary and mesothelial cell layers be-

tween intercellular gaps. In contrast, solute flow across the interstitium occurs through pores or channels within its matrix. The sum of all resistances across the peritoneal membrane will determine its total permeability and solute flow during dialysis.

The permeability of an individual solute across the peritoneal membrane is determined largely by its charge and size. Highly charged solutes such as phosphate are much less permeable than less charged solutes such as Na^+ or K^+. Smaller and lower molecular weight substances are also much more permeable than larger and higher molecular weight substances. For instance, as seen in Fig. 168-2, small solutes such as urea diffuse across the peritoneal membrane into dialysate much more rapidly than larger compounds such as creatinine or inulin. Very large macromolecules such as proteins have an even lower permeability.

Fig. 168-2 also underscores and illustrates an important principle of peritoneal dialysis. The transfer rate of small solutes is biphasic, that is, high early in the cycle and low later in the cycle. In contrast, the transfer rate of large solutes is lower and more uniform throughout the entire dialysis cycle. For instance, as seen in Fig. 168-2, the initial steep portion of the curve for urea reflects the very high initial transfer rate of urea from plasma to dialysate; the later flatter portion of the curve reflects the much lower transfer rate of urea occurring near equilibration. Thus the majority of plasma clearance of small molecular weight compounds such as urea occurs early during the dialysis cycle. Therefore the most effective way to achieve maximal clearance of urea is to perform frequent and short dwell time dialysis exchange cycles. This keeps the rate of urea clearance within the rapid and steep portion of the curve at all times and avoids the slower rates of removal. This same principle is applied when rapid clearance from the plasma of any small solute is desired, for example, when potassium or ammonia levels are high.

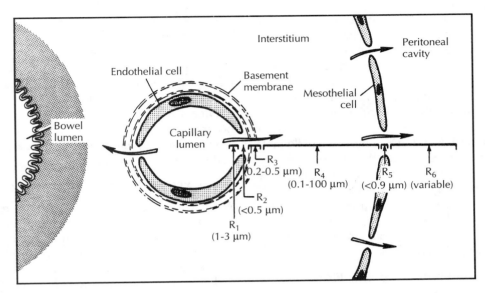

Fig. 168-1 Structure of the peritoneal membrane (see p. 1576). (Modified from Nolph KP, Sorkin MI. In Brenner BM, Stein JH, eds. CAPD in Chronic Renal Failure. New York: Churchill Livingstone, 1981, p 197.)

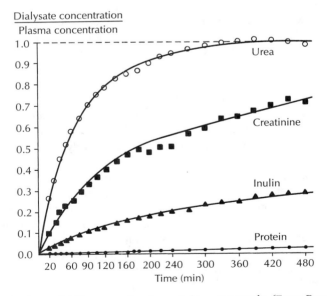

Fig. 168-2 Solute profiles of different molecular weight compounds. (From Popovich RP, Moncrief JW, Nolph KP. Continuous ambulatory peritoneal dialysis. Ann Intern Med 88:449-456, 1978.)

In contrast to urea, the overall transfer rate of much larger molecular weight compounds such as creatinine is much slower and lacks the initial very high transfer rate. Instead the initial transfer rate of creatinine is only modestly higher than its later transfer rate. Thus the clearance of larger compounds depends more on the *total time* on peritoneal dialysis than on the *frequency* of dialysis exchanges. Clearance of "middle molecules," an ill-defined group of larger compounds with a molecular weight of 1000 to 3000 daltons, would be expected to depend on time on peritoneal dialysis. Clearance of middle molecules may be important since they have been postulated to contribute to the symptoms of clinical uremia. Many nephrologists believe that peritoneal dialysis provides superior middle molecule clearance over conventional hemodialysis since total time spent on dialysis is actually greater in peritoneal dialysis than in hemodialysis.

Peritoneal Blood and Lymphatic Flow

Peritoneal capillary blood vessels are the primary source of solute and fluid for removal through dialysate. Although only a small fraction of the peritoneal vasculature is perfused at any given time, peritoneal blood flow is not a rate-limiting factor during dialysis. Even with hypotension and subsequent decreases in peritoneal blood flow, urea clearance is only moderately reduced.

The permeability of the peritoneal capillary varies along its length. In the early proximal portion of the vessel, ultrafiltration of water from capillary to dialysate is high, whereas solute transport in the same direction is poor. Ultrafiltration of water is high because of initial high hydrostatic pressure and solute transport is low because of small intercellular endothelial gaps. In contrast, in the more distal portion of the vessel, ultrafiltration of water is much lower and solute transfer is much greater. Lower hydrostatic pressure and higher plasma oncotic pressure decrease ultrafiltration of water, whereas larger intercellular gaps permit a much greater solute transfer.

The removal of fluid and solute is also affected by peritoneal lymphatic drainage. Lymph fluid from the peritoneal cavity drains either through the mesenteric lymphatic channels or through the stomas (specialized pores) on the caudal surface of the diaphragm. Lymph channels arising from the stomas coalesce and eventually drain into the right lymphatic duct. Systemic absorption of lymphatic drainage from the peritoneal cavity actually decreases net fluid ultrafiltration during dialysis. In previous studies on peritoneal dialysis, 50% of the total or gross capillary ultrafiltration was reabsorbed through the lymphatic system. The peritoneal lymphatic system is also the major route of absorption of high molecular compounds. This has limited the use of high molecular weight osmotic agents within dialysis solution, such as glucose polymers, since systemic absorption would readily occur. The accumulation of such compounds in the bloodstream via peritoneal lymphatic vessels has limited their safety and utility.

INDICATIONS AND CONTRAINDICATIONS

When choosing a modality for renal replacement therapy, all three possible treatments (hemodialysis, peritoneal dialysis, or continuous veno-venous hemofiltration) must be carefully considered. The choice depends on the experience of the physician and nursing personnel and the patient's particular clinical situation. For hemodynamically unstable patients such as children with heart failure, peritoneal dialysis is usually the modality of choice. The gradual correction of excessive extracellular volume and electrolyte abnormalities associated with peritoneal dialysis is well tolerated. Continuous veno-venous hemofiltration is also well tolerated but often is much more labor intensive and more prone to error than peritoneal dialysis. In contrast, hemodialysis corrects excessive extracellular volume and abnormal serum electrolytes over a very short interval of less than 3 to 4 hours. Consequently hemodialysis is not well tolerated by many patients, especially those who are hemodynamically unstable.

Alternatively, hemodialysis is the preferred modality when rapid clearance is desired and rapid changes in extracellular volume and serum electrolytes are better tolerated. For example, a patient with significant extracellular volume overload or severe hyperkalemia who is otherwise not hemodynamically compromised is a good candidate for hemodialysis. In addition, otherwise healthy individuals with drug intoxication are also excellent candidates for hemodialysis.

Peritoneal dialysis or hemodialysis can also both be used to treat inborn errors of metabolism such as hyperammonemia of the newborn, propionic acidemia, or maple syrup urine disease. Of all such disorders, hyperammonemia of the newborn is perhaps the one most frequently confronted by the nephrologist. It results from any one of several enzymatic defects in the urea cycle, all leading to accumulation of toxic plasma levels of ammonia. Patients present with lethargy, seizures, and coma, all resulting from the direct toxicity of ammonia on the CNS. All dialysis therapy is therefore aimed at both quickly lowering the ammonia level and sustaining a low ammonia level. Hemodialysis is most efficient at clearance of ammonia. However, because hemodialysis is intermittent and much less well tolerated hemodynamically by newborns, peritoneal dialysis with short dwell times is often the modality of choice. Peritoneal dialysis removes ammonia gradually and continuously, although at a slower rate than hemodialysis. Since many urea cycle defects are fatal, dialysis can often be used to prolong the child's life until an accurate diagnosis is made.

Contraindications to peritoneal dialysis are rare and include gastroschisis, omphalocele, necrotizing enterocolitis, and diaphragmatic hernias. In all of these instances the integrity of the peritoneal membrane or peritoneal cavity has been compromised. Even children who have recently undergone vesicostomy, gastrostomy, or other bowel surgery can be treated with peritoneal dialysis. The presence of a ventriculoperitoneal shunt, however, is a relative contraindication to peritoneal dialysis. Here the bacteria responsible for peritonitis may ascend the shunt and ventriculitis may develop.

TECHNIQUE
Catheters

All peritoneal dialysis solution is introduced into the peritoneal cavity through an indwelling catheter. Such catheters may be temporary (Cook) or more permanent (Tenckoff). Temporary catheters are often easily placed at the bedside using strict aseptic technique. The peritoneum is entered 2 to 3 cm lateral to the umbilicus using a percutaneously introduced 14- to 16-gauge polyethylene (over-the-needle) catheter. After filling the peritoneum with a small volume of dialysate to distend the abdomen, a guidewire is introduced through the catheter and the dialysis catheter is subsequently inserted over the wire using the Seldinger technique. Filling the peritoneal cavity with dialysis solution to distend the abdomen reduces the risk of bowel perforation with the dialysis

catheter. Temporary catheters for small infants weighing <2000 g may include a 14-gauge IV polyethylene catheter, although a special neonatal Cook catheter is now available. Associated complications include a high risk of peritoneal infection, especially after 72 hours of continuous use. Skin flora gain access to the peritoneal cavity through the catheter exit/entry site. Because of the risk of infection, peritoneal dialysis in children is now usually performed with a permanent catheter that has been placed in the operating room. Such catheters carry a much lower risk of infection. Since pediatric dialysis is commonly performed at a tertiary care center, a pediatric surgeon is usually readily available.

Permanent peritoneal catheters are made of soft silicone rubber and have a Dacron cuff near the skin entry site. Once they penetrate the skin, such catheters traverse a subcutaneous tunnel before entering the peritoneal cavity. The cuff is embedded under the skin in the subcutaneous tissue and allows ingrowth of fibrous tissue to form a seal around the catheter. Both the long subcutaneous tunnel and the seal around the cuff serve to reduce the risk of skin flora contamination and infection. Currently the most commonly used peritoneal catheter is the Tenckoff catheter (straight or curled).

The catheter, once placed, appears as a coil lying in the anterior plane of an abdominal plain radiograph. A coil positioned more perpendicular to the anterior plane is likely to entangle loops of bowel or omentum. A straight catheter lies within the peritoneal cavity, usually along the pelvic floor. Because a well-placed curled catheter is much less likely to physically disturb the bowel, it is preferred over the straight catheter. With either catheter, the omentum can wrap around the catheter and impede the flow of dialysate. For this reason many surgeons will perform either a partial or total omentectomy at the time of catheter placement.

Manual vs. Automated Peritoneal Dialysis

Whether peritoneal dialysis is performed manually or with an automated cycler, the basic steps are the same.

1. The peritoneal dialysis catheter is inserted, preferably a permanent cuffed catheter.
2. Dialysate is instilled into the peritoneal cavity. Usual volumes (exchange volume) are 40 ml/kg of body weight up to a maximum of 2 L. Small-

er volumes of dialysate are initially used after surgical catheter placement and gradually increased to full volumes. Dialysate is warmed to 37° C before use.

3. The dialysate is allowed to remain within the peritoneal cavity for a period of time (dwell time). Equilibration of solutes and removal of uremic toxins occur across the membrane during this phase.

4. The dialysate is drained out of the peritoneal cavity (drain time) and the volume of dialysate is recorded.

5. New and fresh dialysate is reinstilled into the peritoneal cavity for the next cycle.

Because of its simplicity, manual peritoneal dialysis can be performed in both inpatient and outpatient settings. Indeed, when manual peritoneal dialysis is performed at home, the modality is known as chronic ambulatory peritoneal dialysis (CAPD). CAPD involves 4 to 5 evenly spaced exchanges of dialysate per day, with a full volume of dialysate in the peritoneal cavity between each exchange. Peritoneal dialysis can provide, at best, a urea clearance rate of approximately 7 to 10 ml/min/1.73 m².

Peritoneal dialysis can also be performed with an automated cycler machine. Such machines are used not only in hospitalized patients but also at home in patients on chronic dialysis, a modality known as continuous cycler peritoneal dialysis. These cyclers deliver a programmed volume of dialysate, allow the dialysate to dwell for a programmed length of time, drain the peritoneal fluid, and record the individual and cumulative volumes of dialysate outflow. The fill time and drain time are also programmed into the machine. Numerous safety features prevent overfilling of the abdomen and detect obstruction of dialysate flow. The major advantage of a cycler is reduction in nursing and labor time.

Aseptic Techniques

Because one of the major complications of peritoneal dialysis is peritonitis, strict adherence to aseptic technique is crucial to its success. The following are guidelines for reducing the risk of infection:

1. Wear a face mask and thoroughly wash hands for 3 minutes with an antibacterial soap such as Hibiclens prior to manipulation of the dialysis catheter and tubing. No gloves are needed if the hands are washed thoroughly.

2. Provide for a clean area with little or no traffic to perform the dialysate exchanges. The surface on which dialysis supplies will rest must be cleaned with isopropyl alcohol prior to every use.

3. Inspect all new dialysate bags for clarity of the solution and for leaks or breaks in the lines. Inspect the outflow of fluid for turbidity, fibrin, or blood.

4. Examine the catheter exit site daily for crusting, discharge, or erythema. The tunnel must be nontender and nonerythematous. Daily care for a well-healed noninfected catheter exit site consists of gentle cleaning with Hibiclens and thorough drying.

Given that the primary route of peritonitis is bacterial contamination during connection of the dialysate bag to the peritoneal dialysis catheter, strict adherence to the preceding guidelines will keep the risk of infection to a minimum. Over the past several years a number of techniques have emerged to help reduce the risk of peritoneal infection.

One such method uses ultraviolet (UV) light to sterilize a portion of tubing before connecting it to the peritoneal dialysis catheter dialysate bag. A small portable UV-generating device is generally used for this purpose. This device has been demonstrated in clinical trials to be effective in reducing the rate of infection. However, the drawbacks include the need for extra equipment, the cost involved, and the extra time necessary to sterilize the tubing (2 to 5 minutes).

Perhaps the most effective and simplest of such devices is the Y-set tubing (Fig. 168-3). The three arms of the Y-set tubing are each connected to a different component of the dialysis setup, including the dialysis catheter, a fresh dialysate bag, and a drain bag. A small amount of fresh dialysate is used to flush the catheter prior to drainage of the peritoneal fluid. Subsequently new dialysate fills the peritoneal cavity. This "flush before fill" technique is believed to wash away any potential bacterial contaminants before they are introduced into the peritoneal cavity. The Y-set is an inexpensive yet extremely effective method for reducing the risk of peritonitis.

Dialysate

Sterile premixed dialysate solutions are readily available from many commercial vendors. The composi-

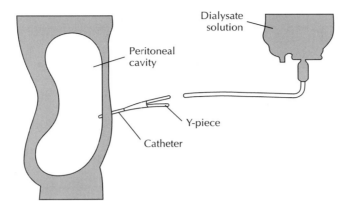

Fig. 168-3 Y-set catheter. (Modified from Schoenfeld P. Care of the patient on peritoneal dialysis. In Cogan M, Schoenfeld P, eds. Introduction to Dialysis. New York: Churchill Livingstone, 1991, p 204.)

tion of a typical peritoneal dialysate solution is listed in Table 168-1. The glucose is available in three premixed concentrations: 1.5, 2.5, and 4.25 g/dl solutions. At such high concentrations glucose acts as an osmotic agent and causes plasma water to ultrafilter across the peritoneal membrane into the peritoneal cavity. This ultrafiltration of water results in fluid loss from the patient and helps to maintain fluid balance. Ultrafiltration of water and fluid balance are especially important in anuric patients. The net ultrafiltration of water achieved over time varies with different dextrose concentrations. As shown in Fig. 168-4, higher glucose concentrations ultrafilter more water because of greater osmotic strength. Maximal ultrafiltration of volume usually is achieved at approximately 120 minutes of dwell time, the exact time depending on the glucose concentration used. Thereafter the systemic absorption of dialysate dextrose reduces the glucose osmotic gradient and decreases the rate of ultrafiltration of water. If enough glucose is absorbed, peritoneal water may similarly be systemically absorbed and decrease net ultrafiltration. The appropriate glucose concentration is guided by the patient's fluid status and any residual urine output. Intermediate dialysate glucose concentrations can be used to achieve the appropriate volume of ultrafiltration desired. Such intermediate glucose concentrations may be mixed using any of the preceding commercially available concentrations. Patients with renal diseases that result in high urine output (i.e.,

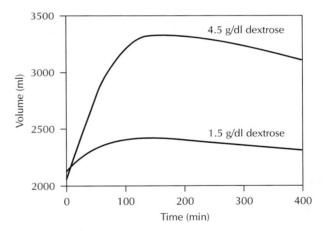

Fig. 168-4 Water ultrafiltration over time. (From Schoenfeld P. Care of the patient on peritoneal dialysis. In Cogan M, Schoenfeld P, eds. Introduction to Dialysis. New York: Churchill Livingstone, 1991, p 192.)

Table 168-1   Dialysate Composition

Components (mEq/L)	PD-1	PD-2	Low Ca
Na	132	132	132
Ca	3.5	3.5	2.5
Mg	1.5	0.5	0.8
Cl	102	96	95
Lactate	35	40	40

Table 168-2   Peritoneal Dialysis Solution Containing Bicarbonate*

	ml	Na$^+$ (mEq)	Cl$^-$ (mEq)	Mg^{++} (mEq)	SO$_4^-$ (mEq)	HCO$_3^-$ (mEq)	Hydrous Dextrose (g)
NaCl (0.45%)	896.0	69	69				
NaCl (2.5 mEq/ml)	12.0	30	30				
NaHCO$_3$ (1.0 mEq/ml)	40.0	40				40	
MgSO$_4$ (10%)	1.8			1.5	1.5		
D$_{50}$W	50.0						25
	999.8	139	99	1.5	1.5	40	25

Calculated osmolality = 423 mOsm/kg H$_2$O.
*From Nash MA, Russo JC. Neonatal lactic acidosis and renal failure: The role of peritoneal dialysis. J Pediatr 91:101-105, 1977.

obstructive uropathy) may need only the lowest glucose concentration, 1.5% solution. Use of higher concentrations of glucose in such a case may ultrafilter excessive amounts of water and lead to hypovolemia and hypotension. In contrast, anuric or hypervolemic patients may need a 2.5% dextrose concentration or more to increase the amount and rate of water ultrafiltration.

Nearly all dialysate solutions contain a sodium concentration (132 mEq/L) lower than that of serum sodium to help avoid potential hypernatremia. Hypernatremia can occur as a result of the sieving effect of solute with rapid fluid removal during peritoneal dialysis. During the ultrafiltration process water moves across the peritoneal membrane much faster than sodium, a charged species, thus leaving the serum relatively more hypernatremic. With a lower dialysate sodium concentration, serum sodium will more quickly diffuse into the dialysate and thus reduce the risk of hypernatremia.

The dialysate calcium concentration (3.5 mEq/L) is higher than that of serum ionized calcium to help promote net calcium absorption. When this high dialysate calcium is used with low glucose concentrations (1.5 g/dl), calcium is absorbed by the patient. However, when high glucose concentrations (4.25 g/dl) are used, calcium is lost. This loss of calcium results when the higher ultrafiltration volumes increase the convective removal of serum calcium and overcome the gain in calcium from diffusion of dialysate calcium.

Peritoneal dialysate solutions are also available in a lower calcium concentration of 2.5 mEq/L. A lower calcium dialysate concentration is used to help avoid the hypercalcemia that may result from use of Rocaltrol (1,25[OH]$_2$-D$_3$) or calcium-containing phosphate binders (i.e., Os-Cal or Titralac). Use of Rocaltrol and calcium-containing phosphate binders is essential in all dialysis patients to prevent secondary hyperparathyroidism and renal osteodystrophy.

To maintain a normal serum bicarbonate level, most dialysate solutions use lactate at 35 to 40 mEq/L. Once absorbed into the systemic circulation, lactate is quickly metabolized by the liver into bicarbonate. Bicarbonate is not directly added to dialysate solution because calcium carbonate would form and precipitate. Some critically ill infants and children with liver disease may not tolerate the lactate present in commercial dialysates. Such infants will benefit from reformulated bicarbonate dialysate (Table 168-2). Calcium cannot be added to this mixture. It is a good practice to measure the electrolyte composition of such fluids to avoid mixing errors. At one time dialysate solutions contained acetate instead of lactate. However, acetate is no longer used because of its association with progressive loss of ultrafiltration and development of sclerosing peritonitis.

The magnesium concentration in the standard dialysate (1.5 mEq/L) is kept at levels lower than serum to avoid hypermagnesemia. Despite this, however, in some patients mild hypermagnesemia will develop. A dialysate preparation with a lower magnesium level of 0.5 mEq/L is available for such patients.

Peritoneal Dialysis Prescription

The peritoneal dialysis prescription varies with each patient, depending on the specific clinical situation. In the 24- to 48-hour period immediately following surgical catheter placement, low volumes of dialysate (20 ml/kg) are used initially to flush the catheter and later to dwell in the peritoneal cavity for up to approximately 45 minutes. The fluid is subsequently drained and fresh dialysate is instilled to begin another cycle. A low volume of dialysate reduces the risk of fluid leakage from around the exit site. In this way a minimal degree of dialysis is actually performed. However, low volumes of dialysate are sometimes absorbed systemically and can contribute to hypervolemia. To avoid this, dialysis is begun with 2.5 g/dl of dialysate, which can be increased to an even higher glucose concentration, if necessary. Low dextrose concentrations (1.5 g/dl) are always absorbed. Heparin is also added to the dialysate at 500 units/L to decrease the fibrin formation that commonly occurs with a new catheter. Exchange volumes of dialysate are gradually increased over a 2-week period up to a maximum of 40 ml/kg per exchange or 2 L maximum. Dialysis may be continued indefinitely while awaiting the return of normal renal function.

Some nephrologists prefer to "cap off" the newly placed peritoneal dialysis catheter and avoid using it for the first 1 or 2 weeks. This capping off is done only after the catheter has been flushed for the first 24 to 48 hours, as previously described. In many clinical studies the tissue around the catheter exit site had healed and reduced the risk of peritoneal fluid leakage. Such an approach, however, can only be used in those patients who do not need immediate dialysis.

In the setting of acute renal failure the primary goals of dialysis are control of systemic blood pressure and extracellular volume and correction of electrolyte abnormalities. In the typical hypervolemic, hypertensive, and azotemic patient, frequent (every 1 hour) exchanges with high glucose concentrations (2.5 to 4.25 g/dl) will maximize fluid removal by means of ultrafiltration and thereby help to decrease the extracellular volume and lower systemic blood pressure. In addition, frequent exchanges will optimize correction of hyperkalemia, acidosis, and azotemia. Frequent exchanges are also especially important when initial dialysate volumes are low and thus suboptimal for efficient dialysis and ultrafiltration. The increase in the frequency of exchanges partially compensates for the low dialysate volume.

In contrast, the hypotensive and azotemic patient must first be treated to maintain systemic blood pressure and tissue perfusion before any consideration is given to dialysis therapy. If necessary, crystalloid or colloid solutions can be given to expand extracellular volume and raise systemic blood pressure. Dialysis is initiated only when the patient is more hemodynamically stable. To avoid excessive ultrafiltration, a low glucose dialysate concentration (1.5 g/dl) in conjunction with longer dwell times (every 2 to 3 hours) is used initially. Caution must also be exercised to ensure adequate correction of hyperkalemia and azotemia.

Once the patient has stabilized, the frequency of exchanges can be decreased and dwell time increased. If native renal function does not return quickly, either chronic ambulatory or continuous cycler peritoneal dialysis may be initiated. With CAPD, the dwell times are lengthened such that 4 to 5 full volume exchanges are performed per day. Thus the peritoneum is in contact with dialysate for nearly 24 hours of the day to maximize efficiency. In continuous cycler peritoneal dialysis usually 6 to 10 exchanges, each lasting 1 hour, are performed during sleep using an automated cycler machine. During the day, a lower volume of dialysate is left in the abdomen and allowed to continue to dwell until continuous cycler peritoneal dialysis is begun again at night.

RISK AND COMPLICATIONS
Infection

Peritonitis remains the most frequent complication of peritoneal dialysis. In fact, 65% of all patients will have an episode of peritonitis within the first year. As a rule, peritonitis occurs in nearly all patients with *temporary* catheters that have been in place for more than 72 hours. This well-known rate of infection has influenced many centers to switch to permanent or cuffed catheters. However, even with permanent catheters, peritonitis still occurs at a very high rate. Peritonitis is more likely to occur early after initiation of dialysis, when the patient is still unfamiliar with the technique.

Most cases of peritonitis probably occur as a result of touch contamination when connecting the tubing between the dialysis catheter and the dialysate solution. Other common routes of infection include entry and migration of skin flora from the catheter exit site or from an accidental break in the tubing. Occasionally bacteria migrate across the bowel wall to cause peritonitis.

One possible reason for the frequent occurrence of peritonitis is that host defense mechanisms within the peritoneal cavity are impaired in the presence of hyperosmotic and acidic dialysate. In such an unphysiologic milieu the peritoneal macrophage is unable to efficiently phagocytize and kill the invading bacteria. However, macrophage phagocytosis does improve somewhat late in the dialysis cycle as glucose is absorbed from the dialysate and the hyperosmolarity is reduced. In addition to impaired phagocytosis, peritoneal macrophages, which normally exist in only 150 ml of peritoneal fluid, are now greatly diluted in a much greater volume of dialysate, thus making phagocytosis much more difficult. There is also evidence that opsonic antibodies, which bind bacteria and aid in their removal, are lost in the dialysate effluent as a result of the nearly continuous peritoneal lavage performed.

The diagnosis of peritonitis is based on the features presented in Table 168-3. Fever and abdominal pain accompanied by cloudy dialysate effluent are the hallmarks of peritonitis. Microscopic examination of the infected peritoneal fluid will reveal >100 WBCs/ml with >50% polymorphonuclear leukocytes. A Gram stain of the peritoneal fluid, however, will only demonstrate bacteria 25% to 50% of the time. This low rate of Gram staining results from dilution of a small number of bacteria in the large volume of dialysate. Culture results are far more reliable and are positive in >95% of cases. However, such dialysate cultures must be handled by an experienced microbiology laboratory to maximize the sensitivity of culture results.

Staphylococcus aureus and *Staphylococcus epidermidis* are responsible for up to 70% of all cases of peritonitis. Because these microbes are part of the normal skin flora, they are likely inoculated into the peritoneal fluid through either touch contamination during the tubing connection or a localized infection of the tunnel or catheter exit site. Gram-negative organisms, including *Escherichia coli, Klebsiella,* and *Pseudomonas,* account for approximately 25% to 30% of all cases of peritonitis. These organisms likely originate through transmural migration of bowel flora or through fecal contamination of peritoneal fluid. *Pseudomonas* is particularly difficult to eradicate since

Table 168-3 Clinical Manifestations of Peritonitis*

Symptoms and Signs	Percent
Symptoms	
Cloudy dialysis effluent	98
Diffuse abdominal pain	78
Fever	35
Nausea	29
Vomiting	25
Chills	18
Poor outflow	15
Constipation	10
Diarrhea	7
Signs	
Abdominal tenderness	76
Temperature >37.5° C	50

*From Fox L, Tzamalookas A. In Heinrich WL, ed. Principles and Practice of Dialysis. Baltimore: Williams & Wilkins, 1994, p 441.

it can grow directly into the peritoneal catheter itself, rendering antibiotic therapy ineffective.

Peritonitis resulting from multiple organisms usually indicates fecal peritonitis. Fecal peritonitis develops when bowel perforation occurs and multiple bowel flora seed the peritoneal fluid. Although uncommon in children, fecal peritonitis is associated with a high mortality rate and immediate surgical intervention is needed for bowel repair and peritoneal cavity lavage.

Treatment of peritonitis usually begins with the evaluation of the peritoneal fluid for cell count, Gram's stain, and culture. Intraperitoneal antibiotics are given empirically before identification of the offending microorganism and include coverage for *Staphylococcus* sp (first-generation cephalosporins or vancomycin) and gram-negative organisms (aminoglycosides or third-generation cephalosporins). Once culture results have been obtained, the choice of antibiotics can be tailored specifically for the particular organism. Table 168-4 outlines some commonly used intraperitoneal antibiotics and their dosages. Antibiotics are typically used for a total of 10 to 14 days. When the infection persists despite appropriate antibiotic treatment, the catheter has likely become colonized with bacteria. A catheter colonized with bacteria (i.e., *Pseudomonas*) is impossible to sterilize and will continue to seed the peritoneal fluid and lead to

Table 168-4 Antibiotic Dosing Guidelines for the Treatment of Peritonitis and Pediatric Patients Receiving Continuous Peritoneal Dialysis*

	Half-Life (hr)			Dose‡		
				Initial		Maintenance
	Normal	ESRD	CAPD	mg/kg	mg/L of Dialysate	mg/L of Dialysate
Vancomycin and others						
Vancomycin†	6.9	161	83	15 IP/IV	—	25-30
Clindamycin	2.8	2.8	ND	—	150	150
Erythromycin	2.1	4.0	ND	—	150	75
Metronidazole	7.9	7.7	11	7.5 PO/IV	—	ND
Rifampin	4	8	ND	10 PO	—	5-10 mg/kg/dose q12h PO
Trimethoprim/ sulfamethoxazole	14/10	33/13	34/14	4/20 PO/IP	—	20-40/100-200
Antifungal						
Amphotericin B	360	360	ND	0.25 IV	—	0.5-1.0 mg/kg/dose q25h IV
Flucytosine†	4.2	115	ND	12.5 PO/IP	—	12.5 mg/kg/dose q12h PO *or* 50-100 mg/L IP
Ketoconazole	2	1.8	2.4	2-5 PO	—	2-5 mg/kg/dose q12h PO
Miconazole	24	25	ND	—	50	50
Aminoglycosides						
Amikacin†	1.6	39	ND	5.0-7.5 IV/IP	—	6-7.5
Gentamicin†	2.2	53	32	1.5-1.7 IV/IP	—	4-6
Netilmicin†	2.1	42	ND	1.5-2.0 IV/IP	—	4-6
Tobramycin†	2.5	58	36	1.5-1.7 IV/IP	—	4-6

ESRD = end-stage renal disease as defined by creatinine clearance <10 ml/min/1.73 m², patient not on dialysis; NA = not applicable; ND = no data; IP = intraperitoneal.

*Modified for pediatric patients from recommendations in Keane WF, Everett ED, Fine RN, et al. CAPD-related peritonitis management and antibiotic therapy recommendations. Peritoneal Dial Bull 7:55-68, 1987.

†Monitoring by frequent serum drug levels recommended.

‡The route of administration is intraperitoneal unless otherwise stated.

These data should only be used as initial guidelines. Individualized dosing is recommended when possible. Initial IP doses are based on a 2- to 4-hour dwell, single exchange.

The pharmacokinetic data and dosing recommendations presented here are based on published literature reviewed through January 1987 and personal experience. Those dosage recommendations that differ from product labeling are based on more recent experience. There is no evidence that mixing different antibiotics in dialysis fluid (except for aminoglycosides and penicillins) is deleterious for the drugs or patients. Do not use the same syringe to mix antibiotics. *Continued.*

Table 168-4 Antibiotic Dosing Guidelines for the Treatment of Peritonitis and Pediatric Patients Receiving Continuous Peritoneal Dialysis—cont'd

| | Half-Life (hr) | | | Dose‡ | | |
| | | | | Initial | | Maintenance |
	Normal	ESRD	CAPD	mg/kg	mg/L of Dialysate	mg/L of Dialysate
Cephalosporins						
Cefamandole	1.0	10	8.0	—	500	ND
Cefazolin	2.2	28	27	—	250-500	125-250
Cefoperazone	1.8	2.3	2.2	—	1000	500
Cefotaxime	0.9	2.5	2.4	—	1000	250
Cefoxitin	0.8	20	15	—	500	100
Ceftazidime	1.8	26	16	—	500	125
Ceftizoxime	1.6	28	11	—	500	125
Ceftriaxone	8.0	15	13	—	500	ND
Cefuroxime	1.3	18	15	—	750	250
Cephalothin	0.2	3.7	ND	—	1000	250
Moxalactam	2.2	20	16	—	500	ND
Cephradine	0.9	12	ND	—	250	125-250
Cephalexin	0.8	19	9	12.5 PO	—	12.5 mg/kg/dose q8h PO
Penicillins						
Ampicillin	1.2	15	ND	—	250	50
Azlocillin	0.9	5.1	ND	—	250	250
Ticarcillin	1.2	15	ND	75 IV	—	75 mg/kg/dose q12h IV

persistent peritonitis. Catheter removal is imperative and is followed by replacement with a new catheter after parenteral antibiotic therapy. Other infections in which catheter removal is necessary include tunnel infection, tunnel abscess, and fecal peritonitis.

Fungal peritonitis, although accounting for <5% of all cases of peritonitis, is especially devastating and commonly occurs in children who have recently received broad-spectrum antibiotics. *Candida* peritonitis is the most common fungal infection and, similar to *Pseudomonas,* can also colonize the catheter and make sterilization impossible. In addition, *Candida* elicits a very intense inflammatory response with a purulent exudate that ultimately leads to excessive scarring and adhesion formation of the peritoneal membrane. Such scarring renders the peritoneal membrane much less effective for fluid and solute exchange. Indeed peritoneal membrane failure after *Candida* peritonitis is not uncommon.

The treatment of *Candida* peritonitis is controversial. Most dialysis centers will remove the catheter and treat the infection with IV amphotericin for 21 days, after which a new peritoneal dialysis catheter is placed. During this period the patient is dialyzed via hemodialysis. Since peritoneal scarring and adhesion formation are very common, some centers have experimented with the replacement of a new peritoneal dialysis catheter after only a short period (4 to 5 days) of amphotericin B. With such an approach it was anticipated that the early use of full volumes of dialysate within the peritoneal cavity would prevent the formation of adhesions. Unfortunately, however, results are still poor with high rates of peritoneal membrane failure. The route of amphotericin B administration must be limited to the IV route; intraperitoneal administration must be avoided at all times. Amphotericin B itself can cause sclerosis of the peritoneal membrane and render it ineffective for fluid and solute transport.

The use of flucytosine and fluconozole has been reported but is still experimental. Studies have demonstrated questionable efficacy in adults. No studies have been conducted in children to date.

Catheter-Related Complications

As mentioned, the catheter exit site may become infected with local skin flora. Exit site erythema, tenderness, swelling, and exudate are the hallmarks of infection. Poor hygiene and prolonged continuous trauma or traction of the catheter all increase the risk of such infections. Proper hygiene includes daily cleansing of the skin around the exit site with an antibacterial soap and removal of the crust that normally forms around the catheter. The catheter must also be secured well, usually with tape, to prevent accidental traction. Any exudate from the catheter site must be sent for culture and sensitivity testing. Exit site infections are usually treated with intraperitoneal antibiotics that cover skin flora. Thus first-generation cephalosporins or vancomycin is the antibiotic of choice. Occasionally *Pseudomonas* is cultured, necessitating an antipseudomonal antibiotic such as ceftazidime. Infections refractory to antibiotic therapy, as evidenced by persistent exudate or erythema, will necessitate removal of the catheter followed by its replacement after a course of antibiotics.

Tunnel infections occur in the subcutaneous tissue between the exit site and the Dacron cuff. Tunnel infections are difficult to treat, and almost always necessitate catheter removal and a course of antibiotics. Since skin flora are involved, first-generation cephalosporins or vancomycin is used.

Leakage. Leakage of the dialysate fluid from around the catheter site occasionally occurs, especially when exchange volumes have been rapidly advanced early after catheter placement. Small leaks can be dealt with by cessation of dialysis for 24 hours followed by smaller exchange volumes. For larger leaks, however, surgical intervention is needed to either place the catheter in a different site or, more commonly, retie the suture around the catheter-peritoneal site. Leaks are more common in small infants with thin abdominal walls or malnourished children with poor wound healing.

Malposition. Even with the best surgical technique, catheters can migrate out of position and result in poor catheter drainage or filling of dialysate fluid. Diagnosis is usually made by radiography (an anterior and a lateral view of the abdomen). Improperly positioned catheters are often entangled within the loops of bowel or the omentum. If the catheter does not fill or drain properly, attempts can be made to reposition it under fluoroscopy with a guidewire in the catheter. However, this technique is often unsuccessful and the catheter must be revised surgically. A well-functioning malpositioned catheter is left alone.

Fluid and Electrolyte Abnormalities

Peritoneal dialysis, if not carefully monitored, can cause potentially serious and life-threatening fluid and electrolyte abnormalities. Although children of all ages can be similarly affected, young infants are particularly susceptible to such abnormalities. Their small size, limited dietary intake, and lack of reserve make them prone to hypovolemia and hyponatremia. With meticulous monitoring of vital signs, weight, and electrolytes, most such fluid and electrolyte abnormalities can be anticipated and avoided.

Hypovolemia and hypervolumia. Patients become hypovolemic when aggressive ultrafiltration has greatly exceeded the fluid intake. This typically occurs with prolonged use of high dextrose dialysate (i.e., 4.25 g/dl) or overuse of frequent (hourly) exchanges. Clinically patients present with the usual signs and symptoms of volume depletion, including hypotension, tachycardia, poor skin turgor, and dry mucous membranes. Despite hypotension, ultrafiltration will continue unabated since peritoneal blood flow is only slightly decreased.

Patients become hypervolemic when poor ultrafiltration results in excessive fluid retention. An inappropriate low dextrose concentration dialysate or infrequent exchanges can all lead to poor ultrafiltration. Hypervolemic patients present with the usual signs of volume overload, including hypertension and edema. Fluid retention can also occur when the peritoneal dialysis catheter is mechanically obstructed and leads to poor dialysate drainage. Alternatively, loops of bowel, omentum, or fibrin clots can all also occlude the peritoneal catheter.

To prevent hypovolemia and hypervolemia, meticulous attention must be paid to fluid balance. All tabulations of ultrafiltration and urine output must be recorded carefully and compared to all fluid intake, including oral IV fluids. Patients need to be weighed at least once daily. Care must be taken to subtract the weight of the peritoneal fluid to accurately reflect the patient's "dry" weight. The amount of peritoneal fluid in the peritoneal cavity is most easily determined at the end of a cycle after drainage (no fluid) or at the beginning of a cycle (full volume exchange). Once the fluid balance and the weight of the patient are known, appropriate adjustments in the dextrose concentration of dialysate or frequency of exchanges can be made to correct for any over- or underfiltration of fluid.

Hyponatremia and hypernatremia. Hyponatremia develops in patients undergoing peritoneal dialysis when peritoneal sodium losses (via ultrafiltration) exceed sodium intake. Sodium is lost in peritoneal ultrafiltrate as isotonic saline solution. Hyponatremia is commonly seen in infants and small children whose dietary intake consists primarily of hypotonic fluids. Older children and adults who usually ingest adequate amounts of dietary sodium rarely develop hyponatremia. To prevent hyponatremia, infants can be given supplemental sodium chloride, either orally or intravenously. The amount of supplemental sodium can be estimated by multiplying the daily ultrafiltrate volumes by the serum sodium concentration.

Hypernatremia is rare except in cases where successive rapid exchanges are performed. As discussed previously, hypernatremia results from the sieving effect of solute removal across the peritoneal membrane. Decreasing the frequency of exchanges will generally correct hypernatremia. More rarely, hypernatremia can result from an error in the formulation of dialysate composition. Such errors usually occur in dialysate solutions prepared by individual hospitals or pharmacies rather than those commercially available.

Hypokalemia and hyperkalemia. Hypokalemia typically occurs after prolonged dialysis without adequate intake of potassium. Correction of hypokalemia is simply accomplished by adding potassium chloride to the dialysate at the concentration desired

(i.e., 3.5 or 4.0 mEq/L). Prolonged hypokalemia in dialysis patients can lead to cardiac arrhythmias, muscle weakness, or even rhabdomyolysis.

Hyperkalemia usually occurs with inadequate dialysis. Simply increasing the frequency of exchanges or the volume of dialysate will correct hyperkalemia. Certain diseases such as tumor lysis syndrome release large amounts of potassium into the extracellular fluid and rapid removal is necessary. Such situations are better treated by hemodialysis, where rapid correction of electrolyte abnormalities is desired.

Hernias

Hernias can occur in patients on peritoneal dialysis because of increased abdominal pressure resulting from the dialysate. Patients on CAPD carry a full exchange volume of fluid in an upright position nearly all day and are at greater risk than those on continuous cycler peritoneal dialysis who are recumbent during dialysis. Inguinal hernias are perhaps the most common hernias and need to be carefully examined for incarcerated and ischemic bowel. Incisional hernias usually occur along the catheter insertion site and are often accompanied by leakage of dialysate. Other less common hernias include umbilical, epigastric, and diaphragmatic hernias.

All hernias need to be surgically repaired. Dialysate volumes can also be decreased shortly after surgical repair to reduce intra-abdominal pressure and aid healing. Care must be taken to maintain the "dose" of dialysis by increasing the total number of exchanges per day.

ADDITIONAL READING

• Alexander SR. Peritoneal dialysis in children. In Norph KP, ed. Peritoneal Dialysis, 3rd ed. Norwell, Mass.: Kluwer, 1989, pp 343-364.

Alexander S. Peritoneal dialysis. In Levin D, Morriss F, eds. Essentials of Pediatric Intensive Care. St. Louis: Quality Medical Publishing, 1990.

• Balfe JW, Vigneau JW, Hardy BE. The use of CAPD in the treatment of children with end-stage renal disease. Perit Dial Bull 1:35-38, 1984.

Chan JCM. Acute renal failure in children: Principles of management. Clin Pediatr 13:686-695, 1974.

Fine RM, Salusky IB, Ettinger RB. The therapeutic approach to the infant, child, and adolescent with end-stage renal disease. Pediatr Clin North Am 34:789-802, 1987.

Fine RM, Salusky IB, Hall T, et al. Peritonitis in children undergoing continuous ambulatory peritoneal dialysis. Pediatrics 71:806-809, 1983.

Fox L, Tzamalookas A. In Heinrich WL, ed. Principles and Practice of Dialysis. Baltimore: Williams & Wilkins, 1994.

Nolph KP, Sorkin MI. In Brenner BM, Stein JH, eds. CAPD in Chronic Renal Failure. New York: Churchill Livingstone, 1981.

Popovich RP, Moncrief JW, Nolph KP. Continuous ambulatory peritoneal dialysis. Ann Intern Med 88:449-456, 1978.

• Schoenfeld P. Care of the patient on peritoneal dialysis. In Cogan M, Schoenfeld P, eds. Introduction to Dialysis. New York: Churchill Livingstone, 1991.

169 Hemodialysis and Hemoperfusion

Shermine Dabbagh · Bassam Atiyeh

Hemodialysis

BACKGROUND AND INDICATIONS

Dialysis therapy is the process of separating crystalloid from colloid substances in blood, using semipermeable membranes, to replace or augment renal function. Before the advent of the Quinton-Scribner arteriovenous shunt in 1960, hemodialysis was not a realistic option in the pediatric age group. With the development of new dialyzers, dialysis machines, and microvascular surgical techniques and the evolution of vascular access, it became possible to treat 25% to 50% of children with end-stage renal disease by means of chronic hemodialysis. These advances have made hemodialysis an attractive alternative in the PICU for the treatment of acute azotemia, metabolic derangements, and acute poisoning. Many of the principles of hemodialysis have similar applications in all age groups and patient sizes. However, children present a challenge that calls for the expertise of pediatric specialists and nurses and hence is better not attempted without the supervision of a pediatric nephrologist.

Hemodialysis involves two processes: ultrafiltration and clearance across a semipermeable membrane, with blood flowing across one surface of the dialyzer membrane and dialysate fluid flowing across the other side of the dialyzer membrane in a countercurrent fashion. With *ultrafiltration,* fluid moves from the blood to the dialysate compartment under hydrostatic pressure. The amount of fluid removed depends on the pressure difference between the two compartments or the transmembrane pressure (TMP). Since the blood oncotic pressure opposes ultrafiltration, the TMP must exceed the plasma oncotic pressure. The primary source of positive pressure across the dialyzer is the blood pump. The magnitude of TMP gradients within the blood compartment is set by varying the resistance on the venous side of the

dialyzer. The pressures in the dialysate compartment are set by either increasing the speed of the outlet pump draining the dialysate fluid or altering the size of the entry port through which the dialysate enters the dialyzer.

In addition, each membrane is characterized by an ultrafiltration coefficient (K_f), which is defined as the volume of fluid (in milliliters) transferred across the dialysis membrane per hour when 1 mm Hg of TMP is applied. Because the pressure in the blood compartment almost always exceeds the oncotic pressure, there is an obligatory loss of plasma fluid during the process of hemodialysis, even when no ultrafiltration is needed. This is important in the pediatric population since hypovolemia and hypotension may ensue in small patients. The ultrafiltration volume can be estimated as follows:

$$\text{Ultrafiltration (ml)} = K_f \times \text{TMP} \times \text{Dialysis time (hr)}$$

Since the lowest TMP setting on the dialysis machines is approximately 50 mm Hg, and if an infant (weight 3 kg) is hemodialyzed using a dialyzer with a K_f of 0.5, the patient will lose approximately 25 ml of fluid per hour, which could be significant with prolonged hemodialysis in infants dialyzed for urea cycle defects or other metabolic disorders. In practice, it is difficult to predict the exact volume of ultrafiltrate using the preceding formula since the TMP depends on pressures in the blood and dialysate compartments, which are likely to vary during the dialysis procedure because of variations in blood flow or patient position. Thus current dialysis machines continuously monitor ultrafiltrate volume and make adjustments in pressures to remove the desired fluid volume.

The concept of *clearance* during hemodialysis is basically the same process as occurs in kidneys. Thus clearance of a solute is the volume of blood that can be cleared of that solute in a unit of time. Each dialyzer has its own clearances, depending on the type of membrane and size of the dialyzer. Membrane properties determine the mass transfer coefficient (KoA), which represents the ability of a solute to pass through the pores of the membrane. Generally urea clearance represents clearance of small molecules, whereas vitamin B_{12} clearance represents clearance of medium-sized molecules. In addition to dialyzer membrane properties, solute clearance depends on blood and dialysate flow and the ultrafiltration rate. Solute clearance (especially of solutes with low molecular weights) increases with higher blood flow rates. Dialysate flow rates are typically set at 500 ml/min. However, with the advent of high-efficiency and high-flux dialysis, higher rates (700 to 1000 ml/min) are necessary for optimal use of dialyzer surface area for solute transport. Finally, there is a correlation between the ultrafiltration rate and solute clearance whereby ultrafiltration increases clearance by means of convection. In summary, combining a dialyzer with a high KoA and high blood flow rate will effect higher clearances of low- and medium-sized molecular weight solutes.

Peritoneal dialysis is usually the modality of choice for the treatment of acute renal failure since it obviates the need for vascular access, particularly in very small children. Moreover, it does not create the rapid osmolar and fluid shifts that occur with hemodialysis, and it is better tolerated in the presence of hemodynamic instability. However, hemodialysis is indicated when peritoneal dialysis cannot be used (e.g., acute renal failure in a patient who has undergone abdominal surgery) or must be abandoned.

Early recognition of oliguria, defined as urine output <240 ml/m^2, is critical. Generally conservative treatment (fluid and salt restriction and aggressive antidiuretic therapy) may be successful in preventing fluid overload. However, when conservative treatment fails, or if the patient needs large amounts of fluid to maintain hemodynamic stability, it may be necessary to consider dialysis to treat intravascular volume overload.

Hyperkalemia is a major cause of death in children with acute renal failure. The high mortality rate associated with hyperkalemia is related, in part, to the high serum concentrations of potassium and to the associated electrolyte abnormalities, including hyponatremia, hypocalcemia, and acidosis. Conservative management includes correcting the electrolyte abnormalities, administering parenteral glucose and insulin or bicarbonate infusion, and administering a sodium-potassium exchange resin (Kayexalate) orally or rectally. In principle, 1 g of Kayexalate/kg/dose

---

INDICATIONS FOR ACUTE HEMODIALYSIS

Intractable volume overload
Hyperkalemia
Hypocalcemia secondary to massive phosphate retention
Intractable metabolic acidosis
Hyperuricemia
Hyperphosphatemia associated with tumor lysis
Severe azotemia (BUN >150 mg/dl)
Symptomatic uremia (e.g., encephalopathy, pericarditis)
Drug overdose (e.g., ethylene glycol poisoning)
Inborn errors of metabolism

TREATMENT OF HYPERKALEMIA

Stabilization of myocardium

10% calcium gluconate, 100 to 200 mg/kg/dose
Sodium chloride if hyponatremia is present

Transcellular shifts

Sodium bicarbonate, 1 mEq/kg/dose IV
Glucose and insulin, 0.5 g glucose/kg/dose, with 0.1 U insulin/kg/dose IV
β_2-Adrenergic agonists, 4 μg terbutaline/kg over 20 min IV or 2.5 mg albuterol for children <25 kg or 5 mg for children ≥ 25 kg by nebulization

Removal of potassium

Sodium-potassium exchange resins (Kayexalate), 1 g/kg/dose PO or PR
Dialysis: Hemodialysis, peritoneal dialysis, continuous arteriovenous (or veno-venous) hemofiltration, continuous arteriovenous (or veno-venous) hemodiafiltration

lowers the serum potassium concentration by 1 mEq/L. When Kayexalate is administered by retention enema, the onset of action is approximately 1 hour; the onset of action tends to be longer when it is administered orally.

Acute and potentially lethal poisonings are not uncommon in the pediatric age group. Frequently these incidents are treated conservatively. When necessary, hemodialysis or hemoperfusion is preferred to peritoneal dialysis since rapid removal of the toxin is usually necessary. Dialysis of a poison depends on its diffusibility, molecular size, concentration in the extracellular fluid, accessibility in the volume of distribution, and protein binding. Lipid- or protein-bound poisons are inefficiently removed by hemodialysis; however, use of charcoal or resin sorbents with hemoperfusion greatly enhances the elimination of these solutes.

Finally, hemodialysis is considered in newborn infants with inborn errors of metabolism such as urea cycle defects, organic acidemias, or maple syrup urine disease. In these disorders there is an accumulation of low molecular weight, water-soluble substances (e.g., ammonia) that can cause brain damage. Hemodialysis is generally the preferred emergency treatment in addition to the administration of sufficient amounts of carbohydrates and lipids to prevent protein breakdown and the formation of increased amounts of endogenous urea. The urea cycle can be bypassed with the administration of arginine, sodium benzoate, and phenylacetate. These newborn infants may be able to tolerate high blood flow rates because their cardiovascular function is normal. The dialysis circuits are primed with blood since more than 10% of the infant's blood volume will be in the extracorporeal circuit. Continuous infusion of 0.9% sodium chloride solution throughout the dialysis session is necessary to offset obligatory fluid loss occurring with ultrafiltration. Monitoring needs to include frequent weighing of the infant to maintain normal fluid volume status.

TECHNIQUE
Mechanics of the Hemodialysis System
(Fig. 169-1)

The dialysis system is composed of the dialyzer, which contains the semipermeable membrane and the supporting pumps, circuit, and monitoring devices.

Dialyzer. There are two types of hemodialyzers:

hollow fiber and parallel plate. The hollow-fiber dialyzer is the most commonly used and consists of thousands of thin fibers bundled together in a polyurethane casing. Blood flows through the fibers while dialysate fluid bathes the outer surface of the fibers. The blood compartment volume is fixed. Alternatively, the parallel-plate dialyzer consists of sheets of flat plates that are supported in such a manner as to produce injection-molded and folded-membrane cartridges. These dialyzers are compliant; the blood volume varies with the TMP. The advantage of the hollow-fiber dialyzer over the parallel-plate dialyzer includes the low priming blood volume in association with a large surface area. Thus hollow-fiber dialyzers have become the dialyzer of choice, even in smaller infants.

Water supply. A water treatment system is needed to provide water with the fewest contaminants (e.g., calcium, magnesium, chloramine, arsenic, barium, lead, mercury, aluminum, copper, and bacteria) that are known to be toxic to hemodialysis patients. The system must provide this water at the correct temperature, pressure, and flow rate so that it is compatible with the proportioning system (see below) of the dialysis machine. Available water systems include water softening, filtration, reverse osmosis, and deionization. The primary purification method of choice is reverse osmosis, which is capable of removing 85% to 95% of dissolved solutes in water. Generally it is accepted that reverse osmosis removes inorganic contaminants by at least a factor of 10 and bacteria by a factor of 10^3 to 10^5. Although this purification system delivers water to dialysis centers, it may not be available for use in ICUs. In this situation tap water with the appropriate pressures could be used after purification with a portable reverse osmosis system.

Delivery system. The delivery system is a compilation of devices that pump blood and dialysate fluid through the system. Dialysis units use single-patient hemodialysis machines that employ single-pass dialysate circulation, thus offering the nephrologist tremendous flexibility and mobility, which is important in an intensive care situation. All dialysis machines have a heater to warm the dialysate to body temperature, a dialysate pump, and flowmeters and alarms to monitor dialysate pressure, temperature, and conductivity and detect air or blood leaks.

Dialysate fluid is constituted using a proportion-

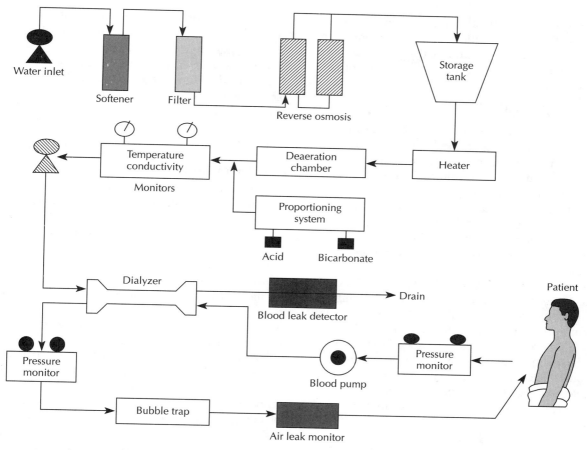

Fig. 169-1   Schematic representation of the various components of a single-patient hemodialysis system.

ing system in which concentrate is diluted in a 35:1 ratio with water to yield the appropriate concentrations of solute: sodium, 138 to 142 mEq/L; potassium, 0 to 4 mEq/L; buffer (acetate or bicarbonate), 30 to 40 mEq/L; calcium, 5 to 7 mg/dl; chloride, 100 to 110 mEq/L; and glucose, 150 to 250 mg/dl. Acetate-containing dialysate remains stable over time and can therefore be mixed in large batches. In addition, it does not cause the precipitation of calcium and magnesium and possesses bacteriostatic properties that prevent the proliferation of bacteria during shipping and handling of the concentrate. Although acetate is tolerated by many patients, select groups of patients (e.g., diabetics and critically ill patients) exhibit hypoxemia and vascular instability when dialyzed against these baths. Bicarbonate-containing dialysates minimize these problems and de-

crease the incidence of associated headache, vomiting, and postdialysis fatigue. In addition, bicarbonate dialysis is mandatory in high-flux or high-efficiency dialysis. The delivery system for bicarbonate dialysate uses an acid concentrate and a bicarbonate concentrate. The bicarbonate concentrate contains the sodium bicarbonate and sodium chloride, whereas the acid concentrate contains the remainder of the solutes, including a small amount of acetic acid (3 to 6 mEq/L). The acetic acid titrates some of the bicarbonate to form carbon dioxide, which is essential to control the dialysate pH and prevent the precipitation of calcium and magnesium.

Dialysate flow is achieved by means of a negative pressure pump. Flows (Q_D) are maintained at 500 ml/min, although systems that deliver 1000 ml/min are available. Blood flow is maintained at a rate that varies from 50 to 600 ml/min, depending on the size of the patient and the efficiency of solute removal required (high-flux vs. high-efficiency vs. traditional dialysis). Blood flow is achieved by means of positive pressure pumps.

Choosing a Dialyzer

Most pediatric dialysis units stock dialyzers in various sizes to fit a range of body weights. The different membranes used include cellulose acetate, cuprammonium-treated cellulose (Cupraphan), and synthetic membranes (e.g., polyacrylonitrile, polypropylene, and polyamide). The choice of a dialyzer depends on biocompatibility, solute clearance, water permeability, and surface area of the dialyzer. The choice of a dialyzer in the pediatric age group depends on two main concepts.

1. No more than 10% of the patient's blood volume is in the extracorporeal circuit. Currently the blood compartment of dialyzers ranges from 19 ml (Gambro mini-minor) to 160 ml (Gambro high-flux IC-6). This volume needs to be added to the volume of the connecting lines, which varies from 30 ml (neonatal lines) to 270 ml (adult circuits). When priming volume exceeds 10% of the patient's blood volume, the circuit is primed with Plasmanate or whole blood.

2. Urea clearance is maintained at approximately 3 ml/kg/min. In cases of prolonged elevations of BUN it is prudent to initiate dialysis using a blood flow that will effect a urea clearance of 1.5 to 2 ml/kg/min.

The most important advantage of parallel dialyzers is the lower dose of heparin needed, which may be important in critically ill patients with bleeding diathesis. However, the disadvantage of using parallel-plate dialyzers is the noted maldistribution of blood and dialysate, which will lead to inefficient removal of solutes, particularly at low flow rates. Table 169-1 lists the commonly used dialyzers in the pediatric age group.

Anticoagulation

Because blood in an extracorporeal circuit will clot, heparinization is necessary in most patients undergoing hemodialysis. Several techniques for heparinization are available, including systemic heparinization, continuous (low-dose) heparinization, regional heparinization, and no heparinization.

The choice of an anticoagulation method depends on the patient's risk of bleeding. Patients who have recently undergone surgery or have active bleeding, hemorrhagic pericarditis, recent head trauma, or bleeding diathesis are considered high risk and merit continuous (low-dose) heparinization or no heparinization when undergoing hemodialysis. Patients with a history of recurrent blood loss or diabetic retinopathy are considered to be at moderate risk for bleeding and merit continuous (low-dose) heparinization.

The primary monitor of heparinization is the whole blood activated clotting time (ACT), which can be assayed at the patient's bedside to produce immediate results. Whole blood is added to a test tube

Table 169-1   Types of Hemodialyzers Used in Pediatric Patients

Dialyzer	Priming Volume (ml)	Compliance (ml/100 mm Hg)	Effective Surface Area (m²)	Ultrafiltration	Type
Asahi AM-03	30	—	0.3	1.4	Capillary
100-HG, Cobe	18	0	0.22	2	Capillary
ExCel 0.3p-Extracorporeal	30	0	0.30	1.4	Capillary
Gambro mini-minor	20	6	0.2	0.4-0.6	Plate
Lundia IC-IL, Gambro	33	10	0.23	0.9	Plate
Baxter, CA-50	38	0	0.5	2.4	Capillary
Baxter, Ca-70	51	0	0.7	2.5	Capillary
Baxter, CA-90	64	0	0.9	4.3	Capillary
F_3, Fersenius	30	0	0.35	1.7	Capillary
F_4, Fersenius	44	0	0.65	2.8	Capillary
F_5, Fersenius	63	0	0.9	4.2	Capillary

that has an activator such as ground glass or earth. The device measures the time from placement of the tube in the machine to the detection of fibrin strands deposited on a pellet in the tube. A normal ACT ranges from 90 to 140 seconds.

Systemic heparinization

During systemic heparinization the goal of anticoagulation is to maintain the ACT at approximately one and a half to three times the normal range. A loading dose of heparin is administered at the start of the hemodialysis procedure. The loading dose used at Children's Hospital of Michigan is 60 units/kg (maximum 5000 units) at the start of hemodialysis. The dialysis lines are primed with 0.9% sodium chloride solution containing no heparin. After the loading dose, heparin is administered proximal to the dialyzer at a rate of 30 units/kg/hr (maximum 1500 units) and is discontinued 60 minutes before the hemodialysis procedure is discontinued. This regimen of heparinization is adjusted according to the patient's ACT, which is determined every 30 minutes while the patient is on dialysis. Systemic heparinization is reserved for stable patients on chronic hemodialysis.

Continuous (low-dose) heparinization

Continuous or low-dose heparinization has been used for more than 20 years in patients who are at increased risk for bleeding. A loading dose of 5 to 10 units of heparin per kilogram of body weight with a continuous infusion of 10 units/kg body weight/hr to maintain the ACT at around 1.25 times the baseline value has been recommended. Alternatively, the loading dose can be eliminated and heparin administered by continuous infusion at a rate of 20 to 30 units/kg of body weight/hr to maintain the ACT at 1.25 times the baseline. This method is used in the hemodialysis of patients who have a tendency toward bleeding but who are not critically ill or are in the immediate postoperative period.

Regional heparinization

This method of anticoagulation involves infusing heparin through the arterial blood line proximal to the dialyzer and protamine into the return line at a rate that will neutralize the heparin (1 mg protamine for every 100 units of heparin infused). Because protamine is more rapidly metabolized than heparin, extra protamine may be necessary a few hours after the termination of dialysis to prevent "rebound." Regional

heparinization has not been shown to be safer than low-dose heparinization and thus has been abandoned for anticoagulation in critically ill patients because of its difficulty.

No heparinization

Despite improved dialysis methods and supportive care, mortality rates remain high in patients with acute renal failure, primarily because of comorbid conditions. Many patients have a coagulopathy that increases the risk of bleeding. Many such patients undergo hemodialysis successfully without anticoagulation. In older patients the method involves maintaining blood flow at 250 to 300 ml/min through the extracorporeal system and examining the circuit every 20 to 30 minutes for signs of clotting by infusing 100 ml of 0.9% sodium chloride solution proximal to the dialyzer. In a review of 50 cases of critically ill patients undergoing acute hemodialysis (total number of treatments = 137) in the critical care unit at Children's Hospital of Michigan, the average blood flow through the circuit was 130 ± 10 ml/min. In all patients the circuit is primed with 0.9% sodium chloride solution containing heparin (100 units/L). A baseline ACT is obtained and follow-up measurements are performed every 30 minutes. The circuit is visually checked for evidence of clotting without the use of 0.9% sodium chloride solution. When the ACT drops below 1.25 times the baseline value, a heparin infusion is begun at a rate of 20 units/kg/hr and the ACT is checked within 15 minutes; the dose of heparin is adjusted to achieve the desired value. Thirty patients were dialyzed with no heparin. In the remaining patients a total of 10 ± 3 units/kg was needed for the duration of the treatment. The incidence of clotting in the circuit was 10%; there was no difference between patients who received heparin and those who did not.

Vascular Access

Vascular access remains a challenge in the pediatric patient, irrespective of whether hemodialysis is performed on a chronic or on an acute basis, particularly in the infant. In the past the Quinton-Scribner external arteriovenous shunt was surgically placed between the radial artery and cephalic vein for acute or chronic dialysis. For acute hemodialysis, catheters placed in large central veins (superior vena cava or inferior vena cava) permit the use of high blood flow rates to achieve better clearance. Double-lumen

Hickman or Quinton catheters are preferred to single-lumen catheters since they provide better solute clearance. These catheters can be left in place for months and can serve as permanent access in infants. At the end of dialysis each catheter port is filled with 1 to 1.5 ml of heparin (1000 units/ml).

Although centrally placed double-lumen catheters can be used for chronic hemodialysis, particularly in infants, permanent access using direct arteriovenous fistulas (Brescia-Cimino) or bridging grafts is preferred. The Brescia-Cimino arteriovenous fistula is preferred when possible since it provides the safest long-term blood access for hemodialysis. As in adults, these fistulas are created between the radial artery and the cephalic vein or the brachial artery and the cephalic vein. At the completion of the procedure a thrill is palpable at the site; however, complete arterialization of the vein is not achieved for 4 to 6 weeks, delaying the initiation of hemodialysis for that period. Alternatively, a bridging graft made of Gore-Tex is placed in the femoral or brachial area; the access is ready for use within 10 to 14 days after placement.

RISKS AND COMPLICATIONS

The process of hemodialysis is associated with a number of problems that are unique to the procedure and are generally independent of those related to the underlying disease or end-stage renal disease. Some of these complications will be discussed in detail.

Catheter-Related Problems

Complications of indwelling catheters include local pain, local hematoma, thrombosis within the catheter, infection, thrombosis of central veins, ipsilateral and contralateral hemothorax, pneumothorax, mediastinal hematoma, and pericardial tamponade. However, there is agreement in the literature that these complications are becoming less frequent. On reviewing our experience with long-term indwelling, centrally placed double-lumen catheters used for chronic hemodialysis we found the complications to be surprisingly low. The most common complication was clotting and malfunction of the catheter, with an incidence of 18%. These episodes were resolved with the use of urokinase, which lysed 73% of the clots, or surgical thrombectomy or catheter revision, which was used in 27% of the cases. In the 98 centrally placed catheters over the past 12 years there were four catheter-related infections, one case of hemo-

thorax, and one case of pneumothorax. The double-lumen Hickman catheter was used for access in 69% of patients. One factor that may have contributed to the relatively low complication rate may be related to the fact that one pediatric surgeon was dedicated to placing the majority of these catheters (84%).

Hypotension

Hypotension remains the most frequently encountered complication of hemodialysis and is reported to occur in 20% to 30% of hemodialysis treatments. It may result from acute blood loss, excessive or too rapid removal of fluid, autonomic nervous system dysfunction, or the use of acetate-containing baths. Excessive ultrafiltration remains the most common cause of hypotension. During the process of ultrafiltration, fluid initially removed from the plasma volume must be replaced by fluid from the interstitial space. High ultrafiltration rates may not be reciprocated by a similar rate of fluid replacement from the interstitial compartment for various reasons, including poor myocardial function, poor peripheral vascular resistance, and low intravascular oncotic pressures (e.g., patients with hypoalbuminemia). These factors may be intrinsic to the underlying disease process and can be compounded by acetate baths, which may affect myocardial function and peripheral vascular resistance. Patients who convert acetate to bicarbonate at a lower rate (e.g., patients with sepsis or liver disease) are prone to hypotension when acetate-containing dialysate is used, particularly when dialyzers with large surface areas and high blood flow rates are needed. Hyponatremia, whether due to the underlying disease or the use of low sodium–containing baths, may lead to hypotension resulting from alteration of the ratio of extracellular to intracellular water.

The best treatment for hypotension secondary to ultrafiltration is prevention. In chronically dialyzed patients these episodes tend to occur in those who gain more than 5% of their estimated dry body weight between treatments. Thus adherence to fluid restriction is stressed. Bicarbonate-containing dialysis baths are currently used in most pediatric units, thus eliminating acetate as a causative factor in ultrafiltration-induced hypotension. Treatment of acute episodes includes reduction of the ultrafiltration rate and blood flow as well as the infusion of volume. Most patients respond to an infusion of 1.5 to 3 ml/kg of 0.9% sodium chloride solution. However, because the infused volume has to be removed to achieve the desired weight loss, some clinicians prefer to administer 0.15 to 0.3 ml/kg of 3% sodium chloride solution or 0.5 g/kg of 20% mannitol. These hypertonic solutions expand the intravascular volume by increasing intravascular and extracellular osmolality, which results in the redistribution of fluid between the intracellular and extracellular compartments. The frequent use of mannitol can cause hyponatremia secondary to the movement of water into the extracellular space and hyperosmolality with its attendant effects on the CNS. These complications result from the elevated levels of mannitol that persist between dialysis treatments since 80% of the solute is normally excreted by healthy kidneys. Patients with hypoalbuminemia respond to 0.5 g/kg of 25% albumin.

Blood loss is the other cause of dialysis-related hypotension. Bleeding may occur internally (e.g., GI hemorrhage) or externally. External blood loss is usually secondary to breaks in the extracorporeal circuit, especially in the dialyzer, or to clotting of the circuit; in both of these situations the dialyzer and/or the circuit needs to be replaced. The decision to perform a blood transfusion depends on the patient's symptoms, the magnitude of the blood loss, and the baseline hemoglobin value.

Dialysis Disequilibrium Syndrome

Dialysis disequilibrium syndrome is a complex of symptoms that include irritability, restlessness, lethargy, nausea, vomiting, headache, and backache; it may progress to twitching, tremors, myoclonic asterixis, hypertension, disorientation, visual disturbances, seizures, coma, and death. The etiology of the syndrome is not clear but appears to be related to rapid correction of the uremia. It is more likely to occur during initial treatments in newly diagnosed patients, with a higher incidence in children than in adults because of the use of large surface area dialyzers.

It has been shown in animals that rapid dialysis results in an increase in CSF pressure as well as a decrease in CSF pH and bicarbonate concentrations. Since the elevated intracellular osmolality in brain tissue resolves more slowly than the elevated serum osmolality, cerebral edema develops. The cerebral edema may result from a transient osmotic disequilibrium related to rapid removal of urea from the blood as compared with the CSF or the brain and is followed by movement of water from the extracellular compartment to the relatively hyperosmolar cells of

the brain, an effect known as reverse urea effect. Alternatively, other investigators have suggested a role for the accumulation of "idiogenic osmoles" in the brain as a cause of dialysis disequilibrium syndrome. The mechanism of intracellular brain acidosis is unknown, but it does not seem to be related to decreased cerebral blood flow, changes in arterial or CSF P_{CO_2}, or increased CSF lactic acid concentrations. Strong organic acids ("idiogenic osmoles") may increase intracellular osmolality directly or indirectly by displacing Na^+ and K^+ from intracellular protein buffers.

In patients with dialysis disequilibrium syndrome EEG findings are characterized by increased slow wave activity, increased spike wave activity, loss of alpha waves, and bursts of delta wave activity.

It is easier to prevent dialysis disequilibrium syndrome than it is to treat it. In patients with high BUN concentrations shorter treatments, use of dialyzer urea clearance rates of 1.0 to 1.5 ml/min/kg, and infusion of 0.5 to 1.0 g/kg of 25% mannitol over the course of the treatment can be used. However, experimental evidence supporting the use of mannitol is lacking, and the accumulation of mannitol stimulates thirst and may lead to the above-noted complications as well as to increased interdialysis weight gain. At Children's Hospital of Michigan the regimen for new patients with high BUN levels includes the use of low urea clearance rates, concurrent dialysate flow for the first two or three dialysis sessions, and short dialysis times, which are increased with each consecutive session until adequate and efficient dialysis is achieved.

When major symptoms develop, dialysis is immediately discontinued and the necessary investigations (e.g., blood chemistry levels, EEGs, and CT scans of the head) are performed. IV diazepam or phenobarbital can be used to treat the seizures. The value of infusing hypertonic urea solutions is questioned.

Air Embolism

Life-threatening and fatal air embolism is rare with the use of modern dialysis machines with detectors that use ultrasound to detect air bubbles and foam. Sources of air entry include the prepump tubing segment, IV infusion sets, other parts of the dialysis circuit, and air bubbles in the dialysate fluid. Central venous catheters are potential sources of air entry into the right side of the heart. Air embolism impairs cardiac output and results in hypoxia and cardiopulmonary arrest with involvement of the pulmonary circulation. When a patient is in a sitting position air entry through a peripheral vein may cause venous emboli and increased outflow resistance in the cerebral circulation, which may lead to seizures and coma. When a patient is in the Trendelenburg position, air may migrate to the lower extremities, resulting in venous obstruction, limb cyanosis, numbness, and pain.

Air embolism is suspected when a patient develops acute dyspnea, hyperpnea and collapse, CNS symptoms, or acute lower extremity ischemic symptoms. Once embolism is suspected, dialysis is discontinued and the blood lines are clamped. For central catheter/right ventricle emboli, the patient is placed on his left side with the head in the down position to trap the air in the apex of the right ventricle followed by aspiration through the dialysis catheter or a separately placed right atrial catheter. Endotracheal intubation may be needed and treatment with 100% oxygen may be necessary.

Acute Biochemical Changes

Biochemical changes in monovalent and divalent ion concentrations during the procedure of hemodialysis can be life threatening. Rarely these perturbations result from incorrect dialysate composition due to technical or human errors. Complications from improper concentrate composition are avoided if the conductivity alarm is functioning properly and correctly set. In machines with conductivity-controlled mixing systems, where the composition of the solutions is automatically adjusted when the conductivity changes, testing the pH of the dialysate becomes an essential step in preventing complications such as metabolic acidosis from low concentrations of bicarbonate in the dialysate bath.

Generally hyponatremia and hypernatremia are the result of technical failures in the proportioning system of the dialysis machine or the conductivity alarm system. The clinical manifestations of hypernatremia are related to hyperosmolality and intracellular volume depletion as water moves from the cells into the extracellular compartment. Symptoms include headache, profound thirst, nausea, vomiting, seizures, coma, and death. Treatment includes discontinuation of dialysis and infusion of 5% dextrose solution to reduce the hyperosmolality. Some clinicians recommend resuming dialysis with a different machine, using dialysate containing a sodium concentration that is 2 to 3 mEq/L lower than that of the plasma while infusing 0.9% sodium chloride solution. The symptoms of hyponatremia include restlessness, anxiety, cramps, chest pain, headache, nausea, vomiting, and seizures, and they result from the movement of water intracellularly with resulting cerebral edema. In addition, patients may develop hemolysis and associated hyperkalemia. Treatment includes discontinuing hemodialysis, clamping the circuit, discarding the hemolyzed blood in the circuit, and providing supportive therapy (e.g., treatment of hyponatremia).

Since potassium clearance by hemodialysis does not conform to single-pool kinetics, it is difficult to predict the rate of potassium removal in a patient. Approximately 100 mEq of potassium is removed during a typical hemodialysis treatment in an adult. In addition, plasma potassium levels may rebound by as much as 30% within 5 hours after hemodialysis is discontinued. Thus immediate posttreatment determination of the serum potassium concentration is not used to assess the effectiveness of potassium removal in a patient with hyperkalemia. Life-threatening muscular weakness and arrhythmias have been observed in patients with hypokalemia during hemodialysis, particularly in those with marginal potassium stores and severe metabolic acidosis, since correction of the acidosis augments the intracellular movement of potassium. Patients maintained on digitalis or who have hypocalcemia or hypomagnesemia are particularly prone to the effects of hypokalemia. Prevention of this complication includes the use of dialysate baths containing 2 to 4 mEq/L of potassium.

Pulmonary Dysfunction

A decrease of 10 to 15 mm Hg in Pao_2 occurs during the process of hemodialysis, which may assume clinical significance in patients with cardiopulmonary disease. It is not unusual for some patients maintained on ventilators and undergoing acute hemodialysis to need an increase in oxygen administration during the procedure. The pathogenesis of the hypoxemia is attributed to the use of acetate baths because of the loss of carbon dioxide from the blood to the dialysate with resulting hypoventilation; a change in Pao_2 may occur independent of any changes in systemic pH. These observed changes are related to dialyzer membrane biocompatibility, with Cupraphan membranes causing more hypoxemia than other types of membranes. There is a decrease in the pulmonary diffusion capacity and transthoracic impedence, widening of the alveolar-arterial oxygen tension gradient, and an increase in the dead space to tidal volume ratio. In addition, the degree of peripheral leukopenia correlates with the severity of hypoxemia. Leukopenia occurs within 15 to 30 minutes of the initiation of hemodialysis and involves granulocytes, which are observed on the dialyzer membrane; however, the majority of the cells are sequestered in the pulmonary circulation. The pathogenesis of leukopenia and pulmonary sequestration involve complement activation, particularly C5a and $C5a_{desArg}$.

Hemostasis

Patients with end-stage renal disease are at increased risk for bleeding and clotting. Bleeding is due to uremia-related platelet defects, including impairment in adhesion, aggregation, and release reactions. Such factors as increased parathyroid hormone, uremic toxins (phenolic acid, guanidinosuccinic acid, and other medium-sized molecules), increased synthesis of nitric oxide, and reduced von Willebrand's factor (vWF) have all been reported to increase the bleeding diathesis in uremia and have been implicated as the cause of uremic hemorrhagic diathesis. The bleeding time may be improved by increasing the concentration of vWF with infusion of desmopressin (DDAVP), which releases endogenous vWF from endothelial cells, or by infusing cryoprecipitate. Other treatments have been used to ameliorate the bleeding diathesis in uremia and include administration of conjugated estrogens, transfusion of red blood cells, and injection of recombinant human erythropoietin. Often the site of bleeding involves vascular access needles or venous catheter or internal organs affected by comorbid conditions. GI bleeding, hemorrhagic pericarditis, hemorrhagic pleural effusion, mediastinal, retroperitoneal, and subcapsular liver hemorrhage, and intracerebral and subdural hemorrhages may be seen.

In contrast to the bleeding diathesis, some patients are prone to hypercoagulability related to increased activation of thrombotic mechanisms. Some patients may present with an increased incidence of vascular access clotting, systemic venous thrombosis, arterial thrombosis, and priapism. An acquired functional deficiency of protein C, heparin-induced antibodies, and recombinant human erythropoietin have been implicated in the pathogenesis of this phenomenon. Recombinant human erythropoietin has been shown to reduce the bleeding time, increase

platelet aggregation, and reduce protein C and antithrombin III acvitivy.

COMPOUNDS REMOVED BY HEMOPERFUSION

Acetaminophen	Diazepam
Adriamycin	Digoxin
Amanitin	Mercury
Amitriptyline	Methotrexate
Ammonia	Nitrostigmine
Ampicillin	Paraquat, diquat
Aromatic amino acids	Pentobarbital
Carbon tetrachloride	Phenobarbital
Chloramphenicol	Phenytoin
Chlorpromazine	Procainamide
Cimetidine	Theophylline

Hemoperfusion
BACKGROUND AND INDICATIONS

Hemoperfusion, a detoxification technique used to remove endogenous or exogenous agents from the blood, has been successful in children and neonates. It is most effective in removing substances that are tightly protein bound, poorly distributed in plasma water, and lipid soluble and works by passing blood through adsorbent materials such as charcoal or resins. Thus it is a useful adjunct in the treatment of children who have ingested lethal quantities of toxins such theophylline, amitriptyline, phenobarbitol, phenytoin, and paraquat. Solutes ranging from 60 to 21,000 daltons in mass can be removed by hemoperfusion. Table 169-2 compares the efficacy of hemoperfusion with respect to hemodialysis in removing frequently ingested compounds. In addition to removing exogenous toxins, hemoperfusion has been used in hepatic failure, with survival rates ranging from 13% to 40% in patients with stage IV hepatic coma. It is viewed as adjunct therapy in patients who are waiting for a suitable liver donor.

Controversy continues as to the effectiveness of hemoperfusion in reducing morbidity and mortality in patients with acute poisonings. There is agreement that hemoperfusion reduces coma time in laboratory animals and that the duration of the coma direct-

Table 169-2   Efficacy of Hemoperfusion in Poisonings

Toxin	Hemodialysis	Charcoal Hemoperfusion	Resin Hemoperfusion
		Extraction Ratios	
Acetaminophen	0.4	0.5	0.7
Paraquat	0.5	0.6	0.8
Phenobarbital	0.27	0.5	0.9
Theophylline	0.5	0.7	0.85
Tricyclics	0.35	0.35	0.8

Adapted from Winchester JF. Active methods for detoxification. In Haddad LM, Winchester JF, eds. Poisoning and Drug Overdose. Philadelphia: WB Saunders, 1990, p 148.

ly affects the mortality rate. Thus the following criteria have been adopted:

1. Severe clinical intoxication that results in abnormal vital signs (i.e., hypotension, hypothermia, and respiratory compromise)
2. Ingestion of a potentially lethal dose
3. Blood concentration within the fatal range
4. Prolonged coma associated with complications such as pneumonitis
5. Presence of significant concentrations of metabolites resulting from metabolism of the ingested toxin
6. Impairment of the organ system responsible for the elimination of the toxin
7. Progressive clinical deterioration despite aggressive conservative management

TECHNIQUE

The most widely used adsorbents in hemoperfusion are activated charcoal microencapsulated with acrylic hydrogel (Hemacol; membrane thickness 3 to 5 μm) or cellulose acetate (Adsorba 300C; membrane thickness 3 to 5 μm) or bed fixed with chlorosulfonated polyethylene (B-D hemodetoxifier). These adsorbents are effective in preventing particle embolization. However, the varying thickness of the polymer coats affects the rate at which the toxins are removed and blood solutes are adsorbed on the charcoal particles. Other adsorbing agents such as nonionic microporous resins (Amberlite) are used to remove lipid-soluble toxins.

Cartridge sterilization by the manufacturer results in a limited shelf life. Many dialysis units stock unsterilized cartridges and autoclave them at 250° F for

Table 169-3   Hemoperfusion Cartridges Available in the United States

Cartridge	Priming Volume (ml)
Adsorba (Gambro)	140
	260
Hemokart (Erika)	66
	85
	155
Biocompatible perfusion systems (Clark)	50
	100
	250

no more than 30 minutes when hemoperfusion is needed for detoxification. Rapid drying is not to be used to avoid cracking of the cartridge. After sterilization, the cartridge is rinsed with heparinized 0.9% sodium chloride solution to eliminate microparticulate matter, and the system is tested under a pressure of 300 mm Hg to detect any leaks. The cartridge is placed between pressure monitors and bubble traps with the blood pumped in an antigravity direction. The size of the hemofilter and extracorporeal circuit depends on the size of the child. Table 169-3 lists the hemoperfusion cartridges available in the United States. Blood flow rates of 2 to 3 ml/kg/min (maximum 100 ml/min in adolescents and adults) are sufficient to achieve good results. Heparinization is prescribed according to the guidelines described for hemodialysis. Vascular access must be established similar to that described for hemodialysis. If hemodialysis is needed in addition to hemofiltration, the dialyzer is placed on the arterial limb of the circuit so that blood is dialyzed prior to detoxification. Such a circuit entrails higher priming volumes and heparin requirements.

RISKS AND COMPLICATIONS

Patients undergoing hemoperfusion are at risk for developing many of the complications associated with hemodialysis. Depending on the cartridge used, patients may develop thrombocytopenia, with platelet counts reduced by 10% to 53%. Patients need to be monitored for bleeding tendency, and those with thrombocytopenia prior to the initiation of hemoperfusion are transfused with platelets to reduce the risk of hemorrhage.

Hypoglycemia may occur because of the adsorption of glucose by the activated charcoal. Some manufacturers recommend rinsing the cartridge with 5% dextrose solution prior to use to coat the adsorbing sites with glucose and reduce the risk of hypoglycemia. All patients need to have a dextrose-containing IV solution administered at the time of hemoperfusion, with frequent blood sugar monitoring or Dextrostix testing. Hypocalcemia is a rare complication, but when it does occur, appropriate supplementation with calcium gluconate or calcium chloride is indicated.

ADDITIONAL READING

Arieff AI. Dialysis disequilibrium syndrome: Current concepts on pathogenesis and prevention. Kidney Int 45:629, 1994.

Better OS, Brunner G, Chang TMS, et al. Controlled trials of hemoperfusion for intoxications. Ann Intern Med 91:925, 1979.

DeBroe ME, Heyrman RM, DeBacker WA, et al. Pathogenesis of dialysis-induced hypoxemia: A short overview. Kidney Int 33:S57, 1988.

Gruskin AB, Baluarte HJ, Dabbagh S. Hemodialysis and peritoneal dialysis. In Edelmann CM Jr, ed. Pediatric Kidney Disease. Boston: Little, Brown, 1992, pp 827-916.

Nissenson AR, Fine RN, Gentile DE, eds. Clinical Dialysis. Norwalk, Conn.: Appleton & Lange, 1995.

Papadopoulou ZL, Novello AC, Calcagno PL. Hemoperfusion in therapeutic medicine. In Fine RN, Gruskin AB, eds. End-Stage Renal Disease in Children. Philadelphia: WB Saunders, 1984, p 77.

Papadopoulou ZL, Novello AC, Gelfand MC. et al. The use of charcoal hemoperfusion in children. Int J Pediatr Nephrol 1:187, 1980.

Ross EA, Nissenson AR. Acid-base and electrolyte disturbances. In Daugirdas J, Ing T, eds. Handbook of Dialysis. Boston: Little, Brown, 1994, p 401.

Vanherweghem J-L, Caboler P, Dhaene M, et al. Complications related to subclavian catheters for hemodialysis. Am J Nephrol 6:339, 1986.

Winchester JF. Active methods for detoxification. In Haddad LM, Winchester JF, eds. Poisoning and Drug Overdose. Philadelphia: WB Saunders, 1990, p 148.

170 Continuous Veno-Venous Hemofiltration

Catherine L. Headrick · Steven R. Alexander

BACKGROUND AND INDICATIONS

The most recent addition to renal replacement therapies is continuous veno-venous hemofiltration (CVVH), a promising advancement in the treatment of acute renal failure that offers several advantages over traditional dialysis methods when used in critically ill, unstable patients. CVVH entails the same basic convection and hemofiltration concepts as continuous arteriovenous hemofiltration (CAVH) but with the added benefit of a pump-driven circuit. With a pump-driven circuit, blood is propelled by a roller head pump from the venous access site through the filter and extracorporeal circuit and returned to the patient. Unlike nonpump-assisted CAVH, CVVH is operated independent of the patient's mean systemic arterial pressure.

Basic Concepts

For purposes of this text, the different methods of hemofiltration are defined in Table 170-1. Although the literature on the use of CVVH in adults is substantial and rapidly increasing, reported experience with CVVH in children is sparse. The CVVH guidelines and suggestions offered in this chapter necessarily reflect to a large degree the authors' experience with CVVH in approximately 50 infants and children over the past 3½ years. The specific techniques described are primarily those currently used in our center, and many are certain to be modified as our experience with this new treatment grows. The indications for the use of CVVH in children must be considered tentative, at best. Much more experience will be needed before clinical criteria can be identified in which CVVH would be preferred over hemodialysis or peritoneal dialysis. Currently the decision to use CAVH, CVVH, or another renal replacement therapy in infants and children with acute renal failure largely depends on vascular access, availability of equipment, and the experience of the nephrologist and PICU staff. It appears that CVVH is important in intensive care, but its role is evolving and has yet to be clearly defined.

At least three basic configurations exist for clinical application of continuous hemofiltration (Table 170-2): continuous hemofiltration (CAVH or CVVH), slow continuous ultrafiltration (SCUF), and continuous hemofiltration with dialysis (CAVHD or CVVHD). Selected characteristics of hemodialysis, peritoneal dialysis, and isolated ultrafiltration are also included in Table 170-2 for comparison with hemofiltration techniques.

Continuous hemofiltration as designed by Kramer et al. is intended to be a complete renal replacement therapy and requires large volumes of ultrafiltrate and filtration replacement fluid. The basic components of the CVVH circuit are shown in Fig. 170-1. When continuous hemofiltration is used only to remove excess fluid, as in diuretic-unresponsive oliguria (with or without uremia), the process is SCUF. The circuit used for SCUF is the same as for CVVH except that no replacement fluid is administered. When dialysate is allowed to flow through the ultrafiltrate compartment of the hemofilter, thereby increasing solute removal by addition of diffusive transport, the process is CAVHD or CVVHD; the CVVHD circuit is diagrammed in Fig. 170-2.

Hemofiltration performed through venous access alone requires a blood pump to propel blood through the circuit. When performed continuously, with relatively slow blood flow rates as compared with hemodialysis, the procedure is CVVH. Much of the inherent simplicity and convenience of CAVH is lost when CVVH is used. However, pump-assisted hemofiltration (CVVH) offers an alternative in infants and small children who have severe systemic hypotension and do not have the mean systemic arterial pressure necessary to propel blood through a

Table 170-1   Hemofiltration: Definition of Terms

Type of Hemofiltration	Components and Equipment Required	Principles of Operation	Considerations in Hemodynamically Unstable Child
Continuous arteriovenous hemofiltration (CAVH)	Extracorporeal circuit, including hemofilter and tubing Filter replacement solution Arterial access Venous access	Convection Ultrafiltration	Systemic mean arterial pressure may not be adequate to propel blood through circuit and achieve desired clearance and water removal Alteration in circuit blood flow may increase clot formation and shorten life of circuit
Continuous arteriovenous hemofiltration with dialysis (CAVHD)	CVVH components Dialysate infusion	Convection Ultrafiltration Diffusion	Same as for CVVH
Continuous veno-venous hemofiltration (CVVH)	Extracorporeal circuit including hemofilter and tubing Filter replacement solution Venous access Blood pump	Convection Ultrafiltration	If vessel size does not accommodate one double-lumen catheter, two single-lumen venous catheters may be needed
Continuous venovenous hemofiltration with dialysis (CVVHD)	CVVH components Dialysate infusion	Convection Ultrafiltration Diffusion	

Table 170-2   Renal Replacement Therapies in Acute Renal Failure

Method	Goals	Solute Transport	Uremia Control	Tolerance by Unstable Patient
Hemodialysis	Complete renal replacement therapy	Diffusion + convection	Excellent	Poor
Peritoneal dialysis	Complete renal replacement therapy	Diffusion + convection	Good	Fair to good
Isolated ultrafiltration	Isotonic plasma volume contraction prior to hemodialysis	Convection	Inadequate	Good
Slow continuous ultrafiltration	Continuous removal of plasma water and solutes without replacement	Convection	Poor	Excellent
Continuous arteriovenous hemofiltration (CAVH)	Continuous removal of uremic plasma water; replaced with balanced electrolyte solution	Convection	Good only when large volumes are replaced	Excellent
Continuous arteriovenous hemofiltration with dialysis (CAVHD)	Combines CAVH and hemodialysis without use of blood pump	Convection + diffusion	Good to excellent	Excellent
Continuous venovenous hemofiltration	Same as CAVH	Convection	With high-flow filtration replacement fluid, good to excellent	Excellent
Continuous venovenous hemofiltration with dialysis	Same as CAVHD but with blood pump	Convection + diffusion	Good to excellent	Excellent

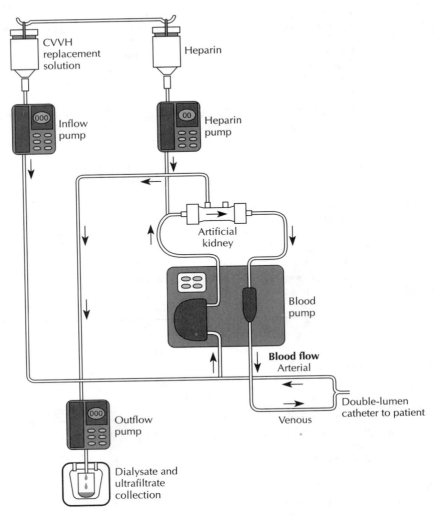

Fig. 170-1   Basic continuous veno-venous hemofiltration design. (Modified and reprinted with permission of Baxter HealthCare, Renal Division, McGaw Park, Ill.)

CAVH circuit. The benefits of CVVH, which include no arterial access and lack of dependence on mean systemic arterial pressure, outweigh the disadvantages of the increased technical and clinical support needed.

Basic System Design

The inherent logic of the CVVH system is striking: a filter that is highly permeable to water and small solutes but impermeable to plasma proteins and the formed elements of blood is placed in a pump-driven extracorporeal circuit. As the blood perfuses the hemofilter, an ultrafiltrate of plasma is removed in a manner analogous to glomerular ultrafiltration. The water and solutes (ultrafiltrate) that are removed are concurrently replaced with a fluid with an electrolyte composition either similar to that of normal plasma or specifically designed to correct the patient's electrolyte abnormalities. A portion of the ultrafiltrate volume can be replaced with total parenteral nutrition (TPN) solutions. In patients with fluid overload a portion of the ultrafiltrate volume is simply not replaced, resulting in predictable and controllable negative fluid balance.

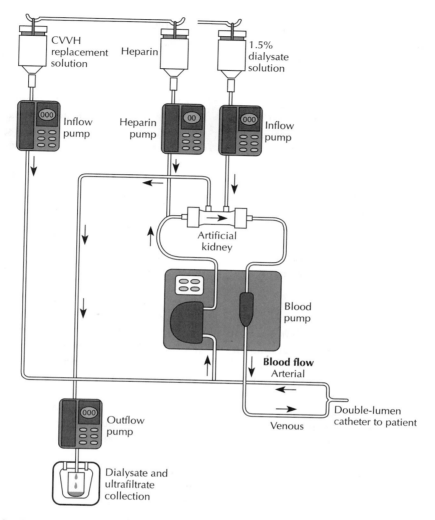

Fig. 170-2 Basic continuous veno-venous hemofiltration with dialysis (CVVHD) design. (Modified and reprinted with permission of Baxter HealthCare, Renal Division, McGaw Park, Ill.)

CVVH provides continuous renal replacement therapy, thus allowing removal of solutes and modification of the volume and composition of the extracellular fluid evenly over time. Hemodynamically unstable patients, who are often intolerant of the abrupt fluid and solute changes that accompany standard hemodialysis, can usually be treated safely with CVVH. The most notable characteristic of CVVH, and its advantage over CAVH, is its independence of mean systemic arterial pressure.

The precision and stability with which fluid and electrolyte balance can be maintained with CVVH is unmatched by any of the alternative dialysis therapies; even continuous peritoneal dialysis (see Chapter 168) does not allow the physician to control the ultrafiltration rate, as can be done with CVVH. Only with CVVH can electrolyte balance be corrected independent of changes in the volume of total body water. CVVH can be initiated rapidly in the PICU setting and a dialysis nurse is not needed.

History

CVVH can be traced to the early days of the development of long-term hemodialysis. In the mid-1960s

Henderson described a renal replacement therapy that relied solely on the process of ultrafiltration, using membranes that were much more permeable to water and small solutes than the usual hemodialysis membranes. The technique was termed diafiltration, and later, more appropriately, hemofiltration.

Henderson et al. showed that by pumping blood at high flow rates through an extracorporeal circuit containing a highly permeable filter, large volumes of an ultrafiltrate of plasma could be generated. This "uremic" ultrafiltrate could be replaced concurrently with fluid with an electrolyte composition similar to that of normal plasma. Hemofiltration is thus technically similar to hemodialysis: both methods require vascular access, an extracorporeal circuit, a semipermeable membrane, and a blood pump. There are differences, however, in the manner in which solutes are removed from the blood.

Henderson et al. proposed hemofiltration as an alternative to long-term hemodialysis. To be effective in long-term treatment of uremia, hemofiltration must generate a very large volume of ultrafiltrate: 25 to 50 L per treatment for the average adult with end-stage renal disease (ESRD) receiving 3-hour hemofiltration treatments three times per week. All but about 2 of the nearly 50 L of ultrafiltrate generated during a single hemofiltration treatment must be continuously and accurately replaced with a sterile, pyrogen-free replacement fluid. The replacement fluid is costly; thus hemofiltration is substantially more expensive to perform than hemodialysis. High cost and the technical problems involved in precise measurement and rapid replacement of very large volumes of ultrafiltrate stifled interest in hemofiltration as a long-term renal replacement therapy in all but a few centers treating ESRD.

Several early investigators noted that hemofiltration had at least one potentially important advantage over hemodialysis: when long-term hemodialysis was changed to treatment with chronic hemofiltration, patients consistently experienced a marked reduction in the number of episodes of symptomatic hypotension during treatments. In 1976 Bergstrom et al. reported that unstable patients undergoing hemodialysis because of either acute or chronic renal failure tolerated fluid removal better if ultrafiltration alone was performed before initiation of standard diffusion hemodialysis. Henderson et al. had originally suggested that hemofiltration might be a safe method

with which to remove fluid from unstable patients with oliguria who had acute congestive heart failure. Thus the stage was set for continuous hemofiltration as a technique especially well suited for use in critically ill, unstable patients.

The conceptualization of continuous hemofiltration as a treatment for acute renal failure was the work of Peter Kramer, a nephrologist in Göttingen, Germany, familiar with the use of intermittent pumped hemofiltration in patients with acute and chronic renal failure. In fact, CVVH actually preceded the development of CAVH: CAVH was the result of a complication during CVVH. One of Dr. Kramer's former students tells that in May 1977, as Kramer was preparing to perform a 3-hour pumped hemofiltration treatment in an unstable adult ICU patient, one of the vascular access catheters intended for the femoral vein was inadvertently placed in the femoral artery. Seizing the moment, Kramer placed the second catheter in the contralateral femoral vein and connected the hemofilter between the arterial and venous blood lines. To his delight, he observed that the patient's cardiac function alone was a sufficient driving force to produce large volumes of ultrafiltrate from this simple arteriovenous hemofiltration circuit. By allowing the circuit to operate continuously 24 hours a day, Kramer demonstrated that his "CAVH" system could generate enough ultrafiltrate to serve as complete renal replacement therapy in adults with anuria. He also showed that the CAVH system could be safely and successfully maintained in continuous operation for many days. (One of Kramer's early patients received CAVH for 38 days and eventually recovered normal renal function.)

It is a sad footnote to the history of CAVH that Dr. Kramer died suddenly in 1984 before he could fully appreciate the effect his contributions would have on the management of acute renal failure in patients of all ages throughout the world. Over the past 10 years CVVH has reemerged as a leading method for continuous hemofiltration.

Indications

The clinical indications for CVVH in pediatric patients have not been clearly defined. In general CVVH can be an effective renal replacement therapy in patients with acute renal failure; diuretic-resistant fluid overload from poor cardiac output, with or without renal failure; electrolyte or acid-base disturbances; and he-

Table 170-3 Hemodynamic Response to Fluid Removal With Different Renal Replacement Therapies

	Acetate Hemodialysis	Bicarbonate Hemodialysis	CVVH
Cardiac output	Decreased	Decreased	Much increased
Peripheral resistance	Much decreased	Increased or no change	Decreased
Blood pressure	Much decreased	No change	Increased

modynamically unstable chronic renal failure that cannot be treated with hemodialysis or peritoneal dialysis. In most patients acute renal failure can be successfully treated with either hemodialysis or peritoneal dialysis. However, patients with multiple organ system failure are often intolerant of standard dialysis therapies because of hemodynamic instability. They usually have hypercatabolism and need large volumes of TPN and other parenteral fluids. In these patients CVVH may become the treatment of choice.

CVVH may also be preferred in patients with fluid overload and hemodynamic instability refractory to diuretics because of poor cardiac output. Fluid removal by hemodialysis is poorly tolerated by such patients, and peritoneal dialysis may be ineffective because of inadequate perfusion of the peritoneum. Neonates and other small infants with these problems may do particularly well with CVVH.

It is unclear why CVVH is so well tolerated by hemodynamically unstable patients. The hemodynamic response to fluid removal with different renal replacement therapies is summarized in Table 170-3. Note that cardiac output decreases during fluid removal by hemodialysis but not during CVVH. Peripheral resistance also decreases during hemodialysis when acetate is used as the buffer, often resulting in marked hypotension. Hemodialysis with bicarbonate buffer produces stable to slightly increased peripheral resistance and more stable systemic arterial blood pressure. During CVVH peripheral resistance decreases and cardiac output increases; the net result is usually an increase in systemic arterial blood pressure and slight decrease in heart rate because of overall improvement in myocardial function. Peripheral vasodilation and afterload reduction may explain, in part, the improvement

in cardiac function in patients treated with CVVH. Other possible explanations include the removal of cardiotoxic factors (e.g., myocardial depressant factors) from the circulation.

CVVH seems particularly effective in the following pediatric patients:

1. Infants and small children with congestive heart failure who also have diuretic-unresponsive oliguria despite inotropic support
2. Neonates with fluid overload that can be difficult to treat with peritoneal dialysis because of poor perfusion of the peritoneal membrane
3. Patients with oliguria who need large volumes of TPN or other fluids (e.g., blood products in patients with disseminated intravascular coagulopathy), perhaps because fluid balance is maintained continuously during CVVH
4. Patients with combined renal and hepatic failure, both before and after liver transplantation
5. Children with hemodynamic instability after cardiac surgery
6. Patients receiving prolonged extracorporeal membrane oxygenation (ECMO) who develop renal insufficiency or fluid-electrolyte disturbances or need large volumes of TPN
7. Patients maintained on cardiopulmonary bypass for prolonged periods during cardiac surgery
8. Patients with septic shock
9. Patients with tumor lysis syndrome with electrolyte abnormalities unresponsive to pharmacologic therapy or requiring continuous therapy to maintain solute or electrolyte balance

Contraindications

Active bleeding is a relative contraindication to CVVH, especially if peritoneal dialysis can be performed. A recent CNS hemorrhage that might be extended with heparinization is also a relative contraindication unless alternative anticoagulation methods or no anticoagulants are used. The presence of a severe coagulopathy is not considered a contraindication to CVVH. These patients usually do not need heparinization, and CVVH can be remarkably successful in patients in whom coagulopathy prevents the filter from clotting. Such patients, however, are at increased risk for local bleeding during catheter placement.

CVVH must not be considered emergency treatment for life-threatening hyperkalemia. Potassium removal by means of CVVH is slow compared with hemodialysis or even peritoneal dialysis. However, if the patient with hyperkalemia is not a candidate for dialysis or tolerates it poorly, CVVH may be attempted with one of the techniques designed to increase solute clearances (e.g., CVVHD or high-flow predilution, see p. 1617).

Principles of Hemofiltration
Transfer of solutes

During any renal replacement therapy two transport mechanisms can be involved in the transfer of solutes across a semipermeable membrane: diffusion and convection. Diffusive transport is driven by the solute concentration gradients that exist between blood and dialysate. Solute molecules are transferred across the membrane in response to a concentration gradient. Solutes move in the direction of the lower solute concentration and at a rate inversely proportional to their molecular weight. For example, during peritoneal dialysis urea diffuses across the peritoneal membrane from blood to dialysate, whereas dextrose diffuses from dialysate to blood.

Convective transport occurs when a solute molecule is swept through the membrane by a moving stream of solvent, a process also called "solvent drag." Solutes are transferred across the membrane in response to a pressure gradient. Convective transport is independent of any solute concentration gradient that might be present across the membrane. Only the direction and force (or rate) of transmembrane solvent flux are important determinants of convective transport.

During hemodialysis solute movement across the dialysis membrane from blood to dialysate is primarily the result of diffusive transport. Convective transport also occurs during hemodialysis when fluid is removed from the blood, but convection accounts for only a small fraction of the total solute removed during a hemodialysis treatment (see Chapter 169). Because no dialysate is used during CVVH, diffusive transport cannot occur. Solute transfer depends entirely on convective transport. The relative inefficiency with which solutes are removed from the blood by means of convective transport alone is one of the most distinctive features of hemofiltration.

Transfer of water

Extracellular free water is removed by the process of ultrafiltration. The rate of removal is determined by the surface area of the filter membrane, the permeability coefficient of the membrane to water, and the transmembrane pressure gradient. With pump-assisted hemofiltration, it is easier to maintain a consistent, optimal blood flow rate and maximize ultrafiltration rate.

CVVH extracorporeal circuit

The standard CVVH system (see Fig. 170-1) consists of venous access, blood tubing that contains multiple ports for blood sampling and attachment of the heparin and filter replacement fluid lines, a hemofilter, and an ultrafiltrate tube from the hemofilter to a collection device. Blood flowing from the catheter into the circuit is joined by continuous heparin infusion before it passes through the hollow fibers of the hemofilter. As the anticoagulated blood perfuses the filter, an ultrafiltrate is formed and collected in the space within the filter that surrounds the hollow fibers. The ultrafiltrate flows out through the ultrafiltrate tubing to a collection device. Filter replacement fluid may be administered into the circuit tubing through the access port on the arterial side of the circuit, before the filter, or on the venous side, after the filter. Filter replacement fluid delivered before the filter is referred to as predilution fluid, and that delivered after the filter is called postdilution fluid.

Approximate extracorporeal tubing and filter volume for the standard circuit currently used at our center is 140 ml. This large volume is not ideal for use in infants and small children. Manufacturers are currently seeking FDA approval for a smaller pediatric tubing set. However, until a smaller volume circuit is available, precautions must be taken with regard to thermoregulation and other considerations for the hemodynamically unstable infant or child. The circulating blood volume–circuit blood volume ratio must be evaluated for every patient. Priming with reconstituted blood, whole blood, albumin, or sodium chloride solution may be necessary (see p. 1623).

CVVH membranes

The CVVH membrane is a composite structure consisting of (1) an inner thin layer adjacent to the blood path, which contains pores of equal diameter and length and which is surrounded by (2) a supporting superstructure ("exoskeleton") that provides mechanical integrity without restricting the passage of water or any solutes small enough to first pass through the pores of the inner layer. The hemofiltration membrane superstructure is responsible for the membrane's high permeability to water. Unlike hemodialysis membranes, which contain long interconnecting pores of different sizes that extend throughout the full thickness of the membrane, resulting in high resistance to fluid flow, the hemofiltration membrane superstructure consists of channels of ever-increasing diameter that offer little resistance to fluid flow (Fig. 170-3).

CVVH membranes from different manufacturers may have different pore sizes, but all pores in any one membrane tend to be of similar size. Most hemofiltration membranes offer no impediment to transport of solutes with a molecular mass less than 500 to 1000 daltons (e.g., urea, creatinine, uric acid, sodium, potassium, ionized calcium, and almost all drugs not bound to plasma proteins), and all CVVH membranes are impermeable to albumin and other solutes with a molecular mass greater than 50,000 daltons.

Several synthetic materials have been developed for use in hemofiltration membranes, including polysulfone, polyacrylonitrile, and polyamide. All of these materials are much more biocompatible than those currently used in hemodialysis membranes, such as cupruphan or cellulose acetate. For example, complement activation, which is common during hemodialysis (see Chapter 169), does not occur during hemofiltration. Similarly, leukopenia, which occurs early during hemodialysis treatment and may be associated with hypoxemia, does not occur during hemofiltration. The high degree of biocompatibility demonstrated by hemofiltration membranes is an essential feature of a treatment that requires that the membrane remain in constant contact with the blood for prolonged periods (days to weeks).

With the ability to control blood and ultrafiltration pump flow rates, use of multiple sizes of hemofilters

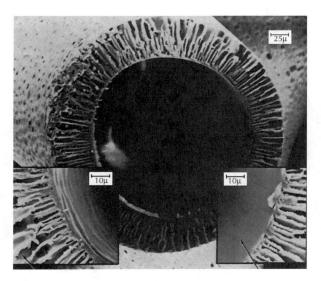

Fig. 170-3 Scanning electron micrograph shows a transection of a typical hollow-fiber hemofiltration membrane (inner diameter, 200 μm). Inset shows the inner thin layer, pockmarked by pores of equal diameter and length. Note the ever-increasing diameters of the channels that traverse the outer superstructure of the membrane. (From Lysaght M, Boggs D. Transport in continuous arteriovenous hemofiltration and slow continuous ultrafiltration. In Paganani EP, ed. Acute Continuous Renal Replacement Therapy. Boston: Kluwer, 1986, pp 43-50.)

is not necessary to control circuit blood flow and ultrafiltrate removal. The CVVH blood pump controls blood flow rate and thus, if vascular access is adequate, ensures a consistent desired hydraulic pressure. Water and solute removal can be controlled with the addition of an IV pump on the ultrafiltrate tube to regulate the volume entering the collection device. The same size of hemofilter can be standardized for CVVH in a small infant or a large adolescent. The blood tubing available for the pump currently used at our institution does not directly fit with the smaller filters (Amicon Minifilter or Minifilter Plus, Menntech, Minneapolis, Minn.) without modification of the tubing. For technical considerations in choosing a hemofilter that meets the patient's needs, see p. 1616.

Factors that govern ultrafiltration in CVVH

The ultrafiltration rate (Qf) in CVVH is a function of the surface area of the membrane participating in ultrafiltration (Ap), the permeability coefficient of the membrane to water (k), and the transmembrane pressure gradient (TMP).

$$Qf = Ap \times k \times TMP$$

As in the glomerular capillary, for ultrafiltration to occur in CVVH or SCUF there must be a transmembrane pressure gradient ("filtration pressure") that favors movement of water from the blood to the opposite side of the membrane. The filtration pressure is primarily determined by the net sum of three pressures: positive hydraulic pressure of the blood, negative hydrostatic pressure exerted by the ultrafiltrate column, and oncotic pressure within the filter fibers. This relationship can be approximated with the following equation:

$$TMP = \frac{(Pi + Po)}{2} + Pf - \frac{(pi + po)}{2}$$

where TMP is the filtration pressure or transmembrane pressure gradient; Pi and Po are the hydraulic pressures of the blood at the inlet (Pi) and outlet (Po) of the filter, Pf is the negative hydrostatic pressure exerted by the ultrafiltrate column, and pi and po are the oncotic pressures at the inlet (pi) and outlet (po) of the filter. A more rigorous calculation of TMP is beyond the scope of this text.

The relationship between oncotic, hydraulic, and hydrostatic pressures is extremely important in CVVH. Although in theory the same forces are involved in determining TMP during standard hemodialysis, additional positive or negative pressure can be mechanically applied to the hemodialysis circuit to maintain the net TMP favoring ultrafiltration as high as 300 to 400 mm Hg. Plasma protein concentration and the resulting oncotic pressure that opposes ultrafiltration during hemodialysis is inconsequential compared with the mechanically applied TMP and thus may be ignored.

Several factors keep the TMP low during CVVH. Blood flow rates are less with CVVH than with hemodialysis. Large-bore tubing minimizes hydraulic pressure losses. Additional hydraulic pressure loss occurs within the filter fibers, depending in part on the resistance to flow inherent in the design of each filter. Currently available CVVH filters and tubing are designed to minimize hydraulic pressure losses; thus pressure loss in the arterial limb of the circuit is almost always the consequence of inadequate, kinked, or thrombosed vascular access. The insertion of a stopcock or any other flow-restricting device into the arterial limb of the circuit will also have an undesirable effect on Pi.

If ultrafiltrate rate removal is determined by gravity drainage, the negative hydrostatic pressure (Pf) is generated by the weight of the column of ultrafiltrate. It is determined by the height of the filter above the collection device according to the following formula:

$$Pf \text{ (in mm Hg)} = \text{Height (in cm)} \times 0.74$$

When the height of the filter is 40 cm above the collection device, Pf is approximately 30 mm Hg. Hydraulic pressure continues to fall as the blood encounters the resistance of the filter. Therefore, by the time the filter's ultrafiltrate outlet is reached, Pf is usually the predominant pressure favoring ultrafiltration.

Ultrafiltration is opposed by the oncotic pressure within the filter fibers, which is a function of plasma protein concentration. Oncotic pressure can be estimated using the following formula:

Oncotic pressure (in mm Hg) =
$$[2.1 \times c] + [0.16 \times c^2] + [0.009 \times c^3]$$

where c is the total serum protein concentration in grams per deciliter. When total serum protein concentration is between 6 and 8 g/dl, oncotic pressure at the filter inlet (pi) ranges between 20 and 35 mm Hg. At this point (Pi + Pf) > pi, and ultrafiltration occurs. However, as blood perfuses the filter, ultrafiltrate is removed, and the plasma protein concentration and its corresponding oncotic pressure increase accordingly.

A point of "filtration pressure equilibrium" is reached in most hemofilters at which the rising oncotic pressure (pe) equals the sum of the falling hydraulic pressure (Pe) and the stable hydrostatic pressure: (pe = Pe + Pf). When filtration pressure equilibrium is reached, ultrafiltration abruptly ceases.

The filter blood flow rate (QB) is also critical in the development of filtration pressure equilibrium. The rate at which the oncotic pressure rises is determined by the filtration fraction (FF), which is that fraction of plasma water removed by ultrafiltration. For any given filtration pressure, FF is determined by QB. When QB is high, FF remains low, oncotic pressure rises slowly, and filtration pressure equilibrium is reached slowly if at all. When QB is low, FF is increased, and with it the oncotic pressure. Filtration pressure equilibrium is reached earlier in the filter, resulting in a decrease in the ultrafiltration rate and pre-

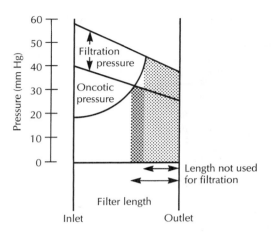

Fig. 170-4 Schema of filtration pressure equilibrium. Two filtration pressures are shown. Shaded areas represent the filter length not used for ultrafiltration because of filtration pressure equilibrium. At the lower filtration pressure, filtration pressure equilibrium occurs nearer the filter inlet, resulting in an increase in the length not available for ultrafiltration. (Modified from Bosch JP, Ronco C. Continuous arteriovenous hemofiltration: Operational characteristics and clinical use. In Maher JF, ed. Replacement of Renal Function by Dialysis, 3rd ed. Boston: Kluwer, 1989, pp. 347-359.)

disposing the filter to clotting. These concepts are presented schematically in Fig. 170-4.

The blood beyond the filtration pressure equilibrium point is characterized by higher hematocrit, protein concentration, and viscosity. The movement of highly viscous blood through a long segment of the filter not used for filtration leads to increased resistance to blood flow within the filter and a further decrease in hydraulic pressure. Eventually a self-perpetuating process develops that ultimately results in clotting of the filter.

Many of the problems associated with filtration pressure equilibrium in pediatric hemofiltration have been alleviated with the use of CVVH and the addition of a blood pump to propel blood through the circuit and maintain hydraulic pressure. With the ability to control pump speed and blood flow rate, it is not necessary to regulate the size of the hemofilter to control filter pressure. Administration of filter replacement fluid on the arterial side of the filter ("predilution" mode) helps to keep oncotic pressure low. (These maneuvers are discussed in detail on p. 1618.)

Factors that govern filter blood flow through the hemofilter

Adequate filter blood flow is a prerequisite to successful CVVH. Blood flow (QB) is determined primarily by pump speed, vascular access site (e.g., femoral vein or subclavian vein), and the internal diameter, configuration (tapered vs. straight), and length of the venous catheter. QB is also influenced by blood viscosity (hematocrit and protein concentration), length and internal diameter of the hemofilter tubing, patency of the hemofilter blood pathways (i.e., how many of the filter's hollow fibers have clotted or are obstructed by entrapment of air), and backflow pressure in the venous limb of the circuit, which is determined by the resistance generated by the return path of the venous catheter. Maximum QB yields maximum spontaneous ultrafiltration rate (Qf).

QB at the filter inlet can be easily estimated by obtaining simultaneous blood samples for hematocrit from the sampling ports located on the arterial (Hct_{inlet}) and venous (Hct_{outlet}) lines while measuring Qf (in milliliters per minute) from a timed volumetric collection:

$$QB = \frac{Qf \times Hct_{outlet}}{Hct_{outlet} - Hct_{inlet}}$$

Plasma flow at the filter inlet (QP) is calculated from the QB and hematocrit at the inlet:

$$QP = QB - \text{Red blood cell mass}$$

where red blood cell mass at the inlet = $QB \times Hct_{inlet}/100$ and Hct_{inlet} is expressed as a percentage.

Indicators of Circuit Efficiency
Filtration fraction

The filtration fraction (FF) is an important indicator of the efficiency of the CVVH system and reflects that fraction of plasma water being removed by ultrafiltration. The FF can be calculated from the following formulas:

$$FF(\%) = \frac{QF}{QP} \times 100$$

or

$$FF(\%) = 1 - \frac{pro_{inlet}}{pro_{outlet}} \times 100$$

where QF is the ultrafiltration rate (in milliliters per minute), QP is the plasma flow rate (in milliliters per minute) at the inlet, and pro is the blood total protein concentration (in grams per deciliter) measured

Table 170-4   Concentrations of Selected Solutes in Ultrafiltrate and Plasma During CAVH With Corresponding Seiving Coefficients

Solute	Ultrafiltrate Concentration	Plasma Concentration	Seiving Coefficient
Sodium (mEq/L)	135.3	136.2	0.993
Potassium (mEq/L)	4.05	4.11	0.985
Chloride (mEq/L)	103.7	99.3	1.046
CO_2 (mEq/L)	22.13	19.78	1.124
BUN (mg/dl)	82.9	79.1	1.048
Creatinine (mg/dl)	6.63	6.5	1.020
Uric acid (mg/dl)	7.54	7.35	1.016
Phosphorus (mg/dl)	4.15	3.94	1.044
Glucose (mg/dl)	173.0	164.5	1.043
Total proteins (g/dl)	0.13	6.21	0.021
Albumin (g/dl)	0.02	2.65	0.008
Calcium (mg/dl)	5.12	8.08	0.637
Total bilirubin (mg/dl)	0.44	12.1	0.030
Direct bilirubin (mg/dl)	0.26	7.35	0.030
Creatine phosphokinase (IU/L)	66.5	80.9	0.676
Magnesium (mEq/L)	1.53	1.74	0.879

Reproduced with permission from Kaplan AA, Longnecker RI, Folkert VW. Continuous arteriovenous hemofiltration: A report of 6 months experience. Ann Intern Med 100:358-367, 1984.

at the arterial (pro_{inlet}) and venous (pro_{outlet}) sampling ports.

Optimum FF is high enough to provide an adequate ultrafiltration rate to meet the solute and fluid removal needs of the patient but not so high that it leads to increased blood viscosity, increased oncotic pressure, an earlier filtration pressure equilibrium point, and consequently to filter clotting. When conditions allow, FF should probably be kept around 30%. Higher FF is possible, and may be unavoidable if QB is low, but such high FF usually is associated with frequent filter clotting.

Composition of ultrafiltrate

The ultrafiltrate formed during CVVH has essentially the same small solute composition as plasma water. Representative plasma and ultrafiltrate concentrations for several solutes are listed in Table 170-4. Note there is a small but detectable difference in the handling of cations and anions. This is due to the Gibbs-Donnen effect created by accumulation of anionic proteins on the plasma side of the membrane, which tends to retard passage or cations and encourage passage of anions. This difference is not clin-

ically important. It is important to note the lower ultrafiltrate concentration of calcium that results from protein binding of a portion of total plasma calcium. Ultrafiltrate calcium concentration is a reasonable approximation of plasma ionized calcium concentration.

Solute clearance and sieving coefficients

CVVH relies entirely on convective transport for clearance of solutes from the blood. In the absence of a gradient for diffusion, the ratio between ultrafiltrate and plasma concentrations of a given solute (X) is called the sieving coefficient (S):

$$S = \frac{X_{Uf}}{X_{plasma}}$$

where X_{Uf} is concentration of X in ultrafiltrate and X_{plasma} is concentration of X in plasma.

Sieving coefficients are also given for the solutes listed in Table 170-4. When S is known for a given solute, the concentration of the solute in the ultrafiltrate is simply

$$X_{Uf} = S \times X_{plasma}$$

Therefore solute clearance (C_X) in CVVH can be calculated as follows:

$$C_X = \frac{X_{Uf} \times Qf}{X_{plasma}}$$

$$= S \times Qf$$

Because S for most small solutes is approximately 1 (see Table 170-4), the clearance of these solutes closely approximates Qf. For example, urea clearance (C_{urea}) obtained with CVVH is simply:

$$C_{urea} - Qf$$

TECHNIQUE
Equipment and Technical Considerations
CVVH circuit

The current configuration used at Children's Medical Center of Dallas for CVVH uses the BM11 pump (Baxter HealthCare, Renal Division, McGaw Park, Ill.). Infusion of the filter replacement fluids (FRF) is shown in the "predilution" mode (see Fig. 170-1). The circuit begins and ends at the venous access catheter. The circuit assembly used for hemofiltration may vary slightly to accommodate the individual needs of each patient, but the main components are similar.

Vascular access. The first and most important circuit component is the vascular access catheter. The size and placement of the catheter are critical to the success of therapy. The catheter and vessel size determine blood flow rate capabilities. Achieving adequate venous access in infants and young children can be particularly difficult. A double-lumen catheter will allow the largest amount of blood flow without compromising vessel integrity or peripheral blood flow. In infants and children the preferred catheter placement is in the subclavian vein. Placement in the femoral vein is possible, but not best because of the potential for contamination and the need to prevent extremity movement.

Catheters of several different designs and sizes have been used for CVVH in pediatric patients, with varying success rates. The following general observations and suggestions may be helpful:

1. Avoid using long, tortuous central venous lines for CVVH venous access; the resistance in these lines is too high to permit adequate blood flow. Catheters used for hemodialysis function well for CVVH.

2. Short, large-bore catheters provide the best blood flow. Percutaneous sheaths may be used as single access lines but may bend easily with active movement of the lower extremities. Brief periods of hip flexion can result in dramatic reduction in filter blood flow and blood pump stopping. A more flexible sheath is ideal as long as increased flexibility is not achieved at the expense of substantially increased wall thickness.

3. The catheter must not be so large that it completely occludes the vessel. The ideal catheter is a double-lumen venous catheter, no smaller than 7 F, which provides maximum blood flow without occluding the vessel; it is difficult to achieve adequate blood flow with a double-lumen venous catheter smaller than 7 F.

4. Infants who weigh <4 kg may need two single-lumen 5 or 6 F catheters, one in the femoral and one in the subclavian vein. When possible, avoid using both femoral veins. Perfusion in cannulated lower extremities must be monitored on a regular basis. In older children adequate blood flow may be achieved by using catheters smaller than the maximum allowable by the size of the vein.

5. Femoral access may be difficult to maintain in the infant or young child who is not comatose or paralyzed. Simply flexing the leg at the hip can partially obstruct blood flow in many catheters and result in filter clotting. Femoral access in alert, older children is tolerable without paralysis or restraints but necessitates prolonged immobility and heavy sedation.

When selecting catheters, it is important to know the manufacturer's specifications for catheter lumen diameter and expected flow rates. Few catheter manufacturers offer short, large-bore, double-lumen catheters smaller than 10 F that are appropriate for CVVH in the infant or small child. Simple, short, double-lumen venous catheters are currently available in sizes 7, 8, and 9 F (VasCath, Medcomp, and Cook).

Although the catheter internal lumen design is constructed to optimize blood flow, knowledge of the catheter's internal design is important in anticipating or diagnosing mechanical problems. For example, in a small infant or child, if the catheter diameter is almost the size of the internal diameter of the vessel, it may be necessary to reverse the catheter blood flow by withdrawing from the lumen at the tip (i.e., the venous lumen) what was the "venous" lumen and returning through the proximal lumena (arterial) on the side of the catheter. The arterial (withdrawal) lumena are on the sides of the catheter; the venous lumen is at the tip of the catheter. If flow is reversed, some degree of recirculation will occur, but the benefits of better blood flow capability usually outweigh the minimal loss in circuit efficiency from recirculation.

The Bunchman catheter (Cook) has a different internal lumen design in an effort to decrease problems of adequate blood flow. This 8 F double-lumen catheter for CVVH is a modified percutaneous sheath. The side port is available to be used for arterial access, pulling blood into the circuit. A short, single-lumen catheter is incorporated in the central port of the sheath for use as a venous line for blood return.

Blood pump and flow rate. The ideal blood pump would allow blood flow rates to be adjusted within a range of 10 to 300 ml/min in increments of 5 ml/min. A wide range of blood flow rates is necessary to accommodate limited vascular access in the small infant as well as high rates of solute clearance and water removal necessary in the large adolescent. The pump is equipped with an air detector, blood leak detector, clot trap, and prefilter (arterial) and postfilter (venous) circuit pressure monitors.

Ideally, it would be possible to monitor the resistance to blood being pulled into the circuit (prefilter, prepump), the resistance to blood returning to the patient, and the pressure gradient between prefilter (arterial) and postfilter (venous) pressure. A wide prepump (arterial) pressure range allows for differentiation in catheter blood flow capabilities but must not be so extreme as to create a pressure great enough to pull air from solution or potentially cause damage to the vessel wall.

Ideal circuit volume, including filter volume, is <50 ml. A small circuit volume will minimize thermoregulation difficulties and decrease the amount of colloid substance used for circuit priming.

No equipment is presently available that completely fulfills these ideal criteria. Many pediatric and adult treatment centers have modified dialysis equipment and assembled their own modified circuits with a blood pump attached. Presently two commercially assembled blood pumps are FDA approved for CVVH use (BM-11, Baxter HealthCare, and BSM-21, Cobe Renal Intensive Care, Lakewood, Colo.). The pumps are similar in overall operation. One has an additional roller head pump for the delivery of dialysate and a syringe pump for continuous heparin infusion. The basic circuit setup, alarms, and other pump features are similar. An advanced CVVH pump designed to be more user friendly and sensitive to the needs of infants and children is currently available in Europe, and manufacturers are working to bring this technology to the United States.

For purposes of this text, the following discussion is focused on the BM-11 pump used for the past 4 years in the PICU at Children's Medical Center of Dallas (see Fig. 170-5). This pump is equipped with prepump (arterial) and postfilter (venous) circuit pressure alarms, air and clot trap, air detector, and blood leak detector. Blood flow rate ranges from 30 to 300 ml/min. Pump speed is most often determined by the blood flow capacity of the catheter. If the blood flow is not restricted by the capability of the catheter, blood flow rate is determined by estimating the amount of blood flow per minute needed to pass through the filter to give the desired solute clearance and water removal. Consult the filter manufacturer's recommendations for blood flow rate and ultrafiltration rate.

When starting the blood pump and initiating CVVH, it is important to consider several important points. First, determine minimum speed required to maintain adequate circuit venous pressure. Circuit venous pressure measures resistance to returning blood to the patient. Venous pressure must be >10 mm Hg for the pump to run. The larger the catheter diameter the higher the minimum speed required. For example, an 11 F catheter may require a minimum pump speed of 150 ml/min, whereas an 8 F catheter may be able to run at as low as 30 ml/min. Inadequate pump speed will be indicated by low venous pressure while arterial pressure remains adequate.

Second, initial blood flow rate is set to the minimum pump speed for adequate catheter blood flow. Once the patient is stable, pump speed is increased slowly (as the patient can tolerate) to the desired continuous blood flow rate. When the circuit has been primed with a blood product containing citrate preservative, it is especially important to initiate circuit blood flow slowly to prevent hypotension secondary to calcium sequestration by the citrate.

Third, circuit arterial and venous pressures are observed to determine adequate catheter blood flow. Low circuit arterial pressure with high venous pressure indicates difficulty pulling blood into the circuit and high resistance to returning blood to the patient. In the infant or child in whom the catheter fits closely against the vessel wall, this problem may be resolved by reversing the arterial blood flow to pull from the distal port and reversing the venous flow to flow through the proximal side ports. If this action does not resolve the problem, the pressure alarms will continue to signal, indicating low arterial and high venous pressure. If blood flow is reversed, the catheter ports and the pump tubing are labeled to indicate reversal and prevent inadvertent administration of medication or other fluids through the arterial side of the circuit. Such labeling will also remind the team at the next circuit change that reversal of flow is necessary.

Pressure alarm interpretation. Consult the manufacturer's information regarding specific error codes or alarm interpretation and recommended actions. In

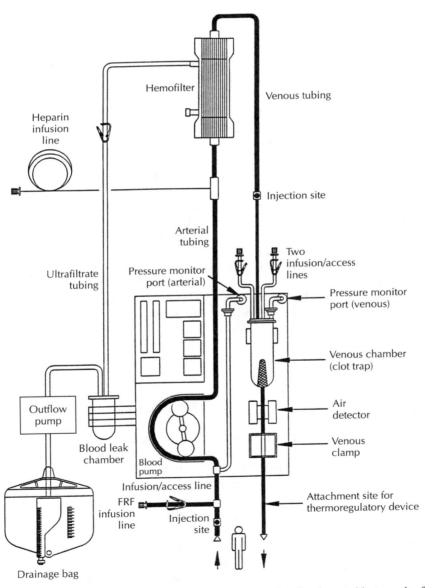

Fig. 170-5 Configuration used at Children's Medical Center of Dallas for predilution, ultrafiltration-controlled CVVH with the BM-11 pump. (FRF = Filter replacement fluid.) (Adapted and reprinted with permission of Baxter HealthCare, Renal Division, McGaw Park, Ill.)

Table 170-5 Comparison of Hemofilters

Hemofilter	Priming Volume (ml)	Membrane Surface Area	Comment
Menntech			
HF 400	28	0.30	
HF 700	53	0.71	
HF 1200	83	1.25	
Asahi Medical			
Pan-06	63	0.60	Special adapters for ultrafiltrate and dialysate ports on filter

general pressure alarms can be interpreted using the following guidelines:

1. Arterial pressure is an indication of the amount of resistance to pulling blood into the circuit.
2. Venous pressure is an indication of the resistance to returning blood from the circuit to the patient.
3. Low arterial pressure indicates low blood flow into the circuit, possibly related to catheter kink or clot, circuit tubing obstruction, or the catheter positioned against the vessel wall.
4. High arterial pressure is rare. Complications that increase arterial pressure generally affect venous pressure first.
5. Low venous pressure is critical and may indicate a disconnection in the circuit, a leak or loose connection, filter clotting, or pump blood flow rate too low for the catheter used.
6. High venous pressure may indicate a clot in the venous access or the circuit venous drip chamber, a kink in the catheter, or obstruction in the circuit tubing.

Hemofilter. Several of the currently available hemofilters that have been used in children are listed in Table 170-5. All of these filters are of the hollow-fiber design. As in hemodialysis, it is also possible to build a hemofilter for CVVH that has the parallel-plate membrane configuration. To date, available parallel-plate hemofilters are too large to be practical for use in small pediatric patients.

No controlled studies have compared hemofilters in pediatric patients. Multiple hollow-fiber filters are available for CVVH use that directly fit with this tubing. The smaller filters (Minifilter, Minifilter Plus) may be used with ECMO in patients undergoing CVVH.

An additional pump for CVVH is not needed: the CVVH circuit is attached to the ECMO circuit, which has sufficient pump pressure to drive the CVVH circuit. The smaller filters restrict blood flow rate, minimize inappropriate shunting of blood away from the ECMO circuit, and decrease the potential compromise of ECMO flow rates.

We currently use the HF 400 filter (Menntech) as the standard CVVH filter. As with all ECMO in children, it is important to minimize the total volume of the filter and extracorporeal circuit, ideally to ≤10% of the child's estimated blood volume (i.e., ≈8 ml/kg). The filter chosen must be the smallest volume filter that fits the tubing connections and provides the clearance and ultrafiltration necessary. With the ability to control blood flow and ultrafiltration rates, it is not necessary to use multiple sizes of hemofilters to control circuit pressures and ultrafiltrate removal. One hemofilter can be standardized for use in small infants as well as adolescents.

Filling volume of the HF 400 hemofilter is 28 ml. Larger filters (e.g., Pan-06 [Asahi Medical, Tokyo] and HF 700 and HF 1200 [Menntech]) fit the BM-11 circuit without adaptation. The larger filters have a greater surface area and greater solute removal capability. These filters have been used in an effort to find a filter with a longer average filter life than the HF 400 and in larger children in whom greater solute and water removal is needed. The larger filling volume limits the use of these more efficient filters to the older pediatric population.

The hemofilter is secured to the pump apparatus with a clamping filter holder attached to the top of the blood pump. The filter is tilted 30 to 60 degrees, venous end up, to trap any small air bubbles in the top corner of the venous end. The filter must be in full view at all times. Any external heating sources used must not obscure the view of the filter or be so close as to damage the filter.

Tubing. The tubing we use is specifically designed for use with the BM-11 pump by the manufacturer. The tubing is packaged in three sections: arterial (prefilter), venous (postfilter), and ultrafiltrate tubing. Tubing blood volume is 110 ml. The availability of smaller volume tubing is pending final modifications and final approval for patient use.

CVVHD adaptations. The hemofilter includes two ultrafiltrate ports, one of which remains capped during standard CVVH or SCUF. To perform CAVHD, peritoneal dialysate is infused into the ultrafiltrate port on the venous end of the filter and collected along with the ultrafiltrate formed. Early CVVHD techniques devised by Ronco et al. used gravity to drip peritoneal dialysate (1.5% dextrose) through the Amicon Minifilter at 1 to 3 ml/min. The optimum dialysate flow rate for CVVHD has not been determined.

CVVHD with controlled ultrafiltrate rate can be set up as follows:

1. Peritoneal dialysate (1.5% dextrose) is pumped into the hemofilter ultrafiltrate compartment at a defined rate (usually 500 or 1000 ml/hr). Dialysate flows in the compartment external to the blood flow compartment, countercurrent to the flow of blood. Dialysate flow acts as an exchange mechanism and does not directly mix with the blood flowing through the circuit.
2. The ultrafiltrate line, attached to an IV pump, is set at the dialysate rate plus desired negative balance (in milliliters per hour).
3. If combined desired ultrafiltrate and dialysate rates exceed 1500 ml/hr, ultrafiltrate rate of removal is regulated by gravity, not a pump.
4. Desired negative output is the sum of dialysate, IV intake, and medications plus desired hourly fluid loss.

Anticoagulant. Heparin or other anticoagulant may be added to the circuit tubing at a port located between the roller pump and the filter. Alternative sites for heparin administration may be selected as long as heparin enters the circuit before the filter. The heparin solution is prepared with 0.9% sodium chloride solution at a heparin concentration of 10 or 100 units/ml. The concentration is determined on the basis of that needed to infuse heparin at a minimum of 5 to 10 ml/hr. More concentrated heparin solutions

running at slower infusion rates may be used but must be delivered by a syringe pump to prevent intermittent heparin administration at such slow infusion rates. Heparin given in small volumes may not adequately mix with the blood before reaching the hemofilter.

Ultrafiltrate. The ultrafiltrate tube from the hemofilter is intended to be inserted into any closed container. It is preferable to control ultrafiltrate rather than only monitor it. Control of ultrafiltrate is achieved by attaching the ultrafiltrate tube to the inlet port of a volumetric IV infusion pump by means of a small adapter and setting the IV pump at the desired rate. A urine collection device can be attached to the end of the IV pump tubing to capture the ultrafiltrate. A 5% to 10% error in actual measured ultrafiltrate vs. the programmed pump rate of the IV pump is not uncommon. Therefore ultrafiltrate is measured hourly in a graduated cylinder or other accurate measuring device, especially if ultrafiltration rate is <500 ml.

A significant decrease in ultrafiltration or repeated alarm signals from the IV pump alert the nurse to a period of inadequate ultrafiltration, which may indicate need for filter replacement. Air bubbles in the ultrafiltrate line also alert the nurse to the potential for inadequate ultrafiltration. Fluid overload may occur if FRF rates are not adjusted to account for decreased or interrupted ultrafiltrate output. When "delivered" ultrafiltrate begins to be less than that "prescribed," either the prescribed rate must be reduced to an amount the filter can deliver or the filter must be replaced.

In Europe devices with volumetric scales are available to continuously monitor spontaneous ultrafiltrate by weight. A digital readout allows the nurse to note the volume of ultrafiltrate formed during the previous period (usually 15 to 30 minutes) and to adjust FRF infusion rate accordingly. However, devices currently available in the United States are not ideal for CVVH ultrafiltration control. Pumps that operate discontinuously have short bursts of negative pressure that quickly fill the small chamber in the pump tubing cassette regardless of the prescribed infusion rate. The rate at which the chamber is emptied is modulated by the pump infusion rate setting. When the chamber is filling, high pressure can be generated in the ultrafiltrate circuit. Hemofilter membranes are capable of withstanding pressures of ≥500 mm Hg and have not ruptured at maximum pump settings

(>1000 ml/hr). The intermittent application of negative pressure to the filter results in short periods of maximum Qf alternating with longer periods during which Qf (ultrafiltrate) is 0 as the pump chamber is emptied.

The high pulling pressures of the discontinuous pumps often create air in the tubing. Constant pump alarm signals can be prevented by placing a piece of fluid-filled tubing in the air-detecting device to "block" the air detector. Because this fluid is not going to the patient and is being measured each hour by another device, this "blocking" mechanism is acceptable.

A continuous pump is preferred for ultrafiltrate control since it can deliver large volumes without the problems of a discontinuous type of device. However, presently no pumps are available that deliver at a rate >999 ml/hr to accommodate high-flow predilution or dialysate infusion needs. At Children's Medical Center of Dallas we use the Gemini IV pump (IMED, San Diego, Calif.) for flow rates <1000 ml/hr. Tubing assembly and connection to the ultrafiltrate line requires IMED Gemini syringe tubing, a male-to-male adapter, and a "blue Christmas tree" catheter adapter. IV tubing is connected to urine collection device tubing by cutting off the top two thirds of the urine collection device tubing and using the "Christmas tree" adapter.

Filter replacement fluid, predilution. The composition of FRF must reflect the needs of the patient. No commercially available CVVH FRF solutions are available in the United States.

In smaller children a formula modified from that used at the University of Michigan is used at Children's Medical Center of Dallas. Four 1 L bags are prepared by the pharmacy and hung simultaneous-

---

FILTER REPLACEMENT FLUID FORMULATIONS*

Physiologic FRF

Bag No. 1: 1000 ml 0.9% NaCl + 7.5 ml 10% $CaCl_2$ (10.35 mEq Ca)
Bag No. 2: 1000 ml 0.9% NaCl + 1.6 ml 50% $MgSO_4$ (6.4 mEq Mg)
Bag No. 3: 1000 ml 0.9% NaCl
Bag No. 4: 900 ml sterile H_2O + 100 ml $NaHCO_3$ (100 mEq $NaHCO_3$) + 10 ml $D_{50}W$ (5 g dextrose)
Final FRF composition: Na = 140 mEq/L
Cl = 120 mEq/L
HCO_3 = 25 mEq/L
Ca = 2.6 mEq/L
Mg = 1.6 mEq/L
Dextrose = 124 mg/dl
K = 0

FRF with additional bicarbonate

Bag No. 1: 1000 ml 0.9% NaCl + 7.5 ml 10% $CaCl_2$
Bag No. 2: 1000 ml 0.9% NaCl + 1.6 ml 50% $MgSO_4$
Bag No. 3: 850 ml sterile water + 150 ml $NaHCO_3$ (150 mEq $NaHCO_3$)
Bag No. 4: 900 ml sterile water + 100 ml $NaHCO_3$ (100 mEq $NaHCO_3$) + 10 ml $D_{50}W$ (5 g dextrose)
Final FRF composition: Na = 139 mEq/L
Cl = 82 mEq/L
HCO_3 = 62 mEq/L
Ca = 2.6 mEq/L
Mg = 1.6 mEq/L
Dextrose = 124 mg/dl
K = 0

*Modified from the University of Michigan FRF.

ly, attached to a five-pronged tubing manifold normally used for automated (cycler) peritoneal dialysis (5C4426, Baxter HealthCare). The FRF infusion line is attached in the predilution position to an access tube off the arterial limb of the CVVH circuit. A similar arrangement on the venous limb allows FRF to be infused in the postdilution mode.

As long as the bags are hung at the same level above the manifold and are filled equally, they each will contribute 25% of the final FRF that reaches the patient. The goal is to provide a physiologic solution to replace plasma water. The use of the cycler tubing manifold allows delivery of Ca and Mg in the same final solution with bicarbonate without the precipitation that would occur if these solutes were combined in the same bag. The brief period of mixing that occurs within the final tubing segment before the solution reaches the patient is too short to allow precipitation.

Occasionally superphysiologic concentrations of bicarbonate in the FRF are needed to correct severe metabolic acidosis. When the high bicarbonate formula is used, care must be taken to avoid overcorrection, with resulting metabolic alkalosis.

Potassium is usually not included in the initial FRF formula in patients with renal failure, although eventually most patients need some potassium supplementation. Potassium and phosphate are usually administered in the TPN solution. When this route cannot deliver sufficient amounts for the patient's needs, potassium salts can be added to the FRF solution. It is safer, although less convenient, to add a physiologic concentration of potassium (e.g., 4 mEq/L of KCl or K_2HPO_4) to each of the four FRF bags. If 16 mEq of KCl is added to a single bag and that bag is hung higher than the others or lines from the other bags become occluded, serious hyperkalemia can develop with terrifying rapidity. For related reasons, hypokalemia must never be treated with KCl in the FRF at final concentrations >4 mEq/L. In pediatric patients the capacity of the CVVH system to rapidly reconstitute the extracellular fluid to be the same as the FRF must be recognized.

Many adults can be successfully treated with CVVH using Ringer's solution as the FRF. Serum lactate and electrolyte levels, however, must be monitored routinely. The advantages of Ringer's solution are convenience and reduced cost as well as no need to worry about a pharmacy error, as in formulation of one of the Michigan bags, a problem that may re-

sult in the development of hyponatremia. Lactated Ringer's solution has been used successfully at our center, and Bosch and Ronco have reported that the high lactate administration rates needed when Ringer's solution is used as FRF have been well tolerated by their adult patients. No controlled studies have been done to compare the two FRF methods (Michigan formulation vs. Ringer's solution) in either adults or children. The Michigan solution may be preferred in critically ill pediatric patients, especially those with hepatic dysfunction, but we have not examined this question systematically.

Thermoregulation therapy and devices. A significant amount of heat is lost in an extracorporeal circuit with an approximate volume of 140 ml. For all patients with CVVH who weigh <10 kg a thermoregulation device needs to be attached to the circuit or available at all times for immediate use. The large extracorporeal circuit and subsequent heat loss may make assessment difficult in the febrile patient.

Thermoregulation devices must be added according to the patient needs. In-line heat exchanger units are expensive and difficult to attach, and external heat sources such as warming light or blanket can obscure the view of the circuit and increase the risk of damage to skin integrity. A blood or fluid warming device is optimal and is easily attached to the FRF bag or directly to the venous blood catheter. The Hot Line (Level One Technologies, Rockland, Md.) is one fluid warming device. The benefits of this device are ease of operation, and unlike warming blankets, its use does not obscure visualization of the circuit or filter. If this device is interpositioned in the circuit tubing, it adds 17 ml to the total circuit volume. Therefore adding this device to the FRF line is preferred.

Other pumps and equipment. IV infusion pumps and tubing are needed for administration of FRF (predilution), dialysate, and anticoagulant. It is important to monitor for problems related to the use of multiple infusion pumps with a CVVH circuit. For example, when an infusion pump is used for both dialysate delivery and ultrafiltrate removal, it is possible that the pumps will work antagonistically, resulting in transference of fluid across the membrane and to the patient rather than out into the ultrafiltrate. This has occurred at dialysate rates in excess of 1000 ml/hr. When total ultrafiltrate rate, including dialysate, exceeds 1500 ml, the ultrafiltrate line is removed from the IV pump and ultrafiltrate output is regulated by gravity.

Clinical Considerations

Anticoagulation. The need to anticoagulate the CVVH circuit can present substantial risks to some patients. Heparinization must be accomplished with great caution, and the heparin dose must be tightly controlled with close monitoring of activated clotting time (ACT). Patients with coagulopathies may not need any heparin other than that used to prime the filter. Often these patients need increasing heparin doses as the coagulopathy improves.

If ACT is >200 seconds before treatment, heparin is not initiated until ACT spontaneously improves or the filter clots. Often these events occur simultaneously. In patients without coagulopathy, a loading dose of heparin similar to that used in hemodialysis must be given (e.g., 20 to 50 units/kg). This dose is best given at least 3 to 5 minutes before the CVVH circuit is connected to ensure that the filter does not clot when it is first perfused. Additional heparin is given as a continuous infusion into the arterial limb of the CVVH circuit.

The initial infusion rate is 5 units/kg/hr and is adjusted until ACT of the blood drawn from the venous limb of the circuit (postfilter) is one and one-half times baseline (approximately 180 to 200 seconds). Usually a heparin infusion rate can be found that keeps the postfilter ACT at one and one-half times baseline without increasing arterial (prefilter and preheparin) ACT more than 5% to 10% above baseline, thereby anticoagulating the filter without severely anticoagulating the patient.

Such "tight" heparinization necessitates close monitoring of ACT and no doubt reduces the average filter life. However, this seems a reasonable price to pay for minimizing the risk of bleeding complications. Unlike hemodialysis, in which the bleeding risk from heparinization is confined to a few hours each day during and for a short time after dialysis treatments, CVVH uses *continuous* heparinization and thus presents a much greater bleeding risk.

Alternatives to standard heparinization are currently being developed. The use of high-flow rates of FRF infused into the arterial limb of the circuit (high-flow predilution) reduces heparin requirements, probably by diluting clotting factors, improving the mixing of heparin with the blood, and decreasing blood viscosity and protein concentration before the blood reaches the filter. Studies are under way at Children's Medical Center of Dallas to confirm these observations.

Regional heparinization of the CVVH circuit with protamine to "reverse" the heparin has been reported in adults and has been used at Children's Medical Center of Dallas. This technique increases the technical support needed from the nursing staff, the amount of equipment used, and the number and amount of medications delivered. It has been our clinical experience that this technique does not significantly affect the risk for bleeding or the life of the circuit any differently than tightly controlling ACT. Tight control of ACT or not using heparin may be preferrable in a child at risk for bleeding. CVVH may be initiated without heparin. Depending on the life of that circuit and the patient's condition, the team may choose to continue not to use heparin or to start heparin with tight control of ACT.

Sodium citrate has been used for regional heparinization of the CVVH circuit, a modification of the technique used in hemodialysis. At Children's Medical Center of Dallas, use of citrate has been limited and unsuccessful. Citrate anticoagulates blood by binding available calcium ions; this effect must be reversed with constant calcium infusion before the blood is returned to the patient. The average filter life span in patients treated with citrate is the same as in patients treated with tight heparinization. The side effects of citrate include hypercalcemia, hypercitratemia, and metabolic alkalosis. More experience with citrate anticoagulation is needed before this method can be recommended as an alternative to standard CVVH heparinization.

Routine rinsing of the circuit with sodium chloride solution or FRF solution has been reported in adults. At our center this method has not proved clinically advantageous in increasing filter life or decreasing clot formation.

Hemodynamic stability. One of the most important factors to consider in anticipating hemodynamic instability is the CVVH circuit volume in relation to the child's circulating blood volume. In small infants and children it may be necessary to prime the circuit with albumin, whole blood, or another colloid substance to avoid hypotension when CVVH is begun. Because of drug clearance by the hemofilter, it may be necessary to titrate any infusion of vasopressor just before and/or in the first few minutes after initiation of CVVH. If these precautions are taken, the incidence of hemodynamic instability in relation to CVVH is rare. Unlike CAVH, pump-assisted hemofiltration and CVVH are able to function independently of the child's mean arterial pressure and can therefore be used in times of low cardiac output.

Hypotension during initiation of circuit blood flow and before initiation of ultrafiltration is most often the result of hypocalcemia secondary to the citrate preservative in the blood prime binding with the patient's calcium. For example, as the blood pump is started, the infant receives a large volume of blood product with citrate preservative very rapidly. The circuit volume and amount of blood administered are often a significant portion of the child's circulating blood volume. Caution must be taken to deliver this volume slowly at blood flow rates of 30 to 50 ml/min. Serum ionized calcium levels are monitored before circuit initiation, and additional calcium is administered if necessary. Other techniques such as those used to prepare the circuit for ECMO are being explored for use in this situation.

Replacement of drugs removed by CVVH. The continuous nature of CVVH has raised concerns about the loss into the ultrafiltrate of a substantial amount of circulating pharmacologic agents (see Chapter 182). Methods for drug dosing during CVVH are based on attempts to estimate and predict the amount of drug removed over time. The amount of any drug appearing in the ultrafiltrate at any moment is determined by the concentration of the drug in plasma and the sieving coefficient for that drug specific to the hemofilter used. Most drugs are well below 500 to 1000 daltons and thus can be considered to pass freely through the pores of all of the CVVH membranes currently in use. Only that fraction of the total plasma concentration of a drug that is bound to protein will be restricted by the membrane. Sieving coefficients for different drugs must be related to the degree of protein binding of each drug.

Golper has used readily available data on protein binding of different drugs obtained in normal subjects in an attempt to predict sieving coefficients for a number of commonly used agents. Protein binding can be highly unpredictable, especially in critically ill patients. When sieving coefficient has been measured in patients treated with CVVH, it has been found to be, at best, only a rough approximation of the predicted sieving coefficient based on protein binding data. Direct measurement of sieving coefficient is still the only reliable way to determine these data.

Much more work needs to be done to better understand the pharmacologic aspects of CVVH and to develop convenient models for drug dosing during treatment. In addition, the effects of CVVH on infusions of inotropes and other agents commonly used in PICU patients have not been defined.

Fluid balance. It may be necessary to begin with zero fluid balance and slowly adjust it as the patient can tolerate. The formula to determine hourly FRF rate is as follows:

FRF = Total fluid out − Total fluid in −
Hourly fluid balance

In a child receiving multiple blood products or fluid boluses it is important to determine what is to be included in the formula as fluid to be "taken off" and what fluid is given to maintain intravascular volume. Strict hourly intake and output measurements and FRF rate determination must be recorded on the patient flowsheet or on a separate flowsheet (Fig. 170-6).

Extracorporeal circuit. Plasma-free hemoglobin levels are measured before initiation and daily to monitor red blood cell destruction by the mechanical trauma in the extracorporeal circuit. Elevated levels indicate accumulation of the end products of red blood cell breakdown. The circuit must be changed when elevated plasma free hemoglobin levels are reported.

Initiation of CVVH
Patient and family preparation

1. Obtain informed consent for the procedure from the family and from the patient if appropriate.
2. Provide educational information to the family and the patient if appropriate about what to expect during CVVH. Pictures of other patients receiving CVVH are helpful.
3. Before initiation of CVVH, obtain baseline laboratory values, including ACT, PT, PTT, platelet count, serum electrolytes, BUN, creatinine, ionized calcium, phosphorus, magnesium, serum albumin, and glucose, and complete blood cell count.
4. Order FRF solutions from the pharmacy to reflect conditions in the individual patient. Use the modified Michigan formula (see p. 1618) to provide a physiologic solution containing 25 mEq/L of bicarbonate or a higher bicarbonate solution if metabolic acidosis is severe. Do not order potassium

Children's Medical Center of Dallas
1935 Motor Street
Dallas, Texas 75235
(214) 640-2000

HEMOFILTRATION INTAKE AND OUTPUT FLOWSHEET

Filter Replacement Fluids (FRF):

Bag #1 _____
Bag #2 _____
Bag #3 _____
Bag #4 _____

Filter: _____
Circuit Prime: _____

Catheter: _____
Site: _____
Filling Volume: _____

Patient Identification

Pend1016 (11/93)

$$FRF = Total\ Out - [(in_{\#2-6}) - (hourly\ change)]$$

Date _____

	intake							output							fluid balance			labs		pump		comments
	FRF	IV Fluids	Meds Flush	Albumin Blood	Heparin u/cc	Other	Total In	Ordered UF	Actual UF	Urine	NG Drains	Blood	Other	Total Out	Ordered Hourly Change	Actual Hourly Change (total in - total out)	Cumulative Fluid Balance	ACT (pre/post)	Other	Speed (ml/min)	Pressures a / v	
	1	2	3	4	5	6	7	8	9	10	11	12	13	14	15	16	17	18	19	20	21	
0700																						
0800																						
0900																						
1000																						
1100																						
1200																						
1300																						
1400																						
TOTAL																						RN
1500																						
1600																						
1700																						
1800																						
1900																						
2000																						
2100																						
2200																						
TOTAL																						RN
2300																						
0001																						
0100																						
0200																						
0300																						
0400																						
0500																						
TOTAL																						RN
0600																						

Fig. 170-6 Example of a flowsheet for recording hourly intake and output measurements.

in the FRF solutions unless the serum K level is already <3.0 mEq/L.

5. Using the baseline ACT and other clotting studies, determine whether initial heparinization will be needed. If baseline ACT is <200 seconds and risk for bleeding is not exceptional, give an IV loading dose of heparin (20 to 50 units/kg) about 5 minutes before connecting the CVVH circuit.

6. Arrange all pumps and equipment at the bedside. Provide thermoregulation support to circuit and patient if necessary.

7. Ensure that a sample from the appropriate FRF solution bags has been sent for measurement of sodium concentration.

Circuit assembly

1. Using sterile technique, assemble the tubing, filter, and any other attachments needed to complete the circuit.

2. Place the assembled circuit on the pump.

3. Attach the priming solution to the arterial side of the tubing. Start the pump, and prime the tubing and filter with heparinized 0.9% sodium chloride solution (5000 units heparin/L) according to the manufacturer's instructions. The amount of fluid necessary to prime the circuit depends on the specifications of the filter and whether it has been prerinsed. Priming removes air trapped in the hollow fibers. Approximately 15 to 30 minutes is needed to set up and prime a filter, depending on the experience of the staff.

4. Air trapped in a hollow fiber retards blood flow and promotes thrombosis. Do not tap the filter with a hard object such as a hemostat; the filter will crack. In fact, tapping may increase the trapped air. Gentle, quick, repeated motions of clamping and unclamping the tubing with a hemostat just beyond the hemofilter brings the air to the top of the hemofilter and allows for easier removal.

5. If heparin administration is contraindicated, a sodium chloride rinse after the heparinized sodium chloride prime will remove any heparin not attached to circuit tubing or membrane.
6. If circuits are primed in advance, primed filters may be refrigerated for 48 hours before use. It is not generally necessary to prime circuits in advance. The life of the circuit in use may extend beyond the life of the refrigerated circuit. Circuit priming is relatively simple and fast with this pump and does not significantly extend the time needed for circuit changes.
7. Refrigerated filters must be allowed to warm to room temperature before being placed in service. A rapid rinse with sodium chloride solution that has been warmed to 37° C may be used to warm the filter. Do not heat the solution beyond 37° C.
8. Venous access catheters can usually be placed during the time needed to prime the filter.
9. Spike FRF solution bags with prongs from the five-prong cycler manifold using appropriate technique. Connect the manifold line to the FRF infusion pump and the line from the infusion pump to the stopcock on the T-connector in the arterial tubing segment for the predilution FRF mode. Be certain that all four FRF bags contain equal volumes and hang freely at the same height above the manifold.

Circuit priming methods

Depending on the need to prime the circuit with blood, the technique used to initiate the therapy may differ. If the patient's blood is used to prime the circuit, initiate therapy with the "prime wasting" method. If the circuit is primed with blood, albumin, or other colloid, use the "blood prime" method.

Prime wasting

1. With sterile technique, connect the end of the CVVH arterial tubing to the proximal (withdrawal) port of the patient catheter.
2. Unclamp and open the CVVH circuit and catheter, arterial limb first. Start the CVVH pump, in priming mode, at 80 ml/min. Keep the ultrafiltrate line clamped. The blood will begin to fill the circuit and push the prime out into the fluid collection bag attached to the venous end of the tubing.
3. As blood flows through the circuit and reaches the point of the venous end of the hemofilter, turn the lever on the BM-11 pump to put the pump into treatment mode. By the time the pump completes

mechanical checks and is in the treatment mode, the blood will have reached the venous end of the CVVH circuit and be ready for patient hookup.

Blood prime

1. After the heparinized 0.9% sodium chloride solution prime, prime the circuit again with blood or colloid substance.
2. When choosing a blood product for priming, consider the following:
   a. Fresh whole blood is the first choice for priming because there is less risk for hyperkalemia. Whole blood can be sterilely "docked" and dispensed in aliquots as needed to minimize donor exposure. However, whole blood is often expensive and difficult to obtain.
   b. If fresh whole blood cannot be obtained, consider using a reconstituted blood product, such as equal amounts of packed red blood cells mixed with fresh frozen plasma.
   c. Instruct your blood bank to take measures to limit donor exposure to patients.
   d. Packed red blood cells, without dilution, have a hematocit of 75% to 80% and are not ideally used as a circuit prime. It is necessary to dilute the packed red blood cells with either fresh frozen plasma or 5% albumin.
3. Once the circuit is primed with blood, use sterile technique to connect both the arterial and venous ends of the CVVH circuit to the appropriate catheter ports. *Keep all lines clamped during the connection process.*

Patient hookup

1. If calcium, bicarbonate, or other solutions are added to the primed CVVH circuit before patient hookup, recirculate fluid in the circuit before connection to the patient. This will allow adequate mixing of the solutions and warming of the circuit contents. Connect the arterial and venous ends of the circuit to each other to create a circuit for recirculation. To minimize red blood cell hemolysis, do not recirculate a blood-primed circuit for longer than 30 minutes. A circuit primed with crystalloid or another noncolloid solution may be recirculated longer if circuit integrity is maintained and the risk for infection is minimal.
2. Prepare the patient catheter and CVVH tubing connections according to hospital protocol and, using sterile technique, attach the CVVH tubing circuit to the venous access catheter ports. Keep the

CVVH circuit clamped *and* the patient catheter ports clamped during this procedure. Eliminate *all* air at the connection between the venous end of the CVVH circuit and the patient before starting the blood pump.

3. *Caution!* Aspirate any heparin solution from the patient catheter before connecting the CVVH circuit. After heparin has been aspirated, flush the catheter ports to demonstrate catheter patency. If blood aspiration or fluid instillation is difficult, *stop* and assess for catheter patency before starting the blood pump.

4. Attach the continuous heparin infusion to the prefilter port on the CVVH circuit and determine the starting heparin infusion rate on the basis of baseline ACT. A starting rate of 5 units/kg/hr is often adequate.

5. Unclamp all lines, patient catheter first, and start the blood pump at the predetermined starting rate.

Initiation of ultrafiltration and circuit maintenance

1. Examine all connections for leaks.
2. When the patient's condition has stabilized, open the clamps on the ultrafiltrate line and begin FRF delivery at the predetermined rate.
3. If the expected ultrafiltration capacity of the hemofilter is not known, a spontaneous ultrafiltration method may be used to determine ultrafiltration rate.
   a. Measure the spontaneous ultrafiltrate rate by carefully collecting the ultrafiltrate produced in the first 5 to 10 minutes of filter operation. Any container can be used as a collection device but needs to be held near the floor to allow full extension of the ultrafiltrate line.
   b. Near the end of the 5- to 10-minute spontaneous ultrafiltrate measurement, draw blood samples simultaneously from the arterial and venous sampling ports to be sent for hematocrit determination.
   c. Clamp the ultrafiltrate line and connect it to the ultrafiltrate control pump. Small patients may not tolerate more than 5 minutes of spontaneous ultrafiltration without marked volume depletion.
   d. Determine the desired ultrafiltration, with the measured spontaneous ultrafiltration as an initial upper limit. Maximum ultrafiltration gives maximum clearance of solutes and correc-

tion of electrolyte and fluid disturbances. Set the desired ultrafiltration rate on the ultrafiltration pump. Do not begin controlled ultrafiltration until FRF infusion is also ready to be started.

4. If heparin infusion is used, monitor ACT every 30 to 45 minutes until stable, then every 1 to 2 hours as needed. If heparin therapy is not used, monitoring ACT once every shift or after determination of PT and PTT may be sufficient.

5. Adjust heparin infusion to keep venous (postfilter) ACT approximately one and one-half times baseline (not >200 seconds). If arterial (prefilter) ACT is monitored, the acceptable range is no more than about 10% above baseline (about 120 to 150 seconds).

6. Monitor actual ultrafiltration hourly and compare with desired rate. If actual measured ultrafiltration is consistently less than desired, reduce the ordered ultrafiltration and FRF rates accordingly. Ultrafiltration rate and FRF rate are considered to operate in tandem. Changes in one must be of equal magnitude as in the other to maintain the same fluid balance. Never change one pump without making an equivalent change in the other pump unless a different fluid balance state is desired.

7. Monitor serum chemistry levels frequently during the first 24 to 48 hours of CVVH and at least every 8 hours thereafter.

8. Weigh the patient at circuit change to minimize risk of catheter dislodgment. More frequent weighing is optimal but often contraindicated.

9. Obtain cultures of blood from the CVVH circuit when symptoms indicate potential infection.

Circuit disconnection

1. If the circuit was primed with the patient's blood (prime-wasting method), attempt to return the blood in the circuit to the patient prior to disconnecting.

2. If the circuit was primed with the blood prime method, stop the pump, clamp all clamps, and disconnect. Any return of blood will be additional volume for the patient.

3. If it is necessary to disconnect the patient from CVVH for a short period (<4 hours), the circuit may be disconnected and recirculated until the circuit can be reconnected, assuming the following:
   a. The circuit is relatively new and the benefits of using the same circuit outweigh those of

changing to a new circuit while the patient is disconnected.

b. The circuit will not be recirculated longer than 30 minutes if it contains blood or longer than 4 hours if the blood has been rinsed out and the tubing contains crystalloid solution.

c. Circuit integrity and sterility are maintained during disconnection, recirculation, and the reconnection process.

RISKS AND COMPLICATIONS

Clotting and filter. Filter clotting is a frequent complication of CVVH. Factors that predispose the filter to clotting include repeated interrupted blood flow, high resistance anywhere in the circuit, high filtration fraction, air pockets within the filter fibers, and inadequate anticoagulation. Of the factors listed, inadequate anticoagulation is probably encountered most often.

Average filter life span varies widely among patients and may also change as conditions change in the individual patient. An average filter life of about 60 hours is a reasonable goal. When more than one filter clots within a 24-hour period, the overall effectiveness and mechanical functioning of CVVH becomes questionable. When a filter clots and the pump stops, if the circuit was primed with the patient's blood, the patient experiences a significant loss of blood equal to the volume in the filter and tubing. The estimated volume lost may need to be returned to the patient. Record any volume loss and volume replacement in the intake and output balance. Renal replacement therapy is suspended until a new filter can be obtained. Thromboembolic and infectious complications are more likely to occur in patients with frequent filter clotting.

Venous trap clotting. Clotting in the venous drip chamber significant enough to stop blood flow is the most frequent complication. BM-11 tubing manufacturers have made attempts to decrease chamber volume and to modify design changes in other ways to decrease clotting. However, this remains the most common reason for circuit change.

Inadequate solute clearance. Hypercatabolic patients may need solute clearance rates in excess of those possible with standard CVVH. The use of the HF 400 hemofilter in infants and children usually provides sufficient urea clearance to offset high urea production. When additional small solute removal is needed, the use of high-flow predilution may be

helpful. Kaplan et al. first observed that urea clearance was increased when FRF was infused into the arterial limb of the circuit tubing before the filter. In this configuration FRF is used to lower the plasma protein concentration and thus decrease oncotic pressure within the filter fibers. Filtration pressure equilibrium occurs later, resulting in an increase in the area of the membrane participating in solute clearance. Dilution of clotting factors also helps by reducing the rate at which filter fibers become occluded by thrombi.

High-flow predilution may have an additional beneficial effect on urea clearance. Kaplan has suggested that when predilution is used, the dilution of the plasma allows urea to diffuse out of red blood cells before reaching the membrane. Predilution CVVH might be effectively removing urea from both intracellular and extracellular urea pools. Studies are under way in several centers to examine this hypothesis.

When high-flow predilution is used, the FRF rate and ultrafiltration rate must be carefully chosen to prevent disturbances in fluid balance. One practical approach to selecting the predilution FRF infusion rate is based on the ordered ultrafiltration rate minus the hourly IV fluid and medication minus the desired negative fluid balance or volume depletion. From that point onward, with any change in ultrafiltration rate due to aging of the filter, FRF rate must be reduced by the same volume. Once the desired patient "dry weight" is achieved and further volume depletion is unnecessary, FRF rate is equal to ultrafiltration rate minus hourly IV fluid and medication rate, to achieve zero fluid balance.

The limits of FRF rate are determined by the maximum ultrafiltration rate achievable with the hemofilter being used. If CVVH clearance is not sufficient, clearances of urea and other solutes can be increased by the use of CVVHD.

Bleeding from excessive heparinization. Tight heparinization is recommended to reduce the risk of excessive heparinization. No heparin is needed when baseline ACT is >200 seconds.

Air embolism. The BM-11 pump contains an air detector system. Air entering the circuit at any point before the venous drip chamber will be eliminated. Air exiting the venous drip chamber will trigger the air detector, which causes an alarm that activates a tubing clamp mechanism and stops the pump.

Thromboembolism. The BM-11 pump has a filter

at the base of the venous drip chamber that is designed to trap any clots from passing directly into the venous circulation. The presence of thrombi in the filter can be detected by simple inspection. In our experience flushing the filter to remove the clots has not been beneficial.

Hypovolemia and hypervolemia. Fluid balance during CVVH is simple: total intake must equal total output. If errors are made in selecting FRF flow rates, intravascular volume status can change rapidly, especially in infants. Patients receiving high-flow predilution rates are at particular risk for hypervolemia if a falling ultrafiltration rate goes unnoticed. All patients receiving CVVH need hourly monitoring of ultrafiltration rate and fluid balance by the PICU nurse. Thorough review of fluid balance and overall circuit function by the responsible physician, advanced practice nurse, and patient care team must be done every 8 to 12 hours to adequately assess the course of CVVH treatment.

Hypernatremia and hyponatremia. Errors in preparation of the Michigan FRF solutions can cause rapid development of severe disorders of serum sodium concentration. The sodium concentration of the final solution reaching the patient must always be 135 to 145 mEq/L. Before dispensing the bags for patient use, the pharmacist sends fluid samples for sodium analysis from all solutions that require the addition of calcium or magnesium to 0.9% sodium chloride solution. For example, sodium concentration is routinely measured on a sample from bag 4 (see p. 1618) each time a new set of FRF bags is prepared by the pharmacy. If 0.9% sodium chloride solution is used in all four bags, the patient's serum sodium concentration will rapidly approach 154 mEq/L.

Hyponatremia may also develop if relatively large volumes of hyponatremic TPN are infused. Sodium balance during CVVH is as straightforward as fluid balance: for every 100 ml of TPN infused, 100 ml of plasma water will be removed. If the TPN contains only 4 mEq of sodium/dl and plasma sodium concentration is 14 mEq/dl, a negative sodium balance of 10 mEq is achieved with every 100 ml of ultrafiltrate formed. This is a prime example of the power of CVVH to change electrolyte concentration while keeping the volume of total body water constant.

Depletion of other electrolytes, minerals, and water-soluble vitamins. Many important substances are lost into the ultrafiltrate. If enteral nutrition is not an option, adequate replacement is thought to be accomplished by the use of complete TPN solutions that contain vitamins and trace elements in addition to major electrolytes and amino acids. Systematic balance studies have not been performed to test this presumption. All patients undergoing CVVH must also be receiving complete nutrition from enteral feedings or TPN.

Anemia. Frequent clotting of the filter may result in substantial blood losses, especially if the circuit is primed with crystalloid, albumin, or solutions other than the patient's own blood. When transfusions are needed, if no other sites are available, blood may be administered through a stopcock at the connection of the venous limb of the CVVH circuit to the catheter. Blood priming methods to prevent further depletion of the hematocrit when a new filter and its tubing are placed in service have been discussed previously. In some pediatric patients administering a transfusion of packed red blood cells when the new filter is attached is an alternative to priming the circuit with blood. The volume of the transfusion can be removed by increasing the ultrafiltration rate by an amount equal to the volume of the packed red blood cell transfusion. It may be necessary to divide this amount and remove it over several hours. More rapid transfusion is possible with CVVH, if volume status remains constant; plasma water is being exchanged milliliter for milliliter with a solution of packed red blood cells that has <50% of its volume as plasma. This is another example of the way CVVH can adjust the composition of the patient's fluids (this time, the hematocrit) while maintaining a constant fluid volume.

Hypothermia. Small infants may become hypothermic when blood perfusing the CVVH circuit is allowed to cool to room temperature. (See Thermoregulation, p. 1619.)

Infection. The CVVH circuit offers many opportunities for invading organisms to enter the central circulation. Only meticulous nursing technique can keep the risk of contamination at an acceptable level. Sterile technique begins with the priming of the filter and extends to include every event that necessitates entering or interrupting the circuit for any reason. Catheter exit site care must be aggressive and uncompromising; protocols based on those used to care for percutaneous hemodialysis catheter exit sites are appropriate. In an effort to decrease risk for infection and maintain circuit integrity, CVVH circuits are changed between circuit day 3 and circuit day 4, and earlier if necessary. Elective circuit changes are performed under optimal staff and patient conditions.

CURRENT RESEARCH AND FUTURE CONSIDERATIONS

The use of prostacyclin has been discussed in the literature, but little clinical data exist. The development of heparin-coated tubing may offer an alternative to heparin infusions. A low molecular weight heparin with high affinity for antithrombin III and minimal effect on PTT value, which can also be completely removed in the ultrafiltrate, has undergone clinical trials in Europe. Little information about its use for this therapy exists. New membrane materials are being developed that contain heparin molecules bound to the surface in contact with the blood. Analogs of PGI_2 are being evaluated that can produce anticoagulation without the potent vasodilatory and hypotensive effects that now characterize the use of PGI_2.

ADDITIONAL READING

• Baldwin IC, Elderkin TD. Continuous hemofiltration: Nursing perspectives in critical care. New Horiz 3:738-747, 1995.

Bellomo R, Tipping P, Boyce N. Continuous venovenous hemofiltration with dialysis removes cytokines from the circulation of septic patients. Crit Care Med 21:522-526, 1993.

Bellomo R, et al. Effect of continuous venovenous hemofiltration with dialysis on hormone and catecholamine clearance in critically ill patients in acute renal failure. Crit Care Med 22:833-837, 1994.

Bommel E, Bouvy N, So K, Zietse R, Vincent H, Bruining H, Weimar W. Acute dialytic support for the critically ill: Intermittent hemodialysis versus continuous arteriovenous hemodiafiltration. Am J Nephrol 15:192-200, 1995.

Bosch JP, Ronco C. Continuous arteriovenous hemofiltration (CAVH) and other continuous replacement therapies: Operational characteristics and clinical use. In Maher JF, ed. Replacement of Renal Function by Dialysis, 3rd ed. Boston: Kluwer, 1989, pp 347-359.

Bosworth C. SCUF/CAVH/CAVHD: Critical differences. Crit Care Nurse Q 14:45-55, 1992.

Golper TA. Continuous arteriovenous hemofiltration in acute renal failure. Am J Kidney Dis 6:373-386, 1985.

Henderson LW. Hemofiltration. Kidney 20:25-30, 1989.

Hendrix W. Dialysis therapies in critically ill children. Crit Care Nurs 3:605-613, 1992.

Kaplan AA, Longnecker RE, Folkert VW. Continuous arteriovenous hemofiltration: A report of 6 months' experience. Ann Intern Med 100:358-367, 1984.

Kierdorf H. Continuous versus intermittent treatment: Clinical results in acute renal failure. Contrib Nephrol 93:1-12, 1991.

Kramer P, Kaufhold G, Grone HJ, et al. Management of intensive care patients with arteriovenous hemofiltration. Int J Artif Organs 3:225-230, 1980.

• Macias WL, et al. Continuous venovenous hemofiltration: An alternative to continuous arteriovenous hemofiltration and hemodiafiltration in acute renal failure. Am J Kidney Dis 18:451-458, 1991.

Price C. An update on continuous renal replacement therapies. Crit Care Nurs 3:597-604, 1992.

Ronco C, Barbacini S, Digito A, Zoccali G. Achievements and new directions in continuous renal replacement therapies. New Horiz 3:708-716, 1995.

Sakarcan A, Karabocuoglu M, Headrick C, Alexander S, Quigley R. The role of continuous venovenous hemofiltration in the nutritional support of critically ill children. J Renal Nutr 5:133-137, 1995.

Smoyer W, Sherbotie J, Gardner J, Bunchman T. A practical approach to continuous hemofiltration in infants and children. Dialysis Transplant 24:633-640, 1995.

Summar M, Pietsch J, Deshpande J, Schulum. Effective hemodialysis and hemofiltration driven by an extracorporeal membrane oxygenation pump in infants with hyperammonemia. J Pediatr 128:379-382, 1996.

• Zobel G, Ring E, Kuttnig M, Grubbauer HM. Five years' experience with extracorporeal renal support in pediatric intensive care. Intensive Care Med 17:315-319, 1991.

XXIII

Gastrointestinal and Nutritional Support Techniques

171 Total Parenteral Nutrition

Robert H. Squires, Jr. · *Charles E. Mize*

BACKGROUND

The goals of total parenteral nutrition (TPN) in the PICU are to temper the catabolic effects of hypermetabolism associated with acute injury and promote nitrogen retention when enteral nutrition is inadequate. In addition, TPN can help ensure the child receives sufficient quantity and quality of calories to promote growth and restore nutritional health. "Total" parenteral nutrition can be a misnomer, because quantities of protein, calories, fluid, or lipids are often inadequate as a result of fluid restrictions in the critically ill child. Although parenteral nutrition is a more realistic term, TPN is used throughout this text, in keeping with traditional terminology. The principles that govern nutritional assessment and nutritional requirements to provide optimal support to the critically ill child are outlined below.

Nutritional Assessment

The clinical impression of malnutrition, derived from a comprehensive history and physical examination, is a useful, valid, and reproducible technique and often all that is necessary for nutritional assessment. Important historical data to evaluate the childs' nutritional status would include evidence and duration of decreased enteral intake, malabsorption, increased requirements, and metabolic dysfunction. Physical signs that are useful include muscle wasting, loss of subcutaneous tissue, edema, hepatomegaly, cheilosis, and abnormalities of the hair, nails, tongue, and gums.

The centile or *z*-score (standard deviation score) of the patient's height, weight, and head circumference is plotted and compared with previous measurements obtained either from the family or the primary care physician. The role of additional anthropometric measurements to assess the critically ill patient is not clearly defined. To review, midarm circumference (MAC), measured in the nondominant arm midway between the acromion and olecranon, is an indicator of muscle and fat content in the upper arm. The triceps skinfold (TSF) is an indicator of fat stores, although errors in measurement are common and this score may not reflect total body fat. The midarm muscle circumference (MAMC) is an indicator of protein status and is calculated as MAMC = MAC − (TSF × 3.14). These tools are likely to be more useful in the preoperative assessment of a stable patient than in the acutely ill metabolically challenged patient.

METHODS OF NUTRITIONAL ASSESSMENT

History
Physical examination
Anthropometric measurements
Laboratory tests
Measurement of body composition

Laboratory measurements commonly used for nutritional assessment include serum albumin, transferrin, prealbumin, and retinol-binding protein, with serum half-lives of 20 days, 8 days, 2 days, and 10 hours, respectively. These measurements have been used to evaluate preexisting nutritional state, and when sequentially measured, help in assessment of response to therapy. Their level in the serum can be affected by increased loss in stool, extravascular extravasation, and dilution from resuscitation, which therefore limits their value in nutritional assessment. Although impaired immune function occurs with malnutrition, the value of skin testing, total lymphocyte count, and serum immunoglobulin levels to assess nutritional status in the PICU patient is unclear.

Indirect calorimetry, derived from a "metabolic cart," can be used to estimate calorie expenditure. This technique measures oxygen consumption and carbon dioxide production at any given moment of metabolic flux and substrate oxidation (e.g., resting, febrile, septic, high-glucose input, and high-fat input states). The expense and expertise needed to operate and maintain this tool limits its general usefulness. However, serial determinations of the respiratory quotient ($RQ = CO_2$ production/O_2 consumption) may aid in management of respiratory insufficiency if carbohydrate overfeeding ($RQ > 1.0$) with resultant hypercarbia could jeopardize the patient's respiratory status.

Route of Administration

Peripheral TPN was made possible with the introduction of a safe lipid infusion. Lipid emulsions provide a concentrated iso-osmolar energy source that enables design of a final TPN solution with a lower carbohydrate concentration. This combination decreases the prevalence of venous thrombosis and extends catheter survival. The peripheral route is preferred if central venous access is not readily available and the anticipated duration of parenteral nutritional support is less than 2 weeks. Frequent visual and physical examination of the IV access site is needed to appreciate signs of infection or infiltration.

To allow infusion of very hypertonic solutions (e.g., 1000 to 1500 mOsm), central venous TPN necessitates placement of a catheter at the junction of the superior vena cava and right atrium or in the inferior vena cava to minimize hyperosmolar injury.

The placement of the tip of the central venous catheter (CVC) must be documented radiographically before beginning the infusion.

INDICATIONS

Parenteral nutrition may be used as the only nutritional source or as a supplement to enteral feedings (see below).

TECHNIQUE
Fluid

Adequate caloric intake cannot be achieved with peripheral TPN at a "maintenance" fluid rate. Maintenance fluids do not equal maintenance calories. For children free of cardiovascular and renal disease, weight-specific fluid rates are given on p. 1631. As progressive increments of fluids are tolerated, the rate can be increased to provide the necessary calories while the patient is monitored closely for evidence of fluid excess (e.g., excessive weight gain or overt edema, tachycardia, increased respiratory effort, or pulmonary crackles). Remember that parenteral nutrition is not a resuscitation fluid and must not be

---

INDICATIONS FOR TPN

Short bowel syndrome
Intractable diarrhea
Respiratory distress syndrome
Surgical GI disorders
   Gastroschisis
   Malrotation with volvulus
   Diaphragmatic hernia
   Multiple intestinal atresias
   Meconium ileus and peritonitis
Pancreatitis
Intestinal pseudo-obstruction
Necrotizing enterocolitis
Trauma
Severe burns
Inflammatory bowel disease
Single or multiple organ failure
Low birthweight
Anorexia associated with chronic disease (e.g., congenital heart disease or cancer)

used for volume expansion or to replace sudden increases in stool, gastric, or urine output.

Protein

Normal protein requirements are outlined in Table 171-1. However, during stress or catabolic illness, nitrogen loss (1 g nitrogen = 6.25 g protein = 30 g wet muscle mass) can approach 20 to 25 g/day during the acute phase of the illness. Therefore increased amounts of protein are needed in critically ill patients. For efficient protein utilization in the stable patient, the ideal ratio between nonprotein calories and

Table 171-1   Age-Related Protein Requirements

Age	Protein (g/kg/day)
Term infant	2.0-2.5
Older infant	2.5-3.0
Older child	1.5-2.5
Adult	1.0-1.5

FLUID ESTIMATES FOR TPN IN CHILDREN WITHOUT CARDIOVASCULAR OR RENAL DISEASE

Initial rate

Weight (kg)	Initial fluid rate
<10	100 ml/kg/day
11-20	1000 ml + 50 ml/kg for each kilogram over 10
>20	1500 ml + 20 ml/kg for each kilogram over 20
Body surface area	1500-1800 ml/m²/day

Advancement rate

Weight (kg)	Rate of increase
<10	10 ml/kg/day (maximum = 200 ml/kg/day)
>10	10%/day (maximum = 4 L/day)

---

grams of nitrogen is 150:1 to 200:1. In critically ill patients the ratio may need to be as low as 100:1 to 125:1.

Energy

Energy (calorie) requirements depend on age, diagnosis, and metabolic stress. For children, caloric needs must provide for basal metabolism and growth. Estimates for additional caloric requirements (e.g., wound healing, recovery from malnutrition, and the hypercatabolism of sepsis, multiple organ dysfunction, and trauma) may be twice basal needs.

Fat

IV lipid emulsions are a safe, concentrated energy source. Their availability and current formulation have virtually eliminated essential fatty acid deficiency as a complication of parenteral nutrition and enabled provision of a mixed calorie source through a peripheral vein. Without previous knowledge of the extent of lipid tolerance, lipid infusions are initiated at a rate of 0.5 to 1.0 g/kg/day and increased by 0.5 g/kg/day to 4 g/kg/day, ideally approaching 30% to 50% of total calories as fat if lipid tolerance and satisfactory plasma triglyceride levels are documented. To prevent bacterial or fungal contamination, only the 24-hour allotment of lipid hangs at the bedside.

ESTIMATED CALORIC REQUIREMENTS

Basal requirements

Age (yr)	kcal/kg/day
0-1	90-120
1-7	75-90
8-12	60-75
13-18	30-60

Increased requirements

Diagnosis	Calories (% increase over base)
Cardiac failure	10-25
Burns	Up to 100
Growth failure	50-100
Malnutrition	50-100
Multiple trauma	25-50

Carbohydrate

The protein-sparing qualities of glucose have been well established over the past 30 years. The monohydrate form of IV glucose used in TPN provides 3.4 kcal/g compared with 3.74 kcal/g for nonhydrated carbohydrate, which is generally used in enteral nutrition. A glucose concentration >12.5% must be delivered through a central vein. The initial glucose infusion rate is 4 to 6 mg/kg/min and can be increased over a few days to a more ideal rate of 8 to 10 mg/kg/min. Higher infusion rates (12 to 15 mg/kg/min) can be tolerated with gradual increases in the infusion rate but may result in significant hyperglycemia (glucose >300 mg/dl) if the increase is too rapid; therefore patients must be monitored carefully.

Hyperglycemia and hypoglycemia may develop in critically ill patients, in large part from alterations in carbohydrate metabolism during stress. Enhanced glucose uptake, likely associated with alterations in specific, noninsulin-responsive glucose transporter functions, occurs in many of the tissues involved in the immune response. Increased glucose use likely results from enhanced glycolysis, which occurs in response to increased metabolic demands. Increased gluconeogenesis and depressed glycogen production,

likely mediated by stress hormones (e.g., glucagon or epinephrine) and cytokines (e.g., tumor necrosis factor), maintain glucose availability to tissues. Finally, relative insulin resistance likely results from alterations in intracellular glucose metabolism or impairment of noninsulin-mediated glucose uptake in tissues.

Vitamins, Minerals, and Trace Elements

Vitamins serve as cofactors to many metabolic pathways and are necessary for critically ill patients. The exact requirements for children under stressed conditions are uncertain. Most vitamin supplements for IV use provide at least the minimum (RDA) recommended daily allowance for children, although this may be insufficient in some patients. Table 171-2 provides a comparison of the RDA in children and adults for the vitamins provided by a commonly used IV supplement. Note that vitamin K is not included in the adult vitamin supplement (MVI-12). In the occasional child receiving anticoagulant therapy who requires IV nutrition, MVI-12 is substituted for MVI-Pediatric.

The requirements of sodium, potassium, chloride,

Table 171-2 Daily Vitamin Requirements and Provisions

| Vitamin | Age <12 Years | | Age 12 Years Through Adulthood | |
	RDA*	MVI-Pediatric (5 ml ampule)	RDA*	Multivitamin Infusion (MVI-12)
A (μg RE)†	375-1000	700	1000	1000
D (μg)‡	10	10	10	5
E (mg α-TE)§	3-10	7	10	10
K (μg)	5-30	200	10	NA
Ascorbic acid (mg)	30-50	80	60	100
Thiamine (mg)	0.3-1.0	1.2	1.0-1.5	3
Riboflavin (mg)	0.4-1.2	1.4	1.2-1.7	3.6
Niacin (mg)	5-17	17	17-20	40
Pyridoxine (mg)	0.3-1.7	1	1.7-2.0	4
Cyanocobalamin (μg)	0.03-2.0	1	2	5
Folic acid	25-150	140	200	400
Pantothenic acid (mg)	2-4	NA	4-7	15
Biotin (μg)	10-20	20	20-100	60

*National Research Council, Recommended Dietary Allowance, revised 1989.
†RE = retinol equivalents; 1 RE = 1 μg retinol or 6 μg β-carotene = 0.3 IU.
‡As cholecalciferol; 10 μg cholecalciferol = 400 IU vitamin D.
§TE = tocopherol equivalents; 1 mg *d*-α-tocopherol = 1 α-TE; 0.74 × *d*-α-tocopherol = 1 mg *dl*-α-tocopherol = 1 IU vitamin E.

magnesium, calcium, and phosphorus are based on summation of the child's maintenance requirements and ongoing losses. If the child has significant ongoing loss (e.g., diarrhea, gastric, or renal loss), a separate, individually tailored replacement fluid can be used and maintenance needs provided in the TPN fluid. The recommended daily intake of electrolytes and other minerals is noted in Table 171-3.

Trace elements known to be essential in humans include iron, zinc, copper, chromium, selenium, iodine, and cobalt. As with vitamins, requirements for trace elements during periods of stress are unknown. Patients with increased GI losses are susceptible to zinc deficiency and may need additional supplementation. Iron is not routinely added to parenteral nutrition fluids because it may affect the stability of other components. IV trace elements are commercially available and are incorporated into the parenteral nutrition regimen, although modifications are necessary for patients with renal and hepatic failure.

Drug Compatibility

In children with limited venous access, nonnutritive solutions such as drugs are given through the CVC. A partial list of compatible medications is given in the next column. In most circumstances the lipid is temporarily discontinued and the catheter below the in-line of the lipid is flushed. The drug is administered below the in-line for the lipid to prevent inappropriate drug-lipid binding. Consultation with a clinical pharmacist is advised before any drug is given along with the TPN.

Ordering TPN

Most institutions have standard infusion protocols or order forms for peripheral and central infusions.

Table 171-3 Recommended Daily Intake of Electrolytes and Minerals for TPN Solutions

Element	Daily Amount
Sodium	2-4 mEq/kg
Potassium	2-3 mEq/kg
Chloride	2-3 mEq/kg
Magnesium	0.25-0.5 mEq/kg
Calcium gluconate	100-500 mg/kg
Phosphorous	1-2 mmol/kg

These "standard" infusions are modified based on the child's needs and tolerance of the infusion. Fluid restriction from renal, cardiac, or hepatic insufficiency, common in critically ill patients, can reduce the nutritional benefit from TPN. Also, the nutritional infusion is often only a fraction of the child's total fluids because of infusions of antibiotics or pressure-support medications. Trace elements are added to all TPN solutions; however, copper is removed and manganese reduced in the TPN infusion for patients with cholestasis (e.g., TPN-related liver disease or primary liver disease) because these potentially hepatotoxic trace elements are poorly excreted from the liver.

In patients who receive TPN for an extended period (e.g., months) or who may be discharged with TPN, the 24-hour infusion can be "cycled" to be infused over 10 to 18 hours. It often takes 3 or 4 days to cycle the infusion, and tolerance varies depending on the rate of carbohydrate infusion, energy needs, and age of the patient. The infusion can be started at the prescribed rate, but the rate is decreased by 50% during the last hour of infusion to prevent hypoglycemia, which can develop with abrupt discontinuation of a carbohydrate infusion >15 mg/kg/min.

Consultation with PICU pharmacy support personnel is useful to assist with questions about TPN composition and medications that are compatible with the infusion.

Monitoring

Specific indices must be monitored to assess clinical progress and to prevent complications if possible

---

PARTIAL LIST OF DRUGS COMPATIBLE WITH AMINO ACID/DEXTROSE/MINERAL COMPONENT OF TPN

Ampicillin	Ranitidine
Carbenicillin	Furosemide
Cefazolin	Heparin
Clindamycin	Hydrocortisone
Cloxacillin	Regular insulin
Gentamicin	Methyldopa
Tobramycin	Methylprednisolone
Cimetidine	Phenobarbitol

Table 171-4 Monitoring Variables in Pediatric Patients Receiving TPN

Variable	Monitoring Frequency
Weight	Daily
Clinical assessment (hydration, alertness)	Daily (minimum)
Height, length, and head circumference	Every 4 weeks
Electrolytes, BUN, glucose, complete blood cell count	Before starting TPN, then weekly
AST, ALT, GGT, Ca, phosphorus, albumin	Before starting TPN, then every 14 days
Triglycerides	Daily until tolerance reached
Urine glucose	Each void for 48 hours, then daily

(Table 171-4). Often the underlying illness dictates the frequency of laboratory measurements. In those patients for whom frequent adjustments of the TPN are necessary, more frequent monitoring is needed compared with that in stable patients receiving long-term TPN.

RISKS AND COMPLICATIONS
Catheter-Related Complications

Complications associated with the CVC can arise from catheter insertion and ongoing use. Those complications related to insertion of the catheter are similar to those associated with the placement of any CVC (see Chapter 131). Venous thrombosis occurs more frequently with polyvinylchloride catheters than with Silastic catheters. Heparin, 1 unit/ml, is used to prevent venous thrombosis, but its value is often debated. Occlusion of the CVC may reflect deposit of fibrin, lipid, or amorphous debris within the catheter or at the catheter tip. Urokinase and streptokinase have been used successfully to dissolve fibrin clot. Ethanol has been used in cases of catheter occlusion from suspected lipid deposits. Hydrochloric acid (0.1 M) is suggested if the amorphous debris is composed of calcium salts.

Catheter-related infections can present as cellulitis at the catheter site or as fever, with or without bacteremia, without an obvious primary source. Subtle signs of sepsis include hyperglycemia or hyperlipidemia in a patient who had previously tolerated the infusion. In all patients receiving TPN through a CVC in whom a systemic infection is suspected, blood for culturing is drawn from the CVC and peripheral vein. Organisms most often responsible for sepsis include *Staphylococcus aureus, Staphylococcus epidermidis,*

CATHETER-RELATED COMPLICATIONS

Insertion	*Prolonged use*
Pneumothorax	Vein thrombosis
Hemothorax	Occlusion
Injury to blood vessel	Migration
Air embolism	Infection
Cardiac perforation	Catheter fracture
Horner's syndrome	
Phrenic nerve paralysis	

Escherichia coli, Enterococcus, and *Candida* species. The catheter can be preserved in some cases if appropriate antibiotics are infused through it. The catheter must invariably be removed in patients with *Candida* sepsis.

Treatment of CVC occlusion

1. Suspected fibrin clot—partial occlusion:
   a. Aseptically instill urokinase (5000 U/ml) to fill the CVC (1 to 2 ml).
   b. Allow 30-minute dwell time.
   c. Aspirate 3 to 5 ml of blood. If not easily obtained, allow 30 more minutes of dwell time.
   d. If still unsuccessful, repeat procedure in 2 hours with fresh urokinase and 3-hour dwell time.
   e. A low-dose urokinase infusion (100 to 200 U/kg/hr) for 24 hours has been used safely.
2. Suspected fibrin clot—complete occlusion:
   a. Sterile technique is needed for this procedure.
   b. Prime a 22-gauge cutdown catheter with urokinase (5000 U/ml).

c. Thread the cutdown catheter into the CVC until resistance is met, but no further than the point where the CVC exits the skin.

d. Instill urokinase until the solution is noted at the hub of the CVC and gradually withdraw the cutdown catheter while infusing urokinase.

e. Allow dwell time of 1 hour before attempting to aspirate 3 to 5 ml of blood.

f. If no blood return is obtained, repeat the procedure with newly reconstituted urokinase and allow dwell time of 4 hours.

g. If successful, aspirate and discard 3 to 5 ml of blood, flush the line with 10 ml of 0.9% sodium chloride solution, and heparin lock the CVC or reconnect to infusion.

3. Suspected occlusion from precipitate formation:

   a. Draw 0.5 ml of 0.1 normal hydrochloric acid into a 1.0 ml syringe.

   b. Aseptically attach the 1.0 ml syringe with 0.1 normal hydrochloric acid to the catheter hub.

   c. Alternate gently pushing and pulling on the plunger for up to 5 minutes.

   d. Once blood return is visualized, clamp the CVC and remove the syringe.

   e. Place an empty 5 ml syringe onto the CVC and aspirate 3 to 5 ml.

   f. Reclamp the CVC and replace the blood-filled syringe with a 10 ml syringe filled with 0.9% sodium chloride solution.

   g. Unclamp the CVC and flush with normal 0.9% sodium chloride solution and heparin lock the CVC or reconnect to infusion.

4. Suspected lipid occlusion:

   a. Break alcohol ampules (dehydrated alcohol injection [USP]) and withdraw 1.5 ml into a 5 ml syringe and then withdraw 0.5 ml of sterile water into the same syringe. This will result in 2 ml of 75% alcohol.

   b. Aseptically attach the syringe containing 2 ml of 75% alcohol to the CVC. When instillation meets resistance, use a repetitive push-pull action on the syringe plunger to maximize solution mixing within the catheter.

   c. Clamp the catheter for 1 hour and aspirate catheter contents.

   d. If resistance has not improved, a second attempt with 75% alcohol may be tried with a dwell time of up to 6 hours.

   e. If resistance has not improved, a third attempt with 75% alcohol may be tried, with a dwell time of up to 16 hours.

   f. If full catheter patency is achieved, aspirate 3 to 5 ml of blood, flush the CVC with 10 ml of 0.9% sodium

Table 171-5 Metabolic Complications Associated With TPN

Complication	Possible Cause
Hyperglycemia	Excessive rate of infusion
	Metabolic stress
	Sepsis
Hypoglycemia	Sudden discontinuation of glucose
Electrolyte abnormalities	Excess loss
Mineral abnormalities	Bowel disease
Trace element abnormalities	Renal disease
	Medication
	Refeeding syndrome
	Excessive infusion
Hypertriglyceridemia	Metabolic stress
	Sepsis
	Pancreatitis
	Multiple trauma
Cholestasis	Prematurity
	Abdominal surgery
	TPN infusion >14 days
	Abdominal sepsis (necrotizing enterocolitis or perforation)
	(?) Protein infusion
	(?) Rate of carbohydrate infusion
	(?) Lipid infusion

chloride solution, and heparin lock the CVC or reconnect to infusion.

Metabolic Complications

The frequency of metabolic complications related to TPN depends on the type and severity of the underlying illness and the nutritional status of the patient. The most common complications and their possible causes are listed in Table 171-5.

Hyperglycemia is associated with either relative peripheral insulin resistance (e.g., sepsis or metabolic stress) or too rapid advancement of the glucose infusion. Hypoglycemia can result from too rapid cessation of the carbohydrate infusion.

Alterations in mineral concentrations result from either inadequate or excessive intake. Increased loss of these elements may be due to disease (e.g., inflammatory bowel disease, chronic diarrhea, malabsorption, or renal tubular injury) or medications (e.g., diuretics, amphotericin, aminoglycosides, or liquid antacids). Hypokalemia and hypophosphatemia have been associated with too rapid nutritional resuscitation ("refeeding syndrome").

Hypertriglyceridemia is associated with sepsis, pancreatitis, renal insufficiency, and insufficient endothelial lipoprotein lipase activity that occur during metabolic stress. Essential fatty acid deficiency has been virtually eliminated with regular fat infusions of at least 1 g/kg for 2 or 3 days a week.

Cholestasis (decreased bile flow) can be a serious complication of TPN. The cause likely is multifactorial and related to protein infusion, prematurity, abdominal surgery, and duration of TPN infusion. Serum bile acids are likely the first biochemical variable to be elevated, but they may not be routinely measured in many institutions. Elevation of serum γ-glutamyl transpeptidase may be more sensitive than aminotransferase or bilirubin levels for early detection of cholestasis. Although biochemical measurements of liver injury may return to normal after discontinuation or cycling of the TPN, histologic evidence of injury (e.g., fibrosis or cirrhosis) may persist. Despite efforts to prevent liver injury, end-stage liver disease can result from prolonged TPN.

ADDITIONAL READING

Benjamin DR. Laboratory tests and nutritional assessment. Pediatr Clin North Am 36:139-161, 1989.

Elia M. Changing concepts of nutritional requirements in disease: Implications for artificial nutritional support. Lancet 345:1279-1284, 1995.

Lelieko NS, Luder E, Fridman M, Fersel J, Benkov K. Nutritional assessment of pediatric patients admitted to an acute-care pediatric service utilizing anthropometric measurements. J Parenter Enter Nutr 10:166-168, 1986.

Mitton SG. Amino acids and lipid in total parenteral nutrition for the newborn. J Pediatr Gastroenterol Nutr 18:25-31, 1994.

Payne-James JJ, Khwawja HT. First choice for total parenteral nutrition: The peripheral route. J Parenter Enter Nutr 12:468-478, 1993.

Pennington CR. Review article: Towards safer parenteral nutrition. Aliment Pharmacol Ther 4:427-441, 1990.

Weinsier RL, Drumdieck CL. Death resulting from overzealous total parenteral nutrition: The refeeding syndrome revisited. Am J Clin Nutr 34:393-399, 1981.

Zoltkin SH, Stallings VA, Pencharz PB. Total parenteral nutrition in children. Pediatr Clin North Am 32:381-400, 1985.

172 Total Enteral Nutrition

Robert H. Squires, Jr. · *Charles E. Mize*

BACKGROUND AND INDICATIONS

Total enteral nutrition (TEN) allows infusion of nutrition directly into the stomach or small intestine. TEN stimulates intrinsic and humoral factors that enhance mucosal integrity and healing. This method of nutritional support is most useful when the child cannot or will not take adequate oral feedings and when the GI tract is functional (If the gut works, use it!).

Ingested macronutrients undergo luminal degradation into absorbable components. The digestive process continues at the mucosal surface, where disaccharidases and peptidases further reduce their specific substrates to monosaccharides and peptides. Specialized transport mechanisms located on the mucosal surface of mature enterocytes allow absorption of salt, water, carbohydrates, peptides, fats, vitamins, and micronutrients.

An intact and healthy intestinal mucosa creates a highly selective barrier to injurious substances. Gastric acid and digestive enzymes provide an initial deterrent to the colonization of bacteria and fungi. Other physical barriers include intestinal mucus and intact tight junctions between cells, which help prevent bacterial translocation to nearby lymph nodes or the liver. In addition, a versatile and effective intestinal immune system provides additional mucosal protection.

Intestinal Adaptation

Stem cells, located near the base of each crypt of Lieberkühn, provide a constant source of immature enterocytes. Over the 5 to 7 days needed for enterocyte migration to the villus tip, the cell undergoes a number of maturational processes that distinguish crypt cells from villus cells. Crypt cells secrete chloride and are not involved in the absorptive process. In contrast, mature villus cells absorb salt, water, glucose, amino acids, and low molecular weight peptides, fatty acids, and monoglycerides, in addition to other nutrients and xenobiotic chemicals. Differences in disaccharidase concentration are noted along the villus; maltase dominates the base of the villus, and lactase is found in greater quantity at the villus tip.

A number of growth factors affect mucosal structure and function. Gastrin and enteroglucagon stimulate mucosal growth and proliferation. Growth hormone and thyroxine (T_4) are important not only in the developing intestinal tract but also in the recovering intestine. Hepatobiliary, pancreatic, and intestinal secretions contain transforming growth factor α, epidermal growth factor, trefoil peptides, and insulin-like growth factor, all of which may influence the development and maturation of the intestinal mucosa. In addition, a number of dietary factors such as short-chain fatty acids, disaccharides, and peptides enhance mucosal recovery. Although denervation of the mucosa may lead to mucosal atrophy, the role of neurogenic influences on mucosal adaptation remains uncertain.

Effect of Critical Illness on GI Tract

Intestinal structure and function are altered as a consequence of direct enterocyte injury, toxin, mucosal invasion, and malnutrition. Rotavirus, an example of direct cell injury, attacks mature absorptive villus tip cells, which results in water-loss diarrhea. Although well tolerated by most healthy children, rotavirus infection can have a devastating effect in malnourished infants. Bacterial toxins affect production of cAMP and cGMP to either increase secretion, decrease absorption, or both, which results in a high volume of watery diarrhea that contains neither blood nor leukocytes. Organisms such as *Shigella, Salmonella,* and enteroinvasive *Escherichia coli* invade the mucosa to produce a symptom complex of fever, abdominal cramps, tenesmus, and bloody diarrhea that contains mucus and leukocytes.

CAUSES OF INTESTINAL MUCOSAL INJURY

Enterocyte injury

Rotavirus
Norwalk-like agent
Giardia

Enterotoxin production

Cholera
Escherichia coli
Staphylococcus aureus
Shigella

Mucosal invasion

Salmonella
Shigella
Clostridium difficile
Amebiasis
Protein allergy

Malnutrition

Fasting status
Hypermetabolism (e.g., trauma, sepsis)
Malabsorption (e.g., pancreatitis)
Inflammatory bowel disease, fistula
Anorexia
Multiple organ dysfunction
Ileus

Starvation alone can result in substantial mucosal alterations. The total weight of the small bowel is dramatically reduced. Crypts and villi become smaller as crypt cell production is reduced and the cell cycle prolonged. Increased intestinal permeability to macromolecules and peptides occurs. When starvation is complicated by hypermetabolism associated with critical illness, the consequences can be devastating, with increased risks for sepsis, delayed wound healing, and altered hormonal responses to stress.

Effect of Critical Illness on General Metabolism

Hypermetabolism is common in the PICU and can cause significant morbidity and mortality. Clinical characteristics include increased oxygen consumption and cardiac output, resulting in increased energy expenditure. Increased use of carbohydrate, protein, and fat as energy substrates occurs concomitantly with increased nitrogen loss in the urine. A primary decrease in systemic vascular resistance occurs. These metabolic and physiologic alterations can resolve over 3 or 4 days if resuscitation and treatment are sufficient. However, a more sustained state of hypermetabolism may result in multiple organ dysfunction, depending on the previous nutritional status of the patient, the nature of the insult, the type of complications that develop, and the quality of the acute care provided.

TECHNIQUE

Early enteral nutritional support can improve the clinical outcome. In the seriously ill patient enteral nutrition may be hindered by gastric and intestinal hypomotility from metabolic alterations, surgery, abdominal trauma, or medications used to sedate or paralyze patients receiving assisted ventilation. However, even small volumes of luminal nutrients may improve mucosal integrity, stimulate maturation of mucosal growth factors and enzymes, and induce biliary and intestinal motility. TEN must be considered early in the course of illness to minimize the consequences of hypermetabolism and preexisting (and possibly ongoing) malnutrition.

Nutrient Requirements

The recommended dietary allowances (RDA) are used as guidelines for enteral nutrition. The RDA (Table 172-1) are estimated to meet or exceed the requirements (except for energy) in 95% of healthy persons and therefore ensure that the needs of most of the population are met; however, they may not meet the requirements for children affected by disease states or medications.

Route of Enteral Feeding

The physiologic responses generated by the smell, taste, and texture of a meal cannot be simulated by direct enteric feeding (e.g., nasogastric, gastrostomy, or jejunostomy tube). If the patient is capable of oral feeding but incapable of taking sufficient calories because of anorexia or weakness, supplemental nasoenteric feeding is recommended.

INDICATIONS FOR ENTERAL SUPPORT

Nasogastric tube

Nutritional needs not met by oral intake
  Anorexia associated with chronic illness
  Short bowel syndrome
  Prematurity
  Protracted diarrhea of infancy
  Swallowing dysfunction
  Crohn's disease
  Gastroesophageal reflux
Prevent hypoglycemia associated with overnight
  fasting
  Glycogen storage disease
  Peroxisomal enzyme defect
  Diverse other genetic-metabolic diseases

Gastrostomy tube

Esophageal obstruction
Complications from nasogastric tube

Jejunostomy tube

Gastric obstruction or atony
Significant risk of aspiration

Nasogastric feeding is indicated for complete or supplemental enteral nutritional support for the patient who is incapable of taking adequate calories by mouth. The ease of placement and low cost make the nasogastric tube the initial method of choice for direct enteral feeding. A soft, polyurethane or silicone nasogastric tube should replace the "plasticized" polyvinylchloride or polyethylene tube used primarily for drainage. The polyurethane tube has a larger internal diameter than a similarly sized silicone tube. These soft tubes can last a month before being changed. Verify placement of the feeding tube within the stomach before initiating feeding; esophageal tube placement predisposes to aspiration of the feeding. While some suggest placement of a gastrostomy tube if enteric feedings are anticipated for longer than 4 to 6 weeks, nasogastric tubes can be used safely for years.

Gastrostomy tubes, placed either surgically or endoscopically, are indicated in patients with complete esophageal obstruction or if complications such as recurrent sinusitis, nasal trauma, or discomfort from the nasogastric tube become prominent. A gastrostomy "button" can replace the bulky tube after the tract matures in 4 to 6 weeks. Experience is increasing with the use of "one-step" gastrostomy buttons.

Jejunal tubes, placed by advancing a designated nasogastric or gastrojejunostomy tube with endoscopic, fluoroscopic, or ultrasound assistance into the small intestine or surgically, are indicated in patients with gastric atony or obstruction. Pulmonary aspiration can occur with jejunal feedings. Although early jejunal feeding may be useful in adult patients with multiple trauma, studies in children are not available.

Selection of Formula

In choosing a formula it is important to first determine whether the child has unique requirements. Premature infant formulas are available for the preterm infant who needs additional calcium and phosphorus. Healthy term infants can be offered either breast milk or a standard 20 kcal/oz formula. Infants with primary or secondary disaccharidase intolerance need to be given lactose-free or sucrose-free formula. If there is evidence of protein intolerance or allergy, casein hydrolysate formulas may minimize the antigenic stimulus and thereby decrease the intestinal inflammatory response. Patients with renal, cardiac, or hepatic dysfunction often need significant fluid restriction; therefore efforts are made to increase caloric density while minimizing the solute load. Children with steatorrhea from pancreatic insufficiency (e.g., cystic fibrosis or chronic pancreatitis) or decreased intraluminal bile acid concentration (e.g., cholestasis or Crohn's disease) will benefit from a formula that contains medium-chain triglycerides (MCTs), which require minimal emulsification and are easily absorbed. MCTs contain no essential fatty acids; therefore, when using MCT-containing formulas, provide sufficient supplemental quantities of long-chain triglycerides as the source of essential fatty acids. Overall, infants with relative intestinal absorptive failure are most likely to tolerate a lactose- and sucrose-free, MCT-containing formula with a protein source of either casein hydrolysate or equivalent amino acid/peptide mixture.

Table 172-1   Food and Nutrition Board, National Academy of Sciences–National Research Council Recommended Dietary Allowances,[a] revised 1989 (designed for the maintenance of good nutrition of practically all healthy people in the United States)

Category	Age (yr) or Condition	Weight[b] kg	Weight[b] lb	Height[b] cm	Height[b] in	Protein (g)	Fat-Soluble Vitamins Vitamin A (μg RE)[c]	Fat-Soluble Vitamins Vitamin D (μg)[d]	Fat-Soluble Vitamins Vitamin E (mg α-TE)[c]	Fat-Soluble Vitamins Vitamin K (μg)
Infants	0.0-0.5	6	13	60	24	13	375	7.5	3	5
	0.5-1.0	9	20	71	28	14	375	10	4	10
Children	1-3	13	29	90	35	16	400	10	6	15
	4-6	20	44	112	44	24	500	10	7	20
	7-10	28	62	132	52	28	700	10	7	30
Males	11-14	45	99	157	62	45	1000	10	10	45
	15-18	66	145	176	69	59	1000	10	10	65
	19-24	72	160	177	70	58	1000	10	10	70
	25-50	79	174	176	70	63	1000	5	10	80
	51+	77	170	173	68	63	1000	5	10	80
Females	11-14	46	101	157	62	46	800	10	8	45
	15-18	55	120	163	64	44	800	10	8	55
	19-24	58	128	164	65	46	800	10	8	60
	25-50	63	138	163	64	50	800	5	8	65
	51+	65	143	160	63	50	800	5	8	65
Pregnant						60	800	10	10	65
Lactating	1st 6 mo					65	1300	10	12	65
	2nd 6 mo					62	1200	10	11	65

[a]The allowances, expressed as average daily intakes over time, are intended to provide for individual variations among most normal persons as they live in the United States under usual environmental stresses. Diets should be based on a variety of common foods in order to provide other nutrients for which human requirements have been less well defined.
[b]Weights and heights of reference adults are actual medians for the U.S. population of the designated age, as reported by NHANES II. The median weights and heights of those under 19 years of age were taken from Hamill PVV, Drizd TA, Johnson CL, Reed RB, Rache AF, Moore WM. Physical growth: National Center for Health Statistics percentile. Am J Clin Nutr 32:607-629, 1979. The use of these figures does not imply that the height-to-weight ratios are ideal.

Breast milk and commonly used infant formulas and enteral feedings are listed in Table 172-2. If given in sufficient quantity to meet energy needs, breast milk or formula will usually provide adequate vitamins and minerals. Breast milk may be obtained by manual or pump expression. If refrigerated, it must be used within 24 hours; if frozen, it can be used for up to 4 months with preservation of nutrients and many desirable immunologic properties, but unless frozen under tightly controlled conditions, freezing inactivates intact leukocytes. Breast-fed infants must receive vitamin D, iron, and fluoride supplements.

The decision to initiate feedings with a full-strength or diluted formula is often left to personal preference. However, even in the injured or shortened intestine, full-strength formula delivered at a slow infusion rate is tolerated in most infants. Healthy infants will voluntarily consume formula to meet their caloric needs but not necessarily their fluid needs. For example, the infant will take twice as much of a 10 kcal/oz formula than a standard 20 kcal/oz formula and less of a 30 kcal/oz formula to achieve the necessary daily calories. Delayed gastric emptying is noted with formulas that have either high osmolarity or increased caloric density (e.g., >24

Water-Soluble Vitamins							Minerals						
Vita-min C (mg)	Thia-min (mg)	Ribo-flavin (mg)	Niacin (mg NE)[f]	Vita-min B$_6$ (mg)	Folate (μg)	Vita-min B$_{12}$ (μg)	Cal-cium (mg)	Phos-pho-rus (mg)	Magne-sium (mg)	Iron (mg)	Zinc (mg)	Iodine (μg)	Sele-nium (μg)
30	0.3	0.4	5	0.3	25	0.3	400	300	40	6	5	40	10
35	0.4	0.5	6	0.6	35	0.5	600	500	60	10	5	50	15
40	0.7	0.8	9	1.0	50	0.7	800	800	80	10	10	70	20
45	0.9	1.1	12	1.1	75	1.0	800	800	120	10	10	90	20
45	1.0	1.2	13	1.4	100	1.4	800	800	170	10	10	120	30
50	1.3	1.5	17	1.7	150	2.0	1200	1200	270	12	15	150	40
60	1.5	1.8	20	2.0	200	2.0	1200	1200	400	12	15	150	50
60	1.5	1.7	19	2.0	200	2.0	1200	1200	350	10	15	150	70
60	1.5	1.7	19	2.0	200	2.0	800	800	350	10	15	150	70
60	1.2	1.4	15	2.0	200	2.0	800	800	350	10	15	150	70
50	1.1	1.3	15	1.4	150	2.0	1200	1200	280	15	12	150	45
60	1.1	1.3	15	1.5	180	2.0	1200	1200	300	15	12	150	50
60	1.1	1.3	15	1.6	180	2.0	1200	1200	280	15	12	150	55
60	1.1	1.3	15	1.6	180	2.0	800	800	280	15	12	150	55
60	1.0	1.2	13	1.6	180	2.0	800	800	280	10	12	150	55
70	1.5	1.6	17	2.2	400	2.2	1200	1200	320	30	15	175	65
95	1.6	1.8	20	2.1	280	2.6	1200	1200	355	15	19	200	75
90	1.6	1.7	20	2.1	260	2.6	1200	1200	340	15	16	200	75

[c]Retinol equivalents, 1 retinol equivalent = 1 μg retinol or 6 μg β-carotene.
[d]As cholecalciferol, 10 μg cholecalciferol = 400 IU of vitamin D.
[e]α-Tocopherol equivalents, 1 mg d-α-tocopherol = 1 α-TE.
[f]1 NE (niacin equivalent) = 1 mg of niacin or 60 mg of dietary tryptophan.

kcal/oz). Thus there is little need to concentrate the formula of a child who tolerates the volume needed to provide adequate calories and is not fluid restricted or needs a small-volume feeding.

Most formulas for tube feeding, designed for adults, are often used for children older than 1 year. Because the volume consumed by a child is less than that of an adult, vitamin and mineral intake may be inadequate. Individual evaluation of nutritional adequacy of adult formulas is therefore necessary. More recently, enteral formulas for infants and children have become available. These newer pediatric formulas have a lower osmolarity, and some incorpo-rate nutrients (e.g., carnitine, nucleotides, and short-chain fatty acids) that may reduce the consequences of acute and chronic illness and hypermetabolism.

Bolus vs. Continuous Feeding

If the intestinal tract is thought to be healthy and un-stressed, the initial feeding can be provided as a bo-lus infusion over 15 to 30 minutes every 4 hours at volumes that will provide individualized fluid needs. Regurgitation may be prevented by allowing the pa-tient to remain in a sitting position 20 to 30 minutes after a feeding. Burping is encouraged after the feed-ing if the child's condition permits. If this volume is

Table 172-2   Commonly Used Formulas*

Product	Formula (per 100 ml)				
	kcal	Protein (g)	Carbo-hydrate (g)	Fat (g)	mOsm/ kg H$_2$O
Breast milk (mature human milk)	71	1.1	7.2	4.6	NA
Casein protein–based formulas: lactose-containing					
Pediatric formulas					
Similac	68	1.5	7.2	3.6	300
Enfamil	68	1.5	7	3.8	300
Good Start (partially hydrolyzed whey)	68	1.6	7.4	3.4	265
Gerber	68	1.5	7.3	3.7	320
SMA	67	1.5	7.2	3.6	300
PM 60/40	68	1.6	6.9	3.8	280
Enfamil Premature	81	2.4	8.9	4.1	300
Similac Special Care	81	2.2	8.5	4.3	280
Next Step	67	1.7	7.4	3.4	270
Adult formulas that can be used in children					
Compleat (blenderized food containing milk)	107	4.3	13	4.3	450
Casein–based formulas: lactose free					
Pediatric formulas					
Lactofree (milk protein isolate)	68	1.5	7	3.7	200
Portagen (86% MCT)	68	2.4	7.8	3.3	220
Pediasure (with or without fiber)	100	3	11	5	310
Kindercal (contains fiber; 20% MCT)	106	3.4	13.5	4.4	Isotonic
Follow-Up (milk-based, but no lactose)	67	1.7	8.8	2.7	N/A
Adult formulas that can be used in children					
Lipisorb (86% MCT)	135	4.6	15.4	6.4	432
Osmolite (good for tube feeding)	106	3.7	14.3	3.8	300
Isocal (good for tube feeding)	106	3.4	13.5	4.4	270
Nubasics (also Nubasics soup and chocolate bars)	100	3.5	13.2	3.7	520
Jevity (with or without fiber)	106	4.4	15	3.6	310
Ensure (with or without fiber; many flavors)	106	3.7	14.3	3.7	470
Sustacal (no fiber; contains sugar)	100	6.1	13.9	2.3	650
Compleat Modified (blenderized foods)	107	4.3	14.1	3.7	300

*Formulas for infants (<1 yr) in bold print; other pediatric formulas are for toddlers (>1 yr) and young children only.

173 Gastroenterology Procedures

Robert H. Squires, Jr.

BACKGROUND AND INDICATIONS

Rapid advances in fiberoptic technology have led to the development of smaller, more versatile endoscopes adapted for use in children. Use of these and other tools to aid in diagnosis and management of GI disorders has increased substantially over the past 10 years. The decision to initiate any procedure can be guided by the following questions: Can the procedure be performed safely? Will the results of the procedure alter therapy? Do the potential risks of the procedure outweigh the potential benefits? This chapter addresses the issues of safety, indications, and risks of various GI procedures.

Sedation

The goals of sedation are to ensure patient safety, provide analgesia and amnesia, control behavior during the procedure, enable successful completion of the procedure, and return the patient to pretreatment level of consciousness. These goals can be accomplished with oral or IV sedation or general anesthesia, depending on the procedure and the condition of the patient.

Proper patient selection is critical to ensure safety of the procedure. After the patient and family are properly informed of the potential risks and benefits of sedation, dietary guidelines for food and fluid intake before the procedure are outlined (Table 173-1). Each patient undergoes a thorough evaluation, including a health history (e.g., allergies, previous experience with sedation or general anesthesia, and current and previous medical problems) and physical examination with attention to any potential airway problems.

For simple procedures that do not require analgesia, an oral sedative may reduce patient anxiety and provide amnesia. Drug combinations with both an amnesic and an analgesic are preferred when pain

---

ASA PHYSICAL STATUS CLASSIFICATION

Class I   Normally healthy patient
Class II   Patient with mild systemic disease
Class III   Patient with severe systemic disease
Class IV   Patient with severe systemic disease that is a constant threat to life
Class V   Moribund patient not expected to survive without surgery

---

Table 173-1 NPO Guidelines for IV Sedation

Age (mo)	Fluids or Food Allowed	Amount	Time Before Procedure (hr)
<1	Clear liquids (e.g., Pedialyte, breast milk)	Usual feeding	2-3
1-12	Clear liquids	≤8 ml/kg	3
	Formula or solid food	Any	6
>12	Clear liquids	Any	3-4
	Milk	Any	6
	Food	Any	6-8

Table 173-2   Characteristics of Commonly Used Medications for Sedation

Drug	Route	Dose (mg/kg)	Onset (min)	Peak (min)	Duration (hr)
Narcotic					
Meperidine	IV	1-2	5-10	5-10	2-4
Fentanyl	IV	0.001-0.002	0.5	2	Variable
Benzodiazepine					
Diazepam	IV	0.5-0.15	1-2	1-2	0.25-1
Midazolam	IV	0.5-0.10	1	1	1-3
Sedative-hypnotic-neuroleptic					
Chloral hydrate	PO only	25-100	15-60		4-11
Phenergan	IM	1	20	120	4-7
Thorazine	IM	1	30	60	3-30
	IV	0.05	1-2		2-4
Propofol	IV	2	1	(for anesthesia use only)	

or discomfort is anticipated (Table 173-2). The decision to use general anesthesia is generally based on objective criteria such as diagnosis, respiratory compromise, and the patient's general condition as classified by American Society of Anesthesiologists (ASA) criteria. For ASA class III, IV, or V, sedation is managed by an anesthesiologist or attending intensivist.

Monitoring

Personnel experienced in the care of sedated children and age-appropriate equipment are critical to ensure the safety of a child who undergoes a GI procedure. A time-based record, similar to that kept by an anesthesiologist during a surgical procedure, is used to document the child's level of consciousness, vital signs, oxygen saturation, and medication record. The endoscopist cannot be responsible for monitoring the clinical status of the patient during the procedure; an assistant, preferably one experienced with pediatric airway management, monitors and cares for the child during the procedure.

DIAGNOSTIC PROCEDURES
Esophagogastroduodenoscopy
Indications

Esophagogastroduodenoscopy (EGD) is generally indicated in the patient with active, persistent, recurrent, or hemodynamically significant upper intestinal hemorrhage. The evaluation of dysphagia, odyno-

phagia, refusal to eat, or persistent noncardiac chest pain may be aided by EGD to rule out viral, fungal, allergic, or peptic esophagitis. EGD can be used to evaluate upper abdominal pain, but only when there are signs or symptoms that suggest serious organic disease (e.g., weight loss, anemia, or anorexia), when it is associated with significant morbidity (e.g., school absenteeism or limitation of usual activities), or when the distress persists despite a course of therapy for suspected acid peptic disease. EGD is useful to evaluate each patient with known or suspected ingestion of a caustic material to look for evidence of esophageal injury. Intestinal graft-vs.-host disease, which develops after bone marrow transplantation, can be diagnosed with an endoscopic intestinal biopsy, as can graft rejection in patients who have received a small intestinal transplant.

EGD likely would not provide useful information in patients with uncomplicated gastroesophageal reflux or functional abdominal pain. EGD is not indicated in patients with congenital hypertrophic pyloric stenosis or a perforated viscus.

Technique

To minimize fear and anxiety, the patient and family must be fully informed of not only the risks and benefits of the procedure but also the technique that will be followed.

Newer, smaller, flexible fiberoptic endoscopes are

now used in infants and children, and the external diameter of these newer endoscopes permits their use in neonates. Larger endoscopes are necessary to allow the use of large biopsy forceps and some therapeutic instruments (e.g., heater probe and through-the-scope balloon dilator). Each instrument has different optic and flexibility qualities. "Therapeutic" endoscopes with large dual suction and biopsy channels are available for use in adolescents and adults.

With the patient adequately sedated and positioned, the endoscope can be passed under direct visualization or "blindly" into the proximal esophagus. Characteristics of the esophageal mucosa are noted. Once in the stomach the endoscope is advanced along the greater curve to the antrum. The pylorus is kept in full view, and gentle pressure may be needed to pass beyond the pyloric channel into the duodenal bulb. Some patients may cough or gag at this point, but these symptoms abate when the scope is advanced into the third portion of the duodenum.

As the endoscope is withdrawn, the tip is moved to carefully inspect the entire surface of the duodenum. Once back in the stomach the scope is maneuvered to visualize the lesser curve, fundus, and cardia. After careful inspection of the gastric mucosa and removal of air and fluid, the endoscope is removed.

Mucosal biopsy specimens are obtained from all suspicious lesions. However, even if the mucosal pattern appears normal, biopsy specimens from the duodenum, antrum, and esophagus can identify mucosal eosinophilia, *Giardia, Cryptosporidium,* and *Helicobacter pylori* in otherwise normal-appearing mucosa.

Risks and complications

EGD is safe when performed by an endoscopist experienced with the procedure in children. Potential problems related to the procedure include perforation of the pharynx, esophagus, stomach, or duodenum, mucosal bleeding, duodenal hematoma, and compromise of the airways. Problems related to IV sedation include hypoxemia, hypercarbia, inadequate sedation, and idiosyncratic reaction to the medication.

Colonoscopy or Flexible Sigmoidoscopy
Indications

Colonoscopy is generally indicated to evaluate inflammatory bowel disease, unexplained hematochezia or iron-deficiency anemia, and clinically significant diarrhea. It is useful to evaluate a clinically significant abnormality found during barium contrast studies (e.g., filling defect or stricture).

Colonoscopy is generally not indicated in patients with acute, self-limited diarrhea, constipation and encopresis, or intestinal bleeding from a demonstrated upper intestinal source. It is contraindicated in patients with fulminant colitis or toxic megacolon, suspected perforated viscus, or recent intestinal resection.

Technique

Patient preparation. Adequate bowel preparation is critical to ensure satisfactory visualization of the colonic mucosa. In one commonly used method a commercially available balanced oral electrolyte solution is given in relatively large quantities over a short time. However, children may have difficulty consuming the liquid voluntarily; therefore administration through a nasogastric tube may be preferred. The other frequently used approach recommends a full liquid diet for 48 hours in addition to administration of an oral cathartic (e.g., magnesium citrate, biscodyl, or senna syrup). If possible, an enema or rectal suppository is not given on the day of the procedure because these can cause visible mucosal irritation and histologic changes that may be confused with colitis.

Instruments. In addition to the standard adult colonoscope, a pediatric colonoscope that is smaller in diameter is available and can be used in most children older than 2 years. For infants and young children, a pediatric upper GI endoscope can be used.

Procedure. The child is initially placed in the left lateral decubitus position after monitoring equipment is secured and IV sedation started. The scope is advanced as quickly as possible to the cecum or area of concern. Discomfort can be reduced if air insufflation of the colon is minimized and unnecessary tension on the sigmoid colon is avoided. Biopsy specimens are best obtained on withdrawal of the instrument.

Risks and complications

Potential risks and complications of colonoscopy include perforation, bleeding, and infection. Perforation has been described rarely, usually in association with polypectomy and connective tissue disorders (e.g., Ehlers-Danlos syndrome). Silent, clinically insignificant mucosal lacerations have been reported. Intestinal bleeding necessitating transfusion is very rare but has been associated with polypectomy. Bacteremia after colonoscopy occurs in approximately 3% to 4% of patients, and the current American Heart Association recommendations for the use of prophylactic antibiotics in susceptible patients does not require that antibiotics be given for colonoscopy with or without biopsy.

THERAPEUTIC PROCEDURES
Endoscopy for Upper Intestinal Bleeding
Indications

Therapeutic upper intestinal endoscopy not only identifies the location of bleeding in the upper intestinal tract but also provides an opportunity to control the hemorrhage and avoid surgical intervention. Upper intestinal endoscopy is indicated in cases of active, persistent, or recurrent bleeding, for assessment of a hemodynamically significant hemorrhage (e.g., anemia necessitating transfusion, hypotension, or shock), or to distinguish between variceal and nonvariceal bleeding. Nonvariceal hemorrhage can arise from a number of sources, including primary or secondary peptic ulcer disease, Mallory-Weiss syndrome, mucosal hemangioma, or tumor. Not every child with upper intestinal bleeding must undergo endoscopy. Patients with a history compatible with an acute self-limited bleeding episode (e.g., pyloric stenosis, recent ingestion of a nonsteroidal anti-inflammatory drug, and vomiting with a presumed Mallory-Weiss tear) with rapid clearance of the nasogastric aspirate may be managed conservatively. If endoscopy is indicated to evaluate the bleeding event, the endoscopist must be prepared to intervene during the procedure to stop or abate the hemorrhage.

Indications for initiating therapeutic hemostasis through the endoscope include active bleeding from a visible vessel, base of an ulcer crater, or under an adherent clot and the presence of a nonbleeding visible vessel. If the suspected lesion has a nonbleeding adherent clot or a clean base, therapeutic intervention can be withheld.

Sclerotherapy or endoscopic variceal ligation (EVL) of esophageal varices is indicated during or after a bleeding episode. Therapeutic intervention for esophageal varices before the first documented variceal bleeding episode is generally not indicated.

Technique

General principles. After the patient has received sufficient volume resuscitation and is hemodynamically stable, therapeutic endoscopy can be considered. The need for blood products, whether packed red blood cells, whole blood, plasma, or platelets, must be anticipated and available for the procedure. Heroic measures may be necessary under some circumstances; however, the risks are greater if the patient's condition is unstable. The benefits of nasogastric lavage with room temperature saline solution remain uncertain. However, this may be useful in reducing the size of the clots that accumulate in the stomach after a significant bleeding episode. Most procedures performed in these critically ill children are done with general anesthesia or with the assistance of the PICU intensivist, who can be responsible for fluid and airway management during the procedure.

The choice of endoscope depends on the size of the patient. The largest endoscope that can safely be placed in the child's esophagus and maximize the suction channel size through which a probe or catheter can be passed is selected. An adult therapeutic endoscope with two suction channels is ideal for both variceal and nonvariceal bleeding and allows a probe or catheter to be placed in one channel while the other is available to aspirate blood or fluid. The external diameter of the adult instruments, however, is too large for many children.

Nonvariceal bleeding. The three commonly used methods of endoscopic hemostasis for nonvariceal bleeding are bipolar electrocoagulation (BICAP, Circon-American ACMI, Stamford, Conn.), heater probe (Olympus Corp., Lake Success, N.Y.), and injection sclerosis. With each method, excess fluid and blood must be washed from the ulcer crater to provide optimal visualization of the vessel to be treated. Bipolar electrocoagulation and the heater probe rely on generation of heat to coagulate the surrounding tissue. Injection sclerosis using epinephrine, absolute alcohol, or sclerosing agents (e.g., polidocanol or tetradecyl) likely achieves hemostasis by a combination of vessel constriction and tissue pressure that results from injecting fluid into the interstitial space. The method chosen usually depends on the equipment and experience available at each institution.

Variceal bleeding. The two methods used to endoscopically control variceal bleeding are injection sclerotherapy and EVL of esophageal varices. Sclerotherapy does not require special equipment and can be performed with a smaller caliber endoscope than is necessary for EVL. Both methods are equally effective in treating esophageal varices. The decision to use sclerotherapy or EVL will depend on the size of the patient, availability of the equipment, and experience of the endoscopist. Once a patient has bled from esophageal varices, the goal with either technique is to totally obliterate all esophageal varices.

Risks and complications

Nonvariceal bleeding. The potential for perforation or precipitation of uncontrolled bleeding are the primary concerns when these techniques are used. Bipolar electrocoagulation and the heater probe are designed to limit the area of tissue injury and minimize the risk of perforation; however, extensive experience with their use in children is not available. Injection sclerotherapy is also thought to be safe based on adult experience, with only one perforation in more than 700 patients.

Variceal bleeding. Clinically significant complications after endoscopic sclerosis of esophageal varices can occur in as many as 20% of patients. Chest pain, likely due to esophageal spasm or chemical mediastinitis, will develop in 25% to 50% of patients. Low-grade fever, usually not related to bacteremia, is present in as many as 50% of patients. Esophageal ulceration develops in virtually all patients within 48 hours of the injection, thereby increasing the likelihood of rebleeding. Esophageal stricture and perforation are rare complications, occurring in 2% to 3% of patients. Although abnormalities on chest radiographs, such as asymptomatic plural effusions, are noted in as many as 80% of patients, acute respiratory failure is rare. Bacteremia occurs commonly enough that patients who are at risk for bacterial endocarditis need to be given prophylactic antibiotics. Paralysis as a result of spinal cord necrosis has been reported. In addition, thrombosis of intra-abdominal vessels associated with infarction of related organs has been described, although the cause remains unclear. Finally, acute pericarditis and cardiac arrhythmias have been reported.

EVL has fewer local and virtually no systemic complications, although the endoscope is often passed in and out of the esophagus as many as 15 times during each procedure to "reload" the apparatus. Recurrent esophageal bleeding, ulceration, and stricture may occur with EVL. Chest pain is noted in most children undergoing the procedure. Recently esophageal perforation and death have been noted after placement of the overtube used to provide a conduit for the endoscope to reach the esophagus. The technical difficulties involved in manipulating the endoscope within a child's esophagus may limit its use to adolescents.

ADDITIONAL READING

• Ament ME, Berquist WE, Vargas J, Perisic V. Fiberoptic upper intestinal endoscopy in infants and children. Pediatr Clin North Am 35:141-155, 1988.

Bell GD. Review article: Premedication and intravenous sedation for upper gastrointestinal endoscopy. Aliment Pharmacol Ther 4:103-122, 1990.

• Cook DJ, Huyatt GH, Salena BJ, Laine LA. Endoscopic therapy for acute nonvariceal upper gastrointestinal hemorrhage: A meta-analysis. Gastroenterology 102:139-148, 1992.

Kahn KL, Kosecoff J, Chassin MR, Solomon DH, Brook RH. The use and misuse of upper gastrointestinal endoscopy. Ann Intern Med 109:664-670, 1988.

Kawamitsu T, Nagashima K, Tsuchiya H, Sugiyama T, Ogasawara T, Cheng S. Pediatric total colonoscopy. J Pediatr Surg 24:371-374, 1989.

Paquet KJ, Kissingen B. Portal hypertension: Sclerotherapy, medical or surgical treatment. Endoscopy 21(Suppl):18S-24S, 1989.

Squires RH Jr, Morriss F, Schulterman S, Drews B, Galyen L, Brown KO. Efficacy, safety, and cost of intravenous sedation versus general anesthesia in children undergoing endoscopic procedures. Gastrointest Endosc 41:99-104, 1995.

• Steffen RM, Wyllie R, Sivak MV, Michener WM, Caulfiend ME. Colonoscopy in the pediatric patient. J Pediatr 115:507-513, 1989.

XXIV
Pharmacology

174 Principles of Drug Administration

Jim Eisenwine · Trina Fabré · Elizabeth Farrington · Christine A. Lindsay

BACKGROUND

In this chapter issues critical to drug delivery are addressed. Not only will this serve to provide administration guidelines but also the rationale behind these guidelines. Several definitions critical to understanding drug administration issues are given below.

osmole Molecular weight of a solute, in grams, divided by the number of ions or particles into which it dissociates in solution. Amount of solute that on dissolution in 1 kg of water will result in an osmotic pressure increase of 22.4 atm under ideal conditions and standard temperature of 0°.

osmolality Osmotic concentration, defined as the number of osmoles of a solute per kilogram of solvent (Osm/kg).

osmolarity Osmotic concentration of a solution expressed as osmoles of solute per liter of solution (Osm/L). This is osmotically equivalent to a mole of an ideally behaving nonelectrolyte.

isotonic Denotes solutions that possess a similar osmotic pressure as human plasma. Limited to solutions in which cells neither swell nor shrink.

isotonicity Property of a solution in being isotonic.

tolerance Also known as tachyphylaxis. Development of decreased response to a pharmacologic agent after repetitive administration. This assumes the drug is being delivered at the same or higher rate and that there has not been an alteration in the pharmacokinetics that would decrease the concentration.

In the PICU IV medications are vital to patient care every day. Concerns of dosing, preparation, delivery, administration, and cost need to be addressed by all health care providers to provide safe, effective, and efficient care. Critically ill children have unique medication needs; thus special dosing and delivery of medications are of great importance.

Intravenous Solutions

One special dosing consideration is the need to maximize concentrations of drugs in patients with fluid restrictions. This can pose problems of solubility of drugs in solution and osmolarity of the final solution.

IV fluids are classified according to the tonicity of the fluids in relation to the osmolarity of normal plasma. The osmolarity of plasma is ~290 mOsm/L (range 270 to 300 mOsm/L). IV fluid that approximates 290 mOsm/L is considered isotonic. Normal saline solution, 0.9% sodium chloride, is said to be iso-osmotic or isotonic with physiologic fluids. IV fluids with an osmolarity >290 mOsm (+50 mOsm) are considered hypertonic, whereas those with an osmolarity significantly lower than 290 mOsm (−50 mOsm) are hypotonic. Parenteral solutions often range from approximately half isotonic (0.45% sodium chloride) to five to 10 times isotonic (25% to 50% dextrose).

Osmole data can be expressed as either osmolarity or osmolality. These two terms differ not only in their definition but also in the final value. Because water has a density close to 1, a liter of water and a liter of dilute solution each weighs close to a kilogram. The osmolarity and osmolality are nearly identical. Osmolality and osmolarity diverge for more concentrated solutions. For example, for dextrose 20%, the difference between 200 g of dextrose per liter (200 g/1000 ml) of solution vs. 200 g of dextrose per gram (200 g/1200 g) of solution is large. The osmolarity and osmolality are approximately 20% different: 1010 mOsm/L vs. 833 mOsm/kg, respectively.

When an IV fluid or drug in solution differs from isotonic, it can become a point of concern. Hypertonic fluids increase the osmotic pressure of the plasma, drawing fluid from the cells, and excessive infusions of such fluid can cause cellular dehydration. Hypotonic fluids lower the osmotic pressure, causing fluid to enter the cells. When such fluid is infused beyond the patient's tolerance for water, water intoxication results. IV fluids <0.45% sodium chloride or 145 mOsm/L have been reported to cause intracellular swelling and hemolysis.

Hypertonic drug solutions or hypotonic IV fluids can be adjusted by mixing them in dextrose 5% and water (D_5W) or normal saline solution. However, hypertonic IV fluids cannot be adjusted so easily. In the PICU, IV hypertonic solutions are administered routinely. Hyperosmolar fluids are infused through veins with a large blood volume to dilute the fluid, prevent trauma to the vessel, and prevent thrombophlebitis. Most literature cites 500 mOsm/L as the highest osmolarity recommended to be infused into a peripheral vein, although higher values have been used occasionally.

Clinically these osmolarity data have been translated so that dextrose 12.5% in water ($D_{12.5}W$) is the maximum dextrose concentration recommended to be given peripherally (630 mOsm/L). The addition of sodium chloride or potassium chloride will increase this value to 700 to 800 mOsm/L. Table 174-1 summarizes the osmolarity of medication solutions commonly used in the PICU. The need to dilute the drug or administer the drug centrally becomes increasingly important with some of these solutions. Infants and children in the PICU may not be able to communicate the burning or pain from a hypertonic IV solution. Thus awareness of the osmolarity of fluids and medications used in the PICU is important.

SPECIFIC PROBLEMS
Intraosseous Infusions

Intraosseous infusions are discussed in detail in Chapter 134. Drug delivery can be efficient when administered short term by means of intraosseous infusions. Because the bone marrow is highly vascularized,

Table 174-1   Osmolarity of Commonly Used Solutions

Solution	Osmolarity (mOsm/L)
Sterile water for injection	0
$D_{2.5}W$	125
0.45% NaCl	154
D_5W	253
0.9% NaCl	308
D_5W, 0.225% NaCl, with 1 mEq KCl/dl	349
D_5W, 0.45% NaCl, with 2 mEq KCl/dl	447
$D_{10}W$	505
D_5LR	525
D_5W, 0.9% NaCl, with 4 mEq KCl/dl	640
$D_{10}W$, 0.45% NaCl	660
10% calcium gluconate	680
10% arginine HCl	950
$D_{20}W$	1010
20% mannitol	1098
25% mannitol	1372
Sodium bicarbonate, 1 mEq/ml	2000
10% NaCl	2040
KCl, 2 mEq/ml	4000
50% magnesium sulfate	4060
Potassium phosphate, 3 mmol/ml	7400
Ammonium chloride, 5 mEq/ml	10,000
Alprostadil injection, 500 μg/ml	>20,000

LR = lactated Ringer's solution.

drugs are absorbed rapidly; however, the peak serum concentration achieved is lower than when a drug is administered intravenously. Concentrations must not exceed those recommended for IV use. Drug extravasation is often a problem, with leakage of the IV fluid into the subcutaneous tissue. The principles of treating intraosseous drug extravasation are the same as when drug extravasates from an IV site.

Concentration of Fluids

Several commonly asked questions pertain to the issue of how concentrated an infusion can be made. This is important for several reasons. PICU patients often have fluid restrictions, and when calculating the total daily fluid requirements, the physician must give medications instead of nutrition.

Numerous factors are involved in drug dilution, including osmolarity, pH, and drug solubility in solution. There is also a factor of potency, which means that if the infusion is too concentrated it is difficult for the nurse to titrate the infusion rate for small infants without making a large increase or decrease in dose. In addition, because of concerns about damaging peripheral veins, limits are placed on concentration that can be administered through peripheral lines.

It is good practice to ask four questions when required to maximally concentrate an infusion.

1. Will the medication be infused through a well-placed central catheter; that is, does the central catheter empty directly into the superior vena cava or right atrium?
2. Does the patient have adequate cardiac function to dilute and circulate the drug effectively?
3. Will the infusion be administered by a syringe pump?
4. Will the infusion rate be constant or be titrated up or down?

When beginning infusion of a specific drug, it is necessary to know the weight of the patient so a suitable concentration can be calculated to provide delivery of an appropriate dose at a rate sufficient that a carrier fluid is not needed but small enough not to cause fluid overload.

For example, in a child weighing 5 kg dopamine is to be started at a dose of 5 μg/kg/min, with the possibility that it will be increased up to 20 μg/kg/min. Here one can use the principles of the rule of six, which states that six times the patient's weight is equal to the amount of drug (in milligrams) that in 100 ml of fluid will result in a solution that when infused at a rate of 1 ml/hr will deliver 1 μg/kg/min. Thus in a 5 kg child 30 mg of dopamine added to 100 ml of fluid and given at a rate of 5 ml/hr will deliver a dose of 5 μg/kg/min. In this example the infusion can be further concentrated simply by multiplying the amount to be added to the bag by 5, so that at a rate of 1 ml/hr the amount delivered is 5 μg/kg/min. Therefore 150 mg of dopamine in 100 ml of fluid infused at 1 ml/hr will deliver the desired amount of drug. The infusion can be started at a rate of 1 ml/hr, with the possibility of increasing it to 4 ml/hr to deliver 20 μg/kg/min.

In larger children the rule of six might produce a concentration that is too strong and that when infused at 1 ml/hr will not deliver a dose of 5 μg/kg/min. For all drugs, this will depend on the weight of the child and the maximum recommended concentration for

administration. For two drugs, epinephrine and isoproterenol, one must use 0.6 in the rule of six. The rule of six can be described by another equation, which often is more versatile and useful for all drugs administered by means of continuous infusion.

$$6 \times \frac{\text{Desired dose } (\mu\text{g/kg/min})}{\text{Desired rate (ml/hr)}} = \frac{\text{Amount (mg) of drug}}{100 \text{ ml of fluid}}$$

Information about the appropriate maximum concentration of commonly prescribed PICU medications is included in Table 174-2. These concentrations have been proven stable for long-term (24 to 48 hours) infusion. Often it is not how much to dilute the drug but how much not to dilute; for example, it is recommended that pentobarbital not be diluted. Also, when multiple drugs are added to the same infusion, the final concentration of the drugs is important. A good example is the arterial catheter fluid used at Children's Medical Center of Dallas. Heparin, 500 units, and papaverine, 60 mg, are mixed with 500 ml of a carrier solution. This solution is stable for at least 24 hours. However, if the undiluted drugs are mixed together (papaverine, 30 mg/ml, and heparin, 1000 units/ml), immediate and serious precipitation will develop. Calcium and phosphate are two drugs commonly infused in the PICU whose solubility is temperature, pH, and concentration dependent. Not only must one be concerned about the calcium and phosphate in total parenteral nutrition (TPN) but also the concentrations in fluids used for replacement and continuous veno-venous hemofiltration.

Infusion Rates

Another problem encountered in the PICU is the need for multiple infusions of various medications in a patient with limited IV access. In many instances a physician may want to increase an infusion rate or give a medication by IV push to decrease time of administration and accommodate administration of other medications. However, several factors must be considered before administering a medication via IV push. Specifically, osmolarity, pH, concentration, and volume to be administered are important considerations when determining whether a vein can physically tolerate a medication to be pushed. (Refer to other sections of this chapter for more in-depth discussion of these topics.) In addition, one must also consider whether administration via IV push results in adverse physiologic changes due to alterations in

Table 174-2 Maximum Recommended Concentrations of Medications Commonly Prescribed in the PICU

Drug	Recommended Maximum Concentrations	Special Conditions*	pH	Osmolality and/or (Osmolarity)
Alprostadil (PGE)	20 µg/ml	Use D₅W or NS; higher dextrose concentrations have precipitated	NA	925 mOsm/kg (20 µg/ml)
Amrinone	5 mg/ml (undiluted)	Dilute in saline solution only	3.2 to 4.0	101 mOsm/kg
Dobutamine	5 mg/ml	Unstable in alkaline solutions	2.5 to 5.5	273 mOsm/kg (12.5 mg/ml)
Dopamine	3.2 mg/ml	Unstable in alkaline solutions	2.5 to 4.5	600 mOsm/kg (40 mg/ml)
Epinephrine	0.1 mg/ml	Unstable in alkaline solutions	2.5 to 5.0	348 mOsm/kg (1 mg/ml)
Esmolol	20 mg/ml		3.5 to 5.5	1063 mOsm/L (25 mg/ml)
Fentanyl	50 µg/ml (undiluted)	D₅W or NS	4.0 to 7.5	<50 mOsm/kg
Furosemide	10 mg/ml (undiluted)		8.0 to 9.3	290 mOsm/kg
Isoproterenol	0.1 mg/ml	Unstable in alkaline solutions	3.5 to 4.5	280 mOsm/kg (0.2 mg/ml)
Labetalol	5 mg/ml (undiluted)		3.0 to 4.0	287 mOsm/kg
Lidocaine	20 mg/ml	D₅W preferred	5.0 to 7.0	352 mOsm/kg (20 mg/ml)
Lorazepam	0.1 mg/ml	Dilute with D₅W and inject immediately	NA	NA
Midazolam	5 mg/ml (undiluted)		3.0	385 mOsm/kg
Milrinone	1 mg/ml (undiluted)	Dilute in saline solution or D₅W	3.2 to 4.0	NA
Nitroglycerin	1.2 mg/ml	In glass; use special tubing; D₅W or NS	3.0 to 6.5	281 mOsm/kg (1 mg/ml)
Nitroprusside	1.17 mg/ml	Protect from light	3.5 to 6.0	214 mOsm/kg (25 mg/ml)
Pentobarbital	50 mg/ml (undiluted)	Do not dilute	9.5	NA
Phenylephrine	0.1 mg/ml		3.0 to 6.5	284 mOsm/kg (10 mg/ml)
Procainamide	50 mg/ml	D₅W, NS	4.0 to 6.0	2000 mOsm/kg (500 mg/ml)
Terbutaline	1 mg/ml (undiluted)	Subcutaneous product given IV	3.0 to 5.0	283 mOsm/kg
Urokinase	5000 U/ml	Reconstitute with sterile water, then dilute with D₅W or NS	6.0 to 7.5	391 mOsm/kg
Vasopressin	1 U/ml	D₅W or NS	2.5 to 4.5	30 mOsm/kg (20 U/ml)
Vecuronium†	1 mg/ml		4.0	292 mOsm/kg (4 mg/ml)

*Unless otherwise specified, these drugs can be mixed in D₅W, dextrose in distilled water, normal saline solution (NS), lactated Ringer's solution, or any combination thereof.

†Vecuronium can be mixed with sterile water for injection to a concentration of 2 mg/ml in severely fluid-restricted patients. No precipitate is noted after 24 hours. Stability is not known.

electrolyte distribution or in an idiosyncratic adverse event.

For some medications, particularly those ions normally found intracellularly, increasing infusion rates may result in increased extracellular concentrations of these ions, leading to intracellular concentration changes. In some cases these effects may be serious. For example, potassium is never administered by IV push or IV retrograde infusion. Fast administration of potassium has resulted in fatal arrhythmias. The recommended rate of infusion is 0.5 mEq/kg/hr, not to exceed 1 mEq/kg/hr in extreme situations. In addition, as an extra precaution at our institution it is policy that any patient in whom the potassium infusion rate exceeds 0.5 mEq/kg/hr will be monitored with a cardiac monitor. Another electrolyte that must be administered slowly is phosphate. The general recommendation is that phosphate be infused over 4 to 6 hours. Case reports have documented severe complications, including hypocalcemia, hypotension, oliguria, and death, associated with faster infusion of phosphate.

Fast infusion of various antibiotics has also been associated with adverse events. Administration of vancomycin over less than 60 minutes is associated with "red man's syndrome," characterized by a sudden, rapid decrease in systemic arterial blood pressure, with or without a maculopapular rash. This histamine-mediated reaction is directly related to the infusion rate of vancomycin.

Acyclovir is an antiviral agent that must not be administered rapidly. Administration over less than 10 minutes can cause crystalluria, elevations in serum urea and creatinine concentrations, renal tubular damage, and acute renal failure.

These are examples of drugs in which adverse events are associated with fast rates of administration. Because there are no set guidelines to assess whether a medication can be administered via IV push, each drug must be researched individually. Questions about administration rates of other drugs can be addressed to a pharmacist to ensure that infusion rates are safe.

Calcium and Phosphate

Calcium and phosphate compatibility guidelines are based on in vitro studies from the literature. Because the major contributing factor for the development of a precipitate is the pH of the solution, any study that evaluates the solubility of calcium and phosphate in TPN solutions is specific for the amino acid product and the amino acid concentration tested. The amino acid product Travasol has a similar pH to Aminosyn and Trophamine, commonly used solutions in the PICU setting; therefore the following guidelines based on Travasol data can be extrapolated to the other two products. The following equation can be used as a guide to check calcium and phosphate solubility in TPN:

mEq of calcium per 100 ml *plus*

mEq of phosphate per 100 ml = X

(To convert mmol/100 ml to mEq/100 ml, multiply by 2.)

X Can Equal	When Protein Concentration Is
4.0	1%
5.0	2%
5.5	3%
6.0	4%
7.0	5%

If the total concentration of calcium and phosphate exceeds these recommendations, a fine, white precipitate will most likely occur. The following options may be considered: (1) increase the protein concentration if therapeutically acceptable; (2) decrease the calcium or phosphate or both to allow increased solubility; or (3) increase the volume of TPN to decrease the concentration of the solution.

Drug Compatibility With TPN Solutions

The addition of drugs to TPN solutions can cause precipitation because the drugs may alter the pH of the TPN solution. This practice is not recommended. Standard practice among nurses is administration of medications in a buretrol or volumetric set, infusing with TPN, or administration via a Y site. However, although the drug is not being added to the TPN infusion bag, precipitation can still occur when these solutions are mixed in the tubing set. We recommend consultation with a pharmacist to determine whether an individual drug can be infused with TPN solution. If the medication and the TPN solution are physically or chemically incompatible, it may be necessary to stop infusion of the TPN to deliver the medication. Many drugs can be diluted in a multitude of diluents to meet the patient's needs, including 0.9% sodium chloride solution, D$_5$W, D$_{10}$W, and lactated Ringer's solution, among others.

Consultation with a pharmacist is recommended if there is any question of physical or chemical incompatibility with simultaneous administration of two or more medications.

Extravasation of Fluids and Medications

Extravasation is the accidental leakage of IV fluids into the interstitial tissue. Both chemotherapeutic and nonchemotherapeutic agents can cause tissue damage from extravasation. The consequences of extravasation or infiltration of some IV fluids or medications may be minimal, but in some cases the consequences may be serious and cause functional impairments and cosmetic defects. Prolonged hospitalization and increased mortality due to extravasation have been documented in the literature.

Extravasation occurs frequently. One study documented that >30% of all peripherally inserted catheters placed in the PICU were removed because of medication infiltration or the development of drug-

related phlebitis. Another study documented a 58% incidence of infiltration in the neonatal population.

Certain properties of drugs make some agents more prone to extravasation. Specifically, hypertonic infusions such as electrolyte solutions and TPN can cause tissue damage from infiltration. Some antibiotics such as nafcillin have irritant properties and can be responsible for tissue injury from infiltration. Extravasation of therapeutic agents that cause local vasoconstriction, such as sympathomimetic agents, can ultimately cause ischemic necrosis. The pH properties such as extreme acidity or alkalinity may cause tissue damage from extravasation. Table 174-3 lists various medications that can cause tissue damage from extravasation.

Extravasation injuries occur commonly in the seriously ill patient and appear to be more prevalent in children and the elderly. The high incidence of extravasation injuries in these populations may be related to the presence of fragile veins and decreased intravascular volume. In addition, critically ill patients may be heavily sedated or unconscious and unable to communicate pain associated with IV fluid infil-

Table 174-3 IV Medications That May Cause Damage From Extravasation

Medication Extravasated	Mechanism of Damage	Antidote
Alprostadil Calcium Dextrose solutions >12.5% Parenteral nutrition Potassium Phenytoin Electrolyte solutions Radiologic contrast media Urea Nafcillin	Hypertonic solution	Hyaluronidase (Wydase): Add 1 ml NS to 150-unit vial to make a final concentration of 150 U/ml
Aminophylline Acyclovir Phenytoin	pH irritant properties	Hyaluronidase: Mix 0.1 ml with 0.9 ml NS in a 1 ml syringe to make a final concentration of 15 U/ml
Dobutamine Dopamine Epinephrine Isoproterenol Metaraminol Norepinephrine Phenylephrine Thiopental Vasopressin	Vasoconstriction	Phentolamine (Regitine): Mix 5 to 10 mg with 10 ml NS; give 0.1 to 0.2 mg/kg (maximum 10 mg) *or* Nitroglycerin topical ointment

tration. Poor cannula insertion technique and the use of steel cannulas and pressurized infusion pumps are also risk factors for extravasation injuries.

Several methods of dealing with extravasation may be used; however, few studies have tested reliable solutions to many infiltration problems. Treatment of extravasation injuries involves the use of specific antidotes. Every episode of infiltration or extravasation does not result in overt tissue damage.

Nonpharmacologic management of extravasation injury

If extravasation or infiltration occurs, the infusion must be discontinued immediately to prevent further tissue damage. Some advocate physical removal of the infiltrated solution after discontinuation of the infusion; however, techniques to achieve this process have not been adequately evaluated. In addition, elevation and splinting of the affected area may prevent serious complications and disability of the extremity.

Use of warm or cold compresses is controversial. Heat can facilitate drug distribution and absorption by causing vasodilation. Moist heat compresses can cause maceration and further tissue necrosis. Conversely, through vasoconstrictive mechanisms, cold compresses may cause local freezing and frostbite. The application of cold compresses may result in more severe tissue damage by localizing the infiltrated drug if no specific treatment is available. This may prove beneficial by localizing the offending agent when a specific treatment protocol is known.

Pharmacologic management of extravasation injury

Hyaluronidase. Hyaluronidase is a proteolytic enzyme that hydrolyzes hyaluronic acid, the so-called cement of connective tissue. This component of connective tissue helps to prevent the diffusion of liquids through the tissues. In the event of extravasation, hyaluronidase can be subcutaneously injected around the site. This proteolytic enzyme breaks down hyaluronic acid, allowing the extravasated fluid to be dispersed over a larger surface and facilitates absorption of the infiltrated solution. Hyaluronidase may help decrease the risk of local tissue damage if used within the first hour after extravasation. A delay in therapy greater than 3 hours has no significant advantage over no treatment.

If used promptly, hyaluronidase may be an effective antidote for various extravasated fluids. These agents are generally hypertonic or possess pH irritant properties (see Table 174-3). Treatment involves preparing a 15 unit/ml solution of hyaluronidase. The solution is subcutaneously or intradermally injected around the extravasated site in five 0.2 ml injections, for a total dose of 15 units of hyaluronidase. Doses of 30 units have been used in cases of severe, large infiltrates, and doses of less than 15 units have been used in infants weighing <1 kg.

Phentolamine. Sympathomimetic agents are vasopressors that can cause severe local ischemia and tissue necrosis after extravasation. Phentolamine is an α-adrenergic receptor antagonist that has been used to minimize the effects of extravasation of vasopressor agents. Phentolamine blocks both pre- and postsynaptic α-adrenergic receptors, causing competitive inhibition of α-adrenergic effects, thus minimizing vasoconstriction. The recommended dose of phentolamine is 0.1 to 0.2 mg/kg (maximum 10 mg) injected into the infiltrated area within 12 hours of the extravasation. Doses of <5 mg have been used in infants.

Topical nitroglycerin has also been used in the treatment of vasopressor extravasation. In neonates topical nitroglycerin ointment (2%) has been used after dopamine extravasation with good results. One inch of ointment applied to the site can reverse ischemic effects.

Each extravasation event must be evaluated individually by assessing the type of agent extravasated and the reliability of a known antidote. In many cases extravasation can be treated by immobilization and elevation of the affected area. Because documentation of extravasation treatment protocols in controlled trials is lacking, most extravasation protocols are limited to case reports and experimental animal models. Therefore the best "treatment" of extravasation is prevention.

Adverse Drug Reactions

An adverse drug reaction is any response to a drug that is noxious or unintended and occurs at doses used in humans for prophylaxis, diagnosis, or therapy. This definition excludes therapeutic failure. Most adverse drug reactions can be described as either predictable or unpredictable. Hypersensitivity or allergic reactions and idiosyncratic reactions are largely unpredictable and unavoidable. Overdosage, extension of pharmacologic effects, side effects, toxic reactions, and drug interactions are considered, for the most part, predictable and preventable.

Table 174-4   Classification of Immunologically Mediated Drug Reactions

	Type I: Anaphylactic	Type II: Cytotoxic (complement mediated)	Type III: Immune Complex Mediated (Arthrus reaction)	Type IV: Hypersensitivity Cell-Mediated or Delayed
Mechanism and cause	Antigen causes release of pharmacologic mediators of anaphylaxis from mast cells. Immediate onset of symptoms.	Antibody combines with tissue antigen to cause activation of the complement system. This in turn causes cytolysis.	Antibody and soluble antigen form insoluble complexes that can deposit in various areas and lead to inflammation and can activate the complement system. Onset of serum sickness is approximately 10 days after exposure.	Initiated by lymphocytes sensitized to deposited antigens. This leads to (1) direct killing of antigenic cells and (2) production of mediators of cell-mediated immune responses. Accumulation of polymorphonuclear cells, monocytes, and liberation of lysosomal enzymes with inflammation occurs.
Examples	Penicillin allergy	Procainamide-induced systemic lupus erythematosus	Cefaclor, barbiturates, hydralazine, penicillins, phenylbutazone, and sulfonamides, among other drugs, are associated with serum sickness–like symptoms. Contact dermatitis from topical drug exposure.	Tuberculin skin test is a well-known example. Transplant rejection.

For a better appreciation of true allergic reactions, it is necessary to discuss the four categories of immunologically mediated adverse drug reactions, as classified by Gell and Coombs in 1975 (Table 174-4). Type I reactions are IgE mediated and traditionally known as anaphylactic reactions. These are immediate hypersensitivity reactions that may lead to anaphylaxis and cardiopulmonary collapse. They must be treated with epinephrine or diphenhydramine. Type II reactions are cytotoxic and cause complement activation. Examples include the development of systemic lupus erythematosus after procainamide use and poststreptococcal glomerulonephritis. Type III reactions (Arthrus reactions) involve the development of toxic antibody-antigen complexes. These complexes can be deposited at various sites and lead to inflammation and activation of the complement system. Type IV reactions are cell-mediated reactions.

Despite this classification system, certain adverse drug reactions can either mimic an immunologically mediated reaction but not fit into the Gell and Coombs schema or not have an immunologic mechanism even though they appear to be anaphylactic. Halothane hepatitis and the allergic reaction seen after administration of radiologic contrast media are two such reactions.

Documentation of adverse drug reactions assists hospitals in detecting potential problems in drug utilization. Any unexpected or significant adverse drug reaction needs to be reported to both the FDA and the manufacturer. The intent of an adverse drug reaction reporting program is to improve the quality of patient care and increase our knowledge base of drug use in critically ill children.

Determining the probability that an adverse or untoward reaction was attributable to a medication is not easy. A few objective measuring tools are often used by pharmacists to determine whether the reaction to a particular drug was doubtful, probable, or definite. Most issues revolve around whether the symptoms resolved after the drug was discontinued and reappeared when the drug was readministered (rechallenge). It would be helpful to know whether similar reactions occurred before and whether there is any objective evidence to confirm the reaction.

CURRENT RESEARCH AND FUTURE CONSIDERATIONS

Drug administration in pediatric patients is often more art than science. Definitive studies have yet to be conducted for the concentrations and commonly used drugs in the PICU. More data need to be collected and analyzed to broaden our knowledge of the aspects of combining the numerous drugs available for IV use. The stability of these solutions also needs to be addressed more rigorously. For example, how does the temperature generated by infant warmers affect the stability of IV solutions?

The future should hold the answers to issues of what to do not only with IV solutions but also blood products and blood substitutes. Better guidelines for concentrating infusions, combining drug products, and minimizing adverse events will allow medications to be prepared more rapidly while minimizing error and enhancing patient care.

ADDITIONAL READING

Brown AS, Hoelzer DJ, Piercy SA. Skin necrosis from extravasation of intravenous fluids in children. Plast Reconst Surg 64:145-150, 1979.

• Flemmer L, Chan JS. A pediatric protocol for management of extravasation injuries. Pediatr Nurs 19:355-358, 424, 1993.

Gatlin L, Kulkarni P, Hussain A. Determining osmolarities: A practical approach for multicomponent intravenous and parenteral nutrient solutions. Am J Hosp Pharm 36:1358-1361, 1979.

Gaze NR. Tissue necrosis caused by commonly used intravenous infusions. Lancet 2:417-419, 1978.

Giuffrida DJ, Bryan-Brown CW, Lumb PD, Kwan KB, Rhoades HM. Central vs. peripheral venous catheters in critically ill patients. Chest 90:806-809, 1986.

Greenlaw CW, Null LW. Dopamine-induced ischemia. Lancet 2:555, 1977.

Isaacs JW, Millikan WJ, Stackhouse J. Parenteral nutrition of adults with a 900 milliosmolar solution via peripheral veins. Am J Clin Nutr 30:552-559, 1977.

Levinson ML. Management of extravasation injuries due to non-cytotoxic drugs. Clin Trends Pharm Pract 8:77-81, 1994.

Maccara ME. Extravasation: A hazard of intravenous therapy. Drug Intell Clin Pharm 17:713, 1983.

Millam DA. Managing complications of IV therapy. Nursing 18:34-43, 1988.

Orlowski JP. Emergency alternatives to intravenous access. Pediatr Clin North Am 41:1183-1199, 1994.

• Patterson R, DeSwarte RD, Greenberger PA, Grammer L. Drug allergy and protocols for management of drug allergies. Allergy Proc 15:239-264, 1994.

Siegel FP, ed. Remington's Pharmaceutical Sciences. Easton, Pa.: Mack Publishing, 79:1481-1498, 1990.

Siwy BK, Sadov AM. Acute management of dopamine infiltration injury with Regitine. Plast Reconstr Surg 80:610-612, 1987.

Tatro DS, Ow-Wing SD. Extravasation due to non-chemotherapeutic agents. Denver: Rumak and Gellman Micromedex, 1995.

Zenk KE. Management of intravenous extravasations. Infusion 5:77, 1981.

Zenk KE. Hyaluronidase: An antidote for intravenous extravasations. CSHP Voice 8:66, 1981.

175 Principles of Pharmacokinetics and Therapeutic Drug Monitoring

Christine A. Lindsay · Barton A. Kamen

BACKGROUND AND INDICATIONS

Therapeutic drug monitoring is based on the concept that pharmacologic response of many drugs correlates better with the blood concentration of drug than with the dose. The dose of most drugs correlates somewhat with the intensity of pharmacologic effects (pharmacodynamics), but because of interpatient differences in absorption, distribution, metabolism, and excretion of drugs, this relationship may vary widely; therefore standard dosages may not always produce predictable drug concentrations.

For certain drugs, studies in patients have provided information on the plasma concentration range that is effective and safe in treating specific diseases. Within this range the desired effects of the drug are seen; below it the therapeutic benefits are not realized; and above it toxicity may develop. For each drug, no absolute boundaries separate subtherapeutic, therapeutic, and toxic drug concentrations. Variability in patient response is influenced by both pharmacodynamic and pharmacokinetic factors. Individual differences in drug metabolism, elimination, and absorption affect therapeutic response. In addition, disease states with altered physiologic status can change pharmacodynamics directly or by influencing pharmacokinetics. Thus pharmacogenetics are important to more completely understand drug metabolism.

Determination of plasma/fluid drug concentrations to optimize a patient's drug therapy is known as therapeutic drug monitoring. The potential advantages of therapeutic drug monitoring are optimization of therapeutic drug benefits and minimization of toxic drug effects. For a therapeutic drug monitoring assay to be clinically useful, however, several criteria must be met. First, the assay method must be specific, sensitive, precise for the intended range of drug concentrations, and able to measure active metabolites if they make a significant contribution to the overall pharmacologic effect of the drug or to differentiate between the drug and its inactive metabolites. Second, a relationship must be established between the drug concentration and its pharmacologic effect. Third, information on the absorption, distribution, metabolism, and rate of elimination must be available. These pharmacokinetic variables determine the sample collection time, the clinical interpretation of drug concentrations, and the means for adjusting dosage regimens based on plasma drug concentrations.

Measurement of drug concentrations is time consuming and expensive. Before routine monitoring of drug concentrations can be justified, the indications for doing so must be carefully considered. The general indications for drug monitoring are as follows:

1. When there is wide interpatient variation in drug plasma concentrations from a given dose. This can be particularly important in children, in whom differences in body weight, extracellular fluid volumes, and elimination rates are great.
2. When saturation kinetics occur, causing a steep relationship between dose and plasma concentration within the therapeutic range (e.g., phenytoin).
3. When there is a narrow therapeutic index, that is, when therapeutic doses are close to toxic (e.g., aminoglycoside antibiotics and digoxin).
4. When the desired pharmacologic effects cannot be assessed readily by other simple means (e.g., blood pressure measurement with antihypertensive agents) or the usual response

is hidden (e.g., anticonvulsant drugs in the patient with neuromuscular blockade).

5. When symptoms occur that might be the result of toxicity or undertreatment of the underlying disease.
6. When prognosis and management are related to blood concentrations after acute overdose (e.g., acetaminophen, barbiturates, and ethanol).
7. When GI, hepatic, or renal disease is present, causing alterations in drug absorption, metabolism, and excretion.
8. When a patient is receiving support with an extracorporeal circuit such as continuous veno-venous hemofiltration (CVVH) or extracorporeal membrane oxygenation (ECMO) and drug removal is suspected.
9. When a drug-drug or drug-food interaction is suspected.
10. During clinical trials of new drugs to establish therapeutic and toxic ranges.

A word of caution is needed, however, because there is always the danger of treating the plasma concentration rather than the patient. With a number of drugs, measurement of the plasma concentration is invaluable but is no substitute for careful clinical assessment of patient response. A plasma concentration that falls outside the appropriate therapeutic range may not warrant dosage adjustment if the patient has shown a satisfactory clinical response to therapy without evidence of toxicity.

BASIC PHARMACOKINETICS

Pharmacokinetics defines the relationship between the dose administered and the concentration of drug reached in the plasma. Knowledge of pharmacokinetic principles is needed to properly order and interpret drug concentrations and calculate dosage regimens based on the concentration values obtained. Without an understanding of these principles, drug concentration monitoring can be ineffective, a waste of time and money, and possibly harmful to the patient.

Definitions and terms used are as follows.

Bioavailability

The bioavailability of a drug is defined as the percentage of the dose that reaches the systemic circulation as unchanged drug after administration by any route. Traditionally, oral bioavailability is a reflection of the fraction of an oral dose, compared to an equivalent IV dose, that reaches the systemic circulation, although any two routes of administration can be compared to obtain relative bioavailability. Bioavailability is calculated by multiplying the dose administered (D) by a bioavailability factor (F). The bioavailability of parenterally administered drugs is considered to be 100% (F = 1.0). However, for a drug administered orally, bioavailability may be <1.0, for several reasons, namely, incomplete absorption or dissolution, metabolism in the gut lumen or gut wall, or a large first-pass phenomenon.

The amount of drug absorbed or drug that enters the systemic circulation will also be affected by the salt form (S) of the drug. The salt form of a drug is important, especially when the drug is measured in the plasma as the base or when doses are being converted from one form to another. Phenytoin sodium is a good example. IV Dilantin is manufactured as phenytoin sodium. Phenytoin sodium is 92% phenytoin base. Therefore the salt factor is S = 0.92. Dilantin capsules are also phenytoin sodium; however, the suspension and chewable tablets are phenytoin base. To convert from IV phenytoin sodium to oral phenytoin suspension, the IV dose needs to be multiplied by 0.92 to achieve an equivalent oral phenytoin base dose.

Drugs administered orally must undergo absorption across the GI cell membranes. Only drugs that are not ionized will cross the membrane. In addition, the blood supply to the GI system empties into the portal vein, which drains directly into the liver. Thus the drug may be metabolized by the liver before it reaches the systemic circulation. This first-pass phenomenon results in lower bioavailability of drug (Fig. 175-1).

Rectal drug absorption produces similar problems. The inferior and middle hemorrhoidal veins bypass the hepatic portal circulation and drain directly into the inferior vena cava. The superior hemorrhoidal vein drains directly into the hepatic portal system and therefore undergoes first-pass metabolism. Variations in the absorption of drug by the rectal route may be attributed to the location from which the drug is absorbed. If a drug is placed high in the rectum, there may be a first-pass effect, whereas a drug placed lower in the rectum may have a more immediate effect.

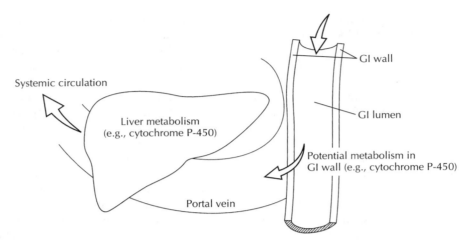

Fig. 175-1   Oral drug absorption and first-pass metabolism.

Plasma Protein Binding

Unless otherwise noted, the plasma concentration of a drug is the total amount of drug (i.e., drug bound to plasma proteins plus drug unbound or free) in the plasma. Because only the unbound portion is pharmacologically active, plasma concentration may be only an indirect reflection of the concentration of active drug available at the site of action.

Two major plasma proteins are responsible for approximately 95% of all drug binding: albumin (acidic drugs) and α_1-acid glycoprotein (basic drugs). Some disease states are associated with decreased plasma proteins (e.g., renal failure, hepatic cirrhosis or hepatitis, burns, malnutrition, stress, and trauma) or with decreased binding of drugs to plasma proteins (e.g., hyperbilirubinemia, hyperuremia, and drug interactions). Changes in the binding characteristics of a drug can affect pharmacologic response to the drug; thus a plasma concentration lower than usual may give the desired therapeutic effect. The effects of altered plasma protein binding in renal and hepatic failure are addressed in detail in Chapter 178.

Signs of drug toxicity may be seen within the therapeutic range. α_1-Acid glycoprotein is known to rise in short-term and long-term inflammatory states, malignancy, stress, and various hematologic conditions. This rise causes increased binding of basic compounds such as lidocaine and quinidine. Therefore, when interpreting plasma drug concentrations, altered protein binding and altered fraction of free drug concentration must be considered. For drugs that are highly protein bound (>90%), minor changes in protein binding can have a substantial effect (see Chapter 178).

Volume of Distribution

The volume of distribution (V_d) relates the amount of drug in the body to the concentration of drug in the blood or plasma. This volume does not necessarily refer to an identifiable physiologic volume but to the fluid volume needed to account for all the drug in the body. A small volume of distribution implies that the drug is largely retained within the vascular compartment (e.g., gentamicin, with V_d = 0.25 L/kg), whereas a large volume of distribution implies distribution throughout the total body water or sequestration in certain tissues (e.g., digoxin, with V_d = 7 L/kg). Volume of distribution is calculated after a bolus dose by dividing the drug dose (D) by the plasma concentration of the drug (Cp) at 0 time.

$$V_d \ (\text{L/kg}) = \frac{\text{Dose}}{\text{Cp in plasma at 0 time}} = \frac{\text{D (mg/kg)}}{\text{Cp0 (mg/L)}}$$

Cp0 is obtained by extrapolating Cp to 0 time to obtain apparent plasma concentration. If the drug is not given parenterally, dose delivered to the body will be modified by the bioavailable fraction (F) (i.e., F × D).

Loading Dose

The volume of distribution and a predetermined (desired) target plasma concentration allow calculation

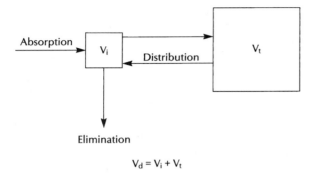

$$V_d = V_i + V_t$$

Fig. 175-2 Two-compartment model.

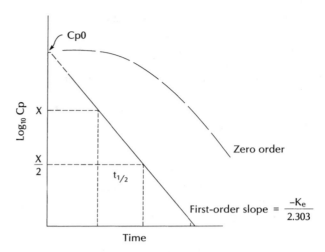

Fig. 175-3 First-order kinetics, half-life ($t_{1/2}$), and elimination rate constant (K_e). Dashed line represents a theoretical zero-order reaction. Note that there is little change in plasma value as a function of time at high drug concentration in a zero reaction. The slope of the line is proportional to $-K_e$.

of a milligram per kilogram loading dose (LD) using the following equation:

$$LD \ (mg/kg) = \frac{Cp \ (mg/L) \times V_d \ (L/kg)}{F}$$

where $F = 1$.

The rate at which a loading dose can be given depends on drug toxicity (i.e., how high can the concentration of drug be before signs of toxicity develop), where the drug is active (plasma or tissue), rate of equilibration of the drug into various body compartments, and degree of plasma protein binding (e.g., diazoxide).

Compartments

Many drugs act as though the body were a single fluid compartment. In some cases a two-compartment model may be more accurate (Fig. 175-2). These compartments can be either by design, meaning the drug exhibits these characteristics in healthy persons, or by disease, meaning the disease process has created an extra compartment into which the drug distributes.

The first compartment is the rapidly equilibrating volume, usually made up of blood and those organs with high blood flow. This is referred to as the initial volume (V_i). The second compartment takes longer to equilibrate with a drug and is referred to as the tissue volume (V_t). The sum of these two volumes is equal to the total volume of distribution. For some drugs there may be multiple compartments. Drugs are assumed to enter into and be eliminated from the initial volume.

Because of the time needed for drug distribution into the tissue volume, a rapidly administered dose

calculated on the basis of $V_d = (V_i + V_t)$ can result in an initial drug concentration larger than predicted because of the smaller initial volume of distribution. For drugs that exert their effects on target organs located in the initial volume, such as lidocaine, the loading dose needs to be administered slow enough to allow for drug distribution into the tissue volume or the total loading dose needs to be given in small increments so the concentration of drug in the initial volume does not reach a toxic level. For drugs with a target organ in the second compartment, such as digoxin, an initial high drug concentration before distribution is expected and is not dangerous.

Half-Life and Elimination Rate Constant

Measuring the drug concentration in plasma (Cp) is generally the only convenient way to obtain data to express pharmacokinetic variables. Because most drugs are eliminated exponentially (first-order elimination), a semilogarithmic plot of plasma concentration vs. time (Fig. 175-3) yields a straight line. The half-life ($t_{1/2}$) is the time it takes for the drug concentration in plasma to decrease by half. The $t_{1/2}$ is related to the elimination rate constant (K_e). Specifically, $t_{1/2} = 0.693/K_e$. Therefore the elimination rate constant $K_e = 0.693/t_{1/2}$. Because $t_{1/2}$ for a given drug is often known or easy to obtain, this relationship is useful in understanding the concepts of clearance, calculations of steady-state plasma concentration (Cp_{ss}, see below), and loading dose.

With the following equation, the concentration at any time (t) can be calculated when the initial concentration (Cp0) and the elimination rate constant (K_e) are known:

$$Cpt = Cp0 \; e^{-K_e \times t}$$

If two concentrations (C1 and C2) and the time elapsed between these concentrations is known (T2 − T1), the elimination rate constant can be calculated with the equation:

$$K_e = \frac{\ln(C1/C2)}{T2 - T1}$$

Half-life can then be calculated with this elimination rate constant.

Most drugs show first-order clearance from plasma. First-order elimination occurs when the amount of drug eliminated from the body is directly proportional to the amount of drug in the body. The fraction of a drug in the body eliminated over a given time remains constant. This concept is different from zero-order elimination, in which the amount of drug eliminated for each time interval is constant, regardless of the amount of drug in the body. In these instances a small increment in dose can result in a more profound rise in drug concentration. Because virtually all drug biotransformation, renal tubular secretion, and certain biliary secretion processes involve enzyme or carrier systems, these systems are capable of being saturated if enough drug is administered. The resulting situation is called zero-order kinetics. Ethanol shows zero-order elimination at such low plasma drug concentrations that it easily accumulates and causes its well-known side effects. Depending on the dose, phenytoin, theophylline, and salicylic acid can be eliminated according to first-order kinetics; however, slight increases may "oversaturate" metabolic clearance and result in zero-order kinetics.

Clearance

Clearance (Cl) is the pharmacokinetic variable that accounts for drug loss from the body. It is a representation of the ability of the body to eliminate a drug. Clearance is expressed as volume of blood (or plasma) cleared of drug per unit time. In fact, it is defined as the product of the volume of distribution (V_d) and the elimination rate constant (K_e).

$$Cl = V_d \times K_e$$

Total drug clearance occurs by two major routes: renal and hepatic (metabolic or biliary elimination). These routes are assumed to be independent and additive ($Cl_t = Cl_h + Cl_r$). Therefore in a patient with renal or hepatic failure, or both, changes in total clearance can be estimated. This adjusted clearance value can then be used to estimate the maintenance dose.

Application of the definition for clearance with previously noted equations generates several useful equations, such as concentration of drug at steady state:

$$Cp_{ss} = \frac{F \times Dose}{Cl \times t} \qquad (1)$$

where F = 1.

$$Cp_{ss} = \frac{Dose}{Cl \times t}$$

where t = time interval between doses.

Because $Cl = V_d \times K_e$, and $K_e = 0.693/t_{1/2}$, if clearance is not known but volume of distribution and $t_{1/2}$ are, clearance can be calculated with the following equation:

$$Cl = V_d \times \frac{0.693}{t_{1/2}} \qquad (2)$$

Thus for IV drug administration, if the dose and interval are known, the steady-state plasma concentration is determined from the following equation:

$$Cp_{ss} = \frac{Dose}{V_d \times \dfrac{0.693}{t_{1/2}} \times t} \qquad (3)$$

When using these equations, units must match (e.g., if $t_{1/2}$ is in minutes, t must be in minutes, not hours). To calculate a dose rate to maintain a specific Cp_{ss}:

$$Dosing \; rate \; (mg/kg/t) = Cp_{ss} \; (mg/L) \times Cl \; (L/kg/t)$$

Dose rate determines absolute concentration at steady state, whereas $t_{1/2}$ determines time to achieve concentration at steady state.

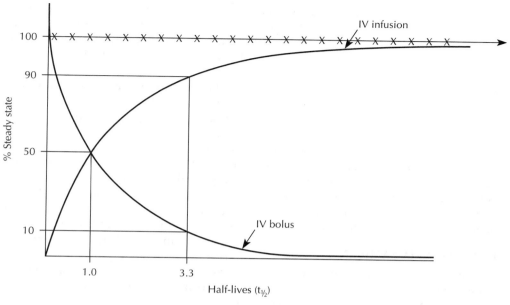

Fig. 175-4   Infusion principles.

Steady State

The time to reach steady state is governed by the $t_{1/2}$ of the drug. The rate of infusion or dosing interval will not affect the time to steady state unless a loading dose or bolus has been given. For first-order rates of reactions, it takes about three and a third half-lives to reach 90% of steady state. By seven half-lives, 99% of steady state has been achieved. With routine monitoring of maximum and minimum plasma concentrations, it is important to wait until steady state has been achieved because of the assumptions made when drawing the minimum concentration ("trough") before the maximum concentration achieved after the dose ("peak"). The ability to use the minimum concentration obtained before the dose and the maximum concentration achieved after the next dose is based on the assumption that with intermittent dosing at steady state all peak and all trough concentrations are the same. Therefore it makes no difference if the minimum concentration is drawn before or after the dose.

Infusion Principles

When an infusion is started, it will still take three to four half-lives to be at >90% steady state (Fig. 175-

4). Once at steady state, the rate of drug input (R_o), or infusion rate, equals the rate of drug output, or clearance (Cl), resulting in the following equation:

$$Cp_{ss}\ (mg/L) = \frac{R_o\ (mg/hr)}{Cl\ (L/hr)}$$

If a bolus is given at the time the infusion is started, it will contribute to the time to achieve steady state because the bolus drug is cleared from the body at the same rate that the infused drug accumulates in the body. In one half-life, 50% of the bolus will have been eliminated, but 50% of the infusion will have accumulated, theoretically resulting in 100% of steady state being achieved. The concentration of both the bolus and the infusion can be calculated at each time point to determine that steady state has indeed been achieved. This underscores the importance of giving a bolus of drug not only when starting infusions but also when adjusting infusion rates, because it will again take three to four half-lives to achieve steady state with changes in infusion rate.

If a bolus is not given and steady state has not been achieved, the concentration of drug in the body can still be calculated if the dosing rate (R_o), elimination rate constant (K_e), and volume of distribution

(V_d) are known. This is done using the following equation:

$$Cp = \frac{R_o}{V_d \times K_e} \times (1 - e^{-K_e \times t})$$

where t is time since start of the infusion.

Extracorporeal Circuits

Measurement of plasma concentrations in a patient maintained with a form of extracorporeal support (ECMO or CVVH) is the most useful means to determine doses and dosing interval. However, these circuits can sometimes have profound effects on the pharmacokinetic parameters of the drug. For a complete discussion of this topic, see Chapter 182.

PRINCIPLES OF PLASMA SAMPLING

To obtain useful drug concentrations, a plan for plasma sampling must consider the route of administration, dosage form, dosing schedule, and pharmacokinetic variables of the drug. Proper interpretation of drug concentrations can be made only if the dose, dosage form, administration times, and sampling time are accurately documented. Without this information, the drug concentrations obtained can be useless or even dangerously misleading.

The timing of the sample must be as close to steady state as possible to assess the efficacy of the current dosage regimen. Blood drawn less than two half-lives after beginning a new drug regimen will allow determination of a volume of distribution but not clearance. Therefore the steady-state concentration cannot be predicted, nor can a maintenance dose be calculated. This is true for intermittent dosing even if a loading dose is given. However, a sample drawn before two half-lives can be useful in some patients to prevent excessive drug accumulation by holding the next scheduled dose if the concentration is too high or to show a loading dose is needed if the concentration is too low. Examples include the patient with renal insufficiency who is receiving a drug that is primarily excreted by the kidneys. Giving a one-time loading dose and obtaining two or three plasma concentrations after dosing allow calculation of volume of distribution and elimination rate. The two plasma samples should be drawn at least one and one-half half-lives apart to ensure the distribution phase is complete and to have the best estimate of half-life for the patient. These two or three samples will then allow the practitioner to more exactly esti-

mate the dose and interval. To obtain information about a drug's steady-state plasma concentration, the sample must not be drawn before three to four half-lives have elapsed (i.e., 87.5% to 92.5% equilibrium reached).

The timing of sampling must also take into consideration the time of dosing and the route of administration. Enough time must be allowed for a drug to distribute from the plasma compartment to its site of action, which may be in the tissues of a specific organ. If a drug concentration is obtained before completion of this distribution phase, it may be significantly higher than expected, and an incorrect adjustment in dosage might be made. For most IV drugs, a sample taken at least 1 hour after the infusion is complete will avoid the initial distribution phase. Two commonly used drugs provide exceptions to this rule. Aminoglycosides may be sampled for maximum plasma concentrations 30 minutes after the infusion is complete, and after an IV dose of digoxin a sample must not be drawn for at least 4 hours because of its very long distribution phase. Drugs administered by means of continuous infusion do not have an appreciable distribution phase, and drug concentrations may be sampled at any time once drug concentration at steady state has been achieved.

Care must be taken not to obtain the blood sample for determination of drug concentration from the same IV line through which the drug is administered. Even if the line is flushed, enough drug may still be present to contaminate the sample and cause a falsely elevated plasma concentration measurement.

For most drugs administered orally, the distribution phase will be shorter than the absorption phase; thus blood may be sampled any time after absorption is complete, usually 1 to 2 hours. Digoxin, again an exception, has a very long distribution phase after oral administration and cannot be sampled sooner than 6 hours after an oral dose.

Table 175-1 shows correct sampling times and therapeutic reference ranges for drugs commonly analyzed at our institution.

INTERPRETATION OF PLASMA DRUG CONCENTRATIONS

To interpret plasma drug concentrations, one must take into account all available clinical information. Therapeutic ranges have been established for many drugs, but these are average values to guide dosing

Table 175-1   Therapeutic Drug Monitoring Collection Guidelines and Therapeutic Ranges

Drug	Optimal Sampling Time	Optimal Serum Concentration Range
Amikacin	Infuse over 30 minutes *Peak:* 30 minutes after end of infusion *Trough:* Immediately before next maintenance dose	*Peak:* 20-30 μg/ml *Trough:* <10 μg/ml
Caffeine	*Peak:* When needed; 2 hours after loading dose *Trough:* Immediately before next maintenance dose	6-20 μg/ml
Carbamazepine	*Trough:* Immediately before morning maintenance dose	8-12 μg/ml
Chloramphenicol	Infuse over 30 minutes *Peak:* 2 hours after end of infusion or 2 hours after oral dose *Trough:* Immediately before next maintenance dose	*Peak:* 10-25 μg/ml *Trough:* 5-15 μg/ml
Digoxin	*Trough:* Immediately before next maintenance dose Sample must be drawn at least 6 hours after most recent IV or PO dose	0.8-2.0 ng/ml
Ethosuximide	*Trough:* Immediately before next maintenance dose	40-100 μg/ml
Flucytosine	*Peak:* 2 hours after dose after at least 4 days of therapy *Trough:* Immediately before next maintenance dose	*Peak:* <100 μg/ml *Trough:* >25 μg/ml
Ganciclovir	Infuse over 1 hour *Peak:* 1 hour after end of 1-hour infusion *Trough:* Immediately before next maintenance dose	Limited data in children *Peak:* 4.7-10 μg/ml *Trough:* 0.2-1.0 μg/ml
Gentamicin	Infuse over 30 minutes *Peak:* 30 minutes after end of infusion *Trough:* Immediately before next maintenance dose	*Peak:* 5-10 μg/ml *Cystic fibrosis:* may require peak of 8-12 μg/ml *Trough:* <2 μg/ml
Lidocaine	6 hours after starting therapy for arrhythmia prophylaxis, then every 24 hours Every 12 hours when there is evidence of cardiac or hepatic insufficiency	1.5-5.0 μg/ml
Phenobarbital	*Trough:* Immediately before next maintenance dose	15-40 μg/ml
Phenytoin	*Trough:* Immediately before next maintenance dose Samples should be drawn at same time each day	10-20 μg/ml (1-2 μg/ml free phenytoin)
Primidone	*Trough:* Immediately before next maintenance dose	5-15 μg/ml
Procainamide	**IV therapy** 2 and 12 hours after starting therapy and every 24 hours for maintenance **PO therapy** *Trough:* Immediately before next oral maintenance dose	4-8 μg/ml *N*-Acetylprocainamide: 7-15 μg/ml
Quinidine	*Trough:* Immediately before next maintenance dose	1-4 μg/ml
Salicylate	*Trough:* Immediately before next oral maintenance dose	150-300 μg/ml
Theophylline	**Infusion therapy** Predose if currently receiving theophylline 0.5-1.0 hour after initial bolus 4-8 hours *and* 24 hours after start of IV drip *and* when rate is changed Every 24 hours for maintenance **Intermittent IV and PO therapy** *Trough:* Just before dose after at least 1 day of therapy	*Asthma:* 10-20 μg/ml *Neonatal apnea:* 5-12 μg/ml
Tobramycin	Infuse over 30 minutes *Peak:* 30 minutes after end of infusion *Trough:* Immediately before next maintenance dose	*Peak:* 5-10 μg/ml *Cystic fibrosis:* may require peaks of 8-12 μg/ml *Trough:* <2 μg/ml
Valproic acid	*Trough:* Immediately before morning oral maintenance dose	50-150 μg/ml
Vancomycin	Infuse over 1 hour; may be infused over 2 hours if clinically indicated *Peak:* 1 hour after end of 1-hour infusion or within ½ hour after end of 2-hour infusion *Trough:* Immediately before next maintenance dose	*Peak:* 25-40 μg/ml *Trough:* <10 μg/ml

and may not apply to all situations. Many factors affect a patient's response to a given concentration of drug at its site of action. Some patients with a seemingly subtherapeutic or toxic drug concentration may receive an adequate therapeutic effect without significant toxicity. Other patients may develop tolerance to a drug after prolonged administration and will need maintenance therapy at a concentration higher than the normal therapeutic limit. Therapeutic ranges of plasma drug concentrations may need to be altered if synergistic or antagonistic drugs are administered at the same time. Changes in drug protein binding or the existence of pharmacologically active metabolites must also be considered in any interpretation of plasma drug concentrations. Recommended therapeutic ranges of drugs are guidelines for dosing. Patient condition and clinical response must also be considered in the total management of each patient's pharmacotherapy.

Unexpected high or low drug concentrations observed in some patients can be caused by several physiologic factors. In addition, one must always consider that an inappropriate dosage might have been given, either because of an incorrect drug order, misinterpretation of an order, or an error in administration. Malabsorption of an orally administered drug in a patient with decreased GI motility from surgery, drugs, or disease will result in reduced concentrations. Changes in bioavailability can occur when drug formulations are changed, yielding unexpected changes in plasma drug concentrations.

When many drugs are administered concurrently in the critically ill patient, the possibility of drug-drug interactions must always be considered. The concentration of one or both of the drugs in question can be affected, and the concentration can be either increased or decreased. Altered plasma drug concentrations can be a result of modification of intestinal absorption of one drug by another, competition for plasma protein binding sites, altered peripheral compartments such as occurs with ascites, or changes in hepatic metabolism or renal excretion of one or both of the drugs. Drugs given intravenously may also be incompatible when administered together, chemically inactivating one and/or the other, with or without an obvious (e.g., visible) physical reaction.

The presence of renal or hepatic disease can decrease the elimination or metabolism of many drugs to varying degrees. Ignoring changes in these organ functions can lead to accumulation of drug with potentially fatal results. If a critically ill patient is known to have renal or hepatic insufficiency, a sampling strategy along with a plan for interpretation of the plasma concentrations is needed before the drug is given to prevent overdosing and maximize drug therapy.

The effects of altered protein binding must be considered in the interpretation of concentrations of any drugs that demonstrate significant binding. In disease states with decreased plasma protein (e.g., hypoalbuminemia) or decreased binding of drugs to plasma (e.g., uremia), the drugs that are usually highly protein bound (>90%) have a larger percent of unbound drug in the plasma. As a result, a greater pharmacologic effect can be expected for a given concentration of total drug in the plasma (which is more commonly measured), and a lower total drug concentration than normal will be needed to obtain the desired therapeutic effect without significant toxicity.

After plasma drug concentrations have been obtained and interpreted, a decision must be made as to whether the dose and dosing interval are appropriate. If a change in dosage is needed, in most cases it can be done by changing the maintenance dose proportional to the change in steady-state plasma concentration desired. If a peak plasma concentration of gentamicin is only 4.5 mg/L when the patient is receiving 40 mg IV every 8 hours, an initial dose increase of 25% (50 mg IV every 8 hours) will be needed to raise the plasma concentration to >5.5 mg/L. With small changes in drug doses, it will take longer to achieve the desired plasma concentration. In critical situations in which a more exact calculation of dosage is needed, a set of plasma drug concentrations can be used to determine individual pharmacokinetic parameters (V_d and K_e), which can then be used for a more precise estimate of the patient's drug dosing regimen. Patients with a large volume of distribution from ascites or another third space often need larger doses to achieve optimal plasma concentrations. At the same time these patients may not need doses as frequently as other children because of concomitant renal or hepatic failure. Taking the time to calculate these simple pharmacokinetic parameters will not only assist in planning optimal therapy in a timely manner but will minimize the number of plasma samples needed and therefore reduce the overall cost of therapy. Blindly obtaining plasma samples and changing dosages on the basis of these measurements is not providing optimal care.

PEDIATRIC PHARMACOKINETICS

Children are not "scaled down adults." Growth rate exceeds that in adults, body proportions are different, and metabolic capabilities are not identical. For example, head circumference of a neonate is nearly 40% that of an adult, but weight (3.5 kg) is approximately 5% of adult weight. Surface-to-volume relationship in infants and adults are so different that in children younger than 1 year (or about 10 kg in weight) dosing based on square meters may result in overdose. Specifically, if dosage is calculated as drug per square meters for a child or adult, and the patient weighs <10 kg, the drug per kilogram dose is calculated by dividing the dose in square meters by 30 (1 m² body surface area equals approximately 30 kg weight) and then multiplying by the infant's weight (in kilograms).

Because pharmacokinetics involves drug absorption, distribution, metabolism, and eventually elimination of the parent compound and metabolites, and significant differences exist between adult and pediatric populations with regard to these variables, age-dependent alterations in drug pharmacokinetics and ultimately pharmacodynamics are common. If these differences are not appreciated, needless drug toxicity or ineffective therapy may result. A thorough review of these considerations for drug dosing is included in Chapter 178.

ADDITIONAL READING

Benet LZ, Massoud N, Gambertoglio JG. Pharmacokinetic Basis for Drug Treatment. New York: Raven Press, 1984.

Clark B, Smith DA. An Introduction to Pharmacokinetics. Oxford, England: Blackwell Scientific Publications, 1981.

DiPiro JT, Blouin RA, Pruemer JM. Concepts in Clinical Pharmacokinetics. Bethesda, Md.: American Society of Hospital Pharmacists, 1988.

Evans WE, Schentag JJ, Jusko WJ. Applied Pharmacokinetics: Principles of Therapeutic Drug Monitoring. Vancouver, Wash.: Applied Therapeutics, 1992.

Morselli PL. Clinical pharmacokinetics in neonates. Clin Pharmacokinet 1:81-98, 1976.

• Peck CC, Conner DP, Murphy MG. Bedside Clinical Pharmacokinetics: Simple Techniques for Individualizing Drug Therapy. Vancouver, Wash.: Applied Therapeutics, 1989.

Rane A, Wilson JT. Clinical pharmacokinetics in infants and children. Clin Pharmacokinet 1:2-24, 1976.

Rowland M, Towzer TN. Clinical Pharmacokinetics: Concepts and Applications, 3rd ed. Baltimore: Williams & Wilkins, 1995.

Steward CF, Hampton EM. Effect of maturation of drug disposition in pediatric patients. Clin Pharm 6:548-564, 1987.

Winter ME. Basic Clinical Pharmacokinetics. Vancouver, Wash.: Applied Therapeutics, 1980, pp 5-67.

176 Receptor Physiology

Grace M. Arteaga · Blair E. Cox

BACKGROUND

A receptor by its most basic definition is any cellular entity that possesses chemical specificity and is able to interact with high-affinity molecules so that functions of a cell are regulated. Cells are protected and isolated from the environment by a plasma membrane, and to survive they must be able to communicate with the external environment. Cell-to-cell communication is accomplished through an elaborate system of proteins that enables a cell to respond to signals received from the surrounding milieu, including other cells. This system includes a variety of cell-surface or membrane-associated receptive proteins, or *receptors,* which are the messengers through which extracellular events are communicated to the intracellular environment.

Cell Signaling

As higher animals evolved, there arose a need for a method whereby cells of a multicellular organism could communicate with one another. Cell communication in eukaryotic animals is mediated by a multitude of different activating or signaling molecules, including amino acids, nucleotides, small peptides, steroids, retinoids, fatty acid derivatives, and dissolved gases such as nitric oxide. Most of these signaling molecules are secreted from the cell by exocytosis, some diffuse through the plasma membrane, and others remain tightly bound to the cell surface and influence only cells that contact the signaling cell. These signaling substances *(ligands)* have high affinity for and bind specifically to specific receptor proteins located mainly in the membranes of targeted cells (Fig. 176-1). The receptor recognition-activation interaction evokes a cascade of biochemical reactions that culminate in regulation of cellular function. Thus cell signaling involves the recognition and binding of a ligand to a receptor followed by transduction of the signal into the targeted cell.

Synaptic signaling is a prime example of local cell communication whereby secreted signaling molecules are rapidly taken up by neighboring target cells to produce regional effects. Synaptic signaling is best characterized by nerve cells. When nerve cells are stimulated, an electrical impulse is sent along the axon, the terminal end of which resides in close contact with target cells. At the terminal end of the axon the impulse stimulates the secretion of a chemical neurotransmitter ligand into the synaptic cleft, where it acts on receptors of the postsynaptic target cell. Another example of cellular communication is endocrine signaling. Endocrine cells secrete their signaling ligand (hormones) into the bloodstream, where it can act not only locally but also be carried to target cells in distant locations. In autocrine signaling the cells stimulate themselves and the similar

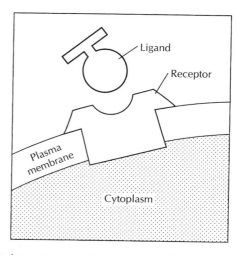

Fig. 176-1   Diagram of receptor-ligand interaction. A target receptor protein binds a signaling molecule with high specificity.

surrounding cells, enhancing local stimulation. The products of arachidonic acid metabolism are a well-defined example. When these products are released to the external environment from within the cell, their effects on the surrounding cells include platelet aggregation and inflammatory responses, among other activities.

Signal Recognition

The ability to biochemically signal and transmit events from outside the cell to the inside distinguishes a receptor from other membrane-associated elements. Any given cell in a multicellular organism is exposed to a multitude of different signals from the external environment, yet cells are capable of responding to these signals selectively because of specific characteristics acquired through cell specialization.

RECEPTOR BINDING THEORY

During the 1920s A.J. Clark pioneered drug-receptor action theory, and his work remains key to understanding the relationship between drug-receptor complexes. The study of receptor binding incorporates the laws of mass action, thermodynamics, and kinetics. The following brief, simplified summary is designed to address some of the more important aspects of drug-receptor interactions.

Drug-Receptor Interaction

To help convey a few important concepts of drug-receptor interactions, a review of the terminology is in order. A ligand that is able to inhibit the action of a drug *(agonist)* while causing no effect itself is an *antagonist*. If the inhibition caused by the antagonistic ligand is reversible with increasing amounts of drug, then the antagonist is said to be surmountable, or *competitive;* that is, it binds reversibly with the receptor. In contrast, a *noncompetitive* antagonist prevents the drug from producing any effect at the receptor as a result of irreversible binding or alteration of the receptor. Thus antagonists may be classified as reversible or irreversible. Because some ligands may bind to receptors better than others do, they are said to have greater *affinity* for the receptor. Furthermore, a ligand that has greater affinity than the drug intended for that receptor, yet produces a lesser effect, is called a *partial agonist*. Finally, although the binding of an agonist to a receptor produces an effect, not all agonists that bind to the same receptor site may produce a maximal effect; that is, ligands also possess the quality of intrinsic activity, or *efficacy*. Thus affinity and efficacy are intimately related in terms of drug or ligand potency.

If we assume a drug interacts reversibly with a receptor, that is, there is constant association and dissociation of the drug with the receptor, and that the effect elicited is proportional to the number of receptors occupied, this equation is expressed as follows:

$$\text{Drug (D)} + \text{Receptor (R)} \underset{k_1}{\overset{k_2}{\rightleftarrows}} \text{DR} \rightarrow \text{Effect}$$

where k_1 = the association rate (DR) and k_2 = the dissociation rate (D)(R). This interaction can be analyzed with the familiar form of the Michaelis-Menten equation:

$$\text{Effect} = \frac{\text{Maximal effect (D)}}{K_D + \text{(D)}}$$

where D = the free drug concentration and K_D = the dissociation constant for the drug-receptor complex. This equation describes a hyperbolic curve where there is no effect when D = 0, a half-maximal effect when D = K_D (i.e., half of the receptors are occupied), and the maximal effect is approached as D further increases. A sigmoidal curve is generated when the effect is plotted against the negative logarithm of the drug dose (Fig. 176-2).

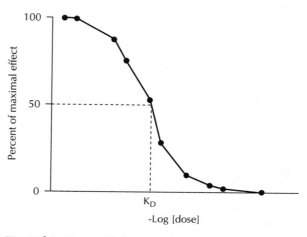

Fig. 176-2 Sigmoidal dose-response curve. The y-axis represents the percent of maximal effect. The x-axis represents the negative logarithmic drug dose. The effect is half-maximal when dose concentration equals K_D.

Mathematical Characterization of Receptors

An identical equation is used in equilibrium saturation studies designed to further characterize the density and affinity of receptors:

$$B_E = \frac{B_{max}\ F}{K_D + F}$$

where B_E = the amount of ligand bound to receptors at equilibrium, B_{max} = the maximum number of receptor binding sites, F = the free ligand concentration, and K_D = the dissociation constant for the ligand-receptor complex.

Finally, by taking the reciprocal of both sides of these equations, that is, using the Lineweaver-Burke format,

$$\frac{1}{Effect} = \frac{K_D}{Maximal\ effect\ (D)} + \frac{1}{Maximal\ effect}$$

we generate a straight line that intersects the y-axis at 1/(maximal effect) and has a slope equal to K_D/(maximal effect) (Fig. 176-3). Extrapolating this line to the x-axis gives the value of the intercept, $-1/K_D$. From this type of graphic representation, the value at which the effect of a drug or ligand is half-maximal (K_D) and the maximal effect of the ligand can be readily calculated. This double reciprocal plot is useful to examine the potency and efficacy of different ligands; however, in examining receptors with radioligand binding studies, a plot described by Scatchard is commonly used. The Scatchard plot describes the relationship between the bound-free ligand ratio vs. the bound ligand:

$$B_E = B_{max} - K_D\frac{B_E}{F}$$

This type of plot yields a straight line with a slope equal to the negative reciprocal of K_D ($-1/K_D$) and an x-intercept equal to the maximum number of receptor binding sites (B_{max}) (Fig. 176-4). Thus the number and affinity of receptors being examined are obtained from a Scatchard plot.

RECEPTOR TYPES

Receptors are either intracellular or cell-surface associated. Once activated, they are able to transmit information to the cell by various mechanisms. Intracellular receptors usually interact with the nuclear DNA and use signaling molecules that are sufficiently small to pass through the plasma membrane, whereas cell-surface receptors use more diverse mechanisms of signal transduction such as modification of

an ion channel, modulation of receptor-associated enzymatic activity, and activation of numerous second messenger systems.

Intracellular Receptors

A family of receptors that resemble each other in structure within the cell is called the intracellular receptor superfamily. Binding of ligands to these receptors, which are located within the nucleus, activates certain gene transcriptions. The signaling molecules for this group include steroid hormones, thyroid hormones, retinoids, and vitamins. All these ligands have in common their small size, hydrophobic characteristics, and ability to bind to blood proteins as carriers for bloodstream transportation and the ability to dissociate from their transfer protein before entering the cell. Intracellular receptors bind to specific sequences (i.e., hormone response elements) that are adjacent to the genes that the ligand regulates. When intracellular receptors are activated by ligand binding, they undergo a conformational change that allows binding of this complex to intranuclear DNA. Alberts et al. describe a dual response within the nucleus after DNA has been activated by the ligand-receptor complex, referred to as the primary and secondary response. The primary response includes direct activation of a specific group of genes (Fig. 176-5, *A*) and the secondary response refers to how the initial transcription products will activate another set of genes in a delayed response (indirect activation) (Fig. 176-5, *B*).

Cell-Surface Receptors

The three well-described classes of cell-surface receptors are ion channel linked, catalytic or enzyme linked, and G protein linked. These cell-surface receptor proteins act as a signal transducer after ligand binding and are located within the plasma membrane.

Ion channel–linked receptors, or transmitter-gated ion channels, allow rapid movement of ions directly into the cell. The conduction system within the heart and neuronal transmission are two systems that use this type of receptor (Fig. 176-6, *A*). These receptors are able to regulate the movement of ions into and out of the cell by assembling as a protein oligomer around a cell membrane pore (channel) to effectively control the gateway to specific ionic flux. Examples of ion channels modified by receptor linkage include sodium channels (nicotinic-cholinergic receptor), chloride channels (γ-aminobutyric acid

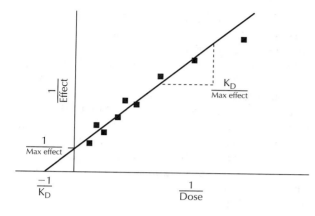

Fig. 176-3   Double-reciprocal plot. The y-axis represents the reciprocal of the percent of maximal effect. The x-axis represents the reciprocal of the drug dose. The extrapolated x-intercept of the line equals the negative reciprocal of K_D. The slope of the line equals K_D/maximal effect.

Fig. 176-4   Scatchard plot. The y-axis represents the ratio of bound/free ligand. The x-axis represents the amount of bound ligand. The x-intercept of the line equals the maximum number of receptor binding sites (B_{max}). The slope of the line equals the negative reciprocal of K_D (i.e., receptor binding affinity).

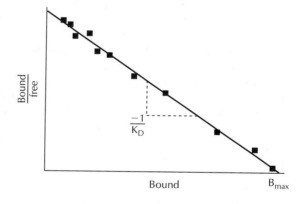

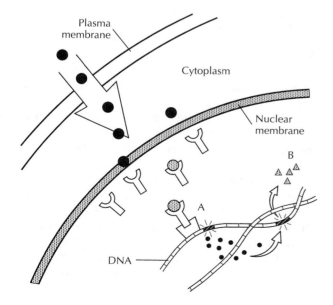

Fig. 176-5   Diagram of intracellular receptors and their actions. Diffusible ligand molecules bind to intracellular receptors. The receptor-ligand complex is then able to bind to specific regions of DNA (hormone response element). This interaction initiates protein synthesis (*A*, primary response or direct activation). The resulting product of gene activation is itself capable of binding to other DNA response elements and inducing synthesis of other gene products (*B*, secondary response or indirect activation).

[GABA], and glycine receptors), and calcium channels (muscarinic cholinergic, angiotensin, and pancreozymin receptors).

Another signaling mechanism that cell-surface receptors use is the modulation of receptor-associated enzymatic activity (see Fig. 176-6, *B*). Enzyme-linked or catalytic receptors have enzymatic activity integrally associated with their intracellular domain. These receptors are transmembrane proteins that span the membrane usually once only, decreasing the exposure of the receptor to membrane lipids and thereby facilitating receptor mobility and internalization. They have a ligand-binding domain exposed to the plasma membrane outer surface and a cytosolic domain with the associated enzyme activity. Their activation leads to enhanced enzymatic activity within the cell that can mediate important events such as phosphorylation-dephosphorylation reactions that are necessary to facilitate signaling cascades. Growth factors such as platelet-derived growth factor (PDGF) bind to this type of receptor causing phosphorylation of tyrosine residues in targeted proteins. Stimulation of this type of receptor can also activate long-term nuclear-mediated events such as cellular differentiation and proliferation. The effects of growth factors (e.g., epidermal growth factor, nerve growth factor, and PDGF) are mediated through activation of receptors of this class. Furthermore, molecular alterations that lead to activation of these receptors can lead to oncogenesis. Some investigators speculate that certain disorders of development may be due to mutations that modify or inactivate selective receptors.

The largest family of cell-surface receptors has the well-described feature of seven transmembrane-spanning regions, each consisting of 20 to 28 hydrophobic amino acids separated by four extracellular and four intracellular domains. These receptors (Fig. 176-6, *C*) indirectly regulate the activity of separate plasma membrane–bound targets (e.g., an enzyme or ion channel) through interactions that are mediated by heterotrimeric guanine nucleotide (GTP)–binding regulatory proteins *(G proteins).*

Trimeric G proteins, identified by Gilman et al., are composed of α-, β- and γ-subunits, which are thought to disassemble when activated. G proteins in the resting stage consist of a complex of the three subunits with dimeric guanine nucleotide (GDP) bound to the α-subunit. With receptor-ligand activation, the receptor changes conformation so that it can bind to

the trimeric G protein, causing the α-subunit to release GDP. GTP immediately binds to this available site, resulting in activation of the α-subunit. The α-subunit–GTP complex now dissociates from the β- and γ-subunits, moving along the plasma membrane until an effector is found (e.g., an ion channel or enzyme) (see Fig. 176-6, *C*). After α-subunit–effector interaction, the α-subunit hydrolyses GTP to GDP and becomes deactivated. The inactivated α-subunit then dissociates from its effector and returns to the resting state, that is, association with the β- and γ-subunits. Alteration of the receptor–G protein–effector mechanism is involved in the pathophysiology of various diseases. Cholera is a prime example in which a bacterial toxin prevents the α-subunit from hydrolyzing GTP to GDP. The α-subunit is unable to dissociate with its ion channel effector, and as a consequence intestinal cells accumulate large amounts of cyclic adenosine monophosphate (cAMP), causing massive secretion of electrolytes and water into the intestinal lumen, which results in severe diarrhea and subsequent dehydration.

SECOND MESSENGER SYSTEMS

Many receptors activate one or more intracellular mediators that are often referred to as *second messengers*. The best described intracellular messengers are cAMP, cyclic GMP (cGMP), calcium (Ca^{2+}), inositol triphosphate (IP_3), diacylglycerol (DAG), and protein kinases. A list of some of the more common receptors and their second messengers is found in Table 176-1. None of these secondary messengers mediates their effects alone but in conjunction with one or more other second messengers.

Cyclic AMP

cAMP (Fig. 176-7, *A*) is synthesized from ATP by an enzyme bound to the plasma membrane, adenylyl cyclase (previously called adenylate cyclase), and is rapidly destroyed by the enzyme phosphodiesterase. The G protein involved in activation of the membrane-bound enzyme is called stimulatory G protein (G_s). The best example of receptors coupled to adenylyl cyclase are the adrenergic receptors, which mediate some of the actions of epinephrine and norepinephrine. When epinephrine binds to a β-adrenergic receptor, adenylyl cyclase is activated, whereas when epinephrine binds to an α_2-adrenergic receptor, adenylyl cyclase is inhibited by an inhibitory G protein (see Table 176-1). Thus the same ligand

Table 176-1   Common Receptors and Their Interaction With Second Messenger Systems

Receptor	Subtype	Second Messenger	Stimulation (+) or Inhibition (−)
ACTH		PI,* Ca^{2+}	
Adenosine	A_1	cAMP	−
	A_2	cAMP	+
Adrenergic	α_1	PI, Ca^{2+}, cGMP	
	α_2	cAMP	−
	β_1	cAMP	−
	β_2	cAMP	+
Angiotensin II	AT_1	cAMP	−
		PI, CA^{2+}	
	AT_2	cGMP	?
Atrial natriuretic factor		cAMP	−
		cGMP	
Bradykinin		PI, CA^{2+}	
Dopamine	D_1	cAMP	+
	D_2	cAMP	−
		PI	
GABA	$GABA_B$	cAMP	+
Glucagon		cAMP	+
Histamine	H_1	PI, Ca^{2+}	
	H_2	cAMP	+
Insulin		cAMP	+
		PI	
Muscarinic cholinergic	M_1	PI, Ca^{2+}, cGMP	
	M_2	cAMP	−
Parathyroid hormone		cAMP	+
Platelet activating factor		cAMP	−
		PI, CA^{2+}	
PGE_1		cAMP	+
PGE_2		cAMP	−
Serotonin	$5\text{-}HT_1$	PI, Ca^{2+}	
	$5\text{-}HT_2$	cAMP	+
Thyrotropin releasing hormone		PI, Ca^{2+}	
Thyroid stimulating hormone		PI, Ca^{2+}	
Vasopressin	V_1	PI, Ca^{2+}	
	V_2	cAMP	+

*PI → PIP → IP_3 + DAG; see p. 1679.

can either increase or decrease the intracellular concentration of cAMP, depending on the type of G protein associated with the receptor.

cAMP-dependent protein kinase or protein kinase A mediates the effects of cAMP by catalyzing the transfer of the terminal phosphate group from ATP to an amino acid, in this case to selective serines or threonines. Protein kinase A is found in all eukaryotic cells; therefore it is currently believed that the bi-ologic action of cAMP is related for the most part to protein phosphorylation.

Signal amplification is one of the important intracellular effects of the cAMP system and involves the phosphorylation (activation) of multiple target proteins. Maintaining a brief and transient activation is important in cellular signaling. The signal ends when the activated (phosphorylated) proteins are dephosphorylated by intracellular phosphatases.

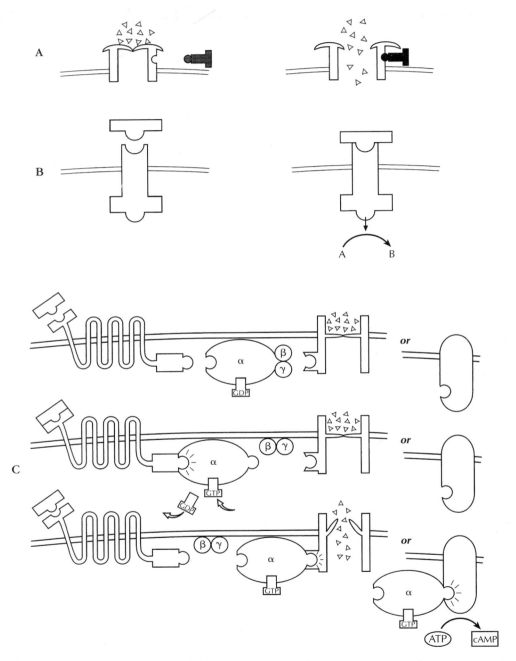

Fig. 176-6 Diagram of cell-surface receptors. **A,** Ion-channel receptors. **B,** Catalytic receptors. **C,** G protein–linked receptors.

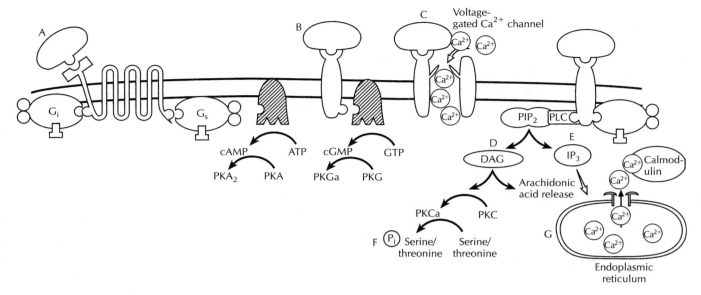

Fig. 176-7 Schema of receptor interactions with second messengers. *A*, cAMP. *B*, cGMP. *C*, Calcium via Ca^{2+} channels. *D*, DAG. *E*, Inositol triphosphate. *F*, Protein kinases. *G*, Calcium via intracellular Ca^{2+} stores. (PK = Protein kinase; PK_a = activated protein kinase; *PKC* = protein kinase C.)

Cyclic GMP

In contrast to receptors that are linked to adenylyl cyclase, receptors linked to cGMP are less well understood. cGMP-linked receptor signaling involves an enzymatic machinery similar to the cAMP second messenger system: (1) an enzyme, guanylyl cyclase, to synthesize cGMP; (2) a second enzyme, cGMP phosphodiesterase, to dephosphorylate the molecule and inactivate it; and (3) a cGMP protein kinase system (protein kinase G) to transmit the information within the cell (see Fig. 176-7, *B*). Recent investigations have revealed that nitric oxide biology and atrial natriuretic factor physiology involve cGMP as the intracellular signal transductor.

Calcium

Calcium is used in receptor signaling by most eukaryotic cells and is even more widely used as a second messenger. The transient increases of intracellular Ca^{2+} cause a vast array of bioactivity, including depolarization and neurotransmitter release (nerve cells), contraction (smooth, skeletal, and cardiac muscle), and hormone secretion. Thus Ca^{2+} function as a second messenger depends not only on the cell type but on the kind of receptor to which it is coupled. To use Ca^{2+} as an intracellular signal, cells must keep resting cytoplasmic Ca^{2+} levels within strict control. The concentration of Ca^{2+} in the cytoplasm of any cell is extremely low (10^{-7} M), whereas its concentration in the extracellular fluid (10^{-3} M) and in the endoplasmic and sarcoplasmic reticulum is very high. Intracellular Ca^{2+} concentrations are kept low by several mechanisms, including sequestration into the endoplasmic reticulum and mitochondria and binding of free Ca^{2+} to binding molecules (i.e., calmodulin). When a cell-surface receptor involved in Ca^{2+} release is activated, intracellular Ca^{2+} concentrations rapidly rise with movement of ions into the cell through surface membrane Ca^{2+} channels (see Fig. 176-7, *C*), as seen in excitable cells such as neurons and cardiac myocytes and mobilization of Ca^{2+} from intracellular stores such as endoplasmic reticulum or sarcoplasmic reticulum, depending on the cell type.

Inositol Triphosphate

It has been well demonstrated that IP_3 is the mediator of Ca^{2+} release (see Fig. 176-7, *E*). The production of IP_3 occurs with activation of G protein–linked receptors that activate phospholipase C (PLC). This enzyme catalyzes the release of IP_3 from phosphatidylinositol 4,5-biphosphate (PIP_2), a phosphorylated derivative of phosphatidylinositol (PI). These phosphorylated substrates of IP_3 are thought to be located in the inner half of the plasma membrane lipid bilayer in all cell membranes. Several cell-surface receptors use this pathway (see Table 176-1). At the same time IP_3 is mediating the release of calcium, the other cleavage product of PIP_2, diacylglycerol, is mediating other cellular effects through a different mechanism.

Diacylglycerol

DAG (see Fig. 176-7, *F*), derived from inositol phospholipids, contributes to important messenger systems. PIP_2, localized at the plasma membrane, hydrolyses into IP_3, which then enhances cellular responses through Ca^{2+} and DAG, activating protein kinase C, an important serine-threonine protein kinase system known to activate gene transcription in many cells.

Protein Kinases

Activation of many proteins involves a process of phosphorylation that is accomplished by protein kinases. A large enzymatic group, while second messengers, are capable of activating a multitude of different protein kinases. A common protein kinase, protein kinase C (PKC; see Fig. 176-7, *G*), is so termed because it is calcium dependent and is stimulated by Ca^{2+}, DAG, and phospholipid. The activation of PKC in many cells can induce proliferation, membrane transport, cellular secretion, or the transcription of specific genes. Knowledge of the various protein kinases and phosphatases and their respective mechanisms of action continues to grow rapidly. In certain disease states our current understanding has led to the use of natural and synthetic compounds that inhibit protein kinases and phosphatases. Some examples include immunosuppressants, tumor suppressants, anti-inflammatory agents, tumor promoters, and herbicides.

RECEPTOR REGULATION

The number of receptor sites available to a ligand at any time is in a state of constant change. Moreover, the intracellular signaling mechanism(s) for the available receptors may or may not be functional. Therefore the total number of *active* receptor sites is dynamic. Cellular responses mediated by receptors, especially those coupled to G proteins, become attenuated from continuous ligand stimulation. This phe-

nomenon is termed desensitization, tachyphylaxis, adaptation, or tolerance. For example, in congestive heart failure, β-adrenergic receptor response to β-adrenergic agonist stimulation is markedly reduced. This occurs by at least two mechanisms: decreased number of physical receptor binding sites, or *down regulation,* and loss of receptor function, or *uncoupling.*

Up Regulation and Down Regulation

Up regulation or down regulation of receptors is a slow adaptation process that generally occurs over hours and results in long-term modification of cellular responsiveness. Receptor up regulation implies an increase in the physical number of available receptor binding sites secondary to either increased synthesis of receptor proteins or removal of receptor-occupying ligand, making that site again available for binding. In contrast, down regulation implies a decrease in available receptor binding sites. One way this occurs is by a decrease in the absolute number of receptors. Ligand-receptor binding occurring on the surface of a target cell is followed by receptor-mediated endocytosis of the receptor-ligand complex into an endosome. Although receptors are usually recycled back to the plasma membrane, a portion fail to release their ligand and end up in lysosomes, where the receptor-ligand complex is degraded, resulting in a gradual loss of receptors. Receptor desensitization also can occur as the result of continuous occupancy of receptors by an antagonist that in effect makes them unavailable for ligand binding and subsequent signaling. Finally, stimulation or occupation of a receptor by a ligand can signal a message specifically directed to the regulation of receptor synthesis (i.e., *feedback message*). Therefore receptor binding sites may increase or decrease as a result of positive or negative feedback messages, respectively.

Signal Uncoupling

Attenuation of cellular responses that occur within seconds to minutes after receptor activation are usually the result of receptor phosphorylation. A good example is the exposure of β-adrenergic receptors to high concentrations of epinephrine, which activates adenylate cyclase by G_s (see Table 176-1 and Fig. 176-7, *A*). These receptors become uncoupled within minutes secondary to receptor phosphorylation. The activated β-adrenergic receptor becomes a substrate for β-adrenergic kinase, which phosphorylates multiple serine and threonine residues on the carboxyl-terminal cytoplasmic tail of the receptor. This phosphorylated tail allows binding of an inhibitory protein, β-arrestin, which interferes with the coupling of the receptor to G proteins, thus blocking the activation of G_s and effectively uncoupling the receptor from its secondary signaling messengers.

Although receptors are becoming fairly well classified, much is still being discovered about how known receptors and newly discovered receptor subtypes function and are regulated. As better understanding in these areas is gained, the role of receptors in normal physiology and various disease states becomes more apparent.

ADDITIONAL READING

• Alberts B, Bray D, Lewis J, Raff M, Roberts K, Watson JD, eds. Cell signaling. In Molecular Biology of the Cell. New York: Garland, 1994, pp 721-785.

Armstrong PW, Moe GW. Medical advances in the treatment of congestive heart failure. Circulation 88:2941-2952, 1994.

Ashcroft FM, Röper J. Transporters, channels and human disease. Curr Opin Cell Biol 5:677-683, 1993.

Beato M. Gene regulation by steroid hormones. Cell 56:335-344, 1989.

Hausdorff WP, Caron MC, Lefkowitz RJ. Turning off the signal: Desensitization of β-adrenergic receptor function. FASEB J 4:2881-2889, 1990.

Hepler JR, Gilman AG. G proteins. Trends Biochem Sci 17:383-387, 1992.

Kleinsmith LJ, Kish VM, Principles of Cell and Molecular Biology, 2nd ed., chaps 6 and 11. New York: Harper Collins, 1995.

Knowles RG, Moncada S. Nitric oxide as a signal in blood vessels. Trends Biochem Sci 17:399-402, 1992.

Linder ME, Gilman AG. G proteins. Sci Am 267:56-65, 1992.

Liu J. FK506 and cyclosporin: Molecular probes for studying intracellular signal transduction. Trends Pharm Sci 14:182-188, 1993.

McConkey DJ, Orrenius S. Signal transduction pathway to apoptosis. Trends Cell Biol 4:370-375, 1994.

Wilson C. Receptor tyrosine kinase signalling: Not so complex after all? Trends Biochem Sci 4:409-414, 1994.

• Williams M, Glennon RA, Timmermans PBMW, eds. Receptor Pharmacology and Function. New York: Marcel Dekker, 1989, p 778.

177 Pharmacologic Support of the Cardiovascular System

R. Phil Barton · Lynn Mahony

BACKGROUND

The cardiorespiratory compromise that is common in patients in the PICU may often be treated effectively with a variety of pharmacologic agents. The goal of treatment is to improve oxygen delivery to vital tissue beds by increasing cardiac index and modulating vascular tone.

Because all of these agents have both beneficial and adverse effects, optimal patient care dictates a rational approach to drug therapy. For example, in pediatric patients drug kinetics and cellular responsiveness may change with age. Therefore, when a diagnosis has been established, knowledge of the mechanism of action and drug dosing and careful monitoring for efficacy and toxicity will improve the bedside clinician's ability to use these agents effectively.

The purpose of this chapter is to review the pharmacology and clinical use of agents commonly used in the PICU. Tables 177-1 and 177-2 provide summary information regarding administration, preparation, dosing, and effects.

SYMPATHOMIMETIC AMINES (CATECHOLAMINES)
Adrenergic Receptor Physiology

Adrenergic receptors constitute a complex group of glycoproteins in the cell membrane, which receives signals from a circulating hormone or neurotransmitter. The three major classifications of adrenergic receptors include α-adrenergic, β-adrenergic, and dopaminergic (DA) receptors. Each receptor class has two clinically important subtypes: α_1- and α_2-, β_1- and β_2-, and DA_1 and DA_2 receptors (Table 177-3). The signals received by adrenergic receptors (except α_1) are transmitted to the intracellular space, in part by G protein–coupled regulation of adenylate cyclase (Fig. 177-1). Stimulation of adenylate cyclase in-

creases the concentration of the second messenger, cyclic adenine monophosphate (cAMP). This activates cAMP-dependent protein kinases that phosphorylate important cardiac and vascular muscular proteins. Phosphorylation of these proteins causes alterations in intracellular calcium transients that lead to tissue-specific cellular responses. Inhibition of adenylate cyclase decreases the concentration of cAMP and thus causes the opposite response.

Transmission of signals received by α_1- receptors is mediated by a G protein (G_q) and results in activation of phospholipase C. The resulting increases in concentrations of the second messengers, inositol triphosphate (IP_3) and 1,2-diacyglycerol (DAG), alter intracellular calcium transients, thereby producing a cellular response.

Many clinical conditions affect the function of adrenergic receptors. β-Adrenergic receptors may be desensitized (down regulated) by prolonged, continuous exposure to catecholamines, myocardial ischemia, chronic congestive heart failure, cardiopulmonary bypass, and severe systemic inflammatory response syndrome (e.g., sepsis or shock). The function of β-adrenergic receptors may also be decreased because of physiologic "uncoupling" at the G protein level. Causes of this uncoupling include hypercalcemia, severe acidosis (pH <7.0), and possibly high circulating cytokine levels. Down regulation of α_1-receptors has been described in congestive heart failure, and resistance to α_1-receptor stimulation occurs in sepsis because of down regulation of the receptors and uncoupling of the receptors to phosphoinositide generation. Finally, age-related changes in receptor density, coupling of receptors, regulation of second messenger concentrations, and effector systems may affect the responsiveness of neonates and young infants to adrenergic agents.

Table 177-1 Administration and Preparation of Inotrope/Vasopressor/Vasodilator Infusions*

Drug	Diluent	Preparation	Infusion Rate
Epinephrine†‡	NS	0.6 mg × body weight (in kg);	1 ml/hr delivers
Norepinephrine†‡	DW	added to diluent to make 100 ml	0.1 μg/kg/min
Isoproterenol‡	NS or DW		
Milrinone§	NS		
Phenylephrine	DW		
Dopamine‡	NS or DW	6 mg × body weight (in kg);	1 ml/hr delivers
Dobutamine‡	NS or DW	added to diluent to make 100 ml	1.0 μg/kg/min
Amrinone†§	NS		
Nitroglycerin‖	NS or DW		
Nitroprusside†	DW		

Rule of six times five: 0.6 mg × body weight (in kg) × 5 added to diluent to make
100 ml, where 1 ml/hr delivers 0.5 μg/kg/min
6 mg × body weight (in kg) × 5 added to diluent to make 100
ml, where 1 ml/hr delivers 5.0 μg/kg/min

NS = normal saline solution (0.09% sodium chloride); DW = dextrose in water.
*Modified from Zaritsky A, Chernow B. Use of catecholamines in pediatrics. J Pediatr 105:341, 1984.
†Photoprotection required because of photochemical degradation.
‡Unstable in alkaline solutions.
§Degradation occurs when directly diluted with dextrose-containing solutions.
‖Must be prepared in glass containers and administered through special sets intended for nitroglycerin.

Table 177-2 Inotropes and Vasoactive Agents

Drug	Dose	Receptor	Effects and Comments
Dopamine	0.5-2.0 μg/kg/min	DA_1	Splanchnic vasodilator
	2-6.0 μg/kg/min	DA_1, β_1	
	6-15 μg/kg/min	$\beta_1 > \alpha_1$	Inotropic effects greater than vasopressor effects
	15-25 μg/kg/min	$\alpha_1 = \beta_1$	Vasopressor effects at higher doses
Norepinephrine	<0.5 μg/kg/min	$\alpha_1 = \beta_1$	Both vasopressor and inotropic effects
	0.5-4.0 μg/kg/min	$\alpha_1 > \beta_1$	Vasopressor effects predominate
Epinephrine	0.05-0.3 μg/kg/min	β_1 and $\beta_2 > \alpha_1$	Inotropic and mild vasodilatory effects
	0.3-2.0 μg/kg/min	$\beta_1 = \alpha_1$	Inotropic and vasoconstrictive effects
Isoproterenol	0.1-5.0 μg/kg/min	$\beta_1 = \beta_2$	Increases cardiac output, mainly from tachycardia; potent bronchodilator; positive inotrope and stimulation cause vasodilation
Dobutamine	2-20 μg/kg/min	β_1	Pure inotrope with mild vasodilatory effects
	>20 μg/kg/min	β_1, α_1	Some α-vasoconstriction effect begins
Phenylephrine	0.1-0.5 μg/kg/min	$\alpha_1 > \alpha_2$	Pure vasoconstrictive effect, no inotropy
Amrinone	0.75-4.0 mg/kg load		Phosphodiesterase III inhibitor; may be used as adjunctive therapy with catecholamines; positive inotropic and vasodilatory effects; long half-life; thrombocytopenia
	5-20 μg/kg/min		
Milrinone	50-75 μg/kg load		Compared with amrinone: more potent, shorter half-life, much less incidence of thrombocytopenia
	0.5-1.0 μg/kg/min		
Nitroprusside	0.5-10.0 μg/kg/min		Arterial and venous vasodilator; potential for thiocyanate and cyanide toxicity, especially in patients with hepatic and renal insufficiency
Nitroglycerin	0.5-20.0 μg/kg/min		Venous dilation and some arterial dilation at high doses

DA = dopaminergic receptor.

Table 177-3   Adrenergic Receptor Profiles*

Receptor	G Protein	Biochemical Action	Physiologic Action
α_1	G_q	Increase IP$_3$ and 1,2-DAG	Vasoconstriction
α_2	G_i	Decrease cAMP	Vasodilation, (−) chronotropy
β_1	G_s	Increase cAMP	Inotropy, chronotropy
β_2	G_s	Increase cAMP	Vasodilation, bronchodilation
DA$_1$	G_s	Increase cAMP	Vasodilation
DA$_2$	G_i	Decrease cAMP	Inhibits prolactin, β-endorphin

DA = dopaminergic; IP$_3$ = inositol triphosphate; 1,2-DAG = 1,2-diacylglycerol.
*Modified from Notterman DA. Pharmacologic support of the failing circulation: An approach for infants and children. Probl Anesth 3:288, 1989.

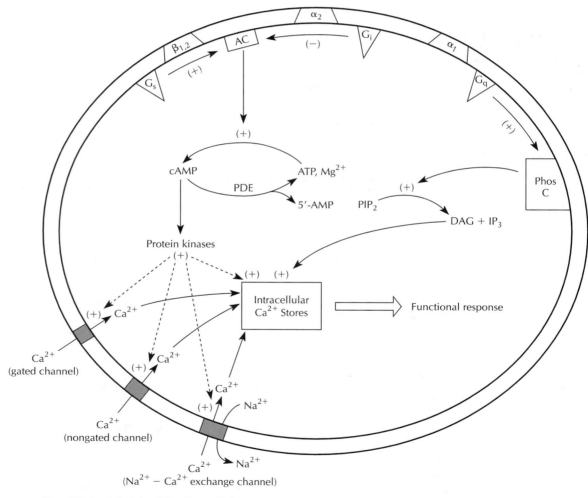

Fig. 177-1   Schema of the intracellular responses to adrenergic receptor stimulation. (α = α-Adrenergic receptor; β = β-adrenergic receptor; G$_s$, G$_i$, G$_q$ = G proteins; AC = adenylate cyclase; PDE = phosphodiesterase; Phos C = phospholipase C; DAG = 1,2-diacylglycerol; IP$_3$ = inositol triphosphate; (+) = positive or stimulatory response or effect; (−) = negative or inhibitory response or effect.)

Endogenous Catecholamines

The catecholamines are classified into endogenous and synthetic groups (Fig. 177-2). Endogenous catecholamines consist of epinephrine, norepinephrine, and dopamine. All endogenous catecholamines originate from the compound tyrosine, and through several enzymatic reactions that involve hydroxylases and decarboxylases, dopamine, norepinephrine, and epinephrine are synthesized. The majority of norepinephrine is produced and acts locally near the presynaptic nerve terminals. In contrast, epinephrine is produced by the adrenal medulla and functions systemically as a circulating hormone. Dobutamine and isoproterenol are the synthetic (exogenous) catecholamines.

Catecholamines may be divided into two functional groups: inotropes and vasopressors. Inotropes improve myocardial stroke volume at a given preload and afterload. Vasopressors increase systemic vascular resistance by increasing peripheral vascular tone.

Dopamine

Mechanisms of action. Dopamine, a chemical precursor of norepinephrine, has direct, dose-dependent, stimulatory effects on the α_1-, β_1-, β_2-, DA, and serotonin receptors. Dopamine's overall affinity for these receptors is DA = $\beta_1 > \alpha_1$ > serotonin (α-like) > β_2. Dopamine differs from the other catecholamines by inducing the release of norepinephrine from presynaptic sympathetic nerves in the heart.

Dosing and effects. At low doses (0.5 to 2.0 μg/kg/min) dopamine affects the DA receptors (vasodilatation of the splanchnic vascular beds) with little adrenergic receptor action. At somewhat higher doses (2 to 6 μg/kg/min) DA receptor stimulation persists and cardiac contractility and heart rate increase because of β_1-stimulation and norepinephrine release from cardiac adrenergic nerve endings that result from β_2-receptor stimulation. At doses of 6 to 15 μg/kg/min dopamine maximally stimulates β_1-receptors. At higher doses (15 to 25 μg/kg/min), β_1-stimulation persists, but α_1-adrenergic receptor stimulation (vasoconstriction) becomes apparent. At doses in this range and beyond the vasoconstrictive α_1-effects predominate.

Clinical indications. Dopamine is used successfully as an inotrope and vasopressor in neonatal and pediatric patients with decreased cardiac output because of depressed contractile function. Poor peripheral perfusion without significant hypotension af-

ter volume resuscitation is a common indication for the use of dopamine. In patients with severe hypotension (with suspected very low cardiac output and either very high or very low systemic vascular resistance), dopamine is somewhat ineffective, and the catecholamine of choice is epinephrine or norepinephrine. In chronic myocardial insufficiency or failure and in severe uncompensated shock, dopamine β-hydroxylase concentrations may be decreased, which results in decreased synthesis of norepinephrine and epinephrine. In these situations a higher than usual dose (>25 μg/kg/min) of dopamine is needed to achieve the desired response, and sometimes high doses are still ineffective. Dopamine is the only inotrope that selectively increases blood flow in the renal and splanchnic vascular beds.

Administration and adverse effects. Dopamine is rapidly metabolized and is therefore given by continuous infusion through a central vein (preferred) or peripheral vein or by means of intraosseous infusion.

Adverse cardiovascular effects of dopamine (usually seen at high doses) include tachycardia, arrhythmias, increased myocardial oxygen consumption, and excessive vasoconstriction with peripheral gangrene. Local infiltration into the skin and soft tissues at the IV site may cause tissue necrosis. Dopamine may depress the respiratory response to hypoxemia and hypercarbia (especially in neonates and premature infants).

Norepinephrine

Mechanisms of action. Formed by the hydroxylation of dopamine, norepinephrine is the primary neurotransmitter of the CNS. Norepinephrine stimulates both α_1- and β_1-receptors, with virtually no β_2-activity noted. This adrenergic receptor stimulation is dose dependent, but α_1-activity predominates over β_1-activity at virtually all doses.

Dosing and effects. Experience with norepinephrine in critically ill infants and children is limited, but the physiologic effects are not different from that reported in adult patients. Low-dose infusions (<0.5 μg/kg/min) produce β_1-stimulation that improves myocardial contractility and equal amounts of α_1-stimulation that cause vasoconstriction. At higher doses (0.5 to 4.0 μg/kg/min) the predominate effect of norepinephrine is vasoconstriction secondary to α_1-stimulation. Although β_1-receptor stimulation still occurs at these higher doses, a positive

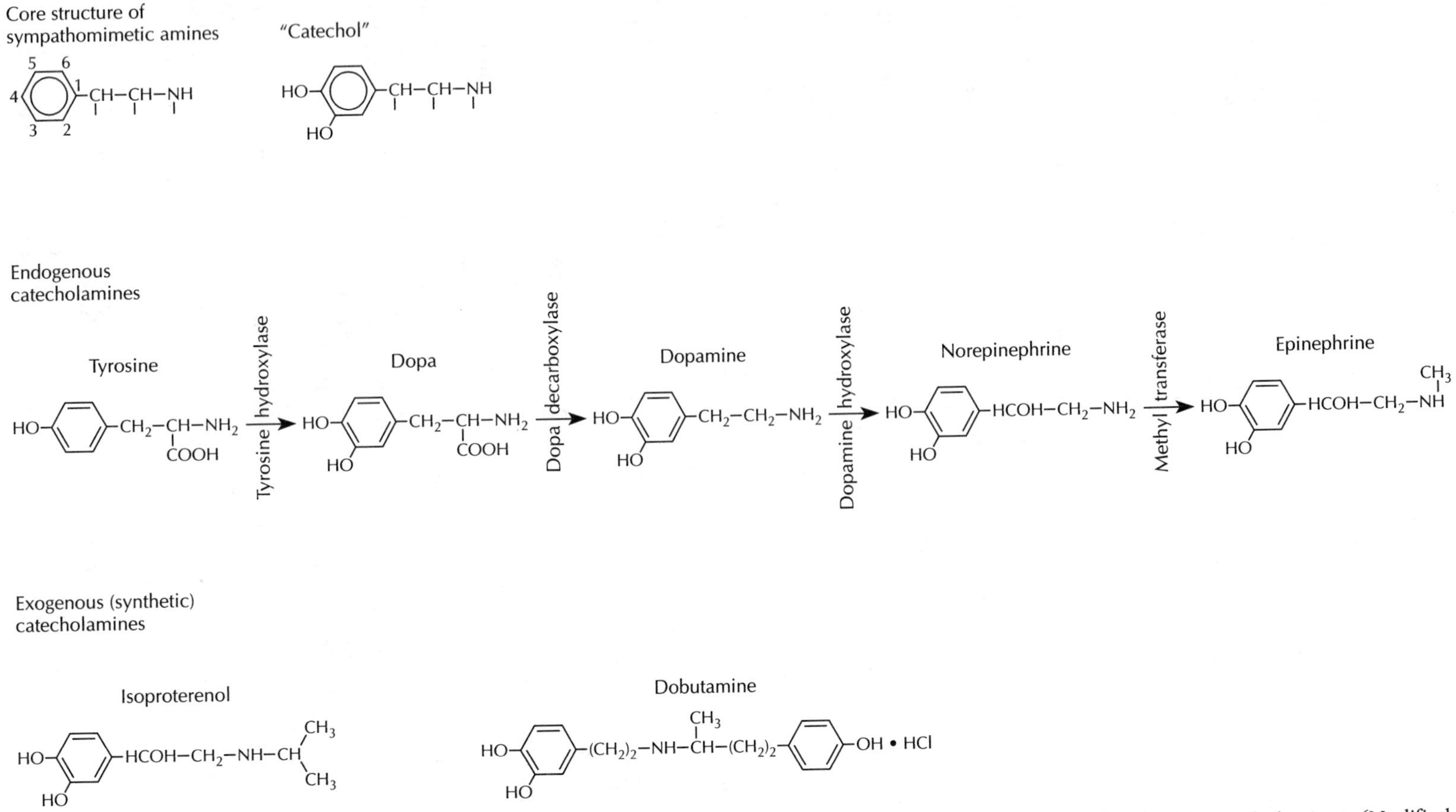

Fig. 177-2   Synthesis and structure of the endogenous catecholamines from tyrosine and structure of exogenous (synthetic) catecholamines. (Modified from Chernow B, Rainey T, Lake R. Endogenous and exogenous catecholamines in critical care medicine. Crit Care Med 10:409-416, 1982.)

inotropic response may not be appreciated clinically because of the cardiac response to the increased afterload. The heart rate may, in fact, decrease as a result of a vagally mediated baroreceptor reflex secondary to the increased afterload.

Clinical indications. The use of norepinephrine is limited because of its severe vasoconstrictive effects. The most common clinical indication is hyperdynamic septic shock, with tachycardia, wide pulse pressure, hyperdynamic (bounding) pulses, warm skin, and prolonged capillary refill due to increased cardiac output and very low systemic vascular resistance. Depending on the severity of shock, hypotension may also be present. In this setting intravascular volume status must be optimized before administration of norepinephrine because of the intense vasoconstriction that occurs in the splanchnic and peripheral vascular beds. If norepinephrine infusions are needed for prolonged periods after an acute resuscitation or if increasing doses are needed, a pulmonary artery catheter is helpful to improve the clinician's knowledge of filling pressures and blood flow characteristics in the systemic and pulmonary circulations.

Administration and adverse effects. Norepinephrine must always be administered through a central venous line because of intense vasoconstrictive effects. Infiltration at a peripheral venous site can cause severe soft tissue and skin necrosis.

Adverse vascular effects of norepinephrine are related to its vasoconstrictive effects. The splanchnic beds, including the renal and GI blood supplies, may be severely compromised. Clinical findings in patients receiving excessive doses of norepinephrine are paleness with acrocyanosis, cool extremities, decreased urine output, and metabolic acidosis.

Epinephrine

Mechanisms of action. Epinephrine is produced by the adrenal medulla and is synthesized from its precursor, norepinephrine. Epinephrine has dose-dependent stimulatory effects on the β_1-, β_2-, and α_1-adrenergic receptors.

Dosing and effects. At initial dosages (0.05 to 0.3 μg/kg/min) virtually pure β_1- and β_2-stimulation occurs, resulting in increased myocardial contractility, increased heart rate, and vasodilation from direct stimulation of the β_2-receptors in the peripheral vascular bed. As the dose is increased, the α_1-effect of vasoconstriction becomes apparent; however, vas-

cular tone is balanced because of continued stimulation of the β_1- and β_2-receptors. As doses approach 1.0 μg/kg/min and higher, stimulation of β_1- and α_1-effects approaches equality, and finally the α_1-effects of vasoconstriction predominate over the β_2-effects.

Clinical indications. Epinephrine infusions are an excellent method of inotropic support in pediatric patients with severe cardiovascular collapse and shock associated with myocardial dysfunction. Epinephrine is most efficacious in the treatment of patients who are severely, acutely, or chronically stressed, with decreased endogenous catecholamine biosynthesis or down regulated β_1-receptors. If volume status has been optimized in critically ill patients who do not respond favorably to other catecholamine infusions (e.g., dopamine or dobutamine), initiation of epinephrine administration must be quick and decisive. Epinephrine is also commonly used for resuscitation and in cardiac arrest. For details concerning the use of epinephrine during cardiopulmonary resuscitation, see Chapter 140.

Administration and adverse effects. Epinephrine must always be given through a central venous catheter except in short-term, emergency situations because local infiltration may cause tissue necrosis.

Epinephrine markedly increases myocardial oxygen demand, which may cause myocardial ischemia and ventricular arrhythmias. The risk of life-threatening arrhythmias is especially important in adult patients because of possible coexisting coronary artery disease, and this must also be considered in pediatric patients with underlying conditions such as myocarditis, hypokalemia, or hypoxemia. Despite the almost pure β-adrenergic effects at low doses, with vasodilation in the skeletal muscle and splanchnic vascular beds, renal and cutaneous vasoconstriction may be significant; therefore urine output and skin perfusion need to be monitored carefully. However, in patients with severe shock epinephrine may improve cardiac output and therefore renal perfusion; thus urine output will improve. Epinephrine increases pulmonary vascular resistance and thus must be used judiciously in patients with pulmonary arterial hypertension. In patients who need high doses (>0.3 μg/kg/min) a pulmonary artery catheter may be considered for close monitoring of hemodynamic variables.

Epinephrine has potentially adverse metabolic effects. Hypokalemia frequently develops because of the stimulatory effect on the sodium-potassium pump in skeletal muscle. Hyperglycemia secondary to enhanced gluconeogenesis and glycogenolysis is observed in patients given epinephrine infusions. Stimulation of α-adrenergic receptors suppresses insulin production and secretion from the pancreas. Epinephrine also activates triglyceride lipases, resulting in increased free fatty acids and glycerol. As a result, serum concentrations of cholesterol, low-density lipoproteins, and phospholipids increase.

Exogenous Catecholamines
Dobutamine

Mechanisms of action. Dobutamine is a synthetic catecholamine that is actually a racemic mixture of two different isomers in solution. One isomer has specific β_1- and β_2-adrenergic receptor stimulatory effects; the other isomer has some α_1-adrenergic effects.

Dosing and effects. At doses of 5 to 20 μg/kg/min dobutamine improves cardiac contractility and has little effect on heart rate. This increased contractility results from stimulation of β_1-receptors. Systemic vascular resistance may also decrease, but the exact mechanism is yet to be delineated. Proposed mechanisms for afterload reduction include direct β_2-adrenergic stimulation, reversal of low cardiac output–associated vasoconstriction, and dobutamine metabolites that are α_1-antagonists. Dobutamine also has direct vasodilatory effects on the coronary vasculature. At doses >20 μg/kg/min α_1-adrenergic receptor stimulation becomes more prominent and the afterload-reducing effects diminish.

Clinical indications. Dobutamine is used to treat a variety of low cardiac output states and normal or high systemic vascular resistance. Patients with myocarditis, dilated cardiomyopathy, and low cardiac output after surgery because of congenital heart disease often benefit greatly from treatment with dobutamine. The use of dobutamine as a first-line inotropic agent in septic shock is somewhat controversial. Inasmuch as dobutamine stimulates β-receptors without a secondary need for endogenous norepinephrine stores, it may be more beneficial than dopamine. This is particularly true in neonates and young infants who have decreased endogenous norepinephrine stores. However, if a patient has hyperdynamic septic shock with a normal to high cardiac output and low systemic vascular resistance, dobutamine is contraindicated and epinephrine or norepinephrine is more appropriate.

Administration and adverse effects. Dobutamine may be administered through a peripheral or central venous catheter. If local infiltration occurs, the effects are not so severe as with dopamine, norepinephrine, or epinephrine.

Dobutamine is generally well tolerated. This agent has a decreased chronotropic effect and is less arrhythmogenic than the endogenous catecholamines. Although all catecholamines may increase intrapulmonary shunting, dobutamine with its vasodilatory effects may potentiate this more than the endogenous catecholamines.

Isoproterenol

Mechanisms of action. Isoproterenol is a synthetically derived catecholamine with very potent β-adrenergic activity and no significant effects on α_1-adrenergic receptors. The β_1- and β_2-receptor stimulatory effects are equivalent.

Dosing and effects. The amount of β-receptor stimulation increases as the dose of isoproterenol increases. The starting dose is 0.05 to 1.5 μg/kg/min. As the dose is increased in this range, β-adrenergic receptor stimulation increases. Usually the dose is increased, as needed, by 0.05 to 0.1 μg/kg/min every 10 to 15 minutes until the desired effect is reached. If heart rate exceeds 200 bpm or diastolic blood pressure decreases to <40 mm Hg, the dose is not increased. Isoproterenol's potent β_1-receptor stimulation increases myocardial contractility, heart rate, and conduction velocity, promotes bronchial dilation, and shortens atrial ventricular nodal conduction. Its potent β_2-adrenergic receptor stimulation in the peripheral vascular bed causes vascular smooth muscle relaxation with vasodilation that can result in reflex tachycardia. If intravascular volume status is optimized, the net result of the β-effects of isoproterenol will be increased cardiac output. If the patient has intravascular volume depletion, the effects of tachycardia and vasodilation may result in decreased cardiac output because of decreased venous return. The isoproterenol-induced increase in cardiac output results more from increased heart rate than from increased myocardial contractility. Stimulation of β_2-receptors also causes decreased pulmonary vascular resistance and bronchial smooth muscle relaxation, producing bronchodilation.

Clinical indications. Isoproterenol was once commonly used to treat low cardiac output secondary to poor cardiac contractility. However, isoproterenol tends to cause a much greater increase in heart rate than dobutamine or dopamine. Inasmuch as many patients with shock are already tachycardic, isoproterenol is now used much less frequently. Myocardial function is extremely preload dependent in septic shock; thus the increased tachycardia and vasodilation produced by isoproterenol may limit venous return and actually compromise cardiac output. In patients in a hyperdynamic phase of septic shock the vasodilatory effects of isoproterenol may be detrimental if systemic vascular resistance is already low. Isoproterenol can be used temporarily to increase heart rate in patients with bradycardia from atrioventricular block or sinus node dysfunction. Isoproterenol infusions may also be used as bronchodilator therapy in patients with severe status asthmaticus and respiratory failure not responding to standard treatments.

Administration and adverse effects. Isoproterenol may be administered safely through a peripheral IV catheter. The major adverse effects associated with the use of isoproterenol include extreme tachycardia, tachyarrhythmias, and increased myocardial oxygen consumption. Myocardial infarction has been reported in both adult and pediatric patients; however, the prevalence is low in children younger than 12 years. Isoproterenol's potent β_2-vasodilatory effects may increase intrapulmonary shunting and therefore increase hypoxemia, especially in patients with diffuse alveolar disease. Other common side effects include nausea, tremors, palpitations, and flushing of the skin.

PHENYLEPHRINE: A NONCATECHOLAMINE VASOPRESSOR

Mechanisms of action. Phenylephrine, a "noncatecholamine" synthetic vasopressor agent, is a powerful direct α_1-adrenergic stimulant with essentially no β-adrenergic stimulatory effects. There is a minimal amount of α_2-effect, but this is not clinically significant. Only a small part of phenylephrine's effect relies on stimulation to release endogenous norepinephrine.

Dosing and effects. Phenylephrine's effect is that of almost pure vasoconstriction without any inotropic activity because of its α_1-adrenergic selectivity. The usual dose is 5 to 20 μg/kg every 10 to 15 minutes as needed. However, some clinicians use 50 to 100 μg/kg doses to treat severe hypercyanotic episodes in patients with tetralogy of Fallot. A continuous IV infusion of 0.1 to 0.5 μg/kg/min is titrated to the desired effect.

Clinical indications. Although known as a nasal decongestant (Neo-Synephrine), phenylephrine has many important uses in the pediatric critical care setting. These include treatment of spinal shock (spinal cord injury in which the patient loses all autonomic control of peripheral vasomotor tone); hyperdynamic, vasodilated septic shock; supraventricular tachycardia (phenylephrine causes vasoconstrictive-induced, baroreceptor vagally mediated bradycardia), and hypercyanotic episodes in patients with tetralogy of Fallot. In patients with tetralogy of Fallot phenylephrine increases systemic vascular resistance, which causes increased left-to-right shunting across the ventricular septal defect and therefore increased pulmonary blood flow. In spinal shock a continuous infusion of phenylephrine is used to control vascular tone. For hyperdynamic septic shock with vasodilation, norepinephrine and epinephrine are usually first-line inotrope/vasopressors of choice because of their additional β_1-adrenergic effects that improve myocardial dysfunction in septic shock. Intermittent doses of phenylephrine are usually sufficient for both supraventricular tachycardia and hypercyanotic episodes, but continuous infusions may be needed for short-term control. Phenylephrine is a last-line therapy for supraventricular tachycardia because more effective therapy is available (e.g., adenosine, digoxin, overdrive pacing, and cardioversion).

Administration and adverse effects. Phenylephrine may be administered orally, subcutaneously, or intravenously, but IV administration is used only in the pediatric critical care setting.

Adverse effects are usually due to phenylephrine's intense vasoconstrictor properties. If the left ventricle is functioning poorly, marked vasoconstriction will increase afterload and may further decrease cardiac output. Decreased renal and splanchnic blood flow result from marked vasoconstriction in these vascular beds.

PHOSPHODIESTERASE INHIBITORS: AMRINONE AND MILRINONE (Fig. 177-3)

Mechanisms of action. Catecholamine stimulation is mediated by increased production of the second

Amrinone

Milrinone

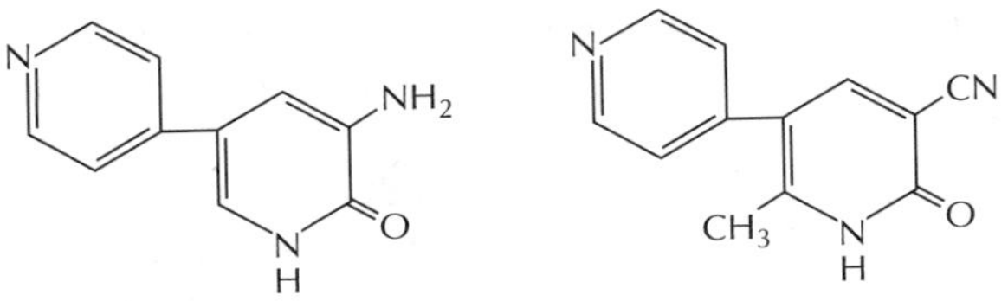

5-Amino (3,4'-bipyridine)
-6(1H)-one

1,6-Dihydro-2-methyl-6-oxo-
(3,4'-bipyridine)-5-carbonitrile

Fig. 177-3 Structure of amrinone and milrinone. (From Alousi AA, Johnson DC. Pharmacology of the bipyridines: Amrinone and milrinone. Circulation 73[Suppl 3]:10-24, 1986).

messenger, cAMP, and degradation of intracellular cAMP is regulated by the phosphodiesterase family of enzymes. Bipyridine agents competitively inhibit the myocardial-specific enzyme phosphodiesterase III, thereby increasing intracellular cAMP concentrations and producing positive inotropic and vasodilatory effects. Clinically, the bipyridine agents are known as "inodilators" because of their inotropic and vasodilator effects.

Dosing and effects. A loading dose of amrinone is necessary, usually 0.75 to 4.0 mg/kg, followed by continuous infusion of 5 to 20 μg/kg/min. The loading dose should be given over at least 10 minutes because rapid infusions cause marked vasodilation and therefore hypotension. The half-life of amrinone is variable and age dependent. In healthy adults the half-life is approximately 4 hours; however, in the presence of poor cardiac output and end-organ insufficiency, the half-life may increase to $\geq$10 hours. In infants and children the half-life is 5 to 8 hours, but in neonates it can be as long as 22 hours.

Milrinone is much more potent than amrinone, but there is little experience in pediatric patients. The initial loading dose in adults is 50 to 75 μg/kg followed by continuous infusion of 0.5 to 1.0 μg/kg/min. The half-life is 30 to 60 minutes in healthy adults but is prolonged in patients with congestive heart failure and end-organ dysfunction. No formal kinetic data for pediatric patients are available.

Amrinone and milrinone increase myocardial contractility and enhance vascular smooth muscle relaxation. Clinically, these effects are manifested as decreased central venous pressure (preload) and vasodilation (decreased afterload). The heart rate increases minimally or stays the same. Some investigators report a more potent pulmonary vasodilatory effect than systemic vasodilatory effect. Amrinone and milrinone may also increase intrapulmonary shunting and therefore lower Pao_2; however, the increase in cardiac output usually compensates for any decrease in systemic oxygen delivery from the increased intrapulmonary shunting. Oxygen delivery may actually increase despite the slight decrease in Pao_2. Unlike catecholamines, amrinone and milrinone increase cardiac contractility without increasing myocardial oxygen demand. In fact, some investigators report a decrease in myocardial oxygen consumption of as much as 50%.

Clinical indications. Although rarely used as a first-line inotrope, amrinone and milrinone may be successfully used in patients with β-receptor down regulation (e.g., chronic congestive heart failure, chronic stress, or septic shock) refractory to escalating doses of catecholamines. Amrinone and milrinone have been used extensively in adults patients with acute and chronic congestive heart failure and acute cardiogenic shock and for immediate support after cardiopulmonary bypass procedures. There are few reports of the use of these agents in pediatric patients. However, amrinone is effective in pediatric patients who have undergone cardiac surgery. An in vitro study demonstrated that amrinone may be effective in inhibiting lipopolysaccharide-induced tumor necrosis factor production; however, the clinical use of amrinone in pediatric septic shock is yet to be proved effective. Nonetheless, anecdotal case reports have been favorable in both adult and pediatric patients with hypodynamic septic shock associated with increased systemic vascular resistance.

Administration and adverse effects. The rate of the IV loading dose has some effect on whether inotropic or vasodilatory effects predominate. If the loading dose is given over 5 minutes, the vasodilatory effect may be more prominent than the increase in inotropy, and hypotension may develop. If the loading dose is given slowly over 10 to 15 minutes, both inotropy and vasodilation occur with equal prominence and hypotension is prevented. Some authors recommend the loading dose be given over 30 minutes. It is imperative to optimize intravascular volume status before administering these agents.

The most common side effect of amrinone is reversible thrombocytopenia (platelet count <100,000/ mm^3) caused by increased peripheral destruction of platelets with decreased platelet survival. In the literature investigations in adult patients show an incidence of thrombocytopenia ranging from 2% to 20%, with the effect being more common as the duration of therapy increases. Thrombocytopenia is a less common complication of milrinone infusion, developing in only about 2% of patients.

Of more concern with the use of milrinone is the prevalence of arrhythmias. In adult patients who have undergone open heart surgery, milrinone-associated asymptomatic ventricular ectopic activity is about 12%, and the incidence of asymptomatic and self-limited supraventricular arrhythmias is 4%. In a recent study by Chang et al. the use of IV milrinone in neonatal patients who had undergone cardiac surgery was not associated with any significant arrhythmias. Few arrhythmias are associated with amrinone administration. Amrinone's relatively long half-life (even more prolonged in neonates and critically ill patients) is not ideal for the critical care setting. Achieving a new steady state may be somewhat difficult, and if the patient's status is rapidly evolving, it may be desirable to discontinue the effects of a vasodilator rapidly. With amrinone's prolonged half-life, this may be difficult to achieve, and use of vasodilatory agents with short half-lives may be more appropriate. Milrinone's shorter half-life and fewer adverse effects may result in this agent being used more commonly than amrinone in the future.

VASODILATORS

Vasodilator agents are important in the management of low cardiac output. Vasodilators may be classified by either cellular mechanism of action or primary vascular action. Seven mechanisms of action have been delineated for vasodilators, including nitrovasodilators (nitric oxide–induced vasodilation), potassium channel agonists, DA_1-receptor agonists, α_1-adrenergic antagonists, central α_2-adrenergic agonists, calcium channel antagonists, and angiotensin-converting enzyme inhibitors. The primary response of the vascular system to these agents is characterized by venous dilation, arterial dilation, or venoarterial dilation.

Nitrovasodilators

Mechanisms of action. The clinically used nitrovasodilators consist of nitroprusside, nitroglycerin, and nitric oxide. This class of drugs causes vascular smooth muscle relaxation (vasodilation) by either directly or indirectly delivering nitric oxide to the vascular smooth muscle cells. Nitric oxide activates intracellular guanylate cyclase, which results in increased production of cyclic guanine monophosphate, leading to dephosphorylation of myosin light chains, which causes vascular smooth muscle cells to relax. Nitroprusside and nitroglycerin will be discussed here; for information on the direct delivery of nitric oxide for treatment of pulmonary arterial hypertension, see Chapter 158.

Nitroprusside

Dosing and effects. Nitroprusside is administered by continuous IV infusion at a rate of 0.5 to 4.0 μg/kg/min. The dose may be increased to 10 μg/kg/min by titrating to clinical effect. Nitroprusside has potent dilatory effects on both the arterial and venous systemic vascular beds. The onset of action is rapid. Atrial pressures (preload), systemic vascular resistance (afterload), and pulmonary vascular resistance all decrease. In patients with impaired myocardial function and compensatory vasoconstriction, stroke volume and therefore perfusion improve primarily because of decreased afterload. With improved stroke volume, the heart rate may actually decrease in some patients.

Clinical indications. Nitroprusside is useful as a vasodilating agent in patients with severe cardiogenic shock (including hypodynamic septic shock) and peripheral vasoconstriction. This agent is also beneficial in patients with severe systemic hypertension (see Chapter 54), pulmonary arterial hypertension, and aortic or mitral valve regurgitation.

Administration and adverse effects. Exposure of nitroprusside solutions to light may cause in vitro production of free cyanide. Therefore delivery systems and tubing that contain the drug must be protected from light.

Hypotension is a potentially severe adverse effect. If hypotension develops, a rapid decrease in infusion rate or temporary cessation of the infusion usually corrects this problem because of the short half-life of nitroprusside. Careful attention to slow titration of the infusion rate and optimization of intravascular volume generally prevent hypotension. Care must also be taken in using this agent in patients with diffuse alveolar disease with intrapulmonary shunting. Vasodilation of the pulmonary vasculature may increase intrapulmonary shunting and decrease Pao_2. Inasmuch as nitroprusside has no direct effect on cardiac output, the slight increase in cardiac output related to decreased afterload may not be sufficient to in-

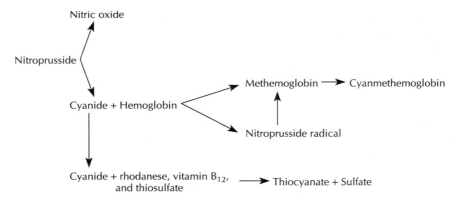

Fig. 177-4   Nitroprusside metabolism in vivo.

crease oxygen delivery enough to offset the decreased Pa_{O_2}. This effect is especially prominent in patients with diffuse alveolar disease. Nitroprusside must be used judiciously in patients with increased ICP, because resulting cerebral vascular dilation may cause an acute increase in ICP.

Treatment with nitroprusside can result in cyanide or thiocyanate toxicity. Nitroprusside is degraded into nitric oxide and cyanide (Fig. 177-4). Free cyanide binds with hemoglobin to form methemoglobin and an unstable nitroprusside radical, which in turn binds to methemoglobin to form cyanmethemoglobin. The remaining cyanide ions react in the presence of rhodanese, vitamin B_{12}, and thiosulfate to form thiocyanate in the liver, which is subsequently excreted by the kidney. Cyanide and thiocyanate toxicity may develop concomitantly, but usually occur separately.

Cyanide toxicity. Thiosulfate is necessary for cyanide metabolism. Thiosulfate stores are decreased in patients with acute or chronic disease states; therefore these patients have less ability to metabolize cyanide. Once thiosulfate reserves are depleted, blood and tissue cyanide concentrations increase. Cyanide binds to cytochrome oxidase complexes and therefore interferes with oxidative phosphorylation. Acidosis results because oxidative phosphorylation is a primary buffer of hydrogen ions.

Cyanide toxicity is characterized by CNS and cardiovascular dysfunction. Unexplained metabolic acidosis often coupled with a need for increasing doses of nitroprusside to maintain the same degree of vasodilatation is an early sign of cyanide toxicity. Other symptoms include altered level of consciousness, seizures, coma, tachypnea, tachycardia, hypertension followed by hypotension, shock, and cardiac arrhythmias. Although usually associated with high doses or long-term use in susceptible patients, cyanide toxicity is a phenomenon for which any patient may be at risk.

Thiocyanate toxicity. Thiocyanate is excreted in the urine with an elimination half-life of approximately 2½ days in normal adults. This prolonged half-life allows thiocyanate to accumulate in patients receiving prolonged nitroprusside infusions, especially in the presence of renal insufficiency. Symptoms of thiocyanate toxicity include skin rashes, abdominal pain, tinnitus, nausea and vomiting, altered level of consciousness, seizures, coma, hypothyroidism, and adrenal suppression. Unlike cyanide toxicity, thiocyanate toxicity is not associated with toxicity-induced metabolic acidosis or altered oxidative phosphorylation.

Nitroglycerin

Dosing and effects. Nitroglycerin may be administered either sublingually, transdermally, or intravenously. The IV route is used most commonly in the PICU. The usual dose for nitroglycerin as a continuous IV infusion is 0.5 to 20.0 $\mu g/kg/min$. In contrast to the arterial and venous dilation caused by nitroprusside, the predominant effect of nitroglycerin administration is dilation of venous vascular smooth muscle, which increases venous capacitance. Higher doses may produce systemic arterial vasodilation. When venodilation is prominent, central venous pressure, pulmonary capillary wedge pressure, and pulmonary arterial pressure decrease. In patients with decreased myocardial function the reduced preload that results from nitroglycerin administration may produce increased stroke volume and cardiac output (Starling curve).

The most common indication for nitroglycerin is in postoperative cardiac patients with low cardiac output, especially those with systemic or pulmonary venous congestion related to increased preload. Nitroglycerin may also be of benefit in congestive heart failure, pulmonary arterial hypertension, and acute cardiogenic shock.

Adverse effects. As with nitroprusside, the most common adverse effect of nitroglycerin is hypotension. This is managed by optimizing intravascular volume status and titrating the dose carefully to clinical effects. Other potential side effects include increased intrapulmonary shunting, especially in patients with diffuse alveolar disease and increased ICP in patients at risk.

Other Vasodilators

Numerous other vasodilators are used in the PICU to treat diseases such as systemic and pulmonary arterial hypertension. Phentolamine and tolazoline (selective α-adrenergic receptor blockers), calcium channel blockers, and various angiotensin-converting enzyme inhibitors are examples of these agents. Refer to other chapters for complete information on these drugs.

CURRENT RESEARCH AND FUTURE CONSIDERATIONS

Appropriate and effective use of inotropic and vasoactive drugs in the pediatric population requires not only an understanding of basic pharmacologic principles but also of age-related changes in drug distribution, effects, metabolism, elimination, and kinetics. Most data regarding vasoactive and inotropic agents are derived from studies in adult patients and are applied to clinical situations for the care of critically ill neonates, infants, and children. Ongoing research on age-related changes in the cellular and subcellular processes that regulate clinical "responsiveness" to these agents will allow optimization of care for all pediatric patients.

ADDITIONAL READING

Allen H, Gutgesell HP, eds. Heart Disease in Infants, Children, and Adolescents, 5th ed. Baltimore: Williams & Wilkins, 1994, pp 375-398.

Alousi AA, Johnson DC. Pharmacology of the bipyridines: Amrinone and milrinone. Circulation 73(Suppl III):III-10–III-24, 1986.

Artman M. Pharmacologic therapy. In Emmanouilides GC, Riemenschneider TA, Allen H, Gutgesell HP, eds. Heart Disease in Infants, Children, and Adolescents, 5th ed. Williams & Wilkins, 1994, pp 375-398.

Artman M, Graham TP. Guidelines for vasodilator therapy of congestive heart failure in infants and children. Am Heart J 113:994-1005, 1987.

Chang AC, Atz AM, Wernovsky G, Burke RP, Wessel OL. Milrinone: Systemic and pulmonary hemodynamic effects in neonates after cardiac surgery. Crit Care Med 23:1907-1914, 1995.

• Curry SC, Arnold-Capell P. Toxic effects of drugs used in the ICU: Nitroprusside, nitroglycerin, and angiotensin-converting enzyme inhibitors. Crit Care Clin 7:555-581, 1991.

Honerjager P. Pharmacology of bipyridine phosphodiesterase III inhibitors. Am Heart J 121:1939-1944, 1991.

Kaufman TM, Horton JW. Characterization of cardiac β-adrenergic receptors in the guinea pig heart: Application to the study of β-adrenergic receptors in shock models. J Surg Res 55:516-523, 1993.

Notterman DA. Pharmacologic support of the failing circulation: An approach for infants and children. Probl Anesth 3:288-302, 1989.

• Notterman DA. Toxic effects of drugs used in the ICU: Inotropic agents. Crit Care Clin 7:583-613, 1991.

• Schremmer B, Dhainaut JF. Heart failure in septic shock: Effects of inotropic support. Crit Care Med 18(Suppl 1):S49-S59, 1990.

• Seri I. Cardiovascular, renal, and endocrine actions of dopamine in neonates and children. J Pediatr 126:333-344, 1995.

Sonnenblick EH. Intravenous milrinone: A new inotropic vasodilator. Resident Staff Physician 39:49-55, 1993.

Zaloga GP, Prielipp RC, Butterworth JF, Royster RL. Circulatory shock: Pharmacologic cardiovascular support. Crit Care Clin 9:335-362, 1993.

• Zaritsky A. Catecholamines, inotropic medications, and vasopressor agents. In Chernow B, ed. The Pharmacological Approach to the Critically Ill Patient, 3rd ed. Baltimore: Williams & Wilkins, 1994, pp 387-404.

Zaritsky A, Chernow B. Use of catecholamines in pediatrics. J Pediatr 105:341-348, 1984.

Zaritsky A, Eisenberg MG. Ontogenetic considerations in the pharmacotherapy of shock. In Chernow B, Shoemaker WC, eds. Critical Care: State of the Art, vol 7. Fullerton, Calif.: Society of Critical Care Medicine, 1986, pp 485-534.

178 Special Considerations in Drug Therapy

Neonates

Trina M. Fabré

BACKGROUND

Neonates are a unique patient population with regard to drug disposition and therapeutic responsiveness. Marked differences in body composition and organ function development have been demonstrated among neonates, infants, and children as compared with adults. Specifically, the immaturity of organs involved in drug metabolism and excretion can alter the pharmacokinetics, therapeutic efficacy, and toxicity of many drugs in neonates. These developmental physiologic changes alter drug disposition and ultimately influence drug therapy. Because alterations in the pharmacokinetics and pharmacodynamics of therapeutic agents in this population are difficult to predict from clinical drug data obtained from older children and adults, caution is necessary in extrapolating dosing guidelines and clinical experience from adults and other pediatric patients to neonates. Physiologic maturational changes in the neonate and how these changes affect drug therapy are discussed.

EFFECTS OF PHYSIOLOGIC MATURATION ON DRUG THERAPY
Absorption

Among the numerous factors that influence intestinal absorption of drugs in the newborn infant are variations in gastric emptying time, gastric pH, and intestinal motility.

At birth gastric pH is similar to that in adulthood (pH range, 1.0 to 3.0). However, over the first 24 hours of life gastric acid production significantly decreases, resulting in increased pH (approximately 6.0 to 8.0). Similarly, in the premature infant gastric pH is relatively alkaline because of immature gastric acid secreting capability. Over the first 2 years of life the gastric acid secreting capacity of the neonate increases, and pH value approaches that in the adult.

Drugs are absorbed through the GI mucosa by means of passive diffusion. Nonionic drugs are absorbed more completely. The higher pH of the neonatal GI tract results in reduced passive absorption of therapeutic agents that are weakly acidic because these drugs are mainly ionic. This may explain in part the lower bioavailability of drugs such as phenytoin and phenobarbital in the neonate. Conversely, weakly basic drugs (e.g., many of the penicillins) will be nonionic at increased gastric pH, which explains their increased bioavailability in the neonate.

Additional factors that alter intestinal absorption of drugs in the neonate are gastric emptying time and intestinal motility. These processes are variable among neonates and appear to be related to factors such as nutritional status, gestational age, and postnatal age. Unpredictable peristalsis of the neonatal GI tract can result in delayed gastric emptying of approximately 6 to 8 hours. The rate of gastric emptying is usually the rate-limiting factor in drug absorption. Delayed gastric emptying means delayed drug absorption. Because most drugs are absorbed from the small intestine, decreased or slowed gastric emptying tends to decrease the rate of intestinal absorption, ultimately achieving reduced peak serum drug concentration. In addition, clinical disease states such as gastroenteritis that increase gastric emptying time and intestinal motility may result in decreased drug absorption.

Bile acids and pancreatic enzymes also affect the absorption of fat-soluble drugs. Because the neonate has a decreased pool of bile acids and decreased production of pancreatic lipase, absorption of fat-soluble vitamins and other drugs can be erratic.

The absorption of therapeutic agents administered intramuscularly is unpredictable in neonates and young infants. In clinical investigations factors such as decreased muscle mass, decreased total body mass, and altered blood flow all affected absorption of drugs given intramuscularly.

Percutaneous absorption of therapeutic agents is increased in neonates. Percutaneous absorption of drugs is inversely related to the thickness of the stratum corneum and directly related to skin hydration. Neonates have a thin stratum corneum and relatively high skin hydration. Premature infants may experience even greater percutaneous absorption of drugs because of a poorly developed epidermal barrier. The use of occlusive dressings may further increase the extent of drug absorption. Caution must be used when applying topical preparations in neonates. Knowledge of the ingredients of topical preparations will prevent neonatal poisonings, which have resulted from use of products such as topical hexachlorophene and boric acid. In addition, transdermal delivery systems are not used in neonates unless specifically designed for this age group.

Distribution

The apparent volume of distribution of therapeutic agents in neonates is influenced by maturational changes. Neonates have a large total body water composition compared with infants and adults (70% to 80% vs. 50% to 60%). Total body water composition is even greater in the premature neonate, approximating 90%. In addition, the extracellular-intracellular water ratio is higher in neonates than in adults. As the infant matures, total body water composition changes and equals that in the adult. Increases in both quantity and distribution of total body water account for the increased apparent volume of distribution of various drugs in this population. It is therefore not uncommon that a larger milligram per kilogram dose of water-soluble drugs is necessary in neonates compared with adults to achieve an equivalent serum drug concentration.

As total body water composition decreases with age to adult proportions, total body fat increases. Because of relatively low fat composition in the neonate, distribution and storage of lipid-soluble drugs are altered. Despite limited fat stores, large volume of distributions has been reported for some lipophilic drugs in the neonate. This is possibly due to the rapid growth of lipid-rich organs relative to total body weight. Lipophilic drugs may distribute to these organs, resulting in increased volume of distribution and increased organ drug concentration. In addition, decreased protein binding may further increase the volume of distribution of highly protein-bound drugs.

Plasma protein binding is important in determining the volume of distribution of many therapeutic agents. It is prudent to remember that the free, or unbound, drug produces the pharmacotherapeutic effect. Changes in the binding capacity of highly protein-bound drugs will alter their distribution.

Albumin, α_1-glycoprotein, and lipoproteins are the major plasma proteins to which drugs bind. Weakly basic drugs can potentially bind to all of these proteins, whereas neutral compounds and acidic drugs bind to albumin. Premature infants and term neonates have a decreased pool of plasma proteins. Serum concentrations of these proteins begin to approach adult concentrations at about 10 to 12 months of age. In addition to decreased albumin concentrations, neonates also have qualitatively different albumin. Fetal albumin has a decreased binding capacity for drugs. This can result in greater free concentration of drug and potential toxicity if these physiologic differences are not considered in dosing regimens. This has been described for anticonvulsant, antibiotic, and analgesic agents. In addition, clinically significant increases in free drug concentrations can result from protein binding–dependent reactions. These reactions occur when a highly protein-bound drug (>90%) is displaced from protein binding sites by agents such as bilirubin and free fatty acids, which can have a greater affinity for protein binding sites than most drugs do.

Hepatic Metabolism

The liver is the primary organ with metabolic capacity. However, full metabolic capacity may take up to 6 months to develop. Many drugs undergo a biotransformation process through phase I or II reactions to facilitate elimination. Phase I reactions alter the molecular structure of a drug, making it a more polar compound, which improves elimination. Phase I reactions include demethylation, hydrolysis, oxidation, and reduction. Of these activities, few are mature at birth; however, adult levels are achieved within 7 to 10 days. Phase II reactions are microsomally mediated and include those that are dependent on cytochrome P-450, cytochrome P-450 reductase, and reduced nicotinamide adenine dinucleotide phosphate (NADPH). These are conjugative or synthetic reactions that greatly decrease the pharmacologic activity of the parent compound. Most conjugative reactions occur with glucuronide, sulfate, acetate, or amino acids. In contrast to phase I biotransformation reactions, these reactions require 4 to 12 weeks before adult levels of activity are achieved (acetate conjugation, 4 weeks; glucuronide conjugation, 8 weeks; and amino acid conjugation, 12 weeks). These metabolic deficiencies in the neonate result in prolonged metabolic half-life for drugs that undergo significant hepatic metabolism. Drugs such as phenytoin, diazepam, theophylline, meperidine, and phenobarbital have increased plasma half-lives in neonates.

Exposure to enzyme-inducing agents may increase the metabolic capacity of the liver. Phenobarbital is a hepatic enzyme inducer that may stimulate or induce metabolic activity of the liver in the neonate. However, altered or decreased hepatic metabolism is already considered in dosing regimens for neonatal patients. (See the next section for a more complete discussion of drug dosing in liver disease.)

Renal Elimination

The kidneys are the primary organs involved in excretion of water-soluble drugs. Like hepatic function, renal function is immature in the newborn infant. The processes of kidney function, including filtration, secretion, and reabsorption, undergo physiologic maturation. Increased renal blood flow and increased number of functioning nephrons contribute to improved glomerular filtration rate (GFR) within the first 2 weeks of life. This function continues to improve over the next 2 years before reaching a clearance rate similar to that in the adult. Renal tubular secretion also matures at a rate similar to GFR; however, tubular reabsorption matures much more slowly.

Pharmacokinetic and pharmacodynamic effects of decreased renal function result in decreased clearance of various therapeutic agents and increased elimination half-life of these agents. Often the dosing interval is prolonged to allow more time for the immature kidney to eliminate the drug. Neonatal drug dosing takes this into account; however, as the infant matures, dosage needs to be adjusted to accommodate functional changes. (See p. 1700 for a more complete discussion of drug dosing in renal disease.)

CONCLUSION

In neonates various maturational changes in the normal physiologic process alter drug disposition. An understanding of these changes will facilitate optimal drug therapy in the neonatal population. Because of these special considerations in the neonate, establishment of safe and efficacious therapeutic regimens is difficult. Maturation occurs over an extended period; thus continued drug monitoring and dose adjustments in the neonate are necessary.

Liver Disease

Trina M. Fabré

BACKGROUND

The liver is one of the major organs that has metabolic clearance capacity, the main mechanism for elimination of drugs from the body. The liver metabolizes compounds by means of biotransformation enzymes that result in inactivation and subsequent elimination of drugs. Not only does the liver provide detoxification, it also activates compounds by converting inactive precursors into pharmacologically active metabolites. Liver dysfunction can significantly alter drug disposition and lead to adverse reactions if appropriate adjustments in dosing are not made.

Drugs are carried to the liver through the portal vein and the hepatic artery and are delivered to the systemic circulation through the hepatic vein. Under steady-state conditions the difference between the amount of drug delivered to the liver and the amount of drug returned to the systemic circulation is the rate of drug extraction by metabolism, and biliary excretion or hepatic clearance is equal to the sum of hepatic metabolic clearance and biliary excretion. Clearance from the liver is based on a perfusion model and assumes that only free drug can be metabolized by the liver and that drug in the liver is in equilibrium with drug leaving the liver.

FACTORS THAT AFFECT DRUG CLEARANCE

Blood flow to the liver, intrinsic clearance by the liver, and the fraction of drug bound to protein are processes that ultimately affect the ability of the liver to extract a drug from the blood.

Hepatic Clearance

Hepatic clearance is a quantitative measure of the liver's ability to eliminate a drug. Hepatic clearance may be defined as the amount of drug cleared from a volume of blood that perfuses the liver per unit of time.

Hepatic clearance can be defined mathematically with the following equation:

$$\text{Hepatic clearance} = \frac{Qh\,(Ca - Cv)}{Ca} \qquad (1)$$

where Qh = sum of hepatic portal and arterial blood flow (in milliliters per minute), Ca = concentration of drug in the hepatic artery, and Cv = concentration of drug in the hepatic vein.

The hepatic extraction ratio (ERh) provides a direct measurement of drug removal from the liver and is expressed as the drug concentration of the blood entering the liver less the relative concentration of drug that leaves the liver and is delivered to the systemic circulation:

$$\text{ERh} = \frac{Ca - Cv}{Ca} \qquad (2)$$

Hepatic clearance may also be expressed in terms of ERh ratio.

$$\text{Hepatic clearance} = Qh \times \text{ERh} \qquad (3)$$

Table 178-1 illustrates the relationship between blood flow, hepatic extraction ratio, and clearance for drugs with high and low extraction ratios.

Drugs with high extraction ratios

Perfusion-limited hepatic elimination. Hepatic clearance is said to be flow dependent or perfusion rate limited for drugs with high hepatic extraction ratios (>0.7). Changes in blood flow or rate of liver perfusion can alter the hepatic clearance of these drugs. Conditions that alter hepatic blood flow such as hypotensive shock, cardiac failure, and extracellular fluid depletion can cause marked reduction in hepatic perfusion. In addition, therapeutic agents, including catecholamines, anesthetics, β-blockers, and histamine-2 receptor antagonists, can reduce hepatic blood flow. These clinical situations may result in significant changes in drug pharmacokinetics and ultimately lead to drug accumulation. Dosage adjustments may be necessary as a result of disease- or drug-induced alterations in hepatic flow.

For drugs with high extraction ratios, changes in protein binding will have no effect on the hepatic extraction ratio or hepatic clearance. However, these changes will affect the hepatic intrinsic clearance of unbound drug and unbound drug concentration. The

liver is capable of removing essentially all drug presented to it, even when the drugs are highly protein-bound. Although only the free, unbound portion of a drug can be cleared, the liver is so efficient at removing drug that the time for reequilibration of bound and unbound drug in the liver has little effect on overall hepatic clearance. The changes in hepat-

---

HEPATIC EXTRACTION RATIOS OF REPRESENTATIVE DRUGS*

Low extraction ratio	*High extraction ratio*
Diazepam	Labetolol
Theophylline	Lidocaine
Phenobarbital	Meperidine
Tolbutamide	Pentazocine
Theophylline	Propoxyphene
Procainamide	Propranolol
Phenytoin	Morphine
Warfarin	Nitroglycerin
Salicylic acid	Isoproterenol
Caffeine	Verapamil
Metronidazole	
Erythromycin	
Chloramphenicol	

*From Rowland M, Tozer TN, eds. Elimination. In Clinical Pharmacokinetics: Concepts and Applications. Philadelphia: Lea & Febiger, 1989.

Table 178-1 Changes in Clearance and Extraction Ratio With Changes in Blood Flow*

Extraction Ratio	Blood Flow	Change in Extraction Ratio	Clearance
High	Increased	No change	Increased
	Decreased	No change	Decreased
Low	Increased	Decreased	No change
	Decreased	Increased	No change

*From Roland M, Tozer TN, eds. Elimination. In Clinical Pharmacokinetics: Concepts and Applications. Philadelphia: Lea & Febiger, 1989.

ic intrinsic clearance of unbound drug will not significantly alter the total or unbound concentrations of the drug because hepatic clearance is rate limited by hepatic blood flow. If blood flow to the liver changes, elimination of these drugs also directly changes.

Drugs with low extraction ratios

If a drug has a very low hepatic extraction ratio (<0.3), the drug concentration gradient across the liver is very small. The concentration of the drug that enters the liver is approximately equal to the drug concentration of the drug that reaches the systemic circulation. Therefore clinical conditions or therapeutic agents that alter hepatic perfusion will have no effect on the concentration, elimination rate, or clearance of these drugs. Consequently, the extraction ratio for drugs with low extraction changes inversely with changes in hepatic blood flow (see equation 3). With decreased hepatic perfusion, there is more time for the liver to extract the drug from the blood, thus maintaining constant clearance. With increased hepatic perfusion the converse is true.

Drugs with low extraction ratios exhibit hepatic clearance that depends on the intrinsic metabolic clearance. Intrinsic metabolic clearance is a measure of hepatocellular activity and reflects the ability of the liver to clear free drug from the blood. Only unbound, or free, drug is available to cross hepatic membranes and be transformed and eliminated. The ability of the liver to clear free drug from the blood depends on a number of factors, including the number and affinity of liver enzymes for a given drug, the concentration of the enzyme, and the mass of the liver.

Conditions that can alter the liver's intrinsic ability to clear a drug can affect the rate of drug removal by the liver. Other factors that affect hepatic intrinsic clearance include age, nutritional status, pathologic factors, and the presence of hepatic enzyme inducers or inhibitors. Alterations in this metabolic capacity affect the rate of drug elimination by the liver. Dosage adjustments for drugs with low extraction ratios are necessary when hepatic disease or drug interactions alter the hepatic intrinsic metabolic clearance of unbound drug.

Capacity-limited, binding-insensitive hepatic elimination. Drugs with low extraction that exhibit protein binding of <75% to 80% will not cause significant changes in the hepatic clearance of a drug if protein binding status changes. These drugs are said to have capacity-limited, binding-insensitive hepatic elimination. The hepatic clearance depends primarily on the hepatic intrinsic clearance of the unbound drug. If the free drug concentration in the liver is greater than the intrinsic metabolic capacity of the liver, protein binding will not affect the hepatic clearance of the drug.

Capacity-limited, binding-sensitive hepatic elimination. Drugs that are highly protein bound (protein binding >85%) and have low extraction ratios are considered capacity limited and binding sensitive. A small displacement of drug from the protein binding site will result in a significant increase in the free drug concentration. Hepatic clearance of these drugs depends primarily on the extent of protein binding and the hepatic intrinsic clearance of unbound drug. However, it is difficult to generalize the effect of hepatic dysfunction on these drugs because the unbound fraction and hepatic intrinsic clearance may be altered, both may be unchanged, or only one may change.

Fig. 178-1 demonstrates the relationship between hepatic blood flow, protein binding, and the hepatic extraction ratio. For a drug that is significantly metabolized by the liver, the drug can be plotted on a graph if the percent of protein binding and the extraction ratio are known. The closer the drug falls to the corners of the triangle, the more likely the drug will demonstrate the characteristic changes in disposition in liver disease as described.

First-Pass Metabolism

To reach the systemic circulation, a drug given orally must first pass through the liver by way of the portal vein. Any drug that escapes elimination from this first pass through the liver is delivered to the general circulation. Liver disease or conditions that shunt blood from the portal hepatic system to the general circulation can potentially cause exaggerated pharmacologic effects and increased systemic blood concentrations by increasing drug bioavailability. This concept is particularly true for drugs with high extraction ratios. As a general rule, the oral doses of these drugs are decreased to 10% to 50% of the normal dose in the presence of liver disease.

Drugs with low extraction ratios have little presystemic metabolism. However, significant dosage reduction of these drugs may still be necessary if overt liver disease is apparent. Table 178-2 describes the changes in pharmacokinetics for various therapeutic agents in liver disease.

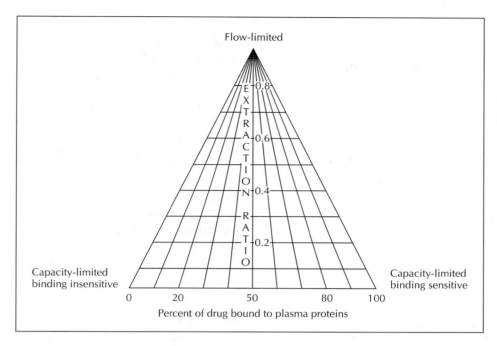

Fig. 178-1 Diagram showing how hepatic extraction ratio and percent protein binding can be used to assign a drug to one of the three categories of hepatic elimination. If the percent protein binding and the hepatic extraction ratio are known, a drug can be plotted on the triangular graph. The closer a drug falls to a corner of the triangle, the more likely it is to display the characteristic changes in drug disposition in liver disease (see text). This information is most significant in drugs primarily eliminated by the liver. (From Blaschke TF. Protein binding and kinetics of drugs in liver diseases. Clin Pharmacokinet 2:32-44, 1977.)

Table 178-2   Changes in Drug Kinetics in Liver Disease*

Drug	Comments
Highly extracted drugs	
Labetolol	Increased oral bioavailability
Metoprolol	Increased oral bioavailability
Propranolol	Increased oral bioavailability
Meperidine	Increased oral bioavailability
Pentazocine	Markedly increased oral bioavailability; reduce dose to 30% of usual
Verapamil	Reduce oral dose to 50% to 75% of usual
Poorly extracted drugs	
Ampicillin	Hepatic clearance reduced by 20%
Chloramphenicol	Hepatic clearance reduced by 60% to 70%
Diazepam	Hepatic clearance reduced by 50%
Cimetidine	Hepatic clearance reduced by 20%
Furosemide	Volume of distribution and terminal half-life increased
Ranitidine	Hepatic clearance reduced by 60%
Theophylline	Clearance reduced by 60%

*Modified from Golper TA, Bennett WM. Altering drug dose. In Schrier RW, Gambertoglio JG, eds. Handbook of Drug Therapy in Liver and Kidney Disease. Boston: Little, Brown, 1991.

DRUGS CONCENTRATED IN BILE*

Ampicillin	Chloramphenicol
Clindamycin	Doxycycline
Metronidazole	Digoxin
Indomethacin	Spironolactone
Steroids	Vincristine
5-Fluorocytosine	

---

*Modified from Golper TA, Bennett WM. Altering drug dose. In Schrier RW, Gambertoglio JG, eds. Handbook of Drug Therapy in Liver and Kidney Disease. Boston: Little, Brown, 1991.

Drugs given intravenously, sublingually, or transdermally escape first-pass hepatic elimination; drugs given rectally may or may not be subjected to first-pass elimination. The inferior and middle rectal veins drain the anus and lower rectum. These vessels drain directly into the superior vena cava, bypassing the portal system. Medications administered in this portion of the rectum bypass first-pass elimination. However, the superior rectal vein, which drains the upper part of the rectum, empties into the portal vein. Rectal administration of medications in the upper portion of the rectum are subjected to hepatic first-pass elimination.

Biliary Excretion

Some drugs are actively secreted into the biliary system. A drug excreted in the bile by the liver enters the small intestine and may be reabsorbed to complete an enterohepatic cycle. If the drug or its metabolite is not reabsorbed, the drug is excreted in the feces. Liver diseases that result in extrahepatic or intrahepatic obstruction can ultimately cause increased serum concentrations of drugs if they are significantly concentrated in the bile. In cholestatic liver disease empiric dose reductions of drugs normally excreted in large amounts in the bile are needed. However, there is little information about the effects of liver disease on hepatic elimination of drugs that are primarily eliminated in bile. A list of drugs that are concentrated in the bile is given above.

CONCLUSION

Several variables can affect hepatic drug clearance. Specifically, one must take into consideration the type of liver disease, pharmacokinetics of the drug, oth-er disease states, and other drugs administered that may alter the pharmacokinetic variables. Modification of drug dosage may be necessary with hepatic dysfunction; however, there are no clear-cut guidelines on dosage adjustment in patients with liver disease. As a general rule, however, when administering IV medications in patients with significant liver disease, constant or continuous drug infusions are not indicated. Because of decreased drug binding (low albumin state), altered hepatic flow, and often altered enzymatic activity in liver disease, increased half-life and higher blood levels may be seen with continuous infusions. Intermittent infusions allow practitioners to evaluate or monitor drug effect and duration of effect in a particular patient.

Renal Failure

Trina M. Fabré

BACKGROUND

The elimination or clearance of drugs by the kidney can be significantly altered in patients with compromised renal function. As a general rule, if >50% of a drug is excreted unchanged by the kidney, dosage adjustments will be necessary when renal function is decreased. Changes in the disposition of drugs affected by decreased renal function may lead to exaggerated pharmacologic responses and potentially significant adverse events. Although it is clear that drug elimination is affected by renal insufficiency, other aspects of pharmacokinetics, including drug absorption, volume of distribution, degree of protein binding, and biotransformation, may also be affected in patients with renal dysfunction. Alterations of these aspects also contribute to the changes seen in drug disposition. Therefore the clinician must have a basic knowledge of pharmacologic, pharmacokinetic, and pharmacodynamic principles as well as the pathophysiologic alterations associated with renal insufficiency. An understanding of these basic principles provides a practical approach for drug dosage regimens designed for patients with impaired renal function.

EFFECTS OF RENAL INSUFFICIENCY ON PHARMACOKINETICS
Drug Absorption

Few data are available on the effects of renal disease on drug absorption and bioavailability. However, bioavailability was once believed to be decreased in renal disease. Theoretical concerns to support this theory were related to the nausea, vomiting, diarrhea, and edematous changes in the GI tract that can be associated with renal failure. Uremic gastritis, colitis, or pancreatitis can affect drug absorption. In addition, the use of antacid therapy to alleviate some of these GI effects may also interfere with drug bioavailability. Altered bioavailability can significantly contribute to erratic absorption of therapeutic agents. With improved dialysis, the number of patients with uremic symptoms has decreased and there may be no change in the absorption and bioavailability of drugs. In some cases, however, the bioavailability of drugs may be increased. It has been demonstrated that some drugs (e.g., propranolol, propoxyphene, and dihydrocodeine) have reduced first-pass or presystemic metabolism in states of renal insufficiency.

Volume of Distribution and Protein Binding

The apparent volume of distribution of drugs in renal insufficiency may increase, decrease, or remain the same. Changes in protein binding states will ultimately affect the volume of distribution of various drugs.

Acidic drugs exhibit decreased protein binding in the presence of uremia. Important drugs that exhibit this characteristic include phenytoin, warfarin, morphine, salicylate, and sulfamethoxazole. Mechanisms of reduced binding capacity include decreased plasma albumin concentrations, accumulation of endogenous inhibitors of binding, and accumulation of drug metabolites that compete for binding. In addition, patients with renal insufficiency may demonstrate qualitative changes in binding sites or alterations in the conformation or structure of albumin. These processes can result in a decreased number of binding sites or decreased affinity of drugs for the binding sites.

Basic drugs may bind to albumin. However, the main binding protein for these agents is α_1-acid glycoprotein (AAG). Concentrations of AAG increase in a variety of clinical conditions, including renal disease. Therefore in patients with uremia, drugs that bind mainly to AAG may demonstrate increased protein binding. It is prudent for the clinician to know the primary binding protein for various drugs to determine the effects of renal disease on changes in protein binding capacity.

The most important and clinically significant change in protein binding status is reduction in protein binding. Altered protein binding affects the apparent volume of distribution of a drug. With phenytoin, decreased protein binding leads to a larger volume of distribution and greater total body clearance in patients with renal insufficiency. In addition, it is likely that changes in protein binding capacity of drugs will result in alteration of total drug concentrations. Only the unbound (free) fraction of a drug is pharmacologically active. However, the measurement of total drug concentration measures bound plus unbound drug. With altered protein binding, the correlation between total serum concentrations and pharmacologic response is perturbed. For example, phenytoin has a therapeutic range of 10 to 20 mg/L in patients with normal renal function. This is a measurement of total drug concentration. The drug is ~90% protein bound, leaving a free fraction of 10% and a therapeutic free concentration range of 1 to 2 mg/L. In patients with significant renal disease the free fraction is increased and the total drug concentration decreased as a result of increased apparent volume of distribution. For example, a 2-fold increase in free drug (10% increased to 20% unbound) results in a measured total phenytoin concentration of 6 mg/L. Although it appears the drug level is subtherapeutic, the free concentration of 1.2 mg/L (20% of 6 mg/L) is therapeutic. The use of "normal" total drug concentrations may result in clinically apparent adverse reactions or exaggerated pharmacologic responses because of increased free drug concentrations. Although it is wise to monitor free drug concentrations for highly (>70%) protein-bound drugs with a narrow therapeutic window, in practice not many drugs can be measured fast enough to allow clinical bedside decisions. Thus clinical judgments must be based on knowledge of the influence of altered binding on drug disposition as well as daily patient monitoring of efficacy and toxicity.

Metabolism

Clinical data show that kidney disease decreases the metabolic capacity of the liver. Although the mechanism is not clearly understood, reduced nonrenal clearance of certain pharmacologic agents probably results from alteration of the enzymatic pathways responsible for drug metabolism.

Although hepatic microsomal oxidation is not generally affected in renal dysfunction, drugs metabolized by acetylation, reduction, and peptide and ester hydrolysis are often metabolized more slowly.

Elimination

In most cases parent drugs are metabolized by the liver to either inactive or partially active metabolites. These metabolites are generally more polar and are better able to be excreted by the kidneys. Impaired kidney function can have a dramatic effect on the kidney's elimination capabilities.

Glomerular function, tubular secretion, and tubular reabsorption are mechanisms involved in the renal handling of drugs. An impairment of any one of these functions can result in altered pharmacokinetics of a drug. Clinically, however, creatinine clearance, an index of glomerular function, is measured to assess renal function.

Drug Clearance and Dosing

To make appropriate dosing recommendations in patients with renal disease, one must have a clear knowledge of how much of a drug is eliminated by the kidney. If >50% of a drug or its metabolite is eliminated by the kidney, dosage adjustments for renal impairment will be needed to minimize the potential for drug- or metabolite-related adverse events. Dosage adjustments may involve decreasing the dose of the drug and/or increasing the dosing interval. Usually the preferred dosage adjustment method is to increase the dosing interval with or without decreasing the dose. By increasing the dosing interval, peak and trough drug concentrations remain similar to those in patients with normal renal function. In addition, the number of doses per day is decreased, resulting in decreased cost and workload. For some drugs with wide therapeutic windows, such as penicillins, decreasing the dose and maintaining the same interval are acceptable and often recommended. This approach maintains average drug concentrations. This method is recognized and accepted; however, the interval-adjustment approach is discussed here.

Dosage adjustment guidelines for drugs with significant elimination by the kidney are based on the degree of renal impairment. GFR is estimated by the creatinine clearance. Renal impairment can be mild, moderate, or severe. In general mild renal insufficiency is classified as creatinine clearance >50 ml/min/1.73 m^2, moderate renal insufficiency as creatinine clearance of 50 to 10 ml/min/1.73 m^2, and severe renal disease as creatinine clearance <10 ml/min/1.73 m^2. The Schwartz equation is commonly used to estimate creatinine clearance in the pediatric population.

$$\text{Creatinine clearance (ml/min/1.73 m}^2) = K \times L/S_{cr}$$

where K = constant of proportionality that is age specific, L = patient length (cm), and S_{cr} = serum creatinine concentration (mg/dl).

K is a constant of proportionality that is a function of urinary creatinine excretion per unit of body size. Therefore calculated creatinine clearances do not need to be corrected to body surface area.

Age (yr)	K
Low birthweight, <1	0.33
Term, <1	0.45
2 to 12	0.55
Female, 13 to 21	0.55
Male, 13 to 21	0.70

It is important to realize the limitations of the Schwartz equation, which assumes that serum creatinine concentration is at steady state (i.e., serum creatinine concentration is neither rapidly rising nor falling but remains constant). Creatinine clearance calculated with the Schwartz equation under non-steady-state conditions are not a good indicator of renal function. In these clinical situations serum creatinine concentrations may lag behind true renal function. Thus, if measured serum creatinine is rapidly rising or deteriorating, calculated creatinine clearance based on non-steady-state serum creatinine values may overestimate true renal function. Conversely, calculated creatinine clearance computed from non-steady-state serum creatinine concentrations that are rapidly falling or improving may grossly underestimate true renal function.

Creatinine clearance is directly proportional to lean body mass. Use of the Schwartz equation assumes that the product of the length and the proportionality constant correctly estimates total creatinine excretion. This may be true for most patients; however, in patients with reduced muscle mass or severe malnutrition, use of the Schwartz equation will greatly overestimate creatinine clearance.

Fong et al. have demonstrated that creatinine clearance estimated with the Schwartz equation does not correspond with measured 24-hour creatinine clearance in critically ill children. The study evaluated the percent difference of creatinine clearance with the two methods. Of 100 critically ill pediatric patients evaluated, 84 had estimated creatinine clearance greater than measured creatinine clearance. In 36 of these patients the discrepancy was >50%. Use of the Schwartz equation to estimate renal function in critically ill patients resulted in gross overestimation of true renal function and could result in potentially detrimental drug overdosage. In this setting and in patients with rapidly changing creatinine values or reduced muscle mass, it is more accurate to calculate creatinine clearance from a 12- or 24-hour timed urine collection. The creatinine clearance is calculated as follows:

$$\text{Creatinine clearance} = U_{cr} \times V/S_{cr}$$

where U_{cr} = urine creatinine concentration (mg/dl) and V = urine flow rate (ml/min).

Unlike the Schwartz equation, this calculated creatinine clearance must be corrected to body surface area with the following equation:

$$\text{Corrected creatinine clearance} = \frac{\text{Calculated CrCl}}{\text{Body surface area}} \times 1.73$$

When used properly, this method will provide a more accurate estimate of creatinine clearance and GFR than the Schwartz equation.

The outline below provides an approach to assist physicians in prescribing drugs for pediatric patients with renal disease. Table 178-3 provides

Text continued on p. 1707.

PRESCRIPTION OF DRUG THERAPY IN RENAL DISEASE

Step 1: Obtain accurate information

An accurate history and physical examination is the first step in assessing the appropriateness of dosing regimens in patients with renal insufficiency. This assessment provides accurate information about a patient's height and weight. Serum creatinine concentration is also determined.

Step 2: Calculate creatinine clearance

Calculate creatinine clearance with the Schwartz equation. Although serum creatinine and BUN levels are used as a crude judgment of renal function, creatinine clearance more accurately approximates GFR.

Step 3: Evaluate creatinine clearance

Evaluate creatinine clearance. Determine if any limitations exist (e.g., rapidly changing creatinine clearance). In this situation the serum creatinine is not a good indicator of renal function. If creatinine clearance is rapidly deteriorating, calculated creatinine clearance may lag behind actual creatinine clearance. This can result in overestimation of true renal function. In this situation one can assume renal function is worse and the dose adjusted accordingly. Conversely, care must be taken not to underdose during the recovery phase of acute renal failure because serum creatinine concentration may remain high even after onset of the diuretic phase of renal recovery.

Step 4: Select appropriate dose

The recommended dosing regimen can be identified in the appropriate creatinine clearance columns. In some columns a dosage range may exist. The larger dose is used in patients with creatinine clearance in the upper range or with severe conditions. Similarly, the lower doses are used in patients with creatinine clearance in the lower range or with mild disease.

If a drug has different dosing regimens for different clinical conditions, the dosing guidelines are expressed as a fraction of the normal dose rather than as specific guidelines based on a milligram per kilogram basis. Refer to other pediatric dosing texts for dosage regimens for various clinical conditions.

Further dosage adjustments for some drugs can be made on the basis of pharmacokinetic serum concentration monitoring. Additional dosage adjustments may be needed if the patient's clinical condition or renal function changes.

Table 178-3   Drug Dosing in Pediatric Patients With Renal Disease

Drug	Creatinine Clearance (ml/min)	
Acyclovir	51->100	Normal dose divided q8h
	21-50	Two-thirds normal dose divided q12h
	11-20	One-third normal dose q24h
	1-10	One-sixth normal dose q24h
Allopurinol	51->100	10 mg/kg/day divided q8h
		or 200-300 mg/m²/day divided q8h
	11-50	5 mg/kg/day divided q12h
		or 100-150 mg/m²/day divided q12h
	1-10	2.5 mg/kg/day q24h
Amantadine		
1-8 yr	51->100	5-9 mg/kg/day divided q12-24h (150 mg max)
9-12 yr		100-200 mg/day divided q12-24h
	31-50	Maximum 100 mg/day
	21-30	Maximum 100 mg qod
	1-20	Maximum 200 mg/week
Amikacin	81->100	15-22.5 mg/kg/day divided q8h
	1-80	Loading dose 5-7.5 mg/kg/dose; obtain two serum concentration measurements after initial dose to determine frequency of subsequent doses consult clinical pharmacist on-call for recommendations
Amoxicillin	51->100	10-50 mg/kg/day divided q8h
	11-50	15-35 mg/kg/day divided q12h
	1-10	7-15 mg/kg/day q24h
Amoxicillin-clavulanic acid	51->100	20-40 mg/kg/day divided q8h
	11-50	15-25 mg/kg/day divided q12h
	1-10	7-15 mg/kg/day q24h
Ampicillin	31->100	100-200 mg/kg/day divided q6h
	11-30	75-175 mg/kg/day divided q8h
	1-10	50-100 mg/kg/day divided q12h
Amphotericin B	Nephrotoxic; GFR decreases 40%-50% in most patients; if decrease is too great (CrCl doubles), hold dose for several days until renal function improves; readminister previous dose	
Atenolol	31->100	1-2 mg/kg/day q24h
	11-30	1 mg/kg/day; maximum 50 mg q24h
	1-10	1 mg/kg/day; maximum 50 mg q48h
Aztreonam	31->100	90-120 mg/kg/day divided q6-8h
	11-30	45-60 mg/kg/day divided q6-8h
	1-10	20-30 mg/kg/day divided q6-8h
Captopril	51->100	0.15-0.5 mg/kg/dose q6-12h; may titrate upward to maximum of 6 mg/kg/day
	1-50	Criteria for dosing in renal failure not clearly defined; some clinicians suggest that patients with CrCl 50-10 ml/min/1.73 m² may tolerate up to 75% of normal dose; patients with CrCl <10 ml/min/1.73 m² may receive 50% of usual dose or usual dose administered q24h
Cefazolin	31->100	50-100 mg/kg/day divided q8h
	11-30	30-65 mg/kg/day divided q12h
	1-10	15-35 mg/kg/day divided q24h

Table 178-3   Drug Dosing in Pediatric Patients With Renal Disease—cont'd

Drug	Creatinine Clearance (ml/min)	
Cefotaxim	21->100	100-200 mg/kg/day divided q6-8h
	1-20	50-100 mg/kg/day divided q12h
Cefoxitin	51->100	80-160 mg/kg/day divided q6-8h
	31-50	60-120 mg/kg/day divided q8h
	11-30	40-80 mg/kg/day divided q12h
	1-10	20-40 mg/kg/day q24h
Ceftazidime	51->100	90-150 mg/kg/day divided q8h
	31-50	60-100 mg/kg/day divided q12h
	1-30	30-50 mg/kg/day q24h
Ceftriaxone		50-100 mg/kg/day divided q12-24h
Cefuroxime	31->100	75-150 mg/kg/day divided q8h
	11-30	50-100 mg/kg/day divided q12h
	1-10	25-50 mg/kg/day q24h
Cephalexin	41->100	25-50 mg/kg/day divided q6h
	11-40	20-40 mg/kg/day divided q8-12h
	1-10	12.5-25 mg/kg/day divided q12-24h
Cimetidine	51->100	20-40 mg/kg/day divided q6h
	21-50	15-30 mg/kg/day divided q8h
	1-20	10-20 mg/kg/day divided q12h
Ciprofloxicin	51->100	20-30 mg/kg/day divided q12h
	21-50	10-15 mg/kg/dose q18h
	1-20	10-15 mg/kg/day q24h
Codeine	51->100	0.5-1.5 mg/kg/dose q4-6h prn; 60 mg/dose max
	11-50	0.375-1.2 mg/kg/dose q4-6h prn
	1-10	0.25-0.75 mg/kg/dose q4-6h prn
Colistin	51->100	5-15 mg/kg/day divided q8h
(polymixin E)	21-50	Avoid use if possible; 3.5-10 mg/kg/day divided q12h
	1-20	Avoid use if possible; 1.5-5 mg/kg/day q24h
Ethambutol	51->100	15 mg/kg/day q24h
	11-50	15 mg/kg/day q36h
	1-10	15 mg/kg/dose q48h
Fluconazole	51->100	3-6 mg/kg/day q24h
		Immunocompromised patients: 10-12 mg/kg/day q24h
	21-50	1.5-3 mg/kg/day q24h
		Immunocompromised patients: 5-6 mg/kg/day 24h
	1-20	0.75-1.5 mg/kg/day q24h
		Immunocompromised patients: 2.5-3 mg/kg/day q24h
Gancyclovir	81->100	Induction: 10 mg/kg/day divided q12h
		Maintenance: 5 mg/kg/day q24h
	51-80	Induction: 5 mg/kg/day divided q12h
		Maintenance: 2.5 mg/kg/day q24h
	31-50	Induction: 2.5 mg/kg/day q24h
		Maintenance: 1.25 mg/kg/day q24h
	1-30	Induction: 1.25 mg/kg/day q24h
		Maintenance: 0.75 mg/kg/day q24h
		or 1.25 mg/kg/dose q48h
		Experience with these doses limited; monitor patient closely for disease progression

Continued.

Table 178-3 Drug Dosing in Pediatric Patients With Renal Disease—cont'd

Drug	Creatinine Clearance (ml/min)	
Gentamicin	81->100	4.5-7.5 mg/kg/day divided q8h
	1-80	Initial dose: 2.5 mg/kg; obtain two serum concentration measurements after initial dose to determine frequency of subsequent doses; consult clinical pharmacist on-call for recommendations
Imipenem	71->100	60-100 mg/kg/day divided q6h
	31-70	30-50 mg/kg/day divided q6h
	11-30	20-40 mg/kg/day divided q8h
	1-10	15-20 mg/kg/day divided q12h
Isoniazid	21->100	10-20 mg/kg/day divided q12-24h
	1-20	5-10 mg/kg/day q24h
Loracarbef	51->100	15-30 mg/kg/day divided q12h
	11-50	7.5-15 mg/kg/day q24h
	1-10	7.5-15 mg/kg/dose q72h
Meperidine	Toxicity appears to result from accumulation of metabolite; kinetics of metabolite not quantified, but it accumulates in uremia; use an alternative agents in patients with renal dysfunction	
Metoclopramide	51->100	0.4-0.8 mg/kg/day in 4 divided doses
	21-50	0.2-0.4 mg/kg/day in 4 divided doses
	1-20	0.1-0.2 mg/kg/day in 4 divided doses
Morphine	Renal disease has no affect on disposition of morphine itself; however, glucuronide metabolite, which may be active, may accumulate in renal insufficiency, which may account for reports of prolonged effects of morphine; dosing intervals may need to be adjusted; monitor patient closely	
Mezlocillin	31->100	200-300 mg/kg/day divided q4-6h
	11-30	150-225 mg/kg/day divided q6-8h
	1-10	75-150 mg/kg/day divided q6-8h
Nadolol	No information about pediatric dosing available in literature; increase dosing interval in renal dysfunction; administer dose q48h if CrCl 50-20 ml/min, and q60-72h if <20 ml/min	
Neostygmine	51->100	Normal dose; refer to drug formulary
	21-50	One-half normal dose
	1-20	One-third normal dose
Penicillin	51->100	100,000-400,000 U/kg/day divided q4h
	31-50	75,000-300,000 U/kg/day divided q6h
	11-30	50,000-120,000 U/kg/day divided q6h
	1-10	30,000-120,000 U/kg/day divided q6h
Pentamidine	Totally dependent on renal elimination; reduce doses in decreased renal function of unknown extent	
Probenicid	51->100	Initial dose: 25 mg/kg/dose as single dose Maintenance: 40 mg/kg/day divided q6h (500 mg max single dose)
	1-50	Avoid; may not be effective if CrCl <50 ml/min
Procainamide	NAPA is active metabolite, and with decreasing renal function NAPA accumulates disproportionately to parent compound; therefore, use of this drug in decreased renal function necessitates great caution and determination of serum levels of both procainamide and NAPA, and assessment of clinical end points of response	

Table 178-3 Drug Dosing in Pediatric Patients With Renal Disease—cont'd

Drug	Creatinine Clearance (ml/min)	
Pyridostigmine	51->100	Normal dose; refer to drug formulary
	21-50	One-half normal dose
	1-20	One-third normal dose
Ranitidine	51->100	PO: 6 mg/kg/day divided q8-12h
		IV: 3 mg/kg/day divided q8h
	21-50	PO: 4 mg/kg/day divided q12h
		IV: 1.5 mg/kg/day divided q12h
	1-20	PO: 2 mg/kg/day q24h
		IV: 1 mg/kg/day q24h
Sotalol	No information about pediatric dosing; adjust dosing interval in renal dysfunction; administer dose q24h if CrCl 30-60 ml/min, q36-48h if CrCl 10-30 ml/min, and individualize dose if CrCl <10 ml/min	
Sulfamethoxazole/ trimethoprim	31->100	Mild to moderate infection: 6-10 mg/kg/day divided q12h
		Serious infection: 15-20 mg/kg/day divided q6h
	1-30	Mild to moderate infection: 3-5 mg/kg/day q24h
		Serious infection: 7.5-10 mg/kg/day divided q12h
Tetracycline	51->100	25-50 mg/kg/day divided q6h
	21-50	8-15 mg/kg/day divided q8h
	1-20	2.5-5 mg/kg/day divided q12h
Ticarcillin	31->100	200-300 mg/kg/day divided q6h
	11-30	150-225 mg/kg/day divided q8h
	1-10	100-150 mg/kg/day divided q12h
Tobramycin	81->100	4.5-7.5 mg/kg/day divided q8h
	1-80	Initial dose: 2.5 mg/kg; obtain two serum concentration measurements after initial dose to determine frequency of subsequent doses; consult clinical pharmacist on-call for recommendations
Vancomycin	81->100	40-60 mg/kg/day divided q6-8h
	1-80	Initial dose: 10-20 mg/kg; obtain two serum concentration measurements after initial dose to determine frequency of subsequent doses; consult clinical pharmacist on-call for recommendations

guidelines for drug dosing with significant renal elimination in pediatric patients with compromised renal function. Dosing guidelines are outlined for each drug over a range of creatinine clearances. The drug is started at a dose that correlates with the degree of renal impairment. More precise dose adjustment based on determination of serum concentrations and evaluation of clinical end points may be needed. These guidelines do not include dosing recommendations for low birthweight infants and neonates; refer to other pediatric dosing handbooks for appropriate starting guidelines for this population.

Respiratory Failure

Patrick C. Sharp

BACKGROUND

Respiratory failure and acute respiratory distress syndrome (ARDS) are commonly seen in the PICU. Drug therapy plays a major role in the support of patients with respiratory failure; however, many physiologic changes are unique to this condition and may influence the pharmacokinetics of the drugs used. Knowledge of these physiologic changes is crucial to the proper pharmacologic management of pediatric respiratory failure.

Diffuse pulmonary endothelial damage is often observed in ARDS, leading to pulmonary capillary leak of fluid and protein even when pulmonary vascular pressure is low or normal. The pulmonary endothelium is the source of vasoactive peptides such as endothelin, cytokines, and metabolic products of arachidonic acid. It also secretes nitric oxide, prostaglandins, and peptides, which have direct effects on pulmonary vascular tone and integrity. The pulmonary endothelium is also responsible for the conversion of angiotensin I to angiotensin II and the degradation of many vasoactive substances. Damage to the pulmonary endothelium increases the release of these factors and disrupts its autoregulating capabilities, which may lead to pulmonary hypertension and other organ dysfunction. Increases in pulmonary vascular resistance lead to increased right ventricular (RV) afterload, which increases RV stroke work until decompensation and finally RV failure occurs.

Organ systems other than the lungs are also involved in respiratory failure. The liver, kidney, GI tract, CNS, and bone marrow may all be involved. Nonpulmonary organ injury is caused by release of endothelial mediators, with increases in vascular injury in all capillary beds. Although there are no specific drug dosing studies for respiratory failure, the clinician needs to be aware that all these factors may lead to alterations in other organ systems.

EFFECTS OF RESPIRATORY FAILURE ON VARIOUS ORGAN SYSTEMS
Renal System

Renal failure occurs in as many as 40% to 50% of patients with ARDS. Decreased renal function in the setting of mechanical ventilation may occur with either decreased or normal cardiac output. The exact mechanism is unclear but probably involves reduction in renal blood flow and afferent renal arteriolar constriction. Humoral mediators may also be involved as atrial natriuretic peptide is decreased with the use of PEEP, whereas levels of plasma renin, aldosterone, and antidiuretic hormone are increased. The decreased renal blood flow causes a decrease in GFR, leading to decreased urine production and sodium excretion. Drugs that rely on renal elimination may all be affected, including antibiotics such as aminoglycosides, vancomycin, and cephalosporins; paralytic agents such as vecuronium and pancuronium;

inotropes such as amrinone, milrinone, and digoxin; and H_2 antagonists such as ranitidine. Use of these drugs must be monitored closely, and dosage may need to be reduced. (See p. 1700 for a more complete discussion of drug dosing in renal failure.)

Hepatic System

In many patients with ARDS increased transaminase and bilirubin levels, prolonged clotting times, and hypoalbuminemia develop. Decreased hepatic blood flow secondary to reduced cardiac output may account for this. Clinically, hepatomegaly and jaundice are frequently observed in patients who need prolonged ventilatory support with high intrathoracic pressure. This may occur secondary to increased hepatic venous and inferior venal caval pressure. Increased hepatic resistance from compression of the liver by the diaphragm may also induce a rise in intravascular portal pressure. This congestive hepatomegaly induced by mechanical ventilation can produce hepatocellular dysfunction similar to that seen in the liver of patients with congestive heart failure. Hepatic elimination of drugs therefore may be decreased during mechanical ventilation. Such drugs may include sedative agents, analgesics, inotropes, neuromuscular blocking agents, anticonvulsants, and antibiotics. (See p. 1696 for a more complete discussion of drug dosing in liver failure.)

Gastrointestinal Tract

Enteral nutrition and oral administration of pharmacologic agents are commonly used in patients with respiratory failure. However, decreased blood flow to the GI tract may reduce GI function and motility, creating delayed or reduced absorption of orally administered medication. If this is suspected, parenteral drug administration may be the preferred route.

Central Nervous System

CNS dysfunction may occur in as many as 30% of patients, producing lethargy, coma, and rarely seizures. Vasodilators, commonly used to reduce afterload or decrease pulmonary vascular resistance in respiratory failure, may also increase cerebral perfusion, compounding the effects of increased ICP from PEEP. The use of CNS-altering drugs such as sedatives and analgesics may hinder the ability to clinically assess increased ICP and therefore need to be closely monitored.

. . .

The physiologic changes seen and treatment methods used in respiratory failure affect not only the lung but other organ systems. Although specific dosing recommendations in respiratory failure have not been studied, the clinician must be aware of potential alterations in pharmacologic response and elimination.

CURRENT RESEARCH AND FUTURE CONSIDERATIONS
Pulmonary Administration of Drugs

Penetration of drugs into diseased lung tissue is poor secondary to general tissue degradation and intrapulmonary shunting. Use of perfluorocarbon (PFC) as a medium to deliver drugs to the lung may overcome these obstacles to drug delivery. This route of administration may also be efficacious for systemic drug delivery when vascular compromise is present. There are many physiologic reasons to support pulmonary administration of drugs by means of PFCs. The lung provides a large surface area for drug exchange since all blood flow passes through the pulmonary capillary bed, and the thin barrier at the alveolo-capillary interface creates a short diffusion distance. The low surface tension of PFCs and their ability to match pulmonary blood flow supports uniform drug distribution. Ventilation can be supported simultaneously, and the biologic inertness of PFCs eliminates any vehicle-drug interactions. PFCs are well suited to deliver both active and inactive agents in treating or diagnosing a wide variety of pulmonary disorders. Exogenous surfactant, antibiotics, steroids, antioxidants, diuretics, vasoactive drugs, and chemotherapeutic agents can all be given via PFC pulmonary administration.

In studies in young cats, acetylcholine, epinephrine, and tolazoline were dispersed in PFC and directly administered through the endotracheal tube during liquid ventilation. Typical dose-dependent cholinergic responses to acetylcholine showed progressive decreases in systemic blood pressure and heart rate and increases in peak tracheal pressure as a function of increasing acetylcholine in the inspired PFC liquid. Characteristic dose-dependent sympath-

omimetic effects of epinephrine and α-adrenergic blockade effects of tolazoline were also noted.

Gentamicin given to newborn lambs by means of direct pulmonary administration during liquid ventilation produced equivalent serum levels at 1 hour, higher lung tissue levels, and uniform interlobar distribution compared with equivalent IV doses.

Finally, visualization of the PFC-filled lung is greatly enhanced over that of the gas-filled lung for plain radiography, ultrasound, or MRI.

In summary, PFC-associated ventilation may not only provide a more efficacious method of ventilation in pediatric patients with respiratory failure but may also provide a better route for drug administration.

Obesity
Christine A. Lindsay

BACKGROUND

Drug doses in children are most commonly based on body weight or body surface area. Although practitioners may note a child is overweight, doses usually continue to be given based on the actual body weight (ABW) of the child. On occasion this may result in elevated serum drug concentrations and untoward effects. The purpose of this section is to identify the drugs most commonly affected by obesity and to provide dosing strategies for these agents.

Obesity is commonly related to two different measurements: ideal body weight (IBW) and body mass index (BMI). A person is usually considered obese when ABW approaches 120% of IBW. To calculate IBW of a child, see equation 1 below. BMI is usually restricted to research applications. Because lean body mass (LBM) and proportion of body fat to total body weight have the greatest effect on the pharmacokinetics of drug dosing, methods or calculations that reflect this disparity are often more useful.

Several clinical methods can be used to determine the percentage of body fat (e.g., skinfold thickness and isoptic dilution methods). However, none of these measurement methods is practical in the PICU. Bioelectrical impedance has also been used in critically ill adults but not extensively in children. Another confounding variable is the introduction of LBM, defined as fat-free weight or total body weight (TBW) minus fat weight. IBW and LBM are related but not identical. However, most practitioners can more readily assess IBW than LBM. Therefore IBW is used more often for drug dosage adjustments.

$$IBW\ (kg) = \frac{Height\ (cm)^2 \times 1.65}{1000} \quad (1)$$

The weight used for dosing hydrophilic drugs that need adjustment for obesity is often called the dosing weight or effective body weight (EBW). EBW is calculated on the premise that fat contains approximately 40% water. IBW is subtracted from ABW to represent the proportion of fat present. Forty percent of this difference is added to IBW to determine EBW:

$$EBW = IBW + 0.4\ (ABW - IBW) \quad (2)$$

Whether a drug is dosed on the basis of IBW, ABW, or EBW depends on the physical properties of each drug.

EFFECT OF OBESITY ON VARIOUS PHARMACOKINETIC VARIABLES
Absorption

It is not surprising that little information is available about the effects of obesity on drug absorption. In studies where this has been examined in obese subjects compared with nonobese subjects, no significant differences were noted.

Distribution

Most of the information about pharmacokinetic parameter changes in obesity focus on distribution characteristics. The alterations in volume of distribution are related to the drug's lipid and water solubility. However, other factors can also play a role.

Binding of drugs to plasma proteins can affect drug distribution. Although some researchers have observed changes in protein binding in obesity, others have failed to confirm these findings.

Regional blood flow is decreased in obese subjects. Under conditions of normal body weight, blood perfusion of fat accounts for only about 5% of cardiac output. Under these same circumstances the viscera receives 73%, and lean tissue 22%. The blood flow per gram of fat is significantly less in obese subjects than in thin subjects. These data suggest that blood flow to fat is proportionally less than blood flow to lean tissue. This hypothesis favors the use of IBW or LBW as a determinant of drug distribution for nonlipophilic drugs.

Metabolism

Few comparative studies of hepatic metabolism of drugs in obese and lean subjects have been published. In adult patients a review of liver biopsy findings was conducted in 1984. Only 12% of specimens were reported as normal. The most common pathophysiologic findings were fatty infiltrates, portal inflammation, and fibrosis. That biotransformation of certain drugs appears altered in obesity may actually be a result of liver damage from these causes, not because biotransformation pathways are induced or inhibited. No study to date has delineated specific changes in biotransformation pathways as a result of obesity.

One drug that appears to have altered metabolism is lorazepam. Total body clearance of lorazepam is more rapid in obese subjects. Usually it is the volume of distribution that is most affected (greater due to the lipophilicity of the drug), thus making the elimination half-life of the drug longer in obese individuals than in lean individuals. Although lorazepam is "cleared" from the systemic circulation faster, it is only being sequestered in fat stores and will take longer to redistribute out of the fat and then out of the body.

Renal Excretion

Glomerular flow rates are elevated in adult women. It was proposed that the increased GFR may actually be a result of increased kidney mass in obese subjects. In addition, proposed equations for calculating creatinine clearance in obese subjects have demonstrated that in healthy obese adults the creatinine clearance was increased in proportion to the estimated free fat mass. No information exists to support an increased active tubular secretion component.

It has been suggested that obese subjects may be at increased risk for aminoglycoside nephrotoxicity. One study demonstrated that when mildly obese persons and individuals of normal weight were given gentamicin or tobramycin over several days, appropriate serum drug concentrations were maintained but creatinine clearance decreased by nearly half in the obese subjects. This observation was tested in an experimental rat model in which obese, overfed rats were given gentamicin. Not only was the kidney mass increased by almost 30% compared with controls, the renal concentration of gentamicin was also 33% higher. With increased kidney mass, more drug can be filtered by the glomerulus, and a large amount of drug is delivered to the tubules. This increases the extent

Table 178-4 Recommendations for Drug Dosing in Obesity

Drug	Recommendations
Aminoglycosides (gentamicin, tobramycin, amikacin)	Initial dose based on EBW; maintenance dose based on specific pharmacokinetic parameters
Alfentanil	Continuous infusions based on IBW
Atracurium	Dosage based on TBW (because of drug hyposensitivity, not altered pharmacokinetic values)
Caffeine	Loading dose based on TBW; maintenance dose based on IBW
Carbamazepine	Time to steady state may be prolonged; maintenance dose may need reduction
Cimetidine	Loading dose based on IBW; maintenance may require an increase with clinical monitoring
Cyclosporine	Dosage based on IBW
Lorazepam	Dosage adjusted to TBW; clearance of lorazepam and diazepam increased in obese subjects
Methylprednisolone	Dosage based on IBW
Ranitidine	Loading and maintenance doses based on IBW
Sufentanil	Loading dose based on ABW; maintenance dose reduced
Theophylline	Initial dose based on EBW; then titrate to serum concentrations
Vancomycin	Initial dose based on EBW; maintenance dose based on specific pharmacokinetic parameters
Vecuronium	Dosage based on IBW
Verapamil	Loading dose based on ABW; maintenance dose based on IBW

of drug uptake by the proximal renal tubules and perhaps explains why the obese individual may develop renal toxicity at a faster rate. To date, no controlled study in children has addressed this issue. The practitioner needs to be diligent about monitoring serum trough concentrations and renal function in the obese child receiving aminoglycoside therapy.

Cimetidine clearance is increased in obese adult subjects, and doses to maintain similar steady-state concentrations were increased 1.6 times that in control subjects. To date, no studies have shown a similar effect with ranitidine.

Dosing Guidelines

Table 178-4 lists dosage adjustment considerations in obesity. This table reflects current dosing information and does not imply that drugs not listed do not need to be adjusted. All recommendations are taken from adult guidelines. Because doses in children are based on kilogram of body weight, it may be even more important to ensure use of the appropriate weight.

For drugs not listed in Table 178-4, the following recommendations apply. For poorly lipid-soluble drugs such as atracurium and β-blockers, distribution is limited to lean tissues. Doses are based on IBW or LBM. For drugs that distribute mainly in LBM and partially in fat (e.g., aminoglycosides, vancomycin, and most antibiotics), doses are calculated on the basis of EBW and adjusted as needed. For the more lipid-soluble drugs that are equally distributed into lean and fat tissues or for drugs that are exclusively distributed into adipose tissues, ABW is used. Chemotherapy drugs and drugs with low therapeutic thresholds are dosed cautiously. Routine use of body surface area for chemotherapy must be examined in obese subjects. LBM or IBW would be more ideal for hydrophilic drugs and may prevent serious toxicity.

CURRENT RESEARCH AND FUTURE CONSIDERATIONS

Although obesity is not common in children, it may affect optimal drug therapy. Practitioners need to study the effects of drugs in obese children to learn more about drug behavior. Although this may not be possible in large studies, even case reports would assist the bedside caregiver in prescribing appropriate therapeutic regimens.

ADDITIONAL READING
Neonates

• Besunder JB, Reed MD, Blumer JL, et al. Principles of drug biodisposition in the neonate: A critical evaluation of the pharmacokinetic-pharmacodynamic interface. Part 1. Clin Pharmacokinet 14:189-216, 1988.

Lopez-Samblas AM, Diaz PR, Binion KH. Drug dosing in the neonate. In Murphy JE, ed. Clinical Pharmacokinetics Pocket Reference. Bethesda, Md.: American Society of Hospital Pharmacists, 1993.

• Reed MJ, Besunder JB. Developmental pharmacology: Ontogenic basis of drug disposition. Pediatr Clin North Am 36:1053-1074, 1989.

Stewart CF, Hampton EM. Effect of maturation on drug disposition in pediatric patients. Clin Pharm 6:548-564, 1987.

Wong AF, Cupit GC. Neonatal therapy. In Koda-Kimble MA, Young LY, eds. Applied Therapeutics: The Clinical Use of Drugs. Vancouver, Wash.: Applied Therapeutics, 1992.

Young SL. Drug disposition in the pediatric patient. J Pharm Pract 2:13-20, 1989.

Liver Disease

• Brouwer KLR, Dukes GE, Evans WE, et al. Influence of liver function on drug disposition. In Evans WE, Schentag JJ, Jusko WJ, eds. Applied Pharmacokinetics: Principles of Therapeutic Drug Monitoring, 3rd ed. Vancouver, Wash.: Applied Therapeutics, 1992.

Golper TA, Bennett WM. Altering drug dose. In Schrier RW, Gambertoglio JG, eds. Handbook of Drug Therapy in Liver and Kidney Disease. Boston: Little, Brown, 1991.

McLean AJ, Morgan DJ. Clinical pharmacokinetics in patient's with liver disease. Clin Pharmacokinet 21:42-69, 1991.

Roland M, Tozer TN, eds. Elimination. In Clinical Pharmacokinetics: Concepts and Applications. Philadelphia: Lea & Febiger, 1989.

Shargal L, Yu ABC. Hepatic Elimination of Drugs. Applied Biopharmaceutics and Pharmacokinetics. Norwalk, N.J.: Appleton-Century-Crofts, 1985.

Renal Failure

Brater DC. Pocket Manual of Drug Use in Clinical Medicine, 4th ed. Philadelphia: B.C. Decker, 1989.

Fong J, Johnston S, Valentino T, et al. Length/serum creatinine ratio does not predict measured creatinine clearance in critically ill children. Clin Pharmacol Ther 58:192-197, 1995.

Gibson TP. Influence of renal disease on pharmacokinetics. In Evans WE, Schentag JJ, Jusko WJ, eds. Applied Pharmacokinetics: Principles of Therapeutic Drug Monitoring. Spokane, Wash.: Applied Therapeutics, 1986.

Matzke GR, Keane WF. Drug dosing in patients with impaired renal function. In DiPiro JT, Talbert RL, Hayes PE, et al., eds. Pharmacotherapy: A Pathophysiologic Approach. New York: Elsevier Science Publishing, 1989.

McEnvoy GK, Litvak K, eds. AHFS Drug Information. Bethesda, Md.: American Society of Hospital Pharmacists, 1994.

Schrier RW, Gambertogilo JG, eds. Handbook of Drug Therapy in Liver and Kidney Disease. Boston: Little, Brown, 1991.

Schwartz GJ, Brion LP, Spitzer A. The use of plasma creatinine concentration for estimating glomerular filtration rate in infants, children and adolescents. Pediatr Clin North Am 34:571-590, 1987.

Swan SK, Bennett WM. Drug dosing guidelines in patients with renal failure. West J Med 156:633-638, 1992.

Taketomo CK, Hodding JH, Kraus DM, eds. Pediatric Dosage Handbook, 2nd ed. Hudson, Ohio: Lexi-Comp, 1993.

Respiratory Failure

Marquez JM, Douglas ME, Downs JB, et al. Renal function and cardiovascular responses during positive airway pressure. Anesthesiology 50:392-398, 1979.

• Paulsen TE, Spear RM, Peterson BM. New concepts in the treatment of children with acute respiratory distress syndrome. J Pediatr 127:163-175, 1995.

Perkins MW, Dasta JF, DeHaven B, et al. A model to decrease hepatic blood flow and cardiac output with pressure breathing. Clin Pharmacol Ther 45:548-552, 1989.

• Prewitt RM, Matthay MA, Ghignone M. Hemodynamic management in the adult respiratory distress syndrome. Clin Chest Med 4:251-268, 1983.

• Richard C, Berdeaux A, Delion F, et al. Effect of mechanical ventilation on hepatic drug pharmacokinetics. Chest 90:837-841, 1986.

• Said SI. Metabolic and endocrine functions of the lung. In Chernick V, Kendig EL, eds. Disorders of the Respiratory Tract in Children. Philadelphia: WB Saunders, 1990.

Sarnaik AP, Lieh-lai M. Adult respiratory distress syndrome in children. Pediatr Clin North Am 41:337-363, 1994.

Pulmonary Administration of Drugs

• Shaffer TH, Wolfson MR, Clark LC. Liquid ventilation. Pediatr Pulmonol 14:102-109, 1992.

Wolfson MR, Greenspan JS, Shaffer TH. Pulmonary administration of vasoactive drugs (PAD) by perfluorocarbon liquid ventilation. Pediatr Res 29:336A, 1991.

Wolfson MR, Shaffer TH. Pulmonary administration of drugs (PAD): A new approach for drug delivery using liquid ventilation. FASEB J 4:1105A, 1990.

Zelinka MA, Wolfson MR, Calligaro I, et al. Direct pulmonary administration of gentamicin during liquid ventilation of the lamb: Comparison of lung and serum levels to IV administration. Pediatr Res 29:290A, 1991.

Obesity

• Blouin RA, Chandler MHH. Special pharmacokinetic considerations in the obese. In Evans WE, Schentag JJ, Jusko WJ, eds. Applied Pharmacokinetics: Principles of Therapeutic Drug Monitoring, ed. 3. Vancouver, Wash.: Applied Therapeutics, 1992, pp 11-1–11-20.

• Cheynol G. Clinical pharmacokinetics of drugs in obesity: An update. Clin Pharmacokinet 25:103-114, 1993.

Morgan DJ, Bray KM. Lean body mass as a predictor of drug dosage: Implications for drug therapy. Clin Pharmacokinet 26:292-307, 1994.

179 Analgesia and Sedation

Gary D. Cieslak · Dorothy C. Foglia

BACKGROUND AND INDICATIONS

The traditional reluctance to prescribe potent analgesic and sedative drugs to neonates and children has been attributed to questions regarding the existence, significance, and assessment of pain in infants and children as well as long-standing concerns about potential harmful effects of opioid analgesics, such as respiratory depression and physiologic dependence or addiction. Early studies of neurologic development concluded that neonatal responses to painful stimuli were decorticate and nonlocalizing in nature and animal studies suggested that neonates may be particularly susceptible to the respiratory depressant effects of potent opioid analgesics. Despite more recent work reevaluating patient responses to painful stimuli and the traditional practices of prescribing analgesics and sedatives to children, considerable resistance to their use persists, especially in those who are particularly young or critically ill. Although the cognitive and emotional experience and interpretation of painful stimuli continue to develop and evolve through childhood, even brief admissions to the PICU can be a terrifying and disorienting experience for a child as well as a wrenching psychological trauma for the entire family. The ethical provision of care for critically ill infants and children mandates the effective and compassionate relief of their pain and anxiety.

The neuroanatomic pathways for the transmission of nociceptive, or painful, stimuli from the periphery to the CNS have been demonstrated to be essentially complete and operational by birth. For example, studies have shown that neonates respond to repeated heel lancings or circumcisions by increased heart rate, systemic blood pressure, and respiratory rate; movement of upper and lower limbs; facial grimacing; palmar sweating; changes in skin conductivity; elevated transcutaneous carbon dioxide readings; and decreased oxygen saturation. These responses are blunted in infants undergoing circumcisions after penile nerve blocks with lidocaine. Furthermore, neonates undergoing circumcisions without analgesia have been shown to exhibit increased irritability and poor feeding behavior for up to 22 hours postoperatively. These studies support the hypothesis that neonates are capable of feeling and reacting to painful stimuli, and as a result, analgesia may be indicated as a part of their medical management.

More recent work has addressed the metabolic and hormonal consequences of minimal analgesia in infants and children undergoing surgical procedures. Such patients exhibit a stress response marked not only by increases in physiologic variables such as heart rate, respiratory rate, and muscle activity but also by increases in oxygen consumption and carbon dioxide production. Hormonal studies conducted in these children report a marked increase in levels of catecholamines, growth hormone, glucagon, cortisol, aldosterone, and other corticosteroids as well as suppression of insulin secretion. These changes reflect a generalized catabolic state and can lead to significant hyperglycemia, lactic acidosis, and increased protein breakdown. In randomized, controlled trials of infants and children undergoing cardiac surgery these changes are inhibited in those infants and children receiving adequate opioid analgesia compared with those receiving minimal anesthesia.

Because cardiorespiratory, hormonal, and metabolic changes are seen in infants and children in response to pain and anxiety, proper use of analgesic and anxiolytic medications may result in physiologic benefits to patients. In addition, adequate relief of pain and anxiety may facilitate the safe and effective conduct of various therapeutic and diagnostic efforts. Excessive patient movement from pain or anxiety can lead to accidental dislodgment of important invasive monitors or artificial airways that can suddenly and significantly compromise care, sometimes at great danger to the patient.

Adequate analgesia and sedation are indispensable

for good care of a patient on a ventilator to relieve anxiety, allow the patient to tolerate otherwise noxious invasion of the airway, and facilitate improved gas exchange. In the paralyzed patient neuromuscular blockade neither alters consciousness nor provides analgesia; therefore adequate sedation and analgesia are essential. For patients in whom the cardiovascular reflexes associated with airway instrumentation and manipulation can be life threatening (e.g., a patient with increased ICP, pulmonary arterial hypertension, or severe airway reactivity), sedation or analgesia must be provided before exposure to such noxious stimuli.

Tracheal intubation and often ventilation in awake neonates can cause significant decreases in transcutaneous oxygen together with increases in systemic arterial blood pressure and ICP, theoretically increasing the risk of intraventricular hemorrhage. The increases in ICP with intubation, however, can be attenuated or abolished in preterm neonates who receive opioid analgesics. The cardiovascular responses of infants to tracheal suctioning, particularly increases in pulmonary artery blood pressures, can be similarly abolished by opioid analgesics.

Sedation is occasionally beneficial for patients with airway obstruction (both upper airway and reactive airways disease) if agitation is further exacerbating the airway compromise. Such treatment of a patient who does not have an artificial airway, however, can be undertaken only if the agitation is not a sign of hypoxia and the increased effort and respiratory rate are not the mechanisms by which the patient is achieving adequate oxygenation and carbon dioxide elimination. In addition, any patient with significant potential for airway obstruction must be cared for in a setting that permits continuous observation and monitoring of the airway and where skilled assistance is immediately available to establish an artificial airway if sedation leads to complete airway decompensation.

Assessment of Pain in Children

Providing effective analgesia and sedation to the pediatric patient depends on accurate and ongoing efforts to assess the intensity of a patient's pain or anxiety and the effectiveness of prior interventions. A child's inability to communicate his or her distress can at times lead caregivers to view such symptoms with skepticism. A patient's underlying personality characteristics, cultural expectations, and parental involvement can also affect a child's response to painful stimuli, and these factors must be considered in assessing the patient.

Since pain and anxiety are not only subjective experiences, the assessment of pain in infants and critically ill children who are unable to communicate relies increasingly on physiologic and behavioral responses. No single standard measure gives a complete quantitative or qualitative measurement of a pediatric patient's painful experience. A number of pain assessment scales and tools have been developed and validated specifically for use in children. Selection of the appropriate assessment tool is based on the child's age, underlying medical condition, and cognitive level. Physiologic scales such as the Objective Pain Scale by Hannallah et al. (Table 179-1) assess hemodynamic variables as well as behavioral characteristics involving motor activity, alertness, agitation, and facial tension. Other scales such as the Children's Hospital of Eastern Ontario Pain Scale (CHEOPS) observe vocal and facial expressions and trunk and limb movements and can be useful in the postoperative period for children 1 to 7 years of age. In the older child or adolescent, patient self-report measures can be very helpful in determining the need for analgesics or sedatives. Children 3 years of age and older are generally able to understand varying intensities of pain, although they may not yet have sophisticated verbal skills to describe it. Simplified versions of more traditional analog scales can be useful. Such scales depict photographs or pictures of children's faces in varying degrees of distress and the child selects the face resembling his or her feelings. Older children and adolescents can generally effectively use linear analog scales to reflect the intensity of their pain. The serial results of any of these tools can be tracked to aid in the assessment of a patient's need for and subsequent response to analgesic and sedative therapies.

TECHNIQUE

Physicians previously treated pain, anxiety, and agitation as a single entity with fixed-dose preparations containing narcotics, antihistamines, and phenothiazines (i.e., the "lytic cocktail"). Such fixed-dose preparations often inadequately address the primary component of a specific child's discomfort and attempt to treat pain with sedation. Instead, the relative degree to which pain, anxiety, and agitation contribute to each patient's discomfort must be identified. Drug therapy is chosen accordingly, considering the

Table 179-1   Pediatric Objective Pain Scale*

Variable	Response	Score†
Blood pressure (systolic)	+10% of control	0
	11% to 30% of control	1
	>30% of control	2
Crying	Not crying	0
	Crying, responds to attentive care	1
	Crying, does not respond to attentive care	2
Movement	None	0
	Restless	1
	Thrashing	2
Agitation	Patient asleep or calm	0
	Mild	1
	Hysterical	2
Verbal evaluation or body language	Asleep or states no pain, preverbal child exhibits no painful posturing	0
	Mild pain or cannot localize, preverbal child flexes extremities	1
	Moderate pain and can localize, preverbal child holds location of pain	2

*Modified from Hannallah RS, Broadman LL, Belman AB, Abramowitz MD, Epwtein BS. Comparison of ilioinguinal/iliohypogastric nerve blocks for control of postorchiopexy pain in pediatric ambulatory surgery. Anesthesiology 66:832-834, 1987.
†A total score of ≥6 signifies intense pain and should be treated accordingly.

age and condition of the patient, the intensity and duration of the noxious stimuli, and any medical contraindications to the use of any particular drug or modality (Table 179-2). No one drug or regimen is appropriate for every patient. Therapy must be tailored to the particular patient and clinical situation (Table 179-3).

Opioids

To control patient pain in the PICU, an opioid is usually the drug of choice. Fentanyl and morphine are used most frequently in pediatric patients since there is extensive experience with their use and considerable support in the literature for dosing recommendations. Other opioids can also be used safely, however. If pain is predictably severe and constant, a continuous infusion of an opioid analgesic may minimize variations in serum drug concentrations and provide better pain relief than an as-needed dosing regimen. For pain associated with a scheduled occurrence such as chest physiotherapy or endotracheal suctioning, a scheduled dose of medication before

the procedure is appropriate. Premedication with systemic analgesics, local anesthetics, or both must be provided before all painful procedures such as central venous catheter or chest tube placements, bone marrow aspirations, or spinal taps.

In small children and infants who are unable to verbalize their pain, either regularly scheduled administration (around the clock) or continuous infusions of opioid may provide optimal pain relief as long as the level of nursing observation and the patient's ventilatory status are adequate. In older children and adolescents, either an as-needed or a regularly scheduled regimen can be used, according to the predictability and intensity of the patient's pain. Alternatively, a patient-controlled analgesia (PCA) regimen, with or without an accompanying continuous infusion, affords the patient greater control over analgesic management and provides more consistent therapeutic serum drug concentrations. In addition, some postoperative patients may benefit from the continuation of epidural analgesia begun in the operating room using opioids, local anesthetics, or both and managed in consultation with the anesthesiology service.

Although the IV administration of opioids is the most reliable, in patients with limited IV access who need significant analgesic medication different approaches to opioid administration may need to be tried. For example, intermittent doses or continuous infusions of subcutaneous morphine have been described in PICU patients. Alternatively, transdermal fentanyl patches allow the continuous administration of fentanyl for up to 72 hours per patch and are available in several different dosages. Caution and close observation must be exercised, however, when using these novel modalities in children because the drug effects are more difficult to control and may lead to excessive CNS depression or other adverse effects.

Mechanism of action

Naturally occurring opiate drugs such as morphine as well as fentanyl and other synthetic analogs act on specific opioid receptors located in areas of the brain and spinal cord involved with pain perception. These areas include the hypothalamus, corpus amygdaloideum, corpus striatum, the periaqueductal gray matter of the brain stem, and the substantia gelatinosa of the spinal cord. Opioids bind to both pre- and postsynaptic sites and act by hyperpolarizing the neuronal membrane and interfering with neurotransmitter release, mimicking the actions of those endogenous peptides that bind to opioid receptors (i.e., endorphins). There are several subpopulations of opioid receptors, including μ_1 receptors, which mediate supraspinal analgesia, and μ_2 receptors, which are thought to mediate ventilatory depression, physical dependence, and other side effects.

Pharmacokinetics

Morphine, as with most other opioids, is metabolized in the liver and its metabolites are excreted by the kidneys. Since clearance may be prolonged in neonates, a single dose has a longer duration of action than in older infants and children. Its metabolites have some pharmacologic activity and patients in renal failure may need to be observed carefully for prolonged effects. However, clinical experience suggests that excessive CNS or respiratory depression is not more common as long as patients are dosed at longer intervals and doses are titrated according to patient response. Alternatively, levorphanol can be used because there does not seem to be significant renal excretion of the parent drug or its metabolites. Meperidine has a pharmacologically active metabolite, normeperidine, which is excreted by the kidneys and has CNS excitatory effects. In high doses or in patients with renal failure its accumulation can cause seizures. The use of meperidine in such situations is contraindicated.

Effects

Cardiovascular effects. Opioids decrease heart rate, an effect that is most prominent with fentanyl. Cardiac output is usually well maintained, especially with synthetic opioids (e.g., fentanyl, sufentanil, and alfentanil). Bradycardia or orthostatic hypotension can occur from decreased sympathetic nervous system reflexes and increased vagal tone. These effects are minimal in euvolemic patients but may become significant in the presence of untreated hypovolemia. Neonates, in whom cardiac output is principally heart rate dependent, may be more prone to developing hypotension from the bradycardic effects of opioids. Nonetheless, fentanyl is often indicated in infants at risk for pulmonary hypertension because it effectively ablates the increase in pulmonary artery blood pressures associated with endotracheal suctioning or airway manipulation.

Morphine causes histamine release and subsequent peripheral vasodilation and venous pooling and can cause hypotension, especially if given rapidly to a hypovolemic patient. Morphine is, however, a safe and effective drug when given to a patient with stable hemodynamics. Meperidine, unlike the other opioids, can cause tachycardia and has a direct depressant effect on the myocardium.

Respiratory effects. Opioids depress ventilation in a dose-related fashion. Opioids directly depress brain stem centers regulating ventilation, leading to decreases in rate, minute volume, rhythmicity, and carbon dioxide responsiveness. The respiratory response to carbon dioxide remains blunted for 3 to 4 hours after a single dose of morphine and for hours longer after larger doses, continuous infusions, or epidural administration. Nevertheless, continuous infusions of 10 to 30 μg/kg/hr can provide adequate analgesia and have not been found to prolong ventilator dependence or interfere with extubation in pediatric patients after undergoing cardiac surgery. However, higher doses of opioids or other sedatives used concomitantly can create cumulative depressant effects on ventilation, necessitating careful titration or

Table 179-2　Pharmacologic Control of Pain, Anxiety, and Agitation

Drug	Dosage	Route	Onset	Duration	Comments
Opioids					
Morphine	Single dose 　Children: 0.1-0.2 mg/kg 　Neonates and infants: 0.05 mg/kg Continuous infusion 　Children: 20-50 μg/kg/hr 　Neonates and infants: 15 μg/kg/hr	IV, IM, PO, SC	IV: 5-15 min IM: 20-30 min	2-3 hr	Histamine release, vasodilation Avoid in asthma, hypotension Usual max dose: 10-15 mg Seizures possible in neonates
Meperidine (Demerol)	PO: 3-5 × IV dose 1-2 mg/kg	IV, IM, PO	IV: 5-10 min IM: 15-20 min PO: 15-30 min	2-3 hr 3 hr	Sustained release available Tachycardia Negative inotropy Metabolite can cause seizures Avoid with monoamine oxidase inhibitors Adult dose: 150 mg
Fentanyl (Sublimaze)	1-5 μg/kg Continuous infusion: 1-3 μg/kg/hr	IV, IM	3-5 min	30-60 min	Bradycardia, chest wall rigidity
Sufentanil (Sufenta)	0.1-0.5 μg/kg Continuous infusion: 0.1-0.3 μg/kg/hr	IV	Immediate; shorter than fentanyl	20-60 min	Bradycardia, chest wall rigidity
Hydromorphone (Dilaudid)	10-20 μg/kg Continuous infusion: 3-5 μg/kg/hr PO: 5 × IV dose	IV, IM, PO, SC	5-10 min	3-6 hr	Less sedation than morphine Adult dose: 2-4 mg
Levorphanol	0.02-0.04 mg/kg	IV	10-15 min	4-8 hr	Adult dose: 2 mg
Methadone	0.05-0.2 mg/kg PO: 2 × IV dose	PO, IV, IM	1 hr	6-24 hr	Usual max dose: 10 mg IV, 20 mg PO
Codeine	0.5-1.0 mg/kg	PO, IM	30-60 min	4-6 hr	Administer with acetaminophen
Anesthetics					
Ketamine (Ketalar)	Single dose 　0.5-2 mg/kg 　3-5 mg/kg 　5-7 mg/kg Continuous infusion: 0.5-1 mg/kg/hr	IV IM PO IV	IV: 30 sec IM: 3-4 min	5-10 min 12-25 min	Releases endogenous catecholamines Avoid emergence delirium with benzodiazepine Increases secretions Bronchodilatation Avoid if raised ICP; catecholamine depletion

Drug	Dose	Route	Onset	Duration	Comments
Benzodiazepines					
Diazepam (Valium)	0.05-0.2 mg/kg	IV	IV: 15 min	4-6 hr	Painful on injection; Thrombophlebitis; Erratic IM absorption
	0.2-0.5 mg/kg	PO	PO: 30-60 min	6-8 hr	
Midazolam (Versed)	0.05-0.1 mg/kg	IV	IV: 3-5 min	2 hr	Max dose: 20 mg
	0.1-0.15 mg/kg	IM	IM: 20-30 min	15 min	
	0.5-0.75 mg/kg	PO	PO: 10-30 min	15-30 min	
	Continuous infusion: 50-200 μg/kg/hr	IV			
Lorazepam (Ativan)	0.05-0.1 mg/kg	PO, IV, IM	IV: 15 min; PO: 30-60 min	8-12 hr	Usual max dose: 4 mg
Barbiturates					
Phenobarbital	2-3 mg/kg	IV, PO	IV: 5 min; PO: 20-60 min	8-12 hr	
Pentobarbital (Nembutal)	2-4 mg/kg	IV	IV: <5 min	2-6 hr	Max dose: 200 mg
	4-6 mg/kg	PO, PR, IM	IM: <20 min; PO: 20-60 min; PR: 30-60 min		
	Continuous infusion: 1-2 mg/kg/hr				
	Pentobarbital coma: Load: 10-15 mg/kg over 2 hr; Maintenance: 1 mg/kg/hr initially; increase to 2-3 mg/kg/hr to maintain EEG burst suppression				
Secobarbital (Seconal)	1-2 mg/kg	PO, PR, IM		2-6 hr	
Sodium thiopental (Pentothal)	4-6 mg/kg (induction)	IV	30-60 sec	5-10 min	Vasodilation, tachycardia
	25-30 mg/kg	PR	5-15 min	60 min	
Methohexital (Brevital)	1-2 mg/kg	IV	30-60 sec	3-5 min	Vasodilation, tachycardia
	25-30 mg/kg	PR	5-15 min	60-90 min	
Other agents					
Chloral hydrate (Noctec)	Sedation: 25-50 mg/kg; Hypnotic: 75-100 mg/kg	PO, PR	30-60 min	6-8 hr	Max dose: 2 g
Etomidate	0.2-0.3 mg/kg (induction dose)	IV	Rapid	5 min	Minimal respiratory depression; Hemodynamic stability; Adrenal suppression after continuous infusions
	Continuous infusion 5-8 μg/kg/min				
	6.5 μg/kg	PR			
Propofol	25-75 μg/kg/min (sedation)	IV	Rapid	5-10 min	Prolonged infusions contraindicated
Droperidol	25-100 μg/kg	IV, IM	5-10 min	6-12 hr	Occasional dysphoria; Antiemetic; α-Blockade

Table 179-3 Contraindications for Common Analgesics and Sedatives

Drug	Contraindication	Alternative
Opioid	Apnea (relative contraindication)	Support ventilation, ketamine
	Hypovolemia (avoid morphine, meperidine)	Fentanyl, benzodiazepine, ketamine
	Asthma (avoid morphine, meperidine)	Ketamine, fentanyl
	Renal failure (avoid meperidine)	Fentanyl, levorphanol
Ketamine	Catecholamine depletion, depressed myocardial function	Fentanyl, etomidate
	Increased ICP	Barbiturate
	Increased intraocular pressure	Barbiturate
	Seizures (relative contraindication)	Barbiturate, benzodiazepine
	Severe systemic hypertension	Benzodiazepine, morphine
	Hepatic dysfunction	Reduce dose, opioid
Benzodiazepine	Hepatic dysfunction (decreased metabolism)	Reduce dose (lorazepam, see text) opioid
	Renal failure (decreased protein binding)	Reduce dose, opioid
Barbiturates	Reduced cardiac reserve, hypovolemia	Fentanyl, etomidate, benzodiazepine
	Porphyria	Benzodiazepine
	Asthma	Ketamine, benzodiazepine, fentanyl
Chloral hydrate	Infant <3 mo of age	Any
	Hepatic dysfunction	
	Gastric or rectal irritation	
Propofol	Reduced cardiac reserve, hypovolemia	Benzodiazepine, fentanyl

lower doses when decreasing a patient's ventilatory support. Opioids also depress the cough reflex and are associated with dose-related decreases in bronchial ciliary activity.

CNS effects. Opioid-induced ventilatory depression can cause increases in ICP if hypercarbia is allowed to develop. If ventilation is unchanged, synthetic opioids generally do not affect ICP, although modest increases in ICP have been reported using these drugs in head trauma patients.

Commonly prescribed doses of opioids have been associated with muscle rigidity and seizure activity in infants but not in older children at commonly administered doses. Although the opioids all have sedating side effects, meperidine is unique in that its active metabolite, normeperidine, can cause CNS excitation and dysphoria. An accumulation of this metabolite from high doses, prolonged administration, or decreased renal clearance can cause tremors, muscle twitches, or overt seizure activity.

Opioids decrease wakefulness, although fentanyl and hydromorphone are typically less sedating than morphine. They can produce pruritus, probably via a centrally mediated mechanism, in addition to the histamine-related effects seen with morphine administration. They cause miosis and can produce either euphoria or dysphoria. In small IV doses (0.25 to 0.5 mg/kg) meperidine can prevent or treat the shivering associated with amphotericin or blood product administration or recovery from anesthesia.

Other effects. High doses of opioids given by rapid IV infusion can cause skeletal muscle rigidity, especially in the thoracic and abdominal musculature. This is most commonly seen with fentanyl and can be severe enough to interfere with ventilation. It can be avoided by administering smaller incremental doses (e.g., ≤ 4 μg/kg of fentanyl) or with simultaneous use of a neuromuscular blocking agent.

Opioids cause nausea and emesis by direct stimulation of the CNS chemoreceptor trigger zone, an effect that is exacerbated by changes in posture. In addition, opioids increase resting GI smooth muscle tone and inhibit motility, which can lead to constipation. Laxatives or stool softeners are sometimes routinely administered to patients expected to receive opioids for more than a few days. Opioids can also

Table 179-4   Special Considerations in Neonates and Premature Infants

Drug	Consideration	Implication
Opioids	Increased sensitivity to respiratory depressant effects (especially morphine): decreased plasma protein binding, blood-brain barrier immaturity, opioid receptor subtype immaturity	Reduce dose
	Prolonged clearance	Increase dosing interval
	Seizures possible with morphine	Use fentanyl
	Fentanyl alone may not adequately blunt stress responses	Supplement with another agent
Ketamine	Larger dose needed in infants <6 mo of age to control movement	Choose alternative agent
	Doses needed for sedation associated with apnea and respiratory depression	Monitor closely and be prepared to control airway and ventilation
	Generalized extensor spasm and opisthotonus	Choose another agent
Benzodiazepines	Prolonged clearance of drug and metabolites (prolonged CNS and respiratory depression)	Decrease dose, increase interval, add fentanyl
	Impaired thermoregulation	Attention to heat-conserving measures
	Propylene glycol and sodium benzoate vehicle	Avoid diazepam
Barbiturates	Greater penetration of blood-brain barrier	Reduce dose, monitor appropriately
	Decreased metabolism	Avoid use of longer acting agents

induce spasm of the sphincter of Oddi, which can lead to increases in biliary duct pressure.

Opioids increase the tone and peristaltic activity of smooth muscle in the ureters, bladder, and bladder sphincter, which can make voiding difficult and cause urinary retention. Dry mouth, sweating, facial flushing, vertigo, bradycardia, orthostatic hypotension, hypothermia, restlessness, and mood changes can also occur. Some patients may suffer severe side effects from one opioid (e.g., morphine) but fare considerably better when changed to another (e.g., hydromorphone).

Special considerations in the neonate

Because of the immaturity of various metabolic and homeostatic mechanisms, neonates who are premature or less than 48 weeks' postconceptual age may exhibit increased sensitivity to both the therapeutic and adverse effects of potent opioid analgesics (Table 179-4).

Immaturity of the cytochrome P-450 hepatic enzyme system responsible for biotransformation of the opioids before their excretion results in decreased elimination and prolonged clearance of opioids in the first few days to weeks of life. This can result in a prolongation of the effects, including ventilatory depression, of a single dose and may lead to drug accumulation after repeated dosing. After several weeks to 2 months of age, however, clearance and elimination of these drugs quickly meet or surpass the rates of older children and adults. Clearance and elimination of opioids in the neonate can be further prolonged if acute illness, abdominal surgery, or increases in intra-abdominal pressure lead to decreases in hepatic blood flow.

Plasma protein binding of morphine is decreased in the neonate, which increases the unbound fraction of drug available for diffusion into the brain. In addition, the immature blood-brain barrier of the neonate may be more permeable to hydrophilic drugs such as morphine, allowing easier penetration of the CNS. Neonates also exhibit marked variability in serum drug levels after a given dose and are reported to be more likely than older children to develop seizures after the administration of morphine. Finally, animal studies suggest that in the newborn it is possible that the early development or function of the μ_1 opioid receptor subtype associated with analgesic effects may lag behind that of the μ_2 receptor that is associated with the respiratory depressant effects of opioids.

These factors contribute to an increased sensitivity in premature infants and neonates to the respiratory depressant effects of commonly administered opioids in commonly used doses. Synthetic opioids such as fentanyl are preferable in these patients, with initial doses one-fourth to one-half the usual dose for older children. Furthermore, the use of these drugs in the term infant less than 2 months of age must be carefully titrated to clinical effect and the patient closely observed in a monitored setting. The use of potent opioids in premature infants less than 48 weeks postconceptual age or term infants in the immediate neonatal period mandates PICU level observation.

Tolerance and dependence

Tolerance to the analgesic and respiratory depressant effects of opioids may develop after repeated or chronic administration over several days or weeks, and subsequent doses may need to be increased to produce similar analgesic effects. Some degree of physical dependence or the need for continuing doses to avoid an abstinence syndrome and its increased sympathetic nervous system activity probably develops in most patients after 7 to 10 days of opioid therapy and more quickly in patients receiving continuous infusions of synthetic opioids. In infants receiving continuous infusions of fentanyl a total dose >2.5 mg/kg or a duration of continuous therapy >9 days has been found to be 100% predictive of an abstinence syndrome developing.

Any patient who has undergone a prolonged course of opioid therapy or exhibits signs of CNS irritability or movement disorders after abrupt withdrawal of the medication is considered to have some degree of physiologic dependence. Such patients are given decreasing doses of opioids over 5 to 10 days or are switched to the longer acting methadone, which can be given orally and decreased over days to weeks. Alternatively, 3 to 5 μg/kg of clonidine given transdermally can be helpful in attenuating many of the withdrawal symptoms (see Chapter 183).

Reversal

Naloxone (Narcan) is a pure opioid antagonist that can reverse both the analgesic and ventilatory depressant effects of opioids. In the child or neonate who has received an opioid overdose 0.01 mg/kg given intravenously can promptly reverse respiratory depression. If analgesia is still necessary, smaller doses (1 to 4 μg/kg) may be used to provide a tolerable level of sedation or to antagonize other undesired opioid side effects and yet minimize the reversal of analgesia. Sympathetic nervous system stimulation manifesting as tachycardia, hypertension, arrhythmias, and pulmonary edema may be seen if the drug is given to patients who have developed physiologic dependence to opioids. It has a short duration of action (30 to 45 minutes), and repeated doses or continuous infusion is needed to reverse the effects of longer acting opioids.

Dosage

The dosing recommendations for the commonly used opioids are listed in Table 179-2.

Patient-controlled analgesia

PCA is a modality by which a programmable infusion pump allows the patient to self-administer small frequent predetermined bolus doses of opioids. Each administered dose is followed by a lockout period during which no further doses can be administered. PCA can be combined with a continuous infusion to provide less variable background serum drug concentrations, easier titration, and improved therapeutic effect. Display screens on the pump allow the current settings and the amounts of medication recently administered to be monitored. Complications of PCA therapy are rare but include all of the usual side effects associated with opioid therapy.

PCA can provide more consistent and satisfactory pain relief by allowing patients to self-titrate drug doses to the level of their own pain, thereby increasing their satisfaction with their analgesic management. It is appropriate in any child sufficiently cognitive and otherwise physically able to operate the drug delivery button when necessary, usually down to 6 years of age. This modality is especially popular and useful with adolescents because it allows them greater control and autonomy over their care.

In all patients the addition of a basal continuous opioid infusion to the PCA regimen can result in a patient who continues to receive drug despite being too sedated or uncomfortable from side effects to push the button. This has been associated with an increased incidence of adverse side effects or even respiratory depression in adults. Nonetheless, significantly increased problems have not been reported in children with continuous infusions of 5 to 10 μg/kg/hr of morphine or its equivalent.

Policies established by the medical and nursing staff must be in place to provide for the safe and effective administration of PCA therapy, including appropriate monitoring and as-needed treatments for possible side effects. Preprinted order forms (Table 179-5) specify the drug formulation, intermittent doses, continuous infusion rates if used, a lockout period, and a cumulative maximum dosage over time. Treatment regimens for common side effects can also be added to the order sheets. Nursing interventions to ensure patient safety include careful checking of dosages and machine programming, frequent assessments of the patient for adverse reactions or side effects to the drug being administered, and frequent documentation of the patient's level of alertness, respiratory rate and pattern, and the amount of drug administered.

Safe and successful implementation of the PCA modality for a patient depends on proper care and selection of the IV access to be used. Using only antireflux IV tubing without side ports (frequently provided by the manufacturer) prevents inadvertent mixing of drugs or the delivery of incorrect drug doses. After a secure and functional IV site is chosen, the PCA delivery tubing is introduced as close to the IV catheter as possible, with a carrier infusion rate sufficient to ensure prompt drug delivery when the PCA pump is activated by the patient. The IV catheter site must be regularly checked for patency and function. Infiltration of the IV infusion prevents proper drug delivery and can itself cause pain and agitation. Once the PCA pump is programmed, a locking mechanism can be activated to avoid any accidental (or deliberate) reprogramming of the dosage settings and any subsequent increased risk for adverse drug effects.

Nonsteroidal Anti-Inflammatory Drugs

Nonsteroidal anti-inflammatory drugs (NSAIDs) are a heterogeneous group of drugs that generally act by blocking the peripheral production of prostaglandins that mediate or modulate the transmission of nociceptive stimuli. In standard doses they are remarkably safe, nonaddictive, and free of respiratory or

Table 179-5   Patient Controlled Analgesia

Drug	Intermittent Dose	Continuous Infusion	Lockout	4 Hr Maximum
Morphine	0.02-0.03 mg/kg to max 0.5-3 mg/dose	0.01-0.02 mg/kg/hr	6-12 min	0.3 mg/kg
Meperidine	0.2-0.3 mg/kg to max 5-30 mg/dose	0.1-0.2 mg/kg/hr	6-12 min	3 mg/kg
Hydromorphone	0.002-0.003 mg/kg to max 0.05-0.3 mg/dose		6-12 min	0.03 mg/kg

Standing nursing orders

No other opioids or sedatives except in consultation with _____ M.D.
Nursing
   Respiratory rates and sedation assessments q1-2h
   Vital signs q2-4h
Monitors: Pulse oximetry and/or cardiac/apnea monitor as indicated
PRN medications
   Bradypnea/inability to arouse
      Turn off PCA pump
      Naloxone, 0.002 mg/kg, and notify anesthesiology on call
   Nausea/vomiting
      Promethazine 0.25 mg/kg IV over 20 min q6h
   Pruritus
      Diphenhydramine, 0.5-1 mg/kg PO or IV over 20 min q6h
Oxygen/bag/mask/naloxone at bedside
Call _____ M.D. on call for problems/questions.

hemodynamic side effects, although many of the agents can inhibit platelet aggregation and functioning via their effects on prostaglandin synthesis. Bronchospasm, anaphylactoid reactions, gastric bleeding, and alterations in glomerular filtration rate have also been reported with these agents. They are indicated for the treatment of mild to moderate pain, especially of bony or soft tissue origin. Unfortunately, these agents exhibit a "ceiling effect" above which increasing doses provide no further analgesia. They are often administered in combination with more potent opioid analgesics to minimize opioid doses and decrease opioid side effects. Acetaminophen, in doses of 10 to 15 mg/kg, can similarly be helpful in the treatment of mild to moderate pain. It is not a NSAID per se, however, and its anti-inflammatory properties are minimal. Aspirin is not prescribed for children because of its association with Reye's syndrome.

Of the various NSAIDs, ketorolac, a new injectible agent, is the strongest analgesic. It can be used either as monotherapy or to augment other more potent analgesics. After an initial IV dose of 1 mg/kg (to a maximum of 60 mg), subsequent doses of 0.5 to 1.0 mg/kg can be given up to every 6 hours (to a maximum of 30 mg/dose). Prolonged use, however, is associated with gastritis and gastric bleeding, and administration of this agent for more than a few days is not recommended.

Ketamine

Mechanism of action

Ketamine is a dissociative anesthetic that probably antagonizes the action of the *N*-methyl-D-aspartate (NMDA) neurotransmitter in the CNS, but it may act on some opioid receptor subtypes as well. It provides profound analgesia of short duration, particularly for pain involving bone and soft tissue. Ketamine can be the sole anesthetic agent for painful diagnostic and superficial surgical procedures when muscle relaxation is not needed and has been used extensively for burn dressing changes, debridements, and pediatric cardiac catheterizations. It is a poorer choice of analgesic for procedures involving visceral pain or when immobilization is needed. Its analgesic effects are terminated by redistribution out of the CNS, and it ultimately undergoes hepatic degradation.

Effects

Ketamine produces a cataleptic or dissociative state in which the patient is noncommunicative but the eyes remain open, exhibiting slow nystagmus and a fixed gaze. Spontaneous verbalizations are common.

Ketamine increases heart rate, systemic arterial blood pressure, cardiac output, myocardial oxygen consumption, and central venous blood pressure by increasing sympathetic nervous system outflow and inhibiting norepinephrine reuptake. It is itself a direct myocardial depressant, however, which occasionally becomes evident in a patient with exhausted endogenous catecholamine stores or diminished myocardial contractility. Although controversial, pulmonary vascular resistance appears to be minimally affected. Ketamine is a potent cerebral vasodilator and may lead to increased ICP independent of other hemodynamic (e.g., increased cardiac output) or respiratory (e.g., increased carbon dioxide tension) effects.

Protective laryngeal and pharyngeal reflexes are better preserved with ketamine than with other agents, but they are not entirely unaffected. Patients receiving ketamine have aspirated radiographic contrast material placed both into the stomach and the posterior pharynx into the lungs. The resting respiratory rate, tidal volume, minute ventilation, and end-tidal carbon dioxide are not changed after ketamine, although the ventilatory response to increases in carbon dioxide is decreased after both bolus dosing and continuous administration.

Ketamine relaxes airway smooth muscle and decreases airway resistance, making it an excellent agent for use in asthmatics, particularly during airway instrumentation or painful procedures.

Side effects

In the septic or severely hypovolemic patient whose compensation has depended on massive catecholamine output and in whom catecholamine stores may be depleted, an injection of ketamine can cause hypotension secondary to its direct negative inotropic effects (see Table 179-3). It must be used cautiously in patients with hypovolemia and only with concomitant and vigorous volume replacement. The decreased inotropy and increased myocardial oxygen consumption also make ketamine contraindicated for use in patients with reduced myocardial reserve or coronary artery disease. It is similarly contraindicated in patients in whom a catecholamine infusion has recently been discontinued. Those patients may have down regulation of adrenergic receptors and diminished endogenous catecholamine stores. Increases in pulmonary arterial blood pressure are probably related to increases in heart rate, systemic arterial blood pressure, or cardiac output. Ketamine can be used cautiously in patients with pulmonary artery hypertension as long as adequate oxygenation and ventilation are maintained. Because of its cerebral vasodilating capabilities, it is not appropriate for patients with closed-head injury or increased ICP.

Ketamine greatly stimulates tracheal and pharyngeal secretions, which can cause airway irritability or obstruction. The concomitant administration of an antisialogogue such as glycopyrrolate or atropine is therefore indicated.

Like all anesthetic agents, ketamine is capable of producing apnea. Infants are more susceptible to the respiratory depressant effects than older children, and premature infants less than 51 weeks postconceptual age are especially prone to episodes of apnea and bradycardia after receiving even small doses of ketamine. Another serious drawback to its use in older children and adults, but not in infants and younger children, is the dose-related association with unpleasant and sometimes terrifying emergence phenomena, including auditory and visual hallucinations, delirium, and agitation. Patients receiving ketamine recover better in a nonstimulating atmosphere (i.e., low light and decreased noise and handling). These reactions are minimized by concomitant use of any benzodiazepine.

There is a high incidence of extrapyramidal muscle activity, fasciculations, purposeless movement of the extremities, and clonic spasms when ketamine is used alone, and these movements can sometimes interfere with procedures or examinations. The epileptogenic potential of ketamine is controversial, but it is relatively contraindicated in patients with seizure disorders if other agents will suffice.

Dosage

Anesthesia of approximately 6 to 10 minutes' duration is rapidly induced with 1 to 2 mg/kg given intravenously. Subsequent incremental doses are usually approximately 50% of the induction dose given at intervals of 8 to 15 minutes, depending on the patient's response to stimuli (see Table 179-2). Recovery occurs within 30 minutes. A continuous infusion can provide excellent hemodynamic and respiratory stability when other agents produce hypotension. An initial dose may be given to induce anesthesia and then administered at a rate of 0.5 to 1.0 mg/kr/hr.

Ketamine lends itself well to use for discrete procedures rather than to control ventilation or treat anxiety. It is a potent anesthetic agent and must be administered by personnel familiar with its properties. Appropriate monitoring of cardiovascular and respiratory variables is essential during its use (airway reflex depression is possible) in a setting in which trained personnel and equipment for airway support, including instrumentation, are immediately available if necessary.

Benzodiazepines

Decreasing anxiety is best achieved with a benzodiazepine. These drugs have amnestic, anxiolytic, and hypnotic effects, with minimal cardiorespiratory depression, and can help allay the fear and sleep deprivation experienced by many PICU patients. Benzodiazepines are also effective as anticonvulsants and muscle relaxants. The various agents differ in their duration of action, preferred route of administration, and degree of amnesia provided (see Table 179-2). Some agents have active metabolites with a longer elimination half-life than the parent compound (e.g., diazepam), making accumulation of the metabolite (e.g., oxazepam) possible with prolonged use. Of the various agents, midazolam is preferred as a continuous infusion since it lacks active metabolites, demonstrates little accumulation, and has a relatively short half-life.

Mechanism of action

Benzodiazepines facilitate the inhibitory effect of γ-aminobutyric acid (GABA) on neuronal transmission at limbic, thalamic, and hypothalamic levels in the CNS by acting on specific GABA receptor sites. Benzodiazepines also augment the inhibitory effects of glycine at the level of the spinal cord.

Pharmacokinetics

Members of this family of drugs are metabolized by hepatic microsomal enzymes (P-450 system) through demethylation. Many metabolites are pharmacologically active and thus may contribute to a prolonged duration of action. Lorazepam differs from midazolam and diazepam in that it is metabolized by glucoronyl transferase. This pathway is better preserved than that of the P-450 system in patients with hepatic dysfunction. The clearance of most benzodiazepines is not altered by renal failure, although decreased protein binding may produce increased levels of unbound drug (see Table 179-3). Cimetidine can inhibit the hepatic enzymes responsible for the metabolism of benzodiazepines and doses must be decreased with concomitant use of this drug.

Benzodiazepines can be given orally, intravenously, or transmucosally, and some are absorbed well intramuscularly. For a brief period of sedation associated with a particular procedure, midazolam may be given orally or rectally. The absorption of intramuscularly administered diazepam is sufficiently erratic and painful to preclude its use via this route. Diazepam also causes venous irritation with pain, erythema, and the development of thrombophlebitis. However, this is not seen with midazolam or lorazepam. Diazepam is dispensed in a solution of propylene glycol and sodium benzoate, which makes it dangerous and contraindicated for use in neonates.

Effects

CNS effects. All degrees of CNS depression occur with administration of benzodiazepines, from anxiolysis to unconsciousness, secondary to action on the reticular activating and limbic systems. They reduce anxiety and aggression and are associated with profound anterograde amnesia, impairing the acquisition of new information. Benzodiazepines have no analgesic properties, but all are potent anticonvulsants. They demonstrate cumulative sedative effects with other CNS depressants. Benzodiazepines cause skeletal muscle relaxation by inhibition of afferent spinal pathways, but they do not affect dose requirements of neuromuscular blocking agents.

Cardiovascular effects. When used alone, benzodiazepines have minimal cardiovascular effects. However, they can contribute to significant hypotension or decreased systemic vascular resistance in the hypovolemic patient or when they are given in conjunction with opioids or barbiturates.

Respiratory effects. In smaller doses benzodiazepines produce minimal depression of ventilation. In larger doses the ventilatory responses to hypercarbia and hypoxia are decreased, although the resting level of carbon dioxide is unchanged. Cumulative depression of ventilation can occur when benzodiazepines are administered concomitantly with opioids or other sedatives, and doses therefore must be reduced or carefully titrated in such situations. Rapid administration of benzodiazepines can rarely cause apnea.

Dependence

Physiologic dependence can develop in patients who receive benzodiazepines for prolonged periods or via continuous infusions. The abstinence syndrome can be as severe as that seen with other CNS depressants and includes tremors, restlessness, tachycardia, choreoathetoid movements (not typically seen with opioid withdrawal), perceptual changes, and generalized seizures. Any patient who has received frequent doses or a continuous infusion of midazolam for more than 1 week can have withdrawal symptoms, which can be minimized by gradually decreasing doses over 5 to 10 days, switching to an agent with a prolonged half-life such as lorazepam, or using 3 to 5 μg/kg transdermal clonidine to treat withdrawal symptoms (see Chapter 183).

Reversal

Flumazenil is a specific benzodiazepine antagonist on the GABA receptor and can reverse the sedative effects of these agents in IV doses of 5 to 10 μg/kg to a maximum of 3 mg/dose. As with naloxone, its duration of action is less than an hour, and continued observation of the patient is indicated and repeated dosing may be necessary.

Dosage

The dosing recommendations for the commonly used benzodiazepines are listed in Table 179-2.

Barbiturates

Although historically barbiturates were used to treat insomnia and agitation, their primary role today is as a hypnotic for nonpainful procedures when movement is not permitted (i. e., during MRI and CT) and as an anticonvulsant. In the PICU barbiturates provide hypnosis for brief procedures such as endotracheal intubation. They may also be effective secondary agents when opioids and benzodiazepines do not provide adequate sedation. All barbiturate compounds are derivatives of barbituric acid and have similar side effects. However, they differ in their onset and duration of action (see Table 179-2). These drugs decrease the excitability of both pre- and postsynaptic membranes. The CNS is the most sensitive organ to the drug effects with the usual doses, and sedation and hypnosis precede cardiac, skeletal, or smooth muscle effects. Barbiturates have no analgesic action and may even increase the reaction to painful stimuli at subanesthetic doses. All barbiturates are potent anticonvulsants, although phenobarbital is the most effective in subhypnotic doses. Barbiturates have a wide range of effects on EEG tracings and decrease the time spent in rapid eye movement (REM) sleep.

Mechanism of action

Although the mechanism of action of barbiturates is unknown, it probably acts via multiple sites and mechanisms. In general barbiturates probably act by facilitating or modulating the actions of GABA and other inhibitory neurotransmitters and inhibiting the synaptic actions of excitatory neurotransmitters.

Pharmacokinetics

Barbiturates are lipid-soluble drugs metabolized by the liver, which converts them to inactive water-soluble products excreted in the urine. Recovery from the effects of barbiturates, however, initially depends on redistribution of the drug out of the CNS rather than on drug metabolism. After equilibration between the blood and high blood flow organs, barbiturates are redistributed to tissues with lower blood flow before ultimately being metabolized. With prolonged or continuous administration, significant drug accumulation is possible in those tissues with lower blood flow. From those sites the drug may redistribute back into the blood, leading to significantly prolonged clinical effects.

Effects

CNS effects. Barbiturates globally depress CNS function, producing the full spectrum of depressed consciousness from drowsiness to coma. They have potent effects on cerebral metabolism and produce dose-related depression of metabolic oxygen consumption and cerebral blood flow, presumably secondary to autoregulation, a desirable effect in patients with increased ICP. Electrical activity is depressed, and in sufficient doses the EEG becomes isoelectric. Decreased membrane excitability and impulse traffic provide the basis for the anticonvulsant effect. Barbiturates have no analgesic effect.

Cardiovascular effects. Barbiturates cause a decrease in myocardial contractility related to decreased bioavailability of calcium to myofibrils. A compensatory (baroreceptor-mediated) increase in heart rate usually occurs, maintaining cardiac output. However, barbiturates can cause profound decreases in cardiac output in patients with hypovolemia or reduced compensatory reserve (see Table 179-3). In addition, peripheral vasodilation and decreases in central venous pressure secondary to histamine release can occur. These effects are most pronounced with rapid IV administration of the short-acting barbiturates methohexital and thiopental. In addition, these agents can produce transient rashes related to histamine release.

Respiratory effects. A dose-related respiratory depression (decreased minute ventilation) occurs with administration of barbiturates in large IV doses. The patient may experience apnea for 3 to 5 minutes, and respiratory depression is cumulative with the administration of other CNS depressants. Airway protective reflexes are preserved, making airway instrumentation with pentothal or methohexital alone hazardous because of hiccups, cough, laryngospasm, or bronchospasm.

Other effects. Most barbiturates induce the cytochrome P-450 enzyme system and may cause a decrease in warfarin, corticosteroid, and anticonvulsant serum concentrations. Barbiturates may increase serum porphyrin and are contraindicated in patients with a history of porphyria.

Dosage

The dosing recommendations for the commonly used barbiturates are listed in Table 179-2.

Chloral Hydrate to Provide Sedation

Chloral hydrate is a nonbarbiturate hypnotic agent that has long been used in pediatrics to provide sedation for painless diagnostic or therapeutic procedures. It is hepatically metabolized to its active form, trichloroethanol, and demonstrates negligible effects on respiration or hemodynamics in recommended doses. An occasional patient can become confused or agitated, and sedation failures are not infrequent. Since tolerance to the sleep-inducing effects of chloral hydrate develops rapidly, it is less suited to repeated or prolonged dosing in the PICU. Its onset is relatively slow and its duration is prolonged. Some patients may still be asleep many hours later. It is not available in a parenteral form, and since it is exceptionally unpalatable, is usually administered rectally. It is not recommended for use in either term or premature infants less than 3 months of age because large or repeated doses in this age group can result in cardiac arrhythmias, myocardial depression, or apnea. It is also contraindicated in patients with hepatic dysfunction because of its prolonged half-life related to decreased metabolism (see Table 179-3).

Dosage

The dosing recommendations for chloral hydrate are listed in Table 179-2.

Sedation of the Nonintubated Patient

Patients who are not intubated and are not expected to undergo airway or ventilatory support frequently need some degree of sedation. Pediatric patients in particular often need relatively deep levels of sedation whether they are being simply monitored and observed or are undergoing a procedure. Since excessive levels of sedation carry the risk of hypoventilation, apnea, loss of protective reflexes, airway obstruction, and subsequent cardiorespiratory impairment, optimal care must include adequate assessment and monitoring of the patient and the ready availability of emergency equipment and trained personnel in case problems arise.

The American Academy of Pediatrics has advanced guidelines for the safe management of sedation in pediatric patients. Although the guidelines are primarily concerned with the sedation of patients for specific discrete procedures, the general principles apply to any setting, including the PICU.

Before sedation

The safe conduct of sedating an infant or child begins before the administration of medications. A pertinent history and physical assessment are essential to elicit underlying illnesses. In particular, the anatomy and adequacy of the child's airway are examined, and baseline vital signs are obtained and recorded. Oral intake of solid foods within the previous 6 hours or clear liquids within the previous 2 hours contraindicates a sedative because compromised protective airway reflexes place the patient at risk for regurgitation and subsequent aspiration.

Monitoring

The type and amount of monitoring necessary depend on the results of the patient's presedation as-sessment and the depth of sedation anticipated. Because of the valuable information that it provides as well as its low cost and noninvasiveness, continuous pulse oximetry is always indicated. Frequent intermittent assessment of other vital signs is also indicated, the most important of which is the sedated patient's respiratory rate and pattern and degree of arousability. IV access must be secured if a significant depth of sedation is anticipated or produced. If a particular procedure is to be performed or a particularly deep level of sedation is anticipated, a separate observer whose only responsibility is to continuously monitor the patient's condition allows others involved in the child's care to focus on their designated tasks. In particularly ill patients or those with complex multisystem disorders, an anesthesiologist may be best equipped to manage the sedation and monitoring of the patient.

Emergency support

Different levels of sedation represent a continuum that extends from minimal drowsiness to obtundation and complete loss of protective airway reflexes. Since any patient can drift into a deeper level of sedation than desired or anticipated, properly trained personnel and emergency equipment must always be readily available to perform interventions and support the airway, ventilation, and hemodynamics of the compromised patient. Oxygen with a bag and mask, a source of continuous suction, a variety of appropriately sized tubes for airway management, and emergency drugs such as epinephrine, atropine, lidocaine, naloxone, and flumazenil must be available (see Chapter 152).

Adherence to these principles when planning and administering medications with sedative effects to the sick infant or child will successfully avoid any unfortunate complications.

Local Anesthetics

Local anesthetic drugs block nerve conduction by reversible blockade of membrane sodium channels involved with depolarization and subsequent impulse transmission. They are weakly basic tertiary amines classified according to the presence of an ester or amide linkage. Their onset and duration of action are affected by a number of factors, including the particular drug's degree of ionization, the surrounding tissue pH, and nerve fiber size and myelinization. The use of epinepherine in a local anesthetic solution causes local vasoconstriction and decreases the rate of systemic absorption, prolonging the duration of nerve blockade. Epinephrine-containing solutions, however, can compromise local blood flow to areas supplied by end arteries and must never be used for digital or penile blocks or in other sites without collateral circulation.

Local anesthetics are generally used in the PICU setting for either local infiltration to allow the performance of painful procedures or to provide continuous analgesia via an indwelling epidural catheter. Patients can benefit from subcutaneous infiltration of a local anesthetic, usually 1% or 2% lidocaine, before procedures such as arterial or IV catheter placement, repair of minor lacerations or surgical wounds, thoracostomy tube placement, or lumbar puncture. The injection of local anesthetic drugs is painful, but it can be minimized by the use of 26- or 30-gauge needles and by buffering the acidic local anesthetic solution in a 10:1 volume ratio with 1% bicarbonate.

Indwelling epidural catheters may be placed either intraoperatively or in the PICU with the assistance of the anesthesiology service. Alternatively, catheters can also be placed within other sites such as the intrapleural space or the axillary sheath. The continuous infusion of local anesthetic drugs in close proximity to somatic nerves can provide blockade of painful impulses transmitted via those nerves. The dosing recommendations for local anesthetic drugs to safely avoid unwanted toxic effects are listed in Table 179-6.

Systemic absorption of local anesthetics and the subsequent risk of toxicity depends on the total dose of drug administered and the rapidity of its absorption into the blood from the particular site of administration. Absorption is most rapid from intrapleural and intratracheal sites, followed in decreasing order by epidural, brachial plexus, distal peripheral, and subcutaneous sites. Accidental IV or intraarterial injection of doses much smaller than those used for various nerve blocks may also produce rapid increases in serum drug concentrations and subsequent toxic effects.

The severity of systemic toxic effects of local anesthetics depends on plasma drug concentrations. Lower concentrations can produce side effects such as tinnitus, perioral numbness, light-headedness, muscle twitching, and restlessness. As plasma concentrations increase, generalized seizures and cardiac arrhythmias may develop and cardiovascular collapse can occur. A child who has recently received a significant dose of local anesthetic or who is receiving a continuous infusion of local anesthetic via an indwelling catheter must be closely observed for complaints of dizziness or numbness or signs of agitation or jitteriness. These signs and symptoms may indicate dangerously increasing serum drug concentrations and any continuous local anesthetic infusions must be immediately discontinued and the child observed closely for more serious problems necessitating emergency supportive measures.

Allergic reactions to local anesthetic drugs are rare with the use of amide local anesthetic drugs such as lidocaine or bupivicaine. Although also rare, allergic reactions to ester-type local anesthetics such as procaine or tetracaine are more likely.

Epidural Analgesics

Epidural administration of opioids, local anesthetics, or both frequently provides excellent analgesia for postoperative patients while producing minimal side effects. The epidural space lies just outside the dura mater from the spinal cord. Administering drugs in the immediate vicinity of the receptors and spinal tracts serving pain perception can decrease the total amount of opioid necessary to provide analgesia and produce less sedation. It may also allow for improved postoperative pulmonary function and earlier ambulation. Placed for anesthesia at the time of surgery, epidural catheters can easily be used postoperatively to provide optimal pain relief. Alternatively, the anesthesiology service can assist with the placement

Table 179-6 Local Anesthetic Dosing Recommendations

Drug	Maximum Dose
Amide type	
Lidocaine (0.5%-2%)	5 mg/kg
With epinephrine	7 mg/kg
Bupivacaine (0.25%-0.5%)	2-3 mg/kg
With epinephrine	0.5 mg/kg/hr
Mepivacaine (1%-2%)	5 mg/kg
With epinephrine	7 mg/kg
Ester type	
Procaine (2%-3%)	7 mg/kg
With epinephrine	8.5 mg/kg

of epidural catheters (or other regional nerve blocks) in the PICU. Contraindications to the placement of such catheters include (1) parental refusal, (2) infection at the puncture site, (3) a bleeding disorder or full anticoagulation, and (4) uncorrected hypovolemia or hemodynamic instability.

Local anesthetics administered epidurally block nerve impulse transmission at the level of the spinal cord and spinal nerve roots. They thus produce somatic nerve blockade but can also block motor and sympathetic nerves as well. This can lead to venous pooling and a subsequent decrease in cardiac preload and is associated with hypotension in adults. However, hypotension is rarely seen in pediatric patients younger than 10 years of age. The accompanying sympathetic blockade may in fact be a desirable effect if vasodilation and enhanced blood flow to a peripheral vascular lesion or anastomosis are needed.

Epidural opioids provide analgesia by binding to receptors in the substantia gelatinosa of the dorsal horn of the spinal cord and modulate somatic nerve transmission at this level. Side effects of epidurally administered opioids include those seen with IV administration. Thus pruritus (especially involving the face), nausea, emesis, constipation, and urinary retention can all occur, although they are usually responsive to symptomatic treatments or small IV doses of naloxone (1 to 2 μg/kg) or a partial agonist such as nalbuphine (25 μg/kg).

The major risk of epidural opioids is respiratory depression, which fortunately is rare, but most commonly occurs when other opioids or sedatives are concurrently administered. It is therefore important to remember that respiratory drive can be depressed for up to 18 hours after a single dose of epidural morphine. Frequent nursing assessments of a patient's respiratory rate and pattern, degree of arousability, and sensory levels if local anesthetics are also being administered epidurally are the primary and most effective means to avoid such a catastrophe.

State nursing boards have established guidelines for the administration of medications via epidural (or intrathecal) catheters for the purposes of pain management. Nurses administering such medications must be knowledgeable about the physiology of epidural analgesia, the pharmacologic effects of the drugs being administered, appropriate monitoring and care of the patient, and emergency procedures. In addition, they must participate in educational activities to acquire and maintain this knowledge.

Proper care of an epidural catheter includes securing it with a transparent occlusive dressing at the skin site and ensuring that the catheter is clearly labeled "epidural catheter." Catheters used for intermittent injections must have a Luer-lok cap attached, whereas catheters for continuous epidural infusions must use tubing without side injection ports and with an in-line bacterial filter. Only preservative-free medications and solutions are injected into the epidural space. If the epidural catheter and injection hub become disconnected, the catheter is cleansed with an iodine solution, the tip cut off with sterile scissors, and the catheter reinserted and tightened into the hub.

It is desirable for patients with epidural catheters in place to be monitored continuously with pulse oximetry and sometimes with cardiorespiratory monitors as well. The single most important monitor of the patient's safety and comfort, however, is the frequent assessment of the child's alertness, arousability, and respiratory rate and pattern. Excessive somnolence or bradypnea mandates immediate discontinuation of any epidural opioid infusion and notification of the anesthesiology or PICU service caring for the patient. In addition, jitteriness, muscle twitching, or ascending levels of sensory or motor blockade may indicate excessive dosing of epidural local anesthetics. Any such continuous infusions must also be immediately discontinued pending evaluation of the patient by the appropriate physician. As with PCA pumps, preprinted epidural order sheets are useful to standardize treatment regimens and provide protocols for treatment of adverse reactions and side effects (Table 179-7).

Other Agents
Etomidate

Etomidate is a unique imidazole hypnotic agent that provides excellent hemodynamic stability, minimal respiratory depression, cerebral protection, and rapid recovery. Since it demonstrates little drug accumulation or prolonged effect, etomidate can be administered as a bolus dose to induce general anesthesia or as a continuous infusion to provide sedation. It is useful to provide brief periods of profound sedation so that invasive procedures can be performed. However, if significant pain is anticipated, additional analgesia is necessary. Etomidate is hepatically metabolized to inactive metabolites that are excreted through the kidney.

Table 179-7   Epidural Analgesia

	Dosing	Maximum Dose	Duration
Intermittent			
Morphine	0.03-0.05 mg/kg/dose	5 mg	8-24 hr
Fentanyl	1-2 μg/kg/dose	100 μg	2-4 hr
Hydromorphone	3-10 μg/kg/dose	0.25-1.0 mg	4-8 hr
Continuous infusion			
Bupivacaine, 0.125% with 2 μg/ml fentanyl	0.2-0.4 ml/kg/hr	0.5 mg/kg/hr bupivacaine maximum	
Bupivacaine, 0.125% with 20 μg/ml morphine	0.2-0.4 ml/kg/hr	0.5 mg/kg/hr bupivacaine maximum	
Bupivacaine 0.125% with 10 μg/ml hydromorphone	0.1-0.3 ml/kg/hr	0.5 mg/kg/hr bupivacaine maximum	

Standing nursing orders

No other opioids or sedatives except in consultation with anesthesiology service
Nursing
   Respiratory rates and sedation assessment q1-2h until stable
   Vital signs and check level of blockade q2-4h until stable
   Ambulate with assistance only
   IV access until 12 hr after last epidural medication
Monitors: Pulse oximetry and/or cardiac/apnea monitor as indicated
PRN medications
   Bradypnea/inability to arouse
     Naloxone, 0.002 mg/kg, and notify anesthesiology on call
   Nausea/vomiting/pruritus
     Naloxone, 0.001-0.002 mg/kg IV
            or
    Nalbuphine, 0.025 mg/kg IV
            or
    Promethazine, 0.25 mg/kg IV over 20 min q6h
   Pruritus
     Naloxone, 0.001-0.002 mg/kg IV
            or
    Nalbuphine, 0.025 mg/kg IV
            or
    Diphenhydramine, 0.5-1 mg/kg PO or IV over 20 min q6h
   Urinary retention
     Input and output catheter once if no output for 8 hr
     If persists, call M.D. on call
Oxygen/bag/mask/naloxone at bedside

Call _____ M.D. on call for problems/questions.

Whether given as a bolus dose or as a continuous infusion, etomidate produces virtually no changes in heart rate, mean systemic arterial blood pressure, cardiac output, or pulmonary vascular resistance. Etomidate has only minimal effects on ventilation, although the patient may experience brief periods of apnea after induction doses, especially when combined with other analgesics or sedatives. Cerebral metabolism and blood flow are reduced with etomidate, thus maintaining or lowering ICP. It has no intrinsic analgesic effects. An IV injection of etomidate can be painful, although this can be minimized by pretreatment with IV lidocaine. Its use can be associated with myoclonic movements, hiccups, nausea and vomiting, and thrombophlebitis.

Unfortunately, etomidate produces dose-dependent reversible inhibition of corticosteroid and mineralocorticoid synthesis. This has not been shown to be clinically significant when given as a single dose or as a short-term (i.e., hours) continuous infusion. However, because of increases in morbidity associated with prolonged infusions, etomidate is indicated only for use during brief procedures.

The dosing recommendations for etomidate are listed in Table 179-2.

Propofol

Propofol is a novel nonbarbiturate hypnotic agent characterized by a rapid onset of action followed by redistribution out of the CNS to other body compartments, resulting in a short duration of action. It has no active metabolites, demonstrates little accumulation, and lends itself well to administration via continuous infusion. Its pharmacokinetics provides rapid control of the depth of sedation produced. It is administered in a lipid emulsion and is associated with significant pain on injection, especially if injected into small veins such as those on the dorsum of a child's hand.

Propofol depresses myocardial function and decreases systemic vascular resistance, typically resulting in modest hypotension. It also increases vagal tone and can cause bradycardia. Its use in hemodynamically unstable patients is therefore contraindicated. In larger doses it is more likely than thiopental to cause apnea but, for sedative infusions, respiratory drive is well maintained. Muscle twitching and choreoathetoid movements have been reported after prolonged infusions of high doses.

Propofol is useful for short-term sedation in the PICU, as when preparing for rapid liberation (within hours) from mechanical ventilation or when prompt reawakening is desirable. Tachyphylaxis develops rapidly, however. Longer term administration has been associated with reports of pronounced abstinence syndromes and unexplained metabolic acidoses in young children that make it unsuitable for prolonged use. Its lipid emulsion also serves as an excellent growth medium for bacteria and therefore strict adherance to aseptic technique must be observed when using it for continuous infusions. Frequent changes of the infusion and tubing are recommended by the manufacturer to avoid bacterial growth, which contributes to increased costs.

The dosing recommendations for propofol are listed in Table 179-2.

Butyrophenones

There is limited reported experience with butyrophenones in the PICU setting, although haloperidol has been used more extensively in adult ICUs. In general droperidol and haloperidol produce sedation via a central dissociative effect and antagonism of dopaminergic receptors. Extrapyramidal side effects and dysphoric reactions may occur, although these side effects are less common with concomitant administration of opioids or other sedatives. Peripheral α-blockade carries the potential for hypotension, especially in hypovolemic patients. Clearance is prolonged in neonates and patients with hepatic dysfunction. Droperidol is also a potent antiemetic via its dopaminergic blockade.

In the child who needs additional sedation despite significant doses of benzodiazepines and opioids, 25 μg/kg droperidol given intravenously in incremental doses up to 100 μg/kg can produce tranquility with minimal depression of respiratory or hemodynamic variables (see Table 179-2).

EMLA

EMLA cream is a eutectic mixture of two local anesthetics, 2.5% lidocaine and 2.5% prilocaine, that allows transdermal absorption of the drugs and produces topical anesthesia at the site of application. It has been shown to significantly decrease the pain associated with needle punctures from a variety of diagnostic and therapeutic procedures, although it does not produce anesthesia of deeper structures. A small amount of cream (typically 2.5 g) is applied on the skin and covered with an occlusive dressing for 60 minutes before significant anesthetic effect is produced. Although transient local skin pallor is common, it is safe for most patients. It is contraindicated in infants less than 1 month of age because of a report of methemeglobinemia associated with its use in this age group.

ADDITIONAL READING

Adams P, Gelman S, Reves JG, Greenblatt DJ, Alvis JM, Bradley M. Midazolam pharmacodynamics and pharmacokinetics during acute hypovolemia. Anesthesiology 63:140-146, 1985.

Alexander CM, Gross JB. Sedative doses of midazolam depress hypoxic ventilatory responses in humans. Anesth Analg 67:377-382, 1988.

• American Academy of Pediatrics, Committee on Drugs. Guidelines for monitoring and management of pediatric patients during and after sedation for diagnostic and therapeutic procedures. Pediatrics 89:1110-1115, 1992.

Anand KJ, Carr DB. The neuroanatomy, neurophysiology, and neurochemistry of pain, stress, and analgesia in newborns and children. Pediatr Clin North Am 36:795-822, 1989.

Anand KJ, Hickey PR. Halothane-morphine compared with high-dose sufentanil for anesthesia and postoperative analgesia in neonatal cardiac surgery. N Engl J Med 326:1-9, 1992.

• Anand KJ, Hickey PR. Pain and its effects in the human neonate and fetus. N Engl J Med 317:1321-1329, 1987.

Anand KJS, Sippell WG, Aynsley-Green A. A randomised trial of fentanyl anaesthesia in preterm neonates undergoing surgery: Effects on the stress response. Lancet 1:243-248, 1987.

Arnold JH, Truog RD, Scavone JM, Fenton T. Changes in the pharmacokinetics of fentanyl in neonates during continuous infusion. J Pediatr 119:639-644, 1991.

Attia J, Ecoffey C, Sandouk P, Gross JB, Samii K. Epidural morphine in children: Pharmacokinetics and CO_2 sensitivity. Anesthesiology 65:590-594, 1986.

Au J, Walker WS, Scott DHT. Withdrawal syndrome after propofol infusion. Anaesthesia 45:741-742, 1990.

• Berde CB. Pediatric postoperative pain management. Pediatr Clin North Am 36:921-940, 1989.

Berde CB, Lehn BM, Yee JD, Sethna NF, Russo D. Patient-controlled analgesia in children and adolescents: A randomized prospective comparison with intramuscular administration of morphine for postoperative analgesia. J Pediatr 118:460-466, 1991.

Bergman I, Steeves M, Burckart G, Thompson A. Reversible neurologic abnormalities associated with prolonged intravenous midazolam and fentanyl administration. J Pediatr 119:644-649, 1991.

Beyer JE, Wells N. The assessment of pain in children. Pediatr Clin North Am 36:837-854, 1989.

Beyer JE, Degood DE, Ashley LC, Russell GA. Patterns of postoperative analgesic use with adults and children following cardiac surgery. Pain 17:71-81, 1983.

Bhat R, Chari G, Gulati A, Aldana O, Velamati R, Bhargava H. Pharmacokinetics of a single dose of morphine in preterm infants during the first week of life. J Pediatr 117:477-481, 1990.

Booker PD, Beechey A, Lloyd-Thomas AR. Sedation of children requiring artificial ventilation using an infusion of midazolam. Br J Anaesth 58:1104-1108, 1986.

Burokas L. Factors affecting nurses' decisions to medicate pediatric patients after surgery. Heart Lung 14:373-379, 1985.

Chamberlain JH, Seed RGFL, Chung DC. Effect of thiopental on myocardial function. Br J Anaesth 49:865-870, 1977.

• Dalens B. Regional anesthesia in children. Anesth Analg 68:654-672, 1989.

Desparmet J, Meistelman C, Barre J, Saint-Maurice C. Continuous epidural infusion of bupivicaine for postoperative pain relief in children. Anesthesiology 67:108-110, 1987.

Doyle E, Robinson D, Morton NS. Comparison of patient-controlled analgesia with and without a background infusion after lower abdominal surgery in children. Br J Anaesth 71:670-673, 1993.

Eland JM, Banner W. Assessment and management of pain in children. In Hazinski MF, ed. Nursing Care of the Critically Ill Child. St. Louis: Mosby, 1992.

Engberg G, Danielson K, Henneberg S, Nilsson A. Plasma concentrations of prilocaine and lidocaine and methemoglobin formation in infants after epicutaneous application of a 5% lidocaine-prilocaine (EMLA). Acta Anaesthesiol Scand 31:624-628, 1987.

Gaukroger PB, Tomkins DP, Van Der Walt JH. Patient-controlled analgesia in children. Anaesth Intensive Care 17:264-268, 1989.

Greely WJ, de Bruijn NP. Changes in sufentanil pharmacokinetics within the neonatal period. Anesth Analg 67:86-90, 1988.

Green SM, Nakamura R, Johnson NE. Ketamine sedation for pediatric procedures: Part I. A prospective series. Ann Emerg Med 19:1024-1032, 1990.

Gross JB, Smith L, Smith TC. Time course of ventilatory response to carbon dioxide after intravenous diazepam. Anesthesiology 57:18-21, 1982.

Hamill RJ, Rowlingson JC. Handbook of Critical Care Pain Management. New York: McGraw-Hill, 1994.

Hamza J, Ecoffey E, Gross JB. Ventilatory response to CO_2 following intravenous ketamine in children. Anesthesiology 70:422-425, 1989.

Hannallah RS, Broadman LL, Belman AB, Abramowitz MD, Epwtein BS. Comparison of ilioinguinal/iliohypogastric nerve blocks for control of postorchiopexy pain in pediatric ambulatory surgery. Anesthesiology 66:832-834, 1987.

Hickey PR, Hansen DD, Cramolini GM, Vincent RN, Lang P. Pulmonary and systemic hemodynamic responses to ketamine in infants with normal and elevated pulmonary vascular resistance. Anesthesiology 62:287-293, 1985.

Hickey PR, Hansen DD, Wessel DL, Lang P, Jonas RA, Elixson EM. Blunting of stress responses in the pulmonary circulation of infants by fentanyl. Anesth Analg 64:1137-1142, 1985.

Hopkins CS, Buckley DJ, Bush GH. Pain-free injection in infants. Use of a lignocaine-prilocaine cream to prevent pain at intravenous induction of general anaesthesia in 1-5 year-old children. Anaesthesia 43:198-201, 1988.

Jaffe JH, Martin WR. Opioid analgesics and antagonists. In Gillman AG, Goodman LS, Rall TW, Murad F, eds. The Pharmacologic Basis of Therapeutics. New York: Macmillan, 1985, pp 495-534.

Katz R, Kelly HW, Hsi A. Prospective study on the occurrence of withdrawal in critically ill children who receive fentanyl by continuous infusion. Crit Care Med 22:763-767, 1994.

· Koehntop DE, Rodman JH, Brundage DM, Hegland MG, Buckley JJ. Pharmacokinetics of fentanyl in neonates. Anesth Analg 65:227-232, 1986.

Koren G, Butt W, Chinyanga H, Soldin S, Tan YK, Pape K. Postoperative morphine infusion in newborn infants: Assessment of disposition characteristics and safety. J Pediatr 107:963-967, 1985.

Krane EJ. Delayed respiratory depression in a child after caudal epidural morphine. Anesth Analg 67:79-82, 1988.

Krane EJ, Tyler DC, Jaconson LE. The dose response of caudal morphine in children. Anesthesiology 71:48-52, 1989.

Kupferburg HJ, Way EL. Pharmacologic basis for the increased sensitivity of the newborn rat to morphine. J Pharmacol Exp Ther 141:105-112, 1963.

Lynn AM, Opheim KE, Tyler DC. Morphine infusion after pediatric cardiac surgery. Crit Care Med 12:863-866, 1984.

Lynn AM, Slattery JT. Morphine pharmacokinetics in early infancy. Anesthesiology 66:136-139, 1987.

Marshall RE. Neonatal pain associated with caregiving procedures. Pediatr Clin North Am 36:885-903, 1989.

Maxwell LG, Yaster M, Wetzel RC, Niebyl JR. Penile nerve block for newborn circumcision. Obstet Gynecol 70:415-419, 1987.

McGrath PJ, Urreh AM. Pain in Children and Adolescents. New York: Elsevier, 1987.

McGrath PJ, Craig KD. Developmental and psychological factors in children's pain. Pediatr Clin North Am 36:823-836, 1989.

McGrath PJ, Johnson G, Goodman JT, Schillinger J, Dunn J, Chapman J. The Children's Hospital of Eastern Ontario Pain Scale (CHEOPS): A behavioral scale for rating postoperative pain in children. In Fields HL, Dubner R, Cervero F, eds. Advances in Pain Research and Therapy, vol 9. New York: Raven Press, 1985, pp 395-402.

Morray JP, Lynn AM, Stamm SJ, Herndon PS, Kawabori I, Stevenson JG. Hemodynamic effects of ketamine in children with congenital heart disease. Anesth Analg 63:895-899, 1984.

Mortenson ME, Rennebohm RM. Clinical pharmacology and use of nonsteroidal anti-inflammatory drugs. Pediatr Clin North Am 36:1113-1139, 1989.

Nabor L, Jones G, Halm M. Epidural analgesia for effective pain control. Crit Care Nurse 14:69-85, 1994.

Olkkola KT, Maunuksela EL. The pharmacokinetics of postoperative intravenous ketorolac tromethamine in children. Br J Clin Pharmacol 31:182-184, 1991.

Owens ME, Todt EH. Pain in infancy: Neonatal reaction to heel lance. Pain 20:77-86, 1984.

Parke TJ, Stevens JE, Rice ASC, Greenaway CL, Bray RJ, Smith PJ, Waldmann CS, Verghese C. Metabolic acidosis and fatal myocardial failure after propofol infusion in children: Five case reports. Br Med J 305:613-616, 1992.

Pasternak GW, Zhang AZ, Tecott L. Developmental differences between high and low affinity opiate binding sites: Their relationship to analgesia and respiratory depression. Life Sci 27:1185-1190, 1980.

Rawlings DJ, Miller PA, Engel RR. The effect of circumcision on transcutaneous pO_2 in term infants. Am J Dis Child 134:676-678, 1980.

Reves JG, Fragen RJ, Vinik R, Greenblatt DJ. Midazolam: Pharmacology and uses. Anesthesiology 62:310-324, 1985.

Rodgers BM, Webb CJ, Stergios D, Newman BM. Patient-controlled analgesia in pediatric surgery. J Pediatr Surg 23:259-262, 1988.

Schecter NL. The undertreatment of pain in children: An overview. Pediatr Clin North Am 36:781-794, 1989.

Schecter NL, Allen DA. Physicians' attitudes toward pain in children. J Dev Behav Pediatr 7:350-354, 1986.

Schecter NL, Allen DA, Hanson K. Status of pediatric pain control: A comparison of hospital analgesic usage in children and adults. Pediatrics 77:11-15, 1986.

· Schechter NL, Berde CB, Yaster M. Pain in Infants, Children, and Adolescents. Baltimore: William & Wilkins, 1993.

Silvasi DL, Rosen DA, Rosen KR. Continuous intravenous midazolam infusion for sedation in the pediatric intensive care unit. Anesth Analg 67:286-288, 1988.

Tobias JD, Deshpande JK, Pietsch JB. Pentobarbital sedation in the pediatric intensive care unit patient. South Med J 88:290-294, 1995.

· Tobias JD, Rasmussen GE. Pain management and sedation in the pediatric intensive care unit. Pediatr Clin North Am 41:1269-1292, 1994.

Tobias JD, Martin LD, Wetzel RC. Ketamine by continuous infusion for sedation in the pediatric intensive care unit. Crit Care Med 18:819-821, 1990.

Tobias JD, Schleien CL, Haun SE. Methadone as treatment for iatrogenic narcotic dependency in pediatric intensive care unit patients. Crit Care Med 18:1292-1293, 1990.

Varni JW, Thompson KL, Hanson V. The Varni-Thompson pediatric pain questionnaire. I. Pain 28:27-38, 1987.

Wagner RL, White PF, Kan PB, Rosenthal MH, Feldman D. Inhibition of adrenal steroidogenesis by the anesthetic etomidate. N Engl J Med 310:1415-1421, 1984.

Watcha MF, Jones MB, Lagueruela R, Schweiger C, White PF. Comparison of ketorolac and morphine as adjuvants during pediatric surgery. Anesthesiology 76:368-377, 1992.

Way WL, Costley EC, Way EL. Respiratory sensitivity of the newborn infant to meperidine and morphine. Clin Pharmacol Ther 6:454-461, 1965.

Welborn LG, Rice LJ, Hannallah RS, Broadman LM, Ruttimann UE, Fink R. Postoperative apnea in former preterm infants: Prospective comparison of spinal and general anesthesia. Anesthesiology 72:838-842, 1990.

Whaley LF, Wong DL. Care of Infants and Children. St. Louis: Mosby, 1991.

White PF, Way WL, Trevor AJ. Ketamine—Its pharmacology and therapeutic uses. Anesthesiology 56:119-136, 1982.

Williamson PS, Williamson ML. Physiologic stress reduction by a local anesthetic during newborn circumcision. Pediatrics 71:36-40, 1983.

Willis WD. The origin and destination of pathways involved in pain transmission. In Wall PD, Melzack R, eds. Management of Pain. New York: Churchill Livingstone, 1985, pp 88-99.

Yaster M, Nichols DG, Deshpande JK, Wetzl RC. Midazolam-fentanyl intravenous sedation in children: Case report of respiratory arrest. Pediatrics 86:463-467, 1990.

180 Neuromuscular Blocking Agents

Stan L. Davis

BACKGROUND AND INDICATIONS

Paralytic agents, or neuromuscular blocking agents, are among the most commonly administered drugs in the PICU. It is appropriate that the discussion of these agents follows the chapter on sedation since only in the most unstable patient is the use of neuromuscular blockade without sedation indicated. The most common indications for neuromuscular blockade in the PICU are to facilitate tracheal intubation and mechanical ventilation or to prevent increases in oxygen consumption, intrathoracic pressure, or intracranial pressure related to the patient "fighting" the ventilator.

Although a detailed review of the physiology of the neuromuscular junction cannot be presented here, an understanding of the basic physiology is necessary before discussing the pharmacodynamics of the neuromuscular blocking agents. The neuromuscular junction consists of the prejunctional motor nerve ending, synaptic cleft, and postjunctional membrane, which contains nicotinic cholinergic receptors (Fig. 180-1). The neurotransmitter acetylcholine is synthesized in the motor nerve terminal and stored in vesicles, which release acetylcholine into the synaptic cleft on the arrival of a nerve impulse. The acetylcholine molecules diffuse across the synaptic cleft and bind to the acetylcholine receptors, initiating a conformational change in the receptor that "opens" a potential channel formed by the receptor subunits (Fig. 180-2). The opening of this channel allows the influx of sodium and calcium ions and the efflux of potassium ions, thereby facilitating the depolarization of the motor endplate and propagation of an action potential that spreads across the skeletal muscle fibers, leading to contraction. The enzyme acetylcholinesterase is responsible for rapid hydrolysis of acetylcholine, which terminates that depolarization of the motor endplate.

All currently available neuromuscular blocking agents exert their activity at the postsynaptic acetylcholine receptor. Skeletal muscle relaxation is achieved by altering the ability of the neurotransmitter acetylcholine to initiate depolarization of the motor endplate. Neuromuscular blocking agents are classified as depolarizing or nondepolarizing agents according to their effect on the motor endplate.

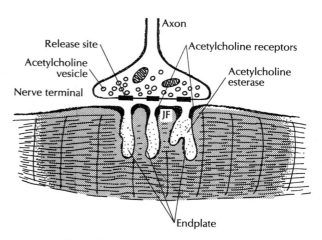

Fig. 180-1 Neuromuscular junction.

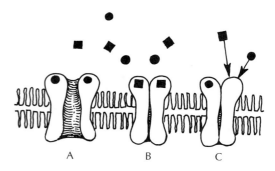

Fig. 180-2 Schematic representation of acetylcholine receptors with the ion channel in open configuration when occupied by acetylcholine molecules (circles) *(A)* and closed when occupied by a neuromuscular blocking agent (squares) in a depolarizing *(B)* or competitive *(C)* fashion.

Depolarizing Neuromuscular Blocking Agents
Succinylcholine

Succinylcholine remains the only depolarizing neuromuscular blocking agent approved for use in the United States. Succinylcholine is formed by the junction of two acetylcholine molecules and acts by binding to the acetylcholine receptor, initiating depolarization of the motor endplates in a random fashion. Neuromuscular blockade develops because the hydrolysis of succinylcholine by plasma cholinesterase (pseudocholinesterase) is much slower than the hydrolysis of acetylcholine; therefore it results in prolonged depolarization of the motor endplate. The major advantage of succinylcholine is its rapid onset of neuromuscular blockade, usually providing intubating conditions within 60 seconds. In addition, succinylcholine is the only neuromuscular blocking agent that may be given intramuscularly for airway emergencies involving patients without venous access.

Nondepolarizing Neuromuscular Blocking Agents

In contrast to succinylcholine, the nondepolarizing neuromuscular blocking agents are large, bulky molecules that bind to one or more of the acetylcholine receptor subunits without initiating a conformational change leading to depolarization of the motor endplate. Instead, these agents block neuromuscular transmission in a competitive fashion by preventing acetylcholine from binding to an occupied receptor (see Fig. 180-2). All of these drugs contain one or more quaternary ammonium groups responsible for binding the acetylcholine receptor and either a steroidal or benzylisoquinolium nucleus, which determines the route of elimination as well as possible cardiovascular side effects. Because they are competitive antagonists, muscle relaxation caused by nondepolarizing agents may be reversed by increasing the amount of acetylcholine available at the receptor site.

TECHNIQUE
Selection of Neuromuscular Blocking Agents

The selection of a neuromuscular blocking agent must be based on the needs of the patient. The four variables that must be considered are time of onset, duration of action, side effects, and route of elimination for the agents chosen (Table 180-1). This choice is not always straightforward, especially when complicated by the need for tracheal intubation without bag and mask ventilation, as in the case of the patient with a full stomach. Succinylcholine remains the gold standard for a rapid-sequence intubation because of the onset of 90% neuromuscular blockade within 60 seconds. Despite a more rapid onset in children as compared to adults, the nondepolarizing relaxants generally take 3 to 4 minutes to reach intubating conditions. If succinylcholine is contraindicated, rocuronium, one of the newer nondepolarizing agents, may be an acceptable alternative, achieving intubating conditions within 45 to 75 seconds at a $4 \times ED_{95}$ dose (which achieves a response in 95% of the population) of 1.2 mg/kg. A useful method for organizing the neuromuscular blocking agents available for use in the PICU is to group the agents by their duration of action, which ranges from ultra short acting to long acting.

Long Duration (60 minutes or greater)
Pancuronium

Pancuronium is a long-acting steroidal, nondepolarizing relaxant with a duration of action of 50 to 60 minutes. Pancuronium causes increases in heart rate, mean systemic arterial blood pressure, and cardiac output secondary to its vagolytic effect and relies on the kidney for 80% of its elimination.

Doxicurium

Doxicurium is a hemodynamicaly stable long-acting agent with a duration of 100 minutes. The primary route of elimination is via the kidneys.

Pipecuronium

Pipecuronium is a vecuronium derivative that offers the same cardiovascular stability but relies more on the renal route of elimination.

Intermediate Duration (25 to 40 minutes)
Vecuronium

Vecuronium, an analog of pancuronium, has a duration of action of 25 to 35 minutes. In addition to its shorter half-life, a major advantage of vecuronium is its lack of vagolytic effects or histamine release, giving this drug very stable cardiovascular characteristics. Elimination of vecuronium is principally hepatic, and renal failure usually necessitates no change in dosage. An unexplained observation is that the

Table 180-1 Neuromuscular Blocking Agents

Agent	Intubation Dose	Infusion Rate	Duration of Action (min)	Elimination	Side Effects
Nondepolarizing					
Long duration					
Pancuronium	0.1 mg/kg	N/A	50-60	Renal	Vagolytic (increased HR and BP)
Pipecuronium	85 μg/kg	N/A	60-70	Renal	N/A
Doxacurium	50 μg/kg	N/A	80	Renal	N/A
Intermediate duration					
Vecuronium	0.1 mg/kg	0.06-0.1 mg/kg/hr	25-40	Hepatic	N/A
Atracurium	0.5 mg/kg	0.3-0.6 mg/kg/hr	25-35	Hofmann elimination/esterase	Histamine release
Rocuronium	0.8 mg/kg	0.5-0.7 mg/kg/hr	30-40	Hepatic	Increased HR with high dose
Cisatracurium	0.1-0.15 mg/kg	2-3 μg/kg/min	25-40	Hofmann elimination	N/A
Short Duration					
Mivacurium	0.15-0.2 mg/kg	12-20 μg/kg/min	15-20	Plasma cholinesterase	Histamine release
Depolarizing					
Ultra short duration					
Succinylcholine	1.5-2.0 mg/kg	N/A	4-6	Plasma cholinesterase	Bradycardia, hyperkalemia, MH trigger

HR = heart rate; BP = blood pressure; MH = malignant hyperpyrexia.

clearance of vecuronium appears to increase slightly in patients with liver disease, although no mechanism has been described.

Atracurium

Atracurium is a relaxant with a benzylisoquinolium ester structure responsible for its spontaneous degradation by Hofmann elimination and ester hydrolysis. Hofmann elimination is a purely chemical process that results in the molecular fragmentation of atracurium to form laudanosine and a monoquaternary acrylate. This results in a duration of action of 20 to 30 minutes, which is independent of hepatic or renal function. Histamine release can be a problem, especially with rapid administration or doses exceeding 2 × ED$_{95}$. An intubation dose of 0.5 mg/kg atracurium induces very minimal histamine release, which becomes significant only with doses >0.6 mg/kg given rapidly. Laudanosine is a CNS stimulant

that may become significant with prolonged use of atracurium in the PICU setting. At present animal studies have demonstrated seizure thresholds for laudanosine but there are no human correlates.

Cisatracurium

Cisatracurium, a steroid isomer of atracurium, is the newest nondepolarizing agent available for clinical use. It is unique in that elimination is totally via the Hoffmann elimination pathway, which requires no hepatic or renal excretion and is not dependent on plasma cholinesterase activity. Unlike atracurium, there is no significant histamine release or hemodynamic changes seen with doses up to 8 × ED$_{95}$.

Rocuronium

Rocuronium is a vecuronium derivative whose chief distinguishing feature is its rapid onset of neuromuscular blockade. With a dose of $4 \times ED_{95}$, rocuronium can provide optimal intubating conditions in 45 to 75 seconds. Elimination is hepatic, and vagolytic effects are seen particularly with doses exceeding 1.5 mg/kg.

Short Duration (15 to 20 minutes)
Mivicurium

Mivicurium is the only true short-acting nondepolarizing agent available. It is metabolized by plasma cholinesterase and therefore can produce prolonged neuromuscular blockade in patients with atypical pseudocholinesterase activity. Like atracurium, histamine release is seen with rapid administration and doses exceeding 0.2 mg/kg.

Ultra Short Duration (4 to 6 minutes)
Succinylcholine

Despite the adverse effects and contraindications to the administration of succinylcholine, it remains a clinically useful agent due to its rapid onset and ultra short duration of action. The primary adverse effects of succinylcholine are hyperkalemia and cardiac arrhythmias, including sinus bradycardia, nodal rhythms, and even asystole. Succinylcholine is absolutely contraindicated in patients with myotonia, muscular dystrophy, burns, and a history of malignant hyperthermia and must be used with the utmost caution in patients with upper motor neuron lesions, denervation injuries, and massive trauma, especially crush injuries. Succinylcholine also causes transient increases in intracranial and intraocular pressures.

Continuous Infusions

Because of the noncumulative pharmacokinetics of several of the nondepolarizing neuromuscular blocking agents, they are uniquely suited to administration by continuous infusion in the PICU. After giving the usual loading dose of the nondepolarizing agent, a continuous infusion can be titrated to provide a consistent level of neuromuscular blockade. This technique provides greater stability and allows for a rapid and predictable recovery, assuming that the depth of neuromuscular blockade has been adequately monitored (see below).

Monitoring Neuromuscular Blockade

The ability to monitor the degree of neuromuscular blockade is extremely useful in titrating continuous infusions of neuromuscular blocking agents and in assessing the recovery of neuromuscular function

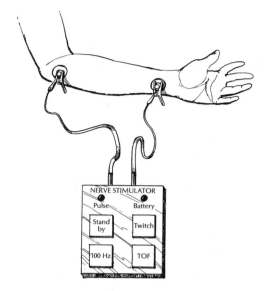

Fig. 180-3   Peripheral nerve stimulator.

after neuromuscular blockade. Two techniques currently available are mechanomyography and evoked electromyography. A simplified version of mechanomyography is discussed here since PICU application is easier and less expensive. A peripheral nerve stimulator is used to apply a transcutaneous electrical stimulus along the course of a peripheral nerve (Fig. 180-3). Attaching the nerve stimulator to ECG pads placed at the wrist over the ulnar nerve yields reliable results as long as the twitch response of the thumb alone is monitored. Finger twitches can sometimes represent artifact caused by direct muscle stimulation rather than stimulation of the ulnar nerve.

The most useful response to monitor in a nondepolarizing block is the train-of-four response. Train of four refers to four stimuli of equal intensity generated at a frequency of two per second. The characteristic pattern for the depression of train-of-four twitch height for depolarizing and nondepolarizing relaxants is shown in Fig. 180-4. Because of the wide margin of safety in neuromuscular transmission, the fourth twitch is not abolished until 95% blockade is achieved. In the PICU the presence of one to two twitches of the train of four provides clinically useful neuromuscular blockade (75% to 90%) and avoids the overdose of relaxant, which can occur when enough drug is used to eliminate all twitch activity. Tetanic stimulation, a supramaximal stimulation

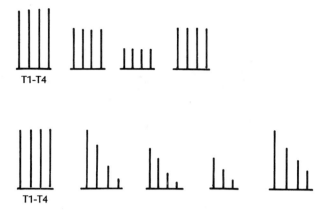

Fig. 180-4 Train-of-four response in depolarizing block (above) and nondepolarizing block (below). The first figure (left) in each row depicts twitch response in the unblocked state. The middle figures represent the progression of blockade. The final figures (right) in each row depict the beginning of recovery. The height of the individual twitch corresponds visually to intensity of muscular contractions.

at a frequency of 50 to 100 Hz applied for 5 seconds, is also useful in the evaluation of an intense neuromuscular block in the absence of a train-of-four response. The posttetanic twitch count correlates with the return of the train-of-four response.

Reversal of Neuromuscular Blockade

The pharmacologic reversal of neuromuscular blockade is achieved by increasing the concentration of acetylcholine at the neuromuscular junction, thus favoring the binding of acetylcholine rather than neuromuscular blocker to the acetylcholine receptors. This is accomplished by the administration of an acetylcholinesterase inhibitor such as neostigmine or edrophonium. The neuromuscular blockade can be too intense for pharmacologic antagonism; therefore, if recovery is not complete after an attempt at reversal, more time must be allowed rather than more antagonist given. It is also necessary to administer an anticholinergic agent before the acetylcholine stimulation of muscarinic receptors. Because of the difference in the time of onset, atropine is usually given with edrophonium and glycopyrolate with neostigmine. The usual doses used for "complete reversal" are neostigmine, 0.07 mg/kg, with glycopyrolate,

0.014 mg/kg, or edrophonium, 1 mg/kg, with atropine, 0.02 mg/kg.

RISKS AND COMPLICATIONS

There are three general areas of concern when giving neuromuscular blocking agents to patients in the PICU. The first is the effect that metabolic abnormalities or concomitant drug administration can have on the action of neuromuscular blocking agents.

Factors affecting the action of neuromuscular blocking agents in the PICU patient

Metabolic states that enhance neuromuscular blockade
    Hypothermia
    Hypokalemia (acute)
    Hypermagnesemia
Drugs that enhance neuromuscular blockade
    Aminoglycosides
    Local anesthetics
    Cardiac antiarrhythmic agents
    Furosemide
    Lithium
    Possibly calcium antagonists
Conditions that decrease neuromuscular blockade
    Hyperkalemia
    Hemiparesis or hemiplegia (affected side shows resistance to nondepolarizing relaxants)
    Burn injuries

The second area of concern is the abnormal response of patients with neuromuscular diseases when given either depolarizing or nondepolarizing neuromuscular blocking agents. The primary concern with the nondepolarizing relaxants is the possibility of increased sensitivity to these agents, resulting in prolonged neuromuscular blockade. Increased sensitivity to nondepolarizing agents occurs in any patient with a disease that affects the prejunctional release of acetylcholine, such as infant botulism, or with a disease that alters receptor morphology, such as myasthenia gravis. A half dose of mivicurium can be useful in these patients until their sensitivity to neuromuscular blockade can be determined. Of greater concern is the abnormal response to the depolarizing relaxant succinylcholine that occurs with a variety of neuromuscular diseases. The common pathologic event in these diseases is the proliferation of extrajunctional acetylcholine receptors, which can be present in large numbers located across the entire muscle membrane and which respond to succinylcholine by maintaining an open ion channel up to four times as long as normal receptors. Disorders that have been associated with hyperkalemic cardiac arrest after succinylcholine administration include:

Upper motor neuron lesions

Hemiparesis

Spinal cord injury

Paraplegia

Massive trauma (especially crush injuries)

Burns

Myotonias

Muscle dystrophies

Guillain-Barré syndrome

In addition, the autonomic dysfunction associated with Guillain-Barré syndrome may lead to an exaggerated response to nondepolarizing agents that decrease peripheral vascular resistance or possess vagolytic properties.

The third concern for PICU patients involves the prolonged administration of neuromuscular blocking agents, particularly without adequate monitoring of neuromuscular blockade. There have been multiple reports of patients with prolonged muscle weakness and even paralysis following the prolonged administration of these drugs. Recovery can be protracted (3 to 12 months) and require lengthy rehabilitation. It appears that both muscle activity and electrical stimulation take part in the regulation of receptor subtype and density and that prolonged paralysis may be associated with neuromuscular blocking agent–induced denervation-like changes at the neuromuscular junction. This effect is highly associated with concomitant administration of steroids and is reported with both the aminosteroids and the benzylisoquinolium drug families of neuromuscular blocking agents.

· · ·

In summary, neuromuscular blocking agents are among the most useful drugs available to the intensivist. By knowing the pharmacodynamic profiles of the multiple agents available, the intensivist can tailor the neuromuscular blocking agent to the needs of the individual patient.

ADDITIONAL READING

· Dodson BA, Kelly BJ, Braswell LM, et al. Changes in acetylcholine receptor number in muscle from critically ill patient receiving muscle relaxants: An investigation of the molecular mechanism of prolonged paralysis. Crit Care Med 23:815-821, 1995.

· Goudsouzian N, Standaert F. The infant and the myoneural junction. Anesth Analg 65:1208-1217, 1986.

Miller RD, ed. Anesthesia, 2nd ed. New York: Churchill Livingstone, 1986.

Miller R, Rupp S, Fisher D, et al. Clinical pharmacology of vecuronium and atracurium. Anesthesiology 61:444-453, 1984.

Segredo V, Caldwell JE, Matthay MA, et al. Persistent paralysis in critically ill patients after long term administration of vecuronium. N Engl J Med 327:524-528, 1992.

Shanks C. Pharmacokinetics of the nondepolarizing relaxants applied to calculation of bolus and infusion dosage regimens. Anesthesiology 64:72-86, 1986.

· Stoelting RK. Pharmacology and Physiology in Anesthetic Practice. Philadelphia: JB Lippincott, 1987.

181 Anticoagulant and Thrombolytic Therapy

Lynn Mahony · Dusit Staworn

BACKGROUND
Coagulation

Blood vessels are lined by endothelial cells, which are nonthrombogenic. Coagulation in vivo is initiated by the transmembrane glycoprotein, or tissue factor. Tissue factor is localized to the blood vessel wall, but when a blood vessel is damaged, blood contacts tissue factor. Coagulation subsequently occurs as a result of a cascade of enzyme-catalyzed reactions (Fig. 181-1). The most important enzyme for thrombus formation is thrombin. Thrombin forms fibrin by removing two small peptides from fibrinogen. The fibrin monomers polymerize to form a fibrin clot. The fibrin is then cross-linked by factor XIII.

Thrombin is generated by two different pathways. In the extrinsic pathway, tissue factor forms a complex with factor VII that converts factor X to its active form. In the presence of activated factor V and activated platelets, activated factor X converts prothrombin to thrombin (activated factor II). In the intrinsic pathway the factor VII–tissue factor complex activates factor IX. In addition, in vitro contact of blood with any negatively charged surface (e.g., glass) activates factor XII (contact phase). Activated factor XII activates factor XI, which in turn activates factor IX.

Age-related changes occur in some of the coagulation proteins necessary for generating thrombin. Plasma concentrations of the vitamin K–dependent factors (II, VII, IX, and X) are about 50% of adult levels in newborn infants and do not reach adult levels until about 6 months of age. In contrast, the concentrations of factors V, VIII, and XIII are not different in newborn infants. The net effect is that the ability of young infants to generate thrombin is about one half that of adults.

Fibrinolysis

The most important enzyme involved in fibrin clot lysis is plasmin. Plasmin degrades fibrin to fibrin degradation products and D-dimers (Fig. 181-2). Activation of plasminogen produces plasmin. Urokinase and tissue plasminogen activator (t-PA) are the principal activators of plasminogen. t-PA diffuses from endothelial cells and converts plasminogen bound to the fibrin clot to plasmin. Plasma concentrations of plasminogen in newborn infants are approximately one half of adult concentrations. Thus plasmin gen-

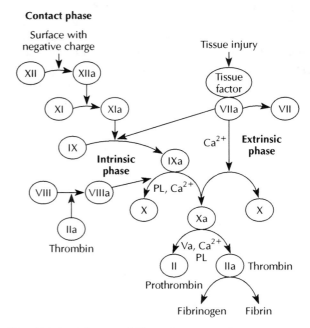

Fig. 181-1 Schema of fibrin formation. (PL = Anionic phospholipid; a = activated coagulation factor.)

eration is relatively impaired in newborn infants as compared with adults.

ANTICOAGULANT THERAPY
Heparin

Heparin, a water-soluble mucopolysaccharide, is a rapidly acting anticoagulant. Heparin is extracted for clinical use from bovine lung or porcine intestinal mucosa and is a mixture of glycosaminoglycan chains of variable lengths (molecular weight 5000 to 30,000 daltons, mean 12,000 daltons).

Heparin acts as an anticoagulant by accelerating the action of a naturally occurring inhibitor of thrombin, antithrombin III (AT-III) (Fig. 181-3). This α_2-globulin is synthesized in the liver and is homologous to the α_1-antitrypsin family of protease inhibitors. AT-III inhibits serine protease coagulation factors (II [thrombin], Xa, and to a lesser extent IXa, XIa, XIIa, and kallikrein) by binding to the serine residue at the active center of the coagulation factor. The reticuloendothelial system clears the AT-III–coagulation factor complex. Binding of AT-III to a coagulation factor is normally a relatively slow process. When heparin binds to AT-III, this reaction and therefore the decay of coagulation factors are greatly accelerated. Heparin also binds to platelets, thereby inhibiting platelet function and contributing to the hemorrhagic effects of heparin. The half-life of the anticoagulant effect of heparin is dose dependent but is about 1½ hours at standard doses.

Indications and clinical effects

Heparin is indicated for the initial treatment of thrombi in large vessels and cardiac chambers in children. Patients with indwelling central venous or arterial catheters are predisposed to vena caval and intracardiac thrombi because blood flow is altered by the catheter, the surface of the catheter is foreign, and the vascular endothelium is damaged by the catheter and infused substances. The thrombus can extend from a central vein to either vena cava and also to the right atrium and right ventricle. Femoral arterial thrombi are associated with vessel puncture for diagnostic procedures such as cardiac catheterization or invasive radiographic procedures and may compromise circulation to the leg. Patients with congenital heart disease (e.g., after a Fontan procedure) who have atrial arrhythmias or severely depressed ventricular function are at risk for intracardiac thrombi because of abnormal blood flow patterns. In theory, heparin treatment will prevent thrombus formation or extension and embolization of existing thrombi, thus minimizing long-term morbidity. Heparin is often administered in conjunction with thrombolytic therapy (see below) to patients with existing thrombi.

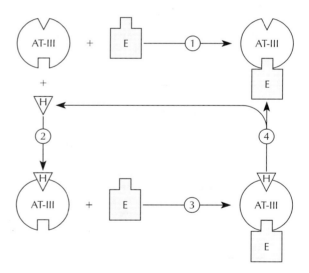

Fig. 181-3 Mechanism of heparin action. The interaction of AT-III, heparin, and serine-active protease. In the absence of heparin the susceptible enzyme is inhibited by a slow time-dependent reaction (step *1*). When heparin interacts with AT-III (step *2*), this reaction takes place instantaneously (step *3*). The AT-III–heparin–enzyme complex may frequently release heparin (step *4*). (H = Heparin; E = serine-active protease.) (From Bitchell TC. Thrombosis and antithrombotic therapy. In Lee GR, Bitchell TC, Foerster J, et al, eds. Wintrobe's Clinical Hematology. Philadelphia: Lea & Febiger, 1993, pp 1515-1551.)

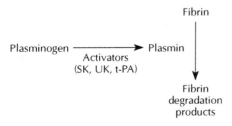

Fig. 181-2 Schema of fibrinolysis. (SK = Streptokinase; UK = urokinase; t-PA = tissue plasminogen activator.)

Therapeutic heparin is also used during interventions such as cardiopulmonary bypass, ECMO, and continuous arteriovenous or veno-venous hemofiltration. The presence of a central venous catheter is one of the most important risk factors for thromboembolic events in children, and heparin is commonly used in prophylactic doses to prevent thrombotic complications in patients with both indwelling arterial and venous catheters.

Administration and monitoring

Heparin is absorbed very poorly from the GI tract and is therefore given subcutaneously or intravenously. Intramuscular injection is avoided because of the risk of hematoma. IV administration is highly recommended because the absorption after a subcutaneous injection is highly variable. Continuous IV infusion may be associated with decreased bleeding as compared with bolus IV (usually every 4 hours) therapy. A suggested protocol for administering therapeutic heparin is shown below. The guidelines are extrapolated from experience in adult patients. Heparinization of premature and newborn infants is difficult in part because of the immaturity of the coagulation system at birth. In addition, there is no documented safe and therapeutic range.

Subcutaneous administration of heparin is indicated for long-term management of patients in whom warfarin is contraindicated (diffuse GI dysfunction and pregnancy). The dose is 200 to 300 units/kg every 8 to 12 hours. The activated partial thromboplastin time (APTT) is measured exactly at the midpoint between doses.

In patients who need long-term anticoagulation heparin is used in therapeutic doses until the patient is stable on warfarin therapy (see below). In some cases (e.g., femoral arterial thrombosis after cardiac catheterization) there is essentially no risk of recurrence and heparin is therefore discontinued after resolution of the thrombus and the patient is not treated with warfarin.

Occasionally it is necessary to perform surgery on patients receiving heparin. The heparin is discontinued 6 hours before surgery. The APTT is checked before surgery to document normalization. If emergency surgery is necessary, heparin is neutralized by protamine sulfate (see Complications section for dose and administration).

PROTOCOL FOR ADMINISTRATION OF THERAPEUTIC HEPARIN TO PEDIATRIC PATIENTS*

1. Before initiation of therapy, obtain blood for CBC, platelet count, and APTT.
2. Loading dose: 75 U/kg (maximum 5000 U) IV over 10 min
3. Initial maintenance dose: ≤1 yr of age, 28 U/kg/hr; >1 yr of age, 20 U/kg/hr (maximum 2000 U/hr)
4. Obtain blood for APTT 4 hr after administration of loading dose and adjust maintenance dose as indicated below:

APTT (sec)	Bolus (U/kg)	Hold (min)	Rate Change (%)	Repeat APTT (hr)
<50	50	0	+10	4
50-59	0	0	+10	4
60-85	0	0	0	24
86-95	0	0	−10	4
96-120	0	30	−10	4
>120	0	60	−15	4

5. Obtain blood for APTT 4 hr after every change in the infusion rate. When APTT values are therapeutic, obtain blood daily to monitor CBC, platelets, and APTT.

*Modified from Andrew M, Marzinotto V, Massicotte P, et al. Heparin therapy in pediatric patients: A prospective study. Pediatr Res 35:78-83, 1994.

All patients receiving heparin are monitored for bleeding. In addition, these patients are not given intramuscular injections or antiplatelet drugs such as aspirin.

The antithrombotic activity of heparin must be monitored carefully because the dose of heparin necessary to achieve clinical efficacy is highly variable among patients. The variability in dose requirement results from the variable binding of heparin to plasma proteins and cell surfaces. The APTT is the test most commonly used for monitoring. It can be performed reasonably rapidly, and at least in adults there is a fair relationship between APTT, actual heparin concentration, and clinical efficacy. The responsiveness to heparin varies considerably among different commercial APTT reagents, and therefore APTT reagents must be standardized against the plasma heparin concentration. An APTT value of 60 to 85 seconds (equivalent to a heparin concentration of 0.2 to 0.4 unit/ml by protamine titration or 0.35 to 0.7 unit/ml as antifactor Xa) is considered therapeutic.

In some patients the APTT will not increase as expected despite high doses of heparin; these patients are called "resistant." Some patients have an accelerated clearance of heparin (seen in children under 1 year of age and in patients with very large thrombi). Alternatively, the baseline APTT may be abnormally short in certain patients because of increased plasma concentrations of factor VIII (released as an acute phase reactant). In these patients the APTT does not reach therapeutic levels (60 to 85 seconds) despite administration of adequate heparin. Adjusting the heparin dose such that the ratio of the treatment to control values of APTT is 1.5 to 2.5 may provide clinical efficacy with minimal risk of bleeding. It is best, however, to measure the heparin level directly (see below).

Another group of patients, especially those with nephrotic syndrome, hepatic cirrhosis, or DIC, may have an acquired deficiency of AT-III (concentration <25% of normal). The APTT does not become prolonged because heparin is not an effective anticoagulant in patients with severely decreased AT-III levels. AT-III levels can be measured in specialized laboratories, and recombinant AT-III is available for transfusion if necessary.

The activated clotting time (ACT) can be measured rapidly. Noncoagulated blood is mixed with a particulate activator, and the time required for clot formation is measured. The therapeutic range varies among the different machines and must be established for each machine. This test is most commonly used when very rapid results are necessary, such as during cardiopulmonary bypass, ECMO, or cardiac catheterization.

Heparin levels can be measured directly by protamine sulfate neutralization (therapeutic range 0.2 to 0.4 unit/ml) or by assaying antifactor Xa activity (chromogenic assay, therapeutic range 0.35 to 0.7 unit/ml). Unfortunately these assays are not universally available.

Contraindications

Contraindications to heparin therapy are listed below. The risk and benefits of heparin in patients with relative contraindications must be considered on an individual basis.

Complications

The risk of intracranial or retroperitoneal bleeding or any bleeding resulting in transfusion or death is about 5% in adult patients treated with therapeutic heparin. The risk is likely lower in pediatric patients, but definite numbers are not available. Generally the patient's overall clinical condition (presence of relative

---

CONTRAINDICATIONS TO ANTICOAGULATION AND THROMBOLYTIC THERAPY

Absolute contraindications

Active bleeding
Cerebrovascular accident within 2 mo

Relative contraindications

Surgery including organ biopsy within 10 days
Serious GI bleeding within 3 mo
Intracranial or intraspinal surgery within 2 mo
Intracranial neoplasm, arteriovenous malformation, aneurysm
Pregnancy
Recent serious trauma/prolonged cardiopulmonary resuscitation (>10 min)
Severe hypertension despite pharmacologic therapy
Chronic liver disease

contraindications) plays an important role in determining the risk of major bleeding. Bleeding is treated by neutralizing heparin with protamine sulfate. One milligram of protamine is administered for each 100 units of heparin given in the preceding 4 hours (maximum dose 50 mg). It is important to infuse protamine sulfate slowly (over 10 minutes) because rapid infusion causes severe hypotension.

Thrombocytopenia, which occurs in 5% to 10% of adult patients, usually begins after 7 to 10 days of therapy but has been reported very early in patients previously exposed to heparin. The platelet count usually returns to normal about 4 days after heparin is stopped. The incidence of thrombocytopenia in pediatric patients is unknown.

Warfarin

The oral anticoagulant warfarin inhibits two enzymes involved in vitamin K metabolism (Fig. 181-4). This results in a marked decrease in the plasma concentrations of the active forms of the so-called vitamin K–dependent coagulation factors (II, VII, IX, and X). The reduction of factor II (prothrombin) activity is the most important in determining the anticoagulant effect. Warfarin also decreases the activity of the coagulation inhibitors protein C and protein S. In general the anticoagulant effects of warfarin outweigh the potential hypercoagulability resulting from decreased protein C and protein S.

Warfarin is rapidly absorbed, and maximum blood levels are attained about 90 minutes after an oral dose. About 97% is bound to plasma proteins and only the free fraction is biologically active. The half-life of the free fraction is 35 to 48 hours. Warfarin is metabolized in the liver and metabolites are excreted in the urine and stool. The rate of metabolism varies widely among patients and also varies to a lesser extent over time in the same patient.

Indications and clinical effects

Warfarin is indicated for any patient who needs long-term anticoagulation. This includes patients with a history of deep vein thrombosis, pulmonary embolism, intracardiac thrombi (or very poor myocardial function and therefore at risk for intracardiac thrombi), atrial arrhythmias, and mechanical heart valves. The relatively high incidence of thromboembolic complications in patients who are not adequately anticoagulated attests to the efficacy of warfarin in these patients.

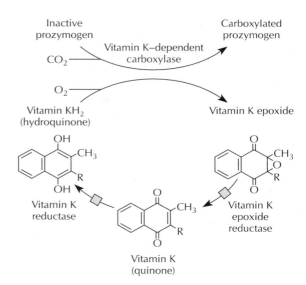

Fig. 181-4 The vitamin K cycle and its inhibition by warfarin. Warfarin inhibits vitamin K epoxide reductase and vitamin K reductase (gray box) and thus blocks the conversion of vitamin K epoxide to vitamin KH_2. Vitamin KH_2 is a cofactor for the carboxylation of inactive proenzymes (factor II, VII, IX, and X) to the carboxylated proenzyme in a reaction that is catalyzed by vitamin K–dependent carboxylase and requires carbon dioxide and oxygen. (From Furie B, Furie BC. Molecular basis of vitamin K–dependent γ-carboxylation. Blood 75:1753-1762, 1990.)

Administration and monitoring

Warfarin therapy is usually initiated with loading doses followed by maintenance doses. Warfarin is always administered once a day. From a practical standpoint, it is convenient to schedule the dose in the late afternoon or early evening. In this way, laboratory data obtained in the morning are available well before the dose is due. Vitamin K must be removed from hyperalimentation fluids, and infants need to be placed on a low vitamin K formula before beginning warfarin. Guidelines for the administration and monitoring of warfarin in infants and children have been extrapolated from experience in adult patients because of the relatively small number of pediatric patients who receive long-term anticoagulation. A suggested protocol for warfarin administration is shown on p. 1747.

Patients receiving warfarin are best monitored by following the prothrombin time (PT). This time is performed by adding a mixture of thromboplastin (a pro-

PROTOCOL FOR ADMINISTRATION OF WARFARIN TO PEDIATRIC PATIENTS*

1. Obtain baseline PT, INR, and liver function tests.
2. Warfarin is always given once daily.
3. Loading doses 1 and 2: If the baseline INR is 1.0 to 1.3, give 0.2 mg/kg. If the baseline INR is >1.3 or there is evidence of liver dysfunction, give 0.1 mg/kg (maximum dose 10 mg).
4. Loading doses 3 to 7 depend on the INR determined after the first two loading doses:

    INR 1.1-1.4   Repeat loading dose
    INR 1.5-2.9   50% of loading dose
    INR 3.1-4.5   25% of loading dose
    INR >4.5   Hold until INR <4.5, then restart at
                   50% less than the previous dose

5. Long-term warfarin maintenance dose guidelines:

If, INR:	INR 2.0-3.0	INR 2.5-3.5
1.1-1.4	Increase by 20%	Increase by 25%
1.5-1.9	Increase by 10%	Increase by 15%
2.0-2.5	No change	Increase by 10%
2.6-3.0	No change	No change
3.1-3.5	Decrease by 10%	No change
3.6-4.0	Decrease by 15%	Decrease by 10%
4.1-4.4	Decrease by 20%	Decrease by 15%
4.5-4.9	Hold one dose, then decrease by 20%	Decrease by 20%
≥5.0	Hold until INR <4.5, then restart at 20% less than previous dose	

*Modified from Andrew M, Marzinotto V, Brooker LA, et al. Oral anticoagulation therapy in pediatric patients: A prospective study. Thromb Haemost 71:265-291, 1994.

tein and phospholipid tissue extract) and calcium to citrated plasma and measuring the time to fibrin formation. The PT is sensitive to a decrease in three of the four vitamin K–dependent coagulation factors (II, VII, and X). Unfortunately the sensitivity of thromboplastins varies according to their source and method of preparation, and this results in considerable variability in PT results. Because this variability complicates monitoring of patients on warfarin, it has been recommended that the reporting of PT ratios (patient PT/control PT) be replaced by the international normalized ratio (INR). The INR incorporates the international sensitivity index (ISI) as a correction factor into the PT ratio to account for the variability in responsiveness of different thromboplastins. Each

batch of thromboplastin is assigned an ISI by calibration against a reference preparation. The INR = [(patient PT/control PT)^{ISI}]. In theory, if a patient has an INR determined simultaneously by three different laboratories, the results will be identical. In practice, some variability persists because of inexactness of assigned ISI values and differences in other reagents and instruments. Calculation of the INR is standard practice in Europe and Canada and is becoming more common in the United States. The INR needs to be maintained between 2.0 and 3.0 for most patients. For patients with mechanical heart valves, the INR needs to be between 2.5 and 3.5.

Warfarin is generally not used to initiate anticoagulation because it takes 3 to 4 days before the patient is effectively anticoagulated. Typically patients are stabilized for several days on heparin and then started on warfarin. Heparin must be continued for at least 3 days and not discontinued until two consecutive INR determinations are in the therapeutic range. The reason for this is that the factor II (prothrombin) concentration decreases within 24 hours, which causes prolongation of the PT. However, a true anticoagulated state is not obtained until after 3 to 4 days of warfarin therapy when the concentrations of the other vitamin K–dependent factors decrease.

In some patients warfarin is used to initiate anticoagulation. For example, administration of therapeutic heparin is contraindicated in patients immediately after placement of a mechanical heart valve. In these patients oral anticoagulation with warfarin is begun on the third or fourth postoperative day. The patient is considered not at risk for serious bleeding by the seventh or eighth postoperative day when a fully anticoagulated state is obtained. For some patients with chronic atrial fibrillation, anticoagulation is considered semielective, and immediate anticoagulation with heparin is not essential.

A large number of drugs have been reported to interact with warfarin, leading to an increase or decrease in the level of anticoagulation. Drugs for which there is evidence of frequent interaction are listed. Many other drugs apparently interact with warfarin in a small minority of patients. It is thus best to measure PT/INR within 5 to 7 days after any medication is added, discontinued, or the dosage has been changed.

Patients with decreased vitamin K levels will have an exaggerated response to warfarin. Decreased vitamin K levels are seen in patients with liver disease, malabsorption, and decreased oral intake (critically ill patients). Prolongation of the baseline PT is often seen in these patients; the loading and maintenance doses of warfarin must be decreased accordingly.

Dietary intake of vitamin K also affects responsiveness to warfarin. This phenomenon is typically seen in hospitalized patients in whom warfarin requirements increase significantly after discharge because of increased food intake. Patients must refrain from eating large quantities of foods known to contain high concentrations of vitamin K.

Warfarin is discontinued for 3 to 5 days in patients undergoing major surgery. Patients with mechanical heart valves are admitted to the hospital 24 to 36

DRUGS THAT INTERACT WITH WARFARIN

Prolongs PT/INR

Amiodarone
Androgens (17-alkyl)
Cimetidine
Clofibrate
Disulfiram
Erythromycin
Metronidazole
Phenylbutazone
Sulfinpyrazole
Tamoxifen
Thyroid hormone
Trimethoprim-sulfamethoxazole

Decreases PT/INR

Barbituates
Carbamazine
Cholestyramine
Rifampin

FOOD HIGH IN VITAMIN K CONTENT*

Beans, mungs, matured
Broccoli spears, raw
Cabbage, raw
Canola oil
Chickpeas, dry
Collard greens
Egg yolks
Liver, raw
Peas, matured seeds, dry
Soybean oil
Soybean, matured seeds, dry
Spinach, raw/frozen
Turnip greens, raw
Wheat, bran, crude

*Modified from Fiore L, Deykin D. Anticoagulant therapy. In Buetler E, Lichtman MA, Coller BS, et al. William's Hematology, 5th ed. New York: McGraw-Hill, 1995, pp 1562-1584. Reproduced by permission of The McGraw-Hill Companies.

hours after warfarin is discontinued and are treated with therapeutic heparin for 2 to 3 days while the INR normalizes. For other patients, the decision to treat with heparin while the INR normalizes must be made on a case-by-case basis by weighing the risk of thrombotic disease against the cost and risks of heparin therapy.

Minor surgical procedures such as dental extractions can be performed without discontinuing warfarin. The dose is reduced so that the INR is about 1.5 at the time of the procedure.

Contraindications

Contraindications to warfarin are listed on p. 1745. The risks and benefits of warfarin in patients with relative contraindications must be considered on an individual basis. Warfarin crosses the placenta and is teratogenic. Women contemplating pregnancy who need anticoagulation must be treated with subcutaneous heparin during conception and throughout gestation.

Complications

Bleeding is the most important complication of warfarin therapy. Major bleeding, defined as intracranial or retroperitoneal bleeding resulting in hospitalization, transfusion, or death, occurs at an annualized rate of about 5% in adult patients. The rate is not defined in the pediatric population but is probably lower because of the relative absence of known risk factors (e.g., hypertension, past GI bleeding, cerebrovascular disease, serious heart disease, and renal insufficiency) in infants and children. The risk of major and minor bleeding in an individual patient rises with the INR.

The risk of bleeding increases in patients who take drugs that interfere with platelet function. The most commonly used agents are aspirin and other nonsteroidal anti-inflammatory drugs. Patients are encouraged to use acetaminophen as an analgesic.

Life-threatening bleeding is treated by administering 5 mg of vitamin K_1 (phytonadione) diluted in 0.9% sodium chloride solution and given intravenously over 10 to 20 minutes while monitoring the patient carefully for anaphylactic shock. In addition, fresh frozen plasma (FFP) (15 to 20 ml/kg) may be given for short-term replacement of coagulation factors. Factor IX concentrate, which contains factors II, VII, IX, and X, 50 units/kg, may be given to patients who cannot tolerate the volume load of FFP, but the expense and risk of viral transmission must be considered. An INR must be obtained immediately after infusion of FFP or concentrate and repeated every 6 to 8 hours. Assuming that vitamin K_1 was administered, two consecutive normal INR determinations document elimination of the warfarin effect.

Treatment of minor bleeding needs to include prompt INR determination and then holding dose(s) and/or dose adjustment as necessary. If bleeding is more than minor but not life threatening, therapy depends on how important it is to maintain some level of anticoagulation. Inasmuch as the half-life of warfarin is 30 to 48 hours, the INR will not decrease for at least 2 days after warfarin is held. Small doses of vitamin K_1, 0.5 to 2 mg administered intramuscularly, will accelerate the decrease in INR, but larger doses will make it difficult to maintain any level of anticoagulation. Infusion of FFP presents similar problems.

Warfarin-induced skin necrosis is a serious but rare complication. Painful, discolored skin presents on the third to eighth day of therapy and typically progresses to necrosis and eschar formation. Patients with hypercoagulable states such as protein S or protein C deficiency are at increased risk.

THROMBOLYTIC THERAPY

Thrombolytic therapy has been used successfully to treat a variety of thrombotic disorders in infants and children. The goal of this therapy is immediate restoration of normal blood flow by dissolution of pathologic intravascular thrombi and emboli. The available agents all act by converting the inactive proenzyme, plasminogen, to the active protease, plasmin. This conversion is critical to the initiation of fibrin degradation. Thrombolytic therapy is now accepted as a first-choice treatment in several conditions because of its demonstrated efficacy, feasibility, and relative safety. Acute myocardial infarction, deep venous thrombosis, and pulmonary embolism are relatively common in adult patients, and thrombolytic therapy has been much better studied in this population. As such, management decisions for pediatric patients are based largely on treatment recommendations for adults. However, the presence of age-related changes in the hemostatic system make it imperative that therapy be individualized for these patients. Optimal doses, choice of agent, method of administration, and duration of therapy for various neonatal and pediatric thrombotic disorders are unknown.

Currently Available Agents (Table 181-1)
Streptokinase

Streptokinase is a single-chain polypeptide that is purified from the secretory products of Lancefield group C β-streptococci. Streptokinase has no intrinsic enzymatic activity; instead, streptokinase forms an equimolar complex with plasminogen, which converts plasminogen to plasmin. Inasmuch as streptokinase activates both circulating plasminogen and plasminogen bound to fibrin at the site of a thrombus (fibrin-associated plasminogen), both local and systemic fibrinolysis are observed. Systemic fibrinolysis degrades fibrinogen, plasminogen, and other coagulation factors. The degradation products increase thrombolysis by enhancing streptokinase-plasminogen complex activity. The half-life of streptokinase is about 12 to 20 minutes; however, the half-life of the lytic effects is 80 to 180 minutes.

Naturally occurring antibodies rapidly inactivate streptokinase, and therefore a loading dose is necessary to inactivate circulating antibodies. The antibodies, which are the result of prior streptococcal infections, are particularly common in school-aged children. Furthermore, streptokinase induces antibody production; sufficient antibodies are produced to neutralize standard doses after 3 to 4 days of treatment. Antibody titers persist for 1 to 2 years. Thus streptokinase must not be used more than once in the same patient within this time period.

In young infants or in older patients with multisystem organ failure who have decreased circulating plasminogen, formation of the initial streptokinase-plasminogen complex may deplete plasminogen to a critical level such that insufficient circulating plasminogen is available for conversion to plasmin. If decreased plasminogen concentration is documented, decreasing the dose of streptokinase by 50% to 75% may increase the amount of circulating plasminogen still available after formation of the streptokinase-plasminogen complex.

Anisoylated plasminogen-streptokinase activator complex (anistreplase)

Anisoylated plasminogen-streptokinase activator complex (APSAC) is a chemically modified derivative of streptokinase in which streptokinase is noncovalently associated with plasminogen and the active site of plasminogen is protected by covalent modification

Table 181-1 Characteristics and Doses of Available Thrombolytic Agents

	Streptokinase	APSAC	Urokinase	t-PA
Source	Strep. culture	Strep. culture	Mammalian cell tissue culture	Mammalian cell tissue culture
Molecular weight (daltons)	47,000	131,000	32,000-54,000	70,000
Plasma clearance time (min)	12-20	40-80	15-20	3-8
Plasminogen binding	Indirect	Indirect	Indirect	Direct
Fibrinolytic activation	Systemic	Systemic	Systemic	Systemic
Fibrin specificity	Minimal	Minimal	Some	Moderate
Antigenic	Yes	Yes	No	No
Allergic reactions/fever	Yes	Yes	No	No
Dose to achieve systemic lytic state				
Loading	3500-10,000 U/kg over 30 min (maximum 250,000 U)		4400 U/kg over 10 min	None
Maintenance	1000-3000 U/kg/h (maximum 100,000 U/h)		4400-8800 U/kg/hr	0.1-0.6 mg/kg/hr*

*Canadian Children's Thrombophila Society regimen: Heparinize patient and continue heparin. Give 0.6 mg/kg t-PA IV over 20 min. Repeat once in 18-24 hr if thrombus persists. If after another 18-24 hr thrombus still persists, give 0.6 mg/kg IV over 20 min followed by 0.6 mg/kg/hr for 6 hr. Follow aPTT to monitor heparin, but otherwise do not monitor coagulation variables.

with a *p*-anisolyl group. As a result of these modifications, ASPAC has a much longer half-life than streptokinase and greater lytic potency.

In practice, the only real advantage of this agent as compared with streptokinase is that it can be administered as a one-time bolus dose. It is considerably more expensive than streptokinase and its use has declined recently. Experience in pediatric patients is limited.

Urokinase

Urokinase, a proteolytic enzyme that converts plasminogen to plasmin, originally was derived from human urine and is now prepared from transformed fetal renal parenchymal cells in tissue culture. Several forms of the enzyme are produced, but only the two-chain form is available in the United States. Urokinase has low fibrin specificity, and IV administration therefore results in systemic lytic effects similar to those observed after streptokinase. Urokinase is not antigenic and can be used repeatedly as needed.

Tissue-plasminogen activator (ateplase)

t-PA is synthesized by vascular endothelial cells. The current preparation of t-PA is manufactured via recombinant technology and is much more expensive than streptokinase or urokinase. The product available in the United States is a single polypeptide chain. t-PA binds to fibrin and activates bound plasminogen much more rapidly than it activates circulating plasminogen. Because of this specificity, t-PA is the first of the so-called second-generation, fibrin-specific agents. This was initially thought to have a significant clinical advantage over streptokinase and urokinase. However, in clinical practice the large doses required for sufficient rapidity of lysis result in systemic plasminemia and a systemic lytic state. Because t-PA binds to fibrin, thrombolysis continues (usually for 2 to 3 hours) after it has been cleared from the circulation.

t-PA does not markedly degrade fibrinogen; therefore it does not generate fibrin degradation products to antagonize thrombin activity or deplete fibrinogen to the same extent as nonfibrin-specific activators. This property may make t-PA–treated patients more prone to formation of new thrombi in the absence of anticoagulant therapy. It is therefore crucial to institute early and effective use of heparin when using t-PA as a plasminogen activator.

Indications and Clinical Effects
Thrombosed central venous catheter

Thrombolytic therapy is used most commonly in pediatric patients to clear indwelling catheters of occlusive thrombi. As many as 25% of patients with indwelling catheters are treated with thrombolytic agents. The success rate is relatively high (80% to 90%). Urokinase is almost always used because of the potential for allergic reactions and development of antibodies with streptokinase and the expense of t-PA.

Arterial thrombosis after cardiac catheterization

Femoral artery thrombosis after cardiac catheterization occurs in infants and young children, especially after interventional procedures in which relatively large catheters are used. Surgical thrombectomy is often not successful in these small infants and may extend vascular damage. Treatment with thrombolytic agents is an excellent alternative to surgery. Treatment is indicated for patients who have a cool leg with absent pulses, low or unmeasurable blood pressure (as compared with the contralateral leg), and decreased capillary refill. Typically, heparin is administered for a variable time period before thrombolytic agents are administered. Success has been reported with streptokinase, urokinase, and t-PA; no agent has been shown to be superior to another. Lysis of the thrombus usually occurs in 4 to 12 hours in more than 90% of patients. Therapy must be monitored by observing skin temperature and pulses and

---

**DISORDERS TREATED WITH
THROMBOLYTIC THERAPY**

Thrombosed central venous catheter
Arterial thrombosis after cardiac catheterization
Superior vena cava syndrome
Intracardiac and cardiac valve thrombosis
Pulmonary embolism
Deep vein thrombosis
Aortic thrombosis
Thrombosed systemic to pulmonary arterial shunt
Acute myocardial infarction

by measuring blood pressures. Bleeding from the catheterization site is common (at least 25% of patients) and is often a signal of reperfusion of the leg. Bleeding can usually be controlled by compression. Rarely, transfusion is needed for large blood losses. Apparent failure of lysis is suggestive of severe arterial damage rather than thrombosis. Rethrombosis does not usually occur, and most cardiologists do not administer heparin after thrombolysis.

Vena caval/intracardiac/mechanical valve thrombosis

Lysis of vena caval and intracardiac thrombi with thrombolytic agents in pediatric patients has been reported. These thrombi may be related to indwelling catheters or abnormal intracardiac blood flow resulting from atrial arrhythmias or congenital heart disease. In addition, although not as common as with adult patients, pediatric patients can develop mechanical valve thrombosis. Although in theory thrombolytic therapy is most efficacious in patients with relatively fresh clots, successful lysis has been documented in patients who have been symptomatic for several weeks.

Pulmonary embolism

Thrombolytic therapy is the initial treatment of choice for patients with massive pulmonary emboli with or without shock. Infusion of the thrombolytic agent directly into a pulmonary artery confers no advantage in terms of rate of lysis or bleeding as compared with infusion into a peripheral vein. The overall success rate for resolution of emboli is 80% to 90%. Recently patients who are hemodynamically unstable as a result of massive central emboli have shown accelerated improvement if treated with a so-called front-loading dosage regimen in which very large doses of urokinase or t-PA are given rapidly at the beginning of treatment.

Deep vein thrombosis

The major sequelae of deep vein thrombosis are subsequent venous insufficiency and pulmonary emboli. Prolonged venous insufficiency can result in postphlebitic syndrome, which is characterized by chronic discomfort, edema, skin discoloration, cutaneous breakdown and possible ulceration, cellulitis, and necrosis. For many years the standard treatment involved anticoagulation with heparin followed by treatment with warfarin. However, this seldom

(<10%) resulted in dissolution of the thrombus and restoration of normal venous flow. In contrast, the success rate with thrombolytic therapy is 55% to 85%. It is preferable to infuse the agent at a site immediately distal to the thrombus. Success is highest if an angiocatheter is passed directly into the thrombus and high concentrations of the thrombolytic agent are delivered into the interior of the thrombus.

Aortic thrombosis

Although an infrequent complication, umbilical arterial catheterization can result in aortic thrombosis. When extensive, this is characterized by systemic hypertension, congestive heart failure, renal failure, and signs of limb ischemia. Administration of thrombolytic agents has been successful in some cases; failures have been attributed to poor overall patient condition and inability to achieve a lytic state, possibly secondary to the low plasminogen concentrations in neonates.

Thrombosed systemic to pulmonary artery shunts

Occasionally patients with systemic to pulmonary artery (e.g., Blalock-Taussig) shunts develop occlusive thrombi within the shunt. Chronic polycythemia, decreased oral intake during a febrile illness, and dehydration associated with gastroenteritis are predisposing factors. These patients present with sudden increased hypoxemia and decreased or absent shunt murmurs. If profoundly hypoxemic, surgical placement of another shunt is the treatment of choice. If the degree of hypoxemia is tolerable, a trial of thrombolytic therapy is justified, especially if the shunt is thought to be of adequate size.

Myocardial infarction

Data from very large controlled clinical trials have shown convincingly that thrombolytic therapy reduces short-term and long-term mortality after myocardial infarction. However, exact clinical indications and contraindications as well as selection, timing, and dosage regimen of thrombolytic agents remain controversial. These issues are beyond the scope of this chapter; the interested reader may refer to several excellent references.

Miscellaneous conditions

The indications for thrombolytic therapy in pediatric patients will continue to expand as more experience is gained. Renal vein thrombosis, intraocular thrombi (local use), and clotted shunts in renal dialysis patients are just a few miscellaneous thrombotic disorders in pediatric patients that eventually may be managed routinely with thrombolytic agents.

Administration and Monitoring

The most common indication for thrombolytic therapy in pediatric patients is occluded IV catheters. Urokinase, 5000 units/ml, is instilled in sufficient volume to fill the lumen of the catheter. This is left in place for 1 to 4 hours before the lumen is aspirated and flushed. This may be repeated with urokinase, 10,000 units/ml, if necessary. Short infusions of low-dose urokinase (150 to 200 units/kg/hr) for 6 to 12 hours may reestablish patency if direct instillation is unsuccessful. Monitoring of coagulation tests is not necessary for these patients.

All patients receiving systemic thrombolytic therapy must be observed physically and monitored closely during administration of these agents. Blood for transfusion must be available. Invasive procedures such as arterial blood gas sampling, intramuscular injections, rectal temperatures, deep venous puncture, and cardiac catheterization are avoided. If the need for thrombolytic therapy is established during cardiac catheterization, venous and arterial sheaths are kept in place until after thrombolytic therapy is completed.

Optimal doses of thrombolytic agents for systemic therapy have not been established for pediatric patients. Dosage ranges used in published reports are given in Table 181-1. In an effort to decrease the incidence of bleeding, various investigators have used relatively low doses. Wessel et al. have reported successful lysis of femoral arterial thrombi after cardiac catheterization with lower doses of streptokinase (1000 units/kg/hr). However, there is some evidence that low-dose regimens require relatively long periods of treatment to achieve lysis; further study is needed to determine if the presumed decreased incidence of bleeding is justified by the costs of prolonged treatment. In addition, some recent findings suggest that a rapid bolus at a fairly high dose results in rapid lysis with a lower frequency of bleeding because a prolonged systemic lytic state is avoided.

Factors that influence lysis of a thrombus include size, age, surface area exposed to circulating blood, and nature of blood flow in the region of the thrombus. Documentation of thrombus lysis or failure to reduce thrombus size determines the end point of ther-

apy. If lysis is not seen after 12 to 24 hours of therapy, consideration must be given to changing the dose of the thrombolytic agent or changing agents. Alternatively, inadequate circulating plasminogen may be a problem, especially in neonates and young infants. Thrombolytic therapy is stopped and FFP given to replete plasminogen followed by measuring plasminogen concentration. In general 20 to 40 ml/kg of FFP given over 4 hours is adequate, but substitution of FFP for maintenance fluids for 24 to 36 hours may be necessary. In these cases concentrated glucose solutions are administered to patients unable to eat to prevent hypoglycemia. Diuretics may be needed to treat fluid overload.

A complete blood count and baseline coagulation profile (PT, APTT, thrombin time, and fibrinogen) are measured in all patients before beginning thrombolytic therapy. In addition, if there is a possibility of a decreased plasminogen concentration (young age or multisystem organ failure), plasminogen must also be measured.

Laboratory monitoring during administration of thrombolytic agents is controversial. In general the PT, APTT, thrombin time, and fibrin/fibrinogen degradation products increase, whereas fibrinogen and plasminogen decrease. None of these variables has been shown to correlate with clinical efficacy or risk of bleeding, although reductions in fibrinogen below 100 mg/dl are associated with increased hemorrhagic risk in adult patients. Inasmuch as coagulation variables are not predictive of lysis or bleeding and sampling is difficult in neonates and young children, some clinicians choose not to monitor coagulation tests during thrombolytic therapy. This is especially true if patients are treated for a relatively short period of time (<4 hours) or with relatively low-dose therapy. Others believe that the thrombin time provides the best estimate of the activity of the fibrinolytic system. If after several hours of treatment the thrombin time is not prolonged as compared with the baseline measurement, thrombolytic therapy may not have activated the fibrinolytic system and dissolution of the thrombus is less likely. Another approach is to assess for the presence of a systemic lytic state. This includes a decrease in fibrinogen (usually by 20% to 50%), production of fibrin/fibrinogen degradation products, or depletion of plasminogen. Unfortunately single or even repeated measurements of fibrinogen or plasminogen are difficult to interpret because synthesis and catabolic rates are unknown. In addition, fibrin split degradation products may interfere with determination of fibrinogen levels. If heparin is given at the same time as a thrombolytic agent (usually t-PA), meaningful interpretation of markers of systemic lysis is not possible. Heparin therapy must be monitored by obtaining serial APPT measurements.

In general patients must be treated with anticoagulants after thrombolytic therapy. Heparin must be administered immediately after treatment with t-PA (some clinicians continue heparin during t-PA). Heparin is given when the thrombin time falls to less than twice the control value after treatment with streptokinase or urokinase. A loading dose of heparin is not given. The patient is switched to oral anticoagulation in the usual manner.

Contraindications

Standard contraindications to thrombolytic therapy are listed on p. 1745. Clearly, active bleeding is an absolute contraindication. The other conditions can be considered relative contraindications. The possible risks and benefits of thrombolytic therapy must be assessed on a case-by-case basis.

Complications

Bleeding is the most important complication of thrombolytic therapy. Bleeding from venipuncture sites and around intravascular catheters is quite common. Although this always creates anxiety on the part of patients, families, and medical staff, this bleeding is excellent evidence of ongoing thrombolysis. It is treated with application of local pressure and also topical thrombin. Rarely, transfusion is necessary for large blood losses.

Major hemorrhagic complications occur in about 1% of patients, and thrombolytic therapy must be discontinued. Although t-PA is relatively fibrin specific, bleeding is just as common with this agent as with the others because t-PA is relatively more effective at dissolving all thrombi. The incidence of important bleeding increases if heparin is used concurrently with thrombolytic agents. In addition, the incidence of bleeding increases as the duration of therapy increases. For example, bleeding is much less common in patients with myocardial infarctions who receive a thrombolytic agent for 1 to 3 hours than in patients with venous thrombosis who are treated for 12 to 72 hours. If severe bleeding occurs, the thrombolytic agent is discontinued. Packed red blood cells, FFP, and cryoprecipitate are administered as needed. If bleeding is life threatening, ϵ-aminocaproic acid is considered. A loading dose of 100 to 200 mg/kg given as an IV infusion is followed by doses of 100 mg/kg given intravenously every 6 hours.

Rapid IV boluses of streptokinase can cause severe hypotension, possibly secondary to breakdown of vasodepressor kinins, and are therefore to be avoided. If hypotension occurs at the recommended infusion rate, it can usually be managed by decreasing the infusion rate. About 20% of patients develop fever and can be treated with acetaminophen. Severe allergic reactions characterized by fever, hypotension, urticarial reaction, and bronchospasm occur in <1% of patients. Premedication with acetaminophen, antihistamines, and/or hydrocortisone has been recommended by some.

CURRENT RESEARCH AND FUTURE CONSIDERATIONS

Low molecular weight heparin (LMWH) has been used for some years in Canada and Europe for prevention of venous thromboembolism and is currently being evaluated in the United States. LMWH is nearly 100% bioavailable because there is minimal binding to serum proteins. The anticoagulant effect is therefore very predictable and frequent APTT determinations are not necessary. In addition, the half-life of LMWH is 2- to 4-fold longer than regular heparin, and therefore only once-a-day subcutaneous dosing is necessary.

Hirudin, which is produced by a medicinal leach, is a very potent and selective thrombin inhibitor. Recently recombinant derivatives, including desulfatohirudin (r-hirudin) and hirulog, have been developed. Because r-hirudin and hirulog bind directly to thrombin, there is no need for an intermediary molecule such as AT-III. In contrast to heparin, r-hirudin and hirulog are not inactivated by components of the platelet release reaction such as platelet factor 4. In addition, r-hirudin and hirulog neutralize clot-bound thrombin and inhibit thrombin-induced platelet aggregation. These agents are thus potentially useful in conditions in which an evolving clot is present despite ongoing anticoagulation with heparin. The results of preliminary studies in animals and human beings suggest that treatment with r-hirudin decreases the incidence of thrombotic events after angioplasty. However, caution is necessary in using these compounds because there is no effective antidote analogous to the effect of protamine on heparin.

Recombinant staphylokinase is a new thrombolytic agent. Because staphylokinase is highly fibrin specific, this agent does not break down fibrinogen. Animal studies show that staphylokinase lyses clots very quickly and produces less bleeding than t-PA. Preliminary studies in human beings are promising; however, staphylokinase is antigenic.

ADDITIONAL READING

· Andrew M. Anticoagulation and thrombolysis in children. Tex Heart Inst J 19:168-177, 1992.

Andrew M, Johnson M. Development of the hemostatic system in the neonate and young infant. Am J Pediatr Hematol Oncol 12:95-104, 1990.

· Andrew M, Marzinotto V, Massicotte P, Blanchette V, Ginsberg J, Brill-Edwards P, Burrows P, Benson L, Williams W, David M, Poon A, Sparling K. Heparin therapy in pediatric patients: A prospective study. Pediatr Res 35:78-83, 1994.

· Andrew M, Marzinotto V, Brooker LA, Adams M, Ginsberg J, Freedom R, Williams W. Oral anticoagulation therapy in pediatric patients: A prospective study. Thromb Haemost 71:265-291, 1994.

Andrew M, Vegh P, Johnston M, Bowker J, Ofosu F, Mitchell L. Maturation of the hemostatic system during childhood. Blood 80:1998-2005, 1992.

Bagnall HA, Gomperts E, Atkinson JB. Continuous infusion of low-dose urokinase in the treatment of central venous catheter thrombosis in infants and children. Pediatrics 83:963-966, 1989.

· Bell WR. Thrombolytic therapy. Med Clin North Am 78:745-764, 1994.

Bitchell TC. Thrombosis and antithrombotic therapy. In Lee GR, Bitchell TC, Foerster J, Athens JW, Lukens JN, eds. Wintrobe's Clinical Hematology. Philadelphia: Lea & Febiger, 1993, pp 1515-1551.

Corrigan JJ, Sleeth JJ, Jeter M, Lox CD. Newborn's fibrinolytic mechanism: Components and plasmin generation. Am J Hematol 32:273-278, 1989.

Fiore L, Deykin D. Anticoagulant therapy. In Buetler E, Lichtman MA, Coller BS, Kipps TJ, eds. William's Hematology, 5th ed. New York: McGraw-Hill, 1995, pp 1562-1584.

Furie B, Furie BC. Molecular basis of vitamin K–dependent γ-carboxylation. Blood 75:1753-1762, 1990.

Habib GB. Current status of thrombolysis in acute myocardial infarction. I. Optimal selection and delivery of a thrombolytic drug. Chest 107:225-232, 1995.

Habib GB. Current status of thrombolysis in acute myocardial infarction. II. Optimal utilization of thrombolysis in clinical subsets. Chest 107:528-534, 1995.

· Hirsh J, Fuster V. Guide to anticoagulant therapy. Part I: Heparin. Circulation 89:1449-1468, 1994.

Jaffe A. Thrombolytic therapy. In Chernow B, ed. The Pharmacologic Approach to the Critically Ill Patient. Baltimore: Williams & Wilkins, 1994, pp 347-364.

· Kothari SS, Varma S, Wasir HS. Thrombolytic therapy in infants and children. Am Heart J 127:651-657, 1994.

· Levy M, Benson LN, Burrows PE, Bentur Y, Strong DK, Smith J, Johnson D, Jacobson S, Koren G. Tissue plasminogen activator for the treatment of thromboembolism in infants and children. J Pediatr 118:467-472, 1991.

Loscalzo J. Fibrinolytic therapy. In Beutler E, Lichtman MA, Coller BS, Kipps TJ, eds. Williams Hematology, 5th ed. New York: McGraw-Hill, 1995, pp 1585-1591.

Majerus PW, Broze GJ Jr, Miletich JP, Tollefsen DJ. Anticoagulant, antithrombotic, and thrombolytic drugs. In Gilman AG, Rall TW, Nies AS, Taylor P, eds. Goodman and Gilman's The Pharmacological Basis of Therapeutics. New York: Pergamon Press, 1990, pp 1311-1331.

Pinto M, Mitchell L, McCusker P, Andrew M. Standardization of prothrombin times in newborn infants. J Pediatr 123:310-312, 1993.

Ries M, Singer H, Hofbeck M. Thrombolysis of a modified Blalock-Taussig shunt with recombinant tissue plasminogen activator in a newborn infant with pulmonary atresia and ventricular septal defect. Br Heart J 72:201-202, 1994.

Silber H, Khan SS, Matloff JM, Chaux A, DeRobertis M, Gray R. The St. Jude valve. Thrombolysis as the first line of therapy for cardiac valve thrombosis. Circulation 87:30-37, 1993.

Wessel DL, Keane JF, Fellows KE, Robichaud H, Lock JE. Fibrinolytic therapy for femoral arterial thrombosis after cardiac catheterization in infants and children. Am J Cardiol 58:347-351, 1986.

Zenz W, Muntean W, Beitzke A, Zobel G, Riccabona M, Gamillscheg A. Tissue plasminogen activator (ateplase) treatment for femoral artery thrombosis after cardiac catheterisation in infants and children. Br Heart J 70:382-385, 1993.

182 Pharmacokinetics in Patients on Extracorporeal Circuits

Raymond Quigley · Christine A. Lindsay

BACKGROUND AND INDICATIONS

Critically ill children are often treated with extracorporeal circulation of blood for life support, which can provide life-sustaining functions but also can remove essential medications and nutrients that are administered to the patient. Pharmacokinetic principles that determine drug removal by exchange transfusion, plasmapharesis, hemodialysis, hemofiltration, hemoperfusion, and ECMO will be reviewed. Drug removal by peritoneal dialysis will not be discussed because it is not an extracorporeal technique. The general principles of drug removal will be reviewed first followed by specific processes for each procedure.

Mechanisms of Drug Removal

Extracorporeal procedures remove drugs and nutrients from a patient by a combination of the following basic processes: convection, diffusion, and adsorption.

Convection

Convection refers to the removal of a substance by removing the bulk fluid in which the substance is dissolved. This can occur as direct removal of whole blood, such as during an exchange transfusion, or of some component of blood. For example, plasmapheresis is a process whereby only the plasma portion of the blood is removed, leaving behind the cellular components of the blood in the patient (see Chapter 166). This can be an important route for elimination of protein-bound drugs.

An ultrafiltrate of blood is formed and removed when hydrostatic pressure (or osmotic pressure in peritoneal dialysis) is exerted to force fluid through a semipermeable membrane. The membrane does not allow passage of proteins or cellular components and thus the ultrafiltrate of the blood is free of protein and cells. The determinants of the ultrafiltration rate (UFR) are the transmembrane pressure (TMP) and the membrane ultrafiltration coefficient (K_{UF}). Thus the UFR is equal to the TMP multiplied by the K_{UF} (UFR = TMP $\times$ K_{UF}). The size and nature of the pores and the electrostatic charge on the membrane will determine if a substance can pass through the membrane. Because blood proteins cannot pass through the membrane, any drug that is highly protein bound will not be removed.

The ability of the drug to pass through the membrane is termed the sieving coefficient (σ). If the drug passes through the membrane readily, the sieving coefficient will be 1. If the drug has a large molecular weight or is highly protein bound and thus cannot pass through the membrane readily, the sieving coefficient will be close to 0. The sieving coefficient of drug X can be estimated by measuring the drug concentration in the ultrafiltrate and plasma and using the following equation:

$$\sigma_x = \frac{UF_x}{P_x}$$

where σ_x is the sieving coefficient of drug X and UF_x and P_x are the ultrafiltrate and plasma concentrations of X, respectively.

Diffusion

Diffusion occurs when there is an electrochemical gradient for a substance to move from one compartment to another. This generally occurs between the patient's blood and a solution known as the dialysate and in practice takes place during the processes of hemodialysis and hemodiafiltration (continuous arteriovenous hemodiafiltration [CAVH] or continuous veno-venous hemodiafiltration [CVVH]). The blood and dialysate compartments are separated by the membrane of the artificial filter. The determinants of diffusion are the blood and dialysate concentrations of the drug and the size and nature of the membrane pores. In general an electrical potential does not exist between the blood and the dialysate so that the gradient is only a chemical gradient. There is no diffusion of drugs in ECMO, hemoperfusion, or hemofiltration because there is no dialysate compartment in which the drug can diffuse.

Adsorption

Drugs may be removed from the body by the process of adsorption, which refers to binding of the drug to the surface of a membrane. This may occur during ECMO where some drugs may bind to the surface of the oxygenator membrane. This also occurs when charcoal hemoperfusion is used. The charcoal particles are prepared so that there is a large surface area for binding of drugs. This technique will remove many drugs that are protein or lipid bound and are thus not amenable to removal by dialysis or hemofiltration. Recent studies have also indicated that there may be some degree of adsorption of molecules to hemodialysis and hemofiltration membranes.

Pharmacokinetic Parameters

The rate at which a drug is removed from the body depends not only on the mechanism of elimination but also on its pharmacokinetic parameters. These include volume of distribution, protein binding, lipid binding, and hepatic and renal clearances. These characteristics have been discussed in Chapter 175 and will only be covered briefly here.

Volume of distribution

After a drug is administered to a patient, it will diffuse through the body into an apparent volume of distribution (V_d). This volume is determined primarily by the drug's water and lipid solubilities, protein and lipid binding, and ability to diffuse into cells. These characteristics can be altered by renal or hepatic failure, changes in acid-base status, or sepsis.

Drugs that have a large V_d tend to be removed more slowly than those with a small V_d. This is because the extracorporeal procedure can directly remove only the fraction of the drug that is in the circulation. As the concentration of the drug in the blood decreases, the drug can diffuse from its V_d into the blood compartment and eventually be re-

moved. The rate at which this occurs will depend on the drug's lipid solubility and ability to move from its V_d to the blood compartment.

Protein binding

The effect of protein binding on the rate of drug removal will depend on the extracorporeal procedure used. In hemodialysis and hemofiltration, where the drug must pass through a membrane for removal, protein binding will inhibit drug removal. However, in charcoal hemoperfusion, where protein- or lipid-bound drugs may adsorb to the charcoal surface more readily than unbound drug, protein binding may enhance drug removal.

Factors that affect the degree of protein binding may in turn affect the rate of drug removal by these extracorporeal procedures. For example, the protein binding of phenytoin decreases in renal failure. Thus its removal rate during hemodialysis will be higher when the patient is more uremic since the unbound fraction of phenytoin will be higher. Bilirubin and lipids may compete for binding sites on albumin and displace drugs that are bound to albumin. The degree of saturation of protein binding may also change with acid-base status and with the patient's protein concentration so that the amount of drug bound in hypoalbuminemic patients may be less.

Lipid binding

The degree of lipid binding of drugs affects drug removal in two ways. The larger effect is its effect on V_d. Drugs that have a high degree of lipid binding are usually highly lipid soluble, will distribute through all the cells in the body, and will accumulate in fat cells. This gives the drug a large V_d and will therefore decrease the rate of removal of the drug. The other effect is that the drug may bind to circulating lipoproteins and will thus be affected by the same factors that affect protein binding.

Renal and hepatic clearances

The clearance of a drug from the body is defined as the volume of blood that is totally cleared of the drug per unit time. It can be expressed by the following equation:

$$\text{Clearance (vol/time)} = \frac{\text{Excretion rate (mass/time)}}{\text{Blood concentration (mass/vol)}}$$

Drugs can be cleared by the kidneys, liver, extracorporeal techniques, or any combination of these routes. The total body clearance is the sum of these clearances:

$$Cl_{total} = Cl_{renal} + Cl_{hepatic} + Cl_{extracorporeal}$$

This is an important concept because the extracorporeal clearance may be only a small fraction of the total body clearance. Thus the impact that the extracorporeal technique has on the drug removal rate will depend on the patient's renal and hepatic function. In general, if the clearance by the extracorporeal procedure is <10% of the total clearance, its contribution can be ignored. This usually means that more attention must be paid to drug elimination by these techniques as the patient's renal and hepatic function deteriorates.

EXTRACORPOREAL TECHNIQUES
Exchange Transfusion

The technique of exchange transfusion has been used to treat severe life-threatening hyperkalemia when dialysis could not be initiated in time. It has also been used to treat hyperbilirubinemia in neonates due to ABO or Rh incompatibility. Partial exchange transfusions are also used to treat patients with polycythemia, severe anemia, or leukocytosis from leukemia. The mechanism by which this technique removes drugs from the patient is convection by direct removal of blood. Considerations for drug dosing during exchange transfusion depend mostly on the V_d of the drug. The smaller the V_d, the greater the likelihood the drug will be removed with the exchange. Antibiotics are the most commonly used agents that fall into this category, and a supplemental dose at the end of the exchange is necessary. For aminoglycosides and vancomycin, plasma concentrations are obtained after the exchange, but before giving the supplemental dose. Less drug is removed in the exchange transfusion if there is a large V_d and doses do not need to be supplemented. However, for drugs that can be measured in the plasma, it is still prudent to obtain plasma concentrations and assess the need for repeat doses.

Plasmapheresis

Plasmapheresis is a process that exchanges the protein-containing plasma of the blood without disturbing the cellular components. Little has been published on the effects of this procedure on drug dosing. Theoretically, any drug that is highly protein bound can be removed by this procedure; however,

two factors probably contribute to the fact that this procedure has little effect on drug dosing. First, the procedure is intermittent. Each plasmapheresis treatment lasts only a few hours and each course of treatment may only be performed over a limited number of days. Second, the procedure can only extract drugs from the circulation, which may represent a small fraction of the drug's V_d and therefore has a very limited capacity for drug removal. In practice, the only drugs that have been noted to need readjusting are antiseizure medications such as phenobarbital and phenytoin.

Hemodialysis

Hemodialysis is discussed in detail in Chapter 169; only the primary features that determine drug removal will be reviewed here. This technique removes drugs from the patient in part by convection but primarily by diffusion. The patient's blood flows through the dialyzer at flow rates up to 5 ml/min/kg body weight (approximately 350 ml/min in adults), and the dialysate flow rates are between 500 and 800 ml/min, depending on the hemodialysis machine in use. With dialysate flow rates in this range, the concentration of the drug in the dialysate remains low, and thus a chemical gradient for diffusion of the drug out of the blood is maintained. For example, if a 20 kg patient is hemodialyzed for 4 hours (240 min) at a blood flow rate of 100 ml/min (5 ml/min/kg), the amount of blood that has passed through the dialyzer is 24,000 ml, but the amount of dialysate (assuming the standard flow rate of 500 ml/min) is 120,000 ml. In other words, it is as though 24 L of the patient's blood was in contact with 120 L of dialysate with the dialyzer membrane between the two. This will allow for the drug to diffuse down its concentration gradient into the dialysate. During the same hemodialysis session the amount of fluid removed may be on the order of 500 to 1000 ml. Thus the amount of drug removed by convection would be minimal compared with the amount removed by diffusion.

The factors that determine whether or not a drug may be removed by hemodialysis are the molecular weight of the drug, the size of the pores in the filter, and the protein binding of the drug. Table 182-1 lists the drugs that are dialyzable by most dialysis filters. Of particular note, the aminoglycosides are dialyzed very well; however, vancomycin is not. Drugs such as cyclosporin A that are highly protein bound are also not removed by hemodialysis. These same factors

Table 182-1   Effect of Hemodialysis on Drugs

Drug	Effect	Recommendation
Aminoglycosides	50% removed	Give 50% of loading dose after dialysis
Penicillins	30%-50% removed	Give dose after dialysis
Nafcillin	Negligible	
Oxacillin	Negligible	
Cephalosporins	30%-50% removed	Give dose after dialysis
Ceftriaxone	Negligible	
Clindamycin	Negligible	
Erythromycin	Negligible	
Ciprofoxacin	Negligible	
Chloramphenicol	20% removed	
Sulfamethoxazole	50% removed	
Trimethoprim	50% removed	
Vancomycin	Negligible	
Amphotericin B	Negligible	
Ketoconozole	Negligible	
Miconazole	Negligible	
Flucytosine	50% removed	
Acyclovir	50% removed	Give dose after dialysis
Amantidine	Negligible	
Cimetidine	10%-20% removed	
Ranitidine	50%-60% removed	
Phenobarbital	10%-50% removed	Give dose after dialysis
Phenytoin	Negligible	
Tricyclic antidepressants	Negligible	
Meperidine	Negligible	
Propoxyphene	Negligible	
Digoxin	Negligible	
Digitoxin	Negligible	
Atenolol	20%-50% removed	
Labetalol	Negligible	
Furosemide	Negligible	
Prednisone	Negligible	
Cyclosporin A	Negligible	

will also determine if the drug will be removed by convection during the procedure of hemodialysis, but as can be seen from the above example, the magnitude of the contribution to drug removal is small compared with diffusion.

Another factor that determines the extent of drug removal during hemodialysis is the V_d of the drug. If the drug easily diffuses through the dialyzer membrane but has a large V_d, the fraction of the drug in the patient that is actually removed may be small. For example, haloperidol is water soluble and can be removed during hemodialysis, but it has a V_d of 14 to 21 L/kg of body weight. Thus the small amount of

drug removed during a hemodialysis treatment will be negligible compared with the amount in the patient. The blood concentration may be low for a short period of time after dialysis, but after the drug has equilibrated, the concentration may be very close to the concentration before hemodialysis.

The duration and frequency of the hemodialysis sessions will affect the drug removal rate. Hemodialysis is usually an intermittent procedure. The removal rate of a certain drug may be very high during dialysis, but once dialysis has stopped, the drug may not be removed for another 24 to 48 hours, depending on when the next dialysis treatment is scheduled. For example, aminoglycosides are readily removed by hemodialysis but are normally excreted by the kidneys. If the patient has acute renal failure, there may be no drug removal when the patient is not on dialysis. Thus the dosing of most aminoglycosides can be done after hemodialysis. Good therapeutic concentrations of the drug will be maintained until the next hemodialysis treatment.

Hemofiltration

The initial form of continuous hemofiltration was CAVH. The driving force for ultrafiltration was the transmembrane pressure, formed across the filter membrane, which was generated by the patient's cardiac output. Thus the ability to ultrafiltrate the patient depended on the patient's cardiovascular stability. When a blood pump was added to the circuit, the need for arterial cannulation was eliminated and CVVH could be performed on patients whose cardiovascular system was not stable enough for CAVH. The driving force for ultrafiltration is still the transmembrane pressure, but it is now generated by the blood pump instead of the patient's heart.

The factors that affect drug removal by hemofiltration are similar to those for hemodialysis. The differences are in the characteristics of the filters and the duration of the treatment. Hemofilters are more biocompatible than hemodialyzer filters and therefore can be used in a continuous fashion. This complicates drug dosing because the drug is being constantly removed from the patient. Another characteristic of the filter that is different is the pore size. The pore size in hemodialysis filters is relatively small and will not allow the passage of many drugs. In contrast, the pore size in hemofilters used for hemofiltration are much larger so that they will have a large K_{UF} and thus allow for ultrafiltration to occur at a lower TMP. The larger pore size also allows for many drugs to be removed that would not be removed by dialysis. Vancomycin is an important example of a drug that is not removed well by hemodialysis but is easily removed by CAVH or CVVH.

Drug removal by hemofiltration (CAVH or CVVH) is via convection. The factors that determine the rate of drug removal are the sieving coefficient and the UFR. The most important factor that is specific for a given hemofilter is the sieving coefficient. The ultrafiltration rate can be changed during the treatment of different patients, but the sieving coefficient is fairly constant. Table 182-2 lists the sieving coefficients

Table 182-2 Sieving Coefficients

Drug	Sieving Coefficient
Amikacin	0.88 ± 0.03
Amphotericin	0.40
Ampicillin	0.69 ± 0.21
Cefoperazone	0.27
Cefotaxime	0.51 ± 0.01
Ceftriaxone	0.71
Cefapirin	1.70 ± 0.49
Clindamycin	0.98
Cyclosporin A	0.00
Digoxin	0.96 ± 0.06
Erythromycin	0.37
Gentamicin	0.81 ± 0.02
Metronidazole	0.86 ± 0.03
Mezlocillin	0.68 ± 0.11
N-Acetyl procainamide	0.92 ± 0.02
Nafcillin	0.54 ± 0.12
Oxacillin	0.02
Phenobarbital	0.86 ± 0.01
Phenytoin	0.45 ± 0.06
Procainamide	0.86 ± 0.02
Theophylline	0.85 ± 0.01
Tobramycin	0.78 ± 0.06
Vancomycin	0.76 ± 0.06

for several common drugs. Because there are always new filters available on the market, these data must always be updated. The sieving coefficient for a particular patient and filter can always be determined by measuring the ultrafiltrate drug concentration (UF_x) and the plasma drug concentration (P_x). The sieving coefficient can be calculated as discussed previously. The clearance of the drug is the product of the sieving coefficient and the ultrafiltration rate.

$$C_x = (\sigma_x)(UFR)$$

The rate of drug removal is the product of the plasma concentration of the drug and the clearance.

$$\text{Drug removal rate} = (P_x)(C_x) = (P_x)(\sigma_x)(UFR)$$

As the drug is removed, the plasma concentration (P_x) will decrease, which will decrease the removal rate. Because the removal rate is directly proportional to the plasma concentration, it has first-order kinetics. The elimination rate constant for hemofiltration can be shown to be $(\sigma_x)(UFR)/V_d$. This calculation can be used as an approximation, but a more accurate elimination rate constant and half-life can be calculated from several plasma concentrations of the drug. Correct dosing amounts and time intervals can be calculated to give appropriate plasma concentrations of the drug.

For example, in the case of a 10 kg patient who needs to be dosed with amikacin, the desired peaks and troughs are 30 and 10 μg/ml, respectively. This patient is on CVVH with an UFR of 500 ml/hr (0.5 L/hr) and the sieving coefficient for amikacin is taken to be 0.9. The V_d of amikacin is approximately 0.25 L/kg body weight. Thus this patient will have a total V_d of 2.5 L. A loading dose of 75 mg (7.5 mg/kg) will give the expected peak of 30 μg/ml. Subsequent doses will need to be 50 mg (5 mg/ml) to increase the concentration from the trough of 10 μg/ml to a peak of 30 μg/ml. The dosing interval can be calculated from the first-order kinetics using $(\sigma_x)(UFR)/V_d$ as the elimination rate constant. This equation will be:

$$\text{Time interval} = \frac{\ln [C(t0)/C(T)]}{(\sigma)(UFR)/V_d}$$

where C(t0) is the peak concentration and C(T) is the trough concentration. The units for UFR and V_d must be kept in mind. If UFR is expressed as liters per hour and V_d is expressed as liters, then the time interval will be in hours. In this particular example the dosing interval would be 6.1 hours.

Several points need to be made regarding the approach to drug dosing in hemofiltration. First, the clearance rate of any drug is directly proportional to the UFR. Once the drug dosing amount and interval have been worked out, the UFR needs to remain constant. If there are changes in the UFR for whatever reason, the pharmacokinetic parameters of the drug will be affected. Second, because all of the pharmacokinetic parameters (e.g., V_d, protein binding, renal and hepatic clearances, and sieving coefficient) of a drug can constantly fluctuate because of the instability of the patient's condition, this approach must be regarded only as an estimate for dosing amounts and intervals. Thus plasma concentrations of drugs need to be monitored carefully when possible. Third, many drugs are used for which it is not possible to measure plasma concentrations. The best estimate for dosing in these situations is to follow the drug dosing guidelines for impaired renal function. The amount of creatinine clearance provided by the hemofiltration procedure can be estimated to be the UFR ($C_{cr} \cong$ UFR).

Hemodiafiltration

Hemodiafiltration is essentially CVVH with the addition of dialysate flowing through the filter to increase clearance. This technique is a recent advancement in hemofiltration and there are few published data on the effects of hemodiafiltration on drug dosing.

The mechanisms by which hemodiafiltration removes drugs are convection and diffusion. The process of convection is essentially the same as for hemofiltration and the process of diffusion is the same as that for hemodialysis. Since the filters used for hemodiafiltration are the same as those used for hemofiltration, the sieving coefficients are the same. The complicating factor is that it is difficult to predict the added effect of the dialysate flow. Until more data are available, the best way to assess this is to measure the drug concentration in the ultrafiltrate. This would contain the drug that was removed by convection (filtration) and the amount that was removed by diffusion (dialysis). This can be used to approximate the drug removal rate. Another approach is to measure timed plasma concentrations and estimate an elimination rate constant so that dosing intervals can be calculated to give the desired drug concentrations.

EXTRACORPOREAL MEMBRANE OXYGENATION

ECMO and the principles of drug administration in a patient receiving ECMO are discussed in Chapter 160. This section is limited to a discussion of the current understanding of drug behavior while a patient is receiving ECMO.

The literature evaluating the effects of ECMO on drug behavior is sparse. Several effects must be considered when determining whether the pharmacokinetics of a drug will be altered in ECMO. The drug is diluted because of the increased V_d contributed by the ECMO circuit. This plays a larger role in altering drug concentrations when a drug has a small V_d or when the patient is small in comparison to the circuit volume (i.e., a neonate).

Adsorption, or binding of drug to the circuit, is another factor to consider. It is known that some drugs will bind to circuit components, such as polyvinylchloride or silicone. If the binding is reversible, the effect is an increase in the V_d; if the binding is irreversible, the effect is increased drug clearance. An increase in both V_d and clearance may also be observed. Several investigators have attempted to determine how much drug is bound to the circuit, and they "prime" the circuit with that quantity of drug in an attempt to saturate the oxygenator membrane. This has been tried for both sedatives and analgesics with no well-documented success. Other investigators have studied the effect of new and used circuits on the adsorption of drug. It was found that used circuits adsorbed less drug. The practitioner must remember this when circuits are changed since drug concentrations may fall more rapidly when a new oxygenator is placed in the circuit, similar to when the patient is first started on ECMO. This can be seen most rapidly with sedatives and analgesics.

The mechanical forces generated by the ECMO pump may also have an effect. Proteins may be denatured in the circuit, and this will ultimately cause an increased clearance of drug. The other factors to consider when adjusting drug doses in ECMO and reviewing the literature relate to the patient. A study in neonates may not necessarily be applicable to large children. This is because neonates are initially dosed differently than larger children because of the immaturity of the neonate's renal and hepatic clearance mechanisms. The circuits used in neonatal ECMO are different than the circuits used in larger children. Numerous physiologic changes occur when a child receives ECMO that will also affect drug distribution, independent of the ECMO circuit. Hepatic and renal insufficiency as well as significant fluid accumulation and shifting will decrease clearance and increase V_d. The ECMO circuit is a small portion of the total picture.

The two areas of greatest research and interest are antibiotic and sedative/analgesic behavior during ECMO. For aminoglycosides and vancomycin, routine monitoring of plasma drug concentrations is recommended in all patients undergoing ECMO. According to the current literature, tobramycin is not sequestered by the ECMO circuit and the prolonged elimination half-life of tobramycin observed during ECMO therapy is a result of an increased V_d, not a change in drug clearance. Since gentamicin and tobramycin have similar pharmacokinetics, it is recommended that larger doses be given and that these doses may need to be given less frequently. This is especially true when ECMO patients have diminished renal function and may also need CVVH. Other antibiotics must be dosed according to age and renal and hepatic function.

Sedatives and analgesics pose the greatest prob-

lem since ECMO patients are rarely given paralytic agents because of the need for frequent neurologic examinations and the need for the patient to remain calm to avoid decannulation. Most ECMO centers report an increased need for sedatives and analgesics while the patient is receiving ECMO. The mechanism surrounding this is unclear, but it is most likely due to adsorption. However, as mentioned earlier, despite early claims that this was a saturable process, investigators have been unable to demonstrate saturation of the membrane. In addition, the silicone partition coefficient is very similar to the partition coefficient of lipids. Therefore drugs that are highly lipophilic, such as certain sedatives and analgesics, may not only adsorb to the membrane surface but may also be sequestered inside the silicone membrane matrix. This would constitute irreversible binding. Not to discount the effects of the oxygenator membrane, children on ECMO also experience significant tolerance of and dependence on analgesics and sedatives due to the high doses used and the duration of the ECMO treatment. This may actually be the reason for the need for increased doses, not the oxygenator interaction.

Dagan et al. studied morphine pharmacokinetics in neonates on and off ECMO and found the concentrations of morphine fell dramatically after the cessation of ECMO despite an unchanged morphine infusion rate. This was not related to changes in renal or hepatic function. The reduction of morphine serum concentrations was accompanied by a clinical picture of withdrawal. The authors do not have an explanation for the changes in pharmacokinetics but state the need for careful observation of these patients for withdrawal symptoms. Further research is needed to assess the changes in hepatic function on and off ECMO and to determine the source of changes in drug metabolism during ECMO.

ADDITIONAL READING

Arnold JH, Truog RD, Orav EJ, et al. Tolerance and dependence in neonates sedated with fentanyl during extracorporeal membrane oxygenation. Anesthesiology 73:1136-1140, 1990.

Bressolle F, Kinowski J-M, de la Coussaye JE, et al. Clinical pharmacokinetics during continuous haemofiltration. Clin Pharmacokinet 26:457-471, 1994.

Cogan MG, Garovoy MR, eds. Introduction to Dialysis. New York: Churchill Livingstone, 1985.

• Dagan O, Klein J, Bohn D, et al. Effects of extracorporeal membrane oxygenation on morphine pharmacokinetics in infants. Crit Care Med 22:1099-1101, 1994.

Dagan O, Klein J, Gruenwald C, et al. Preliminary studies of the effects of extracorporeal membrane oxygenator on the disposition of common pediatric drugs. Ther Drug Monit 15:263-266, 1993.

Golper TA. Drug removal during continuous hemofiltration or hemodialysis. Contrib Nephrol 93:110-116, 1991.

• Green TP. The effect of extracorporeal membrane oxygenation on the biodisposition of drugs. Curr Opin Pediatr 4:473-478, 1992.

Lee CC, Marbury TC. Drug therapy in patients undergoing haemodialysis: Clinical pharmacokinetic considerations. Clin Pharmacokinet 9:42-66, 1984.

Matzke GR. Pharmacotherapeutic consequences of recent advances in hemodialysis therapy. Ann Pharmacother 28:512-514, 1994.

Moller JC, Gilman JT, Kearns GL, et al. Effect of extracorporeal membrane oxygenation on tobramycin pharmacokinetics in sheep. Crit Care Med 20:1454-1458, 1992.

Reetze-Bonorden P, Bohler J, et al. Drug dosage in patients during continuous renal replacement therapy; pharmacokinetic and therapeutic considerations. Clin Pharmacokinet 24:362-379, 1993.

Vos MC, Vincent HH. Continuous hemodiafiltration: Predicting the clearance of drugs. Contrib Nephrol 93:143-145, 1991.

183 Opioid and Benzodiazepine Dependence

Lynn J. Banks · Christine A. Lindsay

BACKGROUND AND PATHOPHYSIOLOGY

Physiologic dependence has been demonstrated to occur in adult and pediatric patients when they are withdrawn from long-term opioid and benzodiazepine medications. The onset of symptoms is directly correlated with the rate of clearance of drug from the body. Since more medications with short durations of action, and therefore short half-lives, are now used in the PICU, increased numbers of patients are experiencing withdrawal symptoms and being diagnosed as being in withdrawal even before leaving the intensive care setting. In this chapter issues surrounding acute, nonaddictive drug dependence and the assessment and treatment of neuroadaptation will be discussed. The following definitions apply:

Tolerance is indicated by the need to increase the dose of a drug to achieve the same drug effect previously achieved with a lower dose. The rate at which tolerance develops depends on the pattern of use. If treatment is intermittent, it is possible to achieve adequate sedative and analgesic effects with standard doses of opioids and benzodiazepines for a longer period of time. However, if the drug is given continuously, significant tolerance can develop more quickly. Although the lethal dose is increased in tolerant individuals, death from respiratory depression is always a possibility. Tolerance to opioids largely disappears when withdrawal has been completed. Tolerance is not related to an increase in the rate of metabolism, but rather to alterations in receptor numbers and/or sensitivities.

Physiologic or physical dependence is a well-recognized phenomenon that occurs after regular drug use, sometimes in just a week. Classically, it is associated with opioid, benzodiazepine, and barbiturate administration. This form of dependence is defined as an altered physiologic state produced by regular, repeated administration of a drug and continued use of the drug is necessary to prevent withdrawal symptoms. Physiologic dependence can exist without any psychological dependence.

Psychological dependence is a syndrome in which the use of a drug is given a much higher priority than other behaviors that once had higher value (compulsive use). No sharp line separates psychological dependence from nondependent but recurrent drug use. Psychological dependence is often associated with the development of tolerance and physical dependence. Addiction can be used to describe a severe degree of drug dependence associated with extreme involvement with drug use. The term conveys a quantitative rather than a qualitative degree to which drug use pervades the total life activity of the drug "seeker" and the range of circumstances in which drug use controls the "seeker's" behaviors. These individuals are obsessed with securing a supply of drug and are more likely to relapse after withdrawal. By these criteria, anyone who is addicted would be considered psychologically dependent. However, not everyone who is drug dependent is addicted. When opioids and benzodiazepines are used appropriately in chronically ill patients, psychological dependence rarely occurs.

Drug abuse is the use, usually by self-administration, of any drug in a manner that deviates from the approved medical or social patterns within a given culture. The term conveys social disapproval, and it is not necessarily descriptive of any particular pattern of drug use or its potential adverse consequences.

Drug dependence, or psychological dependence, is often used to denote a behavioral syndrome, and physical dependence is used to refer to biologic changes that underlie withdrawal syndromes. To make this less confusing, the term "neuroadaptation" has been proposed as a substitute for physiologic de-

Table 183-1 Opioid Receptor Subtypes and Actions

Receptor Subtype	Effects of Agonist at Receptor	Drugs With Agonist Effects	Drugs With Antagonist Effects
Mu	Mu_1: Supraspinal analgesia, physical dependence Mu_2: Respiratory depression, inhibition of GI motility, bradycardia, sedation	Morphine, fentanyl, meperidine, codeine, methadone, hydromorphone, β-endorphins	Naloxone, naltrexone, pentazocine, nalbuphine
Kappa	Spinal analgesia, sedation, miosis, inhibition of antidiuretic hormone release	Morphine, pentazocine, butorphanol(?); nalbuphine has partial agonist effects	Naloxone
Delta	Analgesia, euphoria	Enkephalins	Naloxone
Sigma	Dysphoria, hallucinations, psychomotor stimulation	Pentazocine, butorphanol, nalbuphine; morphine has minimal effects	Naloxone

pendence. Physiologic dependence (neuroadaptation) is an agonist effect of opioids and benzodiazepines. Some degree of dependence can develop within 48 hours of continuous medication administration. Recent studies have shown a significant degree of drug withdrawal after only 5 days of continuous fentanyl administration. There is a high degree of cross-tolerance and cross-dependence among the opioids that act at the same receptor type, but there is little or no cross-tolerance among opioids that act selectively at different receptors. These receptor subtypes, along with the agents that act at each receptor, are listed in Table 183-1.

Mechanisms of Withdrawal
Opioids

Although opioid receptors are distributed widely throughout the brain and spinal cord, these receptors are more highly concentrated in a small nucleus within the brain stem called the locus ceruleus (LC). The LC consists almost entirely of neurons stimulated by norepinephrine (NE) and whose axons project widely throughout the brain. The adrenergic receptors within the LC, which are of the α_2-subtype, mediate inhibitory responses to recurrent LC collaterals and adrenaline input from the lower brain stem. Stimulation of the opiate receptors within the LC by morphine and endogenous opioid peptides has been demonstrated to slow the firing rate of the LC neurons and to block increases in neuronal LC substrate production normally demonstrated after a painful stimulus. Clonidine, an α_2-adrenergic antihypertensive drug, has also been shown to slow the firing of the

LC neurons by stimulating their α-noradrenergic "autoreceptors."

Opioid tolerance and neuroadaptation in animals are accompanied by tolerance of the LC neurons to the slowing effects of opioids but not of clonidine. When opioids are rapidly discontinued in the tolerant animal, the absence of exogenous opiates produces considerable acceleration of the LC firing and a large increase in LC activity and NE release. Anxiety, fear, increased heart rate, increased blood pressure, yawning, diarrhea, nausea, anorexia, insomnia, irritability, increased respiratory rate, restlessness, scratching, pupillary dilatation, and perspiration are some of the symptoms seen in man or primates when given drugs such as piperoxane or yohimbine that markedly activate the LC neurons.

Drugs that inhibit the synthesis of NE theoretically decrease the functional activity of the LC and thus will be useful for treating withdrawal symptoms. Clonidine has the most direct effect on the LC. Clonidine is able to produce the same blockade of LC neuronal activity seen with opioid administration but does not produce the same problems of opioid tolerance. It is a useful alternative to opioid administration without the opioid side effects. Unfortunately other agents have limited use because of their lack of specificity for the LC and adrenergic systems. Benzodiazepines are presumed to block the activity of the LC by interaction with the inhibitory γ-aminobutyric acid (GABA) system and GABA receptors on the pontine LC. These, in particular diazepam, also have an effect on opioid abstinence symptoms.

Recently a strong argument was made for the role

of the nucleus accumbens and selective dopamine-2 receptor effects on opiate withdrawal. In a series of experiments in morphine-treated rats, Harris and Aston-Jones demonstrated the ability of dopamine agonists to reduce somatic symptoms of withdrawal and the ability of dopamine antagonists (haloperidol or flupentixol) to reverse this effect (i.e., precipitate withdrawal symptoms). Reversal of this effect was seen with centrally acting dopamine antagonists but not peripherally acting dopamine antagonists. Although the nucleus accumbens may not be the major site for the initiation of opiate withdrawal symptoms, it may play an important role in regulating circuits that mediate somatic and aversive responses to the discontinuation of opiates. The common practice of using haloperidol to treat agitation in patients in the ICU may actually be precipitating withdrawal in some patients. Further work will need to be done to verify the clinical implications of this research.

Benzodiazepines

Although not as well studied in children in intensive care environments, several hypotheses have been developed to explain the mechanism of benzodiazepine withdrawal. Patrick et al. proposed the mechanism as a functional overactivity of the dopaminergic system, which develops in response to a pharmacologically induced increase in GABA-mediated neuroinhibition. Bergman et al. in 1991 proposed that the choreoathetotic movements observed in their patients were a result of withdrawal from the prolonged action of benzodiazepine agonism on cerebral GABA receptors.

Symptoms of Drug Withdrawal
General principles

Opioids and benzodiazepines with short durations of action tend to produce shorter, more intense abstinence syndromes, whereas those that are more slowly eliminated produce withdrawal syndromes that are prolonged but milder. Most of the literature addresses withdrawal symptoms in adult addicts or neonates born to addicted mothers. Little information is available on the symptoms of withdrawal in the child in the PICU. However, the general principles and time courses are similar and one would expect to observe the same symptoms.

Opioids

The character and severity of withdrawal symptoms when an opioid is discontinued depend on many fac-

tors, including the particular drug, the total daily dose used, the duration of use, and the health and personality of the patient. The total clinical picture of withdrawal involves two types of behavior: purposeful behavior, which is highly dependent on the observer and the environment and directed toward obtaining more drug, and nonpurposeful behavior, which is relatively independent of the observer and the environment.

For agonists such as morphine, nonpurposeful behavior such as lacrimation, rhinorrhea, yawning, and sweating appear within 8 to 12 hours after the last dose. About 12 to 14 hours after the last dose the patient may fall into a tossing, restless sleep that may last several hours but from which the patient awakens even more restless and miserable than before. As the syndrome progresses, additional signs and symptoms appear, including dilated pupils, anorexia, piloerection, irritability, and tremor. With morphine and heroin, the symptoms reach their peak at about 48 to 72 hours. As the syndrome reaches peak intensity, the patients exhibits increased irritability, insomnia, marked anorexia, violent yawning, severe sneezing, lacrimation, and coryza. Weakness and depression are pronounced. Nausea and vomiting are common, as are intestinal spasm and diarrhea. Heart rate and blood pressure are elevated. Marked chills, alternating with flushing and excessive sweating, are characteristic. Pilomotor activity resulting in waves of gooseflesh is prominent. Abdominal cramps and pain in the bones and muscles of the back and extremities are also seen, as are muscle spasms and kicking movements, from which the term "kicking the habit" was coined. The respiratory response to CO_2, which is decreased during opioid use, is exaggerated during withdrawal. Leukocytosis is common in adults and white cell counts above $14,000/mm^3$ can be seen. The failure of an individual to take food and water, combined with the nausea, vomiting, sweating, and diarrhea, results in dehydration, weight loss, ketosis, and alterations in acid-base balance. Rarely is the withdrawal syndrome life threatening, although seizures occur and occasionally cardiovascular collapse may occur. Administration of an opioid at any time in this process will dramatically and completely suppress the symptoms. The further the syndrome has progressed, the smaller the dose necessary to stop the symptoms. Without treatment, the symptoms last about 7 to 10 days.

The early abstinence syndrome, as previously characterized, may be followed by a protracted abstinence syndrome. During this period a number of physiologic values become subnormal. A period of hyposensitivity to the respiratory stimulant effects of CO_2 persists for many weeks after the exaggerated sensitivity of the early abstinence period subsides. Subtle behavioral changes occur, including the inability to tolerate stress, a poor self-image, and overconcern about discomfort.

Meperidine withdrawal occurs within about 3 hours of the last dose and reaches its peak within 8 to 12 hours, declining so that few symptoms are apparent at 4 to 5 days. Less diarrhea, nausea, and vomiting occur and the pupils may be less widely dilated. However, the muscle twitching, restlessness, and nervousness may be more intense than during morphine withdrawal.

Withdrawal in a newborn. Babies born to mothers who have been regularly receiving an opioid prior to delivery will be physically dependent. The signs of withdrawal include irritability and excessive and high-pitched crying, tremors, frantic sucking of fists, inability to nurse, hyperactive reflexes, increased respiratory rate, and increased stooling, sneezing, yawning, vomiting, and fever. These symptoms appear within the first day of life with maternal heroin use but may not appear for several days with methadone use. The intensity of withdrawal does not always correlate with the duration of maternal use or the dose. Concomitant withdrawal from sedatives or alcohol must always be considered. Withdrawal symptoms appear to be more severe in babies born to mothers on methadone than heroin. However, the methadone mothers are often provided better care and intervention, which help identify addiction prior to birth and to decrease the overall fetal mortality and distress. Some mothers are able to have their methadone dose gradually reduced during pregnancy to avoid fetal addiction. However, gradual reduction of the methadone dose and careful observation and monitoring in pregnant women are essential to prevent fetal in-utero withdrawal from opioids, which is potentially lethal.

Opioid antagonists

If an antagonist such as naloxone is given to someone dependent on opioids, a withdrawal syndrome develops within a few minutes and reaches its peak intensity within 30 minutes. Until some of the antagonist is eliminated, even large doses of previously used opioid may not suppress the syndrome. Partial suppression may be possible with very large doses of opioids, but this may lead to respiratory depression as the antagonist effects disappear. Depending on the dose of antagonist used, the abstinence syndrome can be more severe than when the opioid is simply discontinued, especially with longer acting narcotics.

Benzodiazepines

Adverse events associated with benzodiazepine use include paradoxical reactions. Euphoria, restlessness, hallucinations, and hypomanic behavior have all been reported with the use of low doses.

Abuse of and dependence on any of the benzodiazepines is possible. Withdrawal symptoms usually include temporary intensification of the problems that originally prompted their use (i.e., insomnia or anxiety). Dysphoria, irritability, sweating, unpleasant dreams, confusion, hallucinations, seizures, tremors, anorexia, and faintness or dizziness may also occur. As with opioids, drugs with longer half-lives will produce withdrawal symptoms that are less severe and occur later. Therefore the common use of midazolam in the PICU, with its short half-life, has prompted recognition of benzodiazepine withdrawal symptoms before the child is discharged to the floor service.

Tolerance to the sedating effects of benzodiazepines has also been reported in pediatric patients. Tolerance increases the amount of drug necessary to maintain adequate sedation. Children have been reported to awaken even after considerably larger doses than those recommended for initial sedation have been given. With intermittent dosing, it has also been postulated that agitation near the end of the dosing interval may actually be related to the onset of withdrawal in addition to the underlying anxiety and agitation that originally prompted the use of the sedative.

Movement disorders have been noted in infants and small children after opioid and benzodiazepine administration in the intensive care setting. Bergman et al. described these patients as having an encephalopathy characterized by dystonic posturing, choreoathetosis, and decreases in social interaction and visual attentiveness. Another report noted that a 10-week-old infant, who had received pentobarbital and diazepam for sedation, developed choreic movements of the trunk, extremities, and tongue 5 hours after the drugs were discontinued. After 8 days the movements slowly dissipated, with the tongue movements the last to resolve. The severity of these symptoms have often prompted extensive workups for neurologic disorders.

TECHNIQUE
Monitoring

Good clinical assessment skills are essential for monitoring for signs and symptoms of physiologic and psychological dependence. The intensive care nurse at the bedside must monitor for subtle clues indicative of withdrawal while continuing to serve as an advocate for patient comfort. Early recognition and management of withdrawal symptoms are imperative to quality care.

Many of the signs and symptoms associated with withdrawal are similar to those associated with pain or the agitation itself. These signs and symptoms persist despite absence of painful or noxious stimuli or at the point in the patient's disease process that pain is expected to diminish. The practitioner must be alerted to an increasing need for narcotics accompanied by any of the symptoms listed.

Withdrawal is not only extremely uncomfortable for the patient and anxiety provoking for the family, it may further complicate a patient's PICU course. The agitation accompanying withdrawal triggers the release of endogenous catecholamines and other stress hormones such as glucagon and corticosteroids that can lead to cardiovascular compromise. Attempts to withdraw ventilatory support may be disrupted by increasing O_2 consumption and CO_2 production. Withdrawal symptoms expend energy and calories needed for healing and may at times mimic the onset of sepsis.

Use of an objective assessment tool such as the Neonatal Abstinence Scoring Tool (NAST) may assist the caregiver in identifying the presence of withdrawal symptoms since it is easy to overlook these individual symptoms or attribute them to other causes. The NAST was developed in 1975 by Finnegan et al. to assess and manage the narcotic-addicted newborn (Table 183-2). This tool identifies behaviors consistent with withdrawal and assigns a score to each behavior. A score of 8 or greater is indicative of neonatal abstinence syndrome. Although the tool has not been validated for use in older children, it may provide an objective means of assessment for caregivers in the PICU setting.

Treatment
Nonpharmacologic treatment modalities

Many of the methods of treating withdrawal symptoms are consistent with the nonpharmacologic measures to

---

SYMPTOMS STRONGLY ASSOCIATED WITH WITHDRAWAL OF OPIOIDS AND/OR BENZODIAZEPINES

Central nervous system: Irritability, agitation, dysphoria, anxiety, insomnia, restlessness, high-pitched cry, dilated pupils, hallucinations, seizures

Cardiovascular: Tachycardia, hypertension

Musculoskeletal: Tremors with or without stimulation, myoclonic jerks, hyperreflexia, hypertonicity, choreic movements

Gastrointestinal: Diarrhea, nausea, vomiting, feeding intolerance, anorexia, weight loss

Integumentary: Diaphoresis, piloerection, flushing, pruritus, mottling, excoriation due to excess rubbing, skin temperature variation

Respiratory: Apnea, tachypnea, increased respiratory effort, "fighting" the ventilator

Other: Fever, yawning, impaired suck reflex, rhinorrhea, lacrimation, salivation, impaired social interaction, decreased visual attentiveness

---

promote comfort in the PICU patient. These interventions, when combined with protocols for decreasing opioid and benzodiazepine doses, may facilitate the management of withdrawal symptoms but should not be substituted for pharmacologic management.

Develop a trusting relationship with the patient. Establishing a rapport with or understanding of the behavioral patterns of the infant or child enables the caregiver to notice subtle clues that may otherwise be missed. The older child may respond to nonpharmacologic interventions with a more open, positive attitude if he or she feels a bond with the caregiver. Trust also fosters feelings of safety, especially in the absence of parents.

Reduce parental anxiety level. Infants and children are very sensitive to the anxiety level of their parents. An open, honest, and caring approach to the family can assist in reducing their stress level. Encourage parental presence and involvement in the child's care. Praise them for soothing, nurturing behaviors.

Fear of addiction is often a major concern to parents whose children are receiving narcotics for analgesia and/or sedation. Reassure the parents that nei-

Table 183-2   Neonatal Abstinence Scoring System*

Signs and Symptoms	Score	Signs and Symptoms	Score
Cry		Sweating	1
Excessive	2	Fever	1
Continuous	3	100-101° F	1
Sleep after feeding		>101° F	2
<1 hr	3	Mottling	1
<2 hr	2	Nasal stuffiness	1
<3 hr	1	Sneezing	1
Moro reflex		Nasal flaring	2
Hyperactive	2	Respiratory rate (breaths/min)	
Markedly hyperactive	3	>60	1
Tremors		>60 (retractions)	2
Mild disturbed	1	Excessive sucking	1
Moderate to severely disturbed	2	Poor feeding	2
Mild undisturbed	3	Regurgitation	2
Moderate to severely undisturbed	4	Projectile vomiting	3
Increased muscle tone	2	Stools	
Frequent yawning	1	Loose	2
Excoriation	1	Watery	3
Seizures	5		

*Modified from Finnegan LP, Kron RE, Connaughton JF Jr, Emich JP. Neonatal abstinence syndrome. Assessment and management. Addictive Dis 2:141-158, 1975.

ther they nor their child is responsible for the development of physiologic dependence and that psychological dependence rarely occurs with the appropriate use of these agents. Explain the physical basis for the physiologic dependence and communicate to them the PICU team's commitment to managing the withdrawal symptoms and to promoting the comfort of their child.

Provide an environment with minimal stimulation. The frequent and often noxious stimuli inherent in the PICU setting may exacerbate the symptoms of withdrawal. If at all possible keep overhead lighting to a minimum. Provide a darkened environment, especially at night, to promote normal sleep patterns. A small blanket or cloth tented over an infant's head may further diminish light stimuli. Lower the volume on the ventilator, monitor, and infusion pump alarms to an acceptable minimum so as not to startle the child. Minimize additional extraneous noise by partitioning or closing doors. Use a quiet, relaxed tone of voice when approaching the infant or child. Explain all procedures, interventions, and treatments in an age-appropriate manner. Most im-

portant, organize care to allow for maximum periods of undisturbed rest. For example, cluster assessments, medications, and interventions simultaneously.

Use distraction techniques. Distraction is a highly effective method of relieving mild anxiety in a child. If the infant or child is severely restless and anxious, however, distraction techniques may only worsen the distress. Offering a pacifier to a fretful infant will usually facilitate rest and comfort. Use of soothing, familiar music in the form of lullabies or tapes featuring the parents' voices may serve to divert the patient's attention and permit relaxation. If tolerated, age-appropriate toys or activities, including schoolwork, may distract the older child from the irritating symptoms of withdrawal.

Provide comfort measures or use relaxation techniques. Reposition the infant or child frequently to relieve pressure on bony prominences or muscle spasms. Promote comfort through the use of sheepskin or foam mattresses; use soft pillows, toys, or blankets to support extremities. Tactile stimulation in the form of cutaneous rubbing, gentle massage, or passive range of motion may enhance relaxation.

Hold and rock the infant or small child whenever possible; encourage cuddling with a favorite blanket or small toy. When placing the infant in a crib, swaddle him to minimize the motor tremors and jerking associated with withdrawal.

The older child may benefit from deep breathing exercises and guided imagery. Encourage the parent's participation in as many of these activities as possible to promote the infant's or child's level of comfort. In turn, this will enhance the parents' contribution to the well-being of their child.

Establish a routine. Provide for a good night's sleep. Get the child into a routine for going to bed and, if necessary, assist sleep with the use of a mild hypnotic such as pentobarbital or chloral hydrate. Provide for daily activities that will keep the child occupied and provide some sense of normalcy during their stay in the PICU. This routine, along with distraction, can be a useful strategy to eliminate some of the anxiety and fretfulness the child feels in the PICU environment and allows for transition to the inpatient, non-PICU setting.

Pharmacologic treatment modalities

Gradually decreasing doses. Patients who have received a continuous infusion of an opioid or benzodiazepine for longer than 5 days are believed to be more likely to develop withdrawal than those children who have received a shorter duration of the infusion. The appropriate steps for discontinuing these infusions have not been adequately studied in the PICU. The following is offered as a guideline, based on pharmacologic and pharmacokinetic considerations.

Begin decreasing the dose of either the opioid or benzodiazepine as soon as the agent is not physiologically indicated. If there is no need for analgesia, the dose of opioid can be lowered to a minimal level necessary to provide comfort. Decreases of 10% to 20% of the continuous infusion of either fentanyl or midazolam can be made approximately every 12 hours. This provides time for reassessment of the patient and the attainment of a new steady state before the next decrease in dose.

It is also recommended that a simultaneous decrease in both drugs be avoided. Adjust one agent first, then the other. For example, decrease midazo-

lam at 3:00 A.M. and 3:00 P.M. and fentanyl at 9:00 A.M. and 9:00 P.M. Assess the child during each phase and return to the previous infusion rate if signs and symptoms of withdrawal occur. If no symptoms occur, begin decreasing the dose again, but this time more slowly.

Numerous strategies have been tried by various practitioners in an attempt to alleviate the symptoms of withdrawal associated with opioids and benzodiazepines. Strategies have involved the use of other agents or similar agents with longer half-lives. Various pharmacologic options are available for the following drugs.

Clonidine. Clonidine is a centrally acting, α_2-adrenergic agonist that has been shown to inhibit and reverse the effects of stimulation at the LC. Morphine and clonidine seem to act on independent receptors within the LC; however, they have similar depressant effects on overall LC neuronal activity. By inhibiting the increased sympathetic outflow centrally with clonidine, the observed side effects of opioid withdrawal can be eliminated or minimized without having to add another opioid. The most common dosing schedule for clonidine is 3 to 5 μg/kg/dose given orally every 8 hours until the symptoms have stabilized, followed by a daily reduction in dose of 0.1 to 0.2 mg. For in-patients, high cumulative daily doses of clonidine are restricted because of its sedative and hypotensive properties. In outpatient programs 10 μg/kg/day is given in three divided doses. Limited data in newborns of methadone-addicted mothers demonstrated the efficacy of 1 μg/kg/dose of clonidine given orally every 6 hours in treating withdrawal symptoms. Doses may need to be individualized, and the drug must not be otherwise contraindicated because of its side effects. Clonidine transdermal patches have been studied in adults. Until more information is available regarding the use of transdermal clonidine patches in children, their use must be limited.

Methadone. Methadone is a longer acting opioid that can be used to treat iatrogenic opioid dependency in children. Dose for dose, methadone is considered to be equipotent to IV morphine. However, since methadone exhibits better oral bioavailability than morphine, the oral dose of methadone is one half to one third that of the oral dose of morphine. Some authors report success with doses of 0.1

mg/kg of methadone given enterally every 12 hours while gradually decreasing and eventually discontinuing chronic infusions of fentanyl and morphine. When signs of withdrawal abate, methadone can be decreased by 10% to 20% every week and discontinued after 4 to 6 weeks. Other authors state that methadone can be converted to an opioid equivalent and given every 6 hours. The total daily dose is decreased by increasing the dosage interval daily.

Morphine. Morphine is used for the same reasons as methadone administration. Although it has a shorter duration of action than methadone, most practitioners are more accustomed to using morphine. A fentanyl infusion can be converted to a daily morphine equivalent, and the morphine can be given as an intermittent, scheduled dose either intravenously or orally. The dosing interval will be partially determined by the total daily requirements of the patient, but it is given no less than every 4 to 6 hours. The dose is gradually reduced to the low end of the normal dosing range (i.e., 0.1 mg/kg/dose). The dosing interval is extended daily until the drug is given once daily and finally discontinued. This can be helpful if the child is still in pain.

Diazepam. Benzodiazepines are useful for the treatment of withdrawal symptoms based on their presumed interaction with the LC. Opioid withdrawal is purportedly based on increased sympathetic outflow from the LC, and benzodiazepines are presumed to block the activity of the LC by activating the inhibitory GABA receptor system. Therefore the use of benzodiazepines would be expected to block the somatic symptoms of withdrawal from an opioid analgesic. Diazepam is an ideal agent for this use because it is inexpensive and can be given every 6 to 8 hours because of its long duration of action. In addition, diazepam will provide for a gradual decrease in benzodiazepine serum concentrations and assist in the prevention of concomitant benzodiazepine withdrawal symptoms.

Only one study has assessed the use of diazepam for the treatment of heroin withdrawal in adolescents. In this study diazepam was found to be beneficial and reduced the duration of withdrawal symptoms. Since definitive studies are not available for the use of diazepam in treating or preventing withdrawal in the PICU, the following clinical practice guidelines are provided based on experience at Children's Medical Center of Dallas since 1992 (Fig. 183-1).

The most common circumstance in the PICU is a child who has no source of acute pain but has been receiving large doses of fentanyl and midazolam for comfort and sedation while being mechanically ventilated. Initially these patients are converted from IV midazolam to enterally administered diazepam. The conversion to diazepam is not to achieve equipotent doses but rather to obtain a dose of diazepam that will produce similar sedation and comfort for the patient. At our institution using a dose of 0.4 to 0.8 mg/kg/day divided every 6 to 8 hours has been successful depending on the amount of midazolam being administered. The midazolam infusion is decreased by one third 1 hour after the second or third dose of enteral diazepam is administered. The infusion is decreased by another third after the third or fourth dose, and the infusion is discontinued after the fifth or sixth dose of enteral diazepam. The diazepam is usually given every 6 hours except in infants younger than 6 months of age who do not metabolize diazepam as rapidly. These children can be given doses every 8 hours. It may be necessary to give young infants a higher dose of diazepam to control sedation prior to decreasing the dose because of the increased fat to body mass ratio and redistribution of drug, which makes less drug available to the CNS.

Once the child has been converted to enteral diazepam, fentanyl can be decreased incrementally or stopped before or shortly after extubation. The oral or nasogastric dosing interval of diazepam is increased every 2 to 3 days; for example, 2 mg every 6 hours to 2 mg every 8 hours to 2 mg every 12 hours to 2 mg every 24 hours, after which diazepam is discontinued. If the child is uncomfortable or exhibits signs and symptoms of withdrawal at any time during this process, return to the previous dose and increase the interval at a slower rate.

In children who have not received prolonged infusions of midazolam or concomitant opioid infusions, midazolam and fentanyl may be decreased over a 24-hour period while observing for withdrawal symptoms before discontinuing the infusion. Alternatively, midazolam and fentanyl infusions may be discontinued and the patient given 1 or 2 days of oral diazepam. Each patient will have different medication requirements.

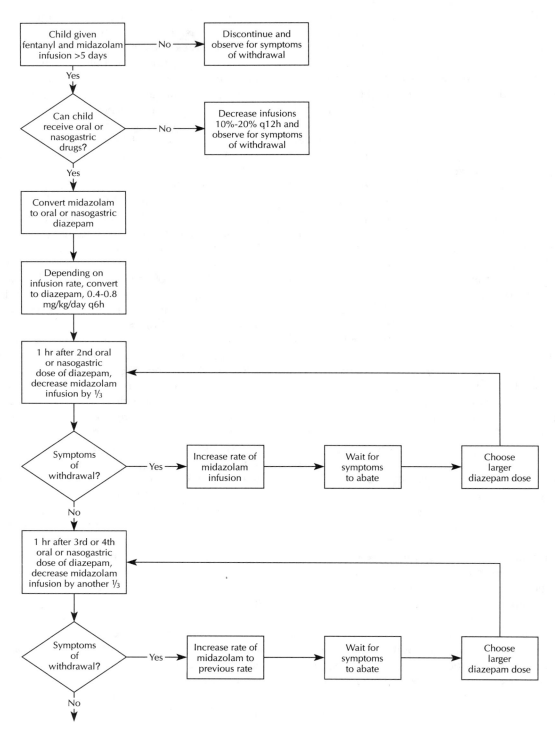

Fig. 183-1 Flow diagram for converting to enteral diazepam and gradually decreasing opioid and benzodiazepine doses to prevent withdrawal symptoms.

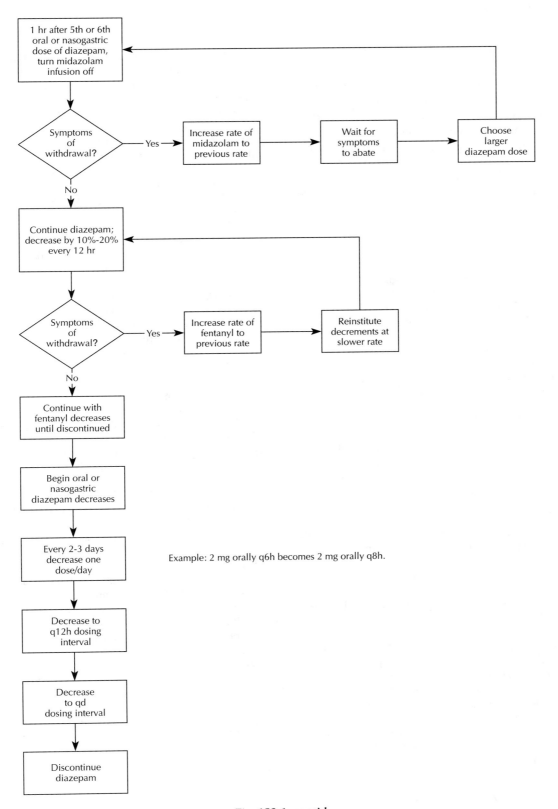

Example: 2 mg orally q6h becomes 2 mg orally q8h.

Fig. 183-1, cont'd

CURRENT RESEARCH AND FUTURE CONSIDERATIONS

A growing number of practitioners are diagnosing withdrawal and using different pharmacologic strategies to manage the problem. The most immediate need is for an objective measurement scale for the diagnosis and monitoring of these patients. When all centers diagnose the condition in the same, objective fashion, sound, scientific strategies for reducing the severity and duration of symptoms can be implemented.

ADDITIONAL READING

Aghajanian GK. Tolerance of locus coeruleus neurones to morphine and suppression of withdrawal response by clonidine. Nature 276:186-188, 1978.

Albeck JH. Withdrawal and detoxification from benzodiazepine dependence: A potential role for clonazepam. J Clin Psychiatry 48(Suppl 10):43-48, 1987.

Ashton H. Guidelines for the rationale use of benzodiazepines: When and what to use. Drugs 48:25-40, 1994.

• Bergman I, Steeves M, Burckart G, Thompson A. Reversible neurologic abnormalities associated with prolonged intravenous midazolam and fentanyl administration. J Pediatr 119:644-649, 1991.

Broome ME, Lillis PP, McGahee TW, Bates T. The use of distraction and imagery with children during painful procedures. Oncol Nurs Forum 19:499-502, 1992.

Cami J, de Torres S, San L, Solé A, Guerra D, Ugena B. Efficacy of clonidine and of methadone in the rapid detoxification of patients dependent on heroin. Clin Pharmacol Ther 38:336-341, 1985.

Charney DS, Kleber HD. Iatrogenic opiate addiction: Successful detoxification with clonidine. Am J Psychiatry 137:989-990, 1980.

Dossey B. Awakening the inner healer. Am J Nurs 91:30-34, 1991.

Finnegan LP, Kron RE, Connaughton JF Jr, Emich JP. Neonatal abstinence syndrome: Assessment and management. Addictive Dis 2:141-158, 1975.

Gold MS, Byck R, Sweeney DR, Kleber HD. Endorphin-locus coeruleus connection mediates opiate action and withdrawal. Biomedicine 30:1-4, 1979.

Gold MS, Pottash C, Sweeney DR, Kleber HD. Opiate withdrawal using clonidine: A safe, effective, and rapid nonopiate treatment. JAMA 243:343-346, 1980.

Harris GC, Aston-Jones G. Involvement of D_2 dopamine receptors in the nucleus accumbens in the opiate withdrawal syndrome. Nature 371:155-157, 1994.

Harris, JM, Ackerman V, Eigen H. Use of midazolam infusions in the pediatric ICU. In Vinik HR, ed. Midazolam Infusion and Intensive Care. Princeton: Excerpta Med, 1989, pp 67-72.

• Hershey L, Weintraub M. Easing morphine withdrawal in children. Drug Therapy 10:57-59, 1980.

Inturrisi CE, Verebely K. Disposition of methadone in man after a single oral dose. Clin Pharmacol Ther 13:923-930, 1972.

Jaffe JH. Drug addiction and drug abuse. In Gilman AG, Rall TW, Nies AS, Taylor P, eds. The Pharmacologic Basis of Therapeutics, 8th ed. New York: MacMillan, 1990, pp 522-573.

Jaffe JH, Martin WR. Opioid analgesics and antagonists. In Gilman AG, Rall TW, Nies AS, Taylor P, eds. The Pharmacologic Basis of Therapeutics, 8th ed. New York: MacMillan, 1990, pp 485-521.

Lennane KJ. Treatment of benzodiazepine dependence. Med J Aust 144:594-597, 1986.

• Levy M, Spino M. Neonatal withdrawal syndrome: Associated drugs and pharmacologic management. Pharmacotherapy 13:202-211, 1993.

Litt IF, Colli AS, Cohen MI. Diazepam in the management of heroin withdrawal in adolescents: Preliminary report. J Pediatr 78:692-696, 1971.

Lloyd-Thomas AR, Booker PD. Infusion of midazolam in pediatric patients after cardiac surgery. Br J Anaesth 58:1109-1115, 1986.

Lopez A, Rebollo J. Benzodiazepine withdrawal syndrome after a benzodiazepine antagonist, Crit Care Med 18:1480-1481, 1990.

Patrick SJ, Snelling LK, Ment LR. Infantile chorea following abrupt withdrawal of diazepam and pentobarbital therapy. Clin Toxicol 31:127-132, 1993.

Pederson C. Effect of imagery on children's pain and anxiety during cardiac catheterization. J Pediatr Nurs 10:365-374, 1995.

Rosen D, Rosen K. Midazolam infusion in the pediatric ICU. In Vinik HR, ed. Midazolam Infusion for Anesthesia and Intensive Care. Princeton: Excerpta Med, 1989, pp 62-66.

• Sury MRJ. Acute benzodiazepine withdrawal syndrome after midazolam infusions in children. Crit Care Med 17:301-302, 1989.

• Tobias JD, Schleien L, Haun SE. Methadone as treatment for iatrogenic narcotic dependency in pediatric intensive care unit patients. Crit Care Med 18:1292-1293, 1990.

• Tobias JD, Rasmussen GE. Pain management and sedation in the pediatric intensive care unit. Pediatr Clin North Am 41:1269-1292, 1994.

XXV
Medical Imaging

184 Plain Films and Contrast Studies

Michael W. Stannard · Marcia A. Pritchard

BACKGROUND

Portable radiographs in the PICU are more difficult to take and to interpret than are films taken in the radiology department. The radiographic technician frequently must negotiate confined spaces and bulky life support equipment to obtain radiographs of patients who often cannot move or cooperate. Radiographs are frequently made at shorter tube-film distances than are usual in the radiology department, resulting in image magnification or distortion compared with standard films. With the standard posteroanterior chest film, for instance, the patient is erect and the heart is closest to the film with minimal magnification. The portable radiograph is usually anteroposterior and the patient supine or semirecumbent so that films of the same patient will show a larger cardiac silhouette. In the supine position the weight of the abdominal viscera pushes the diaphragm cranially so that the lungs are less well inflated and more difficult to assess.

Invaluable as radiographs are in the assessment of the PICU patient, their benefit to the patient depends on interpretation based on adequate clinical information. It is helpful if the requesting physician can formulate specific questions to be addressed by the radiographic study. Since there is more information to be taken into account than is feasible on most request forms, optimal results are usually obtained when PICU staff and radiologist meet to review films together.

With the wide range of imaging techniques now available, it is as difficult for the clinician to keep up to date with available diagnostic options as it is for the radiologist to be knowledgeable about advances in PICU medicine. Much time can be saved by consulting with the radiologist as to the best manner of investigating a specific problem. Would a decubitus film answer this problem? Is a lateral film preferable? Which contrast would be best?

INDICATIONS AND TECHNIQUE
Chest Radiograph

Since the anteroposterior chest film is the most common film taken in the PICU, it is worthwhile to know how to assess it technically.

Film density. Adequate penetration has been achieved if the outlines of the vertebral bodies and disc spaces behind the heart and mediastinum can be seen. A lighter film will not show lobar collapse behind the heart. A film that is much darker will obscure the more subtle shadowing created by lung disease.

Inflation. Merely counting ribs that can be seen above the diaphragm is an insensitive method of assessing lung inflation. Instead, the intercostal spaces need to be observed. If the ribs converge laterally in an otherwise normal chest, underinflation is likely. In a well-inflated hemithorax the ribs tend to be parallel, with the intercostal spaces at least 1½ times the width of adjacent ribs (Fig. 184-1). Underinflation results in loss of lung volume with crowding of lung markings, which can be easily confused with collapse or pneumonia. A minute spent manually ventilating a ventilator-dependent patient with an anesthesia bag to produce well-inflated lungs for the radiology technologist can be worth an hour of discussion about shadows on an underinflated film.

Rotation. Rotation distorts mediastinal and cardiac anatomy, often obscuring at least one lung and producing density differences between the lungs that can hamper interpretation. In adults measuring the distances between the medial ends of the clavicles and the trachea (assuming that the trachea is not displaced) is considered reliable. This will also apply to older children and adolescents. In neonates and infants, however, the rib cage is much more flexible, and the upper chest may be straight while the lower chest is not. A much more useful rule is to compare the lengths of anterior ribs that project over the lung fields on both sides. At any given level the anterior rib length needs to be the same on both sides. If much more rib can be observed on one side than the other in a structurally normal chest, it is usually because the chest is rotated to the other side (Fig. 184-2). This rule has the advantage in that it can be applied to all levels of the chest.

Assessment of the lungs

The plain radiograph displays four radiographic densities: water, fat, air, and bone. It is important (and chastening) to realize that almost the entire spectrum of pulmonary disease is expressed radiographically by the superimposition of water density on air density. In the normal lung the water-density pulmonary vessels and bronchial walls stand out in contrast to the air-density alveoli. It follows that the lung fields can exhibit a limited range of water densities, and these are usually not specific. It is for this reason that clinical correlation is necessary to make an informed judgment of the likely cause of any given shadow within the lungs.

Are the abnormal densities streaky, nodular, or patchy? Are they associated with loss of volume indicated by crowding of ribs, displacement of mediastinum, or crowding of fissure and pulmonary vessels, or are they associated with increased lung volume? Are the changes bilateral or unilateral? Bacte-

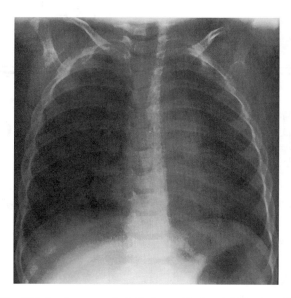

Fig. 184-1   Asymmetric inflation with the right lung well inflated and the left lung not. The right ribs are more horizontal than the left and the intercostal spaces wider.

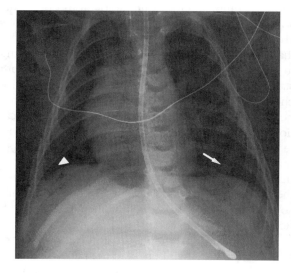

Fig. 184-2   Chest rotation. The upper chest is mildly rotated to the right with more marked rotation of the lower chest. Much more of the anterior ribs is visible on the left (arrow) than on the right (arrowhead).

rial pneumonias tend to be unilateral and lobar in distribution, although they can become bilateral later. Contusion is often unilateral. Bronchial occlusions by masses or foreign bodies are usually unilateral. Vascular processes such as increased pulmonary blood flow and pulmonary edema are usually bilateral, as is the perihilar shadowing of viral pneumonias and acute respiratory distress syndrome (ARDS).

The more advanced the patient's disease the greater the likelihood of multiple superimposed pathologic processes such as aspiration, pulmonary edema, pneumonia, ARDS, and pulmonary collapse. It is usually impossible to distinguish acute from chronic disease on a single film, and it is worth the trouble to track down those elusive previous films or at the very least check the reports for comparison. The sudden appearance of a lobar density in a previously well patient often implies lung collapse; the gradual evolution of the same density over days in a febrile patient is often due to a pyogenic pneumonia; the gradual development of the identical lung shadow over weeks suggests a chronic process such as tuberculous infection or aspiration; and the same shadow present since birth implies a congenital process such as lobar sequestration or bronchogenic cyst.

The same linear streaky shadowing radiating from the hila in an acutely sick patient may be pneumocystis pneumonia; in a patient with congestive heart failure, pulmonary edema; or in the chronically breathless patient, chronic pneumonitis. The patchy perihilar shadowing associated with pneumonia or near-drowning is distinguished only by time from that of ARDS, which is frequently superimposed.

Accumulations of air or fluid within the pleural space may be difficult to assess in the PICU patient who cannot move. On the posteroanterior radiograph of an erect patient made in the radiology department, fluid usually layers laterally and inferiorly and air often rises to the lung apex. On the anteroposterior portable film air will frequently loculate anteriorly and fluid posteriorly and can accumulate in surprising quantities before becoming evident by separating the lung from the chest wall laterally. The smaller the child the greater the relative effect of surface tension and the more likely loculation of air or fluid in non-gravity-dependent sites.

The cross-table lateral film (patient remains supine and the x-ray beam is horizontal) can be useful but superimposes the hemithoraces so that collections cannot be lateralized. If the patient can be rotated into the decubitus position, much more specific information can be obtained.

The lateral decubitus film is described by the side of the patient next to the bed or table. In the left lateral decubitus film the patient lies on the left side.

In the decubitus film four valuable features can be used for diagnostic purposes:

1. The dependent-lung is compressed by abdominal viscera and becomes underinflated. This can be useful in identifying persistent overinflation due to foreign body, lobar emphysema, or pneumothorax.
2. The uppermost lung is relieved of abdominal visceral compression and becomes relatively overinflated. Areas of partial collapse may become reaerated. Basal lung lesions are better visualized.
3. Pleural fluid gravitates medially in the upper hemithorax where it is difficult to see and laterally in the dependent hemithorax where a water-density layer adjacent to the rib cage may provide the best indication of the volume of a mobile effusion.
4. Air rises upward in the upper hemithorax and may become visible between parietal and visceral pleura at the lateral chest wall, whereas it may not be seen in the supine film.

Layering, dependent fluid in the decubitus film is only visible if air contrast is afforded by adjacent aerated lung. If a hemithorax is opaque due to fluid, pulmonary collapse, or pneumonia, the combined water densities are indistinguishable. Ultrasonography or CT are thus necessary to assess the volume and distribution of pleural fluid.

The heart on the anteroposterior supine film is larger in relation to the rib cage than on the standard posteroanterior department film. In children in the first 5 years of life, and sometimes beyond, the thymus blends with the cranial surface of the heart and may extend to the diaphragm. Clear distinction of thymus from heart is impossible. The well-known "thymic wave" and "sail" signs are produced by the normal thymus but give no clue to the total contribution of the thymus to the cardiothymic shadow in the anteroposterior (or posteroanterior) film.

Analysis of cardiac shapes in the diagnosis of chamber enlargement and specific heart disease is unreliable, especially since cardiac lesions are often multiple. The present-day availability of ECG and echocardiography makes such radiographic analysis moot in most cases. Valuable information about heart disease can be accumulated if the observer can determine:

1. Is the heart enlarged and are there any changes from previous studies?
2. Is the heart located within the right or left hemithorax?
3. Are upper abdominal viscera lateralized? (On which side is the major lobe of the liver and on which side is the stomach?)
4. Is the pulmonary vasculature increased, normal, symmetric, or asymmetric? (Undervascularity is difficult to read.)
5. On which side is the aortic arch? The lowermost trachea on a straight film bows away from the aortic arch. A right aortic arch in the presence of congenital heart disease is almost always associated with tetralogy of Fallot or pulmonary atresia with ventricular septal defect. It is also less commonly seen in association with tricuspid atresia, transposition of the great vessels, and truncus arteriosus.

All but the largest pericardial effusions are difficult to detect on a chest radiograph. If suspected, an echocardiogram is diagnostic.

A lateral film of the chest is of good quality if the posterior curvatures of the ribs can be seen overlapping each other behind the spine. If one set of ribs is distinct from the other, the lateral film is rotated. The lateral film of the chest shows the heart separated from thymus. The anteroposterior cardiac diameter seen in the lateral projection is accounted for only by the heart and can reliably be compared with the anteroposterior diameter of the chest to assess heart size. In small children the proportion of heart to anteroposterior diameter can be up to 60% and yet be quite normal. In older children this drops to 50%. If the heart shadow overlaps the spine in the lateral projection in a normally shaped chest, it is usually because of cardiac enlargement or pericardial effusion.

The lateral film is invaluable in assessing pulmonary inflation. Quite a large lung volume lies below the outline of the diaphragm shown on the anteroposterior film and is mostly in the posterior costophrenic sulcus (Fig. 184-3). Pneumonia, atelectasis, and fluid are common in this dependent location in the supine PICU patient and may not be visible on the anteroposterior film.

In the normal patient breathing without assistance the leaves of the diaphragm are convex cranially. If those leaves become flat or inverted, there is a pathologic process. Overinflation is more readily detected on the lateral than on the anteroposterior film. Air trapping is most commonly due to bronchiolitis or re-

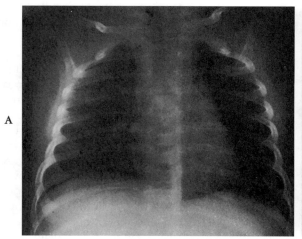
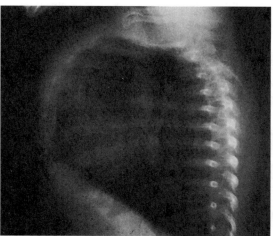

A **B**

Fig. 184-3 **A,** Anteroposterior film shows normal lungs that appear mildly overinflated. **B,** Lateral film shows how much of the lung lies below the highest part of the diaphragm. The diaphragm is flat. There is severe overinflation.

active airways disease. Any cause of reduced lung compliance can cause overinflation, however, and it is commonly seen in viral pneumonia, pulmonary edema, and major pulmonary overperfusion due to intracardiac left-to-right shunts. The three conditions can coexist and be impossible to distinguish. Lobar collapse and pneumonia behind the heart are often best seen on the lateral film, and similar processes involving the middle lobe or lingula, which can be subtle on the anteroposterior film, may be obvious on the lateral projection.

The lateral film can show the pulmonary hila well when they are obscured on the anteroposterior film by a large cardiothymic shadow. Large pulmonary vessels can be recognized in left-to-right shunts, and patchy shadowing with loss of anatomic definitions at the hila is common in the presence of perihilar pneumonia or pulmonary edema. Gas-containing bowel in the chest due to Morgagni and hiatus hernias, which may not be distinguishable on the anteroposterior film, are clearly distinguished on the lateral film. Masses or vascular rings compressing the

trachea or esophagus can be detected on the lateral film, especially if there is air in the esophagus. Such findings should prompt a contrast study of the esophagus (Fig. 184-4).

Location of devices

One of most common indications for a PICU chest film is to monitor the location of the tip of the endotracheal tube since it is difficult to assess clinically. The commonly preferred position is with the tip between the thoracic inlet and above the carina. Since the position of the endotracheal tube depends on head position with flexion of the neck to enable the endotracheal tube to pass down the trachea, extension of the neck elevation of the tube and lateral rotation of the head tend to direct the tip toward the opposite mainstem bronchus. For reproducible assessment of endotracheal tube position, the head needs to be in a standard position for radiography. Placing the patient's head straightforward in the neutral position without flexion, extension, or rotation is the preferred standard.

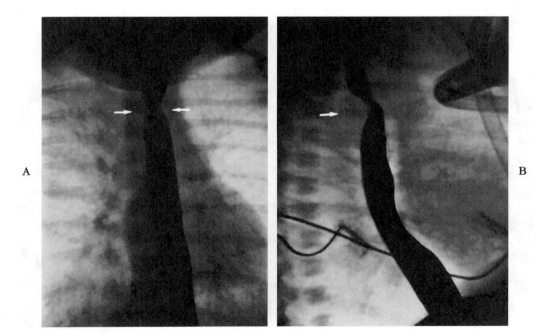

Fig. 184-4 Anteroposterior **(A)** and lateral **(B)** views of the barium-filled esophagus in a newborn with severe respiratory distress relieved by endotracheal intubation. The extrinsic compression at the lateral and posterior aspects of the esophagus (arrows) caused by a double aortic arch would have been difficult to show other than with fluoroscopy in the radiology department.

Radiographs are similarly used to check the position of orogastric and nasogastric tubes. It must be realized that the esophagogastric junction is significantly below the level of the diaphragm in infants and that the tip of a feeding tube can be below the left leaf of the diaphragm and yet not in the stomach, with consequent diminished effectiveness in decompressing the stomach and increased likelihood of regurgitation of feedings delivered into the distal esophagus.

Difficulty is sometimes experienced in distinguishing the feeding tube looped in the stomach from one that lies in the duodenum. If in doubt, a cross-table lateral film readily distinguishes the posterior and retroperitoneal tube in the duodenum from the more anterior tube coiled in the stomach.

Radiographs are commonly obtained after insertion of chest tubes for the relief of pneumothorax and the drainage of effusions. It is not always easy to advance the chest tube in the desired direction, and the anteroposterior film of the chest may not explain failure of fluid or air to resolve (Fig. 184-5). In this situation a lateral film, especially with radiopaque markers to distinguish different tubes, can be invaluable.

Patients frequently return from cardiac surgery with a multiplicity of tubes, the courses of which may be difficult to distinguish on an anteroposterior film alone. A mediastinal tube may look like a medial chest tube. Percutaneous manometer lines may not only enter the heart through the atrial appendages but also through the lower lobe pulmonary veins and even through the anterior wall of the right ventricle.

Finally, internal jugular and subclavian venous catheters normally lie with their tips in the superior vena cava. Catheter tips at the tricuspid value are undesirable, and misplaced higher catheters may pass into the contralateral subclavian vein (Fig. 184-6) or internal jugular vein. They may also lie in the azygos vein or may perforate the wall of a vein (Fig. 184-7).

Abdominal Radiographs

Abdominal radiographs of PICU patients are usually even more difficult to interpret than chest radiographs. Normal patients demonstrate a variety of findings. The sick patient on nasogastric suction with no normal stimulus to bowel function can be expected to have an abnormal gas pattern. With the added effects of electrolyte imbalance, trauma, and surgery with possible bowel resection and anastomoses, interpretation of radiographs can be challenging. As with the chest radiograph, clinical correlation can be critical. What type of trauma was involved? What did the CT show? What was found at surgery and what procedures were performed? Is there a history of ab-

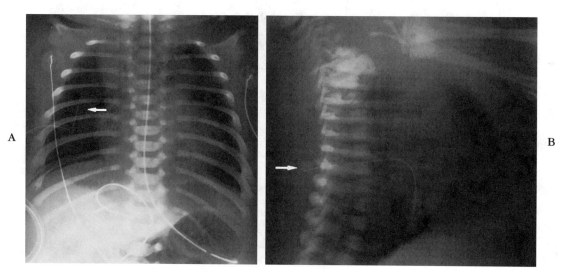

A

B

Fig. 184-5 **A,** Anteroposterior film shows a chest tube on the right (arrow) that did not relieve a pneumothorax. **B,** Lateral film shows the chest tube lying in the soft tissues of the chest wall (arrow). It is entirely extrapleural.

dominal disease? Have there been prior operations? What disease is present elsewhere and what therapy is the patient receiving?

The natural radiographic contrast produced by air is invaluable in revealing the patency and distention

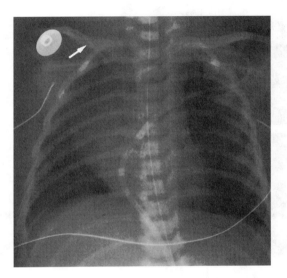

Fig. 184-6   Left subclavian venous catheter with its tip in the right subclavian vein (arrow).

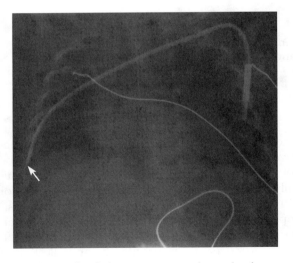

Fig. 184-7   Left subclavian venous catheter that has perforated the superior vena cava and lies in the right pleural space (arrow).

of bowel but is subject to limitations of which the interpreter should be aware. In the first few months of life it is usually impossible to distinguish colon from small bowel on the plain film. Only later do the valvulae conniventes of small bowel and haustra of large bowel develop, making distinction possible. Nasogastric suction, by preventing air from entering intestine, can mask obstruction and other causes of dilated bowel.

Assessment of the abdomen

The gasless abdomen may in itself be an indication of disease and can be seen with severe vomiting and diarrhea in gastroenteritis and in early appendicitis. It may be seen in patients with cerebral depression in whom swallowing is impaired.

The analysis of dilated bowel loops first involves deciding whether they are localized and asymmetric or generalized. Gastroenteritis and paralytic ileus tend to produce generalized and symmetric distention of bowel. Obstruction and local ileus in the vicinity of an abscess or appendicitis tend to produce a pattern of dilation, which is greater in some areas than others. Gastric dilation is seen in pyloric stenosis and gastric volvulus. It can also be seen in duodenal obstruction when the accumulation of fluid immediately proximal to the point of obstruction will mask its level. In distal small bowel obstruction the small gut will be dilated relative to the large gut. In colonic obstruction both large and small bowel are dilated. Generalized dilation of bowel as a result of obstruction can be indistinguishable from ileus in the early stages. Severe distention limited to the colon may be seen in the toxic megacolon, which can complicate various forms of colitis. Dilation of the transverse colon alone may be seen in pancreatitis. Clinical correlation and a knowledge of the quality of the bowel sounds are vital.

When visible, abnormal calcifications in the abdomen may provide vital clues in the acutely ill patient. An appendicolith in the right lower quadrant is diagnostic of appendicitis. Dense, irregular, toothlike calcifications in the female pelvis are characteristic of the ovarian teratodermoid. A careful search must be made for radiopaque gallstones or renal calculi since they may be obscured by bowel content. Ingested materials may be radiopaque. A delayed plain film is useful in showing movement within bowel of an intraluminal density.

If abdominal radiographs are difficult to interpret,

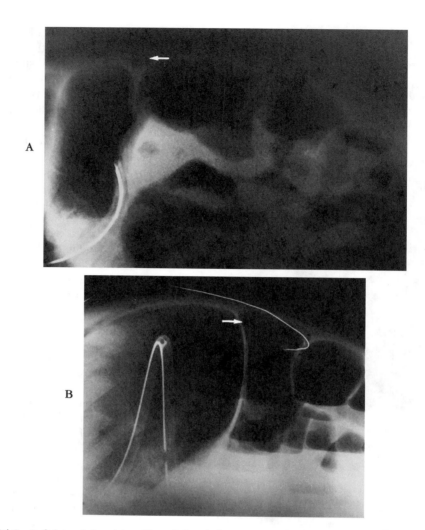

Fig. 184-8 Left lateral decubitus film of the abdomen (**A**) and cross-table lateral (supine) film (**B**) showing a small triangle of free intraperitoneal air (arrow). Recently the patient underwent laparotomy for meconium ileus.

further views can be made with a horizontal beam. These radiographs may either be made with the patient supine (cross-table lateral film) or in the decubitus position (labeled left or right, depending which side the patient lies on). These films are essential to show air-fluid levels and are the easiest way to confirm the presence of free intraperitoneal air.

The cross-table lateral film involves the least disturbance to the patient but superimposes large and small bowel. Free air is seen as a triangular collection between circular bowel loops (Fig. 184-8). In the left lateral decubitus film (left side down) free air can most readily be recognized at the left flank or between the lateral abdominal wall and the right lobe of the liver. Although free air in the abdomen usually follows perforation of bowel, air can persist for 10 days or longer following surgery, masking postoperative perforation. If in doubt, surgical consultation and repeat films are indicated. An increasing volume of free air is considered to be an indication of perforation until proved otherwise.

Displacement of air-containing bowel loops can give useful information about larger abdominal masses. The most common is a distended bladder that is seen as a soft tissue mass arising in the pelvis. Such an appearance must prompt clinical examination and review of the causes of urinary retention or a nonfunctioning bladder catheter. Major enlargement of the liver and spleen will displace bowel; renal and adrenal masses and major lymphadenopathy can produce a similar effect. The appearance of a soft tissue mass in the presence of a ventriculoperitoneal shunt raises the question of a CSF pseudocyst. A soft tissue mass descending from the porta hepatis is often a distended gallbladder, a common finding in patients on total parenteral nutrition. A soft tissue mass in the left epigastrium is commonly a fluid-distended stomach. Finally, a soft tissue density in the periphery of the abdomen with crowding of gas-containing bowel in the central abdomen, especially if those bowel loops are separated from each other, is a typical finding in ascites.

In the PICU patient who cannot be moved to the radiology department the next step in eliminating the cause of an unexpected mass or intra-abdominal fluid is ultrasonography. Since ultrasound cannot pass through air, its role in assessing bowel disease is limited. It may be useful, however, in detecting thickening of bowel wall and inflammatory masses involving bowel.

Location of devices

Plain films of the abdomen are essential in monitoring the positions of CSF drainage catheters, vascular catheters, and surgical drains. Percutaneous jejunostomy and gastrostomy tubes may migrate and can provoke obstruction.

Contrast Studies

Contrast studies may be subdivided into those performed in the PICU itself and those necessitating transfer of the patient to the radiology department. Contrast studies performed in the PICU using serial radiographs are rarely satisfactory. The amount of contrast to be used to establish catheter patency or leak from a viscus, for instance, is difficult to gauge when the study is performed blindly. Too much contrast may obscure more than it reveals. The occasional use of water-soluble contrast to opacify an otherwise invisible intravascular catheter or to confirm the appropriate location of a jejunostomy feeding tube are worthwhile. More ambitious studies in the PICU are feasible if there is mobile C-arm fluoroscopy equipment. For most studies, however, the journey to the radiology department is usually worth the

trouble, and prior discussion with the radiologist who will perform the study is valuable in helping minimize the length of the patient's stay away from the PICU.

The three types of contrast agent available are air, barium, and water-soluble compounds of iodine. Leak of air from bowel will reveal perforation, air in the portal vein may follow necrotizing enterocolitis, and air within the mediastinum can indicate the presence of an esophageal leak. It is now common practice to use air in the diagnosis and pneumatic reduction of ileocolic intussusception.

Barium is an excellent contrast since it is radiodense and chemically inert, but it can only be used in the intact gut. It elicits a strong foreign body reaction in the peritoneal cavity, especially in the presence of bowel content, and cannot be used if there is any question of perforation.

Barium can be used to establish the continuity of the bowel lumen to exclude obstruction, although this can often be assessed from the distribution of bowel gas alone. It is important to bear in mind that barium in the concentrations used for fluoroscopy is too dense to permit an adequate CT scan of the abdomen until it is eliminated and will also interfere with certain radionuclide scans, notably the Meckel scan. When contemplating a subsequent CT or nuclear study, the radiologist needs to be consulted before starting the upper GI series.

Water-soluble iodinated contrast media have evolved rapidly in the past decade. Many radiology departments no longer use the hyperosmolar and irritant agent Gastrografin. Less hyperosmolar media such as Cystografin are still used in cystography and would be used to look for a leak from the bladder. The use of Hypaque is a practical choice when looking for a leak from the colon. Since fluid shift into bowel is associated with hyperosmolar media, electrolytes and hydration will need to be monitored if the patient has retained contrast.

The latest generation of iso-osmolar iodinated media (Isovue and Omnipaque) are well tolerated and almost ideal apart from their high cost. They are nevertheless increasingly becoming the media of choice in studying bowel perforation, sinus tracts, and intravascular catheter position and in studying infants at risk for aspiration. Their radiodensity is less than that of barium. Diagnostic information can usually be obtained in the upper gut, however, if the contrast is delivered to the point of interest through an appropriately positioned nasogastric tube.

Fluoroscopy

Fluoroscopy offers a major advantage in contrast studies since the patient can be moved for optimal demonstration of anatomy and the appropriate volume of contrast to show an obstruction or leak can be gauged (see Fig. 184-7).

RISKS AND COMPLICATIONS

Accidental removal or malpositioning of tubes and catheters are real risks during radiographic procedures that can result in patient instability or even death. Careful attention to monitoring and movement during such procedures is necessary to avoid these complications.

The hazards of plain radiography are few but with conscious effort can be kept to a minimum. The radiation beam must be collimated to the minimum required for any given radiograph, bearing in mind that PICU walls often do not contain lead to absorb secondary scattered radiation. Nursing and medical staff must leave the area at the moment the radiograph is taken. Distance provides far more effective attenuation of x-ray scatter than the lead apron. Above all, staff must avoid being in the line of the primary beam, that is, the radiation emitted in the direction in which the x-ray tube is pointing. Careless radiation safety technique may result in significant exposure during a career spent in the PICU.

More tangible are the risks inherent in maneuvering the x-ray machine in the confined space about the patient. The cooperation of nursing and radiographic staff is needed to see that tubing and lines are not displaced and that electrical cords remain connected. Similar care is necessary when adjusting lines and ventilator equipment away from the areas to be radiographed. Respiratory tubing can make interpretation of the lung fields difficult. When multiple tubes overlie a chest or abdomen, it can be difficult to determine from the radiograph whether they lie outside or within the patient. When possible, they are moved away from the radiographic field.

Radiographs are commonly used to check the position of venous or atrial catheters before they are secured by skin sutures. Rather than risking dislodging the catheter or impairing its sterility by inserting a radiographic cassette beneath the patient in the middle of the procedure, the foresighted clinician will ask the radiographic technologist to place the cassette beneath the patient before starting the procedure.

ADDITIONAL READING

Hauser GJ, Pollack MM, Sivit CJ, et al. Routine chest radiographs in pediatric intensive care: A prospective study. Pediatrics 83:465-470, 1989.

Markowoitz RI. Radiologic assessment in the pediatric intensive care unit. Yale J Biol Med 57:49-82, 1984.

Seibert JJ, Parvey LS. The telltale triangle: Use of the supine cross table lateral radiograph of the abdomen in early detection of pneumoperitoneum. Pediatr Radiol 5:209-210, 1977.

Stark DD, Brasch RC, Gooding CA. Radiographic assessment of venous catheter position in children: Value of the lateral view. Pediatr Radiol 14:76-80, 1984.

• Swischuk LE. Emergency Imaging of the Acutely Ill or Injured Child, 3rd ed. Baltimore: Williams & Wilkins, 1994.

185 Ultrasonography

Michael W. Stannard

BACKGROUND AND INDICATIONS
Head

Head ultrasonography is indispensable in neonates and infants for detecting intracranial pathologic processes, notably hemorrhage, hydrocephalus, and certain cerebral malformations. Since the major sonographic window on the brain, the anterior fontanel, usually does not close until the second year of life, limited but useful information may be obtainable months after the neonatal period. Ventricular size and midline shift, in particular, can often be resolved late in the first year of life. Similar information can be obtained through surgical defects in the skull vault in older patients. Ultrasonography is routine in infants placed on extracorporal membrane oxygenation (ECMO) to detect intracranial hemorrhage to which these anticoagulated patients are prone.

Chest

The role of noncardiac chest ultrasonography is limited, for the most part, to imaging the quality and distribution of pleural fluid. This is valuable in the search for loculated collections for aspiration and in determining how much of a radiopaque hemithorax represents fluid. Although ultrasound studies cannot diagnose infection in pleural fluid, echo characteristics are useful for determining the ease with which a collection can be aspirated. Completely anechoic fluid can usually be aspirated through a medium or broad-gauge needle. The more numerous the internal echoes, however, the more complex the fluid and the greater the likelihood that a chest tube will be needed. A similar appearance may be produced by an effusion that has organized and become solid. Consolidated and collapsed lung can be recognized since it is airless and transmits sound. When possible, it is preferable that the physician planning chest aspiration be present during chest ultrasonography to help select the best site for aspiration and to note the position of the patient. Thoracocentesis performed in a different position runs the risk of failure as a result of mobile fluid gravitating away from the selected aspiration site.

Abdomen

The abdomen is the most commonly examined body region in the PICU (Table 185-1).

Liver

The liver is usually readily accessible to the transducer, and abscesses (Fig. 185-1) and fluid collections in and around it are well demonstrated. Duct dilatation is readily monitored in patients with biliary or pancreatic disease. Diffuse liver disease is difficult to image unless it is severe, when edema and necrosis may be detected. Most uncomplicated hepatitits produces no recognizable change. Gallbladder dilatation with intraluminal sludge is common in patients given total parenteral nutrition. In the trauma patient ultrasonography has some value in following liver lacerations if the patient cannot be moved to the department for CT, although it does not provide as complete a survey of the liver as CT.

Ultrasound scans are crucial in monitoring the liver transplant patient. Hepatic arterial flow can be watched closely during the first few postoperative

Table 185-1 Ultrasound Examinations Performed in the PICU at Children's Medical Center of Dallas in 1994

Head	175
Chest	6
Kidney only (including 29 for renal transplants)	72
Complete abdomen (including 97 for liver transplants)	197
Others (scrotum, neck, extremity)	11
	461

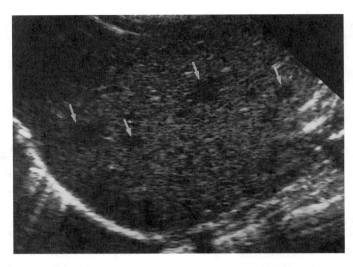

Fig. 185-1 Multiple poorly defined hypoechoic abscesses throughout the liver (arrows) in a patient with miliary tuberculosis.

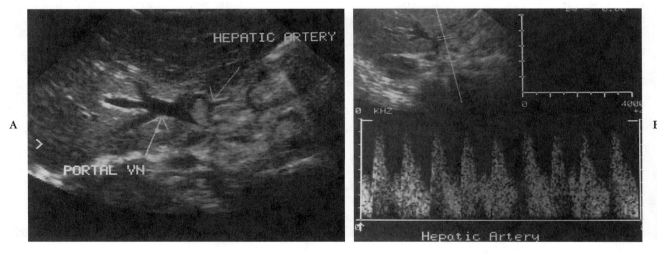

Fig. 185-2 **A,** Transverse sonogram of the liver shows a normal portal vein and hepatic artery (arrows). **B,** A cursor placed on the hepatic artery reveals a Doppler spectrum confirming presence of arterial flow.

weeks (Fig. 185-2), and spectral Doppler ultrasonography assisted by color-flow imaging can confirm normal flow in the hepatic and portal veins and in the inferior vena cava. Hematomas and loculated fluid collections are common around the recently transplanted liver. Although most are absorbed uneventfully, changing ultrasound characteristics in the presence of fever may suggest an infected collection that needs to be drained. Following transplant ischemia, bile leaks from necrotic bile ducts result in loculated bilomas that are frequently first identified by ultrasound scan and are an indication for drainage.

Spleen and pancreas

Abscesses and fluid collections in and around the spleen (Fig. 185-3) can be detected by ultrasonog-

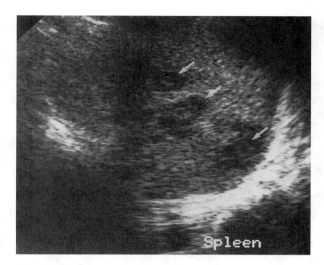

Fig. 185-3   Hypoechoic areas in the spleen (arrows) in a leukemic patient with *Candida* abscesses.

raphy, although in the absence of splenomegaly the complete organ is often difficult to visualize in the PICU patient. This is even more true of the pancreas, which is commonly obscured by air-distended bowel. The skillful sonographer, however, can often see at least the body and head of the pancreas and can detect pancreatic duct dilation and the hemorrhage, pseudocysts, and pancreatic swelling that are common complications of pancreatitis. Since the pancreas may appear normal in pancreatitis, a normal ultrasound does not exclude the disease.

Urinary Tract

Renal failure is not uncommon in PICU patients and ultrasonography is valuable in confirming the number and size of the kidneys and in detecting hydronephrosis and the level of obstruction. Well-established norms for renal size throughout childhood permit diagnosis of renal atrophy and swelling. Renal parenchymal echogenicity can be compared with the adjacent liver and spleen. Nephrotic syndrome and glomerulonephritis can produce an abnormally increased echogenicity of the renal parenchyma (Fig. 185-4).

Obstructed urinary tracts are particularly susceptible to infection. The presence of a fluid-fluid level in hydronephrosis in a febrile patient strongly suggests the diagnosis of pyonephrosis (Fig. 185-5). Depending on the size of the patient, renal calculi of more than a few millimeters in diameter can be de-

tected in the renal parenchyma and collecting system. Nephrocalcinosis is readily detected. Perirenal fluid collections, whether urinary leaks, hematomas, or abscesses, can be shown by real-time ultrasound. Renal lacerations may be seen, although not with the sensitivity of contrast-enhanced CT.

Color-flow and spectral Doppler imaging offers unrivaled methods of viewing the perfusion of kidneys and confirming renal arterial and venous flow. Doppler spectral analysis is used to compare the velocity of flow in systole and diastole and is often expressed as the resistance index

$$\text{Resistance index (RI)} = \frac{\text{Peak systolic velocity} - \text{End-diastolic velocity}}{\text{Peak systolic velocity}}$$

as a method of assessing peripheral arterial resistance within the kidney (Fig. 185-6, *A*). When the resistance index is high, the diastolic flow is relatively low. On occasion, flow may even be reversed during diastole (diastolic reversal) (Fig. 185-6, *B*). Studies to determine the specificity of measurements of the resistance index and spectral waveforms have yielded disappointing results. The interpretation of diminished diastolic flow can only be made after correlation with the patient's clinical condition and is often not entirely explained without renal biopsy. This is especially true in renal transplants, where acute tubular necrosis, rejection, pyelonephritis, tamponade, and cyclosporine toxicity can produce similar Doppler findings.

Doppler imaging is not currently reliable in establishing the presence of renal artery stenosis in native kidneys. It may have a role in assessing narrowing of the renal artery anastomosis in transplanted kidneys, although arteriography is needed to distinguish stenosis from kinking of the renal artery.

In the assessment of the renal transplant patient renal size, urinary obstruction, perinephric collections, urinary leaks, and lymphoceles are readily detected while the integrity of renal arterial and venous flow can be assured. Only in the more serious episodes of rejection will major changes of parenchymal echogenicity, often due to hemorrhage, be recognized. Ultrasonography is useful in selecting an area of the transplanted kidney for biopsy that is not close to major blood vessels, bladder, or bowel. Ultrasound guidance of the biopsy, which is quite feasible in the PICU, is preferred by many nephrologists.

Ultrasound of the urinary tract is incomplete without examination of the bladder. Retention, ure-

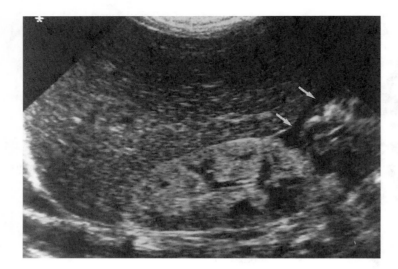

Fig. 185-4 Longitudinal scan through the right kidney, which is hyperechoic compared with adjacent liver. This indicates diffuse parenchymal renal disease. Associated ascites (arrows) is present.

Fig. 185-5 Fluid-fluid level (arrows) in a hydronephrotic kidney in a patient with pyonephrosis. The echoic, dependent fluid is pus.

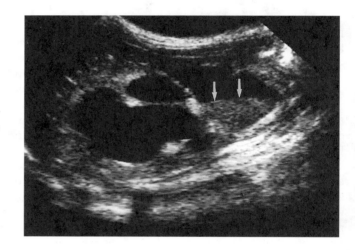

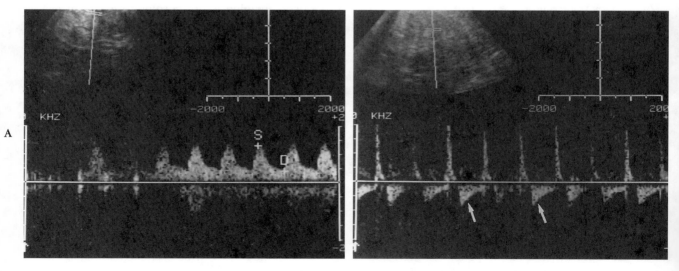

Fig. 185-6 **A,** Normal renal artery spectral Doppler image. Comparison of peak systolic flow velocity *(S)* with end-diastolic flow velocity *(D)* yields a resistance index of 0.66. **B,** Severe rejection of a renal transplant with reversal of diastolic flow (arrows). The kidney had to be removed.

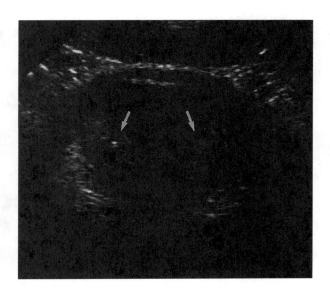

Fig. 185-7 Transverse scan of the bladder showing severe thickening and irregularity of the bladder mucosa (arrows) in a patient with Cytoxan cystitis.

thral catheter malposition, hemorrhage, bladder calculi, and cystitis, either infectious or drug induced, can be recognized (Fig. 185-7). Hydroureter can be detected behind a full bladder, as can ascites and pelvic abscess. As the patient's condition dictates, it may be worth clamping the catheter to allow the bladder to become distended or filling the bladder with saline solution to obtain the sonographic window necessary to show the bladder and pelvis well.

Abscess

Ultrasonography is excellent for detecting abscesses and fluid collections in much of the abdomen. Pelvic ascites, pus, or blood is seen adjacent to the full bladder and can be detected in other dependent sites in the supine patient, the paracolic gutters and the right prerenal space. Such collections may also be detected around the liver and spleen and beneath the leaves of the diaphragm. More difficult to detect are collections high beneath the rib cage and collections surrounded by bowel. Ultrasound cannot distinguish pus from blood or sterile ascites from infected ascites. Correlation with the patient's condition and percutaneous aspiration are necessary. Ultrasound scans can be used to detect psoas hematomas in patients with hemophilia and other bleeding disorders.

Diaphragm

Collections beneath and above the leaves of the diaphragm can be distinguished most easily on the right where the liver provides the larger sonographic window. Ultrasonography can be employed to assess diaphragm function. With the assistance of clinical staff for supervising momentary disconnection from the ventilator, it is usually easy to detect normal, absent, or paradoxical diaphragmatic movement when investigating phrenic nerve paralysis or other causes of a high hemidiaphragm.

Vasculature

Color-flow and spectral Doppler imaging can confirm blood flow in the aorta and inferior vena cava and in the principal vessels of the limbs. Femoral venous catheters are readily recognized in the inferior vena cava. Thrombosis around the catheter can also be seen. Doppler imaging is invaluable in the diagnosis of deep vein thrombosis. It can be used to assess patency of jugular and subclavian veins for venous access, although it is often difficult to guarantee the patency of the brachiocephalic vessels and superior vena cava that lie behind the sternum.

Almost any part of the body in which there is not interposed bone, air, or dressings can be assessed with ultrasound scans. Soft tissue masses, lymph nodes, and abscesses can be located and abscesses located for drainage. Nonradiopaque foreign bodies such as splinters of glass or wood can sometimes be identified.

TECHNIQUE

In many ways ultrasonography is an ideal imaging technique in the PICU. It is mobile, noninvasive, and nonionizing and is able to image anatomic details more precisely than the plain radiograph. As with all diagnostic studies, it will be of most value if it can be performed with specific questions in mind. What is the key information needed and how will it influence the management of the patient? If in doubt, the radiologist will be able to assess the appropriateness of the study or to suggest an alternative.

Ultrasonography is most effective when its shortcomings are taken into account. Not only will ultrasound not pass through air and bone, for instance, but surgical dressings also obstruct ultrasound. The skin over the area to be examined must be uncovered, which may involve discomfort when adhesive dressings are removed. Sonography is more operator dependent than almost any other form of imaging, and resourcefulness and flexibility are critical. It follows that not all sonographers (or sonologists) are created equal. Much may depend on the readiness of the radiologist to go to the PICU to confirm critical aspects of the examination.

RISKS AND COMPLICATIONS

There are few hazards attributable to ultrasonography in the PICU. It is sometimes difficult to maneuver bulky equipment in the confined space near a patient, and care must be taken to ensure that tubing, equipment, and electrical lines are not displaced. Sterile gel such as Lubrifax can be used as a substitute for regular ultrasound gel when scanning areas of skin infections and surgical incisions. Particular care must be taken to sterilize transducer surfaces between patients to avoid transferring infection. Disposable alcohol pads can be used for this purpose.

ADDITIONAL READING

• Han BK, Babcock DS. Sonographic measurements and appearance of normal kidneys in children. Am J Radiol 145:611-616, 1985.
• Hayden CK, Swischuck LE. Pediatric Ultrasonography, 2nd ed. Baltimore: Williams & Wilkins, 1992.
  Kelcz F, Pozniak MA, Pirsch JD, et al. Pyramidal appearance and resistive index: Insensitive and nonspecific indicators of renal transplant rejection. Am J Radiol 155:531-535, 1990.
  Langley DE, Skolnick ML, Zeiko AB, et al. Duplex Doppler sonography in the evaluation of adult patients before and after liver transplantation. Am J Radiol 151:687-696, 1988.
• Siegel MJ, ed. Pediatric Sonography, 2nd ed. New York: Raven Press, 1995.
  Zemel G, Zajko AB, Skolnick ML, et al. The role of sonography and transhepatic cholangiography in the diagnosis of biliary complications after liver transplantation. Am J Radiol 151:943-946, 1988.

186 Computed Tomography

William Banks

BACKGROUND

CT provides a global view of anatomy with excellent anatomic detail, which is neither operator dependent nor limited by bowel gas or bone as is ultrasonography. With contrast-enhanced CT, tissue perfusion and renal function can be assessed. Reconstructed CT images from newer spiral or helical scanners can provide multiplanar imaging that rivals MR imaging. CT is currently faster than MR imaging, resulting in less time away from the PICU, an important consideration for critically ill patients and support staff. Consultation with the radiologist to help coordinate the examination helps ensure the proper study is obtained in the least amount of time. Currently CT is approximately half the cost of an equivalent MR imaging examination.

Oral and IV contrast are essential for optimal abdominal CT. Many pediatric patients have a relative paucity of fat, resulting in poor tissue contrast in the abdomen. Oral contrast permits delineation of the bowel from adjacent viscera and musculature and also distinguishes bowel from pathologic processes (abscesses, adenopathy, and masses that are of similar radiodensity). Other than the risk of aspiration, there are few contraindications to the use of oral contrast. Achieving optimal bowel opacification may take up to 1 or 2 hours, which needs to be taken into consideration in scheduling examinations.

IV contrast shows normal vascular anatomy and organ perfusion and increases sensitivity in the detection of pathologic processes. It is essential for optimal abdominal CT but may not be necessity for all head or chest CT studies. If the use of contrast is in doubt, the radiologist must be consulted to save unnecessary expense and avoid the associated risks of contrast.

INDICATIONS AND TECHNIQUE
Cranial CT

Head CT is the most common neuroimaging modality in acutely ill infants or children. Its advantage over MR imaging is that bone, calcification, and subarachnoid hemorrhage can be visualized. In addition, it has the practical advantages of speed, greater availability, and less sedation. CT, however, is less sensitive than MR imaging in evaluation of the brain stem and posterior fossa.

Trauma

Noncontrasted CT is used in patients with neurologic deficit, loss of consciousness, focal seizures, or mental status changes. Skull films have a limited role in the absence of a depressed fracture. Noncontrasted CT can be used to evaluate extra-axial fluid, edema, cerebral contusion, hemorrhage (both subarachnoid and intraventricular), and fractures. Blood, whether parenchymal or extra-axial, is seen in acute conditions as high density (or white) (Fig. 186-1). CT is less sensitive than MR imaging in the detection of subtle

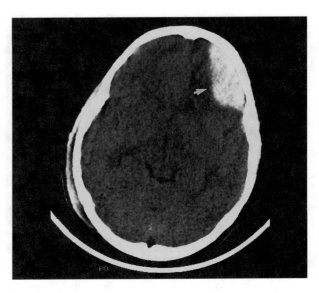

Fig. 186-1 Acute epidural hematoma. Biconvex high-density hematoma in the epidural space (arrow).

contusion or diffuse axonal injury. Cerebral edema, whether secondary to anoxia, metabolic disorder, drugs, or trauma, causes brain swelling that effaces the ventricles, cisterns, and sulci. There is loss of the margin between gray and white matter and diffuse hypodensity (appearing dark on the CT image). The deep gray nuclei may be spared but in severe cases show increased density, creating the "reversal sign" of peripheral low density and central high density (Figs. 186-2 and 186-3).

Infection

CT images of uncomplicated meningitis usually show no abnormality. Contrast-enhanced imaging is indicated when there is suspicion of complications because of (1) elevated CSF protein, (2) positive CSF culture, (3) elevated CSF white blood cell count, or (4) fever. Contrast increases the visibility of ventriculitis, meningeal enhancement, subdural empyema, cerebritis, and abscess.

Encephalitis produces parenchymal hypodensity with a mass effect. Contrast often demonstrates irregular enhancement. Herpes simplex is a common cause and characteristically involves the temporal lobes in older children. In infants, however, involvement tends to be more widespread. Encephalitis may be complicated by abscess or necrosis.

Tumor

Intracranial tumors may present as the result of a local mass effect or increased ICP. Obstruction of CSF flow results in hydrocephalus proximal to the site of obstruction. For suspected brain tumors, CT is per-

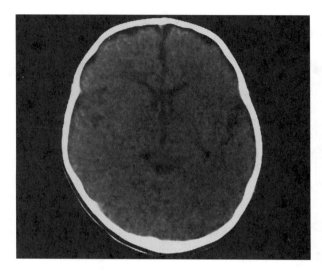

Fig. 186-2 Normal CT of head in a 2-month-old infant. The cortical ribbon of gray matter is of higher density than the adjacent hypodense white matter.

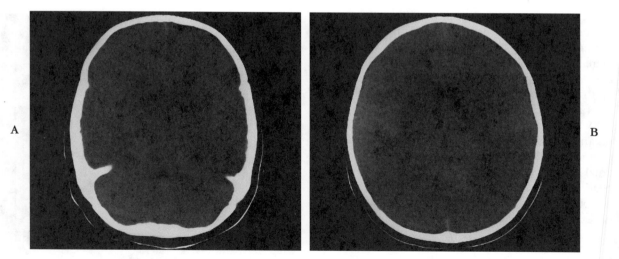

Fig. 186-3 Reversal sign due to profound anoxia. **A,** Peripheral hypodensity with loss of gray-white junction. There is brain swelling with effacement of sulci. Sylvian fissures and basilar cisterns as well as downward transtentorial herniation are seen. **B,** The peripheral low density and central high density represent a reversal of the normal CT appearance. (Note: The scattered peripheral areas of high density represent areas of relative cortical sparing.)

formed with and without IV contrast. The location of the tumor, CT appearance, and patient age are important in establishing the differential diagnosis.

Chest CT

The axial anatomy as depicted by CT is useful in clarifying questions arising from superimposition of structures or total opacification that obscures details on plain films. Lung parenchyma can usually be evaluated without contrast. Evaluation of the mediastinum and pleural space, however, usually necessitates IV contrast.

Trauma

CT is a sensitive method for detection of pulmonary contusion, pneumothorax, and pleural fluid. High density within the pleural space on contrast images indicates hemorrhage. If a cause for hemorrhage (i.e., rib fracture) cannot be found, mediastinal vascular injury needs to be considered. Contrast infusion dynamic or spiral CT has been used to exclude aortic injury but depends on an otherwise completely normal appearance of the mediastinum and aorta. Angiography remains the gold standard in the diagnosis of vascular injury.

Infection

CT helps localize disease in the lung parenchyma or pleural space. This is most helpful when chest radiographs demonstrate an opaque hemithorax or unusual air collection and lung abscess and empyema cannot otherwise be differentiated. IV contrast increases diagnostic sensitivity and can identify fluid within the pleural space by demonstrating enhancement of separated visceral and parietal pleura (Fig. 186-4). CT can also be used to evaluate the position of chest tubes. Placement of chest tubes under radiologic control is limited by the smaller caliber of the tubes used, which predisposes them to obstruction. CT-guided aspiration or drainage of lung abscess offers a less invasive alternative to thoracotomy.

Tumor

Tumors of the mediastinum may present acutely with tracheal or airway compression. CT is useful in localizing tumors to the anterior, middle, or posterior mediastinum, which aids in diagnosis. Specific CT characteristics (fat, calcium, or cystic or solid components) may further define the lesion prior to biopsy. CT-guided biopsy offers an accurate and less invasive alternative to open biopsy.

Abdominal and Pelvic CT

Both oral and IV contrast are necessary for optimal CT examination. Although time may preclude total bowel opacification in trauma patients, a small amount of contrast is administered to distinguish stomach, duodenum, and proximal small bowel from adjacent viscera.

Trauma

CT is the modality of choice for evaluation and follow-up of blunt abdominal trauma. Laceration or fracture of solid abdominal viscera will appear as low-density (dark) bands on both noncontrasted and contrast-enhanced CT. The spleen is the most commonly injured organ subsequent to blunt abdominal trauma (Fig. 186-5). IV contrast increases the detection rate in solid organ laceration.

Trauma is the most common cause of pancreatitis in children. It is important to note, however, that CT findings may be normal in pancreatitis. CT is most helpful in the evaluation of the complications of pancreatitis, most commonly pseudocyst formation (Fig. 186-6) and hemorrhage.

CT is insensitive for the detection of bowel injury. Duodenal hematoma may appear as focal thickening of the bowel wall but is generally better evaluated by an upper GI barium examination. Bowel perforation is suspected in the presence of free air or significant ascites without associated visceral injury.

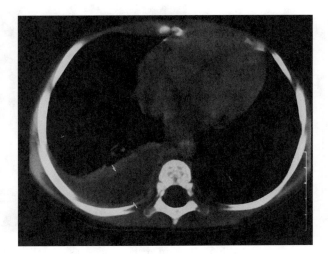

Fig. 186-4 Empyema. Enhancement of separated visceral and parietal pleura surrounding the hypodense pleural fluid collection.

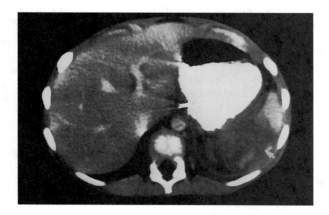

Fig. 186-5   Splenic laceration/contusion. Note marked inhomogeneity and hypodensity of most of the spleen.

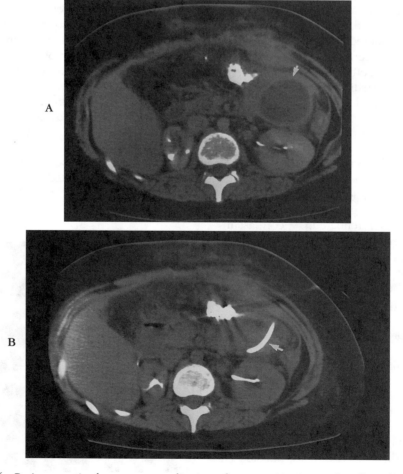

Fig. 186-6   Peripancreatic abscess as complication of pancreatitis. **A,** Peripherally enhancing thick-walled fluid collection (arrow) with inflammatory changes in adjacent soft tissues. **B,** Percutaneous drainage catheter (arrow) placed under CT guidance.

Infection

In abdominal abscess CT is both diagnostic and therapeutic. IV contrast increases diagnostic sensitivity by demonstrating peripheral enhancement in the abscess wall. Abnormal fluid collections can be tapped or drained under CT guidance. Bowel opacification by oral contrast helps to differentiate abscess from bowel.

RISKS AND COMPLICATIONS

Transportation of the critically ill patient between the PICU and the radiology department needs to be carefully planned and coordinated with the radiologist. The patient is often at greatest risk when in transit between departments and must be accompanied by staff able to cope with any untoward event.

Sedation, either conscious or with general anesthesia, carries an inherent risk. CT, especially spiral CT, can often be performed with less or no sedation than conventional CT or MR imaging. The need for and choice of the most appropriate sedation must be discussed with the radiologist.

IV contrast is associated with severe reaction (anaphylaxis or death) in approximately 1 in 100,000 admissions. A history of any contrast reaction needs to be solicited and the radiologist informed. If non-contrast-enhanced examinations cannot provide the necessary information, a 24-hour course of steroids may reduce the risk of severe reaction. The other major contraindication to IV contrast is impaired renal function. Ionizing radiation is used for CT and thus carries a very small risk of cancer and genetic injury.

ADDITIONAL READING

Kaufman RA, Towbin R, Babcock DS. Upper abdominal trauma in children: Imaging evaluation. AJR 142:449-460, 1984.

Kirks DR, ed. Practical Pediatric Imaging Diagnostic Radiology of Infants and Children, 2nd ed. Boston: Little Brown, 1991.

Starshak RJ, Wells RG, Sty JR, Gregg DL. Diagnostic Imaging of Infants and Children, vols I to III. Gaithersburg, Md.: Aspen, 1992.

Swischuck LE. Emergency Imaging of the Acutely Ill or Injured Child, 3rd ed. Baltimore: Williams & Wilkins, 1994.

187 Magnetic Resonance Imaging

Julie A. Mack · Nancy K. Rollins

BACKGROUND AND INDICATIONS

Magnetic resonance (MR) imaging was introduced into clinical practice in 1981 and has since undergone tremendous advances. Current scanners produce images of superb spatial resolution and excellent tissue contrast. Because it is a multiplanar technique, images can be acquired in any anatomic plane. This unique capacity increases its versatility and frequently provides information that cannot be obtained with any other imaging modality.

MR imaging differs from CT imaging in that it does not use ionizing radiation. MR imaging involves the use of a high-strength magnetic field in which hydrogen protons within the body act as magnetic dipoles. When placed in the bore of a scanner, a small number of the patient's hydrogen protons align themselves parallel to the magnetic field. Radio frequency pulses are applied, altering the alignment of the protons. As the protons recover from this deviation, they emit radio signals that are captured by the coils of the scanner. These signals are transformed, via complex computer algorithms, into images.

The most common clinical indications for MR imaging in the PICU are suspected CNS abnormalities. Because of its multiplanar capacity, MR imaging is preferred for the evaluation of most CNS tumors. The tumor, its mass effect, and the surrounding edema are usually well delineated by MR imaging (Fig. 187-1). This imaging modality is also the first choice in pediatric patients with suspected cord compression from neoplastic disease. MR imaging can be especially useful in evaluation of complex congenital anomalies involving the brain or spine as well as in the delineation of primary spinal cord pathology such as myelitis and hydromyelia.

In the evaluation of some pediatric trauma patients MR imaging is clearly superior to CT. In the evaluation of acute injury to the spinal cord it has replaced myelography and follow-up myelogram CT. It also has an important role in the evaluation of the child

| **INDICATIONS FOR MR IMAGING** |

CNS

Neoplasms
Congenital anomalies
Metabolic and storage disorders
Cerebritis and abscess
Subacute or chronic hemorrhage
Cerebral infarction
Vasculitis
Trauma

Spine

Neoplasms
Infection, especially epidural abscess
Congenital anomalies
Trauma, including suspected ligamentous injuries and cord contusion
Myelitis

Thorax

Mediastinal masses
Determination of central vascular patency
Aortic injury and dissection
Vascular rings
Complex congenital heart disease
Vascular malformations of neck and mediastinum
Vascular supply to sequestrations

Abdomen and pelvis

Neoplasms
Patency of inferior vena cava and portal system
Congenital anorectal malformations

Extremities

Musculoskeletal neoplasms
Infection
Trauma
Derangement of joints

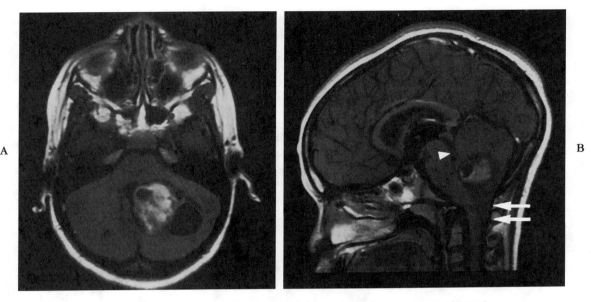

Fig. 187-1   A, T1-weighted contrast-enhanced axial image through the posterior fossa shows an enhancing cystic and solid mass impinging on the fourth ventricle. **B,** Sagittal image shows relationship of fourth ventricle (arrowhead) to tumor. There is downward herniation of the cerebellar tonsils (arrows).

with suspected unstable ligamentous injury to the spine, cord compression, and cord contusion. Although CT continues to be preferred for delineating bony injury of the spine, MR imaging is better than CT in delineating posttraumatic extrusion of intervertebral discs and is superior to CT in detecting subacute or chronic cerebral injury following closed-head trauma. It is less sensitive than CT in detecting acute hemorrhage, however, and for this reason is not to be substituted for CT in the setting of acute closed-head injury, suspected subarachnoid hemorrhage, or other conditions in which acute hemorrhage is suspected.

There are limited indications for MR imaging in CNS infection. Imaging studies are not routinely performed in meningitis since both CT and MR scans are usually normal in uncomplicated cases. MR imaging is reserved for patients who are likely to have complications of meningitis such as hydrocephalus, venous sinus thrombosis, periarteritis, cerebritis, and abscess. It can play an important role in assessing granulomatous meningitis and in the evaluation of herpes encephalitis (Fig. 187-2).

MR vascular imaging is used to study arterial and

venous flow and no contrast agents are needed. The inherent loss of signal from flowing blood results in blood vessels appearing black on conventional imaging. More sophisticated MR techniques in which blood appears bright are referred to as MR angiography sequences. MR vascular imaging is helpful in delineating congenital and acquired abnormalities of major vessels within the neck and chest. It is useful in determining central venous patency in children in whom repeated or prolonged central venous catheterization is necessary, in delineating superior vena cava thrombosis (Fig. 187-3), and in the evaluation of complex congenital heart disease. MR angiography is superb in delineating large vessels and has been widely applied in studying the vessels of the circle of Willis, the base of the brain, and the neck (Fig. 187-4). MR angiography is not sufficiently advanced to allow delineation of small vessels in suspected cases of vasculitis. The role of MR imaging in delineating aortic injury following trauma has not yet been defined, and suspected aortic transsection or posttraumatic pseudoaneurysms are best studied using conventional arteriography.

Indications for MR imaging of the abdomen and

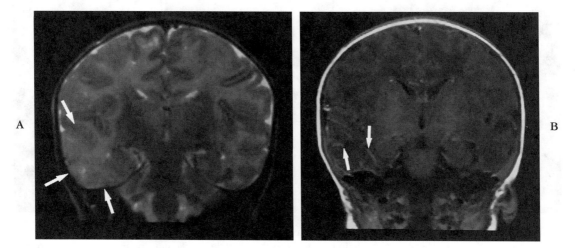

Fig. 187-2   A, T2-weighted image in a 27-day-old child with herpes encephalitis shows edema of the right temporal lobe manifested by loss of the normal cortical ribbon (arrows). **B,** T1-weighted contrast-enhanced image shows typical gyriform enhancement of right temporal lobe (arrows). This patient had unilateral disease, but bilateral involvement is common in the neonatal patient.

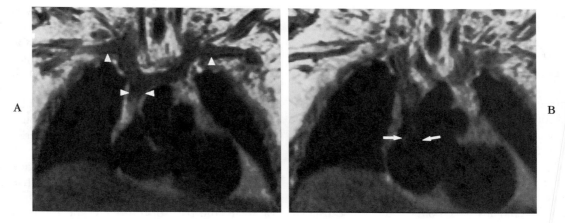

Fig. 187-3   A, Gated T1-weighted image shows abnormally increased signal in the superior vena cava, brachiocephalic veins, and both subclavian veins (arrowheads), indicating thrombosis. **B,** More posterior image shows thrombus extending into the right atrium (arrows).

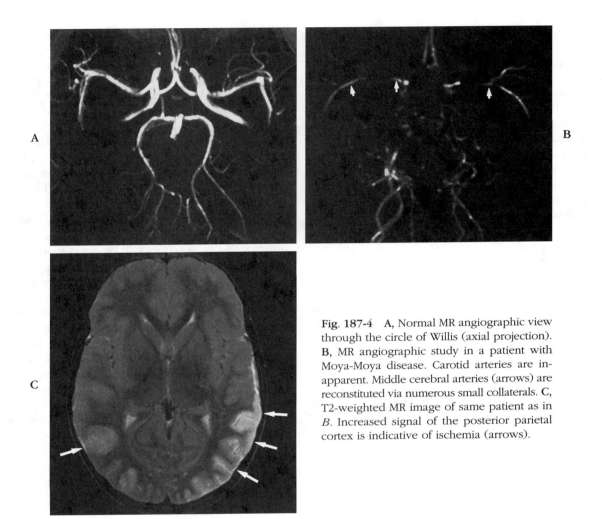

Fig. 187-4 **A,** Normal MR angiographic view through the circle of Willis (axial projection). **B,** MR angiographic study in a patient with Moya-Moya disease. Carotid arteries are inapparent. Middle cerebral arteries (arrows) are reconstituted via numerous small collaterals. **C,** T2-weighted MR image of same patient as in *B.* Increased signal of the posterior parietal cortex is indicative of ischemia (arrows).

pelvis are limited to solid organs where its multiplanar capabilities help to delineate the origin and extent of abdominal tumors. The lack of a satisfactory contrast agent to opacify bowel limits its ability to delineate bowel pathology. CT rather than MR imaging is necessary in patients suspected of having an intra-abdominal abscess. MR imaging is useful, however, in confirming patency of the portal veins, the inferior vena cava, and other large retroperitoneal veins as well as the aorta and proximal renal arteries.

TECHNIQUE

The imaging sequences and parameters are varied according to which part of the body is being studied and the clinical problem being addressed. "Total

body" MR imaging is neither feasible nor desirable. The indications for the MR study need to be clearly stated, and all relevant information communicated to the radiologist so that appropriate sequences and parameters are used.

Because of the time involved in MR imaging, sedation is routinely used in children under 5 years of age. In young infants feeding and warm bundling will usually suffice. For older infants and toddlers under 3 years of age, chloral hydrate is used at doses of 50 to 100 mg/kg orally or per rectum. For children older than 3 years, sodium pentobarbital is administered intravenously beginning with a dose of 2 mg/kg and using a maximum dose not exceeding 6 mg/kg. Patients who fail such attempts at conscious sedation and those at risk for sedation-induced apnea will need a general anesthetic.

As with any patient undergoing conscious sedation, physiologic monitoring is essential. Conventional monitoring equipment cannot be used because it typically contains ferromagnetic components that may be strongly attracted to the scanner. In addition, the electromagnetic field can adversely affect the operation of certain types of monitors, particularly the ECG. A variety of MR-compatible equipment is currently available. Shielded oximetric systems have been developed and provide the most accurate and reliable information about the patient's oxygenation and pulse.

Enough time must be allowed to assemble appropriate resources such as MR-compatible airway support equipment, medication, and personnel to transport the patient to the radiology suite. Personnel accompanying the patient must include at least one individual who is knowledgeable about the patient's condition, usually the bedside nurse. Patients with an unstable hemodynamic status, significant ventilatory support, increased ICP, or difficult airway control must be accompanied by an intensive care physician or anesthesiologist. Any problems with airway patency or with ventilation must be resolved prior to starting the scan. Since monitoring choices are limited, a caretaker must stay in the MR suite with the patient to provide continuous assessment and intervention as necessary. Noise may be a problem and earplugs may be indicated for both patient and personnel.

RISKS AND COMPLICATIONS

The most significant drawback to MR imaging of the PICU patient involves the difficulties encountered in monitoring the patient. The bore of the scanner is long and narrow, restricting observation. Standard monitors and ventilators that contain ferromagnetic materials may be strongly attracted to the MR scanner, becoming potentially dangerous projectiles if placed too close to the magnetic field. In addition, certain types of monitors may be affected by electromagnetic interference from the imager and be rendered inaccurate. Others emit electromagnetic noise that can result in severe image artifacts. There is also the potential for injury to patients by inducing electrical currents in conductive metallic materials, including monitoring leads and wires. Because the intensity of the magnetic field decreases in proportion to the distance from the scanner, some of these prob-

lems can be solved simply by making use of long extension tubing or wires and keeping the equipment a safe distance from the magnetic field. Procedures must be developed cooperatively by both radiology and anesthesiology departments to ensure that only approved equipment is used and all personnel are informed of possible hazards.

An equally important consideration in the imaging of the PICU patient is the time involved in acquiring the image. MR imaging is much more time consuming than CT. CT slices are obtained one at a time, and each slice takes only seconds to acquire; in MR imaging an entire set of slices must be acquired at one time. If the patient moves during the data acquisition, all of the slices will be nondiagnostic. Acquisition of a single MR data set may take up to 10 minutes. Typically, multiple sets are needed to complete a study. Thus, in the unstable or uncooperative PICU patient who cannot be sedated to immobility, alternative imaging modalities must be considered.

MR imaging is contraindicated in patients with certain biomedical implants. These include cardiac pacemakers, cochlear implants, neurostimulators, and implantable drug infusion pumps. Certain cerebral aneurysm clips are ferromagnetic, and movement or dislodgment can occur. The risk of imaging patients with a history of metallic foreign bodies depends on the ferromagnetic properties of the object, the strength of the magnetic field of the scanner, and whether the object is near a vital structure.

ADDITIONAL READING

Barkovich AJ. Techniques and methods in pediatric imaging. In Pediatric Neuroimaging, 2nd ed. New York: Raven Press, 1995, pp 1-8.

Elster AD. Questions and Answers in Magnetic Resonance Imaging. St. Louis: Mosby, 1994.

Holshouser BA, Hinshaw DB, Shellock FG. Sedation, anesthesia, and physiologic monitoring during MR imaging: Evaluation of procedures and equipment. J Magn Reson Imaging 3:553-558, 1993.

Prost R, Czervionke LF. How does an MR scanner operate? AJNR 15:1383-1386, 1994.

Shellock FG, Curtis JS. MR imaging and biomedical implants, materials, and devices: An updated review. Radiology 180:541-550, 1991.

Shellock FG, Kanal E. SMRI safety report: Policies, guidelines and recommendations for MR imaging safety and patient management. J Magn Reson Imaging 1:97-101, 1991.

Sheppard S. Basic concepts in MR angiography. Radiol Clin North Am 33:91-113, 1995.

188 Radionuclide Imaging

Patricia Ann Lowry

BACKGROUND

Although nuclear medicine studies are less commonly performed in the PICU than radiography and ultrasonography, they can provide information not otherwise available.

Nuclear imaging is based on the distribution of various radioactively labeled tracers, or radiopharmaceuticals, in an organ system or body compartment. The usual route of administration is intravenous, although occasionally the tracer is given orally (as in thyroid or GI scans), intrathecally, or by inhalation. Gamma radiation emitted by the radiopharmaceutical is recorded by a gamma camera. The resulting images reflect the distribution of tracer in the area of interest.

The majority of nuclear scans are performed with technetium-99m (^{99m}Tc)–labeled pharmaceuticals. This isotope emits gamma radiation, which is ideal for imaging and has a short (6 hour) half-life, resulting in relatively little radiation exposure to the patient and health care personnel.

In general nuclear medicine provides physiologic information, making it different from other imaging modalities that provide greater anatomic detail. Often the information provided by nuclear scans complements other modalities. For example, a CT scan of the brain in a patient with a closed-head injury may demonstrate intracranial hemorrhage, contusion, or cerebral edema, whereas a nuclear brain flow scan documents the presence or absence of cerebral perfusion but provides little anatomic detail.

Another advantage of nuclear imaging is that the data acquired can be quantitated. Modern digital gamma cameras are equipped with sophisticated computers that measure and display data to aid in interpretation. One example is the renal function curve, which is based on continuous imaging of the kidneys during excretion of a renal radiopharmaceutical to evaluate renal uptake and excretion and compare the function of the kidneys.

Patient Care Considerations

The availability of mobile gamma cameras at many institutions allows some scans to be performed at the bedside. These cameras may be moved and positioned over the patient with relatively little interference with monitors and other support apparatus. Although mobile cameras typically provide a smaller field of view than stationary systems, the field size is adequate for imaging of young children and infants. It may also suffice for imaging smaller organs such as the brain or kidneys in larger patients. If mobile cameras are not available or cannot be moved to the bedside due to limited space in the PICU room, the patient needs to be transported to the radiology department. Any unstable patient must be accompanied by appropriate personnel and monitored closely for the duration of the scan. This is true at all times but is of particular concern during nights and weekends when the nuclear medicine technologist may be working without the usual physician and nursing assistance.

There is usually no special preparation necessary for most nuclear scans. However, all residual radioisotope from a prior nuclear study must be removed since this can interfere with image quality. Most ^{99m}Tc scans must be spaced at least 1 day apart to avoid such interference; some isotopes with a longer half-life such as gallium take longer to decay and clear and more time must be allotted between nuclear studies.

When patient motion is excessive, diagnostic quality scans cannot be obtained and some form of sedation may be indicated. In such cases it is imperative that the sedated patient be closely observed and monitored. Sedation is most often needed when imaging is prolonged, as in bone scans. The need for sedation must be anticipated to allow completion of the scan once tracer has been injected and to expedite the return of the patient to the PICU. If the patient receives sedation and/or pain medication routinely, it is helpful to administer these drugs just before imaging.

Unlike iodinated contrast used in CT and urographic studies, radiopharmaceuticals have no significant toxic effects or allergic reactions and can be used safely in patients with renal insufficiency.

Radiation Safety

Radiopharmaceuticals labeled with ^{99m}Tc do not pose a significant radiation hazard either to the patient or to personnel. The short half-life of this radioisotope results in rapid decay of radioactivity. At the same time excretion of radiopharmaceuticals clears the radioactivity from the patient, often through the urinary tract. Many nuclear medicine studies result in less radiation to the patient than common radiographic studies. A bone scan, for example, results in a radiation dose similar to an IV pyelogram, and much less than that of a barium enema. Furthermore, additional imaging time or extra views do not increase the radiation dose to the patient. Health care personnel obviously receive much less exposure than the patients. However, it is prudent that they minimize unnecessary exposure to radiation. In general this means being aware of urinary, fecal, or biliary excretion and minimizing contact with radioactive waste. Gallium scans result in more prolonged retention of tracer in the patient than the more common scans performed with ^{99m}Tc, and radioactive waste must be handled with care for several days. Health care personnel in close contact with patients over long periods of time must remember that radiation exposure decreases as distance from the patient increases. However, since the amount of radiation exposure to personnel is relatively small, this principle need not interfere with patient care.

INDICATIONS AND TECHNIQUES
Common Scans Performed in the PICU

Cerebral perfusion imaging is often performed to confirm brain death. In cases of severe cerebral insult cerebral edema and increased ICP result in reduction and eventual cessation of blood flow to the brain as ICP approaches systemic arterial pressure. Imaging of the brain as a series of rapid-sequence images following an IV bolus of tracer provides a first-pass "radionuclide angiogram" as the tracer flows through the arterial circulation. A normal cerebral perfusion scan demonstrates flow in the carotid arteries, in the anterior and middle cerebral arteries, and in the

superior sagittal sinus (Fig. 188-1). Intracranial perfusion is absent in brain death, and only a rim of radioactivity is seen around the periphery of the skull, representing scalp perfusion (Fig. 188-2). This scan provides information similar to cerebral angiography, which was used in the past as a confirmatory test for

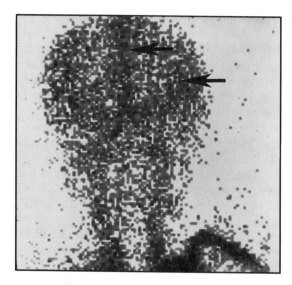

Fig. 188-1 Normal brain flow. Radioactivity is seen in the common carotid arteries, and intracerebral flow (arrows) is present.

Fig. 188-2 Brain death. Tracer activity is seen in the face and scalp, but cerebral perfusion is absent.

brain death. The radionuclide study has the advantage of being noninvasive and readily available and often can be performed at the bedside. The study is usually performed with one of the radiopharmaceuticals used for renal imaging; it is therefore cleared from the circulation rapidly, and if necessary repeat studies may be performed in 12 to 24 hours.

Ventilation-perfusion (V̇/Q̇) lung scans are occasionally indicated for evaluation of pulmonary embolism. Lung perfusion scans are performed using labeled albumin particles that lodge in the pulmonary capillary bed. The distribution in the lungs reflects the regional perfusion of the lungs. Perfusion defects may be due to thromboemboli obstructing pulmonary arterial branches; defects may also result from atelectasis or pneumonia. Therefore specificity for pulmonary embolism is increased by performing a ventilation scan since pulmonary emboli result in a mismatched zone of absent perfusion but normal ventilation. Ventilation scans are often inconvenient to perform on critically ill patients, and therefore a chest radiograph, if clear, may suffice as evidence of normal ventilation. Criteria have been developed for interpretation of V̇/Q̇ scans as high, intermediate, or low probability for pulmonary embolus and take clinical factors into consideration. A normal perfusion scan essentially rules out pulmonary embolus; multiple segmental mismatched defects indicate a high likelihood. In some cases pulmonary angiography is necessary for definitive diagnosis.

Lung scans are generally less helpful in the presence of extensive lung infiltrates. The resulting scans often show matched areas of both ventilation and perfusion abnormality, which occur in a number of conditions, including pneumonia, atelectasis, and pulmonary infarction. Such a pattern is therefore termed indeterminate.

Distribution of pulmonary perfusion may also be evaluated in congenital heart disease. In right-to-left shunts some of the particles bypass the pulmonary capillary bed and can be seen in the kidneys and brain.

Multiple gated acquisition (MUGA) cardiac scans for determination of cardiac ejection fraction are occasionally useful for patients with myocarditis, cardiomyopathy, or congenital heart disease. The circulating red cells are tagged with ^{99m}Tc. Images acquired during the cardiac cycle can be used to calculate the ejection fraction, which is useful for determining the severity of ventricular dysfunction. Images can also reveal chamber size and regional wall motion abnormalities.

Myocardial perfusion imaging with thallium-201, or more recently ^{99m}Tc sestamibi, demonstrates myocardial perfusion. Areas of ischemia or infarct, therefore, appear as "cold" defects in the myocardium. This may be useful in evaluating myocardial ischemia in congenital heart disease or Kawasaki syndrome.

Hepatobiliary imaging is performed using ^{99m}Tc-labeled iminodiacetic acid compounds that are excreted into the bile, demonstrating the bile ducts, gallbladder, and small bowel within 1 hour in normal cases. Hepatobiliary scans are useful in detecting bile duct obstruction or leakage. Bile leaks may follow trauma or surgery and appear as abnormal collections of tracer adjacent to the liver or common bile duct or occasionally free within the peritoneal cavity (Fig. 188-3). In patients with liver transplants biliary scans can confirm the integrity of hepatic perfusion, excretory function, and bile drainage.

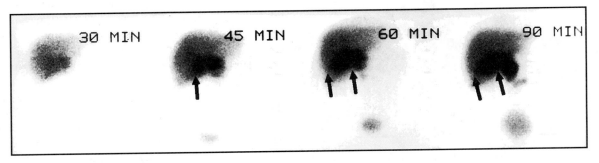

Fig. 188-3   Bile leak. Biliary scan in a patient with biliary atresia and Kasai procedure. A collection of tracer accumulates at the porta hepatis indicating leakage from a ruptured Kasai (arrows).

Acute cholecystitis may occur in patients with or without ultrasound evidence of gallstones. Acute acalculous cholecystitis may occur in critically ill or traumatized patients. Hepatobiliary imaging in acute cholecystitis demonstrates nonfilling of the gallbladder despite adequate visualization of the common duct and bowel, reflecting obstruction of the cystic duct. It is essential that patients be fasted for this study since a recent meal or tube feeding containing fat can cause contraction of the gallbladder, resulting in failure to visualize a normal gallbladder and thus a falsely abnormal scan. Biliary scans are helpful for distinguishing acute cholecystitis from other causes of right upper quadrant pain in patients with sickle cell disease in whom there is a high prevalence of gallstones, which may or may not be related to acute symptoms.

Two different methods of nuclear imaging are used in the study of GI bleeding. *Meckel's scans* employ ^{99m}Tc pertechnetate to identify Meckel's diverticulum, a relatively common cause of intestinal bleeding in children. This tracer accumulates in gastric mucosa. Focal, intense accumulation other than in the stomach suggests ectopic gastric mucosa, such as is found in the majority of Meckel's diverticula and which predisposes to ulceration and bleeding (Fig. 188-4). It should be noted, however, that some Meckel's diverticula do not contain gastric mucosa and will not be detected by this type of imaging. With Meckel's scans, the patient does not have to be actively bleeding at the time of the scan for a positive result.

Tagged red cell imaging must be performed while active GI bleeding is occurring. Red cells labeled with ^{99m}Tc are injected intravenously. When bleeding into bowel occurs, there is accumulation of tracer at the site of hemorrhage. These scans are most useful for localizing small bowel or colonic hemorrhage after gastric or esophageal bleeding has been excluded by lavage or endoscopy. Tagged red cell scans are more sensitive than angiography for small or intermittent hemorrhage since imaging is performed over a longer period of time. Identification of the site of bleeding aids subsequent angiography or surgery. If the patient is not actively bleeding, the tracer remains within the vascular system; a negative study is good evidence that no hemorrhage is occurring at the time of imaging. If both Meckel's and tagged red cell scans are planned, Meckel's scan is performed first. The process of labeling red cells precludes a subsequent Meckel scan by causing the radioisotope to bind to red cells rather than to localize in gastric mucosa.

Renal scans for evaluation of renal perfusion and function are often useful in the PICU. A number of radiopharmaceuticals are available, each with unique properties. The agent most commonly used for renal function imaging is ^{99m}Tc diethylenetriamine pentaacetic acid (DTPA), which is excreted by glomerular filtration. A new agent, ^{99m}Tc mercaptoacetyltriglycine (MAG-3), is excreted by the renal tubules and results in better visualization of the kidneys and collecting systems in the presence of reduced renal function. MAG-3 is thus very useful in patients with anuria or oliguria due to acute tubular necrosis (ATN) in documentating renal perfusion and function. In ATN, scans demonstrate perfusion of the kidneys, uptake of tracer, but poor or absent excretion. Similar findings may occur with renal vein thrombosis. Uptake in the kidneys indicates intact arterial blood supply, and this may provide useful information in anuric or oliguric patients.

Renal transplant patients often undergo a radionuclide renal scan in the early postoperative period to confirm the presence of renal arterial flow and to provide a baseline evaluation of function. Function may be poor initially, especially in cadaver renal transplants, due to ATN. Renal scans can demonstrate urine leaks that may complicate kidney transplantation. Ultrasonography can identify fluid, but it

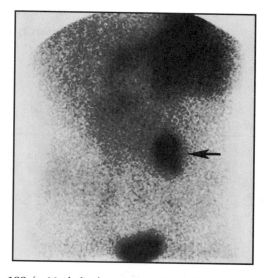

Fig. 188-4   Meckel's diverticulum. Meckel's scan of the abdomen shows normal uptake in the stomach and bladder. The focal collection in the midabdomen (arrow) represents uptake in ectopic gastric mucosa in Meckel's diverticulum.

may not be possible for it to distinguish a urine collection from ascites fluid or hematoma. A focal collection of tracer outside the renal collecting system or bladder confirms urine leakage (Fig. 188-5).

Renal parenchymal imaging using ^{99m}Tc glucoheptonate or dimercaptosuccinic acid (DMSA) is sensitive for detecting renal scarring, which can result in hypertension. Acute pyelonephritis may also result in focal defects on these scans.

Bone scans are the most commonly performed nuclear scan in many institutions. Bone scanning is highly sensitive in the detection of a number of skeletal lesions. Bone scan abnormalities are nonspecific, however, and may result from trauma, infection, tumor, and other conditions. It is primarily used to detect occult trauma or early osteomyelitis when radiographs are normal or inconclusive. Bone scans are performed approximately 2 hours after injection of a ^{99m}Tc diphosphonate compound that localizes in bone but most intensely in areas of increased blood flow or metabolic activity. There are numerous indications for bone scans. In critically ill patients the common indications include detection of occult fracture, differentiation of osteomyelitis and cellulitis, and detection of osteomyelitis as a source of sepsis. It is often not possible, however, to distinguish osteomyelitis from a healing fracture since increased uptake of isotope occurs in both conditions. Patients

must remain immobile during bone imaging and sedation may be needed.

Gallium scans and labeled leukocyte scans are useful in localization of a suspected abscess or inflammatory process. Gallium-67 localizes not only in areas of inflammation but also in some tumors in addition to normal excretion in the urine and bowel. Labeled leukocytes are useful for suspected abdominal abscesses when normal colon uptake might cause difficulty in interpretation of a gallium scan. Leukocyte imaging, however, involves a cell labeling procedure, in which a large volume of blood (60 ml) is needed to provide adequate white cells. Alternatively, donor leukocytes may be necessary for neutropenic patients. Gallium, however, is easily administered without the need for cell labeling and may be used irrespective of the patient's white cell count. Often these imaging techniques are useful to screen the entire body for a suspected focus of infection. Additional evaluation with other modalities may be needed to elucidate an abnormality located by nuclear scan. Whole body imaging is usually performed whatever the area of symptoms since unsuspected foci of infection are not uncommon.

RISKS

There are few risks associated with radionuclide scanning other than the minimal exposure to radiation re-

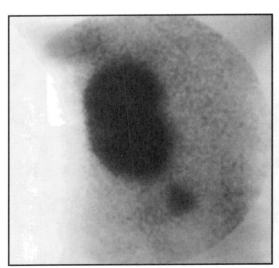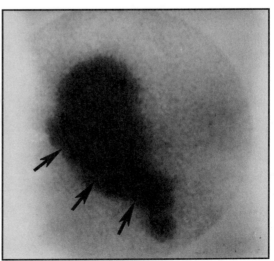

A

B

Fig. 188-5 Renal transplant with urine leak. **A,** Early image of renal scan shows uptake in kidney and some passage to the bladder. **B,** Later image shows an irregular collection lateral and inferior to kidney diagnostic of leakage of urine from the ureter (arrows).

ferred to above. Major problems with PICU patients are most often related to the need for increased care during sedation and transport between the PICU and the radiology department.

ADDITIONAL READING

Alazraki NP. Radionuclide imaging in the evaluation of infections and inflammatory disease. Radiol Clin North Am 31:783-794, 1993.

Buck JR, Connors RH, Coon WW, Weintraub WH, Wesley JR, Coran AG. Pulmonary embolism in children. J Pediatr Surg 16:385-391, 1981.

D'Alonzo WA. Heyman S. Biliary scintigraphy in children with sickle cell anemia and acute abdominal pain. Pediatr Radiol 15:395-398, 1985.

Dubovsky EV, Russell CD. Radionuclide evaluation of renal transplants. Semin Nucl Med 18:181-198, 1988.

Garty I, Delbeke D, Sandler MP. Correlative pediatric imaging. J Nucl Med 30:15-24, 1989.

Gordon I, Helms P, Fazio F. Clinical applications of radionuclide lung scanning in infants and children. Br J Radiol 54:576-585, 1981.

Gupta NC, Prezio JA. Radionuclide imaging in osteomyelitis. Semin Nucl Med 18:287-299, 1988.

Hawkins RA, Hall T, Gambhir SS, Busuttil RW, Huang S, Glickman S, Marciano D, Brown RKJ, Phelps ME. Radionuclide evaluation of liver transplants. Semin Nucl Med 18:199-212, 1988.

Holder LE. Bone scintigraphy in skeletal trauma. Radiol Clin North Am 31:739-781, 1993.

Pjura G, Kim EE. Radionuclide evaluation of brain death. In Freeman LM, Weissmann HS, eds. Nuclear Medicine Annual. New York: Raven Press, 1987, pp 269-293.

Schwartz JA, Baxter J, Brill DR. Diagnosis of brain death in children by radionuclide cerebral imaging. Pediatrics 73:14-18, 1984.

Sfakianakis GN, Haase GM. Abdominal scintigraphy for ectopic gastric mucosa: A retrospective analysis of 143 studies. AJR 138:7-12, 1982.

Sfakianakis GN, Sfakianaki ED. Nuclear medicine in pediatric urology and nephrology. J Nucl Med 29:1287-1300, 1988.

Winzelberg GG, McKusick KA, Froelich JW, Callahan RJ, Strauss HW. Detection of gastrointestinal bleeding with 99m Tc-labeled red blood cells. Semin Nucl Med 12:139-145, 1982.

189 Echocardiography

Jorge A. Garcia · Ellen M. Weinstein

BACKGROUND AND INDICATIONS

Over the past few years echocardiography has become an important noninvasive tool in the evaluation of cardiac anatomy as well as cardiac function and hemodynamics. Two-dimensional and Doppler echocardiography allow accurate noninvasive diagnosis of many congenital heart lesions, in many cases avoiding the need for cardiac catheterization prior to surgery. However, in the PICU echocardiography is used not only to define structural abnormalities but to assess cardiac function, hemodynamics, and pericardial effusions.

Echocardiography uses ultrasound frequencies higher than those audible to the human ear ($>$20,000 Hz or cycles/sec). The ultrasound beam is generated by many independent crystals within the transducers. The transducers generate short bursts of acoustic energy that travel through the tissue, encounter many tissue interfaces, and reflect back to the transducer. The transducer is calibrated to convert elapsed time from transmission of the sound wave to reception into a measurement of distance. The spatial relationship of the reflected echoes with different acoustic densities is processed by the computer to create an image. Each ultrasound pulse generates a line of information that corresponds to the structures encountered along the line of the ultrasound beam. Multiple lines of information produce a two-dimensional image. As ultrasound travels through the tissue, a portion of the energy is absorbed. This absorption increases with frequency. A higher frequency transducer will not penetrate as deeply into the tissue as a lower frequency transducer will. There are several transducers currently available. The high-frequency transducers (5 to 7 MHz) will give better resolution at lower depths, but lower frequency transducers (2 to 3.5 MHz) will have better tissue penetration with less resolution at any given depth. It is necessary to use the highest frequency transducer that will allow adequate penetration to the depth needed.

There are three modalities used in echocardiography. *M-mode echocardiography* (motion-mode or single-plane imaging) is one of the original ultrasound techniques for cardiac evaluation. On the M-mode graphic display a single line of information is plotted against time. This provides a graphic display of the motion of the cardiac structures in real time. Cardiac chamber dimensions and wall thickness are related to changes in weight, height, and body surface area (Fig. 189-1).

Two-dimensional (2-D) echocardiography provides a planar image through the heart and great vessels. This modality is best for evaluation of cardiac morphology and function. It can produce detailed images of intracardiac structures, valves, and myocardium in motion (Fig. 189-2).

Doppler echocardiography provides a quantitative as well as qualitative assessment of the flow of blood within the heart and vessels. It is based on the change in frequency imparted to a sound wave by the movement of erythrocytes. Doppler signals from blood flow directed toward the transducer are displayed as positive (above baseline), and Doppler signals from blood flow directed away from the transducer are displayed as negative (below baseline). The Doppler principle is used to convert the difference between transmitted and received ultrasound frequencies into velocity of blood flow. To obtain a more accurate measurement of flow velocities the ultrasound beam is kept parallel to the flow. The evaluation of hemodynamics, especially pressure gradients between cardiac structures, is accomplished using the modified Bernoulli equation:

$$\text{Instantaneous pressure gradient } (\Delta P) = 4(V_{max})^2$$

where V = velocity of blood flow within the heart or vessels. The most common application of Doppler

USES OF ECHOCARDIOGRAPHIC MODALITIES

M-mode echocardiography

Identify motion of cardiac structures
Measure cardiac dimensions
Measure wall thickness
Evaluate cardiac contractility (percent shortening fraction)
Detect pericardial effusions

2-D echocardiography

Evaluate cardiac structure, including endocardium, myocardium, heart valves, and vessel abnormalities
Detect wall motion abnormalities
Estimate ventricular contractility (EF)
Detect presence of vegetations in endocarditis, usually >2 mm
Detect or assess pericardial effusion
Detect cardiac tumors
Detect thrombus
Evaluate prosthetic valve function
Measure cardiac chamber dimensions

Doppler echocardiography

Detect direction of blood flow
Estimate a pressure difference or gradient between two cardiovascular structures
Detect valvar stenosis or insufficiency
Detect intracardiac shunting (atrial or ventricular septal defects)
Determine patency of proximal coronary arteries
Detect and quantify valvar insufficiency
Quantify ventricular function
Estimate cardiac output

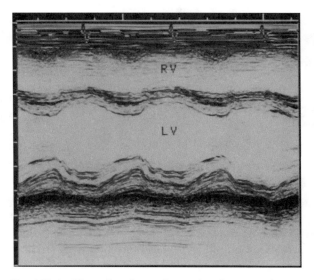

Fig. 189-1 M-mode echocardiography. (RV = Right ventricle; LV = left ventricle.)

techniques is evaluation of valvar stenoses or insufficiency and estimation of pressure.

Currently there are three different Doppler modalities. *Pulsed-wave (PW) Doppler imaging* investigates a relatively small area within the heart. With the use of a single ultrasound crystal serving as the emitter and receiver, a short burst of ultrasound is transmitted to a selected depth and area. The principal advantage of this modality is the ability to measure flow velocity in a defined area and thereby specifically localize any area of abnormal velocity detected. The PW Doppler examination is frequently combined with simultaneous 2-D echocardiography so that the exact location of the sampling within the chamber can be visually displayed. Although areas of high-velocity flow can be detected and localized, there is a limit to the maximum or peak velocity that can be measured with this technique.

In *continuous-wave (CW) Doppler imaging* the ultrasound beam is continuously emitted by one crystal and a second crystal continuously receives the reflected signal. Consequently, an instantaneous Doppler-shift frequency between the emitted wave and the reflected wave can be measured. The principal advantage of CW Doppler imaging is that there is no limit to the maximum velocity that can be measured. CW and PW Doppler imaging complement each other by determining the maximum velocity and as well as location of the flow evaluated, respectively.

Color-flow mapping or *color Doppler imaging* is a more recent development in Doppler technology but is actually an expanded use of PW Doppler imaging. The flow is displayed superimposed on the 2-D echocardiographic image in the form of color. Multiple sample volumes interrogate an area, and Doppler signals are assigned a color based on computer analysis of the velocity, turbulence, and direc-

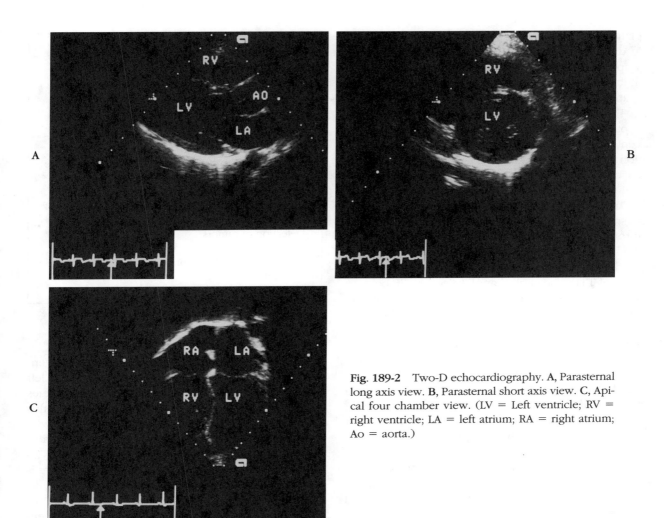

Fig. 189-2   Two-D echocardiography. **A,** Parasternal long axis view. **B,** Parasternal short axis view. **C,** Apical four chamber view. (LV = Left ventricle; RV = right ventricle; LA = left atrium; RA = right atrium; Ao = aorta.)

tion of blood flow. In general red symbolizes flow toward the transducer and blue indicates flow away from the transducer. Greater intensities of color indicate higher flow velocities. Color Doppler imaging does not permit quantitative velocity measurements; however, it provides spatial information about flow that is unavailable with the PW and CW modalities.

TECHNIQUE

Transthoracic echocardiography (TTE). Because echocardiographic diagnosis plays an extremely important role in the management of the patient, very often the child is sedated to allow a complete ex-

amination. Sedation must be appropriate to the clinical condition. Continuous monitoring includes heart rate (ECG) and oxygen saturation (pulse oximetry). Blood pressure is obtained before and after sedation.

TTE is preferably performed in the supine position with the right side elevated to bring the heart closer to the chest wall for better imaging. Planes of echocardiographic views are obtained from four different areas of the body: at the parasternal region on the left (or right in dextrocardia) at the second, third, or fourth intercostal spaces; at the cardiac apex; at the subcostal region; and on the suprasternal notch. Each echocardiographic area of evaluation is not a single plane but rather a family of echocardiographic planes that can be obtained by aiming the ultrasound in different directions. To interpret an echocardiographic study, the interpreter must be familiar with the cardiac anatomy and be able to understand the spatial relations within the different planes.

TTE can be limited by air-filled lungs or a hyperexpanded chest (e.g., patients who are being overventilated or are receiving high-frequency ventilation), obesity, or a dysmorphic chest with bony thoracic structures and in postoperative patients with tissue edema, chest tubes, and bandages.

Transesophageal echocardiography (TEE). With a special transesophageal transducer introduced through the mouth into the esophagus and stomach, the heart and great vessels can be visualized from behind. This technique overcomes many of the limitations of TTE. The clinical application of TEE became widespread in the late 1980s. The greatest advantage of this technique is the superior imaging when TTE is limited. There are different sizes of transesophageal probes (4 to 11 mm), and the smallest may be used in a 3 kg newborn. There are single-plane probes, which are limited to short axis and frontal views of the heart, biplanar probes, and a new multiplane probe with 360-degree rotational capabilities. PW, CW, and color Doppler are available in the newer probes. With the multiplane probes, there are unlimited numbers of imaging planes.

TEE can be invaluable in the PICU and has made a striking change in the management of the critically ill cardiac patient. TEE is safe, but a well-trained and experienced echocardiographer is necessary. Appropriate sedation as well as topical anesthetic in the throat are essential. Continuous monitoring includes heart rate (ECG), oxygen saturation (pulse oximetry), and periodic cuff blood pressure. TEE is clearly superior to TTE for the visualization of the left atrial appendage, atrial septum, thoracic aorta, and some prosthetic valves in older patients. It also often affords superior evaluation of cardiac and aortic anatomy and pathologic lesions such as masses and thrombi.

Ventricular Function

Ventricular function can be assessed by 2-D, M-mode, and Doppler echocardiography. The shortening fraction (%SF) is obtained from M-mode echocardiography and reflects the percent change in the left ventricular diameter.

$$\%SF = (LVEDD - LVESD) \div LVEDD$$

> **SPECIFIC USES OF TRANSESOPHAGEAL ECHOCARDIOGRAPHY**
>
> When transthoracic imaging is poor
> Preoperative examination in the operating room
> Intra- and postoperative monitoring of cardiac function and assessment of surgical results
> Interventional catheterization in the PICU or in the catheterization laboratory
> Evaluation of prosthetic valves
> Detection of vegetations (if there is a suspicion of endocarditis)
> Detection of tumors
> Detection of aortic dissection
> Noninvasive cardiac monitoring in the PICU (estimating ventricular function and cardiac output)

---

where SF is shortening fraction, LVEDD is left ventricular end-diastolic dimension, and LVESD is left ventricular end-systolic dimension. Normal values range from 28% to 44%. This measurement depends on ventricular preload and afterload. In children with increased left ventricular afterload, as in severe aortic stenosis, the shortening fraction is increased. With poor function, as in dilated cardiomyopathy, there is a decrease in the shortening fraction.

Ejection fraction (EF) is assessed by 2-D echocardiography (from the apical views) by tracing the endocardial borders and measuring the left ventricular end-diastolic and end-systolic volumes. The EF is calculated by a variety of different geometric formulas. These techniques correlate well with cineangiography in children and adults. Although there are other measurements of systolic function such as thickening fraction, mean rate of shortening (Vcf_c), peak rate of shortening (dD/dt), wall stress, and E-point septal separation, the use of these measurements is limited in common practice. Stroke volume or cardiac output can be estimated by using the mean velocity across the aortic valve and measuring the cross-sectional area of the aortic valve. This could be useful in the PICU for monitoring patients without having to establish access for more invasive techniques.

Diastolic function can be evaluated from the Doppler spectral display of the mitral valve inflow. The diastolic time intervals reflect the time course of relaxation, peak and mean filling rates of the left ventricle, and the percentage of total filling that occurs in various phases of diastole. Isovolumic relaxation time (the time between minimum left ventricular systolic dimension and mitral valve opening), the mitral inflow peak E and A waves (E = rapid filling, A = atrial contraction), E/A ratio, E-wave acceleration, and deceleration time can all be measured. With abnormal relaxation of the ventricles, there will be a low E velocity, prolongation of deceleration time, and a decreased E/A ratio. These abnormalities occur in patients with hypertensive heart disease, dilated and hypertrophic cardiomyopathy, aortic stenosis, and acute ischemia. Decreased compliance of the ventricles results in restriction to filling, with a high E velocity, a short deceleration time, and an increased E/A ratio. These abnormalities occur in patients with symptomatic dilated, ischemic, and restrictive cardiomyopathy. A normal filling pattern does not exclude intrinsic left ventricular diastolic abnormalities since there can be normalization of mitral inflow patterns by mitral regurgitation and increased left atrial pressure.

Prediction of Intracardiac Pressures

Doppler echocardiography can be used to estimate intracardiac pressures noninvasively. In the presence of valvular regurgitation, stenosis, or intra- or extracardiac shunts, the peak velocity of blood flow between two cardiovascular chambers is proportional to the difference in pressure between the two structures. Thus, if the pressure in one of these chambers is known (on the basis of clinical factors such as systemic blood pressure or central venous pressure), the pressure in the other chamber can be derived.

Right ventricular and pulmonary artery pressures

Right ventricular pressure can be estimated indirectly if there is tricuspid regurgitation. The velocity of the tricuspid regurgitant flow from the right ventricle to the right atrium can then be used to calculate the gradient between the right ventricle and the right atrium. Using the modified Bernoulli equation and an assumed right atrial pressure of 5 to 10 mm Hg or a measured one if available, one can calculate an estimated right ventricular pressure.

$$RVSP = 4(TR)^2 + RAP$$

where RVSP is right ventricular systolic pressure, TR is tricuspid regurgitation velocity (m/sec), and RAP is right atrial pressure. The pulmonary artery pressure will be the same as right ventricular pressure if there is no right ventricular outflow tract obstruction.

By obtaining the velocity of flow across a ventricular septal defect it is also possible to estimate the right ventricular pressure if one knows the systemic blood pressure. This is equal to the left ventricular pressure in the absence of left ventricular outflow tract obstruction.

$$RVSP = SBP - 4(VSD)^2$$

where RVSP is right ventricular systolic pressure, SBP is systolic blood pressure, and VSD is left ventricular to right ventricular peak velocity (m/sec).

Pulmonary artery pressure can be estimated if there is a patent ductus arteriosus (PDA) or a systemic to pulmonary artery shunt. It is important to know the systemic arterial blood pressure for a close pressure estimation. The gradient obtained across the shunt or PDA is subtracted from the systolic blood pressure to estimate pulmonary arterial pressure.

$$PASP = SBP - 4(A\text{-}P)^2$$

where PASP is pulmonary artery systolic pressure, SBP is systemic blood pressure, and A-P is aorta to pulmonary peak velocity (m/sec).

Similarly, the diastolic pulmonary artery pressure can be estimated from the velocity of pulmonary insufficiency flow. The velocity of flow from the pulmonary artery to right ventricle is obtained at end diastole. Assuming the right ventricular end-diastolic pressure is equal to central venous pressure at end diastole, an estimated pulmonary artery diastolic pressure can be calculated.

$$PADP = 4(PI)^2 + RVEDP$$

where PADP is pulmonary artery diastolic pressure, PI is pulmonary insufficiency velocity (m/sec), and RVEDP is right ventricular end-diastolic pressure.

All these noninvasive estimations of the systolic or diastolic pulmonary artery pressure may be useful in monitoring the patient with pulmonary hypertension.

Left heart pressures

The principles used in pressure estimation for the right heart can be used in the left heart. There are some limitations in all these measurements. They are time consuming and for a variety of technical reasons sometimes difficult to measure. However, this approach can be applied successfully in some patients. It is also possible to estimate valve areas as well and to quantitate valvar regurgitation.

Specific Clinical Uses in the PICU

In the critically ill child a complete 2-D and Doppler echocardiogram will assist in distinguishing structural cardiac lesions from myocardial dysfunction secondary to sepsis, hypoglycemia, hypoxemia, or CNS disorder. Myocardial dysfunction from these causes frequently can present with similar clinical symptoms. The differential diagnosis of a neonate presenting with cardiogenic shock includes sepsis, a cardiac malformation with left-sided heart obstruction (hypoplastic left heart syndrome, critical aortic stenosis, or severe coarctation), or severe myocarditis or cardiomyopathy. Echocardiography is helpful in establishing the diagnosis in the neonate with severe hypoxemia when the differential diagnosis is often a primary pulmonary problem (e.g., persistent pulmonary hypertension of the newborn or pneumonia) vs. cyanotic congenital heart disease such as transposition of the great vessels, pulmonary atresia, tricuspid atresia, severe Ebstein's anomaly of the tricuspid valve, or total anomalous pulmonary venous return with obstruction. All patients considered for ECMO need to have a full cardiac evaluation, including an echocardiogram to exclude congenital heart disease, especially in infants less than 2 months of age. In these infants total anomalous pulmonary venous return often has a similar presentation to some pulmonary diseases.

In premature infants a common application of echocardiography is not only to confirm the presence of a PDA before medical or surgical treatment but more important to ensure there is not ductal-dependent congenital heart disease, either severe right or left heart obstructive lesions. In right heart obstruction the ductus will provide a source of pulmonary flow, and in left heart obstruction it will be a source of systemic perfusion.

In cases of infective endocarditis cardiac ultrasound can be helpful in confirming but not necessarily excluding the diagnosis. It will only detect vegetations >2 mm. Thus, if there is a strong clinical picture of endocarditis documented by positive blood cultures, this should be treated as such even if the echocardiogram is negative. Further, since pathologic

diagnosis cannot be made by echocardiograms in the absence of other evidence of endocarditis, abnormal echocardiographic densities detected by ultrasound can represent other cardiac masses, including intracardiac thrombi or tumors. Intracardiac thrombi can be detected by TTE; however, TEE is more sensitive in older children and adults, often permitting better visualization of the atrial appendages. Pericardial effusions are easily identified by echocardiography. With the use of M-mode and 2-D imaging, the size of the pericardial effusion can be easily assessed. Two-D and Doppler evidence that is consistent with hemodynamic compromise in pericardial effusion includes right atrial or right ventricular diastolic collapse and significant (>25%) variation in mitral inflow peak velocity with respiration.

Two-D echocardiography can be used to assist in various procedures. It can be used during pericardiocentesis to localize the effusion. Atrial balloon septostomy can be done under echocardiographic guidance in the catheterization laboratory as well as in the PICU. It aids in catheter and balloon placement, the septostomy itself, and in evaluating the size of the defect.

Contrast echocardiography can sometimes add to the evaluation of intracardiac shunting, although color Doppler imaging is usually superior, especially in children who have adequate echocardiographic windows. Either IV agitated 0.9% sodium chloride solution or albumin solutions will produce microcavitations that are detected by 2-D ultrasound. Since microcavitations ordinarily are cleared in the pulmonary circulation, their presence in the left heart indicates right-to-left shunting.

Echocardiography is most helpful in the evaluation of residual defects in the postoperative cardiac patient, with the findings often affecting medical management as well as identifying patients in whom reoperation is unnecessary.

Potential organ donors need to undergo cardiac evaluation, including echocardiography, to evaluate the anatomy and function of the heart and its suitability for a transplant recipient.

Although cardiac output can be calculated by 2-D and Doppler studies, they are not usually performed on a routine basis. Monitoring critically ill children by 2-D or Doppler ultrasound has not replaced thermodilution determination of cardiac output in most PICUs.

RISKS AND COMPLICATIONS

Diagnostic imaging at standard intensities have not been associated with biologic effects and tissue injury. There is concern about temperature elevation via absorption resulting from interaction of biologic tissue and ultrasound. Beams that are unfocused are more likely to cause temperature elevation in tissues. TEE has some added risks since it is an invasive procedure. Dental or oral mucosal trauma, bleeding, and esophageal tears or rupture as well as airway obstruction are potential complications. False positive or false negative results carry the same risks of misinterpretation as any other diagnostic testing.

CURRENT RESEARCH AND FUTURE CONSIDERATIONS

Some other new techniques that are not used in clinical practice in the PICU at the present time include 3-D echocardiography, intravascular echocardiography, automatic edge detection, myocardial contrast, and Doppler tissue imaging. These developing areas have potential for future clinical application.

ADDITIONAL READING

Chin AJ, Vetter JM, Seliem M, Jones AA, Andrews BA. Role of early postoperative surface echocardiography in the pediatric cardiac intensive care unit. Chest 105:10-16, 1994.

Edelman SK. Ultrasound Physics and Instrumentation. Houston: ESP, 1994, pp 109-110.

Gutgesell HP, Paquet M, Duff DF, McNamara DG. Evaluation of left ventricular size and function by echocardiography. Results in normal children. Circulation 56:457-462, 1977.

Kipel G, Arnon R, Ritter SB. Transesophageal echocardiographic guidance of balloon atrial septostomy. J Am Soc Echocardiogr 4:631-635, 1991.

Lam J, Neirotti RA, Nijveld A, Schuller JL, Blom-Muilwijk CM, Visser CA. Transesophageal echocardiography in pediatric patients: Preliminary results. J Am Soc Echocardiogr 4:43-50, 1991.

Lin AE, Di Sessa TG, Williams RG. Balloon and blade atrial septostomy facilitated by two-dimensional echocardiography. Am J Cardiol 57:273-277, 1986.

Nishimura RA, Abel MD, Hatle LK, Tajik AJ. Assessment of diastolic function of the heart: Background and current applications of Doppler echocardiography. II. Clinical studies. Mayo Clin Proc 64:181-204, 1989.

• Nishimura RA, Miller FA, Callahan MJ, Benassi RC, Seward JB, Tajik AJ. Doppler echocardiography: Theory, instrumentation, technique and application. Mayo Clin Proc 60:321-343, 1985.

Pearson AC, Castello R, Labovitz AJ. Safety and utility of transesophageal echocardiography in the critically ill patient. Am Heart J 119:1083-1089, 1990.

Rein AJJT, Hsieh KS, Elixson M, Colan SD, Lang P, Sanders SP, Castaneda AR. Cardiac output estimates in the pediatric intensive care unit using a continuous-wave Doppler computer: Validation and limitations of the technique. Am Heart J 112:97-103, 1986.

Sahn DJ, Allen HD, George W, Mason M, Goldberg SJ. The utility of contrast echocardiographic techniques in the care of critically ill infants with cardiac and pulmonary disease. Circulation 56:959-968, 1977.

Sanders SP, Yeager S, Williams RG. Measurement of systemic and pulmonary blood flow and QP/QS ratio using Doppler and two-dimensional echocardiography. Am J Cardiol 51:952-956, 1983.

Sanfilippo AJ, Picard MH, Newell JB, Rosas E, Davidoff R, Thomas JD, Weyman AE. Echocardiographic assessment of patients with infectious endocarditis: Prediction of risk for complications. J Am Coll Cardiol 18:1191-1199, 1991.

• Snider AR, Serwer GA. Echocardiography in Pediatric Heart Disease. Chicago: Year Book, 1990, pp 1-135.

• Stamm RB, Martin RP. Quantification of pressure gradients across stenotic valves by Doppler ultrasound. J Am Coll Cardiol 2:707-718, 1983.

• Tajik AJ, Seward JB, Hagler DJ, Mair DD, Lie JT. Two-dimensional real-time ultrasonic imaging of the heart and great vessels. Mayo Clin Proc 53:271-303, 1978.

Wolfe LT, Rossi A, Ritter SB. Transesophageal echocardiography in infants and children: Use and importance in the cardiac intensive care unit. J Am Soc Echocardiogr 6:286-289, 1993.

Index